# Handbook of International Banking

*To Judith and Jullie*

# Handbook of International Banking

*Edited by*

Andrew W. Mullineux

*Professor of Global Finance, University of Birmingham, UK*

and

Victor Murinde

*Professor of Finance, University of Birmingham, UK*

**Edward Elgar**
Cheltenham, UK • Northampton, MA, USA

© Andrew W. Mullineux and Victor Murinde 2003

All rights reserved. No part of this publication may be reproduced, stored in a retrieval system or transmitted in any form or by any means, electronic, mechanical or photocopying, recording, or otherwise without the prior permission of the publisher.

Published by
Edward Elgar Publishing Limited
The Lypiatts
15 Lansdown Road
Cheltenham
Glos GL50 2JA
UK

Edward Elgar Publishing, Inc.
William Pratt House
9 Dewey Court
Northampton
Massachusetts 01060
USA

This book has been printed on demand to keep the title in print.

A catalogue record for this book
is available from the British Library

**Library of Congress Cataloguing in Publication Data**
Handbook of International Banking / edited by Andrew W. Mullineux and Victor Murinde.
  p. cm.
 Includes index.
 1. Banks and banking, International—Handbooks, manuals, etc.
2. International finance—Handbooks, manuals, etc. I. Title: International banking. II. Mullineux, A.W. III. Murinde, Victor.

HG3881 .H2665 2003
332.1'5—dc21                                                          2002032048

ISBN 978 1 84064 093 9 (cased)
      978 1 84542 223 3 (paperback)

# Contents

| | |
|---|---|
| List of figures | ix |
| List of tables | xi |
| List of exhibits | xiii |
| List of contributors | xv |
| Preface | xxix |

### PART I   THE GLOBALIZATION OF BANKING

1  Globalization and convergence of banking systems  3
   *Andrew W. Mullineux and Victor Murinde*

2  Multinational banking: historical, empirical and case
   perspectives  27
   *Elisa A. Curry, Justin G. Fung and Ian R. Harper*

3  Asset-backed securitization, collateralized loan obligations
   and credit derivatives  60
   *Warrick Ward and Simon Wolfe*

### PART II   BANKING STRUCTURES AND FUNCTIONS

4  The new world of euro banking  105
   *Jean Dermine*

5  Competitive banking in the EU and Euroland  130
   *Edward P.M. Gardener, Philip Molyneux and
   Jonathan Williams*

6  How to tie your hands: a currency board versus an
   independent central bank  156
   *Jakob de Haan and Helge Berger*

7  Free banking  173
   *Kevin Dowd*

8  Islamic banking  191
   *Humayon A. Dar and John R. Presley*

| 9 | Universal banking and shareholder value: a contradiction?<br>*Ingo Walter* | 207 |
|---|---|---|
| 10 | Foreign exchange trading activities of international banks<br>*Jürgen Eichberger and Joachim Keller* | 237 |
| 11 | The settlement and financing of international trade<br>*Ayse G. Eren* | 259 |
| 12 | Costs and efficiency in banking: a survey of the evidence from the US, the UK and Japan<br>*Leigh Drake* | 283 |

### PART III   BANKING RISKS, CRISES AND REGULATION

| 13 | Country risk: existing models and new horizons<br>*Sarkis Joseph Khoury and Chunsheng Zhou* | 327 |
|---|---|---|
| 14 | The causes of bank failures<br>*Shelagh Heffernan* | 366 |
| 15 | International banking crises<br>*Alistair Milne and Geoffrey E. Wood* | 403 |
| 16 | Some lessons for bank regulation from recent financial crises<br>*David T. Llewellyn* | 428 |
| 17 | Reforming the traditional structure of a central bank to cope with the Asian financial crisis: lessons from the Bank of Thailand<br>*Andrew W. Mullineux, Victor Murinde and Adisorn Pinijkulviwat* | 486 |
| 18 | Capital flight: the key issues<br>*Niels Hermes, Robert Lensink and Victor Murinde* | 516 |
| 19 | International banks and the washing of dirty money: the economics of money laundering<br>*Kent Matthews* | 546 |
| 20 | The regulation of international banking: structural issues<br>*Richard Dale and Simon Wolfe* | 572 |
| 21 | US banking regulation: practice and trends<br>*Joseph J. Norton and Christopher D. Olive* | 612 |
| 22 | Deposit insurance and international banking regulation<br>*C. Charles Okeahalam* | 637 |

## PART IV  THE EVOLVING INTERNATIONAL FINANCIAL ARCHITECTURE

23  The institutional design of central banks  671
    *Falko Fecht and Gerhard Illing*

24  The International Monetary Fund: past, present and future  699
    *Ian W. Marsh and Kate Phylaktis*

25  Reforming the privatized international monetary and financial architecture  721
    *Jane D'Arista*

26  Globalization, the WTO and GATS: implications for the banking sector in developing countries  751
    *Victor Murinde and Cillian Ryan*

*Index*  765

# Figures

| | | |
|---|---|---|
| 2.1 | US banking and representative operations of international banks, December 1996 | 41 |
| 3.1 | The asset-backed securitization process | 63 |
| 3.2 | Constituents of collateralized debt obligations | 65 |
| 3.3 | Potential CLO market development | 69 |
| 3.4 | Sample of a typical CLO structure | 70 |
| 8.1 | The bank's profits and composition of investments | 197 |
| 8.2 | Organizational structure of a typical Islamic bank | 200 |
| 10.1 | Pole chart | 242 |
| 10.2 | Moving average | 243 |
| 10.3 | Head-and-shoulders pattern | 244 |
| 10.4 | Foreign exchange market | 253 |
| 12.1 | Farrell efficiency | 290 |
| 12.2 | Scale and technical efficiency | 291 |
| 16.1 | Real estate and stock prices in selected Asian countries | 435 |
| 16.2 | Financial sector lending: growth and leverage, 1990–96 | 441 |
| 19.1 | Number of IBCs by jurisdiction | 550 |
| 19.2 | Loan-back scheme | 552 |
| 19.3 | Taxonomy of money laundering | 552 |
| 19.4 | Return–safety–confidentiality trade-off | 554 |
| 19.5 | Loan and deposit markets: partial equilibrium | 559 |
| 19.6 | Loan and deposit markets: effects of an increase in degree of confidentiality | 560 |
| 19.7 | Effect of increase in money laundering on loans and deposits | 562 |
| 19.8 | Effect of increase in money laundering on external sector | 563 |
| 19.9 | Effect of an increase in money laundering | 564 |
| 20A.1 | UK regulatory structure | 598 |
| 20A.2 | Australian regulatory structure | 600 |
| 20A.3 | Japanese new financial regulatory structure | 602 |
| 20A.4a | US regulatory structure | 604 |
| 20A.4b | US depository regulatory structure | 606 |
| 20A.4c | US Glass–Steagall reform: Financial Services Modernization Act 1999 | 608 |
| 20A.5 | New Zealand regulatory structure | 610 |

| 23.1 | A control problem of the central bank: finding a welfare-maximizing monetary policy | 674 |
| --- | --- | --- |
| 23.2 | The time-inconsistency problem | 676 |
| 23.3 | Asymmetric information and inflation expectations | 681 |
| 23.4 | Optimal monetary policy | 684 |
| 23.5 | The effect of a conservative central banker | 688 |
| 23.6 | Central bank independence and average macroeconomic performance, 1961–1990 | 690 |
| 23.7 | The Walsh contract between the government and the central bank | 693 |
| 25A.1 | Clearing function | 745 |
| 25A.2 | Exchange rate adjustment | 746 |
| 25A.3 | Adjustment in reserve holdings | 747 |
| 25A.4a | International open market operations (expansionary) | 748 |
| 25A.4b | International open market operations (contractionary) | 749 |

# Tables

| | | |
|---|---|---|
| 3.1 | European MBS/ABS issuance by asset type, 1997 and 1998 | 62 |
| 3.2 | Some of the major CLOs issued, as at January 1998 | 68 |
| 3.3 | Example of CLOs in facilitating a higher RAROC on investment-grade assets | 75 |
| 3.4 | Comparison of spreads in different types of securitized funding | 76 |
| 3.5 | Breakdown of the SBC Glacier CLO floating rate asset-backed securities | 84 |
| 3.6 | Summary of BIS proposed risk weightings | 96 |
| 4.1 | Currency and home-country relationship in the choice of the bond bookrunner, 1996 | 109 |
| 4.2 | Top underwriters of US debt and equity, January to July 1999 | 110 |
| 4.3a | Mutual funds managers in France, December 1996 | 111 |
| 4.3b | UK league of segregated pension fund managers, 1998 | 111 |
| 4.4 | Interest margins of commercial banks | 116 |
| 4.5 | Domestic bank mergers in Europe | 118 |
| 4.6 | International bank mergers in Europe | 119 |
| 4.7 | Bank rankings | 123 |
| 4.8 | Market concentration | 124 |
| 5.1 | Number of banks: banking system, 1984–1997 | 131 |
| 5.2 | Number of branches, 1984–1997 | 132 |
| 5.3 | Concentration in European banking, 1997 | 133 |
| 5.4 | Net interest margins, 1984–1997 | 134 |
| 5.5 | Non-interest income/gross income, 1984–1997 | 135 |
| 5.6 | Cost–income ratios, 1984–1997 | 136 |
| 5.7 | Return on equity, 1984–1997 | 136 |
| 5.8 | Extent to which strategy has been revised in response to the SMP for broad product areas | 142 |
| 5.9 | Nature of strategic responses to the SMP for broad product areas | 143 |
| 6.1 | Currency boards: an overview | 158 |
| 6.2 | Macroeconomic performance under alternative exchange rate regimes | 161 |
| 10.1 | Foreign exchange market turnover | 238 |

| | | |
|---|---|---|
| 10.2 | Foreign exchange dealers in the United States | 238 |
| 14.1 | Definitions of explanatory variables tested | 390 |
| 14.2 | Panel logit model accepted as superior to its multinomial logit counterpart | 391 |
| 14.3 | Results of multinomial logit regressions using *PROFIT1* | 393 |
| 14A.1 | Banks included in the International Pool | 401 |
| 15.1 | 'Commercial crises', eighteenth and nineteenth centuries | 409 |
| 15.2 | National banking era panics | 410 |
| 15.3 | Recent banking problems in major economies | 412 |
| 16.1 | Stock market prices index | 436 |
| 16.2 | Stock market prices index (property sector) | 436 |
| 16.3 | Private capital flows to Asian countries | 437 |
| 16.4 | Bank lending to private sector (% growth) | 439 |
| 16.5 | Bank lending to private sector (% of GDP) | 440 |
| 16.6 | Banking system exposure to property | 440 |
| 17.1 | Bills, loans and overdrafts of commercial banks, classified by sector | 488 |
| 17.2 | Net private financial flows into Thailand | 491 |
| 17.3 | Movements in interest rates and exchange rates during the reform period | 494 |
| 17.4 | Credit granted by BIBFs | 500 |
| 18.1 | Overview of empirical studies on the determinants of capital flight | 529 |
| 18.2 | Capital flight and policy uncertainty | 537 |
| 18.3 | Stability test results | 538 |
| 20.1 | Targets of regulation | 578 |
| 20.2 | Recent European cross-functional mergers, 1998–1999 | 579 |
| 20.3 | Recent US cross-functional mergers, 1997–1998 | 580 |
| 20.4 | Traditional-style regulatory framework | 585 |
| 20.5 | Structure of financial regulatory agencies | 590 |
| 22A.1 | Design features of explicit deposit insurance systems, 1995 | 666 |
| 25.1 | Assets of institutional investors | 723 |
| 25.2 | Capital flows to developing countries | 725 |
| 25.3 | Debt and the crisis countries | 732 |
| 25.4 | Highly indebted poor countries: a profile | 733 |

# Exhibits

| | | |
|---|---|---|
| 9.1 | Universal bank organization structures | 209 |
| 9.2 | Book, market and potential equity values in universal banks | 211 |
| 9.3 | Estimated major bank IT spending levels | 214 |
| 9.4 | Economies of scale and scope in financial services firms – the evidence | 215 |
| 9.5 | Market-to-book equity value, UK | 219 |
| 9.6 | Price-to-book ratios of US money-centre and major regional banks | 220 |
| 9.7 | Universal banking conflict matrix | 222 |
| 9.8 | Alternative bank–industry linkages | 226 |
| 9.9 | Comparative return analysis: Chase Manhattan Bank, 1991–1995 | 230 |
| 13.1 | Bank sector performance relative to the S&P 500, the Dow, and the NASDAQ | 332 |
| 13.2 | Frequently used variables in qualitative and quantitative models | 337 |
| 13.3 | International transfer risk: examination objectives | 341 |
| 13.4 | Country risk | 343 |
| 13.5 | Country risk analysis: country risk tree | 345 |
| 13.6 | Sovereign ceilings for foreign-currency ratings | 346 |
| 13.7 | Ranking of countries according to level of economic security in 1995 | 347 |
| 13.8 | Statistical release: country exposure lending survey | 349 |
| 13.9 | Summary of proposed country risk model | 361 |
| 13.10 | The extension of the probit model of country risk | 362 |

# Contributors

**Helge Berger** is currently at the International Monetary Fund. At the time of writing he was Research Director, CESifo (Center for Economic Studies and Ifo Institute for Economic Research, Munich, Germany) and Senior Lecturer at the University of Munich (LMU). Berger received his Masters degree and his PhD in economics from the University of Munich. He has been at Princeton University's Woodrow Wilson School as the John Foster Dulles Visiting Lecturer. He has written a number of papers on German monetary policy. He has also worked in several other fields, including German and European monetary policy, central bank independence, regulation and exchange rate systems.

**Elisa A. Curry** was employed as a research assistant at the Melbourne Business School for four years from 1997 to 2001 conducting research into the Australian financial services industry. Her research on financial convergence in the Australian financial services sector (conducted jointly with Professor Ian Harper) was published in the *North American Actuarial Journal* in 2000. Her research into the economic costs of retail payment instruments in Australia was cited in the 1997 Australian Financial System (Wallis) Inquiry. She is currently employed as an investigative officer at the Australian Securities and Investments Commission.

**Jane D'Arista** is Director of Programs at the Financial Markets Center in Philomont, VA. Previously she taught on the graduate programme in International Banking Law at Boston University School of Law and served as Chief Financial Economist for the Subcommittee on Telecommunications and Finance of the House Energy and Commerce Committee. Before that, she served for five years as an international analyst at the Congressional Budget Office and for 12 years as a staff member of the House Banking Committee. Her publications include *The Evolution of U.S. Finance*, a two-volume set published by M.E. Sharpe in 1994.

**Richard Dale** is Professor of International Banking at the University of Southampton, UK, Visiting Professor at the University of Reading and Visiting Professorial Fellow at Queen Mary and Westfield College, University of London. He has written extensively on the subject of financial regulation and is a member of the European Shadow Financial Regulatory Committee.

**Humayon A. Dar** is a lecturer in economics at Loughborough University, UK. His interest in Islamic banking stems from his studies at the International Islamic University, Islamabad. Dr Dar further studied Islamic finance at the University of Cambridge and received his PhD in 1996. Since then he has published many papers on Islamic economics, banking and finance and has advised government and non-government organizations. As a specialist in Islamic economics and finance, he has been involved in organizing seminars and conferences in this field. He is presently a joint director of the MSc programme in Islamic Economics, Banking and Finance at Loughborough University. In addition, he is interested in microcredit financing, factors affecting foreign direct investment in developing countries, and institutional changes in agrarian societies. He is a member of a number of professional organizations, has served as referee for journals on Islamic economics and finance, and is a member of the Advisory Board for the *International Journal of Islamic Financial Services*.

**Jakob de Haan** is Professor of Political Economy, University of Groningen, The Netherlands. He is also Scientific Director of SOM (Systems, Organization and Management, the research school of the faculties of Management and Organization, Economics, and Spatial Sciences of the University of Groningen). He graduated from the University of Groningen, where he gained his PhD. He has published extensively on issues such as public debt, monetary policy, central bank independence, political and economic freedom and European integration. His most recent book is *European Monetary and Fiscal Policy* (jointly written with Sylvester Eijffinger) (Oxford University Press, 2000). He is also on the editorial boards of *Public Choice* and the *European Journal of Political Economy*.

**Jean Dermine** holds a Docteur ès Sciences Economiques from the Catholic University of Louvain and Master of Business Administration from Cornell University, and is Professor of Banking and Finance and Director of the Centre for International Financial Services at INSEAD (the European Institute for Business Administration). Author of numerous articles on asset-liability management, European financial markets and the theory of banking, Jean Dermine has published four books and has had various research papers published in the *Journal of Financial Intermediation*, the *Journal of Money, Credit, and Banking*, and the *Journal of Banking and Finance*, as well as in other academic and professional journals. Laureate of the 1997 European Investment Bank (EIB) Prize for his essay 'Eurobanking, a New World', he is co-author of ALCO Challenge, a computer-based training simulation used in Europe, the Americas and Asia. Jean Dermine has been Visiting Professor at the Wharton School of the University of Pennsylvania, at the universities of Louvain and Lausanne, a Salomon Center Visiting Fellow at New York University, and a Danielsson Foundation Guest Professor of Bank Management at the Göteborg and Stockholm Schools of Economics.

**Kevin Dowd** is Professor of Financial Risk Management at Nottingham University Business School, UK. He previously worked for the Ontario Economic Council, the University of Sheffield, and Sheffield Hallam University. His main research interests are in the areas of financial and monetary economics and, in particular, free banking and financial risk management. His most recent book was *Money and the Market: Essays in Free Banking* (Routledge, 2000).

**Leigh Drake** is Professor of Monetary Economics in the Economics Department at Loughborough University, UK and is Deputy Director of the Loughborough University Banking Centre. He is the author of *The Building Society Industry in Transition* (Macmillan, 1989) and has published widely in the areas of money and banking in journals such as: the *Economic Journal*; *Review of Economics and Statistics*; the *Journal of Money, Credit and Banking*; *Oxford Economic Papers*; *Financial Stability Review*; *Manchester School*; and *Applied Financial Economics*. His main research interests in the field of banking include: costs and efficiency in banking; delivery channels and the pricing of bank services. He has acted as a consultant to a number of leading banks and building societies.

**Jürgen Eichberger** is Professor of Economics at the University of Heidelberg in Germany. He obtained his degrees (Diplom-Volkswirt, Dr. rer. pol.) from the University of Mannheim in Germany. For more than ten years, he taught at the University of Western Ontario in Canada, the Australian National University in Canberra and the University of Melbourne in Australia. In 1995, he returned to Germany and took up a chair at the University of Saarland. His research interests are focused on decision making under uncertainty, game theory and financial economics. His papers have appeared in major economic journals, and he has published several books.

**Ayse G. Eren** graduated in economics and management from Cardiff Business School, University of Wales, Cardiff in 1991. She went on to receive her MSc in international economics, banking and finance from the same university in 1993. She then joined the National Westminster Bank where she worked as a specialist in international trade finance until the end of 1999. Currently, she works as a Senior Relationship Manager at the Development Bank of Singapore, in London, with portfolio responsibility for a range of large corporate clients trading internationally. Since her graduate days, she has continued to contribute to the economics and finance literature.

**Falko Fecht** obtained a Masters degree in economics from the University of Frankfurt, Germany, in 1997, and thereafter worked in the Economics Department of the BHF-Bank. In 1998, he took up a position as Research Assistant at the Economics and Business Administration Faculty of his Alma Mater. Since October 2000, he has been working with the Economics Department at the Deutsche Bundesbank, in Frankfurt am Main, Germany.

**Justin G. Fung** is an Associate in the Melbourne office of The Boston Consulting Group. He specializes in corporate strategy, financial services and telecommunications. He has published peer-reviewed papers on a variety of subjects, including hospital network costs, patents and competition law and Chinese constitutional law. Prior to joining The Boston Consulting Group, he was a Research Fellow with the Department of Economics at the University of Melbourne and a Senior Research Assistant in the Centre of International Finance at the Melbourne Business School.

**Edward P.M. Gardener** is Director of the School for Business and Regional Development (SBARD) at the University of Wales, Bangor. Professor Gardener has published over 200 articles and papers on banking topics. His most recent books (co-authored) include *Investment Banking: Theory and Practice* (Euromoney, 1996), *Efficiency in Banking* (John Wiley, 1996), *European Savings Banks – Coming of Age?* (Lafferty Publications, 1999), *Strategic Challenges in European Banking* (Macmillan, 2000) and *Bank Strategies and Challenges in the New Europe* (Palgrave, 2001). During 1995/96 he co-directed (with economists from Cambridge University) a major EC DG XV project (published by Kogan Page, 1997) on the impact of the European Single Market on the EU credit institutions and banking. Since then he has conducted project research for the World Bank and co-directed (with Cambridge economists) a major banking project input to the HM Treasury Cruickshank Review of Banking Services in the UK.

**Ian R. Harper** is Professorial Fellow in the Melbourne Business School at the University of Melbourne, Australia. From 1993 to 1997, he held the Ian Potter Chair of International Finance in the School. His research interest lies in the field of financial intermediation. His publications include policy-orientated papers on a variety of subjects, including the effects of financial deregulation, the economics of saving, bank supervision, mergers in the financial sector and the role of superannuation. He is co-author with Jürgen Eichberger of a graduate text on financial economics published by Oxford University Press. Prior to joining Melbourne Business School, he was Professor of Monetary and Financial Economics at the University of Melbourne. He has also held positions at the Australian National University in Canberra, Princeton University in the United States and the Reserve Bank of Australia in Sydney.

**Shelagh Heffernan**, BA (Toronto), MPhil (Oxon), DPhil (Oxon) is Professor of Banking and Finance at Cass Business School, City University, London. She was a Commonwealth Scholar at Oxford and has been a visiting professor at several Canadian universities. Grants for research in banking include Leverhulme and HM Treasury. Books include *Sovereign Risk Analysis* (Unwin Hyman, 1986), *Modern International Economics* (co-authored with Peter Sinclair) (Blackwell, 1990), and *Modern Banking in Theory and Practice* (Wiley, 1996); the last book is also published in Chinese, and a new edition is forthcoming. Her research interests include competition in the financial sector, the causes of bank failure, financial regulation, e-cash and the performance of mutual funds. She has published widely in journals, including the *Journal of Banking and Finance*, *Economica*, the *Journal of Money, Credit, and Banking* and the *Journal of Financial Services Research*, with a number of entries in the *International Encyclopedia of Business & Management*.

**Niels Hermes** is Associate Professor at the Department of Management and Organization of the University of Groningen, The Netherlands. His fields of specialization include development economics, international finance and monetary economics. He has published on issues such as finance and development, investment and finance, capital flight, and exchange rate systems in the *Journal of International Money and Finance*, the *Journal of Banking and Finance*, and the *Journal of Development Studies*, among others. He has also co-edited two books.

**Gerhard Illing** is Professor of Macroeconomics in the Department of Economics at the University of Munich. He obtained an MPhil from the University of Cambridge (DAAD scholarship) in 1981, followed by a PhD (Dr. rer. pol.) from the Economics Faculty of the University of Munich, in 1984, after completing a thesis on 'Money and asymmetric information'.

During 1987–92, he was an Assistant Professor at the Economics Faculty of the University of Munich, during which time he completed his Habilitation (1992: Heisenberg Scholarship). He was also Professor of Economics at the University of Bamberg in 1993–95 and Professor in Economic Theory at the Goethe University Frankfurt in 1995–2001, before taking up his current position. He has held visiting professorships at the University of Western Ontario (1986/87; 1998); the University of Pittsburgh Center for Economic Research and Graduate Education (CERGE) in Prague (1992); the University of Freiberg (1991/92); and the Fern Universität Hagen (1994/95). He has published widely in many leading journals, in the area of applications of game theory to monetary theory and policy.

**Joachim Keller** is an economist at the research centre of the Deutsche Bundesbank, where he works on the development of new financial indicators. Prior to joining the Bundesbank he was a student of economics at the University of Pisa, Italy and at the University of Saarland, Germany, where he graduated as an economist in 1995 and where he is completing his thesis 'The effect of new information on the exchange rate' under the supervision of Professor Richter. His research interests lie in the field of monetary and international economics as well as banking and finance.

**Sarkis Joseph Khoury** is Professor of Finance and International Finance and Executive Director of the Foundation for Research in International Banking and Finance at the University of California-Riverside. He is also editor, associate editor and reviewer for many academic journals. He is also a member of the Board of Directors of the Philadelphia Board of Trade. Dr Khoury has authored or edited 22 books and monographs dealing with international banking, international finance, mergers and acquisitions, the stock markets and other investment vehicles. His numerous articles have appeared in some of the leading journals in their field. He has lectured all over the world on a wide range of financial issues, and has served as a consultant to corporations, individuals and academic institutions. Dr Khoury gained his PhD from the Wharton School of the University of Pennsylvania.

**Robert Lensink** is Professor of Finance at the Faculty of Economics, University of Groningen, The Netherlands. He is also an External Fellow of the Centre for Research in International Trade and Development (CREDIT) at the University of Nottingham, UK. His main fields of interest are finance and development, and firm-level investment. He has published widely on these issues, both in international journals and in books.

His most recent book, co-authored with Hong Bo and Elmer Sterken, is *Investment, Capital Market Imperfections and Uncertainty: Theory and Empirical Results* (Edward Elgar, 2001).

**David T. Llewellyn** is Professor of Money and Banking at Loughborough University, UK, and Chairman of the Loughborough University Banking Centre. He has formerly held positions at Unilever (Rotterdam), HM Treasury (London), the University of Nottingham, and the International Monetary Fund (Washington). He has been a Public Interest Director of the Personal Investment Authority (London) and has served as a consultant to banks and regulatory agencies in several countries. His main research interests are in the analysis of financial systems, the theory and practice of bank behaviour, the causes of banking crises and the theory and practice of financial regulation. Recent books include: *The New Economics of Banking* (SUERF, 1999) and *Financial Regulation: Why, How and Where Now?* (with Charles Goodhart) (Routledge, 1998). The chapter in this book is based on a project undertaken for De Nederlandsche Bank on the regulatory implications of banking crises. In 2000, he was elected President of the Société Universitaire Européenne de Recherches Financières (SUERF).

**Ian W. Marsh** holds degrees from Sheffield, London (Birkbeck) and Strathclyde Universities. He is a senior lecturer in finance at Cass Business School and a research affiliate at the Centre for Economic Policy Research. He previously taught at Strathclyde University and has held visiting positions at the universities of Malta, Bolzano and Palermo. He has recent publications in the *Journal of Monetary Economics*, the *Review of Economics and Statistics* and the *Journal of International Money and Finance*, and is co-author of *Exchange Rate Modelling* (Kluwer, 1999).

**Kent Matthews** is the Sir Julian Hodge Professor of Banking and Finance, Cardiff University, UK. He took degrees at the London School of Economics, Birkbeck College, and the University of Liverpool. He has held research and academic appointments at the London School of Economics, the National Institute of Economic & Social Research, the University of Liverpool, the University of Leuven (Belgium), the University of Clemson (USA), the University of Western Ontario (Canada), Liverpool Business School and Humbolt University (Berlin). He has held professional appointments at the Bank of England and Lombard Street Research Ltd. He was the principal forecaster for the Liverpool Macroeconomic Research Group between 1980 and 1989. His research interests cover credit market deregulation, macroeconomic forecasting and aspects of tax evasion and the black economy. He is the author and co-author of eight books, over 40 articles in scholarly journals and edited works, and over 30 articles in professional and popular journals.

**Alistair Milne** is senior lecturer in banking and finance at Cass Business School in London. Previously he has been an economic adviser to the Financial Intermediaries Division of the Bank of England, lecturer in economics at the University of Surrey, a research fellow at the London Business School, and has worked for HM Treasury and the Government of Malawi. He holds a PhD from the London School of Ecnomics, for an econometric thesis on the determinants of inventory investment, and has published papers on a range of academic and policy topics. He is course director of the School's MSc in banking and international finance and is conducting research on: banking competition, especially in the area of securities processing and payment systems; bank capital management and bank regulation; and the impact of capital market frictions on firm and household behaviour and the business cycle.

**Philip Molyneux** is currently Professor in Banking and Finance and Director of the Institute of European Finance at the University of Wales, Bangor. He also holds the Special Chair of Financial Services and Financial Conglomerates at Erasmus University, Rotterdam, The Netherlands. His main area of research is on the structure and efficiency of banking markets and he has published widely in this area, including recent publications in: the *Journal of Banking and Finance*, the *Journal of Money, Credit, and Banking*, *Economica*, *Economics Letters*, the *Journal of Post-Keynesian Economics* and *Applied Economics*. He has authored, co-authored and edited a variety of books, including *Efficiency in European Banking* (John Wiley, 1996), *Private Banking* (Euromoney, 1996), *Investment Banking in Europe* (Euromoney, 1996), *German Banking* (Financial Times, 1996), *Bancassurance* (Macmillan, 1998), *Financial Innovation* (John Wiley, 1999), *European Savings Banks – Coming of Age?* (Lafferty, 1999) and the latest, *European Banking: Efficiency, Technology and Growth* (John Wiley, 2001).

**Andrew W. Mullineux** is Professor of Global Finance and Director of the Global Finance (Research) Group and the MBA (International Banking and Finance) Programme in the Birmingham Business School at the University of Birmingham, UK. He graduated in 1973 with a first class degree in economics and was awarded a Masters in econometrics and mathematical economics by the London School of Economics and Political Science in 1976. He completed his PhD on business cycles in January 1983.

After working for five years as a Lecturer in Economics in the Business Studies Department at Liverpool Polytechnic (now John Moores University) he moved to a research post in the Department of Economics at the University of Birmingham, where he was subsequently employed (apart from spending the 1988/89 academic year at the Cardiff Business School) as Lecturer, Senior Lecturer and Professor of Money and Banking. On 1 May 2001, he moved to the Birmingham Business School to take up his current position. Mullineux has published numerous books and articles in refereed academic and professional journals. He is currently Recorder of Section F (Economics) of the British Association for the Advancement of Science and Managing Editor of the 23rd (October 2001, Brussels) Société Universitaire Européenne de Recherches Financières (SUERF) Colloquium proceedings.

**Victor Murinde** is Professor of Finance as well as Director of the Corporate Finance Research Group at the University of Birmingham, UK, and Hallsworth Senior Research Fellow at the Institute of Development Policy and Management, University of Manchester. He completed his PhD in Economics at Cardiff Business School, University of Wales, Cardiff, in 1990. Thereafter he held positions as Lecturer in Banking at Cardiff Business School, Senior Lecturer in Finance and later Reader in Development Finance at the University of Birmingham. He has also worked as a consultant to the World Bank, the United Nations and UNCTAD (United Nations Conference on Trade and Development) as well as to a number of banks, private companies and governments in developing and transition economies. Professor Murinde has published over 40 articles in many journals, including the *Journal of Banking and Finance*, *Journal of International Money and Finance*, *Review of International Economics*, *Emerging Markets Review*, *Manchester School*, *Journal of Policy Modelling*, *World Development*, *Economic Notes*, *Applied Economics* and *Applied Financial Economics*. His research interests cover corporate finance issues in emerging financial markets, development and international banking, and flow of funds approach to macroeconomic policy modelling.

**Joseph J. Norton** is the James L. Walsh Distinguished Faculty Fellow in Financial Institutions Law and Professor of Law, Southern Methodist University School of Law, Dallas and (dual appointment) Sir John Lubbock Professor of Banking Law at the Centre for Commercial Law Studies, University of London. He currently holds professional positions in banking/financial law in London, the USA and Hong Kong. He is considered one of the leading law experts in international banking and financial law and in finance sector law reform matters. He has published over 35 books and over 120 articles on related subjects, and has lectured on banking and fiance law worldwide. He has practical experience with international and domestic (US) banking and capital markets transactions, international financial regulatory matters, bank corporate and asset restructuring and asset securitization. He is a Senior Research Fellow at the Institute of European Finance (UK). Professor Norton is the Executive Director of the London Institute of International Banking, Finance and Development Law, of the London Forum for International Economic Law and Development and of the Centre for Financial Studies and the Rule of Law (BIICL-London). He currently is actively engaged in emerging financial sector reform consultancies in Africa, South America, Central and Eastern Europe, and East Asia.

**C. Charles Okeahalam** obtained a PhD in economics from the University of London in 1991. Since 1999 he has been a professor at the University of the Witwatersrand, South Africa, where he has held the Donald Gordon Chair in Banking and Finance in the Graduate School of Business Administration (1999–2000) and since 2000, the Liberty Life Chair in Finance and Investment in the Department of Business Economics. He has worked as an investment analyst and served as an adviser to a number of central and commercial banks. During 1999–2000 he led the design, development and implementation process for the establishment of the South Africa Deposit Insurance System.

**Christopher D. Olive** gained a degree in business administration (finance) from the University of Miami, Florida, a J.D. from the Southern Methodist University School of Law and an LL.M. (banking and finance law) from the University of London. He is an Associate, Lending/Structured Finance Group, Jones, Day, Reavis and Pogue, Dallas, Texas; Adjunct Lecturer in Law, Southern Methodist University School of Law; and Fellow, International Banking and Finance Law Unit, Queen Mary and Westfield College, University of London. Christopher Olive's experience includes lending and structured finance and transactions and financial products, including syndicated loan transactions, project, acquisition, aircraft, venture capital and real estate finance and debt securities transactions, synthetic leasing and securitization transactions, structured derivatives transactions, bankruptcy finance and restructuring transactions, and banking and securities regulatory matters.

**Kate Phylaktis** is Head of the Department of Banking and Finance, Professor of International Finance and Director of the Emerging Markets

Group at Cass Business School in London. She has published extensively in the fields of foreign exchange markets, financial markets and financial structures with specific reference to emerging markets. She has written three books: *Financial Data of Banks and Other Institutions* (Pergamon, 1987); *International Finance and the Less Developing Countries* (Macmillan, 1990); and *The Banking System of Cyprus: Past, Present and Future* (Macmillan, 1995). She is an associate editor of *Emerging Markets Review* and the *Greek Economic Review*. She has acted as a consultant to various companies and public bodies, including the Research Department of the International Monetary Fund, the Commonwealth Secretariat, the Cyprus Popular Bank, the Bank of Cyprus, the Ministry of Education of Greece and the Ministry of Education and Culture of Cyprus, and is a member of the Export Guarantees Advisory Council.

**Adisorn Pinijkulviwat** gained a BA in economics at Thammasat University (Bangkok) and an MBA in international banking and finance from the University of Birmingham, UK. He began his career as an assistant analyst in the Department of Bank Examination and Analysis, Bank of Thailand, in 1975. At present, he is a Chief Officer in the Department of Examination and Supervision.

**John R. Presley** has been Professor of Economics in the Department of Economics, Loughborough University, UK, since 1984. He was Head of Department, 1991–96, and Director of the Banking Centre, 1984–89. He is the author of 15 books on European monetary union, the history of economics, banking in the Arab Gulf and Islamic finance. Since 1991 he has been an adviser to the Department of Trade and Industry on Middle East Trade. He is now adviser to Saudi British Bank and a Director of the Arab British Chamber of Commerce as well as Associate Director, Maxwell Stamp plc. He has published articles in most leading economics journals and writes regularly for professional magazines, mainly about the Middle East. He has been an adviser to the Saudi Arabian government (1978–79), visiting professor, Harvard University, and has been an adviser for many international organizations and companies, including the International Monetary Fund, the World Bank, HSBC and British Aerospace plc.

**Cillian Ryan** is Director of the University of Birmingham Jean Monnet European Centre of Excellence, and holder of the Jean Monnet Chair in European Economics. A graduate of University College, Dublin, he received his PhD from the University of Western Ontario. He has been an adviser to various governments on a wide range of trade policy issues, including the North American Free Trade Agreement (NAFTA), the

Uruguay Round, the European '1992' Single Market programme and more recently on financial services, the General Agreement on Trade in Services (GATS) and the World Trade Organization. In addition to the UK, he has held lecturing appointments in Ireland, Canada, the United States, Singapore, France and Hong Kong.

**Ingo Walter** is the Charles Simon Professor of Applied Financial Economics and the Sidney Homer Director of the New York University Salomon Center at the Stern School of Business, New York University. He graduated with an AB in economics (summa cum laude) from Lehigh University in 1962, an MS in business economics from the same university in 1963, and a PhD in economics from New York University in 1966. After working as Assistant Professor of Economics (1965–68) and Associate Professor of Economics (1968–70) at the University of Missouri-St Louis, he became Senior Fellow at the Center for International Studies, New York University (1970–73), before taking up his current Chair at the Stern School of Business. He has authored many leading books and has contributed numerous papers to edited monographs, in addition to publishing widely in many top journals in the area of international banking.

**Warrick Ward** gained a BSc in economics and accounting from the University of the West Indies (Cave Hill), and an MSc in international banking and financial studies from the University of Southampton, UK. He is currently employed at the Central Bank of Barbados as a Banking Analyst in the Governor's Office. Prior to this he has held positions in the Bank Supervision Department and in the Research Department, where he served as an economist. He has served on a number of committees, one of which was mandated to provide input for the enactment of the Electronic Transactions Bill (2000). He is also the Chairman of the Central Bank's E-Banking Committee, and a member of its Investment Committee. Mr Ward has written on a number of topics, including e-banking, life insurance, trade issues, as well as macro-prudential and regulatory topics.

**Jonathan Williams** is a lecturer in banking and finance at the University of Wales, Bangor. His main research interests lie in the area of bank efficiency and organizational structure with particular emphasis on the European savings banks industry. He is also interested in the relationship between financial liberalization and banking sector efficiency in developing countries and is the author of about 50 articles, books and publications on the financial system. As part of the banking research team at Bangor he has contributed to several major studies, including 'Credit Institutions and

Banking', commissioned by the European Commission as part of its Single Market Review initiative, and the recent Cruickshank Review of UK Banking Services. A lecturer at undergraduate and postgraduate levels, he is responsible for delivering modules in the areas of international banking, banking and development, and comparative banking.

**Simon Wolfe** is a lecturer in finance at the University of Southampton, UK. His research interests include asset-backed securitization, long-run performance of convertible bond issuers, financial regulations and Islamic banking. His publications have appeared in such journals as the *European Journal of Finance*, the *Journal of Fixed Income* and the *Journal of Financial Regulation and Compliance*. Dr Wolfe has also contributed to books, for example, *The European Equity Markets: The State of the Union and an Agenda for the Millennium* (edited by Benn Steil) (Royal Institute of International Affairs, 1996).

**Geoffrey E. Wood** is currently Professor of Economics at City University London. He has also taught at the University of Warwick, UK, and has been with the research staff of both the Bank of England and the Federal Reserve Bank of St Louis. He is the co-author or co-editor of ten books, which deal with, among other subjects, finance of international trade, monetary policy and bank regulation. Among his professional papers are studies of exchange rate behaviour, interest rate determination, monetary unions, tariff policy and bank regulation. He has also acted as an adviser to the New Zealand Treasury. He is a Managing Trustee of the Institute of Economic Affairs and of the Wincott Foundation in London.

**Chunsheng Zhou** has been an assistant professor of the University of California at Riverside (UCR), an honorary associate professor of the University of Hong Kong, and a full professor of the Guanghua School of Management, Peking University, Beijing. He has published a number of research articles in leading economics and finance journals and has made numerous presentations to academic researchers, business managers, and financial practitioners, in the United States, Europe, Hong Kong and Mainland China. Dr Zhou has also served as a financial economist in the United States Federal Reserve Board in Washington, DC. In addition, he has served as an economist, consultant and adviser to a number of government agencies, banks and hi-tech companies. He gained his Masters degree in mathematics from Peking University and a PhD in financial economics from Princeton University.

# Preface

## Andrew W. Mullineux and Victor Murinde

The 'internationalization' of banking, which started in the early 1970s, paved the way for the 'globalization' of finance and became more and more evident during the 1990s as international capital flows increased in magnitude. The internationalization and globalization processes have been facilitated by the ongoing communications and information technology (C&IT) revolution and capital flows have increasingly responded to economic and political news. This has created the potential for increased global financial, and consequent economic, instability, of which the 1997/98 Asian financial crisis might only be a precursor.

By allowing countries, whether they are developed, developing, in transition or emerging market economies, to draw on a global capital pool to finance investment, rather than rely entirely on domestically generated savings, a globalized financial system provides great opportunities as well as the aforementioned threat of instability.

The ultimate objective of the monetary authorities must thus be to create a new 'global financial architecture', which ensures that capital flows freely to those who will make the best use of it to enhance the well-being of mankind. To achieve this, risks and benefits (pecuniary and social) and disbenefits (for example, poverty and environmental degradation) must be accurately priced and measured and a regulatory and supervisory system must be put in place to assure price stability without distorting the price mechanism. Much work needs to be done to achieve such a utopia, but good progress is being made on risk, environmental and poverty impact measurement and on the regulatory and supervisory front. Good governance at the international, state and corporate levels is of course essential for the successful conclusion of this global project.

The aim of the *Handbook of International Banking* is to provide a clearly accessible source of reference material, covering the main developments that explain how the internationalization and globalization of banking has progressed over recent decades to its current juncture and to appraise progress with the creation of a new global financial architecture. The Handbook is the first of its kind in the area of international banking.

The chapters contained in the volume have been written by leading specialists in their respective fields, often with remarkable experience in academia and/or professional practice, and have been grouped into four parts. Part I includes chapters dealing with the internationalization and globalization of banking. Part II groups chapters covering structural developments in the international banking industry. The chapters in Part III tackle regulatory and supervisory issues relating to international banking, while the chapters in Part IV assess progress towards the development of a new 'global financial architecture'.

The material is provided mainly in the form of self-contained surveys, which trace the main developments in a well-defined topic, together with specific reference to the relevant frontier research output as contained in recent journal articles and working papers. Some contributions, however, aim to disseminate new empirical findings especially where competing paradigms are evaluated.

The Handbook is designed to serve as a source of supplementary reading and inspiration for a range of courses in banking and finance, including: post-experience and in-house programmes for bankers and other financial service practitioners; Masters and MBA programmes with courses in international banking and finance; and also for practitioners, professional researchers and academics in the field.

The editors (Andrew Mullineux and Victor Murinde) would like to take this opportunity to thank the following people for helping us to bring this project to its successful conclusion: the contributing authors, for the high quality of their chapters; Margaret Ball and Jayne Close, for their excellent secretarial support in helping us to produce the typescript; and Edward Elgar, Alex Minton, Karen McCarthy and their colleagues, for all their encouragement and assistance in helping us produce this Handbook. We all hope that its readers find it useful!

PART I

The Globalization of Banking

# 1. Globalization and convergence of banking systems
## Andrew W. Mullineux and Victor Murinde

## 1  INTRODUCTION

The single global banking space is almost a reality. Nine years ago, analysts named 17 banks that they believed were global banks of the future. All were commercial or universal banks. In a 1998 survey, about the only similarity is the number: analysts still envisage 17 banks as 'global', or with 'global potential', but they describe a very different grouping. Given the changes in banking topography, today's analysts include more investment than commercial banks in the top ranks (see Kahn, 1998). Just as striking, the first two tiers in 1998 are the exclusive realms of US banks. Today's candidates as global banks of the new millennium include Merrill Lynch, Morgan Stanley Dean Witter, Goldman Sachs, J.P. Morgan, Citibank, Chase Manhattan and Deutsche Bank.

During 1999, four banks stood head and shoulders above the rest as global banks: the best global wholesale bank was Chase Manhattan; the best global transaction services bank, and the best global consumer bank was Citigroup; the best global asset management bank was Merrill Lynch; and the best global private bank was Crédit Suisse Private Banking. These banks, no longer content to rule the domestic roost, are joined by an unprecedented number of financial institutions stepping outside their countries' borders to attain true global reach. It seems global reach, perhaps by making overseas acquisitions, is the clearest strategy for independent survival. Alongside the expansion of conventional banks, the last two decades have seen the birth and growth of Islamic banks, which rely on profit and loss sharing rather than the conventional interest rate yardstick to price their operations; see, among others, Murinde et al. (1995), Murinde and Naser (1998), Al-Deehani et al. (1999).

The indications are that financial globalization is broadly beneficial to the world economy (Thiessen, 1998; Murinde, 1996). International financial markets can facilitate access by borrowers to a larger pool of global savings and enhance investment opportunities for savers worldwide. While international capital flows have at times disrupted national financial markets, such episodes more often than not were caused by unsustainable domestic policies and pointed to the need for adjustment. In view of the overall benefits of greater access to global capital markets, it would not serve us well to restrict the free flow of funds. The best way to maximize the benefits of financial globalization and reduce the risks of disruptions to national macroeconomic policies is to ensure that these markets and flows are sound and sustainable. Financial systems need to be prudently managed and supervised – both nationally and internationally. The best policy, therefore, is to support and contribute to global initiatives designed to promote financial market stability worldwide.

In addition, the globalization of financial markets and the development of strategic alliances in regional markets have broadened the horizon for many investors. For example, investment in private capital assets has grown rapidly as investors further diversify portfolios in order to reduce risk and increase returns. In Latin America, for example, growing participation by foreign institutional investors has been a key force in the development of Latin American stock markets since 1990 while accelerating trends of institutionalization and globalization of money management have increased the importance of these investors for the future development of stock markets in emerging economies (Hargis, 1998). There have been some considerable interactions between globalization and institutionalization of money management and the growth of emerging stock markets in Latin America, and elsewhere.

Small, open, developing countries with fragile banking systems have little to lose from globalization and much to gain, provided that globalization is accompanied by policy changes in several areas. First, transaction costs in the banking sector need to be reduced. Second, fiscal policy will have to shift towards the provision of infrastructure and education to prevent local capital from being moved to other countries. Third, a further reduction in foreign trade barriers would improve resource allocation and increase competition.

Knight (1999) argues that the increase in financial globalization and the rise in cross-border financial flows that represents the globalization process could lead, over time, to a more efficient worldwide allocation of savings than was possible in the past. Indeed, the new and growing links between emerging and developed financial markets have been reflected in a spectacular increase in financial flows to developing and transition countries. It is argued that to benefit fully from their growing access to international financing, the developing and transition economies need to strengthen their financial systems. Moreover, given the extremely low level of domestic saving, many developing countries have no option other than to participate actively in the process of financial globalization. Only by participating in the global market will it be possible for the country to share in the surplus savings of the more mature economies (*pace* the US) of the world.

However, some practical outcomes have the potential to delay the process of globalization (Aybar and Milman, 1999). For example, the recent experiences in South East Asia, Russia and Latin America provide ample evidence that countries in the process of integration are increasingly exposed to internal and external economic shocks. The growing vulnerability of developing economies in particular has the potential to undermine decades of development effort. In this context, the Asian crisis clearly demonstrates that we are increasingly unable to predict the triggers of such crises, and certainly lack the institutional arrangements to contain them. Hence, the ability to manage the interaction between domestic and international economic forces is limited or undermined by certain factors; these have the potential to delay the process of globalization and integration of developing economies into the world economy.

Moreover, the recent financial crisis has demonstrated that, through the process of globalization, the financial world has shrunk (Mahbubani, 1999). The financial crisis started in a small, open, developing country in South East Asia (Thailand) and spread through East Asia and on to Russia, Latin America and the developed countries.

Clearly, globalization of finance will engender worldwide, rather than local, competition. In this context, the banking industry should anticipate that the twenty-first century will present it with a considerably more volatile landscape than it faced in the twentieth century (Ludwig, 1999). First, it is expected that computer technology will give financial institutions the ability to analyse market changes more quickly and the ability to react to those changes more quickly. Second, advances in communications technology will transmit market developments more quickly.

This chapter surveys trends in the globalization of banking, focusing primarily on the evolving role of banks and other financial institutions in corporate governance. In what follows, the remainder of the chapter is structured into four sections. Section 2 examines issues surrounding internationalization, securitization and derivatization. Financial system convergence and the issue of banks versus capital markets are discussed in Section 3. Globalization, in the context of the World Trade Organization (WTO) and the General Agreement on Trade in Services (GATS), is discussed in Section 4. Section 5 examines the trends in corporate governance. Section 6 concludes by looking into the future.

## 2 INTERNATIONALIZATION, SECURITIZATION AND DERIVATIZATION

In the last three decades, there has been substantial liberalization of the banking sector and financial innovation. These changes have been facilitated by reregulation of banks, which continue to lie at the heart of all financial systems, and have themselves driven changes in prudential, and monetary, regulation policy. The general trend has been away from proscriptive regulation of financial activities, quantitative control of bank lending in total (in pursuit of monetary control) and to sectors of the economy (in pursuit of development policy), and qualitative controls and guidance; see Hermes et al. (1998, 2000). Quantitative and qualitative controls and guidance have been largely replaced in many countries with a price (interest rate) orientated monetary policy and general regulations. The latter include: risk-related capital adequacy requirements (CARs); deposit insurance schemes (also risk related in the US); rules prohibiting overexposure (to individuals, sectors of the economy, or foreign exchange risk); and rules requiring the holding of adequate reserves to assure liquidity and to make provisions against bad or doubtful debts. To enhance supervision by the authorities, confidential disclosure rules are enforced; and to facilitate monitoring by equity and bond holders, public disclosure and auditing requirements are imposed. Finally, to aid comparison in the increasingly global environment, accounting and disclosure rules are in the process of being harmonized and country-based supervisors are increasingly sharing information about banks and other financial firms. The general trend is towards establishing a set of rules that encourage banks and other financial institutions to manage their asset and liability portfolio risks effectively. If banks achieve an appropriate balance between risk and return, then depositors will be protected while shareholders earn a suitable return; systemic risk, the risk of destabilizing crises in the whole banking system, will be minimized, and capital will be more efficiently allocated.

The banking and wider financial markets are rapidly being 'globalized'. The process started in the 1970s with the internationalization of banking (Pecchioli, 1983). This was followed by a period of rapid innovation in the capital markets, often dubbed 'securitization', in the 1980s. Securitization involves both disintermediation, the growth of non-bank-intermediated or direct (from the capital markets) finance, and a process of 'making loans tradable' on securities markets, or using asset-backed securities. The securitization process has continued into the 1990s, and has been enhanced by the rapid growth in the use of financial derivatives or 'derivatization'.

Also, in the 1990s, there has been a progressive relaxation of capital controls. Some countries moved earlier than others, for example, the UK in

1979, but relaxation of capital controls has been increasingly encouraged by the International Monetary Fund (IMF) as a means of stimulating inward portfolio and direct (in plant and machinery and so on) investment to facilitate economic development. The result has been a rapid growth in overseas portfolio investments by mutual, insurance and pensions funds, with UK and US institutional investors playing a prominent role. Further, the conclusion of the GATS agreement relating to financial services in the mid-1990s encourages the opening of financial sectors in countries around the world to entry by foreign financial institutions. Progress with European financial integration, which has culminated in the European Monetary Union (EMU) and the creation of 'Euroland', is encouraging more cross-border activity in the financial service sector, including bank branching and cross-border alliances and mergers. The merger activity in Europe to date has, however, largely entailed intranational consolidation; leading to greater concentration in national banking systems, but these have increasingly faced greater competition from abroad. The US is probably experiencing the most rapid consolidation, but this is hardly surprising given the highly fragmented banking system it had at the beginning of the 1990s due to strict branching restrictions. At the end of the 1990s, consolidation also began in Japan's banking and wider financial system.

The picture seems to be one of the evolution of global banks competing on a global stage. This is most advanced in the investment banking sphere, but is likely to become increasingly evident as a result of the 'internet revolution'. Banks can now offer services across borders without a branch network. Entry is thus much easier and competition is consequently getting intense. Retail banks, engaged primarily in deposit banking, the provision of payments services and lending, face competition on both sides of the balance sheet and in service provision. Competition in the provision of loans (home, car and so on), including that from credit card companies, is clearly increasing. There is also growing competition in the savings market from internet-based 'banks', mutual funds, and the providers of longer-term savings investments, especially pension providers. The big banks have also seen their share of the supply of debt finance to the larger firms decline as they switch increasingly to direct finance from the capital (bonds) and money (commercial paper) markets. Increasingly, 'commercial' or retail banks are left supplying commercial loans to small and medium-sized enterprises (SMEs). Competition in SME financing is, however, also hotting up in the US as the big banks attempt to 'cherry pick' using mail-shots based on the analyses of their growing databases.

Banks have been forced to refocus their businesses. Many retail-based banks have diversified into investment banking in order to help their large corporate clients access the money and capital markets. In so doing they have boosted their ('broking' and 'market making') fee income to compensate for the lost interest-based earnings from the loans they used to make. The combination of investment and retail banking is sometimes called 'universal banking'. This has long been permitted in parts of Europe, but was not the custom in the UK (or France before the mid-1960s) and was prohibited in the US post-1933, and in post-war Japan. Japan is in the process of relaxing the restrictions imposed by the US administration after the Second World War, and the US has recently repealed the 1933 Glass–Steagall Act restrictions considerably. Universal banking has long been the norm in Germany and Switzerland, for example. In Germany, however, universal banks commonly hold sizeable shareholdings in non-financial firms. Cross-shareholding between Japanese 'city banks' and other '*keiretsu*' member firms are also significant, and cross-shareholding between banks, insurance companies and non-financial firms is also common in France and Italy, for example. EU banking regulations limit the proportion of a bank's capital that can be held as shareholdings in non-financial companies and the current trend is to reduce cross-shareholdings, which raises a number of issues for competition and prudential regulation policy (should banks own non-banks and vice versa?). There are also competition and corporate governance issues and these have come to the fore in the 1990s, leading to pressure on banks to reduce their shareholdings in non-financial firms. The prudential concerns about non-financial firms owning banks relate to the risk of the owning firms exploiting banking depositors by forcing banks to supply cheap finance and the risk that the owning firms might be brought into the lender-of-last-resort and 'too big to be allowed to fail' safety nets. This might also be true in cases where banks own non-financial firms, whose failure would undermine the banks.

It should also be noted that although financial conglomeration is becoming the norm in most national systems, especially among Organization for Economic Cooperation and Development (OECD) countries, there are two approaches to corporate structuring. The integrated firm approach has been common in mainland Europe, while the UK has tended to favour a holding company approach, and the US is set to do so too. Diversification in the US has hitherto been required to take place through separately capitalized subsidiaries in the hope of erecting 'firewalls' between them. These have yet to be tested, but there is considerable doubt about their likely effectiveness in face of 'too big to fail' considerations. There does, however, seem to be an emerging trend towards converting integrated universal banks into holding companies with specialist retail (including telephone and/or internet), corporate and investment, asset management and (see below) insurance subsidiaries.

The banks have sought to diversify their retail financial activities, often hoping to cross-sell products (for example, house insurance on the back of home loans) or simply to exploit the information contained in enlarged databases for marketing and product development purposes. They have thus diversified their loan portfolios, often offering home loans which were traditionally the preserve of specialist savings banks in many countries (savings and loans companies in the US, and building societies in the UK, for example). In addition, they have engaged in offering insurance and pension products, leading to the development of what has been called 'bancassurance' companies. Many insurance companies are also in the process of entering banking; often through the internet or telephone-based services.

The development of global bancassurance firms providing retail banking, insurance, and asset management (pensions and mutual funds and so on), as well as investment banking services worldwide is thus on the verge of a reality. The large financial conglomerates will of course continue to compete with narrower specialist and domestically based institutions, some of which will be 'national champions' formed by domestic mergers. Some big questions remain.

The globalization process has been facilitated by regulatory and supervisory harmonization. Initially this consisted of an attempt to create a 'level playing field' for international banks through the 1988 Basle Concordat on risk-related capital adequacy requirements and subsequent recommendations from the 'Basle Committee'. The creation of the 'single market' in the European Union (EU) required the adoption of the second European Commission (EC) Banking Directive 1989. This consolidated the 'continental European' model of universal banking, which combines investment and commercial banking, and permitted the development of bancassurance. Throughout most of the 1990s, Japan and the US maintained (though progressively relaxed, especially in the US) banking laws that separated investment and commercial banking and banking from insurance. In 1998 Japan introduced 'Big Bang' legislation laying out a phased relaxation of these restrictions, and in 1999 liberalizing legislation was passed in the US. As predicted in Mullineux (1992, Ch. 1), the drive to achieve international competitive equality has led to the adoption of the more liberal, in terms of the scope of banking activity, 'continental' European regime. This has in turn increased the range and intensity of competition among the increasingly globalized large banks. In such a context, does the present, largely nationally based regulatory system provide for adequate regulation supervision of the emerging global bancassurance companies and increasingly interlinked national capital market and the internet-based financial markets and transactions?

Are gaps being left in the provision of financial services to low-income and other minority groups, and is financial exclusion being aggravated by the shrinkage through merger-induced and other closures of costly bank branch networks?

The latter question is beyond the scope of this book, although in the global context the potential financial exclusion of developing countries has become an issue as the Basle II capital adequacy requirements are being finalized. The creation of financial conglomerates or 'wide banks', however, raises the question of how they should be regulated. Commercial banks (banks engaged in lending and deposit-taking businesses with personal and corporate customers) have traditionally been regarded as special. This is because: (i) they are the dominant financial institutions in terms of repositories for savings and providers of finance; (ii) they are the main providers of payments services, which are infrastructural to modern commerce; and (iii) among financial institutions, they alone have liabilities which are money and are thus the most important potential contributors to the inflation-generating process. Thus banks have been regulated separately from other financial institutions in most countries. As banks have diversified, other formerly specialist financial institutions have entered into banking. Hence, the continuing need to regulate banks separately has been questioned. The UK, Sweden and Japan have already introduced FSAs. The letters stand for different words in each country, Financial Services Authority in the UK, Financial Supervisory Agency in Japan, and Financial Supervisory Authority in Sweden, but the approach is similar. All providers of financial services have the same regulator and the regulator is a semi-autonomous government agency, which is not the central bank. Central banks, to the extent that they were responsible for bank and wider financial sector regulation and supervision, are now required to concentrate on inflation control and have been given independent (of the Finance Ministry/Treasury) power to set interest rates in pursuit of this goal, subject to an agreed level of accountability to the legislature. The US, with its complex array of bank and other regulators, each with their own vested interests, has yet to move in this direction, however.

As we move to the global stage, we have noted that the Basle Committee of international bank regulators and supervisors has driven international bank regulatory and supervisory harmonization, while the International Organization of Security Commissions (IOSCO) has led harmonization in the sphere of capital market regulation and supervision. There are numerous gaps in global cooperation, however, and there is no global (or EU-wide) regulatory and supervisory organization. As a response to the Asian finance crisis of the late 1990s, however, the Financial Stability Forum has been established to promote international financial stability through enhanced information exchange and institutional cooperation in financial market supervision and surveillance. The IMF, the International Bank for Reconstruction and Development (World Bank), the Basle Committee (BIS), the OECD, IOSCO and the International Association of Insurance Supervisors (IAIS) are all participating, along with representatives of 'offshore banking' groupings.

In general, banking in the new millennium will be directly influenced by the main developments in the banking space in the last three decades, including the Second EC Banking Directive in 1987, the Basle Concordat in 1988, the Japanese Big Bang in 1998, recently the repeal of the Glass–Steagall Act in the US in 1999, global regulatory harmonization, financial sector liberalization and capital account liberalization, and the computing and information technology (IT) revolutions. All these developments increase the mobility of capital and facilitate the creation of a single global financial space. However, niche players and geographically segregated markets still exist in securities business, retail banking and SME banking.

## 3 PATTERNS OF CORPORATE FINANCING AND FINANCIAL SYSTEMS CONVERGENCE

### A Single Financial Space in Europe?

Murinde et al. (2000) investigate whether there has been some convergence in the EU in terms of the structure of the financial systems as well as the patterns of corporate financing activities by banks, bond markets, stock markets and non-financial corporates (NFCs) themselves through retained earnings. First, a test for convergence is used to investigate the possibility of a shift towards a sustained increase in the relative share of bank financing as a percentage of the overall capital structure of NFCs, given an initial level (say at 1972), in a manner that suggests the economies are moving towards a bank-orientated system as well as a pattern of corporate financing that relies predominantly on bank debt. Second, the convergence test is applied to determine whether there has been a shift towards a sustained increase in the relative share of equity (and/or bond) financing as a percentage of the overall NFC investment financing, given an initial level, in a manner that suggests the economies are moving towards a capital market-orientated system as well as a pattern of corporate financing that relies predominantly on bonds and equity issues. Finally, the convergence test is applied to determine whether there has been a shift towards a sustained increase in the relative share of internal finance as a percentage of the total NFC investment financing, given an initial level, in a manner that suggests the managers of the NFCs behave in conformity with the pecking-order theory of financing choices and hence utilize retained earnings first before they resort to debt, equity or bond financing. The overall results also shed light on whether the financial systems of EU member countries are converging towards a 'bank-orientated' or a 'capital market-orientated' model. See also Chapter 4 by Dermine in this book.

General method of moments (GMM) estimation is applied on a dynamic fixed effects model for convergence on a panel of OECD flow of funds data for seven EU member countries with special reference to the financing of NFCs, hence shedding light on the interaction between the financial and real sectors in the context of the convergence criteria. The study covers the period in which there has been substantial financial innovation, liberalization and regulatory reform; the process started in the 1970s in some of the countries under study here (for example, the UK; see Mullineux, 1987a) and accelerated in the 1980s, particularly from the mid-1980s in the UK and France (Mullineux, 1987b; Bertero, 1994). Broadly, as noted in Section 2, the 1970s can be regarded as the decade of internationalization and the 1980s as the decade of securitization leading into an explosion in the use of derivatives in the late 1980s and early 1990s. During this period, exchange rate controls have been progressively lifted both outside and within Europe, banking systems and stock exchanges have been deregulated and reformed and new regulatory and supervisory systems have been devised through the work of the Basle Committee. The net result of these international processes, combined with the single financial market programme within the EU (Mullineux, 1992), has been an increase of competition within and between member-country banking systems and between these systems and capital markets, particularly with regard to providing finance to NFCs. The process of securitization might be expected to have led to convergence in the EU and, if it continues, to encourage further convergence. The growing competition among alternative financial systems within the EU and between the EU and other countries can also be expected to force convergence. A similar array of financial products has increasingly become available in all countries as 'gaps' in the market are progressively identified and exploited.

However, Brealey and Myers (2000, pp. 383–4) report that for all NFCs in the US over 1981–94, internally generated cash was the dominant source of corporate financing and covered, on average, 75 per cent of capital expenditures, including investment in inventory and other current assets; the bulk of required external financing came from bank debt; net new stock issues were very minimal. The observation is consistent with the findings by Rajan and Zingales (1995) in their international comparisons of capital structures in seven OECD countries, as well as the evidence by Corbett and

Jenkinson (1994), Bertero (1994) and Edwards and Fischer (1994) in selected OECD countries. However, these studies also find some evidence of a shift from bank loans to direct financing from the capital (and particularly the bond) markets as part of the securitization process associated with the financial liberalization of the 1980s.

Nevertheless, in the context of the EU countries, the observed patterns of corporate financing seem to mask the sharp dichotomy in the structure of financial systems. A contrast is drawn between Anglo-Saxon (capital market-orientated) financial systems, as represented by the UK, and continental (banking-orientated) financial systems, as typified by Germany and most of continental Europe (Doukas et al., 1998, p. 10). In a conventional sense, the term 'banking orientated' involves bank lending via the creation of demand deposits in connection with a debt contract between the bank and the borrower, deposit taking and the provision of associated money transmission services to the public. Nevertheless, banks, especially in the EU, are increasingly engaging in both banking and securities business, that is, universal banking, fund management and, more recently, insurance business ('bancassurance' or 'Allfinance'). The term 'bank orientated', therefore, may have various interpretations. It could mean a system in which banks are the dominant institutions providing both indirect (or intermediated debt) finance and access to direct finance from the money and capital markets via instruments such as commercial bills and paper (money market debt finance), bonds and euronotes (capital market debt finance) or shares (capital market equity finance), *inter alia*. The key distinctions here are between direct and indirect finance and between debt and equity financing. Since banking fundamentally involves the provision of indirect debt finance, 'bank orientated' could more narrowly be taken to mean that the most important source of external financing for NFCs is bank loans.

With reference to the EU, therefore, a bank-orientated system could be viewed as one in which banks are the key financial institutions as regards corporate governance by virtue of being both providers of debt finance and the key institutional holders of equity, as in the universal banking system of Germany (and to some extent France; Bertero, 1994). In contrast, in capital market-orientated systems the key institutional shareholders are pension and insurance funds. This is especially true in the UK, where share ownership remains heavily concentrated (see Mayer, 1994). Hitherto, the institutional shareholders in the UK have not exercised their voting rights (including proxy voting rights) as actively as the German *Grossbanken* (Deutsche, Dresdner and so on). The capital markets in the UK also influence management behaviour via the threat posed by aggressive mergers and acquisitions activity. In contrast, in continental Europe, unsolicited takeover bids have, at least until recently, been largely unknown.

The relative merits of the bank- and capital market-orientated systems is integral to the policy debates on the evolution of financial systems in the EU member countries following the Single European Market of 1993. If direct financing is increasing relative to bank financing, the capital markets will have a greater role to play in the future in hitherto bank-dominated financial systems. To the extent that bank-orientated systems are more 'long termist', this trend may lead to a spread of 'short termism' in investment and 'research and development' expenditure decisions. Counteracting this development, and helping to deepen capital markets in previously bank-dominated systems, the privatization of pensions, in response to an ageing population, and the associated budgetary pressures being caused by maintaining 'pay-as-you-go' state pension schemes, will lead to a buildup of pension funds. These funds will increasingly invest in shares (equities) as restrictions requiring large proportions of the funds in domestic government bonds are removed in response to competitive pressures to achieve acceptable returns for the investors. Because pension funds are dealing with long-term savings, they naturally take a strategic view and this should help counteract any bias towards short termism. The creation of the single currency area within the EU (Euroland) has already boosted the development of a European corporate bond market. The continued rapid growth in the euro-based corporate bond market should further reduce the role of bank loans as a source of corporate debt finance.

The question remains, however, whether the different financial systems in the EU have exhibited a tendency to converge over time, following the Single European Market of 1993. In the context of EU financial systems and the patterns of corporate financing, the 'convergence criterion' reflects the expectations of EU member countries that the launching of a borderless Europe in January 1993 would impact on the financial systems of these economies by facilitating the achievement of a single financial space in the EU. This moved a step closer with the decision to proceed with the creation of a single currency adopted by most of the EU states in January 1999. In Euroland, convergence can be expected to accelerate. See also Chapter 4 by Dermine and Chapter 5 by Gardener, Molyneux and Williams in this book.

**Evidence on Convergence in the EU**

Although the data used by Murinde et al. (2000) are different from those used by Corbett and Jenkinson (1994), Bertero (1994) and Edwards and Fischer (1994), the main findings are consistent with the general conclusions in the literature. These authors, as well as Mullineux (1996), find that the level of bank financing is similar in gross terms in Germany and the UK, the two countries that are de facto characterized by different banking systems. Our results do not exhibit convergence perhaps because much further convergence cannot be expected, given the level of similarity in bank financing in these countries as documented by the above authors.

However, Murinde et al. (2000) obtain results which suggest that over time and across the seven EU member countries the NFCs have generally shifted towards the use of equity finance for new investment; the stock markets have also increasingly become important as a means of raising equity finance for new investment by NFCs. However, the UK remains a bit of an outlier. These results are interpreted as providing reliable evidence that the EU member countries are converging towards a capital market-orientated system, in the context of an increase in the relative share of the equity market (compared to that of banks and bond markets) in the overall financing of new investment by NFCs. It is also shown that the nominal exchange rate and the interest rate are not potent monetary policy instruments in facilitating the convergence of the equity markets in the seven EU member countries.

Further evidence suggests that there has been a tendency towards convergence among the EU member countries in terms of the use of company bond finance by NFCs. It is shown that over time and across the seven countries the NFCs have shifted towards the use of bond issues to finance new investment. Moreover, as noted previously, the formation of Euroland can be expected to accelerate the growth of the euro-dominated corporate bond market if the US is any guide.

The evidence on convergence with respect to internal finance is consistent with the results obtained by Corbett and Jenkinson (1994), Bertero (1994) and Edwards and Fischer (1994) who find that high levels of internal financing are confirmed for the UK and Germany, particularly in the net figures and after noting that capital transfers can be regarded as internal sources for publicly owned corporations in Germany. These studies also find that in the Spanish case, perhaps surprisingly given the relatively early stage of financial sector restructuring in that country, internal financing counts for a very high level of investment financing while, in net terms, bank financing and, in the 1990s, equity financing, make a negative contribution.

As they participate in a single market inaugurated in 1993 and as a result of the ongoing restructuring of their banking systems, EU member countries may expect convergence of their financial systems on the evolving 'continental' European model. This model depicts heavy reliance on internal financing with bank-intermediated lending decreasing in importance and increasingly competing with direct financing via equity and bond markets (especially the euronote and bond markets) in the declining market for the external financing of investment. This might be the main plausible interpretation of the evidence obtained in this study. We find that there is a shift towards convergence, conditional as well as unconditional, with respect to equity financing and internal financing of NFCs in seven EU member countries; however, the shift is less pronounced with respect to bond issues, while there is hardly any convergence at all with respect to bank debt (or the banking system). However, a great leap forward has occurred in the development of the corporate bond market following the adoption of the euro in January 1999, further undermining the dominance of bank debt finance and pointing to convergence on the US financial system, where the corporate bond markets are much more developed. In some countries, the banks are also progressively diversifying into the provision of underwriting and brokerage (of financial instruments) services to the NFCs, who previously borrowed from them more heavily via bank loans. The results of this study may be interpreted as suggesting that the 'continental European universal banking' model, in the sense of banks combining lending and securities business, is becoming relevant for the EU as a whole.

All in all, the EU Single Market launched in 1993 and the ongoing restructuring of banking systems in most EU countries are expected to facilitate convergence of the financial systems in the EU towards the 'continental model'. This is also true of the UK, given the virtual disappearance of indigenous independent investment banks. It is only in the US that investment banks flourish as separate entities. It is also argued that convergence will occur in terms of the patterns of corporate financing in the EU. Models are specified for each of the four elements of the capital structure of NFCs, and are estimated and tested using data from the OECD flow of funds tables for the 1972–96 period for seven EU member countries: Finland, France, Germany, the Netherlands, Spain, Sweden and the UK. The study uncovers a number of interesting findings. First, there is no significant evidence of a tendency towards convergence among the EU member countries in terms of the use of bank debt by NFCs. Thus, contrary to the expectations of many policy makers and media pundits, it would appear that over time and across the seven countries the NFCs have not shifted towards the use of bank debt for financing new investment. Nor is there reliable evidence that the EU member countries are converging towards a bank-orientated system, in the sense of an increase in the relative share of the banking system in the overall financing of new investment by NFCs. These results seem to be impervious to a monetary policy stance involving exchange rate or interest rate instruments.

In general, however, the evidence suggests some form of overall convergence of the EU financial systems on a continental variant of the Anglo-Saxon model, depicting heavy reliance on internal financing with bank-intermediated lending decreasing in importance but increasingly competing with direct financing via equity and bond markets in the declining market for the external financing of investment. Following the repeal of the Glass–Steagall Act in 1999, the US financial system may well tend to converge on the same point as large corporations seek both credit lines and the underwriting of securities issues from their 'bankers'.

## 4  GLOBALIZATION, WTO AND GATS

For most of the 1990s, at least until the breakout of the Asian financial crisis, trade in financial services was seen as a necessary step towards globalization. Indeed, the growth rate enjoyed by the Asian 'tigers' had reached miracle status (Murinde, 1996). However, after the crisis and the associated contagion effects, governments and major financial institutions are counting the costs as the collapse of prices and spreads across the emerging markets (Taylor, 1999).

The inauguration of the WTO introduced new and important issues to trade negotiations, mainly pertaining to trade-related intellectual property rights, trade-related investment measures, and trade in services, as represented by the GATS. However, the provisions regarding trade in financial services, as contained in the GATS, have proved to be a source of considerable anxiety for the non-industrialized countries generally. Partly, this may be because the consequences of the GATS are not well understood and there is a sense among these countries that they are being pressurized into signing up for something which may yet turn out to be to their detriment.

Chapter 26 by Murinde and Ryan in this book evaluates the potential effects of the GATS on developing countries. It is argued that developing countries have concerns which differ considerably from the bulk of the developed nations. In general, with respect to the banking industry, there is a general presumption that the GATS will largely enshrine historic comparative advantage and favour the existing market leaders at the expense of other countries with a less developed presence in international financial markets. However, it would be wrong to imagine that the gains from financial liberalization will accrue only to the suppliers of international financial services or indeed that domestic banks will be wiped out, at least on the basis of the evidence from the European Single Market experiment. The recommendation offered by Murinde and Ryan (Chapter 26 in this book) is that the developing economies should respond strategically to the prospect of the GATS in terms of restructuring their domestic banking industry well ahead of the full liberalization required by the WTO and the GATS.

## 5  TRENDS IN CORPORATE GOVERNANCE

The competing financial systems ('Anglo-Saxon' versus 'Germanic', or 'market' versus 'bank-orientated') debate is often couched in terms of implications for corporate governance and indeed society as a whole. The debate is often somewhat confused as a result of the influence of 'financial myths' (Mishkin, 2001, Ch. 1). We have already noted that internal, rather than externally supplied, finance is the major source of investment finance for both large corporates and SMEs. We have also noted that in all countries SMEs are largely dependent on banks for external finance, and that banks are the major suppliers of finance to the non-financial business sector. Only in the US is the corporate bond market a major alternative (to loans) source of debt finance, although the introduction of the euro has resulted in accelerated development of the European corporate bond market. Even in the US, banks remain the main suppliers of debt finance, however, and it is only the large corporates that can tap the traditional bond market, while 'growth firms' in the new technology sectors can increasingly tap the higher-risk 'junk bond' market. Further, the 'equity market' is a market in second-hand stocks through which ownership is transferred. In years of high merger and acquisition activity and share 'buy-backs' the *net* supply of new equity finance through the market is frequently *negative* in the US and the UK. Markets specializing in financing new companies, again usually in the new technology sectors (for example, NASDAQ and the Neur Markt), tend to be net suppliers of equity, but often as a result of replacing and expanding the investments of venture capitalists and other private equity holders. The latter have been growing in importance as an alternative to banks for early-stage 'growth' firms in the technology sector.

In sum, even in Anglo-Saxon systems, banks remain the dominant sources of finance, the more so as the commercial banks diversify from making loans into wider, securities-related, corporate finance. Hence the bank versus market-dominated distinction is outmoded. We have also noted that the, generally liberalizing, reregulation of banks and other financial institutions is also driving to convergence of the scope of 'banks' and other financial institutions (on the 'continental' European model), hence the Germanic versus Anglo-Saxon distinction between financial systems is losing meaning too.

It is, however, true that a larger proportion of indirect finance is, at least for the larger firms, being provided through bond (debt), equity and money (commercial paper and bills and notes) markets. As such, there is convergence on an 'Americanized' continental European system, that is, one in which the main players are diversified bank and insurance companies (and also some specialized investment banks for a while) and mutual and pension funds, but financial markets are becoming increasingly important. The insurance, mutual and pension funds are, however, increasingly becoming the dominant institutional investors as pensions are progressively being privatized and banks disengage from cross-shareholdings in Japan and the EU (particularly Germany).

The convergence of financial systems is leading to a convergence of corporate governance mechanisms. For the, largely private, SME sector there is less change. Banks remain the key players in their governance unless management control is diluted by taking on equity finance from outside (private equity, venture funds). For larger firms that have issued equity to the public and/or taken on bond financing, institutional investors can be expected to play an increasing role in governance relative to banks; but banks will also remain key actors. Given the, seemingly growing, importance of internal finance in larger firms, good management is necessary to ensure that efficient use is made of retained earnings. Here issues pertaining to the structure of management boards, the role of non-executive directors, and whether the roles of chairman and chief executive officer should be separated become increasingly important. Further, stock markets play a role in providing a market for corporate control to keep the managers on their toes. Behind the markets are the institutional shareholders, who must decide which shares to hold in their portfolios and in what proportions.

Through the institutional shareholders, the interests of small investors and pensioners are represented and legislation can be used to encourage investors to take account of ethical and environmental considerations in constructing their investment portfolios (for example, the 1999 pensions fund legislation in the UK).

The interests of stakeholders other than shareholders can also be brought to bear through legislation on management board membership (for example, requiring worker and/or consumer representation, as is the case in a number of countries). By such means the tiger of global capitalization can be tamed and capital will be directed in such a way as to ensure its most efficient (from social as well as financial or economic perspectives) use. Growth will be enhanced and poverty reduced as a result. Social auditing will increasingly complement traditional financial auditing. To achieve this, however, countries must adopt common accounting standards, and adopt best practices in financial sector regulation and, partly as a result of the former, conformable corporate governance (including bankruptcy procedures) systems.

Thus, some important conclusions may be drawn from the above trends in corporate governance in the global financial space. It is noted that the growth in internal finance (retained earnings) exacerbates the principal –agent problem. The growth in direct finance reduces the role of banks in corporate governance and this tendency is enhanced by their declining role as institutional investors through cross-shareholdings (particularly in Germany and Japan). Bondholders (often banks and other financial institutions), not just shareholders, are increasingly important. However, banks remain the key monitors of SMEs. Stock markets, through secondary trading, are markets for corporate control as well as sources of new finance through initial public offerings (IPOs). Institutional shareholders (insurance, pension and mutual funds) are increasingly the key players in corporate governance (though individual shareholdings have increased dramatically in the last five years in the US and continental Europe, but increasingly not in the UK); these shareholders are playing a more active role in ensuring that companies have good management structure and internal controls. However, the increased emphasis on shareholder value may lead to short termism (as opposed to long termism associated with universal banking). If the US is typical, the benefits of greater innovation and flexibility may outweigh any costs of short termism. Further, short termism tends to increase pressure to distribute profits as dividends, reducing capital 'hoarding' for internal investment. Stakeholders other than shareholders may, however, need protecting. This could be done through social auditing (a precursor is recent UK pension legislation).

## 6  WHERE DO WE GO FROM HERE?

### Globalization and Financial Crises

The growing threat of global crisis is fuelling a debate over the means available to contain and resolve it, as well as over the ways in which countries can protect themselves from its consequences (see Guitian, 1999). The world economy has become so closely integrated that not only do countries need to ensure that they manage their own economies well; they must also be ready to anticipate, and adapt to, economic mismanagement elsewhere. The first issue that needs to be addressed is determining what individual countries can do to cope with volatile capital flows. For the orderly liberalization of capital flows, a second issue needs to be addressed: the development of norms and procedures that all countries agree upon and that are flexible enough to cover all potential country situations. A few time-tested principles of international relationships are eminently well suited for the purpose at hand: a provision to allow countries a measure of flexibility; a set of common prudential norms; a principle of temporary international acceptance of restrictive measures; and a provision to allow countries to resort temporarily to controls.

The most pertinent issue, therefore, relates to ways of dealing with financial crises. Clearly, financial crises in Latin America and Asia since 1994 have drawn attention to the potential dangers of globalization of the international financial system (Arner, 1998). In order to prevent the collapse of the financial system of the countries involved and reduce the risk of potential contagion throughout the international financial system, international financial rescues of unprecedented proportions have been organized for Mexico, Thailand, Indonesia and South Korea. The magnitude of these international financial packages and the as yet indeterminate impact that they will have on the international financial system underline a number of ongoing changes in the international financial system. The basic causes of the crises and the nature of the international rescues, beginning with the Mexican peso crisis, are diverse and no uniform rules apply.

Overall, there is need for strengthening the architecture of the international financial system in the wake of these crises. The idea is to explore what can be learned from these events about the opportunities and risks of a global financial market and how the architecture of the international financial system can be strengthened to realize the potential of a twenty-first-century global economy. The time has come for a more systematic approach to strengthening national financial systems that would involve a more intensive assessment of their vulnerabilities and steps to promote reforms.

## Revamping the Tools of Country-risk and Credit-risk Analysis and Management

The traditional country-risk analysis techniques were developed in the 1970s at the height of international bank-lending activities. The motivation was to develop statistical tools which would facilitate the assessment of country risk that could be associated with a given prospective borrower. It was also intended that the models would be applied to forecast the probability of risk associated with future loan transactions. Moreover, the statistical techniques were intended to supplant purely descriptive methods which were being applied by some analysts. Descriptive or informal methods of country-risk assessment relied on political descriptive information to formulate some qualitative judgements on the risk associated with loan obligations with a given country. Some countries were rated as good risks while others were rated as poor risks, without any quantitative indicator of how risk prone these countries were. In general, the main methods of country-risk analysis that have been used in the literature can be classified into four groups; namely, full qualitative methods, structural qualitative methods, checklist methods and quantitative techniques. The main statistical techniques include linear-probability models, logit models, probit models, discriminant analysis, principal components analysis and dynamic programming models. See Murinde (1996, Ch. 9) for details on these methods and their applications.

Consequently, a number of specialist agencies for analysing credit risk, political risk and country risk have emerged over the last two decades. The main ones include Moody's; Standard and Poor's; S.J. Rundt Associates of New York; Multi National Strategies of New York; Political Risk Services of New York; the Institute of International Finance of Washington, DC; International Country Risk Guide of New York; and the Economist Intelligence Unit, London.

Notwithstanding the useful models for country-risk analysis reviewed in this chapter, it is a formidable challenge to accurately assess and predict country risk. The experience of the global debt burden bears testimony to the fact that financial institutions can get country-risk predictions wrong. The main shortcoming of the main models used to predict country risk is that, in general, these models depend on expectations; analysts try to cope with expectations by tempering the models with judgement and knowledge of the underlying structure.

Moreover, the onset of globalization and the end of the cold war have introduced new complications. For example, developing economies will have to compete with one another for external finance. On the side of developing-country governments, there is an increasing awareness of the need to restructure their economies and make them attractive to foreign investors. On the side of investors, there is increasing activity in monitoring the investment climate around the world.

It is therefore necessary to reconsider the traditional tools of country-risk analysis. The series of devaluations and soaring numbers of troubled banks and borrowers in Asia and other countries took many analysts by surprise. In general, the global economy and, especially, the growth and globalization of capital markets have put new strains on the system and created new challenges for risk managers. As recently as January 1996, participants in surveys of country-risk practices still focused on traditional macroeconomic measures in risk-grading country exposure (Hayes, 1998). The future lies in devising more comprehensive tools of risk analysis and management.

**International Coordination of Bank Regulation**

There is urgent need for bank regulators to coordinate regulation following incidents with transnational implications, such as the failure of the UK's Barings Bank and the fraudulent activity at the New York branch of

Japan's Daiwa Bank (Prasad, 1998). At the same time, local bank managers need to put in place programmes for complying with the changing international regulatory environment and international bank management in a rapidly expanding regulatory environment.

**Financial Discipline**

After an empirical assessment of the impact of the globalization of financial markets on developing and transition economies, Knight (1998) argues that imperfectly competitive banking sectors can react perversely to adverse economic shocks. It is found that while non-bank financial markets and institutions can enhance the competitiveness of the banking sector, there are gaps in the institutional and market structures of developing and transition economies. Eliminating these gaps may reinforce financial market discipline in developing and transition economies. Thus, international initiatives for enhancing financial system soundness should emphasize the complementary roles of market discipline and official oversight in an environment of globalized markets.

**The Agenda for Policy Makers**

The question of how to redesign the global financial system is a major issue confronting finance ministers, central bankers, commercial and investment bankers, technocrats at multilateral organizations, and academics.

The issues discussed by the G7 finance ministers at a meeting on 8 May 1998 included ways of strengthening the global financial system, improving cooperation between supervisors of internationally active financial firms, and fighting crime. In regard to strengthening the global financial system, five key areas were identified as requiring action: (i) enhanced transparency and data transmission, (ii) assisting countries in their preparation of integration into the global economy and for free capital flows, (iii) strengthening national financial systems, (iv) ensuring that the private sector takes responsibility for its lending decisions, and (v) enhancing further the role of the international financial institutions and cooperation among them and with the international forums (see Casson, 1998).

**The Age of Internet Banking and Finance**

As a result of very rapid increases in telecommunications and computer-based technologies and products, a dramatic expansion in financial flows, both cross-border and within countries, has emerged. These technology-based developments have so expanded the breadth and depth of markets that governments, even reluctant ones, increasingly have felt they have had little alternative but to deregulate and free up internal credit and financial markets. Still, for central bankers with responsibilities for financial market stability, the new technologies and new instruments have presented new challenges. It should be recognized that, if it is technology that has imparted the current stress to markets, technology can be employed to contain it. Enhancements to financial institutions' internal risk-management systems arguably constitute the most effective countermeasure to the increased potential instability of the global financial system. Improving the efficiency of the world's payment systems is clearly another.

**Concluding Remarks**

In a nutshell, the goal of a single global financial space is to harness the benefits of greater access to external financial markets by developing countries while reducing the risks of sudden reversals of capital inflows. The current initiatives involve strengthening the 'global financial architecture' through institutional, regulatory and supervisory reform (Financial Stability Forum, BIS), and improving country and credit risk analysis (Institute for International Finance, IIF). On the part of developing countries, more fiscal restraint is urged, along with, more controversially, more flexible exchange rates (as, for example, in Argentina, Bulgaria, Estonia and Hong Kong). Proposals to restrict capital outflows (Malaysia) and discourage capital inflows (Chile) have made little progress since neither is effective in the long run and they seem to discourage long-term direct investment. Thus, globalization of finance continues to gather pace, reaching through the internet beyond governments, parastatals, and major corporations into retail (household and SME) banking and finance. An interesting question for future research is: will internet banking and finance remove any remaining scope for regional variation? If so, will there be pockets of financial exclusion as a result of 'cherry picking' and what can be done about it?

# REFERENCES

Al-Deehani, T., R.A.A. Karim and V. Murinde (1999), 'The capital structure of Islamic banks under the contractual obligation of profit sharing', *International Journal of Theoretical and Applied Finance*, **2**(3), pp. 1–39.

Arner, Douglas (1998), 'An analysis of international support packages in the Mexican and Asian financial crises', *Journal of Business Law*, July, pp. 380–96.

Aybar, C. Bulent and Claudio D. Milman (1999), 'Globalization, emerging market economies and currency crisis in Asia: implications on economic reform and development', *Multinational Business Review*, **7**(2), pp. 37–44.

Bertero, E. (1994), 'The banking system, financial markets and capital structure: some evidence from France', *Oxford Review of Economic Policy*, **1014**, pp. 68–78.
Brealey, R.A. and S.C. Myers (2000), *Principles of Corporate Finance*, sixth edition, New York: McGraw Hill.
Casson, Peter (1998), 'G7 meeting: finance ministers discuss international financial stability', *Financial Regulation Report*, May, pp. 23–4.
Corbett, J. and T. Jenkinson (1994), 'The financing of industry, 1970–89: an International Comparison', CEPR Discussion Paper No. 948, May, Centre for Economic Policy Research, London.
Doukas, J., V. Murinde and C. Wihlborg (1998), *Financial Sector Reform and Privatisation in Transition Economies*, Amsterdam: Elsevier Science B.V. (North-Holland).
Edwards, J. and K. Fischer, (1994), *Banks, Finance and Investment in Germany*, Cambridge: Cambridge University Press.
Guitian, Manuel (1999), 'Economic policy implications of global financial flows', *Finance & Development*, **36**(1), pp. 26–9.
Hargis, Kent (1998), 'Do foreign investors stimulate or inhibit stock market development in Latin America?', *Quarterly Review of Economics & Finance*, **38**(3), pp. 303–18.
Hayes, Nicholas L. (1998), 'Country risk revisited', *Journal of Lending & Credit Risk Management*, **80**(5), pp. 61–75.
Hermes, N., R. Lensink and V. Murinde (1998), 'The effect of financial liberalisation on capital flight', *World Development*, **26**(7), July, pp. 1349–68.
Hermes, N., R. Lensink and V. Murinde (2000), 'Capital flight and political risk', *Journal of International Money and Finance*, **19**, pp. 73–92.
Kahn, Sharon (1998), 'The future of global banks', *Global Finance*, **12**(5), pp. 28–30.
Knight, Malcolm (1998), 'Developing countries and the globalization of financial markets', *World Development*, **26**(7), pp. 1185–200.
Knight, Malcolm (1999), 'Developing and transition countries confront financial globalization', *Finance & Development*, **36**(2), pp. 32–5.
Ludwig, Eugene A. (1999), 'The changing nature of risks in the 21st century', *Journal of Lending & Credit Risk Management*, **81**(7), pp. 32–5.
Mahbubani, Kishore (1999), 'Globalization: dangers and opportunities', *Journal of Asian Business*, **15**(1), pp. 82–5.
Mayer, C. (1994), 'The assessment: money and *banking:* theory and evidence', *Oxford Review of Economic Policy*, **10**(4), pp. 1–13.
Mishkin, F.S. (2001) *The Economics of Money and Banking*, sixth edition, New York: McGraw-Hill.
Mullineux, A.W. (1987a), *UK Banking after Deregulation*, London: Croom Helm.
Mullineux, A.W. (1987b), *International Banking and Financial Systems: A Comparison*, London: Graham & Trotman.
Mullineux, A.W. (ed.) (1992), *European Banking*, Oxford: Blackwell.
Mullineux, A.W. (1996), 'The funding of non-financial corporations (NFCs) in the EU (1971–1993): evidence of convergence?' (mimeo) Department of Economics, University of Birmingham.
Murinde, V. (1996), 'Financial markets and endogenous growth: an econometric analysis for Pacific Basin countries', in Niels Hermes and Robert Lensink (eds), *Financial Development and Economic Growth*, London and New York: Routledge, Chapter 5, pp. 94–114.

Murinde, V., J. Agung and A. Mullineux (2000), 'Convergence of European financial systems: banks or equity markets?', in M.M. Fischer and P. Nijkamp (eds), *Spatial Dynamics of European Integration: Regional Policy Issues at the Turn of the Century*, Berlin: Springer-Verlag, pp. 129–42.

Murinde, V. and K. Naser (1998), 'Operationalising the Islamic tenets of banking and finance to accommodate orthodox mortgage finance', *Accounting, Commerce and Finance: The Islamic Perspective Journal*, **3**(2), pp. 1–23.

Murinde, V., K. Naser and R.S.O. Wallace (1995), 'Is it prudent for Islamic banks to make investment decisions without the interest rate instrument?', *Research in Accounting in Emerging Economies*, **3**, pp. 123–48.

Pecchioli, R.M. (1983), *The Internationalisation of Banking*, Paris: OECD.

Prasad, Srinivas B. (1998), 'The global convergence of bank regulation and standards for compliance', *Banking Law Journal*, **115**(6), pp. 550–96.

Rajan, R.G. and L. Zingales (1995), 'What do we know about capital structure? Some evidence from international data', *Journal of Finance*, **50**, December, pp. 1421–60.

Taylor, Bernard (1999), 'The Darwinian shakeout in financial services', *Long Range Planning*, **32**(1), pp. 58–64.

Thiessen, Gordon (1998), 'Globalized financial markets and monetary policy', *Bank of Canada Review*, Summer, pp. 71–7.

# 2. Multinational banking: historical, empirical and case perspectives

## Elisa A. Curry, Justin G. Fung and Ian R. Harper

## 1 INTRODUCTION

One of the paradoxes of multinational banking is that the names of so many of the main players have such strong national or regional connections. BankAmerica, Banque Nationale de Paris, Deutsche Bank, Hongkong and Shanghai Banking Corporation, National Australia Bank,[1] Royal Bank of Canada and Union Bank of Switzerland are but a few instances of this paradox.

This section addresses the paradox by outlining the history and evolution of multinational banking from its parochial roots, and then Section 2 discusses various theories of multinational banking. Empirical support for the theories is examined and illustrative examples are provided. The different ways in which national or regional banks transform themselves into multinational corporations are explored in Section 3. The forms which multinational banks (MNBs) take, the reasons why particular forms are chosen and the various organizational strategies they adopt are the principal focus.

In Section 4, various themes and strands from the preceding two sections are brought together in a discussion of the performance of MNBs. In particular, Section 4 focuses on the performance of foreign MNBs in the US compared with their domestic rivals. Section 5 looks at the future of MNBs and MNB regulatory reform. The challenges to both MNBs and regulators are canvassed, particularly in the context of the ongoing consolidation of the banking and finance sector.

To begin, however, multinational banking and MNBs are defined and distinguished from international banking and international banks.

**Multinational and International Banking**

The terms 'multinational banking' and 'international banking' are often used interchangeably, particularly outside the MNB literature. Similarly, the descriptions 'multinational bank' and 'international bank' are often applied indiscriminately, or at least casually. Although clear delineation is becoming increasingly difficult, it is usual in the literature to find a distinction between 'multinational' and 'international'; these phrases have more specific connotations than in everyday idiom.

Of the two descriptions, international banking is the broader. Lewis and Davis (1987, p. 219), for example, use it to denote the 'cross-border and cross-currency facets of banking business'. They classify international banking into two main activities: traditional foreign banking and eurocurrency banking (p. 221). Traditional foreign banking involves transactions with non-residents in domestic currency to allow trade finance and other international transactions. Eurocurrency banking involves banks participating in foreign exchange transactions with both residents and non-residents. While these aspects of banking may be undertaken by MNBs, and indeed, often are, they need not be. The provision of trade finance, foreign exchange and euromarket loans are activities commonly undertaken by international banks. The international flavour of their business is not the defining characteristic of a multinational bank.

Buckley and Casson (1991, p. 33) define a multinational enterprise (MNE) as an enterprise which 'owns and controls activities in different countries'. Applying this definition to banking, MNBs can be said to 'own and control branches and/or affiliates in more than one country' (Jones, 1992, p. xiii). Robinson (1972, p. 4), Gray and Gray (1981, p. 37) and Lewis and Davis (1987, p. 219) among others, all proffer similar definitions. The defining characteristic of multinational banking is that it involves an element of foreign direct investment, and MNBs are a type of MNE. International banking and foreign banking do not require a physical banking presence offshore and on this basis can be distinguished from multinational banking.

So this chapter concerns itself with banks that have an 'institutional presence in the form of branches in one or more foreign countries' (Cho, 1985, p. 2). These MNBs may focus on multinational retail banking, providing banking services to corporate clients overseas or multinational wholesale banking (Grubel, 1977) but all are essentially involved in credit extension and funding activities and secondary businesses, such as foreign exchange. In fact, '[m]ost multinational banking activities of MNBs are basically an extension of banking activities performed by banks on the domestic level' (Cho, 1985, p. 16). Given this observation, subsequent sections examine why and how regional or domestic banks choose to establish a presence in foreign markets, before proceeding to explore the performance and future of these entities. Prior to this, a brief history of multinational banking is presented to provide the context for the material which follows.

## A Tale of Two Waves

The earliest known examples of 'international' or, perhaps more appropriately, 'inter-civilization' banking, consisted of letters of credit and bills of exchange issued across sovereign boundaries. These date back four thousand years (Walter, 1985, p. 14). 'Multinational' or perhaps 'multi-sovereign' banking, however, is a much more recent development; in the fifteenth century, the great bankers of Florence established subsidiaries or branches in foreign jurisdictions (ibid.). But leaving aside these distant antecedents and focusing on the modern era, the evolution of multinational banking is characterized by two distinct waves.

The first wave of modern multinational banking accompanied and even facilitated the rise of colonialism in the nineteenth century. So in some ways the patterns of development of multinational banking mirror those of the colonial era. Given this symbiosis, it is not surprising that banks based in Britain, the colonial superpower, dominated this wave of multinational banking. The first British MNBs opened branches in the 1830s in the Australian, Caribbean and North American colonies. These were followed two decades later by the establishment of branches in Latin America, South Africa, British India and Asia (Jones, 1992, p. xvi). These early MNBs financed much of the economic development in the British colonies and are often labelled 'British overseas banks' or 'Anglo-foreign banks'; they were headquartered in London, then the global financial capital, but only provided banking services outside the United Kingdom. British MNBs also expanded into the Middle East and continental Europe.

The other colonial powers also engaged in multinational banking on a smaller scale. In the decades following the 1870s, Belgian, French and German MNBs were particularly active, opening branches in their own colonies, Latin America and even in China. They also established a presence in London and elsewhere in Europe. The European MNBs differed in profile from their early British counterparts, however, typically conducting banking businesses in both home and foreign markets. For example, Belgium's largest domestic banking institution at the time, Société Générale, expanded its operations both by foreign acquisition and by setting up foreign subsidiaries. The French MNB, Banque de l'Indochine, was also launched by an existing domestic bank (Jones, 1990, p. 3) and the development of German multinational banking was led by domestic institutions. Nor was multinational banking in the first wave the exclusive preserve of European colonial powers. Both Japan (in the form of the Yokohama Specie Bank) and, more particularly, Canada had strong MNBs.

The decades of war and depression following 1914 effectively ended the first wave. The forces that had hitherto propelled the growth of multinational banking, namely, expanding international trade, colonialism and the strength of the British empire, all fell into decline. At the same time, nationalistic sentiment and competition from local banks in foreign markets intensified, creating further obstacles for MNBs. However, another set of factors was to culminate in the beginning of the second era of dynamic growth for multinational banking in the 1960s. Huertas (1990, p. 261) groups the catalysts for this second wave of multinational banking under three broad headings: macroeconomic, regulatory and microeconomic.

Into the first category fall the renewed vigour with which international trade and investment were pursued during the post-war boom and the return of a relatively stable political environment. With respect to regulatory change, the second wave was also promoted by regulations such as Regulation Q, which effectively limited the ability of US banks to raise funds domestically by capping interest rates payable on US deposits (ibid., p. 254). The consequent emergence of the eurodollar market encouraged many domestic US banks to circumvent the scope of Regulation Q by establishing foreign branches. As MNBs, these banks gained access to the new source of US dollar funds and this in turn allowed them to finance higher levels of domestic loans. In later decades, the gradual liberalization of domestic banking sectors in many countries also drove the second wave.

Huertas (ibid., p. 263) argues that microeconomic forces for multinational expansion were most compelling in the second wave. The startling advances in technology during this period gave internalization of international banking activities a significant cost advantage over traditional correspondent banking networks. A further inducement to expand abroad was the realization that multinational players would be better placed to capitalize on the opportunities presented by the growing importance of institutional investors and the increasing innovation in financial products and services worldwide.

Besides the different factors shaping the two periods, there are other notable distinctions between the modern waves of multinational banking. Allusions to one divergence have already been made: where the first wave was led by British institutions, US banks, minor multinational banking players until then, led the second wave. As already noted, the US MNBs were primarily motivated to expand abroad by the need to increase funding for their domestic businesses. However, they were also driven by a desire to participate in the new global economy, in which the US (and not Britain) was dominant. A second point of difference pertains to geography. Whereas MNBs in the first wave focused largely on developing countries – a consequence of the colonial nature of their growth – their descendants in the second wave were comparatively more interested in expanding into developed economies, where the above microeconomic forces might be used to greater advantage. Finally, there are also differences in the organizational structures and strategies adopted. Many of the MNBs in the nineteenth century conducted retail banking businesses abroad and, particularly for the British MNBs, these businesses were often 'green field' operations. By contrast, with some notable exceptions, such as Citibank, the second wave of multinational banking is characterized by a greater aversion to foreign retail banking, except perhaps where market entry strategies involve foreign bank acquisition. The chapter returns to these issues in Section 3.

Almost four decades having passed since the onset of the second wave, virtually all of the world's largest banking institutions are multinational. The presence of US multinational banking operations has continued to expand. At the end of 1996, the total assets of overseas branches and subsidiaries of US banks exceeded $1.1 trillion (Institute of International Bankers, 1997, p. 12). This represents a significant growth in US multinational banking activity, more than double its 1992 level (ibid., p. 12). Multinational banking entities not only dominate the international aspects of banking but also control a large share of the banking business at the local level in many countries. In the UK, approximately 58 per cent of total UK loans (in all currencies) and 26.7 per cent of sterling loans were made by branches and subsidiaries of non-UK banks at year end 1996 (ibid., p. 2). In Germany, approximately 17 per cent of loans made by private commercial banks were made by branches and subsidiaries of non-German banks at year end 1996 (ibid., p. 2).

While the external climate and influences upon multinational banking and its evolution since the early nineteenth century have been outlined in this section, only passing reference has been made to the largely internal reasons and motivations for domestic banks choosing to become multinational organizations. These theories of MNBs are dealt with explicitly in the next section.

## 2   THEORIES OF MULTINATIONAL BANKING

There are many reasons why domestic banks choose to become MNBs and a few of these have already been touched upon. Indeed, individual banks may decide to expand abroad for multiple reasons, although one or several of the rationales may be more compelling. The drivers justifying or necessitating entry may differ depending upon the specific foreign market under consideration and the external and internal circumstances at particular points in time. Grubel (1977) presents different explanations for multinational banking depending upon whether the activity involves retail, service or wholesale banking.

It is not the objective of this section to propose an overarching, unifying theory of multinational banking, or to enter into the debate between the advocates of eclectic theory[2] and those of internalization theory as frameworks for studying MNBs.[3] This is because '[a]t the level of abstraction represented by internalization theory and eclectic theory, it is not possible to generate empirically testable hypotheses' (Williams, 1997, p. 84) and the aim of this section is not only to canvass the diverse motivations which drive banks towards multinational status but also to gauge the support enjoyed by each theory in the empirical literature and relevant case studies.

The theories are discussed in turn but, for ease of exposition (rather than any claim to mutual exclusivity), they are classified into groups. The first group captures general theories relating to opportunities for growth and profit. The second contains hypotheses concerning the leveraging of strengths throughout a multinational organization; the third includes theories pertaining to bank client activities; the penultimate category groups together theories relating to risk management; and the final group comprises miscellaneous theories of multinational banking.

**Theories Relating to Growth and Profit Opportunities**

If it is assumed that banks seek to maximize growth, profit or income, or to minimize their respective opposites, then to some extent, almost every theory of multinational banking can be said to concern growth or profit opportunities. The hypotheses grouped under this heading, however, pertain to such opportunities at a broad, general level. The more specific theories are addressed in subsequent sections.

Domestic banks may explore offshore options with the general intention of increasing growth, profits or both. These potential MNBs may face mature domestic markets or an intensely competitive domestic banking and financial services sector.[4] According to the foreign market size and foreign market relative growth hypotheses, respectively, large foreign markets and foreign markets with comparatively high rates of growth have more appeal to banks seeking new growth or profit opportunities abroad (Davidson, 1980; Park and Zwick, 1984, p. 32; Nigh et al., 1986). These theories may be particularly apt for banks seeking to attract local business in offshore markets or 'looking to buy into the growth of world trade' (Bailey, 1991, p. 11). These opportunities were certainly important drivers in the Australia and New Zealand Banking Group's ('ANZ Bank') decision to expand into the Asian region in the 1980s (ibid.). While the foreign market size hypothesis has some support in the empirical literature (for example, Terrell, 1979; Davidson, 1980; Goldberg and Grosse, 1994), the relative growth hypothesis has not been extensively tested and the results are equivocal (for example, Goldberg and Saunders, 1981a).

Where the foreign banking market is not intensely competitive and entry barriers are low, growth and profit potential may also be correspondingly higher, irrespective of market size or relative growth. The foreign market competitiveness hypothesis posits that potential MNBs are more favourably disposed towards expansion into less competitive foreign banking sectors. Typically, the competitiveness of foreign banking sectors in econometric work has been gauged by concentration ratios (for example, Cho, 1985) and the theory finds some empirical support (for example, Goldberg and Johnson, 1990).

**Theories Concerning Leveraging of Strengths**

Grubel's (1977) seminal adaptation of the theory of MNEs to the study of multinational banking asserted that potential MNBs must possess (or at least perceive themselves to be in possession of) some advantage over their local competitors in foreign markets. According to this argument, banks would be reluctant to expand abroad in the absence of some competitive edge. This theory can be extended, however, to encompass the scenario where a bank acquires a foreign player with particular technology, for example, with the express intention of applying that technology to improve its own operations. The various theories of multinational banking which involve some leveraging of a bank's competitive advantages are examined in this section.

A bank's ascendancy in some aspect of its business may stem from numerous sources. It may possess or have accumulated superior management skills, knowledge and experience or have developed leading-edge business processes, practices or information technology. It may therefore seek to capitalize upon these capabilities by establishing offshore branches. National Australia Bank, for example, was confident that its 'package of products and services, systems and management [could] be effectively duplicated in other countries' (Argus, 1990, p. 4). These advantages may have been acquired through years of competing in a sophisticated domestic financial sector, through previous experiences of multinational banking or even through past operations in a similar foreign market (Tschoegl, 1982).

The econometric literature has generally found a positive association between the level of sophistication in the domestic market, usually proxied by the size of the domestic market, and the magnitude of the presence in foreign markets (for example, Grosse and Goldberg, 1991; Fisher and Molyneux, 1996; Hondroyiannis and Papapetrou, 1996).

Similarly, the impact of previous multinational experience on multinational operations was positive in Davidson's (1980) sample of MNEs.

Moreover, in Pastre's (1981) survey, more than half of the multinational respondents cited international reputation as an important factor in choosing a bank in a foreign jurisdiction. However, in the literature specific to MNBs, as opposed to MNEs in general, the measures employed to proxy for multinational experience have typically been correlated with MNB size. This has created some difficulties for testing the hypothesis since a bank may have other competitive advantages through its size or through economies of scale or scope, which may be related to size. The empirical problem is further complicated by a question of causality; namely whether large banks tend to become multinational, for example in search of new offshore growth opportunities, or whether multinational status of itself results in banks becoming large.

Of course, the difficulties in testing the multinational experience thesis also afflict tests of whether bank size or scale or scope economies influence the level of multinational banking activity. Clearly, embarking upon a multinational banking business can be a capital-consuming proposition, particularly in the light of capital adequacy requirements and the increasing importance of information technology investments. Furthermore, a large bank may have additional comparative advantages in foreign markets since it may have access to lower-cost capital. So such an enterprise may choose to take advantage of its size or capital and asset strength by expanding its business abroad. While Cho (1985) among others provides some support for the size hypothesis, as noted, isolating size from multinational experience can be problematic. Economies of scale or scope may also provide a competitive advantage which can be leveraged into a foreign market. For example, an MNB with scale economies may be able to operate on tighter interest margins, thus attracting the business of foreign borrowers and depositors. Mahajan et al. (1996) found that US MNBs exhibit economies of scale and are more efficient than their domestic peers but the results of Tschoegl (1983) among others are less definitive on this issue. Again, a question of causality arises such that multinationality may give rise to economies or the presence of economies may motivate multinational expansion.

The size of an MNB is not the sole driver of its cost of capital funds. There are a variety of sources of differences in bank cost of capital, including home-country national saving behaviour, macroeconomic policy, industrial organization, financial policy and taxes (Zimmer and McCauley, 1991, p. 33). Zimmer and McCauley find significant differences in bank cost of capital facing commercial banks in different industrial countries. They find that the increase in the market share of foreign MNBs in the US can be explained by differences in the cost of capital in the MNBs' domestic market. Cost of capital advantages arose from savings and macroeconomic policy, as well as from the relations among corporations, banks and government (ibid., p. 56). McCauley and Seth (1992) investigate foreign bank penetration of the US lending market and also find that foreign MNBs enjoyed a lower cost of capital relative to their domestic US rivals. In both cases, the market share of foreign-owned MNBs with a lower cost of capital has grown relative to rivals with a higher cost of capital.

Finally, banks without a competitive advantage may obtain an edge through the acquisition of foreign businesses, typically in sophisticated markets. For this reason, this can be labelled the 'foreign market sophistication' hypothesis. Under this theory, the objective in becoming multinational is to apply or leverage a newly acquired advantage to domestic banking operations and to any existing multinational operations. If the sophistication of the foreign market is used as a proxy, then the more advanced the market of the foreign target bank in comparison to that of the acquirer, the greater the incentive to become an MNB by making a foreign acquisition in such a market. There is little or no empirical support for this thesis. However, one of the motivations for National Australia Bank's acquisition of the US bank, Michigan National Corporation, was to obtain the potential benefits of having a significant presence in the technologically advanced US market. This strategy of 'reverse leveraging' was even more apparent in National Australia Bank's purchase of the Florida-based mortgage specialist, HomeSide Inc., whose leading-edge mortgage systems and processes were uniformly implemented throughout the bank's multinational businesses.

**Theories Pertaining to Client Activities**

The first of the hypotheses involving the activities of bank clients postulates that when domestic clients look to invest offshore, their domestic banks will establish relevant foreign representation to continue providing services abroad. A decision to become multinational in such circumstances may be defensive in the sense that a failure to do so may result in the loss of a multinational domestic client, not only in foreign markets, but perhaps domestically as well, as the client may choose to bank instead with a foreign MNB with domestic branches or with a domestic MNB competitor of the purely domestic bank. In the words of Hilmar Kopper (1991, p. 9), then spokesman for Deutsche Bank's board of managing directors, '[i]n order to safeguard their strength at home, [banks] had to become . . . global institutions'.[5] This is the defensive expansion hypothesis.

A second and related hypothesis, the trade finance hypothesis, surmises that domestic banks expand abroad to provide banking services for domestic clients' trading, as opposed to investment, activities. For example, early in the twentieth century, US Steel and DuPont both encouraged Citibank to move into South America (Cleveland and Huertas, 1985, p. 77). Expansion in such circumstances, however, need not be purely defensive. Indeed, in Citibank's case, an additional motivation which could be labelled 'offensive expansion' or 'opportunistic expansion', was also a factor. The then president of Citibank expected that the opening of its South American branches might yield 'a very considerable return by offering facilities that other banks cannot offer to exporters, and thus attract their accounts to the City Bank' (ibid., pp. 78–9).

Interpretation of the results of some of the econometric testing of these theories is complicated by the correlation between measures of the size of the foreign market and foreign investment and trade proxies (Jain, 1986). The MNB may have been driven by the attraction of a large new market (a theory already discussed) or by the need to provide existing clients with services abroad, whether for investment or trade purposes. In other words, as a consequence of this correlation, discerning or isolating the drivers for opening foreign branches can be difficult in econometric studies. Nevertheless, both client-related hypotheses have, in general, found support in the considerable empirical literature.[6] Further support for these hypotheses is provided by the statistic that 52 per cent of surveyed US multinationals continued to bank with their domestic MNB with respect to their operations in foreign jurisdictions (Pastre, 1981).[7]

**Theories Relating to Risk Management**

Overseas expansion may bring higher growth rates and greater profits, whether it be through entering large, high-growth markets, by leveraging existing strengths, or by following clients abroad. Of course, considerations relating to risk also influence the decision to become an MNB in two antithetical respects. First of all, investing in foreign jurisdictions is manifestly not without its risks and uncertainties. Second, and in opposition, an offshore investment offers the potential for risk diversification and minimization. The theories of multinational banking which involve risk management are discussed in this section.

Risk averse banks may prefer to expand into overseas markets which are familiar in cultural, linguistic and institutional respects.[8] In this way, any uncertainties may be reduced (Davidson, 1980).[9] Foreign bank acquisition (a subject to which the chapter returns), rather than 'greenfield' development, may also assuage such concerns. Similarly, risk averse banks may avoid investing in politically unstable regions or countries. This is not to say, however, that these banks will altogether eschew foreign economies more risky than their domestic markets. On the contrary, the portfolio diversification hypothesis suggests that by investing in more than one country, an MNB may diversify its business and political risks (Bernal, 1982; Niehans, 1983). In fact, it may even be advantageous for a large, well-known MNB to expand into a less stable economy if, for example, it could build a substantial retail business by offering local depositors a greater level of security than that provided by domestic institutions. Fieleke's (1977) small study of US banks is inconclusive in regard to the portfolio diversification theory and Goldberg and Johnson (1990, p. 124) opine that '[i]nternational diversification benefits have been claimed but supporting evidence is weak'.[10] In contrast, Don Argus, former chief executive officer of National Australia Bank, believes that '[g]eographic diversification of the business reduces that volatility in the bank's performance that arises from total exposure to the domestic economy' (Argus, 1990, p. 8). Similarly, 'Citicorp's world-wide policy of broad diversification of both assets and liabilities helps to maintain stability and reduces risk of excessive concentration in any one particular country' (Citicorp, 1976, p. 25).

From the converse perspective, banks from politically unstable domestic markets may look to establish a more secure income stream and asset base abroad in a more stable political or economic environment (Grosse and Goldberg, 1991). Reversing the example given above, however, Marashdeh (1994) points out that an MNB with such a strategy (and presumably, higher-risk domestic business) may struggle to attract custom in lower-risk markets without providing commensurate returns to foreign depositors. Again, expansion via acquisition of an existing foreign bank may be a more practical approach in these circumstances.

Empirical work on these hypotheses is relatively sparse and the few studies which have been undertaken have yielded conflicting results.[11] In part, this is probably due to the opposing considerations and arguments presented above and in part due to the difficulties inherent in measuring a country's level of risk and, in particular, isolating the proxy for risk from other related attributes such as market size and sophistication.

**Miscellaneous Theories of Multinational Banking**

In this final subsection, three miscellaneous theories are outlined. These concern the impact of regulation, exchange rate movements and distance from the domestic market on the formation of MNBs. Although they are theories or hypotheses in a slightly different sense from those already examined, they have nevertheless attracted the attention of scholars of multinational banking and so are discussed here.

Many have argued that government regulations in both domestic and foreign markets have played an important role in the development of multinational banking (for example, Klopstock, 1973; Brimmer and Dahl,

1975). One example of this influence was cited in Section 1, in the discussion of the impact of Regulation Q upon the evolution of US MNBs. Other restrictions on the domestic banking sector, such as the Glass–Steagall Act,[12] also encouraged US banks to become multinational (Bernal, 1982). Regulation has had an impact upon multinational banking in other countries as well. In order to evade domestic credit restrictions, for example, Japanese banks opened foreign branches in the US to finance loans in Japan (Poulsen, 1986). Of course, regulation is also important from the perspective of receptivity, the degree to which a market is open to foreign investment. In the case of banking, many otherwise receptive jurisdictions have proscribed foreign bank entry altogether, or at least prescribed restricted forms of investment (to be discussed below). The extensive empirical literature provides general support for this regulatory impact theory (for example, Nigh et al., 1986; Goldberg and Johnson, 1990; Hultman and McGee, 1989; Goldberg and Grosse, 1994; Wengel, 1995).

Exchange rate movements can increase or decrease the financial resources required by potential MNBs to enter foreign markets. For example, a depreciation of the currency of the target bank's country relative to that of the acquiring bank's country may make a previously unaffordable takeover feasible, and conversely for a relative appreciation. However, such exchange rate movements have the opposite impact upon the income generated from foreign sources when measured in the domestic currency of the MNB. So the impact of exchange rates upon the incidence of multinational banking is ambiguous. For this reason, and perhaps also because of the complexity of constructing an exchange rate proxy which accurately captures the continuous fluctuations in exchange rates, the modest number of empirical tests in this area provide little guidance or enlightenment (for example, Goldberg and Johnson, 1990).

Some researchers have postulated that the greater the geographic distance between an MNB's domestic and foreign operations, the greater the costs of monitoring foreign borrowers (Ursacki and Vertinsky, 1992) and therefore the lower the likelihood of establishing foreign representation. On the other hand, it has also been proposed that greater distances may require the development of a stronger local supervisory presence in the foreign market and hence lower monitoring costs from the domestic headquarters (ibid.). This would increase the probability of foreign branching from a particular home country. Cultural similarities between, or at least greater understanding of, geographically proximate nations, factors which may influence the likelihood of multinational banking, further confound the testing of this hypothesis (Grosse and Goldberg, 1991). The absence of unequivocal theoretical direction is mirrored in the econometric findings (for example, Fisher and Molyneux, 1996).

## 3  MULTINATIONAL ORGANIZATIONAL FORMS

Banks may invest offshore for greater growth and profit opportunities, to capitalize upon competitive advantages, to follow or lead clients, to manage risk and for other reasons, such as domestic or foreign regulation. Once a decision has been made to expand abroad, the intending MNB must decide on the form its expansion will take and the strategies it will employ. This section is divided into three subsections: in the first one, the different forms of multinational banking representation are explored; factors which influence banks to adopt one particular organizational form over another in foreign markets are examined in the second; and the third subsection discusses multinational strategy for the global integration of products and business systems.

**Types of Multinational Organizational Form**

There are several organizational forms which can provide the vehicle for multinational banking involvement. These forms differ, primarily, in the types of business they are authorized to conduct in offshore markets. Ranked in order of increasing foreign involvement, the organizational forms are: correspondent banking, representative offices, agencies, subsidiaries and branches. The activities of each are outlined below.

Correspondent banking does not in fact constitute multinational banking as defined in Section 1 because it involves no direct foreign investment, or any physical presence in the foreign market. The description of this type of banking is provided merely to contrast with the later discussion of multinational banking. It consists of a correspondent relationship, typically on a reciprocal basis, between domestic banks in different countries. The relationship involves the foreign domestic bank (the correspondent) conducting financial transactions and related activities in the foreign market on behalf of the home bank. Common services include extending foreign currency credit, issuing or honouring letters of credit and providing information about foreign market conditions. The foreign correspondent performs the transactions on behalf of the home bank in return for a fee.

Representative offices are the most limited form of multinational banking and involve MNBs establishing their own commercial premises in foreign countries. Representative offices perform functions which assist and support the operations of MNBs but their activities are restricted. For example, they are not authorized to carry out the general banking functions of deposit taking or lending (Hultman, 1990, p. 5). However, they can collect and forward payments in foreign markets, such as receivables for exporters, on behalf of 'parent'[13] MNBs (Goldberg and Saunders, 1981b,

p. 366). They can also organize loans in foreign markets to be referred to and administered by the 'parent' in the home country (ibid.). Another significant activity of representative offices is the collection of data and intelligence on foreign markets for use by MNBs and their clients.

The establishment of foreign agencies represents a deeper multinational banking presence. Agencies provide a broader range of banking services in foreign markets, with the ability to make commercial, but generally not consumer, loans and the limited power to raise deposits, though deposit taking from foreign residents is also prohibited (ibid.; Hultman 1990, p. 5). For this reason, funds are principally derived from 'parent' MNBs and foreign interbank markets. Another important activity of agencies is the facilitation of foreign trade between home and foreign countries; for example, they issue and honour letters of credit and accept bills of exchange (Goldberg and Saunders, 1981b, p. 367). Through their involvement in foreign capital and money markets, including foreign exchange markets, agencies also play significant roles in the management of the assets of 'parent' MNBs (Heinkel and Levi, 1992, p. 253).

The final two forms of multinational banking, the foreign branch and foreign subsidiary, represent the highest level of multinational banking commitment. Foreign branches and subsidiaries are generally authorized to conduct the full range of banking activities, including the acceptance of deposits and making of loans, as well as providing traditional international banking services. The main activity of a foreign branch is wholesale lending, both within the host country and across its borders (Marsh, 1983, p. 561). Branches also participate in short-term lending to commercial enterprises and the financing of international trade. Although foreign branches are generally permitted to raise retail deposits, close proximity to potential depositors is required in order to attract retail deposits and this in turn necessitates major branch investments. Due to a reluctance to establish large branch networks, the majority of foreign branches raise funds through the wholesale deposit market (ibid., p. 568). Foreign branches also become actively involved in foreign capital, money and foreign exchange markets and so also play a part in managing home-country assets in foreign markets.

Foreign subsidiaries are typically established where an MNB's objective is to compete directly with domestic retail banks or similar MNBs in foreign markets. For this reason, subsidiaries typically control wider foreign branch networks to enable them to participate in both retail and wholesale lending and deposit taking. Hence, a subsidiary tends to operate more like a domestic bank in the foreign host market, in contrast to foreign branches, which, in addition to wholesale financing, perform more specialized functions more closely linked to the activities of 'parent' MNBs (Heinkel and Levi, 1992, p. 254).

In addition to the mainstream types of multinational organizational form there are two specific forms that are unique to the US market, namely, Edge Act Corporations and New York Article XII Investment Companies. Edge Act Corporations are authorized under the US Federal Reserve Act to engage in lending and deposit-taking activities connected with international or foreign business. Both US domestic banks and foreign banks can set up an Edge Act Corporation in the US for the purpose of conducting international business in the US (Levi, 1996, p. 555). New York Article XII Investment Companies are subsidiaries established under New York law that conduct international and wholesale commercial banking operations (Hultman 1990, p. 8). They engage in lending but not deposit-taking activities (Institute of International Bankers, 1997, p. 24).

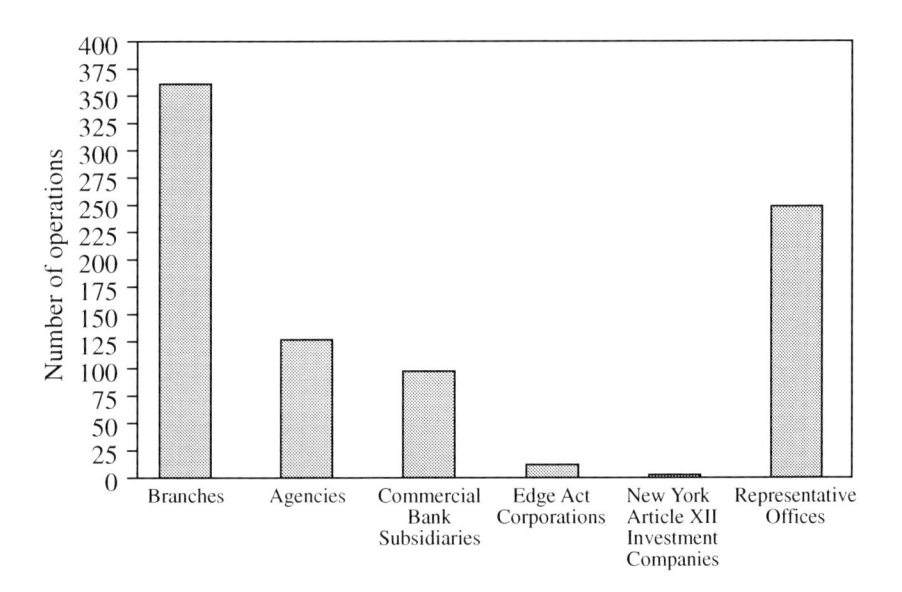

*Source:* Institute of International Bankers (1997).

*Figure 2.1  US banking and representative operations of international banks, December 1996*

Figure 2.1 shows the different types of organizational forms through which multinational banking is conducted by foreign banks in the US. The incidence of multinational banking through a branch structure significantly exceeds that through subsidiaries. Additionally, there are a significant number of representative offices and agencies in the US.

The next subsection examines a bank's choice of multinational organizational form. It investigates the factors that determine why a bank might choose a particular form of organizational structure as opposed to another, to provide the vehicle for its multinational banking activities. It is important also to note that many international banks operate through more than one branch, subsidiary or other kind of office in a particular foreign host market (Institute of International Bankers, 1997, p. 23).

## Choice of Multinational Organizational Form and Multinational Banking Strategy

The choice of an appropriate organizational form for a bank's multinational involvement is dependent not only upon a range of economic and legal circumstances in both foreign and home countries but also upon the individual bank's offshore business strategies. The interaction of these influences means that 'no single route is the best for all countries and all conditions' (Rockefeller, 1964, p. 75). Lees (1974) identifies a list of factors that play a significant role in the choice of organizational form. These can be conveniently grouped into:

- type and volume of foreign business;
- resource requirements; and
- host-country legal and regulatory structure.

Each of these is discussed in turn, followed by an exploration of other influences.

### Type and volume of foreign business

The type and volume of business MNBs hope or expect to conduct in foreign markets are the primary considerations in the choice of organizational form.

Correspondent banking relationships, being an inexpensive method of conducting simple banking transactions, are most suited to relatively infrequent foreign market activity. An increased foreign presence in the form of representative offices may be driven by a desire to increase the amount of referral business from offshore markets to the 'parent' bank. Although referral business may occur through correspondent relationships, correspondents are likely to put their own interests before those of the 'parent' bank. In addition, representative offices provide an important source of foreign market intelligence and may be the first strategic step in establishing a deeper foreign presence while the potential payoff from further commitment is evaluated. Owing to some restrictions on the activities of representative offices, however, it is common for MNBs to maintain concurrent correspondent relationships. Moreover, the existence of representative offices can even improve the quality of such relationships (Robinson, 1972, p. 23).

The decision to pursue a more comprehensive multinational commitment is often motivated by increases in the volume and frequency of cross-border payments and collections (Merrett, 1995, p. 83). In the absence of agencies or branches, the growth of these transactions can generate large cash balances in the hands of correspondents. These balances can typically be more productively employed in trade finance or through cash advances by the establishment of foreign agencies or branches (ibid.). Agencies are an appropriate structure in these circumstances as they are authorized to make loans, finance foreign trade and provide other trade support services. Growth in exporter servicing or lending can also be readily accommodated by expanding the agency as needed (Heinkel and Levi, 1992, p. 259). Establishment of agencies might also be prompted, for example, by the desire to escalate participation in the foreign money and capital markets to assist in the management of home-country assets (ibid.).[14]

Foreign branches are a pertinent organizational form where MNBs wish to further augment involvement in foreign money and capital markets[15] or where increased lending opportunities present themselves (ibid.). The establishment of a foreign subsidiary is considered to be more akin to a financial investment than part of the 'parent' bank's own operations strategy (ibid., p. 260), so the decision to establish a subsidiary is of a different nature to the choice between a representative office, agency or a foreign branch. The latter three provide services which are more closely aligned to the operations of 'parent' MNBs and so comprise elements of a different strategy. For example, the foreign branch, although engaging in deposit taking and lending in the foreign host country, still has many of its functions originating from its 'parent' in managing the 'parent' bank's assets in foreign money and capital markets. The activities of representative offices and agencies are even more closely linked to 'parent' functions. Foreign subsidiaries, on the other hand, resemble domestic banks in the foreign market, providing the full range of banking services and facing the same regulations as domestic banks, except that they are foreign-owned. The activities of a subsidiary are more independent of its parent, and are thus seen as being a financial investment rather than a supporting arm of the parent bank.

Specific to the US market, the establishment of branches in the US is much more common than the establishment of a commercial banking subsidiary. As per Figure 2.1, there were 370 branches compared to 100 subsidiaries at the end of 1996. The benefits of establishing a branch rather than a subsidiary in the US market have been identified as: (i) greater capital flexibility; (ii) lower cost of funding; (iii) access to the worldwide capital base of the parent; (iv) increased freedom to engage in transactions with the parent; and (v) lower transaction costs (US Department of the Treasury and Board of Governors of the Federal Reserve System, 1992, p. 14).

**Resource requirements**
In any business investment decision, the magnitude of resources required is obviously a critical factor to be taken into account. In the case of multinational banking, the resource requirements increase with the depth of foreign involvement and hence the organizational form adopted may depend on the resources available for expansion. While the correspondent banking relationship requires no foreign direct investment, representative offices, agencies, branches and foreign subsidiaries (whether established by acquisition or not) respectively necessitate progressively higher levels of resource commitment.

**Host-country legal and regulatory structure**
The foreign regulatory and legal structure may have a large bearing on the choice of organizational form. Some jurisdictions, such as the UK and Switzerland, allow foreign banking penetration only on condition of reciprocity or, in other words, only if MNBs from the potential host country are guaranteed entry into the intending entrant's home market (Baldock, 1991, p. 205; Widmer and Schmidt 1991, p. 191). Other countries prohibit certain forms of multinational banking outright. The degree to which such regulation reflects political rather than economic motives is debatable. Pauly (1987) argues that the opening of Australia's banking market to foreign banking presence was a decision based heavily on political as well as economic considerations. Even in jurisdictions where the entry of MNBs is welcomed in one form or another, other specific requirements or restrictions may affect the choice of form. For example, minimum capital requirements, possibly different from those applying to foreign domestic banks, may have to be satisfied. In addition, foreign banking licences, grants of which may be subject to political considerations, may have to be obtained in order to engage in branching.

Foreign taxation regimes may also be a crucial factor in the choice of organizational form. For example, the tax treatment of directly controlled foreign branches on the one hand, and foreign subsidiaries on the other, can differ significantly. Common examples of differential treatment of 'stand-alone' branch banking and subsidiary structures can be found in both Switzerland and Germany (Koch, 1991, p. 88; Widmer and Schmidt, 1991, p. 190).

### Empirical evidence on organizational structure determinants

There is a lack of empirical research modelling organizational structure as a choice variable. The exception is Ball and Tschoegl (1982) who find that the main driver of the level of multinational banking commitment is the amount of multinational banking experience the bank has had in the particular foreign host market. If the bank is a relatively new entrant, it is expected to have a more limited multinational banking presence, for example, in the form of a representative office. Additionally, the bank's general experience with multinational banking operations in other host markets is found to be positively related to the level of multinational banking commitment. Ball and Tschoegl's research suggests that a foreign bank with more experience in multinational banking generally and particularly in the specific foreign market is expected to develop a deeper multinational banking presence in the form of a branch or subsidiary. This is, however, an avenue for further empirical research in modelling the determinants of multinational banking organizational form.

### Establishing a multinational banking operation

Another issue in the establishment of a multinational banking presence is how to effect the strategy. A bank that decides to engage in a multinational banking strategy offering the full range of services is faced with the question of whether it should implement that strategy by acquisition, as National Australia Bank chose to do, or by organic growth, the strategy adopted by Citibank. Despite foreign acquisition being the most common method of entry for MNBs into the US market, there has been little empirical research in this area (Hultman and McGee, 1989).[16] Some of the forces which influence this decision have already been mentioned but are drawn together here.

As noted above, foreign regulations can have a significant impact; in some countries, it is not possible to acquire domestic banks, leaving only 'greenfield' strategies. Another reason for establishing branch networks from scratch is to take advantage of international reputation, particularly in less-developed or less-stable economies, where depositors may feel more secure banking with well-known MNBs. Acquiring existing foreign banking operations may also leave MNBs with customer profiles in offshore divisions which are incompatible or at least inconsistent with their overall market positioning. Organic growth, however, allows MNBs to target market segments within foreign economies; one example of this strategy is Citibank with its multinational 'consumer bank' business. Establishing 'greenfield' foreign offices also allows MNBs to extend their existing technology, systems, business practices and processes immediately and seamlessly into their new branches, without the need for the costly integration and retraining which might be associated with foreign acquisitions.[17]

On the other hand, where foreign bank acquisitions are permitted, they offer the opportunity to mitigate some of the difficulties inherent in greenfield approaches. The acquisition of an existing bank in the host market ensures immediate access to core deposits (Shapiro, 1996, p. 786). The foreign bank can engage in local lending more rapidly when it commences from a pre-existing deposit base. However, Peek et al. (1999) find that foreign banks entering the US market by acquisition are more likely to select target banks that have fewer core deposits and more purchased funds. Cultural, linguistic and institutional differences present fewer difficulties for MNBs where the vehicles for multinational expansion are existing foreign businesses with established local staff, knowledge and customer bases. Moreover, where the strategy calls for comprehensive foreign retail networks, acquisition may be the more feasible alternative, particularly if moving quickly is important. Will Bailey, then ANZ Bank's deputy chairman and group chief executive officer, related his bank's experience in the following terms: '[d]eveloping our own networks was slow going, so when the opportunity arose to purchase Grindlays . . . we took it. The acquisition took our overseas representation from 14 to 45 countries at a stroke' (Bailey, 1991, p. 11). Foreign acquisition strategies may also be advantageous for MNBs about which little is known in potential host markets. National Australia Bank's Don Argus argued that '[p]ositioning in a new market against entrenched competition and without an existing customer base as a platform for expansion, forces the newcomer into higher risk lending in its attempt to grow' (Argus, 1990, p. 11).

In the next subsection, some of the themes raised in this brief discussion, particularly those concerning product and systems integration across multinational operations, are explored in greater detail.

**Multinational Organizational Strategy: Multinational to Global**

This subsection focuses on the recent trend of moving from multinational banking to global banking. It draws on the experience of two MNBs, Citibank and National Australia Bank, in integrating their international operations to form global networks. Section 1 of this chapter described the two waves of multinational banking. The most recent trend, which could be termed the 'third wave' in the development of multinational banking, has been the shift over the last decade from multinational to truly global banking operations. The distinction between multinational banking and global banking is that global banking involves the integration of multinational operations to form a globally cooperative network as opposed to a group of largely independently run subsidiaries in different countries. This shift has been driven by the greater sophistication of communications and information technology and the increasing globalization of financial markets. There are many advantages of integrating multinational banking operations. The primary advantages include the realization of global scale economies, reduction of task duplication and global learning.

The major source of efficiency gains from the globalization of operations stems from the adoption of more efficient business division structures. The structure of traditional multinational banking operations is primarily along regional or geographic lines, with subsidiaries essentially run as stand-alone businesses with separate management, products and policies. The integration of these businesses presents broader options for structuring global operations.

A functional business division can be implemented globally both on a product level and on a support function level. On a product level, instead of duplicating product development, manufacture and marketing efforts in each geographic region, a functional division based on product facilitates the manufacture and marketing of core products on a global rather than regional basis. Production and marketing on this scale generates gains in scale economies and reduction of work duplication across subsidiaries in different countries. National Australia Bank (NAB) adopted this strategy. Former Chief Executive Officer, Don Argus, recognized that the banking and financial services industry is truly global in the sense that it is a market where 'the products and services . . . can be manufactured and sold using relatively uniform processes anywhere in the world' (Argus 1998, p. 40). NAB's strategy was to form global core products, identifying mortgages, credit cards and payment services, funds management, wholesale financial services and insurance as products and services that could be produced and marketed on a global basis (National Australia Bank, 1997, p. 2). Core products are modified where necessary to cater for specific regional demands. Citibank has also adopted the strategy of functional business divisions based on product as a part of its globalization strategy. Citibank is moving to a single global platform for manufacturing and marketing products that will ensure standard consistent products across the globe. Such standardization is expected to decrease product manufacture and marketing costs through the realization of global economies of scale, which in turn will enable Citibank to broaden the range of products it offers (Citicorp, 1997, p. 23). An additional advantage of developing core products across regions is the strengthening of brand recognition. This is achieved through the production of consistent products and marketing across regions. In recognition of its global aspirations, National Australia Bank recently adopted a new name, the 'National', for its global financial services to enhance global brand recognition (National Australia Bank, 1998, p. 1). Citibank continues to build its global brand recognition for its 'Citi' brand with Citicard, Citicheck, Citicash and so on (*The Economist*, 1997, p. S34).

The advantages of adopting a business division structure based on product are significant but at the same time certain aspects of a multinational banking business may not be suited to such a division. An alternative structure is one based upon customers or customer groups. Citibank's globalization strategy has involved adopting this form at business division structure within its Global Relationship Banking (GRB) unit. GRB performs transactions for multinational companies and their subsidiaries throughout the world. Citibank has found that it is more appropriate for this business to be managed and measured by customer rather than by region or product (Citicorp, 1997, p. 18). A division based upon customers facilitates a single dedicated relationship team that serves each parent company and its subsidiaries wherever they operate. On the other hand, under a regional business division structure, this is not possible since customers of the GRB operate globally.

In the same way that globalization generates efficiencies through functional business division structures on a product level, integration across regions also presents opportunities to increase efficiency and reduce duplication in the production of core support functions. Rather than having separate support infrastructures for each geographic region, these services can be consolidated to realize scale economies. Citicorp is developing consistent global platforms that involve integrating current systems for processing and other common functions. Credit card processing, customer service centres and general transaction processing will be consolidated across regions to realize significant efficiency gains (Citicorp, 1997, p. 23). Group infrastructure is also being integrated in information and communications. NAB is also adopting a similar strategy as part of its globalization plan, which involves formation of a shared services operation which manages customer support and the common administrative functions. Rather than maintaining separate infrastructures for each local region, shared service divisions will operate more efficiently for functions such as technology, customer services, human resource management, finance and risk management (National Australia Bank, 1997, p. 2).

An important benefit of moving to a global operations structure is to take advantage of group knowledge and expertise through joint learning across subsidiaries. In multinational banking the traditional operations structure is to facilitate a one-way transfer of knowledge and expertise from the parent to the multinational subsidiaries. An integral part of a global operations strategy, however, is a two-way transfer among subsidiaries.

Globalization breaks down the barriers to the flow of information and expertise within a multinational banking group. Learning is facilitated among subsidiaries across national boundaries and best-practice methods can be applied throughout the group. NAB's 1997 acquisition of HomeSide, a leading US mortgage servicer, demonstrates the possibility of learning advantages inherent in a global strategy. The combination of HomeSide's expertise, it being one of the most efficient mortgage services in the world, and NAB's international network has the potential to create a world leader in mortgage services. Senior management from HomeSide assisted with the implementation of HomeSide's systems across the NAB group. Joint or shared learning across international subsidiaries has also been identified as an integral part of Citibank's success. Citibank calls this process 'success transfer'. The aim is to pull together best practices from across the group and implement them in all other subsidiaries. Staff expertise is of course the major source of group learning. Within Citibank's emerging markets group, for example, experienced staff are transferred from one region to another to transfer their expertise across the group (Citicorp, 1996, p. 4).

## 4  THE PERFORMANCE OF MULTINATIONAL BANKS

Section 2 of this chapter outlined the various theories of multinational banking. A subset of those theories was concerned with leveraging of strengths, suggesting that MNBs must possess some competitive edge over local competitors in the foreign market. The sources of such advantages were identified as the MNB possessing superior expertise, processes and practices which it can transfer into the foreign market. Lower cost of capital was also a source of advantage due to size of the MNB or due to factors in the MNB's parent country such as savings rates, macroeconomic and fiscal policy as well as the relationship between corporations, banks and government in the home country. Additionally, an MNB could gain such an advantage by acquiring a foreign bank possessing sophistication in a particular area of business. MNBs that may have initially entered foreign markets to serve the banking needs of the parent's clients under a defensive expansion type motive have increased their presence in foreign markets by actively seeking new business in the host market unrelated to home clients by leveraging such strengths and cost advantages (Terrell, 1993, p. 913).

In practice, however, empirical evidence shows that the performance of MNBs' foreign operations, in some cases, has been disappointing compared to their domestic rivals. A prime example of this finding is in the US market. Various studies have compared the performance of foreign and domestically owned multinational banking operations in the US and have found that despite evidence of foreign banks possessing significant cost advantages, the foreign banks have performed less efficiently compared to US-owned MNBs. DeYoung and Nolle (1996) compare the profit efficiency of foreign and domestic banks in the US and find that although the banks have similar output efficiency, the input efficiency of foreign-owned MNBs is significantly less than that of their domestic rivals, resulting in inferior performance. Peek et al. (1999), consistent with these findings, show that foreign MNBs in the US that enter the market by way of acquisition are also performing less well than their domestic peers. This is attributable to the quality of the target bank pre-acquisition and also to the management strategy post-acquisition. Chang et al. (1998) find that the organizational structure of the MNB plays a key role in its performance in the foreign market. Again, foreign-owned MNBs operating in the US are found to be less efficient than their domestic rivals. The larger the degree of foreign ownership of the MNB, the greater its degree of inefficiency (ibid., p. 695).

Despite a foreign MNB possessing an advantage over its domestic rivals in terms of its cost of capital or its leveraging of other strengths, the evidence above suggests that such advantages do not necessarily translate into superior performance over domestic rivals. DeYoung and Nolle (1996) explain the poor performance of foreign MNBs in the US by reference to inefficiency in the use of inputs. The study finds that while foreign MNBs in the US may have access to lower cost inputs to the production of banking services, they do not operate under an efficient input mix. The source of this inefficiency is heavier reliance on purchased funds than their domestic competitors, who tend to rely more on domestically raised deposits (ibid., p. 632). Peek et al. (1999) also find that foreign MNBs that enter the US market via acquisition of domestically owned US banks tend to acquire banks that have a heavier reliance on purchased funds (ibid., p. 601). Additionally, the reliance on purchased funds continues to persist post-acquisition in the long run (ibid.). An alternative explanation for the poor performance of foreign-owned MNBs in the US is that despite the leveraging of strengths through superior practices and expertise, there may be difficulties in adapting customer service and delivery systems to the foreign host market. Chang et al. (1998) find that organizational structure plays an important part in the ability of an MNB to transfer such advantages to a foreign market (ibid., p. 694).

Despite the empirical evidence that foreign-owned MNBs in the US have performed poorly relative to their domestic rivals, over the same period there has been a marked increase in the level of foreign multinational banking in the US market. Over the period from 1973 to 1992 the reported assets of branches and agencies of foreign banks in the US grew from $25 billion to more than $700 billion (Terrell, 1993, p. 913). Peek et al. (1999) recognize this paradox and attempt to reconcile it. The primary explanation offered is that the foreign 'parent' bank experiences positive externalities from its multinational banking presence in the US. Multinational banking in the US market may assist the foreign bank to service the parent bank's clients abroad and so assist in attracting and retaining domestic business, consistent with the defensive expansion hypothesis. A further positive external benefit from foreign multinational banking presence in the US market is access to new technology and techniques that can be exported back to the home country. National Australia Bank's Don Argus acknowledged the benefits of expansion into the US market from their 1997 acquisition of Michigan National Corporation, describing the US market as being like a 'laboratory for new products' for the NAB Group. International earnings diversification is another positive external benefit for an MNB. The presence of significant positive externalities as a result of multinational banking presence suggests that it may be too simplistic to examine the performance of MNBs in the US market in isolation without considering the overall performance of its corporate banking group. The research therefore identifies an area for further study would be to attempt to quantify such external effects to more comprehensively evaluate the benefits of a multinational banking presence.

## 5  THE FUTURE OF MULTINATIONAL BANKING

More than 160 years after the first wave of multinational banking, it is clear that the future for MNBs will not merely be an 'extension of the past' (Khambata, 1996, p. 286). Powerful forces in the global financial system are producing rapid changes in both the structure of financial markets and the role that banks play within them. Market structure is undergoing significant change driven by the processes of consolidation, conglomeration and specialization in the provision of banking and financial services. Financial disintegration and securitization have changed the very nature of financial intermediation. MNBs have been forced to rethink their strategies as financial markets play an increasing role in channelling funds from net lenders to net borrowers.

Current models of financial intermediaries identify the basis of financial intermediation as the presence of asymmetric information and transaction costs. The models also imply that, where markets are perfect and complete, there is no role for financial intermediaries. Firms interact directly with households through financial markets (Allen and Santomero, 1998, p. 1462). Improvements in the availability of information and in information technology, as well as financial deregulation, have moved the world closer to the textbook model of perfect and frictionless markets. A broad range of substitutes for traditional financial intermediation is now available and banks are increasingly bypassed in favour of direct market participation. Further advances in information technology, communications and openness of markets are expected to accelerate the trend towards disintermediation. In addition, non-bank financial institutions continue to offer bank-like products in competition with banks. This development is set to continue with further deregulation of national financial systems.

The diminishing role of traditional banking is reflected in the increasing migration of financial activity off-balance sheet. Loan securitization is an example. While banks traditionally originated loans and held them on-balance sheet until maturity, the trend is for loans to be on-sold in secondary markets and traded in the same way as other securities.

Despite the growth of loan securitization and other forms of off-balance sheet financing, the role of banks in the lending process is unlikely to be eliminated entirely. Banks will continue to originate the loan transaction which then becomes a tradable commodity. Thus banks will act as 'brokers' of loans rather than traditional balance sheet financial intermediaries. Currently, the growth of loan securitization is limited only by the development of sophisticated secondary markets to facilitate trading. Secondary markets currently exist for the trading of mortgage loans, automobile loans and credit card receivables (ibid., p. 1472).

The phenomenon of loan securitization demonstrates that the underlying basis of financial intermediation is shifting. Nevertheless, the costs of participating directly in financial markets are significant. There are costs in learning about each financial instrument, requiring time and effort on behalf of the investor (ibid., p. 1481). Further, markets must be monitored on a continuous basis in order to adjust the mix of assets for optimal risk management (ibid.). Additionally, there is the cost of trading itself.

Arguably, financial institutions are able to perform these functions at a lower cost than firms or individuals. Provided they continue to enjoy a competitive advantage over firms and households, banks will be free to serve as financial services brokers, interfacing with the market, much as stockbrokers mediate between stockholders and the stock exchange.

In addition to changes in the very nature of financial intermediation, banks are playing a prominent role in the provision of risk management services, trading and managing asset holdings of firms and households. This shift in core business is reflected in the volume of derivatives traded by banks, including futures, swaps and options on financial assets. MNBs and other financial institutions are now in the financial risk business, managing and trading financial instruments to minimize risk for their customers (ibid., p. 1478). The provision of risk management services by financial intermediaries is predicated on the lower market participation costs enjoyed by some intermediaries. If this advantage were to disappear, so too would the role of intermediaries in the business of risk management.

The traditional distinction between banks and financial markets is breaking down (ibid., p. 1474). Balance sheet intermediation is a decreasing part of banks' core business as their involvement in financial markets grows. In this sense, traditional multinational banking is a thing of the past. Banks have become the dominant players in financial markets, with off-balance sheet trading forming the bulk of their core business. A more apt description of such institutions is multinational 'financial services providers' rather than multinational 'banks'.

Competitive pressures are also producing rapid change in the market structure of the banking industry. Conglomeration and consolidation, which began in the 1980s, continue to intensify as banks try to achieve the benefits of increased scale and scope. The underlying causes are varied but include technological progress, excess capacity, globalization and deregulation, and an improvement in the quality of financial institutions (Berger et al., 1999, p. 148). The result is MNBs that are able to offer the full range of banking and financial services. The decline of traditional banking has catalysed the process as banks seek to lower costs and to diversify into other financial services.

Some multinationals defy the trend, however, and remain largely undiversified in their activities, specializing in a particular subset of banking and financial services. A prominent example is J.P. Morgan who specializes in investment banking and funds management services. Competitive pressures are polarizing the industry into specialists at one extreme and universal banks at the other. For the universal banks, conglomeration combined with consolidation is creating one-stop financial services supermarkets able to provide the full range of sophisticated banking and financial services. CitiGroup is a classic example of a financial conglomerate, where loans, risk management services, insurance, pensions, funds management and the like can be obtained from the market through the interface of a single financial services provider.

Rapid change in the provision of financial services presents great challenges to regulators. Existing regulation is increasingly outmoded. First, the growth in securitization and off-balance sheet activity means that the multinational bank of the future will have little need for capital

(Cecchetti, 1999, p. 2). Selling loan assets on a secondary market results in a matching of assets and liabilities of the financial institution and, unlike traditional financial intermediation, no balance sheet risk (ibid.). With the movement of activity/assets away from balance sheets and on to the market, regulation focusing on balance sheets will be rendered redundant.

Second, the globalization of financial services also creates unique problems for regulators. The advance of technology means that national boundaries no longer exist in financial services. A loan can be originated in 'cyberspace' and exist on electronic markets that have no jurisdiction. Such transactions raise issues concerning the most effective form of regulatory regime and appropriate enforcement bodies. Third, the growth of conglomerates raises questions about the most effective way to regulate their different components. Collectively, these changes indicate that regulation needs to be reconfigured and coordinated across the entire global financial system.

With a move to increased off-balance sheet activity, greater reliance will need to be placed on disclosure rather than direct controls. Direct controls that attempt to limit off-balance sheet activity will become ineffective as new instruments continue to evolve (Canals, 1997, p. 319). The most appropriate form of regulation in a market-based environment is to maximize the volume and quality of information available to market participants. This ensures that market prices reflect all available information and effectively disciplines market players (Cecchetti, 1999, p. 4). A complement to market-based discipline is a change in the focus of regulation away from the balance sheet towards evaluation and supervision of internal controls of financial institutions, including audit procedures and other back-office control systems (ibid.).

Globalization and technological advances dictate that regulation must be applied consistently on a global scale. The Basle Accord has already made inroads into this process, introducing minimum capital requirements for MNBs in 1987. These efforts demonstrate that a uniform global regulatory regime is achievable. Although the focus of the Basle Accord is predominantly on the balance sheet, the scheme has been modified to take into account off-balance sheet exposures of MNBs. Again, as the activity of MNBs shifts away from the balance sheet, these regulations will need to be more focused on disclosure of off-balance sheet activity to enforce market discipline. The Basle Committee on Banking Supervision is currently developing a set of recommendations for public disclosure of trading and derivatives activities of banks and securities firms in recognition of this development.[18]

The nature of financial intermediation is changing and the challenge for

MNBs is to find gaps in the market mechanism. As financial markets move closer to perfection, however, such gaps will become fewer and smaller, and the scope for financial intermediaries of the traditional type will inevitably diminish. If MNBs survive at all, it will be as institutions whose role complements that of the market rather than substituting for it.

## NOTES

1. National Australia Bank recently changed its name to the 'National', perhaps partly in acknowledgement of this paradox.
2. Dunning's (1977) eclectic theory proposed that the existence of MNEs can be explained by ownership-specific advantages, internalization incentive advantages and location-specific variables.
3. For a discussion of internalization theory and eclectic theory in the context of MNBs, see Williams (1997).
4. Will Bailey, then deputy chairman and group chief executive of the Australia and New Zealand Banking Group (ANZ Bank) stated that 'fiercer competition in the domestic market . . . made diversification overseas look attractive' (Bailey, 1991, p. 11). National Australia Bank's Don Argus expressed similar sentiments in explaining the Bank's motivations for international expansion: 'initiatives to organically grow our share of the [domestic] market will be vigorously defended by the competition' (Argus, 1990, p. 7).
5. In a similar vein, ANZ Bank's Will Bailey commented that 'to develop, expand or acquire our own international networks would be the best way to head off the threat of the international banks in our domestic markets' (Bailey, 1991, p. 11).
6. See, for example, Nigh et al. (1986); Sabi (1988); Hultman and McGee (1989); and Grosse and Goldberg (1991) with respect to the defensive expansion hypothesis and see, for example, Dean and Giddy (1981); Poulsen (1986); Goldberg and Johnson (1990); Grosse and Goldberg (1991); and Hondroyiannis and Papapetrou (1996) with respect to the trade finance hypothesis.
7. From an MNB's perspective, ANZ Bank's Will Bailey stated that 'opportunities to finance trade' and to 'service the needs of domestic customers abroad' were considerations in entering a new country (Bailey, 1991, p. 11).
8. Deutsche Bank's Hilmar Kopper cited cultural differences as one of the obstacles to becoming a 'global bank' (Kopper, 1991, p. 9). In National Australia Bank's case, the decision to expand into the culturally similar UK, New Zealand and US markets was driven by its strategy of directly transferring its 'formula' for success into overseas markets, a strategy which depended on a degree of cultural affinity (Argus, 1990, p. 10).
9. Davidson's study was with respect to multinational corporations generally, rather than MNBs in particular.
10. For further objections to this thesis, see Walter (1981).
11. For example, contrast Grosse and Goldberg (1991) and Fisher and Molyneux (1996) on the one hand with Marashdeh (1994) on the other.
12. The US Glass–Steagall Act of 1933 provided for the separation of commercial banking and investment banking.
13. Quotation marks are used because the 'parent' MNB is not typically a parent in the strict legal sense of parent and subsidiary.
14. This rationale has been supported empirically by Heinkel and Levi (1992), p. 259.
15. This thesis has also found empirical support in Heinkel and Levi (1992), p. 259.
16. See also Goldberg and Saunders (1981a).
17. In contrast, National Australia Bank 'has been content to grow the NAB formula into [its] UK banks over time and in partnership with existing management, rather than immediately implanting its stamp' (Argus 1990, p. 13).

18. See Basle Committee on Banking Supervision and the Technical Committee of the International Organization of Securities Commissions (IOSCO) (1999).

## REFERENCES

Allen, Franklin and Anthony M. Santomero (1998), 'The theory of financial intermediation', *Journal of Banking and Finance*, **21**, 1461–85.
Argus, Don (1990), 'Global strategies of a major Australian bank', School of Banking and Finance, David Syme Faculty of Business, Monash University, Australia: Banking and Finance Occasional Papers, 90–1.
Argus, Don (1998), 'Global banking', *CEDA Bulletin*, October, 39–41.
Bailey, Will J. (1991), 'Global banking from an Australian perspective', *The World of Banking*, September–October, 10–13.
Baldock, Anne (1991), 'United Kingdom', *International Financial Law Review: International Banking Supplement*, 197–206.
Ball, Clifford A. and Adrian E. Tschoegl (1982), 'The decision to establish a foreign bank branch or subsidiary: an application of binary classification procedures', *Journal of Financial and Quantitative Analysis*, **17**(3), 411–24.
Basle Committee on Banking Supervision and the Technical Committee of the International Organization of Securities Commissions (IOSCO) (1999), 'Recommendations for public disclosure of trading and derivative activities of banks and securities firms', February, <http://www.bis.org/publ/bcbs48.htm> (16 July).
Berger, Allen N., Rebecca S. Demsetz and Philip E. Strahan (1999), 'The consolidation of the financial services industry: causes, consequences, and implications for the future', *Journal of Banking and Finance*, **23**, 135–94.
Bernal, Richard (1982), 'Transnational banks, the International Monetary Fund and external debt of developing countries', *Social and Economic Studies*, **31**(4), 71–101.
Brimmer, Andrew F. and Frederick B. Dahl (1975), 'Growth of American international banking: implications for public policy', *Journal of Finance*, **30**, 341–63.
Buckley, Peter J. and Mark Casson (1991), *The Future of the Multinational Enterprise*, 2nd edn, London: Macmillan.
Canals, Jordi (1997), *Universal Banking: International Comparisons and Theoretical Perspectives*, Oxford: Oxford University Press.
Cecchetti, Stephen G. (1999), 'The future of financial intermediation and regulation: an overview', *Current Issues in Economics and Finance, Federal Reserve Bank of New York*, **5**(8), 1–5.
Chang, Edward C., Iftekhar Hasan and William C. Hunter (1998), 'Efficiency of multinational banks: an empirical investigation', *Applied Financial Economics*, **8**, 689–96.
Cho, Kang Rae (1985), *Multinational Banks: Their Identities and Determinants*, Michigan: UMI Research Press.
Citicorp (1976), *Annual Report*, New York.
Citicorp (1996), 'Focused on global growth in the banking business', *CCInvestor*, June.
Citicorp (1997), *Annual Report*, New York.

Cleveland, Harold van B. and Thomas F. Huertas (1985), *Citibank, 1812–1970*, Cambridge, MA: Harvard University Press.

Davidson, William H. (1980), 'The location of foreign direct investment activity: country characteristics and experience effects', *Journal of International Business Studies*, **11**, 9–22.

Dean, James W. and Ian H. Giddy (1981), 'Strangers and neighbours: cross-border banking in North America', *Banca Nazionale del Lavoro Quarterly Review*, **137**, June, 191–211.

DeYoung, R. and D.E. Nolle (1996), 'Foreign-owned banks in the US: earning market share or buying it?', *Journal of Money, Credit, and Banking*, **28**, 622–36.

Dunning, John H. (1977), 'Trade, location of economic activity and the MNE: a search for an eclectic approach', in Bertil Ohlin, Per-Ove Hesselborn and Per Magnus Wikjman (eds), *The International Allocation of Economic Activity*, London: Macmillan, pp. 395–418.

*Economist, The* (1997), 'Xenophile urges', **343** (8012), 12 April, S32–35.

Fieleke, Norman S. (1977), 'The Growth of US banking abroad: an analytical survey', in Federal Reserve Bank of Boston, *Key Issues in International Banking: Proceedings of a Conference*, pp. 6–40.

Fisher, A. and P. Molyneux (1996), 'A note on the determinants of foreign bank activity in London between 1980 and 1989', *Applied Financial Economics*, **6**, 271–77.

Goldberg, Lawrence G. and Robert Grosse (1994), 'Location choice of foreign banks in the United States', *Journal of Economics and Business*, **46**, 367–79.

Goldberg, Lawrence G. and Denise Johnson (1990), 'The determinants of US banking activity abroad', *Journal of International Money and Finance*, **9**, 123–37.

Goldberg, Lawrence G. and Anthony Saunders (1980), 'The causes of US bank expansion overseas', *Journal of Money, Credit, and Banking*, **12**, 630–43.

Goldberg, Lawrence G. and Anthony Saunders (1981a), 'The determinants of foreign banking activity in the United States', *Journal of Banking and Finance*, **5**, 15–32.

Goldberg, Lawrence G. and Anthony Saunders (1981b), 'The growth of organizational forms of foreign banks in the US', *Journal of Money, Credit, and Banking*, **13**, 365–74.

Gray, Jean M. and H. Peter Gray (1981), 'The multinational bank: a financial MNC?', *Journal of Banking and Finance*, **5**, 33–63.

Grosse, Robert and Lawrence G. Goldberg (1991), 'Foreign bank activity in the United States: an analysis by country of origin', *Journal of Banking and Finance*, **15**, 1093–112.

Grubel, Herbert G. (1977), 'A theory of multinational banking', *Banca Nazionale del Lavoro Quarterly Review*, **123**, December, 349–63.

Heinkel, Robert L. and Maurice D. Levi (1992), 'The structure of international banking', *Journal of International Money and Finance*, **11**, 251–72.

Hondroyiannis, George and Evangelia Papapetrou (1996), 'International banking activity in Greece: the recent experience', *Journal of Economics and Business*, **48**, 207–15.

Huertas, Thomas F. (1990), 'US multinational banking: history and prospects', in Geoffrey Jones (ed.), *Banks as Multinationals*, London, UK and New York, USA: Routledge, pp. 248–67.

Hultman, Charles W. (1990), *The Environment of International Banking*, Englewood Cliffs, NJ: Prentice-Hall.

Hultman, Charles W. and L. Randolph McGee (1989), 'Factors affecting foreign banking presence in the US', *Journal of Banking and Finance*, **13**, 383–96.
Institute of International Bankers (1997), 'Economic benefits to the United States from the activities of international banks: financial services in a global economy', <http//www.iib.org/ben97.pdf> (26 March 1999).
Jain, Arvind K. (1986), 'International lending patterns of US commercial banks', *Journal of International Business Studies*, **17**(3), 73–88.
Jones, Geoffrey (1990), 'Banks as multinationals', in Geoffrey Jones (ed.), *Banks as Multinationals*, London, UK and New York, USA: Routledge, pp. 1–13.
Jones, Geoffrey (ed.) (1992), *Multinational and International Banking*, Aldershot, UK and Brookfield, USA: Edward Elgar.
Khambata, Dara (1996), *The Practice of Multinational Banking: Macro-policy Issues and Key International Concepts*, Westport, CT: Quorum Books.
Klopstock, Fred H. (1973), 'Foreign banks in the United States: scope and growth of operations', *Federal Reserve Bank of New York Monthly Review*, **55**, 140–54.
Koch, Ulrich (1991), 'Germany', *International Financial Law Review: International Banking Supplement*, 87–92.
Kopper, Hilmar (1991), 'A European view of global banking', *The World of Banking*, September–October, 8–9.
Lees, Francis A. (1974), *International Banking and Finance*, New York, USA and Toronto, Canada: John Wiley and Sons.
Levi, Maurice (1996), *International Finance: The Markets and Financial Management of Multinational Business*, New York: McGraw-Hill.
Lewis, M. and K. Davis (1987), *Domestic and International Banking*, Oxford: Philip Allan.
Mahajan, Arvind, Nanda Rangan and Asghar Zardkoohi (1996), 'Cost structures in multinational and domestic banking', *Journal of Banking and Finance*, **20**, 283–306.
Marashdeh, Omar (1994), 'Foreign bank activities and factors affecting their presence in Malaysia', *Asia-Pacific Journal of Management*, **11**, 113–23.
Marsh, Donald R. (1983), 'Foreign branches', in William H. Baughan and Donald R. Mandich (eds), *The International Banking Handbook*, Homewood, IL: Dow Jones–Irwin, pp. 557–79.
McCauley, R.N. and R. Seth (1992), 'Foreign bank credit to US corporations: the implications of offshore loans', *Federal Reserve Bank of New York Quarterly Review*, Spring, 52–65.
Merrett, D.T. (1995), 'Global reach by Australian banks: correspondent banking networks, 1830–1960', *Business History*, **37**(3), 70–88.
National Australia Bank (1997), 'National announces new strategy', *National Australia Bank Media Release*, Melbourne, 6 November.
National Australia Bank (1998), 'National star shines in new brand direction', *National Australia Bank Media Release*, Melbourne, 26 October.
Niehans, Jurg (1983), 'Financial innovation, multinational banking and monetary policy', *Journal of Banking and Finance*, **7**, 537–52.
Nigh, Douglas, Kang Rae Cho and Suresh Krishnan (1986), 'The role of location-related factors in US banking involvement abroad: an empirical examination', *Journal of International Business Studies*, **17**(3), 59–72.
Park, Yoon S. and Jack Zwick (1984), *International Banking in Theory and Practice*, Reading, MA: Addison-Wesley.
Pastre, Oliver (1981), 'International bank–industry relations: an empirical assessment', *Journal of Banking and Finance*, **5**, 65–76.

Pauly, Louis W. (1987), *Foreign Banks in Australia: The Politics of Deregulation*, Sydney, Australia: Australian Professional Publications.
Peek, Joe, Eric S. Rosengren and Faith Kasirye (1999), 'The poor performance of foreign bank subsidiaries: were the problems acquired or created?', *Journal of Banking and Finance*, **23**, 579–604.
Poulsen, Annette B. (1986), 'Japanese bank regulation and the activities of US offices of Japanese banks', *Journal of Money, Credit, and Banking*, **18**, 366–73.
Robinson, Michael J. and Christine Y. Walter (1991), 'Canada', *International Financial Law Review: International Banking Supplement*, 37–46.
Robinson, Stuart W. (1972), *Multinational Banking*, Leiden: A.W. Sijthoff.
Rockefeller, David (1964), *Creative Management in Banking*, New York: McGraw-Hill.
Sabi, Manijeh (1988), 'An application of the theory of foreign direct investment to multinational banking in LDCs', *Journal of International Business Studies*, **19**(3), 433–47.
Shapiro, Alan C. (1996), *Multinational Financial Management*, Englewood Cliffs, NJ: Prentice-Hall.
Task Force on the Future of the Canadian Financial Services Sector (1998), 'Report of the Task Force: challenge, change and opportunity', September, <http://finservtaskforce.fin.gc.ca> (13 March 1999).
Terrell, Henry S. (1979), 'US banks in Japan and Japanese banks in the United States: an empirical comparison', *Federal Reserve Bank of San Francisco Economic Review*, **79**, 18–30.
Terrell, Henry S. (1993), 'US branches and agencies of foreign banks: a new look', *Board of Governors of the Federal Reserve System, Federal Reserve Bulletin*, **79**, 913–25.
Tschoegl, Adrian E. (1982), 'Foreign bank entry into Japan and California', in Alan M. Rugman (ed.), *New Theories of the Multinational Enterprise*, London: Croom Helm, pp. 196–216.
Tschoegl, Adrian E. (1983), 'Size, growth and transnationality among the world's largest banks', *Journal of Business*, Summer, 187–201.
Ursacki, Terry and Ilan Vertinsky (1992), 'Choice of entry timing and scale by foreign banks in Japan and Korea', *Journal of Banking and Finance*, **16**, 405–21.
US Department of the Treasury and Board of Governors of the Federal Reserve System (1992), 'Report to Congress on the Subsidiary Requirement Study', Washington, DC, 18 December.
Walter, Ingo (1981), 'Country risk, portfolio decisions and regulation in international bank lending', *Journal of Banking and Finance*, **5**, 77–92.
Walter, Ingo (1985), *Barriers to Trade in Banking and Financial Services*, Thames Essay No. 41, London: Trade Policy Research Centre.
Wengel, Jan ter (1995), 'International trade in banking service', *Journal of International Money and Finance*, **14**, 47–64.
Widmer, Peter and Judith Schmidt (1991), 'Switzerland', *International Financial Law Review: International Banking Supplement*, September, 183–91.
Williams, Barry (1997), 'Positive theories of multinational banking: eclectic theory versus internalisation theory', *Journal of Economic Surveys*, **11**(1), 71–100.
Zimmer, S. A. and R. N. McCauley (1991), 'Bank cost of capital and international competition', *Federal Reserve Bank of New York Quarterly Review*, **15**, 33–70.

# 3. Asset-backed securitization, collateralized loan obligations and credit derivatives

**Warrick Ward and Simon Wolfe**

## 1 INTRODUCTION

Asset-backed securitization (ABS) can be defined as a process that enables the transformation of illiquid assets into liquid assets (marketable securities) that are sold in the securities markets. Through this process banks can now liquidate assets that were traditionally held on balance sheet until maturity. The set of assets that can be securitized is infinite, for example, residential or commercial mortgages, personal loans, corporate loans, car loans, credit card receivables, aircraft lease receivables, debt obligations, tax receivables, student loans, music receivables and intellectual property rights.

The term 'securitization' is also used to describe the process of disintermediation in the banking sector. This is the continuing loss of banks' prime customers to the securities markets where companies are able to raise capital at more competitive rates than the interest charged by banks for loans (see Berlin, 1992). However, in this chapter we shall be focusing only on ABS.

The objectives of this chapter are twofold. Initially we shall analyse and chart recent trends in the ABS market, specifically focusing on the securitizing of banks' assets – collateralized loan obligations (CLOs). Moreover, we analyse recent innovations in CLO deals, such as the use of credit derivatives. The use of such financial instruments is designed to manage credit risk, and generate payoffs or protection based on an underlying risky debt reference. Second, we shall analyse the regulatory environment surrounding ABS. The focus of our analysis is on capital requirements and transaction reporting standards.

Section 2 provides a brief overview of ABS, notably its theory, concepts and concerns. Here, the rationale behind the use of ABS, and then the developments in such securitizations will be traced with reference to the overriding pressures facing banks in the current environment. Section 3 introduces collateralized obligations, along with a brief description of credit derivatives, thereby providing general insight into their uses, structuring and advantages with respect to balance sheet restructuring. A more specific presentation of credit derivatives in CLO deals will be encapsulated in Section 4. Here, through the use of specific structures and deals, such as the Glacier deal by Swiss Banking Corp. (SBC), we shall demonstrate the uses of credit derivatives. Furthermore, we shall examine the effectiveness of such modifications, in terms of perceived riskiness and capital efficiency. In Section 5 we look at the regulatory issues surrounding ABS. First, we analyse the potential impact of the new Bank for International Settlements (BIS) proposals for capital adequacy. Second, we analyse the new transaction reporting standards developed by the ABS industry under the auspices of the European Securitisation Forum (ESF). Section 6 concludes.

## 2 ASSET-BACKED SECURITIZATION

**Overview**

The securitization of assets, which can be broadly described as the exchange of one type of financial claim for another, is in terms of economic and financial processes a relatively recent innovation.[1] The roots of asset-backed securitization can be traced to the US, where during the 1970s a market for the Government National Mortgage Association (GNMA or 'Ginnie Mae') pass-through securities on mortgages was developed. Although the asset-backed market can be deemed to have been in existence for over two decades, a pure ABS deal was not developed until 1985 when First Boston introduced such a transaction. Albrecht and Smith (1997, p. 1) note that 'it is a form of financing that was initially used to finance relatively simple self-liquidating assets, such as mortgage loans, and has expanded its application [to] more complicated financing structures'. Excluding mortgage deals, the use of ABS with respect to other assets is even more recent – spanning only a decade or so. With the increasing range of securitized assets, such as credit card receivables and loans to the personal sector,[2] there was a rapid rise in the volume of ABS within the US.

The value of asset-backed deals in the US, from an aggregated volume of about $10 billion in 1986, had reached approximately $200 billion in 1993,[3] expanding to $225 billion in 1995, and then $630 billion in 1998.[4] The value of assets securitized by the end of 1996 had reached approximately $2.5 trillion.[5] Such is the growth that within the past decade there has been a growing secondary market outside of the US, reaching about $55.6 billion

Table 3.1  European MBS/ABS issuance by asset type, 1997 and 1998 (in US$ bn)

| Asset type | 1997 | % of total | 1998 | % of total |
|---|---|---|---|---|
| MBS | 11.0 | 24.18 | 22.7 | 48.71 |
| CMBS | 2.6 | 5.71 | 2.6 | 5.58 |
| CBO/CLO | 14.6 | 32.09 | 8.5 | 18.24 |
| Other ABS | 17.3 | 38.02 | 12.9 | 27.68 |

*Notes:*
MBS – Mortgage-backed securitization.
CMBS – Collateralized mortgage-backed security.
CBO – Collateralized bond obligation.
CLO – Collateralized loan obligation.
Other – includes assets such as credit card receivables.

*Source:* Moody's Investor Services.

internationally. In Europe – the largest ABS market outside of the US – market development compared to the US is much more recent. However, the drivers of growth are similar, with both internal and external pressures factoring, and will be discussed later in the chapter. The European market, from annual estimates of less than $10 billion up until 1996, had reached approximately $46.7 billion by 1998 (estimates for 2000 are $100 billion).[6] In this market, mortgages account for the bulk of securitized assets (see Table 3.1), and the outstanding volume is valued at approximately $130 billion.[7]

## Generalized Operation of ABS

Securitization provides an alternative and additional scope for traditional intermediation, which can be observed by briefly examining the securitization process. Typically, the originating institution forms a separate special-purpose, bankruptcy-remote securitization conduit, the special-purpose vehicle (SPV), by providing the initial set of capital. The SPV then purchases part of the originating bank's loan portfolio, or in some cases may even itself originate loans. To finance its portfolio, the conduit issues a varied set of asset-backed market instruments – usually floating rate notes (FRNs)[8] – collateralized by the underlying loan pool (see Figure 3.1). A major portion of the SPV's debt is issued to investors, for example, institutional investors, who, for a variety of reasons, generally require the senior securities to be highly rated investment grade (triple or double A). In order to produce highly rated tranches, the SPV must receive credit enhance-

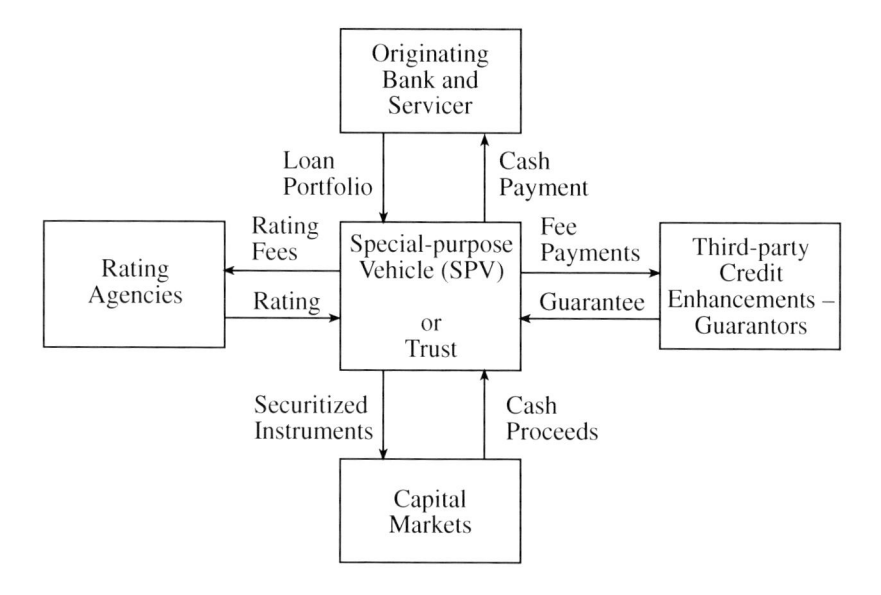

*Figure 3.1   The asset-backed securitization process*

ments that insulate the senior securities from the risk of default on the underlying portfolio. Typically, the originating bank provides the bulk of the enhancements, which can take many forms, ranging from issuing standby letters of credit to the SPV, to repurchasing the most junior securities issued by the SPV.

Many investors are drawn to these high-yielding securities as opposed to those of similar credit quality, for example, corporate and emerging market bonds. They offer higher yields because of a possible prepayment risk, and a liquidity premium due to an underdeveloped European secondary market. The originating bank not only benefits from capital relief, but it also secures origination, servicing and monitoring fees. In addition, it receives the residual spread between the yields on the loan portfolio, and the adjusted interest costs of the conduit, which are all secured by various methods of profit extraction.

## The Rationale behind Asset-backed Securitization

There are a number of perceived reasons for securitizing assets, but these can be segregated into two broad categories, (i) as a means of enhancing performance and (ii) a form of risk management and balance sheet structuring. In respect to the early evolutionary stages of ABS development, the drive by banks to securitize was led by the desire to remove assets off their balance sheet, in an attempt to gain a more efficient use of capital while in the process of transferring risks to investors. Pavel and Phillis (1987), as well as Greenbaum and Thakor (1987), suggested that securitizing provides banks with an alternative method of reducing risk, diversifying portfolios, and funding both their operations and new assets. Furthermore, Lockwood et al. (1996) highlight instances where such innovations lead to wealth effects for the shareholders of the issuing firm.

**Release of Capital: Alternative Source of Funding and Liquidity**

As a result of capital requirements, holding capital against its assets imposes an additional tariff on bank operations, and consequently on its funding costs. These broad requirements set by the Bank for International Settlements have restricted banks' ability to increase leverage, and therefore necessitated the use of innovative techniques in achieving it.[9]

Securitizing provides a vehicle that is used to transform illiquid financial assets – those with a reliable long-term cash flow – into tradable capital market instruments. This represents an efficient conduit to financial markets, producing in many instances a lower cost of funding than that available through debt or equity financing. The issuer can then leverage its portfolio by offloading these securitized assets from its balance sheet and sourcing funds to engage in additional positive Net Present Value (NPV) projects, or even retiring existing debt, which consequently impacts positively on the bank's profit.

To some extent, the originator is provided with greater funding sources, and allows the institution to create larger loan pools than on-balance sheet lending through self-funding permits. In addition to the possibility of increased leverage, originators, through the receipt of asset-servicing fees, effectively add to the wealth effects of securitization. On a wider economic perspective, the presence of a wide-ranging and efficient market for securitized products can lead to a reduced cost of financing in primary lending markets, while broadening its accessibility. This enables a more efficient use of capital, return on capital, and access to a more diverse investor base, while transferring portfolio risk to the financial markets.

**Other Benefits**

To the investor, these securitized instruments provide an opportunity to receive increased yield, as they offer a more attractive return when compared to sovereign issues of similar maturity and credit quality. They also allow investors to diversify their portfolios and associated risks, offering relief in a variety of risks (for example, credit risk[10]) and maturity depending on specific individual risk preferences. Following in this vein, securitization promotes an efficient mechanism for shifting interest rates and other market risks from these financial institutions to the capital markets, thereby reducing the portfolio and systemic risks, *ceteris paribus*. Securitization can – in theory – facilitate efficient allocation of capital by streamlining the credit-granting process based on capital market forces in terms of demand, pricing and valuation. For the diversity of a pool of assets allows an investor to rely not simply on the investigation of a particular loan, but rather on the statistical evaluation of the entire pool. In the next section we analyse the recent development of an important asset type – collateralized obligations – which belongs under the ever-expanding ASB umbrella.

## 3 COLLATERALIZED OBLIGATIONS

### Collateralized Debt Obligations (CDOs)

The generic grouping, collateralized debt obligations, comprise collateralized bond obligations (CBOs) and collateralized loan obligations (CLOs) (see Figure 3.2). However, for the purposes of this chapter the main focus and discussion will be aimed at CLOs.[11] CDOs are securities that are

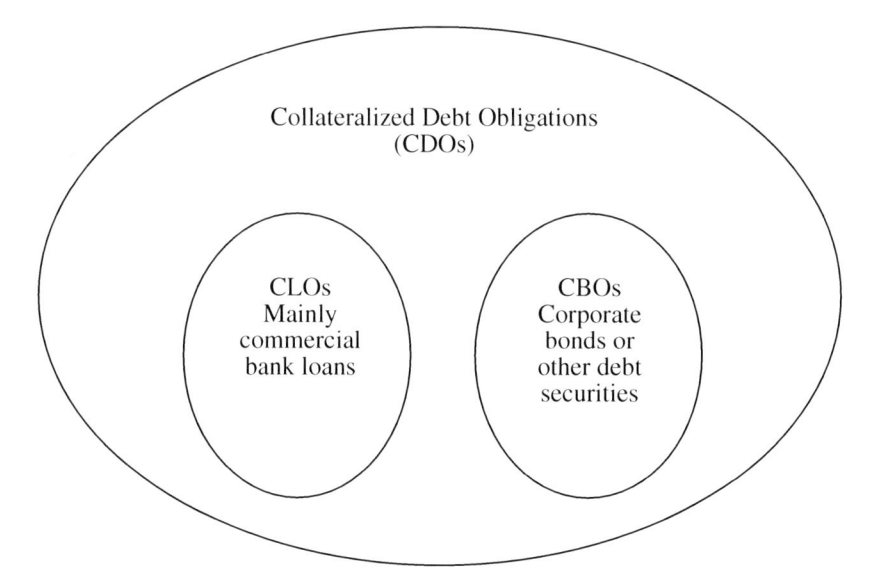

*Figure 3.2    Constituents of collateralized debt obligations*

backed by a pool of debt obligations, ranging from corporate loans to structured finance obligations, and are considered as a relatively recent innovation to the asset-backed securitized market. They are spread into customized security tranches – through which payments are redirected to investors – allowing investors to share in the risks and return of an underlying pool of obligations. Banks use these CDOs to free up regulatory capital by securitizing the layers that encompass the greatest level of risk, and its intrinsic value can be said to lie in its use as a portfolio management tool.

Conceptually, CDO instruments are simply applications of traditional ABS to bonds and commercial loans, and in many aspects are similar to ABS structures. First, they incorporate a bankruptcy-remote SPV, separated from the operating conditions, and on occasion the rating of the originator. Second, instruments issued by the SPV are rated on the basis of the credit quality of the underlying debt/asset pool, along with that of the associated credit enhancements. Third, the SPV brokers the purchase – in some cases synthetically – from the originator and then issues varying tranches of securities. Fourth, investors are dependent on the performance of the underlying asset pool for receipt of principal and interest payments.

However, among the different categories of CDOs, with CBOs and CLOs there are distinct differences. Notwithstanding the difference in the underlying asset, there are usually differences in the structure of these offerings. For instance, in a CBO, there is an issue of a mix of investment and non-investment grade debt collateralized by high-yielding securities – usually US dollar denominated. CLO securities, however, are collateralized by bank loans typically of investment grade, and in some cases with added high-yielding non-investment grade ones. Furthermore, it should be noted that generally the type of collateral pool, to some degree, determines the structure of the CDO. For example, for a pool that consists of bonds all that is required is simply transference to the SPV; however, the transfer of loan assets may require participations or assignments to transfer loans, thereby expanding the structure in the process.[12] This aspect, which will be developed in subsequent sections, can be problematic as it may require the explicit consent of the loan obligors. Next we shall take a more in-depth look at collateralized loan obligations, their history, rationale and structuring.

**Collateralized Loan Obligations (CLOs)**

Initially, the impetus behind the growth in these types of instruments was as a means of repackaging high-yield bonds for investors (Das, 1999). Das further notes that the major driver in this market was insurance companies, which found that the holding of some of its portfolio posed a variety of problems. They encountered a lack of liquidity among some of the securities, compounded by the imposition of weighted reserve requirements. These requirements, which ranged from 1 to 10 per cent, depending on the quality of the security, made them expensive to hold. Countering, the companies repackaged these assets into high-yielding securities, in the process shedding the riskier assets, but retaining the high-quality securitized debt, and consequently achieved a lower capital requirement.

The origin of the banking industry's securitization of its assets follows a similar vein. CLOs originated in the 1990s and were formed from banks' desire to rid their balance sheets of problematic loans. Since the $5 billion Repeat Offering Securitisation Entity (ROSE) Funding transaction in late 1996 by NatWest, international banks have encompassed the idea of securitizing large, diversified portfolios of corporate loans (see Table 3.2). As previously noted, the underlying investment pool comprises investment grade obligations, typically revolving or term loans, but can also include derivatives and standby letters of credit. That deal provided a dynamic solution to one of the greatest hurdles faced by commercial banks to date, the adding of liquidity to commercial loan portfolios.

As a consequence, there has been exponential growth in CLOs, such that CDO transactions combined were more than the amount of credit card loans securitized in 1997. The CLO market is the fastest-growing area in structured finance, outstripping CBO deals in terms of new issues, and according to Moody's this is expected to gain increased momentum as there has never been a rated default of a CLO deal. *EuroWeek* (1999) highlighted that commercial banks through CLO transactions transferred some $60 billion of credit exposure to the capital markets in 1998. Projections are that this is expected to further expand in the near future, fuelled by events such as the euro (see Figure 3.3).

There are varying motives for CLO deals and these determine the market segments and associated structures. The first type of structure, the balance sheet structure, is driven by the originating bank's need to access funding and regulatory capital relief. The underlying portfolio is of largely investment grade and the sponsoring bank generally holds the first loss of the CLO structure. Therefore, the bank focuses on the inclusion of investment grade loans, thereby reducing the equity component or the level of credit enhancements required, thus ensuring favourable regulatory treatment. Irving (1997) noted that instead of placing assets on the balance sheet, resulting in a regulatory capital hit, an originating bank can receive the same upside potential via the purchase of a much smaller CLO junior tranche.

The other type of structure represents what can be considered an arbitrage structure. Usually an investment bank would initiate a CLO

Table 3.2  Some of the major CLOs issued, as at January 1998

| Issuer | Launch date | Estimated amount (in $USm) | Originator | Rating of senior notes (S&P/Moody's) | Average senior credit support (%) | Structure type |
|---|---|---|---|---|---|---|
| ROSE Funding No.1 Ltd | 31.10.96 | 5,094 | NatWest | AA/Aa2 | 4.10 | CLN |
| SBC Glacier Ltd | 08.09.97 | 1,740 | SBC | AA+/Aa1 | 8.50 | CLN |
| NationsBank CLMT | 11.09.97 | 4,346 | NationsBank | AAA/Aaa | 8.50 | De-linked |
| Platinum CLMT | 26.09.97 | 2,700 | LTCB | AAA/Aaa | 10.50 | De-linked |
| ROSE Funding No. 2 Ltd | 09.10.97 | 5,524 | NatWest | AA/Aa2 | 3.64 | CLN |
| Triangle Funding Ltd | 16.10.97 | 5,000 | CSFB | AA/Aa3 | 7.38 | CLN |
| Prime Funding | 29.01.98 | 1,212 | IBJ | AAA/Aaa | 11.97 | De-linked |
| Total | | 25,616 | | | | |

Note:  CLN denotes credit-linked note structure; S&P is Standard and Poor's.

Source:  Merrill Lynch.

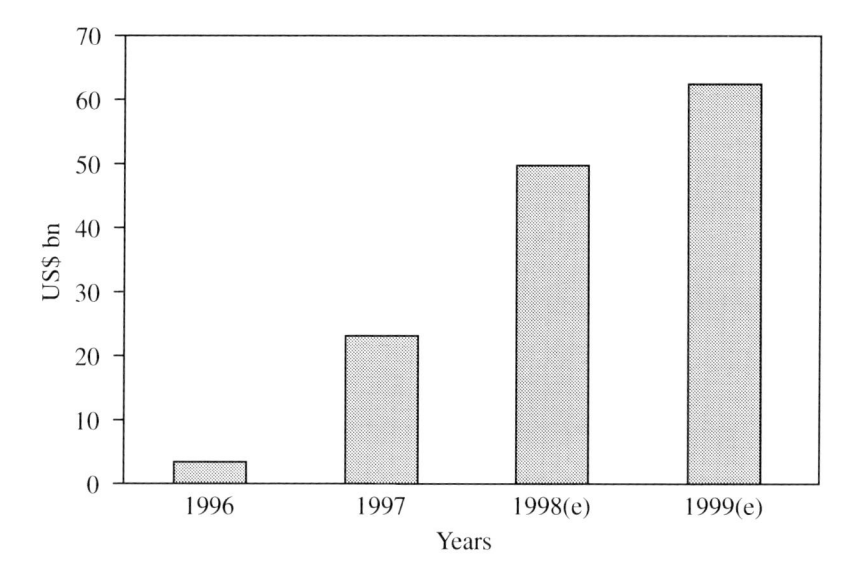

[Bar chart showing US$ bn values approximately: 1996 ≈ 3, 1997 ≈ 23, 1998(e) ≈ 50, 1999(e) ≈ 62]

*Note:* (e) Estimate

*Source:* Merrill Lynch.

*Figure 3.3 Potential CLO market development*

transaction in order to take advantage of value-enhancing opportunities available in the secondary market. The undervalued assets are repackaged with returns derived from the spread between the asset portfolio's cash flow and the servicing requirements of the secondary market asset purchase. These CLOs generally comprise high-yielding loans, including those to emerging markets. Parsley (1997) highlights that this type of financing is popular among overcapitalized banks and those with low return-on-capital hurdles, particularly continental European institutions. With tight spreads, credit protection trades – to be discussed in Section 4 – offer slightly better returns with small additions to risk, mostly illiquidity risk.

**CLO Structuring**

After the formation of the special-purpose vehicle (or trust), a pool of assets is purchased from the originating bank with the proceeds from the sale of debt instruments to investors. In a similar vein to basic ABS deals, the SPV's structure may include a series of tranches backed by the asset pool (see Figure 3.4). These tranches are categorized by their priority of claims on the cash

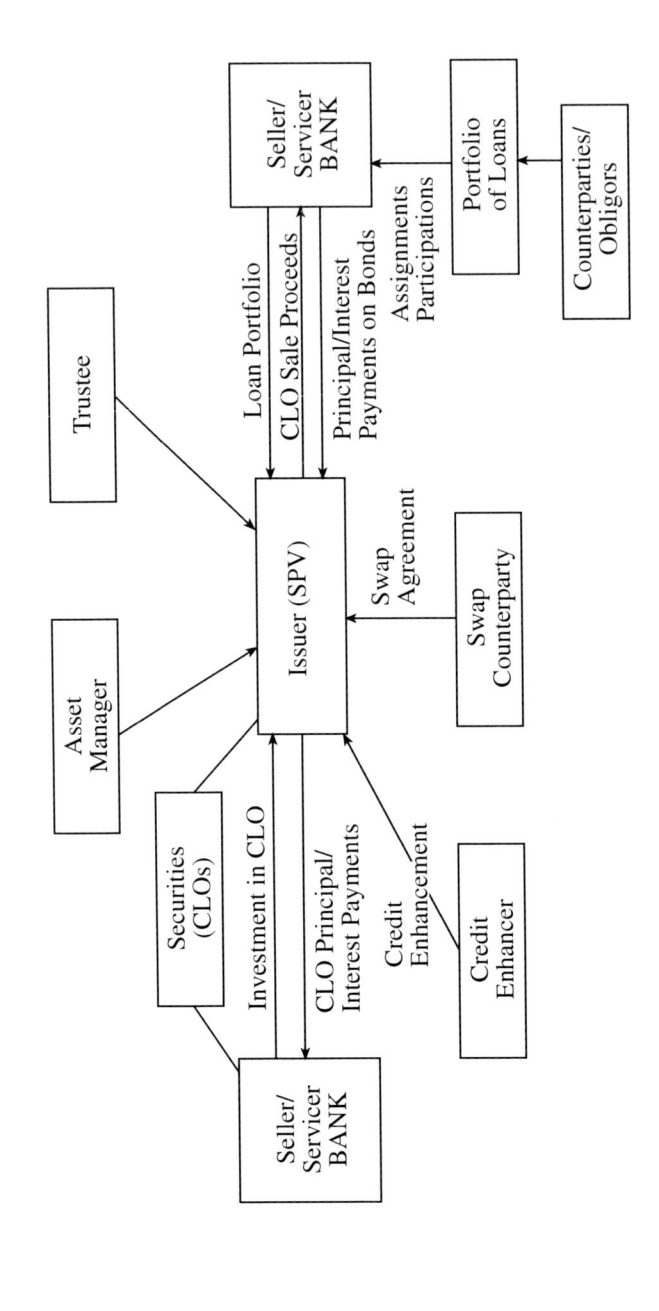

Figure 3.4 Sample of a typical CLO structure

flow of the underlying asset pool, with the deeply subordinated securities treated as an equity investment. The senior investment group, because of its superior credit protection, has the highest credit rating in the CLO structure. It must at this stage be emphasized that the rating of this senior tranche is generally higher than the average rating of the underlying asset pool because of the tiering of claims and through explicit credit enhancements.

The deeply subordinated debt may be unrated or below investment grade. This portion is usually retained by the originating bank or may be transferred to third-party investors who are seeking a higher yield. For example in 1996, according to Moody's Investors Service its speculative grade total return index outperformed US Treasuries by 13 per cent. This junior tranche has characteristics similar to pure equity; it rarely carries a coupon, is usually unrated, and in most instances offers the same risk/return profile. It is, however, a pivotal cog in a CLO transaction as it effectively determines the level of protection – and consequently the rating – the senior tranches can rely upon in the event of default. Irving (1997) noted that the issuer effectively protects the most senior tranches against potential losses by forcing the junior classes to shoulder the risk. He concludes that with subordination the only avenue for providing investment-grade senior tranches is to source and sell the junior tranche, thus guaranteeing at least some credit enhancement.

Obviously, there are a number of structural issues with respect to the offering of CLO instruments. The originator must decide on the number of issues that will be needed, and this will determine whether it uses a single or a master trust structure. A master trust structure allows the issue of a multiple series of collateralized instruments through a single SPV conduit. Similarly, the management of the asset pool, as well as the type of structure – cash flow or market – must also be determined. Although the two are not completely disjoint, with a cash-flow structure the outflow to the investors is met by the funds generated from the underlying asset pool. In contrast, with market-value structures there is greater emphasis placed on the marked to market values, particularly their value with respect to a prespecified threshold value. These are generally associated with CBOs and require active trading unlike the limited trading of cash-flow structures.

Collateral, which is an important aspect of the CLO structure and determines the quality of the issued securities, includes loan participations, various types of loan commitments and default swaps. In most cases, the originator or servicer determines the type, depth and quality of collateral. Although some CLOs may secure an asset manager to maximize the performance and market value of the underlying collateral, typically the role is not that of a portfolio manager but servicer, since CLOs are generally cash-flow transactions.

Irrespective of the number of variants mentioned, the CLO can be either delinked or linked. A number of determining factors influence the type of structure chosen by the originating bank. These are:

- the credit quality of the loans securitized;
- the investment rating of the originating bank;
- the ability of the originator to transfer loans to the SPV without notification of obligors; and
- the preferred capital treatment of the securitized loan or SPV.

There are a few subtle differences between the two, but the fundamental variation relates to the ownership of the securitized assets. In linked CLOs involving the use of credit-linked notes – which will be discussed in the subsequent section – the ownership of the underlying portfolio is retained by the originator, but the cash flow produced is sold to the SPV. However, all or a major portion of the credit risk of this portfolio is transferred to the SPV through the use of credit derivatives. For delinked structures, generally regarded for accounting and other purposes as a true sale, loans are removed from the balance sheet. The projected performance of the loan pool and the quality of the credit enhancement determine the ratings of securities in a delinked structure.

In contrast, ratings on linked CLOs are capped by the credit quality of the originator, since the originator retains ownership of the underlying portfolio. Furthermore, investors are not completely insulated from the credit risk of the originator and therefore face dual exposure (to the originating bank and to the securitized loan pool). Although credit protection is provided through the tranching of debt, default, or in the extreme case, bankruptcy by the originator, can severely disrupt the transmission of the cash flow to investors. In addition to differences cited previously, there are also differences in the accounting and regulatory treatment. In the final analysis, irrespective of the type of basic structure, or even what variation of the CLO is used, the banking sector has realized profound benefits from CLO products.

**Why CLOs?**

Typically, the 'classical' CLO instituted by an originating bank has objectives that can be considered threefold in nature. It seeks to achieve reductions in credit-risk exposures, improved balance sheet management and profitability, as well as diversification in or alternative sources of funding. However, Quinlan et al. (1998) note that there are a number of factors that affect the suitability of the CLO structure. The range of factors includes the cost of Tier 1 and Tier 2 capital, the bank's credit rating, and the cost of unsecured debt. The use of CLOs can provide benefits such as:

- release of core capital and the capping of credit risk;
- illiquid loans converted to liquid securities;
- investors receive access to high-quality corporate risk, repackaged into a variety of tranches to meet differing investor appetites; and
- improvement in the total return on capital employed and profitability.

**Risk management**
Banks are very good at originating credit risk, but very bad at holding it over the long term (Hay, 1998). This is the sentiment among many commercial banks, which directs them towards the use of CLOs. They also have strong links with corporate clients which allows them to have widespread experience in assessing credit risk. Through the reduction of assets there is credit-risk reduction, and consequently an overall reduction in the level of regulatory capital required. The total overall exposure is confined to the level of the equity component – the unrated bonds – retained by the originating bank. Essentially, the active use of such transactions minimizes the bank's exposure to a particular borrower with high concentrations of credit risk. In addition, a bank constrained by internally imposed exposure limits could use the CLO to provide additional loans to a particular, possibly important corporate sector client or sector. Essentially, the CLO allows diversification while not breaching the bank's sector lending limits.

**Bank funding**
The use of CLO transactions can provide access to a new source of funds, particularly in the medium- to long-term bracket. In most CLO deals – provided there are reliable flows from the obligors – the securitized product can potentially achieve a higher credit rating than a plain, stand-alone bond issue. It has even been argued that banks in the US securitize their best assets and achieve a superior rating for their securitized assets, since the liability can be transferred to an underpriced Federal Deposit Insurance Corporation (FDIC) (Greenbaum and Thakor, 1987). Further, the CLO market allows sub-investment or unrated originating banks access to the international financial markets, which was previously unattainable or expensive. Therefore, with a higher credit rating and where there are lower coupon rates, the originator can effectively reduce its funding costs as opposed to bond issues or even interbank loans. In addition, CLOs, through their access to the capital market, provide these banks with increased diversification among their funding sources.[13]

### Improved balance sheet performance

It can be argued that the return on capital represents the major motivation behind commercial banks' use of CLO structures. Smithson et al. (1997) highlighted that until recently, there was a dependence by banks on the return on assets and book equity as performance measures, where simple return on equity and return on assets measures were sufficient. Banks had used regulatory capital as a means of the assigning of capital to various business units. However, with growing complexities, the current focus has shifted to risk-adjusted return measures, and banks are becoming increasingly concerned with economic rather than regulatory capital. Economic capital can be loosely regarded as an earnings-at-risk measurement. Here all types of risk elements, credit, market and operational risks, are aggregated and then discounted by an appropriate interest rate. On a related issue, instituting a CLO deal requires appropriate monitoring and operational capabilities, and this could engender an improvement in the originating bank's efficiency of its risk-management capabilities. The regulatory, sectoral and shareholder pressures have forced banks to focus more intently on business risks, and place profitability targets into risk-related performance measure frameworks.

Since all grades of corporate loans attract the same risk weighting – 100 per cent – under the Basle 1988 Accord, by removing the higher-quality low-yielding assets from the balance sheet a bank can leave the existing bank capital to support higher return activities – increased gearing.[14] Under this Accord, a 100 per cent risk weighting implies that a minimum 8 per cent of the full amount of the bank's loan portfolio is required to cover the risk of losses. Therefore, the bank, essentially through constrained optimization, must increase shareholder value and risk-adjusted returns, but subjected to the constraints of capital requirements. This motive is particularly strong among large banks in control of a large portfolio with a major portion of it containing investment quality loans. Although it can be argued that the origination and execution of the CLO can be more costly than on-balance sheet funding, the risk-adjusted return on capital, RAROC[15] – a measure which is becoming more widespread among banks – is higher with the CLO (see Table 3.3). CLOs therefore provide a dynamic method of balance sheet restructuring and flexibility, along with the boosting of returns on equity and its efficient use.

### Other influences

The investor on the other hand is drawn to these types of issues for a variety of reasons, many of which are proving beneficial in the rapidly developing financial market. First, the credit spreads on structured deals have been attractive in comparison to securities of equivalent or similar type risk. Here

Table 3.3  Example of CLOs in facilitating a higher RAROC on investment-grade assets

| | |
|---|---|
| Assumptions | |
| Amount of loans in CLO | $1 billion |
| Loan portfolio yield | Libor + 50 basis points (bp) |
| Bank funding costs | Libor − 10bp |
| CLO funding costs | Libor + 24bp |
| Bank retains 1% reserve fund | $10 million |
| Before CLO | |
| Yield less funding cost | (L + 50) less (L − 10) = 60bp |
| Net spread earned | 0.006 × $1bn = $6 million |
| Risk-based capital requirements | (8% on $1bn) = $80 million |
| RAROC | $6 million/$80 million = 7.5% |
| After CLO | |
| Yield less funding cost | (L + 50) less (L + 24) = 26bp |
| Net spread earned | 0.0026 × $1bn = $2.6 million |
| Risk-based capital requirements | (100% of Reserve Fund) = $10 million |
| RAROC | $2.6 million/$10 million = 26% |

Source:  Bear Stearns & Co. Inc.

the investor is being compensated for exposure to prepayment or re-investment risk, differences in liquidity relative to highly liquid investments, the complexity of the cash-flow structure, as well as perceived credit risk. Although CLOs are backed by investment-grade loans and naturally low credit risk, the perceived increase in credit risk can be derived from the fact that, for example, the credit-linked note structure can be considered the unsecured risk of the originator overlaid with the portfolio credit risk. Investors are also attracted to the development of what can be considered a limited secondary market that offers an alternative to investing directly into the corporate bond market. Although attractive, a limited secondary market may provide yet another argument for the incremental spread which could stem from the lack of information on a regular basis and transparency at the individual loan level. This issue could hinder the development, liquidity and the formation of an efficient secondary market for CLO securities.[16]

In addition to the attraction in investment yield, investors can use this form of security as a means of producing diversified portfolios of corporate assets without unbalancing the existing portfolio. Complementing the appeal of CLOs to the financial market is the fact that the overall performance history of CLOs has remained favourable, thus further encouraging institutional investor participation.

**Drawbacks**

For some banks, however, there may be some perceived disadvantages with the issuance of CLO products. For instance, the transfer of loans to the SPV without the consent of the obligor may be unattainable and difficult in some jurisdictions. Das (1999) notes that these actions have potential to disrupt client relationships and may in some cases limit the utility of the CLO structure. There may also be a predominance of non-funded types of exposures, for example, revolving credits, unfunded commitments and so on, in the asset portfolios, thus rendering securitization unattractive. Regulatory, and consequently economic, capital may be unchanged, as the originating bank in some transactions may retain a major portion of the credit risk. Furthermore, the actual cost of funding through CLO transactions may be expensive in terms of time and operational costs, making it unattractive for banks with low funding costs (see Table 3.4). Structuring and pricing could be a problem, not only in terms of time consumption, but because of their reliance on large size and fine pricing,[17] they could be vulnerable to market disruptions and volatility.

*Table 3.4  Comparison of spreads in different types of securitized funding*

| Type | Rating | Spread (bp to 3-mth Libor) | Rating | Spread (bp to 3-mth Libor) |
|---|---|---|---|---|
| Collateralized mortgage-backed securities | AA | 25–30 | BBB | 80–90 |
| Corporates | AA | 0–5 | BBB | 50–70 |
| Credit card asset-backed securities | AA | 10–15 | BBB | 100–120 |
| Collateralized loan obligations | AA | 18–23 | BBB | 110–160 |
| Collateralized bond obligations | AA | 35–45 | BBB | 130–180 |

*Source:* Feinne, Papa, Craighead and Arsenault (September 1997), in *CBOs/CLOs: An Expanding Securitisation Product*, J.P. Morgan Securities Inc.

The level of risk that is transferred from the originating bank to the third parties, such as guarantors and investors, is largely dependent on the structure of the CLO transaction (for example, credit enhancements). Directly related, the level of capital relief is also dependent on the variety of enhancements instituted and the extent of the risks reneged. As Irving (1997) highlighted, it is almost impossible to reverse-engineer out of many of these deals without incurring basis risk. He alluded to the fact that many of these structures have no fungible building blocks and it is difficult to replicate the future cash flows, as these are largely unique structures. Furthermore, the limited two-way secondary market would not allow for transparent price discovery.

In addition to the above-mentioned risks and drawbacks, one of the more significant issues with respect to securitizations surrounds the mechanism for the transfer of the lender's rights in the loan to the SPV. Unlike CBOs, where the transfer is relatively simple, as transference can occur through bearer or registered bonds, for CLOs there are a variety of means possible:

- *Assignments*   There is full legal transfer of the rights from the seller of the loan. Here notification and occasionally approval is required from the obligor. There is non-disclosure and, if approved, a direct connection between the SPV and the obligor is established.
- *Participations and sub-participations*   In this transaction the cash flows of a referenced loan are transferred to the SPV. However, if this is undertaken without the consent or knowledge of the obligor, then the contractual relationship is created only between the originating bank and the SPV. Therefore, if the originating bank becomes insolvent then the SPV becomes an unsecured creditor without any direct recourse to the obligor. Clearly, as a stand-alone structure this would have some impact on the credit quality of the collateralized securities issued.

With such issues and pressures, the financial marketplace has progressed to the building of hybrid structures in an attempt to provide the optimal structure. Terms such as contingent assignments – where the originating bank is only obliged to assign to the SPV if there is a degrading in the credit rating below a prespecified level – have emerged. Another hybrid, one that is becoming increasingly popular, involves the use of credit derivatives and credit-linked notes in CLO structures. Here, there is the synthetic transfer of the risk of the underlying portfolio through the use of credit derivative instruments.

## 4   CREDIT DERIVATIVES

### Overview

Since the early to mid-1990s, the use of credit derivatives has become increasingly prominent in various areas of finance. Since Bankers Trust's repo transaction of a commercial loan portfolio, which was broken into tranches, but the loans were retained and the default risk sold, the term 'credit derivative' has been widely used. Duffee and Zhou (1997, p. 1) point out that 'prior to the development of credit derivatives, there were very few ways to trade the credit risk of a given firm other than buying and selling obligations of the firm, such as bank loans, corporate bonds or stock'. Henke et al. (1998) make the point that adverse selection and moral hazard problems resulted in traditional tools (for example, loan sales) being less than successful in transferring credit risk.[18]

Leading in the tradition of financial innovation, credit derivatives evolved from competition among banks, and the differences in individual perceptions of credit risk. They are considered instruments that can literally split and separate the element of risk from an underlying instrument, and itself become a tradable commodity. The ownership and management of credit risk are separated from other aspects of ownership of the financial asset. Masters (1998) notes that 'credit derivatives are bilateral financial contracts that isolate specific aspects of credit risk from an underlying instrument and transfer that risk between two parties'. She adds that these, like many other successful derivative products, have the potential to achieve efficiency gains through the process of market completion.

There are generally a number of key motivations for the use of credit derivatives, such as hedging, speculation or in the case of CLO deals either arbitraging or yield-enhancing purposes. However, traditional credit units, such as investment banks, were concerned with analysis of counterparty credit quality, in addition to the valuation of transactions credit risk and its monitoring. But, with scarce credit resources, finite levels of capital and demanding shareholders, it is clear that investment banks' credit capacity must be utilized most effectively. There are a number of methods to achieve dynamic management of derivative credit exposures. These are (i) the use of credit-risk mitigation techniques to manage the changing exposures, (ii) the use of multiple limits to control different components of credit exposure, and (iii) the use of scenario analysis to determine credit capacity and potential problem areas.

These are of particular interest to commercial banks since, in their daily operations, credit risk forms the major risk category encountered by banks. As such, credit was difficult to isolate, but credit derivatives in most aspects are able to separate and transfer the credit risk as opposed to the economic substance. This gave originating banks the opportunity to trade credit risk and manage it in isolation. Such products provide widespread advantages over traditional credit instruments such as default guarantees. 'By quantifying and pricing each risk-component [duration and so on], credit risk can theoretically be unbundled . . . and parcelled out to the holder able to handle them most efficiently' (McDermott, 1996, p. 1). They encompass a whole family of instruments, ranging from default swaps to credit-linked notes, to spread options:

- *Total return (TR) swaps*   Regarded as a bilateral financial contract built for the transfer of credit risk between the parties involved and produces a synthetic off-balance sheet position in the underlying risky asset for the selling party. For the buying party it provides protection against the deterioration or default of the reference asset. It is distinguishable from the credit swap, as it exchanges the entire economic performance or exposure of the asset for another cash flow. Payments in these transactions are determined by changes in the market valuation of a specific instrument, irrespective of the occurrence of a credit event.[19] For the credit swap a credit event must have occurred before any payments are made. TR swaps are widely used in the formation of new asset classes to investors who are constrained by administrative complexities or investor restrictions that have in the past provided barriers to market entry. Such is the case with insurance companies and fund managers who use these products to gain access to the bank loan markets.
- *Credit default swaps*   Defined as a financial instrument where the protection buyer pays a periodic fee, in return for a contingent payment from the seller following the occurrence of a credit event of the underlying asset. These swaps allow the holder of an exposure to a particular obligor to transfer the risk of default. If there is a credit event there is a predetermined settlement sum or in some cases the physical transfer of the reference asset. Barring such, the protection buyer pays the swap counterparty a spread usually referenced to Libor. This spread could also be tied to that received by an investor in the underlying obligation in either the cash or asset-swap[20] market. The asset-swap market is used as a benchmark largely because the default swap is an unfunded transaction. According to Masters (1998) these credit swaps usually average $25–50 million per transaction, but can range in size from a few million to billions of dollars. Since many of these transactions are derivative over-the-counter (OTC) transactions, there are few limitations; for example, unlike bond issues there is no rating requirement. The greatest hindrance, as in any OTC deal, is the willingness of the counterparties to agree on the credit parameters.

These are the major categories of credit derivative instruments, but there are a number of other derivative instruments such as credit options,[21] downgrade options and dynamic credit swaps, to name just a few. However, since the focus of this chapter is aimed at bank behaviour, those credit derivatives used by banks in securitized issues will be examined in more depth. Total return swaps, for example, provide distinct advantages over the sale of the loan portfolio. First, they allow the originating bank to diversify credit risk, while maintaining the confidentiality of the obligor and its records. Second, the administrative costs of a total return swap are purported to be lower. Third, the use of credit derivatives is less visible to borrowers and competing banks as opposed to an outright loan sale, where information must be transferred and consent received. This third advantage highlights the multi-jurisdictional nature of transactions with respect to the rights of obligors, and thereby compounds the challenges faced by banks in the sale of a loan portfolio. Furthermore, the originating bank may also encounter complex taxing structures.

Combining credit derivatives with traditional elements of ABS, high-profile asset securitizations have been brokered where otherwise not easily possible. With these credit derivative structures, specific balance sheet management goals can be tailored, with credit derivatives aimed at controlling risk, and CDOs that are designed to 'save' on regulatory capital. As earlier mentioned, initially, the desired goal of securitization was clearly aimed at a more efficient use and return on equity capital, that is, capital arbitrage. The overriding argument here surrounds the differences between economic as opposed to regulatory capital. With securitizations, the determining factor should be the difference between regulatory capital and the adjusted[22] economic capital. Taking advantage of anomalies in the financial marketplace, counterparties can also earn incremental earnings, such as fees, and also benefit from lower funding costs on a relatively low-risk basis.

Many credit derivatives are privately negotiated financial products and pose risks such as operational, counterparty, liquidity, operational and basis risks.[23] It is also highly unlikely that such a contract can be reengineered without incurring some costs. Compounding this problem is the absence of a secondary market, as liquidity risk is a vital consideration for market players, leading to the difficulty in offsetting any position before the contract matures. Furthermore, the absence of the secondary market also hinders any ability to hedge the credit exposure in the established position.

**Credit-linked Notes/Credit Derivatives in Securitization**

With innovations it is usually rare to chance upon a totally new concept; it typically involves the modification of an existing idea or process. This same type of reasoning could be applied to the use of CLOs with embedded credit derivative instruments, where there has been a merging of two concepts. For any financial innovation to be successful, it must improve the operational efficiency and completeness of the financial market.[24] In an incomplete market where there is unfulfilled investor desire, an innovation can fuel profit opportunities, effectively exploiting any inefficiency in financial intermediation or incompleteness in financial markets. Evidently, investment banks have seized the opportunity to profit through the formation of CLO securities.

To tackle the pressures from both internal and external sources, banks have instituted credit derivatives. In 1996, credit derivatives entered mainstream structured finance through a number of high-profile securitizations, usually in the form of credit-linked notes (CLNs). Neal (1996) noted that CLNs are a combination of a regular bond and a credit option. They build on the flexibility of a medium-term note issuance mechanism by embedding straightforward credit default swaps via securitization into a note or bond. 'It is a combination of a fixed income security with an embedded credit derivative' (Das, 1999, p. 14). Moreover, the note enables the investor to replicate credit exposure to an underlying reference portfolio, without direct investment into the security itself, capturing the cash flow or movements in the value of the underlying default risk of the instrument. The use of the credit derivative or unfunded guarantees allows the originating bank to transfer virtually riskless senior exposure in the CLO, leaving only the junior levels to be funded in the bond markets. Essentially, CLNs involve the repackaging of portfolios of credit risk into tradable financial instruments.

**Rationale for the Use of CLNs**

The underlying factor for use of credit derivative instruments in CLOs is clearly profit motivated. However, there are many secondary motives, such as credit-risk reduction. When conditions are volatile (for example, inflationary pressures with fluctuating interest rates, or uncertainty in economic conditions), such innovations are designed to reduce exposures to such risks. These economic parameters create a demand for different types of financial products. Clearly, changes in the level of economic activity do stimulate innovation, since in periods of economic prosperity many institutions innovate in the pursuit of corporate growth. However, with steep actual or anticipated recession, the emphasis shifts to risk reduction and liquidity (Van Horne, 1985). Another prominent factor is linked to financial deregulation, which blurs the distinction between financial intermediaries. This increases competition, and the formation of new, attractive investor products may become necessary for survival.

Other motives are derived from the circumvention of regulatory and tax constraints. Here financial innovation is mainly defensive in nature with the main aim focused on the restoration of profitability, risk reduction or both. The fundamental motive for the influx of new banking products stems from risk-reduction or profit motives. These, along with technological advances – which promote process as opposed to product change – allow for the broadening and speed of financial service applications. Credit derivative products in bank-structured instruments are used for a wide-ranging number of reasons, many of which are linked to basic CLO securitization concepts.

Covill (1999, p. 1) noted that 'credit derivatives can be a wonder drug. Widely regarded as a form of Viagra for commercial banks, [they] enable banks to leverage their balance sheets by buying new assets or selling the risk of existing ones.' Traditional motives such as lower funding costs for many lower-rated banks, capital management and credit-risk management have been reinforced by greater emphasis being placed on balance sheet management and the management of client relationships. With contracting credit spreads, and with relatively constant funding costs, banks and investors alike must look for more esoteric assets to trade.

Corporate client relationships have in the past been vitally important to investment banks; however, there exist greater levels of disintermediation within the financial system, leading to some low-yielding loans in many banks' balance sheets. Unlike selling loans as seen in traditional CLOs, this method of securitization through derivative instruments can be considered relationship friendly. By selling a low-yielding loan – usually linked to large corporates – the originating bank can threaten a relationship that has been carefully nurtured. It should be noted that where there are strong relationships with a specific firm or industry, there is the distinct probability that this would create specific concentrations of credit risk.

On the other hand, with reductions in the number of banking relationships by large corporates, the remaining banks may indeed be called upon to lend more, and this could also increase its concentration risk. Credit derivatives allow the bank to repackage the specific credit exposure and pass it on to investors. Therefore the originating bank is able to discreetly shed its credit exposures, while maintaining the client's confidentiality and its security. Importantly, in terms of credit crunches a firm's longevity could be placed in question without a reliable source of packaged funds, through which a long-term relationship would have been forged. Essentially, the bank is able to retain the asset as well as the relationship, while segmenting or managing a portion of the risk. In addition, by maintaining such a relationship, a bank may be able to sell these corporates other more profitable products.

The reference entity, whose risk – in the case of a CLN – is being transferred, need not be aware of a credit derivative transaction. By contrast a loan assignment through the secondary loan market requires obligor notification. Credit derivative instruments are off-balance sheet instruments, except when embedded in structured notes, and as such offer a wide range of flexibility in terms of leverage. The use of a credit derivative instrument allows the user to reverse a possibly skewed credit-risk profile, that is, the earning of a small premium at the risk of a large loss.

Consolidation within the banking and indeed the corporate sector has applied pressure on bank relationships. This, along with the euro's implementation, will have put further emphasis on balance sheet structure and strategic competitiveness. Although the euro will provide greater financial market liquidity, it will also improve transparency and comparability, thereby highlighting any pricing differentials. Linked to the euro is the wave of mergers in the banking sector, and rather than attempting balance sheet shrinkage, the focus will shift to balance sheet stability.

**Some Structural Issues**

Largely as a result of the reasons stated above, this market is considered by many to be one of the fastest-growing areas in structured finance. CLOs with embedded derivative products backed by investment-grade loans appeal to yield-hungry investors. In many cases, they can pick up substantially more yield by purchasing 'synthetic' credit exposure to these CLO structures than they would have in most publicly quoted debt instruments.

Investors purchase the securities from the SPV that pays a coupon – either fixed or floating – during the life of the security. In many of the derivative-enhanced CLOs, the SPV enters a credit default swap where it pays the par value of the security less its recovery rate to the originating bank. The bank meanwhile pays an annual fee to the SPV, which amounts to credit protection, some of which is shunted to the investors to assist in generating the excess yield. At maturity, the note is redeemed at par, unless the underlying referenced asset defaults, in which case the investors receive the recovery value[25] of the asset. It must be further emphasized that the investor is faced with double default risk, that is, the risk of the originating bank defaulting along with that of the underlying referenced portfolio of assets. As highlighted by Irving (1997, p. 9), 'investors' exposure to the underlying reference is . . . the same in the credit linked note as it is in a public bond issued by the reference. There is, however, if remote, [exposure] to the collateral of the trust itself.'

In these structures banks can receive the same or similar regulatory benefits as traditional securitization by transferring risk synthetically. In addition, as largely OTC transactions, the legal and structural risks characteristic of loan sales are avoided, and market and customer confidentiality is maintained. The reference entity, whose credit risk is being transferred, needs to be neither party to nor aware of the credit derivative transaction. Some of these structures can further exploit the unfunded, off-balance sheet nature of CLNs. This allows a bank to purchase credit protection from the SPV, necessary to mimic the regulatory capital treatment of traditional securitization, while preserving a competitive funding advantage. In the final analysis, CLNs provide further stimulus to a rapidly expanding securitization market by extracting and repackaging credit exposures from a large pool of risks. Many of these risks are not conducive to securitized products; because they are unfunded or off-balance sheet, they are not intrinsically transferable, or relationship-wise, they would be complicated.

The CLN structure, such as SBC's 'Glacier' deal (SBC Glacier Finance Ltd, 1997), allows confidentiality, as there is regulatory relief, and no need for disclosure. Risk transfer is usually limited to catastrophe risks, as the excess spread, first loss loan reserves and the lowest rated or unrated tranches absorb most of the risks. There is also the limited effect of an increase in earnings volatility.

### A Credit-linked Structure: SBC Glacier Finance Ltd

The deal involves the CLO of approximately $1.74 billion in five- and seven-year floating rate, bullet notes backed by credit-linked instruments from the underlying portfolio of SBC Warburg (see Table 3.5). The struc-

Table 3.5  *Breakdown of the SBC Glacier CLO floating rate asset-backed securities (rated tranches)*

| Series | Amount $m | Discount margin/ 3-mth Libor | S&P | Moody's | Expected maturity | Final maturity | WAL |
|---|---|---|---|---|---|---|---|
| 1A | 798.225 | +16 bps | AA+ | 100.00 | 10.9.02 | 10.9.04 | 5.0 |
| 1B | 36.105 | +65 bps | na | 100.00 | 10.9.02 | 10.9.04 | 5.0 |
| 2A | 798.225 | +19 bps | AA+ | 100.00 | 10.9.04 | 10.9.06 | 7.0 |
| 2B | 29.58 | +75 bps | na | 100.00 | 10.9.04 | 10.9.06 | 7.0 |

*Note:* Additionally, there were $31.32m – Class C FRN; $36.975m – Class D FRN; $9.57m – Class E Zero coupon notes spread over Series 1 & 2; WAL: Weighted Average Life.

*Source:* The Global Securities Research & Economics Group, Merrill Lynch & Co.

ture of these notes transfers the credit risk of the corporate loans to the investors from SBC Warburg – the originating bank. As a credit-linked structure, the notes are capped by the credit rating of the bank, which was rated AAA. The investors in this transaction assume the risk of both the originating bank and the underlying obligations. Despite a lack of detailed disclosure of underlying corporate obligations, or of obligor characteristics, the portfolio is dictated by strong collateral guidelines. Furthermore, the credit composition of the underlying pool of assets must be broadly maintained, with a ceiling on single industry concentration of 8 per cent and a 5 per cent exposure limit to sovereigns of rating below AA– or Aa3. Although differing environments and jurisdictions can impact on the level of credit exposure to SBC, the consequences from the default probability remain. In the event of default by SBC Warburg, there is a strong likelihood that the CLO-Glacier structure's issues will default.

Since no security has been granted, the CLNs purchased by Glacier from SBC represent senior unsecured obligations of SBC, and rank *pari passu* to other such unsecured obligations. They constitute Libor notes, with the rate of interest on each determined by the referenced Libor rate. The face amount of the CLN is payable on maturity, but this payment may be advanced given defined situations. For example:

1. All or part of the principal amount of the CLN along with any accrued interest should be paid provided there is a change or clarification in the interpretation in tax rules or regulations in the relevant taxing jurisdiction.
2. The CLN holder may simply choose to exercise the option to redeem all or part of each CLN on the predetermined optional redemption date, in which case the principal amount will be paid.
3. Payment is triggered with the occurrence of a credit event, and redemption is set within defined parameters.[26]

Credit enhancement of this structure is through subordination, including the retained equity portion, and through excess spread. Within each series, payments of principal and interest are made sequentially so as to protect the most senior bondholders. Within the agreement with SBC there is an allowance for the purchase of additional CLNs to add to the pool, whose characteristics are expected to vary over the life of the notes.

With this structure, the innovation is found with the use of CLNs to transfer risk to the issuer and then on to the investors, in a fashion different from the use of a sale or sub-participation. In transferring the credit risk, SBC issued one CLN linked to each reference obligor in the underlying portfolio. The CLN in essence securitizes the risk of default for the particular obligor with which it was referenced. Assets are deemed to remain on-balance sheet in accordance with regulatory procedures, but some capital relief is provided to reflect that some risk has been transferred to the SPV. The CLN's principal amount is based on SBC's estimate of credit exposure by each obligor in the securitized portfolio. If there is default of an underlying corporate entity, then the CLN linked to that particular obligor or asset is deemed callable. The recovery values depend on the type of the CLN that was originally issued.

## 5 REGULATION

**Current Overview and Problems**

Banks over the years have used innovative products to combat regulation, among other factors, in order to secure a profitable status and even survival. Until the late 1980s, capital requirements for banks were independently established by regulatory authorities, with little formal regard to one another's approach. With increased globalization of financial markets, this dislocated method of supervision was becoming less relevant, leading to the formation of the Basle Accord. In the banking industry, while competition has intensified, the earlier version of the Basle Accord has reduced banks' incentive to keep investment-grade loans on their balance sheets (see 'Why CLOs?', in Section 3, above).

In recent times there have been additional factors, such as the euro. According to Metcalfe (1999), with the disappearance of currency pairs and consequently fewer trading opportunities, the focus has shifted to credit as an alternative trading opportunity. Further, with the single currency, business and even banks will consolidate and restructure to tackle changes in Europe. Corporate restructuring usually signals increased corporate debt, in the process expanding the credit market, and allowing the use of credit-derivative products to flourish. Financial institutions domiciled within the single industry area will be competing for capital not just domestically, but with other financial institutions throughout the single currency area. This activity will, however, be of concern to regulators, who are usually wary of a surge in such innovative products, along with their impact on capital adequacy and the stability of the financial system overall.

First, however, one must define capital; according to Skora (1998) a broad, technical definition is the bank's *net worth*. In more specific terms, capital can be considered as the cushion against possible losses due to various risks. For if losses exceed this cushion, then the excess loss is transferred to the creditors – such as investors – therefore, capital must be large enough to minimize the likelihood of default. This capital sum can be represented as:

$$\text{Capital} = \text{Expected Loss} + \text{Unexpected Loss}.$$

Here the unexpected loss is a probability measure within a given confidence interval of the uncertainty of loss. Another distinction that must also be clarified relates to that between economic and regulatory capital, both representing some measure of the bank's risks. Economic capital is determined by the bank's internal policies and models, in many cases using sophisticated statistical techniques and historical data which are consistent with the specific bank's activities. On the other hand, regulatory capital is determined by rules set by the authorities, and provides generic application, transmitted through its simplicity and conservatism.

Under the Basle Accord there are stringent definitions of capital, ranging from the most permanent form, Tier 1, to Tier 3, the most fluid, less permanent form of capital which is retained to cover losses on market-related risks. Since the main point of this chapter is not strictly pertaining to the definition of capital, this area will not be examined in great detail. However, it should be noted that there are further definitions of qualifying capital set by Basle. The other side of the capital adequacy calculation is based on assets, where banks must ensure that they have sufficient capital available to absorb the risk of losses should assets fail to perform.

Generally, Tier 1 and Tier 2 capital is intended to buffer against such credit losses, where the credit risk associated with an asset depends on the creditworthiness of the counterparty. Here lies the difficulty for banks in terms of their corporate clients, for currently, claims on a varied spectrum of corporates are all risk weighted at 100 per cent, irrespective of their credit quality. For some credit-risk profiles this may seem prudent but for diversified portfolios of investment-grade credits, this may seem excessive. According to rating agencies – Standard and Poor's (S&P) and Moody's – the default rate on investment-grade credits is low. In a Merrill Lynch (Quinlan et al., 1998) report the average historical cumulative default rate for all investment-grade debt calculated by S&P over a five-year period is 0.81 per cent and 0.84 per cent for Moody's. This represents only default rates, but for loss rates the probability would be lower.

In terms of the structure, as most SPVs are not categorized as banks or financial institutions, claims on SPVs are ordinarily risk weighted at 100 per cent, as with any other corporate entity. This treatment means that, in the absence of cash collateral for the SPV's funding obligation, the originating bank will have the same capital/risk asset ratio requirement in respect of its commitments to lend after the securitization as it had before. However, the usual committed facility will incur no capital cost so long as the facility remains undrawn, thereby negating complicated funding and cash collateralization issues. The originating bank will be aware that an SPV will have a relatively rigid funding structure, and will be less able to exercise discretion in favour of defaulting borrowers than the originator. Alternatively the originating bank may intervene to protect investors in securities issued by the SPV if default levels on the underlying assets prove higher than expected. Such extreme measures are only expected to be executed due to considerations of a possible negative impact on reputation.

The use of CLO transactions allows the originating bank to resist disclosure of its borrowers' identities on both legal and commercial grounds, since any disclosure could be simply offering competitors clear insight into its corporate loan portfolio. The great difficulty with the use of credit derivative instruments stems from the fact that in addition to the clear credit risk, there is also liquidity risk, as many of these structures involve unique instruments that are not widely held. In addition, for many of the bonds or even the underlying portfolio of credits, there is no active, transparent market. For such reasons, the Federal Reserve Board (FRB) cited two examples for limited transfer of credit risk: (i) if the credit derivative agreement adopts a restrictive agreement of a credit event, or (ii) if it establishes a materiality threshold that requires a high percentage of loss to occur before the guarantor is obliged to pay.

Until recently, this has created some level of uncertainty due to the case-by-case nature of the transference of credit risk, as well as the lack of uniform documentation and terms within the financial marketplace. The varying levels of disclosure or detailed information are very much of concern to regulators and investors alike. Various regulators, such as the International Swap and Derivatives Association (ISDA), have all found it necessary to issue some type of documentation on the standardization of these derivative markets. It is also important to note that users of these credit instruments will also be confronted with uncertainty of their regulatory status, since different contracts will fall under the umbrella of, and be regulated by, different agencies, each with different levels of rules. It is believed that with the standardized information flow on returns, defaults and recoveries, parties will be able to identify the precise terms of the transactions from a clearly defined number of alternatives. Clearly, the quality of collateral and ongoing performance information will indeed vary significantly, and the less transparent the information, the greater the possible liquidity risk. With reduced legal and other uncertainties stemming from this lack of information, the market growth should be further enhanced.

In addition to the ongoing effects of the euro in terms of its impact on an increased debt and credit market, the recent proposals by the BIS are expected to be a further incentive for banks to hedge risk, and consequently there will be a demand for credit derivatives. Growth and interest in these new structured credit instruments is not confined to banks, however, for there is growing interest in such products outside of the banking industry, for example, mutual funds and trusts. Theoretically, by giving investors access to bank loan portfolios, credit risk will be more widely and effectively traded among an expanding variety of players. Furthermore, with diversification of credit risk in loan portfolios, there will be greater liquidity in credit markets. These new proposals, along with the major concern, that is, the lack of standardized documentation and transparency in the credit market (which has seriously hindered growth), will be discussed in the following sections.

The 'one size fits all' approach to capital requirements for credit risk is becoming increasingly problematic as banks themselves, in their own internal capital allocation procedures, take into account the widely varying risk characteristics (Yellen, 1996). It can be true to state that both techniques may represent a measure of risk, but where output from the two techniques is diverging, banks will be more motivated to deal with this penalty, such as with the increasing use of CLOs, but how will the regulators respond? More importantly, how should one measure the credit risk associated with CLO activities, and how much capital should be required for a bank also engaged in such activities? Some may look at these structured securitizations and state that they pose no greater threat to other financial activities. Wide-scale overtures to over-regulate derivatives, or even the structured CLO market, would be of little benefit, except to increase the regulatory burden on capital market activities.

**The Cycle of Regulation versus Innovation**

There is an ongoing dilemma between the imposition of regulation and the efficiency, or completeness and profitability, of any market. Van Horne (1985) mentioned that the purpose of financial markets is to channel the savings of the society to the most profitable investment opportunities on a risk-adjusted return basis. There is a dynamic connection between market innovation and regulation. Financial innovation often occurs in response to regulation, especially when regulation makes little economic sense (Meyer, 1998). Economic efficiencies that are potentially associated with financial innovation can be negated by inefficient banking regulation. As regulation is perceived to hinder this process, new variants of financial products would come to the fore. Conversely, advances in the market spur the evolution of regulation. Investment opportunities may originate in the private sector, where the rate of return on the investment is paramount, as opposed to the public sector, where social returns are promoted. Therefore regulation must somehow produce a fine balance between these two positions.

The usefulness of the capital adequacy accord lies in its ability to be used as a benchmark for financial scrutiny by both regulators and counterparties alike. The various shortcomings highlighted previously, along with the ever-increasing levels of financial innovations, undermine the effectiveness of the capital adequacy requirements. With the proliferation of capital arbitrage[27] techniques, securitization included, banks can effectively achieve risk-based capital ratios, which are below the Accord's nominal 8 per cent. Capital arbitrage is fundamentally driven by large divergences between economic risks and that of the risk-weighted measure set by the BIS.[28] This, in addition to its efficiencies, can also give rise to distorted risk-management techniques, and from a safety and soundness perspective, risk-management distortions could be as, or even more, problematic than capital arbitrage.

By contrast, efficient banking regulation not only provides a backdrop for financial advances, but also permits governments to achieve to some extent social objectives which otherwise may have been impossible or incurred at a higher cost. With this current Accord, the phenomenon of capital arbitrage poses some significant policy trade-offs, for the only means available to regulators in limiting such activity is through the imposition of broad restrictions on the use of financial engineering technologies. According to Jones (1999), this would, however, be counterproductive and possibly untenable since capital arbitrage often functions as a safety valve for mitigating the adverse effects of nominal capital requirements which, for some activities, are unreasonably high.

A lack of understanding of the regulatory nature of derivatives could cause an increase in the risk that inappropriate regulations, or ill-conceived regulatory actions, could exacerbate or heighten financial market volatility. Essentially, capital arbitrage permits banks to compete in some activities which they would have been forced to abandon due to insufficient returns on regulatory capital needed. Moreover, securitization and other risk-unbundling techniques to some extent appear to provide significant economic benefits apart from capital arbitrage.

The debate in many instances focuses on whether inefficient or burdensome capital adequacy requirements can reduce the risks in banking. According to Blum (1999, p. 756), 'under binding capital requirements an additional unit of equity tomorrow is more valuable to a bank. If raising equity is excessively costly, the only possibility to increase equity tomorrow is to increase risk today'. Importantly, Gehrig (1995) highlighted that capital requirements greatly influence the nature of strategic competition among banks. Essentially, it must be noted that in a dynamic setting, with incentives for asset substitution, capital adequacy may actually lead to increases in bank risks. Furthermore, if the regulators are concerned with reducing the insolvency risk of banks, then one of the effects of such regulation is reduced bank profits. Theoretically, with lower profits, a bank has a smaller incentive to avoid default, along with the 'leverage effect of capital rules' which raises the value of equity to the bank. For with every dollar of equity, more than one dollar can be invested in a profitable, but risky, asset.

The 1988 Basle Accord is extremely simplistic in terms of credit risk, with banks having to contend with a rather arbitrary capital requirement of 8 per cent, although many of the internal capital allocation procedures have evolved as credit products have evolved. Regulatory requirements for capital have been oversimplified historically and tend to penalize those institutions that invest in sophisticated internal risk-management systems. Regulatory concerns about capital adequacy therefore can best be addressed by allowing qualifying institutions to use their own risk models for determining capital adequacy for credit and market risks, subject to regulatory oversight. This policy can promote innovation, as well as financial market soundness and a more efficient allocation of capital. Currently, regulatory capital rules do not fully capture the economic substance of the risk exposures arising from structured securitizations.

The use of complex derivatives and complex structures has led to difficulties in the measurement of possible risk elements. The major difficulty occurs where regulatory capital requirements are not equipped to capture the complexities of some risk positions being undertaken by banks. However, risk cannot be measured in precise terms, for there are always potential estimation errors, though at some point the measurements will become sufficiently robust to warrant widespread changes in prudential regulations.

Clearly, the growth in CLO transactions, and indeed other forms of arbitrage, has been spurred by the inadequacies in the international standard. This has occurred due to the development of sophisticated models by some banks that quantify risks, including credit risk, which differ substantially from the 8 per cent regulatory standard. As the more sophisticated banks have done through rapid evolution of their system, regulators should follow suit by moving from a ratio-based standard – which says little about insolvency – to a model-based one, especially for the more complex institutions. For such institutions, this standard is inefficient in the objective of limiting bank failure to acceptable levels, since high capital ratios do not necessarily equate to low solvency probabilities. More damaging is the risk of a few institutions failing to keep pace with risk-management practices, which places all banks at risk. The risk is not simply confined to counterparty failures, but the systematic underpricing of credit risk, for example, is damaging to the financial system. Furthermore, it is possible in the long run that the regulated entity could shrink in size when compared to an unregulated one. Therefore, what are the alternatives available to ensure the protection of the banking system and investors alike?

**Inherent Risks and the Way Forward**

There have been a number of concerns associated with the development of these complex-structured CLO transactions. Counterparties and investors alike who are concerned with the possible credit and counterparty risks cite the lack of transparency, standardization and information as a major factor. Participants in the securitization market rely on transaction reporting as the basic source of information necessary to analyse, price and trade asset-backed instruments in the secondary market. The credit and liquidity enhancements that the originating banks provide in these structured deals further complicate the evaluation of risks. These enhancements, which are complex and in some cases indirect in nature, may expose investors to 'hidden' risks that may not become evident until there is deterioration in the assets. Therefore, the availability of quality information enables investors to determine the level of, or indeed whether to invest in, such securities. Quality and consistent information would afford the development of more liquid and efficient securitization markets.

The information could be separated on two different levels. First, collateral-level data, relating to characteristics of the performance of receivables and other assets that provide the source of payments on these transactions. Second, security-level data, which relate to the allocation and distribution of cash flows to the holders of various tranches of securities, according to their differing payment priorities and characteristics (ESF, 1999). However, such information is usually non-existent or not timely, and this generally typifies the opaqueness of the CLO market.

The market for many of the structured derivative CLOs is clearly unregulated, for a large part of the regulatory personnel and associated systems is not equipped to handle many of the complexities involved in these transactions. Such activity must, however, be regulated in some form, but with the ongoing debate and with the continued lack of transparency, the attitude is seemingly 'if no one is providing information of loans and performance, why should we?'. However, the glaring number of deficiencies is evident, with the major drawbacks listed below:

- *A lack of standardization*   It is often the case that no two reports can be directly comparable, as no specific standards are in place with respect to specific reported fields of data.
- *Timeliness of reporting*   If available, the post-issuance reported data are often not produced in sufficient time to allow adequate securities analysis of the information.
- *Availability and adequacy of reported data*   Post-issuance reporting is not usually widely disseminated, being generally limited to the current holders of the securities, effectively blocking further analysis of prospective investors. Furthermore, such information is often inadequate in its scope of reporting necessary to provide an informed investment decision.

These deficiencies must be corrected to ensure the growth, liquidity and soundness of the financial system as it relates to CLOs, or for that matter to securitized transactions. As such, the European Securitisation Forum (ESF, 1999) has attempted to provide guidelines aimed at correcting some of the deficiencies which continue to hamper the continued growth and efficiency of the securitized market. The main recommendations are:

1. Transaction reports should generally be made available to the marketplace, and not limited to current holders. Issuers should make transaction reports through all readily available channels.
2. Regular ongoing post-issuance transaction reporting should be a standard feature of all European securitization transactions.
3. As far as possible, transaction reporting elements and definitions should be standardized, especially for securitization supported by the same type of underlying capital.

Recommendations involved with post-issuance reporting include such important categories as current and cumulative interest shortfalls, drawdowns from credit enhancements or reserves, as well as servicer advances. This level of reporting would definitely provide the investor with some idea of the potential credit risk, and other participants of possible counterparty risk. There are even more 'important' recommendations, such as reporting on current and cumulative defaults, delinquencies, trigger measurements and some idea of ratings movement, with reports on original and current rating by a designated rating agency.

These recommendations are minimum reporting standards constituting a basic set of data, providing consistency as there are developed definitions for each recommended reported category. It is anticipated that market participants would supplement this standard with other relevant information depending on particular features of the individual transactions.

**Self-regulation?**

This is clearly an attempt at the promotion of self-regulation over government or external regulation, such as the BIS Accord, which has recently issued proposals and will be discussed in the next subsection. The urgency for both forms of regulatory authorities to provide guidelines for banking activities provides the backdrop for the growing tensions that exist between regulators and the banking sector. There is a heightened level of discord between the two, following continued concerns being raised by regulators, but from the banking industry's position there is a distinct leaning towards self-regulation. Clearly, in the past, external regulatory authorities have been unable to match the development within the sector, thus placing some members at a distinct disadvantage. Therefore, with the derivative product market there is some indication that instead of external interference, the sector possesses enough internal expertise to operate efficiently within its own specified framework, as well as keep pace with innovative techniques.

Arguably, self-regulation can benefit from industry expertise reinforced by community norms and ethical values. These community norms can be dictated by standards, which if not upheld could involve informal sanction, reputational drawbacks and 'blacklisting' by the community. This set-up stands apart from the rigidity, bureaucracy, costliness and perceived ineffectiveness of external or governmental regulation. However, with self-regulation there is the risk of the formation of a cartel-type organization, which can be difficult to administer. The existence of monopoly power or collusion provides an additional concern that the company or companies found violating rules will not be disciplined. There are also concerns about the operational effects of the non-binding enforcement of industry codes within a global environment, in comparison with the legally binding enforcement of government rules. Furthermore, the question of how the concerns of persons outside of the industry will be included within the industry regulation still remains.

Government rules could be even more protective of the industry than the self-regulatory ones, for the governmental rules must be all-embracing for the collective good of the system rather than a single industry. If indeed self-regulation is more flexible, it may be more flexible for that industry than for others. It is relatively clear that the claimed advantages of industry expertise, community norms and collective good may, on inspection, be less substantial than the industry would hope for. Although it is argued that self-regulation has worked in some industries, there are lingering concerns about its applicability to the financial system, but are these concerns valid? In addition, is it feasible to risk placing the fragile, yet important, financial system largely in the hands of the banking industry, through self-regulation? Some members of the community certainly agree with its feasibility, but so far it remains an open question. The regulators who are concerned with the viability of the industry and financial stability are clearly not swayed by self-regulation's purported merits, as a new proposed framework for external regulation was announced in June 1999.

**BIS 1999 Proposals**

The BIS, although achieving competitive equality to some extent, has recognized the weaknesses – some of which have been addressed previously – in the existing Accord, and issued new proposals in June 1999 for initial consultation aimed at more 'definitive' proposals in 2000. The review of the Accord is designed to improve the way regulatory capital requirements reflect underlying risks. It is also designed to better address the financial innovation that has occurred in recent years (Basle Committee on Banking Supervision, 1999). Innovations such as structured securitizations have made the current Accord – a crude risk measure – less effective in calibrating an institution's true risk profile. The proposed capital framework consists of three 'pillars': minimum regulatory capital requirements, a supervisory review process and effective use of market discipline. However, the scope of this chapter is not to examine the entire set of proposals but only those pertaining to securitizing activity.

According to the report, the Committee recognizes that securitizing serves as an effective and efficient method of redistributing risks and diversifying portfolios. There is concern, however, over the use of structured securitizations to avoid the maintenance of capital consistent with their risk exposures. As such, the new proposals seek to realign the risk weightings of corporate obligors commensurate with their respective credit risk. The capital allocated could therefore be considered appropriate for the credit risk of individual tranches. High-grade securitized paper will now carry a 20 per cent risk weighting, severely reducing the capital requirement to one-fifth of the current standard. Securitized products with a rating A− and higher are those that have received the greatest level of capital relief. Likewise, those below BBB− carry a risk weighting of 150 per cent, a 50 per cent increase in capital adequacy requirements (see Table 3.6).

These proposals are expected to have profound effects on the ABS market. There is expected to be a boost in demand for high-quality securitized products, especially for banks seeking capital relief; such banks with a conservative risk profile could see their capital requirements reduced. There should

Table 3.6  Summary of BIS proposed risk weightings (%)

| Claim | Assessment | | | | | |
|---|---|---|---|---|---|---|
| | AAA to AA− | A+ to A− | BBB+ to BBB− | BB+ to B− | Below B− | Unrated |
| Sovereigns | 0 | 20 | 50 | 100 | 150 | 100 |
| Banks | | | | | | |
|   Option 1[1] | 20 | 50 | 100 | 100 | 150 | 100 |
|   Option 2[2] | 20 | 50[3] | 50[3] | 100[3] | 150 | 50[3] |
| Corporates | 20 | 100 | 100 | 100 | 150 | 100 |
| Securitization products | 20 | 50 | 100 | 150 | Deducted from capital | Deducted from capital |

*Notes:*
[1] Risk weighting based on risk weighting of a sovereign in which the bank is incorporated.
[2] Risk weighting based on the assessment of the individual risk.
[3] Claims on banks of a short original maturity, for example, less than 6 months, would receive a weight that is one category more favourable than the usual risk weight on the bank's claims.

*Source:* Basle Committee, 'A new capital adequacy framework', 3 June 1999.

also be a widening of the gap in prices and consequently yields due to newly proposed differences in ratings. For the market as a whole, the new tiering in capital charges will lead to a more noticeable tiering in spreads among securities in different risk categories, resulting in a steeper credit curve for the international ABS market (Batchvarov et al., 1999). Essentially, there is expected to be greater comparability in prices among spread products, and ABS can benefit from greater transparency in assessing relative values.

The proposals also reward investors with instruments from higher tranches, and effectively penalize those with lower rated ones, thereby pressuring banks to achieve the highest level of ratings possible. The scope for structured securitizations should also increase, as asset-backed securities can be structured in such a way to achieve desired ratings and consequently risk weightings. With the use of internal ratings and greater correspondence with rating agencies, this would provide a means of producing cheaper, quicker and easier packaging of CLOs and further boost the growth in the market. Instead of engaging in widescale capital arbitrage, banks now have further incentive to structure the debt in order to achieve higher rated credit ratings.

Clearly this would entail a greater level of dependence on external credit-rating agencies for providing capital charges for securitizations, as they are even more dependent on provided credit ratings. Implementation of such a proposal could drastically narrow the gap between the current 'crude' capital charges and the economic capital that banks allocate internally. Potentially, this could also provide investors with exposure to high-quality European corporate borrowers which, because they have no public rating, would otherwise be barred to them. Rating agencies will effectively become part of the regulatory mechanism for the financial sector.

This, however, may not be desirable as it also places additional responsibility and pressure on the agencies, and ratings are not foolproof. For example, the junior tranche of the CLO effectively generates the credit rating by guaranteeing the level of overcollateralization in the structure; then the size of that tranche is determined by the losses the asset pool is likely to sustain from defaults. Therefore, at all times the junior tranche must be large enough to absorb any expected losses, but small enough for an issuer to place. These junior and unrated bonds shoulder the major portion of risk, and since they are usually retained by the originating bank, the question of adequate capital and ratings becomes paramount. However, the way the CLO is priced depends largely on how the default data are interpreted; therefore the methodology is open to some extent to basis risk between different proprietary models. Then, arguably, both default and recovery rates could be refined in order to massage down the size of the junior tranche.

Furthermore, some banks using internal ratings may use oversimplifying assumptions due to a lack of long-term data over a series of credit cycles and the infrequency of defaults. These types of scenario would place further pressure on the agencies apropos their 'approval' of the terms of the CLO. For instance, Citibank's C*Star €4 billion synthetic securitization included up to 60 per cent of its portfolio which did not possess a public rating, thus necessitating the mapping of Citibank's internal loan ratings against Moody's. This clearly has implications for the new BIS proposals, allowing in some circumstances the use of internal credit ratings for the calculation of capital adequacy ratios.

Clearly, the provision of 150 per cent on lower-rated securities represents a step in the right direction, but if in these CLO transactions, these bonds bear the majority of the risk of the higher tranches, then the capital charge should be substantially higher. Furthermore, a large portion of these investments is retained by the originator and as such the originator has still not relinquished some portion of risk associated with the CLO transaction. Furthermore, the bands among the levels of ratings in the new proposals are also broad and wide-ranging and can possibly lead to capital arbitrage. Finally, banks must 'get up to speed' quickly with their systems, which would enable them to investigate the possible benefits and drawbacks of the proposed framework for their operations. Likewise, the rating agencies must also determine how the increased demands of ratings will affect the efficiency and quality of their output, thus possibly fuelling the tensions among regulators, bankers and the rating agencies.

## 6 CONCLUSION

Over the last decade, the financial landscape for banks has been altered by a series of innovations. One key innovation has been the development of asset-backed securitization. This chapter focused on the securitization of one asset class – collateralized loan obligations (CLOs) – and its importance for the banking industry. The three key benefits for banks, derived from CLO securitization, are: (i) more flexibility for risk management; (ii) greater diversity among funding sources; and (iii) improvement in balance sheet performance. In an attempt to combat both internal and external pressures, the banking industry has combined the benefits of structured financing with those of basic ABS. These complex structured instruments are typically in the form of credit derivatives, and usually credit-linked notes. The use of credit derivatives, thereby producing synthetic[29] securitizations, allows banks to (i) preserve the confidentiality of their client base, and subsequently its continued business, and (ii) maintain its balance sheet asset position rather than shrinkage (of major significance because of the current wave of merger activity in the sector).

However, the attempt to improve the reporting and regulatory standards proposed by the ESF and the BIS respectively is expected to make a substantial impact. This highlights the underlying 'conflicts' between self- and external regulation. However, the question as to which one is more beneficial is still open to debate. New regulatory changes can provide an incentive to trade in high-grade structured securities, while improvements in reporting standards can contribute to increasing investor comfort levels in structured securitized products. These changes are initially aimed at increasing transparency, consequently leading to soundness and liquidity in the structured finance arena. Such an economically efficient motive should be applauded, but how will the financial market respond? The question then remains, when will the relative 'trickle' in this market turn into a flood?

## NOTES

1. For excellent overviews of ABS, see Aber (1987), Cumming (1987) and Kendall and Fishman (1996).
2. Most recently this area has expanded to many assets, including student loans.

3. Adopted from the Asset Sales Report, 1985–1993, cited in Lockwood et al. (1996).
4. Adapted from the Bond Market Association press release, February 1999.
5. Federal Reserve Bulletin Statistics (1997).
6. The International ABS/MBS Monitor, Merrill Lynch (2000), April.
7. European Mortgages Report, Datamonitor, April 1997.
8. These are usually linked to some reference rate (that is, Libor) offering this rate plus a premium spread.
9. Bank for International Settlements (Basle Accord) (Basle Committee on Banking Supervision, 1988). European banks are also subject to the European Capital Adequacy Directive (CAD) (CEC, 1993).
10. Credit risk is a major aspect in the determination of securitization and can be described as 'the risk of loss on a financial or non-financial contract due to the counterparty's failure to perform on that contract' (Skora, 1998, p. 6).
11. For the year 1997, international asset-backed deals by asset type show CLOs accounting for 29.37 per cent whereas CBOs accounted for just 1.62 per cent of all international ABS (this excludes the US market) (source: International Securitisation Report (ISR) Database).
12. See Financial Reporting Standard (FRS 5) (ASB, 1994) for UK accounting rules for ABS.
13. Traditional funding sources include: expanding retail deposits, accessing the wholesale funds market, and using shareholders' funds (reserves and equity).
14. Capital arbitrage is cited as one of the problems facing the Basle Accord; see Jones (1999) and Jackson (1999).
15. This measure is calculated by the adjusted net income divided by the economic capital measure.
16. However, new transaction reporting standards have recently been adopted by the industry (see European Securitisation Forum, 1999).
17. This aspect of CLOs confines them to maintaining a narrow margin of efficiency.
18. Henke et al. (1998) make this point in relation to small and medium-sized enterprises' (SMEs) commercial loans.
19. A financial occurrence such as a default, which can affect grade and subsequently the value of an underlying reference asset.
20. Credit derivatives are typically priced off of instruments that permit some type of price discovery. The reference credit used to price them is generally a publicly traded bond issued by the same borrower (McDermott, 1996).
21. Put or call options on the price of a floating rate bond, which consists of a credit-risky instrument with any payment characteristics, and a corresponding derivative contract in which there is an exchange of cash-flow streams.
22. Adjusted for the costs involved in securitization.
23. There may be differences, including maturity mismatches in the credit risk and trading characteristics of a widely traded bond and that of the loan-backed security issued by the same obligor.
24. A complete market exists when every contingency in the world corresponds to a distinct security (Hirshleifer, 1970).
25. The rate at which the company's debt trades after default.
26. If the CLN is characterized as a fixed percentage note, then payment is 51 per cent of the face value of the note. Under this transaction, fixed percentage CLNs must comprise at least 25 per cent of the CLN pool. However, if it is a referenced security note, then payment is equal to the average bid price of the referenced security, expressed as a percentage times the face value of the CLN.
27. Defined by Jones (1999) as activities that permit a bank to assume greater risk with no increase in its minimum regulatory capital requirement, while at the same time showing no change or possibly an increase in its capital ratios.
28. Jones (2000, p. 37) states: 'capital arbitrage has attracted scant academic attention. In part, the lack of published research no doubt reflects the scarcity of public data . . . [and] may also reflect the complexity of the underlying transactions.'
29. Allows the retention of the assets, while segmenting or transferring some portion of risk.

# REFERENCES

Aber, J.W. (1987), 'Securitization: promise and opportunity for lenders', *Commercial Lending Review*, Vol. 2, No. 4, pp. 21–30.

Albrecht, Thomas W. and S.J. Smith (1997), 'Corporate loan securitization: selected legal and regulatory issues', Internet Document.

Accounting Standards Board (ASB) (1994), Financial Reporting Standard (FRS) 5, 'Reporting the substance of transactions', April.

Basle Committee on Banking Supervision (1988), 'International convergence of capital measurement and capital standards' (Basle Accord), Basle, July.

Basle Committee on Banking Supervision (1999), 'Proposal to amend the capital accord', Basle, July.

Batchvarov, A., G. Rajendra and M. Yan (1999), 'Regulatory Developments', International ABS Monitor, Merrill Lynch, Global Securities Research and Economics Group, June.

Berlin, M. (1992), 'Securitization', in P. Newman (ed.), *The New Palgrave Dictionary of Money and Finance*, Vol. 3, Basingstoke: Macmillan, pp. 433–5.

Blum, J. (1999), 'Do capital adequacy requirements reduce risks in banking?', *Journal of Banking and Finance*, Vol. 23, No. 5, pp. 755–71.

Council of the European Communities (CEC) (1993), 'Council Directive on the capital adequacy of investment firms and credit institutions', *Official Journal of the European Communities*, L 141, Brussels: CEC, 15 March, pp. 1–26.

Covill, Laura (1999), 'Getting hooked on credit derivatives', *Euromoney Magazine*, February, pp. 1–6.

Cumming, C. (1987), 'The economics of securitization', *Federal Reserve Bank of New York Quarterly Review*, Autumn, pp. 11–23.

Das, Satyajit (1999), 'Credit-linked notes: credit portfolio securitisation structures: Part One', *Financial Products*, Issue 117, July, pp. 14–19.

Duffee, G.R. and C. Zhou (1997), 'Credit derivatives in banking: useful tools for managing risk?', Finance and Economics Discussion Series. Federal Reserve Board, Washington, DC, February.

European Securitisation Forum (ESF) (1999), 'Minimum recommended post-issuance reporting standards for European securitisation transactions', June.

*EuroWeek* (1999), Structured Finance Annual Review, 'CLOs/CBOs: Banks Turn Conduit', January, p. 164.

Gehrig, T. (1995), 'Capital adequacy rules: implications for banks' risk taking', *Swiss Journal of Economics and Statistics*, No. 131, pp. 747–64.

Greenbaum, S.I. and J.V. Thakor (1987), 'Bank funding modes: securitisation versus deposits', *Journal of Banking and Finance*, No. 11, pp. 379–92.

Hay, John (1998), 'CLOs: every bank must have one', *EuroWeek*, International Structured Finance, September, pp. 4–8.

Henke, S., H. Burghof and B. Rudolph (1998), 'Credit securitization and credit derivatives: financial instruments and the credit risk management of middle market commercial loan portfolios', Ludwig-Maximilians University, Munich, CFS Working Paper No. 7, January.

Hirshleifer, J. (1970), *Investment, Interest and Capital*, Englewood Cliffs, NJ: Prentice-Hall.

Irving, Richard (1997), 'Credit notes in record deals', *Risk*, Vol. 10, No. 1, January, p. 9.

Jackson, P. (1999), 'Capital requirements and bank behaviour: the impact of the

Basle Accord', Basle Committee on Banking Supervision Working Papers, No. 1, April.

Jones, David (1999), 'Emerging problems with the Accord: regulatory capital arbitrage and related issues', *Bank of England Financial Stability Review*, June, pp. 103–4.

Jones, David (2000), 'Emerging problems with the Accord: regulatory capital arbitrage and related issues', *Journal of Banking and Finance*, Vol. 24, pp. 35–58.

Kendall, L.T. and M.J. Fishman (1996), *A Primer on Securitization*, Cambridge, MA: MIT Press.

Lockwood, L., R. Rutherford and M. Herrera (1996), 'Wealth effects of asset securitisation', *Journal of Banking and Finance*, No. 20, pp. 151–64.

Masters, Blythe (1998), 'Credit derivatives and the management of credit risk', *The Electronic Journal of Financial Risk*, Vol. 1, No. 2, March/April.

McDermott, Robert (1996), 'The long awaited arrival of credit derivatives', *Derivatives Strategy*, December/January, vol. 2, pp. 1–7.

Metcalfe, Richard (1999), 'CLNs – more than a flash in the pan', *The Financial Times*, March, p. 33.

Meyer, L.H. (1998), 'Financial globalization and efficient banking regulation', Federal Reserve Board Speech, Annual Washington Conference of the Institute of International Bankers, Washington, DC, March.

Neal, Robert (1996), 'Credit derivatives: new financial instruments for controlling credit risk', *Federal Reserve Bank of Kansas City*, Vol. 81, No. 2, pp. 15–27.

Parsley, Mark (1997), 'Credit derivatives – you ain't seen nothin' yet', *Euromoney Magazine*, December, pp. 1–9.

Pavel, C.A. and D. Phillis (1987), 'Why commercial banks sell loans: an empirical analysis', *Economic Perspectives*, Federal Reserve Bank of Chicago, July/August, pp. 3–14.

Quinlan, Jeremy, G. Rajendra and D. Castro (1998), 'Bank collateralised loan obligations: from 0 to 60 in less than 2 years?', Merrill Lynch, Global Securities Research & Economics Group, March.

SBC Glacier Finance Ltd. (1997), 'Offering circular', SBC Warburg Dillon Read, London, September.

Skora, Richard (1998), 'Rational modelling of credit risk and credit derivatives', *Credit Derivatives*, London: Risk Publications.

Smithson, Charles, T. Po and J. Rozario (1997), 'Capital budgeting: how banks measure performance', *Risk*, Vol. 10, No. 6, June, pp. 40–41.

Van Horne, James C. (1985), 'Of financial innovations and excesses', *Journal of Finance*, Vol. 40, No. 3, July, pp. 621–31.

Yellen, Janet L. (1996), 'The "new" science of credit risk management at financial institutions', *The Region*, Federal Reserve Bank of Minneapolis, September.

PART II

Banking Structures and Functions

# 4. The new world of euro banking
## Jean Dermine

## 1 INTRODUCTION

Two main questions are addressed in this chapter. How does the move from national currencies to the euro alter the sources of competitive advantage of banks? What are the main strategic options available to financial firms?

A structural analysis of the banking industry raises the question of the importance of a national currency factor. For instance, the markets for pension funds and mutual funds management, or the euro–franc and euro–lira bond markets, were quite fragmented, with domestic institutions capturing a very large market share. Although this fragmentation is explained in part by regulations and history, it did reflect the importance of national currencies. Another example is the leading role of American investment banks in the dollar-denominated eurobond market. Does the emergence of a new world currency competing with the US dollar help the competitiveness of European banks? This chapter attempts to show how, besides an obvious loss of intra-European currencies' trading business, the introduction of a common currency changes fundamentally the sources of competitive advantage of banks. This calls for a major review of strategic options.

The chapter is structured as follows. In Section 2, the origin of European Monetary Union is briefly reviewed. Eight impacts of the euro are identified and analysed in Section 3. In Section 4, the strategic options available to banks are discussed. Section 5 calls the attention of regulators to the challenge raised by cross-border mergers, and Section 6 concludes.

## 2 THE ORIGIN OF EMU: A REMINDER

Fifteen years ago, in 1985, the European Commission published the *White Paper on the Completion of the Internal Market*, which provides for the free circulation of persons, goods and capital in the European Union (EU). In 1989, the Committee for the Study of Economic and Monetary Union recommended in the Delors Report a three-phase transition spread over ten years. Its conclusions were incorporated in the February 1992 Maastricht Treaty on European Union. Stage I, from 1 July 1990 to 31 December 1993, provided for the freedom of capital flows and the coordination of national monetary policies. Stage II started in July 1994 with the creation of the European Monetary Institute. One of its missions was to prepare the monetary institutions and the European System of Central Banks (ESCB). Finally, Stage III of European Monetary Union (EMU) started on 1 January 1999. The exchange rates between the 11 member countries were irrevocably fixed. The interbank and capital markets operated exclusively in euros, while the retail market continued to use domestic currency until the first two months of 2002, in which euro banknotes and coins replaced national currencies.

The potential economic benefits and costs of EMU were discussed in a European Commission study, 'One market, one money' (Emerson, 1990). The report cited four major benefits arising from the introduction of a single currency: reduction in transaction costs, reduction in risk, increased competition and emergence of an international currency competing with the US dollar. The first benefit is the obvious reduction of transaction costs linked to a reduced need of exchanging intra-European currencies. With intra-European trade representing 61 per cent of the international trade of the EU, the saving was estimated in the Emerson study at €13.1–19 billion, representing 0.3 to 0.4 per cent of European GDP. This reduction in transaction costs will be gained at the expense of financial institutions providing foreign exchange services; it would represent about 5 per cent of banks' value added.[1] The second benefit attributed to EMU is a reduction of foreign exchange risk and of substantial changes in relative prices. The reduction in transaction costs and foreign exchange risk will presumably facilitate the realization of the single market programme, allowing firms to choose the appropriate size and optimal location, facilitating restructuring, investment and economic growth. The third identified benefit is derived from the use of a single denomination measure which will make price comparison easier, increasing competition and consumers' welfare. Finally, the fourth benefit of EMU is the creation of a world currency competing with the US dollar and the assumed (but unidentified) benefits of an international currency status.

A potential cost of EMU has been mentioned by several economists: the sacrifice of national monetary autonomy and the possibility of controlling interest rates or adjusting exchange rates to restore competitiveness. In their reviews of EMU, Eichengreen (1993) and Currie (1997) expressed doubts that the four benefits alone can outweigh the cost linked to the loss of monetary autonomy. In their view, the case for EMU can be argued if a single currency is a necessary concomitant of the single market programme, the benefits of which are likely to be substantial. Resistance to the creation of the single market would be reduced if the single currency could prevent a 'beggar-thy-neighbour' type of competitive devaluation. EMU is therefore the cement of the single market which, by integrating previously fragmented markets, will allow firms to realize gains in productivity and competitivity.

The EU15 population amounts to 372 million (against 263 million in the United States and 125 million in Japan), GDP to €6,602 billion (€5,789 billion in the United States, and €3,371 billion in Japan), and exports to non-EU countries to €591 billion (total exports of €465 billion in the United States, and €353 billion in Japan).

## 3 BANKING WITH A SINGLE CURRENCY[2]

Eight impacts are identified and analysed. The first six concern capital markets, including the government bond market and its fast-growing appendix, the interest rate derivative market, the corporate bond and equity markets, institutional fund management, the euromarket, the foreign exchange market, and the competition between the euro and the US dollar as international reserve currencies. The last two effects concern commercial banking with the impact of the single currency on credit risk and on bank profitability in a low-inflation environment.

### The Government Bond Market, Underwriting and Trading

The government bond market in Europe is very fragmented, with domestic players capturing a large market share of the underwriting and secondary trading business. This raises the question of the sources of competitive advantage for local banks. With regard to the underwriting and trading of government bonds, Feldman and Stephenson (1988), a Federal Reserve Bank of New York study (1991) and Fox (1992) show that the dominance of local players is the result of three main factors. The first is historical, with local players having privileged access to the public debt issuer. The second is domestic currency denomination, which facilitates the access to a large investor home base, providing a significant advantage not only in placing, but also in understanding, the demand/supply order flows. Finally, expertise in the domestic monetary environment provides information essential for operating on the secondary bond market.

Will these sources of competitive advantage survive with a single currency? As domestic currency denomination, the main source of competitive advantage identified for local banks in the literature, disappears, it is quite likely that we shall observe the emergence of a truly integrated

European bond market. If access to a European-wide investor base does facilitate placement and if access to information on the supply/demand order flows seems essential for secondary trading, then very likely operations on a large scale and at a European-wide level will become a necessity[3] and we shall see a consolidation of the government bond underwriting and trading businesses. For instance, both the European Investment Bank and the Kingdom of Belgium have entered the market in 1999 with 'jumbo' issues that can only be underwritten by banks with a large equity base. Bishop (2000) reports that issues of more than one billion euros have increased from 15 per cent to 28 per cent of all euro-denominated issues from the first quarter of 1998 to the fourth quarter of 1999. Moreover, in 1999, the total euro-denominated issue of bonds is 28 per cent larger than the issue of dollar-denominated international bonds.

**The Corporate Bond and Equity Markets, Underwriting and Trading**

As is the case for government bonds, a key issue concerns the sources of competitive advantage of local institutions in corporate bond and equity underwriting and secondary trading. As explained earlier, customer relations, assessment of credit (business) risk, and currency denomination are critical sources of competitive advantage. The eurobond market presents an interesting case. A report by the Federal Reserve Bank of New York (1991), confirmed in Dermine (1996), McCauley and White (1997) and Harm (1998), reports a strong correlation for non-dollar issue between the currency denomination and the nationality of the lead bank manager. This is illustrated in Table 4.1, which shows that, for instance, French banks are the lead managers 86 per cent of the time for French franc-denominated eurobonds issued by French companies, and 75 per cent of the time for similar bonds issued by non-French borrowers. The domestic currency denomination facilitating access to a home-investor base was a key source of competitive advantage not only for placement but also for secondary trading. Indeed, an understanding of local monetary policy would give a competitive advantage to forecast interest rates and price movements. The leading role of American institutions in the dollar-denominated eurobond market is explained not only by large issues by American companies, by their expertise developed in their home corporate securities markets, but also by the important advantage linked to the dollar denomination of many bonds. Indeed, access to home investors and an understanding of US order flows and US monetary policy provide a decisive advantage in secondary trading as they help to predict price movements.

A single currency in Europe changes fundamentally the competitive structure of the corporate bond and equity markets as one key source of

Table 4.1  *Currency and home-country relationship in the choice of the bond bookrunner, 1996 (percentage market share won by bookrunners of indicated nationality)*

| German bookrunners | | | French bookrunners | | |
|---|---|---|---|---|---|
| Borrower | Currency | | Borrower | Currency | |
| | Mark | Other | | French francs | Other |
| German | 44 | 16 | French | 86 | 10 |
| Other | 37 | 2 | Other | 75 | 2 |
| All | 39 | 4 | All | 77 | 2 |

| UK bookrunners | | | Dutch bookrunners | | |
|---|---|---|---|---|---|
| Borrower | Currency | | Borrower | Currency | |
| | Pound | Other | | Guilder | Other |
| UK | 40 | 21 | Dutch | 83 | 26 |
| Other | 48 | 3 | Other | 85 | 2 |
| All | 44 | 4 | All | 84 | 2 |

| US bookrunners | | | Japanese bookrunners | | |
|---|---|---|---|---|---|
| Borrower | Currency | | Borrower | Currency | |
| | Dollar | Other | | Yen | Other |
| US | 86 | 46 | Japanese | 75 | 46 |
| Other | 54 | 13 | Other | 87 | 6 |
| All | 64 | 16 | All | 84 | 8 |

*Source:* McCauley and White (1997).

competitive advantage, namely home currency, will disappear. Indeed, savers will diversify their portfolio across European markets, the exchange rate risk being eradicated. Moreover, a single currency suppresses the secondary trading advantage for domestic banks derived from a better understanding of order flows and monetary policy in the domestic country. Therefore, the two main sources of comparative advantage remaining for local players are historical customer relations and the understanding of credit (business) risk through a better knowledge of the accounting, legal and fiscal (not to mention language) environment. Whenever the business risk embedded in corporate securities can be better assessed by domestic banks, these players will control underwriting and secondary trading.

Local expertise would be particularly valuable for smaller companies, venture capital or the real estate market. However, for larger corporations, worldwide industry expertise will most likely dominate any national advantage. For instance, to serve a Volvo corporation, it is unlikely that Swedish expertise is of great help to local institutions. What is needed is expertise in the global automobile industry.

To conclude this analysis of the impact of a single currency on the corporate bond and equity markets, it seems that customer relations and an understanding of business risk could remain two sources of strength for domestic firms in some segments of the market. But, placing power and trading across Europe coupled with global industry expertise are forces that lead to consolidation in a major part of the securities industry. As a tentative base for comparison, it is symptomatic to observe in Table 4.2 that the top six American underwriters of US debt and equity control 62 per cent of the US market.

*Table 4.2    Top underwriters of US debt and equity, January to July 1999*

| Manager | Market share (%) |
|---|---|
| Merrill Lynch | 14.6 |
| Salomon Smith Barney | 13.4 |
| Morgan Stanley Dean Witter | 9.6 |
| Goldman Sachs | 8.4 |
| CSFB | 8.1 |

*Source:*   Thompson Financial Securities Data.

**Fund Management**

An important segment of capital market business is the fund management industry, pension funds or mutual funds. As Tables 4.3a and b illustrate for France and the United Kingdom, respectively, it is symptomatic to see the dominance of the fund management industry by local firms.[4] In view of this extreme fragmentation, especially in comparison with other segments of the capital markets, what is the impact of the single currency on the fund management industry? In this case too, an understanding of the main sources of competitive advantage needs to be developed. These concern the retail distribution network, the home-currency preference, research expertise and the existence of economies of scale (Kay et al., 1994). The first source of competitive advantage in the retail segment is the control of the distribution network, in the hands of local banks in several countries.

Table 4.3a   Mutual funds (OPCVM) managers in France, December 1996

|  | Euro bn | Market share (%) |
|---|---|---|
| Société Générale | 31.30 | 7.40 |
| Crédit Agricole | 25.10 | 5.90 |
| Crédit Lyonnais | 24.10 | 5.70 |
| BNP | 23.96 | 5.68 |
| CDC-Trésor | 18.50 | 4.40 |
| La Poste | 16.30 | 3.90 |
| CIC-Banque | 14.00 | 3.30 |
| Caisses d'Epargne | 12.90 | 3.10 |
| Banques Populaires | 12.30 | 2.90 |
| Paribas | 8.20 | 1.95 |

*Source:* EuroPerformance, AFG-ASSFI.

Table 4.3b   UK league of segregated pension fund managers, 1998

|  | Total assets under management | |
|---|---|---|
|  | Euro bn | Market share (%) |
| Mercury Asset Management | 105.40 | 17.4 |
| Schroder Investors | 96.10 | 15.8 |
| Phillips & Drew Fund Management | 72.50 | 11.9 |
| Barclays Global Investors | 63.50 | 10.5 |
| Morgan Grenfell Asset Management | 39.70 | 6.5 |
| Goldman Sachs Asset Management | 31.80 | 5.2 |
| Foreign & Colonial Institutional | 20.60 | 3.4 |
| Hill Samuel Asset Management | 20.54 | 3.4 |
| Prudential Portfolio Managers | 20.45 | 3.4 |
| Fidelity Pensions Management | 13.05 | 2.1 |

*Source:* *Financial Times*, 21 May 1999, compiled by author.

Indeed, domestic control of distribution is protected under the current European legislation framework, which gives national authorities the right to regulate the marketing of funds in their own territory. Obviously the advantage derived from the control of the distribution network applies to retail investors only, as it will not be a barrier to entry in the institutional market. A second source of competitive advantage was the customer preference for home-currency assets, often imposed by regulation. A single currency will of course eliminate this factor and reinforce the need for European-wide portfolios. A large part of these will be provided by index-tracking investment funds. A third source of success is excellence in research-based management. As to the existence of economies of scale and scope in the fund management industry, this is still a subject of debate (Bonnani et al., 1998). If scale seems important for index-tracking funds, it could be less relevant for actively managed funds.

A single currency eliminates the obstacle to international diversification. It is likely that there will be very large low-cost European index-tracking funds competing with smaller research-based funds. On the retail distribution side, domestic banks will keep their competitive advantage as long as the branch network remains a significant channel of distribution.

**The Euro-deposit Market**

An extremely efficient euro-deposit market was created 30 years ago to circumvent various forms of domestic regulations.[5] A first issue concerns the size, coverage and remuneration of the reserve requirement on euro-denominated deposits in the future. Indeed, foreign currency-denominated deposits are not subject to reserve requirements in most countries. In October 1998, a reserve ratio of 2 per cent on deposits with a maturity of less than two years was imposed. However, these reserves will be renumerated at the market rate set by the ESCB in its main refinancing operations (Kelly, 1999). A second and more significant issue will be the fiscal treatment of the income earned on these assets in the future.[6]

**Foreign Exchange Markets**

A direct effect of the single currency is that not only intra-European foreign exchange transactions disappear, but the competitive advantage of a particular bank in its home currency *vis-à-vis* third-country currencies changes as well. As an example, a Belgian bank operating in New York is no longer a Belgian franc specialist, but competes with other European banks in the euro/dollar business. As is the case for the government bond markets, for which an understanding of the supply/demand order flows is important to predict the direction of price movements, we are likely to observe a consolidation of the commodity-type low-cost spot foreign exchange business. This conjecture is consistent with the analysis by Tschoegl (1996) of the sources of competitive advantage in the currency market, namely size and the international status of the home currency. Differentiated products based on quality of service or innovations such as options will be another source of competitive advantage.

## The Euro as an International Currency: What Are the Benefits for the Banks?

One of the asserted benefits of EMU is that the single currency will become a challenger to the US dollar as the dominant international currency used for units of accounts, store of value and means of payment (Emerson, 1990; Alogoskoufis and Portes, 1991; and Maas, 1995). But in contrast to a national currency which is imposed as sole tender by national legislation, the role of an international currency is fixed by demand and supply on world capital markets. Two questions are being raised. First, is the euro likely to compete against the US dollar in international financial markets? Second, from the perspective of this chapter, what are the benefits derived for banks of having an international currency status for the euro?

Whether we look at the role of the dollar as a unit of account, a store of value, or a means of payment, it is still by far the predominant international currency. For instance, 60 per cent of the foreign exchange reserves of central banks are denominated in dollars, while US exports represent only 12 per cent of world exports. To assess the euro's chance of accelerating the relative decline in the dollar, it is instructive to have a look at history and the relative fall of sterling and rise of the dollar in the international payment system.

In 1914, on the eve of the First World War, the City of London was indisputably the world's leading international financial centre, with the pound sterling the major international currency. According to economic historians, the pound started to weaken during the First World War. The 1914–18 war saw the emergence of large bond financing in the United States. This was coupled with the events of 1931, the insolvency of the Creditanstalt in Vienna and the inconvertibility of the pound. The Second World War increased the status of the dollar, which was confirmed in its international role by the 1944 Bretton Woods agreement.[7] We can conclude that the rise of the dollar over a 30-year period was very much helped by the two world wars, and that despite abandoning convertibility into gold in 1971 and continuous devaluation, 25 years later the dollar still retains a leading role as an international currency. Based on the last two decades, which have seen a progressive erosion of the dollar and a slow rise of the Deutschmark, in view of the relative economic size of Europe, and building on the potential for growth in the eastern part of Europe, we can extrapolate and forecast that the euro will replace the D-Mark and be a strong competitor to the dollar. Data for the year 1999 indicate that the euro has closed the gap *vis-à-vis* the US dollar. The total issue of euro-denominated bonds amounts to 812 billion, compared to 634 billion of dollar-denominated international bonds (Bishop, 2000).

What are the implications for banks of having the euro as an international currency? Three benefits can be identified. The first one is that an increased volume of euro-denominated assets or liabilities will ease the foreign exchange risk management of bank equity. Indeed, a large part of bank assets will be denominated in the same currency as the equity base, easing the control of currency-driven asset growth and capital management. Second, access to a discount window at the European Central Bank (ECB) will make the liquidity management of euro-based liabilities marginally cheaper. Finally, if third countries issue assets denominated in euros or use the European currency as a vehicle, European banks will be well positioned in secondary trading for the reasons mentioned earlier.

**EMU and Credit Risk**

Many of the channels which have been identified concerned the money and capital markets. An additional impact of the euro is its potential effect on credit risk. There are reasons to believe that the nature of credit risk could change under a single currency. The argument is based on the theory of optimum currency areas and on the objective of price stability inscribed in the Treaty on European Union.

There is an old debate on the economic rationale that leads a group of countries to adopt a common currency.[8] The more that countries are subject to asymmetric economic shocks, the more they would appreciate monetary autonomy to cancel the shock. Indeed, with symmetric shock there would be a consensus among the members of a currency union on economic policy, but with asymmetric shocks a central policy may not be acceptable to all the members of the union. Recent economic developments have strengthened the argument. For instance, has the rapid recovery enjoyed by British banks in 1994 not been helped partly by the 1992 devaluation which reduced the bad debt problem? Similarly, the devaluation of the Finnish markka has helped the restructuring of the country after a major recession. How could the introduction of a single currency affect credit risk? If a bank concentrates its business in its home country, and if that country is subject to asymmetric shocks, it is quite possible that a central monetary policy will not be able to soften the shock. Some have argued that the adverse consequences of such shocks could be dealt with at European level and that, in any case, these shocks would be quite rare. Indeed, severe asymmetric shocks could in principle be mitigated by fiscal transfers across Europe. But this is only a possibility, which remains to be verified. As to the argument that asymmetric shocks are rare events, this is indeed the case, but a fundamental mission of any bank risk-management system is to ensure the solvency of financial institutions on precisely those rare but significant occasions. An indirect and interesting corollary of the optimum currency area theory is that for banks operating in a single currency area, the need to diversify their loan portfolio increases the more their home country is likely to be subject to asymmetric (uncorrelated) shocks. This can be achieved through international diversification or with the use of credit derivatives.

A related effect of EMU on credit risk is that the statute of the ECB will prevent inflationary policies. *Ceteris paribus*, this could increase the potential for losses resulting from default, as we can no longer depend on a predictable positive drift for the value of collateral assets.[9] The inability of a country to devalue and the very strict anti-inflationary policy of the ECB imply that, whenever a need to restore competitiveness arises in a particular region, the only tool available will be a reduction of nominal wages and prices. This will change fundamentally the nature of credit risk as firms and individuals can no longer rely on the nominal growth of their revenue to reduce the real value of their debt. This new world calls for innovative techniques to handle potential deflations.[10]

**Banking in a Low-inflation Environment**

The last effect of a single currency discussed in this chapter concerns the impact on bank profitability of doing business in a low-inflation environment. Indeed, in the last 20 years, higher inflation and interest rates have provided substantial interest margins on price-regulated deposits. For instance, as is documented in Table 4.4 for the 1980–85 period, interest margins on demand deposits were above 10 per cent in Belgium, France, Denmark and Spain. If new products such as money market funds competed with these deposits, then these demand and savings deposits would still represent more than 40 per cent of client resources collected by banks in Belgium or France (Commission Bancaire, 1996; Banque de France, 1996). As Table 4.4 documents, margins on these products have been seriously eroded with the overall decrease in the interest rate level in recent years. We can safely conclude that an objective of monetary stability and low inflation pursued by an independent ECB will reduce the source of profitability on the deposit funding business.

However, if this effect is quite significant in a large number of countries, two additional effects of a low-inflation environment might soften the impact of lower margins on deposits. The first is that a low interest rate environment usually leads to a much higher margin on personal loans because of the relative inelasticity of interest rates on personal loans. For instance, in France, loan rate stickiness has raised the margin on hire purchase (consumer) loans from 6.3 per cent in 1990 to 10.1 per cent in 1996, a period of

Table 4.4  Interest margins of commercial banks

|  | Belgium | Denmark | France | Germany | Netherlands | Spain | UK |
|---|---|---|---|---|---|---|---|
| Average margin on demand deposits* | | | | | | | |
| 1980–85 (%) | 11.2 | 16.2 | 11.7 | 6.5 | 5.6 | 14.5 | 10.8 |
| 1987–92 (%) | 8.7 | 9.0 | 9.7 | 7.2 | 6.8 | 6.0 | 7.0 |
| 1994–95 (%) | 5.0 | na | 6.1 | 4.8 | 4.3 | 3.6 | 3.6 |
| 1996–98 (%) | 3.0 | na | 3.5 | 3.4 | 3.4 | 0.6 | 3.6 |
| Average margin on savings deposits* | | | | | | | |
| 1980–85 (%) | 5.6 | 8.9 | 4.3 | 2.8 | 2.8 | 10.7 | 2.5 |
| 1987–92 (%) | 3.9 | 7.0 | 5.2 | 2.2 | 4.7 | 9.0 | 2.0 |
| 1994–95 (%) | 1.9 | na | 1.6 | 2.9 | 2.8 | 5.0 | na |
| 1996–98 (%) | 0.65 | na | 0 | 0.62 | 1.5 | 1.4 | 1.5 |

Note:   *Current short-term rate minus interest rate paid on deposits.

Source:   Data supplied by Organization for Economic Cooperation and Development.

rapidly declining market rates (Banque de France, 1996). A second positive impact of a low-inflation environment is that the so-called 'inflation tax' will be much smaller (Fisher and Modigliani, 1978). A simple example will give the intuition beyond the inflation tax. Consider a case with no inflation in which equity is invested in a 3 per cent coupon bond. After a 30 per cent corporate tax is deducted, the revenue is 2.1 per cent $((1-0.3)\times 3\%)$. The full profit can be paid as dividend as there is no need for retained earnings and higher capital since there is no growth of assets. If, because of a 10 per cent inflation, the same equity is invested in a 13 per cent coupon bond, the profit after tax is only 9.1 per cent $((1-0.3)\times 13\%)$, a figure too small to finance a necessary equity growth of 10 per cent. No dividend can be paid in this case and equity holders have suffered an inflation tax.

Therefore, the impact of a low-inflation environment on the profitability of banks will depend on the relative importance of reduced margins on deposits, higher profit on personal loans and on the significance of the inflation tax.

## 4 THE STRATEGIC ISSUES

As Table 4.5 shows, a considerable amount of domestic restructuring has already taken place in Europe. This was driven by the creation of the single market in 1992. In most cases, domestic mergers were driven by cost-cutting motives. For instance, White (1998) reports that the restructuring of the Finnish banking system undertaken after a severe financial crisis has reduced employment by 32 per cent.[11] These domestic mergers have increased concentration and produced firms of bigger size, albeit at national level. A first series of cross-border deals, documented in Table 4.6, took place in the merchant banking area, where independent merchant banks (many of them British) were purchased by continental banks. These acquisitions were no doubt motivated by the wish to acquire rapidly a necessary expertise in securities-based corporate finance and asset management. Until quite recently, cross-border mergers of commercial banks of significant size have been rare. The difficulty in merging two national cultures was often put forward as a barrier to cross-border mergers. However, three significant deals have taken place recently in smaller countries: the purchase of the Belgian Banque Bruxelles Lambert (BBL) by the Dutch Internationale Nederland Groep (ING), the merger of the Swedish Nordbanken with the Finnish Meritabank, and the creation of the Belgian–Dutch Fortis Bank. These cross-border deals are noticeable because they involve very large domestic players attempting to create a larger home base. Also, note the creation of Dexia, an international bank

Table 4.5  Domestic bank mergers in Europe

| Country | Year | Mergers |
|---|---|---|
| Belgium | 1992 | CGER–AG (Fortis) |
|  | 1995 | Fortis–SNCI |
|  | 1995 | KB–Bank van Roeselaere |
|  | 1997 | Bacob–Paribas Belgium |
|  |  | CERA–Indosuez Belgium |
|  | 1998 | KBC (KB–CERA–ABB) |
| Denmark | 1990 | Den Danske Bank |
|  |  | Unibank (Privatbanken, Sparekassen, Andelsbanken) |
|  | 1999 | Unibank–TrygBaltica |
| Finland | 1995 | Merita Bank (KOP–Union Bank of Finland) |
| France | 1996 | Crédit Agricole–Indosuez |
|  | 1999 | BNP–Paribas |
| Germany | 1997 | Bayerische Vereinsbank–Hypo-Bank |
| Italy | 1992 | Banca di Roma (Banco di Roma, Cassa di Risparmio di Roma, Banco di Santo Spirito) |
|  |  | San Paolo–Crediop |
|  | 1995 | Credito Romagnolo (Rolo)–Credit Italiano (UniCredito) |
|  | 1997 | Ambroveneto–Cariplo (Intesa) |
|  | 1998 | San Paolo–IMI |
|  | 1999 | Intesa–BCI |
| Netherlands | 1990 | ABN–AMRO |
|  | 1991 | NMB–PostBank–ING |
| Portugal | 1995 | BCP–BPA |
|  | 2000 | BCP–Mello |
|  |  | EspiritoSanto–BPI |
| Spain | 1988 | BBV (Banco de Vizcaya–Banco de Bilbao) |
|  | 1989 | Caja de Barcelona–La Caixa |
|  | 1992 | Banco Central–Banco Hispano |
|  | 1994 | Santander–Banesto |
|  | 1999 | Santander–Banesto–BCH |
|  |  | BBV–Argentaria |
| Sweden | 1993 | Nordbanken–Gota Bank |
| Switzerland | 1993 | CS–Volksbank–Winterthur |
|  | 1997 | SBC–UBS |
| United Kingdom | 1995 | Lloyds–C&G–TSB |

*Note:* List is incomplete; for illustration only.

Table 4.6  International bank mergers in Europe

| Buyer | Target |
|---|---|
| Deutsche Bank | Morgan Grenfell |
| ING Bank | Barings |
| Swiss Bank Corp | Warburg, O'Connor, Brinson, Dillon Read |
| Dresdner | Kleinwort Benson |
| ABN–AMRO | Hoare Govett |
| Unibank | ABB Aros |
| Merrill Lynch | Smith New Court (UK) FG (Spain), MAM |
| Morgan Stanley Dean Witter | AB Asesores |
| CSFB | BZW (equity part) |
| Société Générale | Hambros (UK) |
| Citigroup | Schroder |
| Dexia (France, Belgium, Luxembourg, Italy) | Crédit Communal, Crédit Local, BIL, Crediop |
| Bacob (Belgium) | Paribas (Netherlands) |
| ING (Netherlands) | BBL (Belgium) |
| Générale Bank (Belgium) | Crédit Lyonnais (Netherlands), Hambros (UK, corporate) |
| Fortis (Belgium, Netherlands) | AMEV+Mees Pierson (Netherlands)/CGER/ SNCI (Belgium)/Générale Bank |
| Nordbanken (Sweden) | Meritabank (Finland) |
| KBC | CSOB (Czech Republic) |
| BSCH | Champalimaud (Portugal) |

Note: List is incomplete; for illustration only.

specialized in lending to local authorities, with operations in Belgium, France, Italy, Spain and Luxembourg.

As discussed in Section 3, the arrival of the euro will rapidly change the sources of competitive advantage in various segments of the capital markets, namely government bonds, corporate securities (bonds, shares, asset-backed securities), foreign exchange and asset management. If we accept the argument that size will matter on some of these markets, a question is raised of either exiting (outsourcing) part of these activities, or of reaching the appropriate size. Moreover, an additional, potentially much more significant, change concerns information technology. IT should allow, in principle, the distribution of financial services to retail clients across borders and without a physical presence. Regarding this threat (or opportunity), the key issue is the speed of acceptance of this new delivery channel by customers and their willingness to entrust a significant part of their financial affairs to a foreign supplier. In view of this new eurobanking world, banks face three major strategic options: national champion, European strategy through cross-border acquisition or merger, or European strategy through a cooperative structure.

1. *National (regional) champion* A firm acquires through acquisition a significant market share on its domestic market. It outsources part of its capital market activities to larger international firms. Domestic size will provide the ability to achieve cost efficiency and to offer high-quality services. This strategy can survive until new technology allows large foreign firms to target local clients directly, disintermediating the local financial supermarket. Under such a scenario, the domestic champion will be absorbed sooner or later by a large international player who would benefit from a large low-cost operating platform. Given the loyalty of retail clients and the particular nature of financial services for which trust is an essential element that cannot be acquired so rapidly, we could take the view that significant competition from foreign competitors on the retail market will not take place for several years. This domestic strategy could be adopted by national banks or even by some regional banks, such as the *cajas* in Spain, which have a very strong local retail franchise.
2. *Cross-border merger or acquisition* (top-down approach) This allows the institution to reach size and international coverage rapidly. Corporate control can be efficient as the process is managed with authority from a centre, but the allocation of responsibilities in the newly created entity appears to have been a very difficult process for many financial firms.[12]
3. *The cooperative strategy* (bottom-up approach) Local cooperatives created national centres several decades ago to serve their treasury or international needs (the case of Rabobank in the Netherlands, or Crédit Agricole in France). In a similar way, groups of national institutions could create European centres taking care of asset management and, potentially, large international corporates. This approach has the merit of being decentralized at the national retail level, with an efficient management of capital market activities at the international centre. As history has shown (such as that of European American Bank or European Asian Bank), the danger is a lack of control or speed of decision by the various members. Two examples of cooperation include the creation of the international cash-management system IBOS created by a consortium of banks (including, among others, Royal Bank of Scotland, Banco Santander Central Hispano, Crédit

Commercial de France and Kredietbank–Cera), or the consortium Eureko created by European insurance companies and banks (Friends Provident, Achmea, Banco Commercial Portuguesa . . .).

A premise of the above analysis has been that size will be important in operating on some segments of the markets and that a European coverage will be necessary. This premise demands identification of the major competitive difference between large size at the *domestic* versus the *European* level. Indeed, it could be argued that two large banks of an equal size (one domestic and the other European) could have the same leverage on the bond or currency markets. That question is indeed quite relevant as, no doubt, it will be much more difficult to create an international institution as opposed to a domestic one. It is the author's belief that European coverage dominates a domestic one for two major reasons. The first is that some corporate clients become increasingly international, giving preference to banks with an international coverage. The second, more significant, argument in favour of a European coverage is that it provides a most welcome source of diversification. This is of course necessary to reduce credit risk, but is also relevant to stabilize the demand for services in capital markets. Indeed, if because of a recession or change in the legal–fiscal environment the demand for foreign exchange services, for instance, or pension fund investment in bonds changes dramatically, a large domestic bank would rapidly lose what was deemed necessary to compete: size to analyse the supply/order flows or to have the trading power. A European coverage would be a way to stabilize business flows, allowing an adequate size to be retained permanently.

## 5  CROSS-BORDER MERGERS: A REGULATORY CHALLENGE

Five public policy issues are raised by bank mergers in Europe. These include protection of investors, safety and soundness (systemic stability), concentration, impact on lending to small and medium-sized enterprises (SMEs), and international competitiveness of financial firms.

**Investor Protection**

A first potential source of public concern is investor protection in the case of the acquisition of a domestic bank (let us say a Dutch institution) by a foreign bank. A problem could arise if the Dutch component becomes integrated as a branch of the new group. Indeed, it could be that the new entity supervised by the foreign regulator (home-country control) does not meet the Dutch prudential standards. Such a case would provide an argument for the Dutch regulator to step in to protect 'uninformed' investors (*public interest* argument). Because regulations on conduct of business (such as disclosure of information, liquidity ratios, application of contract law, marketing practices and so on) are controlled by host countries, the issue concerns essentially the solvency of branches of foreign banks.

**Systemic Risk**

Systemic risk could occur because a single bank is deemed too large to fail. Fears of contagion to other banks or fear of negative impact on consumption or investment could create an argument for a bail-out. In the specific context of bank mergers and acquisitions, three separate cases need to be analysed.

First, a Dutch bank becomes very large with a significant portfolio of risks located abroad. This situation raises the difficulty of supervising and assessing the solvency of this international bank. Second, in the case of bank failure and partial or complete bail-out, this could entail a very large cost to the Dutch Treasury or the Dutch deposit insurance. To assess the potential cost of a bail-out, we report in Table 4.7 the level of equity (book value) of the 15 largest European banks as a percentage of the GDP of the home country. Not surprisingly, the highest figures are found in Switzerland and the Netherlands. The equity to GDP ratio is 8.02 per cent for the recently merged United Bank of Switzerland, 4.6 per cent for ABN–AMRO, as compared to 0.89 per cent for Deutsche Bank. For the sake of comparison, the equity of Bank of America and Citigroup represents 0.55 per cent and 0.48 per cent of US GDP. Taking as a reference point that the bail-out of Crédit Lyonnais will cost French taxpayers twice the book value of its 1993 equity (admittedly an arbitrary case), the cost of bailing out the largest Swiss bank could amount to 16 per cent of Swiss GDP, as compared to 1.8 per cent of GDP in the case of the Deutsche Bank.

The second case is the creation of a Dutch financial conglomerate as a bank decides to expand domestically into a set of other financial services. Financial conglomerates of this type create potentially two problems. The first one is that if there is a bail-out, this could again entail considerable cost to the Dutch Treasury. The second is that it can distort competition if the newly acquired business benefits from the implicit bailing-out guarantee. In principle, these effects can be mitigated by creating effective firewalls between the entities, through for instance the creation of separate legal units owned by a holding company. However, this type of separation could prove difficult to implement if one of the subsidiaries fails since, in a world

*Table 4.7  Bank rankings*

| Country | Bank | Equity (book value) €m, 1998 | Equity/GDP (%) |
|---|---|---|---|
| UK | HSBC | 29,352 | 2.12 |
| France | Crédit Agricole | 25,930 | 1.81 |
| France | BNP–Paribas | 23,471 | 1.64 |
| Switzerland | UBS | 20,525 | 8.02 |
| Germany | Deutsche Bank | 18,680 | 0.89 |
| Switzerland | Crédit Suisse | 17,579 | 6.87 |
| Netherlands | ABN–AMRO | 17,471 | 4.60 |
| Germany | Bayerische Hypo | 15,195 | 0.72 |
| Netherlands | Rabobank | 14,688 | 3.88 |
| Spain | Santander–BCH | 14,919 | 2.59 |
| UK | Barclays | 13,495 | 0.98 |
| UK | NatWest | 13,389 | 0.97 |
| Germany | Dresdner | 13,042 | 0.62 |
| Netherlands | ING Bank | 12,961 | 3.42 |
| France | Société Générale | 12,521 | 0.88 |
| USA | Bank of America | 47,030 | 0.55 |
| USA | Citigroup | 40,794 | 0.48 |

*Source:*  *The Banker* (1999), author's calculations.

of imperfect information, a reputation effect could lead to a run on other parts of the group, forcing the bailing out of the entire group.

In the first two cases discussed above – cross-border expansion and domestic across-sector move – diversification of risks could reduce the probability of a (costly) bail-out as long as the level of equity is not reduced and the efficiency of management is not hampered by complexity. Adequate control of risk-management systems (*ex ante* supervision) and frequent and conservative valuation of the equity of the group (*ex post* supervision) would facilitate early intervention and minimize the cost of a bail-out.

The third case involves one large foreign bank buying a Dutch bank. The Dutch Treasury could be forced to bail out for internal stability reasons, but would not have the right to supervise the branch of a foreign bank because of home-country control. Since the Dutch Treasury would retain financial responsibility, it should be able to retain some supervisory control. That is to say, home-country control or even ECB control has to be complemented by some form of host control as long as the cost of bailing out remains domestic. In this last case, since the default of a large international bank could affect many countries, the decision to bail out would demand coordination among these countries. These arguments – the decision to bail out and the sharing of the cost of a bail-out – suggest the need for further fiscal and supervisory measures, a state of the world that cannot be reached as long as nations want to retain full control of their public spending.

**Concentration**

The third public policy issue concerns concentration and the fear of a lack of competition. Data on market shares for deposits and loans are reported in Table 4.8. Not surprisingly, they show relatively high concentration in small countries such as Sweden and the Netherlands, with the five largest banks capturing more than 80 per cent of the market, as compared to 14 per cent for the case of Germany. However, concentration figures should be treated with caution as they might not be a good predictor of market power and large interest margins. Finland is an interesting test case as concentration has increased substantially over the last ten years due to domestic mergers. Margins on deposits have decreased from 8 per cent in 1986 to 1.4

Table 4.8   Market concentration (C5, five largest firms)

|  | Loan | | | | Deposit | | |
| --- | --- | --- | --- | --- | --- | --- | --- |
|  | 1985 | 1990 | 1997 |  | 1985 | 1990 | 1997 |
| Sweden | 62.65 | 64.89 | 87.84 | Sweden | 57.9 | 61.4 | 86.90 |
| Netherlands | 67.10 | 76.70 | 80.60 | Netherlands | 85.0 | 80.0 | 84.20 |
| Greece | 93.16 | 80.75 | 76.90 | Greece | 89.2 | 87.6 | 79.60 |
| Denmark | 71.00 | 82.00 | 75.00 | Portugal | 64.0 | 76.0 | 79.00 |
| Portugal | 60.00 | 73.00 | 75.00 | Denmark | 70.0 | 82.0 | 72.00 |
| Belgium | 54.00 | 58.00 | 66.00 | France | 46.0 | 58.7 | 68.60 |
| Finland | 49.70 | 49.70 | 56.20 | Belgium | 62.0 | 67.0 | 64.00 |
| France | 48.70 | 44.70 | 48.30 | Finland | 54.2 | 64.2 | 63.10 |
| Ireland | 47.70 | 47.50 | 46.80 | Ireland | 62.6 | 52.6 | 50.20 |
| Spain | 35.10 | 43.10 | 42.10 | Austria | 32.0 | 36.4 | 39.00 |
| Austria | 28.90 | 34.00 | 39.30 | Spain | 35.1 | 39.2 | 38.20 |
| Luxembourg | – | – | 28.60 | Italy | 19.9 | 18.6 | 36.70 |
| UK | – | – | 26.00 | Luxembourg | – | – | 28.02 |
| Italy | 16.60 | 15.10 | 25.90 | UK | – | – | 26.00 |
| Germany | – | 13.50 | 13.70 | Germany | – | 11.6 | 14.20 |
| EU | – | – | 52.60 | EU | – | 55.0 | 55.00 |

Source:   ECB (1999).

per cent in 2000, while margins on household loans have increased from 0 per cent in 1990 to 2.7 per cent (Vesala, 1998).

To assess the impact of concentration on margins, we have to analyse the degree of contestability, that is, the ease with which a new player can enter a profitable market segment. For instance, the creation of money market funds has reduced the ability of banks to raise margins on deposits. Similarly, access by large firms to the capital markets with commercial paper or bond issues also reduces the potential impact of concentration on loan margins. However, some specific financial services appear to be less open to contestability. The review of the financial services sector in Canada (MacKay, 1998) points out that the demand for cash and payment services and the access to credit by SMEs is primarily served by local branches of banks. Moreover, although diminishing, there is evidence of 'clustering', that is, consumers acquire products in a bundle rather than individually (for instance, 70 per cent of Canadians buy mortgage and credit cards from the institution in which they do their primary banking services). Vesala (1998) reaches similar conclusions in the case of the highly concentrated market of Finland. An interesting corollary of this analysis (and a proposal in the Canadian MacKay review) is the suggestion to open payment services not only to banks but also to insurance firms and fund managers as a way to reduce concentration and increase competition. Such a move would blur the remaining differences between banks and other providers of financial services.

**Lending to SMEs**

Several countries, such as the United States, Canada and Australia, have feared that the creation of large banks would have a negative impact on the access to bank credit. Although the argument runs against common economic logic, according to which any profitable services would be provided by the market, the perception is that large banks would concentrate their activities on large corporate firms at the expense of SMEs. Peek and Rosengren (1999) and Strahan and Weston (1999) use a 1993–96 data set of mergers to demonstrate that in many mergers the level of small business lending actually increases. In view of this empirical evidence, with competitive products offered by non-bank financial companies or simply trade credit, and in view of the fact that more and more banks are using credit scoring models to evaluate small-business loans (69 per cent of US banks in 1997), is is likely that the impact of bank mergers on small-business lending will not be so significant. To the best of our knowledge, no such study exists in Europe, and a task of central banks should be to monitor both the quantities and prices of services to the retail trade and to SMEs.

**Competitiveness**

A final role for public authorities is to facilitate the creation of competitive domestic firms. The banking literature (Berger et al., 1999 and Dermine, 1999) has reviewed the various arguments for bank mergers. If economies of scale do seem significant in specific segments of the investment banking industry (such as bond and equity underwriting, or custodian activities), scope economies resulting from financial diversification or the search for efficiency through the closure of branches appear relevant in retail banking. Moreover, there is the untested argument that the future with e-banking will demand banks of a larger size. To foster competitiveness, policy makers will want domestic firms to reach an optimal size and European coverage. In this case, there appears to be a trade-off between the benefits of large successful domestic firms and the 'low-probability' event of a very costly bail-out. As discussed above, this trade-off appears particularly acute in smaller countries.

## 6  CONCLUSIONS

The objective of this chapter has been to identify the various ways through which the euro would alter the sources of competitive advantage of European banks and to analyse the various strategic options available. Besides the obvious fall in revenue from intra-European currency trading, the analysis has identified significant and permanent effects on several segments of the industry. A rapid consolidation of commodity-type business is likely: government bonds, interest rate derivatives and spot currency trading. This is motivated by the loss of a main domestic source of competitive advantage, namely the national currency. If domestic expertise in the accounting, legal and fiscal environment gives a competitive advantage to domestic players in some segments of the corporate bond and equity markets, other factors such as trading power across Europe, trading capacity and global industry expertise will lead to consolidation of that industry. On the fund management side, very large European-wide index-tracking funds will compete with specialized funds. Regarding the euro-deposits market, the fiscal rules still have to be known to assess the impact of a single currency on the size and location of this market. On the commercial banking side, the nature of credit risk is likely to change as one of the instruments of monetary policy, devaluation, will not be available. Finally, the impact of a low-inflation environment on bank profitability will work through reduced margins on deposits, higher profits on personal loans, and a lower 'inflation tax'.

Furthermore, we should highlight the obvious but important fact that the single currency makes the creation of a single European banking market *irreversible*. A more predictable environment will facilitate the exploitation of economies of scale and the optimal location of processing units.

If the premises underlying the above analysis are verified in the future, we can anticipate the creation of a new eurobanking world. A major international consolidation of the European banking industry will take place in the capital market business, and further domestic rationalization of commercial banking will be needed. An important premise of the analysis has been that European size would dominate domestic size because of the diversification benefits that would be realized.

A final issue is systemic stability, in particular in small countries that have generated very large institutions, namely the Netherlands and Switzerland. These arguments suggest the need for both a European bail-out authority and a European banking supervisor. However, this cannot be achieved as long as nations want to retain full control of their public spending. In this second-best world, smaller countries will have to carefully balance the benefits of large and competitive financial groups with *low-probability* costly default.

The objective of the 1992 single market programme was to reinforce the efficiency and competitiveness of European firms. Regarding banking, it is a clear conclusion that the introduction of the euro not only makes the creation of a single market irreversible, but that it also, besides the obvious fall in revenue from intra-European currency trading, alters fundamentally the nature of several businesses. A new banking world emerges, with very different sources of competitive advantage. If this challenge is met successfully by European banks, there is little doubt that it will reinforce their competitiveness in the capital markets of third countries such as those of Asia, Latin America or the United States.

## NOTES

1. Gross revenue before provisions and operating expenses.
2. This section draws on Dermine (1997, 1998) and Dermine and Hillion (1999).
3. The relative merits of large domestic scale versus large European scale are discussed in Section 4.
4. Some of these, such as Morgan Grenfell, have been purchased by continental firms.
5. Some creative wording will be needed as we must make a distinction between 'euro-deposits', deposits from non-residents, and 'euro-denominated deposits'.
6. The European Council held in Helsinki in December 1999 was unable to reach unanimity on a 20 per cent withholding tax on interest income.
7. According to McKinnon (1993), a key factor increasing the role of the dollar was the

European Payments Union established in September 1950 for clearing payments multi-laterally, using the US dollar as the unit of account and as the means of payment.
8. The theory of optimum currency areas (Mundell, 1961; McKinnon, 1963).
9. Although an argument can be made that non-inflationary policies will reduce the amplitude of business cycles.
10. A tool could be the creation of securities indexed on regional prices.
11. This has to be compared to a drop in bank employment of 5 per cent in France and 0.3 per cent in Germany (White, 1998).
12. An interesting case in 1998 is that of the highly praised Wells Fargo failing to integrate FirstInterstate successfully, and recently being forced into a merger by Norwest.

# REFERENCES

Alogoskoufis, G. and R. Portes (1991), 'International costs and benefits from EMU', in G. Alogoskoufis (ed.), *The Economics of EMU*, Brussels: European Commission.
Banque de France (1996), *Bulletin Trimestriel*, December.
Berger, A., R. Demsetz and P. Strahan (1999), 'The consolidation of the financial services industry: causes, consequences, and implications for the future', *Journal of Banking and Finance*, **23**, 135–94.
Bishop, G. (2000), *The Euro's Fourth Quarter*, London: Salomon Smith Barney.
Bonanni, C., J. Dermine and L.H. Röller (1998), 'Some evidence on customer "Lock-in" in the French mutual funds industry', *Applied Economics Letters* (5), 275–9.
Commission Bancaire (1996), Annual Report, Brussels.
Currie D. (1997), *The Pros and Cons of EMU*, London: Economic Intelligence Unit.
Dermine, J. (1996), 'European banking with a single currency', *Financial Markets, Institutions & Instruments*, **5** (5), 62–101.
Dermine, J. (1997), 'Eurobanking, a new world', Laureate of the 1997 European Investment Bank Prize, *EIB Papers*, No. 2.
Dermine, J. (1998), *The Euro World, a Strategic Analysis*, Brussels: Video Management.
Dermine J. (1999), 'The economics of bank mergers in the European Union', INSEAD Working Paper 99/35, pp. 1–51.
Dermine, J. and P. Hillion (eds) (1999), *European Capital Markets with a Single Currency*, Oxford: Oxford University Press.
ECB (European Central Bank) (1999), 'Possible effects of EMU on the EU banking systems in the medium to long term', Frankfurt: ECB.
Eichengreen, B. (1993), 'European monetary unification', *Journal of Economic Literature*, **31**, 1321–57.
Emerson, M. (1990), 'One market, one money', *European Economy*, **44**, October, 20–26.
Federal Reserve Bank of New York (1991), *International Competitiveness of US Financial Firms*, New York: Staff Study.
Feldman, L. and J. Stephenson (1988), 'Stay small or get huge – lessons from securities trading', *Harvard Business Review*, May–June, 116–23.
Fisher, S. and F. Modigliani (1978), 'Towards an understanding of the real effects and costs of inflation', *Weltwirtschaftliches Archiv*, **114**, 810–33.

Fox, M. (1992), 'Aspects of barriers to international integrated securities markets', *Journal of International Securities Markets*, Autumn, 209–17.

Harm, C. (1998), 'European financial markets integration: the case of private sector bonds and syndicated loans', mimeo, Copenhagen Business School, pp. 1–26.

Kay, J., R. Laslett and N. Duffy (1994), 'The competitive advantage of the fund management industry in the City of London', London: The City Research Project.

Kelly, J. (1999), 'The minimum reserve system in EMU', *Irish Banking Review*, Summer, 60–72.

Maas, C. (1995), 'Progress report on the preparation of the changeover to the single currency', Brussels: European Commission.

MacKay, H. (1998), The Task Force on the Future of the Canadian Financial Services Sector, Ottawa.

McCauley R. and W. White (1997), 'The euro and European financial markets', Bank for International Settlements Working Paper 41.

McKinnon, R. (1963), 'Optimum currency areas', *American Economic Review*, **53**, 717–25.

McKinnon, R. (1993), 'The rules of the game: international money in historical perspective', *Journal of Economic Literature*, **31**, 1–44.

Mundell, R.A. (1961), 'A theory of optimum currency areas', *American Economic Review*, **51**, 657–65.

Peek, J. and E. Rosengren (1999), 'Bank consolidation and small business lending: it is not just bank size that matters', *Journal of Banking and Finance*, 799–821.

Strahan, P.E. and J.P. Weston (1999), 'Small business lending and the changing structure of the banking industry', *Journal of Banking and Finance*, 821–46.

Tschoegl, A. (1996), 'Country and firms' sources of international competitiveness: the case of the foreign exchange market', Philadelphia: The Wharton School.

Vesala J. (1998), 'Delivery networks and pricing behavior in banking: an empirical investigation using Finnish data', Bank of Finland Discussion Papers 18, pp. 1–47.

White, W. (1998), 'The coming transformation of continental European banking?', Bank for International Settlements Working Paper 54.

# 5. Competitive banking in the EU and Euroland

## Edward P.M. Gardener, Philip Molyneux and Jonathan Williams

## 1 INTRODUCTION

A burgeoning literature and much speculation have already emerged on the impact of European Monetary Union (EMU) on European banking. In this respect at least EMU follows its predecessor, the Single Market Programme (SMP). Banking in Euroland is now involved in a major and far-reaching process of structural and strategic change. The rise of Euroland is not the only important strategic driver of major changes in European Union (EU) banking, but it is certainly one of the most significant together with the impact of new technology and the heightening competitive environment.

This chapter focuses on the rise of Euroland as a major integrating economic event. The chapter is organized as follows. After reviewing broad structure and performance trends in European banking (Section 2), the new strategic environment for banking is explored (Section 3). An examination is then undertaken of the impact of EU regulatory changes such as the SMP and EMU (Section 4); the specific impact of EMU on bank strategies is then considered (Section 5). Section 6 considers the kinds of competitive strategies that banks might pursue in Euroland and the general relevance of recent US experiences with bank consolidation. Section 7 concludes.

## 2 STRUCTURE AND PERFORMANCE TRENDS IN EU BANKING[1]

Increasing competition in financial services has had the result of reducing the number of banks operating in many countries and this trend is common to virtually all European banking markets. It is also apparent across different types of banks, including the mutual savings and cooperative banks as

Table 5.1  Number of banks: banking system, 1984–1997

| Country | 1984 | 1989 | 1992 | 1994 | 1996 | 1997 |
|---|---|---|---|---|---|---|
| Austria | 1,257 | 1,240 | 1,104 | 1,053 | 1,019 | 995 |
| Belgium | 165 | 157 | 157 | 147 | 141 | 134 |
| Denmark | 231 | 233 | 210 | 202 | 197 | 197 |
| Finland | 644 | 552 | 365 | 356 | 350 | 350 |
| France | 358 | 418 | 617 | 607 | 570 | 519 |
| Germany | 3,025 | 4,089 | 4,200 | 3,872 | 3,674 | 3,578 |
| Italy | 1,137 | 1,127 | 1,073 | 1,002 | 937 | 935 |
| Netherlands | 2,079 | 1,058 | 921 | 744 | 658 | 628 |
| Norway | 248 | 179 | 158 | 153 | 153 | 154 |
| Portugal | 18 | 29 | 35 | 44 | 51 | 62 |
| Spain | 369 | 333 | 319 | 316 | 313 | 307 |
| Sweden | 176 | 144 | 119 | 125 | 124 | 120 |
| UK | 598 | 551 | 518 | 486 | 478 | 466 |

*Sources:* Central bank reports (various) and Gardener et al. (1999a).

well as for domestic commercial banks. Nevertheless, there still remain a large number of banks operating in Europe, as illustrated in Table 5.1. All countries (apart from Portugal) experienced a decline in the number of banks since 1992. What Table 5.1 does not reveal, however, is that the number of foreign banks has increased in every banking market over the same period, reflecting the internationalization trend and the opportunities afforded by the EU's Single Market Programme (EC, 1997).

The widespread decline in the number of banks in Europe throughout the 1990s, however, has not been exactly mirrored by a similar trend in branch numbers, as shown in Table 5.2. In fact in many of the larger banking markets (such as Germany, Italy and Spain) branch numbers have proliferated during the 1990s. In the last two cases this has mainly been the result of the removal of branching/territorial restrictions that were in place up to the late 1980s/early 1990s. In Germany, the increase in branch numbers has been mainly a reflection of reunification as well as expansion of the savings banks sector, the latter reflecting increased non-price competition. In Belgium, Finland, Norway, Sweden and the UK there has been a decline in branch numbers. The fall in branches in Scandinavian countries is primarily a consequence of the consolidation and restructuring resulting from the banking crises of 1991/92. Only in the case of Belgium and the UK can it be attributed in large part to the domestic consolidation processes.

*Table 5.2    Number of branches, 1984–1997*

| Country | 1984 | 1989 | 1992 | 1994 | 1996 | 1997 |
|---|---|---|---|---|---|---|
| Austria | 4,005 | 4,378 | 4,667 | 4,683 | 4,694 | 4,691 |
| Belgium | 23,502 | 19,211 | 16,405 | 17,040 | 10,441 | 7,358 |
| Denmark | 3,515 | 3,182 | 2,358 | 2,245 | 2,138 | 2,480 |
| Finland | 2,886 | 3,528 | 3,087 | 2,151 | 1,785 | 1,745 |
| France | 25,490 | 25,634 | 25,479 | 25,389 | 25,434 | 25,464 |
| Germany | 35,752 | 39,651 | 39,295 | 48,721 | 47,741 | 63,186 |
| Italy | 13,045 | 15,683 | 20,914 | 23,120 | 24,406 | 25,250 |
| Netherlands | 5,475 | 8,006 | 7,518 | 7,269 | 7,219 | 7,071 |
| Norway | 1,940 | 1,796 | 1,593 | 1,552 | 1,503 | 1,500 |
| Portugal | 1,469 | 1,741 | 2,852 | 3,401 | 3,842 | 4,645 |
| Spain | 31,876 | 34,511 | 35,476 | 35,591 | 37,079 | 37,634 |
| Sweden | 3,083 | 3,302 | 2,910 | 2,998 | 2,527 | 2,505 |
| UK | 21,853 | 20,419 | 18,218 | 17,362 | 16,192 | 15,253 |

*Source:*   Gardener et al. (1999a).

Tables 5.1 and 5.2 broadly indicate that European banking markets are characterized by a relatively large number of domestic banks which, in some cases, have expanded their branching presence during the 1990s. So while consolidation has undoubtedly been taking place in each banking system, the trend in branch numbers suggests that access to banking services in a range of countries, notwithstanding the introduction of new delivery systems (such as telephone and internet-based operations), has increased.

While access to bank branches in most countries does not appear to have been significantly adversely affected by consolidation and market restructuring during the 1990s, the fall in the number of banks and increased market concentration may have adversely affected customer choice. Table 5.3 illustrates that the top five banks, especially in the smaller European banking markets, tend to dominate overall banking business. A study by the European Commission (EC, 1997) also shows that in every EU country between 1979 and 1995, apart from France, Greece and Luxembourg, the five-firm assets concentration ratio increased. In particular, Denmark, Spain, the UK, Belgium and the Netherlands experienced the largest increases during the 1990s. The EC (1997) study did not cover Finland, Sweden and Norway, but all of these countries experienced large increases in market consolidation resulting from restructuring after the banking crises of the early 1990s.

Overall, European banking markets are (in most cases) characterized by

Table 5.3  Concentration in European banking, 1997

| Country | Five-firm assets concentration (%) | Change in concentration ratio, 1996–97 (%) |
| --- | --- | --- |
| Germany | 16.68 | +3.73 |
| Italy | 24.60 | −3.15 |
| France | 40.30 | −2.18 |
| UK | 28.00 | 0.00 |
| Belgium | 57.00 | +3.64 |
| Portugal | 76.00 | −5.00 |
| Finland | 77.77 | +5.72 |
| Netherlands | 79.40 | +5.31 |
| Denmark | 73.00 | −6.41 |
| Sweden | 89.71 | +4.06 |

Source:   ECB (1999).

a declining number of banks, although most systems have a large number of small local and regional banks with substantial branch operations serving (together with the main commercial banks and specialist lenders) a wide range of banking customers. Market concentration, however, is increasing and in the smaller banking systems the five-firm assets ratio typically exceeds 60 per cent. While the decline in the number of banks and increased market concentration may suggest that banking service choice is declining, the growth in branch numbers in many systems may counter this trend. In addition, increasing foreign bank presence as well as the growth of non-traditional banking service providers, such as retailers and asset-backed financing firms (leasing and factoring companies, consumer finance companies and so forth), make it difficult to state categorically that overall customer choice is declining.

A stronger indication that consolidation and the overall decline in the number of banks have not adversely affected competitive conditions in European banking is reflected in the decline in net interest margins in virtually every banking system, as shown in Table 5.4. While margins obviously vary with the interest cycle and there has been a convergence of money market rates to a lower level during the 1990s (especially in countries aiming to achieve the EMU criteria), the overall trend is downward. As net interest margins have been subjected to increasing competitive pressures – resulting, generally, in downward pressures on earnings streams relative to cost – banks have increasingly focused on growing other, non-interest income sources of earnings. Fees and commissions are

Table 5.4  Net interest margins, 1984–1997 (%)

| Country | 1984 | 1989 | 1992 | 1994 | 1996 | 1997 |
|---|---|---|---|---|---|---|
| Austria | – | 1.73 | 1.85 | 1.90 | 1.43 | 1.35 |
| Belgium | – | 1.57 | 1.51 | 1.33 | 1.32 | 1.46 |
| Denmark | 3.01 | 2.55 | 3.56 | 3.83 | 1.79 | 1.75 |
| Finland | 2.42 | 1.84 | 1.55 | 2.05 | 1.90 | 2.73 |
| France | – | 1.91 | 1.63 | 1.27 | 1.20 | 1.39 |
| Germany | 2.50 | 2.01 | 2.07 | 2.18 | 1.46 | 1.60 |
| Italy | – | 3.28 | 3.17 | 2.63 | 2.42 | 2.57 |
| Netherlands | 2.23 | 2.08 | 1.83 | 1.89 | 1.67 | 1.09 |
| Norway | 3.71 | 3.45 | 3.51 | 3.44 | 2.41 | 2.46 |
| Portugal | 1.86 | 4.12 | 4.11 | 2.78 | 1.95 | 2.14 |
| Spain | 4.15 | 4.05 | 3.59 | 3.00 | 2.54 | 2.66 |
| Sweden | 2.55 | 2.53 | 2.55 | 2.77 | 1.81 | 1.98 |
| UK | 3.00 | 3.10 | 2.60 | 2.40 | 2.10 | 2.20 |

Sources:  BankScope database, Central Bank Reports (various) and Gardener et al. (1999a).

one example of an income stream arising from banks diversifying their activities. The growth of bancassurance and off-balance sheet operations has further fuelled the potential of non-interest income in generating profitability. Table 5.5 shows the trend towards an increase in non-interest income as a proportion of total income in every European banking system.

While the trends in the sources of bank income are clear – a fall in interest margins compensated by an increase in non-interest income – the picture for cost levels is less obvious. It must be remembered that bank efficiency levels can be affected both by endogenous and by exogenous factors. The usual measure for bank efficiency is the cost–income ratio; adverse economic conditions affect the cost–income ratio in the sense that banks do not have total control over their income streams, while restrictive labour laws in many continental European countries hinder staff reductions and productivity improvements on the cost side. In addition, mergers and acquisitions (M&A) activity can add to costs in the short term before all the efficiency savings or/and increased revenue streams are worked through. Also, various income sources, such as those from trading activities, are notoriously volatile. Thus, recent (between 1994 and 1997) increases in the cost–income ratio are just as likely to reflect trends in earnings rather than costs. Nevertheless, the overall trend in European cost–income ratios is expected to be downwards because *inter alia* banks

Table 5.5  Non-interest income/gross income, 1984–1997 (%)

| Country | 1984 | 1989 | 1992 | 1994 | 1996 | 1997 |
|---|---|---|---|---|---|---|
| Austria | – | 27.9 | 33.4 | 28.7 | 38.7 | 32.6 |
| Belgium | – | 22.7 | 21.6 | 23.9 | 35.2 | 35.0 |
| Denmark | 15.5 | 21.8 | 13.1 | 16.7 | 17.7 | 34.5 |
| Finland | 43.2 | 48.5 | 59.6 | 46.9 | 47.7 | 40.2 |
| France | – | 19.7 | 31.3 | 35.7 | 39.4 | 38.4 |
| Germany | 18.0 | 25.6 | 23.9 | 19.4 | 21.5 | 26.7 |
| Italy | – | 22.3 | 18.3 | 23.7 | 30.4 | 34.1 |
| Netherlands | 24.7 | 29.4 | 28.6 | 29.0 | 35.0 | 40.6 |
| Norway | 24.2 | 26.1 | 21.1 | 17.9 | 24.7 | 25.7 |
| Portugal | 39.4 | 16.3 | 24.8 | 27.3 | 34.2 | 36.3 |
| Spain | 14.0 | 17.6 | 20.3 | 21.6 | 24.3 | 25.8 |
| Sweden | 46.2 | 45.0 | 39.6 | 35.7 | 42.0 | 27.5 |
| UK | 35.6 | 37.6 | 42.2 | 43.2 | 44.4 | 43.7 |

*Sources:* BankScope database and Gardener et al. (1999a).

are seeking good-quality business against a background of improving risk controls and enhanced efficiency.

Table 5.6 shows that in the majority of countries the general trend in bank cost–income ratios has been downwards since 1994. The only banking systems, however, which have systematically and most significantly improved their efficiency levels between 1992 and 1997 are Austria, Denmark, Germany, Finland, Sweden and the UK. According to McCauley and White (1997) and White (1998), the UK experienced more M&A activity in its banking sector (in value terms) between 1991 and 1997 than any other European banking market, and these cost improvements could be a partial reflection of this trend. All of the main UK banks have also embarked on aggressive cost-cutting strategies in terms of branch closures and manpower reductions. The improved cost performance of the Scandinavian banks is mainly a consequence of the forced reorganizations following the banking crises of the early 1990s.

The aforementioned income and cost trends feed through into profitability figures, which are shown in Table 5.7. The return on equity (ROE) figures present a mixed picture, although in the majority of countries ROE improved between 1994 and 1997. Given that there is no obvious downward trend in bank performance across countries, some might argue that this is evidence that competition is not increasing in European banking markets.

*Table 5.6    Cost–income ratios, 1984–1997 (%)*

| Country | 1984 | 1989 | 1992 | 1994 | 1996 | 1997 |
|---|---|---|---|---|---|---|
| Austria | – | 65.5 | 64.0 | 65.1 | 61.4 | 57.6 |
| Belgium | – | 66.8 | 66.9 | 71.3 | 61.1 | 67.8 |
| Denmark | 75.6 | 64.9 | 81.4 | 72.5 | 53.5 | 58.1 |
| Finland | 84.0 | 84.8 | 190.4 | 139.9 | 69.3 | 63.6 |
| France | – | 64.6 | 62.5 | 73.5 | 72.8 | 71.2 |
| Germany | 59.3 | 64.6 | 64.5 | 60.7 | 61.2 | 56.2 |
| Italy | – | 61.7 | 63.8 | 65.0 | 69.6 | 72.0 |
| Netherlands | 62.3 | 66.0 | 67.7 | 66.7 | 69.5 | 66.1 |
| Norway | 68.5 | 69.9 | 60.3 | 63.4 | 66.5 | 67.7 |
| Portugal | 67.0 | 46.8 | 53.0 | 58.2 | 56.5 | 63.2 |
| Spain | 64.0 | 60.9 | 60.3 | 59.7 | 63.8 | 63.7 |
| Sweden | 67.6 | 62.7 | 122.2 | 80.0 | 49.3 | 47.0 |
| UK | 66.9 | 64.8 | 65.9 | 64.1 | 60.3 | 60.9 |

*Sources:*    BankScope database and Gardener et al. (1999a).

*Table 5.7    Return on equity, 1984–1997 (%)*

| Country | 1984 | 1989 | 1992 | 1994 | 1996 | 1997 |
|---|---|---|---|---|---|---|
| Austria | – | 10.0 | 6.9 | 7.9 | 9.4 | 5.1 |
| Belgium | – | 6.0 | 6.4 | 8.8 | 20.3 | 14.8 |
| Denmark | 1.0 | 3.0 | −18.3 | −0.9 | 16.4 | 11.8 |
| Finland | 5.1 | 4.0 | −49.5 | −25.7 | 11.9 | 19.8 |
| France | – | 9.4 | 4.3 | −1.4 | 5.8 | 8.5 |
| Germany | 21.1 | 12.4 | 13.2 | 11.9 | 11.9 | 15.8 |
| Italy | – | 14.0 | 9.8 | 4.4 | 6.8 | 5.7 |
| Netherlands | 14.0 | 13.6 | 12.8 | 14.1 | 13.7 | 4.2 |
| Norway | 14.1 | 5.5 | −5.8 | 19.3 | 18.0 | 10.1 |
| Portugal | 5.5 | 9.2 | 8.5 | 6.1 | 9.3 | 11.3 |
| Spain | 8.9 | 14.6 | 10.6 | 8.2 | 14.6 | 14.5 |
| Sweden | 4.6 | 5.9 | 18.5 | 19.1 | 23.9 | 8.7 |
| UK | 20.8 | 3.4 | 10.7 | 19.6 | 21.0 | 25.9 |

*Sources:*    BankScope database and Gardener et al. (1999a).

This viewpoint, however, is too simplistic. It neglects the fact that in all banking markets, traditional margin-based business is probably more competitive than ever before. In addition, banks are increasingly building on non-interest income in areas such as investment banking, brokerage, insurance, pensions, mutual funds and other collective investment product areas (to name but a few) where there are strong established operators; competition, therefore, is likely to be intense in many of these areas. The simplistic argument also neglects the role of technology and the importance of new competitors. For instance, advances in technology allow banks to out-source non-core processing and other activities to scale-efficient, third-party service providers. Customer databases also make the cross-selling and delivery of new types of financial products and services more effective and profitable. Technology has promoted the development of direct banking services and so forth. Non-bank financial intermediaries, retailers and other 'brand name' firms also compete nowadays against banks in the financial services area. These are all important elements that are helping to change the economics of banking business.

## 3   THE NEW STRATEGIC ENVIRONMENT

During the past ten years or so, the banking environment within the EU and globally has altered markedly. In the EU, financial markets have already experienced major changes under the influence of forces such as new regulatory initiatives, competition and technology. Profound shifts are now taking place in banking strategies and many of these are likely to be at least facilitated if not accelerated through the establishment of Euroland.

Banking in this 'new Europe' has a number of distinctive features. Some of the most important of these are listed below:

- efficiency and shareholder value are increasingly emphasized by senior management as the main performance targets;
- banks have de-emphasized traditional banking and re-emphasized their wider financial services role;
- banking markets (both geographically and 'functionally') will become increasingly globalized (integrated), thereby bringing in more competitors;
- deregulation (both *de facto*, via developments like new technology advances and increasing consumer use of these, and *de jure*, as the authorities continue the present deregulatory path) will help to intensify competition by reducing barriers to entry and facilitating the penetration of new competitors;

- in the key areas of asset management and investment banking that are most immediately affected by the euro, EU banks and asset managers face the challenge of the big US asset managers who seek global dominance;
- the arrival of EMU, together with technological advances (like direct banking), has opened up the possibility of longer-term moves towards an EU-wide, more globalized retail banking and financial services marketplace;
- securitization of corporate credit (the increased intermediation of these credit flows through financial markets) is re-emphasizing the importance of higher-margin retail banking;
- banks have become more marketing and strategy orientated; supply-side and demand-side banking strategies need to be 'balanced';
- new kinds of banking alliances and the sharing (even between strong competitors) of competencies are being pursued; and
- technology and virtual banking are everywhere becoming more important strategic drivers.

One of the most pervasive characteristics of the new environment from a bank strategic perspective is 'marketization': see, for example, EC (1997) and Gardener et al. (1997, 1999a and b).

Marketization has many strategic dimensions for banks. From a financial management perspective it implies a much stronger emphasis on shareholder value tests of performance. All banking systems in Europe have become increasingly subject to external, market-determined efficiency tests that are associated with a shareholder value culture and this applies to all banking sectors, not just publicly listed financial firms. Banks are increasingly competing for the same customers so that the most demanding efficiency tests (invariably external, market-orientated ones) correspondingly set the minimum benchmark for all competitors.

Shareholder value maximization requires a shift of bank management emphasis away from traditional, accounting-based measures of performance towards externally orientated market (or 'economic') ones. More banking attention is correspondingly being focused on risk and return trade-offs, economic capital backing (or capital allocation) for banking assets and positions, and new methods of evaluating bank performance. As banking markets become more contestable and the market in bank corporate control is freed up, shareholder value-related performance becomes even more practically important. Maximizing bank productive efficiency is a necessary condition for shareholder value maximization.

The marketization of bank strategies has many other important dimensions. From a customer perspective, it implies a much stronger demand orientation in banking strategies. Strategically, marketing and related aspects like customer service and customer retention assume a higher priority in bank strategies and organizational design. Techniques like data warehousing have become operationally more important as banks increasingly seek to segment and target particular 'customer slices' of the market.

This new market orientation has produced a number of serious strategic challenges for banks. An obvious one, perhaps, is shifting organizational design towards a more market-orientated form (Clarke et al., 1988). A related issue is balancing supply side (emphasizing the bank's own internal resources) and demand side (emphasizing the external market, or customers' demands) within bank strategy (Gardener and Williams, 1996). Banks also have to balance their intensifying internal efficiency demands (cost-cutting) with a continuing and long-term imperative to nurture and facilitate their customer service culture (McLean, 1994).

Another pervasive feature of the new environment is the globalization of banking and financial markets. This has a geographic dimension, where national, previously segmented markets are opened up to foreign competition. It also has a functional dimension in the sense that previously segmented financial markets within a single country (and/or across different countries) or banking strategies (like retail and wholesale) become more closely linked. An example is money market mutual funds, linking retail savers to wholesale money markets (and retail banking with asset management, an investment banking-type function). A globalizing capital market also increases the imperative of shareholder value as a managerial target since capital movements towards higher value are facilitated in this world.

Within this new environment, intensifying competition produces new kinds of competition and new competitors. Securitization is one such example. The increasing disintermediation of the banking system in important segments of corporate banking has incentivized many banks to build up their investment banking capabilities (to follow corporate customers into capital markets), helped to produce an adverse selection problem for banks (which are left with the poorer credit risks on their balance sheets) and re-emphasized the importance of retail banking financial services (as an increasing source of profit).

While securitization is still a comparatively new financial technology for Europe, it looks set to grow in importance. Although the US scale of securitization is unlikely to be replicated in the near future within Europe, the trend towards improved asset productivity is likely to increasingly force European banks to shift low-performing assets off their balance sheets via the technique of asset-backed securitization. This means *inter alia* new markets, new financial instruments and enlarged strategic possibilities (like greater specialization opportunities) for some banks.

The ubiquitous influence of technology affects every key aspect of the new banking environment. The rise of virtual banking, multi-channel delivery systems and increasing use of the internet are leading banks into new areas and creating formidable challenges. Banking in Euroland and beyond will put a premium on banks harnessing technology to increase the quality of their customer service. Already technology is bringing new, more retail-focused competitors into the traditional financial services marketplace.

At a macro level, other fundamental changes are helping to alter the banking map in Europe. The SMP and EMU have been associated with a more market-orientated culture in regulatory and political thinking; there is an apparent sustained movement in many countries and sectors away from more state control and influence. The privatization of social security, ageing populations and the respective necessary reforms of pension schemes throughout Europe (especially in Euroland) open up new opportunities for growth in asset management. But these trends, together with wider globalization developments, bring with them the awesome challenge and financial firepower of the big US asset managers.

The new environment, then, is one of challenges, opportunities and threats for banks in Euroland. What is clear is that relying on historic customer franchises is no longer a wise option for bankers in Euroland. This raises the question of what exactly the launch and development of Euroland itself implies. It will certainly facilitate many key developments within the new environment that have just been outlined. In this sense, the euro is not only a direct cause of change itself, but it is also a kind of catalyst (or facilitator) of many of the key market and strategic changes considered in this section (White, 1998). But what specific effects and strategic adaptations can bankers expect from Euroland itself?

## 4 IMPACT OF REGULATORY CHANGE

The impact of banking regulatory change has stimulated a great deal of policy debate and research. Perhaps rather surprisingly, empirical work has tended to produce much less definitive evidence than the apparent clarity and elegance of the respective theory. There are many reasons for this. One is that even in strongly deregulating financial markets, banking continues to be characterized by several market failures. These include the central bank lender of last resort, the too-big-to-fail doctrine and deposit insurance. While these market failures may not necessarily impede greater (price) allocative efficiency resulting from a deregulation, hypothesized effects on bank productive efficiency, for example, may be lessened.

There are other empirical difficulties. For one thing, deregulation is usually one of a number of factors that impact contemporaneously on bank strategies and key areas such as banking efficiency. As we have seen, other important bank strategic drivers include technology and competition. Disentangling each of their specific effects on bank strategies is a complex task. Another such problem is that a banking deregulation (especially a major one like the SMP and EMU) is invariably accompanied by the re-regulation of supervision (prudential regulation), especially capital adequacy. The respective deregulation, globalization and re-regulation associated with major regulatory changes like the SMP and EMU may each have different impacts (sometimes countervailing) on banking strategies.

Both its predecessor, the SMP, and EMU are major globalizing (or integrating) events. Each primarily aims to create greater integration of banking and financial services. In this respect it is useful to consider the kind of vision of the nature and impact of this kind of regulatory event that was developed in the major EU study by Paolo Cecchini on the SMP (Commission of the European Communities, 1988). The SMP itself was seen as the essential precursor to EMU; Begg (1998, p. 9), for example, refers to it in this context as 'a central plank of the "E" in EMU'.

Cecchini saw the SMP-induced deregulation as a kind of supply-side shock to the system. Deregulation-induced price reductions and output increases stimulate demand; this in its turn leads to further price reductions and output increases (thereby producing a kind of 'virtuous circle' in which this process repeats itself in a self-sustaining way). Within the wider process of completing the EU internal market, Cecchini emphasized the particular strategic importance of the EU financial services sectors in capturing the overall economic gains associated with the entire SMP process. Cecchini saw the productive effects of greater financial services competition as eliminating economic rents (the margin of excess profits or wage rates that result from market protection), lessening X-inefficiencies (those inefficiencies unrelated to the production technology of the firm's investments) and facilitating firms to exploit the benefits of economics of restructuring (scale and scope economies). Cecchini envisaged a substantial increase in cross-border M&A in banking as banks set out to realize potential economies of restructuring.

The famous Cecchini *ex ante* study was an important one, but there were a number of flaws in the methodology used and the practical assumptions drawn from it: see, for example, Gardener and Teppett (1995). For instance, the Cecchini banking model focused primarily on hypothesized deregulation effects on prices and output. No explicit incorporation of the impact of the simultaneous *re*-regulation of supervisory (or prudential) rules was modelled.

Table 5.8  Extent to which strategy has been revised in response to the SMP for broad product areas

| Product area | Ireland | UK | France | Germany | Spain | Portugal | Belgium | Netherlands | Greece | Denmark | Italy | EU |
|---|---|---|---|---|---|---|---|---|---|---|---|---|
| Investment management | 68 | 39 | 55 | 73 | 43 | 54 | 35 | 33 | 56 | 21 | 55 | 55 |
| Off-balance sheet activities | 25 | 39 | 32 | 61 | 49 | 64 | 63 | 32 | 78 | 22 | 67 | 52 |
| Corporate customer loans | 28 | 36 | 46 | 62 | 41 | 54 | 61 | 46 | 74 | 28 | 49 | 51 |
| Other retail saving products | 46 | 34 | 35 | 63 | 52 | 44 | 59 | 32 | 42 | 2 | 57 | 49 |
| Corporate customer deposits | 29 | 36 | 26 | 63 | 36 | 53 | 60 | 46 | 63 | 22 | 38 | 48 |
| Retail deposits (sight and time) | 27 | 36 | 22 | 52 | 48 | 44 | 54 | 47 | 40 | 2 | 39 | 43 |
| Retail customer mortgages | 29 | 36 | 23 | 51 | 50 | 53 | 42 | 47 | 69 | 20 | 36 | 43 |
| Retail customer loans | 11 | 38 | 19 | 51 | 47 | 53 | 42 | 47 | 64 | 4 | 34 | 42 |
| Retail insurance products | 66 | 36 | 35 | 40 | 51 | 52 | 43 | 32 | 48 | 14 | 52 | 41 |

Note:  0 is 'not at all', 25 is 'slightly', 50 is 'to some extent', 75 is 'to a large extent', and 100 is 'totally'.

Source:  EC (1997, Table 4.40, p. 112).

Table 5.9  Nature of strategic responses to the SMP for broad product areas

| Product area | Increased cross-border activity | Product diversification/ innovation | Merger/ alliance/ takeover |
| --- | --- | --- | --- |
| Investment management | 21 | 41 | 10 |
| Off-balance sheet activities | 22 | 46 | 4 |
| Corporate customer loans | 17 | 50 | 4 |
| Corporate customer deposits | 13 | 46 | 4 |
| Retail deposits (sight and time) | 9 | 54 | 6 |
| Retail customer loans | 8 | 51 | 7 |
| Other retail saving products | 4 | 64 | 7 |
| Retail customer mortgages | 4 | 48 | 8 |
| Retail insurance products | 2 | 42 | 20 |

*Note:* All figures are numbers of respondents. Total sample size is 115.

*Source:* EC (1997, Table 4.41, p. 113).

A later and much more detailed empirical study of the *ex post* impact of the SMP on EU banking produced a broader, more in-depth analysis of the impact of the SMP (see EC, 1997). This later study used a range of research techniques (including surveys, case studies and econometric work) to build up a picture of the impact of the SMP on EU banking. EC (1997) found it difficult to separate the impact of the SMP from other key strategic drivers, like competition and technology. It was also found that EU bankers regarded the re-regulation of supervision associated with the SMP as at least as important as the corresponding deregulations of structure and conduct rules. Nevertheless, a number of competition-induced reactions similar to those envisaged by Cecchini were found. In particular, banks in many countries consolidated via M&A in order to strengthen themselves against potential foreign competition.

The apparent strategic reactions by banks to the SMP were also interesting; Table 5.8 shows that the threat of intensified competition provoked strategic revisions in all of the main banking market segments. Over the whole of the EU, this survey confirmed that the SMP had the largest impact in wholesale banking business, especially with respect to off-balance sheet activities, investment management and corporate lending. Retail banking/financial service businesses seemed to be little affected by the SMP.

Table 5.9 shows the nature of the bank strategic response to the SMP. The most common strategic response was product diversification and innovation. This may imply that banks were attempting to consolidate in their domestic markets rather than seeking to penetrate new markets abroad. EC (1997) suggested that this was consistent with the view that non-price competition may be a more common strategic response in an environment where profitability and shareholder value are increasingly prioritized.

Overall, EC (1997) found that the main impact of the SMP was on the strategic thinking and expectations of bankers throughout the EU. In this respect the SMP's general influence was both profound and pervasive. The SMP helped to shift strategic thinking away from historic protection, segmentation and various kinds of collusion towards deregulation, more competition and greater contestability in all areas of financial services. EC (1997) labelled this shift in the EU banking industry frame of reference the 'marketization' of banking strategies. This increased demand (or market) orientation is nowadays apparent in all aspects of key banking strategies.

## 5  GENERAL IMPACT OF EMU ON BANKING AND FINANCIAL MARKETS

The arrival of Euroland represents a watershed in EU (and global) banking. This is not only because of EMU itself, but also because of the positioning in time of EMU and concurrent market developments. The latter 'positioning' reflects the apparently successful launch of EMU closely on the heels of another major and related regulatory initiative, the SMP. EMU has helped to consolidate EU bankers' expectations towards more sustained deregulation and intensifying competition. Contemporaneous market developments embrace trends like globalization, the rise of a shareholder value culture in banking, a related drive to be more efficient, intensifying competition, needed pension reforms throughout much of Europe and, of course, technology. In this context, EMU has a potentially significant and complementary impact on an already strongly integrating and more intensely competitive banking market.

Like its predecessor the SMP, the strategic impact of EMU on banking in the new Euroland is rather complex and with varying time dimensions attached to different possible effects. As explained earlier, disentangling the specific effects of any single bank strategic driver like a major regulatory initiative is also not easy when so many important changes are happening and intensifying at the same time. With these caveats in mind, the strategic impact of EMU is already proving (as expected) to be major.

Broughton et al. (1999, p. 1) point out that in 1998 and 1999 there is strong evidence that the divergence of performance of European bank sectors is narrowing. This phenomenon appears to be associated with a sharp narrowing in divergence of key macroeconomic variables within the EU. The aforementioned authors believe that GDP growth is now the key determinant of performance among EU bank sectors.

EMU is expected to strengthen pressures to reduce excess capacity in banking, bank profits will come under more strain, geographic and market (functional) diversification (both within and outside of EMU) will become more attractive in some segments of banking, and bank M&A activity can be expected to grow. Generally, banking competition is likely to intensify in most sectors. As securities markets become deeper and more liquid, present securitization trends are also likely to be sustained and accelerated.

The immediate and most transparent impact of EMU is on financial markets and on the traditional wholesale banking businesses of foreign exchange, corporate banking and government bond trading. EMU has reduced currency risk and lowered the transactions costs of international trade. Bond and equity markets are expected to become deeper and more liquid; portfolio allocations will become more internationally diversified. Financial services in many countries will become liberalized and more open to foreign competition. EMU and the concurrent rise of internet and direct banking should also help the progression towards a more globalized retail banking market within the EU.

The cost of government debt issues is likely to be lower under EMU. With the removal of currency risk, attention will focus more on the evaluation of credit risk when pricing different EMU countries' debt. The creditworthiness of individual states will be left to the markets. Rating of government debt will become a more important issue; local market underwriting skills will also be increasingly emphasized.

Although fiscal consolidation within EMU is likely to reduce the volume of government debt securities, the market in private securities (bonds and equities) could grow significantly with, for example, more investors and issuers coming to the market in a larger EMU bloc. EMU could boost the corporate bond market; the costs of new bond and commercial paper issues will be lower because of more competitive underwriting and hedging in a market that is no longer segmented by currency. In this new environment, companies are more likely to issue debt than borrow from banks. Some commentators have suggested that up to one-third of EU banks' present corporate lending business could shift into capital markets. Increasing diversification by euro asset managers will correspondingly increase the number of investment portfolios to which these new securities could be marketed. This movement towards increased portfolio diversification will also be stimulated through the needed reform of EU pensions and the resultant boost to asset management along US lines.

However, it seems overly simplistic to assume that Euroland will become 'overnight' a US-style capital market. There are (and will remain) many differences between Euroland and the US. Gros and Lannoo (1999, p. 61), for example, emphasize two such differences. Regional differences are especially important in the EU and these arise from deeply rooted structural and institutional features. A second important difference is that EU banks play a much more important role than market-based forms of financing of investment compared with the US. EMU, however, will certainly facilitate a considerable EU movement along the US-style capital market path in the longer run. This is already apparent in trends like equity market link-ups, the emergence of US-style government bond markets (with a primary focus on credit-risk differentials) and increasing securitization. Also, the movement towards a US style of investment banking is likely to be a more pressing need in some market segments.

As with the SMP, the stronger macroeconomic environment flowing from EMU is expected to increase opportunities for banks. As Spavanta (1999, p. 59) emphasizes, the stimulus to the growth and deepening of financial markets should itself boost EU economies because of the well-documented link between economic growth and financial development. As companies restructure and expand, there should be growing business for banks. The more positive economic environment leading to greater stability and more sustainable higher rates of GDP growth should help to boost bank profits. Although in the shorter term banks appear to face more threats through trends like securitization and the growth of US-style asset management, there are also corresponding increased opportunities for various banks.

Another feature worth emphasizing is that the banking implications of Euroland strictly defined (to include member countries only) clearly extend beyond the Euroland banks themselves. For one thing, other EU and foreign banks compete strongly in the wholesale markets most immediately affected by the EMU initiative. Another strategic feature is that banks in those countries yet to join full EMU need to be prepared strategically. In this general respect it is interesting to note that domestic M&A activity and protecting existing home markets appears to be given a high and more immediate strategic priority by some banks.

## 6  COMPETITIVE STRATEGIES IN EUROLAND

As Davidson et al. (1998, p. 67) note with regard to preparations for EMU:

> Astonishingly, many banks seem ill prepared. Although they have tackled the IT and operational challenges raised by a single European currency, they have failed

to address the more difficult strategic issues. Put bluntly, they have not considered how they will prosper once a single currency wipes out great chunks of profit in their traditional wholesale businesses of foreign exchange, corporate banking and government bond trading.

In the new Euroland environment Davidson et al. argue that the best opportunities are likely to accrue to only a handful of banks.

Bank revenue growth in wholesale banking following EMU is likely to be mainly in investment banking, which spans areas (such as equities, bonds and M&A) where EU banks will find it difficult to match the scale and expertise of the big US investment banks already operating within the EU. Davidson et al. (1998, p. 69) believe that, overall, 'EMU is likely to create more losers than winners in wholesale banking'. EMU, then, poses many serious threats to banks. For example, the 'typical' European bank could lose around 70 per cent of its foreign exchange trading revenues with the abolition of foreign currencies. In other wholesale banking areas, the threats are also apparently as serious (see ibid., p. 70).

In corporate lending, historically 'cheap' bank loans (facilitated by lending overcapacity and less intense competition) are becoming less sustainable. Banks throughout the EU are having to become more shareholder value orientated, allocating their internal capital to support high-performing assets and correspondingly reducing the proportion of low-income assets on their balance sheet. This is not a specific EMU consequence, although EMU certainly facilitates this kind of environment. Governments throughout Europe are generally keen to improve competitiveness through the discouragement of historic close bank/industry link-ups and state subsidies.

At the same time, a single and more liquid European corporate bond market will facilitate more bond issues by companies. The cost of reserve requirements imposed on Euroland banks by the European Central Bank (ECB) may also be passed on to banks' customers, thereby increasing the cost of bank intermediation. Bank lending volumes and margins will be subjected to downward pressures in this new environment. With increasing securitization, banks may find themselves with a growing adverse selection problem in their own lending.

Deposit and money market business is another area of wholesale banking that will come under pressure. In Euroland, volumes may fall since corporate customers will no longer need to hold deposit accounts in each of the EU currencies in which they trade. At the same time, traders will no longer hold different currency-denominated deposit balances in order to exploit interest rate differentials. A countervailing trend is that a deeper, liquid and more standardized EU money market under EMU should boost competition and increase other opportunities for banks. This increased competition, though, will help to reduce margins on this business.

The wholesale payments area will also come under pressure in Euroland. A great deal of this business comes from correspondent banking, but EMU will eliminate intra-European currency payments. The introduction of TARGET (a payments system for processing wholesale Euro transactions) further lessens the need for traditional correspondent banking services. At the same time, cross-border payments are likely to grow with the increased trade expected to flow from EMU. Nevertheless, banking scale and efficiency are likely to be key competitive ingredients of success in this new market environment.

Government bond trading is another key area of wholesale banking that is likely to be a threat to many Euroland banks. As pointed out earlier, increased fiscal discipline by governments will reduce the volume of government bond issues. At the same time, domestic EU banks will no longer be able to rely on their specialist knowledge of domestic monetary and fiscal policy, national currencies and interest rates to win business. Knowledge of country credit risk will be the more relevant driver of successful government bond business in Euroland; distribution capabilities will also be more important.

These threats, together with the more general and inexorable rise of trends like globalization and securitization, are real and immediate. But there are many good opportunities for wholesale banks in Euroland. The development of a broader, more liquid and deeper European capital market should help to stimulate the cross-border consolidation of many industries, thereby generating more M&A business for banks. The municipal, corporate bond and equity markets should all be stimulated by the single currency environment.

The 'privatization' of government debt may help to promote the municipal bond market, which until recently has been virtually non-existent in Europe. The funding of large public infrastructure projects may transfer increasingly to the private sector. Both equity and bond financing are relevant, but bond finance is especially suited to the kind of revenue streams involved. A US-style municipal bond market might eventually emerge as a replacement for present government borrowing. The privatization of social security and pensions is also likely to boost capital markets, investment management and related wholesale banking.

This brief and select strategic overview of threats and opportunities facing banks in Euroland raises many strategic questions. A leading strategic issue is that there appears to be a premium on bank size, although US experience has also demonstrated that in areas like municipal bonds smaller players can compete successfully with the leading investment banks. However, there does appear to be a general strategic view that size may be particularly critical in many important wholesale banking segments.

All of the foregoing leads to the question of what strategies are likely to succeed. This appears to be a much more complex issue than simply focusing on size *per se* (and the benefits of size can often be achieved through various alternative routes). Another, more specific question is whether EU banks (and which kinds of bank) can compete successfully in this new, more globalized marketplace. Once again we are in the realms of 'crystal ball' gazing. One also has the strong impression from many US analysts and consultants that only the giant US investment banks can be expected to dominate in this new, apparently more US style of banking in Euroland.

EMU also has important consequences for retail banking. The stronger macroeconomic environment being facilitated in part by EMU has furthered the downward pressure on interest rates and interest margins in many retail markets; this has exerted pressure on bank profitability. During the 1990s, in the US consolidation and increased penetration of regional and local markets by large national and super-regional banks made these retail banking markets apparently more contestable. Yet, smaller financial institutions in the US regional and local markets are 'surprisingly adept at survival' (Walter, 1999, p. 157). There is evidence from the US 'that retail banking clients remain strongly dependent on financial services firms with a local presence, and where there is a high level of concentration this is reflected in both interest and deposit rates' (ibid.).

Local preferences are a strong feature of individual European banking markets and the proliferation of different types of local and regional banking groups is a characteristic feature of these markets. Furthermore, foreign bank entry into the majority of national markets is relatively low and typically restricted to specialized, niche or wholesale activities (ECB, 1999). Another feature of European banking that is likely to affect the evolving market structure is 'the role of state at national, regional and municipal level' (Walter, 1999, p. 159). Walter makes the point that non-joint stock European banks operate under different performance pressures and that 'when public- and private-sector firms meet in the market, competitive outcomes will clearly be affected' (ibid.). The longer-term outcome, however, is unclear; the immediate impact is to help reduce retail banking profit margins in markets where the commercial banks are subject to competition from public sector banks.

Local banks are thought to possess information advantages. Asymmetric information in bank lending will continue to enable banks to target customer segments even as the level of competition increases. Information about customers and the need to have a link with borrowers means that traditional credit activities are likely to remain substantial (de Bandt, 1999). This scenario will hold particularly true for small and medium-sized enterprises and individual customers, who do not have ready access to securities markets. Local knowledge, therefore, can be argued to provide a sustainable competitive advantage for some retail banks. Nevertheless, the different types of European bank face competition from specialist lenders that have taken advantage of technological developments and are providing lower-cost services. De Bandt summarizes the likely effects of EMU on banks' traditional activities as reducing banks' competitive advantages while intensifying the need for asset transformation and uncertainty management.

In Europe, historical characteristics and the existence of asymmetric information provide an opportunity for the co-existence of a relatively large number of small banks serving local and regional markets, while a few large banks service mainly corporate customers at the pan-European level. There are a number of strategic options for small banks in the post-EMU environment. Specializing in niche areas is one. Another is to build alliances with universal banks, either to protect local markets from potential competitors, or to acquire information technology and a larger distribution network. Yet another strategy might be to try to acquire critical mass through the merger route. Nevertheless, mergers are likely to pressure further those small domestic players who are not efficient and strong enough to match the opposition.

The build-up to a wider Euroland is likely to be accompanied by domestic (protective) consolidation in retail banking; this was a feature of the build-up to the SMP (EC, 1997 and Gardener, 1999a). A wider Euroland also appears to increase the potential for cross-border bank mergers, although most analysts argue that the potential cost savings and synergies need to be targeted carefully. Many also believe that these cost savings and synergies will be hard to find and even harder to sustain.

Walter (1999) argues that the present situation in the EU can be compared in some respects with the US prior to its early 1990s' financial sector restructuring. Before it was restructured, the US financial services industry carried too much capital and employment in the production of financial services; both capital and employment were subsequently reduced through consolidation, a process that has just begun in Europe. Yet, there are several notable differences between Europe and the US. Due to the existence of historical differences in bank ownership, retail market consolidation may be slower in Europe than in the US. Furthermore, the ruthless nature apparent in the US consolidation process is relatively less marked in European banking. Nevertheless, competition is expected to intensify in all European retail markets.

New and more innovative distribution channels will be inevitable features of this new environment. Internet and other forms of direct banking in particular also offer the potential of significant cross-border expansion of much smaller retail financial services firms and those without an established (or any) traditional banking franchise. These technology-led developments are likely to be important strategically in the process (slow to date) of globalizing retail financial servces markets in the EU. EMU will facilitate this process through its likely effect of producing a much greater standardization throughout the EU of the institutional market features (including regulation and taxation) within retail financial services.

What is clear is that the EU banking system is currently in a state of unprecedented change. A great deal of M&A activity has already taken place during the past ten years and this has accelerated recently. As with the SMP, some of this has been in anticipation of the new environment facilitated by EMU. The ECB (1999) believes that in the new environment there is room for further consolidation. Two types of merger have been identified:

- *strategic mergers* – involving at least one large player with the strategic aim of repositioning the merged entity in the EMU market; and
- *mergers to remove excess capacity* – involving mainly smaller banks and being defensive, with the main aim of the new, larger entity being to realize efficiency gains.

The latter has been a major feature of merger activity in Spain, Italy and France during 1999.

A new and still emergent M&A strategy is also worth emphasizing:

- *cross-border mergers between large banks* – Dutch–Belgian bank mergers and the Merita–Nordbanken deal is a good example of what might yet prove to be an important stimulus associated (at least partly) with EMU.

This last type of merger is still rare, although several rumours abound and some potential large cross-border mergers have been recently frustrated. Such mergers were envisaged by Cecchini as a product of the SMP. This Cecchini vision has not been fully realized, but EMU may well further promote these types of mergers.

Drawing comparisons of US experiences with bank consolidation and restructuring must be a cautionary exercise. We emphasized earlier that there are many deep-rooted structural and institutional differences between the US banking market and Euroland. Nevertheless, these comparisons are frequently made and they can help to provide useful insight into what might happen in some market segments. The acquisition of the US Bankers Trust by Deutsche Bank is a clear strategic sign that those Euroland banks that aspire to be global banks recognize the need for US-style investment banking expertise.

A recent comparative study by Hurst et al. (1999) reached the following conclusions about the performance of Euroland banks compared with the US:

- Euroland banks generate a relatively low gross revenue stream and have higher costs.
- Despite higher leverage (due to their better average asset quality), the ROE in Euroland during the 1990s is much lower than for banks in the Anglophone countries.

Hurst et al. (1999) point out that costs are not well managed in many European banks. It is also suggested that this apparent poor performance of Euroland banks can be explained through factors like inadequate product mixes and pricing strategies for corporate clients, and the distorted competitive environment.

There are essentially two ways to improve this apparent poor showing by Euroland banks. One is to improve bank performance via the existing management; the second way is to replace management. In this latter context, the M&A route is the common strategic route and it is in this area that US experiences many give some interesting insights.

The US over the past decade has experienced a 'mega' banking-merger wave, with the number of banks dropping by about 30 per cent. An interesting empirical fact is that analysts to date have not been able to find consistent improvements in the post-merger companies: see, for example, Hurst et al. (1999). European bank M&A activity to date (although much smaller than in the US) also seems to support the view that many bank mergers do not lead to longer-term efficiency gains. Of course, there are many problems in interpreting these apparent results. One set of problems concerns the empirical methodologies used to measure merger-related performance. The other concerns the relevance and practical importance of other, less apparent reasons for bank M&A activity.

In their comparative study (of US and Europe), Hurst et al. (1999, p. 99) conclude that Europe in theory 'should see a merger wave much as has occurred in the US'. Many other analysts and students support this view; recent apparent emergent trends in Europe lend empirical evidence to it. Most of the analysis (both theoretical and comparative) seems to lead to the conclusion of post-EMU excess capacity in banking, followed by inevitable restructuring and consolidation in the new Euroland. Furthermore, with increasing securitization and other trends emphasizing the increased importance of investment banking, bank concentration may be expected to increase with the increased capital expenditures that characterize this kind of banking: see, for example, Danthine et al. (1999, pp. 52–4).

All of this begs two questions (at least). First, why hasn't the present EU merger wave attained US bank proportions? Second, can we really expect the kind of mega bank-merger wave experienced in the US, together with the respective rise in bank concentration? In many respects these questions are interrelated. The answers may also bear directly again on structural and institutional differences between the US and Euroland.

Hurst et al. (1999) suggest that there are still many important barriers to restructuring in Euroland compared with the US. Examples include the high level of public ownership of banks and bank restructuring influenced by non-economic motives (such as preserving national champions). EMU may also prompt increased regulatory rigour and reactions to perceived anti-competitive policies. Other Euro-specific factors include the successful use of sharing arrangements (thereby achieving the economic benefits of bigger size) by important EU bank sectors, such as the savings banks. More rigid labour laws in Europe may also slow down cost-cutting and related M&A activity. The EC (1997) study also confirms that there remain important tax and legal differences, together with linguistic and cultural barriers, within the EU that may impact on banking strategies.

The foregoing might suggest that Euroland bank restructuring and consolidation, while significant, is likely to be a slower process and on a reduced scale (at least in the shorter term) than US experiences might suggest. Furthermore, Hurst et al. (1999, p. 101) conclude that most European banks will generally seek to exploit M&A possibilities in national markets before seeking cross-border opportunities. More bank consolidation, then, will be the likely product of EMU, but it 'may well be a very slow process' (ibid.).

Post-EMU strategies of Euroland banks will take many forms. For those handful that aspire to global status, the challenges (especially from the leading US investment banks) are formidable. Building a significant position in US securities is generally accepted as a necessary step for building leadership in investment banking.

Aspirant regional or multilocal players are also likely to be wholesale driven. Davidson et al. (1998) suggest that in the post-EMU environment, these banks have three basic options: sell all or part of their investment banking business; build a purely pan-European presence; or adopt a niche position. These kinds of banks have to examine carefully and exploit customer and product franchises in which they can sustain competitive advantages.

Local players are essentially retail focused; these banks should consider concentrating primarily on retail financial services. One problem here is that during an era of reform of pensions business, such institutions may want to provide mutual fund products and equity brokerage services to their customers. One option for the smaller players might be to form strategic link-ups. Another option for these kinds of players is to focus more strongly on core specialist and niche products. The latter may also be developed cross-border via internet and direct banking distribution channels.

## 7 CONCLUDING REMARKS

This select survey has emphasized that the rise of Euroland is a particularly important development in the modern evolution of EU and global banking. Although the immediate and more apparently transparent impact is on wholesale banking, there are important implications for retail banking. For one thing, increasing competitive and profit pressures in wholesale banking, together with trends such as securitization, may operate to emphasize the strategic importance of retail banking for many banks. EMU and other developments (such as technology and direct banking) will also increase the pressures towards more globalization in retail banking. US experiences may provide some practical insight into phenomena (such as bank restructuring) that may be expected to be a product of Euroland, but we have also emphasized the structural and institutional differences between the US and Europe. These may operate to reduce the scale and lengthen the time path of the kind of bank-merger wave that is likely to emerge as Euroland becomes more established and expands. At the same time, technological developments (especially internet banking) will facilitate the entry of new players, bringing new forms of competition and presenting serious marketing challenges for the traditional banks.

## NOTE

1. This section draws from Molyneux (1999) and parts of Gardener et al. (1999a and b).

## REFERENCES

Begg, Iain (1998), 'Commentary: The Single Market', *National Institute Economic Review*, April, 2/98, 7–10.

Broughton, Alan, Salveig Babinet and Duncan Farr (1999), 'Fundamental pushes . . . fundamental pulls', 9 July, Morgan Stanley Dean Witter Banks: Europe, London.

Clarke, P.D., E.P.M. Gardener, P. Feeney and P. Molyneux (1988), 'The genesis of strategic marketing control in British retail banking', *International Journal of Banking Marketing*, Vol. 6, No. 2, 5–19.
Commission of the European Communities (1988), *European Economy: The Economics of 1992*, No. 35, March, Brussels: Commission of the European Communities.
Danthine, Jean-Pierre, Francesco Giavazzi, Xavier Vives and Ernst-Ludwig von Thadden (1999), 'The future of European banking', *Monitoring European Integration*, 9, January, London: Centre for Economic Policy Research.
Davidson, Jonathan, Alison R. Ledger and Giovanni Viani (1998), 'Financial institutions', *McKinsey Quarterly*, No. 1, 67–81.
De Bandt, O. (1999), 'EMU and the structure of the European banking system', *The Monetary and Regulatory Implications of Changes in the Banking Industry*, BIS Conference Papers, Vol. 7, March, pp. 121–41.
European Central Bank (ECB) (1999), *Possible Effects of EMU on the EU Banking Systems in the Medium to Long Term*, Frankfurt, February.
European Commission (EC) (E.P.M. Gardener, B. Moore and P. Molyneux) (1997), *The Single Market Review – Credit Institutions and Banking*, Subseries II: Impact on Services, Vol. 3, London: Kogan Page.
Gardener, Edward, Barry Howcroft and Jonathan Williams (1999b), 'The new retail banking revolution', *The Service Industries Journal*, Vol. 19, No. 2, April, 83–100.
Gardener, E.P.M., P. Molyneux and J. Williams (1999a), *European Savings Banks: Coming of Age?*, Dublin: Lafferty.
Gardener, E.P.M., P. Molyneux, J. Williams and S. Carbo (1997), 'European savings banks: facing up to the new environment', *International Journal of Bank Marketing*, 15/7, 243–54.
Gardener, E.P.M. and Jonathan L. Teppett (1995), 'A select replication of the Cecchini microeconomic methodology on the EFTA financial services sectors: a note and critique', *The Service Industries Journal*, Vol. 15, No. 1, January, 74–89.
Gardener, E.P.M. and J. Williams (1996), 'British bank strategies: balancing customer needs and supply side pressures', in Leo Schuster (ed.), *Banking Cultures of the World*, Frankfurt: Fritz Knapp Verlag, pp. 591–612.
Gros, Daniel and Karel Lannoo (1999), 'The structure of financial systems and macroeconomic stability', *Cahiers BEI/EIB Papers*, Vol. 4, No. 1, 61–9.
Hurst, Christopher, Eric Perée and Mirelle Fischbach (1999), 'On the road to wonderland? Bank restructuring after EMU', *Cahiers BEI/EIB Papers*, Vol. 4, No. 1, 83–103.
McCauley, R.N. and W. White (1997), 'The euro and European financial markets', BIS Working Papers, No. 41, Basle: Bank for International Settlements.
McLean, J. (1994), 'Look after the customer', *The Banker*, May, 64–5.
Molyneux, Philip (1999), 'Shareholder value in banking', Lecture delivered at Erasmus University, Rotterdam, Bangor: Institute of European Finance, 1–11.
Spavanta, Luigi (1999), 'Comments on the future of EU capital markets', *Cahiers BEI/EIB Papers*, Vol. 4, No. 1, 59–60.
Walter, Ingo (1999), 'Financial services strategies in the euro zone', *Cahiers BEI/EIB Papers*, Vol. 4, No. 1, 145–66.
White, William R. (1998), 'The coming transformation of continental European banking?', BIS Working Papers, No. 54, Basle: Bank for International Settlements.

# 6. How to tie your hands: a currency board versus an independent central bank

**Jakob de Haan and Helge Berger**

## 1 INTRODUCTION

The proper design of monetary institutions is a very important issue for transition and developing countries alike. There seems to be broad support for the idea that price stability should be the prime objective of monetary policy. How should this objective be realized, that is, what is the proper monetary arrangement? This chapter will compare two options: a currency board and an independent central bank under flexible exchange rates.

Developing and transition countries show considerable diversity in their exchange rate regimes, from very hard currency pegs to free floats and many variations in between. Exchange rate pegs can provide a useful and credible nominal anchor for monetary policy and avoid many of the complexities and institutional requirements for establishing an alternative anchor, such as a functional and credible inflation target backed by an operationally independent central bank (Mussa et al., 2000).

A currency board can be considered as the most credible form of a fixed exchange rate regime as the own currency is convertible against a fixed exchange rate with some other currency(ies), which is codified, be it in a law or otherwise. The anchor currency is generally chosen for its expected stability and international acceptability. There is, as a rule, no independent monetary policy as the monetary base (or in the simplest case: banknotes) is (are) backed by foreign reserves (Pautola and Backé, 1998).[1]

Currency boards are back in fashion (Ghosh et al., 2000). Once they were a common monetary arrangement, especially in the British Dominions. After these countries became independent, currency boards were used by only a handful of small, open economies. However, in recent years quite a number of countries have introduced a currency board or have considered doing so.[2] Argentina (1991), Estonia (1992), Lithuania (1994), Bulgaria (1997) and Bosnia-Herzegovina (1997) are among the countries that have (or had) a currency board. In all of these cases, the currency board was chosen as part of a structural adjustment programme. The countries that adopted currency boards in the 1990s were able to adjust to low inflation levels as rapidly, or more rapidly and lastingly, than other countries in similar situations. Except for Argentina, none of them devalued or was forced to exit the currency board during the various crises (Rivera Batiz and Sy, 2000). Table 6.1, reproduced from Ghosh et al. (2000), presents an overview of currency boards.[3]

A number of recent studies suggest that countries with a currency board have been quite successful. For instance, Ghosh et al. (2000) conclude that currency boards have been instituted to gain credibility following a period of high inflation, and in this regard, have been remarkably successful. Countries with a currency board experienced lower inflation and higher growth compared to both floating regimes and standard pegs.

An alternative to the introduction of a currency board is to have a flexible exchange rate regime and to give the central bank independence and a clear mandate for price stability. It is often argued that a high level of central bank independence coupled with some explicit mandate for the central bank to aim for price stability constitutes important institutional devices to maintain price stability. Indeed, various countries have recently upgraded central bank independence to raise their commitment to price stability. There exists a vast literature showing that a 'conservative' (that is, inflation-averse) and independent central bank will bring lower inflation (see Eijffinger and de Haan, 1996 and Berger et al., 2001a for surveys).

So, an important question is which arrangement should be preferred.[4] This chapter deals with this question. The remainder of our contribution is organized as follows. The next section outlines the working of a currency board. Section 3 presents a very simple theoretical model to compare the welfare benefits of a currency board and an independent central bank. Section 4 discusses some aspects that may be relevant too, but which are not taken up in the model. Finally, Section 5 offers some concluding comments.

## 2  THE ESSENTIALS OF A CURRENCY BOARD

Although not all currency boards are alike, they generally share three features. First (as stated above), there is a fixed exchange rate with some other currency(ies), which is codified, be it in a law or otherwise. In this respect, a currency board differs from a standard peg as the capacity to devalue is severely restricted by requiring parliamentary approval and other

Table 6.1  Currency boards: an overview

| Country | Introduction | Pegged to | Backing rule | Actual backing |
|---|---|---|---|---|
| Argentina | 1991 | $ | 100% of $M_0$ | 139% of $M_0$ |
| Antigua & Barbuda (ECCB) | 1965 | $ | At least 60% of $M_0$ | 86% of $M_0$ |
| Brunei-Darussalam | 1967 | Singapore $ | >70% of demand liabilities | Around 80% |
| Bosnia-Herzegovina | 1997 | DM/euro | 100% of liabilities | 110% |
| Bulgaria | 1997 | DM/euro | 100% of liabilities | 148% |
| Djibouti | 1949 | $ | 100% of currency | 113% of $M_0$ |
| Dominica (ECCB) | 1965 | $ | >60% of $M_0$ | 89% of $M_0$ |
| Estonia | 1992 | DM/euro | 100% of $M_0$ | 122% of $M_0$ |
| Grenada (ECCB) | 1965 | $ | >60% of $M_0$ | 91% of $M_0$ |
| St Kitts and Nevis (ECCB) | 1965 | $ | >60% of $M_0$ | 102% of $M_0$ |
| St Lucia (ECCB) | 1965 | $ | >60% of $M_0$ | 96% of $M_0$ |
| St Vincent and Grenadines (ECCB) | 1965 | $ | >60% of $M_0$ | 96% of $M_0$ |
| Hong Kong | 1983 | $ | 100% of certificates of indebtedness | 110% of $M_0$ (incl. cert. of indebtedness) |
| Lithuania | 1994 | $/euro | 100% of currency and liquid liabilities | 112% of $M_0$ |

*Note:*  ECCB: Eastern Caribbean Central Bank.

*Source:*  Ghosh et al. (2000).

restrictions (Rivera Batiz and Sy, 2000). The anchor currency is generally chosen for its expected stability and international acceptability.[5] A pure currency board arrangement is the strictest possible form of a fixed exchange rate regime, since there is, as a rule, no independent monetary policy (Pautola and Backé, 1998).[6] This is due to the second characteristic of a currency board arrangement, the fact that the monetary base (or in the simplest case: banknotes) is (are) backed by foreign reserves. The assets side of a currency board's balance sheet consists principally of its holdings of the reserve currency, while on the liabilities side there is an equal value of cash held by the public and deposits held by commercial banks. The reserves that a currency board holds are generally low-risk, interest-bearing bonds and other assets denominated in the anchor currency. Unlike many central banks, a currency board does not hold domestic assets, like government debt. Currency boards often hold reserves somewhat exceeding 100 per cent of their liabilities to have a margin of protection should the assets they hold lose value (Schuler, 1992). These excess reserves correspond to the net worth of the currency board. Third, a currency board maintains convertibility between its notes and coins and the anchor currency. A currency board has no responsibility for ensuring that bank deposits are convertible as this is solely the responsibility of banks. Unlimited convertibility means that no restrictions exist on current-account transactions (buying and selling goods and services) or capital-account transactions (buying and selling financial assets, such as foreign bonds).

The consequence of these characteristics of a currency board is that money supply is determined by market forces and, ultimately, by foreign monetary policy. The monetary base increases when the public sells foreign currency to the currency board, or when foreign money flows into the country. Likewise, under a strict currency board interest rates are also fully determined by market forces as monetary operations are not permitted. Changes in the board's foreign exchange reserves are reflected in the availability of domestic liquidity and interest rates (Pautola and Backé, 1998). Under a currency board economic adjustment has to come by way of wage and price adjustments, which can be both slower and more painful if structural rigidities, especially in the labour market, have not been removed.

As pointed out by Schuler (1999), many of the modern currency boards are not orthodox currency boards, but currency board-like systems, that is, central banks that retain some of their old powers, but are constrained by currency board rules regarding the exchange rate and reserves. Under such a modified currency board, the law provides for some flexibility. The currency board may, for instance, provide financial support to banks from its excess reserves, or it can borrow from international capital markets or issue securities to do so. Schuler (1999) argues that, for example, the Estonian currency board-like system has become somewhat more orthodox over time, while the Lithuanian system has maintained a more or less constant level of orthodoxy during its existence.

A number of recent studies suggest that countries with a currency board have been quite successful in bringing down inflation. For instance, Ghosh et al. (2000) conclude that currency boards have been instituted to gain credibility following a period of high inflation, and in this regard, have been remarkably successful. Table 6.2 is reproduced from Ghosh et al. (2000). It shows that the inflation performance under currency boards has been significantly better than under either pegged or floating regimes. This better inflation performance did not come at the cost of lower growth. This outcome could reflect a rebound effect (many currency boards have been established following a crisis) or self-selection (governments willing to accept a currency board are likely to be more reformist). In any case, currency boards have provided an important tool for gaining credibility and achieving macroeconomic stabilization and sustained growth (Gulde et al., 2000).

Likewise, Rivera Batiz and Sy (2000) conclude that currency boards tend to stabilize inflation relative to standard pegs or flexible rates, even for countries that established the currency board under high-inflation conditions such as Argentina, Bulgaria and Estonia. They also find that currency boards tend to align domestic to anchor currency interest rates and show smaller rate volatility than other countries. On the downside, some currency boards showed greater real effective exchange rate appreciation than similar peg regime countries and tended to be more responsive to negative employment shocks.

The lack of discretionary powers of a currency board is often considered to be crucial for its performance. Schuler (1999) argues, for instance, that

> [B]y design, a currency board has no discretionary powers. Its operations are completely passive and automatic. The sole function of a currency board is to exchange its notes and coins for the anchor currency at a fixed rate. Unlike a central bank, an orthodox currency board does not lend to the domestic government, to domestic companies, or to domestic banks. In a currency board system, the government can finance its spending by only taxing or borrowing, not by printing money and thereby creating inflation.

Not everybody is convinced of the working of a currency board. Roubini (1999) argues, for instance, that

> There are countries in which they seem to work for a while; however, these countries are successful not because of the currency board system itself but rather

Table 6.2  Macroeconomic performance under alternative exchange rate regimes (%)

| | Number of observations | Inflation | | | Broad money growth | | | GDP growth | GDP growth per capita | Govt balance |
|---|---|---|---|---|---|---|---|---|---|---|
| | | Mean $\pi$ | Median $\pi$ | Mean $\pi/(1+\pi)$ | Mean $\mu$ | Median $\mu$ | Mean $\mu/(1+\mu)$ | $\Delta y$ | $\Delta y^c$ | $B/y$ |
| Full sample | 1,915 | 29.0 | 8.4 | 10.7 | 33.7 | 14.3 | 14.4 | 3.2 | 1.3 | −4.4 |
| Currency board | 112 | 5.6 | 3.9 | 5.0 | 12.1 | 11.1 | 9.9 | 4.0 | 3.1 | −2.7 |
| Other | 1,089 | 22.3 | 8.4 | 9.1 | 25.1 | 13.7 | 12.3 | 3.3 | 0.9 | −4.6 |
| Pegged float | 714 | 43.1 | 9.2 | 14.2 | 47.4 | 16.0 | 18.2 | 3.1 | 1.7 | −4.3 |

*Source:* Ghosh et al. (2000).

because they follow macroeconomic policies and structural liberalisation policies that are consistent with the maintenance of fixed rates. Fixed rates and currency boards without these good policies lead to currency collapse and economic disaster. Conversely, if you do follow the right economic policies you do not need a currency board: you will do as well without one and adopting one may only hurt you when truly exogenous shocks require an adjustment of your nominal exchange rate parity.

## 3 CURRENCY BOARD OR INDEPENDENT CENTRAL BANK?

A high-inflation problem is an important motivation for countries in transition to consider introducing a currency board or a credible exchange rate peg. However, before a country decides in favour of a currency board, a proper comparison with the alternative of an independent and conservative (that is, inflation-averse) central bank should be made. Both alternatives have advantages and disadvantages and it is not always obvious what the optimum solution would be. Broadly following Berger et al. (2001b), we can illustrate this within a simple model of exchange rate regime choice.

Assume that (the log of) output is given by a simplified Lucas supply curve:

$$y_t = (\pi_t - \pi_t^e) + \varepsilon_t, \tag{6.1}$$

with $\pi$ and $\pi^e$ denoting actual and expected inflation and where $\varepsilon$ is a random output shock with $\varepsilon \sim N(0, \sigma_\varepsilon^2)$. The level of natural output is normalized to zero. The model's demand side is given by the purchasing power parity condition:

$$\pi_t = \pi_t^F + e_t, \tag{6.2}$$

with $\pi^F$ denoting foreign inflation and $e$ the change in the nominal exchange rate towards a possible target country. Under fully flexible exchange rates, $e$ will fully compensate any changes in foreign inflation. In this case inflation will be determined in a process involving both the home country's government and central bank. We can conveniently summarize this process by assuming that a loss function of the following form is minimized:

$$L = \pi_t^2 + [\gamma \chi^{CB} + (1-\gamma)\chi^G](y_t - y^*)^2, \tag{6.3}$$

where $y^* > 0$ is a time-invariant output target giving rise to the well-known time-inconsistency problem for monetary policy. The parameters $\chi^G$ and $\chi^{CB}$ are, respectively, the government's and the central bank's preference put on the real target with $\chi^G$ and $\chi^{CB}$. The weight $\gamma \in (0, 1)$ denotes the degree of *central bank independence*, measuring the extent to which the central banker's preferences affect monetary policy making. If $\gamma = 1$, the central bank fully determines monetary policy. The inverse of $\chi^{CB}$ is often considered a measure of *central bank conservatism*. It is easy to show that the inflationary bias decreases with higher values of $\gamma$ and lower values of $\chi^{CB}$ (see also Eijffinger and de Haan, 2000). Minimizing (6.3) with regard to $\pi$ and introducing rational expectations leads to the following equilibrium inflation:

$$\pi_t = \lambda y_t^* - \frac{\lambda}{1+\lambda} \varepsilon_t, \qquad (6.4)$$

where we have defined $\lambda = \gamma \chi^{CB} + (1-\gamma)\chi^G$. The inverse of $\lambda$ could be interpreted as a measure for the *stabilization culture* prevalent in the home country. The first term in (6.4) is the inflationary bias that has its roots in the inability of monetary policy to commit to a socially optimal inflation rate of zero in the absence of output shocks. The bias is the higher, the less independent and conservative the central bank is and the more output orientated is the government.

Alternatively, the country could opt for a *currency board* to govern monetary policy and credibly fix its exchange rate against a foreign currency of its choice ($e = 0$). In this case the domestic inflation rate will equal the foreign inflation rate. To simplify, assume that the target country's (that is, the foreign) monetary policy suffers from an inflationary bias of size $a$ and reacts to the foreign output shock $u \sim N(0, \sigma_u^2)$ according to the simple linear rule $-bu_t$. In line with the standard model of monetary policy, we can assume that both $a$ and $b$ decrease in the foreign central bank's degree of independence and conservatism. Substituting for foreign inflation we can rewrite equation (6.2) as:

$$\pi_t = \pi_t^F = a - bu_t. \qquad (6.2')$$

Note that, under a currency board regime, the home economy's output shock plays no role in actual monetary policy. The 'imported' policy is aimed at the foreign output shock alone.

The trade-off between a currency board and an independent central bank can be modelled as a comparison of expected welfare under both regimes. Using (6.2'), (6.4) and (6.1), a social planner with a quadratic loss function similar to (6.3) and an output weight of $\bar{\lambda}$ will prefer a currency board if the following inequality is met:

$$(\lambda y^*)^2 - a^2 > \frac{\lambda}{1+\lambda}\left(\bar{\lambda} + \frac{\bar{\lambda}-\lambda}{1+\lambda}\right)\sigma_\varepsilon^2 + (1+\bar{\lambda})b\,\sigma_u^2 - 2\bar{\lambda}b\rho_{\varepsilon,u}\sigma_\varepsilon\sigma_u, \quad (6.5)$$

where $\rho_{\varepsilon,u}$ is the coefficient of correlation between the output shocks in the home economy and the country targeted under a currency board regime. Inequality (6.5) weighs the possible credibility gain from a currency board (LHS) against the expected welfare effects stemming from the loss of a national stabilization policy (RHS). A number of insights and policy recommendations can be derived:

1. *Stabilization culture* Ceteris paribus a currency board becomes more attractive when the home country's central bank is relatively dependent and output orientated compared to the foreign central bank. The same is true when the home country's government is very output orientated. The reason is that a lower $\lambda$ will lower the inflationary bias under a regime of floating exchange rates (first term, LHS). If the social planner is sufficiently conservative, that is, if $\bar{\lambda}$ is low enough, this gain in expected welfare will always outweigh the loss in output stabilization associated with a lower $\lambda$ (first term, RHS).

2. *Conservative and independent foreign central bank* A currency board arrangement is more attractive if the imported foreign monetary policy is in the hands of an independent and conservative foreign central bank. The argument is that a more conservative foreign monetary authority will both lower the inflationary bias under a board (second term, LHS) and the extent to which the imported stabilization policy distorts the home economy (second term, RHS). Note, however, that the last term on the RHS suggests that the latter gain is the lower, the higher is the correlation between the foreign and the home country's output shocks (see below).[7]

3. *Synchronized business cycles* The higher the correlation between the home and foreign country's output shocks, the more attractive is a currency board (last term, RHS). Behind this is the simple fact that a higher $\rho_{\varepsilon,u}$ will ensure that foreign monetary policy is more in line with the needs of the home economy.[8] Of course, this result rests critically on the assumption that imported monetary policy converts output shocks linearly into shocks to inflation without, for instance, non-additive control errors.

## 4 SOME OTHER CONSIDERATIONS

The simple model discussed in the previous section identifies three fundamental arguments that should be taken into account when a country decides about its currency regime. There are of course additional considerations that need to be discussed. Indeed, apart from the credibility benefit and the cost of being vulnerable to foreign shocks, the literature identifies a number of other costs and benefits of a currency board in comparison to an independent central bank.[9]

4. *Transaction costs* An entirely fixed exchange rate will reduce the transaction costs of international trade and investments. Transaction costs are lower since international transactions face less exchange rate uncertainty. If exchange rate uncertainty has a negative impact on trade and international investment, a currency board with a fixed exchange rate regime will lead to a better international allocation of the means of production. However, most empirical studies find hardly any support for a negative relationship between exchange rate uncertainty on the one hand and trade and investment on the other.[10] This transaction costs argument applies to fixed exchange rates in general. A currency board may provide an additional credibility effect as it is a stricter rule-based system which may lead to more capital inflows. The magnitude of the transaction costs depends, of course, on the size of (future) international transactions with the pegging country. Other relevant considerations for the choice of the currency to peg to are the denomination of the pegging country's exports and imports and the denomination of its international debt. The domestic acceptance of a foreign currency may also be taken into account (Enoch and Gulde, 1997).

5. *Political support* Currency boards do not require sophisticated money markets and monetary policy operations to be effective (Kopcke, 1999).[11] Furthermore, to make an independent central bank work requires time. Credibility has to be earned and therefore a currency board may be preferred in a situation of a severe credibility problem and/or crisis. Indeed, currency boards have often been adopted at the end of a prolonged crisis. Still, a currency board is not an easy way out. At the outset, it may be difficult to gather sufficient currency reserves to back the monetary base (Pautola and Backé, 1998). Not least, it requires broad political support (Ghosh et al., 2000). A lack of popular support may result in a self-fulfilling speculative attack (see below). Finally, the introduction of a currency board also takes time as the fixed exchange rate is established in the law and the authorities may first have to clear up a legacy of monetary, fiscal and financial failures of the past (Enoch and Gulde, 1997).

6. *Lender of last resort* A currency board implies that the central bank cannot (fully) act as lender of last resort. As this safety net for the

financial sector is missing, a prerequisite for a currency board is a reasonably healthy financial system. The authorities should ensure that financial institutions have adequate capital, proper reserves for losses, and that they provide full disclosure of their financial accounts and have access to credit markets abroad. This is all the more important as in the past decades, except for the Eastern Caribbean Central Bank, all existing currency boards have experienced at least one banking crisis (Santiprabhob, 1997). Roubini (1999) argues that a monetary tightening when a currency board is subject to a speculative attack can bankrupt the domestic financial system and the domestic banks as tight base money means that, given required reserve ratios, banks are forced to recall loans and firms may go bankrupt.

There is, of course, another side to this coin as a currency board can be seen as a precommitment for a no-bail-out of distressed banks. In other words, it reduces the moral hazard problem of banking supervision. Especially if banking crises result from poor management and supervision, a currency board may be beneficial.

7. *Misalignments* A currency board runs the risk of a real misalignment. If a country's inflation remains higher than that of the pegging country, the currency can become overvalued (Pautola and Backé, 1998). While fixing the exchange rate is a fast way to disinflate an economy starting with a higher inflation rate, pegging the exchange rate will not necessarily reduce the inflation rate instantaneously to that of the pegging country. There are several reasons why inflation will not fall right away (Roubini, 1999). First, purchasing power parity does not hold exactly in the short run since domestic and foreign goods are not perfectly substitutable and the mix of goods and services in the countries concerned may differ. Second, non-tradable goods prices do not feel the same competitive pressures as tradable goods prices, thus inflation in the non-traded sector may fall only slowly. Third, as there is significant inertia in nominal wage growth, wage inflation might not fall right away. Often wage contracts are backward looking and the adjustment of wages will occur slowly. Finally, differing productivity growth rates may be reflected in differences in price increases (Samuelson–Balassa effect). If domestic inflation does not converge to the level of the pegging country, a real appreciation will occur over time. As Roubini (1999) points out, such a real exchange rate appreciation may cause a loss of competitiveness and a structural worsening of the trade balance which makes the current account deficit less sustainable.

Indeed, Rivera Batiz and Sy (2000) report that currency boards experienced substantial real effective exchange rate variability. The currencies of the Latin American and Baltic countries that introduced a currency board showed substantial appreciations. Still, this appreciation could, apart from the reasons outlined above, also be caused by real undervaluation of the currencies concerned. For instance, Richards and Tersman (1996) attribute the real appreciation of the currencies of the Baltic countries to the initial undervaluation. Also, the appreciation of the currency board countries, Estonia and Lithuania, was at the time not greater than that of Latvia. More recently, the IMF (1999) also concluded that appreciation of the Estonian kroon, the Lithuania litas and the Latvian lat was inevitable as the currencies were undervalued when the peg regimes were established. In addition, appreciation is due to the large depreciation of the Russian rouble (see also Keller, 2000).

8. *Financial crises* Recent financial crises have led various observers to conclude that pegged exchange rate regimes are inherently crisis prone for emerging markets and that these countries should therefore be encouraged to adopt floating exchange rate regimes (Eichengreen et al., 1998). It is often argued that those countries that were most severely affected by the recent financial crises had *de jure* or *de facto* exchange rate pegs or had otherwise severely limited the movement of their exchange rate. In contrast, emerging market economies that maintained more flexible exchange rates generally fared much better. As Mussa et al. (2000, pp. 21–2) conclude:

> There is an undeniable lesson here about the difficulties and dangers of running pegged or quasi-pegged exchange rate regimes for emerging market economies with substantial involvement in global capital markets, as evidenced by the fact that only the emerging markets with the hardest pegs were able to maintain their exchange rates. . . . The likelihood of prolonged speculative attack and, indeed, of a downturn in sentiment is reduced to the extent that the credibility of the peg is high; this is most obvious in the case of a currency board.

Although it is sometimes claimed that speculative attacks cannot occur under currency boards, recent experience shows otherwise (Roubini, 1999). Still, most of the countries that introduced a currency board recently were not forced to devalue or to exit the currency board (Rivera Batiz and Sy, 2000). It therefore seems that currency boards may be better able to deal with financial crises and speculative attacks than other pegged exchange rate regimes.

9. *Seigniorage* The seigniorage benefits of an independent central bank and a currency board differ. It is sometimes argued that a currency board will not bring any seigniorage. This is wrong, as a

currency board generates profits from the difference between the interest earned on its reserve assets and the expense of maintaining its liabilities (notes and coins in circulation). Still, although not zero, under a currency board system the seigniorage that a country can collect is limited.[12] As Kopcke (1999, p. 30) puts it: '[the] principal seigniorage offered by a currency board is the option it gives to its economy to create its own central bank'.

10. *Fiscal policy* As a currency board cannot provide credit to the government, this could encourage sound fiscal policy making. If the fiscal authorities know that a budget deficit will not be monetized, their incentives to have large deficits will be reduced. However, that disciplining effect should not be taken for granted, especially not if a country has lacked fiscal discipline in the past (Pautola and Backé, 1998). Indeed, Roubini (1999) argues that the choice of the exchange rate regime does not determine inflation or fiscal deficits. On the contrary, the choice of the exchange rate regime might be determined by the fiscal needs of the country. In other words, like a healthy financial system, sound public finances may be considered as a prerequisite for the successful operation of a currency board (Kopcke, 1999).

A similar case of possible reversed causality exists regarding central bank independence. On the one hand, it has been argued that CBI may enhance sound fiscal policies. On the other hand, causality may also run the other way, that is, a country will grant its central bank an independent status only if the fiscal need for seigniorage is low (Roubini, 1999). There is, however, only weak evidence suggesting that CBI and fiscal policy outcomes are correlated. Sikken and de Haan (1998), using data for 30 less-developed countries over the 1950–94 period, report for instance that some proxies for CBI are significantly related to central bank credit to government but that CBI is not related to budget deficits (see Eijffinger and de Haan, 1996 for a further discussion).

## 5 CONCLUDING COMMENTS

The median inflation rate in developing countries fell to about 5 per cent in the late 1990s from the 10 per cent or more prevailing in the early 1990s. While this decline partly reflects positive supply shocks and the anti-inflationary environment in industrial countries, it also reveals the broad acceptance of the view that the key objective of monetary policy should be to deliver low inflation (Mussa et al., 2000).

In this chapter we have discussed two alternative routes to price stability:

a currency board and a conservative and operationally independent central bank in a flexible exchange rate regime. Our analysis suggests that under certain circumstances a currency board may be beneficial, in others it may not. More specifically, the answer to the question of whether the introduction of a currency board is a good idea for a country seeking to stabilize inflation might depend on a number of criteria other than expected inflation in the target area. For instance, the anchor currency should be issued in a region which has a positively correlated business cycle with the home economy to ensure that imported monetary policy is in line with the stabilization needs of the pegging country. Currency boards may give a new currency a quick start (in some cases more than in others), but it is likely that the balance of costs and benefits will change over time if only because the circumstances may change. Currency boards are neither a quick fix nor a panacea. Low inflation and interest rates are the immediately obvious advantages of a credible currency board. They have also proved to be very resilient: apart from Argentina there have been no involuntary exits. But currency boards can prove limiting, especially for countries with weak banking systems or too lax fiscal policies (Gulde et al., 2000).

So far, most attention from academics and policy makers alike has focused on how to start up a currency board and how to operate it. However, a currency board may not exist indefinitely. This brings up the issue as to how to exit a currency board. In general, if a currency board has functioned for quite some time in a credible way, it may be transformed into an independent central bank. However, the circumstances have to be right for such a transformation. One of the key concerns is to design and implement the exit process in a manner which does not impair the credibility of the monetary policy makers (Pautola and Backé, 1998). As Kopcke (1999) points out, a country should prepare for its potential departure, that is, the monetary authorities should create a capacity to undertake policy analysis and conduct policy, and money markets and financial institutions should develop. However, a currency board does not encourage these developments: 'the art of conducting monetary policy can atrophy for lack of application, and credit markets can remain thin as banks become accustomed to dealing with the currency board and to holding many of their marketable financial assets abroad' (Kopcke, 1999, p. 32). Furthermore, the specification of the exit mechanism may undermine the credibility of the currency board (Enoch and Gulde, 1997).

Gulde et al. (2000) argue that an exchange rate regime for Central and Eastern European countries that may enter EMU in the future should satisfy a number of requirements: facilitating nominal convergence; allowing a market test for exchange rate stability; helping to ensure that countries enter the euro zone at an appropriate exchange rate; and preparing central banks for operating within the euro zone. After considering the pros and cons, these authors come to the view that (i) a currency board can in principle satisfy all these requirements, and (ii) if policies and circumstances remain right, a direct transition from a currency board to EMU without any transitional period of greater exchange rate is the proper policy for the countries concerned.

# NOTES

1. Currency boards often hold reserves somewhat exceeding 100 per cent of their liabilities to have a margin of protection should the assets they hold lose value (Schuler, 1992). Excess foreign exchange reserves can be used to conduct monetary operations or to provide lender-of-last-resort support.
2. Moreover, currency boards have been suggested as the proper exchange rate regime for potential EU and Economic and Monetary Union (EMU) entry countries (Sinn, 1999).
3. This table is not undisputed. Schuler (1999) argues that the Eastern Caribbean Central Bank should not be regarded as being a currency board-like system because in principle it has considerable discretion to lend to commercial banks and member governments.
4. Of course one can argue that these two options can be considered as the extremes and that intermediate positions are possible. However, there is a growing consensus both in the literature and among policy makers that these intermediate positions may not be viable. As Frankel (1999, p. 29) argues, this view 'which is rapidly becoming a new conventional wisdom . . . maintains that countries are increasingly finding the middle ground unsustainable and that intermediate regimes such as adjustable pegs, crawling pegs, basket pegs and target zones are being forced toward the extremes of either a free float or a rigid peg'. In Section 2 we shall discuss the differences between a currency board and a standard peg in some detail.
5. As Schuler (1992) points out, the anchor currency need not be issued by a central bank. In the past, a few currency boards have used gold as the anchor currency.
6. Rivera Batiz and Sy (2000) discuss the choice between a standard peg and a currency board, using a similar approach as employed in Section 3 of this chapter. Currency boards can be welfare improving due to their inflation stabilization and credibility properties. They can be costly because they are limited in their use of unexpected devaluation to offset shocks. The peg versus currency board choice thus depends on whether or not the flexibility value of the peg (that is, the possibility to devalue) dominates the negative welfare effects arising from actual inflation and unrealized anticipated devaluation. Because these effects work in opposite directions, regime choice will depend on country-specific parameters. In contrast to the analysis in Section 3, Rivera Batiz and Sy (2000) do not explicitly pay attention to the characteristics of the anchor country. As we shall show, however, this is important when deciding about regime choice.
7. It is even possible that the second effect prevails. The intuition is that, if the correlation is very high, imported monetary policy will be in line with the home country's stabilization needs (see the following paragraph). In this case a *non*-conservative foreign central bank will produce a better outcome.
8. Somewhat surprisingly perhaps, higher output volatility at home and abroad *as such* is not necessarily an argument against a currency board. As Berger et al. (2000) show, a more volatile economy in combination with a sufficiently high correlation among both economies might actually help the case for currency boards.
9. See also Bennett (1994), Williamson (1995) and Baliño et al. (1997) for a general discussion of the pros and cons of a currency board.
10. Various possible explanations for this rather counterintuitive result come to mind. For

one thing, in most empirical studies exchange rate uncertainty is proxied by observed exchange rate variability, which is not necessarily a good approximation. Another explanation for the lack of a negative impact of exchange rate uncertainty could be the level of aggregation of most studies. See Eijffinger and de Haan (2000) for a further discussion.
11. See Enoch and Gulde (1997) for an exposition of the technicalities of a currency board.
12. This is an important difference with outright dollarization, where seigniorage goes to the country of the anchor currency, unless special arrangements are made. Dollarization represents an even more complete renunciation of sovereignty than a currency board does, including the loss of an 'exit option' that is preserved under a currency board (Mussa et al., 2000).

# REFERENCES

Baliño, T, C. Enoch, A. Ize, V. Santiprabhob and P. Stella (1997), 'Currency board arrangements: issues and experience', IMF Occasional Paper, No. 151.
Bennett, A. (1994), 'Currency boards: issues and explanations', IMF Paper on Policy Analysis and Assessment, 94/18.
Berger, H., J.-E. Sturm and J. de Haan (2000), 'An empirical investigation into exchange rate regime choice and exchange rate volatility', CESifo Working Paper, No. 263.
Berger, H., S.C.W. Eijffinger and J. de Haan (2001a), 'Central bank independence: an update of theory and evidence', CEPR Discussion Paper, 2353, *Journal of Economic Surveys*, **15**(1), 3–4.
Berger, H., H. Jensen and G. Schjelderup (2001b), 'To peg or not to peg? A simple model of exchange rate regime choice in small economies', *Economics Letters*, **73**(2), 161–67.
Eichengreen, B., P. Masson, H. Bredenkamp, B. Johnston, J. Hamann, E. Jadresic and I. Ötker (1998), 'Exit strategies. Policy options for countries seeking greater exchange rate flexibility', IMF Occasional Paper, No. 168.
Eijffinger, S.C.W. and J. de Haan (1996), 'The political economy of central-bank independence', Princeton Special Papers in International Economics, No. 19.
Eijffinger, S.C.W. and J. de Haan (2000), *European Monetary and Fiscal Policy*, Oxford: Oxford University Press.
Enoch, C. and A.-M. Gulde (1997), 'Making a currency board operational', IMF Paper on Policy Analysis and Assessment, 97/10.
Frankel, J.A. (1999), 'No single currency regime is right for all countries or at all times', Princeton Essays in International Finance, No. 215.
Ghosh, A.R., A.-M. Gulde and H.C. Wolf (2000), 'Currency boards: more than a quick fix?', *Economic Policy*, October, 269–321.
Gulde, A.-M., J. Kähkönen and P. Keller (2000), 'Pros and cons of currency board arrangements in the lead-up to EU accession and participation in the euro zone', IMF Policy Discussion Paper 00/1.
International Monetary Fund (IMF) (1999), 'The Baltics – exchange rate regimes and external sustainability', SM/99/282.
Keller, P.M. (2000), 'Recent experience with currency boards and fixed exchange rates in the Baltic countries and Bulgaria and some lessons for the future', Paper presented at a seminar organized by Eesti Pank, May 2000.
Kopcke, R.W. (1999), 'Currency boards: once and future monetary regimes?', *New England Economic Review*, May/June, 21–37.

Mussa, M., P. Masson, A. Swoboda, E. Jadresic, P. Mauro and A. Berg (2000), 'Exchange rate regimes in an increasingly integrated world economy', IMF Occasional Paper, No. 193.
Pautola, N. and P. Backé (1998), 'Currency boards in Central and Eastern Europe: past experience and future perspectives', Oesterreichische Nationalbank, *Focus on Transition* 1/1998, 72–113.
Richards, A.J. and G.H.R. Tersman (1996), 'Growth, nontradables, and price convergence in the Baltics', *Journal of Comparative Economics*, **23**, 121–45.
Rivera Batiz, L.A and A.N.R. Sy (2000), 'Currency boards, credibility, and macroeconomic behavior', IMF Working Paper, 00/97.
Roubini, N. (1999), 'The case against currency boards: debunking 10 myths about the benefits of currency boards', http://www.stern.nyu.edu/~nroubini/asia/AsiaHomepage.html.
Santiprabhob, V. (1997), 'Bank soundness and currency board arrangements: issues and experience', IMF Paper on Policy Analysis and Assessment, 97/11.
Schuler, K. (1992), 'Currency boards', Dissertation, George Mason University, Fairfax, Virginia, http://users.erols.com/kurrency/webbdiss1.htm.
Schuler, K. (1999), 'Introduction to currency boards', http://users.erols.com/kurrency/intro.htm.
Sikken, B.J. and J. de Haan (1998), 'Budget deficits, monetization and central-bank independence in developing countries', *Oxford Economic Papers*, **50**, 493–511.
Sinn, H.-W. (1999), 'Currency boards for the new EU member states', *ifo Viewpoint*, 10.
Williamson J. (1995), *What Role for a Currency Board?*, Policy Analyses in International Economics, 40, Washington, DC: Institute for International Economics.

# 7. Free banking
## Kevin Dowd*

## 1  INTRODUCTION

A free banking system is a financial system with no central bank or other financial or monetary regulator, and no government intervention. It therefore allows financial institutions to operate freely, subject only to the discipline of market forces and the rules of 'normal' commercial and contract law. Free banking is thus equivalent to financial *laissez-faire*. Although the idea is strange to most modern economists, there are in fact many instances of (relatively) free banking in the historical record,[1] and there were vigorous controversies about it in a number of countries in the early nineteenth century (see, for example, Smith, 1936, ch. 6; White, 1984, ch. 4). The notion of free banking was then largely forgotten, even among economists favourable to *laissez-faire*,[2] and was only rediscovered in the last quarter of the twentieth century after Friedrich Hayek resurrected the idea in a famous pamphlet in 1976 (Hayek, 1976). Hayek's proposal attracted considerable attention, and subsequently gave rise to a substantial literature on the topic.[3]

The argument for free banking is essentially an application of the general argument for free trade: if free trade is generally desirable, as most economists agree, then presumably free trade is also desirable in individual sectors of the economy, including financial services, and free trade in financial services is free banking. And if free banking is desirable, the whole panoply of government intervention into the financial sector – central banks, government-sponsored deposit insurance, and government regulation of the financial system – should be abolished.

Most opponents of free banking accept the general argument for free trade, but argue that free banking is (somehow) an exception to this general argument. To defend this position, they must be able to demonstrate that there is something wrong with financial *laissez-faire* – they should show that free banking leads to some sort of market failure. They – the opponents of free banking – must also bear the burden of proof. If we agree that free trade is generally beneficial, as most of us do, then there is at least a prima facie case in favour of free banking: we must presume that free trade applies to any specific case, including the financial services sector, *unless* a clear reason can be established against it. The onus of proof is therefore on those who *oppose* free banking to demonstrate its undesirability.[4]

So the key issue is this: starting from a presumption in favour of free banking, can we establish any case for a market failure that would justify some sort of government intervention to suppress free banking? There is also an important corollary. If we are to justify the kinds of government intervention we see in the real world, we also need to show why one or more market failures would lead to the *particular* types that we see in the world around us, such as central banks, deposit insurance systems and financial regulation.

To develop this rather general argument further, the next section of this chapter sets out the case for free banking in more detail. It gives an idea of what a free banking system might look like, explains why we might expect it to be stable, and examines the impact of state intervention into the financial sector. It also looks at some of the empirical evidence and suggests that the main predictions of free-banking theory are in fact consistent with the evidence from the historical record. Sections 3 and 4 then examine the arguments put forward for the two arguably most important forms of modern state intervention in the financial system – deposit insurance, which insures depositors against loss in the event that their banks fail; and capital adequacy regulation, which is the imposition by regulators of minimum capital standards on financial institutions. Readers can then draw their own conclusions over whether these arguments for state intervention are persuasive enough to overturn our initial presumption in favour of free banking.

## 2 THE CASE FOR FREE BANKING

### A Free-banking System

Imagine a *laissez-faire* regime in a hypothetical 'imperfect' economic environment – information is scarce and asymmetric, there are non-trivial agency and coordination problems and so on.[5] These problems give rise to a financial system characterized by the presence of intermediaries that enable agents to achieve superior outcomes to those they could otherwise achieve (for example, by cutting down on transactions and monitoring costs).

Perhaps the most important intermediaries are banks, which invest funds on behalf of client investors, some of whom hold the bank's debt and others its equity. Most bank debts are deposits of one form or another, and most of these can be redeemed on demand. Many deposits are also used to make payments by cheque. The equity-holders are residual claimants, and their capital provides a buffer that enables a bank to absorb losses and still be able to pay its debt-holders in full.

The banking industry exhibits extensive economies of scale, but *not* natural monopoly,[6] and there are typically a small number of nationwide branch banks, with a larger number of specialist banks that cater to niche markets. The industry is also competitive and efficient by any reasonable standard.[7]

But how stable is the banking system? With no lender of last resort or state-run deposit insurance system, depositors would be acutely aware that they stood to lose their deposits if their bank failed. They would therefore want reassurance that their funds were safe and would soon close their accounts if they felt there was a significant danger of their bank failing. Naturally, bank managers would understand that their long-term survival depended on their ability to retain their depositors' confidence, so they would pursue conservative lending policies, submit themselves to outside scrutiny and publish audited accounts. They would also provide reassurance by maintaining adequate capital: the greater a bank's capitalization, the more losses a bank can withstand and still be able to pay off depositors in full. If the bank's capital is large enough – if the bank is adequately capitalized – the bank can absorb any relatively 'normal' losses and still repay depositors, and depositors can be confident that their funds are safe. The precise amount of capital is then determined by market forces: the more capital a bank has, other things being equal, the safer it is; but capital is also costly, and depositors need to pay shareholders to provide it (for example, by accepting lower interest on deposits). Competition between banks should then ensure that banks converge on whatever levels of capital (or safety) their customers demand (and, by implication, are willing to pay for): banks will be as safe as their customers demand.[8] Consequently, if bank customers want safe banks – as they surely do – then market forces will ensure that they get them.

The conclusion that banks under *laissez-faire* would maintain high levels of capital is consistent with the empirical evidence. For example, US banks in the period before the US Civil War were subject to virtually no federal regulations and yet had capital ratios in most years of over 40 per cent (Kaufman, 1992, p. 386). US banks were subject to more regulation at the turn of the century, but even then their capital ratios were close to 20 per cent, and capital ratios were still around 15 per cent when federal deposit insurance was established in the early 1930s (ibid.). The evidence is also consistent with the associated prediction from free-banking theory that *laissez-faire* banks are very safe. For example, US banks appear to have been fairly safe before the Civil War (Dowd, 1993, ch. 8) and, afterwards, bank failure rates were lower than the failure rates for non-financial firms (Benston et al., 1986, pp. 53–9). Losses to depositors were correspondingly low (Kaufman, 1988). Failure rates and losses were also low for other relatively unregulated systems such as those in Canada, Scotland, Switzerland and various others (see, for example, Schuler, 1992 or the case studies in Dowd (ed.), 1992).

Nor is there any reason to expect banking instability to arise from the ways in which banks relate to each other, either because of competitive pressures, or because of 'contagion' from weak banks to strong ones. It is frequently argued that competitive pressures produce instability by forcing 'good' banks to go along with the policies of 'bad' ones (for example, Goodhart, 1988, pp. 47–9). The underlying argument is that if the bad banks expand rapidly, they can make easy short-term profits which pressure the managers of good banks to expand rapidly as well, with the result that the banking system as a whole cycles excessively from boom to bust and back again. However, a major problem with this argument is that it is not in the interest of bank managers or shareholders to engage in aggressive expansion of the sort this argument envisages. A bank can expand rapidly only by allowing the average quality of its loans to deteriorate, and a major deterioration in its loan quality will undermine its long-run financial health and, hence, its ability to maintain customer confidence. It is therefore hard to see why a profit-maximizing bank would choose to undermine itself this way, even if other banks appeared to be doing so. Indeed, if a bank believes that its competitors are taking excessive risks, the most rational course of action is for it to distance itself from them – and perhaps to build up its financial strength further – in anticipation of the time when they start to suffer losses and lose confidence. The bank is then strongly placed to win over their customers and increase its market share at their expense, and perhaps even drive them out of business. The bank would have to forgo short-term profits, but it would win out in the long run. In sum, there is no reason to suppose that competitive pressures as such would force free banks into excessive cycling.[9]

Then there is the contagion argument that the difficulties of one bank might induce the public to withdraw funds from other banks and threaten the stability of the financial system. The conclusion normally drawn from this argument is that we need a central bank to prevent 'contagion' by providing lender-of-last-resort support to a bank in difficulties (for example, Goodhart, 1989). However, this argument ignores the earlier point that good banks have a strong incentive to distance themselves from bad ones. If the good banks felt there *was* any serious danger of contagion, they would take appropriate action – they would strengthen themselves and curtail credit to weak banks – to help ensure that contagion did not in fact occur. Indeed, as discussed already, they would position themselves to offer the customers of weaker banks a safe haven when their own banks got into difficulties. A serious danger of contagion is thus inconsistent with equilibrium. When runs occur, the typical scenario is a flight to quality, with substantial inflows of funds to the stronger banks, and there is no evidence that runs are seriously contagious (see, for example, Benston et al., 1986, pp. 53–60). The contagion hypothesis is implausible and empirically rejected.

**The Impact of State Intervention**

What happens to this system if the government intervenes in it? There is no space here to consider all the ways in which governments intervene in the financial system, but we should at least consider the impact of the more important forms of state intervention – deposit insurance and capital adequacy regulation.[10]

Suppose then that the government sets up a system of deposit insurance. Assume, too, that this is a fully comprehensive system (that is, with 100 per cent insurance cover) along North American lines.[11] Once it is established, depositors would no longer have any incentive to monitor bank management; managers would therefore have no further need to worry about maintaining confidence. And, since the main point of maintaining capital strength – to maintain depositor confidence – no longer applies, a bank's rational response to deposit insurance would be to reduce its capital. Even if an individual bank wished to maintain its capital strength, it would be outcompeted by competitors who cut their capital ratios to reduce their costs and then passed some of the benefits to depositors in the form of higher interest rates. The fight for market share would then force the good banks to imitate the bad. Consequently, deposit insurance transforms a strong capital position into a competitive liability, reduces institutions' financial health and makes them more likely to fail. It also encourages more risk taking at the margin: if a bank takes more risks and the risks pay off, then it keeps the additional profits; but if the risks do not pay off, part of the cost is passed on to the deposit insurer. The bank therefore takes more risks and becomes even weaker than suggested by its capital ratio alone.[12]

In short, deposit insurance encourages the very behaviour – greater risk taking and the maintenance of weaker capital positions – that a sound banking regime should avoid. Indeed, someone who observed this excessive risk taking might easily attribute it to the market itself, and falsely believe that the banking system actually *needs* the deposit insurance system that is, in reality, undermining it. A major *cause* of banking instability (that is, deposit insurance) could easily be mistaken for its *cure* – and, unfortunately, often is.[13]

The imposition of capital adequacy regulation also tends to have undesirable consequences. If the regulation is binding (that is, imposes a minimum capital requirement that exceeds the capital the bank would otherwise choose to maintain), then the bank's only rational response to it is to find ways to reduce – and preferably, eliminate – the burden associated with the capital regulation. The regulation is a burden because it would make the bank safer than its management themselves prefer, and so reduce their opportunities for profitable risk taking. A bank will therefore respond to this sort of regulation by finding other ways of increasing risk and/or reducing its regulatory capital requirement – by switching to more risky assets, such as riskier loans; by exploiting loopholes or inconsistencies in the capital regulation to reduce its capital requirement; and by resorting to off-balance sheet transactions. Off-balance sheet positions – derivatives positions especially – are very useful means for banks to increase their leverage (and hence their risk), as well as a very convenient way of getting around awkward regulatory and tax obstacles. Thus, a bank will respond to capital regulation by trying to frustrate it, and the net effect of the regulation will be very hard to assess. If there are many opportunities to avoid the regulation, as is increasingly the case, then the chances are that the regulation will become no more than a nuisance: the bank will end up taking similar risks to those it would have taken anyway, and the regulation will do nothing to make it any safer. Indeed, it is quite possible that the regulation will be counterproductive, and induce responses from banks that will make them even weaker than they would otherwise have been (see, for example, Koehn and Santomero, 1980).[14]

## 3 THE CASE FOR DEPOSIT INSURANCE

### Traditional Arguments for Deposit Insurance

We turn now to consider the arguments put forward for government intervention in the financial services sector, and we begin with the arguments put forward for state-sponsored deposit insurance – systems to insure depositors against losses they would otherwise suffer if their banks failed. Deposit insurance was first introduced in nineteenth-century America, and is a now a key feature of most countries' financial regulatory systems.[15]

One common traditional argument is that deposit insurance is needed to protect 'small' depositors or vulnerable people who might lose their savings if their bank failed, and this argument is widely accepted, particularly outside the United States (see, for example, Dewatripont and Tirole, 1993). The standard objection to this argument is that protecting depositors undermines the market discipline that would otherwise force banks to be strong (for example, Kane, 1985 or Kaufman, 1988). However, for the most part, this type of argument is fundamentally one of social philosophy (that is, the merits or otherwise of paternalism) and, apart from the objection just made, largely stands or falls on such grounds.

But perhaps the main argument traditionally put forward for deposit insurance is that it is needed to counter alleged instability of the banking system. If banking is unstable, so the argument goes, then government support is needed to reassure depositors who would otherwise be prone to run on their banks. This argument has been around in one form or another for many years, and was often used to justify the establishment of federal deposit insurance in the United States after the banking collapses of the early 1930s. Indeed, after the 1930s, this argument came to be so widely accepted that Milton Friedman and Anna Schwartz accepted it without question in their monumental *Monetary History of the United States* (1963), and it only came under serious scrutiny again in the early 1980s.

**The Diamond–Dybvig Analysis**

This argument was subsequently formalized in the early 1980s in a classic paper by Diamond and Dybvig (1983). Given the influence of this paper and the issues at stake, it is worth looking at the Diamond–Dybvig analysis in some detail.[16] Let us therefore initially suppose that we have a large number of identical individuals, each of whom lives for three periods, 0, 1 and 2. In period 0, each individual is endowed with a unit of a good and decides how to invest it. He/she faces an investment technology which, for each unit invested in period 0, yields 1 unit of output in period 1 or, if left until then, $R > 1$ units of output in period 2. When period 1 arrives, each agent receives a signal telling him/her the period in which he/she will want to consume, with the type I agents wishing to consume only in period 1, and the type II agents wishing to consume only in period 2. The type Is will therefore liquidate and consume all the proceeds of their investment in period 1, but the type IIs have to decide whether to retain their initial investments until period 2 or liquidate their investments in period 1 and keep the proceeds until the next period. Storage from one period to another is costless and unobservable. An agent's type is not publicly observable, but the proportion of type I agents, $t$, is initially assumed to be fixed and known. We also assume that agents maximize expected utility, and have a utility function that exhibits constant relative risk aversion.[17] Finally, following Wallace (1988, p. 9), we also assume that agents are isolated from each other in period 1, in the sense that those who collect their returns in period 1 do so at random instants during that period.[18]

One option is for agents to plant their endowments in their backyard, and consume them when they need to. However, since they are risk averse, agents would value an opportunity to insure themselves in period 0 against type risk. Given that the proportion of type Is, $t$, is known in advance, we can deduce that there is an 'optimal insurance arrangement' that enables our agents to diversify this risk among themselves, and one way to provide this insurance is for agents to form a financial intermediary in period 0. Agents would deposit their endowments with the intermediary, and the intermediary would invest them on their behalf. When agents' types are revealed in period 1, the intermediary would pay out more to those withdrawing in period 1 than the one unit they would have received had they invested in their backyard, with the remainder being paid out to those who withdraw in period 2, and all these payments would be contingent on $t$, the proportion of type I agents.[19] This arrangement also satisfies a self-selection constraint (that is, it induces type Is to withdraw (only) in period 1, and type IIs to withdraw (only) in period 2): no type I agent would ever wish to keep his/her deposit until period 2, because he/she only benefits from consumption in period 1. At the same time, no type II agent would withdraw prematurely, because the return from premature withdrawal would be less than the return from withdrawing later. Note, too, that the intermediary also operates under a sequential service constraint (that is, it deals with requests for redemption in period 1 in a random order, until it runs out of assets). This constraint arises because of agents' isolation in period 1: since agents collect their returns/deposits at random times within period 1, the intermediary must deal with their requests for redemption 'separately, one after the other' (Wallace, 1988, p. 4).

Unfortunately, this intermediated arrangement only works if $t$ is known in advance. If $t$ is random, contractual payments cannot be made conditional on the realized value of $t$ because the sequential service constraint requires that depositors must be dealt with sequentially, and the realized value of $t$ cannot be known until all period 1 withdrawals have been completed. The intermediary does not know what to pay each depositor until they have all gone and it is too late to do anything about it. It is therefore not possible to condition any insurance arrangement on the realized value of $t$. The obvious alternative is to condition payments on the *expected* value of $t$, but if the subsequently realized value of $t$ exceeds its expected value, the intermediary's promised payments will exceed the return on its investments, and the intermediary will not be able to make its contractual payments. A stochastic $t$ therefore undermines the intermediary's ability to offer credible insurance.[20] This implies, in turn, that a type II depositor cannot be confident of his (or her) promised return if he waits until period 2 to redeem his deposit, so he may decide to 'play safe' by redeeming his deposit in period 1 and keeping it under the mattress until he consumes it in period 2. In other words, the self-selection constraint no longer holds, and type II investors may run on the intermediary in period 1.

The Diamond–Dybvig solution to this problem is for an outside party, the government, to guarantee the intermediary's payments to those withdrawing in period 2 (Diamond and Dybvig, 1983, pp. 413–16). Type II agents would then have no reason to run; the self-selection constraint would be satisfied and the intermediary could provide optimal insurance – and, hence, the Diamond–Dybvig analysis can be interpreted as providing a rationale for government deposit insurance. However, this 'solution' is not feasible if we take investors' isolation seriously: if the deposit insurance guarantee is to work, the government must credibly promise that depositors who keep their deposits until period 2 will get repaid in full. Yet the only available resources are those the intermediary has already paid out to agents who have withdrawn in period 1, and the government can only get access to these resources if it has some means of overcoming the sequential service constraint – which implies that the government has the means to overcome the period-1 isolation that gives rise to this constraint in the first place.[21] If we take the isolation assumption seriously, the government has no way of providing credible deposit insurance – and the Diamond–Dybvig solution is not feasible. In short, the Diamond–Dybvig justification for deposit insurance is a failure.

## 4  THE CASE FOR BANK CAPITAL ADEQUACY REGULATION

### Traditional Arguments for Capital Adequacy Regulation

We now turn to the arguments put forward to justify capital adequacy regulation, or the imposition by government regulators of minimum capital standards (or minimum capital ratios) on banks. We find three traditional arguments for capital regulation in the literature.

The first is that capital adequacy regulation is needed for 'prudential' reasons. However, many advocates of this position take the argument no further and fail to explain why the central bank/financial regulation needs to impose 'prudential' regulation in the first place: they fail to explain why banks would not be strong enough or responsible enough in the absence of regulatory pressure. A deeper defence of this position points to agency problems – conflicts of interest between managers and different types of investors – to suggest that these might constitute some sort of 'market failure' to which government intervention is a solution (see, for example,

Stiglitz, 1984). However, the counterargument is that agency problems are ubiquitous, and markets have evolved many ways of dealing with them. So why should these *particular* agency problems be a justification for government intervention, when agency problems in other industries are (according to free-trade principles) usually accepted as problems that markets *can* adequately deal with on their own? This prudential argument is therefore incomplete, at best.

The second argument is that capital adequacy regulation is needed to protect 'small' depositors in the absence of deposit insurance. However, this argument is open to various objections – that depositors would rarely lose their money anyway under *laissez-faire*, because it would deliver the strong banking system that depositors want; that if depositors want their deposits to be very safe, they should pay for it (for example, by putting their money in very safe banks that pay low deposit interest rates); and that protecting depositors undermines the market discipline that would otherwise force banks to be strong (Kaufman, 1988).

The third argument is that capital adequacy regulation is needed to counter the moral hazard problems created by other regulatory policies, such as deposit insurance or a lender-of-last-resort policy to support institutions in difficulties (see, for example, Benston and Kaufman, 1996). These other policies are taken as given, so the natural solution to the problems they create – to abolish these policies and establish *laissez-faire* – is ruled out by assumption. One can argue over this assumption, but for present purposes it suffices to observe that this argument merely defends capital adequacy regulation given the presence of other interventions, but cannot defend it in their absence (that is, from first principles, by reference to a failure of *laissez-faire*). In other words, advocates of this position concede that *laissez-faire* is best, at least in theory, but rule it out on political or other extraneous grounds.

**The Miles Argument – Capital Adequacy Regulation Counters Asymmetric Information**

A fourth and more detailed argument for capital adequacy regulation has recently been put forward by David Miles (1995). His argument is significant because it appears to be the first rigorous attempt to justify capital adequacy regulation from first principles, given that traditional attempts to justify capital adequacy regulation are either incomplete (for example, the prudential or paternalistic arguments) or else argue that capital adequacy regulation is required to counter the effects of other interventions. The essence of his argument is that *if* depositors cannot assess the financial soundness of individual banks, then banks will maintain lower than optimal capital ratios – information asymmetry thus leads to a capital adequacy problem. His solution is for a regulator to assess the level of capital the bank would have maintained in the absence of the information asymmetry, and then force it to maintain this level of capital.

Miles's starting point is the need to justify 'restrictions on the lending and financing activities of deposit taking financial intermediaries when there are no limits on the balance sheet structure of car companies, hotel chains or computer manufacturers' (Miles, 1995, p. 1366). So what is 'special' about banks that might justify regulating their capital adequacy, *given* that we agree that non-financial firms should *not* be subject to such regulation?

Yet, having accepted the need to base a theory of bank regulation on factors that are *specific* to banks, Miles then has very little to say on what those factors might be. His formal analysis is very general, and his model has nothing in it to make his firm specifically a bank and nothing else. In fact, the only explicit difference between banks and other firms identified by Miles is that the average size of bank debt contracts (relative to the balance sheet) is small (ibid., p. 1376, n. 2), and he uses this piece of evidence only to suggest that this lower relative size gives bank debt-holders (that is, depositors) less incentive to overcome information problems than debt-holders at other firms.

The response is that problems of monitoring incentives are not unique to banking (for example, they arise whenever we have large public firms with many small shareholders) and, in any case, usually have natural market solutions (for example, investors can specialize among themselves so that some have a strong incentive to monitor and others can rely on that incentive to avoid the need to monitor themselves). Miles thus fails to explain what is special about banks that justifies bank-specific regulation. The justification for capital adequacy regulation that he puts forward must therefore apply to many non-financial firms as well as banks – or not at all.

So does it apply or not? I believe not. A crucial link in Miles's analysis is his claim that depositors cannot assess the capital strength of individual banks. He accepts that this assumption might appear 'unusual' (ibid., p. 1375), but defends it in part by suggesting that 'in practice it is not easy' for depositors to evaluate bank capital because doing so requires valuation of the banks' assets.[22] He also defends it by suggesting that 'depositors cannot depend on stock market valuations of a bank to assess the value of shareholders' capital (or equity) backing their deposits; the stock market value may be increased by gearing up and stock market participants also face the problem of valuing the underlying assets (loans) of the bank' (ibid., pp. 1375–6).[23]

However, I would suggest that the depositor monitoring problem is not as difficult as Miles makes out, and depositors *can and do* assess the capital strengths of individual banks. To some extent, this problem is solved by depositors relying on shareholders to value bank capital, and depositors can reasonably assume that their funds are safe if the shareholders give the bank a sufficiently high capital value.[24] The point is that shareholders are residual claimants who can only be paid *after* all the depositors have been paid in full, should the bank default on its debts. Shareholders as a group therefore have strong incentives to value the bank carefully, and if they believe that the bank has a high positive net worth (that is, is well capitalized), *then* depositors can reasonably assume that their own funds (which have prior claim on bank assets) must be fairly safe. The typical depositor's monitoring problem is thus considerably simplified and, in practice, it frequently suffices for him/her to check that his/her bank maintains a fairly high capital valuation and watch for signs of trouble in the media. Moreover, under free banking there would be fierce competition for market share, and banks would have a strong incentive to make monitoring easier for depositors (and shareholders). Banks would have to maintain their confidence if they were to remain in business, and one of the ways in which they could maintain that confidence is by making it relatively easy for depositors to satisfy themselves that their banks are sound.

The claim that depositors cannot assess individual banks' balance sheets is also empirically falsified, at least under historical circumstances where the absence of deposit insurance or other forms of bail-out gave depositors an incentive to be careful where they put their deposits. There is much evidence that depositors *did* discriminate between banks on the basis of their relative capital strengths (see, for example, Kaufman, 1988). The Miles position is also refuted by the empirical evidence on bank-run contagion. If Miles is right and depositors cannot distinguish between banks, then a run on one bank should lead to runs on *all* the others as well (that is, we should observe *universal* contagion): if one bank is in difficulty, and I cannot tell the difference between that bank and mine, then mine must be in difficulty too, so I had better get my funds out. Yet the evidence *overwhelmingly* indicates that bank runs do not spread like wildfire in the way that the Miles hypothesis predicts (see, for example, Benston et al., 1986, ch. 2).

Finally, there is the issue of whether regulation can improve on the *laissez-faire* outcome: can a regulator formulate a feasible rule to make banks hold socially optimal levels of capital, assuming – for the sake of argument – that depositors cannot assess the capital strength of individual banks? I would suggest that they cannot. *If* the information exists (or could exist) for the regulator to formulate a feasible capital adequacy rule, that *same* information could *also* be used to convey credible signals to depositors about the capital strength of their banks, and thereby enable them to distinguish one bank's capital strength from another's.[25] The market failure then disappears, and capital regulation is unable to improve on the free-market outcome. If this information *cannot* be collected, on the other hand, then the regulator cannot collect it either, and in that case Miles's capital adequacy regulation is not feasible. In short, capital regulation is either feasible but unnecessary, or just not feasible. Once again, state regulation is unable to improve on *laissez-faire*.

## 5 CONCLUSIONS

Although the notion of free banking appears to many to be exotic, and even bizarre, free banking is no more than free trade or *laissez-faire* in financial services. If we examine the case for free banking more carefully, we find that there are good grounds to believe that a free-banking system would be both efficient and stable – both of which are obviously very desirable properties. Furthermore, if we accept that free trade is generally beneficial, then we should also accept that there is – at the very least – a prima facie case in favour of free banking. It is therefore up to the critics of free banking to establish that it is flawed – that there is some sort of market failure that justifies government intervention into the financial system. This chapter has looked at the arguments put forward to justify the most important forms of state intervention – namely, deposit insurance and capital adequacy regulation – and readers can draw their own conclusions.

## NOTES

\* This chapter draws heavily from material in Dowd (1996a, 1999, 2000). The author thanks Andy Mullineux for helpful comments, but the usual caveat applies.
1. Schuler (1992) found about 60 historical examples of relatively free banking systems in his overview of world free banking, and there are probably others he overlooked; some specific case studies are collected together in Dowd (ed.) (1992).
2. The two most prominent supporters of *laissez-faire*, Milton Friedman and Friedrich Hayek, both rejected free banking in no uncertain terms (Friedman, 1960, pp. 4–9; Hayek, 1960, p. 324): the idea of free-banking seemed too radical even for them. Both writers have since retracted their earlier arguments against free banking, and Hayek went on to champion the idea in the 1970s and afterwards.
3. For surveys of this literature, see Dowd (1996b, ch. 9) and Selgin and White (1994). The reader interested in pursuing the free-banking literature further might also look at the free-banking homepage at http://www.nottingham.ac.uk/~lizkd/free-banking-homepage.html.
4. The idea that the onus of proof rests with the supporters of central banking appears not to be controversial; one of the most prominent supporters of central banking, Charles Goodhart, clearly accepted the burden of proof in his book, *The Evolution of Central Banks* (Goodhart, 1988, p. 13), and I am not aware of any other supporter of central banking who has disagreed with him. I would therefore argue that it is up to them to

make a convincing case against free banking, rather than up to me to provide a convincing case in favour of it.

5. It is worth emphasizing that the case for free banking does *not* depend on assumptions of perfect competitive markets, full information and so on, as critics of free banking have sometimes claimed. The trouble with such 'perfect' economic environments is that they assume away the 'frictions' that actually underlie much of the economic structure we are seeking to explain. If we work with a model environment that is too 'perfect', we throw the baby out with the bathwater. For example, if we have a model that assumes away all 'frictions' and so gives banks no socially useful purpose, then we should not expect our model to produce any useful insights about banking or bank regulation.

6. There is considerable evidence of economies of scale in banking, but no evidence that these economies of scale are so large that the industry is a natural monopoly. It follows that one cannot defend the central bank's monopoly privileges over the currency supply on the grounds that free banking would lead to a currency monopoly anyway. Nor should natural monopoly be confused with the use of a single economywide unit of account. There will typically be one generally used unit of account (for example, the pound), but the use of a single unit of account reflects economies of standardization (or economies in use) and not natural monopoly, which necessarily involves economies of production. For more on these issues, see, for example, Dowd (1993, ch. 5).

7. Since my focus of interest here is on banking, I skip over issues related to the issue of currency, the unit of account, the monetary standard, price-level determinacy and so on. For more on these, see, for example, Dowd (1996b, chs 10–14).

8. The cost of safe banks is not just that depositors will earn lower returns on their deposits, but also that credit and liquidity are more costly. The optimal arrangement necessarily involves a trade-off between the benefits of bank safety, on the one hand, and the benefits of bank leverage (greater deposit interest rates, and cheaper credit and liquidity), on the other.

9. Proponents of the excessive cycling theory sometimes look to examples such as the excessive bank lending to less-developed countries (LDCs) in the late 1970s and early 1980s (for example, Goodhart, 1988, pp. 48–9). However, episodes like these are not examples of free banking and can hardly be held up as examples of what would happen under it. Many national authorities were actively encouraging their banks to make loans to LDCs, and banks could reasonably expect some form of bail-out if things went bad. In the circumstances, it was therefore hardly surprising that they over-reached themselves.

10. One other important form of state intervention is the central bank's lender-of-last-resort function, which has some of the same effects as deposit insurance. (For more on the specific impacts of the lender-of-last-resort function, see, for example, Selgin, 1989 or Dowd, 1996b, ch. 16.)

11. Admittedly, these systems also typically involve ceilings on the insured amount, but these are largely ineffective because investors can easily divide large deposits into smaller ones, each one of which is fully insured.

12. These claims are also borne out by the evidence: the claim that banks reduce their capital ratios is confirmed by the observation that US bank capital ratios more than halved in the 10 years after the establishment of federal deposit insurance (Kaufman, 1992). There is also abundant evidence that US deposit insurance has increased failure rates and associated losses.

13. The impact of deposit insurance is ameliorated in countries such as the UK where the deposits are only partially insured. The fraction uninsured then gives depositors some incentive to monitor their banks. However, this monitoring incentive is also undermined by the lender-of-last-resort function and by the widespread perception that the central bank will (or even might) bail out institutions in difficulties, particularly large ones. So depositor incentives to monitor banks are still fairly poor in countries such as the UK despite the absence of comprehensive deposit insurance cover. In any case, the political economy of deposit insurance tends to lead to expanding cover over time, so countries such as the UK may well be heading for comprehensive deposit insurance cover in the long run.

14. Bank capital regulators are of course aware of some of the problems that capital regulation can create, particularly the problems associated with the 'building block' approach enshrined in the Basle Accord (1988). They have responded by allowing banks to use their own risk models (so-called 'internal models') to help determine their capital requirements. However, this internal models approach to capital adequacy regulation also has its own problems, and I would in any case prefer here to focus on general principles of capital adequacy regulation rather than the specifics of particular approaches to implement it.
15. State-sponsored bank liability insurance schemes were apparently first introduced in New York in 1829, followed by a number of other northern US states in the period before the US Civil War. However, these schemes were failures (Calomiris, 1989). National (that is, federal) deposit insurance schemes were only set up much later in the US in the aftermath of the banking collapses of the early 1930s. Other countries followed later (for example, Canada in 1967 and the UK in 1983).
16. The discussion that follows is based on a modified version of the Diamond–Dybvig model set out by Dowd (2000), rather than on Diamond and Dybvig's original framework in its entirety. The principal difference is that this modified framework invokes Wallace's 'isolation assumption' (see note 18) to derive the sequential service constraint on which the existence of financial intermediation depends in this sort of environment. The original Diamond and Dybvig framework is less satisfactory because it assumes the sequential service constraint rather derives it.
17. We need our agents to be risk averse if they are to derive any benefit at all from financial intermediation in this environment, since the benefits of intermediation take the form of insurance. The assumption that the utility function exhibits constant relative risk aversion is fairly innocuous and makes the formal analysis easier.
18. This 'isolation assumption' provides a 'friction' in the economic environment that gives an intermediary an advantage over a credit market in period 1 (see, for example, Jacklin, 1987; Wallace, 1988, p. 9). Without it, or something similar, the outcome obtainable by an intermediary can also be obtained by the credit market. There would then be no reason for agents to prefer an intermediary, and therefore no reason to suppose that one would arise. In addition, as noted already, the isolation assumption provides a motivation for the sequential service constraint that Diamond and Dybvig assume rather than derive (Diamond–Dybvig, 1983, p. 408; see also Wallace, 1988, p. 3). This is important because the sequential service constraint turns out to be inconsistent with the government deposit guarantee that Diamond and Dybvig sought to justify (see, for example, Wallace, 1988, pp. 3–4, and Dowd, 2000).
19. Since the liabilities issued by the intermediary are identical, the intermediary itself should be regarded as a mutual fund – albeit an unusual one in that the repayments in each period are known in advance. The Diamond–Dybvig intermediary cannot therefore be interpreted as a bank, because a bank issues more than one type of liability (that is, at a minimum, deposits and equity). The relevance of this mutual fund model to banking is therefore unclear, to say the least.
20. When $t$ is stochastic, the liability of the Diamond–Dybvig intermediary becomes even stranger: it appears to offer fixed repayments, conditional on expected $t$, to those who withdraw in period 1, and residual payments to those who withdraw in period 2. Such a liability is neither debt (which promises specified repayments outside of bankruptcy) nor equity (which promises a residual payment only). So the Diamond–Dybvig intermediary is not just an ordinary mutual fund, but one that issues a very strange liability. I am not surprised that such a mutual fund runs into problems, but fail to see the relevance of these problems to real-world bank regulatory issues.
21. If there is to be any feasible insurance arrangement, we clearly need to introduce at least one additional agent who can pledge his/her resources as collateral and make the insurance arrangement credible. The natural outcome is then for this additional agent to become an equity-holder in the financial intermediary, and for the intermediary itself to become a proper bank (that is, an intermediary with both equity- and debt-holders). We then find ourselves discussing capital adequacy conditions, and so forth – which, apart from anything else, is a good sign that we are dealing with 'real' banking issues. Deposit insurance is

theoretically feasible in this sort of environment, but there is no reason to want it, because free banking in this environment is stable and the private sector can achieve any Pareto optimal arrangement on its own (Dowd, 2000). So deposit insurance is either not feasible, as in the original Diamond–Dybvig model, or pointless (as in the stylized Diamond–Dybvig framework discussed in the text). The advocate of deposit insurance loses either way.

22. He also suggests that evaluation of bank strength is made difficult because it requires information about bank deposits, and obtaining this information is difficult because it 'would require depositors to try to work out the flows of funds in and out of the bank since the last published report' (Miles, 1995, p. 1375). However, there is in fact no need for depositors to 'work out' a bank's flow of funds: all that is required is for the bank to publish (every so often) the total (face) value of its outstanding deposits (and any other relevant information). All that depositors then need to do to be confident of the safety of their deposits is periodically check that their bank does not face a run.

23. One response to the stock valuation claim is that shareholders do indeed face valuation problems, but they choose to take on such problems when they buy shares in the first place. Valuing shares is by no means easy, but shareholders effectively solve it when they decide for themselves the prices at which they are willing to buy and sell their shares. As for the claim that the stock market value can be increased by gearing, there are already strong pressures on shareholders to act in ways that maximize the value of shareholder equity and therefore rule out the possibility that firms can increase shareholder value any further, by gearing up or by any other means. This is the case even in Miles's own model. If shareholder wealth is not already maximized in neoclassical equilibrium, it should be.

24. There also exist rating agencies that scrutinize banks and rate their debt issues, and so simplify the task of assessing banks' financial conditions. Ratings are widely trusted by third parties, and evidence suggests that bank ratings are fairly good indicators of their financial soundness (see, for example, Berger et al., 2000).

25. Miles considers the possibility of banks providing adequate information, but dismisses it on three grounds. (1) He doubts that banks have the 'right incentives' to provide it and claims that, *given* his information asymmetry, banks would have an incentive to play up the size of their capital positions (Miles, 1995, pp. 1376–7). (2) He acknowledges the possible role of private rating agencies, but instead of seeing it as restoring the optimality of *laissez-faire*, he dismisses it on the grounds that it 'is much harder to show' how such an equilibrium becomes established (ibid., p. 1377). (3) Finally, he suggests that regulation 'cuts through' these problems of 'establishing the right incentive for banks to reveal their true default risks by using the legal system' (ibid.).

In response: (1) Banks *do* have strong incentives to signal their individual capital strengths, as explained in the text, and the fact that banks have an incentive to exaggerate their strength if the public cannot tell them apart proves nothing. The relevant issue is *not* whether banks have an incentive to play up their capital positions, given that the public cannot tell them apart; the real issue is whether an individual bank would wish to signal its true capital position, *if* it had the means to do so. (2) Miles still fails to explain why a rating agency could not (or would not) provide the information that enables depositors to assess their banks, assuming that they could not otherwise assess them and that the information is technologically attainable as Miles assumes. (3) The incentives to provide information already exist in the free market, since good banks will always want to signal their quality. I therefore deny that regulation 'cuts through' any problems, in a way that could not otherwise be done.

# REFERENCES

Benston, G.J., R.A. Eisenbeis, P.A. Horvitz, E.J. Kane and G.G. Kaufman (1986), *Perspectives on Safe and Sound Banking: Past, Present, and Future*, Cambridge, MA: MIT Press.

Benston, G.J., and G.G. Kaufman (1996), 'The appropriate role of banking regulation', *Economic Journal*, **106**: 688–97.

Berger, A.N., S.M. Davies and M.J. Flannery (2000), 'Comparing market and supervisory assessments of bank performance: who knows what when?', *Journal of Money, Credit, and Banking*, **32**: 641–67.

Calomiris, C.W. (1989), 'Deposit insurance: lessons from the record', Federal Reserve Bank of Chicago, *Economic Perspectives*, **14** (May–June): 10–30.

Dewatripont, M. and J. Tirole (1993), *The Prudential Regulation of Banks*, London: MIT Press.

Diamond, D.W. and P.H. Dybvig (1983), 'Bank runs, deposit insurance, and liquidity', *Journal of Political Economy*, **91**: 401–19.

Dowd, K. (ed.) (1992), *The Experience of Free Banking*, London: Routledge.

Dowd, K. (1993), *Laissez-Faire Banking*, London: Routledge.

Dowd, K. (1996a), 'The case for financial *laissez-faire*', *Economic Journal*, **106**: 679–87.

Dowd, K. (1996b), *Competition and Finance: A New Interpretation of Financial and Monetary Economics*, Basingstoke: Macmillan; and New York: St. Martin's Press.

Dowd, K. (1999), 'Does asymmetric information justify bank capital adequacy regulation?', *Cato Journal*, **19**: 39–47.

Dowd, K. (2000), 'Bank capital adequacy vs. deposit insurance', *Journal of Financial Services Research*, **17**: 7–15.

Friedman, M. (1960), *A Program for Monetary Stability*, New York: Fordham University Press.

Friedman, M. and A.J. Schwartz (1963), *A Monetary History of the United States, 1867–1960*, Princeton, NJ: Princeton University Press.

Goodhart, C.A.E. (1989), *The Evolution of Central Banks*, Cambridge, MA: MIT Press.

Hayek, F.A. (1960), *The Constitution of Liberty*, Chicago: Chicago University Press.

Hayek, F.A. (1976), *Denationalisation of Money*, Hobart Paper Special Paper No. 70, London: Institute of Economic Affairs.

Jacklin, C.J. (1987), 'Demand deposits, trading restrictions, and risk sharing', Chapter 2 in Edward C. Prescott and Neil Wallace (eds), *Contractual Arrangements for Intertemporal Trade*, Minneapolis, MN: University of Minnesota Press, pp. 26–47.

Kane, E.J. (1985), *The Gathering Crisis in Federal Deposit Insurance*, Cambridge, MA: MIT Press.

Kaufman, G.G. (1988), 'Bank runs: causes, benefits, and costs', *Cato Journal*, **7**: 559–87.

Kaufman, G.G. (1992), 'Capital in banking: past, present, and future', *Journal of Financial Services Research*, **5**: 385–402.

Koehn, M. and A.M. Santomero (1980), 'Regulation of bank capital and portfolio Risk', *Journal of Finance*, **35**: 1235–44.

Miles, D. (1995), 'Optimal regulation of deposit taking financial intermediaries', *European Economic Review*, **39**: 1365–84.

Schuler, K. (1992), 'The world history of free banking: an overview', in Dowd (ed.), pp. 7–47.

Selgin, G.A. (1989), 'Legal restrictions, financial weakening, and the lender of last resort', *Cato Journal*, **9**: 429–59.

Selgin, G.A., and L.H. White (1994), 'How would the invisible hand handle money?', *Journal of Economic Literature*, **32**: 1718–49.
Smith, V.C. (1936), *The Rationale of Central Banking*, London: P.S. King.
Stiglitz, Joseph E. (1984), *The Role of the State in Financial Markets*, Washington, DC: The World Bank.
Wallace, N. (1988), 'Another attempt to explain an illiquid banking system: the Diamond and Dybvig model with sequential service taken seriously', Federal Reserve Bank of Minneapolis *Quarterly Review*, **12** (Fall): 3–16.
White, L.H. (1984), *Free Banking in Britain: Theory, Experience, and Debate, 1800–1845*, New York: Cambridge University Press.

# 8. Islamic banking
## Humayon A. Dar and John R. Presley

## 1 INTRODUCTION

Banking and finance witnessed a major rethinking in Muslim countries during the second half of the twentieth century. The new view rejects the conventional interest-based banking and proposes an interest-free model of banking based on Islamic modes of financing. The idea was first put into practice with the establishment of a rural bank in Egypt in 1963, and later a cooperative bank in Pakistan in 1965.[1] Since the establishment of the Islamic Development Bank (IDB) in 1975, a number of Islamic banks and financial institutions have been established all over the world (Brunei and Bangladesh in the east, Los Angeles in the west, Denmark in the north, as well as in South Africa). At present, 166 such institutions exist throughout the world (*Directory of Islamic Banks and Financial Institutions*, 1996). Pakistan, Iran and Sudan have announced the abolition of interest-based banking in favour of Islamic alternatives of banking and finance. In other countries like Malaysia and Indonesia, Islamic banking has been a policy issue for many years. Some Western banks have also started offering Islamic financial products to tap the savings of the oil-rich Middle Eastern countries.

Funds managed by Islamic banks and financial institutions are estimated to have now reached $100 billion. Twenty-three countries, including 16 developing and emerging market countries, are increasingly involved, with varying intensity, in Islamic banking. The funds, however, are highly concentrated in the Middle East. Over 80 per cent of the funds managed by Islamic financial institutions are located in the Middle East and the Gulf Cooperation Council (GCC) countries (ibid.). Although Islamic finance has attracted practitioners in Europe and the United States, the market is still very small but growing. The average annual growth of assets under the management of Islamic financial institutions worldwide was estimated to be about 15 per cent during the 1990s. It has, however, slowed down recently. Moreover, most of these institutions are small investment companies or banks that primarily rely on fixed return modes of financing. The average annual net profits of Islamic financial institutions in most Muslim countries fall below $10 million (ibid.).

How does Islamic banking differ from Western banking styles? Are the banks as efficient as other financial institutions in responding to the needs of their clients and earning good returns for their depositors? These questions are important for the future development of Islamic banking as billions of dollars, entrusted to these institutions, are at stake. In this brief chapter, we shall describe the theory of Islamic banking and compare it with its current practice. The next section provides an overview of the historical development of Islamic banking. Section 3 provides a simple theoretical model of Islamic banking. Section 4 discusses the practice of Islamic banking. Section 5 briefly describes profit and loss sharing (PLS) as an alternative to interest-based financing. Section 6 provides some suggestions for the future development of Islamic banking.

## 2 HISTORICAL DEVELOPMENT OF ISLAMIC BANKING

Islamic banking is a post-Second World War phenomenon. Two pioneering institutions that paved the way for further development of this type of banking are worth mentioning here, as they provide a good understanding of the idea behind Islamic banking: Mit Ghamr Village Bank in Egypt and Muslim Pilgrims Savings Corporation in Malaysia. Two international groups that form the core of Islamic banking are the Dar al-Mal al-Islami Group and the Al-Baraka Group.

**Mit Ghamr Village Bank**

Mit Ghamr Village Bank combined the idea of German savings banks with the principles of rural banking within the general framework of Islamic values. The advocates of Islamic banking have viewed Mit Ghamr Village Bank as a success, and many argue that the future of Islamic banking in this form of banking in Muslim countries lies in this early model.

Mit Ghamr Village Bank was a primitive form of banking in a rural society where the majority of the population had never dealt with financial institutions before. Basically rural and religious, they tended to distrust the bankers operating in the Western style and, what is more, there were few local branches of such banks that they could patronize. Since a substantial part of their income was not spent immediately, but put aside for social events, emergencies and the like, this idle capital could not be used for productive investments. A precondition, however, of any change of behaviour from hoarding and 'real asset saving' to 'financial saving' was the creation of a financial institution which would not violate the religious principles of a large segment of the population. Only then could the majority of the population be integrated into the process of capital formation.

The bank offered three types of accounts, namely, savings, investment and *Zakah*[2] accounts. There was an impressive growth in deposits of the bank between 1963 and 1966 (just before it was nationalized), and it can safely be said that Mit Ghamr Village Bank succeeded in mobilizing the savings of the rural population to some productive use. The bank would collect deposits from account holders and would lend to small businesses on a PLS basis. Investment in trade and industry was also a major activity.

**Muslim Pilgrims Savings Corporation**

Muslim Pilgrims Savings Corporation was set up by the government of Malaysia in 1963 as a non-bank financial institution to provide an interest-free (or 'clean') mechanism to save for meeting the expenses of the pilgrimage (*hajj*) to Mecca. Later this was converted to the Pilgrims Management and Fund Board (commonly known as Tabung Hajj) in 1969. Its basic objectives were: (i) to help Muslims to save to meet their expenses for promoting the *hajj* or for other expenses beneficial to them; and (ii) to enable Muslims, through their savings, to participate in investment in industry, commerce and plantations, as well as in real estate, according to Islamic principles. It also provides social welfare services to Muslims on the *hajj*.

Working on the principle of absolute power of attorney by depositors, Tabung Hajj invests its deposits on PLS and leasing bases. Since its inception, it has grown into a large organization but has yet to reach its potential size. Starting with just one branch in 1963, Tabung Hajj has a growing number of branches in the country.

**Dar al-Mal al-Islami Group**

The Dar al-Mal al-Islami (DMI) Trust was founded in the Commonwealth of the Bahamas in July 1981 with an authorized capital of US$1 billion. Since its inception, it has played a pivotal role in the global development of Islamic banking. It has invested heavily in Islamic investment companies, insurance companies, banks and other Islamic businesses all over the world. It has established banks and other Islamic financial institutions not only in the Muslim world but also in the Western world.

**The Al-Baraka Group**

In contrast to the DMI Trust, the Al-Baraka Group has its roots in a small company in the city of Riyadh, which started its operations with a capital of

300,000 Saudi riyals. Starting with the Al-Baraka Company for Investment and Development, set up in Jeddah (Saudi Arabia) in 1982, it has become one of the two leading giants in the Islamic banking industry worldwide. Like the DMI Trust, it has helped a number of Islamic financial institutions throughout the Muslim world. Apart from its major businesses in agriculture, trade and commerce, industry, transport and health, it has donated huge sums for research and development in the field of Islamic banking and finance.

**Other Developments in Islamic Banking**

There were a number of other developments that encouraged Islamic banking. Mit Ghamr Village Bank was merged with the Nasser Social Bank,[3] which started its operations in 1972. Impressed by the experiment of Tabung Hajj, an Islamic bank in the Philippines was set up to cater for the *hajj* needs of the Muslim community in the country. The most notable development, however, was the establishment of the Islamic Development Bank, a Jeddah-based intergovernmental bank for the members of the Organization of Islamic Conference. It was set up in 1974 and started operations in 1975.

Islamic banking in the private sector took a new turn when Dubai Islamic Bank was set up in 1975 with an initial capital of 50 million UAE dirhams. Since then there has been a continuous growth in Islamic banking worldwide. Now there are a number of Muslim countries willing to Islamize their banking systems, particularly Malaysia and Indonesia, following the traditions set by Pakistan, Iran and Sudan.

## 3 ISLAMIC BANKING IN THEORY

Islamic banking is based on the idea of profit and loss sharing (PLS) between bank and depositors, and between the former and borrowers. Islamic PLS is based on trust financing and financial partnership.[4]

Earlier models of Islamic banking suggest that an Islamic bank should function on the principle of a two-tier PLS in which the bank accepts deposits on a PLS basis to lend in turn to entrepreneurs on a PLS basis. Profits of an Islamic bank accepting only PLS deposits can be calculated as an administrative cost-adjusted differential of profit receipts from the PLS loans extended to business clients and profit distribution to deposit-holders.

In addition to the PLS deposits, Islamic banks may offer interest-free current accounts and other banking services that involve no interest charging. Deposit mobilization based on trust financing and partnership is suitable for savings and long-term investment accounts while current accounts are proposed on the basis of safe custody.

On the assets side, there is a wide spectrum of modes of financing that may be used by Islamic banks as a substitute for interest. These are classified as: (i) investment-based modes, (ii) sale-based modes, (iii) rent-based modes, and (iv) service-based modes. The investment-based modes are trust financing and financial partnership. The sale-based financing comprises trade bills, mark-up,[5] and buy-back arrangements. The rent-based financing includes hire-purchase, rent-sharing and leasing. The service-based business is not actual financing; rather it includes fringe banking services such as safe custody, provision of lockers and issuance of (interest-free) credit cards. Apart from the above, Islamic banks have been increasingly involved in financing based on commissioned manufacturing.

Calculation of return on individual deposits by the bank customers and investments by the bank is straightforward once we have specified the nature of deposits and investments. This is what we describe in the next sub-section.

**Deposits and Investments**

Suppose a spectrum of deposits – $\Phi(\Phi_v, \Phi_i)$ – is available to depositors/customers, where $\Phi_v$ represents PLS deposits[6] and $\Phi_i$ denotes interest-free (current) or conditional interest-free depository accounts.[7]

Banks offer a range of fixed-return and variable-return modes of financing to borrowers (businesses and consumers): $I(I_f, I_v, I_i)$, where $I_f$ stands for fixed-return investments such as mark-up-based financing, leasing, commissioned manufacturing and so on, $I_v$ are the PLS-based investments, and $I_i$ are the interest-free loans to the holders of conditional interest-free deposit accounts.

If $\alpha = k_f/K$, $\beta = k_v/K$, and $\gamma = k_i/K$ are respective investments in the three types, then the income the bank receives on all its investments is:

$$Y = \alpha r_f + \beta r_v + \gamma r_i \tag{8.1}$$

where $r_f$, $r_v$ and $r_i$ are the rates of return on the fixed-return, variable-return and interest-free loans,[8] respectively.

The bank's profit is:

$$\Pi = Y - C \tag{8.2}$$

where $C$ represents all the costs that the bank incurs to receive $Y$.

Unlike conventional banks, the Islamic banks, however, have to adopt a detailed accounting system that should differentiate among different income streams. This is an important requirement as the banks share profit with the holders of PLS accounts. Let us decompose the total profit of a bank into two components according to its investments on the fixed- and variable-return bases:

$$\Pi = \Pi_f + \Pi_v \qquad (8.3)$$

where:

$$\Pi_f = \alpha r_f - c_f \qquad (8.4)$$

$$\Pi_v = \beta r_v - c_v \qquad (8.5)$$

Profit from the fixed-return investments, $\Pi_f$, is independent of the profits of the projects in which the borrowers use these funds. Hence, we can treat them as a fixed amount.

$r_v$ is the aggregate of returns on all the individual investments on the PLS basis. The Islamic banks invest in different projects on the PLS basis and the rates of return they require from the borrowers are not necessarily the same. If there are $n$ projects they invest in, receiving $\gamma_{2i}$ profit shares, then the total return from the PLS investments is $\Sigma b_i(\gamma_{2i}\pi_{vi})$. Thus equation (8.5) can be rewritten as:

$$\Pi_v = \Sigma b_i(\gamma_{2i}\pi_{vi}) - c_v \qquad (8.6)$$

Thus, total profits of the bank can be rewritten as:

$$\Pi = A + \Sigma b_i(\gamma_{2i}\pi_{vi}) \qquad (8.7)$$

where $A = \alpha r_f - c_f - cv$, $b_i = \beta_i/\beta$ such that $\Sigma\beta_i = \beta$.

Equation (8.7) is fundamental to the practice of Islamic banking and finance. The presence of a fixed-return component ($A$) in the profits to be apportioned has interesting implications for dealing with the agency problem that is considered to be inherent to the PLS.[9] Furthermore, this also explains why Islamic banks extend funds on the basis of the fixed-return modes of financing. El-Gamal (1999) shows that Islamic banking will survive in an environment in which both the fixed-return and the variable-return modes of financing co-exist.

We, however, take a different stance here. Equation (8.7) has strong similarities with the capital asset pricing model (CAPM). If we suppose that the bank invests equal amounts of funds on the fixed- and variable-return bases, then the CAPM implies that $\Sigma b_i(\gamma_{2i}\pi_{vi}) > A$. In terms of Figure 8.1,

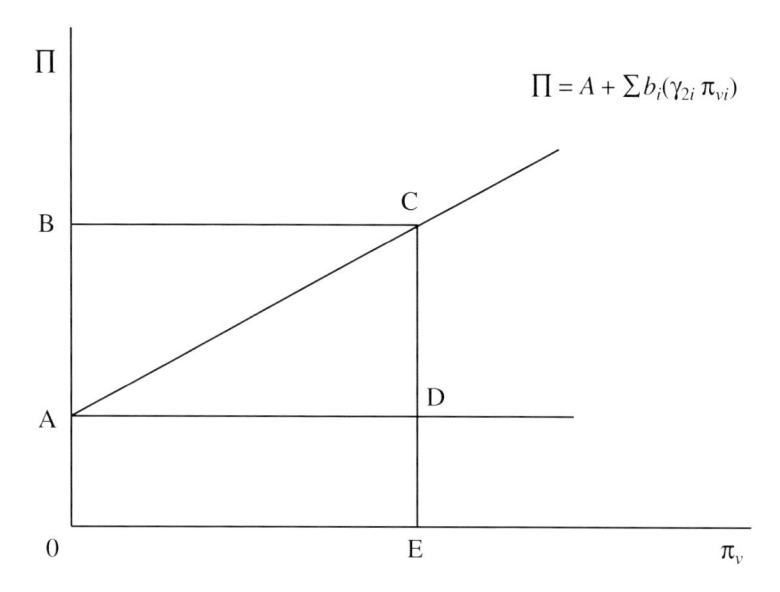

*Figure 8.1 The bank's profits and composition of investments*

this implies that funds should be invested on the variable-return basis such that ACD>0ADE, suggesting that only those investments accruing profits to the right of point C (on the profit line) are feasible. This may imply that the proportion of the variable-return investments be greater than the fixed-return investments in the total portfolio.

**Profit Distribution**

As mentioned earlier, a bank functioning on a two-tier PLS system accepts deposits on a PLS basis to invest them in various projects on the same basis. The bank's profit is determined by the difference between the profit-sharing ratios offered to the depositors ($\gamma_1$) and to the borrowers ($\gamma_2$). For profitable banking, $\gamma_2 - \gamma_1 > 0$. A typical deposit of amount $d = D_i/\Sigma D_i$ into a PLS account should realize $[\gamma_1 \Sigma b_i(\gamma_{2i} \pi_{vi})]d$ if $\Pi - A = \Sigma b_i(\gamma_{2i} \pi_{vi}) > 0$.

An Islamic bank facing a profit function similar to the one given in equation (8.7) will, in equilibrium, demand a profit share ($\gamma_2$) from the individual borrowers (businesses) that equates its marginal profit from each business. This means, in equilibrium,

$$\frac{\partial \Pi}{\partial \gamma_{21}} = \frac{\partial \Pi}{\partial \gamma_{22}} = \ldots = \frac{\partial \Pi}{\partial \gamma_{2n}}, \tag{8.8}$$

or, equally,

$$b_1\pi_{v1} = b_2\pi_{v2} = \ldots = b_n\pi_{vn}. \qquad (8.9)$$

This, however, does not imply that the bank's profit share in each individual project is the same. The profit share will be the same across the board only if: (i) the bank lends an equal amount to all the borrowers, and (ii) the expected profit from the individual projects is the same. In practice, this seems unlikely if not impossible. Thus, it appears as if the bank will have to spend some extra resources to determine an individual project's profitability for ensuring an adequate profit share. This makes it relatively more expensive (as compared to the lending on a fixed-return basis) to invest on a PLS basis. Mirakhor (1987) asserts that the relative ease of the fixed-return modes and the regulators' encouragement have led to an overwhelming dominance of the fixed-return investments in the Islamic banks' portfolios worldwide (to be discussed in the next section).

## 4 PRACTICE OF ISLAMIC BANKING

There are many variants of Islamic banking practices. While in theory, the main emphasis is on the PLS, Islamic banks have failed to practice this principle to the satisfaction of scholars of the Islamic Shariah. There are various explanations for this lack of PLS.

First, PLS contracts are inherently vulnerable to agency problems as entrepreneurs have disincentives to put in effort and have incentives to report less profit as compared to the self-financing owner–manager. This argument is based on the idea that parties to a business transaction will shirk if they are compensated less than their marginal contribution in the production process, and as this happens in the case of PLS, the capitalists hesitate to invest on a PLS basis. The argument further goes back to a different world-view of ownership under PLS as compared to the capitalistic world-view that allows only those who own certain crucial means of production to be legitimate residual claimants in the production process. Entrepreneurs claim on residual income (profit). Capitalists, on the other hand, put an emphasis on the productivity of capital and, hence, show reluctance to bear any losses incurred in production. The unwillingness to bear risk on the capitalists' part and the entrepreneurs' tendency to exclude others from sharing profits has resulted in a less favourable response to PLS from the financial and business community.

Second, PLS contracts require well-defined property rights to function efficiently. As in most Muslim countries property rights are not properly defined or protected, PLS contracts are deemed to be less attractive or to fail if used.

Third, Islamic banks and investment companies have to offer relatively less risky modes of financing as compared to PLS in the wake of severe competition from conventional banks and other financial institutions, which are already established and hence more competitive.

Fourth, the restrictive role of shareholders (investors) in management and, hence, the dichotomous financial structure of PLS contracts make them non-participatory in nature, which allows a sleeping partnership. In this way, they are not sharing contracts in a true sense; the transacting parties share financial resources without participatory decision making (Choudhury, 1998).

Fifth, PLS is not feasible for funding short-term projects due to the ensuing high degree of risk. This makes Islamic banks and other financial institutions rely on some other debt-like modes, especially mark-up, to ensure a certain degree of liquidity.

Sixth, unfair treatment in taxation is also considered to be a major obstacle in the use of PLS. While profit is taxed, interest is exempted on the grounds that it constitutes a cost item. This legal discrimination and its associated problem, tax evasion, make PLS less reliable as a tool for reward sharing.

Seventh, secondary markets for trading in PLS instruments are virtually non-existent. Consequently, they have so far failed to effectively mobilize financial resources.

**Organization of Islamic Banks**

Islamic banks have an organizational set-up similar to their conventional counterparts. Figure 8.2 shows the organizational structure of Bank Muamalat, the first Islamic bank in Indonesia, to give an example of how a typical Islamic bank is organized and how it operates in the market.

The Board of Commissioners takes on the traditional role of a board of directors. However, decision making is constrained by a Shariah Supervisory Board which sanctions or rejects any proposals in the light of the Islamic law. This supervisory board comprises eminent religious scholars who, although appointed by the Board of Commissioners, are independent and have authority to reject any proposals deemed to be against Islamic law. Management of business operations rests in the hands of a 'Board of Directors',[10] headed by a president director who is directly responsible to the Board of Commissioners, the Shariah Supervisory Board and the Board of Auditors. Financial monitoring of the organization is the responsibility of the Board of Auditors, which comprises a team of auditors, with at least one member being a member of the Board of Commissioners, and is appointed by the latter.

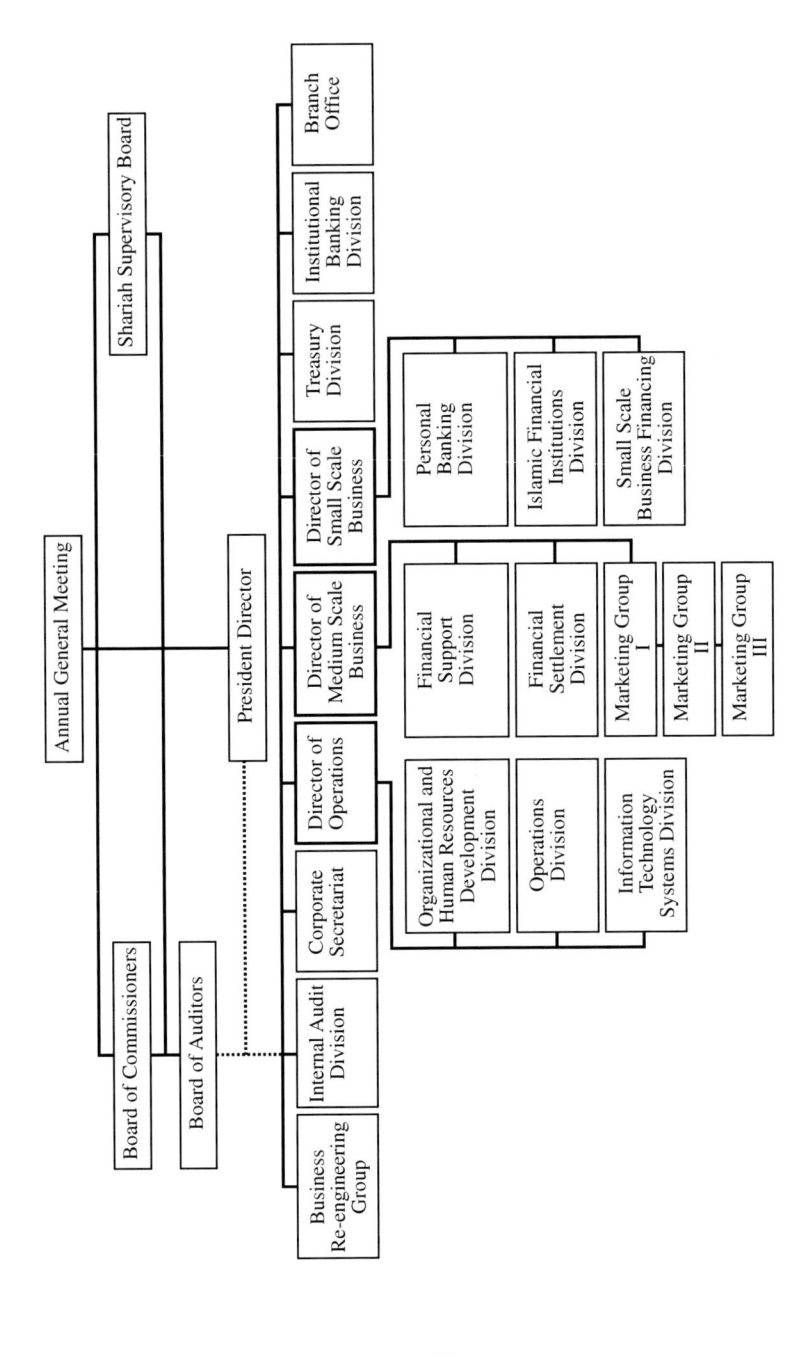

*Figure 8.2 Organizational structure of a typical Islamic bank*

## Mark-up Financing

The most popular mode of finance among Islamic banks has been mark-up financing. An estimated 70 per cent or more of investments by Islamic banks worldwide are financed on this basis (Iqbal, 1998, p. 8). Banks in Pakistan rely heavily on mark-up (decreasing marginally from 86.7 per cent in 1984 to 80.2 per cent in 1995), mainly in commodity and trading operations (Dar, 1996, p. 182).[11] There are some countries where PLS is common and reliance on fixed-return modes is minimal. For example, most Islamic financial institutions (including Islamic banks) in Iran and Switzerland do not use mark-up as their primary mode of financing. Rather, they prefer PLS. Interestingly, IFIs in these two countries on average earn more profit than in other countries (*Directory of Islamic Banks and Financial Institutions*, 1996).

Cost plus mark-up is commonly used in inter-profit centre transactions in multi-divisional firms.[12] When it is difficult to determine the market price of an intermediate good, internally produced by one division to be transferred to another, a cost plus mark-up method is used. This method allows a gross margin to the cost of production of the intermediate good to cover overheads and to provide a profit to the selling division. There may be at least four approaches for determining the gross margin, including:

1. some arrangement for sharing the profits of the venture in which the purchased good is employed;
2. a fixed percentage determined on an arbitrary basis;
3. a mark-up that yields the same return as an interest-based investment in the market; and
4. a mark-up that yields a gross margin equal to the average profit on an equal investment in a particular industry.

Islamic banks in practice determine the mark-up with reference to the market rate of interest. However, mark-up financing can be made a profit-sharing technique by determining the gross margin based on an arrangement for sharing the profits of the borrowing party (the manager).

Many scholars would argue that mark-up-based financing as used by Islamic banks is a fixed-return arrangement. If so, it provides no risk sharing between borrower and lender. This invalidates the asymmetric risk criticism of interest-based financing. Furthermore, mark-up maintains the dichotomy of functions between entrepreneur and financier. Like the fixed interest rate, it allows lenders to avoid the costs of monitoring the behaviour of the borrower. The lender has no incentive to press for management and control rights in the project in which funds are invested, as long as his capital sum is guaranteed with a mark-up.

Impressed by such similarities,[13] many would criticize the mark-up-based financing as being, in effect, no different from the interest as used in most conventional financial transactions. Being a fixed-return arrangement it is as risk free as interest-based financing. Others would criticize it on moral grounds as it maintains the exploitative nature of interest-based financing. In practice, there is no difference between interest and mark-up except that the former is explicit while the latter is implicit in the sale contract. Arguing against this aspect of mark-up financing, the critics see the mark-up as playing no potential role in income redistribution in Muslim countries, most of which are among the least-developed countries of the world.

Furthermore, mark-up financing incurs more transaction costs than interest. It is based on two separate contracts, which make it relatively expensive as compared to interest-based financing. Mortgage financing based on mark-up provides a good example of higher transaction costs of mark-up financing.

Nevertheless, financial intermediation based on mark-up is a *real* phenomenon as it depends on trading in goods and services while the interest-based intermediation is essentially a monetary phenomenon (Khan, 1997, p. 67).

Moreover, even if we maintain the basic criticism of the excessive use of mark-up, its use as a short-term mode of finance makes it a potential substitute for interest if combined with PLS. In this way, mark-up may help mobilize resources in a socially desirable way, especially in developing countries.

## 5  TOO MUCH EMPHASIS ON PLS?

Although mark-up financing is now seen as a legitimate mode of financing, many Islamic economists still view the future of Islamic banking in terms of growth of PLS. The contracts underlying PLS, especially *Mudaraba*, provide no management rights to the financier but allow him to exert some control in terms of supervision and right to access necessary information (for example, accounts). Islamic scholars do not allow collateral to be used as a control device in *Mudaraba* finance. On top of that, no indemnity is permissible unless deliberation on the part of the entrepreneur is proved in the case of a project failure. *Mudaraba* thus tilts the balance of power in favour of the entrepreneur. Apparently, this seems to be a hostile relationship in which concentration of management and control in the entrepreneur's hands makes it a less attractive choice for financiers. Furthermore, *Mudaraba* finance does not provide any additional mechanism to control the agency problem inherent in PLS.[14]

It can be shown that *Mudaraba* finance is socially efficient if the operating profits are divided between the financier and entrepreneur in proportion to the value of their individual contribution in terms of financial and human capital. Using a *Mudaraba*-type arrangement, Miller et al. (1998) show that the right to control the project is an irrelevant issue if the two parties share the profit in proportion to the values of their individual contributions (p. 498). If the entrepreneur's share in profit is greater than the value of his share in investment, this will trigger an early initiation of the project if both rights of management and control lie with him, and vice versa. In such a case, delegating to the financier the right to control (ratification and supervision) may prevent unwise investment by the entrepreneur. However, the separation of management and control may not solve the agency problem completely. In case of a loss, the entrepreneur is not liable financially in *Mudaraba*. Making him share the loss in proportion to the value of his investment in terms of human capital will reduce the agency problem to a large extent.[15]

Islamic jurists do not allow sharing of loss in a proportion other than of individual financial contributions. There is a need for rethinking on this issue. In practice, entrepreneurs are much better off than investors are in the case of a decrease in dividends and even if there is some annual loss. Referring to the practice of *Mudaraba* in Pakistan, the *Mudaraba* management company is largely run by the promoters of *Mudaraba*, who receive salaries and other benefits in addition to the 10 per cent management fee in case of profit, and lose only the management fee if loss accrues. Hence, in the contemporary practice of *Mudaraba*, the entrepreneur's interests are quite secure as he receives a fixed remuneration irrespective of loss or profit, and loses the management fee in case of loss. In such a framework, the entrepreneur has added incentives to overinvest or underinvest than in a simple *Mudaraba* contract. Making him share in loss according to the value of his contribution in terms of human capital (management) should reduce the extent of moral hazard. In the extreme case of loss, that is, bankruptcy, the entrepreneur may not be held liable financially.

Having said this, PLS has a limited role to play on the assets side of Islamic banks, and the evidence so far favours this assertion. Islamic commercial banking can only develop in a sustainable way if it is kept as simple as possible, at least in the beginning. PLS, though more Islamic in its nature, does not fit well in the practice of Islamic commercial banking and hence should only be practised by specialized Islamic investment banks.[16]

## 6  ISLAMIC BANKING IN THE FUTURE

As argued above, Islamic commercial banking has a future in adopting a model that relies on PLS on the liabilities side but invests on the basis of some fixed-return modes of financing acceptable to Islam, particularly leasing and mark-up. For Islamic investment banking, it is vital to use PLS for both liabilities and assets. For development of such banking, the following may prove to be helpful.

First, PLS works best in small and medium-sized projects with relatively low expected profits (Dar et al., 1999). Governments in Muslim countries, almost all of them developing countries, spend huge amounts in encouraging the establishment of small and medium-sized industries as part of their industrial planning. Islamic banks and other non-bank Islamic financial institutions have great scope in such environments.

Second, some Islamic banks should be set up as specialized banks catering for specific sectors. This will help in monitoring the investments in the projects relatively cheaply. The current phase of privatization and the shrinking role of the public sector in resource mobilization should help Islamic banks as they can fill the post-privatization vacuum in development finance. Governments in almost all developing countries, including the Muslim ones, are pulling back from development finance and are gradually introducing private finance initiatives. The Islamic banks have a role to play if they target traditional industries that have enjoyed comparative advantage in the past but now face financial constraints to expand or modernize their operations.[17] Specialized financial institutions can play a pivotal role in the development of these industries.

Third, the Islamic investment bank should target small but growing industries as the firms in such industries are in need of outside capital more than the established firms that in general have access to credit on an interest basis. This is expected to encourage the use of PLS.

Finally, Islamic banks may play a role similar to that of institutional investors. This requires adequate changes in business operations and investment strategies of the Islamic banks to accommodate their dual role of investors and shareholders in the business of the borrowing firms.[18] Furthermore, banking regulations are in need of serious overhauling. In most Muslim countries, banks are either prohibited from taking controlling rights in corporations (regulated so that taking block control would be costly) or structured so that managers of the borrowing firms control their decision making. These laws, along with the hostile attitude of the *Mudaraba* contract towards capitalists, have been a major hindrance in the adoption of PLS by Islamic banks (Dar and Presley, 1999). Hence reforms in banking regulations are required to balance the management and control rights between Islamic banks and the managers of the companies they invest in.

# NOTES

1. Mit Ghamr Local Savings Bank was set up by Ahmed El Naggar in Egypt and a cooperative bank was established by S.A. Irshad in Karachi (Pakistan).
2. *Zakah* is a kind of tax on savings, and its payment is viewed as a religious duty.
3. An interest-free bank with a charter with no reference to Islam or Shariah.
4. The trust financing and partnerships in the context of Islamic banking are based on two pre-Medieval contracts called *Mudaraba* and *Musharaka*, respectively. *Mudaraba* is a contractual arrangement between two or more parties in which one party provides capital to another that contributes entrepreneurship in a business to share profits according to a pre-agreed ratio. The losses are borne by the capitalist with no financial liability on the entrepreneur. In a *Musharaka*, two or more parties wishing to start a joint venture pool their resources to be residual claimants on the income stream of the business. While the profits in a *Musharaka* may be distributed in any ratio, the loss should be borne by the parties involved according to their capital shares.
5. Mark-up combines two contracts, namely, a deferred payment contract with a sale contract that allows a price mark-up on the market price (*Murabaha*).
6. These deposits may be based on *Musharaka* or *Mudaraba* contracts.
7. The conditional interest-free depository accounts require the customers to maintain a minimum deposit for a specified period. The bank pays no return on such deposits but the customers can get interest-free loans from the bank if and when they require after fulfilling the initial depository requirements. Ahmad (1952) proposed a time multiple counter loans scheme for such deposits: a customer who maintains an $X$ amount of deposit with a bank for a time period $t$ qualifies for a loan worth $X \times t$. For example, if a customer maintains a deposit of £100 with the bank for a period of 1 year (12 months), he qualifies for a loan of 1200 units. These units may be borrowed for various time periods. The customer has an option to borrow £100 for one year, or £200 for 6 months, or £400 for 3 months, or £36,500 for one day. No interest is charged on such loans. However, this scheme has by and large failed to appeal to Islamic scholars/bankers.
8. Although there is a possibility of positive returns from such investments, we here assume that the return on them is zero. Hence, $Y = \alpha r_f + \beta r_v$.
9. Many studies in the context of sharecropping in agriculture prove that a mixed portfolio is efficient on risk-sharing grounds (see the references cited in Dar, 1996).
10. This Board of Directors is in fact a management team headed by a chief executive officer (president director in this case).
11. The Pakistani banking system is perhaps the worst example of the use of mark-up financing. The banks have retained the accounting system previously used for calculation of interest. They simply calculate interest on loans and declare it as a 'mark-up' on loans, which is essentially no different from interest.
12. Cost plus contracts are also used in transactions between firms. A buying firm predetermines a supplier, for example, when the supplier manufactures a proprietary good that alone can satisfy the buying firm's needs.
13. And by the misuse of mark-up financing (see note 11).
14. In Pakistan, this vacuum is filled by government regulation. The Registrar of *Mudarabas* (a regulatory authority for Islamic investment companies (called *Mudaraba* companies) doing business on a *Mudaraba* basis) is endowed with wide discretionary powers to supervise *Mudaraba* business and intervene if necessary.
15. Mirakhor (1987) suggests internal monitoring by the financier, who should be represented in the managerial decision making of the venture. However, whereas joint management may help in *Musharaka*, it restricts the role of *Mudaraba* in resource mobilization in an interest-free economy. *Mudaraba* can be used as an effective tool of resource mobilization if complete specialization of management in favour of the entrepreneur is maintained.
16. Mirakhor (1987) and many others share this view.
17. Fishing and forestry in Malaysia and Indonesia, agricultural tools, leather products,

handicrafts and farming in Pakistan, carpets and rugs in Iran, and numerous other industries in all countries need support to compete in the world market.
18. In the Anglo-Saxon world, this suggestion can easily be dismissed, since in the UK and the US, banks face severe restrictions on intervening in the management of the businesses they invest in. However, German and Japanese models of banking are relevant here.

# REFERENCES

Ahmad, S.M. (1952), *Economics of Islam: A comparative study*, Lahore, Pakistan: Islamic Foundation.
Choudhury, M.A. (1998), 'Islamic venture capital', Memo School of Business, University College of Cape Town, Sydney.
Dar, H.A. (1996), 'A comparative analysis of sharecropping and Mudaraba business in Pakistan', PhD Dissertation, University of Cambridge.
Dar, H.A., Harvey, D. and Presley, J.R. (1999), 'Size, profitability and agency problems in profit loss sharing in Islamic finance', *Proceedings of the Second Annual Harvard University Forum on Islamic Finance*, Cambridge, MA: Centre for Middle Eastern Studies, Harvard University, pp. 51–62.
Dar, H.A. and Presley, J.R. (1999), 'Lack of profit loss sharing in Islamic banking: management and control imbalances', Paper presented at the Sixth Annual Conference of the Economic Research Forum, Cairo, Egypt, October.
*Directory of Islamic Banks and Financial Institutions* (1996), Jeddah, Saudi Arabia: International Association for Islamic Economics.
El-Gamal, M. (1999), 'The survival of Islamic banking: a micro-evolutionary perspective', *Proceedings of the Second Annual Harvard University Forum on Islamic Finance*, Cambridge, MA: Centre for Middle Eastern Studies, Harvard University Press, pp. 63–76.
Iqbal, M. (1998), 'Challenges facing Islamic banking', Paper presented at the 6th Orientation Course in Islamic Economics, Banking and Finance, The Islamic Foundation, UK, 17–21 September.
Khan, T. (1997), 'An analysis of risk sharing in Islamic finance with special reference to Pakistan', PhD Dissertation, Loughborough University.
Miller, M., Ippolito, R. and Zhang, L. (1998), 'Shareholders and stakeholders: human capital and industry', *Economic Journal*, **108**, 490–508.
Mirakhor, A. (1987), 'Analysis of short-term asset concentration in Islamic banking', IMF Working Paper No. 67, Washington, DC.

# 9. Universal banking and shareholder value: a contradiction?*

**Ingo Walter**

## 1 INTRODUCTION

In their historical development, organizational structure and strategic direction, universal banks constitute multi-product firms within the financial services sector. Certainly within their home environments, universal banks effectively target most or all client segments, and make an effort to provide each with a full range of the appropriate financial services. Outside the home market, they usually adopt a narrower competitive profile, in the majority of cases focusing on wholesale banking and securities activities as well as international private banking – occasionally building a retail presence in foreign environments as well.

This stylized profile of universal banks presents shareholders with an amalgam of more or less distinct businesses that are linked together in a complex network which draws on a set of centralized financial, information, human and organizational resources – a profile that tends to be extraordinarily difficult to manage in a way that achieves an optimum use of invested capital. The key issue for the investor is whether shares in a universal bank represent an attractive asset-allocation alternative from a perspective of both risk-adjusted total return and portfolio efficiency. The answers to this question, in turn, have an important bearing on the universal bank's cost of capital and therefore its performance against rivals with a narrower business focus in increasingly competitive markets.

This chapter considers these issues within a straightforward conceptual framework. I begin by adding to presumptive adjusted book value of a universal bank's equity a number of building-blocks that ultimately determine the market value of its equity. I then ask whether that market value of equity is in fact the *maximum* value attainable from the perspective of the shareholder. Finally, I outline some of the strategic and tactical alternatives, inside and outside the bank, that are open to management in order to achieve a hypothetical maximum value of shareholder equity. Whatever empirical evidence is available in the literature is brought to bear in the course of the discussion.

## 2 STRUCTURE OF THE UNIVERSAL BANK

Universal banking organizations may take a number of more or less distinct forms.[1] These are stylized in Exhibit 9.1.

- A fully integrated universal bank (Type A) provides a broad range of financial services (banking, securities and insurance) under a single corporate structure supported by a single capital base. There are, at present, no good examples of this particular model.
- A partially integrated universal bank (Type B) conducts both commercial and investment banking within the same entity, but undertakes insurance underwriting and distribution, as well as mortgage banking, asset management, lease-financing, factoring, management consulting and other specialized activities through separately capitalized subsidiaries, either because such activities are separately regulated, or because they involve significant potential for exploitation of conflicts of interest, or a combination of such factors. Deutsche Bank AG would be a good example of this type of universal banking structure.
- In a Type C universal bank the commercial bank, whose core business is taking deposits and making commercial loans, is the parent of subsidiaries engaged in a variety of other financial services ranging from investment banking to insurance. An example would be Barclays plc.
- A final universal banking structure (Type D) involves creation of a holding company which controls affiliates engaged in commercial banking, investment banking, insurance, and possibly other types of financial and non-financial businesses. An example would be Citigroup.

The specific structures that universal banks adopt are driven by regulatory considerations, by the production-function characteristic of financial services, and by demand-side issues relating to market structure and client preferences. American regulation, for example, mandates a Type D form of organization, with the Glass–Steagall provisions of the Banking Act of 1933 and later the Gramm–Leach–Bliley Act of 1999 requiring functional separation of banking and insurance (taking deposits and extending commercial loans) and most types of securities activities. Each type of business

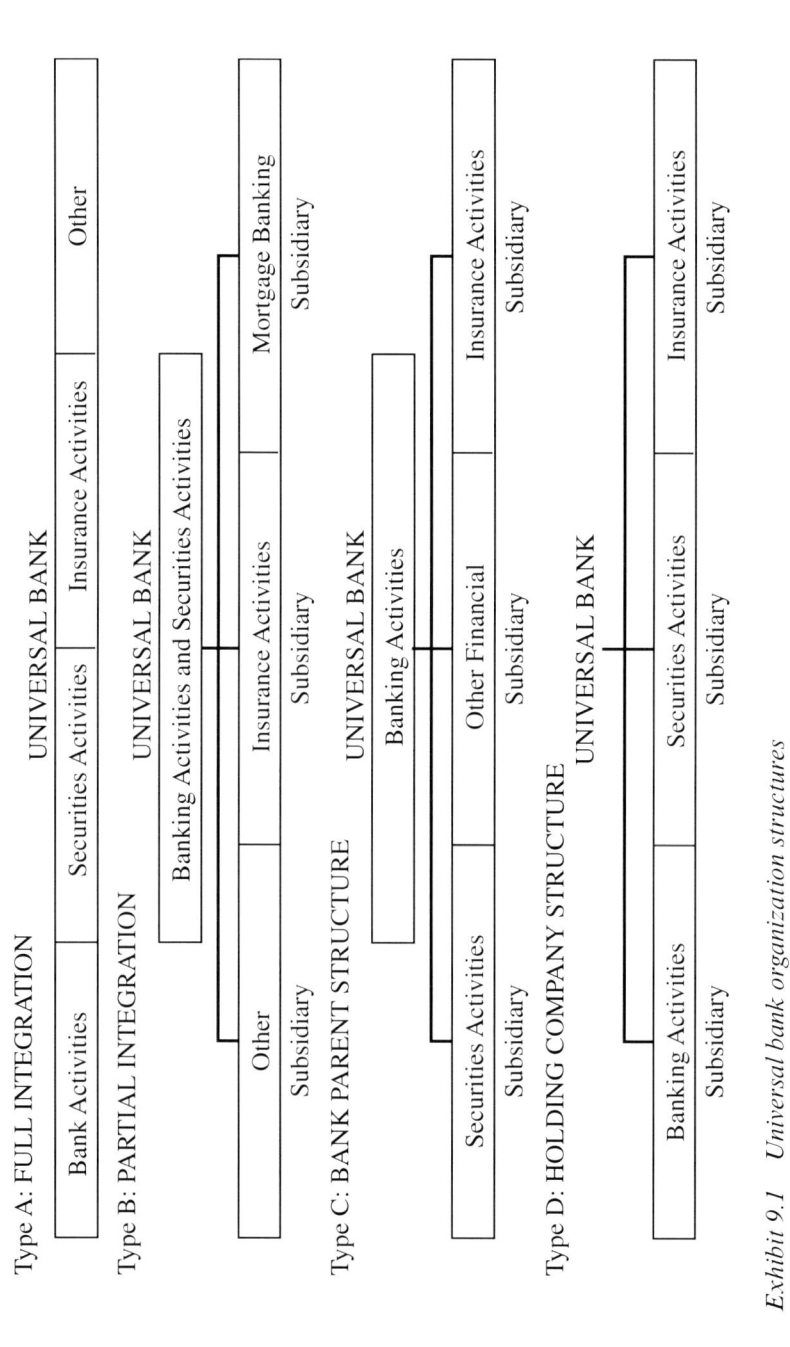

Type A: FULL INTEGRATION

UNIVERSAL BANK

| Bank Activities | Securities Activities | Insurance Activities | Other |

Type B: PARTIAL INTEGRATION

UNIVERSAL BANK

Banking Activities and Securities Activities

| Other Subsidiary | Insurance Activities Subsidiary | Mortgage Banking Subsidiary |

Type C: BANK PARENT STRUCTURE

UNIVERSAL BANK

Banking Activities

| Securities Activities Subsidiary | Other Financial Subsidiary | Insurance Activities Subsidiary |

Type D: HOLDING COMPANY STRUCTURE

UNIVERSAL BANK

| Banking Activities Subsidiary | Securities Activities Subsidiary | Insurance Activities Subsidiary |

*Exhibit 9.1   Universal bank organization structures*

must be carried out through subsidiaries under a qualified holding company structure. British universal banking follows the Type C model, with securities and insurance activities carried out via subsidiaries of the bank itself. Most continental European countries seem to follow the Type B model, with full integration of banking and securities activities within the bank itself (despite functional regulation), and insurance, mortgage banking and other specialized financial and non-financial activities carried out through subsidiaries. As noted, the Type A universal banking model, with all activities carried out within a single corporate entity, seems not to exist even in environments characterized by a monopoly regulator such as, for example, the Monetary Authority of Singapore.

From a production-function perspective, the structural form of universal banking appears to depend on the ease with which operating efficiencies and scale and scope economies can be exploited – determined in large part by product and process technologies – as well as the comparative organizational effectiveness in optimally satisfying client requirements and bringing to bear market power.[2]

## 3 FROM BOOK VALUE OF EQUITY TO MARKET VALUE OF EQUITY

Realization of shareholder value can begin by tracing the sources of value increments in excess of book value of equity (BVE). For universal banks, the BVE is the sum of: (i) the par value of shares when originally issued; (ii) the surplus paid in by investors when the shares were issued; (iii) retained earnings on the books of the bank; and (iv) reserves set aside for loan losses (Saunders, 1996). Depending on the prevailing regulatory and accounting system, BVE must be increased by unrealized capital gains associated with assets such as equity holdings carried on the books of the bank at historical cost and their prevailing replacement values (hidden reserves), as well as the replacement values of other assets and liabilities that differ materially from historical values due to credit and market risk considerations – that is, their mark-to-market values.

We thus have the presumptive adjusted book value of equity (ABVE), which in fact is not normally revealed in bank financial statements due to a general absence of market-value accounting across broad categories of universal banking activities – with the exception of trading-account securities, derivatives and open foreign exchange positions, for example.

As in non-financial firms such as McDonald's, Coca-Cola or any other publicly traded firm, shareholder interests in a universal bank are tied to the market value of its equity (MVE) – the number of shares outstanding times the prevailing market price. MVE normally should be significantly in excess of ABVE, reflecting as it does current and expected future net earnings, adjusted for risk. The MVE/ABVE so-called 'Q' ratio can, however, be either higher or lower than 1, and is clearly susceptible to enhancement through managerial or shareholder action. If it is significantly below 1, for example, it may be that breaking up the bank can serve the interests of shareholders – if ABVE or more can be realized as a result – in the same way as restructurings have raised shareholder value under appropriate circumstances in industrial companies.

Assuming a universal bank's MVE exceeds ABVE, what factors can explain the difference? Exhibit 9.2 begins with ABVE and sequentially identifies incremental-value sources to arrive at MVE, which are explained in the following sections.

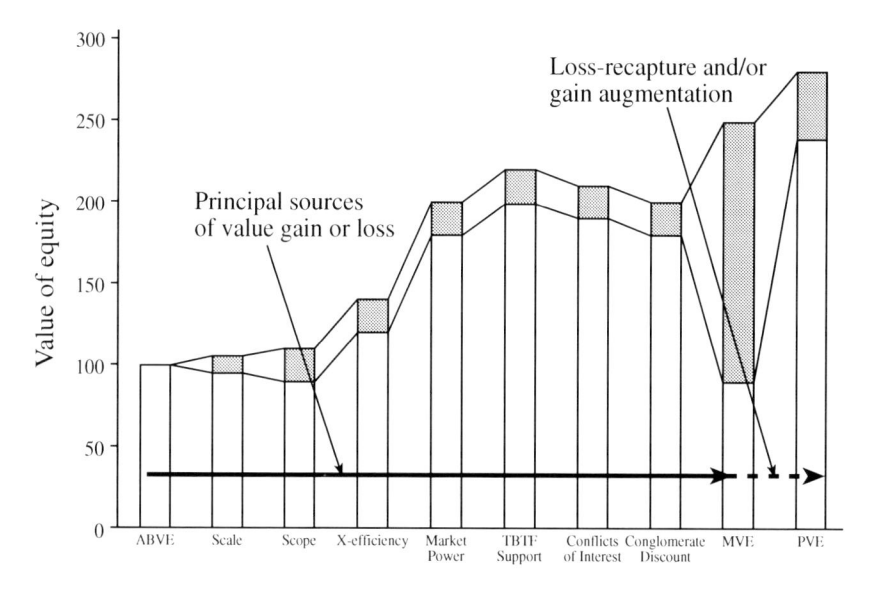

*Exhibit 9.2   Book, market and potential equity values in universal banks*

**Economies of Scale**

Whether economies of scale exist in financial services has been at the heart of strategic and regulatory discussions about optimum firm size in the financial services sector – can increased size increase shareholder value? In an information- and distribution-intensive industry with high fixed costs, such as financial services, there should be ample potential for scale economies – as well as potential for diseconomies of scale attributable to administrative overheads, agency problems and other cost factors once very large firm size is reached. If economies of scale prevail, increased size will help create shareholder value. If diseconomies prevail, shareholder value will be destroyed. Bankers regularly argue that 'bigger is better' from a shareholder-value perspective, and usually point to economies of scale as a major reason why.

**Economies of Scope**

There should also be ample potential for economies and diseconomies of scope in the financial services sector, which may arise either through supply- or demand-side linkages.[3]

On the supply side, scope economies relate to cost savings through sharing of overheads and improving technology through joint production of generically similar groups of services. Supply-side diseconomies of scope may arise from such factors as inertia and lack of responsiveness and creativity that may come with increased firm size and bureaucratization, 'turf' and profit-attribution conflicts that increase costs or erode product quality in meeting client needs, or serious cultural differences across the organization that inhibit seamless delivery of a broad range of financial services.

On the demand side, economies of scope (cross-selling) arise when the all-in cost to the buyer of multiple financial services from a single supplier – including the price of the service, plus information, search, monitoring, contracting and other transaction costs – is less than the cost of purchasing them from separate suppliers. Demand-related diseconomies of scope could arise, for example, through agency costs that may develop when the multi-product financial firm acts against the interests of the client in the sale of one service in order to facilitate the sale of another, or as a result of internal information transfers considered inimical to the client's interests. Management of universal banks often argues that broader product and client coverage, and the increased throughput volume this makes possible, represents shareholder-value enhancement.

Network economics associated with universal banking may be considered a special type of demand-side economy of scope (Economides, 1995). Like telecommunications, banking relationships with end-users of financial services represent a network structure wherein additional client linkages add value to existing clients by increasing the feasibility or reducing the cost of accessing them – so-called 'network externalities' which tend to increase with the absolute size of the network itself. Every client link to the bank potentially 'complements' every other one and thus potentially adds value through either one-way or two-way exchanges through incremental information or access to liquidity. The size of network benefits depends on technical compatibility and coordination in time and location, which the universal bank is in a position to provide. And networks tend to be self-reinforcing in that they require a minimum critical mass and tend to grow in dominance as they increase in size, thus precluding perfect competition in network-driven financial services. This characteristic is evident in activities such as securities clearance and settlement, global custody, funds transfer and international cash management, forex and securities dealing, and the like. And networks tend to lock in users in so far as switching costs tend to be relatively high, creating the potential for significant market power.

**X-efficiency**

Besides economies of scale and scope, it seems likely that universal banks of roughly the same size and providing roughly the same range of services may have very different cost levels per unit of output. There is ample evidence of such performance differences, for example, in comparative cost-to-income ratios among banks both within and between national financial services markets. The reasons involve efficiency differences in the use of labour and capital, effectiveness in the sourcing and application of available technology, and perhaps effectiveness in the acquisition of productive inputs, organizational design, compensation and incentive systems – and just plain better management.

X-efficiency may be related to size if, for example, large organizations are differentially capable of the massive and 'lumpy' capital outlays required to install and maintain the most efficient information technology and transactions processing infrastructures. Exhibit 9.3 shows information technology spending levels that only large banks can afford. If such spending levels result in higher X-efficiency, then large banks will gain in competition with smaller ones from a shareholder-value perspective. However, smaller organizations ought to be able to pool their resources or outsource in order to capture similar efficiencies. From a shareholder-value point of view, management is (or should be) under constant pressure through their boards of directors to do better, to maximize X-efficiency in their organizations, and to transmit this pressure throughout the enterprise.

**Empirical Evidence of Economies of Scale, Scope and X-efficiency**

What is the evidence regarding economies of scale, economies of scope and X-efficiency with regard to bank performance?

Individually or in combination, economies (diseconomies) of scale and scope in universal banks will be either captured as increased (decreased)

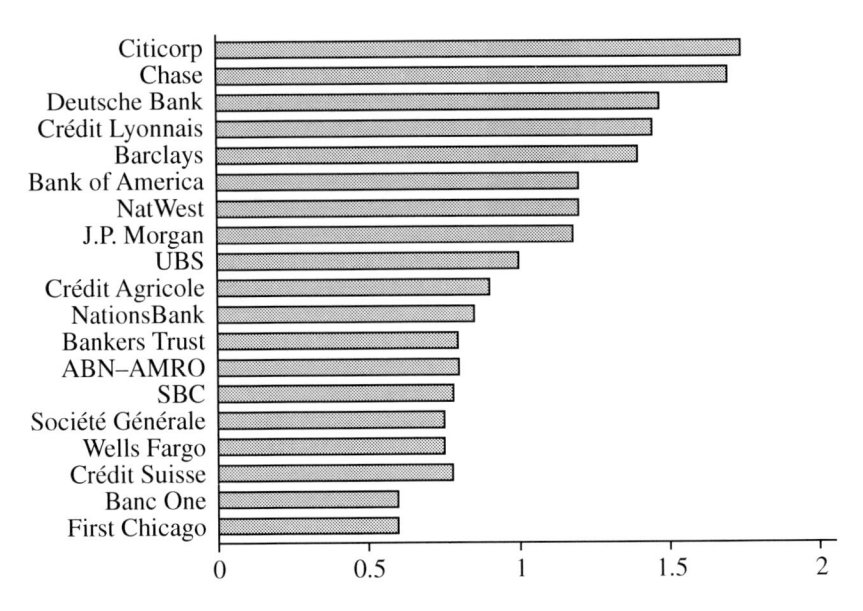

*Source:* The Tower Group, 1996.

*Exhibit 9.3  Estimated major bank IT spending levels ($ billions)*

profit margins or passed along to clients in the form of lower (higher) prices resulting in a gain (loss) of market share. They should be directly observable in cost functions of financial services suppliers and in aggregate performance measures.

Studies of scale and scope economies in financial services are unusually problematic. The nature of the empirical tests used, the form of the cost functions, the existence of unique optimum output levels, and the optimizing behaviour of financial firms all present difficulties. Limited availability and conformity of data present serious empirical problems. And the conclusions of any study that has detected (or failed to detect) economies of scale and/or scope in a sample selection of financial institutions does not necessarily have general applicability.

Many such studies have been undertaken in the banking, insurance and securities industries over the years (see Exhibit 9.4). Estimated cost functions form the basis of most of these empirical tests, virtually all of which found that economies of scale are achieved with increases in size among small banks (below $100 million in asset size). More recent studies have shown that scale economies may also exist in banks falling into the $100 million to $5 billion range. There is very little evidence so far of scale

*Exhibit 9.4*  Economies of scale and scope in financial services firms – the evidence

|  | Economies of scale beyond small levels of output (size) | Economies of scope among outputs |
|---|---|---|
| **Domestic Banks** | | |
| Benston et al., 1983 | No | No |
| Berger et al., 1987 | No | No |
| Gilligan and Smirlock, 1984 | No | Yes |
| Gilligan et al., 1984 | No | Yes |
| Kolari and Zardkoohi, 1987 | No | No |
| Lawrence, 1989 | No | Yes |
| Lawrence and Shay, 1986 | No | No |
| Mester, 1990 | Yes | No |
| Noulas et al., 1990 | Yes | ? |
| Shaffer, 1988 | Yes | ? |
| Hunter et al., 1990 | Yes | No |
| McAllister and McManus, 1993 | No | ? |
| Pulley and Humphrey, 1993 | ? | Yes |
| **Foreign Banks** | | |
| Yoshika and Nakajima, 1987 (Japan) | Yes | ? |
| Kim, 1987 (Israel) | Yes | Yes |
| Saunders and Walter, 1991 (worldwide) | Yes | No |
| Rothenberg, 1994 (European Community) | No | ? |
| **Thrifts** | | |
| Mester, 1987 | No | No |
| LeCompte and Smith, 1990 | No | No |
| **Life Insurance** | | |
| Fields and Murphy, 1989 | Yes | No |
| Fields, 1988 | No | ? |
| Grace and Timme, 1992 | Yes | ? |
| **Securities Firms** | | |
| Goldberg et al., 1991 | No | No |

*Source:* Saunders (1996).

economies in the case of banks larger than $5 billion. An examination of the world's 200 largest banks (Saunders and Walter, 1994) found evidence that the very largest banks grew more slowly than the smaller among the large banks during the 1980s, but that limited economies of scale did appear among the banks included in the study. Overall, the consensus seems to be that scale economies and diseconomies do not result in more than about 5 per cent difference in unit costs. So, for most universal banks scale economies seem to have relatively little bearing on shareholder value in terms of Exhibit 9.2.

With respect to supply-side economies of scope, most empirical studies have failed to find such gains in the banking, insurance and securities industries, and most of them have also concluded that some diseconomies of scope are encountered when firms in the financial services sector add new product ranges to their portfolios. Saunders and Walter (1994), for example, found negative supply-side economies of scope among the world's 200 largest banks – as the product range widens, unit costs seem to go up.

As shown in Exhibit 9.4, scope economies in most other cost studies of the financial services industry are either trivial or negative. However, the period covered by many of these studies involved institutions that were rapidly shifting away from a pure focus on commercial banking, and may thus have incurred considerable costs in expanding the range of their activities. If this diversification effort involved significant sunk costs – which were listed as expenses on the accounting statements during the period under study – that were undertaken to achieve future expansion of market share or increases in fee-based areas of activity, then we might expect to see any strong statistical evidence of diseconomies of scope between lending and non-lending activities reversed in future periods. If the banks' investment in staffing, training and infrastructure in fact bears returns in the future commensurate with these expenditures, then neutrality or positive economies of scope may well exist. Still, the available evidence remains inconclusive.

It is also reasonable to suggest that some demand-related scope economies may exist, but that these are likely to be very specific to the types of services provided and the types of clients involved. Strong cross-selling potential may exist for retail and private clients between banking, insurance and asset-management products (one-stop shopping), for example. Yet such potential may be totally absent between trade-finance and mergers and acquisitions (M&A) advisory services for major corporate clients. So demand-related scope economies are clearly linked to a universal bank's specific strategic positioning across clients, products and geographic areas of operation (Walter, 1988). Indeed, a principal objective of strategic positioning in universal banking is to link market segments together in a coherent pattern – what might be termed 'strategic integrity' – that permits maximum exploitation of cross-selling opportunities, and the design of incentives and organizational structures to ensure that such exploitation actually occurs.

With respect to X-efficiency, a number of authors have found very large disparities in cost structures among banks of similar size, suggesting that the way banks are run is more important than their size or the selection of businesses that they pursue (Berger et al., 1993a, 1993b). The consensus of studies conducted in the United States seems to be that average unit costs in the banking industry lie some 20 per cent above 'best practice' firms producing the same range and volume of services, with most of the difference attributable to operating economies rather than differences in the cost of funds (Akhavein et al., 1996). Siems (1996) finds that the greater the overlap in branch-office networks, the higher the abnormal equity returns in US bank mergers, while no such abnormal returns are associated with increasing concentration levels in the regions where the bank mergers occurred. This suggests that shareholder value in the mega-mergers of the mid-1990s was more associated with increases of X-efficiency than with reductions in competition.

Specifically with respect to X-efficiency in universal banking, Steinherr (1996) has assessed the profit performance and earnings variability of segmented and universal financial institutions worldwide during the late 1980s. Segmented and universal banks are found to have achieved roughly the same profit levels, but universal banks were found to have both lower cost levels and (interestingly) lower credit losses, which the author attributes to better monitoring of their clients based on private (non-public) information that universal banks may enjoy over their segmented counterparts. One explanation for this finding may be that *Hausbank* relationships, which represent an important aspect of universal banking in some countries, include the periodic conversion of bank debt to equity as part of credit workouts of non-financial clients in trouble, thus obviating the need to realize the extent of credit losses.

Taken together, these studies suggest very limited scope for cost economies of scale and scope among major universal banks. Scope economies, to the extent that they exist, are likely to be found mainly on the demand side, and tend to apply very differently to different client segments. It is X-efficiency that seems to be the principal determinant of observed differences in cost levels among banks.

Perhaps contrary to conventional wisdom, therefore, there appears to be room in financial systems for viable financial services firms that range from large to small and from universal to specialist in a rich mosaic of institutions, as against a competitive landscape populated exclusively by 800-pound gorillas.

## Absolute Size and Market Power

Still, conventional wisdom may win out in the end if large universal banks are able to extract economic rents from the market by application of market power – an issue that most empirical studies have not yet examined. Indeed, in many national markets for financial services suppliers have shown a tendency towards oligopoly but may be prevented by regulation or international competition from fully exploiting monopoly positions. Financial services market structures differ widely among countries, as measured for example by the Herfindahl–Hirshman index,[4] with very high levels of concentration in countries such as the Netherlands and Denmark and low levels in relatively fragmented financial systems such as the United States. Lending margins and financial services fees, for example, tend to be positively associated with higher concentration levels. So do cost-to-income ratios. Shareholders naturally tend to gain from the former, and lose from the latter.

Exhibit 9.5 shows the impact on market-to-book values of British banks after the UK clearing cartel was created in the 1920s, followed by market-to-book erosion after the cartel was abolished in the 1970s. Differences in competitive structure are also illustrated in Exhibit 9.6, which compares the price-to-book ratios of US money-centre banks to major regional banks, with the latter operating in substantially less-competitive markets than the former.

## The Value of Income-stream Diversification

Saunders and Walter (1994) carried out a series of simulated mergers between US banks, securities firms and insurance companies in order to test the stability of earnings of the 'merged' as opposed to separate institutions. The authors evaluated the 'global' opportunity-set of potential mergers between existing money-centre banks, regional banks, life insurance companies, property and casualty insurance companies and securities firms, and the risk characteristics of each possible combination. The results were reported in terms of the average standard deviation of returns, along with the returns and risk calculated for the minimum-risk portfolio of activities. The findings suggest that there are potential risk-reduction gains from diversification in universal financial services organizations, and that these gains increase with the number of activities undertaken. The main risk-reduction gains appear to arise from combining commercial banking with insurance activities, rather than with securities activities. In the two-activity case, the best (lowest-risk) merger partners for US money-centre banks were property and casualty insurers. In the three-activity case, the

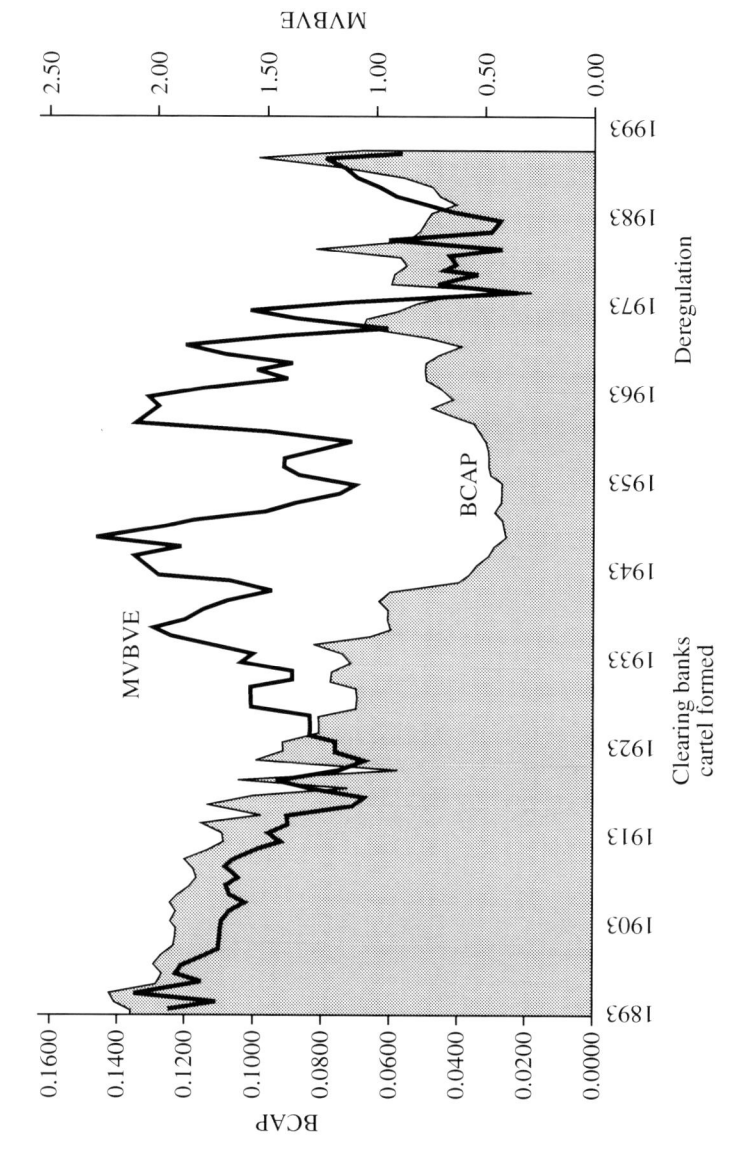

*Source:* Anthony Saunders and B. Wilson, *Bank Capital Structure: A Comparative Analysis of the U.S., U.K. and Canada*, New York: University Salomon Center Working Paper, June 1996.

*Exhibit 9.5  Market-to-book equity value, UK*

*Exhibit 9.6* Price-to-book ratios of US money-centre and major regional banks

|  | 3Q/96 | 2Q/96 | 1Q/96 | 4Q/95 | 3W95 |
|---|---|---|---|---|---|
| Money-Centre Banks Average | 191 | 166 | 165 | 152 | 150 |
| BankAmerica | 172 | 159 | 151 | 134 | 135 |
| Bank of Boston | 222 | 170 | 163 | 153 | 173 |
| Bankers Trust | 157 | 138 | 135 | 124 | 123 |
| Chase Manhattan | 196 | 169 | 170 | 155 | 137 |
| Citicorp | 246 | 214 | 216 | 186 | 174 |
| First Chicago | 183 | 149 | 161 | 150 | 149 |
| J.P. Morgan | 164 | 162 | 160 | 159 | 156 |
| Major Regional Banks Average | 221 | 188 | 217 | 205 | 199 |
| Banc One | 219 | 178 | 185 | 179 | 179 |
| Corestate Financial | 258 | 219 | 220 | 226 | 229 |
| First Union | 218 | 193 | 187 | 179 | 153 |
| Fleet Financial | 200 | 169 | 187 | 174 | 144 |
| Nations Bank | 199 | 181 | 174 | 147 | 158 |
| Norwest Corp. | 276 | 228 | 250 | 229 | 225 |
| Wells Fargo | 177 | 150 | 313 | 299 | 308 |

*Source:* Goldman Sachs & Co., 1996.

lowest-risk merger combination turned out to be between money-centre banks, regional banks and property and casualty insurers. In the full five-activity case (an average of 247,104 potential merger combinations among financial firms in the database), the standard deviation of returns was 0.01452, well below the average risk level for money-centre banks (0.02024) on a stand-alone basis.[5]

Such studies, of course, may exaggerate the risk-reduction benefits of universal banking because they ignore many of the operational costs involved in setting up these activities.[6] Moreover, to the extent that these *ex post* risk measures reflect existing central-bank safety nets, they may underestimate the *ex ante* risk in the future. At best, such results may be viewed as illustrative of the risk-reduction potential of universal banking.[9] It seems unlikely that the diversification benefits in terms of risk reduction outweigh the negative earnings implications of less-than-optimum intra-firm capital allocation from the perspective of universal bank shareholders.

## Access to Bail-outs

It is certainly possible that the purported advantages of universal banking structures can result in a competitive landscape that is dominated by a small number of large institutions. In such a case, failure of one of the major institutions is likely to cause unacceptable systemic problems, and the institution will be bailed out by taxpayers – as happened in the case of comparatively much smaller institutions in the United States, Switzerland, Norway, Sweden, Finland and Japan during the 1980s and early 1990s. If this turns out to be the case, then too-big-to-fail guarantees create a potentially important public subsidy for universal banking organizations and therefore implicitly benefit the institutions' shareholders.

On the other hand, 'free lunches' usually do not last too long, and sooner or later such guarantees invariably come with strings attached. Possible reactions include intensified regulation of credit- and market-risk exposures, stronger supervision and surveillance intended to achieve early closure in advance of capital depletion, and structural barriers to force activities into business units that can be effectively supervised in accordance with their functions even at the cost of a lower level of X-efficiency and scope economies. The speed with which the central banks and regulatory authorities reacted to the 1996 Sumitomo copper trading scandal signalled the possibility of safety-net support of the global copper market, in view of major banks' massive exposures in highly complex structured credits. The fact is that too-big-to-fail guarantees are alive and well for all large banks – not only universal banks – as is public concern about what restrictions on bank activities ought to accompany them.

## Conflicts of Interest

The potential for conflicts of interest is endemic in universal banking, and runs across the various types of activities in which the bank is engaged. The matrix presented in Exhibit 9.7 provides a simple framework for a taxonomy of conflicts of interest that may arise across the broad range of activities engaged in by universal banks. The major types of conflicts include the following:[7]

- *Salesman's stake*  It has been argued that when banks have the power to sell affiliates' products, managers will no longer dispense 'dispassionate' advice to clients. Instead, they will have a salesman's stake in pushing 'house' products, possibly to the disadvantage of the customer.

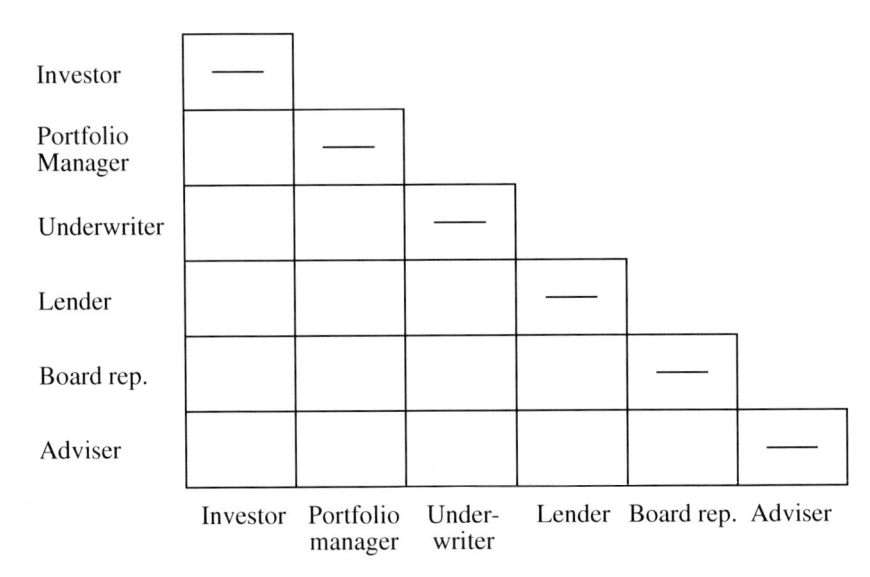

*Exhibit 9.7  Universal banking conflict matrix*

- *Stuffing fiduciary accounts*  A bank that is acting as an underwriter and is unable to place the securities in a public offering – and is thereby exposed to a potential underwriting loss – may seek to ameliorate this loss by 'stuffing' unwanted securities into accounts managed by its investment department over which the bank has discretionary authority.
- *Bankruptcy-risk transfer*  A bank with a loan outstanding to a firm whose bankruptcy risk has increased, to the private knowledge of the banker, may have an incentive to induce the firm to issue bonds or equities – underwritten by its securities unit – to an unsuspecting public. The proceeds of such an issue could then be used to pay down the bank loan. In this case the bank has transferred debt-related risk from itself to outside investors, while it simultaneously earns a fee and/or spread on the underwriting.[8]
- *Third-party loans*  To ensure that an underwriting goes well, a bank may make below-market loans to third-party investors on condition that this finance is used to purchase securities underwritten by its securities unit.
- *Tie-ins*  A bank may use its lending power activities to coerce or tie in a customer to the 'securities products' sold by its securities unit. For example, it may threaten to credit ration the customer unless it purchases certain investment banking services.

- *Information transfer*   In acting as a lender, a bank may become privy to certain material inside information about a customer or its rivals that can be used in setting prices or helping in the distribution of securities offerings underwritten by its securities unit. This type of information flow could work in the other direction as well – that is, from the securities unit to the bank.

Mechanisms to control conflict of interest – or more precisely, disincentives to exploit such conflicts – may be either market based, regulation based, or some combination of the two. Most universal banking systems seem to rely on market disincentives to prevent exploitation of opportunities for conflicts of interest. The United States has had a tendency since the 1930s to rely on regulations, and in particular on 'walls' between types of activities. In most countries, however, few impenetrable walls exist between banking and securities departments within the universal bank, and few external firewalls exist between a universal bank and its non-bank subsidiaries (for example, insurance).[9] Internally, there appears to be a primary reliance on the loyalty and professional conduct of bank employees, both with respect to the institution's long-term survival and the best interests of its customers. Externally, reliance appears to be placed on market reputation and competition as disciplinary mechanisms. The concern of a bank for its reputational 'franchise' and fear of competitors are viewed as enforcing a degree of control over the potential for conflict exploitation.

Shareholders clearly have a stake in the management and control of conflicts of interest in universal banks. They can benefit from conflict exploitation in the short term, to the extent that business volumes and/or margins are increased as a result. On the one hand, preventing conflicts of interest is an expensive business. Compliance systems are costly to maintain, and various types of walls between business units can have high opportunity costs because of inefficient use of information within the organization. Externally, reputation losses associated with conflicts of interest can bear on shareholders very heavily indeed, as demonstrated by a variety of recent 'accidents' in the financial services industry. It could well be argued that conflicts of interest may contribute to the MVE/ABVE ratios of universal banks falling below those of non-universal financial institutions.[10]

**Conglomerate Discount**

It is often alleged that the shares of multi-product firms and conglomerates tend (all else equal) to trade at prices lower than shares of more narrowly focused firms. There are two reasons why this 'conglomerate discount' is alleged to exist.

First, it is argued that, on balance, conglomerates use capital inefficiently. Recent empirical work by Berger and Ofek (1995) assesses the potential benefits of diversification (greater operating efficiency, less incentive to forgo positive net present value projects, greater debt capacity, lower taxes) against the potential costs (higher management discretion to engage in value-reducing projects, cross-subsidization of marginal or loss-making projects that drain resources from healthy businesses, misalignments in incentives between central and divisional managers). The authors demonstrate an average value loss in multi-product firms of the order of 13–15 per cent, as compared to the stand-alone values of the constituent businesses for a sample of US corporations during the 1986–91 period. This value loss was smaller in cases where the multi-product firms were active in closely allied activities within the same two-digit standard industrial code (SIC) classification.

The bulk of the value erosion in conglomerates is attributed by the authors mainly to overinvestment in marginally profitable activities and cross-subsidization. In empirical work using event-study methodology, John and Ofek (1994) show that asset sales by corporations result in significantly improved shareholder value for the remaining assets, both as a result of greater focus in the enterprise and value gains through high prices paid by asset buyers. Such findings from event studies of broad ranges of industry may well apply to the diversified activities encompassed by universal banks as well. If retail banking and wholesale banking are evolving into highly specialized performance-driven businesses, one may ask whether the kinds of conglomerate discounts found in industrial firms may not also apply to universal banking structures as centralized decision making becomes increasingly irrelevant to the requirements of the specific businesses themselves.

A second possible source of a conglomerate discount is that investors in shares of conglomerates find it difficult to 'take a view' and add pure sectoral exposures to their portfolios. Shareholders in companies like General Electric, for example, in effect own a closed-end mutual fund comprising aircraft engines, plastics, electricity generation and distribution equipment, financial services, diesel locomotives, large household appliances, and a variety of other activities. GE therefore presents investors who may have a bullish view of the aircraft engine business – which they would like reflected in their portfolio selection – with a particularly poor choice compared with Rolls Royce, for example, which is much more of a 'pure play' in this sector. Nor is it easily possible to short the undesirable parts of GE in order to 'purify' the selection of GE shares under such circumstances. So investors tend to avoid such stocks in their efforts to construct efficient asset-allocation profiles, especially highly performance-driven managers of institutional equity portfolios under pressure to outperform equity indexes.

The portfolio logic of the conglomerate discount should apply in the financial services sector as well, and a universal bank that is active in retail banking, wholesale commercial banking, middle-market banking, private banking, corporate finance, trading, investment banking, asset management and perhaps other businesses in effect represents a financial conglomerate that prevents investors from optimizing asset allocation across specific segments of the financial services industry.

Both the portfolio-selection effect and the capital-misallocation effect may weaken investor demand for universal bank shares, lower equity prices, and produce a higher cost of capital than if the conglomerate discount were absent – this in turn having a bearing on the competitive performance and profitability of the enterprise.

**Non-financial Shareholdings**

The conglomerate issue tends to be much more serious when a universal bank owns large-scale shareholdings in non-financial corporations, in which case the shareholder obtains a closed-end fund that has been assembled by bank managers for various reasons over time, and may bear no relationship to the investor's own portfolio optimization goals. The value of the universal bank itself then depends on the total market value of its shares, which must be held on an all-or-nothing basis, plus its own market value.

There are wide differences in the role banks play in non-financial corporate shareholdings and in the process of corporate governance (Walter, 1993) (these are stylized in Exhibit 9.8):

- In the equity-market system, industrial firms are 'semi-detached' from banks. Financing of major corporations is done to a significant extent through the capital markets, with short-term financing needs satisfied through commercial paper programmes, longer-term debt through straight or structured bond issues and medium-term note programmes, and equity financing accomplished through public issues or private placements. Research coverage tends to be extensive. Commercial banking relationships with major companies can be very important – notably through backstop credit lines and short-term lending facilities – but they tend to be between *buyer and seller*, with close bank monitoring and control coming into play mainly for small and medium-sized firms or in cases of credit problems and workouts. Corporate control in such 'Anglo-American' systems tends to be exercised through the takeover market on the basis of widely available public information, with a bank's function limited mainly

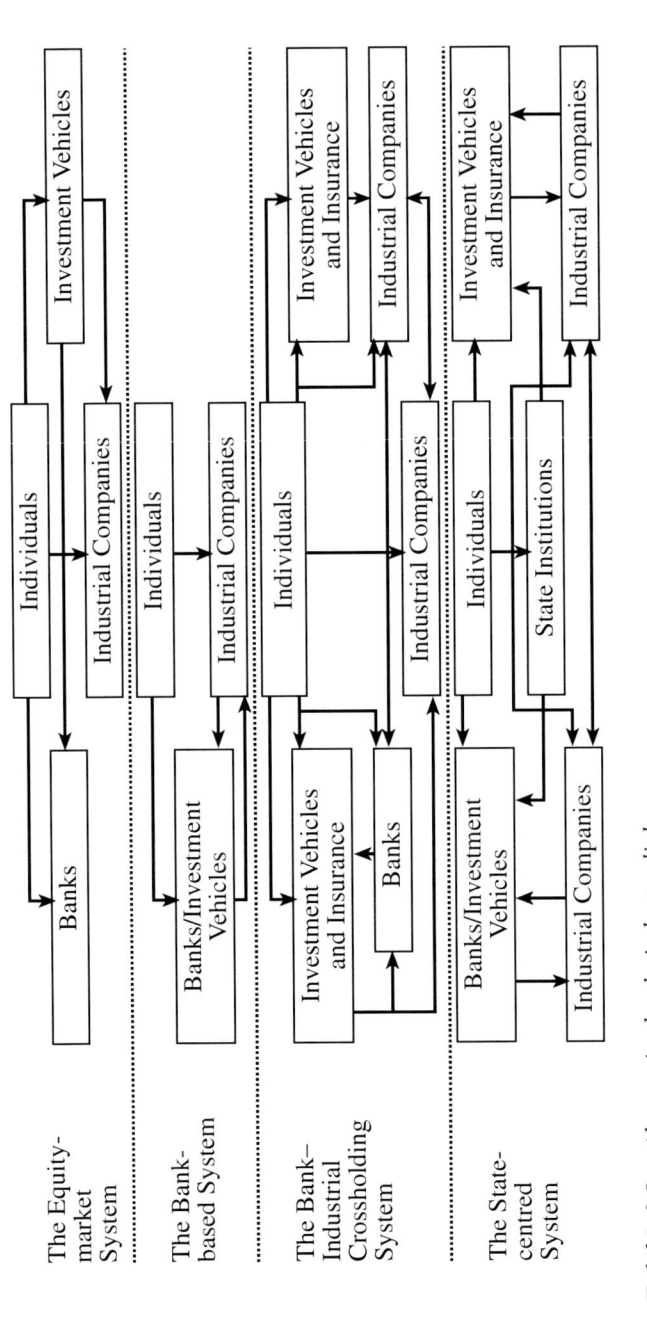

*Exhibit 9.8 Alternative bank–industry linkages*

to advising and financing bids or defensive restructurings. The government's role is normally arm's length in nature, with a focus on setting ground rules that are considered to be in the public interest. Relations between government, banks and industry are sometimes antagonistic. Such systems depend heavily on efficient conflict-resolution mechanisms.
- The second, bank-based approach centres on close bank–industry relationships, with corporate financing needs met mainly by retained earnings and bank financing. The role of banks carries well beyond credit extension and monitoring to share ownership, share voting and board memberships in such 'Germanic' systems. Capital allocation, management changes, and restructuring of enterprises is the job of non-executive supervisory boards on the basis of largely private information, and unwanted takeovers are rare. M&A activity tends to be undertaken by relationship universal banks. Capital markets tend to be relatively poorly developed with respect to both corporate debt and equity, and there is usually not much of an organized venture capital market. The role of the state in the affairs of banks and corporations may well be arm's length in nature, although perhaps combined with some public sector shareholdings.
- Third, in the so-called 'crossholding approach', interfirm boundaries are blurred through equity cross-links and long-term supplier–customer relationships. Banks may play a central role in equity crossholding structures – as in Japan's *keiretsu* networks – and provide guidance and coordination as well as financing. There may be strong formal and informal links to government on the part of both the financial and industrial sectors of the economy. Restructuring tends to be done on the basis of private information by drawing on these business–banking–government ties, and a contestable market for corporate control tends to be virtually non-existent.
- The state-centred approach – perhaps best typified in the French tradition – involves a strong role on the part of government through national ownership or control of major universal banks and corporations, as well as government-controlled central savings institutions. Banks may hold significant stakes in industrial firms and form an important conduit for state influence of industry. Financing of enterprises tends to involve a mixture of bank credits and capital market issues, often taken up by state-influenced financial institutions. Additional channels of government influence may include the appointment of the heads of state-owned companies and banks, with strong personal and educational ties within the business and government elite.

These four stylized bank–industry–government linkages make themselves felt in the operation of universal banks in various ways. The value of any bank shareholdings in industrial firms is embedded in the value of the bank. The combined value of the bank itself and its industrial shareholdings, as reflected in its market capitalization, may be larger or smaller than the sum of their stand-alone values. For example, firms in which a bank has significant financial stakes, as well as a direct governance role, may be expected to conduct most or all significant commercial and investment banking activities with that institution, thus raising the value of the bank. On the other hand, if such 'tied' sourcing of financial services raises the cost of capital of client corporations, this will in turn be reflected in the value of bank's own shareholdings, and the reverse if such ties lower client firms' cost of capital. Moreover, permanent bank shareholdings may stunt the development of a contestable market for corporate control, thereby impeding corporate restructuring and depressing share prices which in turn are reflected in the value of the bank to its shareholders. Banks may also be induced to lend to affiliated corporations under credit conditions that would be rejected by unaffiliated lenders, and possibly encounter other conflicts of interest that may ultimately make it more difficult to maximize shareholder value.

**Franchise Value**

The foregoing considerations should, in combination, explain a significant part of any difference between the adjusted book value of equity and the market value of equity of a universal bank. But even after all such factors have been taken into account and priced out, there may still be a material difference between the resulting 'constructed' value of equity and the banks' market value (see Exhibit 9.2). The latter represents the market's assessment of the present value of the risk-adjusted future net earnings stream, capturing all known or suspected business opportunities, costs and risks facing the institution. The residual can be considered the 'franchise' value of the bank. Much of it is associated with reputation and brand value. Franchise value may be highly positive, as in the case of Coca-Cola for example, or it could be significantly negative, with the firm's stock trading well below its constructed value or even its adjusted book value – for example, if there are large prospective losses embedded in the bank's internal or external portfolio of activities.

Demsetz et al. (1996) argue that the franchise value of banks also serves to inhibit extraordinary risk taking – they find substantial evidence that the higher a bank's franchise value, the more prudent management tends to be. This suggests that large universal banks with high franchise values should serve shareholder interests (as well as the interests of the regulators) by means of appropriate risk management as opposed to banks with little to lose.

## 4 FROM MARKET VALUE OF EQUITY TO POTENTIAL VALUE OF EQUITY

The market capitalization of a universal bank is what it is, a product of a broad spectrum of quantifiable and not-so-quantifiable factors such as those discussed in the previous section. Looking ahead, managing for shareholder value means managing for return on investment, in effect maximizing the 'potential value equity' (PVE) that the organization may be capable of achieving. In the merger market this would be reflected in the 'control premium' that may appear between the bank's market capitalization and what someone else in a position to act thinks the bank is worth.

**The Chase is Dead. Long Live the Chase**

Take the case of Chase Manhattan. The bank had suffered for years from a reputation for underperformance and mediocrity, despite some improvement in its results, better strategic focus, improved efficiency levels and a cleaned-up balance sheet. In January 1995, Chase's stock price was $34, with a return on assets a bit under 1 per cent, a return on equity of about 15 per cent, a price-to-book ratio of about 1.2 and a price to earnings multiple of 7.0. Exhibit 9.9 shows Chase's stock price performance relative to the S&P 500 and the S&P Money Center Banks during 1991–94.

In April 1995, investment manager Michael Price, Chairman of Mutual Series Fund, Inc., announced that funds under his management had purchased 6.1 per cent of Chase's stock, and that he believed the Chase board should take steps to realize the inherent values in its businesses in a manner designed to maximize shareholder value. At the bank's subsequent annual meeting, Price aggressively challenged the bank's management efforts: 'Dramatic change is required. It is clear that the sale of the bank is superior to the company's current strategy . . . unlock the value, or let someone else do it for you'.[11] Chase's Chairman, Thomas Labreque, responded that he had no intention of selling or breaking up the bank. By mid-June 1995 the Mutual Series Fund and other institutional investors, convinced that Chase stock was undervalued, were thought to have accumulated approximately 30 per cent of the bank's outstanding shares and the stock price had climbed to about $47 per share. Labreque announced that the bank was continuing its efforts to refocus the bank's businesses and to reduce costs.

During June and July of 1995, Chase and BankAmerica talked seriously

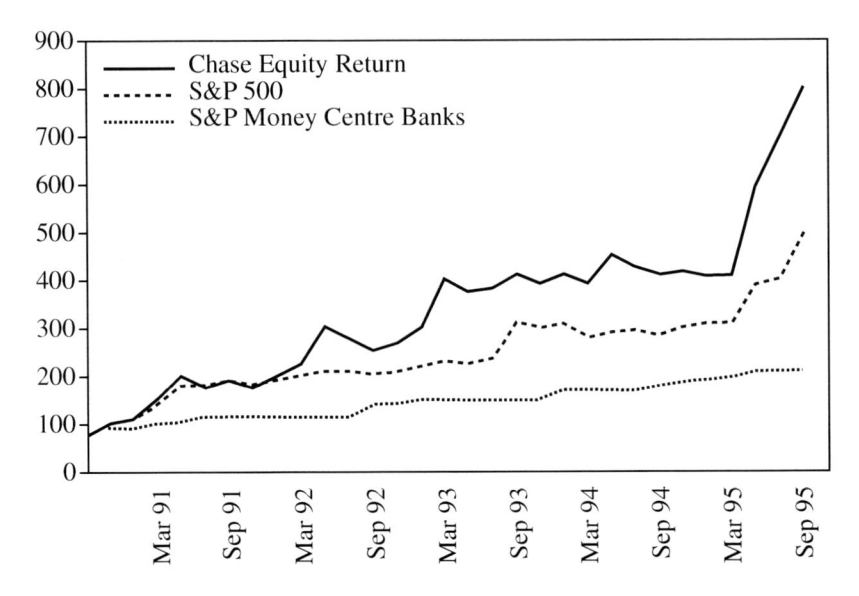

*Exhibit 9.9  Comparative return analysis: Chase Manhattan Bank, 1991–1995*

about a merger in which the BankAmerica name would be retained. Then BankAmerica suddenly backed out for reasons that were not totally clear to outsiders at the time.[12] Chemical Bank followed quickly with a proposal for a 'merger of equals'. According to Chemical's chairman, Walter Shipley, 'This combined company has the capacity to perform at benchmark standards. And when we say benchmark standards, we mean the best in the industry.'[13] Labreque agreed, and the negotiations were completed on 28 August 1995. Chemical would offer to exchange 1.04 shares of its stock for every Chase share outstanding, an offer reflecting a 7 per cent premium over the closing price of Chase shares on the day before the announcement.

The combined bank retaining the Chase name thus became the largest bank in the United States and 13th largest in the world in terms of assets. The new Chase also became the largest US corporate lending bank, one of the largest credit card lenders, and the largest player in trust, custody and mortgage servicing. Shipley became chief executive, and Labreque became president. Substantial cost-reduction efforts were quickly launched (including large-scale layoffs and branch closures) aimed at reducing the combined overhead of the two banks within three years by 16 per cent. In the month following the announcement of the merger, Chemical Bank's stock rose 12 per cent.

Labreque denied that shareholder pressure had anything to do with the merger. Michael Price asserted that he had not played a major role, but was happy to have been in the 'right place at the right time'. Nevertheless, adjusting for the exchange offer and the post-merger run-up in Chemical's share price, Chase shares more than doubled their value in a little over six months based on the market's assessment of the potential value embedded in the merger. What was the source of the added value?

**Realizing the Potential Value of Equity**

Clearly, merger transactions in contestable markets for corporate control are – as in the case of Chase Manhattan – aimed at unlocking shareholder value. The intent is to optimize the building-blocks that make up potential value of equity as depicted in Exhibit 9.2 – realizable economies of scale, economies of scope, X-efficiency, market power and too-big-to-fail (TBTF) benefits, while minimizing value losses from any diseconomies that may exist as well as avoiding to the extent possible conflict-of-interest problems and any conglomerate discount. Evidently the market agreed in this case, amply rewarding shareholders of both banks, especially those of the old Chase.

At least in the United States, bank acquisitions have occurred at price-to-book-value ratios of about 2.0, sometimes as high as 3.0 or even more. In eight of the eleven years in a recent study (Smith and Walter, 1996), the average price-to-book ratio for the US banking industry acquisitions was below 2.0, averaging 1.5 and ranging from 1.1 in 1990 to 1.8 in 1985. In two years, the price-to-book ratio exceeded 2.0 – in 1986 it was 2.8 and in 1993 in was 3.2. These values presumably reflect the opportunity for the acquired institutions to be managed differently and to realize the incremental value needed to reimburse the shareholders of the acquiring institutions for the willingness to pay the premium in the first place. If in fact the value-capture potential for universal banks exceeds that for US-type separated commercial banks, this should be reflected in higher merger premiums in banking environments outside the United States.

Pressure for shareholder value optimization may not, of course, be triggered by an active and contestable market for corporate control, but it probably helps. Comparing cost, efficiency and profitability measures across various national environments that are characterized by very different investor expectations and activism suggests that external pressure is conducive to realizing the potential value of shareholder equity in banking. In terms of Exhibit 9.2 and the empirical evidence available so far, the management lessons for universal banks appear to include the following:

- Don't expect too much from economies of scale.
- Don't expect too much from *supply-side* economies of scope, and be prepared to deal with any diseconomies that may arise.
- Exploit *demand-side* economies of scope where cross-selling makes sense, most likely with retail, private and middle-market corporate clients.
- Optimize X-efficiencies through effective use of technology, reductions in the capital intensity of financial services provided, reductions in the workforce, and other available operating economies.
- Seek out imperfect markets that demonstrate relatively low price elasticity of demand, ranging from private banking services, equity transactions that exploit 'fault lines' across capital markets, and leading-edge emerging-market transactions that have not as yet been commoditized, to dominant 'fortress' market-share positions in particular national or regional markets, with particular client segments, or in particular product lines. The half-lives of market imperfections in banking differ enormously, and require careful calibration of delivery systems ranging from massive investments in infrastructure to small, light, entrepreneurial and opportunistic SWATs (Special Weapons Action Team). The key managerial challenge is to accommodate a broad array of these activities under the same roof.
- Specialize operations using professionals who are themselves specialists.
- Where possible, make the political case for backstops such as underpriced deposit insurance and TBTF support. Although this is a matter of public policy, shareholders clearly benefit from implicit subsidies that don't come with too many conditions attached.
- Pay careful attention to limiting conflicts of interest in organizational design, incentive systems, application and maintenance of Chinese walls, and managerial decisions that err on the side of caution where potential conflicts arise.
- Minimize the conglomerate discount by divesting peripheral non-financial shareholdings and non-core businesses, leaving diversification up to the shareholder. The gain in market value may well outweigh any losses from reduced scope economies and earnings diversification. Pursuing this argument to its logical conclusion, of course, challenges the basic premise of universal banking as a structural form.

- Get rid of share-voting restrictions and open up shareholdings to market forces.
- Pay careful attention to the residual 'franchise' value of the bank by avoiding professional conduct lapses that lead to an erosion of the bank's reputation, uncontrolled trading losses, or in extreme cases criminal charges against the institution. It is never a good idea to cut corners on compliance or building an affirmative 'culture' which employees understand and value as much as the shareholders.

Exhibit 9.2 shows some of these as a 'recapture' of shareholder-value losses in universal banks associated with diseconomies of scale and scope, conglomerate discount not offset by the benefits of a universal structure, and potential conflict of interest and reputational losses. The balance of any further potential gains involves ramping up key elements of the production function of the bank, capitalizing on market opportunities, and an intense focus on maximizing franchise value and reputation.

If a strategic direction taken by the management of a universal bank does not exploit every source of potential value for shareholders, then what is the purpose? Avoiding an acquisition attempt from a better-managed suitor who will pay a premium price, as in the case of Chase Manhattan, does not seem as unacceptable today as it may have been in the past. In a world of more open and efficient markets for shares in financial institutions, shareholders increasingly tend to have the final say about the future of their enterprises.

# NOTES

* Based on Ingo Walter, 'Universal banking: a shareholder value perspective', *European Management Journal*, August 1997. Reprinted in *Finanzmarkt und Portfolio Management* (Switzerland), No. 1, 1997; and in *Financial Markets, Institutions and Instruments*, Vol. 7, No. 5, 1997.
1. For a detailed discussion, see Saunders and Walter (1994).
2. In this context, Switzerland presents an interesting case study, with the three major universal banks operating under a single set of domestic regulatory parameters having adopted rather different structural forms in the past but with more recent signs of substantial convergence.
3. This market profile can be depicted as covering the full state-space of the domestic arena of the Client–Arena–Product (C–A–P) taxonomy presented in Walter (1988) and using that as a platform to target a narrower range of (usually wholesale) financial services and clients in offshore and national markets abroad.
4. The Herfindahl–Hirshman index is the sum of the squared market shares ($H = 3s^2$), where $0 < H < 10,000$ and market shares are measured, for example, by deposits, by assets, or by capital. H rises as the number of competitors declines and as market-share concentration rises among the largest firms among a given number of competitors.
5. Much the same conclusions as these have been reached by Boyd et al. (1990) using a similar methodological approach.

6. That is, only the financial firms in existence for the full 1984–88 period are considered.
7. For a detailed discussion, see Saunders and Walter (1994), ch. 6.
8. A recent example is the 1995 underwriting of a secondary equity issue of the Hafnia Insurance Group by Den Danske Bank, distributed heavily to retail investors, with proceeds allegedly used to pay down bank loans even as Hafnia slid into bankruptcy. This case is now before the courts. See Smith and Walter (1997b).
9. For a comprehensive catalogue of potential conflicts of interest, see Gnehm and Thalmann (1989).
10. A detailed discussion is contained in Smith and Walter (1997a), ch. 8.
11. *The Wall Street Journal*, 19 May 1995.
12. *Institutional Investor*, November 1995.
13. *ABC Evening News,* 28 August 1995.

# REFERENCES

Akhavein, Jalal D., Allen N. Berger and David B. Humphrey (1996), 'The effects of megamergers on efficiency and prices: evidence from a bank profit function', Paper presented at a Conference on Mergers of Financial Institutions, New York University Salomon Center, 11 October.

Benston, George (1994), 'Universal banking', *Journal of Economic Perspectives*, **8**(3), Summer.

Benston, George, G. Hanweck and D. Humphrey (1982), 'Scale economies in banking', *Journal of Money, Credit and Banking*, **14**.

Berger, Allen N., Diana Hancock and David B. Humphrey (1993a), 'Bank efficiency derived from the profit function', *Journal of Banking and Finance*, April.

Berger, Allen N., G. Hanweck and D. Humphrey (1987), 'Competitive viability in banking', *Journal of Monetary Economics*, **20**.

Berger, Allen N., William C. Hunter and Stephen J. Timme (1993b), 'The efficiency of financial institutions: a review of research past, present and future', *Journal of Banking and Finance*, April.

Berger, Philip G. and Eli Ofek (1995), 'Diversification's effect on firm value', *Journal of Financial Economics*, **37**.

Clark, Jeffrey A. (1988), 'Economies of scale and scope at depository financial institutions: a review of the literature', *Federal Reserve Board of Kansas City Review*, October.

Demsetz, Rebecca S., Marc R. Saidenberg and Philip E. Strahan (1996), 'Banks with something to lose: the disciplinary role of franchise value', *Federal Reserve Bank of New York Policy Review*, October.

Economides, Nicholas (1995), 'Network economics with application to finance', *Financial Markets, Institutions and Instruments*, **2**(5).

Fields, Joseph A. and Neil B. Murphy (1989), 'An analysis of efficiency in the delivery of financial services: the case of life insurance agencies', *Journal of Financial Services Research*, **2**.

Gilligan, Thomas and Michael Smirlock (1984), 'An empirical study of joint production and scale economies in commercial banking', *Journal of Banking and Finance*, **8**.

Gilligan, Thomas, Michael Smirlock and William Marshall (1984), 'Scale and scope economies in the multi-product banking firm', *Journal of Monetary Economics*, **13**.

Gnehm, A. and C. Thalmann (1989), 'Conflicts of interest in financial operations: problems of regulation in the national and international context', Working Paper, Swiss Bank Corporation, Basle.

Goldstein, Steven, James McNulty and James Verbrugge (1987), 'Scale economies in the savings and loan industry before diversification', *Journal of Economics and Business*.

Hawawini, Gabriel and Itzhak Swary (1990), *Mergers and Acquisitions in the U.S. Banking Industry*, Amsterdam: North-Holland.

John, Jose and Eli Ofek (1994), 'Asset sales and increase in ficus', *Journal of Financial Economics*, **37**.

Kellner, S. and G. Frank Mathewson (1983), 'Entry, size distribution, scale and scope economies in the life insurance industry', *Journal of Business*.

Kim, H. Youn (1986), 'Economies of scale and scope in multiproduct financial institutions', *Journal of Money, Credit, and Banking*, **18**.

Kolari, James and Ashghar Zardkoohi (1987), *Bank Cost Structure and Performance*, Lexington, MA: Heath Lexington.

Lawrence, Colin (1989), 'Banking costs, generalized functional forms, and estimation of economies of scale and scope', *Journal of Money, Credit, and Banking*, **21**(3).

Mester, Loretta (1987), 'A multiproduct cost study of savings and loans', *Journal of Finance*, **42**.

Mester, Loretta (1990), 'Traditional and nontraditional banking: an information theoretic approach', Federal Reserve Board Working Paper, No. 90-3, February.

Murray, John D. and Robert S. White (1983), 'Economies of scale and economies of scope in multiproduct financial institutions', *Journal of Finance*, June.

Noulas, Athanasios G., Subhash C. Ray and Stephen M. Miller (1990), 'Returns to scale and input substitution for large U.S. banks', *Journal of Money, Credit, and Banking*, **22**.

Saunders, Anthony (1996), *Financial Institutions Management*, 2nd edn, Burr Ridge, IL: Irwin.

Saunders, Anthony and Ingo Walter (1994), *Universal Banking in the United States*, New York: Oxford University Press.

Saunders, Anthony and Ingo Walter (eds), (1996) *Universal Banking: Financial System Design Reconsidered*, Burr Ridge, IL: Irwin.

Shaffer, Sherrill (1988), 'A restricted cost study of 100 large banks', Federal Reserve Bank of New York Working Paper.

Siems, Thomas F. (1996), 'Bank mergers and shareholder value: evidence from 1995's megamerger deals', *Federal Reserve Bank of Dallas Financial Industry Studies*, August.

Smith, Roy C. and Ingo Walter (1996), 'Global patterns of mergers and acquisitions in the financial services industry', Paper presented at a Conference on Mergers of Financial Institutions, New York University Salomon Center, 11 October.

Smith, Roy C. and Ingo Walter (1997a), *Global Banking*, New York: Oxford University Press.

Smith, Roy C. and Ingo Walter (1997b), *Street Smarts: Leadership and Shareholder Value in the Securities Industry*, Boston, MA: Harvard Business School Press.

Steinherr, Alfred (1996), 'Performance of universal banks: review and appraisal', in Saunders and Walter (eds).

Tschoegl, Adrian E. (1983), 'Size, growth and transnationality among the world's largest banks', *Journal of Business*, **56**(2).

Walter, Ingo (ed.) (1985), *Deregulating Wall Street*, New York: John Wiley.

Walter, Ingo (1988), *Global Competition in Financial Services*, Cambridge, MA: Ballinger–Harper & Row.
Walter, Ingo (1993), *The Battle of the Systems: Control of Enterprises in the Global Economy*, Kiel: Kieler Studien Nr. 122, Institut für Weltwirtschaft.
Yoshioka, Kanji and Takanobu Nakajima (1987), 'Economies of scale in Japan's banking industry', *Bank of Japan Monetary and Economic Studies*, September.

# 10. Foreign exchange trading activities of international banks

### Jürgen Eichberger and Joachim Keller*

## 1 INTRODUCTION

After the Bretton Woods system of fixed exchange rates was abandoned in 1973, foreign exchange trading increased exponentially. Two trends characterized the developments. On the one hand, a rapid increase in the total number of transactions in the foreign exchange market was observed. Over the past ten years, turnover in foreign exchange markets has nearly tripled (see Table 10.1). On the other hand, a major change in nature of the instruments traded took place. Trade in forward contracts and currency swaps increased more than proportionally. In 1989, forwards and swaps were roughly 40 per cent of total foreign exchange transactions. A decade later, these transactions account for 60 per cent of foreign exchange turnover.[1] Although spot transactions, that is, exchanges of currencies which have to be settled within two days, have declined as a proportion of total transactions, they are still the main type of transactions (more than 70 per cent) for currency pairs which do not involve the US dollar (BIS, 1999, p. 13). International asset management and trade in derivatives, however, gained growing importance in the foreign exchange market.

Transactions in the foreign exchange market typically consist of bilateral trade agreements between counterparties at preannounced prices. One party is usually a professional dealer or market maker[2] who quotes bid and ask prices for a specific foreign currency contract. The other side of the bargain may be a trader with an immediate need for exchange, a liquidity trader, or another dealer who wants to close an open position from a previous trade.

Most foreign exchange trading involves only a small number of currencies (US dollar, German mark, Japanese yen) and takes place in a few financial centres[3] (London, New York, Tokyo, Singapore). It is carried out by dealers working for international banks and international funds with representation in these trading centres. Some banks run their own foreign exchange trading departments, while others work through subsidiaries or agencies. A recent survey of foreign exchange dealers in the United States

*Table 10.1  Foreign exchange market turnover*

|                          | 1989 | 1992 | 1995  | 1998  |
|--------------------------|------|------|-------|-------|
| Total turnover           | 590  | 820  | 1,190 | 1,500 |
| Spot transactions (%)    | 59   | 48   | 43    | 40    |
| Forwards and swaps (%)   | 41   | 52   | 57    | 60    |

*Note:* Daily averages in billions of US dollars (April).

*Source:* BIS (1999), Table A-1.

*Table 10.2  Foreign exchange dealers in the United States*

| Dealers working for a bank | | | |
|---|---|---|---|
| With headquarters in | % | With daily turnover of (US$m) | % |
| United States | 47 | below 100 | 21 |
| Europe | 40 | 100–999 | 48 |
| Other | 13 | over 1000 | 31 |

*Source:* Cheung and Chinn (1999a), Figures 1.c, 1.d.

(Cheung and Chinn, 1999a) provides further information on the characteristics of foreign exchange dealers (see Table 10.2).

In this study, more than 50 per cent of all responding dealers belonged to a bank with headquarters in a foreign country and more than 30 per cent were banks with turnover of more than one billion US dollars. A similar study of foreign exchange dealers in Germany by Menkhoff (1997) finds approximately 70 per cent of foreign exchange dealers working for banks and 30 per cent for international funds.

An increasing proportion of foreign exchange trading, in particular spot trading, is conducted through automated order-matching systems (BIS, 1999, p. 15). Cheung and Chinn (1999b, Table 1) report that, on average, electronic brokers were involved in 47 per cent of the respondents' transactions, and only 17 per cent worked through traditional brokers. The remaining transactions took place between banks directly.

Foreign exchange trading plays a major role in international bank business. Approximately 64 per cent of the reviewed dealers' trade concerned interbank business and only 36 per cent was related directly to customer business (Cheung and Chinn, 1999a). Thus, the influence of international banks on foreign exchange trading appears to have grown over recent decades.

Dealers, as market makers in the foreign exchange market, face a difficult problem. They must quote bid and ask prices for foreign exchange contracts without knowing to what extent their offer will be taken up by traders in the market. In contrast to long-term investors, foreign exchange dealers usually enter open positions in foreign currency contracts which they need to close quickly. Profitability of their trade depends on the precision of their predictions of the movements of exchange rates.

Reliable exchange rate predictions and good trading strategies are more important for foreign exchange dealers than for investors in stocks and fixed-interest securities. Drawing on experiences in other asset markets, foreign exchange dealers have applied methods of security analysis to their business. *Security analysis* has influenced asset management for many decades. We can distinguish between *technical analysis*, which tries to extract information about current and future prices from time series of past prices, and *fundamental analysis*, which bases its predictions on forecasts of variables which are known to influence asset prices.

At the same time as such techniques were increasingly applied to foreign exchange trading in the wake of the transition to flexible exchange rates in the mid-1970s, security analysis was challenged by the *efficient markets hypothesis*. Markets are *informationally efficient* if all available systematic information about a market is already embodied in the market price. The *weak form* considers only information from the past, while the *semi-strong form* also includes current information which is known to influence prices. The efficient markets hypothesis in its weak form negates the value of gleaning information from past prices, which is the backbone of technical analysis. In its semi-strong form the efficient markets hypothesis is inconsistent with fundamental analysis.

The argument for informationally efficient markets rests on an informal appeal to arbitrage possibilities. If dealers could extract information from past prices, they would be able to make unlimited profits from this information. In a formal model, Grossmann and Stiglitz (1980) show that this argument assumes the absence of information acquisition costs. If costs are required in order to obtain and process information, then markets cannot be informationally efficient. Although information costs cannot be ignored in general, the efficient markets hypothesis has been widely accepted in the academic profession, at least as a benchmark case.

It seems ironic that precisely the market makers who are to establish these informationally efficient prices should be in such need of good predictions of these same prices. The academic controversy has led to an acrimonious debate about the 'irrationality' of all security analysis. In his well-known book *A Random Walk Down Wall Street*, Malkiel (1990, p. 254) writes:

> Technical strategies are usually amusing, often comforting, but of no real value. We love to pick on it. Our bullying tactics are prompted by two considerations: (1) The method is patently false; and (2) it's easy to pick on. And while it may seem a bit unfair to pick on such sorry targets, just remember: it's your money we are trying to save.

Such strong claims about the worthlessness of security analysis stand in stark contrast to the widespread practice of technical and fundamental analysis.

## 2  SECURITY ANALYSIS TECHNIQUES

Trading practices in the foreign exchange market are similar to those in other asset markets. Based on forecasting techniques, traders decide to enter or leave the market once the actual exchange rate crosses certain critical threshold levels. Dealers make buying offers when the exchange rate[4] falls to a level from which they expect the exchange rate to rise and offer to sell the currency when the exchange rate rises to a level where it is expected to fall. To determine such critical values, traders use information from past data of the exchange rate process and information about other variables which are thought to influence the exchange rate.

By analogy with security analysis in stock markets, methods to analyse the exchange rate process fall into two groups. *Fundamentalists* base their predictions of future exchange rate movements on their predictions of 'fundamental' variables. In stock market analysis, fundamental analysis tries to predict the future earning potential of the firms whose stock is considered. For the foreign exchange market, macroeconomic variables which are assumed to determine the exchange rate are the 'fundamentals'. Relative purchasing power of the currencies and interest rate differentials are the most commonly used fundamental variables. The former rests on the presumption that, at least in the long run, the purchasing power of a currency is a fundamental determinant of its value. Interest rate differentials between countries are considered as the main factor determining capital flows between countries. Fundamental analysts use information about macroeconomic and monetary policy variables in order to predict price levels and interest differentials. In contrast to stock market analysts, who deal with data about firm and industry earnings, exchange rate analysts have to rely on macroeconomic models of the foreign exchange market.

The second group of analysts, *technical traders*, study data on past exchange rate movements. Their methods range from sophisticated econometric time-series models to simple rules about how to find patterns in the data which, they expect, will be repeated in the future. This search for patterns has led to these traders also being called *chartists*. A few typical techniques of technical analysis are considered in the following subsection.

**Technical Analysis**

Technical analysis is a combination of prediction and decision rules. In a large number of books and manuals various trading rules based on the analysis of past prices have been suggested. These manuals advise traders on how to construct indicators and how to reach good buying and selling decisions. Many variations of the basic methods exist, so this chapter considers only a few typical methods.

All trading rules extract trends from historic price data which may then allow the analyst to predict future price movements. Moreover, they usually also suggest when to buy and when to sell the asset. Some of these techniques use diagrams, or charts, for the analysis, others compute *moving averages* and similar indicators. We usually distinguish between *trend recognition* and *pattern recognition* methods which are based on explicit analysis of past exchange rate movements and *momentum rules* which suggest some previous value as a signal for buying and selling decisions.

**Trend recognition**
Trend recognition methods determine price ranges. Usually, daily maximal and minimal values of the exchange rate are recorded, and critical levels which have not been exceeded or undercut for some while are identified. Drawing lines connecting such critical values, we can obtain a band to which, at least in the short run, exchange rate movements should be confined. Such critical lines are often supplied by financial analysts employed by banks or other institutions. Figure 10.1 gives an example of such a chart. Vertical lines mark the range of exchange rate variation within a period, where a period may be an hour, a day, or even a longer period. The critical lines, called *resistance* or *support* lines, respectively, specify a corridor of most likely evolution of the exchange rate. If the exchange rate transgresses the boundaries of these trend lines, this will be interpreted as a buying or selling signal. Suppose, for example, that the exchange rate (domestic currency/foreign currency) crosses the resistance line from below; this is interpreted as a signal to buy foreign exchange. Similarly, a deviation below the support line is taken as a recommendation to sell. As a typical example, Curcio et al. (1997) study hourly exchange rate movements using resistance and support lines provided online by Reuters.

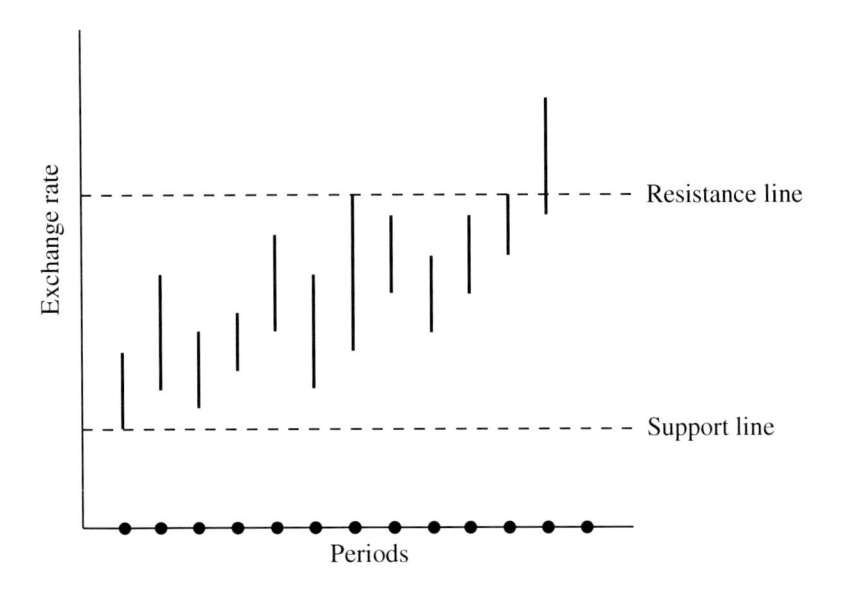

*Figure 10.1  Pole chart*

**Moving averages**
Another method is based on moving averages. For this purpose, moving averages of a particular length, for example, 60 days, 90 days, 200 days, are computed. The moving average is supposed to identify a trend which is purged of short-term erratic movements. Once again, the moving average is compared with the actual exchange rate movements on a chart. A change in the market position is due whenever the actual exchange rate crosses the moving average. If, for example, the exchange rate breaks through the moving average curve from below (see Figure 10.2), then a purchase of the currency in question is recommended; a sale is indicated as soon as the actual exchange rate falls below the moving average curve. Traders do not use such critical values mechanically. In order to avoid too frequent changes in position, the rule may be modified so as to change a position only if the actual exchange rate falls below (or rises above) the moving average by a certain margin.

**Pattern recognition**
Pattern recognition methods seek to identify typical patterns of exchange rate movements from past data. Patterns which point to a trend reversal are distinguished from other patterns which suggest a trend reinforcement. When a particular pattern has been established, buying or selling recommendations can be deduced.

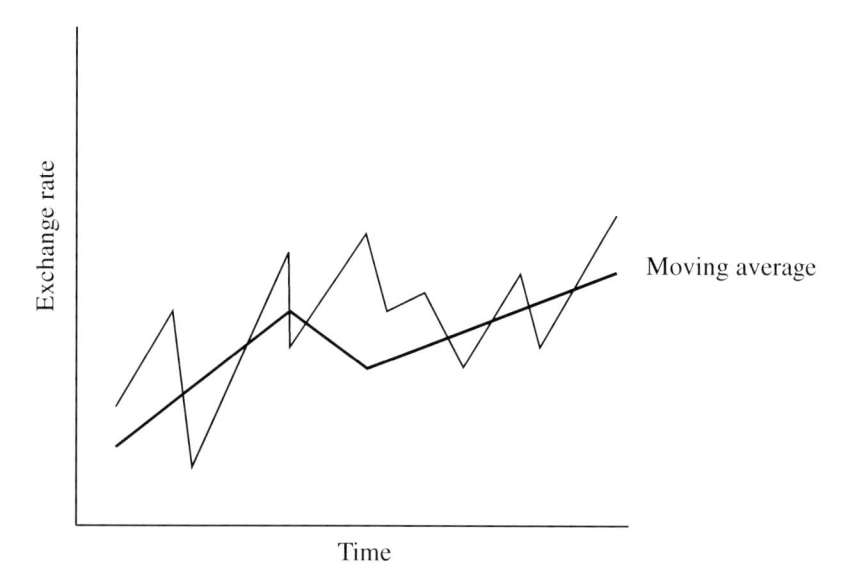

*Figure 10.2  Moving average*

From eight manuals of technical analysis, Chang and Osler (1999) extract a typical example of a reversal pattern. The *head-and-shoulders* pattern tries to find local peaks (or, *mutatis mutandis*, troughs). To this end, the time series of exchange rate data are scanned for a succession of three peaks: a high middle peak, the 'head', and a lower peak on either side, the 'shoulders'. Drawing a line through the troughs on both sides of the central peak, the 'neckline' completes the pattern. Figure 10.3 shows a typical head-and-shoulders pattern. A peak has to be a certain number of percentage points higher than the preceding trough. The number of head-and-shoulders patterns which are identified in a given time series depends, therefore, on the chosen scale for the height of a peak.

Trading strategies based on the head-and-shoulders pattern recommend entering a position after the exchange rate penetrates the neckline. In Figure 10.3, at the time when the exchange rate falls below the neckline after passing the right shoulder, the trader should sell foreign exchange.

**Momentum rules**
Momentum rules compare the actual exchange rate with a reference level of the exchange rate in a previous period, for example 1, 5 or 10 days, earlier. If the actual rate rises above the reference value by a predetermined margin, this is interpreted as a signal to buy. On the other hand, if it falls below the reference value, selling is suggested. The greater the margin by

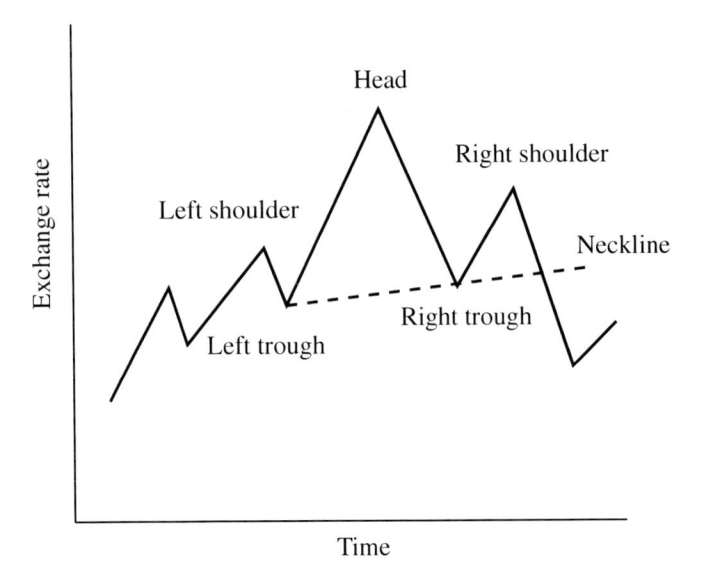

*Figure 10.3  Head-and-shoulders pattern*

which the actual exchange rate exceeds the reference rate, the higher the momentum. There are many similar rules, each distinguished by a different reference rate. One rule, for example, compares the exchange rate with the previous maximum or minimum value over a predetermined period of 5 or 10 days.

**Selection of rules**
More recently, there have been attempts to select among the large number of technical rules in a systematic way. Allen and Karjalainen (1999) use genetic algorithms in order to choose among alternative trading rules. The programme starts with a basic set of trading rules which it combines according to a mechanism. Applying them to a time series of foreign exchange rates, the success of these rules according to a risk-return criterion is assessed, and poorly performing rules are eliminated. The aim is to select successful rules for use in actual trading.

**Fundamental Analysis**

Fundamental analysis seeks to predict asset prices by studying the factors influencing their fundamental value. In the stock market, the appropriately discounted cash flow which a stock generates determines its value.

Fundamental analysts focus therefore on the earning capacities and risk characteristics of firms whose stock price they want to predict.

For exchange rates, in practice, fundamental analysis is based on macroeconomic data, including inflation rates, unemployment rates, trade deficit data, and monetary and fiscal policy indicators. The exact relationship between this information and the exchange rate is often unclear. Open economy macroeconomic models of the exchange rate may inspire the choice of indicators and the regular availability of these data may provide an additional reason for focusing on such variables. Although economics offers explicit formal models of the exchange rate, they seem rarely to be used in practice.

The two most common formal models are the *purchasing power parity* theory and the *interest parity* theory. Both rest on an arbitrage argument. Purchasing power parity (PPP) appeals to the law of one price, assuming that tradable goods and services in one economy are essentially the same as those in another. Hence, in the long run, the ratio of the price indices of these two economies should equal the exchange rate; otherwise profitable arbitrage should be possible. Interest parity theory postulates the equality of rates of return on international assets. According to uncovered interest parity theory, domestic investors who can earn the domestic interest rate on an investment in the home country must earn the same return from a foreign investment allowing for expected movements of the exchange rate. The return on the foreign investment equals the foreign interest rate plus the expected rate of change of the exchange rate. Interest parity therefore determines the expected rate of change of the exchange rate.

Economists readily admit that these theories need to be modified appropriately before they can be applied to actual data, since the theories ignore transaction costs in international trade and investment. Moreover, for PPP and uncovered interest parity to hold, decision makers have to be risk neutral (see Eichberger and Harper, 1997, ch. 1). Risk neutrality is a strong assumption and therefore casts doubt on the practical application of these two approaches.

Few economic theories, however, have been so extensively empirically tested. Despite such efforts a major controversy about the contribution of these theories to the explanation and prediction of exchange rate movements remains unresolved. A special issue of the *Economic Journal* (Vol. 109, November 1999) deals with 'Controversy: Exchange rates and fundamentals'. In the introductory article, Dixon (1999) acknowledges that 'the role of traditional macroeconomic variables in explaining exchange rate movements has been a hotly contested issue' (p. F652). In the same issue, Flood and Rose (1999) propose a model based on uncovered interest parity which seems to perform somewhat better. Yet, the contributions to this symposium fail to demonstrate convincingly that fundamental analysis can contribute more to explaining exchange rate movements than a random walk model, a suggestion put forward by Meese and Rogoff (1983).

## 3 IMPORTANCE OF TECHNICAL ANALYSIS

How widely used is security analysis, in particular technical analysis, by foreign exchange traders? From the late 1970s onwards, newspapers like *The Wall Street Journal* and *Euromoney* surveyed exchange rate forecasts issued by professional dealers. These surveys often included questions on the forecasting method. Hence, it became known that technical analysis was used by a large number of dealers. Based on a survey published in *Euromoney*, Frankel and Froot (1990) report, for example, that the proportion of traders applying technical analysis increased from 13 per cent in 1978 to almost 60 per cent in 1988.

The first systematic survey of trading practices was conducted by Taylor and Allen (1992) in 1988 in cooperation with the Bank of England. They undertook a questionnaire survey on the use of technical analysis by foreign exchange traders in the London market. Their main findings were:

- most dealers use fundamental and technical analysis simultaneously and
- technical analysis appears to dominate in short-run forecasting, while
- fundamental analysis was used for long-run forecasting.

More than 90 per cent of traders give technical analysis some weight. Moving averages and trend-following schemes, the most popular methods, were used by 64 per cent of the respondents. A large majority of traders obtained their information from online chartist computer services.

In 1992, Menkhoff (1997) conducted a similar study for Germany. He confirms the prevalence of technical analysis for short forecasting horizons. Although technical analysis is widely used in Germany, fundamental analysis is generally given a greater weight (44.9 compared to 37.2). From his more detailed questionnaire, Menkhoff (1997) tries to draw conclusions about dealers' motivations for using chartist methods. Dealers who preferred technical analysis tended to believe that 'psychology' was more important than fundamentals for predicting exchange rate movements. Hence, technical analysis may be considered as a strategy to stay in touch with market sentiment. From his observations Menkhoff (1997) conjectures that technical analysis may become a self-fulfilling prophecy.

In a recent survey of US foreign exchange traders, Cheung and Chinn (1999b) find that 30 per cent of the respondents to their questionnaire use predominantly chartist techniques, 25 per cent rely on fundamentals, 22 per cent act mainly on customer orders, and 21 per cent try to make profits in small increments by trading continuously ('jobbing'). This observation underlines the importance of technical trading but it also shows also the importance of customer orders and frequent speculative trading, for which no clear principle can be identified.

In contrast to other studies, Cheung and Chinn (1999b) investigate fundamentalists' behaviour in more detail. Asked how quickly they think traders adjust to new information about fundamental macroeconomic variables, they find an almost unanimous belief among dealers surveyed that such information is absorbed in less than a minute. On the other hand, a question about the relative importance of various macroeconomic variables shows a marked shift over time. While in 1992, 'trade deficit', 'interest rates' and 'unemployment' (in this order) were considered to be the most important fundamental macroeconomic variables, in 1997 this had changed to 'unemployment', 'interest rates' and 'inflation'. A direct question on the meaning of the PPP concept reveals that many dealers see it as 'purely academic jargon', and only 16 per cent know what the proposition actually means.

A third interesting aspect of the survey concerns the role of speculation. Nearly 75 per cent of the traders surveyed believe that excessive speculation is the main reason for exchange rates not reflecting the fundamental value of a currency. Speculation is seen as a source of high volatility but also of high liquidity. More than 60 per cent of these dealers believe that speculation moves exchange rates towards their fundamental value and improves market efficiency. Overall, speculation is viewed as a positive activity.

The picture which arises from this self-evaluation by dealers in the foreign exchange market is quite consistent. Fundamental values of exchange rates are difficult to determine. Hence, being pragmatic individuals, traders often use technical analysis while keeping an eye on the evolution of fundamental variables. Only if several methods give consistent buying or selling recommendations do traders act on them. Technical analysis is widely used, though often viewed as a second-best strategy, valuable in particular in the short run when speculation keeps the exchange rate away from its fundamental value.

## 4 PROFITABILITY OF TECHNICAL ANALYSIS

Given the scepticism of academic economists, empirical tests of the profitability of technical trading rules seem to be a sensible response. Since technical analysis was first developed to deal with financial assets other than exchange rates, tests were conducted initially on stock market data. As early as 1961, Alexander (1961) showed that, after accounting for transaction costs, no significantly higher returns could be obtained with technical trading rules. This became the dominant view despite the growing use of technical analysis by dealers and fund managers.

In the 1980s, a number of articles found profitable charting rules in a variety of asset markets (Lucac et al., 1988), in particular in futures markets (Cabral and Guimares, 1988; Taylor and Tari, 1989). A recent study by Mills (1997) tests a moving average and a trading range rule for the London Stock Exchange with daily data ranging from 1935 to 1994. Profitability of these rules can be established for the sample period and subsample periods before 1980. For the period from 1980 to 1994, however, profitability fails and a buy-and-hold strategy would have yielded a higher return.

For the foreign exchange market, profitability of technical trading rules was first established by Sweeny (1986), a result which was confirmed by Taylor (1992a and 1992b). More recently, Curcio et al. (1997) studied several technical trading rules in the foreign exchange market with hourly data. In contrast to previous studies, these authors imposed the condition that traders had to close their positions at the end of a trading day. They justified this constraint by the fact that, in surveys, traders claimed to use technical analysis mainly for short horizons. Taking into account transaction costs, Curcio et al. (1997) find no evidence for the profitability of the rules which they investigated. Chang and Osler (1999) test the head-and-shoulders pattern for foreign exchange trading with daily data from 1973 to 1994. The authors take great care in following the instructions of popular trader manuals for correctly identifying buying and selling signals. They find that the head-and-shoulders pattern is not profitable for the UK pound, the Swiss franc, the French franc and the Canadian dollar, but is profitable for the German mark and the Japanese yen. Trading in all these currencies yielded a significant net profit, however, and Chang and Osler (1999) conclude that profitability of this rule has to be accepted. This brief survey of empirical tests suffices to show that evidence for profitability of technical trading rules is mixed.

A technical trading rule is usually considered profitable if a trader using this rule obtains a return which exceeds the return from buying the currency and holding it at the going interest rate by more than the transaction costs. Therefore, most studies compare the excess return of the trading strategy over the return of a buy-and-hold strategy. Simple and straightforward as this procedure may appear, there are, however, major differences in the way profitability is measured in the literature. Chang and Osler (1999), for example, measure profitability 'as the cumulative percent change in the exchange rate between entry and exit, adjusting the sign to reflect whether the simulated speculator was long or short' (p. 642). No comparison is made to a return from some reference activity. In contrast, Curcio et al. (1997) compare the mean return from the trading rule with the mean exchange rate return over the respective period. There are no interest differentials considered but, within the context of hourly trading, their approach is equivalent to a comparison with a buy-and-hold strategy.

Even if we can find agreement on the appropriate concept of profitability a number of issues which influence the result of the tests remain unresolved.

1. *Distributional assumptions*   In order to perform statistical significance tests, it is necessary to know the probability distribution of the return rates generated by the trading strategies. Since the distribution from which these return rates are drawn is unknown, different assumptions can be found in this literature. Curcio et al. (1997) simply assume a normal distribution for all return rates and use a $t$-statistic to test for a null hypothesis. Other authors, for example, Cornell and Dietrich (1978) and Logue et al. (1978), argue that returns from technical analysis follow a stable Pareto distribution. With a Pareto distribution, it would be harder to reject a null hypothesis of zero profitability of technical trading strategies. Given ignorance of the underlying probability distribution, bootstrap methods seem most appropriate, a technique used, for example, by Chang and Osler (1999) and Mills (1997).

2. *When to close an open position?*   An important issue concerns the length of period for which traders can hold open positions. Chang and Osler (1999) report average holding periods of up to 22 days. Neely (1997) applied one rule to daily data and made a 30 per cent loss over five months. This raises questions about the appropriate period before an open position must be closed. Most studies choose the maximal length of the holding period arbitrarily. Yet it is hard to imagine that the trading room of a major international bank could accept massive losses from strict adherence to a technical trading rule. Chang and Osler (1999) discuss exiting rules in great detail. They experiment with closing dates between a day and two months. Curcio et al. (1997) argue that dealers have to close their positions by the end of a day.

It is clear that the length of a holding period and the loss which a trader is allowed to make within this period influence the overall profitability of trading strategies. There seems to be a widespread belief that exchange rates deviate from their fundamental value because the holding period of a speculative position on this fundamental value is unacceptably long. Yet open positions of substantial length may also be necessary before technical rules make a profit.

3. *Transaction costs* Direct transaction costs arise because bid and ask prices deviate from each other. Hence, buying foreign exchange is more expensive than selling the same amount. When evaluating the profitability of trading rules, some studies neglect these transactions costs completely (for example, Mills, 1997). Yet, when transaction costs are considered, they vary widely. Neely (1997) assumes transaction costs of 5 basis points (0.05 per cent). Sweeny (1988) considers 0.1 to 0.2 per cent as adequate transaction costs for institutional traders, and Chang and Osler (1999) work with 0.1 per cent.

   In these studies the transaction costs are simply deducted from the calculated profit. Curcio et al. (1997) deal with this problem by using bid and ask prices to determine the buying and selling signals. They will buy and sell only if the ask price rises above the critical level for a buying decision or the bid price falls below the critical level for selling. Thus, transaction costs are implicit in the calculated profits from the trading rule.

4. *Risk premia* A further problem in interpreting the profitability results relates to the riskiness of the trading strategies. Technical trading rules may involve diversifiable risk. Hence, we could interpret the profit from using a trading rule simply as an adequate risk premium. Some studies of foreign exchange trading consider risk premia explicitly. Using the capital-asset pricing model (CAPM) to determine risk premia, Cornell and Dietrich (1978) conclude that risk premia can explain the excess returns from technical trading. Other authors, for example Sweeny (1986), reject such a conclusion.

   In a recent study, Chang and Osler (1999) compute Sharpe ratios for the head-and-shoulders pattern. For the German mark, they compute a ratio of 1.00 and, for the Japanese yen, 1.47. This suggests a much smaller risk than the Standard & Poor's stock market index, which had a Sharpe ratio of 0.32 for the same period. It is doubtful, however, whether these comparisons give an adequate picture of the relative riskiness of technical trading rules.

It appears fair to summarize the evidence on the profitability of technical trading rules as ambiguous. Given the methodological differences, the empirical studies supporting or rejecting profitability of technical trading rules are not comparable. At a deeper level, it must be asked whether it is even possible to draw conclusions about the profitability of trading rules by studying *ex post* exchange rate data without a clear hypothesis about what drives the exchange rate process and how trading behaviour affects this process. This leads, finally, to a review of theoretical approaches.

## 5 TRADING STRATEGIES AND ECONOMIC THEORY

The questionnaire surveys of foreign exchange market dealers in different countries show consistently that technical analysis is important for their trading decisions, though a set of fundamental variables also has a role to play. The variety of these responses suggests substantial uncertainty on the part of these market makers about the factors determining the exchange rate over short and long horizons. A stylized picture extracted from these surveys reveals a belief that in the short run, exchange rates are heavily dependent on speculative trade, while in the long run, fundamental factors become more important.

According to these surveys, traders in the foreign exchange market do not trust the efficient markets hypothesis that all information is immediately incorporated in the exchange rate. Although they seem to be convinced that generally available information about macroeconomic variables will be incorporated in the exchange rate very quickly, in fact within less than a minute, the same is not thought to be true of other kinds of information not based on commonly observable variables. Missing information includes, in particular, speculative behaviour of other traders in the market. Short-term trading profits are believed to be possible by joining the bandwagon of other traders. In this light, technical analysis may be a mechanism coordinating traders' beliefs and inducing self-fulfilling prophecies, a perspective suggested by Menkhoff (1997) based on his questionnaire survey and by Levin (1997) and Flood and Marion (1998) from a theoretical perspective.

Speculative trading, that is, trading without any other motive but the exploitation of arbitrage opportunities, can be judged in two opposing ways. Following Friedman (1953), speculation can be viewed as a necessary mechanism for eliminating arbitrage opportunities and, thus, helping to restore equilibrium faster. By contrast, speculative behaviour may be seen as creating its own momentum at the expense of non-speculative traders, a view held, among others, by Stein (1987) and Flood and Marion (2000).

In a recent article, Carlson and Osler (2000) provide an interesting interpretation of these opposing views of speculation. They consider foreign exchange market equilibria which are disturbed by random shocks. If more speculators reduce the equilibrium price effects of these shocks, then speculation enhances market stability, reduces volatility and helps restore equilibrium. By contrast, if the effects of such shocks on the exchange rate are magnified with more speculators, then speculation is destabilizing and increases volatility.

Carlson and Osler (2000) develop a simple model of foreign exchange trading which distinguishes these effects. A slightly modified version of their model is presented here, showing that speculation makes the excess demand for foreign currency more elastic and, thus, reduces volatility in response to demand and supply shocks originating on the fundamental side of the economy. If shocks affect speculators' decisions directly, however, then the volatility of the exchange rate is increased.

Consider a population with two groups of traders. There are $N$ risk-averse speculators, technical traders, who choose a position $d_t$ in the foreign exchange market in each period $t$. If they are long in foreign exchange, then $a_t > 0$, and if they are short in it, $a_t < 0$. Speculators are traders in the foreign exchange market who are motivated by short-run profit opportunities. The following demand for a position $a_t$ can be derived from a one-period portfolio choice problem (see Carlson and Osler, 2000, pp. 236–7):

$$a_t = B \cdot [\epsilon_t(e_{t+1}) - e_t + (i_t^* - i_t) + \eta_t],$$

where $e_t$ (domestic currency/foreign currency) denotes the logarithm of the exchange rate and $i_t^*$, $i_t$ the foreign and domestic interest rates, respectively. These variables are assumed to be known at period $t$. The parameter $B$ depends on the speculators' risk aversion and the variance of the exchange rate which is assumed constant. $\epsilon_t$ is the expectations operator based on information in period $t$. Information held by a trader includes trading rules and data on the exchange rate. In addition, a white-noise process of signals from trading rules, $\eta_t$, is assumed, affecting the predicted return from buying or selling foreign exchange. This implies that buying and selling signals from trading rules are not correlated with the actual exchange rate process.

There is a second group of $M$ traders in the foreign exchange market who demand and supply foreign exchange for non-speculative reasons. These traders comprise foreign importers, exporters, foreign subsidiaries of domestic firms, and other 'liquidity traders'. Following Carlson and Osler (2000), the excess demand for foreign currency from these traders is denoted as *net current account*, $CA_t$, and assumes the following simple form:

$$CA_t = C + S \cdot [\varepsilon_t - e_t].$$

The parameters $C > 0$ and $S > 0$ and the white-noise random variable $\varepsilon_t$ reflect trade-related demand and supply behaviour with some unsystematic random effect. In this extremely simplified model, $CA_t$ is the fundamental side of the exchange rate process. The fundamental value of the exchange rate is obtained from current account equilibrium, $CA = 0$:

$$e_t = \frac{C}{S} + \varepsilon_t.$$

We could easily model the fundamental traders more realistically without changing the results in regard to the effects of speculative behaviour.

These assumptions about traders yield the following aggregate excess demand for foreign exchange:

$$\begin{aligned} D_t(e_t): &= N \cdot [a_t - a_{t-1}] + M \cdot CA_t \\ &= N \cdot B \left[ \epsilon_t(e_{t+1}) - \epsilon_{t-1}(e_t) + (\Delta i_t^* - \Delta i_t) + e_{t-1} - \bar{\eta}_{t-1} + \eta_t - e_t \right] \\ &\quad + M \cdot [C + S \cdot (\varepsilon_t - e_t)] \\ &= Z + N \cdot B \cdot \eta_t + M \cdot S \cdot \varepsilon_t - [N \cdot B + M \cdot S] \cdot e_t, \end{aligned}$$

where $Z := N \cdot B \left[ \epsilon_t(e_{t+1}) - \epsilon_{t-1}(e_t) + (\Delta i_t^* - \Delta i_t) + e_{t-1} + \bar{\eta}_{t-1} \right] + M \cdot C$ collects all parameters and variables known at $t$. Note that $\bar{\eta}_{t-1}$ is the realized shock of period $t-1$ which is known in period $t$, while $\varepsilon_t$ and $\eta_t$ are random variables. Figure 10.4 illustrates the demand function. The excess demand function has a slope of $-[N \cdot B + M \cdot S]$. Hence, the more speculators there are in this market, the steeper the excess demand function will be. With many speculators excess demand becomes more elastic and shocks on the fundamental system have less of an impact.

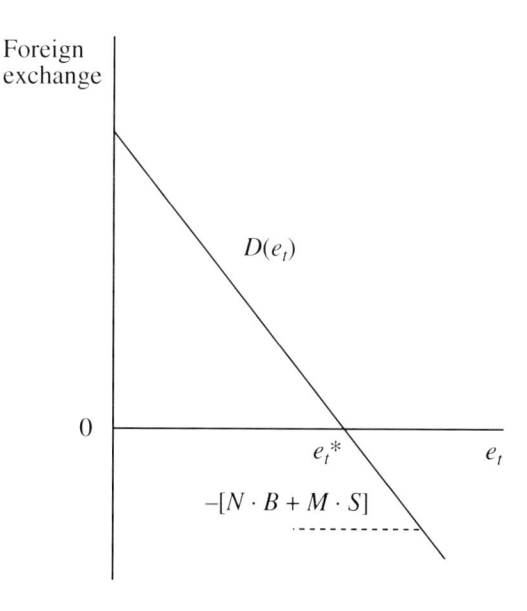

*Figure 10.4  Foreign exchange market*

The equilibrium condition $D_t(e_t^*)=0$ yields the equilibrium exchange rate:

$$e_t^* = \frac{Z}{N \cdot B + M \cdot S} + \frac{N \cdot B}{N \cdot B + M \cdot S} \cdot \eta_t + \frac{M \cdot S}{N \cdot B + M \cdot S} \cdot \varepsilon_t.$$

An increase in the number of speculators $N$ increases the multiplier of $\eta_t$ but decreases the multiplier of $\varepsilon_t$. Hence, fundamental shocks $\varepsilon_t$ will be diminished, while speculative shocks $\eta_t$ will be magnified. Volatility of the exchange rate will be decreased if its cause lies in fundamental changes. On the other hand, volatility will increase when the speculators' signals drive it.

The simple model of Carlson and Osler (2000) sheds some light on the interaction between purely speculative and fundamental trade. On the one hand, speculators give the market more depth and, thus, reduce fluctuations in the demand and supply of liquidity traders. This enhances the efficiency of the market as Friedman (1953) had predicted. On the other hand, speculators may bring their own problems to the market. Through the process of trading signals they may generate extra volatility.

Carlson and Osler (2000) derive the full rational expectations solution of this model. As in all rational expectations models, explosive solutions also exist. Such speculative bubbles correspond to the self-fulfilling prophecy argument, as advanced by Menkhoff (1997) in the context of his survey studies. An interpretation of explosive solutions as bubbles suffers from the problem that such bubbles never burst. In a similar model, which also distinguishes fundamentalist and chartist behaviour, Levin (1997) interprets the unstable solutions of his model in this way and appeals to exogenous 'fears of speculators' in order to conclude that bubbles might eventually burst. Levin's model belongs to a group of models building on the macroeconomic framework of Dornbusch (1976). In a number of articles, Frankel and Froot (1987, 1988, 1990) introduce a distinction between fundamentalists and chartists by modifying the exchange rate expectations in the interest parity condition of the Dornbusch model. Though cast in a more macroeconomic framework, their approach and argument are similar to those of Carlson and Osler (2000). Their dynamic analysis focuses, however, on the multiplicity of instable bubble solutions. From this perspective, they see speculative activities of traders in the foreign exchange market as destabilizing.

This section concludes with an opposing view about speculative behaviour in the foreign exchange market, which has not been formally modelled so far. In order to explain why fundamental variables appear to have so little influence on exchange rates, Sweeny (1986) and Curcio et al. (1997) argue that there may be too little speculation in the foreign exchange market. Due to regulatory and institutional constraints, speculative traders cannot keep positions open long enough to profit from the slow drift of exchange rates towards their fundamental value. Foreign exchange traders are usually not authorized by the international banks for which they work to keep open positions beyond a certain period of time. Curcio et al. (1997) suggest periods as short as one trading day for many dealers. Hence, they may be unable to keep open positions long enough to benefit from a reversal of the exchange rate to its fundamental value.

## 6 CONCLUDING REMARKS

The foreign exchange trading activities of international banks are inextricably linked to the international financial investment strategies of these same banks. Thus, exchange rate risk is closely linked to interest rate risk and credit risk. In 1974, the Herstatt bank in Germany was closed by regulators because of losses from trading in forward foreign exchange contracts. This was the first collapse of a major bank in Germany since the Second World War and it was related to foreign exchange trading in the wake of the transition from fixed to flexible exchange rates. The risks of trading in the foreign exchange market became obvious. Since then, other bank collapses, for example, the collapse of Barings Bank in the United Kingdom in early 1995, have also been connected with foreign exchange trading.

Given these risks, it appears quite reasonable for international banks to devote special attention to their exposure to foreign exchange risk. Such exposure may arise from direct loans to customers in foreign countries, from investment in financial assets, or from speculative trading in the foreign exchange market. Useful as the distinction between 'liquidity trading' and 'speculative trading' may be, in practice, a bank's activities in the foreign exchange market cannot be easily distinguished along such lines. Loans to foreign customers usually involve credit and foreign exchange risk. By making loans in domestic currency, foreign exchange risk can be reduced at the expense of higher credit risk, since the foreign debtor now bears all foreign exchange risk.

Reducing foreign exchange risk by denominating loans in domestic currency seems to have become a common strategy among international banks. In a recent contribution to *Foreign Affairs*, reprinted in the *Australian Financial Review*, Baily et al. (2000) blame the Asian crisis of 1997–98 on the lending practices of international banks. Partly due to capital adequacy requirement regulations, international banks made mostly short-term loans denominated in US dollars which they regularly rolled over. When market risk and country risk increased, they stopped extending these credits and withdrew funds in order to reduce their exposure to these risks. In this way, they aggravated the Asian crisis. Mutual funds and other institutional investors were more resilient to changes in the economic situation facing these countries and much slower to adjust their investment portfolios.

Baily et al. (2000) conclude from this experience that bank loans will become less important as an instrument of international finance. They predict the growing importance of investment finance through international capital markets. How such a change, if it eventuates, will affect the foreign exchange dealings of international banks remains an open question.

## NOTES

* We would like to thank Ian Harper for many helpful comments. The views in this chapter represent the authors' personal opinions and do not necessarily reflect the views of the Deutsche Bundesbank.
1. Even more spectacular was the growth in over-the-counter (OTC) trading. For more details, see BIS (1999), pp. 16–27.
2. We do not distinguish here between market makers and dealers. The latter are often seen as intermediaries between market makers (or bargain hunters) and liquidity traders who are interested in immediate transactions.
3. The Bank for International Settlements *Central Bank Survey of Foreign Exchange and Derivative Market Activity 1998* provides a more detailed description of the pattern of foreign exchange trading (BIS, 1999, pp. 5–15).
4. Exchange rates are quoted as domestic currency units per one unit of foreign currency.

## REFERENCES

Alexander, S.S. (1961). 'Price movements in speculative markets: trends or random walks?', *Industrial Management Review* **2**, 7–26.

Allen, F. and Karjalainen, R. (1999), 'Using genetic algorithms to find technical trading rules', *Journal of Financial Economics* **51**(2), 246–71.

Baily, M.N., Farell, D. and Lund, S. (2000), 'The colour of hot money', *Australian Financial Review*, 10 March, Review Section 1, 2, 6.

Bank for International Settlements (BIS) (1999), *Central Bank Survey of Foreign Exchange and Derivative Market Activity 1998*, Basle: BIS.

Cabral, J.S. and Guimares, R.M.S. (1988), 'Are commodity futures markets really efficient?' A Purchasing-oriented Study of the *Chicago Corn Future Market* **7**, 598–617.

Carlson, J.A. and Osler, C.L. (2000), 'Rational speculators and exchange rate volatility', *European Economic Review* **44**, 231–53.

Chang, P.H.K. and Osler, C.L. (1999), 'Methodological madness: technical analysis and the irrationality of exchange-rate forecasts', *Economic Journal* **109**, 636–61.

Cheung, Y-W. and Chinn, M.D. (1999a), 'Traders, market microstructure and exchange rate dynamics', NBER Working Paper 7416.
Cheung, Y-W. and Chinn, M.D. (1999b), 'Macroeconomic implications of the beliefs and behavior of foreign exchange traders', NBER Working Paper 7417.
Cornell, W. and Dietrich, J.K. (1978), 'The efficiency market for foreign exchange under floating exchange rates', *Review of Economics and Statistics* **60**, 111–20.
Curcio, R., Goodhart, Ch., Guillaume, D. and Payne, R. (1997), 'Do technical trading rules generate profits? Conclusions from the intra-day foreign exchange market', *International Journal of Finance & Economics* **2**, 267–80.
Dixon, H. (1999), 'Controversy: exchange rates and fundamentals', *Economic Journal* **109**, F652–F654.
Dornbusch, R. (1976), 'Expectations and exchange rate dynamics', *Journal of Political Economics* **84**(6), 1161–76.
Eichberger, J. and Harper, I. (1997), *Financial Economics*, Oxford: Oxford University Press.
Flood, R.P. and Rose, A.K. (1999), 'Understanding exchange rate volatility without the contrivance of macroeconomics', *Economic Journal* **109**, F660–F672.
Flood, R.P. and Marion, N.P. (2000), 'Self-fulfilling risk predictions: an application to speculative attacks', *Journal of International Economics* **50**(1), 245–68.
Frankel, J. A. and Froot, K. (1987), 'The dollar as an irrational speculative bubble: a tale of fundamentalists and chartists', NBER Reprint 959, December.
Frankel, J.A. and Froot, K. (1988), 'Chartists, fundamentalists and the demand for dollars', *Greek Economic Review* **10**(1), 49–102.
Frankel, J.A. and Froot, K. (1990), 'Exchange rate forecasting techniques, survey data, and implications for the foreign exchange market', IMF Working Paper, WP/90/43, May.
Friedman, M. (1953), *Essays in Positive Economics*, Chicago: University of Chicago Press.
Grossmann, S.J. and Stiglitz, J.E. (1980), 'On the impossibility of informationally efficient markets', *American Economic Review* **70**, 393–408.
Levin, J.H. (1997), 'Chartists, fundamentalists and exchange rate dynamics', *International Journal of Finance & Economics* **2**, 281–9.
Logue, D.E., Sweeny, R.J. and Willet T.D. (1978), 'The speculative behavior of foreign exchange rate during the current float', *Journal of Business Research* **6**, 159–74.
Lucac, L.P., Brorsen, B.W. and Irwin, S.H. (1988), 'A test of futures market disequilibrium using twelve different trading systems', *Applied Economics* **20**, 623–39.
Malkiel, B.G. (1990), *A Random Walk Down Wall Street*, 5th edition, New York: W.W. Norton.
Meese, R.A. and Rogoff, K. (1983), 'Empirical exchange rate models of the seventies: do they fit the sample?', *Journal of the International Economics*, February, 3–24.
Menkhoff, L. (1997), 'Examining the use of technical currency analysis', *International Journal of Finance & Economics* **2**, 307–18.
Mills, T.C. (1997), 'Technical analysis and the London Stock Exchange: testing trading rules using the FT30', *International Journal of Finance & Economics* **2**, 319–31.
Neely, C. (1997), 'Technical analysis in the foreign exchange market', *Review of the Federal Reserve Bank of St. Louis*, September/October.
Stein, J.C. (1987), 'Informational externalities and welfare reducing speculation', *Journal of Political Economy* **95**, 1123–45.

Sweeny, R.J. (1986), 'Beating the foreign exchange market', *Journal of Finance* **41**, 163–82.

Sweeny, R.J. (1988), 'Some new filter rule tests: methods and results', *Journal of Financial and Quantitative Analysis* **23**, 285–300.

Taylor, M.P. and Allen H. (1992), 'The use of technical analysis in the foreign exchange market', *Journal of International Money and Finance* **11**, 304–14.

Taylor, S.J. (1992a), 'Rewards available to currency futures speculators: compensation for risk or evidence of inefficient pricing?', *Economic Record* **68**, 105–16.

Taylor, S.J. (1992b), 'Trading futures using the channel rule. A study of the predictive power of technical analysis with currency examples', The Management School, Lancaster University, UK.

Taylor, S.J. and Tari A. (1989), 'Further evidence against the efficiency of futures markets', in R.M.C. Guimaraes, B.G. Kingsman and S.J. Taylor (eds), *A Reappraisal of the Efficiency of Financial Markets*, Heidelberg: Springer-Verlag, 603–5.

# 11. The settlement and financing of international trade

## Ayse G. Eren

## 1 INTRODUCTION

International trade activities involve such issues as the exchange of goods and services, the activities of exporters and importers, international payments and exchange rates, and the role of international banking and finance. Exporters and importers tend to prevail on their banks to obtain for them the most cost-effective methods of payment and settlement. Banks and other financial institutions play an important role in identifying from the existing financial markets the most suitable instruments that could be used to finance international trade. Export financing, therefore, can be simply defined as a mechanism for financing export sales. On these grounds, the financing of international trade can be considered as an integral element of international banking (see Murinde, 1996, ch. 8).

In general, international trade finance refers to the provision of bank credit facilities to meet a company's borrowing needs in relation to its international trade activities. For example, international trade financing techniques can be used to bridge the funding gap between any credit provided in the trade contract and the need to finance stock and debtors. Historically, within commercial banks in the UK this funding gap has been financed by overdraft facilities. Furthermore, it is fully acknowledged that in many instances traditional internal working capital finance continues to offer a perfectly adequate solution to customers involved in international trade. However, a major advantage of trade finance products and techniques is the additional assurance which banks can gain through transactional control; and hence the banks' ability to grant lending facilities where they would not be able to do so otherwise.

The dominant mode of international trade finance, which gives a clear view of potential areas of risk, is structured loans. Trade finance structured loans typically have rolling limits and maturity dates set to coincide with the borrower's cash flow generated by the sales of goods, thus offering the banks some considerable advantages. Use of trade finance instruments (for example, documentary collections, letters of credit and so on) enables the bank to exercise transactional control and mitigate risks. Credit facilities are more closely matched to the customer's transactional requirements and trade cycle. For example, repayment is more closely linked to the sale of underlying goods. Any delay in repayment gives an early warning of liquidity problems. Structured facilities increase the quality of account information for banks, which therefore improve the ability to monitor risk. In certain circumstances banks will have a prior security interest in the goods financed, enabling banks to sell the underlying goods.

The increased levels of assurance that banks can acquire through trade finance techniques have a positive effect on the willingness to make credit facilities available to the customers involved in international trade. Thus, the use of trade finance products by commercial banks in the UK offers a number of advantages for the customers. First, banks may be prepared to make trade finance facilities available even if the customer's normal credit facilities are fully extended or the customer's balance sheet does not support the level of limits requested. Second, specific facilities for individual transactions enable the customer to evaluate the profitability of individual transactions, including financial costs. Third, for the customer with a strong credit standing and balance sheet, banks may be prepared to offer a lower margin than on a conventional overdraft, in recognition of the superior transactional control and improved risk profile.

The operational framework that links all the elements of international trade finance in this chapter is the inverse relationship between the risk faced by the importer versus the risk facing the exporter. To understand this framework, we need to bear in mind that importers and exporters have naturally opposing views of risk in international trade. A payment structure which is totally satisfactory for an importer invariably involves a high element of risk for the exporter and vice versa. It is possible to consider this inverse relationship as a risk ladder on which the risks for the importer gradually increase as you go higher, while the corresponding risk for the exporter gradually decreases.

The method of payment used will usually depend on two important aspects. First, the negotiations between the exporter and importer before the sales contract is signed. An importer who is very keen to obtain goods from a particular source (perhaps due to quality or price) may have little choice other than to accept the exporter's request for a certain type of payment method. Second, the commercial practice in the countries involved is important. For example, open account trading is normal practice for trade between the UK and EU countries and North America, while for trade between the UK, the Middle East and many Asian countries, documentary credits are widely used.

When negotiating the method of payment the exporter/importer should bear in mind that his/her decision on this matter will affect not only the risk of payment but also the alternative trade financing structures available.

This chapter focuses on the financing of international trade by specifically dealing with the various settlement methods commonly used in short-term (whereby the settlement is made typically within a maximum 12-month period) international trade. These methods are then evaluated from the importer's as well as the exporter's perspective. The settlement methods and structures that are used in longer-term international trade fall outside the scope of this chapter. Funding mechanisms for medium-to-long-term international trade typically involve the government bodies or substantial guarantor agencies.

In what follows, the remainder of the chapter is structured into four sections. Section 2 examines the main terms of payment and settlement under open account trading. Section 3 deals with documentary collections. Two main types of financing are discussed in Section 4: these are recourse loans against collections and non-recourse finance. Section 5 explores the main types of documentary credits. Section 6 summarizes and concludes.

## 2 OPEN ACCOUNT TRADING

Open account trading means that there is no bank involved in settlement of trade financing and in enforcing the payment between the exporter and the importer. This method of trade financing is based on complete trust between the importer and the exporter. Thus, under these terms of payment, the documents of title (such as bills of lading) are sent directly to the importer. The importer endorses the payments, effectively agreeing to pay after a specified credit period.

This settlement method is widely used in trade between the UK, North America and Europe because the legal framework and political structure provide the safeguard to ensure that the exporter and importer keep their side of the transactions. The settlement document used could simply be an invoice. From the importer's point of view, this is the best method because it does not involve any costly bank charges, which are associated with other settlement methods. Banks could be used, not necessarily to ensure fulfilment of settlement obligations by both parties but generally to provide short-term finance or to provide some other traditional working capital facilities.

However, open account trading may be problematic and risky if the exporter and importer do not have an established relationship. The main risk is that the exporter loses control of the goods. It is therefore recommended that the terms be used only where the exporter–importer relationship and trust have been well established.

# 3 DOCUMENTARY COLLECTIONS

**Introduction**

The collection service provided by a bank is a means whereby a creditor (usually an exporter) in one country obtains payment from a debtor (generally an importer) in another country. Standard international rules governing the role and responsibilities of banks in collections have been established by the International Chamber of Commerce. These are known as the Uniform Rules for Collection (URC). The URC are internationally recognized and have been adopted by all UK banks and most banks worldwide.

In general, two types of document may be handled by the bank when it arranges a collection on behalf of a customer. The first type consists of financial documents, such as a bill of exchange, promissory note and so on. The second type comprises important commercial documents, such as a bill of lading; invoices, insurance policy and possibly other documents such as a certificate of inspection or certification of origin. When commercial and financial documents are present, the collection is known as a documentary collection, whereas a clean collection consists only of financial documents.

The collection service of the banks in the UK can be classified into two, namely export/outward collections and import/inward collections. Under the former, the bank undertakes to obtain payment of financial or commercial documentation from an overseas party on behalf of a UK exporter. The exporter may or may not be a customer of a commercial bank in the UK. Under the latter, the bank assists a correspondent bank abroad to obtain payment of a bill of exchange or promissory note or cheque from a UK importer on behalf of a foreign supplier. It is noteworthy that the UK debtor may or may not be a customer of a commercial bank in the UK.

The traditional parties to a collection are fourfold. The first party is the principal. This is either the customer, the UK exporter who entrusts an outward collection to commercial banks in the UK, or a foreign supplier who entrusts the collection to a bank in his/her country for obtaining payment from a debtor in the UK. The second party is the remitting bank. This is where documents are sent from the bank. The third party is the collecting bank; this is usually a correspondent bank of the remitting bank or the bank specified by the principal in his/her instructions to the remitting bank. Also involved here is the presenting bank, which presents the documents to the debtor for acceptance/payment. Often the collecting bank and the presenting bank are the same bank. The fourth party is the debtor; this is usually the importer.

In general, the two main sources from which commercial banks in the

UK typically receive instructions to handle collections are a bank customer who is an exporter (an outward collection) and a foreign correspondent bank acting on behalf of an exporter in its own country (an inward collection).

**Collection Process (Outward Collections): Exporters**

This section briefly explains how the collection process works in practice, on the side of the exporter. Initially, the customer (the exporter) negotiates a commercial contract with a foreign buyer and ships his/her goods. Then, the exporter submits his/her financial documents and commercial documents to his/her bank in the UK (that is, the remitting bank). Although there is no legal obligation to scrutinize any documents, the remitting bank undertakes a prima facie check of documents to ensure that everything appears to be in order. The remitting bank forwards documents to the collecting bank. Upon receipt, the collecting bank acts in accordance with the instructions of the remitting bank. When handling a documentary collection the collecting bank arranges for the importer to inspect the documents. Strictly speaking this should be done on the bank's premises although practice varies from one bank to another. If the importer considers the documents are in order, the collecting bank releases them against payment or acceptance of the bill or the issuing of a promissory note.

When handling a clean collection the collecting bank either obtains payment from the debtor or his/her acceptance to pay at a future date. Between the date of acceptance of the bill and the maturity date, the bill itself will remain overseas in the custody of the collecting bank. When the bill is paid, the collecting bank should without delay send the proceeds to the remitting bank (less charges if appropriate). The remitting bank then credits proceeds to the account of the exporter (again less charges if applicable).

**Documents against payment versus documents against acceptance**
An exporter should always specify in his/her instructions how the importer should settle a bill of exchange. This should be in one of two ways. The first involves documents against payment (D/P). This means that the bill is payable at sight by the importer. The collecting bank hands over the shipping documents only when the importer has paid the bill. The second involves documents against acceptance (D/A). This means that the exporter is allowing credit terms to the importer. The period of credit is the 'term' of the bill, also known as 'usance'. The importer/drawee is required to accept the bill, that is, to sign the bill as a promise to pay it at a set date in the future. When the bill has been signed by way of acceptance, the

importer can take the documents and clear his/her goods. The bill of exchange is then held by the collecting bank until its maturity and will be presented again at that time for payment by the drawee.

Usually, under the D/P terms the exporter keeps control of the goods (through the presenting bank) until the importer pays. If the importer cannot pay or refuses to pay, the exporter can protest the bill and take the importer to the local court (which may be expensive and difficult to control from another country); find another buyer; and arrange for the sale of the goods at an auction.

**Advantages of collections for the exporter**
Documentary collections provide a method of settlement in international trade, which (like documentary credits) offers a compromise between payment in advance (which favours the exporter, who receives payment before the goods are shipped) and trading on open account (which favours the importer, who usually pays after the goods are received). By using banks as intermediaries to collect payment from the importer for goods which the exporter has already sent, the use of collections reduces the risks for both exporter and importer and the delay in receipt of payment by the exporter and the receipt of goods by the importer.

In the case of documentary collections the exporter can retain control over the goods until the buyer accepts the bill. The latter arrangement is more secure for the exporter. The customer (the exporter) may be able to raise finance against the collection by obtaining an advance against the security of the bill. Obtaining bank finances enables the exporter greater flexibility in the payment terms offered to the buyer overseas. The collecting bank may have greater influence over the foreign debtor and might be more able to obtain payment than if trade were on open account terms. Collections are cheaper than documentary credits (which nevertheless do offer a more secure means of obtaining payment from the overseas buyer). A bill of exchange, used under documentary collections, once accepted, is legally binding on the drawee, and a promissory note once issued and delivered is also legally binding. Accepted term bills and promissory notes therefore provide a form of security to the exporter, while at the same time allowing a period of credit to the buyer. Documentary collections speed up the remittance of funds to the exporter compared with open account trading for the following reasons. The collection bank is under an obligation to present documents without delay and to present an accepted bill for payment not later than its maturity date. The collecting bank ensures that the documents are released to the buyer only on acceptance or payment of bills. In normal circumstances this will encourage the importer to pay or accept the bill promptly in order to gain access to the goods. When payment has been received, the collecting bank can remit the proceeds to the exporter by urgent transfer if this is specified in the collection order.

An important advantage of documentary collection which includes a full set of bills of lading (less one original) is that the customer, the exporter, can keep control of the goods until the foreign buyer has either paid for them or accepted the bill of exchange. This is because the bill of lading is a document of title, and providing that a full set of originals is retained by the collecting bank until the foreign buyer pays for the goods, accepts a bill of exchange or issues a promissory note, then the bank on behalf of its customer has constructive control over title to the goods. The collecting bank must only release this title when the debtor complies with the requirements of the exporter as specified in the collection order. If a waybill (for example an air waybill), rather than a bill of lading, is included in the commercial documents of a collection, the situation is not the same because a waybill is not a document of title. However, the exporter can still keep control over the goods with the help of the collecting bank, by consigning the goods to that bank or to the order of that bank, that is, by specifying the bank in the buyer's country as consignee of the goods. Thus with the consent of the collecting bank overseas, the goods can be dispatched to their destination into the custody of the collecting bank, which will only release the goods when the foreign buyer pays for them or accepts a bill of exchange. Goods should only be consigned to a bank if the bank agrees in advance to be the consignee.

**Possible disadvantages of collections for the exporter**

In general, there are four main disadvantages associated with collections for the exporter. First, the overseas buyer might refuse to pay or accept a bill on presentation of the documents. The exporter will therefore have to decide whether to abandon the merchandise, arrange warehousing or re-ship the goods.

Second, remittance of documents and collection times can be relatively slow (that is, there may be a time lapse due to delay in the importer viewing the documents and providing the necessary payment instructions) and an exporter may have to wait for the resultant funds. To add to the delay it is common practice in some countries to defer presentation of documents for payment or acceptance until the goods have arrived. In the event of delays or difficulties (for example, having to warehouse goods at the port of destination until the buyer takes delivery) the costs are borne by the exporter.

Third, the use of term bills enables the exporter to offer credit terms to the importer (that is, provides a buyer credit mechanism to induce a sale). Although the exporter may be able to raise finance against the collection from his/her own bank, this will nevertheless be at a cost to him/herself, unless this expense is factored into the value of the commercial sales contract with his/her buyer.

Fourth, any expenses incurred by a collecting bank in connection with protesting a bill are charged to the exporter, who should therefore instruct the bank in his/her collection order to protest only if the likely benefits from the protest justify the costs (that is, value of goods versus alternative sale value, solvency of buyer and so on).

**Collection Process (Inward Collections): Importers**

This section briefly explains how the collection process works in practice, for the importer. In general, in an inward collection, commercial banks in the UK assist the bank abroad to obtain payment of a cheque, bill of exchange or promissory note from a UK importer on behalf of a foreign supplier. In these circumstances, a commercial bank in the UK (as collecting bank) is the agent of the overseas remitting bank and must act strictly in accordance with instructions conveyed by the remitting bank which are in fact the overseas exporter's instructions.

The UK debtor may or may not be a customer of the collecting bank in the UK. Where the debtor is a customer of the bank, it must be remembered that the collecting bank in the UK must act in the interests of the remitting bank and the foreign exporter. Bank customers in this situation might expect the bank to be prepared to 'bend the rules' to help them, which may to some degree give rise to a conflict of interests.

In general, the collecting bank's role and obligations can be summarized to comprise four aspects. First, the collecting bank acts as agent to the remitting bank and explicitly follows the instructions in the remitting bank's covering schedule. Second, the collecting bank advises the importer that the collection has been received and seeks his/her acceptance or payment of the bill of exchange in order to obtain the shipping documents. Third, the collecting bank advises the fate of the bill of exchange by informing the remitting bank whether the importer has paid or accepted the bill or whether the importer has refused it. Fourth, the collecting bank may on receiving payment from the importer (that is, the UK customer) remit the proceeds promptly to the remitting bank less charges.

**Advantages of collections for the importer**
In general, there are a number of key advantages of collections for the importer. For example, the use of term bills provides the buyer with a period of credit from the exporter. In addition, the importer can inspect the documents (but not the goods themselves) before accepting a bill (D/A) or paying a bill of exchange (D/P). Moreover, in the case of clean collections

the buyer can take possession of the goods before paying for them. It is also possible to defer payment/acceptance, subject to the exporter's approval, until arrival of the goods. It may also be argued that collections are cheaper and simpler for the importer than documentary credits. This is because the collecting bank does not have any financial interest or risk commitment, so there are fewer formalities and costs. Finally, an importer does not require a credit limit from his/her bank if he/she imports on collecting terms, unlike other methods of international trade settlement where a suitable credit facility is required.

**Disadvantages of collections for the importer**
Legal action might be taken against the importer if he/she dishonours an accepted bill of exchange regardless of the condition of the goods. Refusal to accept or pay a bill could also lead to a protest for non-acceptance or non-payment, which might seriously damage the importer's financial reputation and the relationship with the exporter.

## 4   FINANCING

**Recourse Loans against Collections**

An exporter who is arranging a collection through his/her bank in the UK might want to obtain finance to fund the overseas sale until payment is received. In particular, when extended credit terms are offered to the importer, the exporter might have to wait a considerable time before receiving the payment.

Commercial banks in the UK may be prepared to consider granting a loan against the collection in order to make available to the exporter a part or all of the sale proceeds. Generally, loans against collections are subject to full recourse to the exporter. Therefore if the buyer fails to pay the bill, the bank has the right to debit the exporter's account.

**Non-recourse Finance against Collections**

A number of circumstances may warrant the use of finance against collections without recourse to the exporter. This may happen where the bills are 'avalized' by an overseas bank. This may also be the case where the bills are accepted by a foreign company with a strong credit rating.

'Avalization' is the process whereby a bank guarantees a bill of exchange. This is achieved by the bank endorsing the accepted bill 'pour aval'. At the exporter's request, the UK bank may specify that the documents are not ready to be released until the importer has accepted the bill of exchange and the importer's bank has avalized the bill.

In the case of a bill of exchange avalized by an overseas bank (that is, the importer's bank) it is not necessary to establish a credit limit in the name of the exporter, since the liability is marked against the overseas bank. Generally, the avalized bill would be held on behalf of the presenting/collecting bank (which may also be the avalizing bank) for presentation and payment at maturity. The exporter's bank in the UK would then obtain authenticated confirmation from the overseas bank that the bill has been avalized and that an unconditional undertaking to pay at maturity has been given.

In the case of an avalized bill, the UK bank effectively has an overseas bank guarantee of payment at a fixed date. It is therefore in a position to discount the bill and make the net proceeds (less interest charges) available to the exporter.

Opportunities to provide non-recourse finance to the exporter occasionally arise where the overseas importer has a particularly strong credit rating. In this situation a credit limit would need to be established in the name of the overseas importer.

## 5 DOCUMENTARY CREDITS

**Introduction**

A documentary credit, also known as a letter of credit (L/C), is a written undertaking by a bank on behalf of a buyer/importer to pay the seller an amount of money within a specified time provided the seller presents documents strictly in accordance with the terms laid down in the L/C. It is useful to assume that the banks only handle irrevocable L/Cs, since revocable L/Cs are hardly used these days given that under a revocable L/C the importer can amend or even cancel it without prior notice to the exporter. Thus, revocable L/Cs are extremely rare because they do not provide a satisfactory guarantee of payment for the exporter. This right can be exercised at any time until a payment is made to the exporter. Accordingly the exporter is exposed to a substantial risk that a revocable L/C might be cancelled after he/she has produced and shipped the goods. The exporter would then face the problem of obtaining payment direct from the buyer.

An irrevocable L/C, once issued, cannot be amended or cancelled without prior agreement of the beneficiary (the exporter). An irrevocable L/C therefore gives greater security to the exporter because the issuing bank and confirming bank continue to guarantee payment to the exporter even if the importer changes his/her mind.

An irrevocable L/C can be a very effective means of settlement with overseas parties, offering extra security for both the importer and the exporter: the exporter receives an undertaking from the buyer's bank that he/she will be paid, providing that documents are submitted strictly in accordance with the L/C; and the buyer/importer is able to stipulate the exact documentation that the seller must provide in order to be paid. In addition, the L/C includes an expiry date and a latest date for shipment to prompt the seller to dispatch both goods and documents expeditiously.

The importer/buyer, known as the applicant, negotiates a sales contract with the exporter providing for payment by L/C. The importer's bank is instructed to issue an L/C in favour of the exporter, specifying details of the documents required together with all the terms and conditions of the L/C. The buyer's bank, known as the issuing or opening bank, issues the L/C to a bank in the exporter's country; this will generally be the exporter's own bank and is known as the advising bank. The advising bank informs the exporter of all the terms and documents required and authenticates the genuineness of the L/C. The advising bank may agree to handle the L/C without giving any financial commitment itself to pay the exporter. On the other hand, the issuing bank may request the advising bank to add its confirmation to the L/C, which means that the latter bank adds its own conditional guarantee of payment to the guarantee already provided by the issuing bank. In this case the exporter's bank is known as the confirming bank.

The exporter/supplier, who is also known as the beneficiary of the L/C, is informed by the advising/confirming bank that an L/C has been opened in his/her favour with all the terms and documents required in order to receive payment. Once the exporter has shipped the goods, he/she submits the documents to the advising/confirming bank, or occasionally to a bank known as a nominated bank which has agreed to negotiate the L/C on his/her behalf, to receive payment. The bank checks the documents received very carefully to ensure that they are exactly as stipulated in the L/C. In general, the documents will include transport documents, such as a full set of bills of lading, copies of the invoice, a certificate of insurance (where the insurance is paid by the exporter) and a bill of exchange drawn on the issuing bank or the advising bank. If the documents are found to be in order, the exporter will be able to obtain payment. The advising/confirming or nominated bank then forwards the documents to the issuing bank and receives payment either at sight (immediate payment) or term (if a credit period is granted), providing documents are found to be in order by the issuing bank.

Finally, the issuing bank makes the documents available to the importer and receives reimbursement from the importer.

### Advantages of L/Cs for the exporter

There are many benefits of using L/Cs for the exporter since this is the most secure way of trading from his/her point of view, especially for trading with unknown parties for the first time or trading with less-developed countries. L/Cs can be particularly useful in the early days of a trading relationship, since the exporter may be reluctant to release the goods until he/she is confident of being paid.

First, L/Cs provide a strong degree of security and confidence in international trade, especially since the UCP (Uniform Customs and Practice for Documentary Credits) rules are internationally recognized. Second, they provide a greater security of payment than say a documentary collection, since the exporter has a bank guarantee of payment provided that he/she complies with the terms of the L/C. Thus on receipt of an advice of an L/C the exporter can confidently begin to assemble and ship the goods. Later on it will be explained that the exporters can then use this advice to raise pre-shipment finance locally, which is very common in the Far East. Third, the buyer risk is eliminated since the buyer's agreement to purchase is replaced by a bank guarantee conditional on presentation of specified documents. Banks are concerned only with documents, not goods, and payment will be forthcoming against correctly tendered documents, irrespective of any damage which might occur to the goods themselves in transit. Fourth, payment can be arranged through a bank in the exporter's own country. Fifth, if the exporter does not know the bank which has issued the L/C or has any possible doubts about its ability to pay, then he/she can arrange for the L/C to be confirmed by his/her own bank locally. Confirmation of the L/C is very important as it overcomes any possible country risk and removes risk of non-payment. Sixth, UCP provides a set of internationally recognized rules and procedures which reduces the risk of unpleasant surprises.

### Advantages of L/Cs for the importer

Although L/Cs are more beneficial and convenient for the exporters, they also bring many benefits to the importers. First, the importer can obtain help and advice from the issuing bank (usually his/her own regular bank which was prepared to issue the L/C in the first place and which will be subject to the importer's credit rating) in calling for appropriate documents to be presented under the L/C. Second, the importer can insist on shipment of goods within a reasonable period of time by fixing a last date for shipment and presentation of documents. Third, payment will not have to be made unless documents are presented in accordance with L/C terms and conditions; this feature is often misused. Fourth, the importers may be able to obtain a longer period of credit or a better price under the commercial contract when using an L/C rather than with a less secure method of payment for the exporter. Fifth, depending upon the contract between the importer and exporter, it may be possible for the buyer to pass on all or some of the costs to the exporter. Again this depends on the bargaining strength of the two parties. It could also be said that the importer increases his/her credibility in the eyes of the exporter by being able to arrange with his/her bank to issue an L/C.

**Possible disadvantages for the importer**
The most secure way of trading for the exporter may also mean some disadvantages for the importer under the L/C method of trading. First, banks deal with documents, not goods. Therefore payment under the L/C is made provided the exporter presents the stipulated documents in accordance with the terms of the L/C, regardless of the condition of the goods themselves. Second, as mentioned above, the importer will require a credit limit to be approved by the bank before issuing an import L/C. This may restrict the other credit facilities available to the importer. Third, usually it is the importer who ends up paying the L/C costs (which are normally influenced by his/her credit rating), which can make the L/C method rather costly from the importer's point of view.

**Ways of overcoming disadvantages**
The importer should obtain a status report on the foreign supplier's technical capacity to produce the goods to be ordered. Performance risk of the exporter is an important consideration for the importer and therefore it is better to trade with suppliers of well-known reputation or tested reliability. The documents requested under the L/C might include a third party certificate of inspection which provides the importer with additional assurance that the goods shipped are as specified and in good condition prior to shipment. The L/C could also specify that a particular shipping company known and trusted by the importer should transport the goods.

**Confirmed L/Cs**

The exporter may not know the foreign bank which has issued the L/C. Similarly, the exporter might be concerned that exchange control difficulties or political risks or even the possible liquidation of the issuing bank might mean that the exporter will not receive payment under the L/C. The exporter may therefore prefer to seek additional security in the form of a bank confirmation (that is, additional guarantee) from a bank in the exporter's country, preferably the exporter's own bank. When an advising bank in the exporter's country confirms an L/C, the instrument is known as a confirmed L/C. With a confirmed L/C the supplier is assured of payment provided he/she complies with the terms of the L/C since he/she has conditional guarantees from two banks, one of which is in the supplier's own country. Confirmed L/Cs are commonly used when trading with the Middle East and Latin America.

**Deferred Payment L/Cs**

Normally the terms of an L/C include an instruction to the exporter to draw a bill of exchange and the issuing bank guarantees that such a bill will be honoured provided all other terms of the L/C are fulfilled. However, in a deferred payment L/C there is no need for the exporter to draw a bill of exchange. Rather, the issuing bank simply guarantees that payment will be made at a fixed determinable future date (for example, 30 or 60 days after the date of the bill of lading) provided the conditions of the L/C are met.

A deferred payment L/C will specifically nominate the bank which is to effect payment under the L/C after presentation to it of the stipulated documents. By nominating a bank in the L/C as the paying bank, the issuing bank authorizes the said bank to effect payment under the L/C at the fixed or determinable date indicated in the L/C and undertakes to reimburse the paying bank on the due date.

In order to function smoothly, L/Cs require cooperation between banks in different countries. Internationally agreed standards procedures have therefore been drawn up by the International Chamber of Commerce, known as the Uniform Customs & Practice for Documentary Credits, or UCP 500. Most countries and territories subscribe to UCP 500 either on a collective country basis or on an individual bank notification basis.

When an L/C is opened, the fact that it is subject to UCP is included in the instructions. L/Cs therefore provide a strong degree of security and confidence in international trade since the rules are internationally recognized. However, it is noteworthy that UCP 500 is not legally binding. If legal proceedings arise, national law takes precedence although the UCP rules can be taken into consideration in arriving at a judgment.

**Risk Considerations for Banks when Issuing L/Cs**

When commercial banks issue L/Cs they guarantee payment provided the documents are presented in accordance with the terms of the L/C. The issuing bank is obliged to honour the L/C if its terms have been fulfilled irrespective of whether the applicant has funds in his/her account. As a result, L/Cs are viewed in much the same way as any other credit facility and it is therefore essential for the issuing bank to obtain approval for a suitable credit limit from its credit committee before issuing an L/C.

As with any credit facility, the bank's prime considerations are the creditworthiness (that is, ability to repay) and integrity of the customer. However, it is significant that the underlying goods can be used as a form of 'security' provided correct formalities are observed. Normally in signing the bank's standard application form for an L/C the customer, the importer, gives a pledge to the issuing bank, giving rights over the documents and therefore the goods themselves. If the importer fails to meet his/her obligation to the bank then the issuing bank in the UK has the right to sell the goods. However, in a worst case scenario, banks would not recover all their costs.

**General Types of L/Cs**

There are various types of L/Cs, some more widely used than others. For the purposes of this section only a brief description is given for the different types of L/Cs.

*Transferable L/Cs* are globally used instruments in international trade. A transferable L/C is one which can be transferred in whole or in part by the original beneficiary/exporter to one or more second beneficiaries in either the same country or different countries. This structure is normally used when the first beneficiary does not supply all the goods him/herself but acts as an intermediary between the supplier(s) and the buyer. The first beneficiary might even be an agent in one country for an overseas buyer, responsible for placing a number of purchase orders for the buyer. In these circumstances the L/C is usually for a large amount and the first beneficiary is responsible for distributing the portions of the L/C to various suppliers/second beneficiaries. The intermediary would ask the buyer to arrange a transferable L/C so that the ability to present documents for payment/acceptance/negotiation can be transferred to the supplier(s). Thus the rights and obligations of the first beneficiary under the transferable L/C are extended to a second beneficiary, without any need for a second L/C to be issued.

A transferable L/C does not use up any of the intermediary's credit facilities (he/she does not need to apply to the bank for an import L/C). This is probably the most important feature of this type of L/C. A transferable L/C can be used in such a way that the buyer/importer does not know the identity of the original supplier. There are of course certain limitations of these types of L/Cs and certain risk considerations will still apply for the banks that are transferring the documents.

Another commonly used type of L/C is *back-to-back L/Cs*. These are often used by traders and merchants in buying goods and on-selling them to another party. Therefore back-to-back L/Cs are widely used by commodity traders such as in the steel industry. They consist of two separate

L/Cs but to a limited extent the first L/C acts as a form of 'security' for the second L/C in so far as it is a potential source of reimbursement. Under a back-to-back structure the first L/C is issued in favour of an intermediary who is not supplying the goods him/herself. Instead, the intermediary becomes the applicant for a second L/C to be issued in favour of the supplier of the goods which will be on-sold to the intermediary's client. This type of L/C allows the intermediary, who may have only limited financial resources, to purchase goods from a supplier who is only prepared to sell on L/C terms. An advantage for the intermediary is that the importer and supplier are not aware that they are dealing through a third party.

Back-to-back credits can be complex to administer, time consuming and involve a high degree of risk for the banks. For example, the first L/C is a separate instrument to the second and therefore the issuing bank of the second L/C runs the risk of not getting paid under the first L/C, having already made payment under the second one, and if the terms of the second L/C differ significantly from those of the first, this might result in the supplier meeting the terms of the second L/C and being paid, but the intermediary will then be unable to fulfil the conditions of the first L/C.

Where back-to-back credits are requested, clearing banks in the UK may be reluctant to issue such L/Cs and would normally encourage the use of a transferable L/C where possible. Therefore for most UK banks, such L/Cs are generally issued only for those customers of undoubted integrity where there is a good established relationship and these types of transaction are considered normal. Due to the high risks involved, back-to-back L/Cs are more commonly issued by specialized niche banks.

In many ways back-to-back L/Cs are similar to transferable L/Cs. First, they both involve an intermediary as seller. Second, the intermediary substitutes his/her invoices in place of those provided by the supplier of goods. Third, certain terms and conditions might vary between the first and second legs of the transaction, for example, amount and unit price might be reduced, expiry date and shipment date might be brought forward, date for presentation of documents might be curtailed and the insured amount might be increased to reflect cost, insurance and freight value plus 10 per cent of the sales contract with the end buyer.

The differences between these two types of L/Cs can be summarized as follows. First, back-to-back L/Cs involve two L/Cs, whereas a transferable credit involves only one L/C. Second, transferable L/Cs must be designated at the outset as specifically 'transferable', whereas a back-to-back credit arrangement may work, in principle, with any L/C. Third, transferable credits are transferred without any responsibility by the advising bank, but the second L/C under a back-to-back arrangement is issued under the full responsibility of the issuing bank. Fourth, transferable credits must specifically comply with Article 48 of UCP 500. Back-to-back credits are not specifically referred to in UCP 500 as they involve two separate L/Cs and, finally, an intermediary seeking a back-to-back arrangement needs a credit limit for the amount of the second L/C. An intermediary who is a beneficiary of a transferable credit does not require a credit limit to be approved, which is the most notable difference between back-to-back and transferable L/Cs.

**Other Types of L/Cs**

A *standby L/C* is a guarantee from the issuing bank that a sum will be paid to the beneficiary upon demand in the event that the latter submits a signed statement to the effect that there has been a default or non-performance by the applicant of the L/C. A standby L/C therefore enables an exporter and importer to trade on open account terms against the security of a bank guarantee in the background. A standby L/C has the following characteristics. First, it is typically issued for a fixed term (for example, one year) covering a series of shipments during this period. Second, the maximum value of the standby L/C would normally cover one or two shipments. Third, if trade between the exporter and importer runs smoothly, payments would be made on open account. Thus the standby L/C can remain dormant in the background as security for the exporter in case of need. Fourth, on receiving documents in accordance with the L/C, the issuing bank would make payment to the beneficiary and claim reimbursement from the importer/applicant. Fifth, it is only if the importer/applicant defaults on a payment that the standby L/C would be called upon. In this event, the standby L/C would provide for the supplier to present certain documents which would typically include documents such as a bill of exchange drawn on the issuing bank, a copy of the commercial invoice and a signed statement that payment has not been received within a stated time after the due payment date.

Standby L/Cs are used widely today due to their many advantages and simplicity. For example, they reduce the total commitment of the issuing bank, since the amount typically represents the value of only one or two shipments, rather than the overall number of shipments anticipated during the validity of the standby L/C. A standby L/C reduces the level of credit limit required by the applicant, which can be very useful where the applicant's balance sheet would be inadequate to support the value of the full commercial contract (however, it is still a contingent liability and would be viewed by the bank as the same as an ordinary L/C for facility purposes). It acts as a guarantee for trade conducted on open account terms as well as avoiding the production of the specific documentation normally required for each shipment under a conventional L/C. Furthermore, it can be used where banks are restricted by local legislation from issuing normal guarantees. For example, in the United States, banks are not permitted to issue guarantees and standby L/Cs are therefore used as an alternative. Indeed, in practice they are commonly used instead of advance payment guarantees, performance bonds and so on in the UK.

There are other less widely used types of L/Cs such as *red clause L/Cs* (pre-shipment finance). A red clause L/C allows the beneficiary to obtain pre-shipment finance from the advising/confirming bank. It contains an instruction, inserted at the request of the importer, for the advising bank to make an advance of a percentage of the L/C to the exporter prior to shipment and before he/she presents the required documentation. The red clause will specify how much security the exporter must give to the advising /confirming bank. When the exporter subsequently presents the documents, the amount of the advance plus interest will be deducted from the proceeds of the L/C. The advance to the exporter will usually be made in his/her local currency. Any currency exchange risk resulting thereby will be borne by the exporter unless the terms of the L/C state otherwise.

Historically, red clause L/Cs have been used to cover shipments of primary goods (for example, wool or metals) where the exporter needs finance to buy/manufacture the goods or make cash payments for goods purchased from another supplier. They are now relatively rare, although they can become useful tools under complicated trade structures. Originally such clauses were written in red ink, to draw attention to the special nature of the L/C; hence the name.

*Receipt and undertaking L/Cs* (pre-shipment finance) is another form of pre-shipment finance where an advance is made to the exporter against a receipt and undertaking signed by the exporter. The request for such must be made by the applicant when the L/C is issued. The advance can be made by the advising/confirming bank against a beneficiary's/exporter's receipt and an undertaking signed by the beneficiary or a third-party bank to refund the loan if the beneficiary later fails to present documents in accordance with the L/C.

The difference between receipt and undertaking L/Cs and red clause L/Cs is that under a receipt and undertaking L/C once the advising/confirming bank has made the loan, it can claim immediate repayment from the issuing bank. The bank does not have to wait for the documents to be presented after shipment of the goods. Furthermore, the issuing bank is responsible for initiating claims against the exporter if he/she fails to meet his/her obligations under the signed undertaking.

*A revolving L/C* is one which states that the amount is renewed or reinstated automatically without specific amendments. A revolving L/C allows for flexibility in commercial dealings between importers and exporters, particularly where there are regular shipments of the same type of goods, thereby avoiding the need for repetitive single value/shipment L/Cs to be issued. It is emphasized that an L/C which is available for a certain amount and calls for specified quantities of goods to be shipped within a given period is not a revolving L/C. Rather it is an L/C available by instalments as provided for under UCP 500. These types of L/Cs are widely used today.

**Using L/Cs as a Means of Finance**

L/Cs are extremely useful in international trade not only because they are a secure method for exports but also because they can be structured in such a way as to provide short-term finance to both the exporter and the importer. In this section, the most widely used means of L/C finance are examined.

**Post-shipment finance for exporters**
The most typical method of providing bank finance for the exporter is discounting the bill of exchange under the L/C. This means that a bank pays the net proceeds, that is, the face value of the bill less an interest charge for the period of funding.

In this way the exporter receives immediate payment of the account due to him/her (less charges) instead of having to wait until the end of the period of trade credit. Similarly the importer obtains a period of credit before having to pay for the imported goods.

There are several advantages for the exporter. L/Cs are one of the most effective methods of trading when it comes to raising post-shipment finance. In today's highly competitive trading conditions, the exporters have to offer extended credit terms at times in order to enable the importers to buy. An exporter who can offer credit terms, thus improving the importer's cash flow, will always be more competitive against its peers.

The biggest advantage of obtaining finance by means of discounting L/Cs is the fact that the finance is obtained on a non-recourse basis. This then frees up the exporter's facilities and will also be off-balance sheet. It is a very quick way of obtaining funding from banks since there is no requirement for a credit limit to be put in place for the exporter. The exporter may be able to access the funds at a cheaper rate than other conventional means of funding, such as an overdraft.

**Pre-shipment finance for exporters**
Exporters in some countries are also able to use the L/Cs to obtain pre-shipment finance to assist them with the actual manufacturing costs. This is

typically observed in trade between the UK and the Far Eastern countries. The Far Eastern suppliers/exporters are able to use the L/Cs of which they are beneficiaries and obtain funding from their local banks. In this case the local banks view the L/C issued by a Western bank of high standing as a robust security against which funding may be extended at a more favourable rate. The local banks may extend facilities to their customer (the Far Eastern supplier) prior to shipment in order for him/her to manufacture his/her goods. This is the most important reason why the lead times are typically longer for trade between the UK importer and his/her Far Eastern suppliers.

**Post-shipment finance for importers – import/produce loans**
Although on the whole import loans can be used as a stand-alone funding vehicle and essentially they are not much different from other loans, they are more likely to be used in close connection with a settlement product such as an L/C or a documentary collection.

There are generally two forms of import loans, documentary import loans and clean import loans. The former provide short-term finance for an importer seeking finance to bridge the gap between payment to the exporter and receipt of funds from the sale of goods to a third party. Between receipt of goods by the importer and delivery to the ultimate buyer, goods are held either in an independent warehouse or on trust by the importer/borrower him/herself. Finance is made available against the security of a general letter of pledge and subsequent trust receipts, covering documents of title, for example, bills of lading and warehouse warrants. The documentary import loan structure can be used to finance settlement of L/C and documentary collection (inward bill) transactions, that is, when payment to the exporter falls due. This type of funding is ideal for goods or raw materials that are being or have been imported into the UK and when the funding bank requires constructive possession of the underlying goods.

Clean import loans are appropriate where the funding made available needs to be structured (with clear expiry date and granted at the back of an L/C or documentary collection) but transactional control is not required/available. Security documentation such as trust receipts is not effective under clean import loans since the banks do not have constructive possession in this case. A clean import loan is a short-term finance against evidence of import and/or goods pre-sold (that is, there is an underlying sales agreement/contract between the importer and his/her end customers). Banks will also take the view of granting clean import loans where the customer relationship is fully established, balance sheet is strong, modus operandi is robust and whereby both parties would wish to keep the paperwork to a minimum as documentary import loans involve a lot of administration.

The type of corporates that mostly benefit from this form of financing in the UK are corporates which import goods that are expected to be resold quickly and readily by the importer (for example, basic commodities, foodstuffs, other raw materials or finished consumer products). Import loans are particularly suited to situations where the imported goods are already pre-sold to a third party. The type of business in which a suitable customer may be involved would include distribution as well as merchanting/commodity trading.

Generally, documentary import loans are required by banks when their assurance, the importer, has a weaker balance sheet and therefore transactional control is preferred.

*Security documents used with documentary import loans* One of the major advantages of the documentary import loan is the greater degree of assurance the banks obtain from control of the underlying goods and resultant sale proceeds compared to lending on an unstructured basis.

This mitigation of risk can be achieved by using a combination of certain security documentation such as a general letter of pledge, shipping documents (bills of lading, air waybills), warehouse warrants and trust receipts.

A *general letter of pledge* is in effect an all-moneys pledge and must be executed prior to the granting of facilities. A pledge is a possessory security over goods and it is not a charge. The existence of a pledge is dependent upon possession of the goods, either actual (through physical possession) or constructive (through documents of title). Loss or surrender of possession extinguishes the security, except where a trust receipt has been issued. A pledge is created by the pledgor in favour of the pledgee by way of a transfer of possession (either actual or constructive) with the intention of making a pledge. Thus while banks may hold a general letter of pledge, it is obtaining possession either actual or constructive for a consideration that constitutes and perfects the pledge and therefore a mere agreement to make a pledge is of no effect. The goods must be clearly identifiable, either through shipping marks or by segregation and marking as the subject of the pledge in a warehouse. While the pledgee does not acquire ownership of the goods, it does have a legally recognized security interest which confers property rights. In particular, a pledge confers a power of sale upon default in payment after reasonable notice to the pledgor.

*Shipping documents* may give title of evidence that goods have been consigned to a bank's order. Constructive and in due course physical control of goods may be achieved by calling for shipping documents which provide title (bills of lading) or evidence that the goods have been consigned to the bank's order (for example, air waybills). A *bill of lading* has the unique quality of being a shipping document that is also a document of title. Bills of lading are the most important shipping documents since the importer cannot take possession of goods shipped to him/her without presenting an original bill of lading. In order to obtain constructive possession of goods, the bank would normally insist on a *full* set (that is, three copies) of 'clean on board' bills of lading issued to 'order', that is, to the order of the shipper.

These days a significant portion of goods are delivered by air, where the goods are normally consigned to the importer. In this case *air waybills* are used. An air waybill is not a document of title. However, banks can obtain control over the goods by arranging for them to be consigned to the bank, that is, the bank is shown as 'consignee' on the waybill. However, it must be remembered that there are disadvantages to these arrangements as the banks become party to the carriage arrangements and, in the event of customer failure, can become liable for the payment of associated costs.

A *warehouse warrant* is issued by a warehouse keeper who acknowledges receipt of goods which are held in the bank's name. The warehouse warrant is also a document of title which may be used to transfer title endorsement. Alternatively, a delivery order may be issued by the banks to instruct the warehouse to release goods to the importer and/or the end buyer.

*Trust receipts* are instruments which preserve the pledgee's security rights under the pledge despite the loss of actual or constructive possession of the goods. Typically this will arise when the pledgee releases the documents of title to allow the collection of sales proceeds by the pledgor. The trust receipt is essentially a declaration of trust by the recipient of the title documents (usually the pledgor) whereby such a recipient acknowledges that it holds the goods covered by the documents and the proceeds of their sale on trust for the pledgee. It is of crucial importance that a trust receipt will only be valid if the pledgee has a valid pre-existing right of pledge. Trust receipts are not free from risk in that if the pledgor uses the documents fraudulently to dispose of the goods or to raise new moneys against them, then its act will bind the banks as it is deemed to act as a mercantile agent on behalf of the banks. Trust receipt arrangements get complicated when another bank holds a mortgage debenture (a fixed and floating charge over companies' assets) and therefore priority must be agreed prior to permitting drawdown of any facilities.

*Advantages of documentary import loans for the banks* Although the involvement of extra documentation means more administration work for banks, the advantages are significant enough to outweigh the extra work involved. First, the ability to structure a facility means that the banks are in some cases able to lend more or consider those cases where normally the customer's balance sheet does not support the level of limits requested.

# 12. Costs and efficiency in banking: a survey of the evidence from the US, the UK and Japan
## Leigh Drake

## 1 INTRODUCTION

The aim of this chapter is to provide a selective summary of some of the main academic research into the issue of costs and efficiency in banking, and to set this analysis within the context of the major changes taking place in banking markets around the world. To facilitate this, we focus on three important banking markets, the US, the UK and Japan. We also present a brief overview of some of the alternative methodologies employed by researchers in the study of various aspects of bank efficiency.

## 2 A BRIEF OVERVIEW OF TRENDS IN THE UK, US AND JAPANESE FINANCIAL MARKETS

Banking markets around the world have been subject to an enormous degree of structural change since the early 1980s. This structural change has been associated with: increasing competition, both within and across sectors, and from the capital market; the impact of new technology, which is facilitating competition from new entrants; deregulation; increased diversification and merger activity and, more recently in the UK, the demutualization of segments of both the life assurance and building society industries.

These trends have impacted forcefully on the UK banking sector. Following the intensification of competition in both corporate sector lending and international banking in the late 1970s, UK banks sought to diversify their business in order to maintain their profitability. In 1981, for example, UK banks entered the mortgage market in a significant way as part of an increased focus on the domestic retail banking market, and in 1986, following 'Big Bang' in the London stock exchange, a number of the large UK clearing banks diversified into investment banking activities. More recently UK banks have diversified into insurance, and particularly into life assurance as part of a worldwide trend towards bancassurance. In common with banks around the world, UK banks have dramatically increased the contribution to profits emanating from 'off-balance sheet' business and fee income.

At the same time as banks have been diversifying into other areas of the financial services marketplace, however, other institutions have simultaneously been diversifying into areas which were hitherto the exclusive preserve of banks. Following the deregulation associated with the 1986 Building Societies Act, for example, UK building societies were able to offer unsecured loans, credit cards and money transmission services as well as life and general insurance, unit trusts (mutual funds) and so on. The recent 1997 Building Societies Act has removed most of the remaining restrictions on building societies' activities. More recently, insurance companies such as Standard Life and the Prudential have obtained banking licences, as have a number of large supermarkets and retailers. Furthermore, relatively new 'non-financial' entrants into the financial services marketplace, such as Virgin and Marks and Spencer, are now offering a range of financial services such as credit cards, unit trusts, pensions and so on.

The competitive pressures operating in banking markets have produced a wave of mergers and consolidations in recent years. In the UK we have witnessed the mergers of Lloyds Bank and the Trustee Savings Bank (TSB) and the contested takeover of the NatWest Bank by the Royal Bank of Scotland. Hence, against this backdrop of increasing competition and a trend towards diversification, consolidation and rationalization, the study of costs and efficiency, and in particular economies of scale and scope, is clearly very relevant in the context of UK banking.

It is also highly relevant to US banking, as it is in the US where the consolidation movement has been most pronounced. Between 1980 and 1998, for example, there were 8,000 bank mergers involving $2.4 trillion in acquired assets, and the total number of banks in the US declined from 14,407 to 8,697 over the period (Rhoades, 2000).

The 1980s also witnessed a trend towards so-called megamergers in the US banking industry, that is, mergers and acquisitions in which both banking organizations have more than $1 billion in assets. This trend was stimulated by the removal of many of the previous intrastate and interstate banking restrictions and continued through the 1990s. Towards the late 1990s, however, a trend towards even larger-scale mergers emerged. Berger et al. (1998) refer to these as 'supermegamergers' and define them as mergers and acquisitions (M&As) between institutions with assets of more than $100 billion each. As Berger et al. point out: 'Based on market values, nine of the ten largest M&As in US history in *any* industry occurred during 1998, and four of these – Citicorp–Travelers, BankAmerica–Nations Bank, Banc One–First Chicago and Norwest–Wells Fargo – occurred in banking' (p. 3).

Perhaps the highest profile of these supermegamergers was that between Citicorp and Travelers, which is also symptomatic of a trend towards mergers across different sectors of the financial services marketplace. The merger created a banking group with total assets of about $700 billion and an estimated customer base of over 100 million customers in about 100 countries. Furthermore, this merger has been hailed by many analysts as a new model in the form of the first truly global universal bank, where the term 'universal banking' refers to a bank which provides a full range of commercial banking, investment banking and insurance services. In terms of the relative contributions of the two parties to producing this global universal bank, Travelers offered investment services, asset management, life insurance, property and casualty insurance, and consumer lending. Citicorp on the other hand was a well-established large US commercial bank which also boasted the industry's largest credit card portfolio at more than $60 billion after acquiring AT&T Universal Card Services.

A further significant feature of the Citicorp–Travelers merger was that it was approved by the US regulators despite the fact that it breached the spirit of the 1933 Glass–Steagall Act. This legislation was enacted in the wake of the banking crises of the Great Depression and effectively prohibited universal banking by preventing commercial banks, investment banks (securities firms) and insurance companies from participating in each other's business. Although Congress had considered the repeal of the 1933 legislation many times over the last 20 years or so, and even though the legislation had been partially circumvented via the bank holding company legislation, this supermegamerger provided the impetus for a concerted attempt to overturn the depression era restrictions, given that a US commercial bank – Citicorp – was allowed to merge with the second-largest securities firm in the US – Travelers.

The final result was the Financial Services Modernization Act 1999. A key feature of this legislation is that it repeals the restrictions on banks affiliating with securities firms contained in Sections 20 and 32 of the Glass–Steagall Act. Furthermore, it provides for the creation of new 'financial holding companies' under Section 4 of the Bank Holding Company Act. Once created, these holding companies can engage in a statutorily provided list of financial services including insurance and securities underwriting and merchant banking activities. It seems highly likely that this legislation will pave the way for further large-scale universal bank mergers in the future. Indeed, the recently announced merger between J.P. Morgan and Chase Manhattan is a $30 billion deal creating the third largest bank in the US after Citicorp–Travelers and Bank of America with combined assets of about $660 billion. The merger will also push the combined bank towards the so-called 'bulge-bracket' of large investment banks.

Furthermore, the global nature of recent and prospective US universal banking mergers is likely to prompt similar mergers in other countries around the world. In recent years, for example, we have witnessed the merger of Union Bank of Switzerland (UBS) (which had previously acquired the UK securities firm Phillips and Drew) and the Swiss Bank Corporation, and future European financial sector mergers may well involve cross-border acquisitions, given the impact of the euro and the single European market in financial services.

The Japanese financial system is also currently experiencing a phase of significant structural change and consolidation. In part this reflects a legacy of relatively poor profitability and the problem loans associated with the bursting of the 'bubble economy' of the late 1980s. It also reflects the impact of deregulation and increasing competition from abroad. These pressures have produced a wave of mergers, both across hitherto fragmented segments of banking and financial markets and across the traditional *keiretsu* structures. During 1999, for example, a planned three-way amalgamation was announced between the Long Term Credit Bank, Industrial Bank of Japan, and two large city banks, Dai-Ichi Kangyo and Fuji Bank. The resultant single holding company (Mizuho) will represent the world's largest banking group (by assets) with combined assets in excess of ¥ 141,800 billion, and will account for about 25 per cent of the Japanese retail and corporate banking market. Mergers have also been announced between Sumitomo Bank and Sakura Bank, Bank of Tokyo–Mitsubishi and Mitsubishi Trust and between Sanwa, Asahi and Tokai Banks.

The poor performance of Japanese banks in recent years was caused by the interaction of a banking system which had focused on volume (growth in assets) rather than profitability up to the early 1990s, and the impact of major asset-quality problems which arose following the collapse of the Japanese bubble economy in 1990. For a full exposition, for example, see Hoshi and Kashyap (1999), Harui (1997), Craig (1998) and Hall (1999). In brief, the banking sector was used as an instrument of industrial policy by the Japanese government, recycling Japan's savings in order to provide Japanese industry with very low-cost investment funds. The quid pro quo to the banks for providing low-cost funds was the infamous 'convoy' system, whereby any bank facing financial difficulty could rely on the government to organize a rescue by other financial institutions. This created significant moral hazard in the banking system – Japanese banks largely ignored borrowers' credit quality when making loans and did not price loans according to risk. With low margins prevalent, the focus of Japanese banks was on the volume, rather than the quality, of their loan book. Furthermore, as a large proportion of bank shares were owned by Japanese corporations (who were also borrowers), there was little pressure from shareholders for banks to improve their profitability. A lax regulatory regime, poor disclosure standards and a weak culture of corporate governance also contributed to Japanese banks' ability to maintain their poor performance.

By the early 1990s, however, the Japanese banks began to feel the impact of the collapse of the bubble economy in Japan. They had undertaken a large amount of collateralized lending during the 1980s and the collapse of the asset bubble drove many borrowers into bankruptcy and eroded the value of collateral held against the loans. This led to severe asset-quality problems at Japanese banks. Unfortunately, the low levels of profitability meant that Japanese banks were unable to make adequate provisions against these bad loans. The initial response from banks and the regulatory authorities was one of forbearance, hidden behind weak disclosure standards. Only as time progressed and asset prices failed to recover did the Japanese banks begin to admit the true extent of their bad-loan problems.

The interest in analysing costs and efficiency in the Japanese banking sector is therefore driven, in part, by the need for the sector to increase its profitability. The need for Japanese banks to increase profitability is almost self-evident. On almost any measure, their profitability is low. For example for the years 1993/94 to 1997/98, the return on assets at major Japanese banks averaged −0.1 per cent, compared to an average of +1.2 per cent for the 22 largest US banks. Core profitability (operating profits before provisions) over total assets over the same period was +0.7 per cent at Japanese banks, but +2.1 per cent at the US banks.

Pressure on the Japanese banking sector to increase profits is also coming from reforms to the Japanese financial sector, commonly known as 'Japanese big bang'. This is a series of reforms designed to open up and modernize the entire Japanese financial system. The deregulation and increased disclosure will lead to more pressure from shareholders on banks (and indeed all other Japanese companies) to increase returns.

The Japanese government is also putting pressure on Japanese banks to increase their profitability. In March 1999, the Japanese government injected capital totalling ¥7.5 trillion ($60 billion) into 15 of the largest Japanese banks. One condition of the capital injection, however, was that the banks were required to draw up plans to show how they would increase profits (out to 2002/03). The Japanese government expects the banks to repay these funds within about ten years.

The ability of Japanese banks to take advantage of any potential economies of scale in order to increase profitability has improved dramatically, however, since the change in the regulatory regime in June 1998. Under the old regime, the role of each type of bank within the financial system was tightly defined, and little competition occurred between banks. The government maintained the structure of the system using the convoy system. As such, it was extremely rare for banks to merge, or to fail. As a result, Japan is commonly viewed as 'overbanked'. Under the new regulatory regime, however, the Japanese authorities are much more willing to see banks break out of their traditional role. They have encouraged the merger of some of the larger banks, and have allowed other banks to fail. They have indicated that further failures (particularly of smaller banks) would not be stopped.

Finally, in 2000, at the time of writing, the Japanese financial system is witnessing the first cross-sector alliances. In October 2000, for example, Dai-Ichi Mutual and Yasuda Life Assurance (in itself a unique link-up) announced that they would be asking other Japanese financial companies, including banks such as the newly created Mizuho, to join their planned alliance.

## 3  METHODOLOGY

In academic studies of costs and efficiency in banking, two main approaches have been adopted, a parametric and a non-parametric approach. Both require the specification of a cost or production function or frontier, but the former involves the specification and econometric estimation of a statistical or parametric function/frontier, while the non-parametric approach provides a piecewise linear frontier by enveloping the observed data points. Hence, this latter technique has come to be termed data envelopment analysis (DEA). Unlike the parametric approach, DEA does not require the specification of a particular functional form for the cost or production function. Hence, the derived efficiency estimates are not functional form dependent. In contrast, the accuracy of the efficiency estimates in the parametric approach is conditional on the accuracy of the chosen functional forms approximation to the cost or production function.

A potential drawback of the DEA approach, however, is that, being a non-parametric technique, there is no random error term specified as there would be in an econometric approach. This implies that any deviation above the cost frontier, for example, would be attributable to inefficiency, rather than to a combination of inefficiency and random error, as in the parametric approach.

In order to contrast the two approaches, begin by defining the variables:

$y_{it}$ – a vector of outputs of bank $i$ at period $t$, $y_{it} \in R_+^s$
$x_{it}$ – a vector of input quantities, $x_{it} \in R_+^m$
$w_{it}$ – a vector of input prices, $w_{it} \in R_+^m$, and
$t$ – an index of technological change.

The firm's total cost function is:

$$C(y_{it}, w_{it}, t) = \min_{x_{it}} \left[ \sum_{m=1}^{M} w_{mit} x_{mit} : y_{it} = F(x_{it}, t) \right], \quad (12.1)$$

where $F(x_{it}, t)$ is the firm's input requirement set of feasible input bundles $x_{it}$, which can be used to obtain a predetermined output vector, $y_{it}$ (such as consumer loans). The production function is also at least twice continuously differentiable, increasing and concave in $x_{it}$.

The two approaches to efficiency measurement essentially consist of constructing, for each individual bank in the data sample, either the left-hand side or the right-hand side of this definition (12.1). Models which construct the right-hand side from the observed sample comprise non-parametric frontier models of relative efficiency, such as DEA, while those which construct the left-hand side comprise parametric stochastic frontier models.

**Non-parametric Frontier Models**

Within the DEA framework it is possible to decompose relative efficiency performance into the categories initially suggested by Farrell (1957) and later elaborated by Banker et al. (1984) and Färe et al. (1985). The constructed relative efficiency frontiers are non-statistical or non-parametric in the sense that they are constructed through the envelopment of the DMUs (decision making units), with the 'best practice' DMUs forming the non-parametric frontier. Farrell's categories are best illustrated, for the single output–two input case in the unit isoquant diagram, Figure 12.1, where the unit isoquant ($yy$) shows the various combinations of the two inputs ($x_1$, $x_2$) which can be used to produce 1 unit of the single output ($y$). The firm at E is productively (or overall) efficient in choosing the cost-minimizing production process given the relative input prices represented by the slope of WW'. A DMU at Q is allocatively inefficient in choosing an inappropriate input mix, while a DMU at R is both allocatively inefficient (in the ratio 0P/0Q), and technically inefficient, (in the ratio 0Q/0R) because it requires an excessive amount of both inputs, $x$, compared with a firm at Q producing the same level of output, $y$.

The use of the unit isoquant implies the assumption of constant returns to scale. However, a firm using more of both inputs than the combination represented by Q may experience either increasing or decreasing returns to scale so that, in general, the technical efficiency ratio 0Q/0R may be further decomposed into scale efficiency, 0Q/0S, and pure technical efficiency, 0S/0R, with point Q in Figure 12.1 representing the case of constant returns to scale. The former arises because the firm is at an input–output combination that differs from the equivalent constant returns to scale situation. Only the latter pure technical efficiency represents the failure of the firm to

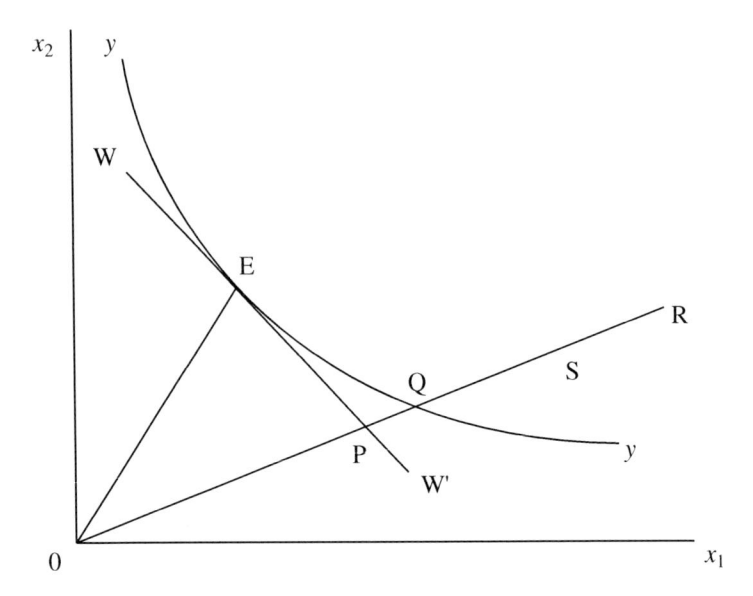

*Figure 12.1   Farrell efficiency*

extract the maximum output from its adopted input levels and hence may be thought of as measuring the unproductive use of resources. In summary,

$$\text{productive efficiency} = \text{allocative efficiency} \times \text{scale efficiency} \times \text{pure technical efficiency}$$
$$0P/0R = (0P/0Q) \times (0Q/0S) \times (0S/0R). \tag{12.2}$$

Hence, concentrating on overall technical efficiency, Farrell suggested constructing, for each observed DMU, a pessimistic piecewise linear approximation to the isoquant, using activity analysis applied to the observed sample of DMUs in the organization/industry in question. This produces a relative rather than an absolute measure of efficiency since the DMUs on the piecewise linear isoquant constructed from the boundary of the set of observations are defined to be the efficient DMUs.

Subsequent developments have extended this mathematical linear programming approach. If there are $n$ DMUs in the industry, all the observed inputs and outputs are represented by the $n$-column matrices: X and Y. The input requirement set, or reference technology, can then be represented by the free disposal convex hull of the observations, that is, the smallest convex set containing the observations consistent with the assumption that having less of an input cannot increase output. We do this by choosing weighting vectors, λ (one for each firm) to apply to the columns of X and Y in order to show that firm's efficiency performance in the best light.

For each DMU in turn, using $x$ and $y$ to represent its particular observed inputs and outputs, pure technical efficiency is calculated by solving the problem of finding the lowest multiplicative factor, θ, which must be applied to the firm's use of inputs, $x$, to ensure it is still a member of the input requirements set or reference technology. That is, choose:

$$\{\theta, \lambda\} \text{ to minimize } \theta \text{ such that: } \quad \theta x \geq \lambda' X$$
$$y \leq \lambda' Y$$
$$\lambda i \geq 0, \Sigma \lambda_i = 1, i = 1, \ldots, n. \quad (12.3)$$

To determine scale efficiency, we solve the technical efficiency problem (12.3) without the constraint that the input requirements set be convex; that is, we drop the constraint $\Sigma \lambda_i = 1$. This permits scaled-up or -down input combinations to be part of the DMU's production possibility set. Figure 12.2 illustrates this for the case of a single input and a single output. In Figure 12.2, the production possibility set under constant returns to scale is the region to the right of the ray, 0C, through the leftmost input–output observation. Any scaled-up or -down versions of the observations are also in the production possibility set under this assumption of constant returns to scale.

Imposing the convexity constraint, $\Sigma \lambda_i = 1$, ensures that the production

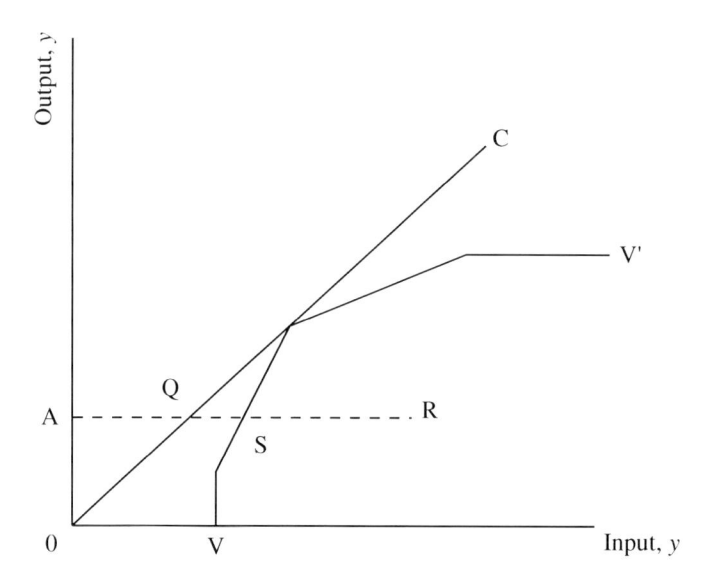

*Figure 12.2  Scale and technical efficiency*

possibility set is the area to the right of the piecewise linear frontier VV′, which does not assume constant returns to scale, but allows for the possibility of increasing returns to scale at low output levels and decreasing returns at high output levels. The resulting overall technical and pure technical efficiency ratios, AQ/AR and AS/AR, are illustrated for one of the observations. Scale efficiency is the ratio of the two results.

In the case of programme (12.3), the efficiency ratios with and without the convexity constraint may be labelled $\theta_p$ and $\theta_o$, and scale efficiency, $\theta_s$ is then $\theta_o/\theta_p$. In the subsequent results we refer to overall technical efficiency as OE, pure technical efficiency as PTE and scale efficiency as SE. As explained above, it follows that:

$$OE = PTE \times SE, \text{ and } SE = OE / PTE. \qquad (12.4)$$

### The Free Disposal Hull (FDH) Technique

It is clear from the previous analysis, and particularly the diagramatic analysis, that in respect of the inputs required to produce given output levels, DEA assumes that linear substitution is possible between the observed input combinations on an isoquant. In turn, these isoquants are derived in a piecewise linear fashion from the DMUs in the sample, which form the efficient frontier. Hence, in DEA each DMU is evaluated in turn relative to this piecewise linear isoquant or efficient frontier. An alternative non-parametric approach to DEA which has been applied in banking efficiency studies, however, is the free disposal hull (FDH) approach. FDH does not permit such linear input substitution. Hence, the isoquant is represented by a step function through the observed input combinations. In the words of Berger and Humphrey (1997):

> The free disposal hull approach (FDH) is a special case of the DEA model where the points on lines connecting the DEA vertices are not included in the frontier. Instead, the FDH production possibilities set is composed only of the DEA vertices and the free disposal hull points interior to these vertices. (p. 177)

### Stochastic Frontier Models

An alternative approach to the non-parametric frontier methodology is that of stochastic frontier models suggested by Aigner et al. (1977). In the context of cost functions, the Aigner et al. procedure is directed to the left-hand side of the cost function definition (12.1). This typically involves the specification of a stochastic production or cost frontier. In the context of the latter, for example, we might write the cost function as follows:

$$\ln C_{it} = \ln C(y, w)_{it} + \varepsilon_{it}, \quad (12.5)$$

where $C$ represents total costs, $y$ is a vector of outputs, $w$ is a vector of input prices and $\varepsilon$ is a composed error term that reflects both statistical noise and the X-inefficiency of the firms in the sample:

$$\varepsilon_{it} = u_{it} + v_{it}; \; u_{it} \geq 0.$$

The component $v_{it}$ is assumed to be symmetrically distributed around a zero mean but $u_{it}$ is assumed to be non-negative (non-positive in the case of a stochastic production frontier). Hence, $u_{it}$ represents the deviations above the minimum cost frontier (X-inefficiency) associated with either technical inefficiency (excessive use of inputs in the production of outputs) and allocative inefficiency (the failure to utilize the cost-minimizing input bundle given input prices and the level of outputs).

Estimation of such models has largely followed Aigner et al. (1977). By specifying particular density functions for the composed error terms, maximum likelihood estimation can be used (see Bauer, 1990, for details of the likelihood functions). Conventionally we assume that $v_{it}$ is normally distributed, while $u_{it}$ has the truncated half-normal distribution:

$$v_i \sim N(0, \sigma_v^2); \; u_{it} \sim |N(0, \sigma_u^2)|.$$

Aigner et al. write the likelihood function in terms of two critical parameters, the ratio of the error term standard deviations, and the sum of their variances, $\sigma^2$:

$$\lambda = \sigma_u / \sigma_v; \; \sigma^2 = \sigma_u^2 + \sigma_v^2.$$

Determining the observation-specific measures of inefficiency is problematic, however, because the components of the errors are not separately observed. In this context, Jondrow et al. (1982) suggest using either the mean of the $u_{it}$ conditional on the known distribution of the $\varepsilon_{it}$, or the conditional mode as shown below:

$$M(u_{it}/\varepsilon_{it}) = \varepsilon_{it}(\sigma_u^2/\sigma^2) \quad \text{if } \varepsilon_{it} \geq 0$$
$$= 0 \quad \text{if } \varepsilon_{it} < 0.$$

The standard techniques described above, however, impose essentially arbitrary assumptions concerning the distribution of the X-efficiency error term, $u_{it}$. As outlined above, this is often the half normal or truncated normal distribution but other distributions such as the gamma distribution have also been used.

### Distribution Free Approach

Berger (1993) has proposed the distribution free approach (DFA) as an alternative to the conventional stochastic frontier technique. Berger points out that the $v_{it}$ component of the composed error term is by definition random and would be expected to average out to zero over time in the context of a panel data sample. Hence, the DFA involves the estimation of a cost function (such as the translog) separately for each year of the panel data sample. The associated error terms will necessarily be the composed error terms, $\varepsilon_{it}$. If these error terms are then averaged over each year of the sample for each firm, assuming that the random error terms average out, this will produce a measure of the average levels of X-inefficiency across the sample of firms. Berger suggests that a period of five years is typically appropriate for this purpose. These efficiency measures are then typically normalized relative to the most efficient firm in the sample.

### Thick Frontier Approach

A further alternative to the stochastic frontier approach is the thick frontier approach (TFA). As with the distribution free approach, TFA attempts to simplify the problem of separating out the two components of the composite error term. Rather than averaging out the observed errors over a number of years, as in DFA, TFA assumes that deviations from predicted costs within the lowest average cost quartile of banks in a size class represent random error, while deviations in predicted costs between the highest and lowest quartiles represent X-inefficiencies. This approach has been used *inter alia* by Berger and Humphrey (1991, 1992a) and Berger (1993).

### The Cost Function Specification

A potential drawback with any parametric frontier methodologies such as the stochastic frontier approach or the distribution free approach is that they require the specification of a particular functional form for the cost (or production) function. Hence, the derived efficiency estimates are inherently functional form specific and their accuracy depends on how well the specified functional form approximates to the true underlying cost (or production) function.

In order to maintain as general a specification as possible, the multi-input, multi-output translog cost function has frequently been adopted by researchers. The appeal of the translog cost function is that it is a so-called flexible functional form. Hence, the translog functional form can provide a second-order approximation to any underlying function, such as a cost function. This implies that scale economies can be estimated accurately as the flexible functional form imposes no a priori restrictions on elasticities. In contrast, earlier function forms, such as Cobb–Douglas and the constant elasticity of substitution (CES), placed severe restrictions on the nature of the unit cost curve, for example.

The standard second-order translog cost function can be written as follows:

$$\ln TC = \alpha_0 + \sum_i \alpha_i \ln Y_i + \sum_j \beta_j \ln P_j + \tfrac{1}{2} \sum_i \sum_k \sigma_{ik} \ln Y_i \ln Y_K$$

$$+ \tfrac{1}{2} \sum_j \sum_h \gamma_{jh} \ln P_j \ln P_h + \sum_i \sum_j \delta_{ij} \ln Y_i \ln P_j + v_i, \quad (12.6)$$

where ln denotes the natural logarithm. Following Young's theorem, the second-order parameters of the cost function must be symmetric, that is:

$$\sigma_{ik} = \sigma_{ki} \text{ for all } i, k, \quad \text{and } \gamma_{jh} = \gamma_{hj} \text{ for all } j, h.$$

Using Shephard's Lemma (Shephard, 1970) and partially differentiating (12.6) with respect to the factor prices $\ln P_j$, the following cost share equations are obtained:

$$S_j = P_j X_j / TC = (\partial TC / \partial P_j)(P_j / TC) = \partial \ln TC / \partial \ln P_j$$

$$= \beta_j + \sum_h \gamma_{jh} \ln P_h + \sum_i \delta_{ij} \ln Y_i + \tau_{jB} \ln B + \eta_{jT} T + \ln u_n. \quad (12.7)$$

To ensure linear homogeneity in factor prices, the following restrictions are typically imposed during estimation:

$$\sum_j \beta_j = 1; \quad \sum_{jh} \gamma_{jh} = 0; \quad \sum_{ij} \delta_{ji} = 0.$$

As the cost shares sum to unity, one share equation must be omitted from the estimation in order to avoid a singular covariance matrix. Maximum likelihood estimates are, however, invariant to the choice of the omitted share equation.

Once the cost function has been estimated, it is then possible to calculate measures of economies of scale. In the case of the translog, for example, the cost function (12.6) is differentiated with respect to output (Panzar and Willig, 1977),

$$OES = C(Y, P, B) / \sum_i Y_i MC_i = \partial \ln TC / \partial \ln Y_i$$

$$\xi = \alpha_i + \sum_i \sigma_{ik} \ln Y_k + \sum_j \delta_{ij} \ln P_j + \eta_{Ti} T, \qquad (12.8)$$

where $MC_i$ is the marginal cost with respect to the $i$th output and $\xi = \delta \ln TC/\delta n\, Y_i$ is the cost elasticity of the $i$th output. If $\xi > 1$, the bank in question experiences diseconomies of scale, if $\xi < 1$, it exhibits increasing returns and if $\xi = 1$, this is indicative of constant returns to scale. These results imply that if an equal proportionate increase in all inputs leads to a less than proportionate increase in costs, there are economies of scale in banking.

An alternative functional form which has been utilized in more recent empirical work incorporates the semi-non-parametric Fourier flexible functional form (see, for example, Berger and Humphrey, 1997, and Altunbas et al., 2000). This will be discussed in more detail subsequently, but the cost function typically specified and estimated by researchers supplements the usual translog cost function with a truncated Fourier expansion in outputs but not input prices. This hybrid translog/Fourier cost function is illustrated below:

$$\ln TC = \alpha_0 + \sum_i \alpha_i \ln Y_i + \sum_j \beta_j \ln P_j + \tfrac{1}{2} \sum_i \sum_k \sigma_{ik} \ln Y_i \ln Y_k$$
$$+ \tfrac{1}{2} \sum_j \sum_h \gamma_{jh} \ln P_j \ln P_h + \sum_i \sum_j \delta_{ij} \ln Y_i \ln P_j$$
$$+ \sum_i [a_i \cos(Z_i) + b_j \sin(Z_j)]$$
$$+ \sum_i \sum_j [a_{ij} \cos(Z_i + Z_j) + b_{ij} \sin(Z_i + Z_j)] + v_i, \qquad (12.9)$$

where $Z_i$ = the adjusted values of the log output $\ln Y_i$ such that they span the interval $[0, 2\pi]$.

## 4 MODELLING THE BANKING FIRM

In order to investigate efficiencies/inefficiencies in financial institutions such as banks using either the parametric or non-parametric frontier methodologies, it is clearly necessary to develop a model of the productive process. That is, it is necessary to specify the inputs and outputs of the depository institution in the production process. Unfortunately, this is not as straightforward in the case of a financial institution, particularly a depository institution, as with a manufacturing firm. Indeed, the classification of inputs and outputs is still a contentious issue in the banking literature, both with respect to cost function studies and the parametric and non-parametric frontier methodologies.

In general, however, two main approaches to the classification of inputs and outputs can be discerned in the literature. The intermediation approach assesses deposit-taking institutions as financial intermediaries which raise retail deposits and/or borrow wholesale funds (managed liabilities) to be transformed into loans and other earning assets. Under this methodology, therefore, outputs are defined as the values of the various categories of interest-bearing assets on the balance sheet while deposits and borrowed funds are included with capital and labour as inputs (see Sealey and Lindley, 1977; Drake and Weyman-Jones, 1992, 1996; Drake, 1992, 1995). Total costs in this approach (which are relevant in cost function and parametric cost frontier studies) are defined inclusive of total interest costs.

In contrast, in the production approach, deposit-taking institutions are characterized as producers of services associated with individual loan and deposit accounts, these services being produced by utilizing capital and labour inputs. Under this approach, therefore, the number of accounts of different loan and deposit categories are generally taken to be the appropriate definitions of output (see Ferrier et al., 1993; Berg et al., 1993; Drake, 2001), and interest costs are excluded from total operating costs.

## 5 EMPIRICAL EVIDENCE

### Scale Economies and X-efficiency: An Overview

Most of the earlier academic research into costs and efficiency in banking tended to concentrate on the issue of economies of scale. That is the shape of the average cost curve in banking and, in particular, the location of the minimum efficient scale or the scale which achieves minimum unit costs. This is clearly an important issue given that banking markets around the world are becoming increasingly competitive. Any bank which is not operating at close to minimum efficient scale would, by definition, be operating above the minimum attainable cost to assets ratio. Furthermore, the increasing trend towards mergers and consolidation in banking has increased the focus on economies of scale, particularly given the emergence of so-called megamergers and supermegamergers in the US and large-scale mergers in the UK, Japan and elsewhere. Clearly, the cost implications of such mergers depend crucially on the nature of economies of scale in banking. If, for example, academic research indicates the presence of diseconomies of large scale in banking, then such large-scale mergers could only be justified on either revenue grounds or on the basis of cost savings, via diversification and economies of scope, and via rationalization.

Most of the earlier academic work focusing on economies of scale implicitly assumed cost-minimizing behaviour on the part of banks. In other words, cost inefficiencies were assumed to be attributable to scale inefficiencies (failure to operate at the minimum efficient scale) rather than to X-inefficiency (failure to minimize costs at the given scale of output). As Berger et al. (1993a) point out, however:

> While scale and scope efficiencies have been extensively studied, primarily in the context of US financial institutions, relatively little attention has been paid to measuring what appears to be a much more important source of efficiency differences – X-inefficiencies, or deviations from the efficient frontier. (p. 222)

Berger et al. found that X-inefficiencies were much more significant than scale inefficiencies in US banking, with mean inefficiencies of about 20 per cent. This contrasted with potential cost savings from scale efficiency of only about 5–6 per cent.

Hence, a good deal of the more recent research has focused on measuring the extent of X-inefficiencies in banking in various countries. Clearly, the greater the extent of X-inefficiencies in given banking markets, the more vulnerable will these institutions be to competitive entry and increasing competition.

It was emphasized previously that both DEA and parametric/econometric techniques can be used to examine issues relating to costs and efficiency in banking. With respect to the measurement of X-inefficiency using the parametric approach, however, a difficulty arises in the context of separating deviations above the cost frontier attributable to inefficiency from those attributable to the random error term, as these are not individually observable. As outlined above, three distinct approaches have emerged in recent years to deal with this problem: the stochastic frontier approach, the distribution free approach and the thick frontier approach. With respect to contrasting the results obtained from these parametric approaches with those obtained from non-parametric approaches, such as DEA, however, a further problem emerges. Specifically, the X-inefficiency measures obtained from parametric estimations are composed of both allocative and technical inefficiency. In contrast, while techniques such as DEA can be used to calculate measures of allocative efficiencies, most studies have tended to concentrate on technical efficiency and its decomposition into pure technical and scale efficiency. This implies that the results from many parametric and non-parametric studies are not directly comparable unless one assumes that the majority of X-inefficiency in banking is technical rather than allocative in nature. It should be noted, however, that this assumption is in fact supported by empirical evidence, for example, Berger et al. (1993a).

## Costs and Efficiency in US Banking

### Economies of scale

Most of the earlier research into scale economies in US banking used data up to the 1980s and typically utilized the translog cost function, as outlined previously. The surprising feature of much of this research was the finding that scale economies were fairly modest and were exhausted at relatively low asset levels. As Berger et al. (1998) point out:

> The consensus finding was that the average cost curve had a relatively flat U-shape with medium sized banks being slightly more scale-efficient than either large or small banks. Only small banks had the potential for economically significant scale efficiency gains and the measured inefficiencies were relatively small, on the order of 5% of costs or less. The location of the scale-efficient point – the bottom of the average cost U – differed among studies, but was usually between about $100 million and $10 billion in assets, with a larger scale-efficient point generally being found when the banks in the sample were larger. (p. 20)

These results were particularly surprising in the context of the merger wave which has characterized US banking during the 1980s and 1990s, and in particular, the trend towards mega- and supermegamergers which has emerged during the 1990s. The studies detailed above suggested that there were no significant scale efficiency gains to be made from mergers, and that there may well be efficiency losses in the context of mergers between relatively large banks. Not surprisingly, these types of results spawned a good deal of research which emphasized alternative motives for mergers and drew on the literature of managerial theories of the firm/expense preference behaviour and so on.

The ambiguity surrounding the evidence on the minimum efficient scale in US banking, however, served to highlight a potential problem with the translog cost function. McAllister and McManus (1993), for example, showed that, even though the translog cost function is a flexible functional form, it may provide a poor approximation to the true cost function when applied to banks of all sizes. In essence, the translog approximation forces large and small banks to lie on a symmetric U-shaped ray average cost curve. It is now well established that these problems emanate from the fact that the translog is only a locally flexible functional form. In other words it can only provide an accurate local approximation to an arbitrary function, which implies that the translog may perform poorly away from the mean product mix. As large banks often tend to have product mixes which are very different from the average bank, this may explain why the US results were relatively sensitive to the particular size range of banks in the sample.

These types of problems have resulted in a recent shift towards semi-nonparametric techniques, such as the Fourier flexible form (detailed above), which can produce global approximations to arbitrary functions such as cost functions. As will be emphasized later in this chapter, more recent research into scale and X-efficiencies in banking has also tended to utilize panel data sets rather than cross-section data sets. In turn, this has facilitated the incorporation of dynamic technological change effects into efficiency analysis, which is clearly not possible in the context of cross-section data. The consequence of these types of innovation in respect of US research has been results which are generally much more positive in respect of potential scale economies and the cost implications of large-scale bank mergers. Berger and Mester (1997), for example, found, using 1990s data, that the results displayed substantial cost scale economies of the order of about 20 per cent of costs, for banks up to between $10 billion and $25 billion in assets.

While these substantial potential cost savings for banks with assets up to $25 billion can provide a rationale for the megamergers in the US (where each bank has assets of over $1 billion each), they do not explain the more recent trend towards supermegamergers (where each bank has assets of over $100 billion each). To provide a rationale for this type of merger, it seems likely that we will need to examine the literature and empirical evidence pertaining to diversification, economies of scope and universal banking. We turn to these issues in a subsequent section in the context of US banks.

**X-efficiency**
With respect to X-efficiency studies in US banking, Berger and Humphrey (1997) survey the results from efficiency studies of 50 US banks incorporating both parametric and non-parametric studies. Given that many studies produce results for more than one year, however, this amounts to no less than 188 annual efficiency estimates. It should be noted that in order to ensure as much comparability as possible, Berger and Humphrey utilize DEA efficiency scores based on variable returns rather than constant returns. This ensures that the DEA efficiency scores relate only to technical efficiency and exclude scale effects. As mentioned, however, many parametric studies report X-efficiencies (allocative and technical) which may not be directly comparable to the technical efficiency levels reported in DEA studies.

With these caveats in mind, Berger and Humphrey find that the mean efficiency score over all studies (parametric and non-parametric) is close to 80 per cent. It is interesting to note, however, that the mean and median efficiencies for the non-parametric techniques are 0.72 and 0.74, respectively.

This contrasts with figures of 0.84 and 0.85 for the parametric approaches. The non-parametric studies were also found to produce a greater dispersion in estimated efficiency ratios, with a standard deviation of 0.17 and a range of 0.31–0.97. This contrasts with the corresponding figures from the parametric studies of 0.06 and 0.61–0.95, respectively. These discrepancies are perhaps to be expected, however, given that DEA attributes all deviations from the frontier as inefficiency, whereas the parametric approaches attribute some of the deviation (that is, from the fitted cost function) to statistical noise and the remainder to X-inefficiency.

Notwithstanding the disparity between the parametric and non-parametric results, however, the consensus is that US banking is characterized by considerable X-inefficiency. Indeed, the mean level of 20 per cent X-inefficiency clearly swamps the inefficiencies associated with scale effects, which have typically been estimated at about 5 per cent of costs. As was mentioned previously, however, more recent studies such as Berger and Mester (1997) have established cost economies amounting to about 20 per cent of costs, for bank sizes up to between $10 billion and $25 billion in assets. This suggests that relatively small US banks could face severe cost (and hence profitability) pressures as a result of the combination both X-inefficiencies and scale inefficiencies. This hypothesis is reinforced by the finding of Berger et al. (1993b) that X-inefficiencies tend to be lower for larger banks. As Berger et al. argue: 'larger banks appear to be substantially more efficient than smaller banks. This does not appear to be a quirk related to comparing very large banks with very small banks, but rather appears to be a significant relationship throughout the range of the data' (p. 344). It is also worth pointing out that, although most studies to date have focused on cost X-inefficiencies, the consensus from the limited studies into profit X-inefficiencies suggests average profit X-efficiency levels of only 50 per cent in US banking (Berger and Humphrey, 1997).

Clearly, these types of X-efficiency results, combined with the generally more positive results which have emerged recently concerning potential scale economies, suggest that we shall see continuing consolidation in US banking. Furthermore, this is likely to encompass both further so-called mega- and supermegamergers, but also increasing M&A activity involving the relatively smaller banks.

**Diversification, economies of scope and post-merger performance**
Although we have made the case for continuing consolidation in US banking via M&A activity, based on the available scale and X-efficiency evidence, it must be recognized that the merger wave in the US has been taking place against the backdrop of the increasing diversification of business by US banks. Indeed, many US bank mergers have combined different aspects

of the financial sector, such as commercial banking and investment banking, commercial banking and insurance (bancassurance), and so on. Furthermore, as was emphasized previously, the recent supermegamergers in the US cannot be justified on the basis of the available economies of scale evidence but must be rationalized in terms of the alleged benefits of diversification associated with universal banking.

The trend towards diversification in US banking is not only a product of the gradual deregulation introduced into US banking (detailed above), but also due to the competitive threats posed to the core banking business by the capital market and by mutual funds. This threat has induced US banks to diversify, at the margin, away from core 'on-balance sheet' margin business and into increasingly into non-traditional 'off-balance sheet' and fee income business. This trend clearly raises the issue of economies of scope; that is, are there sufficient synergies, via joint production cost savings, additional revenue streams, and possibly reduced risk, to justify such diversification?

Furthermore, as this growth and diversification often involves M&A activity, it is relevant to examine the available empirical evidence in order to establish whether M&A activity does deliver the potential benefits in terms of economies of scale (for the relatively smaller banks), economies of scope and reduced costs and enhanced profitability.

We examine these two issues in turn in the subsequent sections.

**Diversification and economies of scope in US banking**
The early empirical evidence on economies of scope in US banking was generally drawn from the same studies which produced the early economies of scale estimates. Hence, the results were based on the translog cost function specification, the potential problems of which were documented in a previous section. Further problems emerge in the context of the measurement of economies of scope, however, since this involves the comparison of the costs of the joint production of a multiple set of outputs with the cost of specialized production, that is, producing each output independently. In most banking data sets, however, there are very few, if any, specialist producers, with most banks tending to produce the joint set of outputs. The usual solution to this problem in the context of the early translog cost function studies was to simulate the costs of specialized production using the parameters of the estimated cost function by setting all the outputs but one to zero. This is problematic in the case of the translog cost function, however, as it is logarithmic and hence is not defined for zero outputs. Hence, a compromise was typically adopted in which the outputs were allowed to be positive but 'close to zero'. A further problem with the early studies, however, was that economies of scope were typically meas-

ured relative to the best-practice cost frontier (the estimated cost function). In reality, however, many firms may have been exhibiting X-inefficiencies and operating above the cost frontier. As the early studies were cost function studies rather than cost frontier studies, however, it may be that the economies of scope estimates were 'contaminated by X-inefficiencies'.

As Berger et al. (1998) point out, the combination of the problems outlined above often resulted in measured economies of scope estimates that were 'erratic and beyond credible levels' (p. 21).

In those studies which provided more credible scope economy estimates, however, the results echoed those obtained from the economies of scale estimates in the sense that they implied very little cost savings from joint production (Berger et al., 1987; Hunter et al., 1990; Pulley and Humphrey, 1993; Ferrier et al., 1993). Furthermore, unlike the empirical evidence on economies of scale in US banking, more recent research using data into the 1990s has failed to produce unambiguous evidence of significant economies of scope. Berger et al. (1993b), for example, found that joint production is optimal for most banks, but that specialization is optimal for others. Berger et al. (1996), however, found little or no revenue scope efficiency between deposits and loans in terms of charging customers for joint benefits.

A potential criticism of the aforementioned research into economies of scope in US banking, however, is that the analysis tended to focus on economies of scope across what might be termed traditional bank outputs such as securities, different types of loans, deposits and so on. As has been emphasized previously, an important feature of US banking in recent years has been the diversification into non-traditional areas in the form of off-balance sheet fee income business, but also via securities and insurance affiliates. Hence, much of the most recent empirical research into US banking has focused on the impact of this diversification into non-traditional business.

A recent study by Rogers and Sinkey (1999) analyses the characteristics of US banks which diversify into non-traditional activities using a sample period covering 1989 to 1993. Not surprisingly, they find that it is the larger US banks that have tended to diversify into these non-traditional activities. Interestingly, however, they find an inverse relationship between the size of the net interest margin and diversification. This is taken to be evidence that banks under the greatest competitive pressure in their traditional intermediation business are resorting to non-traditional business as a means of bolstering profits. They also find that banks with higher levels of non-traditional business tend to exhibit lower risk. This is clearly evidence of economies of scope in respect of risk since more highly diversified firms exhibit less risk than more specialized firms. Furthermore, this supports previous empirical evidence which indicated the potential gains from diversification due to the lack of correlation between the revenue flows in different segments of the business. Kwan (1997), for example, found, using 1990s data, that securities subsidiaries provided diversification benefits due to the low correlations of returns with those in the rest of the bank holding company (BHC). Similarly, an earlier study by Saunders and Walter (1994) found that risk could be reduced by combining banks with non-bank financial firms, especially insurance companies.

In summary, therefore, the empirical evidence to date indicates that economies of scope in US banking are most prevalent when banks combine traditional commercial banking with non-traditional business such as investment banking and insurance in the trend towards bancassurance and universal banking. Furthermore, most of the benefits seem to accrue via additional revenue streams and reductions in risk rather than via cost savings associated with joint production.

**Post-merger performance of US banks**
As has been emphasized previously, the early empirical evidence on economies of scale and economies of scope suggested that there was little scope for cost efficiency improvements from M&As and particularly from large-scale mergers. Subsequent research using data extending into the 1990s, however, indicated potentially significant scale economies for banks with assets up to $25 billion. Furthermore, the empirical evidence on X-inefficiency in US banking suggested that mean X-inefficiency levels were of the order of 20 per cent. It was also established that larger US banks appeared to be more X-efficient than their smaller counterparts. Hence, the empirical evidence would suggest that there are significant post-merger gains to be had in respect of improved cost efficiency. This would clearly be enhanced if the capital market performed as it should in the sense that the acquiring banks were, on average, more X-efficient than the acquired banks. This would suggest that a superior management team could achieve significant reductions in costs by reducing X-inefficiency levels in the acquired bank. It is interesting to note in this respect that a number of studies have indeed found that the acquiring banks do tend to be more X-efficient than the acquired banks (see, for example, Berger and Humphrey, 1992b).

In spite of these apparent potential merger gains, and in contrast to the typical perspective of the media and consultants, the vast majority of the academic research in the US has found that the potential for cost efficiency gains has not been realized in practice. A number of these studies used basic cost ratios, such as operating costs to total assets, and tended to find no significant change in such cost ratios following bank mergers (Rhoades, 1986, 1990; Srinivasin, 1992; Srinivasin and Wall, 1992; Linder and Crane, 1992;

Pilloff, 1996). Even when more sophisticated cost frontier approaches were used, however, the studies typically found little or no improvement in cost efficiency on average (as measured in terms of deviations from the efficient cost frontier) following bank mergers (Berger and Humphrey, 1992a; Rhoades, 1993; Peristiani, 1997; DeYoung, 1997).

In their 1992 study, for example, Berger and Humphrey (1992b) found around a 5 percentage point improvement in X-inefficiencies on average, but found that this was not statistically significant. Similarly, Houston and Ryngaert (1993) found, using a recent sample of bank mergers, that the overall gains (the weighted average of gains to the bidder and target firms) are slightly positive, but statistically indistinguishable from zero. The results of the early research into the impact of US bank mergers (over the period from 1980 to 1993) is summarized by Rhoades (1994) as follows:

> The nineteen operating performance (OP) studies provide consistent evidence that bank mergers have not generally resulted in efficiency gains. The twenty one event studies yield mixed results showing generally positive abnormal returns to stockholders of targets and negative or no abnormal returns to stockholders of bidders following announcement of a merger. Even a simple weighting of the two sets of results would lead one toward an overall conclusion that bank mergers do not tend to result in efficiency gains. (p. 8)

Leaving aside the event studies, the early studies of operating discussed above tended to focus on the potential improvements in cost efficiencies following mergers. As Akhavein et al. (1997) point out, however:

> Mergers and acquisitions could raise profits in any of three major ways. First, they could improve *cost efficiency*, reducing costs per unit of output for a given set of output quantities and input prices . . . Second, mergers may increase profits through improvements in profit efficiency that involve superior combinations of inputs and outputs. Profit efficiency is a more inclusive concept than cost efficiency, because it takes into account the cost and revenue effects of the choice of output vector, which is taken as given in the measurement of cost efficiency . . . Third, mergers may improve profits through the exercise of additional market power in setting prices.

In order to capture these three potential impacts of bank mergers on profitability, Akhavein et al. use a profit function approach rather than the more common, but more restrictive, cost function approach. Furthermore, they control for any industrywide changes in profits or efficiency over time by estimating the profit efficiency of all large US banks (assets over $1 billion) over the period from 1980 to 1990 irrespective of whether or not they were involved in mergers during the period. Akhavein et al. then calculate the improvement in efficiency of each megamerger as the efficiency rank of the consolidated bank after the merger less the weighted average of the acquiring and acquired banks before the merger.

The results obtained by Akhavein et al. are much more favourable to bank mergers than previous empirical research in the sense that they find that the megamergers of the 1980s significantly improved profit efficiency on average. Specifically, 'the average profit efficiency rank of merging banks increased from the 74th percentile to the 90th percentile of the peer group of large banks with complete data available over the same time periods, a statistically significant 16 percentage point increase'.

The results are, however, consistent with previous results in the sense that Akhavein et al. used the same data set as used in a previous cost efficiency study (Berger and Humphrey, 1992b). As in the previous study, Akhavein et al. found no significant cost efficiency improvements, on average, following bank mergers. Hence, the pessimistic results on the efficacy of bank mergers evident in the earlier academic studies appears to have been a consequence of the reliance on the overly restrictive concept of cost efficiency.

Akhavein et al. (1997) also provide some important insights into the sources of improvements in profit efficiency and into those factors (variables) most likely to predict successful merger outcomes. With respect to the former, the results suggest that merging banks tend to change their output mixes from securities and towards loans. This tends to raise profitability since issuing loans creates more value than purchasing securities. Akhavein et al. argue that this finding may support the so-called diversification hypothesis if the change in the mix occurs because merging banks have improved the diversification of risks, thus facilitating a higher loan to asset ratio. Furthermore, they assert that this appears to be the case as '[the] shift appears to occur without any increase in the equity/asset ratio (which in fact declines slightly), supporting the diversification hypothesis, since capital markets typically restrict banks from taking substantial additional risks without increases in equity'.

With respect to the factors which can predict successful mergers, Akhavein et al. claim that their prediction model explains about 80 per cent of the variance of the change in profit efficiency rank. Furthermore, they argue that their results support two particular hypotheses concerning the profit efficiency improvement from mergers. First, the *relative efficiency hypothesis* asserts that *ex post* merger efficiency gains depend upon the difference in the *ex ante* efficiency levels of the two banks since the acquiring bank will seek to raise the efficiency level of the acquired bank towards its own level. In turn, this hypothesis is consistent with earlier evidence that acquiring banks tend to be more efficient than acquired banks. The second hypothesis is the *low efficiency hypothesis*. This asserts that *ex post* improvements in efficiency are greater if either, or both, of the banks have low *ex ante* efficiency. In the words of Akhavein et al.: 'Here, the merger event itself may have the effect of "waking up" management or be used as an "excuse" to implement substantial restructuring or other changes to improve efficiency.'

Rhoades (1998) takes a different approach to Akhavein et al. by presenting an analysis of nine case studies of US bank mergers. The case studies were selected in a non-random fashion on the basis of mergers which, a priori, would be most likely to yield efficiency gains. Specifically, the mergers were horizontal (in-market) mergers involving relatively large-scale banks with a high degree of office (branch) overlap. Furthermore, the mergers typically involved a more cost-efficient bank (on at least one measure) acquiring a less efficient bank, and with the merger plans all expressing a strong commitment to cutting costs. Hence, the latter characteristic is consistent with Akhavein et al.'s relative efficiency hypothesis which has been shown to be a good predictor of post-merger performance.

Rhoades makes the distinction (which is typically not made in the media) between cost reductions and gains in cost efficiency. While all nine banks were found to exhibit significant cost reductions in line with the pre-merger plans, only four out of the nine banks exhibited gains in cost-efficiency levels relative to their peers. The results with respect to profitability, however, were more favourable, with seven out of nine mergers generating improvements in return on assets relative to their peers. This emphasizes the point made by Akhavein et al. that any examination of bank mergers should study the impact on revenues as well as costs.

Finally, Rhoades examines the net wealth effects of the mergers, based on the share price reaction to the merger announcement, and finds that this was positive in five out of the seven mergers for which data were available.

In summary, therefore, the nine case studies indicate that, even in cases where the success of mergers seems most favourable, bank mergers do not unambiguously produce post-merger gains. Furthermore, Rhoades argues that the most important factors explaining the relative success of some bank mergers relative to others are not clear-cut. Nevertheless, the more recent evidence provided by studies such as Akhavein et al. (1997) and Rhoades (1998) are much more positive in respect of the outcomes of large bank mergers than was earlier research. Both suggest that the impact of mergers is likely to be more pronounced on profitability than cost efficiency, which is the issue typically highlighted, *ex ante*, in respect of potential merger. Both studies do suggest, however, that *ex ante* relative efficiency levels are important determinants of *ex post* efficiency improvements. Simulation studies also suggest that large X-efficiency gains are possible if the best-practice acquirers reform the practices of inefficient targets (Shaffer, 1993). In turn, these results suggests that the capital market, and

## Costs and Efficiency in UK Banking

In spite of the significant structural change that has taken place within the UK financial services industry in recent years, it remains relatively under-researched in comparison to the vast amounts of research into the efficiency of North American institutions referred to previously. This is probably attributable to the very large numbers of banks in the US and the availability of high-quality official data. In contrast, there are relatively few commercial banks operating in the UK and there are very few official data on individual banks, with most data being drawn from individual institutions' annual reports and accounts.

One of the few studies into costs and efficiency in UK banking is Drake (2001). This paper utilizes the non-parametric technique DEA to analyse the overall technical efficiency of the UK banking sector using a panel data sample, and to decompose this concept of efficiency into its constituent components, pure technical and scale efficiency. The paper also presents estimates of productivity growth in UK banking over the sample period (1984–95) derived using Malmquist productivity indices. Furthermore, the sources of this productivity growth are established by decomposing the Malmquist productivity indices into their constituent components. These components indicate the extent to which the productivity change for each bank was due to a shift in the efficient frontier or to a process of moving closer to, or further away from, the efficient frontier. These components are often referred to as the 'frontier shift' and 'catch-up' elements of productivity change, respectively.

Given the lack of consensus in the literature concerning the appropriate production model to be employed for depository institutions (alluded to in Section 4), Drake (2001) proposed an agnostic view of the appropriate specification of inputs and outputs in order to investigate the implications of differing specifications for the analysis of efficiency in UK banking. Model 1 represents a modified form of the intermediation approach which recognizes that banks in recent years have increasingly been generating income from off-balance sheet business and fee income generally. Drake argues that these forms of revenue-generating activities would not be captured by focusing on the value of earning assets on the balance sheet. Hence, the category of 'other income' is included as an output along with two categories of earning assets, loans and liquid assets plus investments. With respect to inputs, capital is proxied by the value of fixed assets while labour is proxied by the total number of staff. The final input specfied is the total value of deposits (both retail and managed funds).

Model 2 is a modified form of the production approach. Due to the fact that consistent details on the number of individual loan and deposit accounts were not available for all banks in the sample, however, the total value of deposits is included as an output in addition to the earning assets and 'other income' categories specified in Model 1. Hence, the inputs in Model 2 comprise solely capital and labour.

The panel data set utilized in the study consisted of a sample of nine UK banks over the years from 1984 to 1995. These banks are listed below:

| | | |
|---|---|---|
| Barclays | NatWest | Standard Chartered |
| Lloyds | TSB | Bank of Scotland |
| Midland | Abbey National | Royal Bank of Scotland (RBS) |

Barclays, Lloyds, NatWest and Midland (now HSBC) represented the so-called 'big four' UK clearing banks, while Standard Chartered, the Bank of Scotland and the RBS are much smaller UK banks. TSB is the former Trustee Savings Bank which was owned by the government but privatized in 1986. The TSB subsequently merged with Lloyds Bank in 1995. The Abbey National was formerly a building society, but shed its mutual status and converted into a public limited company (plc) (stock) bank in 1989 following a stock market flotation under the provisions of the 1986 Building Societies Act. It is significant to note that a number of other large building societies have subsequently followed the lead of the Abbey National and converted from mutual to plc bank status in the mid-1990s. Hence, the inclusion of the Abbey National alongside the traditional clearing banks represents an interesting feature of the analysis. A more detailed analysis of the mutuality versus plc debate in the context of UK banks and building societies is provided in Drake (1989, 1997), Llewellyn (1997a, b), and Drake and Llewellyn (1998).

Drake (2001) finds clear evidence of increasing returns to scale for smaller banks such as the Bank of Scotland and the RBS (particularly in the early years of the sample), while the big four UK clearing banks exhibit strong evidence of decreasing returns to scale throughout the sample period. This is an interesting result given the recent battle between the two Scottish banks to take over NatWest. The evidence provided by Drake suggests that the consolidation between the RBS and NatWest will eliminate the scale cost efficiency advantage previously enjoyed by RBS and will worsen the diseconomies of scale evident at NatWest. Clearly, therefore, the justification for this merger must be sought in the area of the scope for cost savings via rationalization. As such, this type of merger is a classic response to the problem of excess capacity evident in UK banking and alluded to previously.

Although Drake does find that the use of alternative input/output specifications does produce some differences in the scale efficiency results, it appears that the minimum efficient scale of operation in UK banking (in terms of exhausting IRS [increasing returns to scale]) is in the real asset range from £18.5 billion to £25 billion (measured in 1984 prices). However, Drake maintains that the precise nature of the average cost curve in UK banking remains uncertain. His evidence suggests that most banks run into decreasing returns well before real assets reach £35 billion. The results for the Abbey National (and to a lesser degree Standard Chartered), however, indicate that the onset of decreasing returns may well be strongly dependent upon the precise nature of the production process and possibly on the degree of business/product diversification. With a business structure more similar to that of large UK building societies than large banks, it was found that the Abbey National (which converted to a plc bank in 1989) continued to operate with DRS (decreasing returns to scale) at real asset levels beyond £60 billion. In contrast, all the large UK clearing banks had run into decreasing returns at real assets well below this level.

Unlike the evidence that has emerged from US banking studies, Drake's results indicate that scale inefficiencies are potentially a more severe problem in UK banking than X-inefficiencies (pure technical inefficiency), particularly for very small and very large banks. Having said that, some tentative evidence did emerge to suggest that very large banks may be more X-efficient than their smaller competitors, particularly in the latter years of the sample period. This is in line with the evidence from US banking studies and supports the evidence cited elsewhere in this chapter suggesting that the impact of new technology may well be changing the nature of the size–efficiency relationship in many banking markets.

Finally, the evidence from the Malmquist productivity indices suggested that, on the whole, UK banks have exhibited positive productivity growth over the period, although the estimates based on the production approach (Model 2) were considerably larger than those based on the intermediation approach (Model 1). For most banks the productivity growth was the net result of a mixture of positive frontier shifts and negative catch-up. Based upon the evidence provided by the Abbey National, however, Drake argues that much of the frontier shift may be attributable to attempts by banks to eliminate excess capacity in the face of a significant intensification of competition in the UK financial services marketplace.

**Evidence from the UK building society sector**
Although evidence on costs and efficiency in UK banking has been relatively limited due to the restricted data samples, some relevant research has been conducted in respect of building societies.

UK building societies are mutual institutions regulated by statute and historically were restricted, in the main, to raising funds from retail deposits and intermediating these funds into mortgage lending. The Building Societies Act 1986, however, enabled building societies to diversify into a much wider range of housing-related and retail financial services and to diversify their assets, within limits, away from the traditional (Class 1) mortgage lending. The powers to hold so-called Class 2 and Class 3 assets enabled building societies to undertake commercial and second mortgage lending, unsecured consumer lending, and to make investments in subsidiaries and associated bodies. The more recent 1997 legislation removed most of the remaining restrictions and building societies can now effectively be viewed as mutual retail banks or mutual retail financial services organizations.

In addition to the diversification powers outlined above, the UK building society movement has also undergone considerable consolidation in recent years, both as a consequence of mergers within the mutual building society sector, and due to the conversion of a number of the larger building societies to plc bank status. In 1992, for example, there were 86 UK building societies, but by 1997 this number had fallen to 70. This consolidation phase in the UK building society sector echoes the trend towards rationalization and mergers evident in UK and US banking and indeed in financial services markets around the world. Although the converted building societies (or so-called mortgage banks) did receive five years' protection from take-over following plc conversion, it seems likely that we will ultimately see further consolidation in UK banking, following the recent examples of Lloyds–TSB and the RBS and NatWest, and some of this may well involve the new mortgage banks.

Against this backdrop of consolidation and increased merger activity, it is clear that the issue of economies of scale is extremely important in the context of both building societies and UK banking and retail financial services more generally. Despite the recent decline in numbers, UK building societies do represent a reasonable sample size for academic research, especially in the context of panel data samples. Furthermore, the diversification of building societies in recent years, coupled with the conversion of a number of the larger societies into plc banks, implies that this sector can provide a highly informative case study of the nature of scale economies and the size-efficiency relationship in the UK retail financial services market.

Although previous empirical work has been conducted into UK building societies by, for example, Hardwick (1989), Drake (1992) and Drake and Weyman-Jones (1996), the data utilized were typically cross-section and related to the 1980s. In general, these studies tended to indicate that only modest economies of scale were present and that they were exhausted at relatively low asset levels. Hardwick (1989), for example, concludes that 'societies with assets of less than £280m can achieve statistically significant economies of scale, but that there are no significant economies to be achieved by the growth of larger societies' (p. 1303). Similarly, Drake (1992) maintains that 'scale economies are evident only for the C class societies, i.e., building societies with assets of between £120m and £500m. For all other asset groups the evidence suggests that constant returns prevail as the scale economy measures are not significantly different from unity' (p. 215).

These results echoed the type of evidence emerging from the US banking literature in the 1980s and implied that alternative explanations should be sought for large-scale mergers. As outlined previously, however, evidence has recently emerged from the US which suggests that scale economy estimates can be sensitive to the particular cost function specification and to the impact of technological innovation on costs (see Berger and Mester, 1997). The latter point also suggests that scale economy estimates may also be sample specific. In particular, it may be the case that the results obtained using data from the 1990s may be very different from those obtained during the 1980s, due to the significant impact of new technology over the last decade or so.

In the light of these developments, a recent paper by Drake and Simper (forthcoming) aims to reappraise the evidence on scale economies in UK building societies, thereby providing some important insights in respect of the market for retail financial services in the UK. In order to do this, Drake and Simper specify and estimate a translog cost function using a panel data set drawn from the 1990s. Particular attention is paid to the robustness of the cost model and to the possibility of mis-specification which could bias the scale economy estimates. A particular innovation, for example, is the incorporation of both Hunter and Timme's (1991) technological change specification and Dionne et al.'s (1998) entry–exit equation, together with the application of a general to specific testing procedure applied to the translog cost function specification. The specification of an entry–exit model may be particularly appropriate for the building society sector given the propensity for exit via mergers and conversion.

Using the general to specific modelling technique, Drake and Simper find that the particular form of cost function specification can have a significant impact upon the resultant economies of scale estimates. The statistically preferred model was the most general specification, which included the log of the number of branches as an additional regressor (together with the associated translog cross-product terms) as well as the entry–exit and technological change specification. This model produced a measure of scale economies at the sample mean of 0.907. This is a highly significant result as it suggests that the UK building society industry is characterized by very substantial economies of scale. Furthermore, this level of scale economies greatly exceeds both those found in previous studies of UK building societies and the findings for financial institutions in general across many different countries. With respect to UK building societies, for example, Drake (1992) finds evidence of only modest economies of scale at the sample mean. The measure of economies of scale used is the inverse of the one used in Drake and Simper (forthcoming). Hence, the scale economy measure of 1.02 found by Drake (1992) would translate into a figure of 0.98.

Interestingly, Drake and Weyman-Jones (1996) found evidence of constant returns at the sample mean using a cross-section translog cost function without the incorporation of branching. Similarly, Drake and Simper (forthcoming) find that when they move to a more restrictive model (via the elimination of the branching variables), the scale economy measure changes from 0.907 to 0.970, which is indicative of much more modest economies of scale at the sample mean. A further interesting result is that when the technological change parameters are eliminated from the cost model, the scale economy estimate changes from 0.970 to 0.985. This finding suggests that the economies of scale evident for UK building societies may be attributable, at least in part, to the impact of new technology in banking and retail financial services. Hence, the failure to incorporate this impact may bias the economies of scale estimates upwards, with the attendant possibility of erroneous policy implications. Indeed, the use of cross-section samples, and the consequent failure to allow for technological change, may go some way to account for the very modest levels of economies of scale found in previous studies.

**The size–efficiency relationship in UK building societies**
Of potentially greater interest than the mean scale economy estimates, from a strategic and policy perspective, is information concerning the relationship between scale efficiency and the size of building societies. In order to facilitate the analysis of this size–efficiency relationship, Drake and Simper subdivided their sample of building societies in terms of their total asset size. Group A societies were defined to have assets over £5 billion, group B had assets between £0.5 billion and £5 billion, group C, £0.12–0.5 billion, group D, £0.05–0.12 billion, and finally, asset group E were building societies with total assets up to £0.05 billion.

Using the preferred model (as outlined above), Drake and Simper found the expected result that the largest potential economies of scale are available to the smallest societies (OES [overall economies of scale] $E = 0.899$ and OES $D = 0.894$) and that the potential scale economies declined with size (OES B = 0.925). A particularly interesting feature of the results, however, was the finding that potential scale economies began to increase again with asset size from group B to group A (OES A = 0.916). This latter result suggests that some of the larger building societies may actually experience more significant economies of scale than their smaller competitors.

Drake and Simper hypothesize that a possible explanation for this type of result is the impact of new technology. Furthermore, this hypothesis is given some credence by the fact that the measure of scale-biased technological change is found to be negative and significant. This suggests that technological change causes larger building societies to become more efficient over time relative to their smaller competitors and hence is a potential source of the observed economies of scale.

In summary, the finding of significant economies of scale for UK building societies appears to be consistent with other more recent research, especially the results emerging from the US. Furthermore, unlike the earlier empirical evidence, these results are entirely consistent with the recent merger and consolidation wave in banking and financial services, as Drake and Simper find evidence of substantial and pervasive economies of scale for all sizes of building societies. They also find evidence that technological progress tends to reduce the costs of larger societies relative to their smaller competitors, thereby enhancing potential economies of scale. These results suggest a strong cost-reducing rationale for mergers even with respect to relatively large building societies with assets of over £5 billion.

Hence, in the light of this recent empirical evidence, we would expect to see further mergers/consolidation within the UK retail financial services sector, particularly when the evidence concerning economies of scale and technology effects is combined with the rationalization potential which mergers bring. With the arrival of new delivery channels such as telephone and internet banking, many financial services organizations are finding that the rationalization of branches, infrastructure and staff is more easily accomplished following a merger in which the costly duplication of resources can be eliminated.

The very limited empirical evidence on the impact of mergers in the UK building society industry does support the notion that mergers can significantly enhance efficiency levels. Furthermore, the results do tend to mirror the findings obtained in the US. Haynes and Thompson (1999), for example, argue that:

> In contrast to much of the existing merger literature, which for the most part uses financial performance data, our results *DO* indicate significant and substantial productivity gains following acquisition. These are consistent with an acqui-

sitions process in which less efficient firms are acquired and reorganized. The post-merger gains appear to increase substantially in the post-deregulation period, when pressures to minimize costs are widely considered to have increased. (p. 825)

Finally, there has been considerable debate in the literature, and among analysts, concerning the future of smaller building societies. One view is that these institutions can survive by being highly focused on a narrow range of products, and by cultivating their local presence. This view, however, rests on the assumption that a narrow focus can deliver a relatively low cost base. While this may facilitate X-efficiency (although this is not supported by the available empirical evidence) it can do nothing to alleviate the problems of scale inefficiency. Previous results have suggested that this is not a serious problem as only modest economies existed and these were exhausted at relatively low asset levels.

The more recent evidence, however, suggests that smaller building societies may be in a much more vulnerable position. Considerable scale economies appear to prevail at all asset sizes and the smallest building societies appear to have the largest unexploited economies of scale. Hence, other things equal (such as X-efficiency), these smaller societies would be expected to exhibit the highest unit costs. The evidence suggests that these societies will also benefit less, in a dynamic context, from the cost-reducing potential of new technology. Clearly, these pressures are likely to intensify in an increasingly competitive financial services marketplace and may well result in an increased numbers of mergers involving the smaller building societies.

## Costs and Efficiency in Japanese Banking

Given the problems experienced by the Japanese financial system (and banks in particular) in recent years, and the recent pressures for consolidation, surprisingly little academic research has been undertaken into the costs and efficiency of Japanese banks. This contrasts markedly with the wealth of research into the performance of US financial institutions detailed previously.

Tachibanaki et al. (1991) estimated a two-output translog cost function using a sample of 61 banks between 1985 and 1987 and found evidence of economies of scale for all sizes of banks in all three years of the study. It should be noted, however, that the outputs were proxied by revenues produced from earning assets. Hence, it is possible that these revenue-based measures of output may have been influenced by market power in respect of the setting of output prices.

Fukuyama (1993) used the non-parametric technique, DEA, to analyse the overall technical efficiency (OE) of Japanese commercial banks and to decompose this into its two constituent components, pure technical efficiency (PTE), and scale efficiency (SE). The cross-section sample consisted of 143 banks for the financial year 1990/91. The mean level of OE for the whole sample was found to be 0.8645 which, compared to a maximum level of unity, implies that banks could, on average, have produced the same levels of outputs with about 14 per cent fewer resources or inputs. Unlike other studies, Fukuyama found evidence of only mild economies of scale, with the mean level of SE being 0.9844. Hence, most of the observed inefficiency was associated with pure technical (mean PTE score, 0.8509), rather than scale, inefficiency. Interestingly, however, only 7 per cent of the sample exhibited constant returns to scale. Furthermore, of those banks exhibiting scale inefficiencies, 81 per cent exhibited increasing returns and only 12 per cent exhibited decreasing returns to scale.

McKillop et al. (1996) used the composite cost function developed by Pulley and Braunstein (1992) to analyse costs and efficiency in giant Japanese banks. The data relate to annual data from five very large Japanese city banks over the 1978–91 period and McKillop et al. use the intermediation approach in a three-output, three-input model. The specification of a composite cost function permits the estimation of four model variants, including the translog and generalized translog. However, for all the models estimated, McKillop et al. find evidence of statistically significant economies of scale for all banks at the sample mean. Furthermore, the estimated values of the economies of scale parameter were found to range between 1.08 and 1.28 (indicating economies of scale), very similar to the values found by Tachibanaki et al. (1991). It is interesting to note, however, that McKillop et al. found that this pattern of economies of scale holds for all years of the sample 'except for the late 1980s onwards where the results suggest that constant returns pertain for all models' (p. 1665). This accords with Fukuyama (1993) who finds that, based on 1990/91 data, 'the majority of the city banks exhibit constant returns to scale, implying that the city banks seemingly operate close to the minimum efficient scale' (p. 1107).

McKillop et al. (1996) refer to 'the persistent, and somewhat surprising, finding of increasing returns to scale for *all sizes* of Japanese banks' (p. 1652). Indeed, as detailed above, until recently the vast majority of empirical studies in other countries have found that economies of scale are exhausted at relatively low output levels. Hence, in this context, the Japanese results are indeed surprising. It is also clear, however, that both McKillop et al. (1996) and Fukuyama (1993) find some evidence that large city banks operating in the late 1980s/early 1990s exhibited constant returns to scale. Clearly, given the current consolidation wave sweeping

Japan, the precise nature of economies of scale in Japanese banking is extremely important, both from an academic and a policy perspective.

Some recent papers, however, have attempted to shed fresh light on the scale economy puzzle in Japanese banking. Altunbas et al. (2000) utilize the hybrid Fourier/translog cost function/frontier outlined previously to investigate both scale economies and X-efficiencies in Japanese banking. They specify three outputs (total loans, total securities and off-balance sheet items) and three inputs (labour, capital and total funds). In addition to the usual cost function specification, however, Altunbas et al. also test for the impact of risk and quality factors on costs, scale economies and X-efficiency. The ratio of loan-loss provisions to total loans is included in the cost frontier to capture loan quality, while risk is modelled via the inclusion of financial capital and the ratio of liquid assets to total assets. The incorporation of risk and quality factors is clearly potentially very important given the recent banking crisis in Japan. It should be noted, however, that Japanese banks were renowned for concealing the true scale of their bad-debt problems for a number of years during the 1990s.

The sample consists of about 136 Japanese banks and covers the years from 1993 to 1996. Furthermore, Altunbas et al. allow for the possibility of technical change over the period via the inclusion of a simple time trend.

Altunbas et al. find that economies of scale in Japanese banking tend to be overstated when risk and quality factors are not incorporated, particularly for the larger banks. Specifically, they find that 'diseconomies of scale become much more widespread and optimal bank size falls from around Yen 5–10 Trillion to Yen 1–2 Trillion when risk and quality factors are taken into account' (p. 1614). X-inefficiencies are found to range between 5 and 7 per cent, in contrast the levels of about 20 per cent typically found in studies of US banks. Interestingly, the X-efficiency estimates are found to be much less sensitive to the exclusion of risk and quality factors than the economies of scale estimates.

Drake and Hall (forthcoming), using DEA on a 1997 cross-section sample, also find that the largest city banks exhibit clear evidence of decreasing returns to scale with a mean SE level of 91.27. They do, however, find evidence of considerable potential economies of scale for most banks as the mean level of SE for the overall sample is only 92.78, with the vast majority of banks exhibiting increasing returns to scale.

In contrast to Altunbas et al. (2000), Drake and Hall find an indicative MES (minimum efficient scale) in the total lending range of ¥6 trillion to ¥10 trillion, and which is relatively invariant to controlling for lending quality (via the inclusion of loan-loss provisions). Furthermore, Drake and Hall find that the measures of pure technical efficiency are more sensitive to the latter than are the scale economy measures.

Interestingly, Drake and Hall (forthcoming) find important efficiency differences across the various subsectors of Japanese banks. Specifically, the trust banks and LTCBs (long term credit banks) are found to be by far the most efficient banking sectors in Japan. Both sectors exhibited mean SE and PTE scores of 100, in contrast to the sample mean levels of 92.78 and 78.11, respectively. Furthermore, this result pertains whether or not lending quality is controlled for. This is an interesting result in itself, but also in the context of the subsequent failures of a number of the LTCBs. The fact that most of these were associated with unrecorded bad debts appears to confirm that many banks continued to hide the true scale of their bad-debt problems for long periods during the 1990s. Hence, any efficiency results for Japanese banks using official 1990s data may not be totally reliable, even if they control for risk and lending quality (using reported loan-loss provisions). The results may also reflect the fact alluded to previously, however, that the major problem facing many Japanese banks was low profitability (and high bad debts) rather than high cost ratios. Hence, it is quite possible that the LTCBs and trust banks were highly cost efficient but neverthelesss suffered from asset quality and profitability problems.

## 6  CONCLUSIONS

Although there are important differences between the banking markets in the US, the UK and Japan (due to historical regulations, the differential pace of deregulation, differential degrees of government intervention, cultural and corporate differences, and so on), there are nevertheless common trends and features which can be observed in these banking markets. Indeed, many of these trends are features of numerous banking markets around the world. There are also important similarities and contrasts that have emerged from the plethora of empirical work which has analysed cost and efficiency issues in these banking markets. This chapter has attempted to provide a selective survey of some of the important research in this area and a brief summary of some of the main findings of the research into cost and efficiency in the banking markets of the US, the UK and Japan is provided below:

1. In the US and the UK, early research tended to indicate that economies of scale were prevalent only for relatively small banks. This was at odds with the emerging trend towards large-scale mergers, particularly in the US.
2. In contrast, the early research in Japan indicated the existence of pervasive economies of scale for all size ranges of banks.

3. Subsequent research in the US and the UK indicated that economies of scale prevailed up to much higher asset sizes than previously thought. This evidence provided support for the megamergers taking place in the US, but could not be used to justify the supermegamergers which took place during the 1990s. Furthermore, evidence has more recently emerged which suggests that technology can have a powerful impact on economies of scale in banking. This is an important result given the trend towards direct, technology-driven, banking and a tendency for banks to increasingly contract out aspects of their business (loan screening, loan administration, and so on). These are both trends which are likely to enhance potential economies of scale. Conversely, there is a limited amount of evidence which tentatively suggests business structure may also have an impact on economies of scale in banking. Hence another major trend in banking, towards conglomeration (bancassurance, universal banking, and so on) and away from a focused, narrow businesss structure, may well impact adversely on economies of scale in banking.
4. More recent research into Japanese banking suggests that, although significant economies of scale persist for many smaller banks, the largest city banks appear to operate unambiguously above the minimum efficient scale. This clearly places question marks against the recent large-scale merger movement evident in Japanese banking.
5. The consensus of evidence from the US suggests that X-inefficiency is a much more serious problem than scale inefficiency. Whereas the latter results in cost inefficiencies of about 5 per cent on average, X-inefficiencies average about 20 per cent. The evidence also suggests that larger banks are typically more X-efficient than smaller banks. This latter result is also found in respect of UK banks, although the UK evidence tends to suggest that scale inefficiencies are much more serious than X-inefficiencies, especially for banks at either end of the size spectrum.
6. The very limited evidence suggests that X-inefficiency averages about 5–7 per cent in Japanese banks, based upon the cost function evidence of Altunbas et al. (2000). Using DEA, however, Drake and Hall (forthcoming) find mean levels of pure technical inefficiency of about 22 per cent, which is closer to the typical levels of X-inefficiencies found in the US.
7. Despite the pronounced recent trends towards large-scale mergers and financial conglomeration via bancassurance and universal banking, the empirical evidence in banking has tended to be very pessimistic concerning both the gains from mergers and the potential economies of scope from diversification. Mergers in particular have often been advocated on the basis of their cost benefits. The evidence suggests,

however, that while many mergers produce cost reductions, few produce any significant gains in cost-efficiency levels.
8. More recent empirical evidence has broadened the scope of the analysis, however, by allowing for revenue/profitability and risk-reduction benefits following mergers and diversification, rather than purely cost-efficiency benefits. This more recent evidence confirms the lack of significant cost-efficiency gains, but establishes significant profitability gains from mergers and significant gains in respect of both profitability and risk reduction following diversification via moves into bancassurance and universal banking. The latter benefits come from diversifying, at the margin, out of intermediation business, where interest margins are under pressure, and into additional revenue streams that are not highly correlated with those of traditional on-balance sheet banking.

In all three of the countries surveyed in this chapter, the catalysts of deregulation and increasing competition are relatively recent phenomena in banking and financial services. In turn these catalysts are producing pronounced ongoing structural changes relating to: business diversification (bancassurance and universal banking); increased merger activity, often large scale and often involving different segments of the financial system; the rationalization of infrastructure and staff; and the increasing use of new technology. As these powerful trends are still ongoing at the time of writing, however, it is not possible to fully analyse their potential impact on costs, efficiency and profitability in banking. In particular, there are still relatively few studies that have attempted to evaluate the impact of the trend towards bancassurance and universal banking. Only when further years of data become available for banks which have engaged in cross-sector mergers or significant business diversification will we get a clearer picture of the impact of these trends. It is hoped, however, that this chapter has provided some tentative insights into the potential impacts of these powerful trends sweeping across banking markets around the world.

# REFERENCES

Aigner, D.J., Lovell, C.A. and Schmidt, P. (1977), 'Formulation and estimation of stochastic frontier production function models', *Journal of Econometrics*, **6**, 21–37.

Akhavein, J.D., Berger, A.N. and Humphrey, D.B. (1997), 'The effects of megamergers on efficiency and prices: evidence from a profit function', *Review of Industrial Organisation*, **12**, 95–139.

Altunbas, Y., Liu, M.-H., Molyneux, P. and Seth, R. (2000), 'Efficiency and risk in Japanese banking', *Journal of Banking and Finance*, **24** (10), 1605–28.

Banker, R.D., Charnes, A. and Cooper, W.W. (1984), 'Some models for estimating technical and scale inefficiencies in data envelopment analysis', *Management Science*, **30** (9), 1078–92.

Bauer, P.W. (1990), 'Recent developments in the econometric estimation of frontiers', *Journal of Econometrics*, **46**, 39–56.

Berg, S.A., Forsund, F.R., Hjalmarsson, R. and Suominen, M. (1993), 'Banking efficiency in the Nordic countries', *Journal of Banking and Finance*, **17** (2–3), 371–88.

Berger, A.N. (1993), '"Distribution-free" estimates of efficiency in the U.S. banking industry and tests of the standard distributional assumptions', *Journal of Productivity Analysis*, **4**, 261–92.

Berger, A.N., Demsetz, R.S. and Strahan, P.E. (1998), 'The consolidation of the financial services industry: causes, consequences and implications for the future', Federal Reserve Bank of New York, Staff Reports, 55, December.

Berger, A.N., Hancock, D. and Humphrey, D.B. (1993b), 'Bank efficiency derived from the profit function', *Journal of Banking and Finance*, **17**, 317–47.

Berger, A.N., Hanweck, G.A. and Humphrey, D.B. (1987), 'Competitive viability in banking: scale, scope and product mix economies', *Journal of Monetary Economics*, **20**, 501–20.

Berger, A.N. and Humphrey, D.B. (1991), 'The dominance of X-inefficiencies over scale and product mix economies in banking', *Journal of Monetary Economics*, **28**, 117–48.

Berger, A.N. and Humphrey, D.B. (1992a), 'Measurement and efficiency issues in commercial banking', in Zvi Griliches (ed.), *Measurement Issues in the Service Sectors*, Chicago: National Bureau of Economic Research, University of Chicago Press.

Berger, A.N. and Humphrey, D.B. (1992b), 'Megamergers in banking and the use of cost efficiency as an antitrust defence', *Antitrust Bulletin*, **37**, Fall, 541–600.

Berger, A.N. and Humphrey, D.B. (1997), 'Efficiency of financial institutions: international survey and directions for future research', *European Journal of Operations Research*, **98**, 175–212.

Berger, A.N., Humphrey, D.B. and Pulley, L.B. (1996), 'Do consumers pay for one-stop banking? Evidence from an alternative revenue function', *Journal of Banking and Finance*, **20**, 1601–21.

Berger, A.N., Hunter, W.C. and Timme, S.G. (1993a), 'The efficiency of financial institutions: a review and preview of research past, present and future', *Journal of Banking and Finance*, **17**, 221–49.

Berger, A.N. and Mester, L.J. (1997), 'Inside the black box: what explains differences in the efficiencies of financial institutions?', *Journal of Banking and Finance*, **21**, 895–947.

Craig. V.C. (1998), 'Japanese banking: a time of crisis?', *FDIC Banking Review*, **11**(2).

De Young, R. (1997), 'Bank mergers, X-efficiency, and the market for corporate control', *Managerial Finance*, **23**, 32–7.

Dionne, G., Gagne, R. and Vanasse, C. (1998), 'Inferring technological parameters from incomplete panel data', *Journal of Econometrics*, **87**, 303–27.

Drake, L. (1989), *The Building Society Industry in Transition*, London: Macmillan.

Drake, L. (1992), 'Economies of scale and scope in UK building societies: an application of the translog multiproduct cost function', *Applied Financial Economics*, **2**, 211–19.

Drake, L. (1995), 'Testing for expense preference behaviour in UK building societies: the implications for measures of scale and scope economies', *The Service Industries Journal*, **15**(1), 50–65.

Drake, L. (1997), 'The economics of mutuality', LUBC – BSA Project Paper No. 3, London: BSA.

Drake, L. (2001), 'Efficiency in UK banking', *Applied Financial Economics*, **11**, 557–571.

Drake, L. and Hall, M.J.B. (forthcoming), 'Efficiency in Japanese banking: an empirical analysis', *Journal of Banking and Finance*.

Drake, L. and Llewellyn, D.T. (1998), 'Mutuals in the financial system', *Financial Stability Review*, **5**, Autumn, 33–45.

Drake, L. and Simper, R. (forthcoming), 'Economies of scale in UK building societies: a reappraisal using an entry/exit model', *Journal of Banking and Finance*.

Drake, L. and Weyman-Jones, T.G. (1992), 'Technical and scale efficiency in UK building societies', *Applied Financial Economics*, **2**, 1–9.

Drake, L. and Weyman-Jones, T.G. (1996), 'Productive and allocative inefficiencies in U.K. building societies: a comparison of non-parametric and stochastic frontier techniques', *Manchester School of Economic and Social Studies*, **114** (1), 22–37.

Färe, R., Grosskopf, S. and Lovell, K.C.A. (1985), *The Measurement of the Efficiency of Production*, Boston, MA: Kluwer–Nijhoff.

Farrell, M.J (1957), 'The measurement of productive efficiency', *Journal of the Royal Statistical Society*, Series A (part III), 253–81.

Ferrier, G.D., Grosskopf, S., Haynes, K.J. and Yaisawarng, G. (1993), 'Economies of diversification in the banking industry', *Journal of Monetary Economics*, **31**, 229–45.

Fukuyama, H. (1993), 'Technical and scale efficiency of Japanese commercial banks: a non-parametric approach', *Applied Economics*, **25**, 1101–12.

Hall, M.J.B. (1999), 'Current banking problems in Japan: how serious are they and how might they be resolved?', *Research in Financial Services: Private and Public Policy*, **11**, 3–33.

Hardwick, P. (1989), 'Economies of scale in building societies', *Applied Economics*, **21**, 1291–304.

Harui, H. (1997), 'Japan's financial problems: causes and prospects', Loughborough University Banking Centre Research Paper, No. 108/97.

Haynes, M. and Thompson, S. (1999), 'The productivity effects of bank mergers: evidence from the UK building societies', *Journal of Banking and Finance*, **23**, 825–46.

Hoshi, T. and Kashyap, A. (1999), 'The Japanese banking crisis: where did it come from and how will it end?', NBER Working Paper No. W7259.

Houston, J.F. and Ryngaert, M.D. (1993), 'The overall gains from large bank mergers', *Journal of Banking and Finance*, **18** (6), 1155–76.

Hunter, W.C. and Timme, S.G. (1991), 'Technology change in large U.S. commercial banks', *Journal of Business*, **64** (3), 339–62.

Hunter, W.C., Timme, S.G. and Yang, W.K. (1990), 'An examination of cost subadditivity and multiproduct production in large US banks', *Journal of Money, Credit, and Banking*, **22**, 504–25.

Jondrow, J., Lovell, C.A., Materov, I.S. and Schmidt, P. (1982), 'On estimation of technical inefficiency in the stochastic frontier production function model', *Journal of Econometrics*, **19**, 233–8.

Kwan, S.H. (1997), 'Securities activities by commercial banking firms' Section 20 subsidiaries: risk, return and diversification benefits', mimeo, Federal Reserve Bank of San Francisco, October.

Linder, J.C. and Crane, D.B. (1992), 'Bank mergers: integration and profitability', Working Paper, Harvard Business School, Cambridge, MA, February.

Llewellyn, D.T. (1997a), 'Reflections on the mutuality v. conversion debate', LUBC –BSA Project Paper No. 1, London: BSA.

Llewellyn, D.T. (1997b), 'The mutuality v. conversion debate', LUBC–BSA Project Paper No. 2, London: BSA.

McAllister, P.H and McManus, D. (1993), 'Resolving the scale efficiency puzzle in banking', *Journal of Banking and Finance*, **17**, 389–405.

McKillop, D.G., Glass, J.D. and Morikawa, Y. (1996), 'The composite cost function and efficiency in giant Japanese banks', *Journal of Banking and Finance*, **20**, 1651–71.

Panzar, J.C. and Willig, R.D. (1977), 'Economies of scale in multi-output production', *Quarterly Journal of Economics*, **91**, 481–94.

Peristiani, S. (1997), 'Do mergers improve the x-efficiency and scale efficiency of US banks? Evidence from the 1980s', *Journal of Money, Credit, and Banking*, **29**, 326–37.

Pilloff, S.J. (1996), 'Performance changes and shareholder wealth creation associated with mergers of publicly traded banking institutions', *Journal of Money, Credit, and Banking*, **28**, 294–310.

Pulley, L.B. and Braunstein, Y.M. (1992), 'A composite cost function for multi-product firms with an application to economies of scope in banking', *Review of Economics and Statistics*, **74**, 221–30.

Pulley, L.B. and Humphrey, D.B. (1993), 'The role of fixed costs and cost complementarities in determining scope economies and the cost of narrow banking proposals', *Journal of Business*, **66**, 437–62.

Rhoades, S.A. (1986), 'The operating performance of acquired firms in banking before and after acquisition', Staff Economic Studies, 149, Board of Governors of the Federal Reserve System, Washington, DC.

Rhoades, S.A. (1990), 'Billion dollar bank acquisitions: a note on the performance effects', Working Paper, Board of Governors of the Federal Reserve System, Washington, DC.

Rhoades, S.A. (1993), 'The efficiency effects of horizontal bank mergers', *Journal of Banking and Finance*, **17**, 411–22.

Rhoades, S.A. (1994), 'A summary of merger performance studies in banking 1980–1993, and an assessment of the "Operating Performance" and "Event Study" methodologies', Board of Governors of the Federal Reserve System, Staff Study No. 167, Washington, DC, July.

Rhoades, S.A. (1998), 'The efficiency effects of bank mergers: an overview of case studies of nine mergers', *Journal of Banking and Finance*, **22**, 273–91.

Rhoades, S. (2000), 'Bank mergers and banking structure in the US, 1980–98', Board of Governors of the Federal Reserve System, Staff Study No. 174, Washington, DC, August.

Rogers, K. and Sinkey, J.F. Jr. (1999), 'An Analysis of non-traditional activities at US commercial banks', *Review of Financial Economics*, **8**, 25–39.

Saunders, A. and Walter, I. (1994), *Universal Banking in the United States*, New York: Oxford University Press.

Sealey, C.W. and Lindley, J.T. (1977), 'Inputs, outputs and the theory of production and costs at depository financial institutions', *Journal of Finance*, **32** (4), 1251–65.

Shaffer, S. (1993), 'Can megamergers improve bank efficiency?', *Journal of Banking and Finance*, **17**, 423–36.
Shephard, R.W. (1970), *Theory of Costs and Production Functions*, Princeton, NJ: Princeton University Press.
Srinivasin, A. (1992), 'Are there cost savings from bank mergers?', *Federal Reserve Bank of Atlanta Economic Review*, March/April, 17–28.
Srinivasin, A. and Wall, L.D. (1992), 'Cost savings associated with bank mergers', Working Paper, Federal Reserve Bank of Atlanta, Atlanta, GA, January.
Tachibanaki, T., Mitsui, K. and Kitagawa, H. (1991), 'Economies of scope and shareholding of banks in Japan', *Journal of the Japanese and Institutional Economies*, **5**, 261–81.

# PART III

# Banking Risks, Crises and Regulation

# 13. Country risk: existing models and new horizons

**Sarkis Joseph Khoury and Chunsheng Zhou\***

## 1 INTRODUCTION

The meltdown in East Asia, Russia, and Latin America (partial) has compounded the concerns about systemic risk[1] and country risk. The latter can exist without causing systemic failure. In fact, recent research by Khoury (2001) demonstrated that systemic risk is largely a myth, as the probability of systemic failure is practically zero under all conceivable and realistic circumstances. An extensive simulation was used to 'prove' the hypotheses of the model. This does not imply, however, that the country risk under discussion in this chapter does not produce limited systemic risk, reflecting itself in a burst of the asset price bubble and/or in a significant reduction of liquidity. Bordo et al. (1995) referred to this as 'pseudo systemic risk'. This is really what most researchers refer to as systematic risk.

Country risk is the likelihood of a financial loss generated by macroeconomic, political, social and/or natural disasters within a given country. It is produced by natural or by manufactured (mismanagement) factors. Country risk is focused on the value of assets (portfolio and direct investment related) held by foreign entities within the country under examination, and is broader than sovereign risk. The latter deals with the inability of a sovereign borrower to pay back its debts to foreigners. The most recent suspension of payments on Russian debt (1998) is an example of sovereign risk, as were the suspensions of payments by a large number of countries in the early 1980s. The repudiation of debt by a sovereign country is the ultimate form of sovereign risk, as was the case of Cuba. A recent article by Wynn et al. (1999) contains a systematic discussion of sovereign risk.

The country risk may stem either from the country, or the country's institutions' inability to pay under current conditions, or simply from the country's unwillingness to pay. The risk, therefore, includes the inability of a privately owned firm to pay its debts as a result of economic mismanagement by the home country.

The most often used definition of country risk is that of transfer risk (restriction on capital transfers and on currency convertibility). In the wake of the Asian crisis (summer 1997), default risk by private entities, caused by macroeconomic conditions, has been added to the concerns of a typical international banker. The Russian case in 1998 added sovereign default as a concern, as did the default by Ecuador on its Brady bonds in 1999.

The exposure of lenders to country risk continues to expand, creating a growing need for country risk measurement and management models. By the end of 1996 'the outstanding stock of sovereign debt issued or guaranteed by developing countries amounted to $1.5 trillion, or 25 percent of their total GNP and to 300 percent of their foreign currency reserves'. Even countries that were thought to be unassailable, in terms of financial strength, are suddenly sources of concern. The downgrading of the Japanese government debt by Moody's in 1998 was not predicted. Red ink is all over the Japanese financial landscape:

> Corporate Japan has a 4:1 debt-to-equity ratio, and borrowing by the central and the regional governments was at 105 percent of GDP and is likely to reach 130 percent by the next fiscal year, after accounting for the combined cost of the bank bailout, the Japan Railway debt assumption, an eight trillion yen ($68 billion) revenue shortfall and three huge supplementary stimulus packages. (*The Wall Street Journal*, 23 October 1998)

It is worth noting that country risk is different from political risk, although it may be a byproduct of it. Political risk stems from political instability or from conscious political decisions that fundamentally change the characteristics of a foreign investment, with expropriation being the most extreme of actions. The capital controls imposed by Malaysia in 1998 represent one form of political risk.

This study provides a perspective on country risk analysis, reviews the existing models for assessing country risk, and proposes new ideas in modelling country risk.

## 2 A PERSPECTIVE ON COUNTRY RISK

The developments of 1997 to 1998 in Asia, which followed the very critical developments in Mexico in 1994 to 1995 and the accompanying tequila effects, have heightened the need for rigorous models capable of generating a probability function for the estimation of country risk under various states of the world. The model would allow the lender to assess the risk and impose, consequently, a justifiable risk premium.

The uniqueness of the events in the late 1990s lies in the unexpected explosion of country risk outside any reasonable range that could have been incorporated in any analysis. The jump in riskiness of borrowing governments and institutions required dramatic actions by governments of developed countries, notably the United States, and by the International Monetary Fund (IMF). A huge political controversy ensued in the United States as a result of the campaign by the Clinton administration to meet the US commitment to the IMF. The $18 billion commitment was finally approved in late 1998 as part of the budget deal, but not without considerable rancour and acrimony. The critics argued that the IMF has not only wasted over $170 billion in loans, but also generated the necessary conditions for moral hazard. The latest $5 billion commitment to Russia in 1998 and the way it was squandered were used as the *cause célèbre*. This led the IMF on 27 January 1997 to approve a new arrangement to borrow 'to provide supplementary resources to the IMF'. Despite all of this, President Bill Clinton got the G7 countries to agree to a new 'reserve fund' to prevent country crises from occurring. This will ultimately result in more regulations in the financial markets. The 4 October 1998 meeting of the G7 countries in Washington DC called, among other things, for 'promotion of soundly based capital flows . . . improved regulatory focus . . . stronger supervisory and regulatory regimes . . . sustainable exchange rate regimes in emerging market economies . . . better transparency and disclosure'. How all of this will be achieved and who will be responsible for it remains unclear.

The best plans can be overtaken by events, however. Almost overnight, the country risk profile of Thailand in 1997 was turned on its head. Its problems became so pronounced that there was a devaluation of the baht and a massive restructuring within the Thai economy. The Indonesian stock market almost disappeared after the Indonesian economy was also affected. The problems were further compounded by the South Korean fiasco, requiring almost $60 billion in IMF bail-out, the largest one ever. Taiwan and the Philippines were also shaken but did not break. The country of Malaysia implemented what was thought to be an extreme policy of capital control in order to 'protect' its economy from speculators. The net results were a massive drop in portfolio and direct investment in Malaysia. Interestingly, a recovery is under way in all of these countries, illustrating the need for dynamic modelling.

This episode in recent economic history illustrates how interdependent country risk analysis is. No country is an oasis. The correlation structure and its stability across national economies must be a part of any country risk modelling to capture the regional or the 'contagion effects'.

These analytical problems are not limited to developing countries. The economic policy histories of France and Italy, for example, do not give much solace to those who wish to ignore country risk. For developed economies such as France a shift occurred overnight from conservative to socialist control. Italy witnessed the ascension of a former communist to the prime ministership. The situation in Germany was no different in the wake of the Kohl defeat, with an ultra leftist minister of finance, and a chancellor who redefined what the 'New Middle' of the political spectrum really means. It translated into 'ecological renewal . . . higher energy taxes' and the undoing of the limited reforms that the Kohl administration had won after extended, difficult battles. The question here is whether such changes significantly increase country risk or simply change the character of the country. Those willing to jump the gun by simply saying 'no' should recall the draconian capital control measures imposed by France in the 1980s.

The interesting lesson from this is that while countries can experience long periods of instability, they do recover. Economic setbacks do not wash countries away. Indeed, they *may* cleanse them and pave the way for reformist governments that set the stage for solid growth patterns built on a firm foundation. However, lenders do not need to bear the cost of cleansing any system and are well aware of the admonishments of John Maynard Keynes: 'in the long run we are all dead', and the bank manager will be out of a job.

It can be said, therefore, that the concern in country risk is largely in the liquidity (broadly defined) of the investment, followed by the likelihood of an interruption in the cash flow owed to lenders, and then by the probability that the loan principal may have to be written off. The Malaysian case extends the risk to that of capital controls. The case of Hurricane Mitch and its devastating effects on El Salvador and on Honduras, washing away 50 years of progress in three days, speak of the difficulty of robust long-term forecasts. It may offer justification for a form of catastrophic insurance by developing countries or by international institutions sold to business firms and to investors. The relief aid and debt forgiveness are indirect and incomplete forms of insurance.

In the light of this reality, the sources of country risk must be identified, measured, have a probability attached to them and must be effectively managed by lending institutions and international agencies. In addition, country risk analysis may be classified in different ways: by the assets or the liabilities of the financial institution, by country, by the nature of the event, by type of borrower and by its degree of severity. We opt here for classification by country.

The analysis of country risk depends on one's degree of cynicism and ideological perspective. The cynic would argue that the US government, the IMF with its large set of programmes, the Bank for International Settlements (BIS), the World Bank and other entities provide a form of insurance policy to bankers which is incorporated into the banker's decision function. Therefore, any country risk analysis represents a façade to satisfy regulators and to coerce borrowers into paying a risk premium on what otherwise is a risk-free loan. This view is shared by an increasing number of economists who watch the behaviour of the IMF and the creation of the new reserve fund at the IMF with great consternation. The safety net that is being constructed turns the IMF effectively into a lender of last resort and encourages suboptimal lending by banks (excessive borrowings by countries). However, this is not our thesis, despite its intellectual attraction and increased empirical support.

Judging by the performance of the stocks of American banks with heavy lending to developing countries during the late 1990s, when most recent rescheduling took place, it appears that the stock market believes that country risk is not as serious a phenomenon as thought by some, reinforcing in the process the belief that bankers may have learned their lessons and/or that the safety mechanisms for the international financial system are quite adequate, as manifested (partially) by the expansion in the IMF lending capacity. Compared to the performance of the Dow Jones 30 Industrials, the Dow Jones 65 Composite, and the S&P 500 Index, bank stocks performed reasonably well (Exhibit 13.1). These results hide the fact that the financial markets tend to overreact to any global situation. For a period, the stock values of American banks were hit severely in the wake of the Russian crisis, despite the fact that the Russian economy represents only 1 per cent of the world GDP and that American banks, especially when compared with their German counterparts, had limited exposure to Russia.

## 3  COPING WITH THE CHANGES

Country risk analysis is an attempt to deal with a large set of uncertainties. The massive number of variables the researcher must grapple with and the range of areas they cover (for example, political, economic, or legal) make the attempt seem futile at first glance. Judging by its results, the attempt was indeed futile in most of the cases. Ingo Walter accurately summarized the problems of country risk analysis:

> In the absence of an efficient market whose data can be analyzed, the delivery of effective country risk assessment ideally requires the employment of a true 'Renaissance person', exceedingly intelligent, a holder of doctorates from respectable institutions in economics, political science, sociology, psychology, and perhaps a few other fields as well, totally objective, with a great deal of common sense. (Walter, 1981, p. 85)

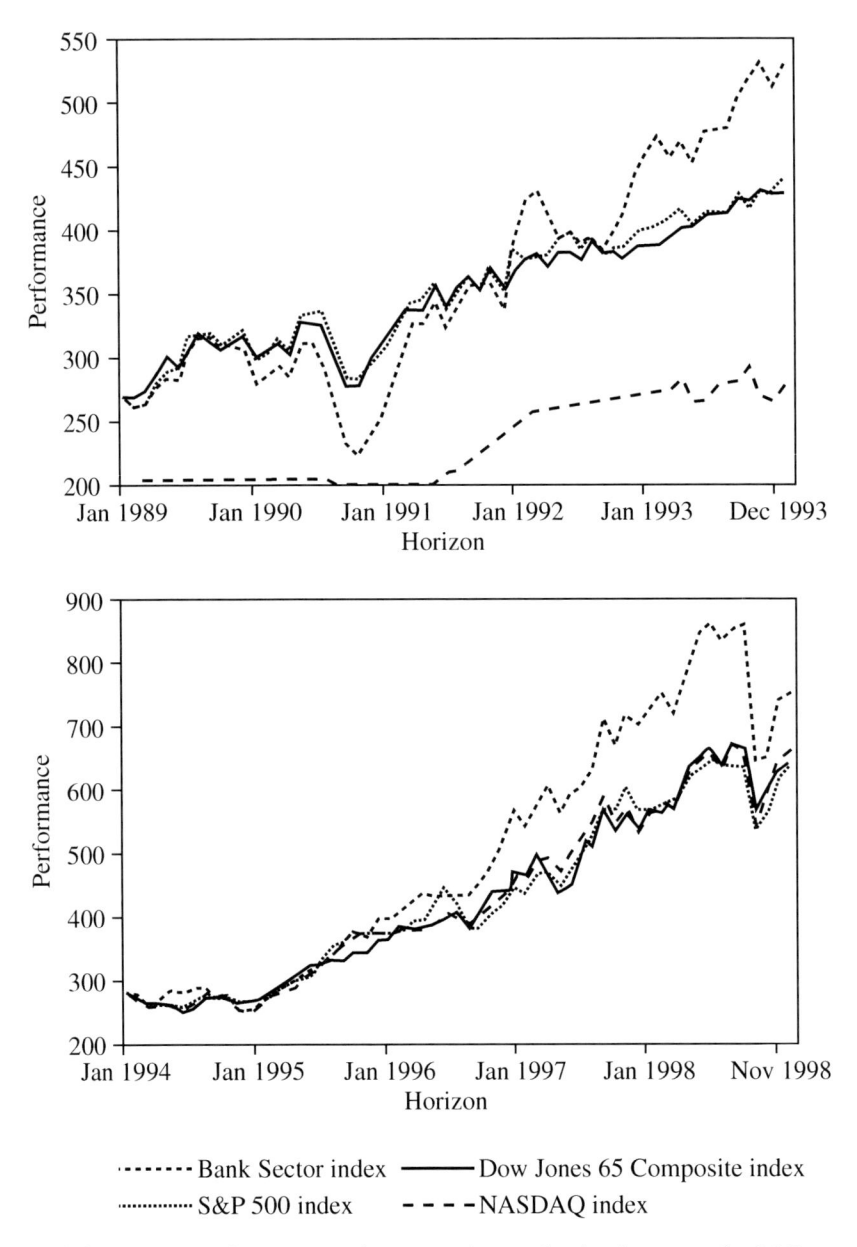

*Exhibit 13.1* *Bank sector performance (upper line) relative to the S&P 500, the Dow, and the NASDAQ*

Bankers have recently proved that they are not renaissance people either as individuals or as a group. Country risk appears to be very unsystematic in nature and thus very unpredictable. Agencies with vast resources and intelligence networks like the CIA failed to predict the invasion of Afghanistan, the overthrow of the Shah of Iran, the toppling of President Somoza in Nicaragua, the invasion of Kuwait by Saddam Hussein, the explosion of the atomic bomb by India and Pakistan and many other embarrassing cases. This shifting sand undermines any analysis no matter how carefully constructed. The same loan could be almost without risk under one set of conditions and very risky under different world economic conditions, world political conditions, a different government in the borrowing country or different policies by the same government in the borrowing country. However intricate and forbidding this may appear, bankers have tried and continue to find better ways to assess country risk and update their country ratings one to four times per year.

Country risk analysis usually begins with a look at the available data and moves towards building reasonable and comprehensive models that would utilize the data and produce forecasts about defaults and their probability of occurrence. The data currently available to banks are less than adequate. Their quality is largely, if not totally, uncontrollable by banks. Some of them may be 'managed', incomplete, or fundamentally flawed. Several governments, East European in particular, are not very forthcoming. The ability of banks to extract additional information is limited. The release of certain data may be deemed inconsistent with the national interest. Yet the data set continues to expand, as does the frequency of its release, thanks to the efforts of the Institute of International Finance, the BIS and large commercial banks.

Some banks have found rather novel ways to extract data from unwilling countries, such as reducing country lending limits and requiring higher spreads unless certain information is released, or simply refusing to make a loan.

The timing of the data is also a source of concern. Take, for example, the case of Bank A wishing to book a loan in Brazil in late 1998. The outstanding loans of that country and the performance against them are obviously of great concern to Bank A, but the latest figures available on the country's total indebtedness are as of March 1998. More up-to-date figures would be of great help. This may become possible. What is not possible is to obtain data on how many banks are trying simultaneously to book loans in Brazil at that point in time and the size of each loan under consideration. If the number of banks is very large, as are the loans being considered, the risk of Bank A's loan will be considerably higher than it would be had Bank A been the only foreign bank booking loans in Brazil. One method for avoiding this problem is to estimate Brazil's borrowing needs during a given period and relate that to the loan under consideration. But since when has Brazil borrowed only what it needed, and who determines what is needed or what is unnecessary?

These are the problems at the macro level. The problems at the micro level are even more serious, as are their consequences. Countries cannot go bankrupt and the access to whatever collateral is backing their borrowing depends on local law and authority, which the borrowing country controls. This led the Interim Committee of the Board of Governors of the IMF in April 1998 to adopt a 'Code of Good Practice on Fiscal Transparency: Declaration of Principles'. This included requirements as to the clarity of roles and responsibilities, timely and comprehensive disclosure of fiscal information, open budget preparation, execution and reporting, and public and independent scrutiny of fiscal information. These goals are commendable. The reality is that there is no one to enforce the new rules. One of the authors has had extensive experience in analysing data from two countries in the Middle East in 1998. The quality of the data could only be described as dismal, despite the presence of many Western trained PhD graduates in the institutions responsible for the production of the data.

Another issue dealing with the completeness of the data is the definition of what is an obligation of a foreign government. All loans, acceptances and placements of securities irrespective of currency or denomination must be included. Aliber (1980) suggested that foreign direct investment should also be included because any subsidiary to parent transfer is a charge on foreign exchange earnings. Yet another problem arises out of the decision on whose obligations are to be included, that is, out of the attempt to determine where the final risk lies. Should private debt be added to public debt? Should credit to branches of foreign banks located in the lending bank's own country be included? The answer is yes, but much of the data remains incomplete and in many cases impossible to complete. Some recent evidence is indeed worrisome. It is reported that Sudan had to survey its bankers to determine how much it owed. Poland hired an accounting firm to work out its amortization schedule. *The Wall Street Journal* reported in its 7 October 1983 issue a $10.8 billion gap in Argentina's debt. Investigators appointed by the federal court could not explain $10.8 billion of $40 billion. The reason appears to be that some private firms paid their debt without informing the government so they could continue to draw dollars from the central bank at the preferential rate. It was also discovered in 1983 that the Philippines had apparently overstated its reserves by $600 million in its attempts to 'reassure' bankers. The Russians admitted in 1998 that they had no idea what happened to the money loaned to them by the IMF. Nor did the IMF. Even European countries attempted, not always successfully, to massage their national data in order to meet the Maastricht criteria.

The various adjustments applied to the debt data have also been subject to controversy. Some economists prefer to speak of net instead of gross debt, where net means gross borrowing adjusted for external reserves of the borrowers. Other economists prefer to speak in real terms instead of nominal terms. They adjust the debt level and thus the real size of the principal amortization to balance the increase in interest payments resulting from higher actual or expected inflation. Most economists break down sovereign loans into their component parts by type of borrower and by maturity. This is necessary as the maturity structure in relation to available net cash flow at a point in time could change the risk profile of the country. Witness the Russian case in 1998 and the default on its domestic obligations.

The breakdown between private and public debt is becoming increasingly fuzzy, however, as governments decree for themselves preferential access to foreign exchange earnings both private and public. *The Wall Street Journal* reported on 7 November 1983 a Philippine government order for banks to 'turn over all their foreign exchange receipts to the government'. The independent source of funds available to private enterprises for debt repayment is suddenly made irrelevant by government fiat. A not too dissimilar case was witnessed in Mexico in 1994.

As they currently stand, the available data are largely acceptable and are getting better, particularly on private debt not publicly guaranteed. The data on long-term, public, non-military debt, of developing countries are quite adequate. The creditor reporting system of the Organization for Economic Cooperation and Development (OECD) Development Assistance Committee, the World Bank and the biannual survey of the maturity of international bank lending by the BIS contain valuable and reliable sources of information. The bulk of the data is on economic variables. Political and sociological data, while available, are not as accurate and certainly not as carefully scrutinized by bankers. That is why the common wisdom is that bankers are good at assessing economic risk but very poor at assessing political risk.

Furthermore, it would be dangerous to assume that the political factor can be ignored in developed countries. Britain under the Tories is not the Britain under the Labour Party. Britain and Italy experienced serious erosions in their ability to repay debt in the late 1970s and borrowed heavily from the IMF. Therefore, while developed countries are generally more stable, more accountable and have higher levels of diversification in their exports, both in terms of markets and exported products, their country risk is not negligible.

## 4 CURRENT COUNTRY RISK MODELS: GENERAL CHARACTERISTICS

A survey by the Export Import Bank classified country risk models into four categories:

- fully qualitative;
- structured qualitative with some statistical data;
- structured qualitative plus checklist qualitative with some quantitative techniques added; and
- econometric approach – highly structured and mathematically based. An example of this is the logit model, which predicts the probability of default.

The early country risk assessment models built on the original work of Avramovic (1964). Frank and Cline (1971), followed by Feder and Just (1980), first explored logit analysis. Ratio analysis was emphasized, as far as academic research shows, by Sofia (1981), the checklist of selected variables by Thompson (1981), and market spread rate analysis by Haegele (1981). More recently, Solberg (1988), Kaminsky et al. (1997), Wynn (1995, 1997), Ul Haque et al. (1996) and Wynn et al. (1999) provided further analyses of various factors that contribute to the sovereign risk or country risk in general. The factors investigated in these studies, which often use a linear regression model, include several categories of indicators, such as debt variables, balance of payments variables, income and expenditure variables, monetary variables and credit market supply-side variables.

In many cases, the factors used in each model included a wide array of variables. How one can carefully weigh each variable (over 100 in some cases), each with its own dynamics, and come out with a consistently accurate prediction remains a big puzzle. This did not discourage banks from trying. The frequently used variables in a qualitative or a quantitative model appear in Exhibit 13.2. All the analyses assume, of course, that the past is a guide to the future. This can lull the naive banker into believing that the presence of a model is sufficient grounds for setting loan rates that are consistent with the estimated underlying risk. *Euromoney* has developed a new rating system that assigns points to each country. The system reflects 'access to market rather than economic rating'. Some misgivings have, however, been raised by Cantor and Packer (1995) as to the usefulness of the ratings. They point particularly to (i) disagreements between the relative sovereign risks implied by the rank orders of market yields on sovereign bonds, and to (ii) differences between the ratings themselves from different agencies for a number of countries, especially those countries with lower ratings.

*Exhibit 13.2  Frequently used variables in qualitative and quantitative models*

I   Economics
A. Background
    (1) natural resources
    (2) demographics
    (3) other
B. Current indicators
    (1) Internal
       a. GNP
       b. inflation
       c. government budget
       d. consumption
       e. investment
    (2) external
       a. trade account
       b. current account
       c. capital account and/or foreign debt analysis
       d. other
        i. export diversity
        ii. import compressibility
        iii. main trading partners
C. Long-run indicators
    (1) managerial capability
    (2) investment in human capital
    (3) long-run projections
       a. internal economic indicators
       b. external economic indicators
II  Politics
A. Stability
    (1) type of government
    (2) orderliness of political successions
    (3) homogeneity of the populace
B. External relations
    (1) quality of relationships with major trading partners
    (2) quality of relationships with the United States
C. Long-run social and political trends

Statistics frequently used
I   Internal economy
A. GNP (per capita)
    (1) absolute
    (2) rate of growth
B. Inflation rate
C. Money supply growth
D. Net budget position
II  External economy
A. Balance of payments
    (1) trade balance
       a. exports and export growth
       b. imports and import growth
    (2) current account balance
    (3) long-term capital flows
B. External ratios
    (1) debt service ratio
    (2) reserve to imports ratio
C. International reserves

What all the models, regardless of sophistication, ignore or cannot incorporate are these important considerations:

1. The compounding effects a bad loan can have on the bank balance sheet. Bad debt begets more bad debts as banks attempt to bail out client states.
2. Banks with a heavy commitment to a country lose their flexibility. The old adage by Keynes is most appropriate here. Paraphrasing: 'If you lend someone a dollar, you own him; if you lend him a million, he owns you.' The use of bank loans is frequently beyond the control of the bank. Non-productive uses increase future debt service requirements but not debt servicing capacity. An example of a loan for financing consumption is a balance of payments adjustment loan.
3. The importance of and the price one has to pay for penetrating a market can be very substantial. Several of the toeholds in international lending, by regional banks in particular, were achieved through loan syndications where the lead bank had excessive leverage.
4. The lack of vigour of regulatory agencies may very well influence the type, size and other characteristics of the loan. Political pressures in the country of domicile could supersede country risk considerations.
5. The hardened mentality regarding a critical economic variable can be very problematic. The dramatic increase of bank loans to the Organization of Petroleum-Exporting Countries (OPEC) in the late 1970s was based on the pervasive faith that oil prices cannot but go upward. This was the 'consensus' which proved disastrous. The scenario was repeated in 1998 when oil prices took a tumble, destabilizing many economies, especially that of Russia and of other non-diversified oil-producing countries.
6. As banks charge higher interest rates to reflect higher country risk, they may be increasing that risk. Higher interest rates increase the probability of default. A significant portion of current less-developed country (LDC) debt represents accumulated interest on debt. Furthermore, higher interest rates in the world markets make for more attractive investment opportunities, encouraging capital flight out of LDCs, which decreases their ability to pay.
7. A new loan by a given bank will have a different impact on the total riskiness of the bank's portfolio, depending on how much is already outstanding in this type of loan or for this type of borrower. The current diversification rules, which limit lending to a single borrower to 5 per cent of capital, do not apply to categories of borrowers. This means that a bank can have exposure in a given country equal to several times its capital.

8. Lenders are not capable of monitoring either the economies of debtor countries or the total indebtedness of these countries. They lack both the legitimacy and the expertise. The upper limit on country risk is, therefore, not controllable by the bank unless country exposure is limited to the worst possible scenario, which effectively negates the usefulness of country risk analysis. The data, while available, may not be sufficiently revealing. From a banker's perspective, a balance of payments surplus, for example, resulting from cash or near cash deals is superior to one resulting from barter-type deals. A significant portion of Brazil's current surplus is barter related. We should note in this regard that a country that mismanages its economy and produces, for example, hyperinflation, will produce the same reaction by investors as one that imposes capital controls and that overtly and directly expropriates wealth. Hyperinflation is but a slower (mildly) way for wealth expropriation. It is a form of tax which rises exponentially and scares in the process both lenders and investors (*Euromoney*, 1998, World Bank Issue).

Country risk analysis, irrespective of the evidence, was and remains strongly dependent on human judgement. That is the nature of the beast.

The country risk we have been discussing deals with single loans and single borrowers. The portfolio effects cannot be ignored, however. Ingo Walter (1981) dealt with this issue. He argued that several problems are encountered when the portfolio approach is considered. Among them are:

1. The dispersion in portfolio preferences between bankers, investors and regulatory authorities. Each of these agents has a different objective function to maximize.
2. The illiquidity of sovereign debt held by banks, which reduces their ability to adjust their portfolio. This risk has been reduced by debt restructuring involving third-party guarantees such as those provided by the US government in the form of the Brady bonds. The Brady bonds were an attempt to resolve the sovereign debt crisis of the 1980s. They translate the non-forgiven portion (typically 85 per cent) of commercial bank debt owed by a given country into a bond form while extending the maturity of the debt. The resulting bonds are collateralized in terms of principal only, typically, by US government securities. The first country to complete a Brady plan restructuring was Mexico in March 1990. This market is now about $140 billion strong and has become the most liquid market for sovereign debt issues.
3. The asymmetry in the variance of returns on international loan portfolios: 'The variance of these returns may be entirely on the downside.'

Upside variances that would favour the bank are typically treated as equally significant as those on the downside.
4. The lumpiness of changes in country exposure makes portfolios 'difficult to adjust at the margin'.

All of these factors contribute further to the difficulty of assessing and dealing with country risk. The problem is compounded by the eternal optimism with which banks treat troubled loans. Loans are classified (reluctantly) as 'non-performing' while in reality they are bad debt. The US IRS (Internal Revenue Service) encouraged this by limiting the tax deductibility of reserves against troubled loans. Loan-loss reserves, which are tax deductible, are limited to 0.6 per cent of the bank's portfolio. Any reserves in excess of these limits must be taken from post-tax earnings. The Interagency Country Exposure Review Committee proposed, in October 1983, two additional reserves to deal with this problem. The first is special prudential reserves for certain countries (bad situations) and basket-type reserves for problem countries. Both of these reserves will be identified on the balance sheet as 'Allocated Transfer Risk Reserves' and will not be considered part of the bank's capital. Other recent regulatory interventions such as those required by FIRREA (Financial Institution Reform, Recovery and Enforcement Act), the various international agreements under the aegis of the BIS and by the accounting profession (FASB 15 requires troubled loans to be distinguished from normal loans) are steps in the right direction, as are the requirements by supervisory authorities, such as the US Federal Reserve and the German Supervisory Authority, requiring commercial banks to be vigilant in assessing country risk and in limiting exposure where it is prudent to do so. The unduly high exposure of German banks in Russia and in some East European countries indicates that the 'supervision' is not as tight as implied. Country risk assessment is further complicated by the nature of the contract between a commercial entity and a sovereign government. Sovereign risk emanates from the legal dimension of the problem. There are serious legal issues which need to be addressed. We shall refrain from this discussion because of space constraints. Suffice it to say that the contract with a sovereign country gives the lending agency very limited leverage. Some described it as 'the smile of a Cheshire cat' (Walter, 1981, p. 85).

The seriousness of regulatory authorities in dealing with country risk is reflected in the detailed reporting requirements shown in Exhibit 13.3. That is why the banks must have explicit ways for measuring and managing country risk.

*Exhibit 13.3   International transfer risk: examination objectives*

Section 7040.2

*Selected Country Exposures*
1. To determine if the bank is properly preparing the Country Exposure Report (FFIEC 009), which is required to be filed quarterly with the respective Reserve Banks.
2. To identify and report individual country exposures considered significant in relation to the bank's capital and the economic performance of the country.

*Classifications Due to Transfer Risk*
3. To evaluate the portfolio to identify those credits in countries considered subject to classification by the Interagency Country Exposure Review Committee.
4. To determine if the bank has adequately provided the required special reserves for those international assets included in the country exposures classified value-impaired.
5. To develop information on the composition of those exposures subject to classification.
6. To prepare report pages on all transfer risks subject to classification.
7. To determine the effect of total transfer risk classifications on the overall quality of the international loan portfolio, as well as that of the total bank.

*Nonclassified Credits Warranting Attention – Other Transfer Risk Problems*
8. To identify and report any exposures to countries identified as 'other transfer risk problems.'
9. To develop information on the composition of those exposures so identified, for report page.

*Nonclassified Credits Warranting Attention – Concentrations of Transfer Risk Warranting Special Comment*
10. To identify and report any concentrations of transfer risk warranting special comment.
11. To develop information on the composition of those concentrations for report page.

*Analysis of the Country Exposure Management System*
12. To determine if the bank's policies, practices, procedures, and internal controls for the management of transfer risk are adequate.
13. To determine if bank officers are operating in conformance with established guidelines.
14. To prepare narrative commentary on the bank's country exposure management system and on any noted deficiencies in a concise reportable format.

*Source:   Commercial Bank Examination Manual* (May 1996).

## 5 CURRENT COUNTRY RISK MODELS: QUALITATIVE

The overwhelming number of financial institutions do not use sophisticated country risk measurement and management models. Some rely on country risk limits to control risk while others use largely externally generated models to measure country risk and to set their spreads.

We begin our review of country risk models with a streamlined, well-circulated and fundamentally qualitative model developed by *Euromoney*. The latest available output of the *Euromoney* model was published in its IMF/World Bank Issue, 1998.

Country risk may be calculated or inferred from market data. The latter could be done by looking at spreads over Libor that borrowers pay, the forfaiting rates and their spreads from a benchmark rate, from the futures and options prices on options and futures contracts, or from bonds such as the Brady bonds. The *Euromoney* approach emphasizes the direct method and develops categories each having a maximum score and a weight in the overall development of a country risk index.

The results of the model are published in table format shown in Exhibit 13.4. The exhibit makes it immediately obvious that country risk must be a dynamic process. The Russian case represents the drama in the changes that can take place. Russia dropped 51 places in just one year, demonstrating the importance of constant monitoring and of the advantage that is inherent in being the first in finding the exit door. But everyone finds the information at the same time; hence the importance of 'connections', leading indicators and aggressive modelling.

The scores are the results of a weighting scheme developed by *Euromoney*. Its elements are:

1. economic performance derived from the magazine's Global Economic Projections. The weight is 25 per cent;
2. a series of net indebtedness ratios such as debt service to exports. The weight is 10 per cent;
3. debt is defaulted on or rescheduled. The highest score (10) goes to the country that had no non-payments. The weight is 10 per cent;
4. credit rating of a country using a weighted average of the country ratings provided by Moody's, Standard and Poor's and Fitch IBCA. The weight is 10 per cent;
5. the variables of access to bank finance, access to short-term finance, access to capital markets, and discount on forfaiting using the US data as a benchmark. The weight for each is 5 per cent.

*Exhibit 13.4   Country risk*

Country risk ranking by *Euromoney* (Sept. 1998)

| Rank Sept. 98 | Dec. 97 | Change Sept.–Dec. | | Total score | Political risk | Economic perform-ance | Debt indica-tors | Debt in default or rescheduled | Credit ratings | Access to bank finance | Access to short-term finance | Access to capital markets | Discount on forfeiting |
|---|---|---|---|---|---|---|---|---|---|---|---|---|---|
| | | | Weighting | 100 | 25 | 25 | 10 | 10 | 10 | 5 | 5 | 5 | 5 |
| 1 | 2 | 1 | Luxembourg | 98.90 | 24.76 | 25.00 | 10 | 10 | 10 | 5 | 5 | 5 | 4.14 |
| 2 | 1 | −1 | United States | 97.85 | 24.97 | 22.88 | 10 | 10 | 10 | 5 | 5 | 5 | 5.00 |
| 3 | 6 | 3 | Germany | 97.06 | 24.89 | 22.21 | 10 | 10 | 10 | 5 | 5 | 5 | 4.96 |
| 4 | 3 | −1 | Netherlands | 96.92 | 24.84 | 22.57 | 10 | 10 | 10 | 5 | 5 | 5 | 4.5 |
| 5 | 10 | 5 | Austria | 96.79 | 24.19 | 22.65 | 10 | 10 | 10 | 5 | 5 | 5 | 4.95 |
| 6 | 7 | 1 | Switzerland | 96.43 | 25.00 | 21.45 | 10 | 10 | 10 | 5 | 5 | 5 | 4.99 |
| 7 | 11 | 4 | France | 95.87 | 24.22 | 21.69 | 10 | 10 | 10 | 5 | 5 | 5 | 4.96 |
| 8 | 4 | −4 | Norway | 95.83 | 22.91 | 23.03 | 10 | 10 | 10 | 5 | 5 | 5 | 4.89 |
| 9 | 5 | −4 | United Kingdom | 95.01 | 25.00 | 20.04 | 10 | 10 | 10 | 5 | 5 | 5 | 4.97 |
| 10 | 12 | 2 | Ireland | 94.87 | 23.02 | 22.61 | 10 | 10 | 9.57 | 5 | 5 | 5 | 4.66 |
| 11 | 13 | 2 | Finland | 94.52 | 22.54 | 22.47 | 10 | 10 | 9.57 | 5 | 5 | 5 | 4.93 |
| 12 | 14 | 2 | Belgium | 94.25 | 23.72 | 21.01 | 10 | 10 | 9.57 | 5 | 5 | 5 | 4.95 |
| 13 | 15 | 2 | Sweden | 93.39 | 23.25 | 21.49 | 10 | 10 | 8.72 | 5 | 5 | 5 | 4.93 |
| 14 | 8 | −6 | Canada | 93.02 | 22.98 | 21.21 | 10 | 10 | 8.94 | 5 | 5 | 5 | 4.89 |
| 15 | 19 | 4 | Spain | 92.01 | 22.24 | 21.33 | 10 | 10 | 9.15 | 5 | 4.64 | 5 | 4.64 |
| 16 | 20 | 4 | New Zealand | 91.34 | 22.23 | 19.86 | 10 | 10 | 9.36 | 5 | 5 | 5 | 4.89 |
| 17 | 22 | 5 | Italy | 91.10 | 21.66 | 20.57 | 10 | 10 | 8.94 | 5 | 5 | 5 | 4.93 |
| 18 | 17 | −1 | Australia | 90.91 | 22.60 | 20.51 | 10 | 10 | 8.72 | 5 | 5 | 5 | 4.07 |
| 19 | 21 | 2 | Portugal | 90.73 | 21.76 | 21.34 | 10 | 10 | 8.94 | 5 | 4.64 | 5 | 4.04 |
| 20 | 9 | −11 | Denmark | 89.67 | 23.74 | 21.91 | 10 | 10 | 9.36 | 5 | 5 | 0 | 4.66 |
| 21 | 16 | −5 | Singapore | 89.17 | 23.29 | 19.24 | 10 | 10 | 9.68 | 5 | 4.64 | 4.3 | 3.02 |
| 22 | 24 | 2 | Iceland | 89.03 | 21.38 | 21.17 | 10 | 10 | 7.77 | 5 | 4.64 | 5 | 4.07 |
| 23 | 18 | −5 | Japan | 88.02 | 23.39 | 15.85 | 10 | 10 | 10 | 5 | 5 | 5 | 3.79 |
| 24 | 23 | −1 | Taiwan | 86.49 | 22.28 | 19.52 | 10 | 10 | 8.72 | 5 | 4.64 | 3.3 | 3.02 |
| 25 | 26 | 1 | Cyprus | 81.92 | 18.69 | 18.22 | 10 | 10 | 7.45 | 5 | 4.64 | 5 | 2.92 |

The weighted results are tabulated and a rank ordering from the highest (the best) to the lowest score is reported as shown in Exhibit 13.4. Luxembourg, the tiny European country, received the best rating (*IMF Survey*, 1998, vol. 27).

The second model we discuss is that developed by German Investment and Development Company (DEG). The model is fundamentally qualitative and distinguishes between country risk that affects a single project in a country and the other risk, which affects all projects in a given country. The results of the model are used for 'provisions in the balance sheet, country ceiling lending, pricing, decision on and planning of projects, and portfolio controlling'. The model measures risk in terms of four risk areas and 14 risk indicators. The model uses infrastructure risk: sociological factors, such as level of education, level of entrepreneurship, corruption, quality of the legal system; and political risk as two of the four risk areas. The other two are risks of foreign direct investment (FDI) policy, and administration and macroeconomic risk.

The end results of the model are the country risk tree shown in Exhibit 13.5 and the accompanying country risk analysis (score) table.

Moody's Investors Service also provides a rather widely quoted country risk rating system, which is based on qualitative variables. The ratings are provided for bonds and for bank deposits (Exhibit 13.6). They are arrived at using economic and political factors with a decided emphasis on the quantitative and the heuristic approach. The approach is decidedly long term. Moody's provides, in addition, 50 country-specific reports on an annual basis. The rating by Moody's and the corresponding one by Standard and Poor's have a significant effect on the observed spreads on sovereign debt. In a paper by Cantor and Packer (1994) the effects were measured and the conclusion was that: 'ratings appear to provide additional information beyond that contained in the standard macroeconomic country statistics incorporated in market yields'.

The IMF publishes what is referred to as an index of economic security. It uses different sources for arriving at the index: Political Risk Services Group for ten economic variables, and the Gastil Index published by Freedom House, New York for arriving at the values of two political risk variables. The 12 variables are then aggregated into components: 'the level of political stability, the democratic character of the political system, the quality of the bureaucracy, the quality of the legal system and the level of violence'. The resulting score, based on largely qualitative analysis is between 0 and 10 (best). The results are published as shown in Exhibit 13.7 (*IMF Survey*, 1998).

The Federal Reserve System, the Office of the Comptroller of the Currency and the Federal Deposit Insurance Corporation started a

# Country risk

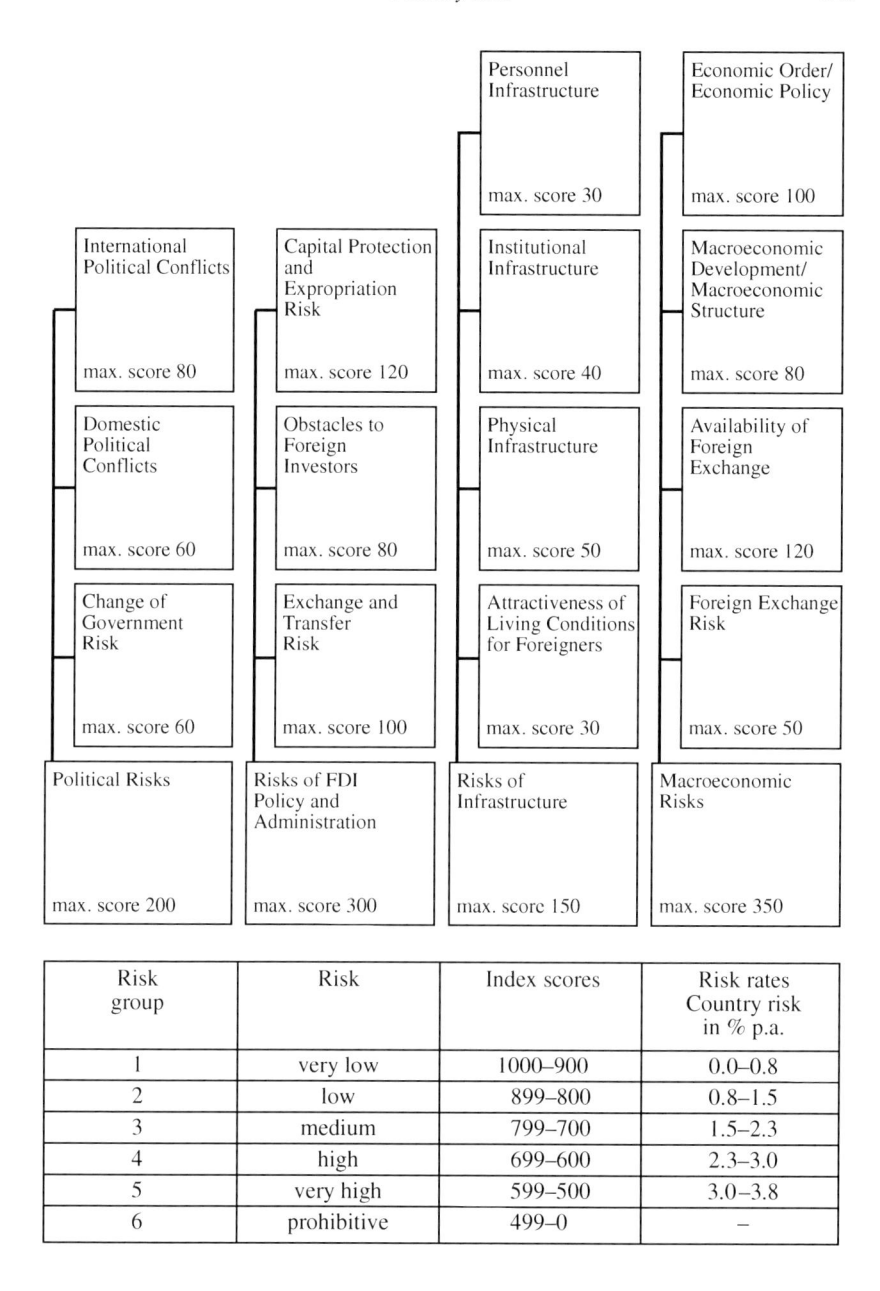

| | | Personnel Infrastructure  max. score 30 | Economic Order/ Economic Policy  max. score 100 |
|---|---|---|---|
| International Political Conflicts  max. score 80 | Capital Protection and Expropriation Risk  max. score 120 | Institutional Infrastructure  max. score 40 | Macroeconomic Development/ Macroeconomic Structure  max. score 80 |
| Domestic Political Conflicts  max. score 60 | Obstacles to Foreign Investors  max. score 80 | Physical Infrastructure  max. score 50 | Availability of Foreign Exchange  max. score 120 |
| Change of Government Risk  max. score 60 | Exchange and Transfer Risk  max. score 100 | Attractiveness of Living Conditions for Foreigners  max. score 30 | Foreign Exchange Risk  max. score 50 |
| Political Risks  max. score 200 | Risks of FDI Policy and Administration  max. score 300 | Risks of Infrastructure  max. score 150 | Macroeconomic Risks  max. score 350 |

| Risk group | Risk | Index scores | Risk rates Country risk in % p.a. |
|---|---|---|---|
| 1 | very low | 1000–900 | 0.0–0.8 |
| 2 | low | 899–800 | 0.8–1.5 |
| 3 | medium | 799–700 | 1.5–2.3 |
| 4 | high | 699–600 | 2.3–3.0 |
| 5 | very high | 599–500 | 3.0–3.8 |
| 6 | prohibitive | 499–0 | – |

*Exhibit 13.5   Country risk analysis: country risk tree*

*Exhibit 13.6  Sovereign ceilings for foreign-currency ratings**

|  | Bonds and Notes | | Bank Deposits | |
| --- | --- | --- | --- | --- |
|  | Long-term | Short-term | Long-term | Short-term |
| Alderney | Aaa | P-1 | Aaa | P-1 |
| Andorra | Aa2 | P-1 | Aa2 | P-1 |
| Argentina | Ba3 | NP | B1 | NP |
| Australia | Aa2 | P-1 | Aa2 | P-1 |
| Austria | Aaa | P-1 | Aaa | P-1 |
| Bahamas | A3 | P-2 | A3 | P-2 |
| Bahamas – Off Shore Banking Center | Aaa | P-1 | Aaa | P-1 |
| Bahrain | Ba1 | NP | Ba2 | NP |
| Bahrain – Off Shore Banking Center | A3 | P-2 | A3 | P-2 |
| Barbados | Ba1 | NP | Ba2 | NP |
| Belgium | Aaa | P-1 | Aaa | P-1 |
| Bermuda | Aa1 | P-1 | Aa1 | P-1 |
| Bolivia | B1 | NP | B2 | NP |
| Brazil | B2 | NP | Caa1 | NP |
| Bulgaria | B2 | NP | B3 | NP |
| Canada | Aa2 | P-1 | Aa2 | P-1 |
| Cayman Islands | Aa3 | P-1 | Aa3 | P-1 |
| Cayman Islands – Off Shore Banking Center | Aaa | P-1 | Aaa | P-1 |
| Chile | Baa1 | P-2 | Baa1 | P-2 |

*Note:* * Current as of 25 Nov. 1998, 05:57 EST.

*Source:* Moody's Investors Service.

programme in 1978 to improve their supervision of country risk. The premise was that the burden of proof for prudent lending and the risk-management function are decidedly the responsibility of the banking institution, and the purpose of the regulatory intervention is to set the rules of the game and the performance guidelines through supervision. The International Lending Supervision Act of 1983 compelled all banks with $30 million or more in foreign lending to file with the Fed the Country Exposure Report, which covers 24 different items. The aggregate of these reports is published on a quarterly basis in the *Federal Reserve Bulletin* (Exhibit 13.8). The three agencies do not assign a lending limit per country or for all countries. They simply examine the lending levels per lending

Exhibit 13.7  Ranking of countries according to level of economic security in 1995

| First Quintile | | Second Quintile | | Third Quintile | | Fourth Quintile | | Fifth Quintile | |
|---|---|---|---|---|---|---|---|---|---|
| Somalia | 1.60 | Liberia | 2.03 | Algeria | 4.07 | Nicaragua | 6.03 | Hong Kong, China | 8.02 |
| | | Sierra Leone | 2.13 | Togo | 4.15 | Panama | 6.07 | Poland | 8.15 |
| | | Zaire | 2.40 | Guinea-Bissau | 4.22 | Dominican Rep. | 6.10 | Korea, Rep. | 8.20 |
| | | Sudan | 2.58 | Haiti | 4.35 | Qatar | 6.10 | Cyprus | 8.22 |
| | | Iraq | 2.60 | Myanmar | 4.40 | Suriname | 6.12 | Czech Rep. | 8.23 |
| | | Angola | 3.27 | Guinea | 4.52 | Colombia | 6.13 | United Kingdom | 8.23 |
| | | | | Niger | 4.58 | Ecuador | 6.18 | Portugal | 8.32 |
| | | | | Gambia | 4.65 | Pap. N. Guinea | 6.20 | Hungary | 8.32 |
| | | | | Yugoslavia | 4.67 | Bolivia | 6.22 | Belgium | 8.40 |
| | | | | Nigeria | 4.72 | India | 6.25 | Malta | 8.40 |
| | | | | Cameroon | 4.77 | El Salvador | 6.38 | France | 8.50 |
| | | | | Senegal | 4.82 | Philippines | 6.38 | Japan | 8.58 |
| | | | | Ethiopia | 4.85 | Oman | 6.40 | USA | 8.68 |
| | | | | Korea, DPR | 4.87 | Malawi | 6.43 | Ireland | 8.75 |
| | | | | Guatemala | 4.93 | Brazil | 6.47 | Canada | 8.82 |
| | | | | Congo | 5.03 | Bahrain | 6.48 | Australia | 8.83 |
| | | | | Burkina Faso | 5.07 | Kuwait | 6.52 | Germany | 8.83 |
| | | | | Yemen, Rep. | 5.07 | Romania | 6.53 | Sweden | 8.90 |
| | | | | Uganda | 5.07 | Venezuela | 6.53 | Austria | 8.92 |
| | | | | Russia | 5.12 | Thailand | 6.55 | Iceland | 8.95 |
| | | | | Mali | 5.20 | Paraguay | 6.57 | Denmark | 9.00 |
| | | | | Peru | 5.27 | Albania | 6.58 | Finland | 9.00 |
| | | | | Vietnam | 5.30 | Morocco | 6.63 | Norway | 9.03 |
| | | | | Cuba | 5.37 | Uruguay | 6.65 | Netherlands | 9.08 |
| | | | | Sri Lanka | 5.37 | Mongolia | 6.68 | New Zealand | 9.08 |

Exhibit 13.7 (continued)

| First Quintile | Second Quintile | Third Quintile | | Fourth Quintile | | Fifth Quintile | |
|---|---|---|---|---|---|---|---|
| | | Indonesia | 5.40 | Trinidad & Tobago | 6.87 | Switzerland | 9.17 |
| | | Mozambique | 5.42 | Malaysia | 6.97 | Luxembourg | 9.25 |
| | | Cote d'Ivoire | 5.43 | Guyana | 7.00 | | |
| | | Tanzania | 5.45 | Jamaica | 7.15 | | |
| | | Gabon | 5.47 | Argentina | 7.22 | | |
| | | Honduras | 5.47 | Jordan | 7.22 | | |
| | | Madagascar | 5.47 | Botswana | 7.22 | | |
| | | Bangladesh | 5.52 | Bulgaria | 7.22 | | |
| | | Kenya | 5.53 | Brunei | 7.28 | | |
| | | Zambia | 5.55 | Slovak Rep. | 7.37 | | |
| | | Saudi Arabia | 5.58 | Singapore | 7.42 | | |
| | | Turkey | 5.58 | Israel | 7.43 | | |
| | | Libya | 5.62 | Spain | 7.48 | | |
| | | New Caledonia | 5.73 | Bahamas | 7.55 | | |
| | | Pakistan | 5.73 | Chile | 7.57 | | |
| | | Lebanon | 5.75 | South Africa | 7.57 | | |
| | | Iran | 5.77 | Costa Rica | 7.63 | | |
| | | Egypt | 5.82 | Greece | 7.73 | | |
| | | Tunisia | 5.83 | Namibia | 7.77 | | |
| | | Mexico | 5.88 | Italy | 7.82 | | |
| | | UAE | 5.92 | Taiwan, Prov. of China | 7.92 | | |
| | | Zimbabwe | 5.92 | | | | |
| | | Ghana | 5.95 | | | | |
| | | Syria | 5.97 | | | | |
| | | China, PR | 5.98 | | | | |

*Source:* The IMF.

Exhibit 13.8 *Statistical release: country exposure lending survey*

Table I. *Amounts owed U.S. Banks by Foreign Borrowers (Includes Adjustments to Reflect Guarantees and Indirect Borrowings) ($ Millions)*

| E.16 (126) | (A)<br>Total Amount Owed by Country of Borrower After Adjustments for Guarantees and External Borrowings (Except Derivative Products) | (B)<br>Cross Border Exposure Resulting from Revaluation Gains on Foreign Exchange and Derivative Products After Adjustments for Guarantees and External Borrowings | (C = A + B)<br>Total Outstanding Adjusted Cross Border Exposure Excluding Local Country Claims | (D)<br>Net Local Country Claims/2 | (E = C + D)<br>Total Outstanding Cross Border Exposure |
|---|---|---|---|---|---|
| G-10 and Switzerland | | | | | |
| Belgium | 9,781 | 2,809 | 12,590 | 491 | 13,081 |
| Canada | 16,144 | 4,279 | 20,423 | 1,445 | 21,868 |
| France | 23,288 | 8,950 | 32,238 | 471 | 32,709 |
| Germany | 30,804 | 13,936 | 44,740 | 3,105 | 47,845 |
| Italy | 13,756 | 8,251 | 22,007 | 4,457 | 26,464 |
| Japan | 19,981 | 14,186 | 34,167 | 2,364 | 36,531 |
| Luxembourg | 4,558 | 1,435 | 5,993 | 0 | 5,993 |
| Netherlands | 13,408 | 6,357 | 19,765 | 175 | 19,940 |
| Sweden | 5,258 | 1,676 | 6,934 | 52 | 6,986 |
| Switzerland | 14,699 | 4,658 | 19,357 | 463 | 19,820 |
| United Kingdom | 21,167 | 12,731 | 33,898 | 2,937 | 36,835 |
| | 172,844 | 79,268 | 252,112 | 15,960 | 268,072 |

Exhibit 13.8 (continued)

| | All Banks | | | | |
|---|---|---|---|---|---|
| | (A) Total Amount Owed by Country of Borrower After Adjustments for Guarantees and External Borrowings (Except Derivative Products) | (B) Cross Border Exposure Resulting from Revaluation Gains on Foreign Exchange and Derivative Products After Adjustments for Guarantees and External Borrowings | (C = A + B) Total Outstanding Adjusted Cross Border Exposure Excluding Local Country Claims | (D) Net Local Country Claims | (E = C + D) Total Outstanding Cross Border Exposure |
| E.16 (126) | | | | | |
| Non G-10 Developed Countries | | | | | |
| Australia | 4,522 | 4,364 | 8,886 | 2,720 | 11,606 |
| Austria | 2,046 | 986 | 3,032 | 62 | 3,094 |
| Denmark | 2,703 | 1,612 | 4,315 | 66 | 4,381 |
| Finland | 2,411 | 1,224 | 3,635 | 0 | 3,635 |
| Greece | 2,365 | 130 | 2,495 | 126 | 2,621 |
| Iceland | 90 | 5 | 95 | 0 | 95 |
| Ireland | 2,387 | 1,032 | 3,419 | 1 | 3,420 |
| New Zealand | 1,041 | 439 | 1,480 | 519 | 1,999 |

*Source:* Federal Financial Institutions Examination Council, 30 June, 1998.

institution in the light of economic analyses submitted by economists from the US Treasury, the Federal Reserve Bank of New York and by the Board of Governors. The focus of the analyses is transfer risk and it ranks countries as 'strong', 'moderately strong' or 'weak' in terms of that risk. Based on these criteria, the bank loans will be classified as 'losses', 'value impaired', 'substandard' and 'other transfer risk problems'. The first category requires that the loan be written off, and the second category requires an allocation of transfer risk reserve ranging from 10 to 100 per cent of capital. The Interagency Country Risk Review Committee evaluates transfer risk in judging the overall quality of the institution's assets and adjusts the above categories of transfer risk for commercial risk factors. In addition, the committee evaluates the procedures and the models used by banks in the evaluation of their international lending programmes.

## 6 CURRENT COUNTRY RISK MODELS: QUANTITATIVE

One of the early rigorous studies on modelling country risk is the one by Jeffrey Sachs (1984), which suggests that a bank's return on a loan to a specific country can be expressed as:

$$E(R) = \alpha + f(L_i/B_i), \qquad (13.1)$$

where a bank expects a given rate $\alpha$ (a spread above Libor) on its loans when its exposure to country $i$ is low, and a premium over $\alpha$ when its loan exposure $L_i$ increases as a proportion of its total capital $B_i$.

Sachs then defined the bank managers' utility function in terms of return and risk:

$$E(U) = E(R_p) - \beta[\sigma(R_p)], \qquad (13.2)$$

where $E(R_p)$ is the expected return of the bank's loan portfolio and $\sigma(R_p)$ is the volatility of the portfolio return. This utility function suggests that bank managers are made better off by increased returns, but worse off by increased variability of those returns. The variability is reduced via portfolio diversification. An equilibrium condition was achieved when the first derivative of the utility function is set equal to zero, or when the marginal rate of substitution of risk and return equals the market price of risk.

Sachs (1984) develops a mathematical model which can predict the maximum and optimum levels of debt of a sovereign borrower. The maximum debt is given by:

$$(1+r)D_t \leq \max \sum_{i-1}^{\infty} (1+r)^{-(i-t)} (Q_i - I_i), \qquad (13.3)$$

where $D_t$ is the debt in period $t$, $r$ is the real interest rate (assumed to be constant), $Q_i$ is the country output in time $i$ and $I_i$ is the investment outlay in period $i$. The author also argues that the above constraint plays a role in the consumption utility maximization of the borrowing country. The function is:

$$\text{Max } U(C1, C2, C3, \ldots), \qquad (13.4)$$

subject to:

$Q_t = (K_t, L_t)$ (production equation)
$K_{t+1} = K_t(1-d) + I_t$ (capital accumulation, $d$: rate of depreciation)
$C_t = (Q_t - rD_t) - I_t + (D_{t+1} - D_t)$ (consumption constraint)
$(1+r)D_t \leq \max \Sigma (1+r)^{-(i-t)}(Q_i - I_i)$ (debt constraint).

The maximum level of debt that can be attained also depends on the ability of the borrowing country to tax its citizens, the uncertainty in output level $Q$, and many other factors.

In a more recent paper, Sachs et al. (1996) create a model for determining the likelihood of a financial crisis in a country. The model is based on three major factors: significant appreciation in the real exchange rate, weak banking system and low foreign currency reserves. The authors state that countries with sufficient foreign reserves, strong banks and insignificant real rate appreciation were less vulnerable to a foreign currency crisis than countries with less strong fundamentals.

The authors state that sharp devaluations of the domestic currency of a country are more likely where the country's banking system is weaker and the exchange rate is overvalued. High reserve levels may preclude a currency crisis, since in that case investors will not perceive the country's financial instrument to be as risky as when no reserves exist to maintain the exchange rate peg. It is also assumed that, unlike the case of the country with strong fundamentals, multiple equilibria exist for the economically disadvantaged country; hence this model will have no predictive power. Here currency risk is assumed to constitute a leading indicator for financial difficulties.

The authors run a multiple regression to estimate the value of a crisis index ($IND$ – a measure of the extent of financial crisis), based on the following equation:

$$IND = \beta_1 + \beta_2(RER) + \beta_3(LB) + \beta_4(D^{LR} \times RER)$$
$$+ \beta_5(D^{LR} \times LB) + \beta_6(D^{LR} \times D^{WF} \times RER) + \beta_7(D^{LR} \times D^{WF} \times LB), \qquad (13.5)$$

where *RER* represents the percentage change in the real exchange rate index for a period of time compared to a base period, and *LB* is the lending boom factor. *LB* is measured using a ratio of banks' claims on the private sector (*B*) as a percentage of GDP for a period of time. (Sachs et al., 1996 use $LB = (B/GDP_{1994})$.) $D^{WF}$ is a dummy variable for economic fundamentals, such as $D^{WF}$ is equal to one for weak fundamentals and equal to zero for strong fundamentals. $D^{LR}$ is the reserve level indicator, which is equal to one for low reserves and equal to zero for high reserves. The coefficients $\beta_2$ and $\beta_3$ capture the effects of the fundamentals on the crisis index IND in countries with high reserves ($D^{LR}=0$). The coefficients $\beta_2+\beta_4$ and $\beta_3+\beta_5$ capture the effects on countries with low reserves ($D^{LR}=1$) and weak fundamentals ($D^{WF}=0$). The regression results of Sachs et al. (1996) indicate that more than 50 per cent of the variation in the crisis index might be explained by movements in the real exchange rate, lending boom and the dummy variables.

Other possible causes for financial crises were identified as:

- the composition of excessive capital inflows (excessive inflows alone do not explain the crisis);
- large current account deficits;
- loose fiscal policy;
- different absorption of capital inflows (the paper focuses on sterilization of inflows and fiscal contraction);
- differences in the underlying productive structure among countries; and
- nominal exchange rate policy.

Balkan (1995) started from a different premise that all bank managers are risk averse and will make their decisions in accordance with a Sachs-type utility function. We present an extensive discussion of the Balkan model as it is thorough and as it presents the various aspects of country risk analysis in easy to follow steps using both economic and political data.

Generally speaking, a default event associated with the country risk has two states, that is, default happens or default does not happen. In econometrics, such an event can be described with a qualitative response (QR) model. Denote the probability of default as $P_d$. The QR model of $P_d$ can be specified as follows:

$$P_d = F(Z), \qquad (13.6)$$

where $F$ is certain pre-specified (probability) function and $Z$ is a function of certain independent variables.

The functional forms of $F$ most frequently used in application are the following:

$$\text{Linear probability model:} \quad F(Z) = Z. \quad (13.7)$$

$$\text{Logit model:} \quad F(Z) \equiv \Lambda(Z) = \frac{e^z}{1 + e^z}. \quad (13.8)$$

$$\text{Probit model:} \quad F(Z) = N(Z) = \frac{1}{(2\pi)^{1/2}} \int_{-\infty}^{Z} \exp(-u^2/2) du. \quad (13.9)$$

The linear probability model has an obvious defect in that $F$ for this model is not a proper distribution function as it is not constrained to lie between 0 and 1. Probit models are based on underlying quantitative variables and use the cumulative normal distribution. Logit models by contrast rely on qualitative variables and use binomial distributions. Although the two models typically yield the same results, probit models are easier to track and to interpret.

Balkan developed a probit model which estimates the default probabilities of sovereign countries based on a series of economic and political factors. Balkan's probit model is then tested in the context of the capital asset pricing model (CAPM) to determine whether banks make their pricing decisions in accordance with CAPM stipulations. The conclusion is that the probit model has the capability of default estimation, while international loans are priced according to the CAPM, but not in its pure form.

Balkan based his study on a set of assumptions: banks make lending from excess capital, a risk-free asset exists, and a loan that yields Libor with certainty can be made. International loans are risky, and risk-averse bankers choose to invest in a portfolio of assets which also includes the risk-free asset. There is perfect competition on the eurocurrency market, as no single bank can significantly affect the rates and spreads charged on the market. The expected return depends on mutually exclusive and exhaustive set of events (states of the world).

Country risk stems from both political and economic factors. Economic circumstances like current account deficits and economic downturns may create solvency problems for the borrowing country, while political turmoil may endanger debt repayment despite the country's ability to cover its payments.

Country risk can, consequently, be separated in three levels: temporary delay in payments, debt rescheduling or moratorium on payments for a certain period of time and repudiation of the debt. All three events pose a threat to the liquidity and profitability of the lender, and, therefore, are termed as default and should be avoided by risk-averse bank managers. Earnings decreases, lower capitalization ratios, reduction in trade financing opportunities, and reduced deposit transactions with the defaulting country are among the possible risks that a defaulting nation can impose on a lending institution.

The probit model was utilized to predict the likelihood of default of a nation in a given year. It is assumed that the probability of default $P_d$ is related to a vector of economic and political variables:

$$P_d = F(Z) = \frac{1}{(2\pi)^{1/2}} \int_{-\infty}^{Z} \exp(-u^2/2) du, \quad (13.10)$$

where $Z$ is a linear combination of the $X_i$, given by:

$$Z = F^{-1}(P_d) = \alpha + \beta_i X_i. \quad (13.11)$$

The value of $Z$ in the preceding equation is a linear function of the exogenous variables $X_i$, but its rate of change is not constant. The coefficient $\beta$ determines the direction in which each $X_i$ will affect the default probability. The chosen independent variables may be divided in two categories – economic and political. The desire to meet the obligations is assumed to be explained in the political variables. Most variables have been proved to be statistically significant by prior research. The economic variables of the model include: debt service, reserves/imports (the higher the reserves relative to imports, the more reserves are available to meet debt payments), imports/GNP, amortization rate (the rate at which a borrower repays loans), interest/exports (measures the decreased liquidity due to pending interest payments), debt outstanding/GNP, export growth (a proxy for the availability of foreign exchange funds), GNP growth rate, current account deficit/exports (the amount that the country overspent relative to its foreign currency income), domestic saving/GNP (a relatively higher savings rate makes a country better able to find internal financing, therefore reducing the risk of default) and OECD growth rate (measures the growth in availability of capital to developing countries).

The political indicators include: a democracy index (computed on a point basis where a given number of points are assigned for the competitiveness level in the executive, legislative and political systems of a country. The democracy index in this case ranges from 3 to 20, 20 being the most democratic), political instability variables (given by the following formula $\Sigma \beta_i V_i$, where $\beta$ is a coefficient of instability and $V$ is the instability variable).

Regressing on the basis of the above-mentioned independent variables yielded the probability of default. In this case the author has chosen to define default as the occurrence of any of the three levels of country insolvency, since the ultimate case – borrower's repudiation of debt – is a quite rare event. The author proceeded to develop a ranking of countries based on the probit model for 33 major debtor nations over the period from 1970 to 1984. The political variables were significant, suggesting that political variables play a major role in determining default probabilities.

The author suggests two ways of testing the model. First he assumes that if a country's probability of default is bigger than a given probability $P^*$, the country is denied credit and vice versa. In that case two types of errors are possible:

Error I  Probability lower than $P^*$, but default occurs.
Error II Probability higher than $P^*$, but default does not occur.

It is assumed that risk-averse bankers will prefer to limit the type I error, regardless of the fact that it is economically sound to try minimizing the amount of total error.

The model was tested at three levels of $P^*$ and the probability of type I error was significantly lower when political variables were incorporated in the analysis. In addition, as suggested before, including political factors improves the explanatory capability of the model and increases its $R^2$ from 0.62 to 0.79.

Balkan then compared the rankings of the probit model to those of three publications, *The Institutional Investor*, *Euromoney Ratings*, and *International Country Risk*. In all three cases it is shown that the model's prediction is significantly better than the rankings given by the three publications.

Wynn et al. (1999) provide some additional insights into the prediction power of sovereign risk of rankings given by rating agencies. They conclude that much remains to be done for these rankings in improving both the methods of forecast evaluation and the models used to produce predictions.

**Extension of Probit Model (I): Currency Risk**

We have mentioned the independent variables used by Balkan (1995) in his probit model of country risk. These variables range from debt service, GNP growth, to political instability indicators. However, one critical variable that is closely related to a country's ability for debt payments was ignored in Balkan's model. This variable is the currency stability of a country, which measures the stability of the exchange rates of a country's currency against major international currencies, such as the US dollar and the German mark. The stability of a currency can be measured in two ways. One measure is the volatility of the currency's exchange rate against US dollar or some other major international currency units. The volatility can be estimated either unconditionally from the historical data or conditionally by using ARCH-type time-series models. Another measure is the likelihood of a major currency depreciation or currency crisis.

A currency crisis exists when there is *abrupt* currency depreciation (see, for example, Esquivel and Larrain, 1998). Based on this, we believe that a jump process is useful for capturing a currency crisis. For instance, on 2 July 1997, the Thai baht was made to float because of financial and economic pressures. This led to a 40 per cent fall of the baht against the US dollar. This is an obvious case of jump risk in exchange rates. The other example is Hurricane Mitch and its devastating effects on El Salvador and on Honduras, cited earlier. For a comprehensive empirical study on jump risk in exchange rates, see Jorion (1988).

Mathematically, the jump risk can be incorporated in the following jump-diffusion process in continuous time (Zhou, 1998a, 1999):

$$\frac{dE}{d} = \mu \cdot dt + \sigma \cdot dW + \delta \cdot dq, \tag{13.12}$$

where $E$ is the exchange rate, $\mu$ is the drift term in exchange rate that is related to the expected percentage change in $E$ (the expected return on foreign currency without jumps), $\sigma$ is the volatility of diffusion component of the exchange rate (the average historical risk without jumps), $W$ is a Wiener process (a particular case of random processes), $dq$ is a Poisson process (representing the big change in exchange rate in a very short time) with a constant intensity, $\lambda$, where $\lambda$ can be interpreted as the expected number of jumps in a year. The parameter $\delta$ is the random jump size, and has the following distribution:

$$\ln(\delta + 1) \sim N(\mu_\delta, \sigma_\delta^2). \tag{13.13}$$

All the parameters can be estimated empirically, as shown in Jorion (1988).

There are many economic and non-economic causes for currency crises, including seigniorage, current account imbalances, low foreign exchange reserves, real exchange rate (RER) misalignment, political unrest, speculative attacks, investors' sentiment deterioration, international and/or regional contagion and so on. Esquivel and Larrain (1998) find that high rates of seigniorage, current account deficits, low foreign exchange reserves, real exchange rate misalignment, negative income growth and a contagion effect all help to explain the presence of currency crises.

Seigniorage is defined as annual change in reserve money as a percentage of GDP. According to Krugman (1979), seigniorage is useful for predicting currency crises because the government had no access to capital markets and therefore had to monetize the deficit. The monetization of the government deficit is key to explaining exchange rate collapses. Many authors have emphasized that currency crises are usually preceded by periods of exchange rate overvaluation or misalignment.[2] As we mentioned earlier, in a recent article, Sachs et al. (1996) use the significant appreciation in the real exchange rate of a country's currency as one of three major factors determining the likelihood of a financial crisis in a country. They state that keeping other conditions unchanged, countries with significant real exchange rate appreciation are more vulnerable to a foreign currency crisis (asset bubble effect). Many authors construct an RER index as an explanatory variable for currency crises. In Esquivel and Larrain (1998), an RER misalignment variable is constructed as the negative of the percentage deviation of the RER from its average over the previous 60 months. The intuition for the linkage between other mentioned variables and currency crises is well known and straightforward.

Currency crises often have a self-fulfilling feature. When a currency crisis occurs, investors quickly lose confidence in the currency, which leads to a large-scale capital outflow and a further currency depreciation. Using their theoretical models, Solnik (1974) and Zhou (1998b) show that either expected currency depreciation or a high currency uncertainty discourages international investors from investing in a country.

The stability of currency is important because it is directly related to a country's wealth measured in US dollars. On the one hand, a sharp depreciation of a country's currency will substantially reduce the country's wealth and therefore its ability for fulfilling its debt obligation if the debt is denominated in US dollars or other major international currencies. On the other hand, substantial currency depreciation will lead to a significant financial loss to an international investor if his/her investments are not protected from currency depreciation, no matter whether there is a default or not. The recent (1997–98) experience of South Korea, Indonesia, Malaysia and other countries has clearly shown the importance of currency stability in evaluating country risk.

**Extension of Probit Model (II): Contagion Effect**

A spate of recent financial crises, the international crisis of Mexico in 1995, the still unfolding effects of the Asian crisis and the more recent financial crisis in Russia have been accompanied by episodes of financial market contagion in which financial markets of many countries have experienced increases in volatility. Using a panel data set with annual information for 30 countries during the period from 1975 to 1996, Esquivel and Larrain

(1998) find that the contagion effects in currency crises among countries in the same regions are both economically and statistically significant. Theoretically, economists have identified two main explanations for contagion effects. The first one focuses on trade linkages and in the loss of competitiveness associated with devaluation by a main trading partner, which in turn leaves the domestic currency in particular and the domestic financial market in general more vulnerable to a speculative attack (Gerlach and Smets, 1995). The second is related to multiple equilibrium of the economy, and suggests that a crisis in one country may raise the odds of a crisis elsewhere by signalling that currency devaluation or a financial trouble is more likely as a result of the initial crisis. The signal may then lead to a self-fulfilling speculative attack (Mason, 1998).

The following is a partial list of economic factors that can contribute to the contagion effect or cross-correlations among countries:

- trading interdependence; this can be measured by the ratio of cross-country trade to regional trade, or to the total trade of a country;
- cross-border capital flows for portfolio and direct investment purposes;
- cross-labour flows (Mexican–American labour sending earnings back);
- membership in regional economic organizations (for example, NAFTA (North American Free Trade Agreement) and APEC (Asia-Pacific Economic Cooperation)); and
- direct and reverse direct investment.

The contagion effect among countries has many important implications for investments and risk management. For instance, financial contagion implies high correlation between some financial markets during bad times. Therefore, portfolio diversification across financial regions that have different contagion patterns is of great importance.

Because financial contagion is important, it should be incorporated in country risk models. Balkan's (1995) probit model assumes the independence of default risk between countries. That is, the default or financial crisis in one country does not provide any information about the financial status of other countries. This is inconsistent with our observation on financial contagion.

In this section, we incorporate the contagion effect into the probit model. Define a random variable $y_i$ for country $i$ such that $y_{it} = 1$ if a default occurs in country $i$ at time $t$ and zero otherwise. Using Balkan's notation, we can write:

$$y_{it} = 0 \mid X = X_{it} \text{ if } \alpha + \beta_i \cdot X_{it} + \varepsilon_{it} \leq 0$$

and

$$y_{it} = 1 \mid X = X_{it} \text{ if } \alpha + \beta_i \cdot X_{it} + \varepsilon_{it} > 0,$$

where $X_{it}$ is the vector of economic and political indicators observed at time $t$ for country $i$ and $\varepsilon_{it}$ is an i.i.d. normal variable associated with country $i$ ($i = 1, 2, \ldots, n$).

To allow for financial contagion among countries, we assume that the error term $\varepsilon_{it}$ is determined by a factor model such that:

$$\varepsilon_{it} = \gamma_{i1} u_{1t} + \ldots + \gamma_{im} u_{mt} + e_{it},$$

where $\gamma_{i1}, \ldots, \gamma_{im}$ are constant coefficients and $u_{1t}, \ldots, u_{mt}$ are standard normal variables that are i.i.d. over $t$. The residual term $e_{it}$ is assumed to be i.i.d. over $t$, be independent of $u_{1t}, \ldots, u_{mt}$, and be independent of $e_{jt}$ for all $j \neq i$. For simplicity, we can assume that factors $u_{1t}, \ldots, u_{mt}$, are mutually independent.[3]

The factors $u_{1t}, \ldots, u_{mt}$ have quite a few economic interpretations. The simplest case is a one-factor model where $m = 1$. In this case, a common factor can affect the whole world economy. A factor can also be interpreted as a regional economic variable that affects countries in a particular economic region or countries sharing certain common financial characteristics. In this case, we may impose some restrictions on $\gamma_{i1}, \ldots, \gamma_{im}$. For instance, if $u_{1t}$ is a regional factor for Asian countries, we can set $\gamma_{i1} = 0$ for all non-Asian countries.

By assumption, the vector of $\varepsilon_{it}$, $\Phi_t = [\varepsilon_{it}]_{i=1}^n$, has the following joint normal distribution:

$$\Phi_t \sim N(0, \Sigma).$$

The $(i, j)$ cell of matrix $\Sigma$ is given by

$$\Sigma_{ij} = \sum_{k=1}^m \gamma_{ik} \cdot \gamma_{jk}.$$

The above probit model can be estimated by employing the standard maximum likelihood econometric methodology. The likelihood function is

$$L = \prod_{t=1}^T F[\Psi_t *(2Y_t - 1); \Sigma *(2Y_t - 1)(2Y_t - 1)^n]. \tag{13.14}$$

where * denotes the Hadamard product,[4]

$$\Psi_t = [\alpha + \beta \cdot X_{1t}, \ldots, \alpha + \beta \cdot X_{nt}]^n, \tag{13.15}$$

and

$$Y_t = [y_{1t}, \ldots, y_{nt}]^n. \tag{13.16}$$

The expression $F[x; \Omega]$ denotes the cumulative distribution function of $N[0, \Omega]$.

Exhibit 13.9 shows a summary of the full model we are proposing.

*Exhibit 13.9   Summary of proposed country risk model*

---

Based on previous research results and our analysis, we believe that the following adjusted probit model is a more comprehensive model of country risk. The points marked with an asterisk (*) are added by the authors of this chapter.

- *Economic Indicators: Debt Service Capacity*
    - Debt service
    - Reserves/imports
    - Imports/GNP
    - Amortization rate
    - Interest/exports
    - Debt outstanding/ GNP
    - Export growth
    - GNP growth rate
    - Current account deficit/exports
    - Domestic saving/GNP
    - OECD growth rate

* *Economic Indicators: Currency/Financial Crisis Index*
    * Seigniorage
    * Real exchange rate misalignment
    * Soundness of banking system
    * Conditional volatility and/or jump probability in exchange rates

The last variable is related to other economic variables. The conditional volatility of exchange rates can be estimated by using ARCH or GARCH type models. The probability of jump in exchange rates can be estimated by using historical jump frequency in exchange rates or by compiling a subjective index.

- *Political Indicators*
    - Democracy index
    - Political instability variables

* *Contagion Effect*   The contagion effect can be incorporated in a probit model as discussed in the previous section.

---

In short, we propose a new probit model that is based on Balkan's (1995) original work and takes two additional important factors, currency risk and contagion effect, into account. Mathematically, the model can be summarized as shown in Exhibit 13.10. We let $y_{it} = 1$ if default occurs in country $i$ at time $t$, and zero otherwise.

*Exhibit 13.10   The extension of the probit model of country risk*

---

*The Probit Model*

$$y_{it} = 0 \mid X = X_{it} \text{ if } \alpha + \beta_i \cdot X_{it} + \varepsilon_{it} \leq 0$$

and

$$y_{it} = 1 \mid X = X_{it} \text{ if } \alpha + \beta_i \cdot X_{it} + \varepsilon_{it} > 0,$$

where $X_{it}$ is the vector of economic and political indicators listed above.

*Adjustment for Jump Risk and Currency Risk*
Exchange rate following the jump-diffusion process

$$\frac{dE}{E} = \mu \cdot dt + \sigma \cdot dW + \delta \cdot dq.$$

The estimates of the parameters in the above jump-diffusion process are used as input variables ($X_{it}$) in the probit model.

*Adjustment for Contagion Effect*
The contagion effect is incorporated in the probit model by letting the residual terms $\varepsilon_{it}$ be correlated and be governed by a factor model

$$\varepsilon_{it} = \gamma_{i1} u_{1t} + \ldots + \gamma_{im} u_{mt} + e_{it}.$$

The residual term $e_{it}$ is assumed to be i.i.d over $t$, be independent of $u_{1t}, \ldots, u_{mt}$, and be independent of $e_{jt}$ for all $j \neq i$.

---

## 7   CONCLUDING REMARKS

This chapter defined country risk and differentiated it from other forms of macro risks that are faced by international investors. The pitfalls in measuring the size and the impact of country risk were then discussed, as were the effects of the participation of governments and international agencies in the lending function and/or in the lending guarantee function (implicit or explicit).

The chapter considered the intellectual and operational premise for modelling country risk by lending institutions. The model then reviewed the most used quantitative and qualitative models. The probit model developed by Balkan (1995) was discussed extensively in the quantitative section.

This study added two important dimensions to the probit model proposed by Balkan (1995) based on the recent lesson from the financial markets. These are the currency risk effect and the contagion effect. The resulting model is robust and quite inclusive of the concerns of international investors. It allows for the determination of the likelihood of default taking into consideration internal and external shocks.

Much research remains to be done. We hope that there will be better data sets available, and more cooperative governments.

The best advice we can give bankers is: 'Analyse, analyse, analyse; limit, limit, limit exposure; and diversify, diversify, diversify.'

## NOTES

\* The research assistance of Hristo Stefanov and Alisa Marnell is gratefully acknowledged.
1. Systematic risk was defined by Kaufman (1996) as 'the probability that cumulative loss will occur from an event that ignites a series of successive losses along a chain of institutions or markets comprising a system'.
2. See, among others, Connolly and Taylor (1984), Edwards (1989), Dornbusch et al. (1995), and Sachs et al. (1996).
3. This assumption is not restrictive because we can always transform the factors to make them orthogonalized.
4. The Hadamard product of two matrices is defined as follows. Let $A = \{a_{ij}\}$ and $B = \{b_{ij}\}$ be matrices of the same size. Then the Hadamard product $A*B$ is defined by $A*B = \{a_{ij} \cdot b_{ij}\}$.

## REFERENCES

Aliber, R.Z. (1980): 'A conceptual approach to the analysis of external debt of the developing countries', World Bank Staff Paper No. 421, Washington, DC.

Avramovic, D. (1964): *Economic Growth and External Debt*, Baltimore, MD: Johns Hopkins University Press.

Balkan, E.M. (1995): *International Bank Lending and Country Risk*, Commack, NY: Nova Science.

Bordo, M.D., B. Mizrech and A.T. Schwartz (1995): 'Real versus pseudo international systemic risk: some lessons from history', National Bureau of Economic Research, Working Paper, 5371.4005236198, Cambridge.

Cantor, R. and F. Packer (1994): 'The credit rating industry', *Federal Reserve Bank of New York Quarterly Review*, **19**(2), Summer–Fall.

Cantor, R. and F. Packer (1995): 'Sovereign credit ratings', *Current Issues in Economics and Finance*, Federal Reserve Bank of New York, **1**(3), 1–6.

Connolly, M. and D. Taylor (1984): 'The exact timing of the collapse of an exchange rate regime and its impact on the relative price of traded goods', *Journal of Money, Credit, and Banking*, **16**, 194–207.

Dornbusch, R., I. Goldfajn and R. Valdes (1995): 'Currency crises and collapses', *Brookings Papers on Economic Activity*, **1**, 219–70.
Edwards, S. (1989): *Real Exchange Rates, Devaluation and Adjustment: Exchange Rate Policy in Developing Countries*, Cambridge, MA: MIT.
Esquivel, G. and F. Larrain (1998): 'Explaining currency crisis', Working Paper, Harvard University.
*Euromoney*: Various issues, especially 1998.
Feder, G. and R.E. Just (1980): 'A study of debt servicing capacity of developing countries', *Journal of Development Studies*, **16**, 25–38.
Frank, C.R. Jr. and W.R. Cline (1971): 'Measurement of debt serving capacity: an application of discriminant analysis', *Journal of International Economics*, **1**, 327–44.
Gerlach, S. and F. Smets (1995): 'Contagious speculative attacks', *European Journal of Political Economy*, **11**, 45–63.
Haegele, M.J. (1981): 'Using market determined spread as a guide', in R. Ensor (ed.), *Assessing Country Risk*, London: Euromoney Publications, pp. 75–9.
Jorion, P. (1988): 'On jump processes in the foreign exchange and stock markets', *Review of Financial Studies*, **1**, 427–45.
Kaminsky, G.L., S. Lizondo and C.M. Reinhart (1997): 'Leading indicators of currency crises', *IMF Staff Papers*, **45**, 1–48.
Kaufman, G. (1996): 'Bank failures, systemic risk, and bank regulation', Working Paper, 96-1, Federal Reserve Bank of Chicago.
Khoury, S.J. (2001): 'A more vigorous and realistic simulation', with S. Gould and S. Maftilan, in Laurent L. Jacques and Paul M. Vaaler (eds), *Financial Innovation and the Welfare of Nations*, New York: Kluwer Academic Press.
Krugman, P. (1979): 'A model of balance of payments crises', *Journal of Money, Credit, and Banking*, **11**, 311–25.
Mason, P.R. (1998): 'Contagion effect: monsoonal effects, spillovers, and jumps between multiple equilibria', Working Paper, International Monetary Fund.
Sachs, J.D. (1984): *Theoretical Issues in International Borrowing*, Princeton, NJ: International Finance Section Section, Department of Economics, Princeton University.
Sachs, J.D., A. Tornell and A. Velasco (1996): 'Financial crisis in emerging markets: the lessons from 1995', *Brookings Papers on Economic Activity*, **2**.
Sofia, A.Z. (1981): 'Rationalizing country risk ratios', in R. Ensor (ed.), *Assessing Country Risk*, London: Euromoney Publications, pp. 49–68.
Solberg, R.L. (1988): *Sovereign Rescheduling: Risk and Portfolio Management*, London: Unwin Hyman.
Solnik, B.H. (1974): 'An equilibrium model of international capital markets', *Journal of Economic Theory*, **8**, 500–524.
Thompson, J.K. (1981): 'An index of economic risk', in R. Ensor (ed.), *Assessing Country Risk*, London: Euromoney Publications, pp. 69–71.
Ul Haque, N., M.S. Kumar, N. Mark and D.J. Mathieson (1996): 'The economic content of indicators of developing country creditworthiness', *IMF Staff Papers*, **43**, 688–724.
Walter, I. (1981): 'Country risk, portfolio decisions and regulation in international bank lending', *Journal of Banking and Finance*, **85**, 77–92.
Wynn, R.F.K. (1995): 'Tabular comparisons of specifications, samples, estimates and forecast results relating to the statistical analysis of sovereign risk', Discussion Papers in Economics, No. 68, University of Liverpool.

Wynn, R.F.K. (1997): 'The statistical analysis of sovereign ratings: results from new evidence, indicators, and forecast evaluations', Research Papers in Economics, Finance, and Accounting, No. 97121, University of Liverpool.

Wynn, R.F.K., E. Nowell and S.C. Blackman (1999): *The Current State of Economic Science, Vol. 1: Evaluating Statistical Sovereign Ratings: Results for Turning Points and Individual Developing Countries*, Delhi: Spellbound Publications.

Zhou, C. (1998a): 'The term structure of credit spreads with jump risk', mimeo, University of California, Riverside.

Zhou, C. (1998b): 'Currency risk, borrowing constraint, and international portfolio diversification', mimeo, University of California, Riverside.

Zhou, C. (1999): 'Path-dependent option valuation when the underlying path is discontinuous', *Journal of Financial Engineering*, **8**, 73–98.

# 14. The causes of bank failures
## Shelagh Heffernan*

## 1 INTRODUCTION

This chapter considers the causes and effects of bank failures. Normally failure of a profit-maximizing firm is defined as insolvency, that is, the company's assets exceed its liabilities, making its net worth negative. In the case of banks, for reasons which will become apparent, the definition is expanded to include not only insolvent banks which are closed, but banks which would have failed but for government intervention, and banks that are merged with healthy banks under central bank/government pressure and/or with state assistance.

Section 2 discusses the policy controversies surrounding bank failures. There is a spectrum of academic thought ranging from the view that they should be treated the same as the failure of a firm in any industry, to the other extreme that bank failure(s) or the possibility of failure require government protection of the banking system in the form of a 100 per cent safety net, because of the potential for devastating systemic effects on an economy. In between is support for varying degrees of intervention, including deposit insurance, a policy of ambiguity as to which bank should be rescued, merging failing and healthy banks and so on.

The debate among academics is reflected in the different government policies around the world. Governments in Japan (after a brief reversal of policy in the mid-1990s) and France believe that virtually every problem bank should be bailed out, or merged with a healthy bank. In Britain, there is a policy of ambiguity but most observers agree that the top four commercial banks[1] and all but the smallest banks would be bailed out. The United States has, in the past, tended to confine rescues to the largest commercial banks. However, since 1991, legislation[2] has required the authorities to adopt a 'least-cost' approach (from the standpoint of the taxpayer) to resolve bank failures, which may, in the future, mean that most troubled banks will be closed, unless a healthy bank is willing to engage in a takeover, including the bad loan portfolio or other problems that got the bank into trouble in the first place.

The question of what causes failure will always be of interest to investors, unprotected depositors, and the bank employees who lose their jobs. However, if the state intervention school of thought prevails, then identifying the determinants of bank failure is of added importance because public funds are being used to single out banks for special regulation, to bail out/merge banks, and to protect depositors. For example, the rescue of failing American thrifts in the 1980s is estimated to have cost the US taxpayer anywhere up to $300 billion. In Japan, the authorities avoided intervention in the early years of the banking problems because of a hostile, taxpaying public. However, the recent extension of deposit insurance to cover all deposits to an unlimited amount (1998), together with the provision of public funds to bail out banks, puts the total cost of the bail-out at 60 trillion yen ($540 billion), which could rise by another 10 trillion yen.[3]

Section 3 considers methods by which the factors contributing to bank failure can be identified. It begins with a qualitative survey of the causes of bank failure. After a review of related empirical studies, this section employs multinomial and conditional (for panel data) logit models to identify the significant variables contributing to bank failure, from an international sample of failed and healthy banks. The quantitative results are compared to the qualitative contributors, identified by looking at the backgrounds of a wide range of failed banks from around the world. Section 4 conducts econometric tests on the factors causing bank failure, and Section 5 concludes.

## 2 BANK FAILURE: THE CONTROVERSIES

Most academics, politicians (representing the taxpayer), depositors and investors accept the idea that the banking sector is different. Banks play such a critical role in the economy that they need to be singled out for more intense regulation than other sectors. The presence of asymmetric information is at the heart of the problem. Bankers, their customers, regulators and investors have different information sets on the health of a bank. Small depositors are the least likely to have information and, for this reason, they are usually covered by a deposit insurance scheme, creating a moral hazard problem (see below for more detail). Regulators have another information set, based on their examinations, and investors will rely on the results of external audits.

Managers of a bank have more information about its financial health than depositors, regulators, shareholders or auditors. The well-known *principal–agent* problem arises because of the information wedge between managers and shareholders. Once shareholders delegate the running of a firm to managers, they need to monitor them to ensure managers take decisions to maximize shareholder value added rather than, say, maximizing short-term sales revenue to boost their personal power and remuneration. However, agency problems are not unique to the banking sector.

The difference in the banking sector, it is argued, is that asymmetric information, agency problems and moral hazard, taken together, can be responsible for the collapse of the financial system, a *negative externality*. To see how a bank run might commence, recall a core banking function, intermediation. Put simply, banks pay interest on deposits and loan out the money to borrowers, charging a higher rate of interest to include administration costs, a risk premium and a profit margin for the bank. All banks have a liquidity ratio, the ratio of liquid assets to total assets, meaning that only a fraction of deposits are available to be paid out to customers at any point in time. However, there is a gap between the optimal liquidity for safety and the ratio a profit-maximizing bank will choose.[4]

Governments may also impose a reserve ratio, requiring banks to place a fraction of non-interest-earning deposits at the central bank. It is treated as a tax on banking activity. The effective tax the bank pays is obtained by multiplying the interest forgone by the volume of funds held as reserves. Since the nominal rate of interest incorporates inflation expectations, the reserve ratio is often loosely thought of as a source of inflation tax revenue. Over the past 20 years, many Western governments have reduced or eliminated this reserve ratio. For example, in the United Kingdom, the reserve ratio has been reduced from 8 per cent in the 1971 to just 0.4 per cent in 2002. In developing and emerging markets, the reserve ratio imposed on banks can be as high as 20 per cent, because it is a means of earning revenue in poorer countries.

The reserve ratio can also be used as a tool in monetary policy: raising a reserve ratio will take money out of the economy, so reducing the money supply. It was a common tool of monetary policy in most countries until the late 1970s, and then largely abandoned. However, in certain key countries, such as Japan, the central bank authorities continue to use it as an integral part of their monetary policy.

Returning to the liquidity ratio, given that banks, even healthy ones, only have a fraction of their deposits available at any one time, an unexpected sudden surge in the withdrawal of deposits will mean that they soon run out of money in the branches. Asymmetric information means rumours (ill-founded or not) of financial difficulties at a bank will result in uninsured depositors withdrawing their deposits, and investors selling their stock. *Contagion* arises when healthy banks become the target of runs, because depositors and investors, in the absence of information to distinguish between healthy and weak banks, rush to liquidity.

In the absence of intervention by the central bank to provide the liquidity necessary to meet the depositors' demands, a bank's liquidity problem (unable to meet its liabilities as they fall due) can turn into one of insolvency, or negative net worth. Normally if the central bank and/or other regulators believe that but for the liquidity problem, the bank is sound, it will intervene, providing the necessary liquidity (at a penalty rate) to keep the bank afloat. Once depositors are satisfied they can get their money, the panic subsides and the bank run is stopped. However, if the regulators decide that the bank is insolvent and should not be rescued, the run on deposits continues, and it is forced to close it doors.

If the authorities do intervene but fail to convince depositors that the problem is confined to the one bank, contagion results in systemic problems, affecting most or all banks, and the sector is in danger of collapsing. In the extreme, the corresponding loss of intermediation and the payments system could reduce the country to a barter economy. A 'bank holiday' may be declared in an effort to stop the run on banks, using the time to meet with the stricken banks and decide how to stem the withdrawals, usually by an agreement to supply unlimited liquidity to solvent banks when their doors open after the holiday.

If the bank holiday agreement fails to assure depositors, or no agreement is reached, the outcome is a classic negative externality because what began as a run on one bank (or a few small banks) has resulted in the collapse of the country's financial system. The economic well-being of all the agents in an economy has been adversely affected by the actions of less than perfectly informed depositors and investors, who, with or without good reason, decided that their bank was in trouble and sought to get their money out. The negative externality is a type of market failure, as is the presence of asymmetric information. Market failure is a classic argument for a sector to be singled out for government intervention and regulation.

Another argument for intervention arises because of the utility-maximizing behaviour of individuals. Senior management are normally the first to recognize that their bank is, or will be, in serious trouble. They have the option of taking no action, letting it fail, and losing their jobs. However, if they are the only ones with information on the true state of the bank, downside risk is truncated. Returns are therefore convexified, encouraging gambling to increase their survival probability and resurrect the bank. Thus, they will undertake highly risky investments, even with negative expected returns. Likewise, 'looting' (see below for more detail) may be seen as a way of saving the bank, and if not, to provide a comfortable payoff for the unemployed managers. Given the presence of contagion in the sector, such behaviour should be guarded against through effective monitoring.

Lack of competition will arise in a highly concentrated banking sector and can also be a source of market failure. However, anti-competitive behaviour can arise in other sectors, and is referred to a government body with the power to act, should the behaviour of firms or firms be deemed uncompetitive.

To summarize, the banking system needs to be more closely regulated than other markets in the economy because of the presence of market failures, as evidenced by asymmetric information, and the negative externality caused by the systemic collapse of the financial system. The special regulation can take a number of forms, including deposit insurance (funded by bank premiums being set aside in an insurance fund), the licensing and regular examination of banks, intervention by the authorities at an early stage of a problem bank, and lifeboat rescues.

In fact, the complete collapse of a country's banking or financial system is rare. The best example is that of the United States, where the collapse of the banking sector in 1930–33 threatened the entire financial system, and was a contributory factor to the deep depression. Going further back in history, we can identify a British financial crisis in 1866. Proponents of special regulation of banks, and timely intervention if a bank or banks encounter difficulties, would argue that it is the presence of strict regulation of the banking sector which has headed off any serious threats to financial systems of the developed economies. Additionally, there have been many bank failures and crises in emerging markets, most recently in some Asian countries. Contagion spread from problems in Thailand and Indonesia to the economies of a number of countries in the region.

Unfortunately, there is a downside to the regulation of banks. The key problem is one of *moral hazard*. A term borrowed from the insurance literature, it means that incentives of the insured party may be altered once the insurance contract is entered into. The classic example is that of a comprehensive house contents insurance policy. The insured individual may be less concerned about security than in the absence of a contract. The insurer will attempt to counter the problem by introducing conditions attached to the insurance. For example, an unsecured house (doors unlocked, windows open) may cancel the contract if the house is burgled. No-claims bonuses also help to reduce moral hazard.

In banking, moral hazard arises in the presence of deposit insurance and/or because a central bank is willing to intervene should a bank encounter difficulties. If a deposit is backed by insurance, then the depositor is unlikely to withdraw the deposit if there is some question raised about the health of the bank. Hence, bank runs are less likely, effectively putting an end to the possibility of systemic failure of the banking system. The deposit insurance has to cover 100 per cent of deposits to guarantee the absence of any systemic risk. However, deposit insurance is costly, and normally, governments limit its coverage to the retail depositor, on the grounds that this group lacks the resources to be fully informed about the health of a bank. For example, in the United States, the amount of deposit insurance is considered generous, at $100,000, and through the practice of deposit brokerage[5] it is effectively much higher.

The problem with restricted deposit insurance is it that it does not eliminate the possibility of bank runs because wholesale depositors and others (for example, non-residents, or those holding funds in foreign currencies) can initiate a run. For example, in 1998, the Japanese authorities had to extend the insurance to cover all deposits after the collapse of insurance firms led to a run on products such as pension funds. In 1984, Continental Illinois Bank suffered a withdrawal of funding by uninsured wholesale depositors.

On the other hand, the more extensive the deposit insurance coverage, the more pronounced the problem because depositors have little incentive to monitor the banks, making it easier for senior management to undertake risks greater than they might have in the absence of closer scrutiny by their customers. This argument applies in particular to bank managers who know their bank is in trouble, and undertake highly risky investments in an attempt to rescue themselves from the problem.

A counter-argument made by proponents of deposit insurance is that even in its presence, the incentives of senior management are not altered to such a degree that they undertake riskier investments. Management is still answerable to shareholders, who do have an incentive to monitor their investments, which are unprotected in the event of failure. Also, if the bank does fail, it is the managers and employees who lose their livelihoods.

A final argument relates to the fund itself. Normally it is the banks that pay the insurance premia to fund the deposit insurance. In most countries, all banks pay the same premium but in the United States, regulators rank banks according to their risk profile, which is kept confidential. The riskier the bank, the higher the premium paid. Being answerable to shareholders, linking the deposit insurance premium to banks' risk profiles, and loss of employment will help to reduce the consequences of moral hazard on the part of bank management.

While most economists accept the need for some special regulation of the banking sector, a minority advocate a return to *free banking*. The interpretation of this term varies widely, but essentially, it means banks are left to regulate themselves to some degree. A model of nineteenth-century free banking was the Scottish system. Between 1716 and 1844, banks were allowed to operate with virtually no government regulation. Cameron (1972) argues that in the absence of regulation, the banking sector promoted economic growth because intense competition forced banks to innovate; they were the first to introduce overdrafts, interest-earning deposit accounts and overdraft facilities.

Modern-day free bankers argue that government regulation or the presence of a central bank is undesirable because of the possibility of collusion among the regulators and regulated. While recognizing the desirability of protecting the small depositor, avoidance of collusive behaviour by banks has been one of the principal objectives of much of the banking legislation passed in the United States, beginning with the National Bank Act (1863; amended in 1864) and the 1913 Federal Reserve Act. Even so, as will be seen in the next section, 'regulatory forbearance'[6] has been a costly problem associated with the large number of thrift and bank failures in the 1980s in the United States, the ongoing Japanese banking problems, and in the United Kingdom.

According to proponents of free banking, it is in the collective interest of the banks to prevent bank runs, so they will establish a private deposit insurance scheme. The sector could also form a private clearing house which would intervene in much the same way as a state central bank does, to prevent a run on one bank turning into a systemic problem. However, a fund and/or a clearing house is not going to eliminate the market failures arising from the presence of asymmetric information and the negative externality associated with systemic collapse. Individual bank managers will still have an incentive to free ride on the system, hiding problems from the rest of the banking community, and if the bank is in serious trouble, going for broke by investing in highly risky assets.

There is no reason to expect a private clearing house to be able to prevent bank runs on healthy banks any better than a central bank. In fact, the clearing house's fund would have a finite amount for rescuing illiquid banks, whereas the government which controls the money supply has, in theory, an infinite amount.

Prudential regulation in New Zealand was similar to systems found in most industrialized economies until January 1996, when the government radically altered its regulation of the banking sector, moving to a limited form of free banking in January 1996. The key idea is a 'partnership between supervision and market disciplines' (Don Brash, Governor, Reserve Bank of New Zealand). The main regulatory reforms are:

1. Each bank is required to produce a quarterly 'Key Information Summary', with a summary of the bank's credit rating, capital ratios (using the Basle definitions), and information on exposure, concentration, asset quality, profitability, and, if applicable, shareholder guarantees. All branches must display the summary prominently. Thus, the public has easy access to this information, and can make informed decisions on where to keep their deposits.
2. A more extensive disclosure document is produced for professional

analysts and the media, including comprehensive financial statements, detailed information on capital adequacy, exposure concentration, loans to controlling shareholders, asset quality and exposure to market risk.
3. Disclosure statements are subject to external audit twice a year.
4. Bank directors (or appointed agents) are required to confirm that the bank is meeting the licence conditions set by the Reserve Bank and has adequate risk management systems which are being used properly. They must disclose a bank's exposure to controlling shareholders if it is contrary to the interests of the bank.
5. Should a disclosure statement prove to be false or misleading, bank directors face personal liability for creditors' losses, and up to three years in jail.

At the same time, the Reserve Bank removed regulations on lending exposures to individual customers or groups of closely related borrowers, open foreign exchange positions, and its audit requirements in relation to a bank's risk control systems. However, *supervision* of the banking system remains the responsibility of the Reserve Bank. It licenses any firm wishing to call itself a bank, imposing a capital requirement of NZ$15 million for bank registration. Banks incorporated in New Zealand are subject to limits on lending to major shareholders and must conform to the Basle risk assets ratio requirements. Although the Reserve Bank continues to monitor banks on a quarterly basis, the information comes from the disclosure statements, not private information passed from bank to supervisor. The Bank also consults with senior management, typically on an annual basis. There is no deposit insurance scheme.

The disclosure system was introduced to provide the public with information about the health of a bank. Placing a burden of responsibility on directors of banks to produce accurate information is a strong incentive for banks to employ adequate risk-management systems. The absence of private information flows between banks and the regulator reduces the likelihood of a problem with regulatory forbearance. Although the Reserve Bank acts as lender of last resort, it has made it clear that problem banks, no matter what their size, will not be bailed out.

The banking system in New Zealand consists of subsidiaries of foreign banks. At the time of writing in 2000, one small retail bank, the Taranaki Savings Bank, is domestically owned, and it is a (largely) mortgage bank operating in one region, though it does offer a banking service to small-business clients. With a recent takeover (see below), there are six (foreign-owned) bank subsidiaries offering universal banking services.

The extensive foreign ownership of banks has given rise to accusations that New Zealand is 'free riding' on the costly prudential regulatory systems of the home countries of its key banks – it effectively imports its regulation at a considerable saving to the government of New Zealand. The supervision of insolvent foreign subsidiaries is the joint responsibility of the host and home countries under the revised Basle Concordat (1983). Were it not for their unique situation, assigning sole responsibility for disclosure to the banks might have encouraged increased risk taking and looting by managers. In refusing to bail out any bank, the government knows that the parent bank is likely to inject capital if it wants to maintain a presence in New Zealand. On the other hand, the changes are consistent with other radical reforms of New Zealand's economy which began in the early 1980s.

This section reviewed the controversies related to bank failures. Proponents of government intervention are by far the majority, though bankers and regulators alike are watching the New Zealand reforms with interest. Those who support special regulation of the banking sector expect governments/regulators to use the determinants of bank failure to achieve an optimum where the marginal benefit of regulation/rescue is equal to its marginal cost. More recently, some researchers have gone further and argued that the benefits should exceed any costs. Free bankers also have an interest in what causes a bank to fail, if only because investors and depositors lose out when a bank goes under. Either way, it is an important question, and the next section attempts to answer it.

## 3  THE DETERMINANTS OF BANK FAILURE

The causes of bank failure can be examined using either qualitative or quantitative approaches. In this section both are employed, with a view to providing the reader with a comprehensive review of the determinants of bank failure. The section begins by reporting the results of qualitative studies of bank failure. Based on 'case studies', it is possible to identify common causes of bank failure. Having reviewed the qualitative results, the findings of econometric models used to identify the determinants of bank failure are reported. In a final exercise, the quantitative and qualitative findings are discussed and compared.

**Bank Failure: A Qualitative Review**

This author has reported the details of individual bank failure cases from around the world elsewhere (Heffernan, 1996). Based on those cases, together with some failures which have occurred since, it is possible to identify the major features of failure. The list of causes, as it appears below, is for ease of exposition – it is rare for a bank failure to be due to one single factor. Usually, there are a number of contributing factors. For example, poor management can be the source of a weak loan portfolio, or sloppy supervision and regulatory forbearance can make conditions ripe for rogue traders and fraud.

**Weak asset management**
Weak asset management consists of a weak loan book, usually because of excessive exposure in one or more sectors, even though regulators set exposure limits. When these are breached, the regulators may not know it or may fail to react. Examples of excessive loan exposures that regulators failed to control effectively are numerous. In Japan, there were many instances from 1990 onward, especially in the property market. As early as 1990, the Ministry of Finance (MoF) instructed all banks and agricultural cooperatives to cease lending to the *jusen*, specialized mortgage lenders. The banks complied and the cooperatives did not, but no punitive action was taken by the MoF, the key regulator at the time.[7] The failure of the MoF to act is attributed to close links between one of the major (and ruling) political parties and the cooperatives.

By December 1995, the seven *jusen* were insolvent in all but name, and the government announced a $6.5 billion bail-out of these firms. The banks and agricultural cooperatives had been the key lenders to the *jusen*; loans to them made up 17 per cent of the top 20 banks' dud loans. The MoF announced that most of the *jusen* lending was to property companies controlled by Japanese Mafia known as the *Yakuza*. A new body was created to buy the bad assets from the *jusen*, the purchases to be funded by new loans from the banks and cooperatives. These assets were to be sold off, but to date, very few have been. The banks (but not the cooperatives) were required to write off all loans made to the *jusen*.

The larger Japanese banks successfully entered the international loan market by using competitive pricing to attract new borrowers. Any bank determined to increase size by expanding its assets is bound to end up with borrowers who would not otherwise have been given loans. It was not long before the banks were highly exposed in Latin American lending. When they had made the loans, in many cases, at or below market rates, Latin American debt became a serious millstone. The MoF discouraged banks from writing off this debt, to limit tax credits and to encourage banks to exercise more discipline.

These Japanese examples are a consequence of a burst financial bubble. Preceding these problems was an investment strategy known as '*zaitech*', prevalent in Japan from 1984 to 1989. Its beginnings were innocent enough.

Many large Japanese corporations realized they had credit ratings as good as or better than the banks from which they borrowed. It was cheaper to raise finance by issuing their own bonds, instead of borrowing from banks.

It soon became apparent to most firms that it was more profitable to follow the *zaitech* strategy by borrowing funds to invest in financial assets instead of manufacturing. At first, these firms relied on borrowed money but, over time, began to issue bonds with a low cash payout, using the money to speculate in risky stocks, options, warrants and the booming real estate sector. Even though *zaitech* was a form of disintermediation, the banks did not discourage it because they were earning fee income by underwriting new issues and guaranteeing the payment of principal and interest on the bonds. In addition, as was noted earlier, many banks had turned their attention to international lending.

By the late 1980s, a bubble economy was present, as illustrated by the high degree of speculation in the financial markets, financed by margin loans and bond issues. Bubbles add to uncertainty because no one is sure when they will burst, and asset management is made more difficult because of increased marginal borrowers on domestic and international markets. The bubble burst in December 1989, when the Nikkei index began to fall, having risen sixfold over more than ten years. Within two years, share prices had declined by an average of 62 per cent, and the property market was near collapse. Government inaction has led to long-term asset price deflation, massive bad debts and a credit squeeze. Between 1992 and 1999 over 60 banks (30 in 1999),[8] consisting largely of credit cooperatives but also City, *sogo* (regional), and *shinkin* (local credit associations) banks, were given assistance by the Deposit Insurance Corporation of Japan, mainly through subsidized mergers, with any distressed loans being purchased by the Cooperative Purchasing Credit Association. In 1998, deposit insurance was extended to *all* deposits[9] to discourage bank runs, which were further undermining an already weakened banking sector.

It is possible to look at almost any Western country and find examples of excessive exposure by banks in one particular market which eventually led to failure. In other cases, such as the collapse of Barings (February 1995), the failure was not caused by the excessive loan exposure, but by uncovered exposure in the derivatives market. Usually, the regulatory authorities knew guidelines (or rules) on exposure were being exceeded but took no action. Internal and external auditors also failed to detect any problem. All of these countries tightly regulate their banking sectors, yet no system has managed to resolve this problem. In some cases, such as the thrifts, some banks in regions of the United States (for example, Texas), the Scandinavian countries (Denmark, Norway, Finland) and Spain, the problem was widespread and resulted in large sums of taxpayers' money being used to protect the banking system from systemic collapse. In other countries, such as France and Canada, the problem has been confined to just a few banks.

Weak asset management often extends to the collateral or security backing the loan, because the value of the collateral is highly correlated with the performance of the borrowing sector. In Japan, both regulators and the banks themselves are reluctant to declare bad loans because the majority are secured by the property sector, and calling in the loans would send a weak market into a price free-fall. In the case of the Continental Illinois Bank, new loans had been secured by leases on underdeveloped properties, where oil and gas reserves and production had not even been proved. Texan state banks provide another example. Key banks, namely First Republic Bank, (1988), First City (1988) and MCorp (1989), all required large amounts of federal support; some were merged with healthy banks. In the late 1980s, 25 per cent of failing banks in the US were based in Texas. Although there were other contributory factors to their problems, a key one was lending to the energy sector in Texas, and accepting Texan real estate as collateral for these loans. The correlation between the two sectors was so high that the collapse of the energy sector was quickly followed by plummeting real estate prices.

**Managerial problems**
Deficiencies in the management of failing banks is a contributing factor in virtually all cases. The Crédit Lyonnais case is a classic example of how poor management can get a bank into serious trouble. Jean Yves Harberer was a typical French meritocrat. He earned an excellent reputation at the Treasury, heading it in his forties. In 1982, after the newly elected socialists had nationalized all the key banks, President François Mitterrand asked Harberer to take charge of Paribas, where he was responsible for one of the worst fiascos in Paribas's history. Removed from office when Paribas was re-privatized in 1986, Harberer was appointed chief executive of Crédit Lyonnais (CL), despite his poor track record. Harberer's principal goal was growth at any cost, to transform the bank into a universal, Pan-European bank.

This rapid growth caused CL to accumulate a large portfolio of weak loans, which could not survive the combination of high interest rates and a marked decline in the French property market. By 1993, Harberer had been dismissed and made the head of Crédit National, but the post was terminated after the CL 1993 results were published later that year.

Although weak management was the key problem, it is difficult to untangle it from government interference in the operations of the bank. The government, through its direct and indirect equity holdings, had a tradition of intervention by bureaucrats in the operational affairs of state-owned firms, commonly known as *dirigisme*. It is consistent with French industrial policy, where a proactive government role in the economy is thought to be better than leaving it to the mercy of free market forces. Crédit Lyonnais did not escape; the best-known example was when Prime Minister Edith Cresson asked CL to invest FF 2.5 billion in Usinor-Sacilor, in exchange for a 10 per cent stake in the ailing state-owned steel company. By late 1992, 28 per cent of CL's capital base was made up of shares in state-owned firms, many of them in financial difficulty.[10] The problem escalated over time because the bank's fate was linked to the deteriorating performance of these firms.

By March 1994, the first of four rescue plans was announced, and the government was committed to privatizing Crédit Lyonnais by 2000.[11] It is difficult to calculate the total cost of the bail-out because of other aspects of the rescue plans, including creating a 'bad bank' which took on CL's bad loans, thereby removing them from the bank's balance sheet.

Although state interference in CL partly explains why the bank got into such difficulties, it is one of the best examples where poor management, based on a strategy of growth at any expense, is the main reason why the bank ended up effectively insolvent.

Barings was brought down by a 'rogue trader', but the underlying problem was bad senior management. For example, head office allowed a trader in Singapore to run the front and back offices simultaneously even though a 1994 internal audit report had recommended that Nick Leeson give up running the back office. His simultaneous control of the two offices allowed him to hide losses in the '5-eight' account. Nor did managers question how huge weekly profits could be made on arbitrage, which is a high-volume, low-margin business. Finally, senior management sanctioned a huge outflow of capital from Barings, London. For example, the bank transferred £569 million (its total capital was £440 million) to Barings Singapore in the first two months of 1995.

Leeson subsequently claimed that his actions were driven by the imminent decision on bonuses. Had he been able to keep up the charade for only a few more days, he would earn a large bonus, along with his office colleagues. The size of the bonus was a function of net earnings, so Leeson had every incentive to hide losses until they were paid. There have been other instances where bonus-driven behaviour was at the expense of the bank in question. For example, there is a tendency to promote individuals associated with innovation or rapid growth in assets. Although this problem also exists in non-financial sectors, it has more serious consequences in the financial sector because of the maturity structure of the assets, both on- and off-balance sheet – what is profitable today may not be so in the future. It suggests that management should seek out more incentive-compatible bonus schemes. For example, group responsibility would be encouraged by group bonus schemes. Salomons introduced bonuses determined by a specified post-tax return on profits. A percentage is withheld should the firm do badly in subsequent years. The result was the loss of some of their top performing traders to other firms which continued with schemes to reward the individual. Even ING, the Dutch concern that bought Barings after its collapse, had to pay out bonuses totalling $100 million to prevent Barings staff from going to rival firms.

Senior bank management are also prone to mimicry, copying untested financial innovations by other banks in an effort to boost profits. Again, the source of the problem is asymmetric information in this sector. One consequence is that whereas in other sectors, managers strive to differentiate their product, bankers seem to rush to copy the actions of other banks, the success of which is attributed to financial innovations.

Continental Illinois, a US bank, would have collapsed in 1984 had it not been for a government rescue. Its problems, too, can be traced back to managerial deficiencies. Managers were unaware that one of the senior officers at Continental had a personal interest in Penn Square – he had arranged a personal loan of half a million dollars. There was no change in the internal credit review process even though there had been repeated criticisms by the Comptroller of the Currency, one of several bank regulators in the United States. Furthermore, Continental's internal audit reports of Penn Square never reached senior management. Finally, management's strategy was growth by assets despite very narrow margins. Continental also relied on the wholesale (interbank) markets for most of its funding, partly explained by an Illinois rule which restricted a bank's branches to one.

**Fraud**

Benston and Kaufman (1986) note that the Comptroller of the Currency cited fraud or law-breaking as the most frequent cause of bank failures in the US between 1865 and 1931, and the Federal Deposit Insurance Corporation (FDIC) reported that about one-quarter of bank failures in the 1931–58 period were due to financial irregularities by bank officers. Benston (1973) noted that 66 per cent of US bank failures from 1959 to 1961 were due to fraud and irregularities, a percentage backed (and indeed higher, at 88 per cent) by Hill (1975) for the 1960–74 period.

Barker and Holdsworth (1994) cited a study published by a US government house committee[12] which found that about 50 per cent of bank failures and 25 per cent of the thrift failures between 1980 and mid-1983 were principally due to fraud. The authors also cite a US Interagency Fraud Working Group finding of fraud in a substantial percentage of failures between 1984 and the first half of 1986.

Outside the United States, there is hard evidence of fraud in the failures of the Bank of Credit and Commerce International, Bankhaus Herstatt, Banco Ambrosiano[13] and Barings. There were suggestions of fraud in relation to the collapse of Johnson Matthey Bankers,[14] but no one was ever prosecuted. However, it is rare to be able to identify fraud as the principal cause of bank failure – even BCCI had a low-quality loan book. In the case of Barings, the Leeson fraud was only possible because of problems with senior management. In Japan, there were Mafia links to property firms which borrowed from banks and cooperatives. Illegal activities have been proved in only a handful of cases, though they are thought to be widespread. Securing a conviction is problematic because of the fine line between fraud and bad management.

The 'looting' hypothesis illustrates this very point. Akerlof and Romer (1993) argue that managers know that their bank is in serious trouble long before the authorities do. This information advantage prompts them to adopt strategies to boost short-term profits, from which they benefit through dividends, cashing in stock options, and so on. They know that these actions have a very small chance of rescuing the bank but a high probability of far greater losses when the firm does go bust. For example, according to Akerlof and Romer, many thrift managers bought risky debt (junk bonds) to profit from short-term high interest payments, when they knew default was likely in the longer term. The authorities had relaxed accounting rules in the early 1980s to encourage wider diversification, which meant that managers could move into little-known product areas. Finally, thrift managers took advantage of customers using brokered deposits (see note 5), by offering very high deposit rates to attract funding, thereby contributing to short-term profitability.

**The role of regulators**

Bank examiners, auditors and other regulators missed important signals and/or were guilty of 'regulatory forbearance'. In many cases of failure, subsequent investigation shows that stated exposure limits were exceeded, with the knowledge of the regulator. Examples include Johnson Matthey Bankers, Banco Ambrosiano, most of the US thrifts, Barings and some of the Japanese banks/financial institutions.

Like all firms, banks pay for external private auditing of their accounts. In every Western country, with the exception of the UK, banks are also subject to audits by regulators. For example, in the United States and Japan, banks are regularly examined by more than one independent regulator. In the UK, where there is no formal examination by the Bank of England/Financial Services Authority, the role of the private auditor assumes greater importance. However, Johnson Matthey Bankers, BCCI and Barings had been examined by private external auditors. Some firms are being sued by these banks' liquidators for signing off a bank in good health when in fact it wasn't. The official report[15] into the collapse of Barings criticized Coopers and Lybrand, London, for failing to detect the discrepancy between the large outflow of funds to Singapore and the claim that the Singapore office was responsible for three-quarters of the bank's profits. Coopers London has refused to accept any blame because the bank collapsed before they could conduct its 1994 audit, and it had questioned the documentation for a £50 million receivable. However, Coopers Singapore had audited the subsidiary in 1994 but did not raise any concerns.

These failures indicate communication difficulties between the auditor and the Bank of England. Despite official reports calling for a resolution of the problem (after Johnson Matthey, BCCI and Barings), no explicit solution has been tabled. However, it is worth emphasizing that other countries with multiple regulators conducting regular examinations either ignore or miss important signals of trouble.

Part of the failure to report irregularities may be due to the problem of regulatory forbearance, when regulatory bodies put their interests and those of the regulated firms ahead of the taxpayer. The best example is in relation to the thrifts. In 1981–82, the Federal Home Loan Bank Board (since abolished) tried to ease the problems of the thrifts by allowing these firms to report their results using the Regulatory Accounting Rules, which were more lenient than the Generally Accepted Accounting Rules. They also lowered net worth requirements for thrifts in 1980 and again in 1982. The Federal Savings and Loans Insurance Corporation (FSLIC – also since abolished) issued income capital certificates which the thrifts could use to supplement their net worth because they were treated as equity. Effectively, the FSLIC was using its own credit to purchase equity in insolvent thrifts. Thus, both institutions had a vested interest in keeping thrifts going long after they were insolvent. It was this sort of activity which prompted US legislators to impose a legal requirement on all regulators to adopt a 'least-cost approach'.

There is also evidence of regulatory forbearance in the 1984 Continental Illinois case. The Comptroller of the Currency failed to follow up its own criticism of Continental's internal review process and concentration in wholesale funding. The regulator also denied newspaper reports in May 1984 that Continental faced collapse, even though it was true. However, had it admitted that the bank was in trouble, it may not have given the authorities time to put together a rescue package.

A final problem with regulators is confusion over which ones are in charge. For example, BCCI was a Luxembourg holding company. UK operations were through BCCI SA, a Luxembourg bank subsidiary of the holding company. The Bank of England argued that it was not the lead regulator because BCCI was headquartered in Luxembourg. Under the Basle Concordat (1975, revised 1983), the principal regulator was the Luxembourg Monetary Institute, even though 98 per cent of its activities took place outside its jurisdiction. In 1987, in an attempt to resolve the problem, the Luxembourg Monetary Institute, together with regulators from Britain, Switzerland and Spain, formed an unofficial College of Regulators for BCCI. However, hindsight showed that the College proved unequal to its task, largely because of the massive web of subterfuges and inter-subsidiary transactions, involving many jurisdictions, that concealed the systematic looting of depositors' funds.

**Too big to fail**
The policy of 'too big to fail' applies in all countries, to some degree. In France and Japan, the safety net is close to 100 per cent, rarely letting any but the smallest banks fail. In Britain, and most other countries, the regulators operate a policy of deliberate ambiguity with respect to bank rescues. Lifeboat rescues, whereby regulators pressure healthy banks for capital injections before agreeing to organize and contribute to the bail-out, became the norm. Lifeboats have largely replaced the traditional lender of last resort,[16] which involved the central bank (as regulator or via the regulator) providing a very large proportion (up to 100 per cent) of the capital required to shore up a bank. Even though the central banks try to operate a policy of ambiguity, it is normally clear to analysts which banks will be bailed out. For example, Fitch IBCA, a private rating agency, provides its clients with a 'legal rating' for each bank, indicating the likelihood, on a scale of one to five, of a bank being rescued by the authorities. In the UK, the Bank of England has tried to put together lifeboats even when it is unlikely that the failure would have systemic effects. Examples include Johnson Matthey Bankers and Barings. In the case of Barings, however, the Bank of England failed to assemble a lifeboat. This outcome may indicate an increasing reluctance on the part of healthy banks to accede to requests by the central bank, unless they think their own banks might be threatened by the failure.

Before the introduction of the 'least-cost approach' for dealing with bank failures, US regulators successfully launched a lifeboat rescue of Continental Illinois in 1984, and several large (for example Texan) banks since. The argument in favour of bailing out key banks is to prevent runs and systemic failure of the banking system, but it creates moral hazard problems (managers have an incentive to make the bank big), aggravates looting tendencies, and can contribute to regulatory forbearance, points discussed at length elsewhere. It also means supervisors may concentrate on the health of these banks at the expense of smaller banks. Finally, it effectively gives the large banks a competitive advantage over the smaller ones. For example, when BCCI collapsed, there was a flight to safety (the key high street banks) by local authorities and other investors at the expense of perfectly healthy smaller banks and building societies.

**Lack of experience with relatively new financial products**
This problem is a global one, and typically involves international transactions. Bankhaus Herstatt and Franklin National Bank collapsed[17] in 1974 after huge losses arising from trading in the (relatively new) foreign exchange markets. In Denmark, several banks got into severe difficulty because of inexperience in the securities markets in the 1980s. The US thrifts had little experience with junk bonds or mortgage-backed securities but used them to boost short-term profits. Barings did not seem to understand the difference between arbitrage and gambling, and some of the Japanese banking problems were exacerbated because banks allowed borrowers to engage in *zaitech* financing.

However, in all of these cases, the real problem can be traced back to senior management, who either did not understand the exotic new forms of trading, or failed to monitor less senior employees. Also, in many of these cases, there was an element of fraud.

**'Clustering': bank failures tend to be clustered around a few years**
Looking at failures across a number of countries, there appears to be a clustering effect in relation to bank failures. In the United States, there were serious banking problems in the 1931–39 and 1981–90 periods. In Spain, 48 banks failed between 1978 and 1983, and in Japan, banking problems have persisted through the 1990s. The presence of a herd instinct among depositors and investors would explain a run on several banks over a relatively short period, and more recently, this has been coupled with a flight to quality or to banks thought to be too big to fail. However, it does not explain why banking problems last for up to a decade, suggesting that macroeconomic factors are at work.

An alternative, but related, reason for clustering may be the failure of timely intervention by the government.[18] Japan is the best recent example. Although the stock market collapsed in 1989, there were no immediate injections of liquidity into the economy, prompting a decade-long recession, which, as has been noted earlier in the chapter, included the collapse of substantial numbers of financial firms, threatening the soundness of the financial system. The government succumbed to pressure for an overhaul of the financial system by the second half of the 1990s. The result was the announcement of three 'big bangs' in 1997, with the reforms in place by 2001.[19] The market reforms are based on 'FREE' (emphasizing free market entry, free price movements and the removal of restrictions on financial products), 'FAIR' (introduction of transparent markets and rules, with an investor protection scheme), and 'GLOBAL' (all financial markets to be opened up to global players, with adherence to international legal, accounting, and supervisory standards). The authorities also agreed to 100 per cent deposit insurance cover.[20]

To conclude this section, seven factors have been identified as the contributory factors to bank failure. However, the discussion itself illustrates that most failures are explained by an interaction of the various causes listed above. A more precise answer can be supplied by quantitative models.

**Bank Failure: Quantitative Models**

While a qualitative review of bank failure provides some insight into what causes a bank to fail, these ideas must be subjected to more rigorous testing. Any econometric model of bank failure must incorporate the basic point that insolvency is a discrete outcome at a certain point in time. The outcome is binary: either the bank fails or it does not. The discussion in the previous section shows that banks (or, in Japan, almost the entire banking sector) are often bailed out by the state before they are allowed to fail. For this reason, the standard definition of failure, insolvency (or negative net worth), is still extended to include all unhealthy banks which are bailed out as a result of state intervention, using any of the methods outlined in earlier sections, such as the creation of a 'bad bank' which assumes all the troubled bank's unhealthy assets and becomes the responsibility of the state, and a merger of the remaining parts with a healthy bank.

Some of the methodology employed here is borrowed from the literature on corporate bankruptcy, where a firm is either solvent (with a positive net worth) or not. In situations where the outcome is binary, two econometric methods commonly used are discriminant or logit/probit analysis. Multiple discriminant analysis is based on the assumption that all quantifiable, pertinent data may be placed in two or more statistical populations. Discriminant analysis estimates a function (the 'rule') which can assign an observation to the correct population. Applied to bank failure, a bank is assigned to either an insolvent population (as defined above) or a healthy one. Historical economic data are used to derive the *discriminant function* that will discriminate against banks by placing them in one of two populations. Early work on corporate bankruptcy made use of this method. However, since Martin (1977) demonstrated that discriminant analysis is just a special case of logit analysis, the multinomial logit model is used here.

The logit model has a binary outcome. Either the bank fails, $p=1$, or it does not, $p=0$. The right-hand side of the regression contains the explanatory variables, giving the standard equation:

$$z = \beta_0 + \beta' \mathbf{x} + \varepsilon, \tag{14.1}$$

where:

$p = 1$ if $z > 0$
$p = 0$ if $z \leq 0$
$z = \log[p/(1-p)]$
$\beta_0$: a constant term
$\beta'$: the vector of coefficients on the explanatory variables
$\mathbf{x}$: the vector of explanatory variables
$\varepsilon$: the error term.

It is assumed that var $(\varepsilon) = 1$, and the cumulative distribution of the error term is logistic; were it to follow a normal distribution, the model would be known as probit.

Readers are assumed to be familiar with logit analysis; if not they are referred to any good textbook in introductory econometrics. In a simple application of equation (14.1), should $\mathbf{x}$ consist of just one explanatory variable (for example capital adequacy), the logit model becomes a two-dimensional sigmoid-shaped curve.

However, there are problems with much of the published literature as it stands. The first is that virtually every econometric study of bank failure is based on US data, because it is only in the US that the sample of bank failures is large enough to allow quantitative tests to be conducted. The problem with interpreting the results relates to the structure of the American banking system, which is very unlike banking structures typical of most other Western countries, with the possible exception of Japan.[21]

With reference to the US, the most important difference is the absence of a national banking system, dominated by four or five banks, with branches located across the country. US banking regulations have, historically, focused on discouraging the concentration of banks, and it is only in the late 1990s that severe branching restrictions across (and sometimes within) states have been removed. With such a different banking structure, empirical results based on US data should be treated with caution if applied to other Western countries. An added problem is the difficulty in testing for the effects of macroeconomic variables when only one country is studied.

A final, potential problem relates to the use of the multinomial logit function in estimating bank failure. These studies rely on a cross-section of failed banks either in a given year, or over a number of years. They are using panel data, and for this reason, an alternative model could be a panel data logit specification first described by Chamberlain (1980). The 'conditional' logit model for panel data is:

$$z = \alpha_i + \beta' x + \varepsilon, \qquad (14.2)$$

where:

$\alpha_i$: captures individual group effects, and is separate for each group; $i$ = failed or non-failed
$\beta' x$: as in equation (14.1).

Chamberlain shows that if a multinomial logit regression is used on panel data, and the number of observations per group is small (except in the US, where the number of failed banks was very high in the early 1930s and throughout the 1980s), the result is inconsistent estimates, arising from omitted variable bias. Furthermore, the $\alpha_i$ allow a test for group effects, addressing the question of whether there is something unique to the group of bank failures. In equation (14.2), the $\alpha_i$ are not considered independent of $x$.

None the less, the results of key studies which use a multinomial logit model are reviewed to identify the statistically significant variables causing bank failure.[22]

Espahbodi (1991), Martin (1977) and Thomson (1992) employ US financial ratio data based on a cross-section of bank failures. Their observations are confined to the US, and, with one exception, these studies did not test for macroeconomic influences on bank failure. Thomson used a two-step logit model, and a sample of FDIC-insured failed and healthy banks. He tried to capture the effects of macroeconomic variables using state gross domestic product, state-level personal income, and county-level employment data. He found a number of variables to be statistically significant with the right sign. These were a proxy for net worth or solvency, non-deposit liabilities/(cash + securities), overheads/total assets, net income after taxes/total assets, loans to insiders/total assets, dummies for unit banking state and bank holding companies, the log of total assets, and the log of average deposits per banking office.

Espahbodi's (1991) data consisted of 48 banks[23] that failed in 1983, matched with another 48 healthy banks. The matching was based on the FDIC's membership status, bank size and geographical location. He finds two sources of fund measures (the ratio of loan revenue to total income and interest income on US Treasury securities to total operating income), a use of funds variable (interest paid on deposits/total operating income) and a deposit composition (total time and savings operations/total demand deposits) measure to be significant and right-signed. However, various measures of liquidity, capital adequacy (total loans/total equity capital), efficiency (total operating expenses/total operating income), loan quality (reserve for possible loan losses/total loans) and loan volume were found to be insignificant as explanations for why banks fail.

Martin's (1977) data set consisted of 58 US banks that failed between 1970 and 1976, and different combinations of 25 financial ratios, classified into four groups: asset risk, liquidity, capital adequacy and earnings. In his best regression, using 1974 data, he found measures of profitability (net income/total assets), asset quality (commercial loans/total loans and gross charge-offs/net operating income), and capital adequacy (gross capital to risky assets) to be significant and right-signed.

Avery and Hanweck (1984) report results from one of the largest samples employing a logistic function. They used 100 failed US banks from the 1979–83 period, and for non-failed banks, a 10 per cent random sample of all insured commercial banks, totalling 1,190 banks. They find earnings after taxes on assets, the ratios of capital to assets and loans to assets, and a bank's percentage of industrial and commercial loans to be statistically significant variables in explaining bank failure. The higher the percentage of commercial and industrial loans, the greater the probability of failure. Likewise, Barth et al. (1985) and Benston (1985), employing US data, report various financial ratios as significant variables in explaining bank failure.

Barker and Holdsworth (1994), in an unpublished research paper, conducted an extensive study of 859 failed and 12,364 non-failed institutions for the 1986–91 period using six logit specifications. They divided the possible causes of bank failure into three categories: risk taking, mismanagement and fraud, and external and systemic factors. There was some statistical support for all three categories, but the best explanation of bank failure was risk taking by banks, measured by concentration of loans in specific areas (namely, real estate). Mismanagement and systemic factors (such as local real estate market conditions) contributed to bank failure. The authors attempted to measure the extent to which fraud contributes to bank failure, but their proxies, loans to insiders (significant and positive) and the ratio of non-interest expenses to total assets (significant and negative – 'wrong-signed', according to the authors) are not necessarily indications of fraud. Non-interest expenses could be interpreted as a sign of diversification and, therefore, may have the right sign.

Heffernan (1995) is the first published work to employ an international database and to estimate a conditional logit model and the more standard, multinomial logit model. The fact that several countries are included made it possible to test for macroeconomic variables, in addition to financial ratios and bank-size variables.

This global study of the causes of bank failure was made possible by access to financial ratio data for banks reporting to IBCA, a ratings firm based in New York and London.[24] Since this firm is rating banks from around the world, one of its principal aims is to ensure that the financial ratio data reported to its clients are comparable across banks.

The countries included in the sample were Australia, Finland, France, Norway, Sweden and the United States. All had financial ratio data on healthy and failed banks. Other variables tested were various measures of bank size and a number of macroeconomic indicators.

The potential for multicollinearity problems, arising from lack of independence among the variables, made a stepwise (forward and backward) procedure appropriate. Variables were dropped from or added to the model one at a time based on their contribution to the overall fit of the model, as measured by pseudo or McFadden $R^2$ ($MR^2$).[25]

The period of estimation ran from 1989 to 1992. The sample was pooled across countries and a total of 88 regressions were run, but of these, only 28 were worth reporting, based on the size of the $MR^2$ and the significance of coefficients as measured by $t$-ratios. The number of observations for these 28 regressions ranged from 155 to 205.[26] Even among the 28 equations, the $MR^2$ ranged from 0.23 to 0.784.

The key findings of the 1995 paper are as follows. The financial ratio, net income/total assets, a measure of profitability, was available for most of the banks in the sample. It is correctly signed (that is, as profitability rises, the probability of failure falls) and statistically significant at the 99 or 95 per cent confidence levels in 11 of the 15 regressions which tested this variable. Other measures of profitability, such as net interest revenue/total assets or the ratio of net income to equity, were correctly signed but either insignificant or weakly significant.

The risk-weighted capital assets ratios were, during this period, reported by only a few banks in the sample, and for this reason, could not be tested. However, the ratio of equity to total assets is widely reported. Any measure of capital adequacy should have a negatively signed coefficient. Of the 26 regressions testing this variable, six were wrong-signed but insignificant, and, of the 21 remaining regressions, eight were statistically significant and correctly signed at the 99 or 95 per cent confidence levels. The other financial ratios tested, including measures of liquidity and internal capital generation (retained profit), yielded inconclusive results.

Four measures of bank size were tested, all involving the banks' assets, measured in US dollars. Only one, the log of (bank $i$'s assets in US$/US nominal GDP) had any explanatory power. In the nine regressions tested, four had negatively signed coefficients significant at the 99 or 95 per cent confidence levels. One regression had a positively signed coefficient (significant at 0.95) and the other four (two of which had positive signs; two negative) were insignificant. This would suggest that the larger the bank, the lower the probability of failure, which may be due to 'too-big-to-fail' intervention by the authorities, resulting in closer regulatory scrutiny of these banks compared to smaller ones. Or it may indicate that larger banks have a lower probability of failure because their portfolios are more diversified.

Five macroeconomic variables were tested for significance, including the growth rate of real GDP, the nominal and real effective exchange rates, nominal and real interest rates, a price index and the rate of inflation. The coefficients on all the variables had the expected sign,[27] and except for real GDP growth rate, were significant, at the very minimum, at the 90 per cent level of confidence. The coefficient on the real interest rate variable was positively signed and significant at the 95 per cent level of confidence, but in only one of the nine regressions testing this variable. Of the eight regressions testing the nominal interest rate, two were positively signed but insignificant; the coefficients on the other five were significantly positive at the 95 per cent level of confidence. From these tests, we can conclude that the state of the macro economy can often contribute to bank failures, and the nominal interest rate in particular is an important explanatory variable: as interest rates rise, the probability of bank failure also increases.

The IBCA individual rating for each bank ranges from 5 (A – excellent) to 1 (E – the bank has a serious problem and is likely to require external support). The firm rates a bank based on financial ratios, size, macroeconomic variables (to a lesser extent), and on the knowledge of its field experts. To avoid problems of multicollinearity, the model was run in a separate regression, and the coefficient on the rating variable was significantly negative at the 99 per cent level of confidence, with a very respectable McFadden $R^2$ of 0.56.

Multinomial logit regressions were run on the same pool of banks. However, the overall performance of the model was poor compared to the conditional logit model, with $MR^2$s ranging from 0.16 to 0.32, though the significance of the coefficients on the individual explanatory variables was similar, and the constant term significant at confidence levels of 99 or 95 per cent.

An updated version of the above models was recently tested by this author.[28] The number of countries included in the data set was increased to include Spain, an expanded data set for France, Italy and the United Kingdom, with the period of estimation running from 1982 to 1995. Table 14A.1 in the appendix lists the healthy and failed banks used in the sample. Unlike many studies, there was no pairwise grouping of data (matching a healthy bank with a failed one) because of the possibility of sample bias, given the low frequency of bank failure. The criterion for including banks was based on the availability of financial ratio data from Fitch IBCA.

Rather than conducting logit regressions on every combination of variables as was done in the 1995 paper, the variables found to be significant or near-significant in that study were tested. These included internal capital generation, three measures of profitability, capital adequacy, liquidity and bank size. It was also possible to include a loan-loss measure: the ratio of loan-loss reserves to total loans. The macroeconomic variables include effective exchange rates and interest rates, real and nominal. The definitions for these variables may be found in Table 14.1. The Fitch IBCA rating was also tested in a separate regression.

A total of 21 regressions were run for the different combination of variables, using both multinomial and conditional (for panel data) logit models. With an updated version of the software package, it was possible to employ a more powerful test of model superiority. The Hausman[29] test was devel-

Table 14.1  Definitions of explanatory variables tested

| Variable | Definition |
| --- | --- |
| INT K GEN | Internal capital generation, or an increase in bank equity from retained profit |
| PROFIT1 | Net income/total assets (average) |
| PROFIT2 | Net interest revenue/total assets (average) |
| PROFIT3 | Net income/equity (average) |
| CAP ADEQ | Equity/total assets (average) |
| LIQUIDITY | Liquid assets/(customer + short-term funding) |
| LLOSS | Loan-loss reserves/loans |
| SIZE | Log of US$ assets for bank $i$/US nominal GDP |
| RINT | Average annual real interest rate for country $i$* |
| NINT | Average nominal real interest rate for country $i$ |
| REE | Average annual real effective exchange rate for country $i$: as the real exchange rate rises, the real value of the home currency rises |
| NEE | Nominal effective exchange rate |
| INF | Annual inflation rate for country $i$ |
| IND | Annual consumer price index for country $i$ |
| RGDP | Annual real GDP growth rate for country $i$ |
| RA | IBCA rating for bank $i$ |

*Note:* *Annual average computed from monthly market rate.

*Sources:* Financial ratios (all data are year-end, unless otherwise stated), size variable, and RA: Fitch IBCA; macroeconomic variables: IMF, *International Financial Statistics*, various years.

oped to test for specification error, and can be used to compare a given model with a hypothesized alternative. If there is no misspecification, there exists a consistent and asymptotically efficient estimator, but that estimator is biased and inconsistent if the model is misspecified.

In the conditional panel logit model, recall that the $\alpha_i$ are different for the failed and healthy bank groups. The $\alpha_i$ cannot be identified but are common to banks that fail, for example, rogue traders or bank managers looting a bank before it fails. The Hausman test, applied here, is asking whether the $\alpha$s for the failed and healthy groups are the same or not. They are homogeneous if the same, heterogeneous if substantially different. The Hausman test discriminates between these two hypotheses.

Of the 21 regressions, there was only one where the conditional logit for panel data model could be accepted as superior with a 99 per cent level of confidence, thereby rejecting the hypothesis of homogeneous $\alpha$s in this one case.[30] The results are reported in Table 14.2.

As can be seen from Table 14.2, while the Hausman test confirms the panel logit regression to be superior, all the coefficients are rendered insig-

*Table 14.2  Panel logit model accepted (using the Hausman test) as superior to its multinomial logit counterpart*

| Independent variable | Conditional logit | Multinomial logit |
|---|---|---|
| | Coefficient (*t*-ratio) | Coefficient (*t*-ratio) |
| Constant | n.a. | 2.45 (2.00**) |
| INT K GEN | −0.0222 (−0.679) | 0.0138 (2.21**) |
| PROFIT1 | −4.31 (−1.84*) | −0.960 (**4.26**) |
| CAP ADEQ | −0.876 (0.71) | −0.183 (1.44*) |
| LIQUIDITY | −0.11 (−0.77) | −0.560 (**3.50**) |
| LLOSS | 0.0335 (0.06) | −0.0403 (−0.53) |
| SIZE | 16.2 (1.71*) | −0.351 (1.60*) |
| INF | 0.400 (0.70) | 0.258 (**2.54**) |
| Hausman/MR² | Hausman: 49.33 (7d.f.) | MR²: 0.500 |
| Observations | 335 | 335 |

*Notes:*
p = 1 (bank failure); p = 0 (healthy bank).
Abbreviations: See Table 14.1.
Levels of significance:
**Bold:** significant at (at least) 99% level of confidence.
**significant at 97.5% level of confidence.
*significant at 90% level of confidence, except profit measure, which is significant at 95% level of confidence.
Hausman = 49.33, which, with 7 degrees of freedom, is significant at the 99.95% level of confidence, using the cumulative $\chi$-square distribution.

nificant, with the exception of the profitability and bank size coefficients, which are significant at the 95 per cent level of confidence. The sign on the coefficient for the size variable changes, from negative to positive, suggesting the probability of failure rises with bank size. Also, the significance level for profitability drops, compared to a 99.95 per cent significance level in the multinomial logit model. The internal capital generation (*INT K GEN*), capital adequacy, and loan-loss variables are all wrong-signed.

Only one of the 21 regressions passes the Hausman test with a high level of confidence, and, at the same time, most of the coefficients on the explanatory variables are insignificant, sometimes with the wrong signs, with the exception of profitability variable. The implication to be drawn is that the hypothesis of homogeneity of the αs cannot be rejected, and therefore the conditional panel logit model is not generally superior to the multinomial logit model.

This finding contradicts previous (1995) results but they were obtained with less sophisticated software (which relied upon a comparison of the $MR^2$ because the Hausman test was not available) and a smaller sample size.

The details of the results of the 21 multinomial regressions are reported in the working paper, but a summary of the findings appears in Table 14.3. It is sensible to concentrate on the regressions run using *PROFIT1*, defined as the ratio of net income to total assets, with the other financial ratios (capital adequacy, liquidity, loan losses), bank size and the sequence of macroeconomic variables listed in Table 14.1. The results of the first seven regressions are reported in Table 14.3. In terms of $MR^2$ (with one exception), measuring the overall fit of the model and the significance of *PROFIT1* (as compared to the other two measures of profit employed in the subsequent 14 regressions), it is quite clear that the regressions employing the *PROFIT1* variable were superior.

The coefficient on the ratio of net income to total assets (*PROFIT1*) is very highly significant (at the 99.95 per cent level of confidence), with the expected negative sign. The same is true of the internal capital generation variable (the use of retained profits to increase bank equity) and liquidity. The coefficient on loan losses was negative and nearly significant at the 95 per cent confidence level in the first seven equations. At first this result may appear counterintuitive, but it may be that banks which set aside reserves are explicitly acknowledging loan-loss problems and take appropriate action, thereby avoiding failure.[31] The measure for bank size, the rate of growth of the bank, had a significantly negative coefficient (95 per cent level of confidence) in only two equations, suggesting that as bank size increases, the probability of failure falls.

The inflation and real exchange rate coefficients were, in their respective

Table 14.3  Results of multinomial logit regressions using **PROFIT1**

| Dependent variables | Coefficient | t-ratio | Dependent variables | Coefficient | t-ratio |
|---|---|---|---|---|---|
| (a) | | | (e) | | |
| INT K GEN | −0.138 | **−2.46** | INT K GEN | −0.137 | **−2.34** |
| PROFIT1 | −0.798 | **−3.63** | PROFIT1 | −0.819 | **−3.62** |
| CAP ADEQ | −0.165 | −1.29 | CAP ADEQ | −0.155 | −0.15 |
| LIQUIDITY | −0.493 | **−3.16** | LIQUIDITY | −0.503 | **−3.22** |
| LLOSS | −0.157 | −1.58 | LLOSS | −0.134 | −1.34 |
| SIZE | −0.286 | −1.38 | SIZE | −0.269 | −1.29 |
| NINT | −0.303 | −0.74 | INDEX | −0.876 | −0.40 |
| Constant | 1.260 | **2.85** | Constant | 4.060 | 1.71 |
| MR² | 0.450 | | MR² | 0.439 | |
| (b) | | | (f) | | |
| INT K GEN | −0.140 | 2.18* | INT K GEN | −0.138 | −2.21* |
| PROFIT1 | −0.873 | **−3.91** | PROFIT1 | −0.958 | **−4.26** |
| CAP ADEQ | −0.192 | −1.48 | CAP ADEQ | −0.184 | −1.44 |
| LIQUIDITY | −0.631 | **−3.51** | LIQUIDITY | −0.576 | **−3.48** |
| LLOSS | −0.110 | −1.19 | LLOSS | −0.403 | −0.53 |
| SIZE | −0.293 | −1.41 | SIZE | −0.351 | −1.60 |
| RINT | −0.303 | −1.91* | INF | 0.257 | 2.54* |
| Constant | 1.260 | **3.33** | Constant | 2.440 | 2.00* |
| MR² | 0.491 | | MR² | 0.500 | |
| (c) | | | (g) | | |
| INT K GEN | −0.143 | **−2.62** | INT K GEN | −0.138 | **−2.40** |
| PROFIT1 | −0.786 | **−3.71** | PROFIT1 | −0.958 | **−3.60** |
| CAP ADEQ | −0.144 | −1.14 | CAP ADEQ | −0.184 | −1.26 |
| LIQUIDITY | −0.454 | **−3.92** | LIQUIDITY | −0.518 | **−3.16** |
| LLOSS | −0.149 | −1.54 | LLOSS | −0.139 | −1.44 |
| SIZE | −0.327 | −1.55 | SIZE | −0.258 | −1.21 |
| NEE | −0.531 | 1.31 | RGDP | −0.257 | 0.33 |
| Constant | −2.160 | **−4.24** | Constant | 3.220 | **2.80** |
| MR² | 0.455 | | MR² | 0.440 | |
| (d) | | | | | |
| INT K GEN | −0.142 | **−2.65** | | | |
| PROFIT1 | −0.888 | **−4.19** | | | |
| CAP ADEQ | −0.810 | −0.64 | | | |
| LIQUIDITY | −0.588 | **−3.74** | | | |
| LLOSS | −0.122 | −1.31 | | | |
| SIZE | −0.263 | −1.23 | | | |
| REE | 0.135 | **2.51** | | | |
| Constant | −9.910 | −1.89* | | | |
| MR² | 0.516 | | | | |

*Notes:*
P = 1 (bank failure); p = 0 (healthy bank).
Abbreviations: See Table 14.1.
Number of observations (a) to (g): 335.
**Bold *t*-ratio:** coefficient significant at 99% (2.326) or 99.99% (3.291) levels of confidence;
* *t*-ratio: coefficient significant at 95% (1.645) level of confidence.

equations, highly significant (99 per cent level of confidence), and positive, suggesting that as the rate of inflation increases or real value of the home currency rises, the probability of failure also increased. Surprisingly, the real interest coefficient was significantly negative, suggesting that bank failures rise as the real interest rate falls. The nominal interest and exchange rate coefficients were insignificant, so too was the country's annual growth rate.

These findings contradict some of the 1995 results, where nominal interest rates had a significantly positive coefficient, and the sign on nominal (and real) exchange rates was significant and negative in some regressions. A possible explanation for the unexpected negative sign on real interest rates might be as follows. The central bank is the first to know when some banks are beginning to experience difficulties. They may be prepared to allow a brief period of lower interest rates, and hence lower real rates, to allow the banking sector to regain control over problem loans. Sometimes the troubled banks recover. In other cases, they do not, with the failure occurring more often than not during the period of lower real interest rates. More generally, banks' loan difficulties may begin in a period of high rates, and build up slowly before generating failure at a point in the cycle when the real interest rate has started to fall. The positive sign on the inflation rate is consistent with the idea that higher inflation rates prompt fears of future recession, and a rise in problematic banks.

The coefficient on capital adequacy had the expected negative sign in all 21 equations, but was insignificant in the equations where *PROFIT1* was included. However, when run with *PROFIT2* it is highly significant in all seven regressions; and significant in two of the seven *PROFIT3* equations. *PROFIT2* is the ratio of net interest revenue to total assets; *PROFIT3* is net income to total equity. Although the coefficient on net interest revenue is negatively signed it is insignificant, as is the positively signed *PROFIT3* variable. This suggests that in the absence of a reliable measure of profitability, such as net income, the capital adequacy measure becomes an important variable in explaining bank failure. However, using the ratio of equity to total assets as a measure of capital adequacy may be less accurate than, for example, the Basle risk assets ratio, which weighted total assets, albeit crudely, according to risk. All international banks and European Union credit institutions (1993 Directive) are required to report and adhere to the minimum ratios, 8 per cent for Tier 1 capital and 4 per cent for Tier 2. Unfortunately, there are not enough data on the Basle ratio (which international banks were required to report from January 1993) to allow tests.

The Fitch IBCA ratings variable was also tested in a separate regression and, again, had the expected negative sign, and was highly significant ($t$-

ratio of –5.56). With an MR² of 0.723, it did better than any of the models above, even though the number of observations fell to 270 because not all the banks in the sample had been assigned ratings in all years. The finding suggests users of this service are getting value for money when it comes to identifying troublesome banks which could fail.

**Summary of Qualitative and Quantitative Findings**

In this subsection, the degree to which the qualitative review and quantitative studies of the causes of bank failure are compatible is discussed. The results of quantitative studies show, overwhelmingly, that profitability, defined as the ratio of net income to total assets, is one of the key determinants of bank failure. That is, as profitability rises, the probability of failure declines. Management is responsible for a bank's profit, making this finding consistent with the case study findings that poor management is one factor explaining bank failure, though bad luck or other exogenous influences could also reduce profitability. Recall that in virtually all the cases reviewed, poor asset quality was evident among failed banks, but in the econometric tests, the loan-loss coefficient was negatively signed and insignificant, though it was nearly significant when run with the *PROFIT1* variable. There is no variable to test for collateral, so it is not possible to comment on the anecdotal finding that bank problems seemed to be aggravated by the value of collateral being correlated with asset performance.

Although fraud and/or 'looting' are often cited as important causes of bank failure, there was a proven case of fraud in only one of the banks in the sample used for the econometric study (Barings). As for looting, the negative relationship between profits and the probability of bank failure rejects the idea that the management of failing banks boost profits by undertaking risky activities because they know the bank is likely to fail at some future date. However, it may be that the data used were too aggregated. To conduct a proper test of the looting hypothesis, it would be necessary to divide short- and long-term profits; no such division was made in the quantitative studies.

In the econometric models, it was found that the larger the bank (in terms of assets), the less likely it is to fail. The finding is consistent with the too-big-to-fail hypothesis, which often results in these banks being singled out for close scrutiny by regulators. It could also indicate that large banks engage in greater diversification, which makes them less likely to fail.

Although it was not possible to test the role of bank examiners, auditors and other regulators, the econometric studies do suggest that they need to concentrate on some relatively simple financial variables, especially operating profits and liquidity. There is a weaker case for monitoring capital adequacy (though recall that this variable is not risk weighted) and loan losses. However, since all of these financial variables are monitored by the authorities and private auditors, the important lesson from the case studies is the need to scrutinize banks more closely as these variables start to decline, especially operating profits. Regulators should be using their considerable power (or even regulatory authority vested in them) to influence bank behaviour *ex ante* with respect to the quality of the loan portfolio.

The finding that macroeconomic variables play a statistically significant role in explaining why banks fail is consistent with the qualitative observation that bank failures appear to be clustered around certain years. However, different macroeconomic variables were found and some of the signs changed if these results are compared to those from the 1995 paper. More research is needed, possibly with a larger database. Even though the findings are mixed, regulators and investors should treat the macroeconomic environment as important, and perhaps encourage banks to be more cautious than they might otherwise be during economic upturns.

It is worth commenting on the problems associated with the two studies by Heffernan. First, while there are advantages to using an international data set, the main disadvantage comes in the small sample size, limited by the reporting of different financial ratios by countries. This has meant that only developed economies could be included, and the data set restricted the study to only a few countries. The Basle Committee (and various commissions, reporting in different countries) has been advocating the use of standard accounting procedures since it was formed in 1974 to coordinate the regulation of international banks, but, to date, there has been little progress on this front.

## 4 CONCLUSIONS

This chapter began with a discussion of the controversies on the economic impact of bank failures and reviewed the different schools of thought. The vast majority of economists, civil servants and politicians accept the need for government intervention in the banking sector, and believe that banks should be subject to close scrutiny by regulators. There is a more divided opinion on which banks, if any, should be rescued to prevent systemic failures. There is also debate over the extent and amount of deposit insurance coverage, and whether prudential regulation should be conducted by a body independent of the central bank. A very small group advocate free banking and self-regulation of banks.

One puzzling observation is that despite special and intense regulation of the banking sector compared to any other industrial or financial group in most Western countries, banks do fail. In the United States and Japan, with reputations for stringent supervision of their banking and financial sectors, there have been serious, costly (to the taxpayer) banking problems in, respectively, the 1980s and 1990s.

In this chapter it was argued that whatever the view taken on the consequences of failure, it is useful to explore the causes, if only to provide bank regulators, investors, employees and taxpayers with a means of monitoring banks. Section 3 began with a qualitative case survey to identify factors contributing to bank failure, though it was stressed that the listing was somewhat arbitrary, and in most cases several factors were responsible for failure.

The second subsection concentrated on econometric models of bank failure, where the objective was to identify the statistically significant factors contributing to failure. After a review of key econometric studies of bank failure, the results of the multinomial logit regressions were reported. Employing an international data set, it was possible to test the role of macroeconomic variables as determinants of bank failure. It was found they are influential in causing banks to fail, along with bank size and financial ratios, especially profitability, when defined as the ratio of net income to total assets. If other measures of profitability are employed, capital adequacy coefficients become significant, indicating it is an important ratio to monitor. A more accurate measure of capital adequacy (such as the ratio of capital to risk-weighted assets) may have done better.

It was established that the macroeconomic environment is a significant contributor to bank failure, especially real exchange and inflation rate coefficients, which were positive and significant. The negative sign on the real interest rate may be explained by a lag; although banks suffer from rising rates, the actual failure may not occur until rates have started to decline. More research on the contributory role of macroeconomic variables is needed. Also, it is clear that the rating agency tested here adds value; regulators and auditors should consider private rating agency findings in their bank examinations. However, a study of the performance of a number of these agencies would shed more light on their potential contribution.

It appears that the multinomial logit model is superior to the conditional model for panel data as an estimating procedure, but again, more work is required before any definitive conclusions can be drawn.

# NOTES

\* Thanks go to Ameet Wadhwani, a BSc Banking and International Finance undergraduate in his final year, who helped with the database and regressions. I am also grateful to

Mr Robin Munro-Davies of Fitch IBCA, for supplying the financial ratio data. An anonymous referee made some helpful suggestions, which have been incorporated. All errors are my responsibility.

1. HSBC, Barclays, Lloyds–TSB and the new bank that will emerge from the takeover of National Westminster Bank by the Royal Bank of Scotland, in February 2000. The policy of ambiguity adopted by the Bank of England is not as straightforward as it was because of the creation of the Financial Services Authority (FSA) by the Labour government in June 1997. Official legal status was conferred in June 2000, when Parliament passed the Financial Services and Markets Act. It gives the FSA wide regulatory powers over banks, building societies and other financial institutions. Any lender-of-last-resort intervention would involve the Bank of England.
2. This rule is part of the Federal Deposit Insurance Corporation Improvement Act, 1991.
3. Sources: 'Notes', *The Financial Regulator*, **4**(4), 2000, p. 8 and *The Banker*, January 1999, p. 10.
4. For example, in the United Kingdom, mutually owned building societies maintain quite high liquidity ratios, on the order of about 15–20 per cent, compared to about 10 per cent for profit-orientated banks.
5. In the United States, deposit brokers advise clients to place up to $100,000 in banks or savings and loans firms offering the highest deposit rates around the country, knowing that should any one of the banks fail, the full amount of the deposit is covered by the Federal Deposit Insurance Corporation.
6. The term 'forbearance' was first coined by Kane and Yu (1994), who defined it as 'a policy of leniency or indulgence in enforcing a collectable claim against another party' (see p. 16 for a complete definition).
7. Regulation of financial institutions in Japan has, since 1997, been the responsibility of an 'independent' government body, the Financial Supervision Agency, though the key employees have been transferred from the MoF and the Bank of Japan.
8. Source: Deposit Insurance Corporation of Japan, supplied by the Fuji Research Institute Corporation, London. These figures exclude the large number of securities houses and insurance firms which have also had to be rescued.
9. The change in policy to 100 per cent deposit insurance was a departure from the earlier rule imposed in 1971. Then, deposits of up to 10 million yen were covered.
10. By forcing state-owned banks to invest in these industries, the state continued to play an indirect role in the management of these firms, even if they were privatized.
11. The rescue plans led to a formal complaint of unfair competition by other French and European banks. In response, the European Commission sanctioned the rescue plans, conditional upon Crédit Lyonnais being privatized by 2000.
12. The House Committee on Government Operations.
13. Bankhaus Herstatt collapsed in 1974 due to losses in the foreign exchange market; a decade later the then chairman was convicted of fraud for hiding these losses. Banco Ambrosiano collapsed in 1982 – fraud was cited as the main cause, and its chairman was found hanging from a bridge in London ten days after he disappeared when the Italian authorities announced he was wanted for questioning. BCCI operations were shut down simultaneously in July 1991 by a number of regulatory authorities in different countries, led by the Bank of England. After a large number of fraudulent and illegal dealings came to light, it came to be known as the 'Bank of Criminals and Cocaine International'.
14. Johnson Matthey Bank was rescued by a lifeboat, arranged by the Bank of England. It was argued that the rescue was necessary to protect the parent, Johnson Matthey, gold bullion dealers, and to ensure that London remained a key centre for trading gold.
15. The Board of Banking Supervision Report (Bank of England), July 1995.
16. A lender of last resort is still used to inject liquidity into fragile economies when systemic collapse threatens. For example, on Black Monday (October 1987), when stock markets around the world appeared to be going into free fall, the central banks of most Western countries injected liquidity to prevent the world economy from slipping into depression. Likewise, when the UK withdrew from the Exchange Rate Mechanism (September 1992)

and Barings failed (February 1995), the Bank of England stood ready to inject liquidity should there be a run on shares.
17. What was left of Franklin National Bank was taken over by a consortium of European banks. Bankhaus Herstatt was closed.
18. I am grateful to an anonymous referee for this point.
19. That three 'big bangs' are necessary reflects the high degree of segmentation of Japanese financial markets. The reports were produced by the Financial System Research Council, the Securities and Exchange Council and the Insurance Council, respectively.
20. See Ito et al. (1998) for more detail.
21. The Japanese banking system has some features of the US structure because it was, to a degree, modelled after the US system during occupation following the Second World War. For example, Article 65 (of the 1948 Securities and Exchange Law) was an attempt to separate commercial and investment banking (like the Glass–Steagall Act, one of four parts of the US Banking Act, 1933). On the other hand, although there is a significant degree of functional segmentation in Japan, it does have a national banking system, unlike the US.
22. Studies using discriminant analysis identify certain financial ratios as statistically significant in explaining bank failures. All of these studies employ US data. Altman (1977), looking at thrift failures in the 1966–73 period, found different measures of capital adequacy, asset quality and earnings to be important. Sinkey (1975) uses multiple discriminant analysis to identify the causes of bank failure. Financial ratios are taken from year-end balance sheets between 1969 and 1972, and 110 problem banks in 1972 and 1973 are analysed, each one matched with a control bank.
23. Lack of data reduced the sample size by a small amount, though the exact amount is not reported by the author.
24. The firm is now called Fitch IBCA after a merger in October 1997.
25. The McFadden $R^2$ is a pseudo $R^2$ and is defined as: $1 - (\text{log-likelihood}) \div (\text{restricted (slopes} = 0)\text{log-likelihood})$. See McFadden (1974).
26. The number of observations varied because not all countries report the same financial ratios. For example, for loan-loss provisions, loan-loss reserves/loans is reported by Australia, Finland, France, Norway and Sweden, but not the United States, which reports, among other ratios, reserves/non-performing loans, and net charge-offs/average loans. Likewise, when the IBCA ratings variable, RA, was used, some banks were excluded because of the absence of ratings for some banks in certain years, resulting in 175 observations. More generally, given the use of a stepwise procedure, the number of observations would vary.
27. The signs for the real GDP growth rate, real and nominal effective exchange rates, and inflation were negative; the signs were positive for the nominal and real interest rates, and the price index.
28. Heffernan, 'Bank failure – mark two' (forthcoming as a City University Working Paper).
29. See Hausman (1978), and Maddala (1988).
30. Four regressions were accepted at the 50 per cent level of confidence, eight at the 75 per cent level of confidence, and the rest (eight) were rejected because they would only converge to permit a Hausman test to be run by dropping the macroeconomic variable, either the real or nominal interest rates or the inflation index.
31. When run with *PROFIT 2* and *PROFIT 3*, the coefficient on loan losses was negative but insignificant.

# REFERENCES

Akerlof, G. and P. Romer (1993), 'Looting: the economic underworld of bankruptcy for profit', *Brookings Papers on Economic Activity*, **2**, 1–73.
Altman, E.I. (1977), 'Predicting performance in the savings and loan industry', *Journal of Monetary Economics*, October, 443–66.

Avery, R.B. and G.A. Hanweck (1984), 'A dynamic analysis of bank failures', in *Bank Structure and Competition: Conference Proceedings, Federal Reserve Bank of Chicago*, Chicago: Federal Reserve Bank of Chicago, 380–401.

Barker, D. and D. Holdsworth (1994), 'The causes of bank failure in the 1980s', Federal Reserve Bank of New York, Research Paper No. 9325, New York: Federal Reserve Bank of New York, 1–59.

Barth, J.R., R. van Brumbaugh, D. Sauerhaft and G.H.K. Wang (1985), 'Thrift institution failures: causes and policy issues', in *Bank Structure and Competition: Conference Proceedings, Federal Reserve Bank of Chicago*, Chicago: Federal Reserve Bank of Chicago.

Benston, G.J. (1973), 'Bank Examination', *Bulletin of the Institute of Finance*, New York University Graduate School of Business Administration, May, 89–90.

Benston, G.J. (1985), 'An analysis of the causes of savings and loans failures', Monograph Series in Finance and Economics, New York University.

Benston, G.J. and G.G. Kaufman (1986), 'Risks and failures in banking: overview, history, and evaluation', *FRB Chicago Staff Memoranda*, 1–27.

Cameron, R. (ed.) (1972), *Banking and Economic Development: Some Lessons of History*, New York: Oxford University Press.

Chamberlain, G. (1980), 'Analysis of covariance with qualitative data', *Review of Economic Studies*, **47**, 225–38.

Espahbodi, P. (1991), 'Identification of problem banks and binary choice models', *Journal of Banking and Finance*, **15**, 53–71.

Hausman, J. (1978), 'Specification tests in econometrics', *Econometrica*, **46** (6), 1251–71.

Heffernan, S.A. (1995), 'An econometric model of bank failure', *Economic and Financial Modelling*, Summer, 49–82.

Heffernan, S.A. (1996), *Modern Banking in Theory and Practice*, Chichester: Wiley.

Hill, G.W. (1975), *Why 67 Insured Banks Failed: 1960–1974*, Washington, DC: Federal Deposit Insurance Corporation.

Ito, K., T. Kiso and H. Uchibori (1998), 'The impact of the big bang on the Japanese financial system', Fuji Research Paper No. 9, Tokyo: Fuji Research Institute Corporation.

Kane, E.J. and M.T. Yu (1994), 'How much did capital forbearance add to the tab for the FSLIC mess?', in *The Declining Role of Banking: Conference Proceedings, Federal Reserve Bank of Chicago*, Chicago: Federal Reserve Bank of Chicago.

McFadden, D. (1974), 'The measurement of urban travel demand', *Journal of Public Economics*, **3**, 303–28.

Maddala, G.S. (1988), *Introduction to Econometrics*, New York: Macmillan.

Martin, D. (1977), 'Early warning of bank failure: a logit regression approach', *Journal of Banking and Finance*, **1**, 249–76.

Sinkey, J. (1975), 'A multivariate statistical analysis of the characteristics of problem banks', *Journal of Finance*, **30**, March, 21–36.

Thomson, J.B. (1992), 'Modelling bank regulators' closure option: a two-step logit regression approach', *Journal of Financial Services Research*, **6** (1), May, 5–23.

# APPENDIX 14A

*Table 14A.1  Banks included in the International Pool*

| Country | Healthy banks | Failed banks (year the bank failed) |
|---|---|---|
| Australia | Australia & New Zealand Banking Group (1985–94)<br>National Australia Bank (1985–94)<br>Commonwealth Bank of Australia (1985–94)<br>State Bank of New South Wales (1987–94)<br>Westpac (1985–94) | State Bank of Victoria (1990) |
| Finland | Okobank (1988–89) | Kansallis-Osake Pankki (1992)<br>Skopbank (1991) |
| France | Banque Paribas (1985–93)<br>Crédit Commercial de France (1986–88); (1991)<br>Société Générale (1985–93)<br>Banque Worms (1989–91)<br>Banque Indosuez (1987–93)<br>Banque Nationale de Paris (1986–93)<br>Banque Française du Commerce Extérieur (1985–93)<br>Banco Portugues de Investimento (BPI) (1988–93) | Banque Arabe et Internationale d'Investissement (1989)<br>Union de Banques Arabes et Françaises (UBAF) (1989)<br>Crédit Lyonnais (1994) |
| Italy | Banca Nazionale Del Lavoro (1980–83)<br>Banca Nazionale Dell'Agricoltura (1981–83)<br>Banco Ambrosiano Veneto (1979–83)<br>Banco Di Napoli (1978–83)<br>Credito Italiano (1978–83) | Banco Ambrosiano (1982) |
| Norway | Union Bank of Norway (1988–93) | Christiana Bank OG Kreditkasse (1991)<br>Fokus Bank (1991)<br>Den Norske Bank (1991) |
| Spain | Banco Atlantico (1989–94)<br>Banco Santander (1988–94)<br>Banco Guipuzcoano (1988–94)<br>Banco Herrero (1988–94)<br>Banco Popular Español (1988–94)<br>Banco Urquijo (1988–94) | Banco Español de Credito (Banesto) (1993) |

*Table 14A.1 (continued)*

| Country | Healthy banks | Failed banks (year the bank failed) |
|---|---|---|
| | Banco Zaragozano (1988–91) <br> Banco Bilbao Vizcaya (1988–94) <br> Bankinter (1988–94) <br> Banca March (1989–94) <br> Banco de Valencia (1988–91) | |
| Sweden | Scandinaviska Enskilda Banken (1986–93) <br> Svenska Handelsbanken (1986–93) <br> Swedbank (Sparbanken Sverige) (1988–93) <br> Foreningsbanken (1991–93) | Gota Bank (1991) <br> Nordbanken (1991) |
| United Kingdom | Guinness Mahon Holdings (1992–94) <br> Kleinwort Benson Group (1992–94) <br> Lazard Brothers & Co. (1992–94) <br> Morgan Grenfell Group (1992–94) <br> N.M. Rothschild & Sons (1993–94) <br> Schroders (1992–94) | Barings plc (1995) |

*Note:* For the failed banks, data going back four years were used.

# 15. International banking crises

**Alistair Milne and Geoffrey E. Wood**

## 1 WHAT IS AN INTERNATIONAL BANKING CRISIS?

In many industries, competition has become increasingly global over the past two decades. Banking and financial services are no exception. Rapidly falling costs of transaction due to technological innovation and the removal of capital controls, in the industrial countries in the late 1970s and early 1980s and in many developing countries thereafter, have together led to a huge increase in the volume of short-term international financial flows. Core investment and commercial banking services – syndicated lending or underwriting of bond and equity issues to give just two examples – are now worldwide markets centred on the major international financial centres. Many of the world's largest banks are looking to cross-border market penetration and cross-border acquisition as a means to achieving significant revenue growth in products such as mortgages, credit cards, personal lending and corporate banking services. On top of all this the 'internet revolution' is having an impact on many aspects of banking and promises to accelerate the trend towards internationalization of banking.

This internationalization raises new concerns about financial stability. Might financial problems, perhaps originating in some obscure part of the globe far from the major financial centres, lead to major solvency problems among the world's banks and threaten the functioning of the world's financial markets? The objective of this chapter is to examine whether globalization of banking does indeed bring with it increased risks of an international banking crisis of this kind.

Addressing this issue requires first a clarification of what constitutes a banking crisis and, in particular, of what constitutes an international banking crisis. As we note in Section 2, where we discuss the theory and history of banking crises, it is advisable to restrict the term 'banking crisis' to cases where widespread bank failure threatens the stability of the banking system and the operation of the payments system. Banking crises are thus to be distinguished from other financial problems by their severity and their impact on the functioning of the financial system as a whole. Financial losses, collapse of asset prices, even a series of bank failures, do not necessarily constitute a banking crisis. Only where the integrity of the banking system is threatened do we have a banking crisis and only then is there an obvious case for intervention to protect failing institutions. Banking crises, thus defined, have at least in developed countries been relatively rare occurrences, even in recent years, when the rate of bank failures has risen sharply in comparison to the early post-war decades. By this standard, in recent years among developed countries only Spain in the early 1980s, and Scandinavia and perhaps also Japan in the 1990s, can be said to have experienced a domestic banking crisis. Banking crises have been more widespread in emerging markets, including the well-known problems of Venezuela, Mexico and Thailand.

This strict definition of a banking crisis is appropriate and widely accepted. What then can we mean by an international banking crisis?[1] A natural definition, based on this definition of a banking crisis, is a situation where financial problems are transmitted internationally and trigger banking crises in a number of different countries. We might also classify as an international banking crisis a case where international transmission of financial problems triggers a banking crisis in a single country, although such an occurrence would be primarily of domestic rather than international concern.

On either of these definitions international banking crises have been rarer even than domestic banking crises – indeed it does not seem possible to point to a single example of a genuine international banking crisis ever having taken place. What the record reveals is a number of near, or sometimes not so near, misses – episodes where losses or liquidity problems on international exposures appeared, at least at the time, to threaten domestic banking crises in other countries. These cases include the failure of Credit Anstalt in the 1930s, the Herstatt failure of 1974, the losses on sovereign lending in the early 1980s, and most recently problems in emerging markets in 1997 and 1998.[2] Otherwise even major international financial problems, such as the collapse of Bretton Woods, problems in the European Exchange Rate Mechanism (ERM) in 1992 and 1993, and stock market collapses of 1929 and 1987, did not threaten to trigger banking crises in other countries.

This then is what we mean by an international banking crisis. The way we address our central question – whether or not the risks of an international banking crisis are increased by the internationalization of banking – is historical and comparative. Section 2 examines the theory and history of banking crises. Section 3 then looks at the origins and transmission of banking crises, discusses their international transmission, assesses whether the likelihood of an international banking crisis has increased or reduced in recent years. Finally, Section 4 considers and dismisses the case for an international lender of last resort to cope with international banking crisis, should one emerge. Section 5 summarizes and concludes.

## 2  BANKING CRISES: THEORY AND HISTORY

The theory and history of banking crises developed interconnectedly and almost simultaneously. It seems probable that the reason for this was that the theory developed in the nineteenth century, and was developed largely by those who had been or still were practical bankers, or, most notably in the case of Walter Bagehot, commentators on current financial arrangements and events.

Certainly until this century, only problems in the banking system were seen as financial crises. Crashes of financial or other asset markets were the consequence of prior 'manias', a result of human gullibility and folly, a proper subject of study by the disinterested observer but not requiring any policy action. This attitude is vividly summarized in the title of Charles McKay's (1845) classic, *Extraordinary Popular Delusions and the Madness of Crowds*.

Crises in the banking system, however, were regarded as serious, even dangerous, occurrences. Anna Schwartz (1986, p. 11), in a recent statement of this view, described such events as 'real' crises. 'Such a crisis is fuelled by fear that means of payment will be unavailable at any price, and in a fractional reserve banking system leads to a scramble for high-powered money.' In contrast to these 'real' crises are 'pseudo' crises. These involve 'a decline in asset prices, of equity stock, real estate, commodities, depreciation of the exchange value of the national currency; financial distress of a large non-financial firm, a large municipality, a financial industry, or sovereign debtors' (p. 24). Such loss of wealth causes distress, but is not in itself a financial crisis. A 'pseudo crisis' is simply an unusually large case of mistaken investment, and mistaken investments are inevitable in an uncertain world. A 'real' financial crisis is when the stability of the whole banking system is threatened.

Such 'real' crises have been quite rare, although more prevelant in recent times (Scandinavia, Japan, and in some developing countries such as Venezuela). Certainly, on this definition, episodes frequently described as international crises – such as Latin America in the early 1980s and Russia in 1998 – were not crises outside these countries, and were not always crises in the sense in which Schwartz uses the term inside these countries.[3]

According to Schwartz no such crisis has occurred in Britain since 1866[4] and in the United States since 1933.

Schwartz's definition says nothing of the cause of the crisis. In that regard, as in the definition itself, it follows in the tradition of Thornton (1802) and Bagehot (1873). Their approach aimed at clarifying a problem and then going on to propose a solution. A 'real' crisis in the Schwartz sense is dangerous because it can lead to an unanticipated and undesired collapse in the stock of money, and such an unanticipated squeeze will cause a recession, perhaps a depression. The monetary squeeze is produced both by a fall in the money multiplier (as cash shifts from the banking system to the public) and as bank deposits fall. To prevent this squeeze, Thornton, Bagehot and Schwartz, and other writers in this tradition, suggested the following course of action.

The central bank of whichever country experiences such a shock should lend freely on collateral. It should not restrict lending to the classes of security (usually quite narrow) that it would accept for discount in normal times. Advances should be made without limit, on demand, but at a rate of interest above the pre-crisis rate. These loans should be made to the market – that is, to anyone who brings in acceptable security. In addition (and argued in particular by Bagehot) it should be made clear that the central bank will act in that way should there ever be a crisis: this reduces the likelihood of runs because knowledge that the central bank will supply liquidity makes it seem less urgent to scramble for it.

What can trigger such a 'real' crisis? Palgrave (1894), under the heading 'Crises, commercial and financial', provides first a definition of crises and then a description of the development of several nineteenth-century crises: 'Times of difficulty in commercial matters are, when pressure becomes acute, financial crises.' His description of the events of 1825 is a good example:

> The next serious crisis occurred in 1825, one of the most severe through which the commercial *and banking* [emphasis added] systems of the country had ever passed. At this date speculation ran very high, for the most part in loans and mining adventures, and other investments abroad. The foreign exchanges were so much depressed as to be the cause of a nearly continuous drain on the bullion of the Bank. Many and heavy banking failures, and a state of commercial discredit, preceded and formed the earlier stage of the panic. The tendency to speculation, and the undue extension of credit, was preceded, probably caused, and certainly favoured and promoted, by the low rate of interest which had existed for some time previously; and this low rate of interest was apparently prolonged by the operations of the Bank of England. (Palgrave, 1894, p. 457)

Palgrave gives several examples of such chains of events, and refers to Tooke (1838) and to Levi (1888) as providing many more details.

To summarize so far, the view developed in the nineteenth century, and restated in the twentieth by Schwartz and others, is that crashes in financial markets are not in themselves crises. They can lead to runs on the banking system, and thus produce 'real' crises. One can lead to the other by starting a scramble for liquidity.[5] But to quote Palgrave (1894, p. 457) again, 'Commercial crises may take place without any reference to the circulating medium as has been exemplified in Hamburg and elsewhere.'

Were – and are – such crises random events? The famous Diamond and Dybvig (1983) model of a banking crisis would certainly suggest that they are. That model sees crises as being triggered by an unpredictable random shock – a sunspot theory of crises. There is of course criticism of that famous paper. But rather than simply looking at these, it is helpful to consider whether the classic banking crises they model actually were random. There is a good amount of evidence on this, examining both the seasonal and the cyclical pattern of crises.

Seasonal regularity has been noted both by present-day and by nineteenth-century writers. Miron (1986, pp. 125–40) observes that financial panics in the nineteenth century displayed a seasonal pattern in both Europe and the United States. For US data, a $\chi^2$ test rejects at the 0.001 per cent confidence interval the hypothesis that crises were distributed randomly across the seasons. Examination of Kemmerer's (1910) listing of 29 banking panics between 1873 and 1908 shows 12 to be in the spring (March, April, May) and a further ten in September or December.

Kindleberger's (1978) enumeration of panics in Europe between 1720 and 1914 yields similar results. A $\chi^2$ test rejects the hypothesis of uniform distribution across the year; as in the United States, a marked preponderance fell in the spring or the autumn (Miron, 1986).

The still accepted explanation for this seasonality is that given by Jessons (1866). He observed a seasonal pattern in interest rates associated with the agricultural cycle in asset demands. Reserve/deposit ratios for banks fell in the spring and the autumn when there was a seasonal upturn in the demand for both currency and credit. So it was in spring and autumn that banking systems were at their most vulnerable. The seasonal pattern in interest rates largely vanished when central banks started smoothing the interest rate cycle.[6]

Was there a cyclical as well as a seasonal regularity in the occurrence of crises? Seasonal regularity certainly need not imply cyclical regularity; it is necessary to look afresh at the data. Numerous writers in the nineteenth century noted the regularity with which 'commercial crises' occurred. Palgrave (1894) lists 1753, 1763, 1772–73, 1783, 1793, 1815, 1825, 1836–39, 1897, 1866, 1875 and 1890. 'An examination of recorded years of acute commercial distress suggests periodicity. During the 140 years trade and banking have been carried on in war and peace, with a silver standard, with a gold standard, under a suspension of cash payments, in times of plenty, and in times of want; but the fatal years have come round with a considerable approach to cyclical regularity' (Palgrave, 1894, p. 466). Periodicity was also remarked on by Langton (1858), Jessons (1866), Mills (1868), and Chubb (1872), among others.

Table 15.1 shows the main 'commercial crises' listed by Palgrave (1894), with a brief description of each from a contemporary or near-contemporary source. Of these 'commercial crises', only that of 1847 was not at a business cycle peak according to the Burns and Mitchell (1946) chronology of British business cycles. This appears to suggest a close association with subsequent recessions.

Unfortunately it is not clear how much weight that finding can bear. The reason for this arises from how Burns and Mitchell determined their cyclical chronology. Their method was to inspect a large number of series for different aspects of the economy, and, on the basis of this inspection, reach a judgement on the length of each cycle. This causes a problem because one of the series they examined was for financial panics and they regarded the occurrence of one of these as suggesting the economy was at or around a business cycle peak. Further doubt about the finding is created by comparing the Burns and Mitchell chronology with that which Capie and Mills (1991) developed by estimating a segmented trend model. Capie and Mills's work goes back only to 1870, but between that year and 1907 (their last peak) they differ from Burns and Mitchell in the timing of three (out of five) peaks and one (out of five) troughs.

Turning next to the United States, analysis has been carried out by Gary Gorton (1988). His approach was to consider whether banking crises ('real' crises) are random events, 'perhaps self-confirming equilibria in settings with multiple equilibria', or alternatively, whether they were systematic, linked to 'occurrences of a threshold value of some variable predicting the riskiness of bank deposits' (p. 751). Table 15.2 provides the basic data for the early part of the period in the United States. Crises were usually at business cycle peaks, but were not by any means at every business cycle peak.

Deposit behaviour changed after 1914 (the founding of the Federal Reserve) and again after 1934 (the start of deposit insurance), but despite that, crises remained systematic, linked to the business cycle. 'The recession hypothesis best explains what prior information is used by agents in forming conditional expectations. Banks hold claims on firms and when firms begin to fail, a leading indicator of recession (when banks will fail), depositors reassess the riskiness of deposits' (Gorton, 1988, p. 248).[7]

It might be thought that Gorton's result gives support for the similar

Table 15.1  *'Commercial crises', eighteenth and nineteenth centuries*

| Year(s) | Commercial crises |
|---|---|
| 1792–93 | Followed 'investments in machinery and in land navigation ... Many houses of the most extensive dealings and most established credit failed' (McPherson, 1805) |
| 1796–97 | 'Severe pressure in the money market, extensive failures of banks in the North of England, great mercantile discredit' (Palgrave, 1894, p. 43) |
| 1810–11 | '[T]he fall of prices, the reduction of private paper, and the destruction of credit, were greater and more rapid than were before, or have since, been known to have occurred within a short space of time' (Tooke, 1838, p. 10) |
| 1825 | '[O]ne of the most severe through which the commercial and banking systems of the country had ever passed' (Palgrave, 1894, p. 168). Palgrave quotes Huskinson as saying 'that we were within a few hours of a state of barter'. This crisis followed a steady and very substantial fall in yields. Palgrave gives the price of 3% public funds.<br><br>1823  3rd April       $73\frac{1}{2}$ (the lowest)<br>       1st July         $80\frac{3}{4}$<br>       3rd October      $82\frac{1}{2}$<br>1824  1st January      86<br>       2nd April        $94\frac{1}{2}$<br>       28th April       $97\frac{1}{4}$ (the highest)<br>       November         $96\frac{1}{2}$<br>1825  January          $94\frac{1}{2}$<br>1826  14th February    $73\frac{7}{8}$<br><br>'Though the period of pressure in 1825 was so short, it had been preceded by considerable and extravagant speculations in foreign loans and shares of companies, mining and commercial' (Palgrave, 1894, p. 180) |
| 1847 | '[A] considerable period of speculative activity, fostered by a low rate for money, preceded this crisis also' (Palgrave, 1894, p. 200). Palgrave also notes that Peel's Bank Act came into effect on 2 September 1844, and this 'took away from the directors [of the Bank of England] alike any power or any responsibility for the "regulation of the currency" so far as this consisted of their notes'. Interest rates fell, and there was, as in 1825, considerable speculation, this time in 'railways and other improvements at home' (p. 202) |
| 1857 | '[I]t is very clear that during the years 1855 to 1856 the extension of credit was enormous and dangerous ... [In 1857] the reserve of the Bank of England may be said to be continually at a danger point ...' (Palgrave, 1894, p. 204) |
| 1866 | Failure of Overend, Gurney and Co. |
| 1890 | Baring crisis |

*Table 15.2  National banking era panics*

| National Bureau of Economic Research cycle Peak–Trough | Crisis date |
|---|---|
| Oct 1873–Mar 1879 | Sept 1873 |
| Mar 1882–May 1885 | Jun 1884 |
| Mar 1887–Apr 1888 | No panic |
| Jul 1890–May 1891 | Nov 1890 |
| Jan 1893–Jun 1894 | May 1893 |
| Dec 1895–Jun 1897 | Oct 1896 |
| Jun 1899–Dec 1900 | No panic |
| Sep 1902–Aug 1904 | No panic |
| May 1907–Jun 1908 | Oct 1907 |
| Jan 1910–Jan 1912 | No panic |
| Jan 1913–Dec 1914 | Aug 1914 |

*Source:* Gorton (1988).

Palgrave/Burns and Mitchell view. But caution is necessary, for the structures of the banking systems of the two countries differed (and still differ) greatly. The importance of banking structure is discussed subsequently.

It would appear, therefore, that there is sufficient regularity in crises – regularity in the sense of their being associated with prior causal or at the least facilitating events – as to imply that it is a useful exercise to look for underlying causes and for ways of preventing crises. They are not, in other words, random events – such as meteor strikes or sunspots – over which we have no control.

The above does of course refer to classic liquidity crises. Banking crises in even the comparatively recent past were the consequence of a shortage of liquidity, not a shortage of capital. Even in the Great Depression in the United States, this was true. Now, this certainly represents a marked contrast with some recent events – notably the Japanese banking crisis and that in the Scandinavian economy.

Why shortage of capital emerged as a mid-twentieth-century problem is in large part a consequence of aspects of regulation and governance and is explained in some detail in the following section of this chapter.

## 3  THE ORIGINS AND TRANSMISSION OF BANKING CRISES

In this section we discuss, briefly, the principal forces that have played a role in triggering bank crises, covering the macroeconomic policy background, structural and regulatory features, and international transmission. We then consider to what extent these forces may have changed over recent years, and increased the likelihood of an international banking crisis.

**The Macro Policy Background**

It was observed above that one compelling item of evidence against crises being purely random events is when they occurred both seasonally and over the cycle. Further support for the non-random nature of crises, and also guidance on how to make them less likely, is provided by consideration of the macroeconomic conditions when they are most likely to occur.

Over the past two decades, banks in a number of countries have experienced severe problems. In some cases the institutions would have failed without taxpayer support, and in others whole sectors of the financial system would have failed without a period of low interest rates in which they could restore profits and rebuild capital. Such episodes appear to require a double trigger – macroeconomic instability along with a period of financial deregulation. The effects of these seem to be transmitted through rapid growth in bank credit and asset prices.

There are various explanations for this linkage. One is quite simply that deregulation allows banks and other institutions to enter new areas of business, where they have no experience. Some maintain that problems have been exacerbated by an increase in the variability of asset prices, while others (for example, Hellwig, 1996) suggest that economies have become more volatile. It has also been claimed that deregulation affects stability not simply by promoting bank expansion, but by changing institutional and ownership structures. This affects attitudes to risk, and the consequent changes may well be not only frequently unpredicted but actually unpredictable.

How does the evidence bear on these explanations of why the combination of liberalization and macroeconomic instability may lead to a period of financial instability? Recent unpublished Bank of England work has made cross-country comparisons drawing on the experience of developed countries. Table 15.3 sets out an overview (derived from that study) of financial problems and associated economic conditions. Certain features stand out from this table. Most important, financial liberalization was a necessary although not a sufficient precondition for banking problems. A downturn in the economy, usually accompanied by a severe downturn in asset prices across a range of markets, also seems to be required.

This is consistent with two wide-ranging studies of developing economies and of smaller industrial ones. Lindgren et al. (1996) analysed eight countries which faced systemic banking problems in the 1980s – six

Table 15.3  *Recent banking problems in major economies*

(1) *Systemic*

| Country | Year | Pre-crisis | | | During crisis | |
|---|---|---|---|---|---|---|
| | | Macroeconomic | Type of financial liberalization | Asset price bubble? | Macro-economic downturn | Induced by higher interest rates? |
| Finland | 1991–94 | Boom; loosening in monetary policy | Credit quantities; foreign banks | Equities, residential and commercial property | Yes | Yes |
| Norway | 1987–93 | Boom; loosening in monetary policy | Credit quantities; interest rates | Equities, residential and commercial property | Yes | No – oil price fall |
| Sweden | 1990–93 | Boom; loosening in monetary policy | Credit quantities; interest rates | Equities, residential and commercial property | Yes | Yes |
| Japan | 1992–present | Boom; loosening in monetary policy | Credit quantities; interest rates | Equities, residential and commercial property | Yes | Yes |

(2) *Bank loan losses*

| Country | Year | Pre-losses | | | During losses |
|---|---|---|---|---|---|
| Australia | Early 1990s | Boom; loosening in monetary policy | Credit quantities; interest rates | Equities and commercial property | Yes | Yes |
| United Kingdom | Early 1990s | Boom; loosening in monetary policy | Credit quantities; interest rates | Commercial and residential property | Yes | Partially |
| United States | Early 1990s | | Banking licensing made easier (intense competition) | Commercial property | Yes | |

(3) *No real problems (late 1980s–early 1990s)*

| Country | Lessons from past | | Late 1980s/early 1990s | | During late 1980s/early 1990s |
|---|---|---|---|---|---|
| Canada | Yes, 1985 | Boom | No recent changes; foreign banks faced capital controls | Commercial property | Yes | Partially |
| Netherlands | Yes, late 1970s/early 1980s | Boom; loosening in monetary policy | No recent changes | No | Modest | Yes |
| Germany | | Boom* | No recent changes; limited new entrants | Commercial property | Yes* | Yes* |

*Note:* * Following German unification.

developing ones (Argentina, Chile, Ghana, the Philippines, Uruguay and Venezuela) and two developed ones (Norway and Finland). In every case, an economic downturn accompanied the crisis and liberalization preceded it. Kaminsky et al. (1998) sought to provide leading indicators to warn of an approaching crisis on the basis of a study of previous crises in 25 larger emerging and industrial countries over the years 1970–95. They found the best indicators to be a rise in broad money relative to the monetary base (a proxy for financial liberalization), a rise in real interest rates, and declines in the growth of output and in equity prices.[8]

This certainly does not, however, imply that financial liberalization produces instability. A number of economies which were liberalized for some time before an economic downturn, including Germany, did not experience banking problems when an economic downturn came. Most, indeed, appear to have banking systems with well-developed methods of containing risks. The picture rather seems to be that there is vulnerability *during the process* of liberalization, a process in the course of which new entrants, both domestic and foreign, fare worse than already established institutions. Another feature of Table 15.3 is the key role property prices appear to play in triggering financial problems. This was highlighted again in 1997 in the financial crises in east Asia.

In summary it is fair and unsurprising to say that cross-country comparisons indicate most episodes of large-scale banking sector problems have been associated with preceding financial liberalization *in combination with* a period of loose monetary policy. A very frequent transmission channel has been property prices – an unsustainable rise followed by a collapse seems important in triggering major losses of bank capital. It does, all in all, seem inescapable that monetary policy stability facilitates banking sector stability; and monetary policy volatility encourages banking sector instability.

**Moral Hazard, Looting and Failures of Governance and Supervision**

The scale of losses in individual institutions and the overall severity of domestic banking crises also depend upon microeconomic or structural factors. It is well understood that failing institutions may be subject to both excessive risk taking and fraud. The US savings and loan crisis (not incidentally a banking crisis under our definition, since while of substantial magnitude it did not threaten the integrity of the US banking system or payment mechanism) illustrates how the management and owners of failing institutions can have considerable incentives to shift bank investments into highly risky assets (see, for example, White, 1991). Owners and management protected from further loss by limited liability, and able to continue in business because of the presence of deposit insurance or simply the ignorance of depositors of the plight of the bank, stand to gain substantially if such a 'gamble for resurrection' succeeds. Even more crudely, management and owners are likely to 'loot' the failing bank, using a variety of admittedly fraudulent devices to transfer value out of a doomed enterprise (Akerlof and Romer, 1993).

Fraud and excessive risk taking have played a role in other banking crises, although primarily as a triggering mechanism. Fraud was at the root of the 1984 collapse of Herstatt bank, which led to the subsequent liquidity crisis in CHAPS, the New York interbank payment system. But fraud was not the cause of this crisis. The liquidity crisis occurred because of a combination of unfortunate timing (the decision by the German authorities to close Herstatt while CHAPS was still open) and inadequate risk controls in the CHAPS system itself. A bank failure occurring for some quite different reason at the same stage of the payments cycle might well have triggered a similar chain of events. Moreover other failures of moderately sized internationally active banks (Banco Ambrosiano, BCCI, Barings in 1995), arising from fraud and from other circumstances, have not led to problems in payment systems.

While institutions as a whole can be subject to 'moral hazard' or looting by owners, it is more common to find, at the heart of banking crisis, that it is failures of internal control that allow excessive risk taking or fraud by individual loan officers. There are many examples. The sovereign debt crisis that erupted with the 1982 Mexican default arose in large part because of inadequate systems for control of the lending decisions within individual banks (Congdon, 1988; Kuczinski, 1988). Bank executives making lending decisions were well aware of the misuse of the loans they were approving, but salary and career incentives pushed them to maximize the volume of lending regardless of risk, and there were no effective systems for monitoring or controlling the exposures of financial institutions.

Similar weaknesses of internal control have magnified bank exposure to other credit risks, for example in many cases of widespread bank credit losses in the early 1990s. Reckless expansion of lending played a role in the bank crises of Norway and Sweden, and in losses on commercial property in both New England and in London. This is not to say that weaknesses of internal control always lead to banking crises, since of these examples it is only the Scandinavian cases that qualify as banking crises.

In these cases it must also be asked, why it is that bank owners allow them to operate without adequate risk controls? Little systematic research has been done on this point; but among several factors, the following seem to be important. Controls are often weakest when, following periods of financial liberalization, banks enter new and unfamiliar markets. Weaknesses of governance and hence of internal control are often associated with state ownership (for example, Crédit Lyonnais, South Korea, Indonesia) or non-profit structures (Barings).

Finally, it is often asserted that weaknesses of financial regulation and lack of resources devoted to supervision are an important factor in exposing banks to excessive credit risk. Again, this is another assertion on which there seems to be relatively little persuasive evidence. Severe banking problems have occurred in the US during the 1980s and early 1990s, despite its extensive and generously resourced systems of bank supervision. It is certainly true that regulation and supervision were lax in, for example, the banking problems that emerged in South East Asia in 1997. But as we discuss further below, these banking problems also reflected deep-seated problems of governance and control, with much lending politically directed, and a lack of adequate internal controls. Moreover both domestic depositors and international creditors believed (in the event correctly) that local governments would support the liabilities of their banks. It is questionable whether additional resources and training for supervisory agencies could have done much alone to avert these problems.

**International Transmission**

It is now widely accepted in the area of international finance that in the presence of a reasonable degree of international capital mobility only a freely floating exchange rate or a rigidly fixed one, such as a currency board or even a monetary union such as the European Monetary Union (EMU), is sustainable. This was first pointed out by Milton Friedman in 1958, and his arguments have been formalized more recently by a number of authors; a good recent review can be found in McCallum (2002). However, it is only starting to be noticed that there are somewhat similar implications for the banking system of the choice of exchange rate regime. In this subsection we first summarize how the choice of exchange rate regime affects the channels of transmission of crises from one country to another and then show how a particular regime can, if not promote instability, then certainly exacerbate the effects of a shock.

With regard to transmission, under a fixed exchange rate a country (unless it is the lead country in a monetary union) has no monetary independence. Under a floating rate, domestic monetary conditions not only can be but must be domestically determined. This in turn implies that a banking liquidity crisis will spread from country to country with a fixed rate, and cannot – except by pure contagion – under a floating system.

The first is well exemplified by the Great Depression. The waves of bank failures, and consequent monetary contraction, in the United States had no banking sector impact in either Britain or Canada. Neither of these countries had any banking sector crisis in that episode, despite being the major trading partners of the US. In both cases, they insulated themselves by breaking the link between their currencies and the US dollar (and gold).

What are the dangers of an adjustable peg system? How can it exacerbate banking crises? East Asia in 1998 is a good example here. The East Asian crises were certainly not all identical, but they did have common features. There were asset price booms, followed by crashes, followed by problems in banking systems and flight from currencies.

That is not a new story. Commentators who expressed surprise at crises arising in the absence of public sector problems had formed their expectations on a narrow slice of history. Why the asset price crash led so rapidly to large-scale banking problems and then to problems with currencies has been neatly summarized by Ronald McKinnon (1999, p. 3): 'banks and other financial institutions were poorly regulated but their depositors were nevertheless insured – explicitly or implicitly – against bankruptcy by their national governments. The resulting moral hazard was responsible for the excessive build up of short-term foreign-currency indebtedness.'

This build-up of foreign currency indebtedness was encouraged by the pegged exchange rate regime. Because of the guarantees, there was undiversified lending as well as undiversified borrowing by banks. In addition, and again because of the guarantees, the problem was large in scale, and the banks had little collateral to offer in exchange for liquidity from the central bank. These problems, themselves substantial, were exacerbated by many of the banks involved having to make loans on the direction of government rather than according to commercial criteria.

In short, the system could not have been worse designed either to provide stability or to facilitate lender-of-last-resort action; and even had such action been feasible, the fall in value of the East Asian currencies undermined the capital position of the banks via their net foreign currency indebtedness. Crash turned into crisis.

**Are the Risks of an International Banking Crisis Increasing?**

First, let us restate our definition. An international banking crisis is the international transmission of financial problems that, without policy intervention, would have threatened the stability of the banking system and the operation of the payments system in a number of different countries. On this definition, events that come even close to being classified as international banking crises have been extremely rare. Over the past century there has been Credit Anstalt, Herstatt, and the problems of Sovereign Debt lending, and none of these can really be categorized as a fully fledged international banking crisis.

Moreover, on balance we can argue that, the globalization of banking notwithstanding, the risks of an international banking crisis in the early part of the twenty-first century have diminished rather than increased, relative to the situation in the second half of the twentieth century. Our argument runs as follows. First we consider again, and in turn, the main forces underlying banking crises previously discussed in this section, establishing that the risks of bank crisis, domestic or international, have diminished. Second, we consider whether increased international exposure has increased the risk of a domestic crisis transmitting internationally and becoming international. We find that it has not.

Macroeconomic policy making, especially monetary policy, is now much more stable than was the case a decade or more ago. The shift towards greater independence of central banks in the industrial world, together with the widespread adoption of inflation targeting, is a profound change. The UK is a prime example of the acceptance of monetary discipline, beginning with the espousal of monetarist policies by the Conservative government of Margaret Thatcher in the early 1980s and culminating in the 1997 decision by the Labour government of Tony Blair to give the Bank of England operational independence in monetary policy.

For some of the more inflation-prone countries of southern Europe, monetary policy discipline has been attained by an alternative route, through the creation of the euro and the substitution of politically independent European Central Bank monetary policy in place of a more politically controlled domestic monetary policy. This is not to say that no financial problems lie ahead. Again the UK provides a good example, where the control of inflation and consequent lowering of interest rates during the 1980s was followed by an asset price and consumption boom. Some countries within the eurozone, including Portugal and Ireland, have experienced similar asset price and consumption booms in the late 1990s, and the possibility of them. But these cases are to a large extent problems of transition from a regime of high and variable to low and stable inflation. Once the new regime is widely understood and accepted, the acceptance of monetary discipline promises to bring about greater banking sector stability in all the developed countries, making the possibility of an international banking crisis even more remote.

Internal controls and the external governance of banks have also, generally, improved over recent years. In France, Italy, Greece and elsewhere there have been major programmes of bank privatization. At a global level there have been improvements in risk management as a response to the experience of portfolio losses and of loan default. Virtually all investment banks now use 'value at risk' modelling to monitor their exposure to market risk. While value at risk is not an exact measure, it is a good deal better than having no measure of risk exposure at all. Commercial banks in Scandinavia, France, the US, the UK and elsewhere now generally operate much tighter controls over all their credit exposures than was customary a decade ago.

Experience of exchange rate problems such as in the European ERM in 1992 and 1993, or in South East Asia in 1997, has reinforced the point that pegged exchange rates are not sustainable in a regime of capital mobility. Thus in all the major countries the choice has been made between either permanent exchange rate fix (in the eurozone) or a floating exchange rate. In consequence banks are either less exposed to foreign exchange risk, or the foreign exchange risks are so obvious that they have to be almost entirely hedged.

A number of developments have also strengthened both domestic and international payments systems, and come close to removing the possibility of an international or even domestic payments breakdown. Most large value payment systems, including the euro TARGET system linking the payment systems of the euro area, now operate on a real time gross settlement basis. This development, not without cost because someone has to provide liquidity, removes the threat that the failure of a single institution could cripple payments activity. Where systems still operate on a net basis, for example, the New York CHAPS, stringent operating standards are now applied, again effectively removing the possiblity of a systemic crisis. In the foreign exchange markets the introduction, early in 2002, of continuous linked settlement will further reduce systemic risk. While central bankers on the Bank for International Settlements committee on payment and settlement systems remain vigilant, it can be fairly safely asserted that a Herstatt crisis could only happen in today's payment systems if some cataclysm were first to wipe out the majority of the world's financial institutions. Nowadays payments breakdown might be a consequence of, but could not be a contributory cause to, an international banking crisis.

It is thus clear that all these principal factors, macroeconomic, structural and international financial arrangements have shifted so as to reduce (although not eliminate) the risk of banking crises. Still, it might be argued, increased international exposure may have increased the risk of an international banking crisis, even if the risks of domestic banking problems have receded. We can make a number of points to refute this position.

First, globalization of the banking industry has not in fact proceeded very far in commercial banking. With the exception of a handful of institutions with substantial international corporate and trade finance business (including Citigroup, HSBC, Deutsche Bank, Barclays and ABN–AMRO), commercial banking exposures remain overwhelmingly domestic. This is true even within the euro area, where cross-border banking activity is still relatively unimportant. This fact means that the risk of a domestic banking crisis remains relatively high (because many institutions have considerable exposure to their own country) but that the threat of a bank failure leading to the collapse of banking systems and payment mechanisms in several countries is very low.

Second, were commercial banking exposures to become international, as may well happen in the euro area over the next few years once a genuine single market in financial services is established, there will be two offsetting impacts. While international transmission of bank difficulties will have increased, bank portfolios will be increasingly diversified. In the event of much greater globalization of commercial banking, and with country and industry risks unchanged, the probability of an individual bank failure occurring is greatly diminished. In such a situation a banking crisis if it occurs will be international simply because banking systems have become international. But the likelihood of crisis is greatly diminished.

Third, as commercial banking becomes a truly international activity, it will be accompanied by increased international banking competition and, most importantly, a growing international market for the control of banks via mergers and acquisitions. Provided governments do not seek to protect their own local institutions, this will in turn promote better governance and improved standards of risk management and internal control, since a clear focus on profitability and appropriate risk-adjusted returns to shareholders will be the only effective defence against acquisition. Where acquisition does take place it will generally result in a transfer of better practice into the target bank.

Internationalization has proceeded rapidly in global investment banking. Here the nature of risk is entirely different from that in commercial banking. Investment banks' exposure to market risks is now tightly controlled. What the major investment banks face instead are substantial business risks, especially the very real possibility at this point in time of a worldwide decline in securities issuance and trading. But suppose there were a serious collapse of these businesses, with ensuing problems of overcapacity and the need for contraction and even liquidation of major international investment banking operations. This would no more be an international banking crisis than would be a collapse in the market for steel or motor cars. Nowadays, with investment banking activity income shifted so substantially from trading to fee-based issuance and market making, there would not be a direct impact on the pricing and liquidity of financial assets. And contraction or liquidation of the investment banking sector does not threaten bank depositors, payments activity, or the integrity of the financial system. Such developments would not qualify as an international banking crisis.

## 4 THE SUPERFLUITY OF AN INTERNATIONAL LENDER OF LAST RESORT

We have argued that the risks of an international banking crisis have actually diminished over recent years. But we still need to consider the case for an international lender of last resort (LOLR) to cope with the risk of an international banking crisis. If the risk of such an internationally transmitted crisis really is as low as we judge, then no one would need to make the case for such an international LOLR. But suppose that we are wrong, and the risks of an international banking crisis in the early part of this century are actually rather high. Some might then argue that an international LOLR is needed to avert the threat of such a crisis.

This final section of this chapter argues to the contrary, that even if the risk of an international transmission of banking crises is high, very much higher than we suppose, an international LOLR is superfluous. This is because, in the event of an internationally transmitted banking crisis, the role of LOLR in supplying liquidity is fully satisfied by the domestic LOLR.

**The Origins and Domestic Role of the Lender of Last Resort**

The concept has its origins in a problem which can occur in a domestic banking system in a scramble for liquidity as follows. Suppose one bank fails. This gives rise to fears on the part of other depositors about the soundness of their own banks, and they go to get cash accordingly (in the nineteenth century in the form of gold or in Britain as Bank of England notes). But banks do not hold all funds deposited with them as cash, so all banks together cannot cope with a mass withdrawal. One bank could, by getting cash from other banks; but the only and ultimate source of cash for the whole system in a system with a central bank is the central bank.

The problem and the solution were both described well by two eminent nineteenth-century writers on monetary economics. First, the problem: 'If any bank fails, a general run upon the neighbouring banks is apt to take place, which if not checked in the beginning by a pouring into the circulation of a very large quantity of gold, leads to very extensive mischief' (Thornton, 1802, p. 97); and then the solution: 'What is wanted and what is necessary to stop a panic is to diffuse the impression, that though money may be dear, still money is to be had. If people could really be convinced that they would have money . . . most likely they would cease to run in such a mad way for money' (Bagehot, 1873, p. 106).

Acting in the way Bagehot prescribed could, it was asserted, prevent the problems associated with a banking system collapse. These problems are many, but most basic is the unanticipated collapse in the stock of money which it would produce. Such collapses cause severe recession, of which the Great Depression in the United States is the archetype. These can be prevented by taking the following action.

The central bank that experiences such a shock should lend freely on collateral. It should not restrict lending to the classes of security (usually quite narrow) that it would accept for discount during normal times. Advances should be made without limit, on demand, but at a rate of interest above the pre-crisis rate. These loans should be made to the market – that is, to anyone who brings in acceptable security. In addition (and argued in particular by Bagehot) it should be made clear that the central bank will act in that way should there ever be a crisis: this reduces the likelihood of runs because knowledge that the central bank will supply liquidity makes it seem less urgent to scramble for it.

That is the theory. Does it work in practice? There can be no doubt that it does. One often cited item of evidence is that there has been no such banking crisis in Britain since 1866 – by 1875 the Bank had accepted Bagehot's advice. The Governor of the Bank from 1875 to 1877, H.H. Gibbs, described the 1866 crisis as 'the Bank's only real blunder in his experience'; but he did not criticize the then Governor, for 'the matter was not as well understood then as it is now' (Gibbs, 1877, p. 15).

The other example is the Great Depression in the US. There were several contributing factors, but the major one was undoubtedly the failure of the recently established Federal Reserve System to act adequately as lender of last resort in the waves of bank failures from 1930 to 1933. The Federal Reserve's failure led in 1934 to the establishment of deposit insurance – a perhaps unhappy precedent to which we return.

Less well-known examples are France and Italy. In both countries LOLR action prevented bank runs, and its absence allowed them.

That, then, is the essence of domestic LOLR action. It is rapid, involves the abundant supply of domestic money on the basis of provision of collateral, and does *not* involve bailing out individual institutions.[9]

**An International Role?**

Now we come to dealing directly with the international LOLR concept. Unless the International Monetary Fund (IMF) or some other body can issue any currency it wishes on demand and without limit, it cannot act as international LOLR. Many of the advocates of this scheme come close to recognizing this, and urge that the IMF should be given more reserves to enable it to lend more freely. The trouble with that, apart from its ignoring the fundamental point that an international LOLR has not yet been justified, is that the more resources it has, the more it will need. Only when it has enough to be able to replace on demand the entire money stock of an economy with US dollars (assuming that to be the money demanded) will it have enough.

But why should there be such a body in any event? A domestic one is needed because banks cannot suddenly declare that (for example) dollar deposits are no longer redeemable in dollars, but only in a currency of the bank's own issuing which floats against the dollar. That option is always available to a country; a country can always float its exchange rate.

Can there be such a thing as an international lender of last resort? Certainly it has often been asserted that there can be, with some talk of the IMF or some such body behaving in this fashion. When the Bank for International Settlements was established in 1929, hopes were expressed by some that it would go on to become a central bank. Or, for example, there has been the view that the Bank of England was the effective LOLR to the world in the classical gold standard years, 1880–1914. Rockoff (1986) even goes further in saying that any national bank that acted as an LOLR was forced by the gold standard to act as an international LOLR.

But the dominant view of the operation of the gold standard is that if there is a shortage of funds in one participating country, funds will be drawn in from other countries and in this particular case from the Bank of England, the 'conductor of the orchestra', in one smooth and continuous process of arbitrage. The process would have been encouraged by adherence to the 'rules of the game'. We do not dissent from that. Our argument is that a financial crisis is different. It is more than the normal ebb and flow of funds. A financial crisis requires prompt injection of liquidity. We place principal emphasis on the fact that the LOLR is the ultimate source of the means of payment. The only currency the Bank of England supplied was sterling. Thus if there were a financial crisis in, say, the United States, interest rates would rise there and that might have the effect of drawing cash from England and from other countries. But the Bank of England was not able to supply dollars in quantities in excess of the base money of the system. And indeed all the evidence is that the US suffered repeated banking panics and financial crises while England was relatively free of them. That was one of the reasons why the US set up the Federal Reserve.

Furthermore, the gold standard was the long-run rule that provides long-term price stability. The LOLR is in some respects the antithesis of this. Hawtrey was one of the few writers who seems to have been clear on this and made it explicit: 'An international central bank can only help so long as an international medium is required; it cannot supersede the ultimate remedy of an emergency issue, which remains a matter of national not international jurisdiction' (1962, p. 274). Kindleberger has argued that there has been a need for an international LOLR. He argued first (and correctly) that financial crises could be, and often were, internationally transmitted. He then produces a *non sequitur*: 'It follows from the international propagation of financial crises . . . that a case can be made for an international lender of last resort' (1978, p. 201). We reject that for the reasons given above.

## 5  SUMMARY AND CONCLUSION

In this chapter we have examined the concept of an *international* banking crisis and discussed whether the risks of such a crisis have been increasing. Our findings can be briefly summarized. We point out that for there to be a banking crisis proper, not only must banks face financial losses but the scale of these losses must be sufficiently great so as to threaten the integrity of the entire banking system or national payment system. An international banking crisis is where financial difficulties are transmitted internationally and produce such a banking crisis in a number of countries.

We examined the principal forces that have triggered past banking crises, emphasizing the roles of macroeconomic and especially monetary instability, and of weaknesses of governance and of internal control. We also examined the international transmission of financial crises, focusing on the example of Asian crisis of 1997 and 1998, and pointing out that the severity of these problems was due to an important degree to the pursuit of an unstable exchange rate regime.

With this discussion in mind we then assessed whether there has indeed been any increase in the risk of an international banking crisis. On the contrary, we find that improved monetary discipline and standards of bank governance and risk management, together with a moderate degree of portfolio diversification arising from the slowly increasing internationalization of commercial banking, has reduced the likelihood of an international banking crisis. The macroeconomic environment is more stable. Banks are better run. International diversification of income streams affords a further degree of protection.

There are still potential problems of adjustment. Individual institutions entering into new markets in other countries face a difficult challenge in managing both financial and business risks. Resulting losses could in turn impact on their domestic banking systems. The expectation of unlimited state support may allow banks that get into difficulties to take excessive risks, or even to effectively defraud the state through the looting of bank assets. The risks of some international banking crisis cannot therefore be said to be entirely negligible. But these are risks that need to be dealt with through improvements in corporate governance and clearer delimitation of the scope for state support of failing banks. In order to ensure international financial stability it is necessary neither to impose limitations or restrictions on the internationalization of the banking industry nor to extend the role of lender of last resort so as to provide a general protection against the possibility of losses on international financial exposures.

## NOTES

1. It would no longer be necessary to ask this question if, in the long-term future, we reach a situation where banks themselves are largely international institutions taking deposits from many countries, and where payment systems between banks all operate at an international rather than national level. In such a global banking system a banking crisis would, in order to qualify as a crisis, have to be international. Despite the rapid internationalization of banking, we are still some way from a truly global banking system of this kind, and the question remains a pertinent one for the forseeable future.
2. Other prominent bank failures such as Banco Ambrosiano, BCCI or Barings were international but were clearly not banking crises. These episodes, while central to any discussion of the appropriateness of international supervisory arrangements, therefore fall outside the scope of our analysis.
3. This is not to say they were not severe problems for the countries concerned.
4. In this she follows Palgrave (1894, p. 462): 'One of the most remarkable and instructive facts is negative, viz., that there has been really no panic in England since 1866.'
5. This theory of the origin of banking panics is clearly related to what Calomiris and Gorton (1991) call the 'asymmetric information approach'.
6. This could not be done before 1914, as it was a worldwide interest rate cycle and would have required concerted worldwide action by central banks. This was not possible as the United States, a major agricultural producer, did not have a central bank until 1914.
7. Gorton also tests whether the Fed was an improvement on previous stabilizing devices – private clearing houses – by running his pre-1914 equations on post-1914 data and comparing the the forecast out-turn with events. The hypothetical outcome was much preferable.
8. In addition, they found two external factors important – an appreciation of the real exchange relative to trend and a decline in the growth of export volumes.
9. Even so, there is some degree of moral hazard. This was pointed out by Thomson Hankey, Deputy Governor of the Bank of England, at the time Bagehot was writing. Hankey maintained that without LOLR, banks would hold larger reserves. This is undoubtedly true; but subsequent writers have judged this modest increase in moral hazard a price worth paying to insure against crises.

## REFERENCES

Akerlof, G.A. and P.M. Romer (1993), 'Looting, the economic underworld of bankruptcy for profit', *Brookings Papers on Economic Activity*, **2**, 1–60.
Bagehot, Walter (1873), *Lombard Street: A Description of the Money Market*, Reprinted 1962, Homewood, IL: Irwin.
Burns, A. and W. Mitchell (1946), *Measuring Business Cycles*, New York: NBER.
Calomiris, C.W. and G. Gorton (1991), 'The origin of banking panics: models, facts and bank regulations', in R.G. Hubbard (ed.), *Financial Markets and Financial Crisis*, Chicago, IL: University of Chicago Press.

Capie, F.H. and T.C. Mills (1991), 'Money and business cycles in the US and the UK, 1870–1913', *Manchester School*, **59**, 38–56.
Chubb, H. (1872), 'Bank Act and Crisis of 1866', *Journal of the Statistical Society of London*, **35**.
Congdon, Tim (1988), *The Debt Threat*, Oxford: Basil Blackwell.
Diamond, D.W. and P.H. Dybvig (1983), 'Bank runs, deposit insurance, and liquidity', *Journal of Political Economy*, **91** (3): 401–19.
Gibbs, H.H. (1877), Correspondence with Professor Bonamy Price on the Reserve of the Bank of England, pamphlet printed for private circulation.
Gorton, Gary (1988), 'Banking panics and business cycles', *Oxford Economic Papers*, no. 40, 751–81.
Hawtrey, R.G. (1962) [1932], *The Art of Central Banking*, London: Longmans, Green & Co.
Hellwig, M. (1996), 'Financial innovations and the incidence of risk in the financial system', in F. Bruni, D.E. Fair and R. O'Brien (eds), *Risk Management in Volatile Financial Markets*, Boston: Kluwer, pp. 25–39.
Jessons, S.C. (1866), 'The frequent pressure in the money market', *Journal of the Statistical Society of London*, **29** (235).
Kaminsky, G., S. Lizondo and C. Reinhart (1998), 'Leading indicators of currency crises,' *IMF Staff Papers*, Vol. 45, March.
Kemmerer, E.W. (1910), *Seasonal Variations in the Relative Demand for Money and Capital in the United States*, National Monetary Commission, Washington, DC: Government Printing Office.
Kindleberger, Charles P. (1978), *Manias, Panics and Crashes*, New York: Basic Books.
Kuczinski, Pedro-Pablo (1988), *Latin American Debt*, Baltimore, MD: Johns Hopkins University Press.
Langton, W. (1858), Observations on a table showing the balance of account between the mercantile public and the Bank of England, *Transactions of the Manchester Statistical Society*.
Levi, L. (1888), *History of British Commerce and of the Economic Progress of the British Nation, 1763–1870*, London: John Murray.
Lindgren, C.J., G. Garcia and M.I. Saul (1996), *Bank Soundness and Macroeconomic Policy*, Washington, DC: International Monetary Fund.
McCallum, B.T. (2002), 'The choice of exchange rate regime', in F.H. Capie and G.E. Wood (eds), *Monetary Unions: Theory, History, Public Choice*, London: Routledge.
McKay, Charles (1845), *Extraordinary Popular Delusions and the Madness of Crowds*, London: Richard Bentley.
McKinnon, Ronald (1999), 'The East Asian dollar standard, life after death?' (Typescript).
McPherson, D. (1805), Manufactures, Fisheries, Navigation, etc., *Annals of Commerce*, Vol IV.
Mills, J. (1868), Credit cycles and the origin of commercial panics, *Transactions of the Manchester Statistical Society*.
Miron, J.A. (1986), 'Financial panics, the seasonality of nominal interest rates, and the founding of the Fed', *American Economic Review*, **26**, 125–40.
Palgrave, R.H.I. (1894, 1896, 1898), *Dictionary of Political Economy*, London: Macmillan.
Rockoff, Hugh (1986), 'The Bagehot problem', in F.H. Capie and G.E. Wood (eds), *Financial Crises and the World Banking System*, London: Macmillan.

Schwartz, Anna J. (1986), 'Real and pseudo financial crises', in F.H. Capie and G.E. Wood (eds), *Financial Crises and the World Banking System*, London: Macmillan, pp. 11–31.

Thornton, Henry (1802) *An Enquiry into the Effects of the Paper Credit of Great Britain*, Reprinted 1978 (with Introduction by F.A. Hayek), Fairfield, NJ: Augustus Kelley.

Tooke, Thomas (1838, 1840, 1848), *A History of Prices*, London: Longman, Brown, Green & Longman (becomes Tooke and William Newmarch for Vol. V, pub. 1858).

White, Lawrence J. (1991), *The S&L Débâcle: Public Policy Lessons for Bank and Thrift Regulation*, Oxford: Oxford University Press.

# 16. Some lessons for bank regulation from recent financial crises

David T. Llewellyn*

## 1 INTRODUCTION AND OUTLINE

Our objective is to consider the experience of recent banking crises in both developed and developing countries, and to draw lessons most especially with respect to the regulation and supervision of banks, and the design of an optimum 'regulatory regime'. This will be done by setting out a series of general principles designed to lower the probability of banking distress. Just as the causes of banking crises are multidimensional, so the principles of an effective *regulatory regime* also need to incorporate a wider range of issues than externally imposed rules on bank behaviour. What will be termed a 'regulatory regime' also includes the arrangements for intervention in the event of bank distress and failures. This is because they have incentive and moral hazard effects which potentially influence future behaviour of banks and their customers and the probability of future crises.

The focus of the chapter is a consideration of alternative approaches to achieving the objectives of regulation: systemic stability and consumer protection. A central theme is that what are often regarded as 'alternatives' are in fact complements within an overall regulatory strategy. As the regulatory regime is wider than the rules and monitoring conducted by regulatory agencies, the skill in constructing a regulatory strategy lies in how the various components of the *regime* are combined.

When a particular regulatory problem emerges, the instinct of a regulator is often to create new rules. This implies an *incremental approach* to regulation by focusing upon the rules component of the regulatory regime. The chapter argues that there are serious problems with such an incremental rules approach in that it may blunt the power of the other mechanisms and may, in the process, reduce the overall effectiveness of the regime in achieving its core objectives.

Although there is considerable academic debate about whether or not banks should be regulated at all, this issue is not addressed. Some studies (notably those of Benston and Kaufman, 1995) argue that the economic rationale for bank regulation has not been robustly established and that, in some cases, banking problems have their origin in regulatory rather than market failure. In particular, emphasis is given to the moral hazard effects of safety-net arrangements. A similar approach is found in Schwartz (1995).

The general economic rationale for financial regulation (in terms of externalities, market imperfections, economies of scale in monitoring, gridlock problems, and moral hazard associated with safety nets) has been outlined elsewhere (Llewellyn, 1999). For purposes of the present chapter, the economic rationale for regulation is taken as given.

A central theme is that the various components of the regulatory regime need to be combined in an overall regulatory strategy, and that while all are necessary, none is sufficient. While external regulation has a role in fostering a safe and sound banking system, this role is limited. Equally, and increasingly important, are the incentive structures faced by private banking agents, the efficiency of the necessary monitoring and supervision of banks by official agencies and the market, and corporate governance arrangements within banks. External regulation is only one component of regimes to create safe and sound banking systems which, if it is pressed too far, may blunt other mechanisms and in the process compromise the impact of the overall regime.

A sustained theme is that the regulatory regime is defined more widely than externally imposed regulation on financial institutions. In current conditions it would be a mistake to rely wholly, or even predominantly, on external regulation, monitoring and supervision by the 'official sector'. The world of banking and finance is too complex and volatile to be able to rely on a simple set of prescriptive rules for prudent and compliant behaviour. There is a danger of thinking only in terms of incremental change to regulation, rather than strategically with respect to the overall regime. This needs to be set in the context of trade-offs between the various components. In some circumstances the more emphasis that is given to one of the components (for example, regulation), the less powerful becomes one or more of the others (for example, market discipline on financial firms, or the effectiveness of corporate governance arrangements) and to an extent that may reduce the overall impact.

The skill in formulating regulatory strategy lies not so much in choosing between various options, but in combining the seven components of the regime. The objective is to move towards an optimum mix, combined with careful choice of regulatory instruments within each. It is not, therefore, a question of choosing between either regulation or market disciplines; or between regulation and supervision on the one hand or competition on the other. The concept of a *regulatory strategy* is that these are not alternatives but components of an overall approach to achieve the objective of systemic stability. A key issue for the regulator is how its actions can not only contribute to the objectives directly, but how they impact on the other components of the regime: in particular, the issue is how regulation affects incentive structures within firms, and also the role that can be played by market discipline and monitoring.

The optimum mix of the components will change over time. It is argued that, over time and as the market environment in which banks operate becomes more complex, four structural shifts within the regulatory regime are desirable: (i) external regulation needs to become less prescriptive, more flexible and differentiated as between different institutions, (ii) more emphasis needs to be given to incentive structures and the contribution that regulation can make to creating appropriate incentive structures, (iii) market discipline and market monitoring of banks need to be strengthened, and (iv) corporate governance mechanisms for banks need to be strengthened.

The outline of the chapter is as follows. It begins with a brief overview of recent banking crises. Section 3 considers some common elements in banking crises. This is followed in Section 4 by a discussion of the multidimensional nature of recent crises. Section 5 reviews the impact of liberalization, where a distinction is made between the transitional effects associated with the shift from one regime to another, and the steady-state characteristics of a deregulated financial system. Section 6 discusses the nature of a regulatory regime and the trade-offs between its components, and proceeds to draw together the implications of the nature and origin of banking crises by setting out some principles designed to lower the probability of distress in the banking sector. Section 7 offers conclusions and an overall assessment.

## 2 RECENT BANKING CRISES

Given their incidence and variety over the past 15 years, banking crises (in both developing and industrial economies) are clearly not random or isolated events. Around the world, banks have had high levels of non-performing loans, there has been a major destruction of bank capital, banks have failed, and massive support operations have been necessary. The failure rate among banks has been greater than at any time since the great depression of the 1920s. In the case of Indonesia, Malaysia, South Korea and Thailand, non-performing loans of banks recently amounted to about 30 per cent of total assets. Banking crises have involved substantial costs. In about 25 per cent of cases the cost has exceeded 10 per cent of GNP (for example, in Spain, Venezuela, Bulgaria, Mexico, Argentina, Hungary). Evans (2000) suggests that the costs of crises amounted to 45 per cent of GDP in the case of Indonesia, 15 per cent in the case of Korea and 40 per cent in the case of Thailand. These figures include the costs of meeting obligations to depositors under the blanket guarantees that the authorities introduced to handle systemic crises, and public sector payments to financing the recapitalization of insolvent banks.

Almost always and everywhere banking crises are a complex interactive mix of economic, financial and structural weaknesses. Lindgren et al. (1996) give an excellent survey of the two-way link between banking systems and macro policy. The trigger for many crises has been macroeconomic in origin and has often been associated with a sudden withdrawal of liquid external capital from a country. As noted by Brownbridge and Kirkpatrick (2000), financial crises have often involved triple crises of currencies, financial sectors and corporate sectors. Similarly, it has been argued that East Asian countries were vulnerable to a financial crisis because of 'reinforcing dynamics between capital flows, macro-policies, and weak financial and corporate sector institutions' (Alba et al., 1998, p. 38). The link between balance of payments and banking crises is certainly not a recent phenomenon and has been extensively studied (for example, Kaminsky and Reinhart, 1998; Godlayn and Valdes, 1997; Sachs et al., 1996).

Almost invariably, systemic crises (as opposed to the failure of individual banks within a stable system) are preceded by major macroeconomic adjustment, which often leads to the economy moving into recession after a previous strong cyclical upswing. While financial crises have been preceded by sharp fluctuations in the macro economy, and often in asset prices, it would be a mistake to ascribe financial instability entirely to macroeconomic instability. While macro instability may be the proximate cause of a banking crisis, the crisis usually emerges because instability in the macro economy reveals existing weaknesses within the banking system. The seeds of a problem (for example, overlending, weak risk analysis and control and so on) are usually sown in the earlier upswing of the cycle: mistakes made in the upswing emerge in the downswing. The downswing phase reveals previous errors and overoptimism. In South East Asia, for instance, a decade of substantial economic growth up to 1997 concealed the effects of questionable bank-lending policies.

A common experience in countries that have experienced banking crises is that expectations have been volatile, and asset prices (including property) have been subject to wild swings. A sharp (sometimes speculative) rise in asset prices is often followed by an equally dramatic collapse. An initial rise in asset prices has often induced overoptimism and euphoria, which in turn have led to increased demand for borrowed funds and an increased willingness of banks to lend (Llewellyn and Holmes, 1991).

## 3 SOME COMMON ELEMENTS IN BANKING DISTRESS

Analysis of recent financial crises in both developed and less-developed countries indicates that they are not exclusively (or even mainly) a problem of the rules being wrong (see, for instance, Brealey, 1999; Corsetti et al., 1998; and Lindgren et al., 1996). Five common characteristics have been: weak internal risk analysis, management and control systems within banks; inadequate official supervision; weak (or even perverse) incentives within the financial system generally and financial institutions in particular; inadequate information disclosure; and inadequate corporate governance arrangements both within banks and their large corporate customers. An unstable or unpredictable macroeconomic environment is not a sufficient condition for banking crises to emerge: it is an illusion to ascribe such crises to faults in the macro economy alone. The fault also lies internally within banks, and with failures of regulation, supervision and market discipline on banks.

While each banking crisis has unique and country-specific features, they also have a lot in common. Several conditions tend to precede most systemic banking crises. A period of rapid growth in bank lending within a short period, and unrealistic expectations and euphoria about economic prospects, often form the backdrop to subsequent crises. These are frequently aggravated by sharp and unsustainable rises in asset prices (part of euphoria speculation), which lead to unrealistic demands for credit and a willingness of banks to supply loans. In the process, inadequate risk premia are often incorporated in the rates of interest on loans. This is a version of the standard Fisher and Minsky thesis: debt accumulation in the upswing leading to problems for banks in the downswing.

During the period of substantial growth in bank lending, concentrated loan portfolios (often with a high property content) often emerge. This is partly because, in periods of rapid asset-price inflation, property appears to be either an attractive lending proposition or a secure form of collateral against bank loans. However, it is in essence speculative lending and the bubble bursts when the overcapacity in the property sector becomes evident. This means that, while individual project risks may be accurately assessed, overall portfolio risks are often not. It is also the case that, in periods of rapid growth in bank lending, insufficient attention is given to the value of collateral, most especially in periods of asset-price inflation.

Banks do not always operate as totally independent agents and in many crisis countries bank decisions have involved political influences and insider relationships. Such government involvement in lending decisions has the effect of weakening incentive structures, and eroding discipline on lenders through the perception of an implicit guarantee.

The origins of crises have been both internal to banks and external. To focus myopically on one side misses the essential point that systemic crises have both macro and micro origins. In the final analysis, weak internal risk analysis, management and control systems are at the root of all banking crises. Instability elsewhere should not conceal, or be used to excuse, weaknesses in this area of bank management.

It is also the case that banking crises often follow major changes in the regulatory regime which create unfamiliar market conditions. Periods of rapid balance sheet growth, most especially when they occur after a regime shift and in a period of intense competition, almost inevitably involve banks incurring more risk. There are several reasons for this: banks begin to compete for market share by lowering their risk thresholds; risks are under-priced in order to gain market share; internal control systems tend to weaken in periods of rapid balance sheet growth; growth itself generates unwarranted optimism and a growth momentum develops; and portfolios become unbalanced if new lending opportunities are concentrated in a narrow range of business sectors. When, as is often the case, fast-growth strategies are pursued by all banks simultaneously, borrowers become overindebted and more risky, which in turn increases the vulnerability of the lending banks.

## 4  A MULTIDIMENSIONAL PROBLEM

The recent banking crises in South East Asia have, as always, been complex and the causes have been multidimensional. While evident macro-policy failures and volatile and structurally weak economies have been contributory factors, fundamentally unsound banking practices, perverse incentive structures and moral hazards, and weak regulation and supervision have also been major contributory factors. A myopic concentration on any single cause fails to capture the complex interactions involved in almost all banking and financial crises.

This suggests that the response to avoid future crises also needs to be multidimensional, involving macro policy, the conduct of regulation and supervision, the creation of appropriate incentive structures, the development of market discipline, and the internal governance and management of financial institutions. As a prelude to a consideration of the principles to reduce the probability of future banking fragility, the remainder of this section briefly considers the main components of recent banking crises. While the experience of each country varies in detail, there is a remarkable degree of commonality, including the experience of financial fragility in some developed economies. A discussion of the factors behind the Scandinavian banking crises of the early 1990s is given in Andersson and Viotti (1999) and Benink and Llewellyn (1994).

Reflecting the multidimensional aspect of financial distress, the main causal factors are considered under eight headings: (1) volatility in the macro economy; (2) the inheritance of structural weaknesses in the economy; (3) bad banking practices; (4) hazardous incentive structures and moral hazard within the financial system; (5) ineffective regulation; (6) weak monitoring and supervision by official agencies; (7) the absence of effective market discipline against hazardous bank behaviour due partly to the lack of transparency and the disclosure of relevant information; and (8) structurally unsound corporate governance mechanisms within banks and their borrowing customers.

We find that the recent distress of banks in South East Asia is a product of a volatile economy (with strong speculative elements) combined with bad banking practices, weak regulation, ineffective supervision both by official agencies and the market, and hazardous incentive structures. All of this induced excessive lending and risk taking by banks.

**The Macro Economy**

Although growth in the countries of South East Asia had been strong for many years before the onset of recent crises, structural weaknesses in some of the region's economies were also evident. In many cases, exceptionally high investment rates concealed inefficiencies in the allocation of investment funds in the economy. Investment plans were often undertaken without reference to realistic assessment or measurement of expected rates of return. The financial and solvency position of many large investing companies was also seriously overstated by inaccurate accounting procedures.

Many financial crises have been preceded by sharp and speculative rises in real and financial asset prices (see, for instance, the experience of Indonesia, Malaysia, the Philippines and Thailand in Figure 16.1 and Tables 16.1 and 16.2). Such sharp and unsustainable rises in asset prices have a bearing on subsequent financial distress through several channels. As already noted, the main route is through the effect on the demand and supply of bank credit. There is something of an accelerator effect in this: a rise in asset prices produces an increase in the value of collateral, which raises the borrowing capacity of agents and a greater willingness of banks to extend credit. This in turn re-reinforces the rise in asset prices.

Figure 16.1 (charts for Indonesia, Malaysia, Philippines, Thailand showing stock prices, office prices, residential prices from 1988–1998)

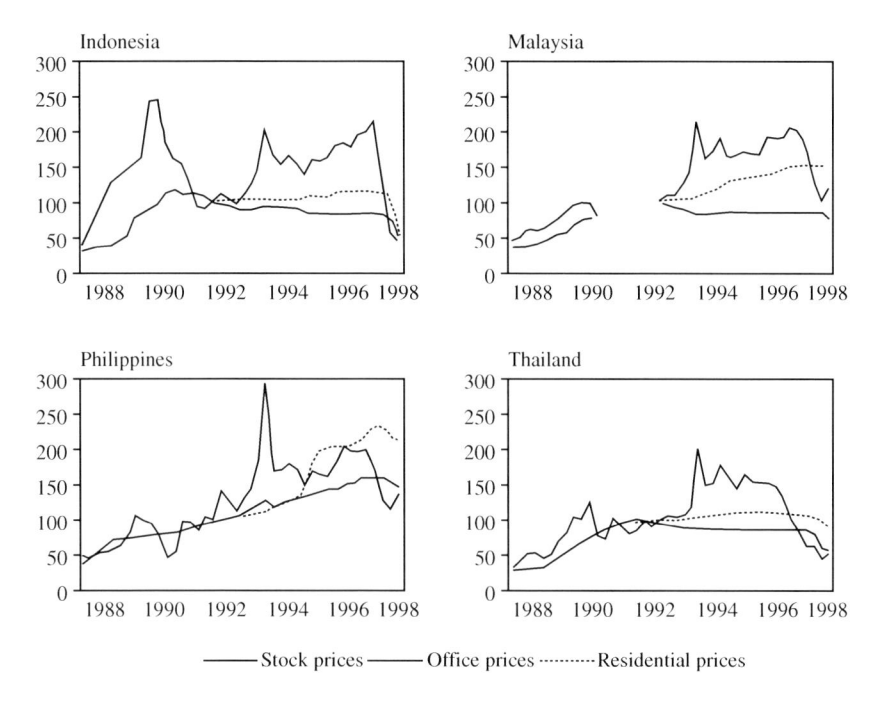

*Note:*
Indices, March 1992 = 100
[1] Real estate and stock prices in local currencies, except for Indonesia, where prices are in US dollars.

*Sources:* International Finance Corporation; and Jones Lang Wootton.

*Figure 16.1 Real estate and stock prices in selected Asian countries[1]*

A key factor in the macroeconomic background to recent banking crises has been the dependence on short-term capital inflows intermediated via the banking system. Table 16.3 shows the pattern of private capital flows to Asian countries over the 1990s and the dependence of the crisis countries (Indonesia, Korea, Malaysia, the Philippines and Thailand) on volatile banking flows (the dominant component of the 'other' category in Table 16.3). The vulnerability to such volatile flows is shown in the $73 billion turnaround in 1997 with a net inflow of $41 billion in 1996 followed by a $32 billion net outflow in the following year. A substantial proportion of the short-term capital inflow was intermediated by domestic banks incurring short-term liabilities against foreign banks. The vulnerability of the crisis countries to an external illiquidity problem became substantial, and

*Table 16.1    Stock market prices index*

|  | 1990 | 1991 | 1992 | 1993 | 1994 | 1995 | 1996 | 1997 |
|---|---|---|---|---|---|---|---|---|
| Korea | 696.00 | 610.00 | 678.00 | 866.00 | 1027.00 | 882.00 | 651.00 | 376.00 |
| Indonesia | 417.00 | 247.00 | 274.00 | 588.00 | 469.00 | 513.00 | 637.00 | 401.00 |
| Malaysia | 505.00 | 556.00 | 643.00 | 1275.00 | 971.00 | 995.00 | 1237.00 | 594.00 |
| Philippines | 651.00 | 1151.00 | 1256.00 | 3196.00 | 2785.00 | 2594.00 | 3170.00 | 1869.00 |
| Singapore | 1154.00 | 1490.00 | 1524.00 | 2425.00 | 2239.00 | 2266.00 | 2216.00 | 1529.00 |
| Thailand | 612.00 | 711.00 | 893.00 | 1682.00 | 1360.00 | 1280.00 | 831.00 | 372.00 |
| Hong Kong | 3024.00 | 4297.00 | 5512.00 | 11888.00 | 8191.00 | 10073.00 | 13451.00 | 10722.00 |
| Taiwan | 4350.00 | 4600.00 | 3377.00 | 6070.00 | 7111.00 | 5158.00 | 6933.00 | 8187.00 |

*Table 16.2    Stock market prices index (property sector)*

|  | 1990 | 1991 | 1992 | 1993 | 1994 | 1995 | 1996 | 1997 |
|---|---|---|---|---|---|---|---|---|
| Indonesia |  | 119.00 | 66.00 | 214.00 | 140.00 | 112.00 | 143.00 | 40.00 |
| Malaysia | 113.00 | 113.00 | 126.00 | 369.00 | 240.00 | 199.00 | 294.00 | 64.00 |
| Philippines | 32.00 | 34.00 | 39.00 | 81.00 | 80.00 | 87.00 | 119.00 | 59.00 |
| Singapore | 230.00 | 280.00 | 250.00 | 541.00 | 548.00 | 614.00 | 648.00 | 357.00 |
| Thailand | 74.00 | 82.00 | 168.00 | 367.00 | 232.00 | 192.00 | 99.00 | 7.00 |
| Hong Kong | 312.00 | 453.00 | 554.00 | 1392.00 | 862.00 | 1070.00 | 1682.00 | 941.00 |
| Taiwan | 61.00 | 71.00 | 57.00 | 137.00 | 109.00 | 59.00 | 55.00 | 55.00 |

this was a pattern evident in crises faced by several other countries (see Cole and Kehoe, 1996 and Sachs et al., 1996). In this context one interpretation of the origin of the crises is that they were precipitated by a change of view by international investors about the economic prospects of the region, (for example, Corbett et al., 1999). The issue is discussed in more detail in Corsetti et al. (1998).

Overall, strong economic growth was, at least at the margin, intermediated by domestic banks incurring foreign currency liabilities to foreign banks on the basis of short-term interbank loans. Strategies based on funding high interest rate loans in domestic currency through low interest rate foreign currency deposits created a substantial interest rate and exchange rate exposure for banks.

### The Inheritance

Many of the crisis countries had a long tradition of intrusive government involvement and ownership in the banking system and elsewhere in the

Table 16.3 Private capital flows to Asian countries

| | 1990 | 1991 | 1992 | 1993 | 1994 | 1995 | 1996 | 1997 |
|---|---|---|---|---|---|---|---|---|
| Asia | | | | | | | | |
| Total net private capital inflows | 19.1 | 35.8 | 21.7 | 57.6 | 66.2 | 95.8 | 110.4 | 13.9 |
| Net foreign direct investment[1] | 8.9 | 14.5 | 16.5 | 35.9 | 46.8 | 49.5 | 57.0 | 57.8 |
| Net portfolio investment | −1.4 | 1.8 | 9.3 | 21.6 | 9.5 | 10.5 | 13.4 | −8.6 |
| Other | 11.6 | 19.5 | −4.1 | 0.1 | 9.9 | 35.8 | 39.9 | −35.4 |
| Net external borrowing from official creditors | 5.6 | 11.0 | 10.3 | 8.7 | 5.9 | 4.5 | 8.8 | 28.6 |
| Affected countries' net private capital inflows[2] | 24.9 | 29.0 | 30.3 | 32.6 | 35.1 | 62.9 | 72.9 | −11.0 |
| Net foreign direct investment[1] | 6.2 | 7.2 | 8.6 | 8.6 | 7.4 | 9.5 | 12.0 | 9.6 |
| Net portfolio investment | 1.3 | 3.3 | 6.3 | 17.9 | 10.6 | 14.4 | 20.3 | 11.8 |
| Other | 17.4 | 18.5 | 15.4 | 6.1 | 17.1 | 39.0 | 40.6 | −32.3 |
| Affected countries' net external borrowing from official creditors | 0.3 | 4.4 | 2.0 | 0.8 | 0.7 | 1.0 | 4.6 | 25.6 |

Notes:
[1] Net foreign direct investment plus net portfolio investment plus net other investment.
[2] Indonesia, Korea, Malaysia, the Philippines, and Thailand.

Sources: International Monetary Fund, *International Financial Statistics* and *World Economic Outlook* database.

economy. This frequently meant that funds were channelled to ailing industries under overt or covert political pressure. Bisignano (1998) argues that such selective credit allocation was a factor retarding the development of effective risk analysis and management systems in banks. In many South East Asian countries directed lending in the pre-liberalization phase often carried explicit or implicit guarantees (see Corbett et al., 1999; Stiglitz, 1999; Rodrik, 1999). In effect, banks have not always acted as market-orientated financial intermediaries but as a channel for the public policy support of industries that would not have received the scale of support through market mechanisms. In addition, the close connections between banks and industrial corporations, and the general influence of government in the economy and the support of certain industries, created a climate in which neither borrowers nor banks would be allowed to fail. This in turn aggravated a tendency towards imprudent lending. These issues are discussed further in Martinez (1998).

This is not a problem restricted to the less-developed countries of South East Asia. With respect to Japan, Suzuki (1986) has argued that heavy involvement of government in the financial intermediation process carries three potential hazards: capital may be allocated inefficiently and on non-market criteria, it may undermine the effectiveness of monetary policy, and it may undermine fiscal discipline.

The 'inheritance problem' also included weak corporate structures with powerful links between companies in a way that enabled them to avoid normal market discipline on corporate behaviour. This in turn was often aggravated by weak corporate governance arrangements, and the non-feasibility for the market in corporate control to operate. Both of these weaknesses muted normal market disciplines.

Before financial liberalization was instigated, many of the crisis countries operated on the basis of fairly rigid public control and/or direction. Some of the subsequent problems emanated from losses (which were often concealed) incurred during the previously repressed financial regime. It is also evident that the true financial condition of many banks had been concealed in the pre-liberalization period through weak loan classification standards and an expectation that banks would be supported in the event of difficulty. In many Latin American countries, accounting standards were lax, to an extent that banks were reporting positive net income even during a banking crisis (Rojas-Suarez and Weisbrod, 1995). Such questionable accounting practices are not exclusive to developing countries (Kim and Cross, 1995). In some cases, banks seem to have been able to determine loan-loss provisions on the basis of managing the level of declared capital rather than to reflect the true quality of loans (Beatty et al., 1993).

## Bad Banking Practices

Several elements of 'bad banking' which were concealed during the optimism generated during the previous period of rapid economic growth also played a central role in the emergence of financial fragility and the subsequent failure of banks. Common examples of 'bad banking' include:

- Banks operating on the basis of low capital ratios which were sometimes below minimum capital adequacy standards set by the regulatory authorities, and which were not addressed by the regulators.
- Substantial foreign currency exposures incurred because foreign currency borrowing appeared to be cheap, because the alleged commitment to a fixed exchange rate was not questioned, and because of the general expectation of 'bail-outs' in the event of difficulty.
- Rapid growth in bank lending in a short period. As already noted, a common feature of bank crises (including in advanced economies) is that they are preceded by a period of rapid growth in bank lending. This is indicated for the crisis countries of South East Asia in Tables 16.4 and 16.5, which show the high rates of growth in lending to the private sector. Rapid growth of bank lending is not in itself hazardous. However, periods of rapid growth frequently conceal emerging problems: it is more difficult to distinguish good from bad loans (Hausmann and Gavin, 1998); it often involves banks lending in areas with which they are not familiar; herding behaviour develops; credit standards are weakened in a phase of euphoria, and some lending is based on speculative rises in asset prices. This has also been noted in the Scandinavia banking crises of the early 1990s (Benink and Llewellyn, 1994).

*Table 16.4   Bank lending to private sector (% growth)*

|  | 1991 | 1992 | 1993 | 1994 | 1995 | 1996 | 1997 |
|---|---|---|---|---|---|---|---|
| Korea | 20.78 | 12.55 | 12.94 | 20.08 | 15.45 | 20.01 | 21.95 |
| Indonesia | 17.82 | 12.29 | 25.48 | 22.97 | 22.57 | 21.45 | 46.42 |
| Malaysia | 20.58 | 10.79 | 10.80 | 16.04 | 30.65 | 25.77 | 26.96 |
| Philippines | 7.33 | 24.66 | 40.74 | 26.52 | 45.39 | 48.72 | 28.79 |
| Singapore | 12.41 | 9.77 | 15.15 | 15.25 | 20.26 | 15.82 | 12.68 |
| Thailand | 20.45 | 20.52 | 24.03 | 30.26 | 23.76 | 14.63 | 19.80 |
| Hong Kong |  | 10.17 | 20.15 | 19.94 | 10.99 | 15.75 | 20.10 |
| China | 19.76 | 20.84 | 43.52 | 24.58 | 24.23 | 24.68 | 20.96 |
| Taiwan | 21.25 | 28.70 | 19.46 | 16.18 | 10.00 | 6.00 | 8.92 |

Table 16.5  Bank lending to private sector (% of GDP)

|             | 1990   | 1991   | 1992   | 1993   | 1994   | 1995   | 1996   | 1997   |
|-------------|--------|--------|--------|--------|--------|--------|--------|--------|
| Korea       | 52.54  | 52.81  | 53.34  | 54.21  | 56.84  | 57.04  | 61.81  | 69.79  |
| Indonesia   | 49.67  | 50.32  | 49.45  | 48.90  | 51.88  | 53.48  | 55.42  | 69.23  |
| Malaysia    | 71.36  | 75.29  | 74.72  | 74.06  | 74.61  | 84.80  | 93.39  | 106.91 |
| Philippines | 19.17  | 17.76  | 20.44  | 26.37  | 29.06  | 37.52  | 48.98  | 56.53  |
| Singapore   | 82.20  | 83.34  | 85.06  | 84.14  | 84.21  | 90.75  | 95.96  | 100.29 |
| Thailand    | 64.30  | 67.70  | 72.24  | 80.01  | 91.00  | 97.62  | 101.94 | 116.33 |
| Hong Kong   |        | 141.84 | 134.20 | 140.02 | 149.00 | 155.24 | 162.36 | 174.24 |
| China       | 85.51  | 87.87  | 86.17  | 95.49  | 87.12  | 85.83  | 91.65  | 101.07 |
| Taiwan      | 100.41 | 108.99 | 126.43 | 137.23 | 146.89 | 149.49 | 146.05 | 146.23 |

- Weak risk analysis, management and control systems within banks.
- Concentrated loan portfolios often with a substantial exposure to property and real estate, either directly in the form of loans, or indirectly through the collateral offered by borrowers. The exposure to property of seven countries of South East Asia is given in Table 16.6.

Table 16.6  Banking system exposure to property

|             | Property exposure | Collateral valuation |
|-------------|-------------------|----------------------|
| Korea       | 15–25%            | 80–100%              |
| Indonesia   | 25–30%            | 80–100%              |
| Malaysia    | 30–40%            | 80–100%              |
| Philippines | 15–20%            | 70–80%               |
| Singapore   | 30–40%            | 70–80%               |
| Thailand    | 30–40%            | 80–100%              |
| Hong Kong   | 40–55%            | 50–70%               |

Source: J.P. Morgan 'Asian Financial Markets', January 1998.

- Bank lending on the basis of an unsustainable rise in asset prices.
- Substantial connected lending by banks to companies within the same group and on the basis of poor (or non-existent) risk assessment and non-market criteria.
- The failure to incorporate risk premia in interest rates on loans. The Bank for International Settlements (BIS) has noted that in many crisis countries the lending margin was low (and was declining during the period of rapid growth), which indicates that insufficient risk premia were being charged (BIS, 1998).

- Inaccurate accounting standards and weak loan classification and provisioning, which had the effect of overstating the value of bank loans and hence the true capital position of banks.

An interesting perspective on the effect of excessive bank lending is given by an International Monetary Fund (IMF) team (Adams et al.,1998). The growth of lending was substantially in excess of the growth of GDP in the distress countries of South East Asia (Figure 16.2). This produced high leverage ratios (ratio of credit to the private sector relative to GDP). The study notes that in many of the countries where bank distress was most marked (Korea, Malaysia and Thailand) loan leverage ratios rose to levels that were higher than those in industrial countries with more developed financial

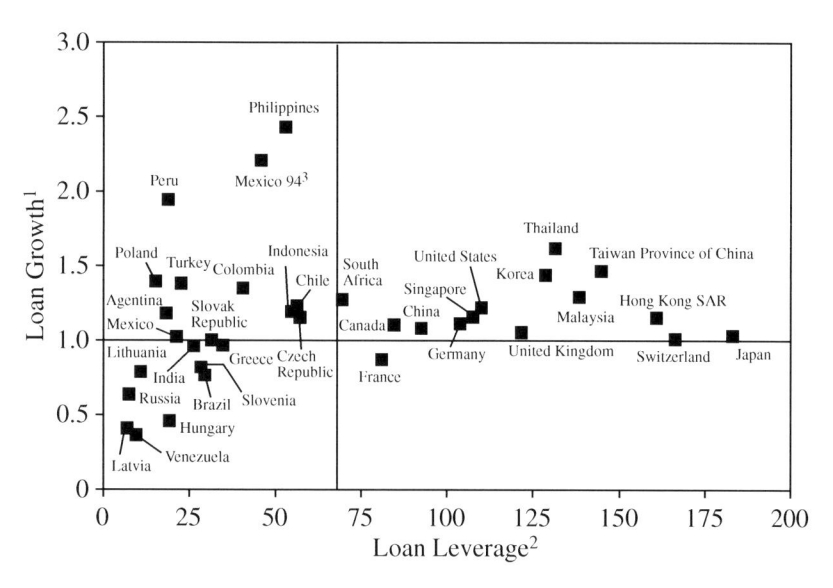

*Notes:*
Loan growth of the following countries and regions started in different years: Hong Kong SAR, Poland, and Slovenia (1991); Malaysia (1992); and Russia, the Czech Republic, Latvia, Lithuania, and the Slovak Republic (1993).
[1] Loan growth is the ratio of growth in loans to private sector (bank and non-bank) versus nominal GDP growth from year-end 1990 to year-end 1996.
[2] Loan leverage is defined as the ratio of loans to private sector versus nominal GDP as of year-end 1996.
[3] Loan growth from 1990–94 and loan leverage is as of year-end 1994.

*Sources:* International Monetary Fund, *International Financial Statistics*, and *World Economic Outlook*.

*Figure 16.2 Financial sector lending: growth and leverage, 1990–96*

infrastructures (Figure 16.2). Several studies (for example, Demirguc-Kunt and Detragiache, 1998; Kaminsky and Reinhart, 1998; Benink and Llewellyn, 1994) show that rapid credit growth and high and sharply rising leverage are significant factors in banking crises in both developing and developed countries.

The authors of the IMF study suggest that, with respect to Figure 16.2, countries in the early stages of economic development are normally in the north-west quadrant (high loan growth with low leverage) but as they advance in their development they are expected to converge to the border between the south-east and north-east quadrants. The figure shows, however, that Korea, Thailand and Malaysia each had both high growth rates of bank lending and high leverage ratios. A somewhat different picture emerges for the Philippines (very high growth rate of bank lending but comparatively low leverage ratio) and Indonesia, with a modest growth rate of bank lending and a modest leverage ratio.

**Incentive Structures and Moral Hazard**

A maintained theme of this chapter is that incentive structures and moral hazards faced by decision makers (bank owners and managers, lenders to banks, borrowers and central banks) are major components of the regulatory regime. This means that the regulator needs to consider the impact its own rules have on regulated firms' incentive structures, whether they might have perverse effects, and what regulation can do to improve incentives. Incentive structures are at the centre of all aspects of regulation in that if they are perverse it is unlikely that other mechanisms in the regime will achieve the desired objectives. Regulatory strategy needs not only to consider how the various components of the regime impact directly on the objectives, but also how they operate indirectly through their impact on the incentives of regulated firms and others. Some analysts ascribe recent banking crises in part to various moral hazards and perverse incentive structures such as fixed exchange rate regimes, anticipated lender-of-last-resort actions, what have been viewed as bail-outs by the IMF, and safety-net arrangements.

Schinasi et al. (1999) argue that banks have complex incentive structures, including internal incentive structures (that is, incentives that motivate key decision makers involved with risk), corporate governance mechanisms (such as accountability to shareholders), the external market in corporate control, market disciplines which may affect the cost of capital and deposits, and accountability to bank supervisors. The presence of regulation and official supervision adds a particular dimension to the structure of incentives faced by decision makers. The key is to align incentives of the various stakeholders in the decision-making process: between the objectives set by regulators and supervisors (systemic stability and consumer protection) and those of the bank; between the overall business objectives of the bank and those of actual decision makers in the management structure, and between managers and owners of banks. Conflicts can arise at each level, which complicates incentive structures. A central role of regulation is to create incentives for managers and shareholders to behave in a way consistent with the objectives that are set for regulation when these may not always be in the immediate interests of either managers or owners of banks.

Several potential adverse incentive structures can be identified in many of the countries that have recently experienced distressed banking systems:

- The expectation that the government's commitment to the exchange value of the domestic currency was absolute may have induced imprudent and unhedged foreign currency borrowing both by banks and companies.
- Expectations of bail-outs or support for industrial companies (which had at various times been in receipt of government support) meant that the bankruptcy threat was weak.
- A belief in the role of the lender of last resort and expectations that banks would not be allowed to fail. The IMF notes that the perception of implicit guarantees was probably strengthened by the bail-outs in the resolution of earlier banking crises in Thailand (1983–87), Malaysia (1985–88) and Indonesia (1994).
- Close relationships between banks, the government, other official agencies and industrial corporations often meant that relationships (for example, lending) that would normally be conducted at arm's length became intertwined in a complex structure of economic and financial linkages within sometimes opaque corporate structures. This also meant that corporate governance arrangements, both within banks and with their borrowing customers, were often weak and ill defined.

It has frequently been argued (for example, Drage and Mann, 1999) that in the recent case of South East Asia, the expectation and actual injection of funds by the IMF and the World Bank (which in effect replaced private finance) effectively bailed out investors and, by shielding them from the full losses of their actions, may have the effect of encouraging imprudent capital inflows and bank lending in the future. It has also been claimed that the aftermath of the Mexico crisis sent a signal to investors that they are less likely to sustain losses by investing in short-term securities.

However, this view has been challenged on the grounds that, in the case of South East Asia, investors did in fact lose value, and that governments are reluctant to resort to IMF facilities because of the resultant conditionality that is applied (Brealey, 1999). It is relevant in this regard that in the years before the crisis, the countries of this region had grown at a faster rate, and for longer, than any countries in history. There were, therefore, powerful economic reasons for capital inflows irrespective of any expectation of bail-outs in the event of sovereign problems. International fund managers were also motivated by a desire to develop globally diversified portfolios including assets in fast-growing regions. In addition, a substantial proportion of the inflows were in forms that could not expect any rescue. Overall, the idea that capital inflows were motivated largely by the expectation of a bail-out in the event of distress is less than convincing (Adams et al., 1998). While potential moral hazard effects may be exaggerated, this is not to deny the central importance of identifying the incentive structures implicit in regimes, and the potential moral hazards that can arise.

If incentive structures are hazardous, regulation will always face formidable difficulties. There are several dimensions to incentive structures within banks: the extent to which reward structures are based on the volume of business undertaken; the extent to which the risk characteristics of decisions are incorporated into the reward structures; the nature of the internal control systems within banks; internal monitoring of the decision making of loan officers; the nature of profit-sharing schemes and the extent to which decision makers also share in losses, and so on. High staff turnover, and the speed with which officers are moved within the bank, may also create incentives for excessive risk taking. A similar effect can arise through herd behaviour.

It is clear that some incentive structures can lead to dysfunctional behavioural responses (Prendergast, 1993). This may often emerge when incentives within regulated firms relate to volume rather than their risk-adjusted profitability, that is, there is a clear bias towards writing business. Thus, bank managers may be rewarded by the volume of loans made. Many cases of bank distress have been associated with inappropriate incentive structures creating a bias in favour of balance sheet growth, and with moral hazard created by anticipated lender-of-last-resort actions. Dale (1996) suggests that profit-related bonuses were an important feature in the Barings collapse.

One potentially hazardous feature of bank management is the tendency towards herd behaviour. Fink and Haiss (2000) argue that there is often an unwillingness on the part of managers to risk rejection by the 'in-group' within the bank. They also argue that it is necessary to curb herd behaviour by altering the incentive structures faced by various stakeholders.

Some analysts find that, under some circumstances, there can be a negative relationship between risk and return within banks. This may be because banks in distress seek risky projects (Bowman, 1982). According to Prospect Theory, bankers have an asymmetric view of risk taking and risk avoidance. Performance expectations may raise the need or desire to take excessive risk (Kahneman and Tversky, 1979).

There is a particular issue with respect to the incentive structure of state-owned, or state-controlled, banks as their incentives may be ill defined, if not hazardous. Such banks are not subject to the normal disciplining pressures of the market, their 'owners' do not monitor their behaviour, and there is no disciplining effect from the market in corporate control. Political interference in such banks, and the unwitting encouragement of 'bad banking' practices, can itself become a powerful ingredient in bank distress. Lindgren et al. (1996) found, for instance, that banks that are, or were recently, state owned or controlled were a factor in most of the instances of unsound banking in their sample of crises.

**Ineffective Regulation**

In all crisis countries, banks have been regulated and supervised and, in principle, most countries nominally adopted standard international norms of regulation. However, the adoption of such standards was often weak and uncertain. There are many elements of weak regulation in the origin of banking crises in recent years which aggravated the effect of other dimensions of distress:

- Capital adequacy regulations were often either not fully in place or were not effectively enforced.
- Regulatory requirements for capital, while nominally conforming to the letter of international agreements, were nevertheless set too low in relation to the nature of the risks in the economy and the risks being incurred by banks. Capital adequacy regulation often did not accurately reflect banks' risk characteristics (BIS, 1998).
- Rules with respect to classification of loan quality and provisions were often too lenient and ill specified, with the result that provisions were insufficient to cover expected losses, and earnings and capital were overstated (Brownbridge and Kirkpatrick, 2000; Folkerts-Landau et al., 1995).
- Rules with respect to exposure to single borrowers were often too lax (or not enforced).
- Regulation and supervision with respect to concentrated exposures (for example, property) were often too lenient.
- Poor accounting standards enabled banks to evade prudential and other restrictions on insider lending (Rahman, 1998).

- Many governments and regulatory authorities were slow and hesitant to act in the face of impending solvency problems of banks. Such regulatory forbearance was often due to regulatory authorities having substantial discretion as to when and whether to intervene, and often being subject to political pressure of one kind or another.

**Weak Monitoring and Supervision**

As with all companies, banks need to be monitored. In addition to the standard principal–agent issues, banks are universally monitored and supervised by official agencies (for example, central banks). In practice, 'some form of supervisory failure was a factor in almost all the sample countries' (Lindgren et al., 1996, p. 52). In many countries supervisory agencies did not enforce compliance with regulations (Reisen, 1998). In Korea and Indonesia in particular, banks did not comply with regulatory capital adequacy requirements or other regulations (UNCTAD, 1998). Moreover, connected lending restrictions were not adequately supervised partly because of political pressure and the lack of transparency in the accounts of banks and their corporate customers.

There has often been a lack of political will on the part of supervisory agencies to exercise strong supervision. This may be associated with adverse incentive structures faced by politicians and others who may gain from imprudent banking (Fink and Haiss, 2000). While prudent banking is a public good, hazardous behaviour can be beneficial to some stakeholders. Others have noted the lack of political will to exercise strong supervision in the transitional economies of Eastern Europe (Baer and Gray, 1996).

A further dimension to supervisory failure has been that supervisory intensity has often not been adjusted in line with liberalization in financial systems and the new business operations and risk characteristics of banks that emerged in a more deregulated market environment. This is discussed in more detail in the next section. This was also the case with Scandinavian countries when, in the second half the 1980s, banks responded aggressively to deregulation. The nature and intensity of official supervision needs to reflect the nature of the regulatory environment. In practice, while the latter changed, this was often not accompanied by sufficiently intensified supervision.

**Weak Market Discipline on Banks**

Monitoring is not only conducted by official agencies whose specialist task it is. In well-developed financial regimes, the market also monitors the behaviour of financial firms. The disciplines imposed by the market can be as powerful as any sanctions imposed by official agencies. However, in practice, the disciplining role of markets (including the interbank market, which is able to impose powerful discipline through the risk premia charged on interbank loans) was weak in the crisis countries of South East Asia. This was due predominantly to the lack of disclosure and transparency of banks and the fact that little reliance could be placed on the quality of accountancy data provided in bank accounts. In many cases standard accounting and auditing procedures were not rigorously applied, and in some cases there was wilful misrepresentation of the financial position of banks and non-financial companies. Market disciplines can work effectively only on the basis of full and accurate disclosure and transparency.

A further dimension relates to the potentially powerfully disciplining power of the market in corporate control which, through the threat of removing control from incumbent managements, is a discipline on managers to be efficient and not endanger the solvency of their banks. As put in a recent IMF study: 'An open and competitive banking market exerts its own form of discipline against weak banks while encouraging well-managed banks' (Lindgren et al., 1996, p. 60).

**Unsound Corporate Governance Arrangements**

In the final analysis, all aspects of the management of a bank are corporate governance issues. This means that if banks behave hazardously this is, to some extent, a symptom of weak internal corporate governance. This may include, for instance, hazardous corporate structures of banks' lack of internal control systems, weak surveillance by (especially non-executive) directors, and ineffective internal audit arrangements. Corporate governance arrangements were evidently weak and underdeveloped in banks in many of the distressed countries. Moral hazard can be created through lack of owner accountability and weak accountability of regulatory agencies (Krugman, 1998).

Some bank ownership structures tend to produce ineffective corporate governance. In some cases, particular corporate structures (for example, banks being part of larger conglomerates) encourage connected lending and weak risk analysis of borrowers. This was found to be the case in a significant number of bank failures in the countries of South East Asia and Latin America. Some corporate structures also make it comparatively easy for banks to effectively conceal losses and unsound financial positions.

**Assessment**

The central theme of this section has been that recent banking crises have been multidimensional and a complex mix of several interacting pressures and weaknesses. A myopic focus on particular causal components is likely to produce a distorted picture and also to produce inadequate policy and reform proposals. The experience of many countries has demonstrated the lethal cocktail of fundamental and structural weaknesses in the economy, hazardous incentive structures, weak and ineffective regulation, inadequate official supervision, and an inability or unwillingness of the market to impose discipline on banks. It follows that reform needs to proceed along several channels simultaneously, which in itself makes the reform process more demanding and challenging. We return to this issue in Section 6.

## 5 LIBERALIZATION: STOCK ADJUSTMENT VERSUS STEADY STATE

Many financial crises have been associated with changes in the regulatory regime and a process of liberalization. For decades, the economies of South East Asia were highly regulated with interest rate ceilings, limitations on lending growth by financial institutions, restrictions on foreign entry into the banking system and so on. At various times during the 1990s, these restrictions were relaxed, and the pace of financial liberalization accelerated.

Williamson and Mahar (1998) show that almost all of their sample of 34 economies (both industrialized and developing) that undertook financial liberalization over the 1980s and 1990s experienced varying degrees of financial crisis. Similarly, Kaminsky and Reinhart (1998) found that in the majority of cases in their sample of countries that had experienced banking crises, the financial sector had been liberalized during the previous five years. They conclude that financial liberalization helps predict banking crises across a range of countries. Goldstein and Folkerts-Landau (1993) observe a general pattern of deregulation inducing more competition being followed by increasing financial fragility.

Demirguc-Kunt and Detragiache (1998) find that financial liberalization increases the probability of a banking crisis. However, they also find that the probability is reduced the stronger are the institutional preconditions for liberalization and market discipline in terms of contract enforcement, lack of corruption, bureaucratic interference in lending decisions and so on. This reinforces the established wisdom that liberalization involves a significant change in the market environment and that, for the new regime to be stable and efficient, certain basic prerequisites of a well-functioning market system need to be in place. The key is that institutional structures and mechanisms need to be consistent with the prevailing market regime. Problems arise when a change to the market regime is made without there also being corresponding changes in institutional mechanisms.

While in both developed and less-developed countries banking distress has often followed periods of deregulation and liberalization, a distinction needs to be made between the *transitional* effect of moving from one regulatory regime to another, and the characteristics of a *steady-state* liberalized financial system. The instabilities that may occur in the transition period do not necessarily carry over into the new steady state.

**The Transitional Phase**

The universal evidence is that financial liberalization enhances efficiency in the financial system, and that financial repression distorts the incentives for saving and investment. However, financial liberalization often creates instability, most especially in the transition period:

- One effect of increased competition that results from liberalization is an erosion of the economic rents enjoyed by financial firms associated with the previously uncompetitive environment. The subsequent lower profitability may induce financial institutions into taking more risk.
- As discussed earlier, and noted by Corbett et al. (1999, p. 201), 'A key mistake, which led to the vulnerability of the financial system, appears to be that the old-style financial system continued into the new era of liberalization.' This often included the continuation of old-style guarantees which are described in detail in Krugman (1999).
- In the stock-adjustment phase (that is, during the period when the new regime is being introduced) uncertainty is created as financial firms are unfamiliar with the characteristics and management requirements of the new regime. Previously protected institutions need to adapt behaviour though this may occur only with a considerable time lag. New behaviour patterns need to be learned. Some mistakes during the process of financial liberalization occur because banks do not adjust quickly enough to the new regime. Behaviour which is appropriate under one regime may be totally inappropriate in another (see Benink and Llewellyn, 1994 for a more formal discussion).
- In the first instance, liberalization may increase inflationary pressure as banks' balance sheet restraints are lifted and financial firms increase their lending rapidly in a relatively short period. This is often associated with a sharp rise in asset prices. The implication is that financial liberalization needs to be accompanied by an appropriate stabilization policy to reduce the potential impact on inflation, which can distort lending decisions.

- In many countries that liberalized their financial systems after decades of controls, banks responded in a remarkably similar way by substantially increasing the volume of lending in a short period. As a result of increased competitive pressures, banks lowered *equilibrium* and *disequilibrium* credit rationing and risk thresholds (Llewellyn and Holmes, 1991); bank lending margins were squeezed, and bank profitability at first rose due to this expansion, but later deteriorated sharply due to massive loan losses.
- The rapid growth in lending during the stock-adjustment phase also increased risks because banks' internal control systems that were weak in the previous regime were carried forward into the new environment. This was compounded when banks adopted market-share strategies in a strongly expanding loans market.
- In general, periods of substantial growth of bank lending are likely to involve banks moving into more risky business and adopting a higher risk profile (OECD, 1992). The removal of controls often unleashes a pent-up demand for credit, and suppliers of credit are freed to compete, which in some cases leads to a relaxation of standards (see also Schinasi and Hargreaves, 1993).
- The same competitive pressures may also make it difficult, in the short run, for banks to incorporate higher risk premia in loan rates, with the result that bank loans are underpriced.
- The initial stock-adjustment reaction often involves a phase of overreaction by lenders as balance sheet structures are taken beyond long-run sustainable positions. There are several reasons for this: reaction times in financial markets are short, adjustments can be made quickly, and financial systems are often characterized by oligopolistic competition. As a result, competitive pressures induce firms to move together: the 'herd instinct'. Some analysts ascribe this to a property of the incentive structure within banks in that, in a world of uncertainty, the desire to avoid personal blame for mismanagement is liable to make risk-averse managers subject to peer-group pressure to follow the same strategy.
- Liberalization may also reveal inherent weaknesses in the banking system with respect both to structure and the traditional way of conducting business.
- In some cases, some basic infrastructure of markets had not been created ahead of liberalization: a strong legal framework to ensure that property rights are well defined and easily exercisable; a legal framework for the pledging of collateral and the ability to take possession of collateral, and clearly defined bankruptcy laws and codes along with enforcement mechanisms.

- If supervision is not intensified in line with liberalization, the financial system is more likely to become crisis prone. When liberalizing their financial systems, the countries of South East Asia ignored the risks posed by rapid liberalization when it is not accompanied by significant strengthening of regulation and supervision of bank behaviour (Furman and Stiglitz, 1998). In this, they followed the earlier experience of the Scandinavian countries. Bisignano (1998) suggests that this experience represents a combination of 'excess momentum' by the private sector and 'excess inertia' by the regulatory authorities. Put another way, there is a trade-off between regulation and supervision in that if regulation is eased to allow banks to conduct more business, there is an increased requirement for effective supervision of the way that business is conducted. The IMF has argued thus: 'bank supervision may need to be restructured before financial market liberalization to cope with the new challenges and risks liberalization entails' (IMF, 1993, p. 8).

These are essentially (though not exclusively) problems of transition. A distinction is made between what happens during a *stock-adjustment* phase of liberalization, and the characteristics of a *steady-state*, deregulated financial system. Although the evidence indicates that a liberalized financial system is more efficient and contributes more substantially to economic development, when moving from one regime to another (especially from a highly controlled financial system to a more market-orientated system) instability may be created as new behaviour patterns need to be learned. The fact that instability may occur during the transitional, stock-adjustment period does not necessarily mean that a deregulated financial system is inherently unstable, or even less stable than a regulated regime. Many of the financial crises experienced in recent years have been associated with the uncertainties and mistakes during the *transitional* phase during which liberalization measures were adopted. Crises have often been a function of uncertainty associated with regime changes (as the system moves from one regime to another) rather than the inherent characteristics of the new regime *per se*.

The policy implication is that care is needed in the process of liberalization, and that supervision of financial institutions needs to move in pace with liberalization. Deregulation without enhanced supervision is likely to be hazardous irrespective of the long-run benefits of liberalization and the erosion of financial repression. Liberalization has often not been accompanied by necessary changes in regulation and supervision, corporate governance reforms, and enhanced market monitoring and control.

## The Steady State

However, while some of the financial distress is associated with the transition from one regime to another, it may also be the case that a more competitive market environment tends to be more risky. This is because the value of the banking franchise is reduced by competition. Keeley (1990), for example, analyses how deregulation and increased competition can induce banks to behave with less regard to risk because they lower the value of the banking franchise. The higher is the expected future value of the banking franchise, the more owners and managers have to lose through excessive risk taking, which raises the probability of the bank failing. An IMF study (Goldstein and Folkerts-Landau, 1993) suggests that risks in banking increased over the 1980s due to a combination of increased competition and the existence of safety nets. Similar conclusions are found in Caprio and Summers (1993), and Demsetz et al. (1997). Using data to proxy bank franchise values, Hellman et al. (1995) examine the relationship between bank franchise values and financial market liberalization as a test of the argument that moral hazard increases as banks' franchise values fall. Their results confirm that banking crises are more likely to occur in countries with a liberalized financial sector, and that franchise values tend to be lower when financial markets are liberalized. Shafer (1987) suggests that deregulation is likely to create financial markets with a permanently greater tendency to instability.

In many cases, previous, highly regulated, regimes acted as a protection to financial institutions by effectively limiting competition. The extent of the economic rents that were created was probably underestimated by the regulatory authorities. In many cases the extent to which deregulation and liberalization would increase competition in the banking industry was underestimated even though that was one of the public policy objectives. These errors inhibited appropriate responses in the areas of prudential regulation and monitoring and supervision.

The potential conflict and trade-off between stability and efficiency is highlighted by Sijben (1999) where efficiency considerations require deregulation and liberalization in financial systems, though by enhancing competition this may compromise the objective of stability. Hellweg (1995) suggests that the low rate of bank failures in Switzerland between the late 1930s and the 1970s was due, in part, to the absence of disintermediation threat and the generally weak climate of competition in the Swiss banking system. The resultant high margins in banking enhanced franchise values and also enabled capital to be quickly replenished following write-downs due to loan write-offs. In the Hellweg analysis, increased competition in the banking industry produces higher levels of risk in banks because it creates incentives for higher risk taking.

## 6 THE REGULATORY REGIME

Having discussed some of the common origins of banking distress, we turn to consider a set of principles to reduce the future probability of crises. Emphasis has been given to inadequate regulation and supervision of banks. In the final analysis, regulation is about changing the behaviour of regulated institutions. A key issue is the extent to which behaviour is to be altered by externally imposed *rules*, or through creating *incentives* for firms to behave in a particular way.

A sustained theme is that a regulatory regime is to be viewed more widely than externally imposed regulation of financial institutions. Regulation is only one of seven key components. Regulation needs to be viewed and analysed not solely in the narrow terms of the rules and edicts of regulatory agencies, but in the wider context of a regulatory regime. This concept has seven components:

- the *rules* established by regulatory agencies (the regulation component);
- *monitoring and supervision* by regulatory agencies;
- the *incentive structures* faced by regulatory agencies, consumers and, most especially, regulated firms;
- the role of *market discipline and monitoring*;
- *intervention arrangements* in the event of compliance failures of one sort or another;
- the role of *corporate governance* arrangements in financial firms; and
- the *disciplining and accountability* arrangements applied to regulatory agencies.

In current conditions, it would be hazardous to rely wholly, or even predominantly, on external regulation, monitoring and supervision by the official sector. The world of banking and finance is too complex and volatile to be able to rely on a simple set of prescriptive rules for prudent behaviour.

The key to optimizing the effectiveness of a regulatory regime is the portfolio mix of the seven core components. All are necessary but none alone is sufficient. Particular emphasis is given to incentive structures because, in the final analysis, if these are perverse or inefficient, no amount of formal regulation will prevent problems emerging in the banking sector.

Regulatory strategy is set in the context of *trade-offs* between the various components. In some circumstances the more emphasis that is given to one of the components (for example, regulation), the less powerful becomes one or more of the others (for example, market discipline on banks), and to an extent that may reduce the overall impact. Thus, while regulation may be viewed as a response to market failures, weak market discipline and inadequate corporate governance arrangements, causation may also operate in the other direction, with regulation weakening these other mechanisms.

Within the regulatory regime trade-offs emerge at two levels. In terms of regulatory strategy, choices have to be made about the balance of the various components and the relative weight to be assigned to each. For instance, a powerful role for official regulation with little weight assigned to market discipline might be chosen, or alternatively a relatively light touch of regulation but with heavy reliance on the other components.

The second form of trade-off relates to how the components of the regime may be causally linked. For instance, the more emphasis that is given to detailed, extensive and prescriptive rules, the weaker might be the role of incentive structures, market discipline and corporate governance arrangements with financial firms. This has been put by Simpson (2000, p. 28) as follows: 'In a market which is heavily regulated for internal standards of integrity, the incentives to fair dealing diminish. Within the company culture, such norms of fair dealing as "the way we do things around here" would eventually be replaced by "It's OK if we can get away with it".' In other words, an excessive reliance on detailed and prescriptive rules may weaken incentive structures and market discipline.

Similarly, an excessive focus on detailed and prescriptive rules may weaken corporate governance mechanisms within financial firms, and may blunt the incentive of others to monitor and control the behaviour of banks. Weakness in corporate governance mechanisms may also be a reflection of banks being monitored, regulated and supervised by official agencies. The way intervention is conducted in the event of bank distress (for example, whether forbearance is practised) may also have adverse incentive effects on the behaviour of banks and the willingness of markets to monitor and control their risk taking.

An empirical study of regulation in the United States by Billett et al. (1998) suggests that some types of regulation may undermine market discipline. They examine the costs of market discipline and regulation and show that, as a bank's risk increases, the cost of uninsured deposits rises and the bank switches to insured deposits. This is because changes in regulatory costs are less sensitive to changes in risk than are market costs. They also show that when rating agencies downgrade a bank, the bank tends to increase its use of insured deposits. The authors conclude: 'The disparate costs of insured deposits and uninsured liabilities, combined with the ability and willingness of banks to alter their exposure to each, challenge the notion that market discipline can be an effective deterrent against excessive risk taking' (p. 14). This type of evidence demonstrates that, under some circumstances, regulatory arrangements can have the effect of blunting market discipline.

The public policy objective is to optimize the outcome of a regulatory strategy in terms of mixing the components of the regime, bearing in mind the possibility of negative trade-offs. However, the optimum mix in a regulatory regime will change over time as financial structures, market conditions and compliance cultures change. For instance, the combination of external regulation and market discipline that is most effective and efficient in one set of market circumstances, and one type of financial structure in a country, may become ill suited if structures change. Also, if the norms and compliance culture of the industry change, it could become appropriate to rely less on detailed and prescriptive regulation, at least for some firms.

Nor does the same approach and mix of components in the regulatory regime need to be the same for all regulated firms. On the contrary, given that banks are not homogeneous in their risk profiles, it would be suboptimal to apply the same approach. A key strategic issue is the extent to which differentiations are to be made between different regulated firms.

Financial systems are changing substantially and to an extent that may undermine traditional approaches to regulation and, most especially, the balance between regulation and official supervision, and the role of market discipline. In particular, globalization, the pace of financial innovation and the creation of new financial instruments, the blurring of traditional distinctions between different types of financial firm, the speed with which portfolios can change through banks trading in derivatives and so on, and the increased complexity of banking business create a fundamentally new – in particular, more competitive – environment in which regulation and supervision are undertaken. They also change the viability of different approaches to regulation which, if it is to be effective, must constantly respond to changes in the market environment in which regulated firms operate.

Having established the general framework of the regulatory regime, the following subsections outline a set of general principles designed to reduce the probability of banking distress. They are focused on each of six of the core components: (i) regulation, (ii) incentive structures, (iii) monitoring and supervision, (iv) official intervention in the event of bank distress, (v) the role of market discipline, and (vi) corporate governance arrangements.

**Regulation**

Four particular issues need to be considered with respect to the regulation part of the regime: the weight to be given to formal and prescriptive rules of behaviour; the type of rules in the regime; the impact that rules may have on the other components of the regulatory regime; and the extent to which regulation and supervision differentiate between different banks.

The first issue concerns *formal and prescriptive rules of behaviour*.

A former US regulator has noted:

> Financial services regulation has traditionally tended towards a style that is command-and-control, dictating precisely what a regulated entity can do and how it should do it . . . generally, they focus on the specific steps needed to accomplish a certain regulatory task and specify with detail the actions to be taken by the regulated firm. (Wallman, 1999, p. 310)

Wallman's experience in the US suggests that the interaction of the interests of the regulator and the regulated may tend towards a high degree of prescription in the regulatory process. Regulators tend to look for standards they can easily monitor and enforce, while the regulated seek standards they can comply with. The result is that regulators seek precision and detail in their requirements, while regulated firms look for certainty and firm guidance on what they are to do. Wallman suggests that: 'The result is specific and detailed guidance, not the kind of pronouncements that reflect fundamental concepts and allow the market to develop on its own' (p. 13).

The arguments against reliance on detailed and prescriptive rules are outlined in Goodhart et al. (1998). Although precise rules have their attractions for both regulators and regulated firms, there are several problems with a highly prescriptive approach to regulation:

- An excessive degree of prescription may bring regulation into disrepute if it is perceived by the industry as being excessive, with many redundant rules.
- Risks are usually too complex to be covered by simple rules.
- Balance sheet rules reflect the position of an institution only at a particular point in time, although its position can change substantially within a short period.
- An inflexible approach based on a detailed rule book has the effect of impeding firms from choosing their own least-cost way of meeting regulatory objectives.
- Detailed and extensive rules may stifle innovation.
- A prescriptive regime tends to focus upon firms' processes rather than outcomes and the ultimate objectives of regulation. The precise rules may become the focus of compliance rather than the objectives they are designed to achieve. In this regard, it can give rise to a perverse culture of 'box ticking' by regulated firms. The letter of regulation may be obeyed but not the spirit or intention.

- A prescriptive approach is inclined towards 'rules escalation' whereby rules are added over time, but few are withdrawn.
- A highly prescriptive approach may create a confrontational relationship between the regulator and regulated firms, or alternatively cause firms to overreact, engaging in excessive efforts at internal compliance out of fear of being challenged by the regulator. In this sense, regulation may in practice become more prescriptive and detailed than originally intended by the regulator.
- Forcing a high degree of conformity on regulated firms causes an information loss. If firms are given leeway in satisfying the regulator's objectives, more may be learned about how different behaviour affects regulatory objectives, and also about the properties of different rules.
- In the interests of 'competitive neutrality', rules may be applied equally to all firms, although firms may be sufficiently heterogeneous to warrant different approaches. Treating as equal firms that in practice are not equal is not competitive neutrality, and a highly prescriptive approach to regulation reduces the scope for legitimate differentiations.
- A highly prescriptive rules approach may in practice prove to be inflexible and insufficiently responsive to market conditions.
- There is a potential moral hazard as firms may assume that, if something is not explicitly covered in regulation, there is no regulatory dimension to the issue.
- Detailed rules may also have perverse effects in that they are regarded as actual standards to be adopted rather than minimum standards, with the result that, in some cases, actual behaviour of regulated firms may be of a lower standard than they would have chosen without the rule. This is most especially the case if each firm assumes that its competitors will adopt the minimum regulatory standard (adverse incentive) or if firms who would adopt a higher standard were to exit the market (adverse selection).

The limitations of a prescriptive rules and rigid formula approach to regulation is highlighted in Estrella (1998), who argues that, while there is a clear role for regulation, what really matters is how the bank behaves and the quality of its risk analysis and management systems rather than whether particular detailed rules are applied within the bank.

A second issue with respect to regulation relates to the *choice about the type of rules*. This may have implications for enforcement as trade-offs are involved. Black (1994) distinguishes different types of rules along three dimensions: *precision* (how much is prescribed and covered in the rule), *simplicity* (the degree to which the rule may be easily applied to concrete situations), and *clarity*. The trade-off is between precision and ease of enforcement, in that the more precise is the rule the easier it is to enforce. On the other hand, the more precise is the rule the less flexibility is created within the overall regime.

A third issue is whether the degree of precision in rules has a *positive or negative impact* on the other components of the regime. For reasons already suggested, precision and detail may have a negative effect on compliance and compliance culture. Conversely, a regime based more on broad principles than detailed and extensive rules has certain advantages: principles are easily understood and remembered; they apply to all behaviour, and they are more likely to have a positive impact on overall compliance culture. It might also be the case (as suggested in Black, 1994) that principles are more likely to become board issues, with the board of financial firms adopting compliance with principles as a high level policy issue, rather than a culture of 'leaving it to the compliance department'. As put by Black, 'it helps chief executives to see the moral wood for the technical trees' (p. 76).

A central issue in regulation for financial stability is the extent to which it *differentiates* between different banks according to their risk characteristics and their risk analysis, management and control systems. Most especially when supervisory resources are scarce, but also in the interests of efficiency in the banking system, supervision should be more detailed and extensive with banks which are considered to be more risky than others. In the UK the Financial Services Authority (FSA) plans to adopt a risk-based approach to supervision.

The objective of 'competitive neutrality' in regulation does not mean that all banks are to be treated in the same way if their risk characteristics are different. With respect to capital adequacy requirements, and reflecting the practice in the UK, Richardson and Stephenson (2000) argue that the FSA (and formerly the Bank of England) treats the requirements of the Basle Accord as minima and requires individual banks to hold more capital than the minima, dependent upon the bank's risk exposure. Capital requirements are set individually for each bank. The authors list the major factors that are taken into account when setting individual banks' capital requirements. These include experience and quality of the bank's management; the bank's risk appetite; the quality of risk analysis, management and control systems; the nature of the markets in which the bank operates; the quality, reliability and volatility of the bank's earnings; the quality of the bank's capital and access to new capital; the degree of diversification; exposure concentrations; the complexity of a bank's legal and organizational structure; the support and control provided by shareholders; and the degree to which a bank is supervised by other jurisdictions. The authors note that:

'these considerations imply that the appropriate margin above the minimum regulatory capital requirements will differ across banks' (p. 51).

Goodhart et al. (1998) argue that, because regulation is not supplied through a market mechanism, the perception is that it is a free good, which means that it is likely to be overdemanded. If this is coupled with risk-averse regulators, there is an inherent danger of overregulation. In this context six main principles for the regulation component of the regime are outlined:

1. *The objectives of regulation need to be clearly defined and circumscribed* Financial regulation should have only a limited number of objectives. In the final analysis the objectives are to sustain systemic stability and to protect the consumer. Regulation should not be overloaded by being required to achieve other and wider objectives, such as social outcomes. Constructing effective and efficient regulation is difficult enough with limited objectives, and the more it is overburdened by wider considerations, the more likely it is to fail in all of them.
2. *The rationale and motivation of regulation and supervision should be limited* The rationale for regulation lies in correcting for identified market imperfections and failures which, in the absence of regulation, produce suboptimal results and reduce consumer welfare: such imperfections include externalities; economies of scale in monitoring; breaking a 'gridlock', and limiting moral hazard associated with safety nets (see Llewellyn, 1999). Regulation in general, and regulatory measures in particular, need to be assessed according to these criteria. In other words, regulation should be limited to correcting identified market imperfections and failures. If they do not satisfy any of these criteria, particular regulatory measures should be abandoned.
3. *Regulation should be viewed in terms of a set of contracts* Laws, regulations, and supervisory actions provide incentives for regulated firms to adjust their actions and behaviour, and to control their own risks internally. They can usefully be viewed as *incentive contracts* within a standard principal–agent relationship where the principal is the regulator and the agent is the regulated firm. Within this general framework, regulation involves a process of creating incentive-compatible contracts so that regulated firms have an incentive to behave in ways consistent with systemic stability and investor protection. If incentive contracts are well designed they will induce appropriate behaviour by regulated firms. Conversely, if they are badly constructed and improperly designed, they might fail to reduce systemic risk (and other hazards regulation is designed to avoid) or have undesirable side-effects on the process of financial intermediation (for example, impose high

cost). At centre stage is the issue of whether all parties have the right incentives to act in a way that satisfies the objectives of regulation.

4. *The form and intensity of regulatory and supervisory requirements should differentiate between regulated institutions according to their relative portfolio risk and efficiency of internal control mechanisms*   While the objective of 'competitive neutrality' in regulation is something of a mantra, this is not satisfied if what in practice are unequal institutions are treated equally. In this respect, 'equality' relates to the risk characteristics of institutions. A hazard of a detailed and prescriptive rulebook approach is that it may fail to make the necessary distinctions between non-homogeneous firms because the same rules are applied to all. In this regard, it reduces the scope for legitimate differentiations to be made.

5. *In some areas the regulator could offer a menu of contracts to regulated firms requiring them to self-select into the correct category*   There is an information, and possibly efficiency, loss if a high degree of conformity in the behaviour of regulated firms is enforced. If, alternatively, firms have a choice about how to satisfy the regulator's stated objectives, they would be able to choose their own, least-cost way of satisfying these objectives. One approach is for regulators to offer a menu of self-selecting contracts rather than the same contract to all institutions. Equally, banks could offer their own contracts. A particular proposal in this regard is the precommitment approach, which gives banks the possibility to preannounce a maximum trading loss and incur regulatory penalties or other incentives in proportion to the extent to which preannounced maximum losses are exceeded (this is discussed below).

6. *Capital regulation should create incentives for the correct pricing of absolute and relative risk*   If differential capital requirements are set against different types of assets (for example, through applying differential risk weights) the rules should be based on actuarial calculations of relative risk. If risk weights are incorrectly specified, perverse incentives are created for banks because the implied regulatory capital requirements are more or less than justified by true relative risk calculations. This in turn distorts the relative and absolute pricing of risks. A major critique of the current Basle capital requirements is that the risk weights bear little relation to relative risk characteristics of different assets, and the loan book carries a uniform risk weight even though the risk characteristics of different loans within a bank's portfolio vary considerably. This is recognized in the BIS discussion document on capital adequacy (Basle Committee, 1999a) which outlines a proposal for a wider range of risk weights attached to bank assets.

## Incentive Structures

A sustained theme is that incentive structures and moral hazard faced by decision makers (bank owners and managers, lenders to banks, borrowers and regulators) are central components of the regulatory regime.

The overall theme is twofold: first, there need to be appropriate internal incentives for management to behave in appropriate ways, and second, the regulator has a role in ensuring internal incentives are compatible with the objectives of regulation. Overall, more understanding is needed about incentive structures within financial firms and whether, for instance, incentive structures align with the objectives of regulation. Research is needed into how regulation impacts positively and negatively on incentives within regulated firms. The possibility that detailed rules may have a negative effect of blunting compliance incentives and other components of the regulatory regime have already been considered.

With respect to internal incentives for owners and management of financial firms, several procedures, processes and structures may reinforce internal risk control mechanisms. These include internal auditors, internal audit committees, procedures for reporting to senior management (and perhaps to supervisors), and making a named board member of financial firms responsible for compliance and risk analysis and management systems. In some countries (for example, New Zealand) incentives faced by bank managers have been strengthened through increased personal liability for bank directors; bank directors are personally liable in cases involving disclosure of incomplete or erroneous information. The FSA in the UK has recently proposed that, under some circumstances, individual directors and senior managers of financial firms should be made personally liable for compliance failures.

Supervisors can also strengthen incentives by, for instance, relating the frequency and intensity of their supervision and inspection visits (and possibly rules) to the perceived adequacy of the internal risk control procedures and internal compliance arrangements. In addition, appropriate incentives can be created by calibrating the external burden of regulation (for example, number of inspection visits, allowable business and so on) to the quality of management and the efficiency of internal incentives.

Evans (2000) suggests several routes through which incentive structures in banks can be improved: greater transparency and information disclosure by financial institutions; subjecting local banks to foreign competition; ensuring a closer alignment of regulatory and economic capital; greater use of risk-based incentives by supervisors; and lower capital adequacy requirements for banks headquartered in jurisdictions which comply with the BIS core principles of supervision.

Deposit insurance has two opposing sets of incentive structures with respect to systemic risk. By reducing the rationality of bank runs (though this is dependent on the extent and coverage of the deposit insurance scheme and the extent of any co-insurance) deposit insurance has the effect of lowering the potential for financial instability. On the other hand, the moral hazard implicit in deposit insurance may increase risk in the system. Given that there is little firm empirical evidence for bank runs in systems without deposit insurance, the second factor probably outweighs the first. This reinforces the case for deposit insurance to be accompanied by regulation to contain risk taking by banks. Reviewing the experience of bank crises in various countries, Demirguc-Kunt and Detragiache (1998, p. 311) argue:

> Our evidence suggests that, in the period under consideration, moral hazard played a significant role in bringing about systemic banking problems, perhaps because countries with deposit insurance schemes were not generally successful at implementing appropriate prudential regulation and supervision, or because the deposit insurance schemes were not properly designed.

Bhattacharya et al. (1998) consider various schemes to attenuate the moral hazard associated with deposit insurance. These include cash-reserve requirements, risk-sensitive capital requirements and deposit insurance premia, partial deposit insurance, bank closure policy and bank charter value.

In its recent consultation document on capital adequacy the Basle Committee recognizes that supervisors have a strong interest in facilitating effective market discipline as a lever to strengthen the safety and soundness of the banking system. It argues: 'market discipline has the potential to reinforce capital regulation and other supervisory efforts to promote safety and soundness in banks and financial systems. Market discipline imposes strong incentives on banks to conduct their business in a safe, sound and efficient manner' (Basle Committee, 1999a, p. 148).

The key challenge, therefore, is how to align the incentives of financial firms with those of the regulatory objectives and at the same time minimize moral hazard for both consumers and regulated firms. Two general principles are outlined.

7. *There should be appropriate incentives for bank owners*  Bank owners have an important role in the monitoring of bank management and their risk taking as, in the final analysis, bank owners absorb the risks of the bank. There are several ways in which bank owners can be appropriately incentivized:

- One route is to ensure that banks have appropriate levels of equity capital. Capital serves three main roles as far as incentive structures are concerned: a commitment of the owners to supply risk resources to the business and which they can lose in the event that the bank makes bad loans; an internal insurance fund; and the avoidance of the bank becoming the captive of its bad debtors. In general, the higher is the capital ratio the more the owners have to lose and hence the greater the incentive for them to monitor the behaviour of managers. Low capital creates a particular moral hazard in that, because of the small amount owners have to lose, the more likely they are to condone excessive risk taking in a gamble-for-resurrection strategy.
- Corporate governance arrangements should be such that equity-holders actively supervise managers.
- Ownership structures should foster shareholder monitoring and oversight. This includes private ownership of banks to strengthen the monitoring of management performance and to minimize adverse incentives for managers.
- Supervisors and safety-net agencies should ensure that owners lose out in any restructuring operations in the event of failure. Failure to penalize shareholders in the restructuring of unsuccessful banks was a major shortcoming in some rescue operations in Latin America.
- In some countries (for example, New Zealand) the incentive on owners has been strengthened by experimenting with a policy of increased personal liability of bank directors.

8. *There should be appropriate internal incentives for management*
Creating the right incentive structures for managers of financial institutions is equally important for owners. Specific measures could include:

- Strong and effective risk analysis, management and control systems to be in place in all financial institutions for assessing risks *ex ante*, and asset values *ex post*. This includes systems and incentives for timely and accurate provisioning against bad or doubtful debts. In the final analysis, most bank failures are ultimately due to weaknesses in this area. Regulatory agencies have a powerful role in insisting upon effective systems of internal management and risk control in financial institutions by strict accountability of owners, directors and senior management.
- Managers should also lose if the bank fails. This requires a high degree of professionalism in bank managers and decision

makers and penalties (including dismissal) for incompetence among bank managers. Remuneration packages may be related to regulatory compliance.
- Mechanisms need to be in place to ensure that loan valuation, asset classification, loan concentrations, interconnected lending, and risk assessment practices reflect sound and accurate assessments of claims and counterparties. This also requires mechanisms for the independent verification of financial statements and compliance with the principles of sound practice through professional external auditing and on-site inspection by supervisory agencies.
- A requirement for large banks to establish internal audit committees.

The key is that there need to be effective internal incentives for management to behave in appropriate ways, and the regulator has a role in ensuring internal incentives are compatible with the objectives of regulation. Combining appropriate incentives for owners and managers contributes to a robust financial system and, in principle, the market would evolve such incentives. However, experience indicates that, in many areas, and most especially when the competitive environment is changing and the regulatory regime is being adjusted, it is hazardous to rely on the market evolving appropriate incentives.

**Monitoring and Supervision**

Because of the nature of financial contracts between financial firms and their customers (for example, many are long term in nature and involve a fiduciary obligation), there is a need for continuous monitoring of the behaviour of all financial firms. The key issue is who is to undertake the monitoring. Several parties can potentially monitor the management of banks: bank owners, bank depositors, rating agencies, official agencies (for example, the central bank or other regulatory body), and other banks in the market. In practice, there can be only a limited monitoring role for depositors due to major information asymmetries which cannot easily be rectified, and because depositors face the less costly option of withdrawal of deposits. Saunders and Wilson (1996) review the empirical evidence on the role of informed depositors. The funding structure of a bank may also militate against effective monitoring in that, unlike with non-financial companies, creditors tend to be large in number but with each having a small stake.

Because most (especially retail) customers, and many other creditors, are not in practice able to undertake such monitoring, and because there are substantial economies of scale in such activity, an important role of regulatory agencies is to monitor the behaviour of financial firms on behalf of customers. In effect, consumers delegate the task of monitoring to a dedicated agency.

However, in the process, adverse incentive effects may emerge in that, given that regulatory agencies conduct monitoring and supervision on a delegated basis, they may reduce the incentive for others to conduct efficient monitoring. The role of other potential monitors (and notably the market) needs to be strengthened in many, including well-developed, financial systems. This in turn requires adequate information disclosure and transparency in banking operations. There need to be greater incentives for other parties to monitor banks in parallel with official agencies. A major advantage of having agents other than official supervisory bodies involved in the monitoring of banks is that it removes the inherent danger of having monitoring and supervision conducted by a monopolist with less than perfect and complete information.

Two principles related to official monitoring and supervision are indicated:

9. *Official agencies need to have sufficient powers and independence to conduct effective monitoring and supervision* This means they need to be independent of political authorities and able to license, refuse to license, and to withdraw licences from banks. They need to have the authority and ability to monitor the full range of banks' activities and business and be able to monitor and assess banks' systems for risk analysis and control. Because of the moral hazard created in some bank structures, the agencies need to have power to establish rules about ownership and corporate structure of banks, and be able to establish minimum requirements for the competency and integrity of bank management.
10. *Less emphasis should be placed on detailed and prescriptive rules and more on internal risk analysis, management and control systems* Externally imposed regulation in the form of prescriptive and detailed rules is becoming increasingly inappropriate and ineffective. More reliance needs to be placed on institutions' own internal risk analysis, management and control systems. This relates not only to quantitative techniques such as value-at-risk (VaR) models but also to the management 'culture' of those who handle models and supervise traders. A shift in emphasis towards monitoring risk-control mechanisms is needed, together with a recasting of the nature and functions of external regulation away from generalized rule setting towards establishing incentives and sanctions to reinforce such internal control systems. The

recently issued consultative document by the Basle Committee on Banking Supervision (Basle Committee, 1999a, p. 197) explicitly recognizes that a major role in the supervisory process is the monitoring of banks' own internal capital management processes and 'the setting of targets for capital that are commensurate with the bank's particular risk profile and control environment. This process would be subject to supervisory review and intervention, where appropriate.'

**Intervention**

A key component of a regulatory regime is intervention arrangements by regulatory agencies in the event of financial distress. The issue focuses on when and how intervention is to be made. The experience of banking crises (in both developed and developing countries) is that a well-defined strategy is needed for responding to the possible insolvency of financial institutions. The way such intervention is made has signalling and incentive effects for the future behaviour of financial institutions. The conditions under which intervention is made, the manner of intervention and its timing may, therefore, have powerful moral hazard effects. Important issues related to the credibility of intervention agencies also arise.

A key issue in this area relates to rules versus discretion in the event of bank distress: to what extent should intervention be circumscribed by clearly defined rules (so that intervention agencies have no discretion about whether, how and when to act), or should there always be discretion because all the relevant circumstances cannot be set out in advance? The obvious prima facie advantage of discretion is that it is impossible to foresee all future circumstances and conditions for when a bank might become distressed and close to (or actually) insolvent. It might be judged that it is not always the right policy to close a bank in such circumstances.

On the other hand, there are strong arguments against allowing discretion and in favour of a rules approach to intervention. First, it enhances the credibility of the intervention agency in that market participants, including banks, have a high degree of certainty that action will be taken. Second, the danger of discretion is that it increases the probability of forbearance, which experience suggests usually eventually leads to higher costs when intervention is finally made. Third, and based on the experience of some countries which have recently experienced banking distress, it removes the danger of undue political interference in the disciplining of banks. Experience in many countries indicates that supervisory authorities face substantial pressure to delay action and intervention. Fourth, it is likely to have a beneficial impact on *ex ante* behaviour of financial firms. A rules-based approach, by removing any prospect that a hazardous bank might be treated leniently, enhances the incentives for bank managers to manage banks prudently so as to reduce the probability of insolvency (Glaessner and Mas, 1995). It also enhances the credibility of the regulator's threat to close institutions. Finally, a rules approach guards against the hazard associated with risk-averse regulators who themselves might be inclined not to take action for fear that intervention will be interpreted as a regulatory failure, and who might be tempted to allow a firm to trade out of its difficulty. This amounts to the regulator 'gambling for resurrection'. In this sense, a rules approach may be of assistance to the intervention agency as its hands are tied.

The BIS has argued as follows: 'Above all, reducing incentives to excessive risk-taking will depend on the credibility of the authorities' commitment to limiting intervention to the necessary minimum in the event of turmoil. In much the same way as the monetary authorities' anti-inflation commitment, it needs to be demonstrated in consistent action' (BIS, 1991, p. 85). The need to maintain the credibility of supervisory agencies creates a strong bias against forbearance. The overall conclusion is that there should be a clear bias (though not a bar) against forbearance when a bank is in difficulty. While there should be a strong presumption against forbearance, and that this is best secured through having clearly defined rules, there will always be exceptional circumstances when forbearance might be warranted in the interests of systemic stability. However, when it is exercised the regulatory agency should be made accountable for its actions.

In some respects there is a trade-off between credibility and flexibility with respect to intervention arrangements. Bruni and Paterno (1994) analyse the trade-off between rules and discretion in bank supervision in a game-theoretic framework. They argue that time consistency and credibility play a central role. They conclude that the optimum arrangement is for a no-bail-out commitment fixed by law but with special exemptions.

The transition to a no-bail-out strategy is unlikely to be a smooth, trouble-free process because of the incentive structures of supervisors. This is partly a reflection of the interaction between the incentive structures of supervisors and those of politicians. Kane (1991) suggests that a conflict of interest can emerge (an 'incentive breakdown') and that this partly explains the bail-out of the US savings and loans institutions in the 1980s. He argues that supervisors intervened under political pressure and that this resulted in a bail-out of insolvent institutions.

Intervention arrangements also have important implications for the total cost of intervention (for example, initial forbearance often has the effect of raising the eventual cost of subsequent intervention), and the distribution of those costs between taxpayers and other agents. Different intervention arrangements may also have implications for the future efficiency of the financial system in that, for instance, forbearance may have the effect of sustaining inefficient banks and excess capacity in the banking sector.

All this amounts to the need for care when devising bank restructuring policies, and the need for appropriate incentives for intervention agencies. Several principles can be established to guide the timing and form of intervention:

11. *The design and application of safety-net arrangements (lender of last resort and deposit insurance) should create incentives for stakeholders to exercise oversight and to act prudently so as to reduce the probability of recourse being made to public funds* It is well established that, dependent upon how deposit insurance schemes are constructed (most especially with respect to which deposits are insured and the extent of any co-insurance), moral hazards can be created: depositors may be induced to act with less care, and under some circumstances they may be induced to seek risky banks on the grounds that a one-way bet is involved. At the same time, insured institutions may be induced to take more risk because they are not required to pay the full risk premium on insured deposits; risk is therefore subsidized, banks may be induced to hold less capital, and the cost of deposit protection is passed to others who have no say in the risk-taking activity of the insured bank.

12. *The extent and coverage of deposit insurance schemes should be strictly limited* Maintaining the integrity of the banking system requires that some bank liability holders are to be protected from the consequences of bank failure. But this should be limited because such protection may create adverse incentives. In particular, and in order to avoid the potential moral hazards emerging, coverage should be explicit (rather than assumed) and restricted to comparatively small deposits. There should always be an element of co-insurance to the extent that less than 100 per cent of any deposit is insured.

13. *There needs to be a well-defined strategy for responding to the possible insolvency of financial institutions* A regulatory regime that avoided any possibility of bank failure would certainly imply overregulation to an extent that would impose economic costs on society and the efficiency of the financial system. Occasional bank failures will always be a part of a well-functioning financial system. This means it is necessary to have a strategy with respect to how to respond to bank failures when they occur or when the predicament of individual banks is evidently deteriorating. A response strategy in the event of bank distress has several possible components:

- being prepared to close insolvent financial institutions;
- taking prompt corrective action to address financial problems before they reach critical proportions;
- closing unviable institutions promptly, and vigorously monitoring weak and/or restructured institutions;
- undertaking a timely assessment of the full scope of financial insolvency and the fiscal cost of resolving the problem.

14. *There should be a clear bias (though not a bar) against forbearance when a bank is in difficulty*  A central issue for the credibility, and hence authority, of a regulator is whether rules and decisions are time consistent. There may be circumstances where a rule, or normal policy action, needs to be suspended. The priors are in favour of a strong case for pre-commitment and rules of behaviour for the regulator. There is also a case for a graduated-response approach since, for example, there is no magical capital ratio below which an institution is in danger and above which it is safe. Other things being equal, potential danger gradually increases as the capital ratio declines. This in itself suggests there should be a graduated series of responses from the regulator as capital diminishes.

    Regulatory authorities need to build a reputation for tough supervision and, when necessary, decisive action in cases of financial distress. Supervisory authorities may, from time to time, face substantial political pressure to delay action in closing hazardous financial institutions. There is an additional danger of regulatory capture, and that a risk-averse regulator may simply delay intervention in order to avoid blame. The need to maintain credibility creates a strong bias against forbearance.

15. *Time-inconsistency and credibility problems should be addressed through precommitments and graduated responses with the possibility of overrides*  Some analysts have advocated various forms of predetermined intervention through a general policy of structured early intervention and resolution (SEIR). Goldstein and Turner (1996) argue that SEIR is designed to imitate the remedial action which private bond holders would impose on banks in the absence of government insurance or guarantees. In this sense it is a mimic of market solutions to troubled banks. An example of the rules-based approach is to be found in the prompt corrective action (PCA) rules in the US. These specify graduated intervention by regulators with predetermined responses triggered by capital thresholds.

    Under a related concept (the 'precommitment approach' to bank supervision) banks' own assessments of their capital needs (as determined by their own internal risk models) are used as the basis of supervision. At the beginning of each period the bank evaluates its need for capital and is subsequently required to manage its risks so that its capital does not fall below the precommitment level. Penalties are imposed when capital falls below these levels. There are several advantages to a precommitment strategy: it avoids the necessity of detailed and prescriptive regulation, it creates powerful incentives for bank decision makers (the choice of an excessive amount of capital imposes costs on the bank, while choosing too low a level of capital risks the imposition of penalties), and it is flexible as it offers scope for each bank to choose a level of capital which is appropriate to its own particular circumstances. On the other hand, Estrella (1998) argues that the precise design of the penalty structure is likely to be complex.

However, even in a precommitment and graduated-response regime there may be cases where predetermined rules are to be overridden. The problem, however, is that if this is publicly known the credibility of the regulator may be compromised, bearing in mind that it is to create and sustain such credibility that the precommitment rule is established in the first place. Can there be any guarantee that such an override would not turn regulation into a totally *ad hoc* procedure? One solution is to make the intervention agency publicly accountable for any actions and decisions not to intervene.

16. *Intervention authorities need to ensure that parties that have benefited from risk taking bear a large proportion of the cost of restructuring the banking system* This implies, for example, that shareholders should be the first to lose their investment along with large holders of long-term liabilities such as subordinated debt. Also, delinquent borrowers must not be given favourable treatment at public expense.

17. *Prompt action should be taken to prevent problem institutions extending credit to high-risk borrowers, or capitalizing unpaid interest on delinquent loans into new credit* Execution of this principle is designed to reduce the moral hazard risk in bank restructurings that arises when institutions with low and declining net worth continue to operate under the protection of public policies designed to maintain the integrity of the banking system. This implies that, when practicable, insolvent institutions should be removed from the hands of current owners, whether through sale, temporary nationalization, or closure.

18. *Society must create the political will to make restructuring a priority in allocating public funds while avoiding sharp increases in inflation. Use of public funds in rescue operations should be kept to a minimum and, whenever used, be subject to strict conditionality* This follows from previous principles in that their execution requires adequate funding to pay

off some liability-holders with negative net worth. Attempts should always be made to recover public funds over a period of time by, for instance, asset sales from resolution trusts, and so on.

19. *Barriers to market recapitalization should be minimized*   A particular barrier that is often encountered relates to the market in corporate control. Governments or regulatory agencies frequently impose rules regarding the ownership of banks and the extent to which banks can be taken over through the market in corporate control. There are often particular limitations on the extent to which foreign banks are allowed to purchase domestic banks, even though this is often a solution for an insolvent bank, which can be effectively recapitalized by being purchased by a stronger domestic or foreign institutions.

20. *Regulators should be publicly accountable through credible mechanisms*   Regulatory agencies have considerable power through their influence on the terms on which business is conducted. For this reason agencies need to be accountable and their activities transparent. In addition, public accountability can be a protection against political interference in the decisions of regulatory agencies, and it can create incentives against forbearance. Difficulties can arise when it may be prudent for a central bank's success in averting a bank failure or systemic crisis to remain secret. One possible approach is to create an audit agency of the regulator, with the regulator being required to report on a regular basis to an independent person, or body. The report would cover the objectives of the regulator and the measures of success and failure. The audit authority would have a degree of standing that would force the regulatory agency to respond to any concerns raised. In due course, the reports of the regulator to the agency would be published.

**Assessment**

In the process of restructuring following a financial crisis, financial market functioning needs to be restored as quickly as possible while minimizing market disruption. Balance sheet assets of weak institutions need to be restructured and placed on a sound footing. This should be designed to ameliorate the moral hazard that weak banks become the captive of their bad customers and, in the process, bad loans drive out good loans. In addition, the management and recovery of loans should be separated from the ongoing activity of banks so that a proper focus can be given to the efficient management of the continuing activity of banks.

Lessons can be learned about how to respond to crises when they emerge. The experience of Mexico, for example, demonstrates how a serious banking crisis can be managed and the banks restored to viability. The experience is instructive as an object lesson in how a banking crisis can be transformed if appropriate measures are taken. Several policy measures were adopted both to restore the banking system and to lower the probability of similar crises recurring:

- Foreign competition in banking was encouraged. There was subsequently a major influx of foreign banks and foreign capital into the banking sector associated with the privatization of banks and the relaxation of entry barriers. As a result, foreign ownership of banks in Mexico now exceeds 20 per cent.
- Consolidation of the banking system was supported and encouraged.
- Regulation and supervision were tightened and made more explicit.
- Accountancy and disclosure standards and requirements were tightened.
- Links between bankers and politics were broken.

When a banking crisis emerges, the policy strategy has to be to reconstitute the banking system (including recapitalizing banks) and to apply measures designed to significantly lower the probability of a crisis re-emerging.

**Market Discipline**

Monitoring is not only conducted by official agencies whose specialist task it is. In well-developed regimes, the market also has incentives to monitor the behaviour of financial firms. The disciplines imposed by the market can be as powerful as any sanctions imposed by official agencies. The disciplining role of the markets (including the interbank market) was weak in the crisis countries of South East Asia in the 1990s. This was due predominantly to the lack of disclosure and transparency of banks, and the fact that little reliance could be placed on the quality of accountancy data provided in bank accounts. In many cases standard accountancy and auditing procedures were not rigorously applied, and in some cases there was wilful misrepresentation of the financial position of banks and non-financial companies.

Within the general framework of monitoring, a particular dimension is the extent to which the market undertakes monitoring and imposes discipline on the risk taking of banks. Given how the business of banking has evolved and the nature of the market environment in which banks now operate, less reliance can be placed on supervision by official agencies, and a greater role needs to be played by the market. Market disciplines need to be strengthened. The issue is not so much focused on market versus agency discipline, but the mix of all aspects of monitoring, supervision and discipline. It has been noted that:

Broader approaches to bank supervision reach beyond the issues of defining capital and accounting standards, and envisage co-opting other market participants by giving them a greater stake in bank survival. This approach increases the likelihood that problems will be detected earlier . . . [it involves] broadening the number of those who are directly concerned about keeping the banks safe and sound. (Caprio and Honahan, 1998)

A potentially powerful disciplining power of markets derives from the market in corporate control which, through the threat of removing control from incumbent managements, is a discipline on managers to be efficient and not endanger the solvency of their banks. As put in a recent IMF study: 'An open and competitive banking market exerts its own form of discipline against weak banks while encouraging well-managed banks' (Lindgren et al., 1996, p. 38).

Some analysts (for example, Calomiris, 1997) are sceptical about the power of official supervisory agencies to identify the risk characteristics of banks compared with the power and incentives of markets. Along with others, he advocates banks being required to issue a minimum amount of subordinated and uninsured debt as part of the capital base. This would involve having private sector funds that could not be withdrawn from the bank and which would effectively be put at risk because the authorities would have no incentive to rescue the holders of such debt. Subordinated debt-holders would therefore have an incentive to monitor the risk taking of banks. Discipline would be applied by the market as the market's assessment of risk would be reflected in the risk premium in the price of traded debt. In particular, because of the nature of debt contracts, holders of a bank's subordinated debt do not share in the potential upside gain through the bank's risk taking, but stand to lose if the bank fails. They therefore have a particular incentive to monitor the risk profile of the bank compared with shareholders who, under some circumstances, have an incentive to support a high-risk profile. Movements in the price of a bank's subordinated debt also serve as a signal to official supervisors.

A scheme along these lines has been introduced in Argentina whereby holders of subordinated debt must be entities of substance which are independent of the bank's shareholders, and it is required that the issue of debt must be in relatively lumpy amounts on a regular basis (Calomiris, 1997). However, while there is a potentially powerful role for market discipline to operate through the pricing of subordinated debt, the interests of holders of such debt do not necessarily precisely coincide with those of depositors or the public interest more generally (Dewatripont and Tirole, 1994). It is not, therefore, a substitute for official monitoring. It is intended as a mechanism to extend the role of market monitoring.

A further mechanism to enhance market discipline is to link deposit insurance premiums paid by banks to the implied risk of the bank as incorporated in subordinated debt yields or classifications of rating agencies.

The merit of increasing the role of market discipline is that large, well-informed creditors (including other banks) have the resources, expertise, market knowledge and incentives to conduct monitoring and to impose market discipline. For instance, it has been argued that the hazardous state of BCCI was reflected in market prices and interbank interest rates long before the Bank of England closed the bank.

Some principles concerning market discipline are:

21. *Regulation should not impede competition but should enhance it and, by addressing information asymmetries, make it more effective in the marketplace* However well intentioned, regulation has the potential to compromise competition and to condone, if not in some cases endorse, unwarranted entry barriers, restrictive practices, and other anti-competitive mechanisms. Historically regulation in finance has often been anti-competitive in nature. But this is not an inherent property of regulation. As there are clear consumer benefits and efficiency gains to be secured through competition, regulation should not be constructed in a way that impairs it. Regulation and competition need not be in conflict: on the contrary, properly constructed they are complementary. Regulation can, therefore, enhance competition. It can also make it more effective in the marketplace by, for instance, requiring the disclosure of relevant information that can be used by consumers in making informed choices.

    Discipline can also be exerted by competition. Opening domestic financial markets to external competition can contribute to the promotion of market discipline. There are many benefits to be derived from foreign institutions entering a country. They bring expertise and experience and, because they themselves are diversified throughout the world, what is a macro shock to a particular country becomes a regional shock, and hence they are more able to sustain purely national shocks compared with domestic institutions. It is generally the case that competition that develops from outside a system has a greater impact on competition and efficiency than internal competition. Foreign institutions tend to be less subject to domestic political pressures in the conduct of their business, and are also less susceptible to local euphoria which, at times, leads to excessive lending and overoptimistic expectations.

22. *Regulation should reinforce, not replace, market discipline; the regulatory regime should be structured so as to provide greater incentives than*

*exist at present for markets to monitor banks* In many countries, market discipline (for example, through disclosure) needs to be strengthened. This means creating incentives for private markets to reward good performance and penalize hazardous behaviour. Regulation and supervision should complement and support, and never undermine, the operation of market discipline.

23. *Whenever possible, regulators should utilize market data in their supervisory procedures* The evidence indicates that markets can give signals about the credit standing of financial firms which, when combined with inside information gained by supervisory procedures, can increase the efficiency of the supervisory process. Flannery (1998) suggests that market information may improve two features of the overall process: first, it permits regulators to identify developing problems more promptly, and second, it provides regulators with the incentive and justification to take action more quickly once problems have been identified. He concludes that market information should be incorporated into the process of identifying and correcting problems.

If financial markets are able to assess a bank's market value as reflected in the market price, an asset-pricing model can in principle be used to infer the risk of insolvency that the market has assigned to each bank. Such a model has been applied to UK banks by Hall and Miles (1990). Similar analysis for countries which had recently liberalized their financial systems has been applied by Fischer and Gueyie (1995). On the other hand, as there are clear limitations to such an approach (see Simons and Cross, 1991), it would be hazardous to rely exclusively on it. For instance, it assumes that markets have sufficient data upon which to make an accurate assessment of the risk profile of banks, and it equally assumes that the market is able to efficiently assess the available information and incorporate this into an efficient pricing of bank securities.

24. *There should be a significant role for rating agencies in the supervisory process* Rating agencies have considerable resources and expertise in monitoring banks and making assessments of risk. It could be made a requirement, as in Argentina, for all banks to have a rating, which would be made public.

**Assessment**
While market discipline is potentially powerful, it has its limitations. This means that, in practice, it is unlikely to be an effective alternative to the role of official regulatory and supervisory agencies:

- Markets are concerned with the private cost of a bank failure and reflect the risk of this in market prices. The social cost of bank failures, on the other hand, may exceed the private cost (Llewellyn, 1999), and hence the total cost of a bank failure may not be fully reflected in market prices.
- Market disciplines are not effective at monitoring and disciplining public sector banks.
- In many countries, there are limits imposed on the extent to which the market in corporate control (the takeover market) is allowed to operate. In particular, there are limits, if not bars, on the extent to which foreign institutions are able to take control of banks, even though they may offer a solution to undercapitalized banks.
- The market is able to efficiently price bank securities and interbank loans only to the extent that relevant information is available. Disclosure requirements are, therefore, an integral part of the market disciplining process.
- It is not self-evident that market participants always have the necessary expertise to make risk assessments of complex, and sometimes opaque, banks.
- In some countries, the market in debt of all kinds (including securities and debt issued by banks) is limited, inefficient and cartelized.
- When debt issues are very small it is not always economic for a rating agency to conduct a full credit rating on the bank.

While there are clear limitations to the role of market discipline (discussed further in Lane, 1993), the global trend is appropriately in the direction of placing more emphasis on market data in the supervisory process. The theme is not that market monitoring and discipline can effectively replace official supervision, but that it has a potentially powerful role which should be strengthened within the overall regulatory regime. In addition, Caprio (1997) argues that broadening the number of those who are directly concerned about the safety and soundness of banks reduces the extent to which insider political pressure can be brought to bear on bank regulation and supervision. The recent consultative document issued by the Basle Committee on Banking Supervision incorporates the role of market discipline as one of the three pillars of a proposed new approach to banking supervision. The Committee emphasizes that its approach 'will encourage high disclosure standards and enhance the role of market participants in encouraging banks to hold adequate capital' (Basle Committee, 1999a, p. 386).

## Corporate Governance

There are several reasons why corporate governance arrangements operate differently with banks than with other types of firm. First, banks are subject to regulation in the interests of systemic stability and consumer protection, which adds an additional dimension to corporate governance arrangements. Regulation is partly a response to limitations in corporate governance mechanisms in banks. Second, banks are also subject to continuous supervision and monitoring by official agencies. This has two immediate implications for private corporate governance: shareholders and official agencies are to some extent duplicating monitoring activity, and the actions of official agencies may have an impact on the incentives faced by other monitors, such as shareholders and even depositors. However, for reasons already outlined, official and market monitoring are not perfectly substitutable. Third, banks have a fiduciary relationship with their customers (for example, they are holding the wealth of depositors), which is generally not the case with other types of firm. This creates additional principal–agent relationships (and potentially agency costs) with banks that generally do not exist with non-financial firms.

A fourth reason why corporate governance mechanisms are different in banks is that there is a systemic dimension to banks and, because in some circumstances (for example, presence of externalities) the social costs of bank failures may exceed private costs, there is a systemic concern with the behaviour of banks that does not exist with other companies. Fifth, banks are subject to safety-net arrangements that are not available to other companies. This has implications for incentive structures faced by owners, managers, depositors and the market with respect to monitoring and control.

All of these considerations have an impact on the two general mechanisms for exercising discipline on the management of firms: internal corporate governance and the market in corporate control. While there are significant differences between banks and other firms, corporate governance issues in banks have received remarkably little attention. A key issue, as noted by Flannery (1998), is that little is known about how the two governance systems (regulation and private) interact with each other and, in particular, the extent to which they are complementary or offsetting.

A key issue in the management of financial firms is the extent to which corporate governance arrangements are suitable and efficient for the management and control of risks. The FSA in the UK has argued as follows: 'Senior management set the business strategy, regulatory climate, and ethical standards of the firm . . . Effective management of these activities will benefit firms and contribute to the delivery of the FSA's statutory objectives' (p. 19). Corporate governance arrangements include issues of corporate structure, the power of shareholders to exercise accountability of managers, the transparency of corporate structures, the authority and power of directors, internal audit arrangements, and the lines of accountability of managers. In the final analysis, shareholders are the ultimate risk takers and agency problems may induce managers to take more risks with the bank than the owners would wish. This in turn raises issues about what information shareholders have about the actions of the managers to which they delegate decision-making powers, the extent to which shareholders are represented on the board of directors of the bank, and the extent to which shareholders have power to discipline managers.

The Basle Committee has rightly argued that effective oversight by a bank's board of directors and senior management is critical. It suggests that the board should approve overall policies of the bank and its internal systems. It argues in particular that: 'lack of adequate corporate governance in the banks seems to have been an important contributory factor in the Asian crisis. The boards of directors and management committees of the banks did not play the role they were expected to play' (Basle Committee, 1999b, p. 164).

Useful insights have been provided by Sinha (1999), who concludes, for instance, that while in the UK the regulatory authorities approve the appointment of non-executive directors of banks, such directors are generally considerably less effective in monitoring top management than is the case in manufacturing firms. Sinha compares corporate governance arrangements in banks and manufacturing firms in the UK and finds that top management turnover in banks is less than in other firms, and that turnover seems not to be related to share price performance. Prowse (1997) also shows that accountability to shareholders, and the effectiveness of board monitoring, is lower in banks than in non-financial firms.

An interesting possibility is the extent to which all this results from moral hazard associated with official regulation and supervision: this is a further example of possible negative trade-offs within a regulatory regime. It could be the case that, as regulatory authorities impose regulation and monitor banks, the incentive for non-executive directors and shareholders to do so is reduced. The presumption may be that regulators have more information than do non-executive directors and shareholders, and that their own monitoring would only be wastefully duplicating that being conducted by official supervisors. Further research is needed into the role of non-executive directors and institutional investors in the effectiveness of corporate governance mechanisms in banks.

The Basle Committee has recognized that different structural approaches to corporate governance exist across countries. While it has not, therefore, taken a view with respect to any particular ideal model, the

Committee encourages any practices which strengthen corporate governance in banks. The general principle should be that:

25. *Corporate governance arrangements should provide for effective monitoring and supervision of the risk-taking profile of banks*   These arrangements would provide for, *inter alia*, a management structure with clear lines of accountability; independent non-executive directors on the board; an independent audit committee; a 'four-eyes' principle for important decisions involving the risk profile of the bank; transparent ownership structure; internal structures that enabled the risk profile of the bank to be clear, transparent and managed; and monitored risk analysis and management systems. According to the Basle Committee, good corporate governance includes:

   - establishing strategic objectives and a set of corporate values that are communicated throughout the banking organization;
   - setting and enforcing clear lines of responsibility and accountability throughout the organization;
   - ensuring that board members are qualified for their positions, have a clear understanding of their role in corporate governance and are not subject to undue influence from management or outside concerns;
   - ensuring that there is appropriate oversight by senior management;
   - effectively utilizing the work conducted by internal and external auditors;
   - ensuring that compensation packages are consistent with the bank's ethical values, objectives, strategy and control environment;
   - conducting corporate governance in a transparent manner.

## 7   CONCLUSIONS AND ASSESSMENT

The concepts of a *regulatory regime* and *regulatory strategy* have been introduced. Seven components of the regime have been identified: each is important but none alone is sufficient for the objectives of regulation to be achieved. They are complementary and not alternatives. Regulatory strategy is ultimately about optimizing the outcome of the overall regime rather than any particular components. Regulation in particular needs to consider that, if it is badly constructed or taken too far, there may be negative impacts on the other components to the extent that the overall effect is diluted. However, there may also be positive relationships between the components, and regulation can have a beneficial effect on incentive structures within financial firms.

Effective regulation and supervision of banks have the potential to contribute to the stability and robustness of financial systems. However, there are also distinct limits to what they can achieve in practice. Although regulation is an important part of the regulatory regime, the other components are equally important. In the final analysis, there is no viable alternative to placing the main responsibility for risk management and general compliance on the shoulders of the management of financial institutions. Management must not be able to hide behind the cloak of regulation or pretend that, if regulation and supervisory arrangements are in place, this absolves them from their own responsibility. Nothing should ever be seen as taking away the responsibility of supervision of financial firms by shareholders, managers and the markets. On the contrary, regulation and supervision can be constructed in a way that enhances this responsibility.

The objective is to optimize the outcome of a regulatory strategy in terms of mixing the components of the regime, bearing in mind that negative trade-offs may be encountered. The emphasis is on the *combination* of mechanisms rather than alternative approaches to achieving the objectives. The skill of the regulator in devising a regulatory strategy lies in how the various components in the regime are combined, and how the various instruments available to the regulator (rules, principles, guidelines, mandatory disclosure requirements, authorization, supervision, intervention, sanctions, redress, and so on) are to be used.

Several shifts within the regulatory regime have been outlined in order to maximize its overall effectiveness and efficiency:

- Less emphasis to be given to formal and detailed prescriptive rules dictating the behaviour of regulated firms.
- A greater focus to be given to incentive structures within regulated firms, and how regulation might have a beneficial impact on incentives.
- Market discipline and market monitoring of financial firms need to be strengthened within the overall regime.
- Greater differentiation between regulated firms.
- Less emphasis to be placed on detailed and prescriptive rules and more on internal risk analysis, management and control systems. In some areas, externally imposed regulation in the form of prescriptive and detailed rules is becoming increasingly inappropriate and ineffective. For instance, with respect to prudential issues, more reliance

should be placed on institutions' own internal risk analysis, management and control systems.
- Corporate governance mechanisms for financial firms need to be strengthened so that owners play a greater role in the monitoring and control of regulated firms, and compliance issues are identified as being the ultimate responsibility of a nominated main board director.

Overall, the lesson of recent banking crises is that there needs to be more effective surveillance of financial institutions by both supervisory authorities and the markets. For markets to complement the work of supervisory agencies, there needs to be good and timely information about banks' activities and balance sheet positions. Regulation, supervision and information disclosure are not alternatives.

## NOTE

\* The author expresses his thanks to Jeffrey Shafer and Jacques Sijben for invaluable comments on an earlier draft of this chapter. The ususal disclaimer applies.

## REFERENCES

Adams, C., Mathieson, D., Schinasi, G. and Chadha, B. (1998), *International Capital Markets*, Washington, DC: IMF.
Alba, P., Bhattacharya, G., Claessens, S., Ghash, S. and Hernandez, L. (1998), 'The role of macroeconomic and financial sector linkages in East Asia's financial crisis', mimeo, World Bank, Washington, DC.
Andersson, M. and Viotti, S. (1999), 'Managing and preventing financial crises', *Sveriges Riksbank Quarterly Review*, 71–89.
Baer, H. and Gray, C. (1996), 'Debt as a control device in transitional economies: the experiences of Hungary and Poland', in R. Frydman, C. Gray and A. Rapaczynski (eds), *Corporate Governance in Central Europe and Russia*, Vol. 1, Budapest: Central European University Press.
Bank for International Settlements (BIS) (1991), *Annual Report*, Basle, June.
Bank for International Settlements (BIS) (1998), *Annual Report*, Basle, June.
Basle Committee (1999a), 'A new capital adequacy framework', Consultative Paper, BIS, Basle, June.
Basle Committee (1999b), 'Enhancing corporate governance for banking organizations', Basle Committee on Banking Supervision, BIS, Basle.
Beatty, A., Chamberlain, S. and Magliola, J. (1993), 'Managing financial reports on commercial banks', Wharton Financial Institutions Centre, Paper No. 94–02, August.
Benink, H. and Llewellyn, D.T. (1994), 'De-regulation and financial fragility: a case study of the UK and Scandinavia', in D. Fair and R. Raymond (eds),

*Competitiveness of Financial Institutions and Centres in Europe*, Dordrecht: Kluwer, pp. 186–201.
Benston, G. and Kaufman, G. (1995), 'Is the banking and payments system fragile?', *Journal of Financial Services Research*, September, 178–210.
Bhattacharya, S., Boot, A. and Thakor, P. (1998), 'The economics of bank regulation', *Journal of Money, Credit, and Banking*, November, 745–70.
Billett, M., Garfinkel, J. and O'Neal, E. (1998), 'The cost of market versus regulatory discipline in banking', *Journal of Financial Economics*, 333–58.
Bisignano, J. (1998), 'Precarious credit equilibria: reflections on the Asian financial crisis', mimeo, Bank for International Settlements, Basle.
Black, J. (1994), 'Which arrow? Rule type and regulatory policy', *Public Law*, June, 228–64.
Bowman, E. (1982), 'Risk seeking by troubled firms', *Sloan Management Review*, Summer, 33–40.
Brealey, R. (1999), 'The Asian crisis: lessons for crisis management and prevention', *Bank of England Quarterly Bulletin*, August, 285–96.
Brownbridge, M. and Kirkpatrick, C. (2000), 'Financial sector regulation: lessons of the Asian crisis', *Development Policy Review*, **17** (3), 243–66
Bruni, F. and Paterno, F. (1994), 'Market discipline of banks' riskiness: a study of selected issues', *Journal of Financial Services Research*, **5**, 313.
Calomiris, C. (1997), *The Postmodern Safety Net*, Washington, DC: American Enterprise Institute.
Caprio, G. (1997), 'Safe and sound banking in developing countries: we're not in Kansas anymore', Policy Research Paper No. 1739, World Bank, Washington, DC.
Caprio, G. and Summers, L. (1993), 'Finance and its reform', Policy Research Paper No. 1734, World Bank, Washington, DC.
Caprio, Gerard and Honahan, Patrick (1998), 'Restoring banking stability: beyond supervised capital requirements', *Journal of Economic Perspectives*, **13**, 43–64.
Cole, H. and Kehoe, T. (1996), 'A self-fulfilling model of Mexico's 1994–95 debt crisis', *Journal of International Economics*, **41**, 309–30.
Corbett, J., Irwin, G. and Vines, D. (1999), 'From Asian miracle to Asian crisis: why vulnerability, why collapse', in D. Gruen and L. Gower (eds), *Capital Flows and the International Financial System*, Sydney: Reserve Bank of Australia, pp. 190–213.
Corsetti, G., Pesenti, P. and Rabini, N. (1998), 'What caused the Asia currency and financial crisis?', Banca D'Italia, *Temi di Discussione*, December, 1–38.
Dale, R. (1996), *Risk and Regulation in Global Securities Markets*, London: Wiley.
Demirguc-Kunt, A. and Detragiache, E. (1998), 'Financial liberalization and financial fragility', World Bank Annual Conference on Development Economics.
Demsetz, R., Saidenberg, M. and Strahan, P. (1997), 'Agency problems and risk-taking at banks', Federal Reserve Bank of New York Research Paper, No. 9709.
Dewatripont, M. and Tirole, J. (1994), *The Prudential Regulation of Banks*, Cambridge, MA: MIT Press.
Drage, J. and Mann, F. (1999), 'Improving the stability of the international financial system', *Financial Stability Review*, June, 40–77.
Estrella, A. (1998), 'Formulas or supervision? Remarks on the future of regulatory capital', *Federal Reserve Bank of New York Economic Policy Review*, October, 1–25.
Evans, H. (2000), 'Plumbers and architects: a supervisory perspective on interna-

tional financial architecture', Occasional Paper, No. 4, Financial Services Authority, London, January.

Fink, G. and Haiss, P. (2000), 'Lemming banking: conflict avoidance by herd instinct to eliminate excess capacity', paper presented at SUERF Colloquium, Vienna, May.

Fischer, K. and Gueyie, J. (1995), 'Financial liberalization and bank solvency', University of Laval, Quebec, August.

Flannery, M. (1998), 'Using market information in prudential bank supervision: a review of the US empirical evidence', *Journal of Money, Credit, and Banking*, August, 273–305.

Folkerts-Landau, D., Schinasi, J., Cassard, M., Ng, V., Reinhart, C. and Spencer, M. (1995), 'Effects of capital flows on the domestic sectors in APEC countries', in M. Khan and C. Rheinhart (eds), *Capital Flows in the APEC Region*, Occasional Paper No. 122, IMF, Washington, DC.

Furman, J. and Stiglitz, J. (1998), 'Economic crises: evidence and insights from East Asia', Brookings Papers, Brookings Institution, Washington, DC.

Glaessner, T. and Mas, I. (1995), 'Incentives and the resolution of bank distress', *World Bank Research Observer*, **10** (1), February, 53–73.

Godlayn, I. and Valdes, R. (1997), 'Capital flows and the twin crises: the role of liquidity', IMF Working Paper, 97/87, Washington, DC, July.

Goldstein, M. and Folkerts-Landau, D. (1993), 'Systemic issues in international finance', World Economic and Financial Surveys, IMF, Washington, DC.

Goldstein, M. and Turner, P. (1996), 'Banking crises in emerging economies', *BIS Economic Papers*, No. 46, Basle: BIS.

Goodhart, C., Hartmann, P., Llewellyn, D.T., Rojas-Suarez, L. and Weisbrod, S. (1998), *Financial Regulation: Why, How and Where Now?*, London: Routledge.

Hall, S. and Miles, D. (1990), 'Monitoring bank risk: a market based approach', Discussion Paper, Birkbeck College, London, April.

Hausmann, R. and Gavin, M. (1998), 'The roots of banking crises: the macroeconomic context', mimeo, Inter America Development Bank (IADB), Washington, DC.

Hellman, T., Murdock, K. and Stiglitz, J. (1995), 'Financial restraint: towards a new paradigm', in K. Aoki and I. Okuno-Fujiwara (eds), *The Role of Government in East Asian Economic Development*, Oxford: Oxford University Press, pp. 70–93.

Hellweg, M. (1995), 'Systemic aspects of risk management in banking and finance', *Swiss Journal of Economics and Statistics*, Special Volume, December, 1–33.

International Monetary Fund (IMF), (1993), 'Deterioration of bank balance sheets', *World Economic Outlook*, **2**.

Kahneman, D. and Tversky, A. (1979), 'Prospect theory: an analysis of decision under risk', *Econometrica*, 263–91.

Kaminsky, G. and Reinhart, C. (1998), 'The twin crises: the causes of banking and balance of payments problems', Board of Governors, Federal Reserve System, International Finance Discussion Papers, No. 554, republished in *American Economic Review*, June 1999, 423–500.

Kane, E. (1991), 'Financial regulation and market forces', *Swiss Journal of Economics and Statistics*, **20**, 326.

Keeley, M. (1990), 'Deposit insurance, risk and market power in banking', *American Economic Review*, December, 1183–201.

Kim, M. and Cross, W. (1995), 'The impact of the 1989 change in bank capital standards on loan loss provisions', mimeo, Rutgers University.

Krugman, P. (1998), 'Asia: what went wrong?', *Fortune*, March, 2.
Krugman, P. (1999), *The Return of Depression Economics*, London: Allen Lane.
Lane, T. (1993), 'Market discipline', *IMF Staff Papers*, March, 55.
Lindgren, C.J., Garcia, G. and Saal, M. (1996), *Bank Soundness and Macroeconomic Policy*, Washington, DC: International Monetary Fund.
Llewellyn, D.T. (1999), 'The economic rationale of financial regulation', Occasional Paper No. 1, Financial Services Authority, London.
Llewellyn, D.T. and Holmes, M. (1991), 'Competition or credit controls?', Hobart Paper No. 117, Institute of Economic Affairs, London.
Martinez, P. (1998), 'Do depositors punish banks for bad behaviour? Examining market discipline in Argentina, Chile and Mexico', World Bank Policy Research Working Paper, February.
Organization for Economic Cooperation and Development (OECD) (1992), *Banking Under Stress*, Paris: OECD.
Prendergast, C. (1993), 'The provision of incentives in firms', *Journal of Economic Literature*, March, 7–63.
Prowse, S. (1997), 'Corporate control in commercial banks', *Journal of Financial Research*, **20**, 509–27.
Rahman, M. (1998), 'The role of accounting and disclosure standards in the East Asian financial crisis: lessons learned', mimeo, UNCTAD, Geneva.
Reisen, H. (1998), 'Domestic causes of currency crises: policy lessons for crisis avoidance', OECD Development Centre, Technical Paper 136, OECD, Paris.
Richardson, J. and Stephenson, M. (2000), 'Some aspects of regulatory capital', Occasional Paper No. 7, Financial Services Authority, London.
Rodrik, D. (1999), *The New Global Economy and Developing Countries: Making Openness Work*, Washington, DC: Overseas Development Council.
Rojas-Suarez, L. and Weisbrod, S. (1995), 'Financial fragilities in Latin America: 1980s and 1990s', Occasional Paper No. 132, IMF, Washington, DC.
Sachs, J., Tornell, A. and Velasco, A. (1996), 'Financial crises in emerging markets: the lessons from 1995', Brookings Papers 1, Brookings Institution, Washington, DC.
Saunders, A. and Wilson, B. (1996), 'Contagious bank runs: evidence from the 1929–1933 period', *Journal of Financial Intermediation*, **5**, 409–23.
Schinasi, G., Drees, B. and Lee, W. (1999), 'Managing global finance and risk', *Finance and Development*, December, 14–30.
Schinasi, G. and Hargreaves, M. (1993), 'Boom and bust in asset markets in the 1980s: causes and consequences', *World Economic Outlook*, IMF, Washington, DC, December.
Schwartz, A. (1995), 'Coping with financial fragility: a global perspective', *Journal of Financial Services Research*, September, 193–240.
Shafer, J.R. (1987), 'Managing crisis in the emerging financial landscape', OECD *Economic Outlook*, No. 9, 55–77.
Sijben, J. (1999), 'Regulation versus market discipline in banking: an overview', mimeo, University of Tilburg, Netherlands.
Simons, K. and Cross, S. (1991), 'Do capital markets predict problems in large commercial banks?', *New England Economic Review*, May, 51–6.
Simpson, D. (2000), 'Cost benefit analysis and competition', in *Some Cost Benefit Issues in Financial Regulation*, London: Financial Services Authority, pp. 40–60.
Sinha, R. (1999), 'Corporate governance in financial services firms', Loughborough University Banking Centre Paper No. 121/98, Loughborough University.

Stiglitz, J. (1999), 'Must financial crises be this frequent and this painful?', in R. Agenor et al. (eds), *The Asian Financial Crisis: Causes, Contagion and Consequences*, Cambridge: Cambridge University Press, pp. 115–40.

Suzuki, Y. (1986), *Money, Finance and Macroeconomic Performance in Japan*, New Haven, CT: Yale University Press.

United Nations Conference on Trade and Development (UNCTAD) (1998), *Trade and Development Report*, Geneva: United Nations.

Wallman, S. (1999), 'Information technology revolution and its impact on regulation and regulatory structure', in R. Littan and A. Santomero (eds), Brookings–Wharton Papers on Financial Services, Washington, DC: Brookings Institution Press.

Williamson, J. and Mahar, M. (1998), 'A survey of financial liberalization', Princeton Essays in International Finance No. 211, Princeton University, Princeton, NJ.

# 17. Reforming the traditional structure of a central bank to cope with the Asian financial crisis: lessons from the Bank of Thailand

**Andrew W. Mullineux, Victor Murinde and Adisorn Pinijkulviwat***

## 1 INTRODUCTION

The Bank of Thailand (BoT) became Thailand's central bank on 10 December 1942, and like all traditional central banks was entrusted with a broad range of traditional functions: to issue currency; to safeguard the value of money; to promote monetary stability and a sound financial structure; to promote economic growth; to act as the bankers' bank and provide lender-of-last-resort facilities; and to act as banker and financial adviser to the government.[1] During most of its history, the BoT played an important role in promoting the development of financial institutions and markets in Thailand. However, following the Asian financial crisis which broke out in 1997, the BoT became vulnerable as Thailand started to experience a severe economic crisis. The crisis derailed all ongoing financial reforms and directly crippled the banking sector, the stock exchange and the foreign exchange market (McKinnon and Pill, 1998). Regarding the banking sector, the major problems associated with the crisis included: failure of financial institutions; insufficient bank liquidity and inadequate capital; high non-performing loans; and loss of momentum in rebuilding confidence among international investors, depositors and economic development organizations, potentially limiting future capital flows into Thailand. In this context, it is interesting to examine how a traditional central bank, like the BoT, is able to cope with a financial crisis of a magnitude far beyond its stipulated role.

This chapter examines the role played by the BoT in trying to cope with the financial crisis that hit Thailand in the summer of 1997. The emphasis is on the banking sector rather than the financial markets, but within the broader context of financial reforms and central bank regulation.

In what follows, the chapter is structured into six sections. Section 2 describes financial liberalization attempts and consequences in Thailand, especially with respect to interest rate and exchange rate liberalization. Section 3 focuses on extensions of the scope of banking and financial institution operations. The Financial System Master Plan, which was conceived before the financial crisis, is discussed in Section 4. Section 5 examines the 1997 financial crisis and its impact on financial reforms. Restructuring and regulatory reform after the crisis are discussed in Section 6. Section 7 concludes.

## 2 FINANCIAL LIBERALIZATION

### The Reregulation of Commercial Banking

Commercial banks dominate the financial system in Thailand, with a 73 per cent share of both household savings and credits extended by all financial institutions. Local commercial banks and branches of foreign banks are governed by the Commercial Banking Act of 1962 together with the amendments made in 1979, 1985 and 1992. The first two amendments were designed to improve and revise the 1962 Act in order to make it more efficient and suitable to changing circumstances so that public interest could be protected. The main aim of the 1992 amendment was to introduce the capital adequacy standards of the Basle Committee (Laurisden, 1998).

Prior to the 1962 Act, foreign banks were allowed to open sub-branches; however, after 1962, the banks were not allowed to extend sub-branches in the Thai Kingdom. In addition, the BoT became very restrictive in terms of granting licences to new local banks. Hence, domestic banks and branches of foreign banks remained low in number; for example, by the end of December 1993, only 15 local banks and 13 branches of foreign banks were operating in the Kingdom.

The major shareholders of domestic commercial banks mostly belonged to a group of families. For example, Bangkok Bank, the largest bank in the country with a market share of 21 per cent, belonged to the Sophonpanich family. The third largest bank with a market share of 13 per cent, the Thai Farmers Bank, belonged to the Lumsum family. The Bank of Ayuthaya, the fifth largest bank with a market share of 8 per cent, belonged to the Ruthanaruk family. There was only one state-owned bank, the Krung Thai Bank, which was the second largest bank in the Kindgom and held a market share of 15 per cent. The fourth largest bank, the Siam Commercial Bank, had a market share of 9 per cent; it was crown property. Family-owned banks were generally managed by a group of family members and mainly extended loans to the businesses of their executives and related persons. However, by 1979 commercial banks had gradually become public companies, although the family group still remained the major shareholders of banks indirectly. By 1994, the local commercial banks had expanded branches to the whole Kingdom with a network of 1,709 branches in 1983 to 2,838 branches in 1994, operating 2,320 automated teller machines (ATMs) throughout the country (Bank of Thailand, 1999).

It is useful to compare the scenario in 1994 with that in 1998. While at the end of 1994, Thai commercial banks held a market share in deposits of 98 per cent, by 1998 the figure was 96 per cent. The market share for creditors was 88 per cent in 1994 but had fallen to 85 per cent by 1998; the branches of foreign banks, however, increased their market share from 12 per cent by 1994 to 15 per cent by 1998, as the confidence in local banks fell. In general, as shown in Table 17.1, commercial bank lending for personal consumption fell; there was also a decline in lending to real estate business, exports, agriculture, other financial services and wholesale and retail trade. However, the share of total lending to manufacturing, construction, imports, and public utilities increased in 1998 compared to the 1994 base level.[2] Moreover, in 1998 commercial banks introduced elec-

Table 17.1 *Bills, loans and overdrafts of commercial banks, classified by sector*

| Sector | Year 1994 | Share % | Year 1998 | Share % |
|---|---|---|---|---|
| 1. Agriculture | 152.3 | 4 | 146.6 | 3 |
| 2. Mining | 15.7 | 1 | 32.2 | 1 |
| 3. Manufacturing | 836.2 | 24 | 1,606.3 | 30 |
| 4. Construction | 142.0 | 4 | 264.8 | 5 |
| 5. Real estate business | 364.2 | 11 | 506.1 | 10 |
| 6. Imports | 115.7 | 3 | 192.5 | 4 |
| 7. Exports | 166.5 | 5 | 174.0 | 3 |
| 8. Wholesale and retail trade | 672.7 | 18 | 867.5 | 16 |
| 9. Public utilities | 86.3 | 2 | 189.7 | 4 |
| 10. Other financial business | 245.2 | 7 | 263.4 | 5 |
| 11. Services | 268.4 | 8 | 418.6 | 8 |
| 12. Personal consumption | 437.5 | 13 | 595.0 | 11 |
| 13. Others | – | – | – | – |
| 14. Total | 3,502.7 | 100 | 5,256.7 | 100 |

*Note:* Loan values are in billions of baht; shares are in sectoral percentages of the total.

*Source:* Bank of Thailand (1999).

tronic banking by providing deposit and withdrawal services through an on-line system to branches in almost all provinces, with over 2,320 ATMs in two pools, namely, BANKNET and SIAMNET; these were used to provide out-of-hours deposit and withdrawal nationwide. Swift, used for the transfer of funds among banks throughout the world, was introduced in 1985.

**Reforming the Exchange Rate System**

The main reform of the Thai exchange rate system can be traced back to immediately after the Second World War when, due to economic difficulties and a serious shortage of foreign exchange, Thailand was forced to adopt a multiple exchange rate system. However, in 1963 the economic situation improved and the exchange rate regime was switched to a par value system such that the value of the baht was fixed in terms of gold. In order to maintain the baht parity, the Exchange Equalization Fund (EEF) was established with the aim of stabilizing exchange rate movements within prescribed margins. The successful operation of the EEF enabled full parity of the baht to be maintained for 15 years or so.

However, in 1978 the volatility of major world currencies forced the BoT to adjust the exchange rate, and the par value system was abolished. A system of pegging the baht to a basket of major currencies (in which the US dollar weight was 0.85) was introduced. The new system allowed greater flexibility in exchange rate adjustments to reflect more accurately economic and monetary conditions. It also facilitated the stability of the baht since the currency was no longer tied to any particular currencies. The system operated smoothly until 1981, when signs of trouble began to emerge due to the strong appreciation of the US dollar relative to other currencies. The baht depreciated rapidly, and although the government devalued the currency twice in mid-1981, public confidence could not be restored. However, in July 1981, a decision on the daily fixing was made, and the EEF fixed the exchange rate of the US dollar at 23 baht. This rate was held fixed until 1984, when the government announced a replacement of the dollar-pegging system by pegging the baht to a basket of currencies.

But it was not until 21 May 1990 that the BoT took the most important step in the process of exchange rate deregulation by accepting the obligations under Article VIII of the Articles of Agreement of the International Monetary Fund (IMF), and implementing the first phase of exchange control relaxation. The aim was to liberalize the foreign exchange system in line with the globalization of the economic and financial systems, and allow freedom of international capital movements. Specifically, exchange rate deregulation was implemented in three main phases. Phase I of the exchange control deregulation began on 21 May 1990 by allowing commercial banks to process customers' applications for the purchase of foreign currency for trade-related transactions, that is, imports and exports without prior approval from the BoT.[3] Phase II of the exchange rate deregulation began on 1 April 1991 by allowing greater flexibility to private businesses and the general public in the purchase or sale of foreign exchange. All exchange controls were abolished and new forms were introduced for reporting purposes only. A limit of US$10 million was allowed for an annual investment for one person and for the acquisition of real estate and stocks overseas. Foreign funds, on the other hand, were allowed to move in and out of the country freely. Phase III began on 30 April 1992 to further provide more convenience for the public, and exporters in particular. Exporters were allowed to receive and make payment in baht in addition to foreign currencies, and to transfer foreign currency deposits for overseas debt payment.[4]

Of all the financial liberalization measures, the development of offshore banking facilities, known as the Bangkok International Banking Facilities (BIBFs), was the most important for developing Bangkok as a regional financial centre. BIBFs were introduced in 1993 when the BoT perceived that the Thai financial system should be developed as a regional financial centre, given its stable economic conditions, liberal exchange rates and interest rates, as well as high international borrowing transactions. The BoT proposed the establishment of BIBFs in order to facilitate and reduce the cost of international borrowing, while encouraging foreign capital inflows to finance domestic investment as well as investment throughout the Indo-Chinese region. Initially, 46 BIBF licences were granted. Licensed banks could use foreign funds raised overseas to lend to their domestic customers (known as 'out–in' operations), or to overseas customers (known as 'out–out' operations). Apart from out–in and out–out operations, which were considered to be the core businesses, BIBFs were also allowed to provide other international banking services, such as cross-currency trading, trade financing on strictly an out–out operational basis, loan syndication arrangements, arranging the issue of debt instruments, and engaging in underwriting in foreign currencies.

Capital flows responded in stylized fashion (Fry and Murinde, 1998). After the floatation of the baht currency in July 1997, net capital outflows peaked in the third quarter of 1997 and the baht currency kept on depreciating against the US dollar until it reached 55 baht per US dollar in January 1998. It then stabilized at around 36–40 baht per US dollar from the fourth quarter of 1998 onward. Although short-term nominal interest rates climbed to more than 20 per cent during the crisis, low confidence and exchange rate uncertainties led to huge capital outflows through non-

Table 17.2  Net private financial flows into Thailand (billions of US$)

|  | 1994 | 1995 | 1996 | 1997 | 1998 |
|---|---|---|---|---|---|
| Banks | 13.9 | 11.2 | 5.0 | −6.4 | 13.9 |
| Commercial banks | 3.8 | 3.1 | 0.4 | −4.7 | −4.3 |
| BIBFs | 10.1 | 8.1 | 4.6 | −1.7 | −9.6 |
| Non-banks | −1.9 | 9.6 | 13.2 | −1.9 | −2.0 |
| Direct investment | 0.9 | 1.2 | 1.5 | 3.2 | 4.7 |
| Other loans | −5.6 | 1.5 | 5.5 | −3.7 | −4.3 |
| Portfolio investment | 1.1 | 3.3 | 3.5 | 4.5 | 0.5 |
| Non-resident baht A/C | 2.0 | 3.4 | 2.9 | −5.9 | −2.7 |
| Trade credits | 0.5 | 0.3 | −0.1 | −0.2 | −0.5 |
| Others | −0.6 | −0.1 | 0.02 | 0.3 | 0.02 |
| Net private capital inflow | 12.0 | 20.8 | 18.2 | −8.4 | −16.0 |

Source:  Bank of Thailand (1999).

renewal and repayment of short-term loans towards the end of 1997 through to 1998. The net outflows of private capital at the end of 1997 accounted for US$8.4 billion and continued to increase to more than US$16.0 billion in 1998. The banking sector, including the BIBFs, shouldered the biggest impact of the financial crisis. The commercial banks recorded a net outflow of US$4.7 billion in 1997, but the net outflow dropped in 1998 to US$4.3 billion. The BIBFs followed with net outflows of US$1.7 billion in 1997, peaking in 1998 at US$9.6 billion. Table 17.2 reports the private financial net flow position in Thailand during 1994–98.

By the end of 1999, the surging volume of foreign exchange activities and derivatives trading made it necessary to strengthen prudential supervision in this area. The BoT imposed net foreign exchange position limits and provided guidelines to reinforce existing internal control procedures and practices widely utilized by commercial banks in monitoring and controlling their foreign exchange activities. In 1999, the required ratio for commercial banks was limited within the range of 15 per cent of the net overbought (asset) position to 15 per cent for the net oversold (liability) position.

Financial liberalization through the BIBF considerably increased short-term debts since most of the credits were on a short-term basis and continually rolled over for long-term use. The deterioration of investor confidence and deceleration of economic growth made foreign creditors unwilling to roll over BIBF credits. The volatile exchange rates motivated borrowers to repay loans, resulting in high net capital outflows throughout the second half of 1997 and 1998.

**Interest Rate Liberalization**

As Lensink et al. (1998) have shown, interest rate liberalization is the key policy instrument used by many developing countries that wish to embark on financial liberalization. In Thailand, the liberalization of interest rates was conceived and implemented as a three-year plan (1991–93) aimed at enabling the banking system to adjust to changing demand and supply, both domestically and externally. With continuous economic expansion since 1987, there was apparent need to mobilize long-term and stable funds for national development. When it was evident that long-term deposits had not expanded in line with borrowing needs, the BoT deemed it appropriate to lift the ceiling rate on term deposits exceeding one-year maturity from the previous ceiling of 9.5 per cent to 10.5–11.0 per cent per annum in June 1989 in order to accelerate the process of savings mobilization. The gradual process of deregulation was aimed at allowing time for financial institutions and the public to make the necessary adjustments without major disruption.

With regard to the ceilings on other types of deposits, the BoT continued the interest rate liberalization policy. Ceilings on deposits for all maturity periods were abolished on 16 March 1990. On 8 January 1992, the BoT announced the removal of the ceiling on savings deposit rates. In June 1992, the BoT fixed the ceiling rate on promissory notes issued by finance companies and *crédits fonciers*. Competition for deposit mobilization in the form of attractive offer rates followed as a result of the liberalization process. This factor increased pressure for the ceiling on lending rates to be freely determined according to the prevailing liquidity positions while also minimizing adverse impacts on borrowers. After 1992, interest rates followed a downward trend and the timing was right to remove the lending-rate ceilings for commercial banks, finance companies and *crédit foncier* companies.

The lifting of the lending-rate ceiling became effective on 1 June 1992, allowing domestic interest rates to fully adjust in accordance with demand and supply conditions. From January 1993, the BoT began to implement measures to encourage commercial banks to reduce their lending rates for general customers in response to changes in the cost of deposits. It managed to do so by requesting cooperation from commercial banks and cutting the bank rate twice, in June and September. As a result, commercial banks responded by reducing both their deposit rates and their lending rates and, thus, narrowing the differential between the lending rate for general customers and the one-year time deposit rate to 6.75 per cent in September 1993. However, the BoT did not wish to lead or intervene in the operation of commercial banks every time, but wanted to establish an adjustment mechanism for the lending rate for retail customers to automatically adjust to the actual cost of funds, as determined by the market mechanism. The BoT and the Thai Bankers' Association set up a working group to study and determine the benchmark for the lending rate for retail customers. Finally, the working group agreed to introduce the minimum retail rate (MRR) as a reference lending rate for retail customers.[5]

The commercial banks and branches of the foreign banks began to announce the MRR from the end of October, and the MRR was adopted by all banks in mid-November 1993. During the month when the MRR became effective, the interest margin between the lending rate for retail customers and the one-year deposit rate rose to 7.5 per cent, as commercial banks cut the deposit rate by more than the lending rate. Nevertheless, since the profit margin for retail customers was set at not more than 2 per cent, banks were forced to adjust by lowering the rates on both loans and deposits. Moreover, the lending at lower interest rates by the BIBF in the domestic market enhanced the stiff competition among banks and enabled borrowers to acquire cheaper loans.

In May 1997 the minimum loan rate (MLR) and the MRR were allowed to move freely according to the market mechanism in order to help stimulate the economy. The BoT asked the commercial banks to set the MLR limit in line with market conditions and the MRR, as well as the cost of funds, to reflect the risk differentials between the wholesale and retail customers. However, as the competition among financial institutions increased and customers were offered higher rates on both deposits and loans, difficulties arose in liquidity management because of the high cost of funds to the banks. In June–July 1997, the BoT temporarily limited the ceiling on time deposit to 12–14 per cent to reduce the high lending and deposit rates in order to maintain stability in the financial system.

Interest rates started to go up by late 1996, when the weakness in economic indicators, especially in the current account deficit, began to appear (see Table 17.3). The BoT was forced to maintain high interest rates to help support the baht currency, and to raise funds to bail out ailing finance companies through the Financial Institutions Development Fund (FIDF). The policy continued until the floatation of the baht in July 1997. Thailand then sought assistance from the IMF and had to follow the advice that high interest rates were necessary to help reverse the outflow of capital and stabilize the currency. As shown in Table 17.3, the interbank rate peaked in the third quarter of 1997 through the second quarter of 1998 at between 18 and 20 per cent, and began to fall to only 3.8 per cent at the end of the fourth quarter of 1998. The interbank rate bottomed out at around 1–2 per cent at the end of 1999.

Nevertheless, in July 1998, when the economy started to cool down, the

Table 17.3  *Movements in interest rates and exchange rates during the reform period*

| Year | Interbank interest rate (%) | Exchange rate (baht per US$) |
| --- | --- | --- |
| 1994 | 6.41 | 24.99 |
| 1995 | 10.17 | 25.12 |
| 1996Q1 | 7.30 | 25.23 |
| 1996Q2 | 7.24 | 25.28 |
| 1996Q3 | 11.41 | 25.30 |
| 1996Q4 | 10.97 | 25.46 |
| 1997Q1 | 11.31 | 25.84 |
| 1997Q2 | 11.99 | 25.87 |
| 1997Q3 | 19.32 | 32.95 |
| 1997Q4 | 20.15 | 40.71 |
| 1998Q1 | 20.64 | 47.11 |
| 1998Q2 | 18.03 | 40.33 |
| 1998Q3 | 9.52 | 41.06 |
| 1998Q4 | 3.84 | 36.05 |

*Source:*  IMF (2000) (Thailand, country pages).

BoT allowed commercial banks to adjust interest rates more freely by using the reference rate.[6] Interest payable on savings deposits was made subject to the reference rate plus not more than a 2 per cent mark-up, while time deposits of over three months were made subject to the reference rate plus not more than a 3 per cent mark-up. All the rates had to be disclosed, and the new rules applied to the head office and all branches. In addition, the central bank issued new long-term government bonds to refinance the liabilities of the FIDF. This helped to support the downward trend of short-term money market rates. Market liquidity improved markedly throughout 1999, allowing market interest rates to decline further. Deposit interest rates peaked at 14–15 per cent in 1998, but fell from 6–7 per cent in early 1999 to 3–4 per cent at the end of 1999 (Vatikiotis and Keenan, 1999).

## 3  EXTENSIONS OF THE SCOPE OF BANKING AND FINANCIAL INSTITUTION OPERATIONS

**Encouraging Banks to Open Branches or Participate in Joint Ventures Abroad**

In order to support Bangkok as the financial centre in the region, the BoT allowed the commercial banks to open branches in Laos, Kampuchea,

Vietnam, Burma, as well as mainland China. These branches could provide banking services not only to the local community, but also to Thai investors or foreign investors who use Thailand as a gateway or springboard to the region. Also, they would gather or collect prime information or data for new investors in Thailand.

On the other hand, in regions where branches are not permitted or where it was quite risky to open them due to the unfamiliar economic systems or the differences in language, joint ventures in banking businesses were encouraged to facilitate entry. In addition, local commercial banks were also allowed to open branches or set up wholly owned subsidiaries in financial centres such as Singapore and the Cayman Islands. These could be used to tap cheap funds for their BIBF offices in Bangkok. This could enable the Thai BIBF offices to compete efficiently with foreign BIBFs.

**Relaxation of Constraints on Financial Institution Portfolio Management**

Since 1970, financial institutions have been required to contribute to rural development and overall development of the economy. Commercial banks, including branches of foreign banks, were required to fulfil the agricultural credit target, and branch opening requirements were imposed on domestic banks. Rural branches of domestic banks were required to extend at least 60 per cent of their deposits as credit to local people, and of this amount not less than 20 per cent must be lent to the agricultural sector. However, from 1990 the structure and economic environment of the country has changed tremendously. Consequently, the BoT deemed it appropriate to diminish its role of intervening in the decision-making process of financial institutions. In retrospect, the intervention policy could be perceived as unfair to the financial institutions concerned as well as to customers and other economic sectors.

During the 1991–93 three-year plan, the BoT streamlined and eliminated certain requirements imposed on financial institutions while retaining only those needed to maintain the stability and solvency of the financial system. This was intended to provide greater flexibility in the management of financial institutions and thereby to reduce their costs of operation, increase the quality of their assets and engender greater competition.

**Streamlining the Rural Credit Policy**

In the past, the BoT set targets for commercial banks, including the branches of foreign banks, to allocate credits in proportion to total deposits for agricultural enterprises. In 1987, however, a new definition and a new set of ratios were imposed on the so-called 'rural credit' policy. After 1987, the structure of the country's agricultural production shifted towards small-scale industries and the services sector. To give commercial banks greater flexibility in asset management and in responding to the government's policy to support regional small-scale industries, the BoT modified the rural credit policy to cover a wider scope of activities than the narrowly defined agricultural activities. Moreover, in January 1991, the BoT broadened the coverage of rural credits to include credits for wholesale trading of agricultural produce and regional industrial estates. In 1992, the definition was further broadened to include credits for the secondary occupation of farmers, and the export of farm products.

**The Change in the Computation of Reserve Requirements**

With effect from 23 June 1991, the BoT relaxed the constraints on commercial banks' portfolio management by replacing the reserve requirement ratio with the liquidity ratio.[7] This provided greater flexibility in relation to investment options and asset management. It should be noted, however, that since the BoT had not made full use of the reserve ratio as an instrument of monetary policy (as distinct from prudential control), the change, in effect, had no significant monetary policy implication.

**Widening the Scope of Operation of Financial Institutions**

In the 1990s, the BoT formulated policies to permit financial institutions to broaden their range of activities and to fully utilize their resources and expertise. Consumers of financial services stand to benefit from the greater variety of financial services as well as greater competition among financial institutions. Under existing conditions, where financial institutions compete on the basis of deposit as well as lending rates, the margin between the lending and deposit rates has narrowed from about 6 per cent in 1990 to 4 per cent in 1994, while the cost for administration is not less than 2 per cent. Financial institutions, therefore, had to seek revenue from fee-based income. Hence, broadening the scope of operation of financial institutions will benefit both the public and the financial institutions themselves. Nevertheless, the policy to broaden the scope of operation of financial institutions was undertaken in gradual steps, with due regard being paid to the efficiency and readiness as well as available expertise of financial institutions. The solvency and stability of the financial system, along with improved procedures for supervision and examination, will also be taken into account, along with customer protection.

With regard to widening the scope of banking business, it is useful to note that financial institutions' supervision in Thailand had always placed great emphasis on prudential control. Commercial banks were therefore not permitted to engage in businesses that were considered highly risky, or in those that required specialized skills. However, the financial liberalization policy increased competition among commercial banks. The new environment forced commercial banks to change their business perspectives and to seek fee-based income to boost their profits. From 1987, the BoT deemed it necessary to allow commercial banks to conduct business related to banking business. Moreover, in 1992, commercial banks were permitted to jointly establish mutual funds management companies with local finance companies and foreign analysts with expertise in managing mutual funds. In the 1992–98 period they were allowed to conduct more businesses: for example, to act as agents to sell the government's and state enterprises' debt instruments such as bonds, debenture and commercial papers; to provide economic, financial and investment information services; to provide financial and advisory services; arranging, selling and trading debt instruments; to act as agents for secured and unsecured debenture holders; to act as trustees to mutual funds, securities registrars and as selling agents of unit trusts; to purchase and sell certificates of deposit; to receive orders to purchase or sell unit trusts to be delivered to the security companies or finance and security companies; allowing foreign branches of domestic banks to manage mutual funds for investment or international development; to manage provident funds and personal funds, to act as agents for collecting loans; to manage the project for securitization to be submitted to the Security Exchange Commission; and to purchase or transfer loan debtors. In addition, in June 1999, the BoT granted permission for commercial banks to act as agents to operate securities borrowing and lending business. Furthermore, in 1999, as a result of debt restructuring, the commercial banks were allowed to engage in the hire purchase and leasing business for a trial period of three years.

In terms of widening the scope of financial conglomerates, it should be noted that, in the past, banks' holding in other companies was strictly limited to 10 per cent of the companies' shares sold. Thai commercial banks have, for various reasons, found it necessary to set up subsidiaries or affiliates to perform non-banking businesses. This has led some banks to shield their stake in the form of holding companies or nominees. In May 1994, the BoT recognized the need for transparency and consolidated supervision and announced that banks could seek the approval to hold shares exceeding the 10 per cent limit in the following cases. A commercial bank was allowed to hold an aggregate share value of up to 20 per cent of its first-tier capital. Once the BoT relaxed the 10 per cent limit on holding shares as well, so as to allow banks wider business opportunities, it became necessary to review this limitation. The BoT therefore allowed banks to hold an aggregate share value of up to 20 per cent of their total capital (instead of Tier 1 capital). In addition, after the financial crisis of 1997, the proportion of non-performing loans in the financial system grew as a result of the economic deterioration and more stringent regulation on the classification of loans (Doukas et al., 1998). Debt restructuring helped contain the problem. As a result of debt restructuring, in November 1998, the BoT permitted financial institutions to hold shares exceeding 10 per cent of shares sold and 20 per cent of the aggregate share value on the condition that they reduce the shareholding to the legal limit within three years.

## 4 THE FINANCIAL SYSTEM MASTER PLAN (1995–2000)

### The Background

The aim of the Financial System Master Plan was to guide the development of the financial system, facilitate policy coordination, and support the national economic development plans. The plan was set to run for five years, from 1 March 1995 to 29 February 2000. It was divided into two phases. Phase I, which included short-term plans, covered the period from March 1995 to February 1997. Phase II covered the medium- and long-term plan up to 2000.

The content of the Financial System Master Plan covered seven major areas.

- The first area was the expansion in the scope of operation of financial institutions in order to operate business in line with international best practice and to strengthen their competitiveness.
- The second area was the improvement of financial system structure. The aim was to ensure proper functioning of the money market as well as the capital market, in order to support the mobilization of savings, fund allocation and economic growth.
- The third area related to enhancing competition and financial liberalization. The idea was to end oligopolistic practices and encourage competition in the financial system, paving the way for adhering to Thailand's agreed commitments under the General Agreement on Trade in Services (GATS).
- The fourth area included measures to support the government's provincial and rural development policy. Specialized financial institutions (SFIs) were to set up a Rural Development Fund to finance projects in the rural areas, particularly for infrastructure and educational projects.

- The fifth area was the improvement of the efficiency of supervision of financial institutions, in terms of both regulatory guidelines and techniques of supervision, in tandem with the process of financial liberalization and administrative expediency.
- The sixth area related to human resource development and promotion of business ethics in the financial industry.
- Finally, in order to transform Thailand into a regional financial centre, efforts were made to promote the BIBFs. However, the BIBFs later became the major contributors to the 1997 crisis.

**Facilitation of New Entry: Licensing of the BIBFs**

BIBFs were most important for developing Bangkok as a regional financial centre and thus enjoyed some tax concessions. For example, there were both reductions in tax rates and exemptions to help promote BIBFs. Corporate income tax was reduced from 30 to 10 per cent and stamp duties were exempted. Although BIBFs were required to maintain capital funds of not less than 100 million baht, they were free to maintain the funds in any form of assets. Also, they were subject to setting provisions of not less than 0.25 per cent of outstanding loans, and were required to maintain the liquidity ratio on short-term borrowings of less than one year at not less than 6 per cent. However, they were allowed greater flexibility in their operations. The BoT relaxed all prudential regulations for commercial banks (including the branches of foreign banks), such as the capital adequacy ratio and the single lending limit. The relaxation was consistent with a view that BIBFs were supervised by the authorities of the country where the parent banks of BIBFs were located. In the early stages, the BIBFs' main operations consisted of out–in corporate finance. This indeed helped to alleviate the negative investment–savings gap, which stood at 7 per cent of GDP during the rapid growth of the economy.

At the end of November 1994, total BIBF loans outstanding stood at 481.8 billion baht (approximately US$19.3 billion), about 14.5 per cent of total loans including commercial banks. Out of that amount, 417.5 billion baht (or about 86.6 per cent) was in out–in activities. The BIBFs of local banks accounted for 39.6 per cent, followed by 20.5 per cent of the BIBFs of foreign banks' branches, and 39.9 per cent of BIBFs previously without branches in Thailand. Among others, the cross-currency business was the most active, followed by the loan arrangement business. At the end of 1996, BIBF lending amounted to 1,289 billion baht, an increase of 80 per cent from the previous year. Out–out lending demonstrated a substantial increase from 165 billion baht in 1995 to 482 billion baht in 1996, while out–in lending increased moderately from 541 billion baht in 1995 to 807

Table 17.4  Credit granted by BIBFs (including Thai Banks, foreign branches and new BIBFs) (billion baht)

|  | 1996 | 1997 | 1998 | November 1999 |
|---|---|---|---|---|
| Thai banks | 330.2 | 513.2 | 211.9 | 108.4 |
| Foreign branches | 222.7 | 691.5 | 431.9 | 328.0 |
| New BIBFs | 254.5 | 206.9 | 121.7 | 90.7 |
| Total out–in | 807.4 | 1,411.6 | 765.5 | 527.1 |
| Thai banks | 16.3 | 35.4 | 28.9 | 21.7 |
| Foreign branches | 9.4 | 264.3 | 89.2 | 38.8 |
| New BIBFs | 456.6 | 171.1 | 30.4 | 12.4 |
| Total out–out | 482.3 | 470.8 | 148.5 | 72.9 |
| Total | 1,289.7 | 1,882.4 | 914.0 | 600.0 |

Source:  Bank of Thailand (1999).

billion baht in 1996, accounting for 17 per cent of overall domestic credits. After the financial crisis in 1997, the out–in lending slowed down and tended to decline due to the cessation of lending to local borrowers (see Table 17.4).

As of 1998, the overall lending of BIBFs had fallen dramatically from 1,289 billion baht in 1996 to 914 billion baht and it further decreased to 600 billion baht by the end of November 1999. Out–out lending dropped sharply from 482.3 billion baht in 1996 to only 72.9 billion baht (a decrease of 85 per cent). Out–in lending also declined to a large extent, from 807.4 billion baht to only 527.1 billion baht (a decrease of 35 per cent), over the same period.

The financial crisis in 1997 was caused, in part, by the operation of BIBFs and could be attributed to the moral hazard induced by the fixed exchange rate system, in the sense that domestic borrowers did not find it necessary to hedge against foreign exchange risk (Abdalla and Murinde, 1997). In addition, the BIBFs were not restricted from lending to domestic borrowers in dollars. Thus, out–in lending exposure grew very fast, from 456.3 billion baht in 1994 to 1.4 trillion in 1997, much of it in dollars. Shackled by the bad debts and with the economy moving into mild recession, banks sought to consolidate their balance sheets, restrict new lending and shore up their capital bases. The deepening economic recession caused the asset quality of all financial institutions to deteriorate further. Sharp declines in credit quality and falling earnings negatively impacted upon the efforts of all financial institutions to recapitalize. Given that most of the lending exposure of financial institutions in Thailand was collateral based, the banking system was badly exposed to the risk of asset price deflation.

## 5 THE 1997 FINANCIAL CRISIS AND ITS IMPACT ON FINANCIAL REFORMS

There is plenty of literature on the causes and symptoms of the Asian financial crisis in general, and the experience of Thailand in particular; see, for example, McKinnon and Pill (1998). Specifically, the poor supervision of commercial banks and finance companies by the BoT is widely seen as a key reason for the Thai economy's rapid collapse after the baht was floated in July 1997 (Vatikiotis, 1998; Vatikiotis and Keenan, 1999), along with the aforementioned build-up of private international debt through the BIBFs. When the property and stock price boom were in full swing, financial institutions did not spend resources on valuing the underlying collateral because they believed that the gains would be substantial should the need for foreclosure arise.

Moreover, in 1998 the BoT tightened the asset classification and provisioning rules, aiming to further strengthen financial supervision and bring supervisory regulations in line with the international standards. The classification criteria would include on- and off-balance sheet items and would adopt '3 months past due loans' as the definition for non-performing loans (Doukas et al., 1998). The provisioning requirement was made such that banks had to set aside provisions of at least 20 per cent in each accounting period, and fully maintain these provisions by 2000. Recognition of accrued interest income was shortened from 12 to 6 months to conform with the new definition of non-performing loans. To facilitate the foreign inflow of funds for recapitalization, the restriction on foreign ownership in Thai financial institutions was relaxed, thereby allowing foreign entities to acquire up to 100 per cent ownership for ten years, after which they would be 'grandfathered' with respect to the absolute amount of their equity holding.

The economic downturn, together with the stringent regulations, made things even worse for the banking system. Heavy losses directly affected the ability to extend credits. Most financial institutions had to recapitalize to cover the increasing amount of non-performing loans. In connection with this, four banks which were financially vulnerable and could not recapitalize on their own had to be nationalized; while the banks' management was replaced, and the existing shareholders' equity written off, to preserve the integrity of the financial system.

In solving the problem of non-performing loans in the financial system, which were continuously rising to an average of over 40 per cent at the end of 1998 due to the new loan classification system and the further economic downturn, new regulations for debt restructuring and collateral appraisal were issued as guidelines for banks. As part of an attempt to monitor the non-performing loans in the system more carefully, financial institutions were ordered to conduct qualitative reviews of their portfolios, both on- and off-balance sheet, and to submit a summary of the results to the BoT on a quarterly basis. In order to assist banks to recapitalize, on 14 August 1998 the BoT offered an assistance scheme for financial institutions which could not find partners for recapitalization. If financial institutions could comply with the new loan provisioning rules immediately, they would have the right to apply for assistance from the BoT to recapitalize their Tier 1 capital. Moreover, financial institutions were allowed to apply for assistance in recapitalizing Tier 2, if they undertook debt restructuring.

Apart from this, at the end 1998, privately owned asset management corporations (AMCs), which were set up by financial institutions solely or jointly with investors, were allowed to segregate their non-performing loans. The Thai Farmers' Bank led the way by setting up its own AMC, followed by Siam Commercial bank.

## 6 RESTRUCTURING AND REGULATORY REFORM

### New Institutions Formed to Cope with the Post-1997 Financial Crisis

#### The Asset Management Corporation (AMC)

The AMC was established on 22 October 1997 in accordance with the Emergency Decree on Asset Management Corporations B.E. 2540. The corporation was established to take over and manage all the assets of the 56 closed finance companies left over from the Financial Restructuring Authority (FRA) auctions or from the Property Loan Management Organization, as well as to purchase or receive non-performing assets from the FIDF. In order to help improve the quality of loans, it could also lend to debtors to enable them to continue in business. Initially, the capital fund of 1,000 million baht came from the Ministry of Finance, and it was given permission by the cabinet to issue bonds worth 12,000 million baht to finance the purchase of assets from the FRA.

In March 1999, the AMC purchased assets from the FRA with a principal outstanding value of 185 billion baht for 31.2 billion baht, which was a steep discount. The AMC issued promissory notes of five years' maturity in exchange for the assets purchased from the FRA. The AMC had a limited number of options in managing the assets, including debt restructuring and debt to equity conversion. It had to follow prescribed steps in order to help liquidate the assets purchased. First, it focused on debt-restructuring deals of about 5–10 billion baht with real estate developers. Second, it sold non-core assets such as vehicles, yachts and resort houses.

Third, it sold factories, developed land plots, and assets which could produce cash as soon as possible. Then it sold low-demand assets. For all the sales, the AMC made sure that all assets were sold to buyers on condition that the debtors could buy them back later. Lastly, the AMC calculated the value of non-collateralized assets in order to estimate the proportion of loans which would be converted to equity, rescheduled or written off.

Until about 2004, the AMC will manage the debts, given that some of the promissory notes mature by that date. Therefore, the AMC needs all the debtors to repay loans by 2004. In some cases, debtors need to issue debentures to cover payment to the AMC, which can then sell the debentures.

**The private asset management companies (PAMCs)**
The Emergency Decree on Asset Management Companies B.E. 2541 allowed a limited company that wished to register as a PAMC to apply for registration as an AMC. The scope of business of PAMCs focused on the purchasing of the non-performing assets from financial institution and related businesses; this was limited to no more than either the outstanding debt in contracts or the appraised value of collateral, whichever value was lower. In order to rehabilitate the debtors, PAMCs were allowed to engage in any related businesses, such as lending, collecting interest and fees, securitization, restructuring, holding shares, debt for equity swaps, renting and leasing, as well as property development, or other businesses approved by the BoT. The sources of funds came from borrowing locally or abroad and the issuance of securities, including shares and debentures as well as debt instruments. The rationale behind the issuance of the Emergency Decree was that financial institutions had a lot of low-quality assets that obstructed their recapitalization and also had an adverse effect on their ability to lend. Full economic recovery was impossible unless non-performing loans were reduced and financial institutions were able to resume lending. So it was deemed appropriate to separate low-quality assets for sale or transfer to other legal entities. This allowed banks to manage non-performing loans more effectively and press borrowers to restructure credits. In order to attract the establishment of such legal entities, in October 1999 the cabinet deemed it appropriate to give waivers on transfer fees arising from debt restructuring and on specific business taxes levied on interest revenues gained from bank lending to management companies. In 1999, the Thai Farmers' Bank started to operate a PAMC called the Thonburi AMC, and this was followed by the Jatujak AMC of Siam Commercial Bank.

The implication of the above experience is that the BoT has to enforce strict regulatory rules and monitor the PAMCs to ensure that their operations and the asset transfers are conducted in line with the regulatory standards. In cases where the commercial banks directly or indirectly hold shares in PAMCs of more than 50 per cent, the commercial banks have to draft consolidated balance sheets, and the assets transferred have to be sold by 2010.

**Radanasin Bank**
Radanasin Bank was established under the Commercial Banking Act B.E. 2505, as amended by the Commercial Banking Act (No. 3) B.E. 2535 on 23 February 1998. The initial registered capital of 4,000 million baht was fully paid by the Ministry of Finance. It was raised finally to 12,500 million baht at the end of December 1998. Radanasin Bank was mandated to purchase the good assets of 56 closed finance companies from the FRA. As well as managing the good assets from the closed finance companies, it could also lend to debtors to enable them to continue their businesses. However, because Radanasin Bank had very limited resources, its main objective was not fulfilled.

In order to efficiently manage and rearrange shareholdings in financial institutions, on 16 March 1999, the cabinet approved the sale of the ordinary shares of Radanasin bank, held by the Ministry of Finance, to the FIDF. The transfer took place on 26 July 1999. Furthermore, on 6 October 1999, the United Overseas Bank of Singapore made a 75 per cent acquisition of Radanasin Bank. Some 43 billion baht worth of non-performing loans were transferred to an AMC in exchange for bonds guaranteed by the FIDF. The AMC was set up by the FIDF and managed under a loss- or profit-sharing agreement by the United Overseas Bank (UOB). Losses of the asset management company would be borne 85 per cent by the FIDF and 15 per cent by UOB; while gains would be shared 95 per cent by the FIDF and 5 per cent by UOB. In return, UOB would receive a management fee equal to 0.1 per cent of the non-performing loans.

As of March 1999, the total assets of the new entity accounted for about 61,000 million baht, mainly comprising credit extensions; while the liabilities mainly consisted of deposits and capital funds (of 19.8 billion baht).

**The Secondary Mortgage Finance Corporation (SMC)**
The SMC was established on 27 June 1997 in accordance with the Emergency Decree on the Secondary Mortgage Finance Corporation B.E. 2540 and the Emergency Decree on the Specific Purpose Juristic Person for Securitization B.E. 2540. The rationale behind the establishment of the SMC was that it was deemed necessary to rectify the problems of real estate businesses in the country, which were in a sluggish stage, by expanding credits on housing. This was considered as one of the measures for the rehabilitation of the national economy as a whole.

The securitization business was an important financial process which could be implemented to rectify the shortage of both short- and long-term capital of businesses. It also helped create a new, highly stable financial instrument, which could facilitate the development of the country's capital market and the mobilization of savings. It was therefore expedient to establish a government agency for the development of the secondary market for housing loans by using the securitization technique to raise funds to accommodate the expansion of demand for housing credit.

The SMC received an initial fund of 1,000 million baht as capital funds from the BoT on 2 February 1998. The major source of funds, however, came from its issuance of bonds, approved by the Ministry of Finance in early 1999, in exchange for the mortgage loans from financial institutions. The mortgage loans were securitized by the issuance of securities to be sold to investors, the returns on which depend on the inflows arising from the assets. By the end of September 1998, the total assets of the SMC amounted to about 1,100 million baht, mainly cash and deposits, with only 300 million baht of credit extension while the liabilities consisted mainly of equity.

**The FIDF and the Deposit Insurance Authority**
At the time when the crisis broke out, there was no formal deposit insurance scheme in Thailand. However, the FIDF was established under the Bank of Thailand Act B.E. 2485, as amended by the Royal Decree B.E. 2528, which took effect on 27 November 1981. The Fund was set up as a separate legal entity managed by the BoT. The rationale behind the establishment of the FIDF was that financial crises had occurred several times in the past 30 years, including the RAJA finance company which was in crisis in 1979 and the 4 April 1984 lifeboat scheme which was launched to save many banks. All these past crises had created deposit runs in the financial system and public confidence had to be restored. Thus the establishment of the FIDF was a combined effort of the private sector and the government and was created within the BoT to rehabilitate the financial institutions as well as to develop the financial system and restore solvency and stability.

The initial capital of 1,500 million baht came from the BoT, with further annual contributions to help cope with the financial crisis. The Fund was empowered to collect annual insurance fees from financial institutions not exceeding 0.5 per cent of total deposits and borrowings. Initially, it began to collect fees of 0.1 per cent but, in 1998, this was raised to 0.2 per cent to compensate for the higher risk in the financial system. In addition, the government was responsible for the loss incurred by the Fund, since the Fund operated in accordance with government policy. As well, the BoT was, from time to time, allocating to the Fund any suitable amount from its reserves.

The FIDF sold four nationalized banks. The first sale, on 10 September 1999, of Nakornthon Bank (which is wholly owned by FIDF) to Standard Chartered Bank, was worth 12.38 billion baht (75 per cent of equity) and was a major success in privatizing the nationalized bank. Furthermore, on 6 October 1999, the United Overseas Bank of Singapore sealed a 75 per cent acquisition of Radanasin Bank for 15.089 billion baht, equivalent to a price of 14.4 baht per share. There were two more nationalized banks which were privatized under the scheme, Siam City Bank and Bangkok Metropolitan Bank.

Since the FIDF had to isssue a general letter of guarantee to all depositors and creditors in order to restore public confidence in the financial system in 1997, the burden directly impacted on the government, which was responsible for the loss by the FIDF. Therefore, the BoT Act was amended to reaffirm the government's commitment to underwrite the FIDF guarantees for depositors and creditors.

In the context of the above, the FIDF has played a complementary role to the traditional role of financial stability played by the BoT. Specifically, the FIDF has been instrumental in revitalizing ailing financial institutions throughout the economic crisis such that the burden of supporting financial restructuring has fallen on the FIDF rather than on the BoT. Some of the FIDF's exposure has been converted into equity as part of the recapitalization of the restructured financial institutions. The government has promised to take full responsibility for the losses of the FIDF, by converting them into government debt. This has been a key component of Thailand's overall economic programme, which is supported by the IMF (IMF, 2000).

### The Financial Sector Restructuring Authority (FRA)

The FRA was established on 24 October 1997 in accordance with the Emergency Decree on Financial Sector Restructuring B.E. 2540. The FRA was created as an independent body to oversee the rehabilitation of 58 finance companies – whose operations were suspended by the orders of the finance minister on 26 June 1997 (16 companies) and 5 August 1997 (42 companies) – and to safeguard the interest of bona fide depositors and investors.

Thus, the FRA provided a support role to the BoT in restoring financial stability to Thailand. Initially, the FRA focused on segregating the good assets from the bad assets of the banking sector. Then the FRA sold most of the good assets to Radanasin Bank in order to continue the operation of businesses. The bad assets were sold to the AMC in order to improve the value of the assets. However, as the government changed, the policy to deal with the assets of the 56 closed finance companies also altered. In order to attract more foreign currency and allow foreign investors to manage the assets, the government had to adopt a new policy to allow foreign investors to bid for the assets. After two years of operation, the FRA auctioned 648 billion of the 924 billion principal value of assets of the 56 defunct companies, with 583 billion baht as core assets and 64 billion as non-core assets. With the six past auctions of FRA, the value of the sold assets raised about 181 billion baht, about 27 per cent of the total principal value of 648 billion baht. Sales of core assets, loan contracts, yielded 25 per cent of the principal value, while the sale of the non-core assets, such as collateral and other property, yielded 53 per cent of the principal value. There were 229 billion baht of assets unsold, of which 219 billion baht were core and 10 billion baht were non-core. The FRA called bids for assets worth 23.8 billion baht on 10 November 1999, and began distributing returns from the sales to creditors in November 1999.

With the financial crisis in Thailand now over, the FRA is expected to close its operations soon after paying creditors the money earned from the auctions of the 56 defunct companies.

**The Property Loan Management Organization (PLMO)**
The PLMO was established on 10 April 1997, in accordance with the Royal Decree on the Property Loan Management Organization B.E. 2540, in order to deal with the property market bubble that had burst in 1996. The oversupply of property was caused by a lack of reliable and comprehensive information on real estate projects, together with fierce competition among the developers. In order to resolve the problem, the BoT stepped in to remedy the property loans in the financial institutions that extended credits to the property sector.

The PLMO was established to purchase property loans with collateral from financial institutions for the purpose of managing and enhancing their value. The aim was to enable the financial institutions to improve the quality of assets while continuing to look after their borrowers through additional credit and loan monitoring processes. The PLMO was not intended to directly extend credits to borrowers but was expected to arrange for a restructuring of debt so that property developers have flexibility to complete their project.

The initial capital of 1 million baht was appropriated from the government budget. Another source of capital was contributed by the 35 participating financial institutions, with an admission fee of 1 million baht for each financial institution. Its working capital, up to 100,000 million baht, was mobilized through the sale of government-guaranteed bonds as approved by the cabinet. The bonds were sold to general investors. The main objectives were to provide facilities for financial institutions to manage their property loans more flexibly, as well as to assist property developers to continue with their projects through a debt-restructuring programme. The PLMO's operating expenses were borne by both financial institutions participating in the scheme and the property developers whose loans had been transferred to the PLMO. Also, a management fee of 0.2 per cent per annum was charged equally to both financial institutions and the property developers.

As of December 1998, the total assets of the PLMO amounted to about 660 million baht, mostly consisting of short-term promissory notes issued by government financial institutions. From the beginning of its operation, the PLMO purchased only three property projects, worth around 500 million baht. Since its members were mostly the 56 closed finance companies, therefore, the business was no longer viable. On 23 March 1999 the cabinet approved the proposal of the Ministry of Finance to revoke the operation of the PLMO.

Thus, the PLMO provided a short-term palliative measure for restoring stability in the mortgage finance market, thus playing a supporting role to the efforts of the BoT in reversing the adverse effects of the financial crisis.

**The Thai Credit Bureau Company**

The Thai Credit Bureau Company was set up in September 1999 as a joint venture between the Government Housing Bank (GHB) and the Processing Centre Co. (owned by commercial banks), to operate under the auspices of the Finance Ministry. The aim of this body was to pool information about borrowers among different financial institutions. The information was expected to cover existing loans, payment and service history, and basic demographic information such as age, assets and dependencies. In the early stage, the bureau focused on consumer loans such as auto leasing, credit cards and personal loans. The bureau relied primarily on information gathered from the GHB's vast pool of mortgage borrowers. Information from other participating banks was expected to be put in the system by the end of 1999, adding to the GHB files already entered in the system. It was believed that the absence of a credit bureau was a major cause of poor credit risk management in the past, contributing to the financial crisis. There was limited customer information and hardly any credit scoring within the Thai banking system.

The Thai Bankers' Association also launched its own credit bureau, with support from the BoT, at the end of 1999. The bureau was owned by 13 Thai commercial banks with starting capital of 26 million baht. The bureau was expected to rely on the information from periodic reports on classified loans filed with the BoT, with the main focus on corporate loans. Banks were not permitted to access the information without authorization from customers. The status of the borrowers was noted in the records, such as if they were under restructuring or in bankruptcy proceedings. The bureau changed banks' lending practices from relationship-based connections and collateral-based values to analysis based on cash-flow projections.

Thus, these credit bureaux have complemented the traditional role of the BoT in restoring financial stability in Thailand. It is expected that the bureaux will eventually lead to stronger financial institutions and increased lending as banks gain increased confidence in selecting promising customers. Access to credit files of the credit bureau is limited to participating financial institutions, and then only in cases where they are considering a new loan application. Customers approaching the banks for new loans will be asked to authorize lenders to access their files from the bureau databases. The credit bureau will help speed up loan requests, reduce costs and improve access to credits for customers with good credit histories. Customers with poor credit histories will also find access to credits more difficult in the future.

**Achieving International Regulatory Standards**

**Basle capital adequacy ratio**
In order to comply with the guideline of the Basle Committee on capital adequacy, the BoT proposed to amend the Commercial Banking Act B.E. 2505, as amended by the Commercial Banking Act B.E. 2528, with the aim of upgrading the local banking standard to the international standard. The new capital adequacy ratio addressed both on- and off-balance sheet items. Since the implementation of the Basle Committee standards in 1993, Thai commercial banks have been permitted to include long-term subordinated debts and asset revaluation surpluses as supplementary capital.

During 1990–95, local commercial banks managed to accumulate their first-tier capital internally through the marked increase of retained earnings. To accomplish this, banks decreased their dividend payout to net profit ratio from 47 per cent in 1990 to 35 per cent in 1995. The banks also succeeded in the accumulation of second-tier capital. The increase in Tier 2 capital could be attributed to two main factors. First, Thai commercial banks were able to issue long-term subordinated debt in foreign currency denominations since early 1993, at a time when the Thai banking sector was very healthy. Second, the rapid expansion of branch networks of Thai banks in the past ten years had yielded a large number of new premises.

The BoT implemented the Basle ratios well before the crisis. The Basle Capital Accord of 1988, which the BoT adopted, assigned weights for various types of assets, with greater capital required for riskier types of loans. Capital to be maintained divides into two categories: first-tier capital, defined as equity and retained earning; and second-tier capital, defined as subordinated debts and revaluation from assets such as bank offices. The Basle Committee on Banking and Supervision, in June 1999, issued a new capital adequacy framework aimed at replacing the 1988 Capital Accord. The objectives of the new Capital Accord were to strengthen the stability of the international banking system and ensure a level playing field among international banks. The minimum capital adequacy ratio was initially set at 7 per cent and was gradually raised to 8.5 per cent; the first-tier capital ratio was also raised to 6 per cent in October 1996. Following the devaluation of the baht currency in July 1997, the commercial banks faced increasing non-performing loans and had to set aside provisions to meet the requirements of the BoT. Thus capital to asset ratios duly fell below the Basle ratio and the commercial banks were forced to try to recapitalize, but the time was not ripe to do so. In order to solve the problem of continuing decreases in capital, especially Tier 1 capital, in August 1998, the BoT reduced the Tier 1 requirement from 6 to 4.25 per cent, but still maintained the overall risk-weighted capital adequacy ratio of 8.5 per cent. In addition, in March and June 1999, preferred shares attached with subordinated debts were allowed to be counted as a part of Tier 1 capital, but subject to a limit of not more than 25 per cent of Tier 1 capital. This was in line with the Bank for International Settlements (BIS) rule. Moreover, the 1 per cent provision requirement set in the case of normal lending was also permitted to be counted as Tier 1 capital, but subject to a limit of 1.25 per cent of risk assets.

**Asset classification, accrued interest and appraisal of collaterals**
In the past, the BoT allowed Thai commercial banks to include as assets accrued interest, in the form of revenues, given that the value of collateral covered total debt outstanding. However, the practice motivated banks to focus and rely on collateral (most of which is real estate) in their credit approval process. In an effort to follow international accounting standards, a more stringent income recognition rule for financial institutions was introduced in July 1995 when the BoT ruled that financial institutions could record accrued interest as income only up to 6 months, and if the loans and interest accrued were fully collateralized, accrued interest could then be recorded up to one year. Consequently, the period was reduced to only 6 months, and since 1999 only 3 months' accrued interest could be recorded in accordance with the '3 months past due' classification.

The classification and provisions of debts were amended. Previously, the BoT classified debts into four categories, namely, 'special mention', 'substandard', 'doubtful' and 'bad'. For doubtful debts, banks were required to set aside provisions of up to 50 per cent. In order to comply with international standards, in 1998 the classification of debts was improved by dividing them into four categories according to the past due date. If within 3 months past due, they were classified as special mention, 3–6 months past due as substandard debts, 6–12 months past due were classified as doubtful debts and over 12 months past due were classified as doubtful loss. In addition, the provisions were also adjusted: for doubtful debts they were raised to 75 per cent (100 per cent in 1995) while provisions of 20 and 100 per cent were levied on substandard debts and doubtful loss in 1997, respectively, with provisions of 1 per cent for normal debts and 2 per cent for special mention were introduced in 1998.

**Other Post-crisis Developments**

**Guidelines for equity holding for foreign investors in Thai financial institutions**
The 1962 Banking Act prohibited foreign nationals from holding shares (or being directors) in Thai commercial banks in excess of one-quarter of the total shares. It also prohibited directors of one commercial bank from becoming directors in another commercial bank. As the financial crisis broke out in 1997, the public had no confidence in the financial system. The quality of assets was also deteriorating rapidly in line with the slowdown in the economy. It was difficult for financial institutions to raise their own capital. Therefore, in order to attract funds from abroad so as to enhance the stability of the financial system, the 1962 Banking Act was amended on 28 June 1997 to allow foreign entities or foreigners to hold shares in excess of the previous limit and to allow directors from one bank to be directors in another bank as well. However, the Ministry of Finance and the BoT also issued guidelines for equity holdings in financial institutions by permitting foreign entities that have a sound financial status and high potential to help increase the efficiency of the management of their financial institution to hold equities in Thai financial institutions of more than 49 per cent of total shares for a period of ten years. After ten years, if the shareholding exceeded 49 per cent, the foreign entities would be allowed to continue such an amount of shareholdings but they could not purchase or exercise the right to purchase any additional shares, unless the amount of shareholdings was less than 49 per cent.

Regarding the policy statement, DBS Bank, ABN–AMRO Bank, Standard Chartered Bank and United Overseas Bank were allowed to acquire shares in Thai banks of more than 49 per cent (and up to 75 per cent). Between 10 and 49 per cent of shares in other banks, such as Bangkok Bank, Thai Farmers' Bank and Siam Commercial Bank, were allowed to be acquired by foreign entities. Many other Thai banks, such as Bangkok Metropolitan Bank and Siam City Bank, were put up for sale.

## Mergers, acquisitions and the privatization of state-owned banks

Following the closure of 56 finance companies in 1997, the persistent economic slowdown and liquidity shortage in the money market caused the asset quality of financial institutions to deteriorate. Moreover, the requirement for financial institutions to set aside provisions against classified assets in line with international best practice resulted in many financial institutions experiencing losses, thus requiring recapitalization in order to strengthen their positions.

In May 1998, the BoT ordered seven finance companies and four banks to write down their capital and reduce their par value per share to 1 satang (100 satang equals 1 baht) to eliminate the loss of the companies. Moreover, in August 1998, the BoT further intervened in two banks and five finance companies using the same criteria. Thereafter, the financial institutions concerned were expected to raise sufficient capital to increase their capital adequacy ratio to 9 per cent, with the new shares to be sold to the FIDF. The BoT also ordered the removal of the board of directors and the appointment of new directors to oversee the management. Thereafter, Krungthai Thanakit Public Company Limited, a state-owned finance company, merged with 12 finance companies and Union Bank of Bangkok and became Bank Thai, while Leam Thong Bank was integrated with Radanasin Bank. Another two banks, Bangkok Bank of Commerce and First Bangkok City Bank, were partially or fully acquired by Krung Thai Bank. Two other banks, including Bangkok Metropolitan Bank and Siam City Bank, were offered for sale by the end of year 2000. These procedures were designed to reduce damage to the FIDF because of the potential profits from selling these shares to the private sector in the future.

Following the government's measures to resolve the corporate liquidity situation and strengthen financial sector soundness, the BoT on 14 August 1998 set the criteria whereby a bank or a finance company would be required: to write down capital to 1 satang per share; to remove management; and to seek recapitalization by the FIDF. The institutions would qualify for FIDF recapitalization if they had incurred large operating losses but they were able to present a clear and credible recapitalization plan.

In addition, due to slim future prospects to raise new capital to meet the Basle capital adequacy ratio, the government initiated the 'capital support scheme' to help recapitalize the financial institutions and provide incentives for the financial institutions (especially large commercial banks) to extend more credit to the corporate sector. The Financial Restructuring Authority Committee (FRAC) was set up with a 300 billion baht budget to help Thai banks recapitalize. The FRAC was expected to support any Thai commercial banks wanting to seek additional Tier 1 capital from the BoT in the form of preferred shares to fulfil their BIS capital adequacy ratio after setting aside the 100 per cent provisions required in year 2000 up front. Should the existing shareholders or management be concerned about the *dilution* effect, they would opt for the Tier 2 scheme in order to boost corporate debt restructuring.

Thus, this scheme is working jointly with BoT in a bid to facilitate the recapitalization of Thai banks.

**Proposed Banking and Finance Act reforms**
The Commercial Banking Act and the Act on the undertaking of finance business, securities business and *crédit foncier* business have been effective since 1962 and 1979, respectively. Both Acts have been improved and amended several times during the 1976–92 period. When the financial crisis broke out in 1997, both Acts were unable to cope with the problems. The main objectives of amending the Commercial Banking Act and the Finance Company Act were as follows:

- Banks and finance companies were separately treated using different supervisory frameworks. This created difficulties in efficiently controlling them. In the amendment to the Acts in 1992, the BoT sought to bring both Acts to the same standard.
- Financial service conglomerates were permitted in order to modernize the regulatory framework for both banks and finance companies. It allowed financial services, such as insurance, leasing and securities companies, to be owned by holding companies. The BoT was responsible for supervising financial institutions while other agencies were involved in regulating the financial services.

Thus, the amendments to the Acts were designed to provide the BoT with more powers to tackle problems in financial institutions at an early stage. They would allow the central bank to tackle problems rather than avoiding them. Previously, the Banking Act had left such matters to the discretion of the central bank governor, but the revised Act called for prompt and thorough action in all cases, thus modifying the traditional role of the BoT in view of the financial crisis.

## 7 CONCLUSIONS AND LESSONS

One important lesson from the financial crisis is that, in Thailand, financial liberalization in an uncontrolled financial sector resulted in misallocation and mismatching of funds. In general, the Thai financial crisis reflected the failure of the banking sector, expressing itself partly in increasing current account problems but mainly in careless lending/borrowing and the accumulation of non-performing loans. By the time the real economy started to show signs of weakening, with sluggish exports and an increase in the current account deficit, 'hot money' flowed in and covered the deficit; but this also led to careless investments. Consistent with the conclusion by Lensink et al. (2000), it may be argued that political instability, indecisiveness and mismanagement at the political and administrative level also contributed to capital flight and the financial meltdown in Thailand.

Lack of effective financial regulation played an important role in aggravating the financial crisis. Thus, the important lesson is that failure to impose proper regulatory and legal control over the operations of banks has serious consequences. In particular, excessive lending by domestic banks (sometimes financed by international investors) and a lack of control over the actions of the borrowers need to be addressed. Poor policy making, both at the central bank and within commercial banks, encouraged overinvestment and hence aggravated the fragility of the banking sector as firms were unable to service their debts.

One inevitable consequence of the financial crisis in Thailand has been the renaissance of informal credit in Thailand (Vatikiotis, 1998). New BoT rules introduced at the end of March 1998 to tighten borrowing have led to sharply higher interest rates. The tougher regulations will mean a fundamental – perhaps painful – change in Thailand's business culture. For generations, Thais have taken out loans using assets, rather than cash flow, as collateral. To change all this may require more than a simple decree from the central bank. The personal nature of banking in Thailand means that local branches often act independently of head offices, setting their own interest rates and managing their own clients.

Another important lesson from this chapter is that, under a liberalized financial system, the central bank's role in supervision and examination of financial institutions is complex and demanding. Prudential regulation must be robust, up to date and well balanced in order not to hinder the future development of financial institutions and innovations. Regulation must also be effective in maintaining stable and sound operation of financial institutions.

## NOTES

\* We thank Malee Sariddikul for useful comments on earlier versions of this chapter. We gratefully acknowledge financial support from the Department for International Development (DFID) under the 'Finance and Development Research Programme', Contract No. RSCI06506. However, the interpretations and conclusions expressed in this

chapter are entirely those of the authors and should not be attributed in any manner to DFID.
1. These responsibilities are stipulated in the Bank of Thailand Act B.E. 2485 (1942).
2. Possibly, the increase in bank lending to some sectors by 1998 compared to 1994 reported in Table 17.1 may be explained by the fact that the general lending practices of Thai banks were not focused primarily on collateral, such as land and premises, but on the feasibility study. If the business plan for the project was well prepared, the amount of the loan granted would be much higher than the value of the collateral.
3. The central bank also raised the limit on foreign exchange purchase for travelling expenses overseas to US$20,000 per trip. Commercial banks were also allowed to approve outward transfers of foreign exchange in small amounts not exceeding US$50,000 for the remittance of loans, the sale of securities, and the liquidation of companies.
4. In addition, on 2 February 1994, further relaxation of the exchange control increased convenience for outward transfer of foreign exchange and baht currency for foreign investments and lending to subsidiaries, with limits being raised from US$5 million to US$10 million; the repayment of foreign debt was also permitted.
5. The calculation of the MRR is based on the total cost of deposits, operational cost, and profit margin of 2 per cent. Every category of lending rate to retail customers must be related to the MRR, and commercial banks have to quote a lending rate for retail customers not exceeding the MRR.
6. This is an average of interest payable on the deposits of the five biggest banks.
7. The liquidity ratio allows commercial banks to substitute other securities for government securities, namely BoT's bonds, and bonds issued by governmental organizations and state enterprises.

# REFERENCES

Abdalla, I.S.A. and V. Murinde (1997), 'Exchange rate and stock price interactions in emerging financial markets: evidence on India, Korea, Pakistan, and the Philippines', *Applied Financial Economics*, **7**, February, 25–35.

Bank of Thailand (1999), *Bank of Thailand Annual Report*, Bangkok: Bank of Thailand.

Doukas, J., V. Murinde and C. Wihlborg (1998), *Financial Sector Reform and Privatisation in Transition Economies*, Amsterdam: Elsevier Science B.V. (North-Holland).

Fry, M.J. and V. Murinde (1998), 'International financial flows and development: Editors' preface', *World Development*, **26** (7), July, 1165–68.

International Monetary Fund (IMF) (2000), *International Financial Statistics*, April, Washington, DC: IMF.

Laurisden, L.S. (1998), 'The financial crisis in Thailand: causes, conduct and consequences?', *World Development*, **26** (8), 1575–91.

Lensink, R. and N. Hermes and V. Murinde (1998), 'The effect of financial liberalization on capital flight', *World Development*, **26** (7), July, 1349–68.

Lensink, R., N. Hermes and V. Murinde (2000), 'Capital flight and political risk', *Journal of International Money and Finance*, **19**, 73–92.

McKinnon, J. and H. Pill (1998), 'International overborrowing: a decomposition of credit and currency risks', *World Development*, **26** (7), July, 1267–82.

Vatikiotis, M. (1998), 'Culture shock', *Far Eastern Economic Review*, **161** (16), 54–6.

Vatikiotis, M. and F. Keenan (1999), 'Princely tradition', *Far Eastern Economic Review*, **162** (22), 44–5.

# 18. Capital flight: the key issues
## Niels Hermes, Robert Lensink and Victor Murinde

## 1 INTRODUCTION

The issue of capital flight has gained much attention in academic as well as policy circles since the early 1980s (see, for example, World Bank, 1985; Cuddington, 1986; Eaton, 1987; Deppler and Williamson, 1987; Dooley, 1988; Diwan, 1989; Mikkelsen, 1991; Hermes and Lensink, 1992; Claessens and Naudé, 1993; Murinde et al., 1996; and Lensink et al., 1998, 2000). Initially, research interest focused on Latin American economies, since the debt crisis that hit these countries stimulated massive outflows of capital.[1] Capital flight from Latin America, in general, appeared to be voluminous in absolute terms; the sheer volume posed a threat to the viability of the domestic banking system, national solvency and economic stability. In addition, the flight of capital – the scarce resource in these economies – occurred at the same time that the countries were in desperate need of foreign exchange to amortize their outstanding debt to commercial banks in industrial countries. In the context of highly indebted countries coexisting with commercial banks ridden with bad loans, the capital flight problem indirectly also threatened the stability of the international financial system.

From the end of the 1980s and early 1990s the debt crisis appeared to be contained and interest in the capital flight phenomenon waned. However, capital flight still remained a serious problem in a number of countries. In particular, several countries in Africa and Eastern Europe still experienced outflows. Yet, many countries in Asia and Latin America were receiving large capital inflows, instead of experiencing massive outflows during this period. However, from the mid-1990s the international financial system was confronted with the outbreak of several major financial and economic crises. First, in 1994–95 Mexico and some Latin American countries experienced the Tequila crisis. Then, in 1997–98 several Asian countries experienced a deep financial and economic crisis, followed by Russia (1998) and Brazil (1999). In all these cases, countries experienced massive withdrawal of capital, which was tantamount to serious capital flight. The financial and economic problems led domestic and international investors to withdraw their money immediately, causing panic in the international financial markets, which was stimulated by herd behaviour of investors as well as contagion effects in the markets. Again, as in the early 1980s, there were fears of massive capital outflows threatening the stability of the international banking system. As of late 1999, the Asian crisis seems to have been solved to a large extent and the international banking system has been prevented from becoming unstable. Yet, the problems in Russia and (to a lesser extent) Brazil may still pose a threat to the international financial system. The Russian case, especially, is currently heavily debated, due to the volume of capital flight involved (estimated at between US$120 billion and US$160 billion in the 1990s; Abalkin and Whalley, 1999; Loukine, 1998), and the potentially explosive relationship with the unstable political situation in the country.

These current and past crisis situations and their consequences for economic conditions in recipient countries, as well as the international banking system, call for more research on the determinants of capital flows and the related behaviour of domestic and international investors. Increased insight into those determinants may help to develop measures to avoid the extreme volatility of capital flows of the past, thereby contributing to the stability of the international banking system. One way of approaching this is to investigate empirically what exactly determines the capital flight phenomenon.

This chapter examines the main issues surrounding capital flight, including the definition, measurement and determinants of the phenomenon. In particular, the chapter focuses on a very important, but until now empirically neglected determinant of capital flight, namely the effects of uncertainty of domestic policies on the flight of capital from developing countries. Before analysing the relationship between policy uncertainty and capital flight, however, the chapter starts by presenting an up-to-date survey of the capital flight phenomenon.

In what follows, this chapter is structured into six sections. Section 2 discusses the concept of capital flight. Section 3 identifies the different methods of measuring capital flight in the existing literature. Section 4 presents estimates of the order of magnitude of capital flight for a large group of developing countries for the 1971–91 period. Section 5 provides an overview of the theory on the determinants of capital flight, as well as the outcomes of empirical studies on these determinants. Section 6 presents new estimates on the relationship between policy uncertainty and capital flight. Section 7 concludes.

## 2 CONCEPTS OF CAPITAL FLIGHT

In the literature on capital flight there is no general agreement on what exactly is meant by the term. In several studies, it is suggested that capital flight should be distinguished from *normal* capital outflows. According to these studies normal outflows are based on considerations of portfolio diversification of residents – for example, in terms of portfolio or direct investment and trade credit – and/or activities of domestic commercial banks aiming at acquiring or extending foreign deposit holdings. In their view, the phenomenon of capital flight is somehow related to the existence of extremely high uncertainty and risk with respect to returns on domestically held assets. Residents take their money and run in order to avoid extremely high losses on their domestic asset holdings. Authors like Deppler and Williamson (1987) argue that capital flight is motivated by the fear of losing wealth, due to, for example, expropriation of wealth by the government, sudden exchange rate depreciation, non-repayment of government debts, (changes in) capital controls and financial market regulations, and (changes in) tax policies. Walter (1987) and Kindleberger (1987) have a similar opinion. These authors suggest that capital flight should be related to the abnormal or illegal nature of certain capital outflows.

One way of dealing with separating normal from abnormal, or illegal, capital flows is to label all capital outflows that do not generate reported interest income as being illegal capital flows. Other attempts to separate normal capital outflows from capital flight simply focus on those outflows that are viewed as being normal, such as long-term portfolios and foreign direct investment. These outflows are then subtracted from total capital outflows to determine capital flight. Yet, as will be discussed more fully in the next section, in practice it is extremely difficult to distinguish empirically between normal and abnormal or illegal capital outflows (see also Gordon and Levine, 1989).

One may question whether it is indeed useful to distinguish capital flight and capital outflows based on the arguments discussed above. For countries struggling with (large) current account deficits – which are thus in need of foreign capital – any capital outflow increases the problems of financing their net imports, thus reducing economic growth. For example, a recent study shows that the cost of capital flight for Mexico amounted to between 0.6 and 1.7 per cent of GDP during 1982–88 (López, 1998). So, the usefulness of distinguishing normal and abnormal outflows also depends on the underlying economic policy question.

Therefore, in this chapter all resident capital outflows leading to a buildup of assets held abroad by residents are labelled capital flight. Capital flight is the result of a private portfolio decision. The individual wealth-holder compares expected rates of return of different domestic and foreign assets. Taking into account portfolio diversification, rates of return differentials, and risk and uncertainty aspects, the individual divides his or her wealth over domestic and foreign assets (Eggerstedt et al., 1995; Collier et al., 1999).

## 3  THE MEASUREMENT OF CAPITAL FLIGHT

Since there is no general agreement on what exactly is meant by capital flight, the measurement of capital flight is difficult. Consequently, several capital flight measures are available in the literature. Not surprisingly, this leads to differences in capital flight estimates for different countries.

In general, the following methods of capital flight measurement can be distinguished in the literature: (i) the residual method; (ii) the hot money method; (iii) the Dooley method; (iv) the trade misinvoicing method; and (v) the asset method (Claessens and Naudé, 1993, pp. 2–9; Murinde et al., 1996, pp. 62–6). Below, we shall briefly describe these different methods of measurement.

**The Residual Method**

This method measures capital flight indirectly by comparing the *sources* of capital inflows (that is, net increases in external debt and the net inflow of foreign investment) with the *uses* of these inflows (that is, the current account deficit and additions to foreign reserves). This approach starts from the standard balance of payments framework. In principle, if the balance of payments statistics were to be used, the uses and sources of funds should be equal. However, since these statistics may not measure flows accurately, and in particular private capital flows, World Bank statistics on the change in the external debt are used instead. If the sources, calculated by using World Bank debt data, exceed the uses of capital inflows, the difference is termed 'capital flight'. The residual method acknowledges the difficulties of separating abnormal from normal capital outflows and, therefore, measures all private capital outflows as being capital flight.

According to the residual method capital flight is calculated as follows:

$$KF_r = \Delta ED + FI - CAD - \Delta FR, \qquad (18.1)$$

where $KF_r$ is capital flight according to the residual method, $\Delta$ denotes change, $ED$ is stock of gross external debt reported in the World Bank data, $FI$ is the net foreign investment inflows, $CAD$ is the current account deficit and $FR$ is the stock of official foreign reserves.

In the literature, the residual method has been widely used, in some cases with (minor) modifications. The standard approach as described above has been used by, among others, the World Bank (1985) and Erbe (1985). Morgan Guaranty (1986) takes into account an additional item, that is, the change in the short-term foreign assets of the domestic banking system ($\Delta B$). This modification is introduced to focus on non-bank capital flight. The Morgan Guaranty variant of the residual method ($KF_m$) can thus be calculated as:

$$KF_m = \Delta ED + FI - CAD - \Delta FR - \Delta B. \tag{18.2}$$

Cline (1986; cited in Cumby and Levich, 1987) also uses the residual method, but proposes to exclude the following items from the current account balances: travel (credit), reinvested earnings on direct investment abroad, reinvested earnings on direct investment domestically, and other investment income (credit). He argues that income from tourism, border transactions and reinvested investment income should not be considered capital flight since these earnings are beyond the control of the authorities (Cumby and Levich, 1987, pp. 33–4). Claessens and Naudé (1993), in contrast to most others, take into account net acquisitions of corporate equities in their measure of foreign direct investment. Zedillo (1987) argues that the standard residual method should be modified with respect to the measurement of external debt and the current account deficit. First, instead of measuring changes in the stock of external debt, Zedillo proposes to look at flows, since this may more accurately report annual capital flows. Second, he proposes to adjust the current account for interest earned and retained abroad. This is estimated by taking the interest on identified deposits of residents held abroad. Brown (1990) and Vos (1992) propose to take into account the unrecorded remittances of workers abroad. These remittances tend to be understated in the balance of payments statistics of developing countries, leading to an overstatement of the current account deficits. This would then result in lower estimates of capital flight. Remittances of workers abroad are important sources of foreign exchange for several developing countries, for instance Egypt, Sudan and the Philippines. Finally, Morgan Guaranty (1988) and Pastor (1990) add interest earnings on the stock of assets held abroad, taking a representative international market interest rate to compute these earnings. This, of course, increases the estimates of capital flight based on the residual method.

**The Dooley Method**

This method aims at distinguishing normal from abnormal, or illegal, capital flows. Dooley (1986) sees capital flight as the total amount of externally held assets of the private sector that do not generate income recorded in the balance of payments statistics of a country. Or, stated otherwise, capital flight is all capital outflows based on the desire to place wealth beyond the control of the domestic authorities. The Dooley method of measuring capital flight starts by computing total capital outflows as reported in the balance of payments statistics, but then makes a number of modifications. First, errors and omissions are taken into account to measure total capital outflows. Second, the Dooley method takes into account the difference between the World Bank data on the change in the stock of external debt and the amount of external borrowing as reported in the balance of payments statistics. If the first is larger than the second, this difference is assumed to be part of capital flight. Third, the stock of external assets that corresponds to the reported interest rate earnings in the balance of payments is computed by using a representative market interest rate (that is, the US deposit rate). The difference between total capital outflows and the change in the stock of external assets corresponding to reported interest income is measured as capital flight. The Dooley method is conceptually different from the residual method. Yet, Claessens and Naudé (1993, pp. 5–7) show that in practice capital flight measured according to the Dooley method and the residual method are fairly similar, since a major part of the data used for calculation are the same in both cases.

According to the Dooley method, capital flight is measured as follows. First, the amount total capital outflows is calculated:

$$TKO = FB + FI - CAD - \Delta FR - EO - \Delta WBIMF, \qquad (18.3)$$

where $TKO$ is total capital outflows, $FB$ is foreign borrowing as reported in the balance of payments statistics, $EO$ is net errors and omissions, and $WBIMF$ is the difference between the change in the stock of external debt reported by the World Bank and foreign borrowing reported in the balance of payments statistics published by the International Monetary Fund (IMF).

The stock of external assets corresponding to reported interest earnings is:

$$ES = (1 + r_{US}) * INTEAR, \qquad (18.4)$$

where $ES$ is external assets, $r_{US}$ is the US deposit rate (assumed to be a representative international market interest rate), and $INTEAR$ is reported interest earnings. Capital flight according to the Dooley method is then measured as:

$$KF_d = TKO - ES. \qquad (18.5)$$

### The Hot Money Method

According to this method, capital flight is measured by adding up net errors and omissions and non-bank private short-term capital outflows. Cuddington (1986, 1987), Ketkar and Ketkar (1989) and Gibson and Tsakalotos (1993) are examples of authors that have used this method of measuring capital flight. Like the Dooley method, this method corresponds to the idea that capital flight goes unrecorded, due to the illegal nature of these capital movements. These unrecorded capital movements are believed to appear in net errors and omissions. Moreover, by concentrating on short-term flows, medium- and long-term outflows are excluded, which are viewed as being normal in character (Gibson and Tsakalotos, 1993, p. 146). Thus, the hot money method ($KF_h$) can be calculated as follows:

$$KF_h = SKO + EO, \tag{18.6}$$

where $SKO$ is the total amount of short-term capital outflows.

### The Trade Misinvoicing Method

Some authors use the amount of *trade misinvoicing* as a measure of capital flight (Claessens and Naudé, 1993). Proponents of this measure stress the fact that abnormal capital outflows of residents may be included in export underinvoicing and/or import overinvoicing, since both these malpractices provide channels to siphon domestically accumulated wealth outside the country. In some cases, those authors using the residual method argue that the measurement of capital flight in this way is inaccurate due to the poor quality of export and import figures resulting from trade misinvoicing. They, therefore, propose to adjust capital flight figures based on the residual method (Gulati, 1987; Lessard and Williamson, 1987; Vos, 1992; Eggerstedt et al., 1995; Collier et al., 1999).

### The Asset Method

Finally, some authors take the total stock of assets of non-bank residents held at foreign banks as a measure of capital flight. This is the so-called *asset method* (Hermes and Lensink, 1992). The asset method is a short-cut measure of capital flight. Data on such bank assets can be obtained directly from IMF statistics. This measure may be seen as an indication of the minimum amount of assets held abroad, since residents may hold their assets in other forms next to bank accounts, for example, in foreign equity holdings.

**The Methods and Their Drawbacks**

The methods discussed above have important drawbacks. In our view, the Dooley and hot money methods are conceptually wrong. As was already argued above, the distinction between normal and abnormal, or illegal, capital outflows is not useful. What really matters is that a country confronted with a lack of financial resources to finance long-term development experiences an adverse impact on its future growth prospects when net capital outflows occur. With respect to the hot money method it may be added that it is unclear why capital flight should consist of short-term capital movements only. Assets of residents held outside the home country based on a longer-term perspective should also be part of capital flight. The asset method may suffer from being too narrow a measure of total capital flight and may leave out potentially large parts of capital flight. Moreover, assets held at foreign banks are not always specified by ownership. Taking into account the inaccuracy of trade data due to misinvoicing may help to improve capital flight estimates. Yet, it has been argued that trade misinvoicing may also occur in the presence of trade taxes. Calculated trade misinvoicing may then be unrelated to the phenomenon of capital flight (Gibson and Tsakalotos, 1993, p. 150). Moreover, Chang and Cumby (1991, p. 167) in a study on the magnitude of capital flight in Sub-Saharan Africa point out that 'the systemic underreporting of trade figures in both directions to avoid trade barriers . . . seems to overwhelm any discernible capital flight through misinvoicing'. Since many developing countries make use of some form of trade barriers, we have every reason to assume that this finding will also apply in the case of other developing countries.

Taking into account the above-mentioned drawbacks of the different methods of calculating capital flight, we are in favour of using the residual method, and in particular the specification proposed by Morgan Guaranty (1986), to measure capital flight. Thus, in the rest of this chapter we shall use this measure to calculate capital flight.

## 4 THE MAGNITUDE OF CAPITAL FLIGHT

A number of empirical studies have reported measures of capital flight on the basis of the main methods used in the literature. For example, Lensink et al. (2000) present the annual flow of capital flight for 84 developing countries during the 1971–91 period, calculated according to three methods of measurement: the Morgan Guaranty method, the hot money method and the Dooley method. It is argued that the Morgan Guaranty method should be used to represent the residual method of measuring capital flight, since the most widely used variation on this measure follows Morgan Guaranty (1986). The other two measures are presented to show the sensitivity of measuring the capital flight phenomenon when using different methods. The annual flows measured according to the Morgan Guaranty and Dooley methods show similar patterns. This may be expected, since as discussed in the previous section, both methods – although conceptually different – measure capital flight using the same data definitions. The annual flows measured according to the hot money method differ in two respects from those based on the other two methods. First, the flows based on the hot money method fluctuate less severely. Second, hot money flows turn negative after 1985, whereas for the other measures this is the case only after 1988. Nevertheless, the general trend of the flows for all the three measures presented in Figure 1 of Lensink et al. (2000) shows a similar pattern for most of the 1971–91 period.

Collier et al. (1999) provide estimates of the stock of flight capital and the total stock of private wealth (measured as the sum of capital flight stock, private real capital stock and quasi money) for 51 developing countries in 1990. It is shown that the total stock of private capital divided by the labour force is very low for the Sub-Saharan African countries (US$1,069) as compared to the countries in Latin America (US$17,424), South Asia (US$2,425), East Asia (US$9,711) and the Middle East (US$3,678). Yet, the capital flight ratio, measured as the capital flight stock divided by the total stock of private wealth, is the highest for the Sub-Saharan African countries. Whereas this ratio is 0.39 for the countries in this region, it is considerably lower for the countries in East Asia (0.06), South Asia (0.03) and even for those in Latin America (0.10). Only the Middle Eastern countries seem to suffer from a similar incidence of capital flight (0.39) by 1990.

## 5 DETERMINANTS OF CAPITAL FLIGHT: THEORY AND EMPIRICAL RESULTS

Stated in a formal way, capital flight is directly related to the behaviour of a risk-averse individual who diversifies their wealth in order to maximize their returns. This emphasizes the decision to hold assets abroad as part of the process of portfolio diversification (Cuddington, 1986; Gibson and Tsakalotos, 1993; Lensink et al., 1998). Differences in rates of return between domestic and foreign asset holdings, the amount of wealth, and risk and uncertainty aspects influence this decision. The following main determinants of capital flight are discussed here: (i) macroeconomic instability; (ii) political instability; (iii) rate of return differentials; (iv) capital inflows; and (v) stock of capital flight (Hermes and Lensink, 1992;

Murinde et al., 1996; Collier et al., 1999). These determinants have a direct influence on portfolio decisions of individuals. As will be shown, in a number of cases the determinants are closely connected. The definition and measurement of these determinants are presented in Appendix 18A.

**Macroeconomic Instability**

Macroeconomic instability occurs when aggregate domestic demand exceeds aggregate domestic supply on a structural basis. The causes of this instability may be manifold, for example political tensions and instability, wrong or lacking incentive structures and institutions to let markets efficiently coordinate demand and supply, and heavy government involvement, which may put markets at the sideline. Whatever the exact reasons, when a country experiences macroeconomic instability this may become manifest in a number of ways: budget deficits will rise, current account deficits increase, exchange rate overvaluation occurs and inflation is growing. Variables describing such factors are often found in studies on the determinants of capital flight.

Exchange rate overvaluation is often found to be an important variable in studies of capital flight and its underlying determinants. An overvalued exchange rate leads to increasing expectations of depreciation in the near future. This in turn will lead to rising prices of foreign goods relative to those of domestic goods and thus to loss of real income. To avoid welfare losses residents hold at least part of their assets abroad. High inflation directly erodes the real value of domestic assets, stimulating residents to hold assets outside the country. Moreover, inflation rates and the exchange rate are closely connected, since high inflation may lead to increasing expectations of depreciation in the future. High current account deficits may have a similar impact on exchange rate expectations, and may thus be a stimulus for capital flight. Government budget deficits may stimulate capital flight, since they raise expectations of residents with respect to future tax increases or increases in inflation tax, as it is anticipated that the government needs to repay its debt. In both cases, the real value of domestic assets is eroded, leading to capital flight.

In all the cases discussed here, macroeconomic instability leads to (indirectly) increasing taxes and tax-like distortions. This will lower returns and increase risk and uncertainty of domestically held wealth (Collier et al., 1999, p. 4). This will increase incentives for capital flight. The large outflows of capital at the beginning of the debt crisis in the early 1980s and at the outbreak of the Asian crisis in 1997–98 support this view. The macroeconomic situation of these countries was highly unstable during these years.

### Political Instability

Whereas macroeconomic instability variables focus on the outcomes of public policies and their impact on capital flight, one may also look at the institutional context in which these policies have been carried out. The institutional context itself may give rise to capital flight. Public sector behaviour may have an impact on the risks and uncertainty regarding the policy environment and its outcomes. More specifically, residents may decide to hold their assets abroad based on a lack of confidence in the domestic political situation and its consequences for the future value of their assets. In these cases, perceived political instability may generate capital flight. Models that illustrate the impact of political instability on capital flight can be found in Alesina and Tabellini (1989), Tornell and Velasco (1992), and Bhattacharya (1999). They show that when different governments with different interest groups supporting them come into office, this will increase the uncertainty with respect to future fiscal policies. Such an unstable political situation may, for example, lead to a political business cycle. Political instability may also turn into political unrest, leading to strikes, riots, assassinations, and so on. Finally, different forms of the regime type (for example, democracy, autocracy) may have a different impact on the degree of uncertainty about future policy and its outcomes.

Political instability may thus have an influence on the possibility that the government may in one way or another erode the future value of asset holdings. The erosion of future wealth is based on the expectation that domestic political instability causes rising macroeconomic instability, leading to rising budget deficits, current account deficits, exchange rate uncertainty and high inflation. Several studies on the determinants of capital flight take into account one or more variables that measure the degree of political uncertainty.

### Interest Rate Differentials

Of course, capital flight may occur simply because the returns on assets are higher abroad as compared to assets held domestically. Most studies on the determinants take this into account by adding a variable that measures the (after tax) real interest rate differential.

### Capital Inflows

Several authors specifically emphasize the role played by foreign borrowing as a determinant of capital flight. The explanations for the relationship between foreign borrowing and capital flight are related to the issues discussed earlier with respect to macroeconomic and political instability. Yet, we spend some time discussing the role played by foreign borrowing, since in the literature several models deal with the issue of the simultaneous occurrence of capital flight and capital inflows. Moreover, as we shall show below, most empirical studies emphasize the role played by capital inflows in explaining capital flight.

Especially during the 1970s and early 1980s, developing countries experienced massive capital inflows and outflows at the same time. Eaton (1987) presents a theoretical model in which he explains why the increase of foreign borrowing may stimulate capital flight. According to the model, residents may borrow on international capital markets and then use the loans (plus potential domestically held assets) to buy foreign assets. This is advantageous if they expect their government to nationalize debt repayments at some point in time, which will release them from the obligation to repay, and if domestic taxes are high. These expectations reflect moral hazard behaviour of residents: they expect to be bailed out by their government. In the early 1980s the moral hazard behaviour of domestic borrowers was rewarded when governments of several developing countries actually nationalized foreign debt repayments.

Under the above-mentioned assumptions, current foreign borrowing increases future repayment obligations of the government when it actually nationalizes debt repayments. If residents perceive that the government will pass the costs of these repayments on to them, for example by using the inflation tax, they may choose to convert their domestic assets into foreign assets. Moreover, the occurrence of capital flight itself stimulates others to hold money abroad, since now the future costs of debt repayment by the government have to be shared by a decreasing number of wealth holders. Similar models by Eaton and Gersovitz (1989) and Ize and Ortiz (1987) show that capital flight is stimulated when the public sector itself borrows in the international capital markets to finance its current expenditures. Fry (1993) stresses that growing government-guaranteed foreign debt may increase expectations about exchange rate devaluations, which provides a stimulus to hold foreign assets.

Other authors stress the importance of differences in perceived risk of investing in the domestic economy to explain the simultaneous inflow and outflow of capital (Khan and Ul Haque, 1985; Dooley, 1988; Diwan, 1989). Residents face a higher risk of a reduction in the value of their domestically held assets as compared to foreign investors. This may lead to a situation where domestic investors buy foreign assets while foreign investors buy domestic assets at the same time. Unlike domestic investors, foreign investors are not hurt by the inflation tax, since they lend in foreign currency. A similar asymmetry in perceived risks holds with respect to currency depreciation following the accumulation of debt obligations. Domestic investors will experience a reduction of the real value of their assets, whereas foreign investors are not hurt by such exchange rate changes.

It has also been argued that in practice the domestic debt obligations of the government are junior to foreign debt obligations (Ize and Ortiz, 1987; Kant, 1996), which reduces the willingness of residents to lend to their own government. Foreigners, instead, are not reluctant to lend to the government due to the seniority of their claims.

Razin and Sadka (1991), Dooley and Kletzer (1994) and Bjerksund and Schjelderup (1995) present models that emphasize differences in tax treatments for domestic and foreign investors, leading to simultaneous capital inflows and capital outflows.

Finally, simultaneous capital inflow and outflow may also be due to asymmetric information about expected returns on domestic assets between domestic and foreign investors.

**The Stock of Capital Flight**

A final determinant of capital flight is the stock of capital flight itself. The argument to take the stock of capital flight as a determinant of the flows of capital flight stresses the spillover effect of large asset holdings abroad on the expected losses on domestically held assets. When residents hold large amounts of foreign assets, the tax base is reduced considerably. Under these circumstances, the tax burden due to increased public expenditures and foreign borrowing has to be shared by a smaller tax base, increasing the burden per unit of domestically held asset. Consequently, this will further stimulate residents to take their money and run. Thus, the larger the stock of capital flight, the higher the incentives to flee (Collier et al., 1999). An entirely different argument to take the capital flight stock as a determinant is given by Vos (1992). He argues that the stock of capital flight reflects the desire of residents to hold foreign assets to satisfy their foreign consumption needs. In this spirit, flows of capital flight may reflect residents' behaviour in targeting a certain stock of foreign asset holdings.

**Evaluating Empirical Studies of the Determinants of Capital Flight**

A number of studies are available in which the determinants of capital flight are analysed empirically. We shall summarize the results of these empirical studies. Table 18.1 provides an overview of these studies, specifying the measure of capital flight used, the determinants of capital flight, the countries or regions of which data have been used, the sample period, and the estimation technique. The summary presented below will focus on

Table 18.1  Overview of empirical studies on the determinants of capital flight

| Author(s) [1] | Methodology [2] | Countries [3] | Sample period [4] | Estimation technique [5] | Main determinants tested [6] |
|---|---|---|---|---|---|
| Cuddington (1986) | Hot money | Argentina, Brazil, Chile, Korea, Mexico, Peru, Uruguay and Venezuela | 1974–1982 | OLS | $REER\,(+/-)$, $FINC$, $RINTR$, $RINTRF$, $INFL\,(+)$ |
| Cuddington (1987) | Hot money | Argentina, Mexico, Uruguay and Venezuela | 1974–1984 | OLS | $REER\,(+)$, $RINTRF$, $INFL$ |
| Dooley (1988) | Dooley | Argentina, Brazil, Chile, Mexico, Peru, Philippines and Venezuela | 1977–1984 | OLS (pooled) with instruments | $INFL\,(+)$, $FINC\,(+)$, $PR\,(-)$ |
| Ketkar and Ketkar (1989) | Hot money | Argentina, Brazil and Mexico | 1977–1986 | OLS | $RINTR$, $RINTRF$, $INFL\,(+)$, $REER\,(+)$, $DUMG\,(+)$, $SPREAD$ |
| Pastor (1990) | Residual | Argentina, Brazil, Chile, Colombia, Mexico, Peru, Uruguay and Venezuela | 1973–1987 | OLS (pooled) | $INFL$, $FINC\,(+)$, $REER\,(+)$, $DEBTGDP\,(+)$, $YG\,(-)$, $TAXGDP$ |
| Mikkelsen (1991) | Weighted average of residual and hot money | 22 LDCs | 1978–1985 | OLS (pooled) | $YG\,(-)$, $\Delta E(FINC)\,(+)$, $\Delta BUDDEF\,(+)$ |
|  | Weighted average of residual and hot money | Mexico | 1976–1985 | OLS | $\Delta E(FINC)\,(+)$, $\Delta RINTR$, $DUMG\,(+)$ |

Table 18.1 (continued)

| Author(s) | Methodology | Countries | Sample period | Estimation technique | Main determinants tested |
|---|---|---|---|---|---|
| Hermes and Lensink (1992) | Residual and asset | Côte d'Ivoire, Nigeria, Sudan, Tanzania, Uganda and Zaire | 1978–1988 | OLS (pooled) | *DEBTGDP* (+), *REER* (+), *FINC*, *YG*, *RINTRF*, *AIDGDP*, *SHDGDP* |
| Vos (1992) | Residual | Philippines | 1971–1988 | OLS | *DEBTGDP* (+), *REER* (+), *CFS* (+), *SPREAD* (+) |
| Henry (1996) | Residual | Barbados, Jamaica and Trinidad and Tobago | 1971–1987 | OLS | *BUDDEF*, *YG*, *TAXGDP*, *REER*, *INFL*, *DEBTGDP* (+), *SPREAD* |
| Murinde, Hermes and Lensink (1996) | Residual | Côte d'Ivoire, Nigeria, Sudan, Tanzania, Uganda and Zaire | 1976–1991 | SUR | *DEBTGDP* (+), *REER*, *FINC*, *INFL*, *YG*, *RINTRF*, *AIDGDP* |
| Collier, Hoeffler and Pattillo (1999) | Residual | 39 LDCs | 1970–1990 | LAD | *DEBTGNP* (+), *REER* (+), *CFS* (+) |
| Hermes, Lensink and Murinde (1999) | Residual | Hungary, Poland and Romania | 1982–1995 | OLS | *DEBTGDP* (+), *REER*, *BUDDEF*, *FINC*, *AIDGDP* |
| Lensink, Hermes and Murinde (2000) | Residual, hot money and Dooley | 84 LDCs | 1971–1990 | EBA and CDF | *BANKL* (+), *AIDGDP* (+) *FDI*, *PINSTAB*, *WAR*, *CIVLIB* (+), *PRIGHTS*, *PARCOM* (+) |

*Notes:*
In all studies listed in the table the dependent variable is capital flight, measured in different ways, however (see Column [2]).
The estimation techniques mentioned in column [5] are: ordinary least squares (OLS), seemingly unrelated regressions (SUR), quantile regressions using least absolute deviation estimation (LAD; see Collier, Hoeffler and Pattillo, 1999), extreme bound analysis (EBA; see Levine and Renelt, 1992), and estimation with cumulative distribution functions (CDF; see Sala-i-Martin, 1997a and 1997b).
Column [6], indicating the 'main determinants tested', shows only those variables of interest to the study of capital flight and its determinants. In several cases the specification of the equations estimated also may contain control variables. These variables have been left out of the table. A (+) or (−) after a variable in this column indicates that this variable is significantly positive (or negative) related to capital flight, that is, $t$-values for this variable are above 1.7 in the majority of the equations estimated in the studies listed.
For abbreviations of variables used in the table, see Appendix 18A.

discussing some of the most interesting features and findings of these studies. Due to limitations of space we cannot discuss the studies in detail. The interested reader is referred to the original articles.

Starting with the measure of capital flight used, the summary in Table 18.1 makes clear that most studies use a version of the residual method. Some studies investigate empirically the determinants of capital flight using the hot money method. In several cases, estimations are presented using different kinds of measures for capital flight to show the sensitivity of the estimation results to the specific measure used. In general, the table shows that estimation results differ, depending on the measure of capital flight used. This indicates the crucial importance of the issue of measurement of the capital flight phenomenon.

The studies summarized in Table 18.1 focus on developing countries. The table shows that most studies focus on capital flight of Latin American countries. Only a few have focused on African countries. The emphasis on Latin America is due to the massive outflows these countries experienced during the 1980s following the debt crisis. As was shown in Section 3, in absolute terms capital flight of these countries was by far the largest. However, the relative burden of capital flight was the largest for countries in Sub-Saharan Africa, emphasizing the need for research with respect to the determinants of capital flight from this continent. In a number of cases estimations have been carried out using individual-country data. This particularly holds for early attempts to investigate the capital flight phenomenon. More recently, one study has investigated the determinants of capital flight using a large sample of developing countries.

In most cases the empirical studies on the determinants of capital flight implicitly use a portfolio model to decide which variables should be taken into account. Almost all studies estimate a reduced-form equation. Consequently, this leads to equations of a rather *ad hoc* nature, which in a way is a shortcoming of the empirical literature on capital flight. Only Lensink et al. (1998) aim at estimating a full portfolio model, in which capital flight is taken into account as one of the assets, which allows for investigating the simultaneity of different effects between different variables. Most studies estimating a reduced-form equation apply ordinary least squares (OLS). In some cases the empirical studies deal with time series, in other cases they use pooled regressions. In Lensink et al. (2000), Barro-type cross-country estimations have been carried out (Barro, 1991), using sensitivity tests such as the extreme bound analysis proposed by Levine and Renelt (1992), or the method proposed by Sala-i-Martin (1997b).

As was already mentioned, in most cases empirical studies implicitly use a portfolio model to decide which variables should be taken into account.

If we take the five categories of determinants of capital flight as discussed in the previous section, the following picture emerges. With respect to *macroeconomic instability*, one or more variables such as exchange rate overvaluation, government deficits, the inflation rate and current account deficits appear in almost all studies. In particular, measures of the degree of exchange rate overvaluation are prominently present in these studies. The results of the empirical investigations indicate that macroeconomic instability causes capital flight. In most specifications variables measuring the extent of macroeconomic instability are statistically significant and positively related to capital flight.

Few studies focus on measures of *political instability* as determinants of capital flight. Several kinds of measures have been used. In some cases, the empirical investigations focus on the regime type as a measure of political instability, using different dummy variables that proxy for the degree of democracy of a country. Other studies use dummy variables to measure issues related to the policy regime, such as indexes of civil rights and liberties. Still other studies use more direct measures of political instability, such as the number of assassinations and revolts, dummies for the fact that a country has been involved in a war situation. In general, the results of the empirical investigations support the view that political instability, measured in various ways, and capital flight are positively related.

Proxies of the *interest rate differential* are used in some studies to measure the relative attractiveness of domestic as compared to foreign assets. In most cases researchers have calculated some kind of exchange rate differential between the domestic interest rate on deposits and a foreign deposit rate, normally the US deposit rate. Another measure proxying for the attractiveness of different assets used is the growth rate of GDP or GNP. Measures of the interest rate differential do not always have a statistically significant relation to capital flight. This may indicate that other determinants, such as macroeconomic and political instability, are more important to explain capital flight.

In many studies *capital inflow* variables are taken into account. In several cases these capital flows have been split into one or more forms of inflows. In particular, research has focused on investigating the impact of long-term versus short-term foreign debt. A few studies have also investigated the role played by aid flows. Among others, Bauer (1981) argued that development aid would be used to finance capital flight. Table 18.1 shows that especially long-term debt inflows have a statistically significant influence on capital flight. The hypothesis put forward by Bauer on the relationship between aid and capital flight is supported in some of the studies surveyed.

Finally, to our knowledge only a few studies focus on the *stock of capital flight* as a determinant of capital flight (Collier et al., 1999). This study finds evidence for a positive relationship between capital flight and the stock of capital flight. Vos (1992) also finds a positive relationship, which he takes as evidence for his hypothesized stock-adjustment behaviour based on satisfying foreign consumption needs of residents.

In conclusion, it appears that foreign debt variables, exchange rate overvaluation and political risk variables do have a statistically significant impact on capital flight in all empirical studies summarized in Table 18.1. It should be added, however, that the studies also show quite diverse outcomes with respect to the determinants of capital flight at the individual-country level. In several cases, other macroeconomic instability variables do have an impact on capital flight. The table shows only general results found.

## 6  POLICY UNCERTAINTY: THE KEY DETERMINANT OF CAPITAL FLIGHT?[2]

**Policy Uncertainty**

As was argued in Section 5, capital flight may be explained by several factors. Public policy behaviour appeared to be one of the main determinants and was related to both macroeconomic and political instability. If the content and direction of current and future public policies are uncertain and/or unstable, domestic investors will be uncertain about the impact of these policies on the real value of domestically held assets in the future. This uncertainty may stimulate them to withdraw their investments from the country and buy foreign assets. One example of a theoretical analysis of policy uncertainty and its influence on capital flight is found in Sheets (1995). Sheets argues that the shock therapy implemented by some transition economies led to substantial capital flight, since the policy reforms initially generated increased uncertainty about policies and their outcomes.

As was discussed above, in the existing empirical studies on capital flight uncertain/unstable public policies are proxied by variables such as high inflation rates, overvalued exchange rates and high budget deficits (see Appendix 18A). However, these variables do not directly measure uncertain public policies. At best they may be indirectly linked to the uncertainty surrounding policy behaviour of the public sector. This section presents the results of a new empirical investigation into the relationship between policy uncertainty and capital flight by focusing directly on uncertainty with respect to government consumption expenditures, taxes, budget deficits, inflation and real interest rates. In the remainder of this section we shall discuss the construction of policy uncertainty measures, the estimation methodology and the outcomes of the econometric investigation.

## The Construction of the Policy Uncertainty Measures

The empirical literature on uncertainty distinguishes between *ex post* and *ex ante* approaches to measure uncertainty (see Bo et al., 2001). The *ex ante* approach is primarily based on the variance derived from survey data. This approach is not useful for our analysis. The most popular *ex post* approaches use measures based on: (i) the variance of the unpredictable part of a stochastic process; or (ii) the conditional variance estimated from a General Autoregressive Conditional Heteroskedastic (GARCH)-type model. The GARCH-type model approach is especially relevant for high-frequency data, such as financial market data, since such data display clustering effects. Since we use annual data, we proxy uncertainty by the variance of the unpredictable part of a stochastic process. More specifically, we first specify and estimate a forecasting equation to determine the expected part of the variable under consideration. Next, the standard deviation of the unexpected part of the variable, that is, the residuals from the forecasting equation, is used as the measure of uncertainty. This approach has also been used by, for example, Aizenman and Marion (1993), Ghosal (1995), and Ghosal and Loungani (2000). Differences in the measurement of the uncertainty variable mostly stem from the way in which the forecasting equation is formulated. We follow the most widely used approach and specify a second-order autoregressive process, extended with a time trend, as the forecasting equation:

$$P_t = \alpha_1 + \alpha_2 T + \alpha_3 P_{t-1} + \alpha_4 P_{t-2} + e_t, \qquad (18.7)$$

where $P_t$ is the variable under consideration, $T$ is a time trend, $\alpha_1$ is the intercept, $\alpha_3$ and $\alpha_4$ are the autoregressive parameters and $e_t$ is an error term. We estimate the above equation for all developing countries in the data set, using data for the 1970–95 period. The uncertainty measure is determined by calculating the standard deviation of the residuals for the entire sample period per individual country. We calculate the following five different types of uncertainty, all related to the uncertainty surrounding public policies: uncertainty with respect to (i) budget deficits (*EBUD*); (ii) tax payments (*ETAX*); (iii) government consumption (*EGOVC*); (iv) inflation (*EINFL*); and (v) the real interest rate (*ERINTR*).

## The Estimation Methodology and Outcomes

The estimation methodology is as follows. We start by estimating a base equation for capital flight, where capital flight is measured using the Morgan Guaranty variant of the residual method. In an earlier study we showed that capital flight is mainly caused by capital inflows and by political risk variables (Lensink et al., 2000). Following the results of this earlier study, the base equation contains measures of different forms of capital inflows and several measures for political risk. With respect to capital inflows, we test the significance of bank lending as a percentage of GDP (*BANKL*), foreign aid as a percentage of GDP (*AIDGDP*) and foreign direct investment as a percentage of GDP (*FDI*). The following political risk variables are used: a measure for the degree of political instability (*PINSTAB*) and an index of civil liberties (*CIVLIB*). The best-fitting base equation is presented in column [1] of Table 18.2. *FDI* does not appear in the base equation, since it is not statistically significant.

Next, we add the different policy uncertainty variables one by one. These estimates are presented in the columns numbered [2] to [6]. It appears that almost all policy uncertainty variables have a highly significant and positive effect on capital flight. *EINFL* is the only policy uncertainty variable that is not statistically significant. In general, the estimation results appear to be quite encouraging. Most importantly, in line with what might have been expected, policy uncertainty appears to be an important determinant of capital flight.

In order to test for the stability of the results presented in Table 18.2 we use a methodology proposed by Sala-i-Martin (1997a and 1997b). Following this methodology, we start by adding four additional variables to the different estimated equations containing the uncertainty measures. The four additional variables are taken from a group of variables that are found to be important for explaining capital flight in other studies. The entire group of additional variables is: two measures for free trade openness (*FREEOP* and *TRADE*); per capita GDP (*GDPPC*); the primary enrolment rate (*PRENR*); credit to the private sector as a percentage of GDP (*CREDITPR*); the investment to GDP ratio (*INVEST*); a dummy variable (from 0 to 5) representing the extent to which non-elites are able to access institutional structures for political expression (*PARCOM*); a dummy variable (from 0 to 10; 0 = low) representing the general openness of political institutions (*DEMOC*); debt service as a percentage of GDP (*DEBTS*); the ratio of money and quasi-money to GDP (*MONGDP*); the debt to GDP ratio (*DEBTGDP*); the interest rate spread (*SPREAD*); the black market premium (*BMP*); terms of trade shocks (*TOT*); government consumption as a percentage of GDP (*GOVCGDP*); the budget deficit of the government to GDP ratio (*BUDDEF*) and the per capita growth rate (*PCGROWTH*). We use all possible combinations of four of the entire set of additional variables and perform regressions in which the base variables, the policy uncertainty measure, as well as four additional variables are included. This implies that for each individual equation containing one of

Table 18.2  Capital flight and policy uncertainty

|  | [1] | [2] | [3] | [4] | [5] | [6] |
|---|---|---|---|---|---|---|
| BANKL | 0.701 | 0.545 | 0.051 | 0.156 | 0.647 | 0.103 |
|  | (1.87) | (1.72) | (0.20) | (0.62) | (1.69) | (0.43) |
| AIDGDP | 0.091 | 0.040 | 0.067 | 0.081 | 0.095 | 0.083 |
|  | (2.71) | (0.92) | (1.55) | (2.19) | (2.79) | (2.10) |
| PINSTAB | 5.244 | 4.791 | 2.474 | 3.032 | 4.248 | 2.559 |
|  | (2.35) | (2.27) | (1.61) | (2.00) | (1.89) | (1.55) |
| CIVLIB | 0.398 | 0.275 | 0.417 | 0.456 | 0.440 | 0.408 |
|  | (2.06) | (1.54) | (2.43) | (3.05) | (2.28) | (2.21) |
| EGOVC |  | 1.040 |  |  |  |  |
|  |  | (2.52) |  |  |  |  |
| ETAX |  |  | 1.237 |  |  |  |
|  |  |  | (4.00) |  |  |  |
| EBUD |  |  |  | 0.824 |  |  |
|  |  |  |  | (4.19) |  |  |
| EINFL |  |  |  |  | 0.002 |  |
|  |  |  |  |  | (1.61) |  |
| ERINTR |  |  |  |  |  | 0.026 |
|  |  |  |  |  |  | (1.81) |
| Constant | −2.541 | −3.012 | −3.101 | −3.575 | −2.729 | −1.828 |
|  | (−2.84) | (−3.26) | (−3.66) | (−4.21) | (−3.02) | (−2.30) |
| Adj. $R^2$ | 0.32 | 0.41 | 0.28 | 0.43 | 0.35 | 0.18 |
| F-statistic | 11.230 | 13.205 | 7.265 | 12.672 | 10.470 | 4.47 |
| Jarque-Bera | 4.364 | 1.553 | 6.852 | 1.835 | 1.947 | 8.738 |
| N | 89 | 89 | 80 | 78 | 89 | 79 |

*Notes:* The dependent variable for all the above equations is capital flight, measured according to the Morgan Guaranty method (Morgan Guaranty, 1986). The capital flight measures are averages over the 1970–90 period (this holds for all estimates in this section). We have tested for the significance of intercept dummies for different groups of countries, such as a dummy for Latin America and a dummy for Sub-Saharan Africa. They all appeared to be insignificant, and are therefore not presented. *t*-values in parentheses. All the t-values are based on White heteroskedasticity-consistent standard errors. $N$ = number of observations. For abbreviations of variables, see Appendix 18A.

*Source:* Hermes and Lensink (2001, Table 2, p. 379).

the policy uncertainty measures 1,365 variants of this equation are estimated. For each individual estimated equation, a coefficient as well as a standard error for the uncertainty measure are obtained. We then calculate the mean estimate for the coefficient and the mean estimate for the standard deviation. In Table 18.3 the mean estimate is given in the column 'coefficient' and the mean standard deviation can be found in the column

*Table 18.3  Stability test results*

|  | $R^2$ | Coefficient | Std error | CDF | %<95 | %<90 |
|---|---|---|---|---|---|---|
| Morgan Guaranty method |  |  |  |  |  |  |
| EGOVC | 0.32 | 0.974 | 0.384 | 0.99 | 14.6 | 0.07 |
| ETAX | 0.27 | 1.150 | 0.314 | 1.00 | 0 | 0 |
| EBUD | 0.40 | 0.831 | 0.193 | 1.00 | 0.6 | 0 |
| EINFL | 0.25 | 0.113 | 0.073 | 0.94 | 66.3 | 52.20 |
| ERINTR | 0.16 | 0.015 | 0.013 | 0.89 | 81.2 | 66.50 |

*Note:* The number of regressions estimated per policy uncertainty measure is 1,365. For abbreviations of variables, see Appendix 18A.

*Source:* Hermes and Lensink (2001, Table 3, p. 380).

'Std error'. Dividing the mean estimate of the coefficient by the mean estimate for the standard error gives a test statistic, which, assuming normality, holds information on the fraction of the cumulative distribution function (CDF) that is on the right- or left-hand side of zero. In Table 18.3, CDF denotes the larger of the two areas. If CDF is above 0.95, we conclude that the variable under consideration has a robust effect on economic growth. Finally, as an additional stability test, we present the percentage of all estimated equations for which the variable under consideration is insignificant at the 95 and 90 per cent levels, respectively, in the last two columns of Table 18.3.

When we evaluate the outcomes of the econometric investigation, the following general picture emerges. To begin with, it appears that *EGOVC*, *ETAX* and *EBUD* have a robust impact on capital flight. The other measures are not robust using the CDF test statistic. However, most of these variables are almost robust (CDF just below 0.95), suggesting that they may have an impact. Overall, the empirical results seem to confirm the importance of policy uncertainty for explaining capital flight. This emphasizes the importance of stable macroeconomic policies and a stable policy environment in developing countries in order to reduce the magnitude of capital outflows.

## 7  SUMMARY AND CONCLUSION

Since the mid-1990s the international financial system has been confronted with the outbreak of several major financial and economic crises, for instance in Mexico, East Asia, Russia and Brazil. In all these cases countries experienced massive withdrawal of capital, that is, capital flight. The financial and economic problems led domestic and international investors to withdraw their money, causing panic in the international financial markets. There were fears of massive capital outflows threatening the stability of the international banking system, as was the case in the early 1980s during the outbreak of the international debt crisis.

We argued that these current and past crisis situations, and their consequences for economic conditions in recipient countries, as well as the international banking system, call for more research on the determinants of capital flows and the related behaviour of investors. Increased insight into those determinants could help to develop measures to avoid the extreme volatility of capital flows of the past, thereby contributing to the stability of the international banking system. We decided to approach this issue by investigating empirically what exactly determines the capital flight phenomenon, emphasizing the role of policy uncertainty, since the existing theoretical and empirical literature appears to suggest that such uncertainty is an important cause of capital flight.

The chapter began by providing an exhaustive overview of the literature on capital flight. In particular, it discussed the definition and measurement of the phenomenon and contained a survey of the available theoretical and empirical studies on its determinants. Thereafter, this chapter continued by presenting a new empirical investigation on the relationship between the uncertainty of domestic policies and capital flight. The outcomes of the econometric investigation support the view that policy uncertainty stimulates capital flight.

The results of the empirical investigation have clear policy implications. In order to reduce capital flight, governments of developing countries should focus on stabilizing their macroeconomic and political situation. In particular, they should follow clear policies with respect to their public finances and monetary policies, affecting both inflation and interest rates. Stable macroeconomic policies and a stable policy environment are also to the advantage of the international banking system, since they reduce the possible threats of increased instability of capital flows. Exactly how governments of developing countries can achieve a more stable macroeconomic and policy environment is beyond the scope of this chapter. Yet, since the stability of the international banking system is involved, developing-country governments should certainly be supported, be it financially or in terms of policy advice, when a stable macro economy and policy environment are to be created. The international financial community, and the IMF and World Bank in particular, should play a crucial role in this respect.

## NOTES

1. However, Hermes and Lensink (1992) and Murinde et al. (1996) have shown that capital flight is also an important problem for Sub-Saharan African countries.
2. This section draws heavily from Hermes and Lensink (2001). We thank Elsevier Science for permitting us to use parts of this article to write this section.

## REFERENCES

Abalkin, A. and John Whalley (1999), 'The problem of capital flight from Russia', *The World Economy*, **22** (3), pp. 421–44.
Aizenman, Joshua and Nancy P. Marion (1993), 'Macroeconomic uncertainty and private investment', *Economics Letters*, **41** (2), pp. 207–10.
Alesina, Alberto and Guido Tabellini (1989), 'External debt, capital flight and political risk', *Journal of International Economics*, **27** (3–4), pp. 199–220.
Barro, Robert J. (1991), 'Economic growth in a cross section of countries', *Quarterly Journal of Economics*, **106** (2), pp. 407–43.
Barro, Robert J. and Jung Wha Lee (1994), Data Set for a Panel of 138 Countries, National Bureau of Economic Research, Internet Site, Cambridge, MA: NBER.
Bauer, Peter T. (1981), *Equality, the Third World and Economic Delusion*, London: Weidenfeld & Nicolson.
Bhattacharya, Rina (1999), 'Capital flight under uncertainty about domestic taxation and trade liberalization', *Journal of Development Economics*, **59**, pp. 365–87.
Bjerksund, Petter and Guttorm Schjelderup (1995), 'Capital controls and capital flight', *FinanzArchiv*, **52** (1), pp. 33–42.
Bo, Hong, Robert Lensink and Elmer Sterken (2001), *Investment, Capital Market Imperfections, and Uncertainty: Theory and Empirical Results*, Cheltenham, UK and Northampton, MA, USA: Edward Elgar.
Brown, Richard (1990), 'Sudan's other economy: migrants' remittances, capital flight and their policy implications', Sub-series on Money, Finance and Development Working Paper, 31, The Hague: Institute of Social Studies.
Chang, P.H. Kevin and Robert E. Cumby (1991), 'Capital flight in Sub-Saharan African countries', in Ishrat Husain and John M. Underwood (eds), *African External Finance in the 1990s*, Washington, DC: World Bank, pp. 162–85.
Claessens, Stijn and David Naudé (1993), 'Recent estimates of capital flight', Policy Research Working Paper 1186, Washington, DC: World Bank.
Collier, Paul, Anke Hoeffler and Catherine Pattillo (1999), 'Flight capital as a portfolio choice', Policy Research Working Paper 2066, Washington, DC: World Bank.
Cuddington, John T. (1986), 'Capital flight: estimates, issues and explanations', Princeton Studies in International Finance, No. 58, Princeton, NJ: Princeton University.
Cuddington, John T. (1987), 'Macroeconomic determinants of capital flight: an econometric investigation', in Lessard and Williamson (eds), pp. 85–96.
Cumby, Robert and Richard Levich (1987), 'Definitions and magnitudes: on the definition and magnitude of recent capital flight', in Lessard and Williamson (eds), pp. 27–67.

Deppler, Michael and Martin Williamson (1987), 'Capital flight: concepts, measurement, and issues', in *Staff Papers for the World Economic Outlook*, Washington, DC: International Monetary Fund, pp. 39–58.

Diwan, Ishac (1989), 'Foreign debt, crowding out, and capital flight', *Journal of International Money and Finance*, **8** (1), pp. 121–36.

Dooley, Michael P. (1986), 'Country-specific risk premiums, capital flight, and net investment income payments in selected developing countries', unpublished manuscript, Washington, DC: International Monetary Fund.

Dooley, Michael P. (1988), 'Capital flight: a response to differences in risk', *IMF Staff Papers*, **35**, pp. 422–36.

Dooley, Michael P. and Kenneth M. Kletzer (1994), 'Capital flight, external debt and domestic policies', NBER Working Paper, 4793, Cambridge, MA: National Bureau of Economic Research.

Eaton, Jonathan (1987), 'Public debt guarantees and private capital flight', *The World Bank Economic Review*, **1** (3), pp. 377–95.

Eaton, Jonathan and Mark Gersovitz (1989), 'Country risk and the organization of the international capital transfer', in Guillermo Calvo, Ronald Findlay, Pentti J.K. Kouri and José Braga de Macedo (eds), *Debt Stabilization and Development, Essays in Memory of Carlos Diaz-Alejandro*, Oxford: Blackwell, pp. 109–29.

Eggerstedt, Harald, Rebecca Brideau Hall and Sweder van Wijnbergen (1995), 'Measuring capital flight: a case study of Mexico', *World Development*, **23** (2), pp. 211–32.

Erbe, Susanne (1985), 'The flight of capital from developing countries', *Intereconomics*, **20**, pp. 268–75.

Fry, Maxwell J. (1993), 'Foreign debt accumulation: financial and fiscal effects and monetary policy reactions of developing countries', *Journal of International Money and Finance*, **12** (4), pp. 347–67.

Ghosal, Vivek (1995), 'Input choices under price uncertainty', *Economic Inquiry*, **33** (1), pp. 142–58.

Ghosal, Vivek and Prakash Loungani (2000), The differential impact of uncertainty on investment in small and large businesses', *Review of Economics and Statistics*, **82** (2), pp. 338–43.

Gibson, Heather D. and Euclid Tsakalotos (1993), 'Testing a flow model of capital flight in five European countries', *The Manchester School*, **61** (2), pp. 144–66.

Gordon, David B. and Ross Levine (1989), 'The "Problem" of capital flight: a cautionary note', *The World Economy*, **12** (2), pp. 237–52.

Gulati, Sunil K. (1987), 'A note on trade misinvoicing', in Lessard and Williamson (eds), pp. 68–78.

Henry, Lester (1996), 'Capital flight from beautiful places: the case of three Caribbean countries', *International Review of Applied Economics*, **10** (2), pp. 263–72.

Hermes, Niels and Robert Lensink (1992), 'The magnitude and determinants of capital flight: the case for six Sub-Saharan African countries', *De Economist*, **140** (4), pp. 515–30.

Hermes, Niels and Robert Lensink (2001), 'Capital flight and the uncertainty of government policies', *Economics Letters*, **71** (3), pp. 377–81.

Hermes, Niels, Robert Lensink and Victor Murinde (1999), 'The magnitude and determinants of capital flight in Eastern Europe', in Andrew W. Mullineux and Christopher J. Green (eds), *Economic Performance and Financial Sector Reform in Central and Eastern Europe*, Cheltenham, UK and Northampton, MA, USA: Edward Elgar, pp. 243–55.

Ize, Alain and Guillermo Ortiz (1987), 'Fiscal rigidities, public debt, and capital flight', *IMF Staff Papers*, **34** (2), pp. 311–32.
Kant, Chander (1996), 'Foreign direct investment and capital flight', Princeton Studies in International Finance, No. 80, Princeton, NJ: Princeton University.
Ketkar, Suhas L. and Kusum W. Ketkar (1989), 'Determinants of capital flight from Argentina, Brazil, and Mexico', *Contemporary Policy Issues*, **7** (3), pp. 11–29.
Khan, Moshin S. and Nadeem Ul Haque (1985), 'Foreign borrowing and capital flight: a formal analysis', *IMF Staff Papers*, **32** (4), pp. 606–28.
Kindleberger, Charles P. (1987), 'A historical perspective', in Lessard and Williamson (eds), pp. 7–26.
Lensink, Robert, Niels Hermes and Victor Murinde (1998), 'The effect of financial liberalization on capital flight in African economies', *World Development*, **26** (7), pp. 1349–68.
Lensink, Robert, Niels Hermes and Victor Murinde (2000), 'Capital flight and political risk', *Journal of International Money and Finance*, **19** (1), pp. 73–92.
Lessard, Donald R. and John Williamson (eds) (1987), *Capital Flight and Third World Debt*, Washington, DC: Institute for International Economics.
Levine, Ross and David Renelt (1992), 'A sensitivity analysis of cross-country growth regressions', *American Economic Review*, **82** (4), pp. 942–63.
López, Julio (1998), 'External financial fragility and capital flight in Mexico', *International Review of Applied Economics*, **12** (2), pp. 257–70.
Loukine, Konstantin (1998), 'Estimation of capital flight from Russia: balance of payments approach', *The World Economy*, **21** (5), pp. 613–28.
Mikkelsen, Jan Ghiem (1991), 'An econometric investigation of capital flight', *Applied Economics*, **23**, pp. 73–85.
Morgan Guaranty (1986), 'LDC capital flight', *World Financial Markets*, **2**, pp. 13–16.
Morgan Guaranty (1988), 'LDC debt reduction: a critical appraisal', *World Financial Markets*, **7**, pp. 1–12.
Murinde, Victor, Niels Hermes and Robert Lensink (1996), 'Comparative aspects of the magnitude and determinants of capital flight in six Sub-Saharan African countries', *Savings and Development Quarterly Review*, **20** (1), pp. 61–78.
Pastor, Jr., Manuel (1990), 'Capital flight from Latin America', *World Development*, **18** (1), pp. 1–18.
Razin, Assaf and Efraim Sadka (1991), 'Efficient investment incentives in the presence of capital flight', *Journal of International Economics*, **31** (1–2), pp. 171–81.
Sala-i-Martin, Xavier (1997a), 'I just ran two million regressions', *American Economic Review*, **87** (2), pp. 178–83.
Sala-i-Martin, Xavier (1997b), 'I just ran two million regressions', unpublished manuscript, New York, Colombia University.
Sheets, Nathan (1995), 'Capital flight from the countries in transition: some theory and empirical evidence', International Finance Discussion Papers, 514, Washington, DC, Board of Governors of the Federal Reserve System.
Tornell, Aarón and Andrés Velasco (1992), 'The tragedy of the commons and economic growth: why does capital flow from poor to rich countries?', *Journal of Political Economy*, **100** (6), pp. 1208–31.
Vos, Rob (1992), 'Private foreign asset accumulation, not just capital flight: evidence from the Philippines', *Journal of Development Studies*, **28** (3), pp. 500–537.

Walter, Ingo (1987), 'The mechanisms of capital flight', in Lessard and Williamson (eds), pp. 103–28.
World Bank (1985), *World Development Report*, Washington, DC: World Bank.
World Bank (1997), *World Development Indicators*, Washington, DC: World Bank.
Zedillo, Ernesto (1987), 'Mexico', in Lessard and Williamson (eds), pp. 174–85.

# APPENDIX 18A  LIST OF ABBREVIATIONS AND VARIABLES USED

| | | |
|---|---|---|
| $\Delta$ | = | change in a variable |
| AIDGDP | = | development aid as a percentage of GDP |
| BANKL | = | bank and trade-related lending as a percentage of GDP |
| BMP | = | black market premium, calculated as [(black market rate/official rate) − 1]. |
| BUDDEF | = | overall budget deficits, including grants as a percentage of GDP |
| CFS | = | stock of capital flight |
| CIVLIB | = | index of civil liberties (from 1 to 7; 1 = most civil liberties) |
| CREDITPR | = | credit to the private sector as a percentage of GDP |
| DEBTGDP | = | the external debt to GDP ratio |
| DEBTS | = | total external debt service as a percentage of GDP |
| DEMOC | = | general openness of political institutions (from 0 to 10; 0 = low) |
| DUMG | = | dummy variable for regime change |
| E(.) | = | expected value of a variable |
| EBUD | = | uncertainty with respect to government budget deficit |
| EGOVC | = | uncertainty with respect to government consumption expenditures |
| EINFL | = | uncertainty with respect to inflation |
| ERINTR | = | uncertainty with respect to real interest rate |
| ETAX | = | uncertainty with respect to taxes |
| FDI | = | foreign direct investment as a percentage of GDP |
| FINC | = | financial incentive variable, i.e. the difference between domestic and foreign interest rate corrected for changes in the exchange rate, based on Pastor (1990). Note that Cuddington (1986), Dooley (1988) and Mikkelsen (1991) use similar but slightly different definitions of this variable |
| FREEOP | = | measure of free trade openness (calculated as $0.528 - 0.026 \log (AREA*0.095(DIST))$), where $AREA$ = size of land; and $DIST$ = average distance to capitals of world 20 major exporters |
| GDPPC | = | GDP per capita in 1970 |
| GOVCGDP | = | government consumption as a percentage of GDP |
| INFL | = | annual domestic inflation rate |
| INVEST | = | average investment to GDP ratio over the 1970–90 period |

| | | |
|---|---|---|
| *MONGDP* | = | average money and quasi money to GDP ratio over the 1970–90 period |
| *PARCOM* | = | extent to which non-elites are able to access institutional structures for political expression (from 0 to 5; 0 = unregulated; 5 = competitive) |
| *PCGROWTH* | = | average real per capita growth rate over the 1970–90 period |
| *PINSTAB* | = | measure of political instability, calculated as 0.5 times the number of assassinations per million population per year plus 0.5 times the number of revolutions per year |
| *PR* | = | political risk variable (specified in Dooley, 1986) |
| *PRIGHTS* | = | index of political rights |
| *PRENR* | = | primary school enrolment rate in 1970 |
| *REER* | = | real (effective) exchange rate |
| *RINTR* | = | real interest rate (per cent) |
| *RINTRF* | = | foreign real interest rate (per cent) |
| *SHDGDP* | = | short-term debt to GDP ratio |
| *SPREAD* | = | interest rate spread (that is, foreign minus domestic real interest rate) |
| *TAXGDP* | = | total taxes as a percentage of GDP |
| *TOT* | = | a variable measuring terms of trade shocks (growth rate of export prices minus growth rate of import prices). This variable is measured over the 1970–85 period |
| *TRADE* | = | exports plus imports to GDP. This variable measures the degree of openness |
| *WAR* | = | dummy variable (1 = country participated in at least one external war during 1960–85; 0 = no participation in external wars) |
| *YG* | = | rate of domestic economic growth |

The source for all variables is *World Development Indicators* (World Bank, 1997, available on CD-ROM), except for *BMP*, *CIVLIB*, *FREEOP*, *PINSTAB*, and *TOT*. These variables have been obtained from the Barro–Lee data set (Barro and Lee, 1994). *PARCOM* is obtained from the POLITY III Code Book (internet site: fttp://isere/colorado.edu/pub/datasets/polity3/polity3.codebook). The uncertainty measures have been calculated by the authors (see Section 6 of this chapter for an explanation of the methodology used).

# 19. International banks and the washing of dirty money: the economics of money laundering
## Kent Matthews*

## 1 INTRODUCTION

The chapters in this book are devoted to issues in banking. By this stage it should be clear to the reader that the nature of banking from its earliest conception of taking in deposits and making loans has altered beyond simple description. The modern bank is a multifaceted financial institution, staffed by multiskilled personnel conducting multitask operations ranging from retail business to corporate business, personal banking to syndicated, and balance sheet to off-balance sheet operations. The modern bank has had to re-engineer in the face of growing competition from the non-bank financial institutions, and fast-moving communication technology. In response, banks have merged, restructured, downsized, and increased productivity by investing in information technology (IT)-driven methods. However, the banking sectors face a further threat from two sources. First, banks have become an important conduit in the process of 'money laundering'. Money laundering (ML) raises the danger that a bank's reputation could be unintentionally harmed by the activities of some of its clients. Second, banks face the threat of prosecution from the law enforcement agencies for not reporting suspicious financial transactions to the supervisory authorities. In the last decade of the twentieth century, the banks have been forced to tread a fine line between confidentiality – a term that is synonymous with banking – and reputational and legal considerations.

The term 'money laundering' conjures up pictures of seedy individuals, mob bosses, Colombian drug barons and Russian mafiosi, in the process of disguising the proceeds of their ill-gotten gains. The picture is not entirely invalid but from a modern perspective it is incomplete. Modern-day money laundering involves sophisticated procedures involving the banks, lawyers, accountants and, at first glance, reputable firms in legitimate businesses. The revelations of the Bingham Report (1993) into the activities of the

Bank of Credit and Commerce International (BCCI) indicate the difficulty and nature of supervision. More recently, the Bank of New York (BONY) has admitted cooperating with an investigation into an alleged $10 billion money-laundering connection with Russian sources, which shows that even the prestigious banks are not exempt from infiltration.

This chapter examines the economics of money laundering, its scope and scale of activity, the motivation, the method, the danger to the financial system and the proposed methods of dealing with it. Section 2 begins with the nature of the activity, the participants and the measured scale of the activity as seen by the various official international agencies. Section 3 outlines the microeconomics of money laundering. It sets out the motivation for conducting money-laundering operations and the choice set faced by the principal players. Section 4 discusses the macroeconomic implications of the activity, in particular how the activity impinges on asset markets, capital flows and the setting of domestic monetary policy. Section 5 presents the international efforts to combat money laundering. Section 6 summarizes and concludes.

## 2  MONEY LAUNDERING: SCALE, SCOPE AND TYPOLOGY

According to Drage (1992, p. 418),

> [M]oney laundering is the process by which criminals attempt to conceal the true origin and ownership of the proceeds of their criminal activities. If done successfully, it also allows them to maintain control over those proceeds, and ultimately to provide a legitimate cover for their source of income.

While such a definition covers the underlying purpose of money laundering it is incomplete because it gives the impression that all such activity is the result of serious criminal activity. While drug trafficking, loan sharking, illegal gambling, embezzlement, extortion, illegal trafficking in arms, prostitution and slavery represent the principal source of proceeds in money laundering, less violent but no less serious activity such as tax evasion, regulatory evasion and smuggling also forms part of the picture.[1] The 1997 report of the Financial Action Task Force (FATF) also refers to bank fraud, credit card fraud, investment, advance fee and bankruptcy fraud.[2] The geographic distribution of money-laundering activity takes in financial crimes from the Scandinavian countries to organized criminal activity in Italy, Japan, Colombia, Russia, Eastern Europe, Nigeria and the Far East.

By its very nature, the scale of money-laundering activity defies measurement. Estimates of its size are necessarily non-rigorous. The FATF report (1997, pp. 6–8) used three indirect methods for estimating the scale of money laundering. The first method is the extrapolation of world drug production based on global crop projections, consumption and export of drugs in each producer country, estimated production of psychotropic substances, street prices of drugs, and financial flows within individual countries. The second method is the extrapolation from the consumption needs of drug users. The third is extrapolation from drug seizures by law enforcement agencies applying multipliers ranging from 5 to 20 per cent. FATF estimate that sales of cocaine, heroin and cannabis amounted to about $122 billion per year in the US and Europe, of which 50–70 per cent (as much as $85 billion) could be available for laundering and subsequent investment. FATF also quote a UN study that the drug trafficking market amounted to $300 billion in 1987. The widely cited figure for the scale of money-laundering activity is $300–$500 billion a year (Quirk, 1996). The *Financial Times* (18 October 1994) reported that according to US and UK officials, money laundering amounts to a global figure of $500 billion (2 per cent of gross world product). Most recently *The Economist* quoted an estimate of money laundering as $1.5 trillion (5 per cent of gross world product) (*The Economist*, 1999, p. 17).

The process of money laundering involves three basic steps:

- *placement* – the introduction of cash into the banking system or legitimate trade;
- *layering* – separating the funds from its criminal origins by passing it through several financial transactions; and
- *integration* – aggregating the funds with legitimately obtained money.

Until the 1970s, banks would generally accept large cash deposits without question, even from unknown customers. In the 1980s, legislation in the US, the UK and other Western economies began to tackle the problem with allowances in their respective laws for the confiscation of proceeds from money laundering.[3] During the 1990s, the authorities increasingly placed the burden on the banks to disclose suspicious transactions to the financial authorities. In the UK and the US, the tension between customer confidentiality and the demands of the financial policing authorities is particularly acute where the banks can be threatened with prosecution for knowingly or unknowingly aiding the money-laundering process. The banks are forced to walk a delicate middle way between the compulsion to disclose and the contractual obligations of confidentiality to the customer. The UK Money Laundering Regulations of 1993 require banks to report any suspicious transactions, and transactions over £10,000. Procedures are to be in place for the verification of the identity of clients. Record-keeping procedures are to be set up and specialized staff concerned with money-laundering matters employed with responsibilities for disclosure (Norton, 1994, p. 45). Failure carries a maximum penalty of two years' imprisonment, a fine, or both.

Guidance notes from the Bank of England (1990, 1993) to banks and building societies under the 'know your customer' rules have driven the deposit-taking institutions to taking a stronger interest in their clients' financial matters. The 'know your customer' principle is reinforced by the Basle Committee on Banking Regulation, 1988. The European Community Directive of 1991 extends money-laundering legislation beyond the narrow confines of drug trafficking by requiring member states to introduce legislation to require banks and financial institutions to carry out checks and make reports on transactions that carry the risk of money laundering (Cullen, 1993).

The response of the money-laundering industry to the regular reporting of large currency transactions has been to divide large deposits into several smaller sums, making deposits in several banks, or even several branches of the same bank. This process is known as restructuring of deposits and referred to as 'smurfing'. Money is smurfed into banks by cash deposits through automated teller machines (ATMs). However, this process is time intensive and launders relatively small amounts of money. Larger sums of money flow through the banking system through electronic communications systems.[4]

The FATF reports refer to the use of 'shell corporations' that are chartered and set up offshore or the use of legitimate businesses with high cash sales and turnover as convenient vehicles for money laundering. Offshore international business companies (IBCs) are relatively easy to set up and can operate in an environment of minimal reporting conditions and cost-effectiveness. A recent UN report, *Financial Havens, Banking and Money Laundering* (see Courtenay, 1999) recognizes that IBCs are at the heart of the money-laundering problem. It recommends that the best way to discriminate good from bad IBCs is not to recognize entities that 'do not have full authority to do business in their same jurisdiction'. Figure 19.1 shows the number of IBCs by jurisdiction. While not all IBCs are involved in dubious activity, the concentration of the 'usual suspects' is strongly indicative. Besides 'shell companies', the businesses that attract money laundering are casinos, *bureaux de change*, bookmaking, and jewellery shops. The laundered funds are mixed in with the revenues of legitimate businesses and then typically invested in real estate or newly privatized industries.

A better method for laundering money is to buy a bank. From the

550   *Banking risks, crises and regulation*

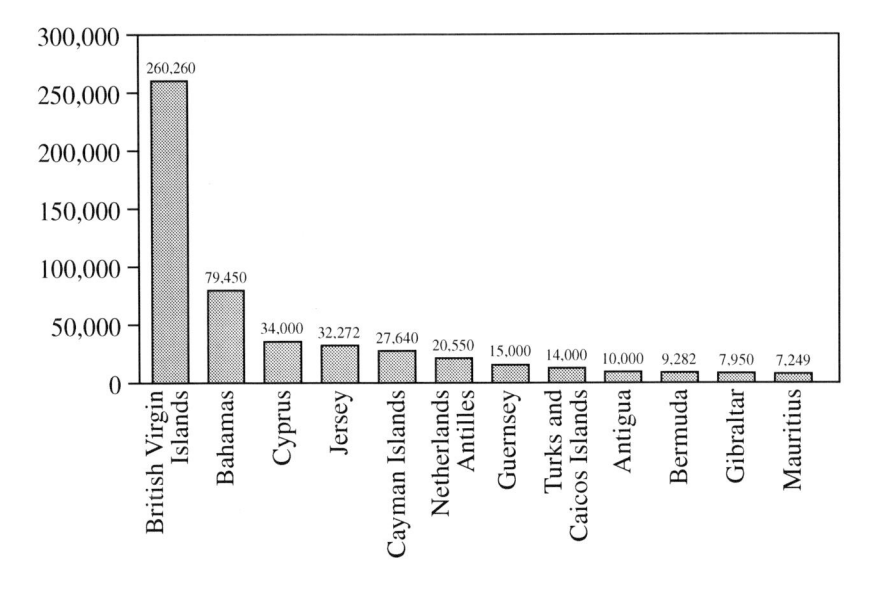

[Bar chart showing number of IBCs by jurisdiction:
- British Virgin Islands: 260,260
- Bahamas: 79,450
- Cyprus: 34,000
- Jersey: 32,272
- Cayman Islands: 27,640
- Netherlands Antilles: 20,550
- Guernsey: 15,000
- Turks and Caicos Islands: 14,000
- Antigua: 10,000
- Bermuda: 9,282
- Gibraltar: 7,950
- Mauritius: 7,249]

*Source:* Courtenay (1999).

*Figure 19.1  Number of IBCs by jurisdiction*

Seychelles in the Indian Ocean, to the Cayman Islands where there are 560 banks with combined assets of $470 billion, several small offshore economies offer relatively low set-up costs for banks.[5] In some countries such as Russia, banks are controlled by criminal organizations.[6] Complicity by bank employees has been noted in the FATF report of 1997. An account is opened with the aid of the bank employee and large deposits and withdrawals conducted, but activity ceases and a few thousand dollars retained in the account a few months before a bank audit. The audit notes an account that has little activity and is deemed less suspicious.

A method that is widely used by ethnic groups from Africa or Asia is the 'collection account'. This takes small credits from different individuals into one account, which is then remitted abroad. Such a method is used legitimately by immigrant workers to remit funds to their home country. The 'payable-through-accounts' poses a particular challenge to the 'know your customer' policy. These are demand deposit accounts in a financial institution maintained by foreign banks or corporations. The foreign bank channels all the deposits and cheques of its customers in the local bank and the foreign customers have signatory authority as sub-account holders. This way they can conduct normal international banking transactions. Many banks that offer such facilities are unable to verify the identity of their customers.

A further method that is popular with ethnic groups from Africa and Asia is the *hawala*, *hundi* or 'underground banking' system. The system involves the transfer of funds between countries but outside the legitimate banking system. Its advantage is that it does not involve any paper records. The process involves a broker that has a correspondent relationship with another broker in another country. The broker, which may be an ordinary grocery shop, has a customer that requires funds abroad. The corresponding broker in the foreign country may have a customer that wishes to remit funds to the home country. The two brokers will match the amounts with their respective correspondent customers and balance their books by transferring the net amount between them. The system depends on considerable trust – records are kept to a minimum. Many of these transactions are not money laundering in the accepted sense but remain outside the conventional banking system for the purpose of avoiding exchange and other regulatory controls.

A common technique of laundering that has potential tax advantages is the method of 'loan-back'. The launderer transfers the illegal cash to another country (usually by currency smuggling) and then deposits the proceeds as security for a bank loan, which is then credited back to the original country. The remittance of the laundered cash in the form of a loan has the appearance of a legitimate international loan with the potential for a reduction in tax liability. The loan-back scheme is illustrated in Figure 19.2. The scheme shows the cash generated from drug transactions being smuggled into the Caribbean and placed with a 'shell company' which deposits the proceeds in a Swiss bank in the name of a Swiss 'shell company'. A legitimate loan is taken from a London bank based on guarantees given by the Swiss 'shell company'. The loan is eventually repaid by the Swiss company.

The laundering process of the loan-back scheme has been made more efficient by the use of electronic funds transfer (EFT). The globalization of financial services has also created a highway of cash transfer that is indistinguishable from legitimate traffic. As in the example of the loan-back scheme described above, much of the cash from drug transactions returns to the US after payment of expenses, bribes and wages, for investment in legitimate enterprises, property or financial securities. 'Payable-through-accounts' is one technique that is used to transfer money in and out of the country. By this method a number of foreign customers are authorized to make cash deposits and withdrawals, including EFT. The 'know your customer' policy of banks is subverted by this process as the foreign customers are known to the bank by a name only. The FATF report also recognizes that the internet affords more opportunities for the money launderer. The lack of traceable transactions and the use of encryption software can make transactions totally secure in the future.

Figure 19.3 provides a graphic taxonomy of money laundering.

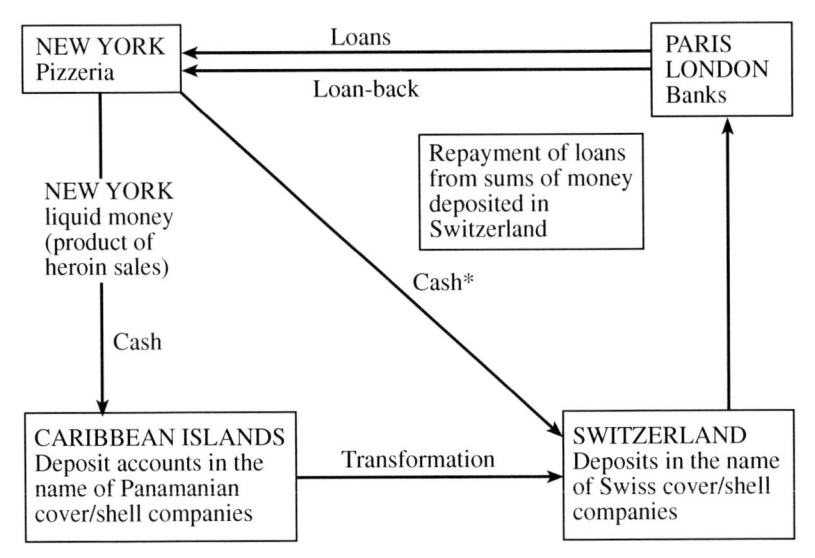

552  *Banking risks, crises and regulation*

*Note:* *Where direct deposit in Swiss accounts is possible (a more dangerous practice).

*Source:* Serge Garde and Jean de Maillard, *Les beaux jours du crime*, Paris: Plon, 1992.

*Figure 19.2  Loan-back scheme*

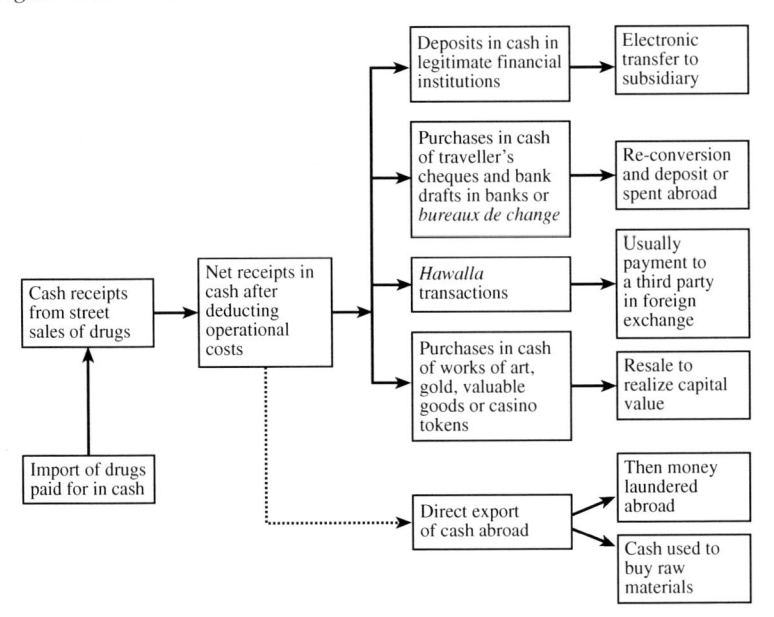

*Figure 19.3  Taxonomy of money laundering*

## 3 THE MICROECONOMICS OF MONEY LAUNDERING

The microeconomics of money laundering is a two-stage decision-making process that parallels the conventional consumption-saving and portfolio selection decision of a utility-maximizing agent. The first stage involves the decision to engage or not engage in criminal activity. The choice is formulated within the conventional framework of choice under uncertainty (as in Becker, 1968 and Ehrlich, 1973). The second stage involves the laundering of the proceeds of criminal activity, trading off risk and return against confidentiality. The two stages are not strictly separable, as the expected return from the risk–confidentiality trade-off will, at the margin, influence the proportion of compliance or criminal activity undertaken.

The results of the crime and punishment analysis suggest that an increase in the probability of detection and/or an increase in the penalty will have a negative effect on criminal activity. The basic framework of Becker (1968) has been extended to the general theory of tax evasion by Allingham and Sandmo (1972) and applied to the firm by Marrelli (1984). The basic results of this literature are that an increase in the probability of detection or an increase in the penalty will increase compliance but an increase in taxes or a reduction in the returns from legitimate activity will have ambiguous effects because of offsetting scale effects.[7]

According to Tanzi (1996), laundered funds are channelled towards financial instruments, real estate, small enterprises and countries where money can be invested without too many questions being asked. Some of the funds are held as bank deposits, especially those banks that respect confidentiality. But other liquid assets are government bonds, and domestic and foreign currency.

Portfolio theory provides some insights into the decision making of the money launderer in the second stage of the decision tree. Conventional theory tells us that holders of financial assets allocate wealth according to expected returns and associated risks. In the case of the money launderer, expected returns are traded off with risk and confidentiality as a separate factor. Banks often provide the appropriate level of confidentiality that a money launderer desires. Confidentiality has value to the money launderer as disclosure increases the probability of detection and penalty. The money launderer pays for confidentiality by accepting a lower expected return or higher risk than the position that prevails if confidentiality was not a consideration (Walter, 1993). The basic model is set out in Figure 19.4.

The vertical axis shows expected return. The axis at 65° to the vertical shows safety, which can be thought of as the inverse of risk. As risk increases, safety declines. The minimum risk portfolio (maximum safety)

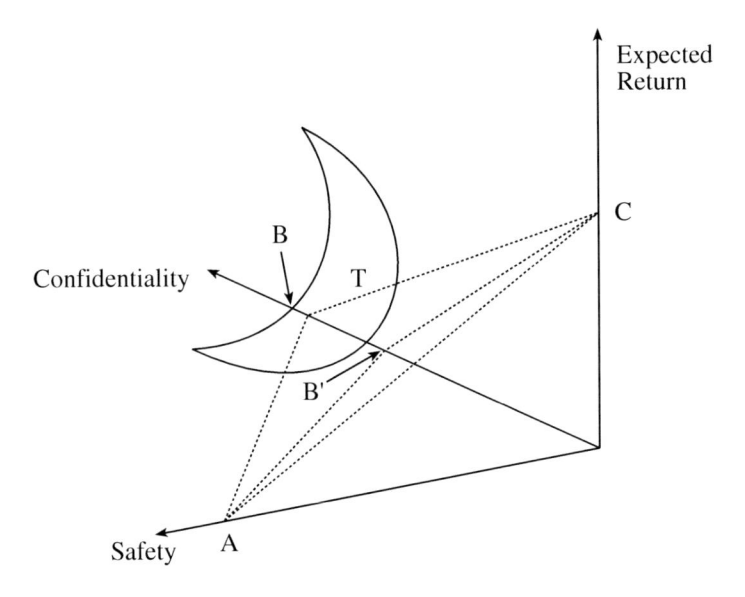

*Figure 19.4  Return–safety–confidentiality trade-off*

position is shown as point A on the safety axis and risk increasing as one moves to the right. Point C on the vertical axis represents the maximum risk–return position for the money launderer and the line AC the conventional opportunity locus between risk (safety) and expected return. The element of confidentiality is shown on the axis at 100° degrees from the vertical. Increased confidentiality is traded off against reduced expected return shown by the line BC, where B represents the minimum return, maximum confidentiality position. Points to the left of B will have negative returns. The line AB shows the confidentiality–risk trade-off, where increased confidentiality is obtained by accepting reduced financial safety (increased risk). Assuming zero covariance, the plane ABC represents the opportunity set for the money launderer. The precise mix of return, risk and confidentiality will depend on the risk preferences of the launderer (or more accurately the bosses). The assumption of risk aversion provides a contour of points of convex preferences for the mix of confidentiality, risk and return. The shape of the preference map will depend on the marginal rates of substitution between the three objectives in the money launderer's objective function. The utility maximum position is shown on the point T on the plane ABC where the convex preference map is tangent to the plane. If confidentiality is a stronger consideration for the money launderer, the equilibrium point will lie closer to point B, indicating lower safety and lower return.

The model can be used to analyse the effects of changes in the environment regarding risk and disclosure. A reduction in confidentiality caused by changes to the legal environment that increase disclosure on the part of the banks and other financial institutions will shift the opportunity-plane ABC to AB'C. The money launderer has a lower welfare position where expected return is commensurately lower for given levels of risk. The results of changes to the law on disclosure have a direct impact on expected return and by implication the decision to engage or not in criminal activity. A further implication is that lower confidentiality may lead to a higher probability of detection and lower criminal activity.

The decision by the banks and other financial intermediaries to knowingly engage in money-laundering practices has been analysed by Masciandaro (1996). The penalty to the banks is not just a fine in excess of the profits made from the laundering activity but the long-term loss of reputation. It follows that banks have to earn high profits to cover the risk from engaging in illegitimate activity. The model of choice under uncertainty of Becker (1968) is applied to the bank to determine the optimal anti-money-laundering policy.

The bank's decision is to choose between engaging in money laundering activity with profit $\pi_y$ if not detected and $\pi_-$ if detected, where $\pi_- < \pi_y$ and profit $\pi_L$ if engaged in legitimate activity only. Clearly $\pi_y > \pi_L$ and:

$$\pi_z = \pi_y - T\pi_y - \pi_L, \tag{19.1}$$

where $T$ is the penalty rate (and can include an element for loss of reputation) for engaging in illegal activity and $T > 1$.

The bank maximizes its expected utility:

$$E[U(\pi_R)] = (1-p)\,U(\pi_y) + (p)U(\pi_-), \tag{19.2}$$

where $p$ is the probability of detection. If the bank decides to engage in money laundering such that the proportion of its profits that comes from legitimate activity is $\alpha$, where $\alpha = \pi_L/\pi_y$, it can be shown that an increase in the penalty rate reduces money-laundering activity, so:

$$\frac{\partial \alpha}{\partial T} > 0.$$

Similarly it can be shown that an increase in the probability of detection reduces money-laundering activity, so:

$$\frac{\partial \alpha}{\partial p} > 0.$$

The model is useful in describing the static equilibrium marginal impacts of improvements in the detection rate, and increases in the penalty rate. However, the effect of reputational loss can only be modelled in an intertemporal setting where the profit from current money-laundering activity is traded off against future detection, and profit loss.

## 4 MACROECONOMICS OF MONEY LAUNDERING

If money laundering is sufficiently large within an economy,[8] then measurement of macroeconomic variables like the money supply can be distorted and could lead to misdiagnosis and incorrect policy setting. Quirk (1996, 1997) suggests that while the erratic behaviour of monetary aggregates in the advanced economies during the 1980s was largely the result of financial innovation, the aggregate growth in money-laundering activity may have also made a contribution. Cross-border laundering leads to inexplicable shifts in money demand between countries, with consequences for interest rate and exchange rate volatility. Large capital inflows and outflows influence movements in interest rates and exchange rates and asset prices.[9] Where the exchange rate is free to fluctuate, in the absence of sterilization, large capital inflows can also lead to an expansion in the monetary base, with consequences for domestic prices (Tanzi, 1996).

A simple portfolio balance model of an open economy, with flexible exchange rates and a banking system, is developed to understand the implications of money-laundering activity on macroeconomic variables such as interest rates and the exchange rate. The model is a portfolio balance framework based on Branson (1977). There are four assets: domestic currency ($C$), bank deposits ($D$), bank loans ($L$) and net foreign assets ($F/S$). The banking sector supplies deposits and loans to the public and the central bank supplies base money.

The private sector allocates its portfolio according to the following asset demand functions.

$$C = c(r_D, r_L, \rho^*, \mu, \phi) W \qquad (19.3)$$

$$D = e(r_D, r_L, \rho^*, \mu, \phi) W \qquad (19.4)$$

$$L = n(r_D, r_L, \rho^*, \mu, \phi) W \qquad (19.5)$$

$$\left(\frac{F}{S}\right) = f(r_D, r_L, \rho^*, \mu, \phi) W, \qquad (19.6)$$

where wealth $W = C + D - L + (F/S)$ which implies the following adding-up condition: $c + e - n + f = 1$.

The variables in the implicit functions are:

$r_D$ = interest rate on deposits
$r_L$ = interest rate on loans
$\mu$ = the degree of confidentiality offered by a bank to its customers
$\phi$ = the degree of money laundering in asset demand
$S$ = the exchange rate of foreign currency per unit of domestic
$\rho^*$ = expected rate of return on foreign assets,
where $\rho^* = r^* + (S - S^e)/S$

For convenience we make the assumption that $r^* = 0$ and that the expected appreciation/depreciation of the exchange rate is mean reverting to equilibrium as in Dornbusch (1976):

$$S^e - S = -\theta(S - \tilde{S}).$$

We can simplify the model by positing the following restrictions:[10]

$$\frac{\partial c}{\partial r_D} < 0, \frac{\partial c}{\partial r_L} = 0, \frac{\partial c}{\partial \rho^*} = 0, \frac{\partial c}{\partial \mu} = 0, \frac{\partial c}{\partial \phi} > 0$$

$$\frac{\partial e}{\partial r_D} > 0, \frac{\partial e}{\partial r_L} = 0, \frac{\partial e}{\partial \rho^*} < 0, \frac{\partial e}{\partial \mu} > 0, \frac{\partial e}{\partial \phi} > 0$$

$$\frac{\partial n}{\partial r_D} = 0, \frac{\partial n}{\partial r_L} < 0, \frac{\partial n}{\partial \rho^*} > 0, \frac{\partial n}{\partial \mu} > 0, \frac{\partial n}{\partial \phi} > 0$$

$$\frac{\partial f}{\partial r_D} < 0, \frac{\partial f}{\partial r_L} < 0, \frac{\partial f}{\partial \rho^*} = 0, \frac{\partial f}{\partial \mu} = 0, \frac{\partial f}{\partial \phi} > 0.$$

Combined with the adding-up restrictions, the above conditions imply the following:

$$\frac{\partial c}{\partial r_D} + \frac{\partial e}{\partial r_D} + \frac{\partial f}{\partial r_D} = 0$$

$$-\frac{\partial n}{\partial r_L} + \frac{\partial f}{\partial r_L} = 0$$

$$\frac{\partial e}{\partial \rho^*} - \frac{\partial n}{\partial \rho^*} + \frac{\partial f}{\partial \rho^*} = 0$$

$$\frac{\partial e}{\partial \mu} - \frac{\partial n}{\partial \mu} = 0$$

$$\frac{\partial c}{\partial \phi} + \frac{\partial e}{\partial \phi} + \frac{\partial f}{\partial \phi} = 0.$$

Following De Grauwe (1982), the banking sector assets consist of loans and required reserves. The liabilities of the banks consist of deposits.[11] If $k$ is the fixed reserve ratio, the balance sheet constraint for the banking sector is:

$$kD + L = D. \qquad (19.7)$$

The banking sector supplies loans in response to the margin of intermediation between loans and deposits:

$$L^S = L(r_L - r_D, k), \frac{\partial L}{\partial r_L} > 0, \frac{\partial L}{\partial k} < 0. \qquad (19.8)$$

Banks supply loans when the profitability from loans increases.[12] From the bank's balance sheet constraint, by similar reasoning as for equation (19.8), the supply of deposits by the banks can be described as:

$$D^S = D(r_L - r_D, k), \frac{\partial D}{\partial r_L} > 0, \frac{\partial D}{\partial k} < 0. \qquad (19.9)$$

By Walras's law we can eliminate one market and we choose to eliminate the market for currency. Equilibrium in the loan market is when the supply of bank loans is equalized with the demand for bank loans:

$$L(r_L - r_D, k) = n\left[r_L, \theta\left(\frac{S - \bar{S}}{S}\right), \mu\right] W. \qquad (19.10)$$

Treating $k$ as a constant, totally differentiating (19.10) and rearranging terms:

$$\left(\frac{\partial L}{\partial r_L} - \frac{\partial n}{\partial r_L} W\right) dr_L = \frac{\partial L}{\partial r_D} dr_D + \frac{\partial n}{\partial \mu} + W d\mu + n dH + \frac{n}{S} dF$$

$$+ \left(\frac{\partial n}{\partial \rho^*} \frac{\theta \bar{S}}{S^2} W - n \frac{F}{S_2}\right) dS. \qquad (19.11)$$

Equation (19.9) describes a positive relationship in $(r_L, r_D)$ space with the slope:

$$\left.\frac{dr_L}{dr_D}\right|_{LL} = \left(\frac{\frac{\partial L}{\partial r_L}}{\frac{\partial L}{\partial r_L} - \frac{\partial n}{\partial r_L} W}\right) < 1.$$

Equilibrium in the bank deposit market is given by equating deposit supply with deposit demand:

$$D(r_L - r_D, k) = e(r_D, \rho^*, \mu, \phi)W. \quad (19.12)$$

Differentiating totally and rearranging equation (19.12) gives equation (19.13):

$$\frac{\partial D}{\partial r_L} dr_L = \left(\frac{\partial D}{\partial r_L} + \frac{\partial e}{\partial r_D} W\right) dr_D + \left(\frac{\partial e}{\partial \rho^*} \frac{\theta}{S^2} W - \frac{eF}{S^2}\right) dS + \frac{\partial e}{\partial \mu} W d\mu$$

$$+ \frac{\partial e}{\partial \phi} W d\phi + eDH + \frac{e}{S} dF. \quad (19.13)$$

Equation (19.13) defines a positive relation in $(r_L, r_D)$ space with the slope:

$$\left.\frac{dr_L}{dr_D}\right|_{DD} = \left(\frac{\frac{\partial D}{\partial r_L} + \frac{\partial e}{\partial r_D} W}{\frac{\partial D}{\partial r_L}}\right) > 1.$$

Figure 19.5 shows the partial equilibrium in both loan and deposit markets. It is worth examining the partial equilibrium implications of an increase

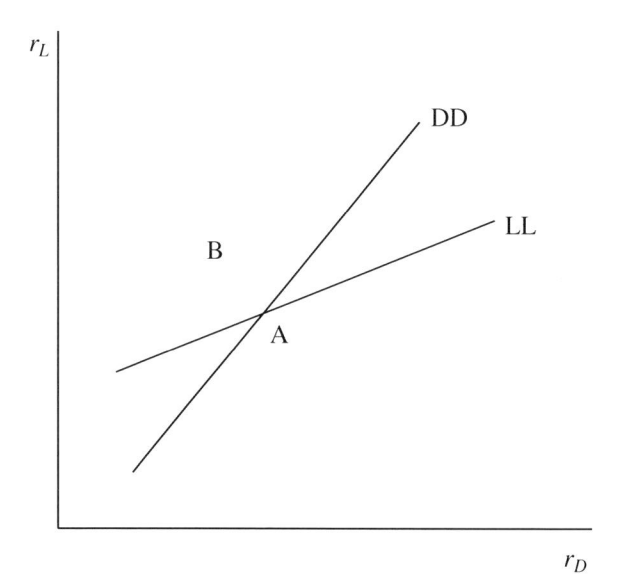

*Figure 19.5  Loan and deposit markets: partial equilibrium*

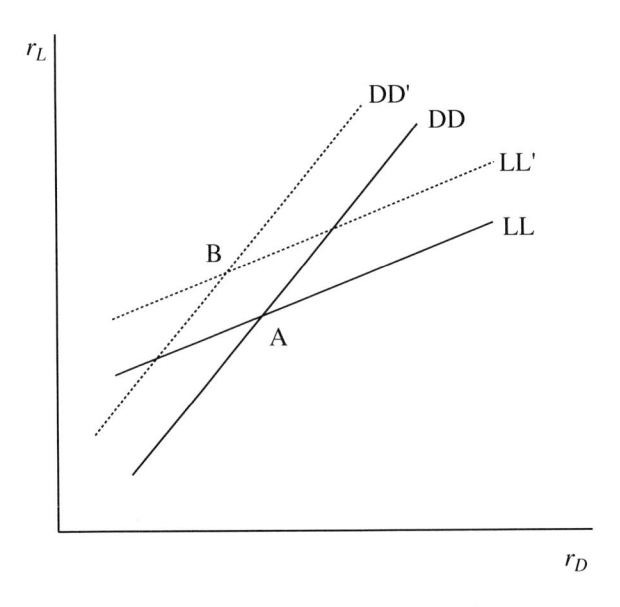

*Figure 19.6  Loan and deposit markets: effects of an increase in degree of confidentiality*

in the degree of confidentiality offered by banks to their customers.[13] Figure 19.6 describes the effects. An increase in confidentiality increases the demand for bank deposits, as money launderers are willing to trade off return for secrecy. The increase in demand for deposits reduces the rate of interest on deposits offered by banks and the DD schedule shifts to the left to DD'. The increase in confidentiality means that launderers feel confident about negotiating 'loan-back' deals for asset purchases at a higher rate of interest. The LL schedule shifts up to LL'. The increase in demand for loans increases the loan rate. The effect on the loan rate is unambiguous but the effect on the deposit is ambiguous. The deposit rate depends on the relative strength of deposit demand to loan demand. If the increase in loan demand were relatively less than the increase in deposit demand (the likely scenario), then the deposit rate would decline. Otherwise it would rise, but in either case, the margin of intermediation (loan rate relative to the deposit rate) will increase as banks demand higher profits to compensate for engaging in illegal activity.[14]

Assuming that substitution effects dominate scale effects, it can also be shown by inspection of equations (19.11) and (19.13) that an appreciation of the exchange rate will shift the LL schedule up and the DD schedule down. This is because an appreciation in the exchange rate, *ceteris paribus*, implies an expected depreciation, which increases the return from offshore deposits and reduces the demand for domestic deposits, which increases the deposit rate for every given loan rate. Banks respond by widening the gap between loan and deposit interest rates, which increases the supply to credit markets and reduces loan rates. Similarly, the expected depreciation of the exchange rate raises the costs of borrowing offshore and increases the demand for domestic bank credit. The overall effect is to raise both loan and deposit rates.

Full equilibrium in asset markets is obtained by solving for the deposit rate in equation (19.13) and substituting into equation (19.11), which gives a positive relationship between the loan rate and the exchange rate, shown in Figure 19.7 as LD, with slope:

$$\left.\frac{dr_L}{dr_S}\right|_{LD} = \frac{\beta_2 + \beta_1 \alpha_2}{1 - \beta_1 \alpha_1} > 0,$$

where:

$$\beta_1 = \left(\frac{\frac{\partial L}{\partial r_L}}{\frac{\partial L}{\partial r_L} - \frac{\partial n}{\partial r_L} W}\right) < 1, \quad \beta_2 = \left(\frac{-\frac{\partial n}{\partial \rho^*} \frac{\bar{S}\theta}{S^2} W - nF}{\frac{\partial L}{\partial r_L} - \frac{\partial n}{\partial r_L} W}\right) > 0,$$

$$\alpha_1 = \left(\frac{\frac{\partial D}{\partial r_L}}{\frac{\partial D}{\partial r_L} + \frac{\partial e}{\partial r_D} W}\right) < 1, \quad \alpha_2 = \left(\frac{-\frac{\partial e}{\partial \rho^*} \frac{\bar{S}\theta}{S^2} W - eF}{\frac{\partial D}{\partial r_L} + \frac{\partial e}{\partial r_D} W}\right) > 0.$$

The effect of an increase in money laundering increases the demand for currency and bank deposits and is described by:

$$\left.\frac{dr_L}{d\phi}\right|_{LD} = \frac{\beta_1 \alpha_4}{1 - \beta_1 \alpha_1} < 0,$$

where:

$$\alpha_4 = \left(\frac{-\frac{\partial e}{\partial \phi} W}{\frac{\partial D}{\partial r_L} + \frac{\partial e}{\partial r_D} W}\right) < 0.$$

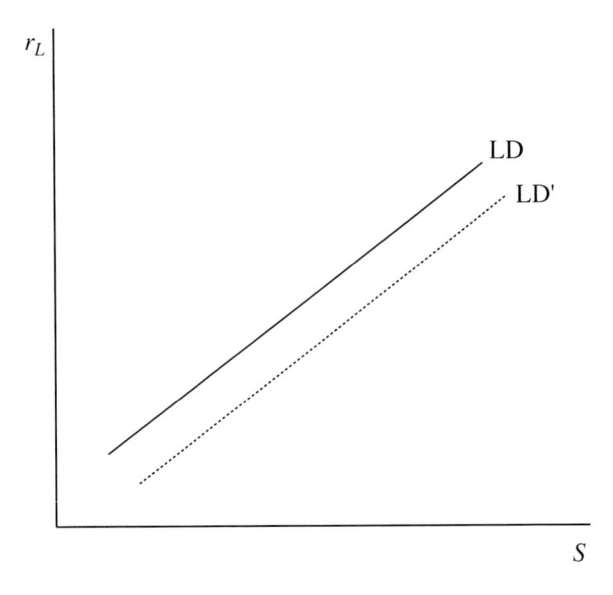

*Figure 19.7  Effect of increase in money laundering on loans and deposits*

The increase in demand for deposits increases the supply of loanable funds and reduces the deposit rate. The increased availability of funds increases the bank's supply of loans and decreases the loan rate. This is shown in Figure 19.7 as a downward shift in LD to LD'.

The increase in money-laundering activity is modelled as a capital inflow in excess of the trade account. The increase in the demand for cash and deposits is matched by a decline in the demand for net foreign assets. An increase in capital inflow represents an increase in foreign liabilities (also implied by the model restrictions). Net wealth is unaffected because, as we shall see, the reduction in the domestic currency value of net foreign assets is obtained through an appreciation in the exchange rate. If the exchange rate does not fully offset the effect of the capital inflow, there is a corresponding expansion of the monetary base, so that:

$$dW = 0 = dH + \frac{1}{S}dF - \frac{F}{S^2}dS.$$

Equilibrium in the external sector is obtained by differentiating equation (19.6) totally and substituting for the deposit rate from equation (19.13). For analytical ease we assume that demand for foreign assets and liabilities responds equally to changes in domestic borrowing and lending rates. In notation:

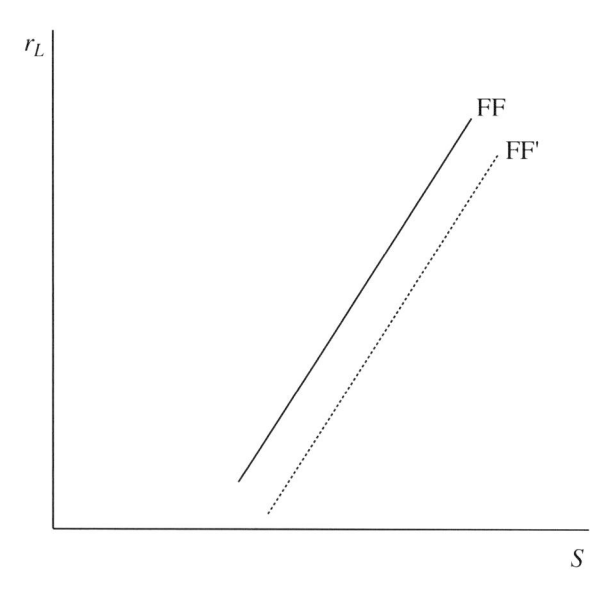

*Figure 19.8  Effect of increase in money laundering on external sector*

$$\frac{\partial f}{r_L} = \frac{\partial f}{r_D}.$$

A positive relation between the loan rate and the exchange rate, shown as FF in Figure 19.8, describes the external sector equilibrium. A rise in the exchange rate (appreciation) reduces the supply value of net foreign assets. To maintain equilibrium, a rise in the loan rate will shift borrowing overseas and reduce the demand for net foreign assets. The slope of FF is given by:

$$\left.\frac{dr_L}{dS}\right|_{FF} = \alpha_2 - \left(\frac{F(1-f) + \frac{\partial f}{\partial \rho^*}\frac{\bar{S}\theta}{S^2}W}{\frac{\partial f}{\partial r_L}}\right) > 0.$$

An increase in money-laundering activity shifts the FF schedule down to the right to FF'. The shift is given by:

$$\left.\frac{dr_L}{d\phi}\right|_{FF} = \left(\frac{\alpha_4 - \frac{\partial f}{\partial \phi}}{\frac{\partial f}{\partial r_L}}\right) < 0.$$

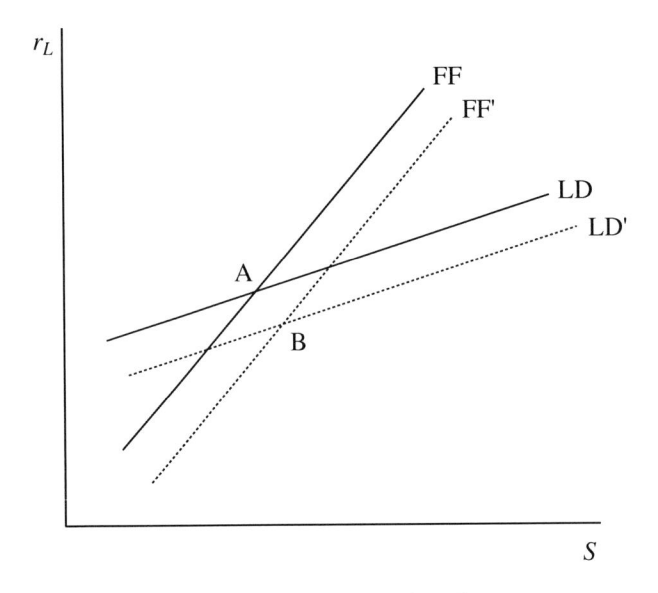

*Figure 19.9  Effect of an increase in money laundering*

An increase in money-laundering activity is reflected in a capital inflow, which reduces the demand for foreign assets (increases foreign liabilities) and increases the demand for bank deposits. Since the trade account is unaffected, the reduction in $F$ can only be achieved by an appreciation in the exchange rate. Another way of thinking about it is that an increase in money-laundering activity reduces the demand for foreign assets over liabilities. The disequilibrium in that sector can only be eradicated by a decrease in the loan rate, which reduces foreign borrowing and increases the demand for the domestic currency value of net foreign assets.

The relative slopes of the LD and FF functions are difficult to evaluate. However, we can hypothesize that the reduction in the domestic currency value of net foreign assets caused by a small rise (appreciation) in the exchange rate is offset by a much larger increase in the loan rate to reduce the net demand for foreign assets. So the FF function is expected to be steeper than the LD function. Figure 19.9 shows the effect of an increase in money laundering. In fact, the relative slopes of the LD and FF functions do not matter for the general conclusion of an increase in money-laundering activity. The comparative statics show a movement from point A to point B, an increase (appreciation) of the exchange rate and a reduction in the loan rate.

The model we have developed supports the notion that if money laundering is a significant component of capital flows for small open economies, then its activity contributes to exchange rate and interest rate volatility. Tanzi (1996) notes that the decision to move laundered capital from one habitat to another is more to do with the avoidance of detection rather than higher return. As a consequence, such movements distort the optimal allocation of resources in the world economy.

The externalities caused by money laundering can create adverse social and economic consequences. The annual total flows of laundered money amount to hundreds of billions of dollars. Clearly the stock of cash and other assets that have been accumulated through illegitimate activity is many times greater. Movements in the stock could be the source of asset price volatility, and put at risk the whole financial system through a loss of investor confidence (see Sherman, 1993, p. 16).

Indirect macroeconomic effects of money laundering can be equally severe. A cause for concern is the penetration of legitimate businesses by criminal organizations. It is recognized that the Mafia probably derives more income from its legal investments than from its illegal investment (ibid., p. 13). Illegal transactions can cause contamination effects and deter legal transactions. Legal transactions with Russian enterprises have become less desirable because of association with criminal activity. Confidence in the efficiency signalling of the financial market is eroded if there is perceived to be widespread corruption, insider trading, fraud and embezzlement.

## 5   COMBATING MONEY LAUNDERING

Money laundering is an international problem and therefore requires a coordinated international policy response. A negative result of deregulation of external trade and currency exchange has been the ease by which illegal flows of currency can be disguised with the daily flows of currency that make up the global capital market. Therefore, funds associated with illegitimate activity will always attempt to exploit the less-regulated financial sectors of the world economy. The microeconomics of money laundering suggests that effective regulation (with appropriate penalties) and monitoring will reduce financial institutions' involvement in illegitimate activity. The loss of confidentiality could reduce the amount of funds allocated to laundering activity and may even reduce illegal activity. However, making regulation more effective in one country (or group of countries) could have the effect of driving the cash receipts of illegal activity to other less-well-regulated areas, underscoring the need for coordinated action.

The last two decades have seen a concerted effort by governments and international agencies in the fight against money laundering. The starting point was the United Nations Vienna Convention against Illicit Traffic in Narcotic and Psychotropic Substances of 1988, followed by the 1990 Council of Europe Convention on Laundering Search, Seizure and Confiscation of the Proceeds of Crime. The Vienna Convention created an obligation of the signatories to criminalize the laundering of money from drug trafficking. It established the important principle that bank secrecy conventions should be secondary to international criminal investigations. The Council of Europe Convention established a common definition of money laundering and a common policy to deal with it.

On a more practical level, the Basle Committee on Banking Regulations and Supervisory Practices issued a 'statement of principles' with which the international banks of member states are expected to comply. These principles cover the identification of customers, the avoidance of suspicious transactions, and the cooperation with law enforcement agencies (Drage, 1992). The European Commission's directive on the 'Prevention of the Use of the Financial System for the Purpose of Money Laundering' in June 1991 was part of the EU's contribution to the war on organized crime and drug trafficking. The imperative for the directive was the internal market that was on track for 1 January 1993. The directive was in response to opportunities for money laundering provided by the liberalization of capital movements within the EU. The Commission stated that 'the Community has the responsibility to impede launderers from taking advantage of the single financial market' (Cullen, 1993, p. 35). The directive obliges member states to outlaw money laundering and to require financial institutions to establish and maintain internal preventive systems.

The main international body engaged in the business of combating money laundering is the Financial Action Task Force. FATF was set up in July 1989 following a decision by the G7 Paris Economic Summit.[15] The Task Force meets about five times a year and has pursued three main tasks:

- monitoring progress in applying anti-money-laundering measures by member states;
- reviewing money-laundering typologies; and
- promoting the adoption of anti-money-laundering measures by non-member states.

The mainstay of the FATF has been the 40 recommendations put forward by the group in 1990. The recommendations address four themes (see Scott, 1995, p. 2):

- The *context*, in which member countries are urged to ratify the Vienna Convention.

- The *legal framework*, which involves the criminalization of money laundering and the promotion of procedures to confiscate assets related to laundered funds.
- The *financial system*, whereby banks and other financial institutions play their part in identifying customers, and setting up procedures and controls. The procedures and controls are to be backed up by a regulatory framework by each member state.
- *International cooperation*, by which the authorities exchange information on currency flows, techniques and suspicious transactions.

Effective action by member states is promoted by means of two mechanisms: self-assessment and peer review. Self-assessment involves the completion of a detailed annual questionnaire designed for the measurement of objective indicators. Peer review involves a team of representatives from at least three member states reviewing the performance of another member state. According to Sherman (1993, p. 19), the value of external pressure has had significant effects on the introduction of anti-money-laundering measures: 'During my presidency in the current year of Task Force activities (1992/93) I noticed a considerable number of member countries are making significant efforts to introduce anti money-laundering measures in anticipation of a visit from the team of evaluators.'

International cooperative action has to be backed up with bilateral and multilateral agreements. As with all international agreements, the potential for 'free riding' exists, whereby signatories to the agreement can effectively renege on treaty promises to benefit from adoption of stricter regulatory rules by other countries. The development of various offshore tax havens in emerging economies in Eastern Europe, the Caribbean and elsewhere is an indicator of this development. The recent OECD report on tax havens (OECD, 2000) and the FATF report on non-cooperative states (FATF, 2000) are attempts to prompt action through the mechanism of 'naming and shaming'.

## 6 CONCLUSION

The microeconomics of money laundering suggests that if the activity becomes more costly, the incentive to engage in such activity will diminish. The imposition of penalties on financial institutions will increase the riskinesss of laundering activity and increase the premium paid by the criminals to launder illegitimate funds. The crime and tax evasion literature suggests that a reduction in the return from illegitimate activities will lead to a tendency towards legitimate activity. Alternatively, if the return from laundering funds offshore is reduced, criminal organizations will turn to laundering from domestic sources, which also increases the probability of detection.

This chapter has examined the various methods that have been used to launder cash obtained from criminal activity. Money-laundering activity covers a wide area of criminal activity – from the concealment of cash from drug trafficking to tax and value-added-tax evasion. The theoretical literature on the microeconomics of money laundering is closely associated with the economics of crime and punishment, tax evasion and the black economy. Traditionally the macroeconomics of money laundering has stemmed from the implications of the underground economy for the demand for money. Unaccountable shifts in the demand for money, unrelated to macroeconomic fundamentals, have been blamed on the ebb and flow of laundered cash. Shifts in the demand for money have implications for interest rates, the exchange rate and, ultimately, inflation and output.

A popular method for estimating the size of the underground economy has been through the estimation of a demand for cash or narrow money. Typically the demand for currency or M1 has been inflated by the need to finance unrecorded economic activity. The literature is full of evidence for a 'black economy effect' on the demand for money. However, Quirk (1996) finds that underground economic activity has led to a decline in the demand for money in the 1990s in the developed economies because of the increasing sophistication of the launderers. He argues that the 1990s saw criminal organizations employing other financial instruments, such as derivatives, and other vehicles such as electronic funds transfer, to launder the gains of illegitimate activity other than simply cash or bank deposits.

The sudden shifts in money-laundering activity, and its implications for capital flows and the demand for money, have implications for exchange rate and domestic interest rate setting. This chapter has developed a model of portfolio balance to examine the implications of money-laundering activity on the exchange rate and the rates of interest set by the banking system on loans and deposits. It has been shown that an increase in confidentiality offered by banks increases the ratio of loan rates to deposit rates and the profits of the banks that engage in illegitimate activity because of the increased risk. It follows that if higher penalties, in the form of criminal charges and reputation loss, occurred, then banks would have to increase their premium on handling laundered funds with the consequence of a reduced return on the money laundered. We demonstrate that an increase in money-laundering activity could lead to an appreciation of the exchange rate, a decrease in interest rates and possibly an increase in the domestic monetary base.

The model has not been extended to examine the implications for output, inflation and asset prices, but if money-laundering activity is significant it can be argued that increased interest rate and exchange rate volatility caused by its activity could have detrimental effects on growth and inflation.

The working of the international financial system is a global public good that requires the authorities of participating financial markets to regulate and police activity that could create negative externalities on the world economy. The 40 FATF recommendations are only recommendations. Many countries have adopted them in law. However, it can be argued that the regulatory framework needs to be extended to establish a minimum set of rules that form the basis of full participation in international financial markets. Such a framework would reduce the potential for regulatory arbitrage in relation to money laundering.

Tanzi (1996) goes further by arguing that penalties should be attached to countries that attract laundered money by imposing punitive taxes on financial transactions that emanate from their respective financial sectors. However, such policies may eventually be difficult to police, with the development of e-money systems. The potential anonymity of digital cash transactions opens up a new avenue of money transport across national boundaries that makes the policing of money-laundering activity a difficult prospect (see Tanaka, 1996). What is clear is that the fight against money laundering is not just about fighting crime but about maintaining the integrity of the international financial order.

## NOTES

\*   I am grateful without implication to the editors for helpful comments and to Jihane Bouizen and Patrick O'Sullivan for assistance in the writing of this chapter.
1.  In Scandinavian countries financial fraud accounts for a larger proportion of laundered proceeds than drug money. Smuggling of alcohol and tobacco also generates large amounts of funds that need to be laundered (FATF, 1997). See also Walter (1990).
2.  The FATF was created during the 15th Annual Economic Summit of G7 countries in Paris 1989 to examine measures to combat money laundering. In 1990 it issued 40 recommendations that were revised in 1996. Members of FATF, which is based at the OECD, comprise 26 governments, the EU Commission and the Gulf Cooperation Council.
3.  In the UK, confiscation and anti-money laundering provisions are contained in the Drug Trafficking Offences Act 1986, and the Criminal Justice Acts 1988 and 1990. The Criminal Justice Act 1993 makes the laundering of non-drugs-related funds a criminal offence for the first time.
4.  There are 700,000 wire transfers a day in the United States, of which about 0.05 to 0.1 per cent represent money laundering. The implied $300 million of money laundered a day is dwarfed by the legitimate transfer of $2 trillion a day.
5.  Some Caribbean governments sell bank licences for as little as $10,000 (*The Economist*, 17 February 1996, p. 90).

6. The Russian Interior Ministry estimates that crime syndicates control half of Russia's banks (see *The Economist*, 1999, p. 18).
7. For a general discussion, see Cowell (1990).
8. A recent survey of the underground economy in the developed countries shows a range from 6.7 per cent of GDP for Switzerland to 18 per cent for Norway (see Schneider and Enste, 2000).
9. For example real estates, shares in privatized industries, and government bonds.
10. It is hypothesized that an increase in money-laundering activity increases the demand for money (currency + deposits) as consistent with much of the literature on the underground economy (see, for example, Bhattacharyya, 1990).
11. Non-deposit liabilities are excluded for simplicity.
12. The reason why banks do not supply an infinite amount of loans for a positive margin of intermediation is because of risk aversion or real resource costs. See, for example, Pyle (1971) and Pesek (1970).
13. Bank secrecy has been the subject of a recent OECD report on harmful tax practices and also an FATF report on non-cooperative countries in the battle against money laundering (OECD, 2000; FATF, 2000b).
14. According to Tanzi (1996), money laundering is an expensive business. Fees in excess of 30 per cent of the amount laundered have to be paid or loss-making enterprises bought.
15. For a detailed description of the activities of the FATF, see Sherman (1993).

# REFERENCES

Allingham, M. and Sandmo, A. (1972), 'Income tax evasion: a theoretical analysis', *Journal of Public Economics*, **1**, pp. 323–38.
Becker, G.S. (1968), 'Crime and punishment: an economic approach', *Journal of Political Economy*, **78**, pp. 526–36.
Bhattacharyya, D.K. (1990), 'An econometric method for estimating the hidden economy', *Economic Journal*, **100**, pp. 661–92.
Bingham Report (1993), *Report of the Inquiry into the Supervision of the Bank of Credit and Commerce International* (chairman Lord Justice Bingham), HC 1992–93, 198.
Branson, W.H. (1977), 'Asset markets and relative prices in exchange rate determination', *Sozialwissenschaftliche Annalen*, **1**, pp. 69–89.
Courtenay, A. (1999), 'Know your IBC', *The Banker*, April, pp. 85–6.
Cowell, F. (1990), *Cheating the Government: The Economics of Tax Evasion*, Cambridge, MA: MIT Press.
Cullen, P. J. (1993), 'The European Community Directive', in H.L. MacQueen (ed.), *Money Laundering*, Hume Papers on Public Policy, Vol. 1, No. 2, Edinburgh: Edinburgh University Press, pp. 34–49.
De Grauwe, P. (1982), 'The exchange rate in a portfolio balance model of the banking sector', *Journal of Money and Finance*, **1**, pp. 225–39.
Dornbusch, R. (1976), 'Expectations and exchange rate dynamics', *Journal of Political Economy*, **84**, pp. 1161–76.
Drage, J. (1992), 'Countering money laundering: the response of the financial sector', *Bank of England Quarterly Bulletin*, November.
*Economist, The* (1999), 'Russian organized crime', 28 August–3 September, pp. 17–19.
Ehrlich, I. (1973), 'Participation in illegitimate activities: a theoretical and empirical investigation', *Journal of Political Economy*, **81**, May–June, pp. 521–65.

European Commission (1997), *Second Commission Report to the European Parliament and the Council on the Implementation of the Money Laundering Directive*, Directorate General XV, XV/1116/97-rev.2-En.

Financial Action Task Force (FATF) (1997), *Financial Action Task Force on Money Laundering, Report on Money Laundering Typologies, 1997–1998*, Paris: OECD, February.

Financial Action Task Force (FATF) (2000), *Financial Action Task Force on Money Laundering, Review to Identify Non-Co-operative Countries or Territories: Increasing the Worldwide Effectiveness of Anti-Money Laundering Measures*, Paris: OECD, June.

Marrelli, M. (1984), 'On indirect tax evasion', *Journal of Public Economics*, **25**, pp. 181–96.

Masciandaro, F. (1996), 'Pecunia olet? Microeconomia del riciclaggio bancario e finanziario', *Rivista Internazionale di Scienze Economiche e Commerciali*, **43**, pp. 817–44.

Norton, J.J. (1994), *Banks: Fraud and Crime*, London: Lloyds Press.

Organization for Economic Cooperation and Development (OECD) (2000), *Towards Global Tax Co-operation: Report to the 2000 Ministerial Council Meeting and Recommendations by the Committee on Fiscal Affairs, Progress in Identifying and Eliminating Harmful Tax Practices*, Paris: OECD, June.

Pesek, B. (1970), 'Banks' supply function and the equilibrium quantity of money', *Canadian Journal of Economics*, **3**, pp. 357–83.

Pyle, D.H. (1971), 'On the theory of financial intermediation', *Journal of Finance*, **26**, pp. 737–47.

Quirk, P.J. (1996), 'Macroeconomic implications of money laundering', International Monetary Fund Working Paper WP/96/66, June.

Quirk, P.J. (1997), 'Money laundering: muddying the economy', *Finance and Development*, International Monetary Fund, March, pp. 7–9.

Scott, D. (1995), 'Money laundering and international efforts to fight it', *Public Policy for the Private Sector*, The World Bank, May, Note 48, pp. 1–4.

Schneider, F. and Enste, D.H. (2000), 'Shadow economies: size, causes, and consequences', *Journal of Economic Literature*, **37** (1), pp. 77–114.

Sherman, T. (1993), 'International efforts to combat money laundering: the role of the financial action task force', in H.L. MacQueen (ed.), *Money Laundering*, Hume Papers on Public Policy, Vol. 1, No. 2, Edinburgh: Edinburgh University Press, pp. 12–33.

Tanaka, T. (1996), 'Possible consequences of digital cash', *First Monday*, www.firstmonday.dk/issues/issue2/digital_cash/.

Tanzi, V. (1996), 'Money laundering and the international financial system', International Monetary Fund Working Paper, WP/96/55, May.

Walter, I. (1990), *The Secret Money Market*, New York: Harper & Row.

Walter, I. (1993), 'The economics of international money laundering', *Papers on Latin America*, Columbia University: Institute of Latin American and Iberian Studies, September.

# 20. The regulation of international banking: structural issues*
## Richard Dale and Simon Wolfe

## 1 INTRODUCTION

Several recent developments – notably, the breakdown of traditional distinctions between different types of financial activity, the globalization of financial markets and increasing emphasis on systemic stability as a regulatory objective – have prompted policy makers to search for an 'optimum' regulatory structure that is adapted to the new market environment. Further impetus has been given to this debate by the radical overhaul of regulatory structures, along quite different lines in the UK, Australia, Japan, the United States and New Zealand.[1]

This chapter examines alternative ways of organizing the regulatory function in the context of the new financial market environment. Section 2 reviews the objectives, targets and techniques of regulation; Section 3 describes the new market environment and the restructuring of the financial services industry; Section 4 assesses the implications of this new environment for the structure of regulation; Section 5 addresses the international dimension; and the final section provides a summary and conclusion.

## 2 OBJECTIVES, TARGETS AND TECHNIQUES OF REGULATION

**Objectives of Regulation**

The case for regulating financial institutions can be made on three broad grounds. First, there is the consumer protection argument. This is based on the view that depositors and investors cannot be expected to assess the riskiness of financial institutions they place their money with, or to monitor effectively the standard of service provided by such institutions. The consumer protection rationale gives rise to three categories of regulation: first, compensation schemes designed to reimburse all or part of losses suffered through the insolvency of financial institutions; second, regulation in the form of capital adequacy requirements and other rules aimed at preventing insolvency; and finally, conduct of business or market practice rules intended to ensure that users of financial services are treated fairly. This last type of regulation reflects market imperfections arising from, *inter alia*, asymmetric information, principal–agent problems, and the fact that the value of a financial product or service may only be determinable well after the point in time at which it is purchased.

The consumer protection rationale for regulation is closely related to another concern. If depositors or investors are to be reimbursed for losses incurred through the insolvency of financial institutions then there will be little or no incentive to exercise care in the choice of depository or investment institution. This in turn means that risky institutions will be able to attract business with the same ease and on the same terms as more prudently run firms, thereby undermining financial market discipline and increasing the incidence of insolvencies. The ensuing losses must then be borne by the deposit insurance scheme, investor protection fund, or, ultimately, the taxpayer. Prudential constraints on financial institutions' risk taking then become necessary in order to limit such losses and to offset the regulatory incentives in favour of excessive risk taking.

A third objective of financial regulation is to ensure the integrity of markets, embracing such diverse matters as money laundering, market manipulation, price discovery, fairness (for instance, in terms of access to information) and, above all, transparency. Market integrity focuses on the organization of the market as a whole rather than on the bilateral relationships between financial institutions and their customers (that is, conduct of business).

Among supervisors themselves the rationale for financial regulation that gives most cause for concern is systemic risk – that is, the risk that the failure of one or more troubled financial institutions could trigger a contagious collapse of otherwise healthy firms. It is, above all, their alleged susceptibility to contagious disturbances that distinguishes financial institutions from non-financial firms. In the words of a member of the Board of Governors of the Federal Reserve System:

> It is systematic risk that fails to be controlled and stopped at the inception that is a nightmare condition . . . The only analogy that I can think of for the failure of a major international institution of great size is a meltdown of a nuclear generating plant like Chernobyl. The ramifications of that kind of failure are so broad and happened with such lightning speed that you cannot after the fact control them. It runs the risk of bringing down other banks, corporations, disrupting markets, bringing down investment banks along with it . . . We are

talking about the failure that could disrupt the whole system. (LaWare, 1991, p. 34)

These, then, are the main considerations behind the regulation of financial institutions: consumer protection, moral hazard (a consequence of consumer protection), market integrity and systemic risk. In addition it should be noted that a further major regulatory objective is to achieve competitive equality – between financial institutions from different countries, between functionally distinct financial firms (banks, securities firms and insurance companies) that carry on the same kinds of business, and between rival financial centres. Concerns about competitive equality do not provide an independent justification for financial regulation but they do often provide an important impetus to international regulatory coordination initiatives. For instance, the European financial market directives have been framed with the explicit objective of achieving a 'level playing field', and the original motivation behind the Basle Accord on minimum capital standards was the perceived need to avoid competitive distortions associated with uneven national capital requirements.

**Targets of Regulation**

Within a financial market regime characterized by specialized financial institutions conducting distinct financial activities, the main *targets* of financial regulation are banks, investment firms, insurance companies, fund management companies and exchanges (incorporating clearing and settlement arrangements). The various rationales for financial regulation described above apply in different ways to these separate segments of the financial services industry, as described below.

Banks are characterized by short-term and unsecured value-certain liabilities (deposits) and illiquid value-uncertain assets (commercial loans). Banks are subject to deposit insurance and other forms of consumer protection, in part because banks' balance sheets are opaque and depositors are therefore not in a position to assess the riskiness of their deposits. Depositor protection in turn gives rise to moral hazard. But the case for bank regulation also rests heavily on systemic risk – that is, the alleged potential for destructive bank runs that can endanger not only individual institutions, but the stability of the banking system as a whole. According to this view, bank runs are caused by depositors seeking to withdraw their funds in response to the fear of bank asset losses that could lead to insolvency. Given the nature of the deposit contract (that is, a fixed nominal claim), those who run first can expect to be repaid in full, while those who delay withdrawals risk losing some or all of their deposit balances.

Therefore, depositors have a (rational) propensity to run at the first sign of trouble.

The more recent academic literature does not rely on any loss in the value of a bank's underlying assets to explain the occurrence of bank runs (see Diamond and Dybvig, 1983, 1986). The focus instead is on a bank's transformation services – specifically the conversion of illiquid assets (bank loans) into liquid claims (bank deposits) – and the fact that a bank's loan portfolio is worth significantly less in liquidation than on a going concern basis. All that is required to make a run possible – and rational – is that the liquidation value of the loan portfolio is less than the value of the liquid deposits. This approach explains how runs can occur even in the case of healthy banks, since the victim institution will be forced to dispose of its assets at liquidation prices, thereby threatening insolvency.

Investment firms, in contrast to banks, are characterized by short-term but (generally) secured liabilities and liquid assets whose value is transparent, albeit subject to fluctuations. For investment firms, the case for regulation has traditionally rested on consumer protection – the idea that investors should bear the market risk associated with their investments but should not be fully exposed to the risk of default by the intermediary through whom they transact.

On the other hand, investment firm failures are much less likely to have systemic consequences than the failure of banks. The assets of a non-bank investment firm consist largely of marketable securities and there will therefore be little difference between their value on a going concern basis and in liquidation, in marked contrast to banking assets – which are worth considerably less in liquidation. This means that a troubled investment firm will generally be able to wind down its business in an orderly manner, meeting its obligations by prompt asset disposals at close to book value. On the liabilities side too, investment firms are generally less vulnerable than banks, because much of their funding is secured and in any case cannot be immediately withdrawn, as can bank sight deposits. To the extent that funding is curtailed, an investment firm will generally be able to contract its way out of trouble. In short, investment firms are much less vulnerable to contagious liquidity and solvency crises than are banks.

Insurance companies are characterized by long-term liabilities of uncertain value and liquid value-certain assets. Among the major categories of financial institution, this balance sheet structure is least likely to give rise to systemic risk, liquidity transformation being in the reverse direction to that of banks. Regulation of insurance companies is based on consumer protection, reflecting the fact that it is difficult for consumers to assess an insurer's financial strength in relation to its prices and quality of service. In addition, insurers may increase their risk after policyholders have purchased a policy and paid premiums. Therefore, in the absence of regulation, imperfect consumer information and agency problems may result in a (socially) excessive level of insolvencies. For similar reasons, conduct of business regulation is also an important aspect of the regulatory framework for insurance companies.

Fund management companies invest not on their own account but on behalf of their customers. This agency role means that investors are protected from a management company's insolvency so long as funds under management are segregated from the latter's own assets. Regulation of fund management companies accordingly focuses on conduct of business (advertising, disclosure, charges, and so on). Systemic risk is not generally a consideration here.

Securities exchanges, as distinct from exchange members, are regulated to ensure market integrity. In general, exchanges have not been viewed as a potential source of systemic risk, although, in respect of securities clearing and settlement, this perception is changing (see below). On the other hand, wholesale interbank payment systems, as the linch-pin of the banking system, have traditionally been subject to rigorous central bank scrutiny to minimize systemic risk (see, generally, Dale, 1997).

In summary, systemic concerns have in the past tended to focus exclusively on banks and payment systems. Consumer protection regulation, on the other hand, is applicable to all categories of financial institution. While deposit protection (and hence moral hazard) has been a particular feature of banking, all institutions providing retail financial services have been subject to conduct of business regulation. Finally, market integrity is the primary regulatory objective for securities exchanges.

It may be noted that so long as the financial activities above are distinct and separate, regulation is both functional *and* institutional. This follows from the fact that particular functions are carried on within specialized financial entities: regulation of the function is tantamount to regulation of the associated entities and vice versa.

It is also worth noting that within the above framework, issues of regulatory neutrality as between different categories of financial firm are *de minimis*. This is because there is relatively little business overlap between different categories of specialist financial firm.

**Techniques of Regulation**

While techniques of conduct of business regulation do not vary significantly across different categories of institution, when it comes to prudential regulation there are important differences that reflect the different risk characteristics of banks, investment firms and insurance companies.

Because bank failures can have systemic consequences, there is traditionally a strong emphasis on *protective* bank regulation in the form of lender-of-last-resort facilities and deposit protection (which in turn gives rise to moral hazard). In this context the extent of deposit protection may be well in excess of the protection offered by deposit insurance schemes, reflecting policy makers' preference for safeguarding banking institutions and not merely depositors. Also reflecting the regulatory goal of sustaining banks as going concerns, *preventive* regulation, aimed at curbing excessive risk taking, has tended to focus on capital adequacy requirements, with assets, for this purpose, valued on a going concern basis.

In contrast to the above, investment firms are regulated with a view to ensuring that they can wind down their business rapidly when they run into trouble. Accordingly, investment firms' assets are required to be liquid and marked to market. In addition, regulators typically require that customer assets be segregated from those of the firm. These key instruments of regulation – asset contraction and insulation of customers – sharply differentiate the traditional regulatory approach of securities and bank regulators.

Insurance companies are different again. Prudential regulation here focuses on long-term solvency based on actuarial principles, taking account of the uncertain value of long-term liabilities. In other words, solvency requirements have to address not only asset risk but also liability/underwriting risk.

Fund management companies are not subject to extensive prudential regulation, while exchanges are typically self-regulated on the basis of membership capital requirements.

**Assessment**

In the traditional financial framework described above the financial services industry is divided into separate pillars (banks, investment firms, insurance companies, and so on), each with its own distinct regulatory regime, reflecting differing regulatory objectives and techniques (see Table 20.1). Regulation is both functional and institutional since institutions are co-extensive with particular activities. At the same time, regulatory neutrality is not a major issue because the separate pillars within the industry do not compete directly with one another. This may be viewed as a dream world for regulators in which regulatory objectives, targets and techniques are neatly compartmentalized and problems of regulatory interface do not arise. However, in the new financial market environment described in the following section, issues of regulatory structure and coordination become much more problematic.

*Table 20.1   Targets of regulation*

|  | Assets | Liabilities | Regulatory objective |
|---|---|---|---|
| 1. Banks | Illiquid, value uncertain (book values) | Short term, value certain, unsecured (deposits) | Moral hazard, depositor protection, systemic risk |
| 2. Investment firms | Liquid, mark-to-market | Short term, secured | Investor protection |
| 3. Insurance companies | Liquid, value certain | Long term, uncertain values | Consumer protection |
| 4. Fund management companies | Agency role | | Investor protection |
| 5. Exchanges | Counterparty risk | | Market integrity |
| 6. Payment systems | Counterparty risk | | Systemic risk |

## 3   THE NEW MARKET ENVIRONMENT

The compartmentalized model of the financial services industry and its regulatory framework has over the past decade or so been transformed by market developments. The traditional pillars of banking, securities business, insurance and fund management are being displaced by a quite different industry structure in which hitherto discrete activities are conducted within the same financial services group (see OECD, 1997a,b).

### Functional Integration

The process of functional integration reflects the perceived efficiency benefits of combining financial services under one corporate roof. Such benefits are of two kinds: firms may realize *internal* economies of scope through joint production and marketing of diversified financial services; and users of financial services may realize *external* economies of scope because they can more conveniently purchase several financial services at a single location or from a single firm (see Litan, 1987, pp. 60–98).

There are various degrees of functional integration which may be associated with different levels of efficiency gains. The first stage of integration is based on ownership linkages between financial firms conducting different types of business (see Tables 20.2 and 20.3).

Table 20.2  Recent European cross-functional mergers, 1998–1999

| Nationality | Institutions | Type | Size $m | Date* |
|---|---|---|---|---|
| Italian/Spanish | Unicredito Italiano / Banco Bilbao Vizcaya | Bank/Bancassurance | 725 | 1999 |
| Dutch/German | ING Group / BHF Bank | Bancassurance/Bank | 2,338 | 1999 |
| UK/French | CGU PLC / Société Générale | Insurance/Bank | 711 | 1999 |
| Italian/Polish | Investor Group / Bank Polska Kasa Opieki | Investment Bank/Bank | 1,082 | 1999 |
| Swiss | Schweizerische Lebensversicher / Banca del Gottardo | Insurance/Bank | 944 | 1999 |
| Dutch/French | ING Group / Crédit Commercial de France | Insurance/Bank | 1,254 | 1998 |
| Belgian | Royale Belge / Anhyp | Insurance/Bank | 645 | 1998 |
| Dutch/Belgian | Fortis International / ASLK-CGER Banque | Insurance/Bank | 1,523 | 1998 |
| Belgian | Fortis Group / Générale de Banque | Bancassurance/Bank | 12,298 | 1998 |
| Dutch/Belgian | ING / Banque Bruxelles Lambert | Bancassurance/Bank | 4,500 | 1998 |
| Spanish/Swiss | Assicurazioni Generali / Banca della Svizzera Italiana | Insurance/Bank | 1,290 | 1998 |
| Belgian | Kredietbank / Almanij-Banking & Insurance | Bank/Insurance | 7,655 | 1998 |
| Swiss | Crédit Suisse / Winterthur | Bank/Insurance | 10,000 | 1988 |
| German | Dresdner Bank / Allianz | Bank/Insurance | n/a | 1998 |
| Italian | Banca Nazionale del Lavoro / Banco di Napoli / INA | Bank/Bank/Insurance | n/a | 1998 |

*Note:* *Date is the announcement year.

*Source:* Thomson Financial Securities Data (January 2000).

*Table 20.3  Recent US cross-functional mergers, 1997–1998*

| Institutions | Type | Size |
|---|---|---|
| BankBoston / Robertson Stephens | Bank / Securities | $800 m |
| Travelers Group / Citicorp | Insurance / Banking | $83 bn |
| US Bancorp / Piper Jaffray Companies | Bank / Securities | $730 m |
| Fleet Financial / Quick & Reilly | Bank / Securities | $1.6 bn |
| First Union / Wheat First Butcher Singer | Bank / Securities | $471 m |
| NationsBank / Montgomery Securities | Bank / Securities | $1.2 bn |
| ING Barings / Furman Selz | Bank / Securities | $500 m |
| Swiss Bank Corporation / Dillon Read | Bank / Securities | $600 m |
| CIBC Wood Gundy / Oppenheimer | Bank / Securities | $525 m |
| BankAmerica / Robertson Stephens | Bank / Securities | $540 m |
| Bankers Trust / Alex Brown | Bank / Securities | $1.7 bn |

*Source:*  Shearlock (1998), p. 17.

The second stage of integration involves exploitation of economies of scope through, for instance, cross-selling of financial services. Such efficiency gains may be significant where banks' branch networks are used to sell fund management, insurance and securities products, possibly under a single brand name.

A third, and crucial stage, of integration occurs when financial conglomerates adopt a centralized approach to risk management. The rationale for such a policy is based, first, on potential economies of scale and scope related to advanced computer technology and highly specialized skills in quantitative risk measurement, and second on the ability to unbundle discrete categories of risk within different parts of an organization and then to monitor and manage those exposures on a consolidated basis for the group as a whole. In the words of Andrew Large, former Chairman of the UK Securities and Investments Board:

> [O]ver the past 5–10 years, the institutional deregulation initiatives in different countries have combined with huge advances in computer power and communications technology, to create a totally new breed of financial intermediary. [They] have embraced the theory of financial risk management which applies portfolio theory to the range of risks associated with the securities business ... The key characteristic of this approach is that it seeks out the common elements of risk wherever they may lie in a portfolio and manages them centrally. These firms no longer respect the traditional boundaries between markets or the old institutional boundaries between banking, securities and insurance. They are in the risk-management business pure and simple, and they operate on a large scale and on a truly global basis. (Large, 1994, p. 1)

The final stage of functional integration is reached if diversified financial activities are conducted within the same legal entity and on the same balance sheet. This is the pure version of the 'universal banking' model. However, in practice, financial conglomerates generally have corporate structures that reflect broad product lines, although such subdivisions may be compatible with a centralized management structure.

**Deregulation and Erosion of Boundaries**

For the purposes of the present discussion, the key development is the integration of hitherto discrete segments of the financial services industry through a combination of ownership linkages and centralized risk management. However, there are other important considerations.

First, the commercial impetus towards financial conglomeration has coincided with a change of regulatory philosophy. The new thinking rejects activity constraints on banks and other financial firms as being inefficient and heavy-handed, and instead focuses on capital adequacy requirements to cover the risks associated with whatever financial activities a group chooses to undertake. The recent dismantling of Japan's statutory separation of banks, securities firms and trust banks, and US regulatory relaxation of the Glass–Steagall restrictions on banks' securities activities are examples of the new regulatory approach.

Second, quite apart from ownership linkages between different categories of financial firm, the distinctiveness of the *business* of banking and other financial activities is gradually being eroded. For instance, on the liabilities side of the balance sheet, internationally active banks have been increasing their secured funding – a form of financing traditionally associated with investment firms.[2] On the assets side of the balance sheet there is also convergence, with the proportion of loans to non-banks in total bank assets (a measure of banks' illiquid assets) tending to decline. For instance, the Bank of England has calculated that for large UK, internationally active, banks the share of such loans is currently about 50 per cent, having fallen from 65–70 per cent five years previously, a decline attributable to the expansion of these institutions' investment banking operations (see George, 1997, p. 10). Furthermore, there is a trend towards increased secondary market trading of bank loans, thereby blurring the traditional distinction between bank loans and securities.[3] Finally, balance sheet data understates banks' securities activities to the extent that banks sell down their loans in the form of securitized assets (for instance, US bank-holding companies are estimated to have removed some $200 billion from their balance sheets through the sale of securitized assets) (George, 1997, p. 10).

Finally, with the advent of new complex financial instruments it is not possible to determine a priori whether these are banking, securities or insurance products: for instance derivative instruments may be categorized in different ways in different jurisdictions.

The above developments, involving financial conglomeration, centralized risk management and the blurring of traditional distinctions between banking and other types of financial activity, have prompted regulators to adapt their approach to supervision. In the words of Alan Greenspan, Chairman of the US Federal Reserve Board:

> Most large institutions in recent years have moved toward consolidated risk management across all their bank and non-bank activities... it is likely that [new non-banking activities by banking organizations] would be managed on a consolidated basis from the point of view of risk-taking, pricing and profitability analysis. Our regulators' position must adjust accordingly, to focus on the decision-making process for the total organisation. Especially as supervisors focus more on the measurement and management of market, credit, and operating risks, supervisory review of firm-wide processes increasingly will become the appropriate principle underlying our assessment of an organisation's safety and soundness. (Greenspan, 1997, p. 8)

**Consolidated Supervision**

Consolidated supervision is one key ingredient of the new regulatory approach. Under this regime the various entities within a financial conglomerate are supervised on a group-wide basis and capital requirements, actual capital and risk exposures are subject to group-wide supervisory assessment. The Joint Forum on Financial Conglomerates, representing bank, insurance and securities supervisors, has described consolidated capital adequacy assessment as follows:

> [S]ubsidiaries are usually consolidated in full... For prudential purposes, regulatory capital in excess of such a subsidiary's own regulatory capital requirements, and which can be regarded as in principle available to support risks in the parent company or other entities in the group should a shortfall arise, can be recognized in a group-wide capital adequacy assessment. (BIS, 1998, p. 11, para. 32)

In other words, under a consolidated supervision regime, both risk exposures and capital available to back those exposures are viewed as accruing to the group as a whole. Risks are no longer to be assessed on a legal entity basis or on the basis of the category of financial activity being undertaken. This holistic approach is consistent with the trend towards centralized risk management within financial conglomerates noted above and brings regulatory risk appraisal into line with financial firms' own risk management practices.

**Assessment**

In recent years there has been a progressive erosion of the traditional demarcation lines that have separated banking from other, non-bank financial activities. This development reflects cross-functional ownership linkages between different categories of financial firm, the blurring of distinctions between banking and non-banking business through 'securitization' and other forms of financial innovation, and the dismantling of legal activity constraints previously applied to banking organizations. At the same time large diversified financial groups have tended to adopt a centralized approach to risk management that ignores traditional boundaries between different financial activities.

In the new financial environment it is no longer possible to identify separate sets of regulatory objectives, targets and techniques covering banking, securities business, insurance and fund management. Banks are no longer 'special' in the sense of being uniquely exposed to systemic risk because their activities and risk exposures have become intermingled with non-bank financial business. The regulatory objective of systemic stability now extends to investment firms,[4] securities and derivatives clearing and settlement systems and even insurance[5] and fund management entities (dramatically underlined by the recent débâcle over the Long-Term Capital Management (LTCM) entity, a $100 billion US hedge fund).[6] The need to curb moral hazard through regulatory action similarly embraces all those activities undertaken within a conglomerate that may benefit, directly or indirectly, from the availability of lender-of-last-resort support.

The targets of regulation are no longer distinct because corporate entities and groupings are no longer co-extensive with identifiable lines of business. At the same time, the consolidated supervision of financial conglomerates, as described above, explicitly recognizes the interdependence of risks and capital resources within diversified financial groups. Furthermore, the techniques of regulation are no longer business specific. Reflecting recent developments in financial technology and risk measurement, regulators are moving away from static, point-in-time balance sheet analysis and focusing instead on the *process* of risk management. This entails an assessment both of management's risk models and internal control procedures. Since the new approach to regulatory risk assessment applies across different categories of financial activity – banking, securities business and insurance – there is no longer a clear justification for separate regulation of these activities on grounds of regulatory specialism. On the contrary, a convergent approach to regulation across functions, together with the observed trend towards centralized risk management, points in the opposite direction. To quote Alan Greenspan again:

> One could argue ... that regulators should only be interested in the entities they regulate and, hence, review the risk evaluation process only as it relates to their regulated entity. Presumably, each regulator of each entity – the bank regulator, the SEC [Securities and Exchange Commission], the state insurance and finance company authorities – would look only at how the risk management process affected their units. It is our belief that this simply will not be adequate. Risks managed on a consolidated basis cannot be reviewed on an individual legal entity basis by different supervisors. (Greenspan, 1998, p. 10)

It may also be noted that the new market environment creates a mismatch between functional and institutional regulation – since previously distinct functions now flow over institutional boundaries. In other words a purely institutional approach to regulation would inevitably have to combine different types of financial activity under one regulatory agency; while a purely functional approach would require regulatory agencies to cut across institutional demarcation lines.

Finally, whereas under the segmented financial structure described in Section 2 competitive equality is not a primary concern, within the more fluid competitive environment of overlapping financial activities (for example banks competing with investment firms in derivatives markets) regulatory parity becomes a major issue.

## 4 IMPLICATIONS FOR REGULATORY STRUCTURE

In considering institutional structures for financial regulation it is necessary to assess alternative models in terms of economies of scope, regulatory parity (the 'level playing field') and (in respect of prudential regulation) what might loosely be termed 'prudential logic'. Prudential logic refers in particular to the importance of aligning the remit of the regulator with the risk management function of the regulated organization, so that in the case of centralized risk management of diversified activities, the regulator's perspective is the same as that of management. A mismatch between the regulator's unit of assessment on the one hand, and management's on the other, is likely to lead to trouble (as suggested in Section 3 above).

In the traditional segmented financial structure described in Section 2 a regime of functionally specialized prudential regulators makes sense because different sets of regulatory objectives, techniques and targets are associated with different financial activities. For instance, a traditional-style regulatory framework covering the main areas of activity is summarized in Table 20.4.

Within this segmented industry structure there are no obvious economies

Table 20.4  Traditional-style regulatory framework

|  | Targets | | |
| --- | --- | --- | --- |
|  | Banks | Investment firms | Insurance companies |
| Objectives | Systemic stability<br>Neutralize moral hazard<br>Depositor protection | Investor protection | Consumer protection |
| Techniques | Lender of last resort/<br>deposit insurance<br>Capital requirements<br>(going concern basis)<br>On-site examinations | Liquid capital<br>mark-to-market<br>valuation<br>(liquidation basis) | Actuarial solvency |
| Regulator | Central bank/bank<br>regulator | Securities regulator | Insurance regulator |

of scope to be gained, nor is there any prudential logic, in combining specialized prudential regulatory functions within a single regulatory agency. Furthermore, regulatory parity is not a serious issue. On the other hand, conduct of business regulation is concerned primarily with fair treatment of retail depositors, investors and savers. Because in this case regulatory objectives and techniques are similar across different categories of financial activity, there is an arguable case for a single conduct of business regulator in terms of both efficiency and regulatory neutrality – regardless of the structure of the financial services industry.

Within the new market environment described in Section 3 above, very different considerations apply. Regulation may in this context be divided up in a number of ways, the most important alternative models being as follows:[7]

1. functional regulation;
2. institutional regulation;
3. systemic versus non-systemic institutions;
4. regulation by objective; and
5. wholesale versus retail.

Under a functional regulation regime, specialist regulators focus on the type of business undertaken irrespective of which institutions are involved in that business. Individual institutions might then be subject to several regulatory agencies; there would very likely be a mismatch between regulators' disaggregated approach to risk assessment and the centralized risk management adopted by financial firms; and consolidated supervision becomes problematical. New Zealand (see Figure 20A.5 in the appendix) may be viewed as an example of functional regulation but problems of regulatory overlap are minimized because of the authorities' emphasis on market forces and strong internal governance incentives as a substitute for detailed official supervision.

A more effective form of functional regulation might be envisaged, however, if regulators were to mandate a corporate structure for diversified firms that seeks to segregate risks associated with different financial activities. Financial conglomerates could be required to operate through a financial services holding company which would conduct its business through specialized operating subsidiaries separated by 'firewalls'. Those subsidiaries could then be subject to functional regulation by specialized regulatory agencies. An element of institutional regulation could then be superimposed in the form of consolidated supervision of the holding company. This model has now been adopted in the US following passage of the Financial Services Modernization Act in 1999 which repealed key provisions of the Glass–Steagall Act. The new US regulatory regime combines umbrella supervision of the consolidated group by the Federal Reserve, regulation of banks by their primary bank regulators and financial regulation of affiliated non-bank entities by their respective specialized regulators (see Figure 20A.5c in the appendix). However, the main drawback to such an approach, apart from potential regulatory confusion, is that attempts to segregate risks within specialized entities may well prove ineffective and are in direct conflict with the observed trend towards centralized risk management (see, generally, Dale, 1992).

Institutional regulation, in contrast to functional regulation, demands that regulation be directed at financial institutions irrespective of the mix of business they undertake. It has been argued that under this regime 'each institutional regulator would need to apply the business rules appropriate for every function – which would be hugely inefficient in terms of regulatory resources' (George, 1996; cited in Goodhart et al., 1998, Chapter 8). However, this view may be overstated: in the context of a single mega-regulator (such as the UK now has – see Figure 20A.1 in the appendix) all regulation is institutional in the sense that the diversified activities of each institution/group fall within the regulatory remit of a single agency which is also responsible for consolidated supervision. On the other hand, in a regime of multiple regulatory agencies specialized by function, 'pure' institutional regulation becomes impossible for the simple reason that institutions are no longer synonymous with functions (although an element of institutional regulation may be introduced through the appointment of a 'lead regulator' for diversified groups).

A third possible regulatory divide is between institutions which give rise to systemic risk and those which do not. Since banks are generally viewed as systemically sensitive this might involve a simple distinction between banks and non-banks. However, as explained in Section 3, changes in the market environment have blurred the risk characteristics of banks and non-banks. An alternative approach would be to identify those institutions, whether banks or non-banks, which are of such a size that their default would pose a systemic threat. The difficulty here is that the failure of even small institutions can in some circumstances have systemic consequences. More generally, given the complexity and fluidity of the present market environment it is impractical to identify systemic risk with some specified subset of financial institutions. On the contrary, the interconnectivity between both institutions and markets means that a systemic threat may originate almost anywhere and be transmitted through a variety of institutional channels.

Another way of dividing up the regulatory function is according to regulatory objective. As noted in Section 2, the relevant prudential objectives in this context are systemic risk, moral hazard and consumer protection, while to these must be added consumer protection in the conduct of business sense as well as market integrity. In assessing the merits of this structural model it is important to stress that there has been a convergence of prudential regulatory *objectives* (in that systemic risk and moral hazard have become a feature of financial activities other than banking) as well as a convergence of prudential regulatory *techniques* (reflecting the new supervisory emphasis on value at risk models and internal management controls for all types of financial business). Therefore there is much greater congruence than previously in the prudential regulatory function as it is applied to banks, investment firms, insurance companies and so on. The implication is that there are important potential economies of scope to be gained from combining the prudential regulatory function under one regulatory agency. Furthermore, a single prudential regulator embracing all financial business is consistent with centralized risk management practised by diversified firms and the matching principle of consolidated supervision. Prudential logic therefore points to the desirability of a single prudential regulator which would also be in a position to apply consistent rules across institutions and activities, thereby ensuring regulatory neutrality.

The above is, broadly speaking, the 'Twin Peaks' approach advocated by Taylor which would divide regulatory responsibilities between a single prudential regulator (Financial Stability Commission) and a single conduct of business regulator (Consumer Protection Commission) (see Taylor, 1995). It may be objected that a single prudential regulator would be dealing with three different objectives, namely systemic stability, which calls for a *higher* degree of risk restraint than the market would provide even without an official safety net; moral hazard which requires regulators to simulate the self-regulatory constraints that would exist in the absence of an official safety net; and consumer protection which is one of the causes of moral hazard. However, since these objectives imply different intensities of prudential regulation, rather than different regulatory techniques, and since systemic risk and moral hazard permeate many areas of financial activity, it would seem neither efficient nor practicable to allocate the objectives to separate regulatory agencies.

It may also be objected that a single prudential regulatory agency would not offer efficiency gains because as a matter of practical necessity there would have to be specialist divisions within the unified agency. Such internal divisions (see for instance the Financial Services Authority's (FSA's) 'functional' divisions in Figure 20A.1 in the appendix) might involve internal transactions costs equivalent to those incurred by separate agencies. While there is no doubt some force in this argument, the key point is that where prudential responsibility lies clearly with a single authority the regulatory function and the group managerial function are much more closely aligned. In other words the *scope* of these two functions is precisely matched, even though the regulatory and managerial objectives may diverge.

Following publication of the findings of the Wallis Committee of Inquiry, Australia has adopted a regulatory structure that closely resembles the Twin Peaks model described above (Financial System Inquiry, 1997). However, the Reserve Bank of Australia retains responsibility for systemic stability and is specifically responsible for safeguarding the payments system. Similarly, following the establishment in the UK of a single mega-regulator, the Bank of England retains responsibility for systemic stability.

A key question that arises in this context is whether a central bank that is deprived of prudential regulatory powers (except, perhaps, in respect of the domestic payments system) can meaningfully be responsible for systemic stability – other than in the narrow sense of crisis management. In any event, the supervisory interface between the central bank and the prudential regulatory authority under such a regime assumes great importance (see Memorandum of Understanding between the FSA and the Bank, summarized in the appendix).

Finally, regulatory responsibilities may be divided according to whether the financial activity concerned is wholesale or retail, on the grounds that retail users of financial services are in greater need of regulatory protection. The differentiation is particularly relevant for conduct of business regulation but since this distinction, too, relates more to the intensity of regulation than to differences in regulatory technique, there would appear to be efficiency gains in combining wholesale and retail business under one regulatory roof.

**Assessment**

It has been suggested that the convergence of prudential regulatory objectives and techniques relating to previously distinct financial activities has created potential economies of scope in the regulation of such activities. Furthermore, a single prudential regulatory agency is better equipped to conduct consolidated supervision that matches the consolidated risk management practised by diversified financial firms. Finally, regulatory neutrality and consistency are best assured under a unified prudential regulator.

The housing of conduct of business and market integrity regulation within a single conduct of business regulatory agency similarly offers efficiency benefits. However, there is no obvious case for combining the prudential and conduct of business regulatory functions within a single all-purpose regulatory agency given that the techniques and skills required for those functions are very different.

Whether the central bank should be the single prudential regulatory for all financial activities is a different issue altogether (Taylor, 1997). There have been various inconclusive analyses of the appropriate role of central banks in the regulatory process (see Goodhart and Schoenmaker, 1993). However, if, as is increasingly the case, the monetary authority is divested of its prudential regulatory role yet retains responsibility for systemic stability, the ability to exercise that responsibility depends very heavily on the central bank's working relationship with the prudential regulatory authority.

The argument in favour of a single prudential regulator must be modified to the extent that some financial systems, typically in emerging markets, retain the traditional institutional and functional distinctions between banking, securities business, insurance and so on (see Taylor, 1998). Furthermore in those systems where regulators seek to separate and subsidiarize such activities carried on within diversified financial groups, there may be a case for preserving the traditional structure of regulation based on specialized agencies. Nevertheless, the predominance of the specialized regulatory agency model (see Table 20.5) does suggest that regulatory structures have yet to adapt to recent and ongoing changes in financial markets.

## 5  THE INTERNATIONAL DIMENSION

The globalization of financial markets has been well documented. There are various dimensions to this process involving the growth of cross-border banking and securities transactions, the rapid expansion of the 'borderless' euromarkets, the proliferation of multinational financial firms straddling

Table 20.5  Structure of financial regulatory agencies

| Regulatory structure | Type | Countries |
|---|---|---|
| 1. Mega regulator Combined banking, securities and insurance regulator | Commission Central bank or Ministry of Finance | Denmark, Japan, Korea, Malta, Norway, Sweden, Taiwan, United Kingdom Austria, Singapore |
| 2. Combined Banking and securities regulator | Banking and Securities Commission Central bank | Belgium, Finland, Mexico, Switzerland Bermuda, Cyprus, Dominican Republic, Ireland, Luxembourg, Uruguay |
| 3. Combined Banking and insurance regulator | | Australia, Canada, Colombia, Ecuador, Macau, Malaysia, Paraguay |
| 4. Combined Securities and insurance regulator | | Chile, Czech Republic, South Africa |
| Individual specialist regulator Banking | Agency Central bank/ monetary agency | Chile, France, Germany, Guatemala, Hungary, United States Algeria, Barbados, Botswana, Brazil, Bulgaria, China, Costa Rica, Czech Republic, Egypt, Greece, Hong Kong, India, Indonesia, Israel, Italy, Jamaica, Jordan, Kenya, Netherlands, New Zealand, Nigeria, Pakistan, Philippines, Poland, Portugal, Russia, South Africa, Spain, Taiwan, Thailand, Turkey, United States |
| Securities | Agency | Argentina, Australia, Bolivia, Brazil, Canada, China, Columbia, Ecuador, Egypt, France, Germany, Greece, Hong Kong, Hungary, India, Indonesia, Israel, Italy, Ivory Coast, Jamaica, Jordan, Kenya, Malaysia, Netherlands, New Zealand, Nigeria, Pakistan, Paraguay, Philippines, Poland, Portugal, Russia, Slovenia, Spain, Sri Lanka, Taiwan, Thailand, Turkey, United States, Venezuela, Zambia |
| Insurance | Agency | Argentina, Belgium, Bermuda, Bolivia, Brazil, Egypt, France, Germany, Hong Kong, Hungary, Italy, Luxembourg, Mexico, Netherlands, Philippines, Poland, Portugal, Russia, Spain, Switzerland, United States |

*Sources:* Taylor (1998), Goodhart et al. (1998) and *Directory of Financial Regulatory Agencies* (1996).

numerous jurisdictions, and, most recently, a surge in cross-functional *and* cross-border financial mergers between banks, investment firms, insurance companies and fund management groups (see Tables 20.2 and 20.3).

The globalization of financial markets calls for international regulatory coordination for two reasons (see, generally, Herring and Litan, 1994). First there are 'externalities' in that financial disorders can no longer be confined to the jurisdiction in which they originate – as amply demonstrated by the East Asian financial crisis. Second, regulatory neutrality between competing financial centres as well as between financial firms of differing nationality has become a major issue in the new global marketplace.

These concerns about systemic risk and regulatory parity have been reflected in the evolution of the Basle Committee on Banking Supervision, the International Organization of Securities Commissions (IOSCO) and, more recently, the emergence of an embryonic cross-functional coordinating group in the form of the Joint Forum on Financial Conglomerates embracing the Basle Committee, IOSCO and the International Association of Insurance Supervisors (see Dale, 1996, pp. 135–51).

Arguments about the institutional architecture of international regulatory coordination follow closely those relating to national regulatory structures. The dangers of having two separate international agencies covering banks and investment firms has, for instance, been illustrated by well-publicized tensions in the recent past between Basle and IOSCO (ibid., pp. 144–6). In the area of prudential regulation, economies of scope, prudential logic and concerns about regulatory neutrality again point to the need for an overarching coordinating body to oversee the full spectrum of cross-border financial activity. It may be that the newly established Financial Stability Forum will have a key role to play here.

There is a particular problem here in connection with emerging financial markets, as underlined by the East Asian crisis. In the banking sector, Basle sets the minimum prudential standards, but the International Monetary Fund (IMF) is increasingly being drawn into a monitoring and enforcement role, both as part of its Article 4 surveillance process and in the conditionality associated with its stabilization programmes. The question here arises as to whether the standard-setting and enforcement roles can be effectively discharged by separate international agencies.

Similarly, the IMF has de facto become the lender of last resort to countries experiencing acute liquidity problems. As in the domestic context, some would argue that the lender-of-last-resort function should be combined with responsibility for prudential standards. Under the pressure of recent events things seem to be moving in this direction, but there is a need to sort out the respective roles of Basle and the IMF.

Finally, there may be a need for a new supranational industry body representing the financial sector's own interest and expertise in risk control. The Group of Thirty has, for instance, suggested that 'core institutions' – embracing large internationally active banks as well as the largest securities firms – should establish a standing committee to work with supervisors in promulgating and reviewing global principles for managing risk. This proposal is based on the increasing scale, speed, complexity and interconnectivity of financial transactions and the observation that 'the global operations of major financial institutions and markets have outpaced the national accounting, legal and supervisory systems on which the safety and soundness of individual institutions and the financial system rely' (Group of Thirty, 1997, p. v).

In summary, the combination of globalization and functional integration of financial markets creates a dangerous potential for both cross-border and cross-functional financial contagion. This has been a painful lesson learned from the East Asian crisis, where the channels for contagious disruption have been both geographic and intermarket (banking, securities and foreign exchange). The implication is that international coordination of prudential regulation should, like domestic regulation, be organized on a multifunctional basis through a single prudential regulatory agency. Arguably, that single agency should be responsible for standard setting, monitoring and enforcement. Whether the same agency should also be the international lender of last resort is, however, a moot question.

## 6 SUMMARY AND CONCLUSION

The main considerations behind the regulation of financial institutions are: consumer protection, moral hazard (a consequence of consumer protection), market integrity and systemic risk. In addition, regulatory neutrality is an important element in the design of any regulatory framework.

In what has loosely been described as the traditional model, the financial services industry is divided into separate pillars (banks, investment firms, insurance companies and fund management companies), each with its own distinct regulatory regime. Since functions and institutions are synonymous, regulation is both functional and institutional; regulatory neutrality is not a major issue; regulatory objectives, targets and techniques are neatly compartmentalized; and problems of regulatory interface do not arise.

Over the past decade or so the traditional demarcation lines between banking and non-bank financial activities have been eroded. Ownership linkages between banks and non-banks, the blurring of distinctions between banking and securities business due to 'securitization' and other forms of financial innovation, and the dismantling of legal activity constraints previously applied to financial institutions, have together transformed the financial landscape. In the new market environment banks are no longer uniquely susceptible to systemic risk and moral hazard; it is no longer possible to identify separate sets of regulatory objectives, targets and techniques covering the main categories of financial activity; and there is an inevitable mismatch between the regulation of functions and the regulation of institutions (since function and institution are no longer synonymous).

A further key factor in the new environment is the centralization of risk management within diversified financial firms, using advanced statistical techniques that 'unbundle' different types of risk at the individual entity level and reaggregate them (again by type of risk) for the purpose of centralized management at the group level. Regulators have meanwhile adopted the principle of consolidated supervision, which broadly aligns the regulatory approach to risk appraisal with that of management.

It has been suggested here that the institutional structure of regulation should be assessed in terms of economies of scope, prudential logic and regulatory neutrality. On this basis the convergence of prudential regulatory objectives and techniques relating to previously distinct financial activities points to the need for a single prudential regulator. In this context there could be regulatory interface problems if the central bank is divested of its responsibility for prudential supervision but nevertheless retains responsibility for systemic stability.

There is a parallel, though less compelling, case for the housing of conduct of business (and market integrity) regulation within a single regulatory agency. On the other hand, there is no such argument for combining the prudential and conduct of business regulatory functions within a single all-purpose regulatory body, given the very different techniques and skills required for those functions.

Finally, arguments relevant to the design of the domestic financial regulatory structure apply with equal force at the international level. Indeed, it has been pointed out that the combination of globalization and functional integration of financial markets creates a dangerous potential for both cross-border and cross-functional financial contagion, as evidenced by the East Asian crisis. This in turn calls for cross-functional international regulatory coordination.

In terms of the present loose international federation of banking, securities and insurance supervisory authorities, there is a strong case for a more integrated overarching coordinating body whose remit is to oversee the full spectrum of cross-border financial activity. Furthermore, in place of the present divided responsibility for international standard setting (Basle) and enforcement (IMF) a single agency should arguably be responsible for both functions.

## NOTES

\* A previous version of this chapter was presented at the World Bank Conference, El Salvador, June 1998.
1. For a summary description of the relevant regulatory structures, see Appendix 20A.
2. For J.P. Morgan and Bankers Trust the proportion of secured funding is as high as 25–36 per cent compared to 55–80 per cent for major US securities firms (cited in George, 1997, p. 8).
3. According to the Loan Market Association – the euromarket's equivalent of the more long-standing Loan Syndication Traders Association in the US – a secondary loan market is developing in Europe (see Edward Luce, 'Europe warms to secondary loan market', *Financial Times*, 4 August 1997).
4. For instance, IOSCO has recently given prominence to the reduction of systemic risk as a primary objective of securities regulation: see IOSCO (1998), p. 8.
5. Insurance should, however, be differentiated for two reasons: first, as explained in the text, systemic risk is less than in banking/securities business and, second, it may not be appropriate to include insurance companies within group-consolidated capital adequacy assessment if under relevant insurance legislation capital cannot be transferred to other financial firms within the group.
6. Since 1990, the US mutual fund industry has grown from $600 billion to over $4 trillion today, while US bank deposits over the same period have remained static at $2.2 trillion. Investment actions by mutual funds could conceivably give rise to systemic instability (see *The Banker*, April 1998, p. 17).
7. See Goodhart et al. (1998), p. 19. Chapter 8 of this study provides a useful discussion of policy issues relating to the institutional structure of regulation.

## REFERENCES

Bank for International Settlements (BIS) (1998), 'Supervision of financial conglomerates', Consultation document by the Basle Committee on Banking Supervision, Basle, February.
Dale, R. (1992), *International Banking Deregulation: The Great Banking Experiment*, Oxford: Basil Blackwell.
Dale, R. (1996), *Risk and Regulation in Global Securities Markets*, New York: John Wiley.
Dale, R. (1997), 'Controlling risks in large value interbank payments systems', *Journal of International Banking Law*, **12** (2), pp. 426–34.
Diamond, D. and P. Dybvig (1983), 'Bank runs, deposit insurance and liquidity', *Journal of Political Economy*, **91** (3), pp. 401–19.
Diamond, D. and P. Dybvig (1986), 'Banking theory, deposit insurance and bank regulation', *Journal of Business*, **59** (1), pp. 55–68.
*Directory of Financial Regulatory Agencies* (1996), London: Central Bank Publications.
Financial System Inquiry (1997), *Financial System Inquiry: Final Report* (Wallis Inquiry), Commonwealth of Australia, March.
George, E. (1997), 'Are banks still special?' Speech at the IMF 7th Central Banking Seminar: 'Banking soundness and monetary policy', Washington, DC, 29 January.
Goodhart, C., P. Hartmann, D. Llewellyn, L. Rojas-Suarez and S. Weisbrod (1998), *Financial Regulation: Why, How and Where Now?*, London and New York: Routledge.

Goodhart, C. and D. Schoenmaker (1993), 'Institutional separation between supervisory and monetary agencies', London School of Economics Financial Markets Group, April.

Greenspan, A. (1997), 'Remarks', at the Annual Convention of the Independent Bankers Association of America, Arizona, 22 March.

Greenspan, A. (1998), 'Statement before the Subcommittee on Financial Institutions and Consumer Credit Committee on Banking and Financial Services', United States House of Representatives, 13 February.

Group of Thirty (1997), *Global Institutions, National Supervision and Systemic Risk*, Washington, DC: Group of Thirty.

Herring, R. and R. Litan (1994), *Financial Regulation in the Global Economy*, Washington, DC: Brookings Institution.

International Organization of Securities Commissions (IOSCO) (1998), 'Objectives and principles of securities regulation', Consultation Draft, June, 3.

Large, A. (1994), 'Speech to the International Organization of Securities Commissions' Conference, Tokyo, cited in the *Financial Times*'s Financial Regulation Report, October.

LaWare, J. (1991), 'Testimony before the Subcommittee on Economic Stabilization of the Committee on Banking, Finance and Urban Affairs', United States House of Representatives, 9 May.

Litan, R. (1987), *What Should Banks Do?*, Washington, DC: Brookings Institution.

Organization for Economic Cooperation and Development (OECD) (1997a), 'Regulatory reform in the financial services industry: where have we been? Where are we going? *Financial Markets Trends*, No. 67, June, pp. 31–96.

Organization for Economic Cooperation and Development (OECD) (1997b), 'Recent regulatory and structural developments in the financial services industries of OECD member countries', *Financial Markets Trends*, No. 68, November, pp. 127–72.

Shearlock, P. (1998), 'The new retail model', *The Banker*, April.

Taylor, M. (1995), 'Twin Peaks: A regulatory structure for the new century', London, Centre for the Study of Financial Innovation, December.

Taylor, M. (1997), *Regulatory Leviathan: Will Super-SIB Work?*, London: CTA Financial Publishing.

Taylor, M. (1998), 'Assessing the case for an integrated financial commission', paper presented at the third High Level Group on Financial Sector Reform in Latin America and the Carribbean, Madrid, May.

# APPENDIX 20A

**Memorandum of Understanding between the UK Treasury, the Bank of England and the Financial Services Authority: Summary of issues addressed**

### 1 Bank of England's responsibilities
The Bank will be responsible for the overall stability of the financial system, involving:
(i) Stability of the monetary system.
(ii) Financial system infrastructure, in particular the payments system.
(iii) Advice on implications for financial stability of domestic and international financial market developments.
(iv) Role as lender of last resort.
(v) Efficiency and international competitiveness of the financial sector.

### 2 FSA's responsibilities
The FSA will be responsible for:
(i) The authorisation and prudential supervision of banks, building societies, investment firms, insurance companies and friendly societies.
(ii) The supervision of financial markets and clearing and settlement systems.
(iii) The conduct of support operations, other than lender of last resort assistance, involving, for instance, changing capital or other regulatory requirements and capital injections into troubled firms by third parties.
(iv) Regulatory policy in the above areas.

### 3 Treasury's responsibilities
The Treasury is responsible for the institutional structure of regulation and the legislation that governs it. It has no operational responsibility for the activities of the Bank or the FSA but it is to be kept informed of problem situations so that the Chancellor may be given the opportunity of refusing support action.

## 4   Cooperation between the Bank and the FSA

The Bank's Deputy Governor will be a member of the FSA's board and the FSA Chairman will sit on the Court of the Bank. The FSA and the Bank will establish information sharing arrangements. There will be a standing committee of representatives of the Treasury, Bank and SFA which will discuss financial stability issues on a monthly basis (and at other times as needed).

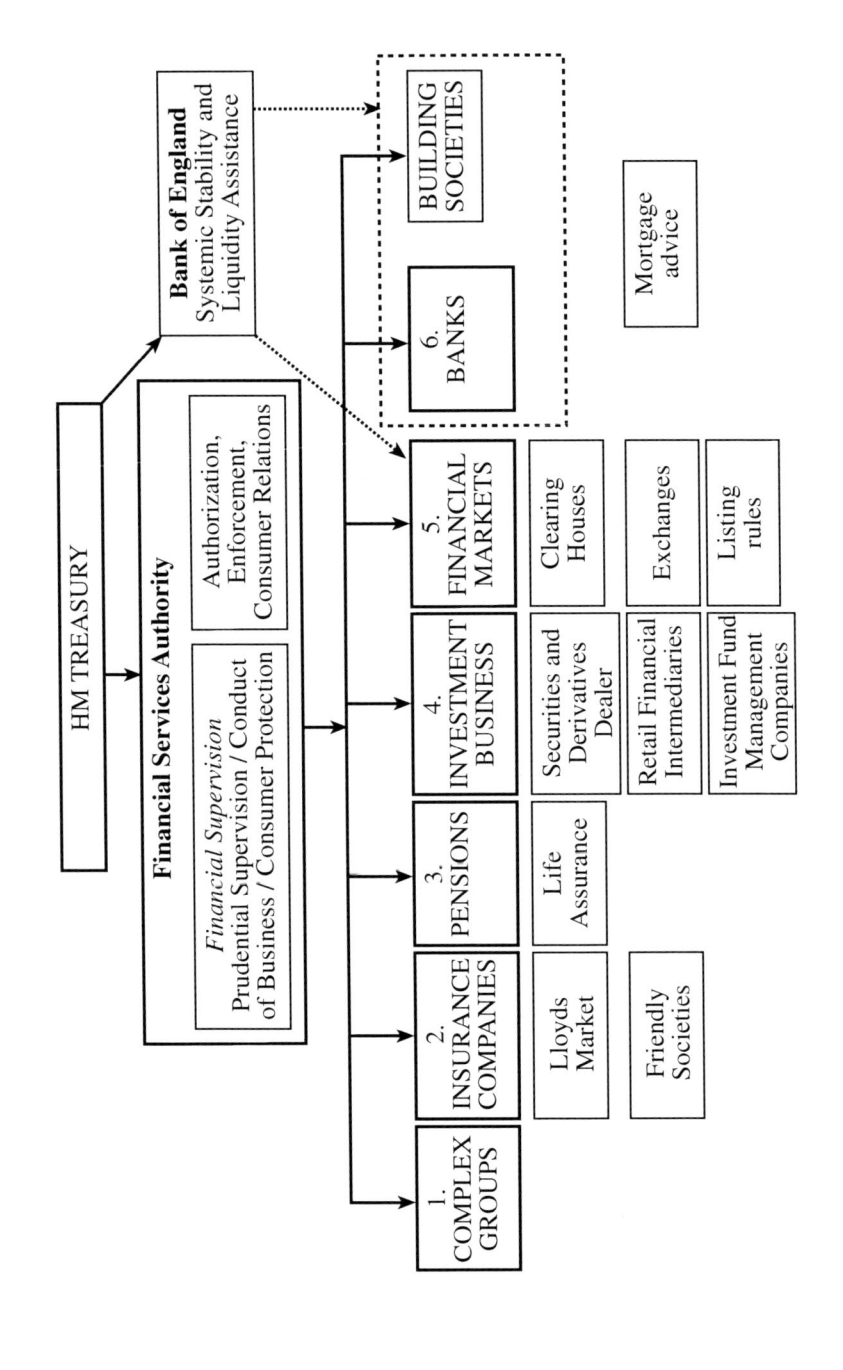

```
                                    HM TREASURY
                                         │
                                         ▼
                    ┌────────────────────────────────────────┐       ┌──────────────────────┐
                    │      Financial Services Authority      │       │   Bank of England    │
                    │ ┌────────────────────────────────────┐ │──────▶│ Systemic Stability and│
                    │ │        Financial Supervision       │ │       │ Liquidity Assistance │
                    │ │ Prudential Supervision / Conduct   │ │       └──────────┬───────────┘
                    │ │ of Business / Consumer Protection  │ │                  ┊
                    │ ├────────────────────────────────────┤ │                  ┊
                    │ │         Authorization,             │ │                  ┊
                    │ │          Enforcement,              │ │                  ▼
                    │ │        Consumer Relations          │ │        ┌───────────────────┐
                    │ └────────────────────────────────────┘ │        ┊                   ┊
                    └────────────────────────────────────────┘        ┊   BUILDING        ┊
      │          │            │            │            │             ┊   SOCIETIES       ┊
      ▼          ▼            ▼            ▼            ▼             ┊                   ┊
   ┌──────┐  ┌────────┐  ┌────────┐  ┌──────────┐  ┌──────────┐  ┌────────┐              ┊
   │  1.  │  │   2.   │  │   3.   │  │    4.    │  │    5.    │  │   6.   │              ┊
   │COMPLEX│ │INSURANCE│ │PENSIONS│  │INVESTMENT│  │FINANCIAL │  │ BANKS  │              ┊
   │GROUPS│  │COMPANIES│ │        │  │ BUSINESS │  │ MARKETS  │  │        │              ┊
   └──────┘  └────────┘  └────────┘  └──────────┘  └──────────┘  └────────┘              ┊
             ┌────────┐  ┌────────┐  ┌──────────┐  ┌──────────┐                          
             │ Lloyds │  │  Life  │  │Securities│  │ Clearing │                          
             │ Market │  │Assurance│ │    and   │  │  Houses  │                          
             └────────┘  └────────┘  │Derivatives│ └──────────┘                          
                                     │  Dealer  │                                        
                                     └──────────┘                                        
             ┌────────┐              ┌──────────┐  ┌──────────┐              ┌──────────┐
             │Friendly│              │  Retail  │  │Exchanges │              │ Mortgage │
             │Societies│             │Financial │  │          │              │  advice  │
             └────────┘              │Intermediaries│└────────┘              └──────────┘
                                     └──────────┘
                                     ┌──────────┐  ┌──────────┐
                                     │Investment│  │ Listing  │
                                     │   Fund   │  │  rules   │
                                     │Management│  └──────────┘
                                     │Companies │
                                     └──────────┘
```

*Notes:*
FSA: Financial Services Authority.
1. Complex Groups regulation will follow the 'lead Supervisor Model'.
2. Insurance Companies: the FSA will have extensive powers over Lloyds of London.
3. Pensions: includes life assurance companies, pension funds, unit trusts.
4. Investment Business: covers all current SFA (The Securities and Futures Authority) firms, PIA (Personal Investment Authority) firms and IMRO (Investment Management Regulatory Organisation) firms.
5. Financial Markets: exchanges includes LIFFE, London Metals Exchange, International Petroleum Exchange, OMLX, London Stock Exchange, Tradepoint, Over-the-counter Markets. October 1999 announcement of the transfer of the UK Listing Authority (UKLA) to the FSA from the London Stock Exchange.
6. Banks: following the new BoE Bill in June 1998, the supervision of banks falls under FSA's remit, and under the Financial Services and Markets Act (November 2000) supervision includes Building Societies, Friendly Societies, Credit Unions, Industrial and Provident Societies.

*Figure 20A.1   UK regulatory structure*

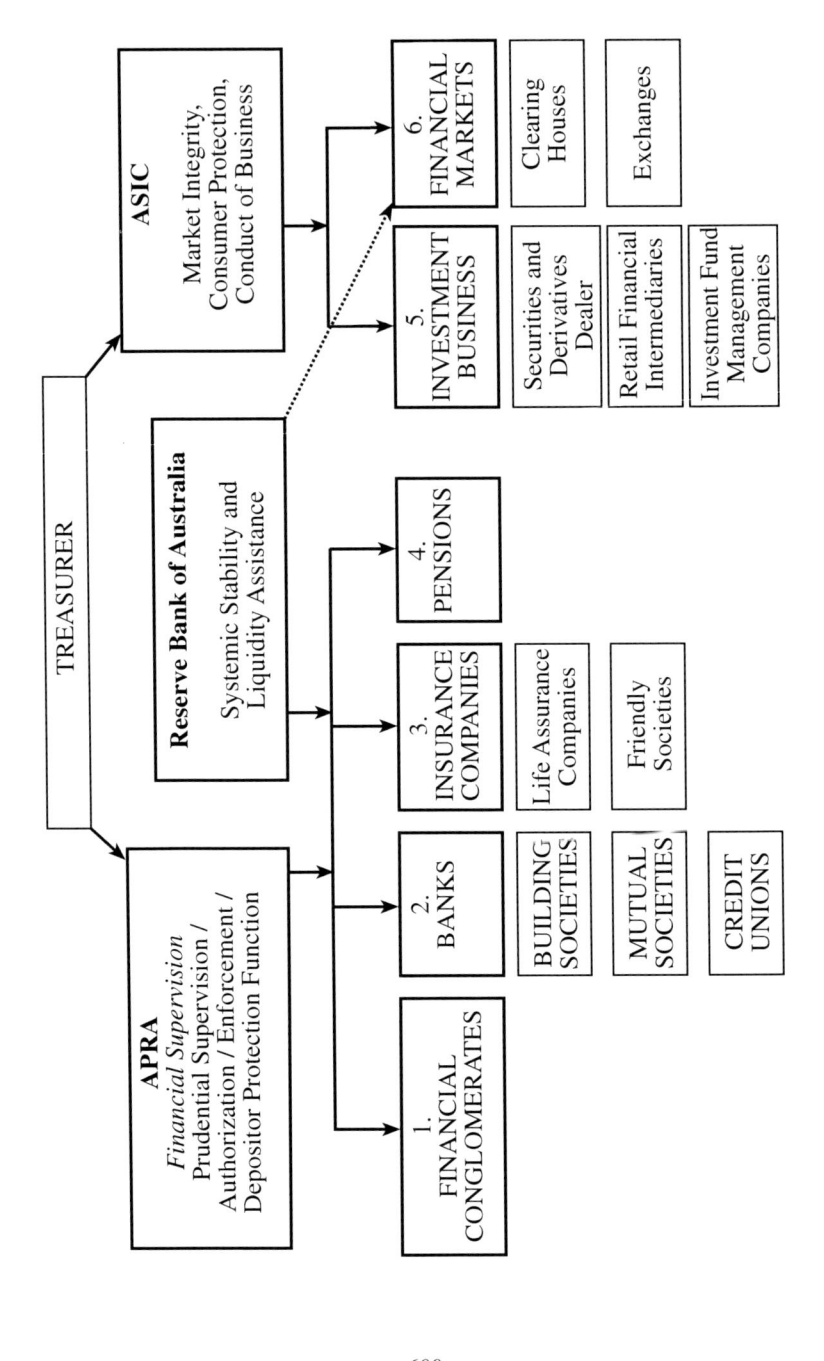

```
                          TREASURER
         ┌───────────────────┼──────────────────┐
         │                   │                  │
┌────────────────┐  ┌──────────────────┐  ┌──────────────┐
│      APRA      │  │ Reserve Bank of  │  │     ASIC     │
│   Financial    │  │     Australia    │  │              │
│  Supervision / │  │                  │  │   Market     │
│   Prudential   │  │ Systemic         │  │  Integrity,  │
│  Supervision / │  │ Stability and    │  │   Consumer   │
│ Authorization/ │  │ Liquidity        │  │  Protection, │
│  Enforcement / │  │ Assistance       │  │  Conduct of  │
│    Depositor   │  │                  │  │   Business   │
│   Protection   │  └──────────────────┘  └──────────────┘
│    Function    │
└────────────────┘
```

| 1. FINANCIAL CONGLOMERATES | 2. BANKS | 3. INSURANCE COMPANIES | 4. PENSIONS | 5. INVESTMENT BUSINESS | 6. FINANCIAL MARKETS |
|---|---|---|---|---|---|
| | BUILDING SOCIETIES | Life Assurance Companies | | Securities and Derivatives Dealer | Clearing Houses |
| | MUTUAL SOCIETIES | Friendly Societies | | Retail Financial Intermediaries | Exchanges |
| | CREDIT UNIONS | | | Investment Fund Management Companies | |

600

*Notes:*
APRA: Australian Prudential Regulation Authority.
ASIC: Australian Securities and Investment Commission.

*Figure 20A.2   Australian regulatory structure*

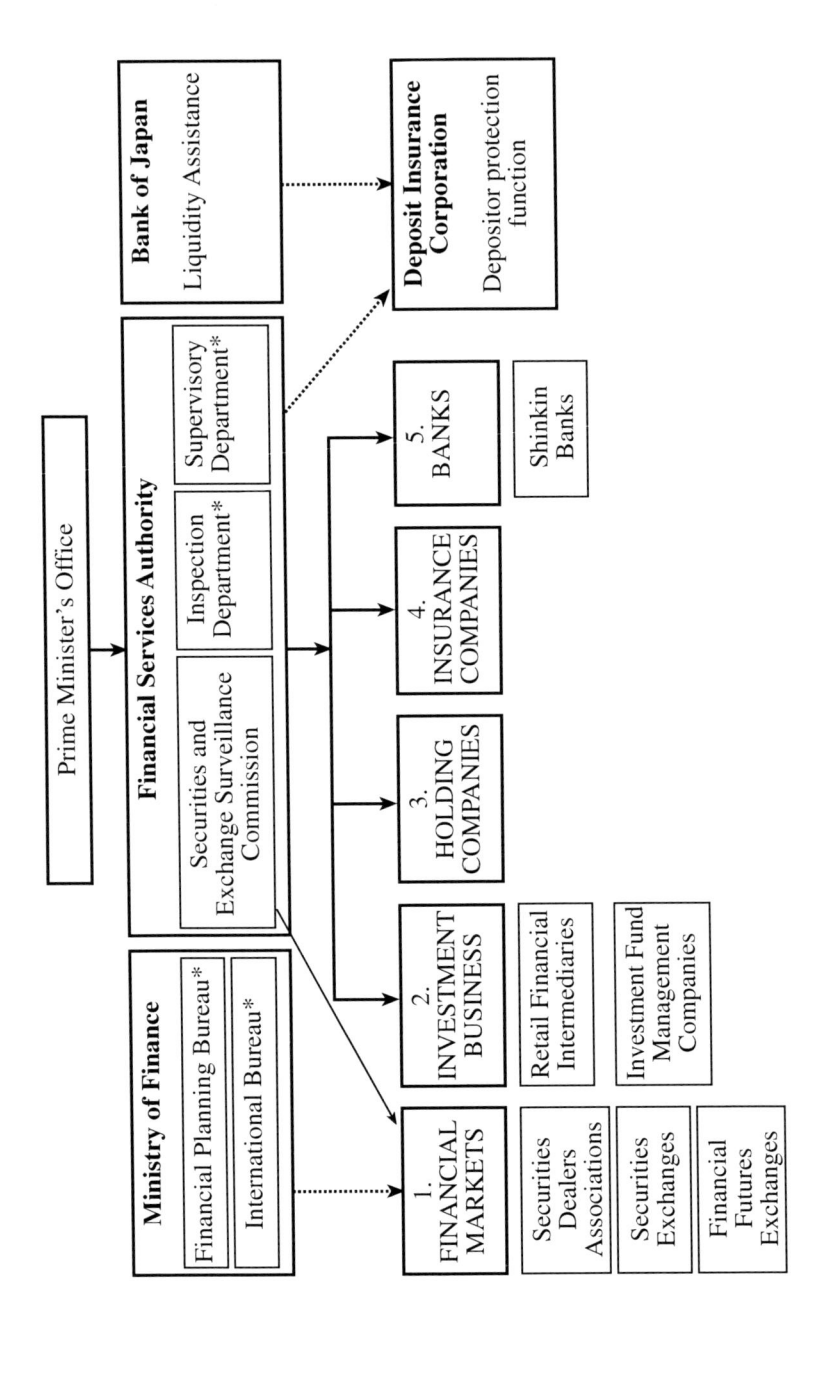

```
                              Prime Minister's Office
                                        |
                                        v
    Ministry of Finance          Financial Services Authority          Bank of Japan
    ┌──────────────────┐    ┌──────────────────────────────────┐    ┌──────────────────┐
    │ Financial        │    │ Securities │ Inspection │ Super- │    │ Liquidity        │
    │ Planning Bureau* │    │ and        │ Department*│ visory │    │ Assistance       │
    ├──────────────────┤    │ Exchange   │            │ Dept.* │    └──────────────────┘
    │ International    │    │ Surveil-   │            │        │
    │ Bureau*          │    │ lance      │            │        │
    └──────────────────┘    │ Commission │            │        │            |
                            └──────────────────────────────────┘            v
                                                                  ┌──────────────────────┐
                                                                  │ Deposit Insurance    │
                                                                  │ Corporation          │
                                                                  │                      │
                                                                  │ Depositor protection │
                                                                  │ function             │
                                                                  └──────────────────────┘

         1.              2.              3.              4.              5.
     FINANCIAL      INVESTMENT        HOLDING         INSURANCE         BANKS
      MARKETS        BUSINESS        COMPANIES       COMPANIES

     Securities    Retail Financial                                   Shinkin
     Dealers       Intermediaries                                     Banks
     Associations

     Securities    Investment Fund
     Exchanges     Management
                   Companies
     Financial
     Futures
     Exchanges
```

*Notes:*
FSA: Financial Supervisory Agency. Responsibilities: Prudential Supervision/Conduct of Business/Consumer Protection/Authorization/Enforcement.
MoF: Responsible for legislation for the whole financial system (banks, securities and insurance companies) and international representation (IMF and G7).
*Denotes a tentative name.

*Figure 20A.3  Japanese new financial regulatory structure*

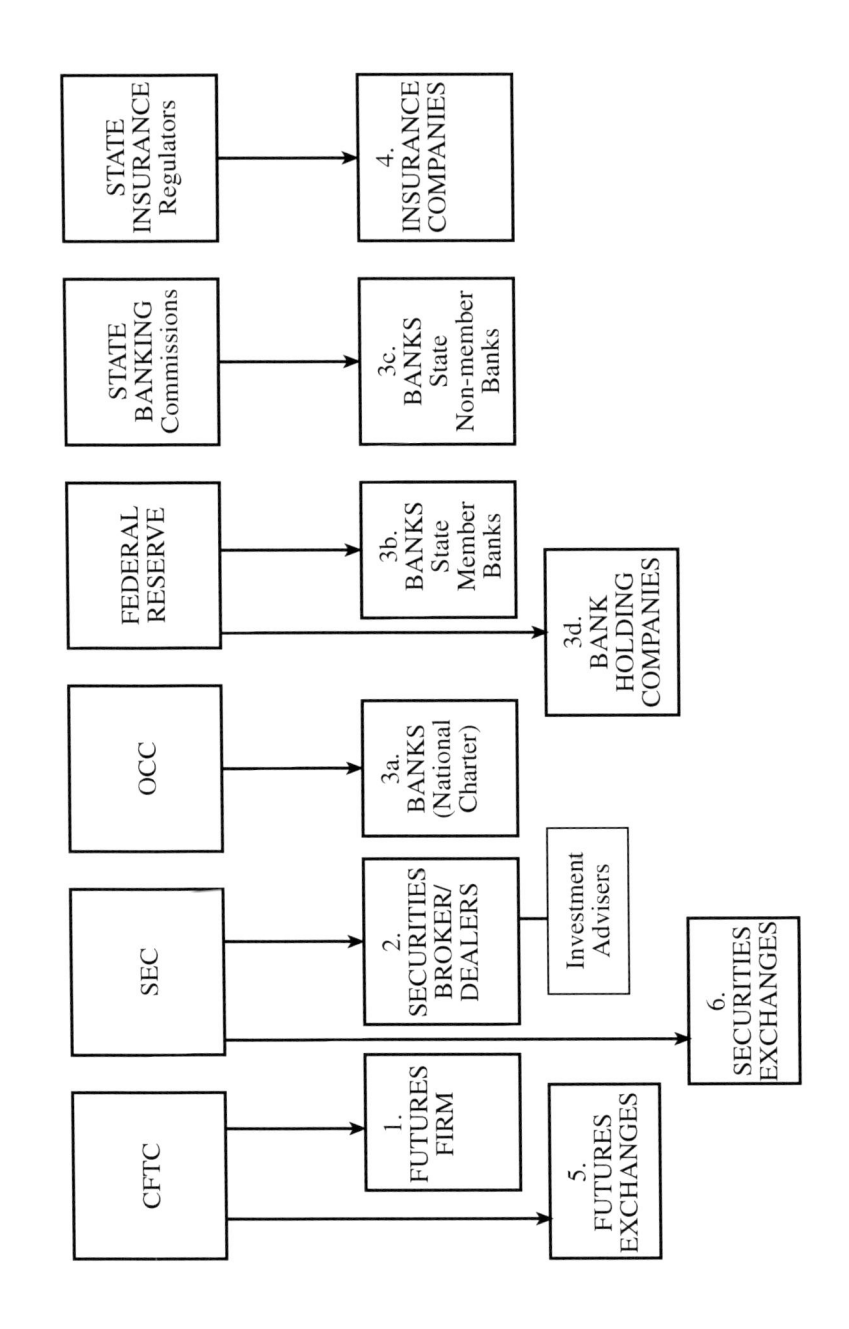

```
┌──────────┐  ┌──────────┐  ┌──────────┐  ┌──────────┐  ┌──────────┐  ┌──────────┐
│   CFTC   │  │   SEC    │  │   OCC    │  │ FEDERAL  │  │  STATE   │  │  STATE   │
│          │  │          │  │          │  │ RESERVE  │  │ BANKING  │  │INSURANCE │
│          │  │          │  │          │  │          │  │Commissions│ │Regulators│
└────┬─────┘  └────┬─────┘  └────┬─────┘  └────┬─────┘  └────┬─────┘  └────┬─────┘
     │             │             │             │             │             │
     ▼             ▼             ▼             ▼             ▼             ▼
┌──────────┐  ┌──────────┐  ┌──────────┐  ┌──────────┐  ┌──────────┐  ┌──────────┐
│    1.    │  │    2.    │  │   3a.    │  │   3b.    │  │   3c.    │  │    4.    │
│ FUTURES  │  │SECURITIES│  │  BANKS   │  │  BANKS   │  │  BANKS   │  │INSURANCE │
│  FIRM    │  │ BROKER/  │  │(National │  │  State   │  │  State   │  │COMPANIES │
│          │  │ DEALERS  │  │ Charter) │  │  Member  │  │Non-member│  │          │
│          │  │          │  │          │  │  Banks   │  │  Banks   │  │          │
└──────────┘  └────┬─────┘  └──────────┘  └──────────┘  └──────────┘  └──────────┘
                   │
                   ▼
              ┌──────────┐
              │Investment│
              │ Advisers │
              └──────────┘

                                          ┌──────────┐
                                          │   3d.    │
                                          │   BANK   │
                                          │ HOLDING  │
                                          │COMPANIES │
                                          └──────────┘

┌──────────┐                 ┌──────────┐
│    5.    │                 │    6.    │
│ FUTURES  │                 │SECURITIES│
│EXCHANGES │                 │EXCHANGES │
└──────────┘                 └──────────┘
```

604

*Notes:*
CFTC: Commodity Futures Trading Commission.
SEC: Securities and Exchange Commission.
OCC: Office of the Comptroller of the Currency.
1. Future Firms: Regulated by the CFTC, and subject to the following self-regulatory bodies (National Futures Association, and Futures Exchanges).
2. Securities Brokers/Dealers: Regulated by the SEC and State Securities Regulators, and also by the following self-regulatory bodies: National Association of Securities Dealers (NASD) and Stock Exchanges.
3. a,b,c,d: Banks: See Figure 20A.4b.
4. Insurance Companies: Regulated by the State Insurance Regulators.
5. Futures Exchanges and futures exchanges' Clearing Houses: Regulated by the CFTC.
6. Securities Exchanges: Regulated by the SEC.

*Figure 20A.4a   US regulatory structure*

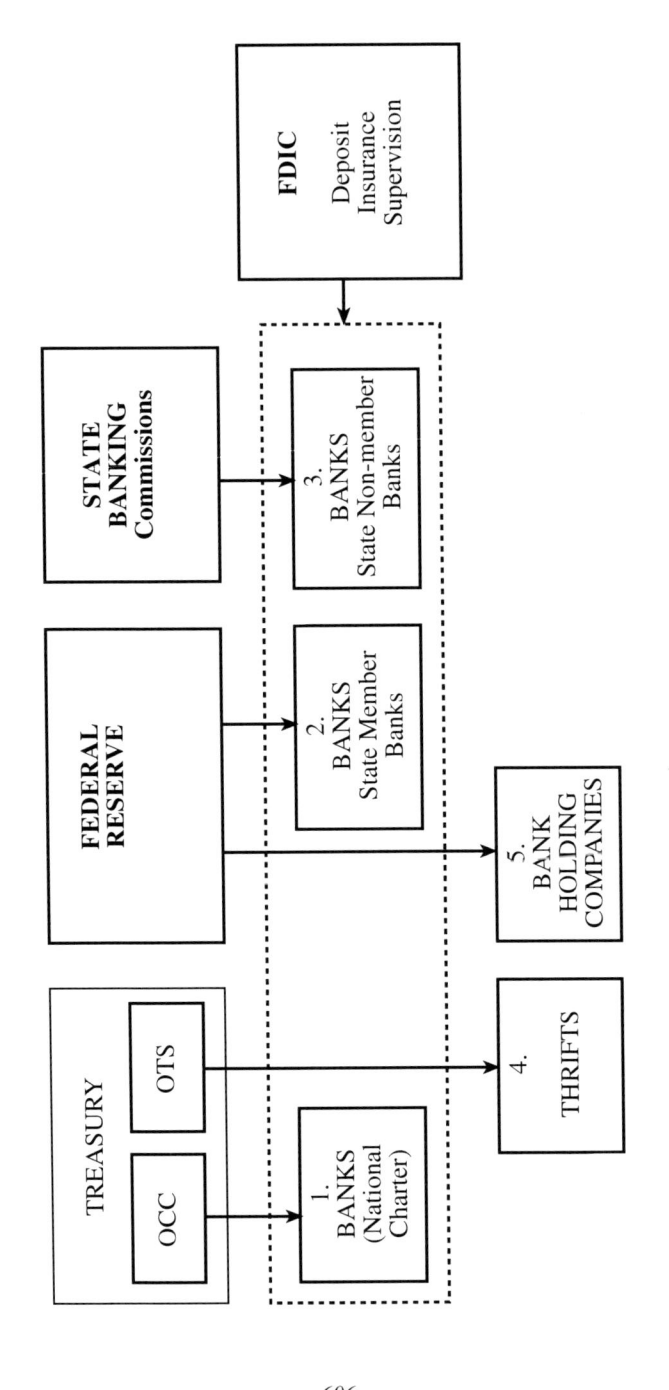

```
                                                        ┌──────────────┐
                                                        │    FDIC      │
                                                        │   Deposit    │
                                                        │  Insurance   │
                                                        │ Supervision  │
                                                        └──────┬───────┘
                                                               │
┌─────────────────┐      ┌──────────────┐    ┌──────────────┐  │
│    TREASURY     │      │   FEDERAL    │    │    STATE     │  │
│ ┌─────┐ ┌─────┐ │      │   RESERVE    │    │   BANKING    │  │
│ │ OCC │ │ OTS │ │      │              │    │ Commissions  │  │
│ └──┬──┘ └──┬──┘ │      └───────┬──────┘    └──────┬───────┘  │
└────┼───────┼────┘              │                  │          │
     │       │     ┌─ ─ ─ ─ ─ ─ ─┼─ ─ ─ ─ ─ ─ ─ ─ ─ ┼ ─ ─ ─ ─ ─┼─ ┐
     │       │     │             │                  │          ▼  │
     ▼       │     │  ┌────────┐ │   ┌────────┐    ┌────────┐     │
  ┌────────┐ │     │  │   1.   │ ▼   │   2.   │    │   3.   │     │
  │   1.   │ │     │  │ BANKS  │     │ BANKS  │    │ BANKS  │     │
  │ BANKS  │ │     │  │(Nat'l  │     │ State  │    │ State  │     │
  │(Nat'l  │ │     │  │Charter)│     │ Member │    │Non-mem │     │
  │Charter)│ │     │  └────────┘     │ Banks  │    │ Banks  │     │
  └────────┘ │     │                 └────────┘    └────────┘     │
             │     └─ ─ ─ ─ ─ ─ ─ ─ ─ ─ ─ ─ ─ ─ ─ ─ ─ ─ ─ ─ ─ ─ ─ ┘
             ▼                     │
        ┌────────┐                 ▼
        │   4.   │            ┌──────────┐
        │ THRIFTS│            │    5.    │
        └────────┘            │   BANK   │
                              │ HOLDING  │
                              │COMPANIES │
                              └──────────┘
```

*Notes:*
OCC: Office of the Comptroller of the Currency.
OTS: Office of Thrift Supervision.
FDIC: Federal Deposit Insurance Corporation.
1. Banks with a National charter are regulated and supervised by the OCC.
2. State-chartered banks that are members of the Federal Reserve System (State Member Banks) are regulated and supervised by the Federal Reserve and their State agency.
3. State-chartered banks that are not members of the Federal Reserve System (State Non-member Banks) are regulated and supervised by their State agency, and supervised by the FDIC if federally insured.
4. Thrifts are regulated and supervised by the OTS. State chartered Thrifts are also regulated by the States.
5. Bank Holding Companies are regulated and supervised by the Federal Reserve, even though in most cases it does not regulate or supervise the subsidiary bank.

*Figure 20A.4b   US depository regulatory structure*

**OPTION 1**

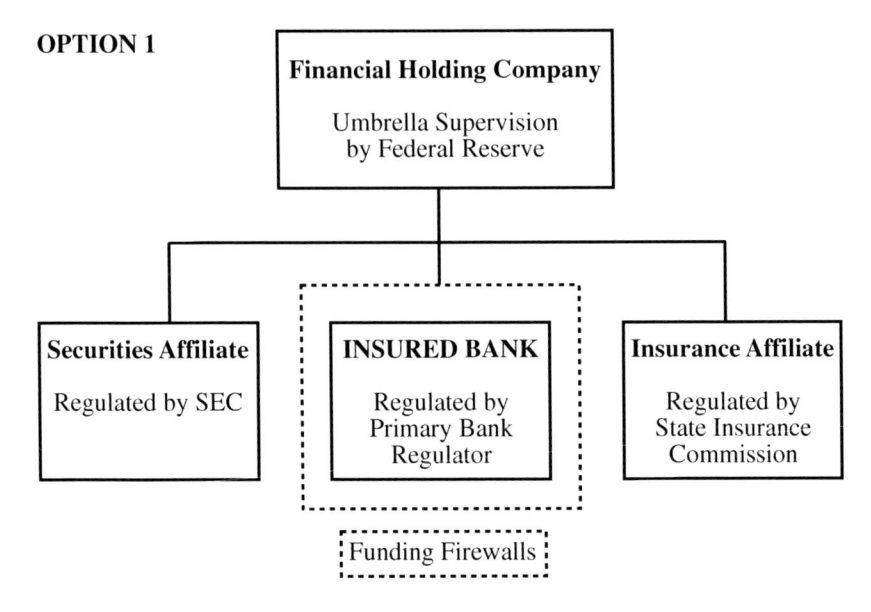

```
                    ┌──────────────────────────┐
                    │ Financial Holding Company│
                    │                          │
                    │   Umbrella Supervision   │
                    │    by Federal Reserve    │
                    └──────────────────────────┘
                                 │
        ┌────────────────────────┼────────────────────────┐
┌───────────────────┐  ┌───────────────────┐  ┌───────────────────┐
│Securities Affiliate│  │   INSURED BANK   │  │ Insurance Affiliate│
│                   │  │                   │  │                   │
│ Regulated by SEC  │  │   Regulated by    │  │   Regulated by    │
│                   │  │   Primary Bank    │  │  State Insurance  │
│                   │  │    Regulator      │  │   Commission      │
└───────────────────┘  └───────────────────┘  └───────────────────┘
                            │ Funding Firewalls │
```

*Notes:*
1. Financial Holding Company (FHC) bank subsidiary must be 'well capitalized' and 'well managed'.
2. Combination of: (i) supervision of consolidated entity by Federal Reserve (ii) regulation of bank by primary bank regulator; (iii) functional regulation of non-bank entities by specialized regulators.
3. Funding firewalls between bank entity and its affiliates (sections 23A and 23B of Federal Reserve Act).

*Figure 20A.4c   US Glass–Steagall reform: Financial Services Modernization Act 1999*

**OPTION 2**

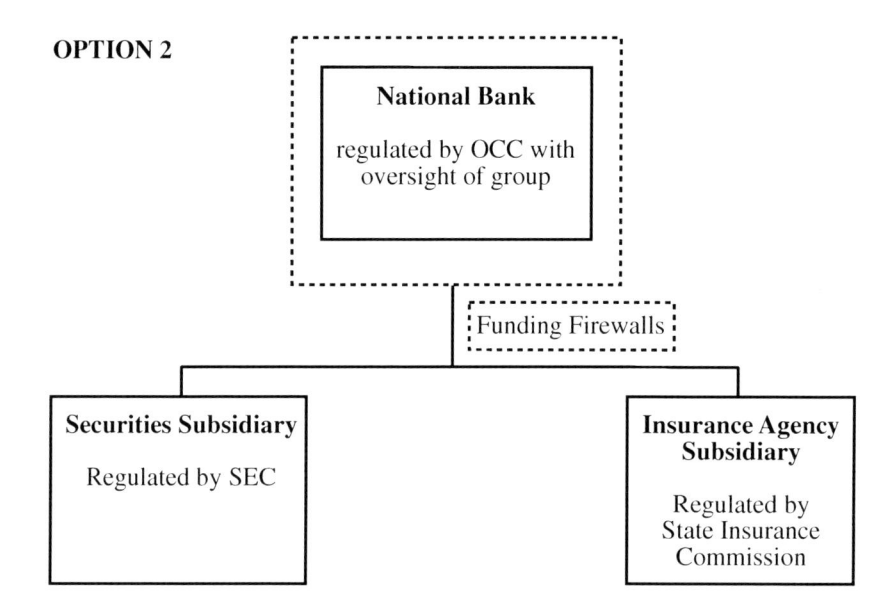

```
┌─────────────────────────────┐
│     National Bank           │
│  regulated by OCC with      │
│  oversight of group         │
└─────────────────────────────┘
         │
    Funding Firewalls
    ┌────┴────┐
```

**Securities Subsidiary**

Regulated by SEC

**Insurance Agency Subsidiary**

Regulated by State Insurance Commission

*Notes:*
1. National bank must be 'well capitalized' and 'well managed'.
2. Functional regulation, subject to OCC having oversight responsibility for group.
3. Funding firewalls between bank entity and its non-bank financial subsidiaries.
4. Restrictions (not applicable to FHC): (i) assets combined of financial subsidiaries must not exceed 45% of parent bank's assets or $50 bn; (ii) financial subsidiaries prohibited from conducting merchant banking, insurance underwriting, insurance portfolio investment and real estate development and investment.

*Figure 20A.4c    continued*

## NZ TREASURY

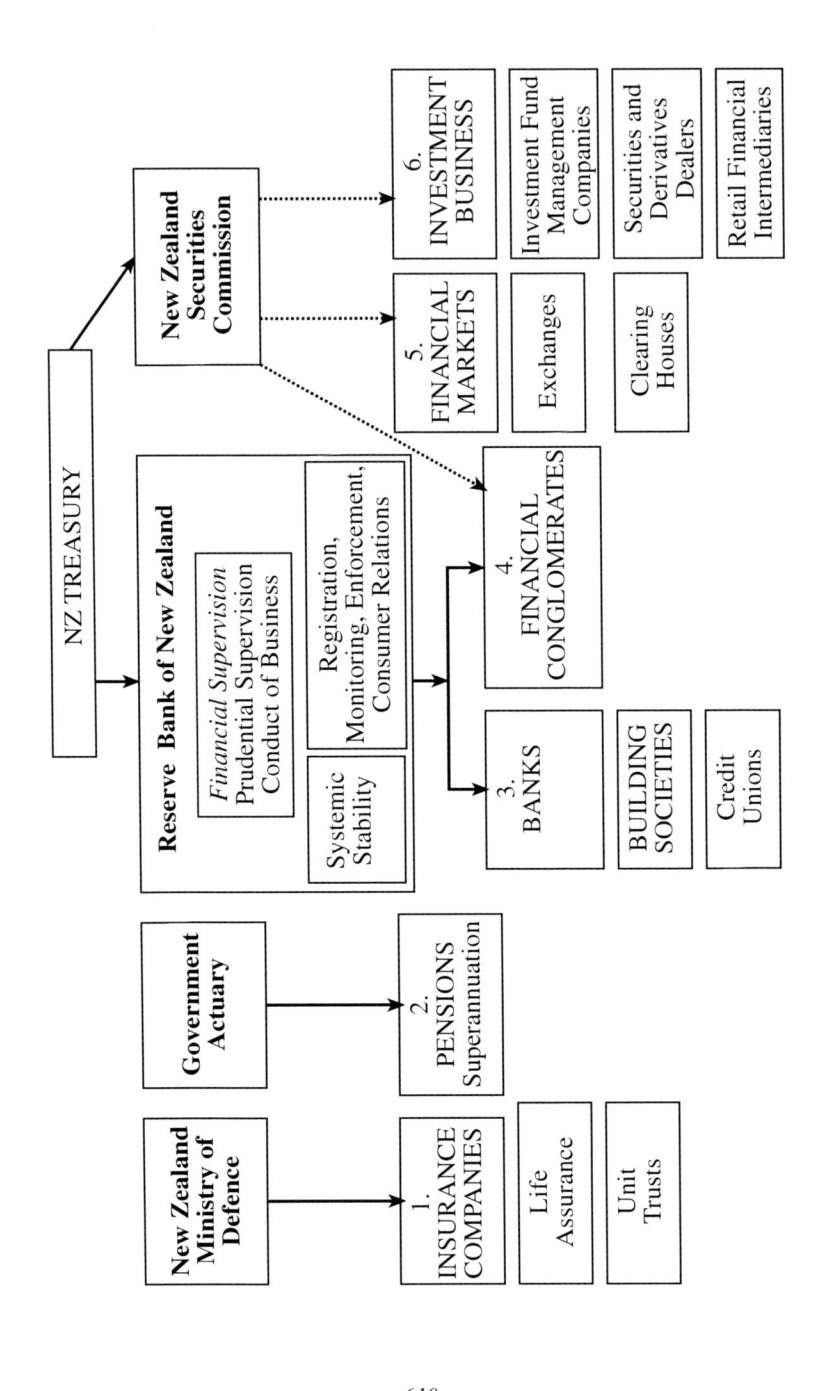

**Reserve Bank of New Zealand**

*Financial Supervision*
*Prudential Supervision*
*Conduct of Business*

- Systemic Stability
- Registration, Monitoring, Enforcement, Consumer Relations

**New Zealand Securities Commission**

**Government Actuary**

**New Zealand Ministry of Defence**

1. INSURANCE COMPANIES
   - Life Assurance
   - Unit Trusts

2. PENSIONS — Superannuation

3. BANKS
   - BUILDING SOCIETIES
   - Credit Unions

4. FINANCIAL CONGLOMERATES

5. FINANCIAL MARKETS
   - Exchanges
   - Clearing Houses

6. INVESTMENT BUSINESS
   - Investment Fund Management Companies
   - Securities and Derivatives Dealers
   - Retail Financial Intermediaries

*Notes:*
RBNZ: Reserve Bank of New Zealand.
NZSC: New Zealand Securities Commission.
1. Insurance Companies: annual audited returns are required to be forwarded to the Secretary of the Ministry of Commerce. Unit trusts are monitored by independent trustee corporations.
2. Pensions: the government Actuary is the authority with jurisdiction over registered superannuation schemes.
3. Banks: New Zealand has a universal banking system. NZ does not have an explicit deposit protection scheme.
4. Financial conglomerates: regulation does not formally follow the 'lead supervisor model'.
5. Financial Markets: securities markets include the stock exchange and the NZ futures and options exchange.
6. Investment Business: the NZSC has responsibility for the functioning of NZ's securities markets.

*Figure 20A.5   New Zealand regulatory structure*

# 21. US banking regulation: practice and trends

Joseph J. Norton and Christopher D. Olive

## 1 INTRODUCTION

The purpose of this chapter is twofold: first to explore briefly a series of selective trends generally impacting upon the shape and face of banking and bank regulation in the United States; and second to focus on three of the more specific and complex bank regulatory trends in the US banking industry as it enters the twenty-first century with respect to bank-HLIs (that is, highly leveraged institutions) relationships, OTC (that is, over-the-counter) derivatives, and banking organization activities following the most recent enactment of the new federal Gramm–Leach–Bliley Modernization Act of 1999 ('GLBA') (FRB, 2000). As to the selective general trends, these will be touched upon in Section 2 and will include (i) the consolidation of banking groups and institutions, (ii) the rise of financial conglomerates, (iii) the redefining of 'banking business' resulting from the rapid technological and product innovations impacting financial markets and services, (iv) the search for a role for community banking institutions, and (v) the protection of the individual users. Section 3 turns to the specific and more complex bank regulatory trends by reviewing defining regulatory reports issued by the President's Working Group on Financial Markets ('Working Group'). The first Working Group Report addressed, among other things, banking organization failures regarding counterparty credit risk management arising from the long-term capital management (LTCM) episode of August–September 1998. The second Working Group Report addressed the OTC derivatives markets, in particular revisions to federal laws to remove perceived 'legal uncertainties' regarding various types of derivatives contracts. Section 4 reviews various aspects of the GLBA relevant to banking organization activities, and the regulatory challenges presented under the GLBA framework for US banking agencies. Section 5 concludes.

For the purposes of this chapter, the US banking agencies primarily consist of the Federal Reserve Board (FRB), regulatory authority for bank holding companies (BHCs), BHC non-bank affiliates, and state banks that are members of the Federal Reserve System ('state FRS member banks') and the Office of the Comptroller of the Currency (OCC), the regulatory authority for federally chartered national banks and their operating subsidiaries, whether within or outside of the BHC framework (see Brown et al., 1998; Myer, 1999, 2000; Norton and Whitley, 1983; Norton and Olive, 1997). The chapter speaks as of early 2000.

## 2 SELECTIVE TRENDS IN US BANKING SUPERVISION

### Banking Consolidation and Financial Conglomerates

The recent US bank developments include a proliferation of mergers involving national scope banking institutions, large regional banking and large thrift institutions. There has even been a combination between a major national banking institution and a major national insurance firm (for example, Citicorp/Travelers Insurance) and various acquisitions/affiliations involving securities firms designed to establish a diversified financial conglomerate. The scale and scope of these merger transactions raises important issues about their implications on domestic and international competition; the preparedness of regulatory authorities to oversee the resulting organizations; and their impact on consumers and local communities. Banks are seeking out merger and acquisition partners to realign their franchises, which, combined with the failures of many banks and thrift institutions in the 1980s and early 1990s, has resulted in a significant consolidation of the banking system (by nearly 40 per cent) to date.

With regard to national bank combinations, the Bank Merger Act requires OCC approval for any merger between insured depository institutions that results in a national bank. The OCC will consider (i) competitive effects; (ii) financial and managerial resources; and (iii) convenience and needs of the communities to be served. The Community Reinvestment Act (CRA) requires the OCC to consider the applicant institution's record of helping to meet the credit needs of its entire community, including low- and moderate-income neighbourhoods, when evaluating certain applications, including mergers. The federal banking laws further require that the OCC ascertain that the merger transaction is in accordance with other laws governing national bank mergers or to determine that those laws do not apply to the proposed merger at issue.

With respect to the merger transition supervision period, the OCC will generally expect that the following actions are carried out:

- tightly controlled merger transition process;
- clear business plans, lines of authority, and accountability in the combination process;
- departure of key management and technical personnel at the time of the merger announcement or shortly thereafter;
- combining operational and information systems without interfering with ongoing operations;
- retention and enforcement of risk management and internal control systems;
- ensuring that management efforts to reduce costs to achieve post-combination operational savings do not weaken bank internal controls and audit functions; and
- allowing selection of the organizational structure which best enables them to operate efficiently and compete effectively (removing artificial constraints).

The trend of banking consolidation has resulted in a further defining trend of bifurcating bank regulation and supervision with regard to 'large' national banks (generally defined in terms of assets and the degree of complexity of each banking institution organization and activities). The OCC has maintained a separate and distinct 'large bank supervision' framework for such institutions which is primarily 'risk based' in nature. The 'supervision by risk' programme for large national banks essentially focuses supervisory resources on various key risk categories and attempts to facilitate close supervisory relationships with such institutions. The OCC essentially assigns 'supervisory teams' to each large banking institution and directs them to focus on the material areas of risk within each banking institution. The supervisory teams are directed to guide their banking institutions to develop risk-management and internal control systems that are appropriately tailored to the respective risk profiles. These national banks typically have various bank subsidiaries that are authorized to engage in the same activities as the parent organization, and to a limited extent in activities that the parent is not authorized to engage in directly. The bank subsidiaries may generally be established in one of many forms; the OCC has approved such forms as corporations, joint ventures, partnerships and limited liability companies.

The growing trend of national bank consolidation in the US is part of a larger trend of financial consolidation through the BHC structure. In this structure, one or more banking institutions (and their respective bank subsidiaries) are owned or controlled within BHC structures that contain other non-bank subsidiaries or 'affiliates' of the bank(s). These BHC financial conglomerates are generally referred to as 'large complex banking organizations' (LCBOs) and are generally subject to FRB regulation and supervision. Prior to the GLBA, the banks within the BHC structure were generally regulated and supervised by either the OCC (national banks) or the FRB (state-chartered FRS member banks) at the federal level. The BHC itself and its non-bank subsidiaries/bank affiliates are regulated and supervised by the FRB. The FRB also maintains separate supervisory programmes and methodologies for institutions qualifying as LCBOs, that is, somewhat similar to the OCC's large bank supervision programme.

The FRB has designated about 30 entities, accounting for nearly 60 per cent of the total US bank assets, as LCBOs, and ten of these are foreign-owned institutions. In particular, the FRB assigns teams of supervisors to thoroughly understand the organization's business strategy, management structure, key policies and risk control systems, similarly to the OCC large bank supervision programme. These teams are headed by a senior examiner, designated as a central point of contact (CPC), and the CPC's team of examiners utilize the services of specialists in risk management, payments, market and credit risk modelling, information technology and other technical areas.

The growing scale and complexity of the largest US banking organizations, and those of other nations, raise new challenges and potential for systemic risk from a significant disruption in or failure of one of these institutions. The LTCM episode, discussed further in this chapter, provides a good example of the scope of this new challenge. The question is whether to address this trend through enhanced regulatory and supervisory frameworks or to increasingly rely on public disclosure, market discipline, and public–private supervisory partnerships in dealing with LCBOs.

The US banking agencies are responding to this new reality. The FRB in particular is working through three primary channels in this regard. First, through the continuous enhancement of the FRB's supervisory framework in cooperation with other banking agencies. Second, through the Basle Committee on Banking Supervision, with banking officials of other G10 countries. Third, through a Federal Reserve System committee called the 'F-6', formed to examine the systemic implications of changing banking markets. In 1999, the F-6 commissioned and reviewed several studies which addressed the potential role of subordinated debentures for regulatory capital purposes, the value of public disclosure, staff resourcing needs to supervise LCBOs, and other issues.

The primary regulatory focus for LCBOs at this stage is capital adequacy, particularly credit-risk-based capital requirements. The evolving consensus of the Basle Committee and primary US banking agencies is to develop a new capital accord based on the three 'pillars' of capital, supervision and market discipline.

**Redefining the 'Business of Banking'**

The trends of banking consolidation and financial conglomeration are facilitated in significant part by trends and practices that have redefined the 'banking business'. Perhaps more ominously, these trends have expanded the scope of banking business to the point where it is more reasonable to identify what is not within the scope of banking business. The evolution of banking business to financial products and services far beyond deposit-taking and lending activities is the result of fundamental changes which have occurred over a period of years, such as:

- the decline in core deposits and proportionate increase in non-deposit liabilities;
- the disintermediation of highly rated corporate borrowers from banks to the capital markets;
- the increased lending to smaller and potentially riskier firms and consumers;
- technological advancements that result in enhanced electronic product delivery;
- the significant increase in off-balance sheet activities, particularly OTC derivatives activities and securitization techniques;
- the continuous search for fee-generating activities to expand and diversify income sources;
- the gradual reduction of statutory barriers and limitations to engaging in securities and insurance activities through deregulatory activism;
- the gradual inclusion of activities considered by the banking agencies to be as 'incidental to' the business of banking or 'closely related to banking so as to be a proper incident thereto';
- the sustained efforts to reduce operating costs and compete more efficiently; and
- the increased intra-banking industry and non-bank competition in the US and global credit markets.

The business of banking has been expanded even further through the removal or reduction of many legislative and regulatory restrictions and burdens on bank operations inherent in the GLBA.

For example, the banking business and limitations on bank securities and insurance activities have been substantially redefined under Title I of the GLBA (discussed further in this chapter). The impact of the GLBA on banking supervision will almost certainly be to facilitate increasing financial conglomeration, through the new 'financial holding company' structure. This new structure presents the opportunity for banks, insurance companies and securities firms to make cross-industry acquisitions to form conglomerates subject to the umbrella supervision of the FRB and functional regulation of respective regulatory agencies for different component activities.

The advances in information technology, financial engineering, and risk-management expertise have accelerated the expansion of the banking business to a dramatic extent in the past decade and will undoubtedly continue to facilitate the consolidation trends previously noted. New electronic payment technologies, global electronic linkages of financial markets, 'high-tech' derivative financial instruments, the spread of asset securitization globally, the internet and the rise of e-commerce and e-finance, the proliferation of the dematerialization of commercial and financial instruments – all these challenge tradition perceptions and usages of banking and other financial institutions. Is the future nature of the banking business tied to creating a symbiotic and efficient series of 'portals' for the harnessing, processing and implementation of such new technologies?

These mutually reinforcing trends will consequentially require continued supervisory enhancements and the establishment of the three pillars of the new capital adequacy framework as banking organizations push the boundaries of financial services and products to new limits.

**Ongoing Role of Community Banking Institutions**

The accelerating trends of consolidation and conglomeration raise important implications for community banking systems. Although community banking institutions are still flourishing, the question arises as to whether the larger banking organizations that acquire them would increasingly limit services and products to low- and moderate-income regions in the United States on profitability concerns. The US Congress enacted the Community Reinvestment Act (CRA) legislation to address this issue.

The FRB and the OCC have articulated concerns about the impact of bank mergers and acquisitions, with regard to application of the CRA to large complex and geographically diverse banking institutions and the impact of bank mergers on low-income communities. The thrust of the CRA is that banks and BHCs are required to maintain strong commitments to community reinvestment through meeting CRA requirements, in order to engage in certain activities, mergers and acquisitions. Banks and BHCs are rated on their CRA performance overall and in each state in which they have a presence, and the CRA is assessed across the entire institution, as part of bank and BHC examinations. Bank and BHC mergers and acquisitions (that is, the acquirer, acquiree and the post-merger institution) are evaluated directly on CRA criteria as a part of the merger and acquisition approval process.

**Effects on Customer Fees and Financial Privacy**

The trends of consolidation and expansion of the business of banking in turn generate various regulatory concerns about the impact of these trends on bank customers. Although many of these concerns are addressed in CRA applications, the banking agencies remain principally concerned with several critical issues. First is the impact of these trends on fees charged to bank customers for services and products. The pricing of bank services and products is often complex, and it is not necessarily easy to identify the precise rationale for differences in pricing bank services and products. Second is the potential for abuse in the marketing and cross-selling of products and services to customers, particularly regarding securities and investment advisory activities.

Lastly, and perhaps most importantly, are regulatory concerns about financial privacy. As banking institutions become larger and engage in more activities, they also gain information on their customers, including medical, credit and investment information. This is potentially quite valuable business information in many respects for bank holding companies and their affiliates, and the potential clearly exists for abuse in this area.

**Furtherance of International Standards**

The US banking regulatory agencies continue to participate in the development and implementation of the ongoing guidance being issued periodically by the Basle Committee on Banking Supervision. For example, the Basle Committee Market Risk Amendment (MRA) authorized (and in the US required) banking organizations with significant trading book activities to develop their own 'internal models' consisting of tailored value-at-risk (VaR) methodologies for the purpose of measuring market risk inherent in such activities to provide a basis for applying market risk-based capital requirements thereto. The dominant theme regarding the MRA is that US banking agencies essentially rely upon banking organizations themselves to measure market risk and develop and test their own financial models. This form of 'regulatory reliance' has continued to evolve into other areas, as the US banking agencies have quite clearly continued to allow banking organizations to develop their own models and controls in various other respects so long as they are subject to certain qualitative and quantitative standards developed by the agencies.

The defining trend in this respect, following the MRA, is that banking agencies are subjecting large complex banking organizations to a separate and distinct risk-based supervisory process that is tailored according to the risks incurred through their activities. The banking agencies essentially require these banking organizations to develop and implement meaningful risk-management programmes and internal control systems following general regulatory principles and prudential measures to meet all risks and challenges presented by new and complex financial products and services. In return for granting banking organizations such discretion, the banking agencies have obtained greater access to bank proprietary information and more frequent contacts with senior management as part of the examination process. As discussed above, the banking agencies have established frameworks for regulating and supervising LCBOs.

## 3 BANKING REGULATION, HEDGE FUNDS AND OTC DERIVATIVES

**The Working Group**

The most significant regulatory actions taken by the US banking agencies in 1999 occurred through the President's Working Group on Financial Markets (Working Group), a forum established in 1990 to address issues of relevance to the entire financial regulatory community. The Working Group consists of the US Treasury Department, the FRB, the Securities and Exchange Commission (SEC), and the Commodity Futures Trading Commission (CFTC). The FRB and OCC ('banking agencies'), acting through the US Department of the Treasury (holding the Comptroller of the Currency, the regulatory agency for the national bank, as one of its bureaus) and the FRB (regulatory authority over the FRS and state-chartered FRS member banks), are the dominant players in this forum. The banking agencies are responsible for regulating and supervising nearly all material banking organizations, and in particular have direct oversight of the banks representing the largest and most influential derivatives dealers in the world. In the decade of blurring entity distinctions and financial activities, and conflicts in regulatory jurisdiction, unanimous regulatory agreement on any issue affecting interests across organization lines is increasingly difficult to come across.

In an unprecedented move, the Working Group issued two very significant reports establishing unified positions on issues of profound significance to the global banking community: bank–hedge fund relationships and OTC derivatives markets. The Working Group issued these reports, entitled *Hedge Funds, Leverage, and the Lessons of Long-Term Capital*

*Management* (the 'Hedge Funds Report') and *Over-the-Counter Derivatives Markets and the Commodity Exchange Act* (the 'OTC Derivatives Report') in April 1999 and November 1999, respectively. The subject that both of these reports have in common is preservation of the OTC derivatives markets and related products and services for the elite US banking organizations, which are the dominant institutions in this extremely lucrative market.

There is little question that OTC derivatives and financial engineering are one of the most significant financial activities that tend to distinguish US global banking organizations from their foreign counterparts in terms of ultimate competitiveness and profitability. OTC derivatives activities consists of derivatives dealing, proprietary trading, investment advisory, hedging for their own accounts, portfolio credit and market risk management, and regulatory capital arbitrage, to name a few applications.

The OTC derivatives markets have evolved through financial innovation, encouraged by the banking agencies, but continuously subject to the scrutiny of the CFTC and the SEC, whose statutory regimes provide exclusive jurisdiction for most exchange-traded futures and options contracts but arguably extend to certain OTC derivatives that are not otherwise expressly excluded from them. In fact, OTC derivatives are essentially not subject to a regulatory framework, except to the extent that banking agencies have jurisdiction to supervise banks' OTC derivatives activities. The supervisory process is designed to ensure that their constituent institutions adhere to safety and soundness principles by engaging in appropriate risk-management measures and developing meaningful internal control systems to maintain adequate capital and manage various risks emanating from derivatives. The supervisory process is therefore ultimately not as concerned with directly regulating the OTC derivatives markets from the dealer–end user relationship perspective, or with ensuring that certain 'regulatory arbitrage' practices engaged in by banks for themselves or on behalf of their customers through derivative structures are curtailed to any meaningful extent. The OTC derivatives market has, however, consistently been plagued by congressional efforts to introduce regulatory frameworks to mitigate perceived abuses and lingering questions over the legal certainty of many contracts, particularly swaps and forward contracts, as being characterized so as to fall within the scope of federal legislation and CFTC regulation.

The OTC derivatives market is the pinnacle linkage between banking organizations and hedge funds with regard to trading activities. Hedge funds are generally defined as private investment vehicles that are incorporated or based in an offshore financial centre or tax haven jurisdiction but hold US principals, and engage in myriad trading activities that are largely not subject to the regulatory or supervisory oversight of any one agency. Hedge funds enjoy a symbiotic relationship with global banking organizations that are heavily engaged in OTC derivatives (and securitization) activities. For instance, hedge funds generally serve as important customers or counterparties for banking organizations actively involved in OTC derivatives activities, particularly for the more exotic structures that earn higher fees as opposed to 'plain vanilla' derivatives that are quickly becoming 'commoditized' (such as basic currency and interest rate swaps and forward contracts).

Hedge funds pursue many different and sophisticated trading strategies which provide banking organizations with much needed liquidity in derivatives contracts; are often willing participants to absorb market or credit risks that banking organizations themselves may not be eager to bear; and are perceived as being able to engage in adequate risk-management practices regarding these activities. Hedge funds are among the most sophisticated traders in financial markets, and provide important information to banking organizations with respect to trading opportunities.

The OTC derivatives business also introduces the ability for banking organizations to provide many other financial services to hedge funds, such as clearing and execution of trades in the exchange-traded markets, which may generate enormous transactional and advisory fees in the process.

**The Hedge Fund Report**

**The report in general**
The FRB and the Treasury Department, among other agencies, ultimately became involved and facilitated a 'private sector' bail-out among these counterparties, which injected billions of dollars into long-term capital management and arranged for its subsequent management as a going concern and the liquidation of some or all of its positions. The LTCM débâcle and the role played by banking organizations and their regulatory agencies in it thereafter came under close scrutiny through multiple sessions of congressional hearings and public scrutiny. The issues raised by the LTCM débâcle in the banking context primarily focused on the fact that the leading banking organizations appeared to have pushed aside prudent risk-management functions required by banking regulatory frameworks to engage in a range of very profitable transactions with LTCM with little or no information about the condition of LTCM as a counterparty, under the watch of the regulatory authorities. These transactions allowed LTCM to achieve extraordinary degrees of non-transparency, risk and leverage. In short, bank and non-bank counterparties, among other things:

- failed to acquire sufficient information to monitor the fund's risk profile and concentration of exposures in certain markets and tolerated non-transparency;
- failed to adequately assess, price, or collateralize the fund's potential future exposures relative to the conditions of market stress and creditworthiness of the fund; and
- failed to adequately manage credit risk in trading relationships by accounting for linkages between market risk, liquidity risk, and credit risk; and relied on VaR and potential future exposures models constructed on recent price data that probably underestimated both the size of potential shocks to risk factors and correlations between them.

The LTCM scenario also raised significant questions about the regulatory agencies' (particularly the FRB's) ability or muster to meaningfully regulate such banking counterparties' activities, and suggested that the 'too-big-to-fail' doctrine was indeed alive and well in the US regulatory framework.

**Working Group recommendations**

The Working Group was commissioned to prepare a study on the 'lessons learned' from the LTCM episode. As such, the Working Group issued a series of recommendations (Working Group, 1999a) aimed at constraining excessive leverage (that is, constraining bank–hedge fund relationships), such as:

- more frequent and meaningful information on hedge funds should be made public;
- public companies, including financial institutions, should publicly disclose additional information about their material financial exposures to significantly leveraged institutions, including hedge funds;
- financial institutions should enhance their practices for counterparty risk management;
- regulatory agencies should encourage improvements in the risk-management systems of regulated entities;
- regulators should promote the development of more risk-sensitive but prudent approaches to capital adequacy;
- regulators need expanded risk-assessment authority for the unregulated affiliates of broker–dealers and futures commission merchants;
- Congress should enact the provisions proposed by the Working Group to support financial contract netting; and
- regulators should consider stronger incentives to encourage offshore financial centres to comply with 'international standards'.

With respect to enhanced supervisory oversight, the Working Group asserted that the banking, securities, and futures regulatory agencies should monitor and encourage improvements in the risk-management systems of regulated entities. The Working Group observed that US banking agencies introduced new guidance on many risk-management issues, such as (i) the credit approval process and ongoing monitoring of credit quality; (ii) limits on counterparty credit exposures and the exposure management process; (iii) improving procedures for estimating potential future credit exposures and stress testing; and (iv) the use of collateral.

The Working Group further observed that banking agencies 'notified' banks that examiners would be looking to ensure that:

- senior management and boards of directors understand the strengths and weaknesses of risk measurement systems, including model risk, liquidity risk and the risk of divergence of historical correlations among different instruments and markets that underscore market risk and credit risk measurement techniques;
- senior management and boards of directors obtain realistic assessments of their tolerance for losses in periods of market stress;
- the linkages of material risks, such as market risk, credit risk and liquidity risk, are integrated into credit and market risk-management decisions;
- operational risk matters such as unconfirmed trades and unexecuted derivatives master agreements are addressed and resolved;
- legal risks such as enforceability of contracts and uncertainties concerning different insolvency and contract law frameworks in different countries are understood and addressed in the risk-management process;
- credit standards applied to trading activities are consistent with overall credit standards imposed by the banking organization; and
- risk oversight functions of banks 'possess independence, authority, expertise, and corporate stature'.

The Working Group guidance and observations in these respects are neither new nor extraordinary in any way. The question is whether banking agencies necessarily take full and complete steps to ensure that such guidance is followed, such as through the use of examination authority, and to require immediate and substantive corrective actions if deficiencies are uncovered. The related question is whether banking agencies should increasingly provide additional specific guidance to certain banking organizations or with respect to certain activities in general. The Working Group suggested that 'additional guidance' could be issued following review of the analysis and recommendations of the Basle Committee on Banking Supervision reports on bank interactions with highly leveraged institutions, and further with respect to regulatory stress testing requirements for credit risk profiles (similarly to those already established for market risk); limiting the permissibility of 100 per cent financing on reverse repurchase agreements; and requiring banks to ensure that counterparties develop meaningful measures of potential future credit exposures.

With respect to enhanced 'private sector practices for counterparty risk management' (that is, 'counterparty discipline'), the Working Group opined that financial institutions should establish and publish counterparty credit risk management standards in the following areas:

- the credit approval process and ongoing monitoring of credit quality, including the availability of information on counterparties and its use in rendering credit decisions;
- procedures for estimating potential future credit exposures, including stress testing to estimate exposures in volatile and illiquid markets, and model validation procedures, including backtesting (similarly to the internal models approach inherent in existing market risk-based capital requirements);
- approaches to establishing limits on counterparty credit exposures, measure leverage and risk, limiting concentration of credit exposures and of exposures to particular markets;
- integrating risk-management practices for linkages between credit, market and liquidity risks;
- procedures for exercising judgement given the inherent limitations of risk measurement models;
- policies regarding the use of collateral to mitigate counterparty credit risks; and
- procedures for valuation of OTC derivatives and collateral, close-out netting and liquidation of contracts and collateral, and considering legal risks in credit decisions (that is, questions concerning legal authority of a counterparty to enter into a contract and the uncertainties regarding differing insolvency laws, commercial codes, and recognition of netting and termination rights).

The Working Group observed that the private sector indeed pursued various counterparty credit risk initiatives in the banking organization context. First, the leading international banks and securities firms formed the Counterparty Risk Management Policy Group (CRMPG), which issued a report consisting of meaningful discussion of counterparty credit risk issues and recommendations for enhancing risk-management practices for such institutions providing credit services to significant counterparties in the derivatives and securities markets. Second, the International Swaps and Derivatives Association (ISDA) issued a review of collateral management practices drawing upon lessons learned from experiences during the LTCM débâcle and other periods of market stress. The ISDA Review provided a series of recommendations for improving collateral management practices and a plan to implement them. Third, the Institute of International Finance (IIF) issued the Report of the Task Force on Risk Assessment in March 1999 just prior to the Hedge Funds Report.

With respect to capital adequacy, the Working Group opined that banking agencies should enhance credit risk-based capital adequacy requirements in the following respects:

- the Basle Committee should revise the Capital Accord in order to 'align' capital requirements more closely with the risks taken by financial institutions through distinguishing among claims, instruments, or counterparties, based on credit quality;
- the capital treatment applied to credit exposures from derivatives transactions should be similar to that of a commercial loan to the same counterparty after accounting for any underlying collateral;
- derivatives that possess identical or similar market risk characteristics as the underlying instruments should have similar capital requirements for market risk;
- counterparty VaR and other risk models should be subjected to validation procedures, including backtesting (to confirm the reliability and stability of model results) and stress testing (to determine the effect of low-probability market outlier events), consistent with the Basle Committee approach on market risk;
- banking agencies in offshore banking centres should be encouraged to impose internationally recognized capital requirements on banks in their jurisdictions; and
- banking agencies should monitor the use of 'double leverage' especially if the borrowing is short term in nature (for instance, borrowing by a holding company that effectively finances an equity position in a non-bank affiliate or subsidiary bank may result in excessive double leverage).

The Working Group underscored that the LTCM scenario clearly suggested that the sudden insolvency of one significant counterparty, as augmented by leveraged trading positions and wide-ranging non-transparent OTC derivatives transactions, could jeopardize banking and financial systems. The Working Group emphasized that the ability to terminate financial contracts upon a counterparty's insolvency (that is, close-out netting) enhances market stability. There is little question that close-out netting allows solvent counterparties to replace terminated contracts without incurring additional market risk, and serves to prevent the failure of one counterparty such as LTCM from causing more serious ramifications for market disruption.

Thus, the Working Group asserted that the LTCM episode raised several issues under the US Bankruptcy Code and recommended the addition of amendments thereto. In this respect, the banking agencies participated with OTC derivatives dealers in crafting a legislative proposal, generally known as the 'Financial Contract Netting Improvement Act', which eliminates ambiguities under the Bankruptcy Code regarding close-out netting and forecloses various opportunities for counterparties to use US ancillary proceedings or offshore bankruptcy regimes to turn the table against actions taken by solvent counterparties.

Finally, the Working Group addressed issues regarding hedge funds and offshore financial centres and tax havens, and explicitly emphasized that one of the possible incentives to encourage offshore centres to adopt and comply with 'internationally agreed upon standards' could include the imposition of higher risk weightings on counterparty transactions for banks doing business with a financial entity operating in an offshore jurisdiction that does not comply with the Basle Core Principles.

**The OTC Derivatives Report**

The Working Group subsequently issued the OTC Derivatives Report in November 1999, which provided specific recommendations for legislative action to Congress in November 1999 (Working Group, 1999b). The OTC Derivatives Report purports to focus on changes to the Commodity Exchange Act (CEA) deemed necessary to promote innovation, competition, efficiency and transparency in the OTC derivatives markets, to reduce systemic risk, and allow the US to maintain leadership in these markets. The principal basis for the report is establishing greater 'legal certainty' for the OTC derivatives markets with respect to contract enforcement, execution and clearing functions.

**US banking regulatory community reactions**
The US banking agencies have consistently taken the position that OTC derivatives markets should not be subject to any separate regulatory scheme or even tightened accounting standards. In the face of highly publicized OTC derivatives losses suffered by non-financial end users in 1994–95, various hearings were held to determine whether OTC derivatives should

be more closely regulated by the CFTC or by a new regulatory entity given the diverse interests involved. The banking agencies, representing their constituent banking organizations, in particular consistently argued in congressional hearings that OTC derivatives should be subject to no separate regulatory scheme, and that the bank regulatory and supervisory framework provides them with adequate oversight into bank derivatives dealing, trading and hedging activities.

The US banking agencies worked through the Basle Committee and public–private partnership groups to issue 'guidance' that addressed public policy questions regarding OTC derivatives arising from significant dealer and end-user losses. The banking agencies essentially deflected congressional attempts to impose additional regulatory constraints on OTC derivatives, and the dealer banks prospered significantly as a result of these efforts. The uniform theme of these efforts was that banking organizations engaging in significant derivatives activities should adopt and implement sufficient risk-management programmes and internal control systems to mitigate credit, market and other risks arising from such activities; and that the agencies should receive access to meaningful and timely information about bank derivatives activities (whether or not otherwise disclosed to the public).

**SEC and CFTC approaches**
The banking agency efforts could be contrasted with other regulatory efforts, notably the SEC with regard to derivatives accounting and disclosure practices by public registrants that were subject to the federal securities laws (that is, major OTC derivatives dealers and their significant end users). Questions regarding the viability of the current US accounting standards with respect to derivatives valuation and in particular 'hedge accounting' continued to plague the banking industry, which lobbied furiously to combat any attempts by the Financial Accounting Standards Board (FASB) and the SEC to tighten accounting and disclosure standards for derivatives.

The FASB and the SEC persevered against a united position of the bank agencies; and the decade-long derivatives accounting debate ended in June 1998 when the FASB voted unanimously to issue the Statement of Financial Accounting Standards No. 133, *Accounting for Derivative Instruments and Hedging Activities* ('SFAS 133'), released two years to the month after publication of the exposure draft (which was thereafter revised in August 1997). SFAS 133 established new hedge accounting and derivatives disclosure standards that came into effect in June 2000.

Also, the CFTC and its Chairperson continues its crusade of asserting or implying that OTC derivatives should be more closely regulated through various public statements and more importantly in congressional hearings regarding the LTCM débâcle and the role of OTC derivatives therein.

**The Working Group's recommendations**
The Working Group predictably concluded that the trading of financial derivatives by eligible swap participants should generally be excluded from the CEA. The Working Group also concluded that legal obstacles should be removed from the development of electronic trading systems to increase market liquidity and transparency, and regulated clearing systems to reduce systemic risk by allowing for the 'mutualization of risks' by market participants and facilitating netting of contracts.

The Working Group issued unanimous recommendations for OTC derivatives, including the following:

- exclusion of bilateral swap and derivative transactions between 'eligible swap participants' (sophisticated counterparties, defined similarly as in the CFTC swaps exemption) from the CEA, other than transactions that involve non-financial commodities with finite supplies (for which the CFTC would retain its current exemptive authority);
- amending the CEA to clarify that a party to a transaction may not avoid performance of obligations under or recover losses incurred on a transaction based solely on the failure of that party or its counterparty to comply with the terms of an exclusion from or exemption under the CEA;
- exclusion of electronic trading systems for derivatives from the CEA, provided that such systems limit participation to 'eligible swap participants' (sophisticated counterparties) trading for their own accounts and are not used to trade contracts involving non-financial commodities with finite supplies;
- elimination of obstacles under federal law to provide a framework for the clearing of OTC derivatives subject to the regulation of the CFTC, the SEC, or banking agencies, depending on the type of OTC derivatives in question;
- clarification of the Treasury Amendment to provide the CFTC with authority to regulate transactions in foreign currency between retail customers and entities other than banks, broker–dealers, and their affiliates, but exclude all other transactions in products within the scope of the Treasury Amendment from the CEA, unless conducted on an 'organized exchange' within the meaning of the CEA;
- modification to the exclusive jurisdiction language of the CEA to provide increased legal certainty to hybrid instruments (that is,

depository instruments such as demand deposits, time deposits, or transaction accounts; or debt or equity securities that have one or more components with payment features economically similar to swaps, forwards, options, or futures contracts); and
- clarification of federal laws regarding the applicability of the Shad–Johnson Accord to hybrid instruments that reference non-exempt securities.

The Working Group also reiterated its support for improvements in the close-out netting framework for OTC derivatives under the Bankruptcy Code and bank insolvency laws recommended in the Hedge Funds Report (discussed above). These improvements would focus on, among other things, expanding and clarifying definitions of financial contracts eligible for netting; authorizing eligible counterparties to engage in netting across different types of contracts, including swaps, repurchase agreements and forward contracts; and addressing the impact of bankruptcy filings by foreign counterparties in a non-US jurisdiction and bank failures regarding termination, netting and liquidation rights.

Interestingly, the Working Group also recognized the issue of 'regulatory and tax arbitrage', or the use of OTC derivatives to circumvent regulatory and tax measures. Most interestingly, the Working Group acknowledged that the derivatives industry (that is, large global banks and securities firms) have been 'quite creative in tailoring particular products to achieve certain regulatory results that were not originally intended'.

## 4 THE GRAMM–LEACH–BLILEY ACT OF 1999

**Overview**

The most significant recent event in US banking and financial services regulation is the enactment of the Gramm–Leach–Bliley Act of November 1999 (GLBA). Title I of the GLBA comprehensively restructured the statutory framework that governs the banking and financial services industry. The GLBA represented several decades worth of legislative jockeying by different financial and congressional interests to modernize the US financial services statutory framework with respect to banking, securities, and insurance activities and affiliations. These activities and affiliations were otherwise limited by legislation such as the National Bank Act of 1864 (as amended), the Glass–Steagall Act of 1933, and the Bank Holding Company Act of 1956 (BHCA) (as amended).

Title I of the GLBA has five critical components for the purposes of banking regulation relevant to this chapter. First, the GLBA eliminates remaining statutory limitations on the financial activities authorized of banking organizations for qualifying bank holding companies. Second, the GLBA establishes restrictions on the channels for carrying on new or expanded non-bank financial activities within the banking organization. Third, the GLBA both reduces and increases existing limitations on commingling banking and commerce activities. Fourth, the GLBA mixes functional supervision of the financial entities with umbrella supervision of the consolidated financial holding companies. Fifth, the GLBA establishes the framework for a regulatory process of determining whether certain financial activities that contain aspects of banking and securities should be subject to banking agency or SEC or CFTC regulation.

With respect to banking regulation, there is little question that banking organizations will continue to expand into securities and insurance activities under the GLBA. The FRB and the OCC have through deregulatory efforts slowly but surely eroded the statutory barriers to conducting expanded securities and insurance activities over the past decade. The FRB has done so through liberalizing the section 20 constraints in 1996 and section 20 firewalls in 1997, respectively, to increasingly authorize BHC affiliates to conduct significant securities activities. The FRB has also liberally construed the Glass–Steagall Act and relevant provisions of the BHCA to consistently authorize new financial activities under Regulation Y for BHCs and their affiliates. The OCC has done so in several significant respects. First, through interpretations of section 24 (Seventh) of the National Bank Act in a liberal manner to authorize national banks to conduct a range of activities as within the business of banking except to the extent that they otherwise directly conflict with other statutory authority (that is, the Glass–Steagall Act). Second, through increasingly liberal interpretations of section 92 of the National Bank Act regarding insurance sales. Third, in developing an extensively liberal framework for national bank operating subsidiary activities. The OCC has interpreted this liberal framework to authorize national bank operating subsidiaries to conduct the same activities as national banks may conduct directly, as well as to conduct activities that are part of or incidental to the business of banking but that are not otherwise permitted for national banks directly so long as certain eligibility criteria and safeguards are maintained. One of the most interesting interpretations in this respect is the *Zions Bank* order which authorized a national bank operating subsidiary to engage in municipal bond underwriting activities, notwithstanding sections 16 and 20 of the Glass–Steagall Act.

These actions have collectively reduced the effect of statutory barriers, introduced cumulative pressure on regulatory agencies to reduce regulatory burdens and on Congress to enact financial services modernization reform legislation. The GLBA will clearly facilitate the combination of banking and securities activities within single financial organizations. At this time, there are 51 active section 20 securities affiliates of BHCs, owned by 25 domestic BHCs and 19 foreign banking organizations. There is little question that some of these securities affiliates will become operating subsidiaries of national banks, while others may remain as BHC affiliates. Moreover, other banks and securities entities not currently related will probably become related in some manner under the new GLBA provisions.

Thus, the GLBA essentially will result in further consolidation of the banking and financial services industry and expand the range of financial activities authorized for banking organizations. The number of US banking organizations has been reduced by nearly 25 per cent since 1990, and this trend of consolidation will probably continue under the GLBA. The GLBA will probably increase mergers among institutions specializing in different financial services to obtain perceived advantages of cost savings and corporate synergies. The net effect of the GLBA will undoubtedly be more consolidation of banks and across banks, securities and insurance firms within the banking and financial services industry. If consolidation results in further perceived diversification, the consolidated entities may achieve certain benefits associated with perceived risk-reduction effects. The mere assumption of increased diversification, however, may not necessarily result in risk reduction *per se*. The critical focus of risk management and disclosure practices must reside in analysis of risks assumed by the individual components of the diversified entity.

The most critical aspect of the GLBA is the provisions of Title I which, among other things, repeals sections 20 and 32 of the Glass–Steagall Act, and is intended to facilitate affiliations among banks, securities firms, insurance firms and other financial companies. In furtherance of this objective, the GLBA amends section 4 of the BHCA to authorize bank holding companies (BHCs) and foreign banks that qualify as 'financial holding companies' (FHCs) to engage in securities, insurance, and other activities that are 'financial in nature' or 'incidental to a financial activity'. The activities of BHCs and foreign banks that are not FHCs would continue to be limited to activities currently authorized under the BHCA and implementing regulations that are deemed to be 'closely related' to banking and permissible for BHCs.

The GLBA defines an FHC as a BHC that meets certain eligibility requirements. In order for a BHC to convert to an FHC, and receive the full benefits of the GLBA, the Act requires that all depository institutions (that is, banks) controlled by the BHC must be 'well capitalized' and 'well managed'. With respect to foreign banks that operate branches or agencies or own or control a commercial lending company in the US, the GLBA requires the FRB to apply comparable capital and management standards that give due regard to the principle of national treatment and equality of competitive opportunity. The GLBA requires BHCs desiring to convert to FHCs to submit to the FRB a declaration that the company elects to be an FHC and a certification that all of the depository institutions controlled by the company are 'well capitalized' and 'well managed'.

The GLBA grants the FRB discretion to impose limitations on, among other things, the conduct or activities of any FHC that controls a depository institution that does not remain both well capitalized and well managed following election to FHC status. The FRB has recently observed that several of the larger securities organizations may be too large to qualify as subsidiaries of banks in FHCs. The question is whether these entities will merge with existing banking organizations and become affiliates in an FHC, remain independent, acquire a bank as part of an FHC that is largely defined by securities activities, or create a new small banking structure.

The FRB has further observed that banking organizations will probably expand into insurance underwriting activities, in addition to insurance sales (marketing) activities, but that many US insurance firms are 'mutual' companies, and this may prevent banks from merging with or acquiring them until they convert to stock companies.

Title I of the GLBA also authorizes national banks to acquire control of or hold an interest in a new type of subsidiary called a 'financial subsidiary'. The GLBA defines a financial subsidiary as a company that is controlled by one or more insured depository institutions, other than a subsidiary that engages solely in activities that national banks may engage in directly (under the same terms and conditions that govern the conduct of these activities by national banks) or a subsidiary that a national bank is specifically authorized to control under federal law. The financial subsidiary may engage in specified activities that are 'financial in nature' and in activities that are 'incidental to financial activities' if the bank and the subsidiary meet certain requirements and comply with certain safeguards. A financial subsidiary may also combine these newly authorized activities with activities that are permissible for national banks to engage in directly.

**Selective Regulatory Observations**

The financial services industry must determine how to take best advantage of the opportunities provided by the GLBA. The regulatory agencies must similarly address the challenges of implementing the framework for regulating and supervising the increasingly diversified financial holding companies authorized under the new legislation. The framework will necessarily consist of 'umbrella' supervision of the consolidated entity by the FRB, oversight of the depository institutions by their respective banking agencies, and functional regulation of various non-bank entities by their respective agencies. The range of activities authorized by the GLBA necessitates increased coordination and cooperation by and between the banking, securities, and insurance regulatory agencies, and the FRB as umbrella supervisory agency. The challenge is to implement the mix of umbrella supervision and functional supervision established in the GLBA. The difficulties inherent in this challenge will depend on the complexities of integration of financial activities within FHCs and the size and scope of bank and non-bank activities within these organizations.

The GLBA will further necessitate enhanced communication, cooperation and coordination between the FRB as umbrella supervisory agency and the primary banking agencies. The GLBA retains the FRB's current role as consolidated supervisory agency of bank holding companies, with FHCs serving as a component. The new regulatory and supervisory framework is an evolution from the changes perceived within the banking and financial services industry. Congress maintained the supervisory framework for consolidated financial institutions that include a bank, but ensured that the FRB would continue to respect the authority of functional regulatory agencies and avoid imposing excessive or duplicative regulatory structures.

There is little question that the FRB has gained some experience as an umbrella supervisor in this sense prior to the GLBA in supervising the affairs of Citigroup, with respect to its grandfathered insurance activities as part of that holding company. The role of the umbrella supervisor is necessarily distinct from the approach of direct supervision of banking institutions themselves. The oversight of risk taking of the consolidated organization is paramount: the supervisor must keep the relevant regulatory agencies informed about overall risk taking by the entity and identify and evaluate the various risks of activities throughout diversified FHCs to determine how the components affect affiliated banks.

**Capital requirements**
The FRB must necessarily focus on the organization's consolidated risk-management processes and overall capital adequacy. The consolidated capital requirements are inherently problematic because banks are affiliated with other financial institutions that have their own regulatory agency and separate capital regulations.

**Moral hazard/safety net**
The FRB will also need to limit extension of the safety net beyond banking institutions within the FHC context to the extent possible. The 'federal safety net' generally refers to deposit insurance and access to the discount

window and other guarantees associated with the Federal Reserve payment and settlement system. The FRB should develop and enhance the concept of 'market discipline' from the regulatory sense to ensure that the federal safety net is not extended to non-bank activities. The GLBA clearly discourages the imposition of bank regulation and supervision to non-bank affiliates and subsidiaries through the functional regulation provisions. The FRB also simultaneously should develop regulatory features that protect the banking institutions from the risks of other non-bank activities conducted in FHC affiliates. These objectives may be conflicting in part, and the FRB will need to balance these interests through relationships with the functional regulators of non-bank affiliates.

**FRB examinations**
The FRB maintains the authority to examine and require reports from any bank holding company, including an FHC, and any subsidiary of the holding company. The GLBA does limit the FRB's authority to examine and require reports from functionally regulated subsidiaries of a BHC, defined as certain entities regulated by the SEC (broker, dealer, investment adviser, or investment company), the CFTC, or state insurance agencies (insurance company, insurance agent). The GLBA requires the FRB to rely on publicly available information to the greatest extent possible in this respect, regulatory reports submitted by a functionally regulated subsidiary to its regulatory agency, and financial statements subject to external audit. The FRB may examine functionally regulated subsidiaries only if (i) the FRB has reasonable cause to believe that the entity is engaged in activities that pose a material risk to an affiliated depository institution; (ii) the FRB determines that an examination is necessary to provide information about the risk-management systems of the company; or (iii) the FRB has reasonable cause to believe the entity is not in compliance with banking laws.

**FRB–functional regulatory agency relationships**
The GLBA does not reduce the complexity of the US regulatory and supervisory framework applicable to financial activities and institutions, but does attempt to clarify relationships between regulatory agencies for diversified financial organizations. The concepts of coordination and information sharing will be paramount in implementing the GLBA. The GLBA clearly opens the door for even larger and more complex diversified financial organizations, and requires the banking agencies to eliminate excessive or duplicative regulatory burdens and de facto extensions of the federal safety net to non-bank activities. The GLBA will also require new relationships between the FRB, the SEC, and insurance agencies regarding the functional regulation of bank securities and insurance affiliates.

## FRB–banking agency relationships

The relationship between the FRB and primary banking agencies is not necessarily changed by the GLBA. The FRB is, with the state banking departments, the primary bank supervisor for state FRS member banks. The OCC is the primary regulatory agency for national banks, and the FDIC is the federal primary regulatory agency for state non-member banks. Thus, the relationship between the FRB as umbrella supervisor and the primary bank regulatory agency would involve the OCC or the FDIC. The practical reality is that the principal relationship for large and complex financial holding companies will involve the FRB and the OCC because the banks in such holding companies are either state FRS member banks or national banks. Most of the organizations that will pursue opportunities under the GLBA have national banks as lead banks. The relationship between the FRB and the OCC, for instance, will necessarily require mutual respect and coordinated information sharing, respectively, beyond mere publicly available information. This relationship may be complex, given the tendency to compartmentalize proprietary information. Thus, the relationship will likely evolve to require joint examination teams from the FRB and the OCC, and other electronic access to information obtained by each agency under terms and conditions as appropriate. The relationship will need to be defined in agreements or memoranda of understanding, at the very least.

## GLBA Implementing Regulations

The GLBA requires the FRB to draft regulations to implement parts of the GLBA, a responsibility that is frequently shared with the Treasury Department. For instance, the FRB and the Treasury are jointly authorized to draft regulations to implement the merchant banking provisions for FHCs, including holding periods for merchant bank investments and limits on transactions between depository institutions and the firms in which the merchant bank invests, including their customers. The FRB and the Treasury are also jointly authorized to draft regulations to determine what other activities that FHCs are authorized to engage in are 'financial in nature' or 'incidental to financial activities'. The FRB is required to adopt regulations addressing the application of sections 23A and 23B of the Federal Reserve Act regarding derivative transactions and intraday credit. The GLBA also has extensive CRA, privacy and third-party disclosure regulatory requirements that will necessitate joint rulemaking and interpretation and resolution of conflicting language in the GLBA and policy interests raised in these areas.

## 5 CONCLUDING OBSERVATIONS

The US banking system, as with most banking systems globally, is undergoing major and ongoing transition and transformation. In large part, this new environment is being forced by the rapidly expanding 'globalization processes' in the interconnected financial and technology sectors. At present, legislative and regulatory developments are trailing the realities of the new financial marketplace – more reacting than directing the shape and face of this new global financial environment. Further, part of the 'push and pull' of this process is countervailing concerns for community responsibilities for financial institutions and protection of the rights and interests of users/consumers.

## REFERENCES

Brown, Stephen J., William N. Goetzmann and James M. Park (1998), 'Hedge funds and the aftermath of the Asian currency crisis of 1997', NBER Working Paper No. 6427, National Bureau of Economic Research, February.

Federal Reserve Board (2000), Bank Holding Companies and Change in Bank Control, Docket No. R-1057 (interim rule for establishing FHCs under the Gramm–Leach–Bliley Act of 1999 with request for public comment), 65 *Federal Register* 3785, 25 January.

Meyer, Lawrence H. (1999), Remarks by Governor Meyer, Federal Reserve Board, 'The implications of financial modernization legislation', before the Symposium on Financial Modernization Legislation, sponsored by Women in Housing and Finance, Washington, DC, 15 December.

Meyer, Lawrence H. (2000), Remarks by Governor Meyer, Federal Reserve Board, 'Implementing the Gramm–Leach–Bliley Act', before the American Law Institute and American Bar Association, Washington, DC, 3 February.

Norton, J.J. and S.C. Whitley (1983), *Banking Law Manual* (US), supplementary annual, 1999.

Norton, J.J. and C.D. Olive (1997), 'The ongoing process of international bank regulatory and supervisory convergence: a new regulating market "partnership"', 16 *Annual Review of Banking Law* 227.

Office of the Comptroller of the Currency (OCC), *Quarterly Journal*, which lists various mergers and acquisitions.

Working Group (1999a), Report of the President's Working Group on Financial Markets, *Hedge Funds, Leverage, and the Lessons of Long-Term Capital Management*, April.

Working Group (1999b), Report of the President's Working Group on Financial Markets, *Over-the-Counter Derivatives Markets and the Commodity Exchange Act*, November.

# 22. Deposit insurance and international banking regulation
## C. Charles Okeahalam*

## 1 INTRODUCTION

Deposit insurance is part of the regulatory mechanism in international banking. Countries have different types of deposit insurance. It is usual to define deposit insurance as either implicit or explicit. Implicit deposit insurance is the lender-of-last-resort (LOLR) guarantee which the central bank or regulatory authorities provides to banks and depositors. Under implicit deposit insurance, deposits are protected by the bank monitoring and regulatory authority – which does so without specifying guarantees regarding the extent of the protection. Usually implicit deposit insurance is not specifically funded. In a country where there is explicit deposit insurance, deposits are protected up to a pre-set limit by the bank monitoring and regulatory authorities. All schemes are designed to provide a mechanism with which the bank regulatory authority can protect deposits in banking institutions. As will be explained in detail below, explicit deposit insurance can be funded publicly or privately or via a combination of public and private funds.

There has been extensive debate regarding the usefulness of explicit deposit insurance. Some countries are convinced that their own financial system can operate an explicit deposit insurance system. Others are not. This chapter reviews the major aspects of the debate on the utility of deposit insurance in general, but places particular emphasis on the key aspects of explicit (funded) deposit insurance design and policy. Section 2 summarizes the costs and benefits of deposit insurance. Section 3 reviews the literature on deposit insurance with particular emphasis on moral hazard and the behaviour of banks under explicit deposit insurance regimes. Section 4 explains the underlying concepts of deposit insurance pricing, how premiums are arrived at in practice and also the difficulty of arriving at fairly priced deposit insurance. Section 5 presents the key features which are necessary for a deposit insurance scheme to work in practice. The final section concludes by suggesting some important steps for the way forward on deposit insurance.

## 2 DEPOSIT INSURANCE: ORIGINS AND BACKGROUND

In principle an explicit deposit insurance scheme (DIS) is a fund to which deposit-taking financial intermediaries (usually banks) make premium contributions. The basic theoretical idea is that banks make these payments into the fund to perform two roles. First, in the event of a bank insolvency, to compensate depositors fully up to a pre-set limit and second, to provide uninformed and unsophisticated depositors with a financial safety net. This instils greater confidence among depositors, which reduces information asymmetry and increases the likelihood of financial stability. If carefully designed, the panoply of regulations and supervisory expectations that are part of explicit deposit insurance can reduce information asymmetry for depositors, engender greater confidence in the banking system and reduce financial instability.[1] To be effective, an explicit DIS needs to establish the level of protection which should be accorded to depositors. To do this, an explicit DIS needs to be able to measure and price the absolute and relative risk of bank insolvency, bank failure and potential loss of depositors' funds, then explicitly relate this to the expected level of public and/or private funding. This partly reduces the forbearance, insurance mispricing and regulatory capture costs of implicit deposit insurance. Accordingly, the basic objectives of deposit insurance are to protect retail deposits, promote financial stability and encourage competitive neutrality.

If one were to rank each of these objectives, then clearly the primary objective of a DIS[2] is to protect small retail deposits in banks. The definition of 'small' usually refers to retail customers but in an international context is country specific. Large depositors and other bank creditors have access to information and the resources to monitor deposit-taking institutions. They are therefore not as vulnerable as small depositors.

By ensuring the protection of small depositors, an explicit DIS supports other bank regulatory agencies in maintaining financial stability. DISs encourage financial stability by ensuring that bank operations are based on sound business and financial policies. Furthermore, DISs support financial stability by bolstering the confidence of depositors that they will be refunded if the bank in which they have their deposits becomes insolvent or fails.

In a retail bank sector with high levels of concentration, a DIS promotes competitive neutrality by reducing the higher perception of risk which depositors would otherwise attach to small and less well-established banks relative to large banks. So a DIS can serve as an implicit competitive subsidy to small banks which is analogous to, or to some extent mitigates, the implicit 'too-big-to-fail' (TBTF) subsidy of the core and larger banks. In essence it increases the likelihood of diversification of deposit mobilization.

Despite all these benefits, there has been significant debate as to the cost–benefit of deposit insurance. Explicit deposit insurance can increase moral hazard and the US savings and loans (S&L) crises of the 1980s are evidence.[3] For example, it has been suggested by Kaufman (1995) and Stern (1998) that if the US explicit deposit insurance system had been more optimally designed this would not have taken place. The Federal Deposit Insurance Corporation Improvement Act 1991 (FDICIA) has helped to make the US banking industry healthier by changing the behaviour of bankers and regulators. One way it has done this has been by moving from a flat-rate system which caused moral hazard to a risk-based deposit insurance premium structure. Although this is an important reform, in a discussion of deposit insurance for small banks and for large banks which are considered TBTF, Stern (1998) makes the point that while FDICIA substantially increased the likelihood that uninsured depositors and other creditors would suffer losses when their banks failed, the level of coverage is still too high. He suggests that, since regulators can provide full protection if they feel that a failing bank is TBTF, there is still a moral hazard problem which FDICIA has yet to address. Several countries have learned from the experience of the US and have made reforms to their systems in line with the FDICIA. It would appear that these countries have taken the view that their regulatory authorities can still play the LOLR role effectively via the constructive ambiguity of an implicit deposit insurance scheme. This controversy has generated significant debate.[4]

The primary anti-deposit insurance view is based on the perspective that the benefits of explicit deposit insurance do not come without potential or real costs. First, as Heifer (1999) points out, inappropriate design and structure of deposit insurance has affected the basic objective of financial stability and confidence and has caused financial instability in some countries, most notably the US. Furthermore, while deposit insurance is basically like any other form of insurance, for reasons which will be explained in Section 4 below, premiums for deposit insurance cannot easily be established in practice. This is because it is difficult to estimate the actual risks that banks take. So if poorly implemented, a deposit insurance scheme can lead to bad bank regulation and supervisory failure, particularly with regard to bank monitoring and licensing. In addition, the nature of the industrial structure of the banking sector in a country can distort members' incentives and create adverse selection (suboptimal decision making) and deposit insurance free-rider problems.

## 3  DEPOSIT INSURANCE AND RISK-TAKING BEHAVIOUR

Before proceeding into more detailed discussion, it would be useful to make three points regarding the literature. The first point is that perhaps as a result of the US savings and loans crises, the literature on deposit insurance is primarily focused on the US and most authors who have contributed are US based. Second, analysing deposit insurance and the specific relationship this has with moral hazard and bank failures has a large and well-developed literature of its own. Third, the literature is large both in breadth (adjacent areas of enquiry) and in depth (detailed analysis of very specific issues); therefore a comprehensive review is beyond the ambitions of this chapter. Instead what is presented herein is a summary of the major aspects of the literature and key contributions.

Explicit deposit insurance has contributed to bank insolvencies in several countries, for example, Norway and Finland, and most notably the US S&L crises of the 1980s.[5] It is now a fairly well-established premise that explicit deposit insurance can act as a double-edged sword. On the one hand, given that bank balance sheets typically have money uncertain assets and money certain liabilities, in the absence of deposit insurance, depositors may seek their funds and cause instability in the system. On the other hand, the presence of explicit deposit insurance may create incentives to excessive risk taking by bankers (moral hazard) which when realized (or even suspected) may lead to bank runs and instability in the system. Moral hazard in banking arises when banks are provided with incentives to take risks, can retain the returns, but at the same time can pass the (potential or realized) costs of the risks to depositors, regulators or the taxpayers. Banks secure in the safety net provided by the government feel free to take on higher levels of risk. Depositors who believe that their deposits are safe do not take as much care as they should in monitoring banks and as a result do not send appropriate market discipline signals, for example, by demanding higher interest rates or withdrawing their deposits. Another way of interpreting the behaviour of depositors in a high-risk banking environment with explicit deposit insurance is to suggest that as result of the high information asymmetries, depositors are incapable of monitoring managers and that managers are aware of this and free ride on depositors and the taxpayer.

The above view of explicit deposit insurance vividly illustrates the difficulties inherent in designing an optimal bank regulatory policy. Accordingly, the debate on optimal bank regulation and whether or not explicit deposit insurance has a role to play within such a framework has been quite extensive; see for example, Giammarino et al. (1993), Thakor

(1993) and Bhattacharya et al. (1998). Seen in one way, as Rajan (1992) points out, given the insider–outsider problem and information asymmetry, optimal bank regulation may only be attainable via an increase in bank self-regulation. Yet the difficulty of implementing such solutions lies in the creation of workable incentives that allows the equilibrium that arises from greater self-regulation to maximize the welfare function for banks, regulators and taxpayers.

Furthermore, it can be argued that as innovations in financial products and services continue to evolve, the level of information asymmetry which bank regulators face increases. This would be the case even if the regulator learnt from previous experiences and attempted to monitor developments. This makes the cost of pure public sector bank regulation prohibitive. It is for this reason that some, such as Mishkin (1996), suggest that some form of public sector optimal bank regulation can only take place if banks are provided with incentives to behave in ways that reduce information asymmetry for regulators. Seen in this light, it is not surprising that whether or not explicit deposit insurance is useful or harmful, is often discussed in the following context: first, the extent to which it creates inappropriate incentives, second, the appropriate pricing of bank risk-taking behaviour and third, how this deviates from optimal bank regulation.

Given the framework under which the discourse is usually held, the literature on explicit deposit insurance is usually embedded within the context of the search for an optimal bank regulation framework; it therefore focuses primarily on moral hazard and the efficacy or otherwise of incentives to avoid moral hazard. Diamond and Dybvig (1983) rigorously explain the way in which moral hazard emanates in the first instance. They suggest that in a production economy with stochastic liquidity shocks, banks primarily serve to provide optimal intertemporal insurance to consumers. Although this is a narrow definition of the intermediation role which banks play, it infers the problem of information asymmetry faced by depositors and regulators – which creates the opportunity for moral hazard to exist. However, von Thadden (1997) suggests that a fuller understanding of the moral hazard problem can be achieved if the definition of banks is extended beyond Diamond and Dybvig's narrow definition. Others have made contributions in this area.[6] For example, the study of Karels (1997) accentuates the potential for moral hazard which the absence of depositor and market discipline creates. Under the present risk-based premium structure, asset risk has the potential to decline when the regulatory agency raises capital requirements.

Yet the ability and temptation to pass downside risk of financial operations is neither limited to the banking industry nor is it new. For example, Brewer et al. (1997) provide further evidence (from outside the banking industry) of the significance of increasing the potential liabilities of creditors, so that they, in turn, increase their monitoring efficiency and reduce moral hazard.[7] Furthermore, the prominence which moral hazard has received as an explanation for the savings and loan problem might suggest that moral hazard is a recent phenomenon. But it is not. Bodenhorn (1996) explains that the first experiment with deposit insurance in the US was the New York Safety Fund. The New York Safety Fund was founded in 1829 and ended nearly as disastrously as the S&L crises of the 1980s for the same reasons. Hooks and Robinson (1996) provide evidence to support the view that moral hazard existed in US Texas state chartered banks in the 1920s. A state-run deposit insurance system was in place at the time and membership was mandatory for all state chartered banks in Texas. Consistent with the role of moral hazard in increasing *ex ante* risk, the individual bank-level data reveal that declines in capitalization were positively correlated with increases in loan concentrations at insured banks. In addition, Gunther and Robinson (1990) explain that after a 60-year period of relative stability, this problem arose again in Texas. They show that the ratio of a bank's capital adequacy is an important factor in determining how likely it is to succumb to deposit insurance moral hazard incentives and take on higher risks. They also show that deregulation and increased competition probably interacted with moral hazard in the recent period of widespread bank insolvencies and failures. This leads to the suggestion that the recent episode of deposit insurance moral hazard may lie behind the transition from the well-balanced bank portfolio characteristics of stable banking periods to the higher-risk portfolios which are a usual characteristic of banks when their capital levels drop below adequate regulatory standards.

To enable further insight on this issue, the extent to which deregulation can be blamed for the large number of failures caused by the moral hazard of deposit insurance has also been tested. But deregulation of the banking industry should not be confused with bad bank regulation and supervision.[8] Fraser and Zardkoohi (1996) test the deregulation hypothesis – which argues that banks and savings and loans associations take on more risk in a deregulated environment. They show that savings and loans take on more risk in a deregulated environment which has inappropriate bank regulation.

This is in keeping with the findings of Grossman (1992), who explains that inadequate implementation of bank regulation and supervision is mistakenly construed as deposit insurance moral hazard. In an analysis of the risk-taking behaviour of insured and uninsured institutions operating under strict and less strict regulatory regimes, he shows that insured institutions which operate under less strict regulatory regimes are more likely to undertake more risky lending activities than those which are more tightly regulated. Although, prima facie, this fits in with moral hazard, the results also suggest that deposit insurance was not the sole culprit of the higher insolvencies and failures that took place among the institutions from the less strict cohort. Rather, the problem was caused by a combination of deposit insurance and inadequate sequencing of deregulation. The results suggest that since deposit insurance still requires careful reform, further bank deregulation should be viewed and undertaken with caution. And most importantly, if the system of explicit deposit insurance is not reformed to remove all the moral hazard loopholes, then the level and quality of on-site and off-site bank regulation and supervision has to improve.

**Incentives, Deposit Insurance and Bank Behaviour**

As noted earlier, the evidence in the literature also suggests that careful assessment and development of appropriate incentives lie at the heart of the attainment of effective explicit deposit insurance. Incentives can yield unexpected positive as well as unexpected negative or adverse outcomes. Wheelock and Khumbakar (1995) analyse the incentive effects of deposit insurance by examining the insurance system of the US state of Kansas over the 1909–29 period in which it operated. They show that while the Kansas system had a number of unique features, such as voluntary membership, which were incorporated to limit risk taking, it also suffered from both adverse selection and moral hazard. In addition, after controlling for the insurance selection effect, the Kansas DIS encouraged insured banks to hold less capital relative to uninsured banks. The premium structure did not provide the appropriate incentives to insured banks to hold more capital – on the contrary, it encouraged them to choose greater leverage than their insured competitors. This is not surprising since the nature and selection of members into a DIS is an important decision which can greatly influence the success or failure of a scheme.

Along the same lines, Mazumdar (1996) analyses the joint impact which the US Federal Reserve Bank System's discount window credit and reserve requirements and the FDIC's deposit insurance have on bank optimal capital structure and asset risk choice. It is found that the presence of the discount window does not always prompt bank risk taking and leverage but it does partially offset such incentives under certain indirect subsidies that may encourage deposit funding. Therefore Mazumdar suggests that regulatory reforms, for example the enactment of the FDICIA of 1991, may not sufficiently resolve banking firms incentives for moral hazard behaviour.

One solution to the difficult objective of providing an appropriate incentive-based deposit insurance framework is provided by Kupic and O'Brien (1998). Their study illustrates that where commonly used modelling stylizations on bank investment and finance choices are relaxed there are difficulties in designing optimal bank regulatory policy. To resolve this, they show that when banks can issue equity at the risk-adjusted risk-free rate, collateralization of deposits with a risk-free asset costlessly resolves some of the factors that encourage moral hazard, such as inadequate pricing of deposit insurance.

Along the same lines, Nagarajan and Sealey (1998) have developed a model of incentive compatible bank regulation. They illustrate that with regulatory instruments which involve *ex post* pricing contingent on the bank's performance relative to the market, conceptually implementable mechanisms can solve each type of deposit insurance incentive problem separately and achieve the first-best outcome. A major aspect of this contribution is that the mechanisms suggested do not involve a subsidy to the bank. When the regulator simultaneously faces moral hazard and adverse selection, conditions are identified under which the same mechanism can achieve the first-best solution.

Yet Stroup (1997), among others, explains that bank debt as a source of debt finance is declining as firms tap the capital (bond) market for debt finance. The corollary is that a substantial transfer of deposits from banks to other parts of the financial system is taking place. The catalyst for these two trends has been the increase in non-bank competition, the reduction in banking industry profits and the perception of increased risk as a result of the high bank failure of the 1980s in the US and 1990s elsewhere. Since one of the stated objectives of deposit insurance is to ensure financial stability, given the trends just stated, the value of explicit deposit insurance in attaining this objective becomes debatable. As assets migrate from insured institutions, deposit insurance exerts less of a stabilizing influence on the overall financial system. In effect an insurance programme which applies to a shrinking segment of the modern financial services market cannot play the role of ensuring the stability of the entire system.

So Gorton and Rosen (1995) explore the incentive role which fixed-rate deposit insurance has played in encouraging the decline of bank intermediation. They test an alternative hypothesis based on corporate control considerations and find that managerial entrenchment provides a better explanation for, and played a more significant role than explicit deposit insurance in encouraging, moral hazard in the recent behaviour of banks.

Gorton and Rosen's finding that moral hazard is not solely a consequence of explicit deposit insurance design is supported by the findings of Crawford et al. (1995), who test the agency theory deregulation hypothesis which posits that bank chief executive officer compensation becomes more sensitive as banks and the action which their management can take become less regulated. Their findings indicate a significant increase in pay–performance sensitivities in the United States over the pre-deregulation period (1976–81) and the deregulation period (1982–88). The increases in pay sensitivities are observed for salary and bonus, stock options and common stock holdings. Furthermore, the increases in the pay–performance relation associated with high capitalization ratio banks were observed to be consistent with providing incentives for wealth creation. In addition, even larger increases in pay–performance sensitivity for lower capitalization ratio banks suggest a deposit insurance moral hazard problem.

In addition to the above, while many of the moral hazard problems of deposit insurance have been related to on-balance sheet risk-taking behaviour, it is important to note that developments in off-balance sheet and derivative finance have also increased incentives and the scope for moral hazard in deposit insurance. Peek and Rosengreen (1997) explain that because of the moral hazard associated with deposit insurance, troubled banks with relatively small capital adequacy cushions with which to absorb losses have an incentive to take speculative positions. If this is the case, then the prevalence of problem banks among those actively engaged in derivatives markets should be of concern to bank supervisors. The derivatives activity at troubled banks should raise the same concerns expressed about banks' on-balance sheet positions; namely that given the presence of explicit deposit insurance, banks may not be fully exploiting hedging opportunities or may be placing their remaining capital at risk. However, Peek and Rosengreen suggest that bank supervisors do not take into account (favourably or unfavourably) the derivatives activities of troubled banks in their decisions to downgrade bank ratings or impose regulatory actions.[9]

Furthermore, despite all the incentives to avoid risk taking and moral hazard explained above, whenever bank insolvencies occur there is still the perceived need for deposit insurance. Thus, as Flood (1996) explains, the history of the demand for introduction of explicit DIS is correlated with the experience of bank insolvencies and although some, for example Calomiris (1990), believe that the financial regulatory authorities can still play the LOLR role effectively via the constructive ambiguity of an implicit deposit insurance, others, for example Garcia (1997), have countered (with the view based on a narrow premise of Diamond and Dybvig) that the presence of an explicit DIS supports the stability of the financial system by providing the ready bank liquidity with which to assure depositors that they will have immediate access to their funds even if their banks fail and that this will reduce the likelihood of a run on banks and prevent a crisis. So, despite the risks of moral hazard, the introduction of explicit deposit insurance is increasing internationally because it is felt that the benefit of deposit insurance outweighs its costs.

Discouraging bank runs can in itself prevent a sense of panic from spreading in the financial system. Panic and threats to systemic stability can choke off liquidity and cause healthy as well as insolvent banks to fail. Careful structuring of the incentives of the managers of the DIS so that they maintain and protect members' funds, augmented by other agencies responsible for bank monitoring and supervision, is essential for effective deposit insurance to provide market discipline to banks.

In sum, a DIS will provide the financial authorities with standby funding and guidance regarding the decision as to which banks to inject liquidity into and which to let fail. Insolvent banks may fail because they are insolvent – this is a market process. However, sometimes banks are illiquid, but not insolvent. By preventing the failure of banks experiencing a temporary liquidity crisis, an explicit DIS can contribute to financial stability. Thus an explicit DIS with the right balance in design, administrative and managerial incentives, in close collaboration with other agencies, will be more able to make this assessment transparently and ensure stability in the financial system. Giles (1996) sums up this issue well by suggesting that the answer to addressing the difficult question of attaining the correct balance between efficiency and financial stability is to tighten regulation dramatically while retaining comprehensive explicit deposit insurance.

## 4  THE PRICING OF DEPOSIT INSURANCE PREMIUMS

The pricing of the premiums which banks should pay is one of the most contentious issues in explicit deposit insurance design. When structured accurately, the premium paid is derived on a risk-adjusted basis and is also a function of the size of deposits which an institution holds on its balance sheet relative to its loan assets and the performance or non-performance of those assets. For example, in the United States the Federal Deposit Insurance Corporation (FDIC) cuts premium rates for well-capitalized banks and increases them almost punitively for weak banks.[10] The premiums collected from the banks are then held within a fund to be used to pay depositors in the event of a bank insolvency or failure.

Several authors (for example, Merton, 1977, 1978; Marcus and Shaked, 1984; Chan et al., 1992; Bond and Crocker, 1993) have illustrated the difficulty of establishing actuarially and consistently accurate deposit insurance premiums. Merton's studies (1977 and 1978) are still the pathbreaking papers. These two papers mathematically illustrate that deposit insurance is analogous to a put-option in that it creates an incentive for bankers to undertake risks with the knowledge that the bank regulator (hence, the taxpayer) will compensate them (write the option) or provide the right to sell for every level of risk which is undertaken. The majority of the papers in this area follow in Merton's footsteps and attempt to use an option-pricing formula to arrive at an appropriate risk-adjusted price or fair price.[11] Despite these contributions, explicit deposit insurance is still difficult to price. This is because, in practice, it is difficult to establish precisely the actual risks that banks take. Given the simultaneity which (as explained above) may exist between incentives to bank risk taking and explicit deposit insurance, the fact that there is an information lag in the full value of actual risk and that such risk is usually only observable *ex post*, in a socially optimal welfare framework, totally transferable and universally 'fair' explicit deposit insurance is difficult to arrive at. Accordingly in this section, the key theoretical factors which are required to determine a fairly priced explicit DIS are presented so as to illustrate why it is so difficult to achieve in practice.[12]

First, let us make the following assumptions. Let us assume that banks in a capital market operate in a public bank regulatory and corporate tax jurisdiction. Now, let us make the rather more restrictive assumption that debt capital is raised entirely via loans from banks and that the industrial structure of this capital market is competitive[13] and two less restrictive assumptions: the risk-free rate is given by $\delta$ and $\delta \geq 1$ and that we have a two-date economy $t_0$ and $t+1$. For an investing company (IC) to make a return it would have to make an investment into a project or vector of projects, the success or otherwise of which could be assessed over the period $t_0$ to $t+1$. Accordingly an IC can be identified by the success or failure probabilities of its investment projects $\sigma \in [1,0]$. At the microeconomic level any investment project undertaken by the company will require capital investment of $1$[14] and will yield a finite constant $\lambda$ if successful (where $\lambda \geq \delta$) and 0 if unsuccessful. The bank can only observe $\sigma$, the *ex ante* probability of success of an IC project at $t_0$, while at $t+1$ the bank observes the actual success or failure of the IC project. $\sigma$ is observable only to the bank and IC company – the bank regulator does not observe this. The bank regulator observes the lending rate $\Delta$ and $\sigma'$ – the bank loan quality report to determine the extent to which the bank is in deficit or otherwise regarding risk-management and capital adequacy compliance. Depending on the outcome of the regulator's evaluation, a bank will be charged an insurance premium of $\rho(\sigma')$ for every money unit deposit and simultaneously bank equity-holders will increase their capital outlay by $\beta(\sigma')$ per money unit loan.

For simplicity we make three further assumptions. First, the deposit insurance cover is assumed to be provided in full; accordingly the interest rate on deposits is the risk-free rate. Second, as in Chan et al. (1992), the interest rate is used as the full price of the bank loan. In reality there would be collateral and default compensation considerations in the loan price terms. Third, this model assumes that collusive agreements regarding side payments between the bank and IC do not occur. This is an important issue because the regulatory cost of preventing such collusion is very high and the monitoring costs required for the bank regulator to reduce the information asymmetry to be able to control this are prohibitive. Accordingly, if this cannot be prevented, then fair pricing of deposit insurance is impossible.[15]

With these assumptions in place it is possible to proceed under the following structure. An IC with project success [0,1] probability $\sigma$ applies for a loan from a bank and is granted a loan at loan rate $\Delta$. The bank informs the DIS $\sigma'$ and then the DIS charges the bank the deposit insurance premium of $\rho$ ($\sigma'$); in addition the bank is then faced with a equity capitalization charge of $\beta$ ($\sigma'$). Given that the bank is aware of $\sigma$, $\sigma'$, $\rho$ ($\sigma'$), $\beta$ ($\sigma'$), the bank charges $\Delta$ and is faced with the task of designing an optimal algorithm of debt ($D$) and equity ($E$) with which to provide the loan to the IC. In the event of a successful project the DIS faces no financial costs. In this case the IC will pay off the $\Delta$ to the bank and make a positive net present value (NPV) of $\lambda - \Delta$ conditional on paying its depositor liabilities $\delta D$, its tax liabilities $\Delta - (\delta - 1)DT$ and shareholder dividends as applicable. In the event of an unsuccessful project where the IC has defaulted completely on the loan and the non-performance of the loan may cause the bank to become insolvent, depositors' contingent claims $\delta D$ are paid by the deposit insurance fund.

Given that the bank has made a loan of quality $\sigma$ at a loan rate $\Delta$, and has reported $\sigma'$ to the reserve bank and, as a consequence, the regulator has allocated a $\rho(\sigma')$, $\beta(\sigma')$, it is possible to define the bank's loan financing constraint as:

$$1 + \rho(\sigma')D + E \text{ and } E \geq \beta(\sigma'), \tag{22.1}$$

where $\beta(\sigma')$ is the equity capital requirement set by the reserve bank. At any risk-free rate $\delta$, the demand for deposits is elastic and the bank can use deposits to pay its deposit insurance premium as long as its equity capital is greater than or equal to the minimum loan equity capital requirement which is set for it by the DIS – thus $E \geq \rho(\sigma')$. Using deposits to do this should not represent a problem as long as the DIS is confident that the reason for allowing this is not that the bank's equity capital is insufficient. This can be discretionary and could be applied to banks according to their level of capitalization.[16] Some countries do not permit this at all.

Like any other business the bank will choose an appropriate capital structure with which to attempt to maximize the NPV of its equity-holders, $NPV^E(\sigma, \sigma')$. Then, formally, in keeping with equation (22.1), the bank's position can be expressed as:

$$\max NPV^E(\sigma, \sigma') \equiv \frac{\sigma[\Delta(1-T) - \delta D + (\delta-1)DT] - E}{\delta}. \quad (22.2)$$

As well illustrated by Diamond (1984, 1991) and Rajan (1992), the first RHS term of (22.2) is observable to insiders (managers and knowledgeable equity-holders) and is the actual value attributable to the bank's current shareholders. The second RHS term is the cost to equity-holders of making the loan to the IC for project $\sigma$. The actual value of bank equity which is conditioned by the loan quality is not observable to the outsiders (less-informed bank equity-holders, and the bank regulator). While it is impossible for the DIS to fully bridge the gap (that is, to receive full information from the banks) since it is unlikely that outsiders will ever be able to observe a bank's true loan quality, it has to be emphasized that for deposit insurance prices to mirror anything that might be called 'fair' it is necessary for the bank regulator to narrow the gap between insiders and outsiders at *all* banks.[17] We need to remember also that some creditors may be better informed than some equity-holders and the DIS.

Now if we define $s[\sigma, \rho(\sigma')]$ as the net value of deposit insurance subsidy[18] per money unit deposit given $\sigma, \sigma'$ then the total net value of the deposit insurance subsidy can be expressed as follows:

$$\frac{(1-\sigma)\delta D}{\delta} - \rho(\sigma')D = [1 - \sigma - \rho(\sigma')]D. \quad (22.3)$$

The first term in the LHS of (22.3) is the present value of the deposit insurer's contingent liability costs given the true probability of the project failing, the loan quality being the same as that reported, and the true bank insolvency rate that would be available given true information of the aforesaid variables. The second term is the total insurance premium the bank pays to the DIS. Accordingly it is possible to obtain a risk-based deposit insurance premium based on $\sigma'$ as long as:

$$\rho(\sigma')D = 1 - (\sigma') \sigma \varepsilon [0, 1]. \quad (22.4)$$

Accordingly, as Chan et al. (1992) have shown, if the bank's management are provided with the incentive to report truthfully the actual loan quality relative to the loan report so that $\sigma = \sigma'$, then the deposit insurance premium would be actuarially fair because $s[\sigma, (\rho\sigma')] = 0$.

Thus truthful reporting of bank to IC project loan quality and the actual loan quality ($\sigma = \sigma'$) have a significant impact on fair pricing of explicit deposit insurance. In practice achieving this is difficult because it is dependent on *all* banks being honest with the bank regulator. This is unlikely. Second, if the banking sector has a high concentration ratio or Herfindahl index (measured by bank assets or deposits) thus bordering on a monopoly or strong oligopoly structure (as is many developing countries), then the core banks are likely to have banking relationships with major ICs with relatively lower risk.[19] The smaller banks will then normally be left with the relatively higher risks of the margins of the market and therefore are more likely to finance relatively higher-risk IC projects and have *ceteris paribus* a higher incentive to falsely report the project loan quality. Given a risk-weighted system (with overt bias to the risk variables) small banks would then pay a relatively higher risk-related premium price because of their size and type of clients they serve. At the same time the larger banks (which pay *lower risk-related* premiums) are aware that smaller banks have higher-risk clients and potential risks. Since via TBTF dictum, the regulator is to some extent hostage to the large banks, the large banks must be prepared to accept a relatively higher level of enquiry into their activities via special off-site and on-site examinations. This level of enquiry is still likely to be less than that which will be faced by small banks when corrected for scale.

Despite these problems – which can be overcome – the main issue is to ensure that costs are allocated fairly; a risk-adjusted premium is still preferable to a flat-rate premium which carries with it much more moral hazard and free-rider problems. In sum, the primary key to making a fairly priced explicit DIS work lies in creating the incentive mechanism for banks to report truthfully.[20]

## 5   DESIGN FEATURES OF A DEPOSIT INSURANCE SCHEME

It can be argued that conditions in the banking industry over the last 20 years are at least partly the result of exogenous sectoral shocks and peculiarities in the competitive and micro-regulatory structure. Whether these factors caused an increase in moral hazard, or are the result of moral hazard, is worthy of debate. Yet relative to the pressing practical concern of reforming deposit insurance – given what we know of the dangers of inadequate design – such debate may be trivial.

As can be deduced, most of the discussion on reforming deposit insurance design has focused on ways of reducing moral hazard via the imposition of tougher public sector bank regulation and monitoring. However, the role of the market as the optimal bank monitor is increasingly gaining ground; for example, see Dowd (1994 and 1996). In their considerations of deposit insurance, the 'free banking school' often cite the problems of moral hazard and adverse selection and state that at the least, if explicit deposit insurance is introduced then it should only be for banks operating in a 'narrow' range of banking activities and that banks which can engage in 'universal' activities should not be members.[21]

Two recent suggestions for reforming explicit deposit insurance which are based on increasing the monitoring and self-regulation role of the market to reduce the possibility of moral hazard are worth mentioning. The first suggestion is based on the narrow banking concept and therefore it is not exactly new. The suggestion is that deposit insurance should be explicitly limited to cover only banks that pay a relatively low rate of interest. In addition, insured deposits should be more than fully backed by relatively safe and liquid assets such as treasury bills and commercial bonds. The main difference in this suggestion to the standard narrow bank idea is that, in effect, it calls for narrow banks within universal banks and so does not require a major restructuring of the banking industry – with separate narrow banking firms.

Although this alteration of the original narrow banking idea makes it more feasible, the main criticism of this approach is that a deposit insurance scheme cannot function well without effective bank supervision. Indeed, the narrow/universal banking split increases the administrative costs and complexity of off-site and on-site bank monitoring and supervision and the expectations placed on the agencies responsible for bank supervision. A further problem with this narrow banking approach is that with costly equity issuance, it can impose large deadweight financing costs and reduce positive NPV investments funded by the banking system. Furthermore, it calls for heavy information requirements which inhibit incentive-compatible designs in obtaining optimal bank-specific results. It is therefore debatable as to whether the narrow/universal limited coverage split will yield benefits (reduction in moral hazard and adverse selection) that outweigh the costs of the increase in complexity which it will bring to bank monitoring and supervision.

The second idea involves the use of subordinated debt. The most detailed exposition of this idea has been put forward by Calomiris (1991) and further expanded in Calomiris (1997) and Haubrich (1998). The suggestion is that a system should be established in which banks issue subordinated debt instruments to each other. This debt should be equal to approximately 2 per cent of assets and it should be junior to deposits. Since the incentives of debt-holders are similar to those of the DIS and therefore of taxpayers – if the bank becomes insolvent or fails – then the debt-holders would lose money.[22] The important contribution of this suggestion lies not in what happens in the event of insolvency or failure, but rather in the fact that unlike bank shareholders, creditors have no incentive to encourage risk-taking behaviour. This is because, irrespective of the returns obtained from taking higher risk, the most they will receive is the value of the yield on their fixed income instrument. Since the yield on this subordinated debt would reflect the market assessment of the risks which the bank is taking, bank regulators would then cap this yield and this would force the bank to cap its risks. An important contribution of this suggestion is that indications of high risk would be provided by the market and not by the regulator.

This is an elegant idea which is being considered seriously by bank regulators, particularly in developed countries. And therein lies its major problem. It is an idea which is likely to work well in countries where the capital market is well developed and market signals are efficient. Given this fact, it would be difficult to use in emerging markets and extremely difficult to use in developing-country markets.[23]

**Practical Deposit Insurance Design Solutions**

Given the practical difficulties associated with the more radical explicit deposit insurance reform suggestions presented above, most practical suggestions, for example Berlin et al. (1991), are based on two approaches. The first approach calls for further use of risk-based insurance premiums, higher capital levels, increased use of market value accounting, non-discretionary forbearance and closure policies to increase discipline on bank equity-holders. The second approach calls for capping the level of coverage provided to depositors and reducing the scope of coverage afforded to creditors so that debt-holder discipline increases.

Accordingly, reforms in deposit insurance design currently taking place in many countries are based on a mix of the first and second approaches. However, given the differences in the structure of financial and legal systems in different countries, it is difficult to envisage a DIS which can be readily transferred internationally. Therefore, while lessons may be learned from international experience, it is not easy to generalize about deposit insurance design, since this is determined by the specific nature of the banking and financial services sector in each country. As can be seen in the appendix (Table 22A.1), DIS design varies by country. However, there are some design features which should be universally applicable to all countries.

The financial health of the banking system should be reflected in the nature and design of the DIS of every country. In fact Kane (1999) uses a minimum–maximum transparency and minimum–maximum deterrence framework to provide a convincing argument for the inclusion of other country-specific variables such as the levels of adherence to international accounting standards, levels of corruption, transparency and protection of property rights. In addition, Stern (1998) suggests that a strong independent central bank is also important for well-structured explicit deposit insurance.

The need for a rationale which underpins explicit deposit insurance should be communicated to all interest groups – banks, regulators, taxpayers and, most importantly, retail depositors. Banks should be encouraged to participate in the communication process to their depositors.[24] Insured banks must understand that the financial implications, licence withdrawal procedures, removal from membership of a DIS and explicit guarantees are based on the specific tenets of the rule of law. Allied to this international prudential regulatory, supervisory, compliance and accounting and valuation principles as outlined in the 1997 Core Principles for Effective Banking Supervision of the Basle Banking Committee must be consistently applied to ensure efficacy of any explicit or implicit DIS. This is taking on great importance as international capital markets become more integrated and capital moves ever more freely.

Membership of a DIS must be compulsory for all retail banks. If membership of a DIS is non-compulsory, it creates loopholes and increases the likelihood that some sections of the industry will attempt to free ride on others. Furthermore, as the findings of Wheelock and Khumbakar (1995) which were noted earlier illustrate, this might lead to a reluctance of some well-capitalized members to participate, which might lead to adverse selection. On the other hand, it may increase moral hazard if they decide to participate.[25] This is likely to undermine public sector deposit insurance schemes. A further point which supports compulsory membership is that the cost of paying for any form of insurance is least when it is spread across a larger number of members. From a risk perspective the cost incurred by members would be increasingly optimal if the size of the membership were homogeneous, the risk profile known and not correlated and the geographical base of member banks well diversified. In theory this would increase the actuarial probability of arriving at a fair insurance cost. Indeed, using the normal distribution, this should improve once the number of members exceeds 30.

However, the reality is that bank failures are not independently distributed, and in many countries bank deposits are highly concentrated in a small number of very large banks. If membership is not made compulsory for all retail banks, it may be limited to the weak, poorly managed and fragile institutions which therefore have the incentive to be members. So banks which the bank regulator assesses as being fragile will have to meet specified monitoring and supervisory targets prior to membership. Using its regular on-site and off-site supervision process, the bank regulator provides the DIS with prudential information on all banks and the potential contribution to DIS liabilities that these banks present and the possibility of the banks being able to meet the specified targets, prior to their membership of the DIS being acceptable. It is also worth noting that in their study of banking in transition economies, Morton et al. (1998) suggest that some banks may exit the industry or choose to change the focus of their business away from the retail sector as a result of the introduction of a tighter regulatory regime of which compulsory explicit deposit insurance may be a facet. While this is not impossible, bank regulatory authorities are not in the position to conjecture what banks will *actually* do if a DIS is introduced. However, if membership is not made compulsory for *all* retail banks, some banks will free ride on others and undermine the entire system. While the primary rationale for making DIS membership compulsory for all retail banks has been provided above, it should also be noted that membership is compulsory in 26 of the 43 countries in the 1995 World Bank survey of explicit deposit insurance systems. The key findings of this survey are summarized in the appendix (Table 22A.1).

**Institutional Efficiency**

The decision-making processes for effective prudential regulation usually become more complex as a result of the introduction of a DIS. This is because the establishment of a separate department for managing the DIS might create a bureaucratic tension between the DIS and other bank regulatory agencies. This can be used effectively to get the best from the different agencies. However, this has to be managed very carefully. Accordingly, there is a need to define and separate the functions of the competing agencies, even if they have to collaborate closely.

In many countries the DIS relies primarily on other agencies to provide it with general bank supervision information. In addition, the other agencies are called upon to carry out specific investigations from time to time as required to enable the DIS to have the level of prudential information it needs to allow for efficient attainment of its mandate, for example establishing risk-based premiums and the stratification of banks into capital-premium categories.[26] The DIS is usually left to concentrate on its primary role, which is to protect depositors' funds by protecting its assets. In short, any bank inspections and prudential investigations which the DIS calls for from the other agencies or undertakes itself usually remain a byproduct of its primary function. The DIS will normally use the standard prudential information provided by the bank regulator to meet its mandate.

## Deposit Insurance Coverage Limits

One of the most important design issues is the coverage limit which can and should be provided by a DIS. Usually all deposits are protected up to a specific cap or limit, and international best practice is that the DIS should provide cover for depositors, not accounts – up to the specified limit. However, in determining the coverage cap or limit for a DIS there is a need to assess the basis on which the limit should be set. It is possible to set the limit on the basis of each separate account at a failed bank. However this is potentially expensive, since depositors would spread their deposits across as many accounts up to the limit as possible. It is also possible to set the limit for all accounts owned by an individual investor at all banks that fail during a specific period. This has a double-edged effect in that on the one hand it would limit the period of time during which the DIS is liable and thus might reduce its potential liability to depositors. However, in the event of widespread crisis the cost to the DIS of meeting all its potential liabilities could be very high.

A further system is one wherein a depositor is allowed to be compensated only up to a specific limit during his/her lifetime. Thus, in such a DIS, if a depositor has been paid out before, from the DIS, up to the pre-set limit and is unfortunate enough to have placed his/her deposits in another bank which subsequently fails, then that depositor will only be compensated up to the pre-set limit. While this places a correct emphasis on individual bank monitoring – in keeping with the views of Kane (1999) (noted earlier) – such a system is likely to be inappropriate in many developing countries given the low level of education and capacity for monitoring which most depositors in those countries currently have. It might, however, be useful in that it would create further incentives for bank corporate creditors and depositors – who by definition have better monitoring and market information – to select their bank more carefully.

In the event of bank failure, given the size and nature of their transactions, corporate depositors tend to seek to move their funds to solvent banks – small depositors will usually run to cash. The last of the four limit criteria is one which covers the sum of all accounts held by any individual depositor at a failed bank. Under this scheme, the DIS would be most exposed in the event of a systemic crisis or if several banks failed at the same time. Garcia (1999) finds that it is becoming widely accepted that this DIS design, in which the limit is capped on the sum of all accounts held by an individual depositor, is best for most countries. This is because it reduces the likelihood of the DIS incurring high costs as a result of depositor fraud, moral hazard and adverse selection. Depositors would still have the right, and may choose, to have deposits in more than one bank, however, the incentive to free-riding by depositors (some would say effective diversification of deposits) is reduced since the limit is placed on the sum of all deposits held per individual at a failed bank.

Moral hazard will also be reduced since, once past the limit, depositors will not benefit from diversifying their deposits in accounts within the same bank. As a result, prudent banks will have less incentive to take risks. Less well-managed, but more risk-prone, banks which may compromise the stability of the financial system will also be less likely to be adversely selected by the market as a result of the provision of a free ride by the DIS.

Having explained the need to avoid creating inappropriate incentives in establishing the level of coverage, it is useful to briefly explain the ways in which the actual financial limit is arrived at in most countries. The financial limit is usually arrived at via two methods – the statistical bank liability method (SBLM) and the GDP per capita method (GDPPCM). The SBLM calls for the bank regulator to analyse the distribution and statistical properties (mode, median, mode) of deposits within the entire banking system. This will indicate the size and structure of deposits within the system and the proportion of total deposits which will be covered if a particular limit is set. This system has the advantage that in theory the limit can be adjusted downwards if the mean of the size of deposits declines. Given the rarity of zero inflation, it is unlikely that this theoretical benefit will accrue – there is likely to be more pressure for the level of coverage to increase given that the average nominal size of deposits is more likely to increase than decrease. The GDPPCM has proved fairly popular in many countries. In this method, the limit is set as a ratio of the country's GDP per capita. This is used as proxy for the level of deposits and avoids the costs and time involved in arriving at a statistical limit structure as explained above. Most countries use a ratio of between one and five times the level of GDP per capita.

An appropriate coverage limit level should be set with the objective of encouraging depositor confidence without compromising financial stability. As explained above, the SBLM is more complex, but may not necessarily be any more accurate in meeting the overall requirements. On close examination of the appendix table, the coverage limit in the 43 DIS summarized therein is fairly well correlated with the income per capita of the countries. The trend indicates that wealthier countries tend to have higher compensation limits and vice versa.

**Deposit Insurance and Failed Institutions**

If banks experience difficulties, there might be political pressure for the regulatory authorities to exercise forbearance. Davies and McManus

(1991) model bank closure policy for risk-averse banks in a flat deposit insurance regime. They find that increasing the net worth at which banks are closed can either increase or decrease risk-aversion, but will most certainly increase the likelihood that weak but still solvent banks will be subject to moral hazard.[27] This is in line with the findings of Acharya (1996) who uses simulations of risk taking to illustrate that an optimal DIS forbearance framework for an insolvent bank alleviates (but does not fully remove) moral hazard, if it leaves the bank with a large enough charter value. In addition, the results of Davies and McManus (1991) and Acharya (1996) imply that more timely (perhaps some form of optimal) closure policies should be imposed in conjunction with greater monitoring of bank portfolio risk and with restrictions on risk taking for weak banks. Indeed, depending on the correlation of asset returns, changes in closure policy can increase or decrease desired leverage. So reducing forbearance may be most effective in limiting the losses of deposit insurance funds, if it is accompanied by restrictions on bank risk taking for banks with low but positive net worth.

Such findings support the argument for enabling legislation for the DIS to have an effective exit strategy. It is important that the DIS has clear, mandatory and universally applicable measures and the availability of criteria for the ultimate sanction of closure. In addition, every DIS should be able to provide quick reimbursement and compensation to all depositors within a specific timeframe. This timeframe needs to be communicated and explained to depositors. International practice varies from between two weeks and 12 weeks depending on the nature and complexity of the bank resolution. Once the DIS closes a bank, it will, in principle, pay off the deposit liabilities of the bank to depositors. Such a bank will usually be insolvent; in other words, its non-performing assets will be larger than its equity capital. By paying off the depositors (creditors) of the bank, the DIS will assume control of the bank by capitalizing the payment made to depositors within the balance sheet of the bank. The DIS will then be responsible for and have control of the workout process, and pursue non-performing assets where appropriate. Only after the funds used to recapitalize the bank to acceptable regulatory limits have been reimbursed and other senior creditors to the bank have been paid will bank equity-holders be considered.

Accordingly, as Tirole (1994) and Benink (1998) point out, there is therefore a need to throw more light and increase objectivity and transparency on the steps taken by regulators, particularly if it emerges that a bank is insolvent. This will enhance the efficiency of industry entry (bank licensing) and exit (licence withdrawal) debate. This debate is very important, particularly if the view is taken that inadequately capitalized and managed 'zombie' banks crowd out well-managed and capitalized banks, present a super-ordinary regulatory cost to bank regulators, carry higher real social welfare costs than any benefits which they may provide by being in existence, and at the mean have a higher probability of destabilizing the system. This is a particular problem if the bank is considered too big to fail and regulatory capture increases.

Finally, since bank supervision and monitoring already requires high financial and administrative costs, every country needs to be sure that the total benefits (economic, social and financial) of an explicit DIS approximates the financial costs. Given the symbiotic relationship between deposit insurance design and bank insolvency, as Caprio and Klingebiel (1996) note, attempts at developing and reforming the DIS will need to weave in the history and to some extent the reasons for bank insolvency. It is only after a detailed analysis of the reasons why banks have become insolvent that meaningful policy can be developed on appropriate DIS design.

## 6 CONCLUSIONS AND POLICY IMPLICATIONS

In conclusion, this chapter has presented a discussion of deposit insurance with particular emphasis on explicit DIS. The demand for and rate of introduction of explicit DIS suggests that more countries are in favour of this form. But as a result of the differences in the structure of financial and legal systems in different countries, it is difficult to envisage a readily internationally transferable deposit insurance system. Therefore, while lessons may indeed be learned by sharing international experience, it is not easy to generalize about deposit insurance design since it would be a function of the nature of the banking and financial services sector, which are in themselves a function of other factors. Put in a welfare context, given that regulation is not costless in all countries, there is a need to design a DIS in which the economic and social benefits of the DIS approximates the financial costs.

The policy implications are that given what we know of the history and consequences of explicit deposit insurance, the main essential ingredients of an effective DIS are that it must be provided with independent, legal and regulatory authority, that it should be empowered to take remedial action against insolvent or failing institutions and that failing institutions need to be resolved quickly. In addition, the amount of each deposit covered by the deposit insurance fund needs to be kept small and retail bank membership of the scheme must be compulsory so as to avoid adverse selection. Finally, insured depositors are to be paid quickly, and most important of all, premiums should be risk based.

It should be emphasized that if care is not taken in the distribution of disciplinary and market incentives to depositors, banks and regulatory agencies, explicit DIS may carry with them more economic (financial and social) costs than benefits. Accordingly, deposit insurance design must attempt to minimize the possibility of moral hazard. In particular, bank regulators need to ensure that the differences in size, length of time of bank charter and the industrial structure of the retail banking sector do not distort the efficacy of prudential regulation. Second, the principle of imposing a limit which covers the bulk of the distribution of retail deposits should be studiously maintained. Therefore a major emphasis in design has to be placed on avoiding excess coverage – recalling that excess coverage (rather than under coverage) is likely to cause moral hazard. Accordingly, the coverage limit needs to be carefully calculated and set at a level which can be met in each country without encouraging increased risk taking by banks. All the moral hazard problems inherent in explicit deposit insurance should be placed in an appropriate context and compared with the cost of not having a ready mechanism or dedicated funds when banks fail. This implies that while it may not be possible to remove the moral hazard component inherent in explicit deposit insurance, attempts should be made to manage it.

There are still unresolved issues in deposit insurance design. From the standpoint of deterrence, the important and as yet unresolved consideration is whether government intervention or incentives to greater market discipline are the better regulators of moral hazard in explicit DIS design. There are also perhaps more subtle issues, which despite their indirectness are of great importance. For example, we are still unclear as to what the best level of public involvement in deposit insurance should be and the extent to which private monitoring can mitigate supervisory failure. Furthermore, we are still unclear as to how the value of bank charters and the structure of the banking industry within a particular regime can distort incentives and create adverse selection. We are also unclear as to whether these factors are additive, multiplicative and, as Kane (1999) suggests, we are unsure as to exactly how (or if) they interact with variables which capture the level of corruption, transparency and inadequate adherence to accounting standards. Other questions which are still unanswered are: given the differences in the structure of financial and legal systems in different countries, is it possible to design an internationally transferable deposit insurance system? If so, is such a system desirable? If not, what is the way forward for deposit insurance design? Providing theoretically sound and practical answers to these issues will enable us to include these findings in DIS design. Any enquiry which attempts to answer these questions will in the process throw light on the important relationship between bank insolvency, financial stability and the economic implications of deposit insurance schemes.[28] Continuing the deposit insurance debate is in the public interest.

## NOTES

\*  I am grateful to Mrs Joan King for very helpful research assistance.
1. Mishkin (1996) presents a useful information asymmetry framework with which to understand the causes of lack of confidence in the banking system and the subsequent instability.
2. I have used the abbreviation DIS, which stands for 'deposit insurance scheme', throughout this chapter. Some countries with explicit deposit insurance have a deposit insurance agency – sometimes referred to as the deposit insurance corporation with full legal body corporate status, for example the United States, Canada and Nigeria. Others, for example, the United Kingdom and Germany, do not have a specific agency. In such cases the DIS is usually housed in one of the other financial institutions' regulators. Accordingly, for simplicity the abbreviation DIS is used herein in a generic sense to describe an explicit deposit insurance scheme and/or deposit insurance agency or fund.
3. This crisis in particular led to the restructuring of deposit insurance in the United States via the enactment in 1991 of the Federal Deposit Insurance Corporation Improvement Act (FDICIA). Kaufman (1995) explains FDICIA attempts to correct two specific deposit insurance problems which in his view contributed to the problems faced by the US banking industry. FDICIA addresses two moral hazard problems – insufficient capital and the agency problems caused by the level of forbearance extended by the Federal Deposit Insurance Corporation (FDIC).
4. Yet Garcia (1993 and 1997) identifies three specific reasons for introducing explicit deposit insurance schemes. First, to enable the banking and regulatory authorities to have the resources available to meet liquidity problems for healthy banks. Second, in the event of bank failures to have the available liquidity to be able to reimburse deposits to their legal owners up to a pre-set limit and to be able to protect small, uninformed and unsophisticated depositors with a financial safety net. Third, to instil greater confidence among depositors and increase the likelihood of financial stability. In addition, Russell (1993), while acknowledging the presence of moral hazard, states that an explicit DIS can serve as an extra source of liquidity, particularly during panics, and that this is an essential contribution to bank regulation.
5. White (1990) explains how an inappropriate incentive regime in the design of the US deposit insurance scheme created moral hazard which led to the failure of numerous savings and loans deposit institutions.
6. Von Thadden (1997) presents a model with several investment opportunities in which banks have the additional function of asset diversification. This pooling of intermediation functions is shown to reduce the moral hazard problem, thereby enhancing the stability of depository contracts and increasing the scope of the banks' deposit insurance function.
7. In their study of risk-taking behaviour of life insurance companies, Brewer et al. (1997) find that risk taking by life insurers is higher in jurisdictions where the state guaranty provides partial protection to life insurance liability holders. In states where taxpayers pay for the costs of resolving insolvencies, life insurers hold portfolios with higher overall stock market risk and higher levels of risky assets. By contrast, in states where the guaranty funds are underwritten by the industry, overall risk is no higher than in states without these funds. However, Karels and McClatchey (1999) have shown that deposit insurance did not increase risk-taking behaviour in the US credit union industry.
8. Marshall (1994) investigates the level of risk taking and the consequences of the deregulation of the Indonesian commercial banking sector which began in 1988. She finds that despite the central bank's efforts to reduce loan refinancing programmes at state banks, the reforms led to a significant increase in the size of bank assets. Given the level of bank insolvencies and failures which have taken place in Indonesia since 1997, with the benefit of hindsight, it would appear that the observers who suggested (at the time the reforms were being introduced) that the expansion was driven by unsound lending practices motivated by deposit insurance moral hazard have been proved correct.

9. Peek and Rosengreen's findings have related implications. First, they augment the bad press which value-at-risk models have received recently, since the level of skill and sophistication of management capacity in banks varies widely. Second, some banks, particularly those in developing countries, lack the capacity and skills to use the system while others are able to and should be further encouraged along this road.
10. In the United States in 1992, the deposit insurance premium paid by banks ranged from 0.23 cents per US$100 of deposits to 0.31 cents per US$100 of deposits.
11. Urrutia (1990) is one of the few papers to use a non-option-price approach to attempt to develop a model for risk-adjusted premium pricing. His model uses coinsurance and deductible clauses for deposit insurance. The model suggests that coinsurance and deductibles reduce the liabilities of the DIS and also reduce the size of the insurance premium which the usual option-price-based model would forecast.
12. Giammarino et al. (1993) have illustrated that three conditions must hold to enable a risk-adjusted socially optimal fair premium. First, asset quality has to be below the first-best level. Second, higher-quality banks should have larger asset bases and therefore also face lower capital adequacy requirements than lower-quality banks. And third, the probability of failure should be equally distributed across banks.
13. The first assumption mitigates the impact of the relationship between loan quality and loan interest rates given the interaction of the non-bank and bank capital markets. The second assumption is tenuous in a market environment where there is a high concentration of loan assets. Monopoly or non-competitive oligopoly power may mean that loan interest rates do not fully reflect loan quality.
14. One (1) monetary unit, for example, dollar, pound and so on.
15. Chan et al. (1992) analyse risk-sensitive, incentive-compatible deposit insurance and explain why fairly priced deposit insurance is impossible in a competitive banking system with private information and moral hazard. They show that the DIS can obtain truthful disclosure regarding the risk structure of bank asset portfolios without intrusive monitoring and that this can be achieved by offering banks capital requirement schedules which are inversely related to deposit insurance premiums, given that each bank is permitted to choose its most preferred combination. However, such a framework will only work in a competitive banking industry if deposit-linked subsidies are provided. (Recent findings by Nagarajan and Sealey (1998) suggest that in an appropriate incentive-compatible regulatory framework, a subsidy to the bank is not necessary.) However, since perfectly competitive DIS does not completely remove deposit subsidies in pricing loans, positive bank charter values are maintained and this makes incentive compatibility feasible. This is an important policy issue, in that prior to the development and introduction of an incentive-compatible deposit scheme, it is necessary to evaluate what the supervisory and monitoring costs of preventing bank–IC collusion might be.
16. If $E \geq \rho(\sigma')$, then this might be allowed – other factors such as the regulatory history of the bank, and in particular evidence relating to *ex post* evaluation of the deviation of its in-house risk management and value-at-risk models will be taken into consideration. Of course if $E \leq \rho(\sigma')$ then this should never be allowed. In addition, Duan and Yu (1994) develop a multiperiod deposit insurance pricing model. They explicitly incorporate capital forbearance and moral hazard into their model and make two useful contributions. First, their model illustrates that a fairly priced premium is not neutral to forbearance policy even in the absence of moral hazard. Second, their model formally explains how excessive risk taking under capital forbearance can cause financial system instability by increasing the liabilities of a DIS.
17. This is one of the reasons why Okeahalam (1998) recommends the establishment of an explicit deposit insurance system in South Africa.
18. If the bank uses deposits to finance its loan portfolio, there is the possibility that it can benefit from two sources of subsidy. First, it can benefit from the classic Modigliani–Miller debt preference capital structure and derive marginal tax benefits on interest payments. Second, it can receive a subsidy by providing a false report on the true loan quality $\sigma'$ of the loan it has made to the IC for project $\sigma$.

19. High concentration levels exist in the banking sectors of developed countries, but as explained earlier, the significance which banks play in the supply of debt finance is decreasing.
20. At times improper sequencing of the bank deregulatory process, particularly when coupled with inadequately designed explicit deposit insurance or an implicit deposit insurance scheme with adverse selection features, results in insufficient monitoring and supervision which distorts risk–reward incentives and encourages free-riding banks to create and benefit from the put-option hypothesized in Merton (1978). Since regulation is not a free good, banks should be provided with incentives to self-regulation. Whether this is via in-house value-at-risk (VaR) management models is debatable – but nevertheless, there need to be further incentives to ensure bank compliance. This has regulatory and moral hazard implications in that it may, in the first instance, determine the level of monitoring which (subject to review) a specific bank should be placed under in a particular regulatory regime and, in the second instance, should reduce the free-rider situation which often arises when a move to greater *laissez-faire* takes place or when deposit insurance is introduced.
21. Under this free market proposal, banks with 'universal' banking charters would not be covered by explicit deposit insurance. Depositors doing business with such banks would be informed of this and the regulator would ensure that banks with such charters informed depositors accordingly as part of the deposit receipt process. Other banks would have limits or a 'narrow' range of products which they could provide to the consumers and the deposits held at such institutions would be fully covered by the deposit insurance fund in line with statutory limits as explained above.
22. If depositors are also considered to be bank debt-holders, then a further related deposit insurance moral hazard reform issue is the extent to which uninsured depositors are made to bear some of the risk in bank failures. Stern (1998) suggests that the moral hazard problem of deposit insurance is caused by the absence of deductibles. The US Congress became aware of this fact and accordingly FDICIA has tried to make the protection of uninsured depositors less likely by giving regulators new tools with which to close a troubled bank before large losses ever develop. This reform places the emphasis on uninsured depositors to increase the monitoring of their banks' activity. If depositors are subjected to limited but meaningful loss, the market for information about the financial condition of banks will certainly broaden and deepen over time – which should influence bank behaviour and commitment to safe and sound practices.
23. A creditor's absolute level of information asymmetry depends on the level of monitoring and search cost which he or she carries out and incurs as part of their risk assessment of the bank. Any *relative* level of asymmetric information advantage should be a function of the level of efficiency of the capital market. The extent of information asymmetry will then be dependent on the extent to which the capital market is efficient in the weak, semi-strong or strong form sense. The evidence suggests that the majority of capital markets in developing (African) countries are not information efficient (see Okeahalam and Jefferis, 1999).
24. Usually after a DIS is established, all member institutions are expected to display the fact that they are insured members in such a way that retail depositors are made aware.
25. It has been suggested that the costs of moral hazard might be less than the cost of providing a resolution to a banking crisis. Sometimes moral hazard is the cause of the crisis, sometimes it is not. It can further be argued that narrow banking carries the cost of reduced liquidity and so is not a costless solution since the benefits of wide availability of bank intermediated credit may outweigh the costs of providing a safety net for it via explicit deposit insurance.
26. In the US there are five categories – well capitalized, adequately capitalized, undercapitalized, significantly undercapitalized and critically undercapitalized. All banks are stratified according to their ability to meet prudential guidelines.
27. In their study of the incentive-compatible role of regulatory forbearance, Nagarajan and Sealey (1995) find that when a bank's asset portfolio has market risk, the regulator can influence the bank's choice of *ex ante* risk by delaying the closure of an insolvent bank. The optimal closure framework is therefore dependent on effective coordination of the

closure decision with market-wide performance variables. Accordingly such a closure framework may alleviate the bank's *ex ante* risk-shifting problem.
28. Demirguc-Kunt and Detragiache (1999) have started on this road. They use limited dependent variable econometrics to explore a panel data set with explanatory variables of deposit insurance design features of 61 countries. Their preliminary findings suggests that explicit deposit insurance has a negative impact on bank stability and that the adverse impact is positively correlated with higher coverage and public management of the scheme.

# REFERENCES

Acharya, S. (1996, 'Charter value, minimum bank capital requirement and deposit insurance pricing in equilibrium', *Journal of Banking and Finance*, **20**, 351–75.
Benink, H. (1998), 'Dealing with problem banks', *The Banker*, August, 24–5.
Berlin M., Saunders, A. and Udell, G.F. (1991), 'Deposit insurance reform: what are the issues and what needs to be fixed?, *Journal of Banking and Finance*, **15**, 735–52.
Bhattacharya S., Boot, A.W.A. and Thakor, A.V. (1998), 'The economics of bank regulation', *Journal of Money, Credit, and Banking*, **30**, 745–70.
Bodenhorn, H.(1996), 'Zombie banks and the demise of New York's Safety Fund', *Eastern Economic Journal*, **22**, 21–33.
Bond, E. and Crocker, K. (1993), 'Bank capitalization, deposit insurance and risk categorization', *Journal of Risk and Insurance*, **60**, 547–69.
Brewer E., Mondeschean, T.S. and Strahan, P.E. (1997), 'The role of monitoring in reducing the moral hazard problem associated with government guarantees: evidence from the life insurance industry', *Journal of Risk and Insurance*, **64**, 301–22.
Calomiris, C. (1990), 'Is deposit insurance necessary?', *Journal of Economic History*, **50**, 283–95.
Calomiris, C. (1991), 'The role of demandable debt in structuring optimal banking arrangements', *American Economic Review*, **81**, 497–513.
Calomiris, C. (1997), *The Postmodern Bank Safety Net: Lessons from Developed and Developing Countries*, Washington, DC: American Enterprise Studies.
Caprio, G. and Klingebiel, D. (1996), 'Bank insolvency: bad luck, bad policy or bad banking?', in M. Bruno and B. Plekovic (eds), *Proceedings of the Annual World Bank Conference on Development Economics*, Washington, DC: World Bank, 79–104.
Chan, Y.S., Greenbaum, S.I. and Thakor, A.V. (1992), 'Is fairly priced deposit insurance possible?', *Journal of Finance*, **47**, 227–45.
Crawford, A.J., Ezzell, J.R. and Miles, J.A. (1995), 'Bank CEO pay–performance relations and the effects of deregulation', *Journal of Business*, **68**(2), 231–56.
Davies, S.M. and McManus, D.A. (1991), 'The effects of closure policies on bank risk taking', *Journal of Banking and Finance*, **15**, 917–38.
Demirguc-Kunt, A. and Detragiache, E. (1999), 'Does deposit insurance increase banking system instability? An empirical investigation', Unpublished Joint World Bank and IMF Research Paper.
Demirguc-Kunt, A. and Kane, E.J. (1998), 'Deposit insurance: issues of design and implementation', World Bank research proposal, February.
Diamond, D. (1984), 'Financial intermediation and delegated monitoring', *Review of Economic Studies*, **51**, 393–414.
Diamond, D. (1991), 'Monitoring and reputation: the choice between bank loans and directly placed debt', *Journal of Political Economy*, **99**, 689–721.

Diamond, D. and Dybvig, P. (1983), 'Bank runs, deposit insurance and liquidity', *Journal of Political Economy*, **91**, 401–19.
Dowd, K. (1994), 'Competitive banking, bankers' clubs and bank regulation', *Journal of Money, Credit, and Banking*, **26**, 289–308.
Dowd, K. (1996), 'The case for financial *laissez-faire*', *Economic Journal*, **106**, 679–87.
Duan, J. and Yu, M. (1994), 'Forbearance and pricing deposit insurance in a multi-period framework', *Journal of Risk and Insurance*, **61**, 575–91.
Flood, M.D. (1996), 'The great deposit insurance debate', in D.M. Papadimitriou (ed.), *Stability in the Financial System*, Basingstoke: Macmillan.
Fraser, D.R. and Zardkoohi, A. (1996), 'Ownership structure, deregulation and risk in the savings and loan industry', *Journal of Business Research*, **37**, 63–9.
Garcia, G.G. (1993), 'Financial reform and the enforcement problem', *Cato Journal*, **13**, 229–42.
Garcia, G.G. (1997), 'Protecting bank deposits', Economic Issues No. 9, International Monetary Fund, Washington, DC.
Garcia, G.G. (1999), 'Deposit insurance: a survey of actual and best practice', IMF Working Paper, Washington, DC.
Giammarino, R.M., Lewis, T.R. and Sappington D.E.M. (1993), 'An incentive based approach to banking regulation', *Journal of Finance*, **48**, 1523–42.
Giles, M. (1996), 'Safe banking', *The Economist*, 27 April.
Gorton, G. and Rosen, R. (1995), 'Corporate control, portfolio choice and the decline of banking', *Journal of Finance*, **50**, 1377–420.
Grossman, R.S. (1992), 'Deposit insurance, regulation and moral hazard in the thrift industry: evidence from the 1930s', *American Economic Review*, **82**, 800–821.
Gunther J.W. and Robinson, K.J. (1990), 'Moral hazard and Texas banking in the 1980s: was there a connection?', Federal Reserve Bank of Dallas Financial Industry Studies, 1–8.
Haubrich J.G. (1998), 'Subordinated debt: tougher love for banks?', Economics Commentary, Federal Reserve Bank of Cleveland, 1–4.
Heifer, R.T. (1999), 'What deposit insurance can and can not do', *Finance and Development*, **36**, 22–5.
Hooks, L. and Robinson, K.J. (1996), 'Moral hazard and Texas banking in the 1920s', Federal Reserve Bank of Dallas Financial Industry Studies, No. 96, 1–35.
Kane, E.J. (1999), 'Designing financial safety nets to fit country circumstances', Paper presented at the Annual Bank Conference on Development Economics, World Bank, Washington, DC.
Karels, G.V. and McClatchey, C.A. (1999), 'Deposit insurance and risk-taking behavior in the credit union industry', *Journal of Banking and Finance*, **23**, 105–34.
Kaufman, G.S. (1995), 'FDICIA and bank capital', *Journal of Banking and Finance*, **19**, 721–2.
Kupic P.H. and O'Brien, J.M. (1998), 'Deposit insurance, bank incentives and the design of monetary policy', *Economic Policy Review*, **4**, 201–11.
Marcus, A. and Shaked, I. (1984), 'The valuation of the FDIC deposit insurance using option-pricing estimates', *Journal of Money, Credit, and Banking*, **14**, 446–60.
Marshall, K.G. (1994), 'Competition and growth: changes in Indonesia's banking sector since 1988', *Journal of Asian Business*, **10**, 11–30.
Mazumdar S.C. (1996), 'Bank regulations, capital structure and risk', *Journal of Financial Services Research*, **19**(2), 209–28.
Merton, R.C. (1977), 'An analytical derivation of the cost of deposit insurance and

loan guarantees: an application to modern option pricing theory', *Journal of Banking and Finance*, **1**, 3–11.

Merton, R.C. (1978), 'On the cost of deposit insurance when there are surveillance costs', *Journal of Business*, **51**, 439–52.

Mishkin F.S. (1996), 'Understanding financial crises: a developing country perspective', in *Proceedings of the Annual World Bank Conference on Development Economics*, M. Bruno and B. Pleskovic (eds), Washington, DC: World Bank, pp. 29–62.

Morton, G., Winton, A. and Claessens, S. (1998), 'Banking in transition economies: does efficiency require instability?', *Journal of Money, Credit, and Banking*, **30**, 621–55.

Nagarajan, S. and Sealey, C.W. (1995), 'Forbearance, deposit insurance pricing and incentive compatible bank regulation,' *Journal of Banking and Finance*, **19**, 1109–30.

Nagarajan, S. and Sealey, C.W. (1998), 'State-contingent regulatory mechanisms and fairly priced deposit insurance', *Journal of Banking and Finance*, **22**, 1139–56.

Okeahalam C.C. (1998), 'The political economy of bank failure and supervision in the Republic of South Africa', *African Journal of Political Science*, **3**(2), 29–48.

Okeahalam, C.C. and Jefferis, K.R. (1999), 'A test of the differential information hypothesis on the Botswana and Zimbabwe stock exchanges', *The Investment Analysts' Journal*, **49**, 31–40.

Peek, J. and Rosengreen, E.S. (1997), 'Derivatives activity at troubled banks', *Journal of Financial Services Research*, **12**, 287–302.

Rajan, R. (1992), 'Insiders and outsiders: the choice between informed and arm's length debt', *Journal of Finance*, **47**, 1367–400.

Russell, S. (1993), 'The government's role in deposit insurance', *Federal Reserve Bank of St Louis Review*, **75**, 3–9.

Stern G.H. (1998), 'Deposit insurance, too big to fail and small banks', *Fedgazette*, 10–11.

Stroup, S.S. (1997), 'Wake up to market realities', *Banking Strategies*, **73**, 43–6.

Thakor, A. (1993), 'Deposit insurance policy', *Federal Reserve Bank of St Louis Review*, **75**, 25–8.

Tirole, J. (1994), 'Western prudential regulation: assessment and reflections on its application to Central and Eastern Europe', *The Economics of Transition*, **2**(2) 129–49.

Urrutia, J. (1990), 'The cost of deposit insurance: derivation of a risk-adjusted premium', *Insurance, Mathematics and Economics*, **9**, 281–90.

Von Thadden, E.L. (1997), 'The term structure of investment and the banks' insurance function', *European Economic Review*, **41**, 1355–74.

Wheelock, D.C. and Khumbakar, S.C. (1995), 'Which banks choose deposit insurance? Evidence of adverse selection and moral hazard in a voluntary insurance system', *Journal of Money, Credit, and Banking*, **27**, 186–201.

White, L.J. (1990), 'The S&L debacle: how it happened and why further reforms are needed', *Regulation*, **13**, 11–16.

Table 22A.1  Design features of explicit deposit insurance systems, 1995

| Country | Membership compulsory? | Management | Premium as % of deposits | Co-insurance? | Limit (US$) | Per deposit? | All deposits? | Only households | Excludes foreign currency or interbank deposits |
|---|---|---|---|---|---|---|---|---|---|
| Argentina | Yes | Joint | 0.36–0.72 | – | 20,000 | No | No | No | Yes |
| Austria | Yes | Private | Unfunded | – | 18,000 | No | No | Yes | Yes |
| Bangladesh | Yes | Public | 0.04 | – | 15,000 | No | No | No | Yes |
| Belgium | No | Joint | 0.02[a] | – | 12,500 | No | No | No | Yes |
| Canada | Yes | Public | 0.16 | – | 42,800 | No | No | No | Yes |
| Chile | No | Public | Unfunded | Yes | 3,000 | No | No | No | – |
| Colombia | Yes | Public | 0.09–0.15 | Yes | 12,000 | No | No | No | Yes |
| Czech Rep. | Yes | Public | 0.5 | Yes | 3,565 | No | No | Yes | Yes |
| Denmark | Yes | Private | 0.2 | – | 41,100 | No | No | No | Yes |
| Dom. Rep. | No | Joint | – | – | 8,000 | No | No | No | – |
| El Salvador | – | – | Unfunded | – | 3,400 | No | No | No | Yes |
| Finland | Yes | – | 0.01–0.05[b] | – | No limit | No | No | No | – |
| France | No | Private | Callable | – | 74,800 | Yes | No | No | Yes |
| Germany | No | Private | 0.03 | – | 30%[e] | No | No | No | Yes |
| Hungary | Yes | Public | 0.2 | – | 9,000 | No | No | No | Yes |
| Iceland | Yes | Public | 0.05 | – | 80%[f] | No | Yes | No | No |
| India | Yes | Private | 0.04 | – | 960 | No | No | No | Yes |
| Ireland | Yes | Public | 0.2 | Yes | 5,440 | No | No | No | Yes |
| Italy | No | Private | Callable | Yes | 526,000 | Yes | No | No | Yes |
| Japan | Yes | Joint | 0.012 | – | 100,260 | No | No | No | Yes |
| Kenya | Yes | Public | 0.4 | – | 2,100 | No | No | Yes | Yes |
| Kuwait | – | – | Unfunded | – | No limit | No | Yes | No | No |
| Lebanon | Yes | Private | 0.05 | – | 18 | No | No | No | – |

| Country | | Administration | Funding | | Coverage | | | | |
|---|---|---|---|---|---|---|---|---|---|
| Luxembourg | Yes | Private | Callable | – | 15,200 | Yes | No | No | Yes |
| Marshall Islands | No | Public | Variable | – | 100,000 | No | Yes | No | No |
| Mexico | Yes | Public | 0.3$^a$ | – | No limit | No | No | No | – |
| Micronesia | No | Public | Variable | – | 100,000 | No | Yes | No | No |
| Netherlands | Yes | Joint | Unfunded | – | 23,050 | No | No | No | Yes |
| Nigeria | Yes | Public | 0.937 | – | 2,270 | No | No | No | Yes |
| Norway | No | Joint | 0.015$^b$ | – | No limit | No | Yes | No | No |
| Peru | No | Joint | – | – | 2,100 | No | No | No | – |
| Philippines | Yes | Joint | 0.2 | – | 3,700 | No | No | No | Yes |
| Portugal | – | Joint | 0.2 | Yes | 100–50%$^f$ | No | No | No | Yes |
| Spain | No | Public | 0.10–0.15 | – | 11,400 | No | No | No | Yes |
| Switzerland | No | Public | Callable | – | 22,875 | Yes | Yes | No | Yes |
| Taiwan | No | Public | 0.015 | – | 38,500 | No | No | No | Yes |
| Tanzania | Yes | Public | 0.1 | – | 480 | No | No | No | Yes |
| Trinidad & Tobago | Yes | Public | 0.2 | – | 8,500 | No | No | No | – |
| Turkey | Yes | Joint | 0.3 | – | 83 | No | Yes | No | Yes |
| Uganda | Yes | Public | 0.2 | – | 3,000 | No | No | No | Yes |
| United Kingdom | Yes | Public | 0.3$^c$ | Yes | 23,100 | No | No | No | Yes |
| United States | No | Public | 0.234$^d$ | – | 100,000 | No | Yes | No | No |
| Venezuela | Yes | Joint | 1 | – | 23,600 | No | No | No | Yes |

*Notes:*
$^a$ of liabilities
$^b$ of assets
$^c$ of maximum
$^d$ average
$^e$ of bank capital
$^f$ of deposits

*Source:* Demirguc-Kunt and Kane (1998).

PART IV

The Evolving International Financial Architecture

# 23. The institutional design of central banks
## Falko Fecht and Gerhard Illing

## 1 INTRODUCTION

The question of how monetary institutions should be designed has attracted considerable attention during the past years. In the context of the Maastricht Treaty, there has been a plethora of papers on the design of the European Central Bank (ECB); the breakdown of the rouble zone created a strong demand for policy advice about what kind of monetary institutions should be adapted in Eastern European countries; finally, after the breakdown of stability of money demand in many countries, there was a need to redesign monetary policy instruments.

For those searching for theoretical foundations of policy advice, game theory has been a popular candidate for obvious reasons: a specific branch in game theory is concerned with the issue of mechanism design (that is, the search for adequate rules). The mechanism design approach has been extremely successful in the theory of industrial organization, yielding important insights into issues such as the optimal regulation of firms under asymmetric information. One of the most spectacular applications was the design of auctions for selling radio waves by the federal government in the US.

It seems natural to try to apply these methods also to monetary policy, and so it is not surprising that game-theoretic models play a major role in the present debate on the design of monetary policy. Indeed, these models provide helpful insights into what rules of the game monetary policy should follow. During the past years, there have been two significant trends in monetary policy: central banks have become increasingly independent across many countries, and inflation targeting has been adapted as a new framework for monetary policy in a growing number of countries.

Game-theoretic analysis gives a theoretical foundation for both trends. In particular, it supports moves to delegate policy to an independent central bank. In the literature, however, different paradigms can be found which give quite contradictory policy advice for essential details. On the one hand,

Rogoff (1985) suggests that monetary policy should be delegated to a conservative central banker. On the other hand, Walsh (1995), in a much-cited paper, argues that monetary policy should be specified in a transparent contract between government and central banker.

In a rough, oversimplified, but provocative way we could argue that these two concepts give theoretical support to two quite different forms of central bank independence, both of which have been hotly debated recently: Rogoff's idea is frequently cited as a justification for the model of the Bundesbank (which is the prototype for the design of the ECB). Crudely speaking, it suggests that the central bank should be independent from government interference both when formulating its goals and when choosing its instruments. On the other hand, the Walsh contract can be interpreted as justifying movements towards inflation targeting as experienced in New Zealand and Great Britain (see Fischer, 1995). According to Walsh, a democratic parliament should specify the final targets that the central bank is supposed to aim for in a contract, and then let the bank itself choose the instruments to implement these goals (the bank gets operational independence). The central bankers should be paid according to the performance achieved, and the contract has to be designed to give the appropriate incentives.

At least in theory, the Walsh contract performs much better than the Rogoff delegation mechanism. Remarkably, it can completely eliminate all inefficiencies caused by a lack of credibility. Thus, the Walsh contract presents a challenge for those who consider incentives for surprise inflation to be one of the major issues for monetary policy. The contract approach is also of interest because it suggests a quite different route from the one chosen by the ECB.

## 2 MONETARY POLICY AS A STABILIZATION DEVICE

After the breakthrough of Keynesian economics one, if not the major, aim of monetary policy was the stabilization of business cycles. And in mainstream economics as well as in economic politics, stabilization policy is still one of the most prominent tasks of central banks. The potential for a stabilizing monetary policy rests on staggered nominal wage and debt contracts.

In short, with staggered nominal contracts, changes in inflation expectations do not immediately affect contract conditions. Thus, in the short run, inflation expectations are more or less given. Consequently, by lowering short-term nominal interest rates, an expansionary monetary policy reduces short-term real interest rates, which proportionally translates into lower long-term real interest rates. Less productive investment objects become profitable. So investment expenditure starts to increase, leading to a stronger demand for goods. Since wages are also sticky in the short run, an increased aggregate demand only partially affects inflation. Output and employment are driven up as well. In the long run, when the effect is fully embodied in all contracts, monetary policy influences only the level of inflation. Thus, monetary policy can stabilize only short-run and unexpected aggregate demand and supply shocks. In the long run, monetary policy should be neutral in that on average it should guarantee price stability.

In this manner, monetary policy is welfare improving, because the private sector's adjustment is limited by sticky contracts and would consequently be accompanied by severe business cycles. From this point of view, finding a welfare-maximizing monetary policy is simply a control problem. If the central bank tries to minimize inflation and deviations of output from its full-employment level simultaneously, interest rates should be set in order to fully compensate for aggregate demand shocks. Since monetary policy can only influence aggregate demand, negative supply shocks should be stabilized by a combination of inflation and deviation of output from its full-employment level. The optimal relation of inflation and output losses depends on the elasticity of aggregate supply and on the marginal social disutility of inflation and unemployment, respectively.

To demonstrate this, consider a central bank that minimizes the social loss function

$$L(\pi; y) = \pi^2 + b(y - y^*)^2$$

subject to the supply curve

$$y = y^* + a(\pi - \pi^e) - \varepsilon,$$

where $\pi$ and $y$ symbolize the actual inflation rate and the actual output, respectively, while $b$ measures the importance attached to full employment. $y^*$ is the full-employment output and $\pi^e$ are the inflation expectations of private sector agents incorporated in their contracts. Thus, a surprisingly high actual inflation rate ($\pi - \pi^e > 0$) leads to an output larger than the full-employment level.

The supply shocks $\varepsilon$ are fully unexpected for the private sector and realized after the private sector contracts are signed. They follow a normal distribution with a zero mean ($E(\varepsilon) = 0$) and a variance of $\sigma_\varepsilon^2$. Consequently, the supply shocks do not influence inflation expectations incorporated in the contracts. Because of this, combined with a monetary policy that is on average neither expansionary nor restrictive, the private sector expects price stability ($\pi^e = 0$).

Thus, for any given supply shock $\varepsilon$ the central bank minimizes social losses, if it sets interest rates to shift the demand curve that intersects the aggregate supply function at an inflation level of

$$\pi = \frac{ab}{1 + a^2 b} \varepsilon.$$

Correspondingly, the optimal deviation of output from its full-employment level is

$$y - y^* = \frac{1}{1 + a^2 b} \varepsilon.$$

Figure 23.1 gives a graphical representation of this control problem of the central bank. Temporary supply shocks cause fluctuations of the short-run supply curve around the expected level $y = y^* + a(\pi - \pi^e) - E(\varepsilon)$. A negative supply shock $\varepsilon_2 < 0$ shifts the curve to the upper left, while a positive shock $\varepsilon_1 > 0$ shifts it to the lower right. The ellipses around the point of price stability and full-employment output are the social indifference curves. Those with a larger distance from the ideal point of price stability combined with

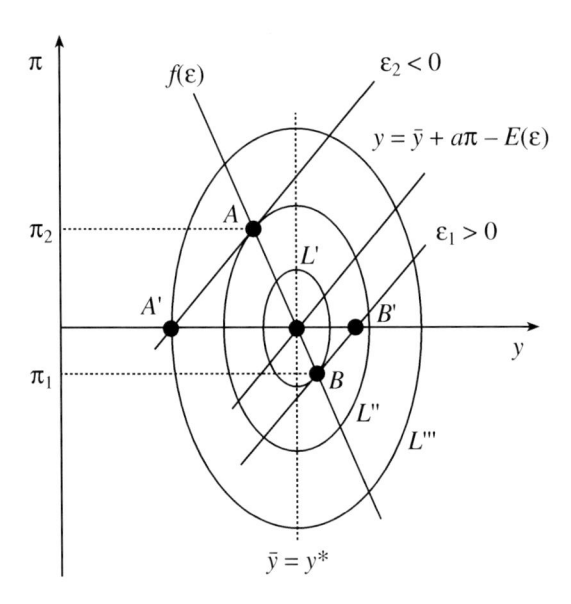

*Figure 23.1  A control problem of the central bank: finding a welfare-maximizing monetary policy*

full employment bear higher social losses. The optimal policy response for a given supply shock is always characterized by a point of tangency between the short-run supply curve and a social indifference curve. Only at that point is the marginal loss of a further increase in inflation equal to the marginal welfare gain of an output expansion caused by that further inflation increase. Thus, the stabilization curve $f(\varepsilon)$ represents for all $\varepsilon$ the optimal combination of inflation and output that monetary policy can reach.

Since on average the ideal point with price stability and full-employment output is reached, the central bank has no incentive to have a permanent expansionary or restrictive monetary policy. Consequently, rules that restrict the ability of the central bank to respond to aggregate shocks reduce social welfare. A commitment to preserve price stability not only on average but also in the short run hinders the central bank from having a beneficial stabilization policy. Inefficiently large fluctuations of output result in higher than necessary welfare losses (compare point $A$ with $A'$ and $B$ with $B'$). In this case discretionary monetary policy is obviously optimal.

## 3 THE TIME-INCONSISTENCY PROBLEM

In contrast to the approach of the previous section, Kydland and Prescott (1977) and Barro and Gordon (1983) assume in their pathbreaking work that central banks have an incentive to deviate systematically from price stability.

This incentive results from structural inefficiencies that cause a shortfall of equilibrium output from its full-employment level. Structural inefficiencies, such as monopolistic competition and proportional income taxes, bring about a situation comparable to the prisoner's dilemma: although everybody would benefit from full employment, individual utility maximization results in an unemployment equilibrium. At zero actual and expected inflation, a central bank that again tries to minimize inflation and unemployment simultaneously could improve welfare by introducing a small surprise inflation, because at that point welfare losses caused by a surprise inflation are smaller than the welfare gains of the corresponding reduction in unemployment from its high level. But a higher than equilibrium output is not efficient on the individual level. Thus, people will try to anticipate the surprise inflation and incorporate it in their contracts. Inflation expectations rise, fully offsetting the overall beneficial effect of the expansionary monetary policy. Therefore in the rational expectations equilibrium the incentive to introduce a surprise inflation results only in an increased actual and expected inflation rate while employment maintains its equilibrium value: an inflation bias occurs. But since everybody dislikes inflation, all agents in the economy would be better off if price stability were a policy commitment.

To illustrate this, consider again a central bank that tries to minimize the social loss function

$$L(\pi; y) = \pi^2 + b(y - y^*)^2.$$

Abstracting from aggregate supply shocks, the restricting supply curve is now given by:

$$y = \bar{y} + a(\pi - \pi^e),$$

where $\bar{y}$ is the equilibrium level of output ($y^* - \bar{y} = \Delta > 0$).

If the private sector anticipated price stability ($\pi^e = 0$), the optimal combination of inflation and output would be given by:

$$\pi_{SI} = \frac{a^2 b}{1 + a^2 b} \Delta \text{ and } y = \bar{y} + \frac{a^2 b}{1 + a^2 b} \Delta.$$

Obviously, although the central bank may undertake to preserve price stability, it would have an incentive to inflate if private agents believed this: central bank promises not to generate inflation are not time consistent. Therefore rational-expectations-forming individuals will not expect price stability under these circumstances. But nor will they expect an inflation rate of $\pi_{SI}$. As becomes obvious from Figure 23.2, an expected inflation

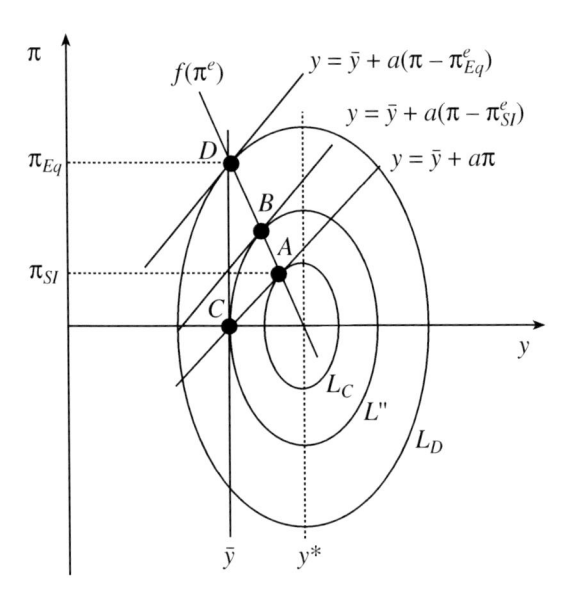

*Figure 23.2 The time-inconsistency problem*

rate of $\pi_{SI}$ shifts the supply curve to the upper left, so that it reaches the equilibrium level of output at an actual inflation rate that equals the expected one. This induces an even stronger incentive for the central bank to raise inflation up to the level of point B. Thus, a rational expectations equilibrium is only reached when the anticipated inflation is as high as $\pi_{Eq}$. At that level the central bank has neither an incentive to choose a higher than expected inflation rate nor an incentive to disinflate. In point D, marginal welfare losses of a further increase of inflation again equal the marginal loss reduction by a rise of employment induced by the marginal surprise inflation.

Game theoretically, the rational expectations equilibrium is a simple subgame perfect equilibrium. On the one hand it is determined by the optimal inflation rate that the central bank can set, given the inflation expectations of the private sector. On the other hand, private sector agents will form their inflation expectations on the basis of the incentive structure of the central bank and will consequently know which inflation rate the central bank will actually choose for given expectations. Thus, the equilibrium conditions are

$$\pi = \frac{a^2 b}{1+a^2 b}\pi^e + \frac{ab}{1+a^2 b}\Delta \text{ and } \pi^e = \pi,$$

leading to an equilibrium inflation rate of $\pi_{Eq} = ab\Delta$. Since there is no surprise inflation in equilibrium, output will be at its natural level $\bar{y}$ and the overall welfare losses will amount to $L_D = a^2 b^2 \Delta^2 + b\Delta^2$.

Apparently, the permanent incentive of the central bank to reduce social welfare losses by an expansionary monetary policy is counterproductive. In the rational expectations equilibrium, welfare losses are even higher than at point C. If the central bank could make a commitment to preserve price stability, inflation expectations would be zero and the inflation bias $\pi_{Eq} = ab\Delta$ could be averted. Although output would still be inefficiently small, the overall welfare losses could be reduced to $L_c = b\Delta^2$.

Interestingly, the welfare gains of such a commitment are the larger, the bigger the gains of a surprise inflation. Since in equilibrium a stronger incentive to introduce a surprise inflation only increases the inflation bias of a discretionary monetary policy, a stronger incentive amplifies equilibrium welfare losses. Consequently, a flatter aggregate supply curve (corresponding to a bigger $a$), and thus a larger impact of a surprise inflation on unemployment, increases welfare losses, just as a higher weight on full employment in the social loss function (a larger $b$) does. Because of the increasing marginal losses induced by unemployment, a larger shortfall of equilibrium output from its full-employment level also increases the incentive to introduce a surprise inflation: with rising $\Delta$, the inflation level at which a further increase of $\pi$ (caused by a surprise inflation) is no longer beneficial, increases.

In sum, the fact that a central bank cannot credibly make a commitment to preserve price stability in the presence of persistent deviations of output from its full-employment level is – under the 'time-inconsistency problem of monetary policy' – a strong and, in the theoretical discussion, well-established argument against discretionary monetary policy. A strict rule for monetary policy to preserve price stability even in the short run would at least lead to the second-best outcome according to that viewpoint.

But is it really necessary to restrict the flexibility of the central bank to avoid an inflation bias? Is the inflation bias not merely a result of the misleading one-shot game that is used in this framework to analyse an ongoing interaction between the central bank and the public? We might expect that in an extended analysis that captures the repetition of the interaction, reputational effects will reduce the incentive of the central bank to inflate the economy unexpectedly. If the public were to increase future inflation expectations in response to an actual surprise inflation, the central bank would have to compare the welfare gains of a surprise inflation today with the welfare losses caused by a high equilibrium inflation rate in the future. Thus, if the future losses were higher than the actual gains, the central bank might refrain from introducing the surprise inflation.

Although this argumentation is intuitively convincing, a deeper analysis shows that it cannot be taken for granted that reputational effects will enforce the right incentives for the central bank. This is most obvious if the interaction period between the central bank and the public is limited. In that case the results of the preceding analysis do not change. This can be shown by backward induction: assume that a central banker is appointed for only a limited number of $n$ periods. Clearly, in the last period the central banker has no benefit from further investing in his/her reputation: since there is no period $n+1$, a surprise inflation in period $n$ will only have a positive output effect today – the effect on inflation expectations is invalid. So the public can anticipate that the central banker will systematically increase inflation at least in the last period. Consequently, private agents will expect an inflation rate of $\pi^e = ab\Delta$ for the last period. But this means that inflation expectations for the last period are independent of the previous behaviour of the central bank. However, if the central bank cannot influence inflation expectations for the last period by his/her monetary policy during period $n-1$, then it can never be beneficial to refrain from introducing a surprise inflation in $n-1$ as well and an inflation bias will also arise in that period. Apparently, this argumentation can be continued and ultimately shows that even in the first period the inflation bias will occur. Thus, the finitely repeated interaction does not change the results of the one-period model.

In contrast, if we assume that the central banker can be dismissed in any period with a given probability $1-\delta$, then there is no distinct final period. Consequently, in any period future gains from reputation will be realized with probability $\delta$. However, to calculate the gains from reputation it is important to know the reaction of the public to a surprise inflation. But there are a multiplicity of conceivable ways in which the public could react. One possibility would be that the private agents at first expect the central bank to preserve price stability. But if the central bank fails to do so they adjust their inflation expectations once and for all to $\pi^e = ab\Delta$.

Abstracting from short-run supply shocks, the central bank could realize $L_C$ in every period if the public reacted in the described manner and the central bank always preserved price stability. The overall welfare losses would in that case amount to

$$L_C + (\delta + \delta^2 + \delta^3 + \ldots)L_C = L_C + \frac{\delta}{1-\delta}L_C.$$

In contrast, by introducing a surprise inflation in the first period, the central bank could reduce the losses at $t=0$ to $L_{SI}$. But this would induce the public to raise inflation expectations to $\pi^e = ab\Delta$ in all consecutive periods. Thus, the minimum welfare losses the central bank could realize in every period from $t+1$ onwards would be $L_D$. The overall losses of that strategy would amount to

$$L_{SI} + \frac{\delta}{1-\delta}L_D.$$

Consequently, if the private sector agents form their expectations as anticipated, a surprise inflation in the first period is only beneficial if the first-period welfare gains overcompensate for the welfare losses of all succeeding periods. Analytically, the central bank will refrain from introducing a surprise inflation if:

$$L_{SI} - L_C < \frac{\delta}{1-\delta}(L_C - L_D).$$

Obviously this is more likely the higher the probability that the central banker stays in office: since an increase of $\delta$ gives the future gains a higher weighting, the larger is the reputational effect on the right-hand side of this inequality. Thus, in a stable monetary constitution the central bank can possibly overcome the credibility problem without a binding commitment.

But these results crucially depend on the presumed reaction of the public to a surprise inflation. For instance, if the public reduced their inflation expectations again a few periods after a surprise inflation, the reputational effect would be much smaller, and even for relatively high $\delta$ the incentive to introduce a surprise inflation in the present period dominates. Thus, depending on the assumed reaction of the public, many more central bank equilibrium strategies are possible – a phenomenon known in game theory as the Folk Theorem. What is even more questionable is the assumption that all private sector agents form their inflation expectations in the same way. If they did not coordinate over how to react to a surprise inflation, the central bank's incentive to enhance its reputation could be further reduced. Consequently, it cannot be taken for granted that the reputational effects in the repeated interaction between the central bank and the public are sufficient to solve the credibility problem.

More convincing is an approach that tries to explain the incentive to refrain from introducing a surprise inflation with a reputational consideration on the basis of incomplete information. Given that the public is uncertain about the weight the central bank devotes to full employment to enhance its reputation means convincing the public to be more concerned about price stability. Since any central bank would benefit from low-inflation expectations, the information asymmetry cannot be overcome by purely verbal declarations. The only way the public can learn about the true loss function of the central bank is by inference from its past monetary policy. If the central bank has preserved price stability at the cost of high unemployment in the past, it is more likely that it is more hawkish. In contrast, a more dovelike central bank can be recognized by a high-inflation record combined with lower unemployment.

But as familiar results from the game-theoretical analyses of situations with incomplete information suggest, strategic considerations may even induce a dovelike central bank to preserve price stability in order not to be exposed. Even if the central bank is more concerned with unemployment – is more dovelike – it may be beneficial not to increase employment by introducing a surprise inflation immediately. If the private sector agents inferred from low inflation that the central bank is a hardliner, they would also expect a restrictive monetary policy in the succeeding period. Thus, by postponing the surprise inflation until the last period even a soft central banker could circumvent the inflation bias in his/her period of office. In game theory this situation in which a dovelike central banker mimics a hawkish one is called a 'pooling equilibrium'.

Unfortunately, although the above intuition seems convincing it overestimates the reputational effect. As the analytical approach shows, the inflation bias is in fact only reduced but cannot be totally avoided in this setting.

To keep the analysis simple, suppose that there are two types of agents from which the central banker is appointed for two periods. The first – the hawkish one – does not care at all about unemployment ($b=0$), while the second shares the preferences of the public ($b>0$). Since the public do not know the true type of the appointed central banker, they can only guess that with a probability of $\mu$ the central banker is a hardliner and with the probability of $1-\mu$ that the banker is soft on inflation.

The hawkish central banker will preserve price stability irrespective of the inflation expectations and the impact of his/her policy on unemployment. In the first period the dovelike central banker will also conduct a monetary policy that yields a zero inflation rate. Since the private sector agents will anticipate that he/she will mimic a hardliner, they will expect price stability. Thus, the banker realizes a welfare loss of $L_C$. In contrast, if the banker conducted a surprise expansionary monetary policy, he/she could reduce the welfare losses of the first period to $L_{SI}$ but only at the cost of revealing his/her preferences. Recognizing the banker as soft on inflation would induce the public to adjust their inflation expectations for the second period to $\pi^e = ab\Delta$. Consequently, the succeeding losses will amount to $L_D$. Contrarily, if the central banker imitates the hardliner, the public cannot update their beliefs concerning the banker's true preferences. But they know with a probability of $\mu$ that the banker is really a hardliner and will conduct a restrictive monetary policy in the second period, too. With the prior probability of $1-\mu$ they expect the banker to be weak, in which case they will anticipate an increase in inflation up to $\pi_W$ – the inflation rate that prevails at the intersection of the actual supply curve with the $f(\pi^e)$-line (see Figure 23.3). Thus, the overall inflation expectations for the second period in the pooling equilibrium will be $\pi_{II} = \mu \cdot 0 + (1-\mu) \cdot \pi_W$.

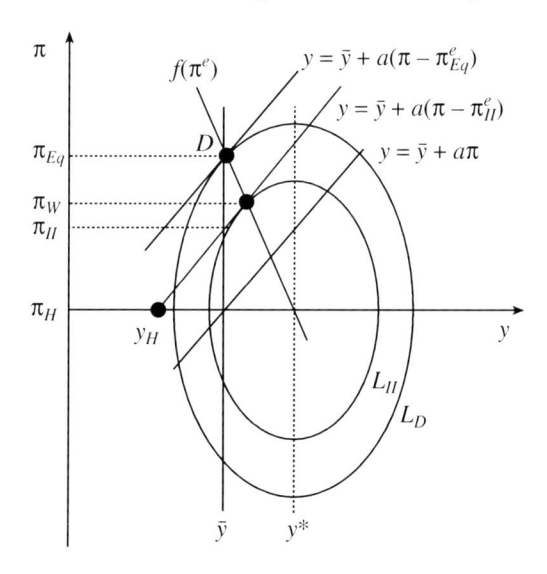

*Figure 23.3   Asymmetric information and inflation expectations*

Thus, in a situation with asymmetric information the inflation bias is overcome by reputational considerations in the pooling equilibrium only at the beginning of the central banker's period of office. Towards the end, inflation expectations increase, leading again to an inflation bias. Nevertheless, as Figure 23.3 shows, even in the second period the inflation bias is smaller in a situation with incomplete information than under a symmetric information distribution as long as there is a positive probability that the central banker is hawkish ($\mu>0$). But while this reduces the overall welfare losses, the uncertainty about the future stance of monetary policy lowers the expected social welfare in comparison with the standard model: because of the increasing marginal losses of unemployment, the welfare costs of the recession that occurs if the central banker turns out to be hawkish always overcompensate for the welfare gains of the surprise inflation and the corresponding boom caused by a weak central banker.

Consequently, even the reputational effect in the situation with uncertainty about the central banker's real preferences cannot implement the second-best solution. The only way to avoid the inflation bias seems to be for the central bank to be committed to preserving price stability under all circumstances.

## 4 THE BASIC TRADE-OFF: FLEXIBILITY VERSUS CREDIBILITY

The two previous sections showed that different approaches to the conduct of monetary policy are preferable for coping with different problems faced by the central bank. But is a discretionary or a rule-based monetary policy better if there is simultaneously a permanent incentive to introduce a surprise inflation and a potential to stabilize short-run aggregate supply shocks? Clearly, the answer to this question depends on the relative importance of welfare losses caused by aggregate fluctuations compared to losses induced by the inflation bias.

To illustrate this, consider a central bank that tries to minimize the standard quadratic social loss function now subject to an aggregate supply function that incorporates both short-run shocks and an equilibrium output that is inefficiently low:

$$y = \bar{y} + a(\pi - \pi^e) - \varepsilon.$$

Since a commitment to preserve price stability under all circumstances signifies a zero inflation expectation of the private sector ($\pi = \pi^e = 0$), the losses this commitment induces can easily be computed by substituting the supply curve into the loss function. Thus, the social welfare losses of a monetary policy that strictly follows a rule of zero inflation amount to $L_C = b(\Delta^2 + \sigma_\varepsilon^2)$.

In contrast, the losses induced by a fully flexible monetary policy are

$$L_D = \frac{b}{1+a^2b}\sigma_\varepsilon^2 + (1+a^2b)b\Delta^2.$$

They can be derived from the optimal inflation rate the central bank can choose for any given inflation expectations. Since the central bank knows the extent of the supply shock before setting the inflation rate, the optimal inflation rate depends on the supply shock. Thus, optimizing the quadratic loss function for a given supply curve yields

$$\pi_D = \frac{ab}{1+a^2b}(a\pi^e + \varepsilon + \Delta).$$

Given that private sector agents do not know the size of the supply shock when signing their contracts, their best guess on future inflation results from

$$\pi^e = E(\pi_D) = \frac{ab}{1+a^2b}(a\pi^e + \Delta)$$

and thus again incorporates an inflation bias of $\pi^e = ab\Delta$.

By comparing the welfare losses induced by the different monetary policy procedures, it becomes clear that the relative merits of a flexible monetary policy stem from the efficient stabilization of supply shocks. If output fluctuations incorporate any welfare losses ($b>0$) and a surprise inflation has any effect on output ($a>0$), the ability of a discretionary monetary policy to reduce those fluctuations by small fluctuations of inflation is beneficial:

$$\frac{b}{1+a^2b}\sigma_\varepsilon^2 < b\sigma_\varepsilon^2.$$

But the drawback of a discretionary monetary policy is obviously the higher average inflation rate. The inflation bias of a discretionary policy leads to additional welfare losses of $(ab\Delta)^2$.

Therefore, a strict commitment of the central bank to preserve price stability under all circumstances is preferable if the central bank has a strong incentive to introduce a surprise inflation, because of large inefficiency of the market equilibrium, for instance. In contrast, if the losses caused by business cycles dominate those stemming from the inflation bias, choosing an optimal inflation rate should be left to the central bank's discretion.

However, neither a discretionary nor a rule-based monetary policy can implement the second-best solution in this setting. Since monetary policy is certainly not able to remove real inefficiencies, it can never implement the first-best solution. Nevertheless, an optimal monetary policy framework should guarantee in a credible way that policy will not give in to the permanent incentive to introduce a surprise inflation stemming from these inefficiencies but has enough flexibility to optimally stabilize short-run aggregate supply fluctuations.

Graphically, the optimal monetary policy is depicted in Figure 23.4. It should combine the optimal stabilization of the discretionary monetary policy given by the slope of the $f(\varepsilon; \pi^e)$-line with the average long-run commitment to price stability of the rule-based monetary policy. Thus, to implement the second-best solution, the central bank should choose output and inflation according to the $f_C(\varepsilon)$-line.

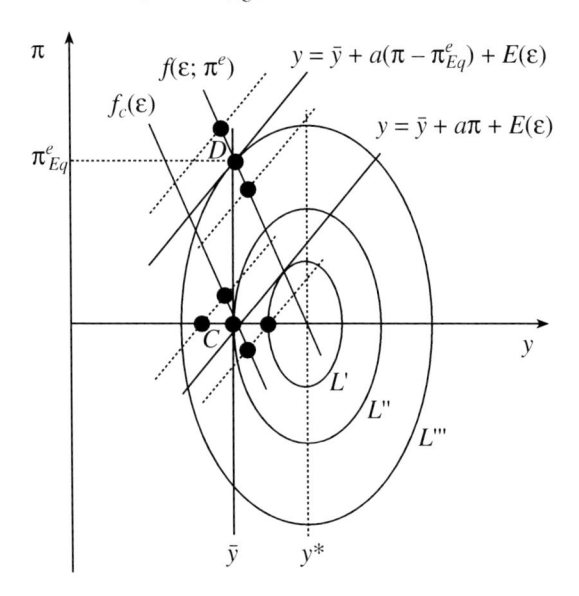

*Figure 23.4  Optimal monetary policy*

Since the monetary policy procedures already analysed could not implement the optimal monetary policy, the immediate question arising is whether it could be realized by any other simple monetary policy rule. First of all we might think of a strict long-run monetary target as proposed by Milton Friedman (1968). Such a strict monetary target prevents the central bank from influencing the aggregate demand curve. But an optimally chosen monetary growth rate should lead to an aggregate demand curve that intersects the expected aggregate supply curve at point C. Thus, the combinations of inflation and output that are realized after short-run aggregate supply shocks are given by the aggregate demand curve. Therefore, if the aggregate demand function has a negative slope, aggregate supply shocks lead to fluctuations of inflation that beneficially reduce output cycles. Nevertheless, from the graphical representation it becomes immediately obvious that monetary targeting can implement the optimal stabilization of supply shocks only if by mere coincidence the demand function has the same slope as the optimal stabilization line ($f_C(\varepsilon)$). But although monetary targeting allows some stabilization of supply shocks, it is not necessarily superior to a strict commitment to price stability, if demand shocks are also taken into account.

Nominal GDP targeting, another simple monetary policy rule proposed by Bennett McCallum (1988), at least circumvents the welfare losses caused by demand fluctuations. In this framework the central bank should be committed to preserving a constant nominal GDP that corresponds to the equilibrium output level at price stability. If the output is below the equilibrium level because of a negative supply shock, the central bank should allow an increase in inflation that is in line with the constant nominal GDP. Graphically this policy rule can be interpreted as a stabilization line with a slope of $-1$ that intersects point C. Thus, although this framework permits the central bank to stabilize demand shocks, it implements the optimal stabilization of monetary policy only if by chance the optimal stabilization line ($f_C(\varepsilon)$) has a slope of $-1$, too. Consequently, neither of the proposed simple monetary policy rules leads in general to the optimal monetary policy.

## 5 OPTIMIZING THE TRADE-OFF: THE CONSERVATIVE CENTRAL BANKER

Obviously, there is no simple monetary policy rule that can simultaneously implement the optimal stabilization of supply shocks and avert the inflation bias; nor can reputational effects in general be expected to induce the right incentives for the central bank. So a monetary policy framework that at least minimizes the combined welfare losses resulting from suboptimal stabilization of supply shocks and from the inflation bias might be preferable. Interestingly, a much-cited paper by Rogoff (1985) shows that having a totally independent conservative central banker is a framework that may exactly optimize this trade-off between losses from inefficient stabilization and those from the inflation bias.

In his approach, in addition to the framework described above, Rogoff assumes that the agents in the economy differ according to their degree of conservatism. Analytically, the conservatism of an individual is expressed by the weight $b_i$ he/she attaches to the deviation of output from its full-employment level. Thus, the density can be described by a function $g(b_i)$ of $b_i$ over all agents $i$. Less conservative agents place a higher weight on full employment, which therefore has a larger $b_i$. Consequently, in a democracy, a government that needs the support of the median voter $m$ will try to minimize the voter's loss function: $L_m(\pi; y) = \pi^2 + b_m(y-y^*)^2$. If the government delegates monetary policy to an individual $k$, leaving the choice of future output–inflation combinations to that individual's discretion, the agent will set inflation according to his/her own preferences: he/she will minimize $L_{CCB}(\pi; y) = \pi^2 + b_{CCB}(y-y^*)^2$ subject to the aggregate supply curve $y = \bar{y} + (\pi - \pi^e) - \varepsilon$.[1]

Since the appointed central banker's choice is not restricted by any rule imposed by the government, an inflations bias will again appear in this setting. The public will expect an inflation rate which the central banker has no incentive to systematically deviate from. Apart from supply shocks at an expected inflation rate of $\pi_{CCB} = b_{CCB}\Delta$, the additional welfare losses of a surprise inflation for the central banker are equal to the welfare gains from the corresponding employment increase. Thus, the only difference to the inflation bias under a discretionary social welfare-maximizing central bank is that in this setting the inflation bias is dependent on the preferences of the central banker: since a more conservative central banker (one with a small $b_{CCB}$) has for any given inflation expectation a weaker incentive to introduce a surprise inflation, the more conservative the central banker is, the smaller are inflation expectations in equilibrium. Consequently, by appointing a conservative central banker the government can reduce the inflation bias.

The inflation bias can even be totally averted if the government delegates monetary policy to an extremely conservative person with a $b_{CCB} = 0$. But in this case the delegation would simply replicate the monetary policy of the strict rule to preserve price stability even in the short run, because the central banker will not respond at all to output fluctuations caused by short-run supply shocks. However, the government will not appoint an extremely conservative central banker. Since the median voter dislikes inflation, he/she prefers a government that will appoint a central banker who will try to stabilize the output on the costs of variable inflation rates.

So the question immediately arising is, how conservative should the central banker optimally be? If the government delegates monetary policy to a modestly conservative central banker ($b_{CCB} > 0$), he/she will use monetary policy to minimize his/her personal loss function. Consequently, an inflation bias occurs, but the central banker will stabilize a given supply shock $\varepsilon$ according to the inflation output combination:

$$\pi_{CCB} = b_{CCB}\Delta + \frac{b_{CCB}}{1+b_{CCB}}\varepsilon \text{ and } y_{CCB} = \bar{y} + \frac{1}{1+b_{CCB}}\varepsilon.$$

Substituting this into the median voter's expected loss function yields:

$$E(L_m) = b_{CCB}^2 \Delta^2 + \frac{b_{CCB}^2 - b_m}{(1+b_{CCB})^2}\sigma_\varepsilon^2 + b_m \Delta^2.$$

The first term determines the losses induced by the inflation bias while the second term measures the expected losses from the supply shocks. The third term represents the unavoidable losses from structural unemployment in equilibrium.

The optimal degree of conservatism of the appointed central banker can be derived from the first-order condition:

$$\frac{\partial E(L_m)}{\partial b_{CCB}} = b_{CCB}\Delta^2 + \frac{b_{CCB} - b_m}{(1+b_{CCB})^3}\sigma_\varepsilon^2 = 0.$$

While the first term shows that losses from the inflation bias can be minimized by an extremely conservative central banker, the second term indicates that the losses from supply shocks are minimized if the median voter is him/herself in charge of conducting monetary policy. Consequently, as long as there are structural inefficiencies and supply shocks ($\Delta, \sigma_\varepsilon^2 > 0$), the overall losses are minimized if a central banker is appointed who is not extremely conservative but more conservative than the median voter. Analytically this can be shown by rearranging the first-order condition to:

$$\frac{b_m - b_k}{b_k(1+b_k)^3} = \frac{\Delta^2}{\sigma_\varepsilon^2} > 0.$$

Hence, policy should be delegated to a more conservative central banker, the lower the variance of supply shocks and the larger the inflationary bias arising from stronger structural inefficiencies. But it should never be delegated to an extreme conservative unless $\sigma_\varepsilon \to 0$ or $\Delta \to \infty$, respectively. On the other hand, if $\sigma_\varepsilon \to \infty$ or $\Delta \to 0$, there is no gain from delegation.

Figure 23.5 illustrates the effect of a conservative central banker graphically. The dotted indifference curves give the preferences of the median voter, whereas the continuously drawn indifference curves $L_k$ represent the preferences of the conservative banker. Since the conservative central banker gives less weight to output stabilization, a larger deviation of output from its full-employment level causes the same welfare losses as a relatively small increase of the price level. So compared with the median voter, the banker's indifference curves are flatter. Consequently, a conservative banker's optimal stabilization line is less steep, average inflation rate is

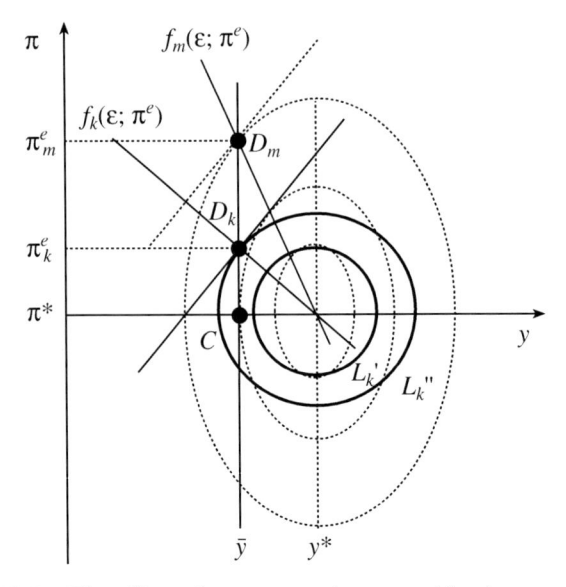

*Figure 23.5  The effect of a conservative central banker*

lower and at the same time the response to output shocks is weaker. Thus, the inflation bias will be reduced at the expense of a stabilization bias.

Rogoff's paper became popular because his ideas conform with intuition about central bank policy: central bankers usually behave in a conservative way, and Rogoff gives a mathematical proof that this is exactly what they should do. So, at first sight, his approach seems to provide a convincing answer to the problem of mechanism design. To make this solution work, the central bank, once appointed, should be given both target and operational independence because obviously there is a strong incentive for the government to renege on the delegation. As soon as private agents have formed their expectations, it would be in the interest of the median voter to cancel the arrangement. Thus, delegation to a conservative banker makes sense only if, once appointed, the banker is free to do what he/she wants. The government should not be allowed to interfere with the banker's policy.

Technically the model shows that the decision about which monetary policy framework to use should not be a decision between the two extreme cases: that is, avoid an inflation bias while accepting a totally inefficient stabilization of supply shocks or give the central bank the opportunity for an optimal response to business cycles while accepting a very high permanent level of inflation. In contrast, Rogoff demonstrates that already existing monetary policy frameworks implement an interior solution to this trade-off between flexibility and credibility.

From the Rogoff approach, two distinct and empirically testable results derive:

1. the more independent a central bank, the lower the average inflation rate; and
2. the lower the variability of inflation, the higher the fluctuations of output.

There are many recent studies that have tested the empirical evidence for both of these hypotheses. In a detailed survey, Eijffinger and de Haan (1996) conclude that in general these studies show that the first hypothesis is empirically evident while the second has to be rejected. Thus, a more independent central bank seemingly leads to lower average inflation but at no real costs in the form of a higher variability of output growth.

Based on the pioneering work of Parkin and Bade (1978), some empirical studies establish indices that try to quantify the degree of independence of the central bank in different countries. For example, the two broadest studies by Cukierman (1992) and Grilli et al. (1991) construct an index consisting of proxies for the personal independence of the chief central banker. Those proxies are:

1. criteria concerning the rules of appointing the chief central banker;
2. tenure of office;
3. the possibility of being reappointed by the government; and
4. the possibility of being dismissed by the government.

Another important aspect is the question of how independent the central bank is in formulating the target of its monetary policy. This goal independence manifests in characteristics such as whether or not price stability as the main target of monetary policy is laid down in the constitution of the central bank, who decides on the prevailing exchange rate regime, whether or not the central bank is involved in financing governmental budget deficits and whether or not the government can veto the monetary policy decision of the central bank.

If the central bank does not have this goal independence it should at least have operational independence, which means that it is free to choose which instruments to use to achieve a target prescribed by the government.

It is essential for the reliability of these studies that their specific index should deliver a consistent ranking of the considered countries concerning their independence. But as Mangano (1998) shows, the correlation of the ranking in Cukierman's study compared with that of Grilli et al. is quite low. This is also true with respect to other studies. Thus, the study-specific classification of a country's central bank independence seems to be heavily dependent on the authors' knowledge of national peculiarities. This is mainly because central bank independence is not just a question of the central bank's constitution but also crucially depends on the personal integrity of the chief central banker and the public support of the central bank, which is very hard to quantify.

Despite the fact that the different studies emphasize different aspects of independence, they in general come to the conclusion that in industrialized countries a higher degree of independence goes along with a lower average inflation rate (see Figure 23.6). Nevertheless, the negative correlation does not necessarily imply that independence *causes* a low average inflation rate. Instead, independence *and* a low average inflation rate could be determined by common characteristics, such as a strong public inflation aversion. Correspondingly, Posen (1995) argues that it might have been the bank dominance in the German financial system that allowed the very inflation-averse financial market participants to assert their interest successfully.

While the inverse relationship between independence and inflation can be regarded as a stylized fact, the effect of independence on output volatility is not empirically verifiable, as already mentioned above. One reason for this could be that business fluctuations are mainly caused by political cycles and not by exogenous supply shocks. Consequently, a more independent

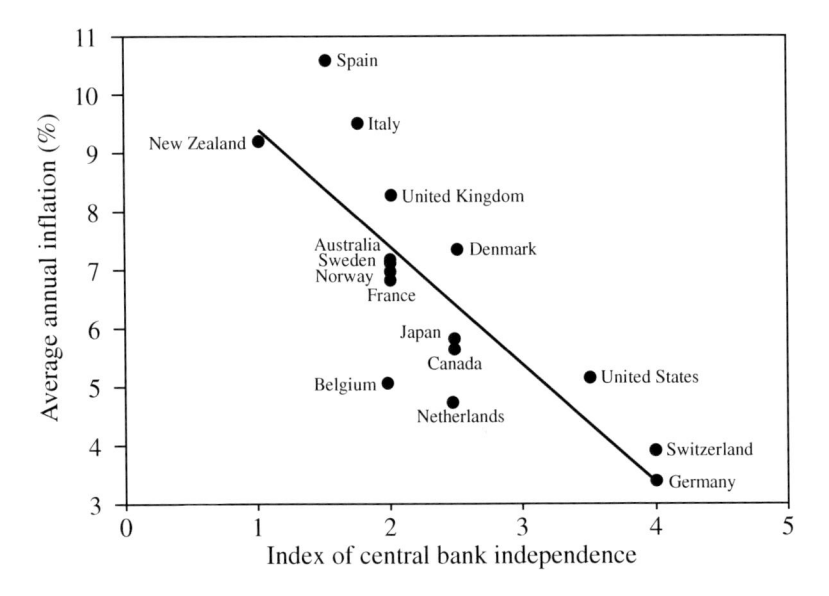

*Figure 23.6  Central bank independence and average macroeconomic performance, 1961–1990*

central bank lowers the potential for political interference and thus reduces the magnitude of business cycles (see Alesina and Gatti, 1995).

Another reason could be that conservatism is not correctly defined by the degree of inflation aversion of a person. Conservativism could instead be reflected in the optimal level of employment ($y_i^*$). Thus, the central banker would be appointed on the basis of his/her personal judgement of the output gap ($\Delta_i$). Since the credibility problem leading to the inflation bias rests on the incentive of the central banker to reduce the output gap, a central banker who is satisfied with the equilibrium level of unemployment will never have such an incentive. Consequently, by appointing a central banker with $\Delta_i = 0$, an inflation bias could be totally avoided. If the central banker has in addition the same inflation aversion as the median voter, then the banker will optimally stabilize output fluctuations. Thus, the appointment of a conservative central banker could eliminate the inflation bias at no cost.

## 6 RESOLVING THE TRADE-OFF: THE OPTIMAL CENTRAL BANK CONTRACT

While an independent conservative central banker optimizes the trade-off between flexibility and credibility, more recent institutional approaches show that this trade-off could be totally avoided.

Applying the theory of optimal regulation of firms, Walsh (1995) models monetary policy as a principal–agent problem between government (the principal) and the central banker (the agent). The problem is to design an efficient contract between the two parties. At first sight, surprisingly, the optimal contract between principal and agent has an extremely simple form, provided that the agent is risk neutral with respect to his/her personal income. It can completely overcome the trade-off between inflation and the stabilization bias. A crucial condition for this result, however, is that the preferences of the central banker are known.

The idea is fairly straightforward. When deciding about policy, central bankers are directed by their preferences regarding inflation and output, but they also care about their own monetary payoffs. For a start, assume that the central banker has the same preferences as the government ($b_i = b_m = b$). Then, even in the absence of any incentive payments, the banker would optimally take care of stabilization of output. The only difference to the commitment solution is that – benevolent as the banker is – he/she cannot resist the temptation to inflate, thus causing an inflationary bias. Intuitively, if the banker gets punished for the social cost imposed by high inflationary expectations, he/she internalizes these costs and refrains from cheating. So, if a contract gives adequate monetary incentives, it may correct for this bias. Actually, payments depending simply on the inflation outcome are sufficient to sustain the commitment outcome. To see why, we analyse the banker's optimization problem:

$$L_i = \pi^2 + b_i(y - \bar{y} - \Delta)^2 - T(\pi, \varepsilon).$$

After observing the shock $\varepsilon$, the first-order condition for discretionary policy is:

$$\pi + b(\pi - \pi^e + \varepsilon - \Delta) - \tfrac{1}{2}\frac{\partial T}{\partial \pi} = 0 \text{ for all } \varepsilon.$$

This gives:

$$\pi = \frac{b}{1+b}(\pi^e - \varepsilon + \Delta) + \tfrac{1}{2}\frac{1}{1+b}\frac{\partial T}{\partial \pi}.$$

Taking the average and imposing $\pi^e = E(\pi)$, this reduces to:

$$E(\pi) = b\Delta + \tfrac{1}{2}\frac{\partial ET}{\partial \pi}.$$

The inflation bias can be eliminated completely if $\partial ET/\partial \pi = -2b\Delta$. If we impose the condition that on average transfer payments should cancel out in equilibrium (for example, $E(T) = 0$), we get the condition for the optimal transfers by integrating the optimality condition for the monetary compensation:

$$T(\pi, \varepsilon) = -2b\Delta\pi.$$

In contrast to Rogoff, according to Walsh, the government should appoint a central banker with the same preferences. In addition, the banker should impose a transfer if actual inflation deviates from the target. If inflation exceeds the target, the banker gets punished, whereas he/she is rewarded if inflation is below the target. These transfer payments are not meant as punishment for misbehaviour; rather they are supposed to correct for the extra welfare cost imposed by higher inflationary expectations.

Graphically, the Walsh contract works by shifting preferences downwards (see Figure 23.7). Since the personal transfers are only connected to the actual rate of inflation and not to current output, the shift is strictly vertical. The measure of the shift is precisely given by the inflation bias. Apart from the shift, the shape of the indifference curves of the central banker do not change. Consequently, the central banker will on average preserve price stability while optimally stabilizing short-run supply shocks. Thus, the

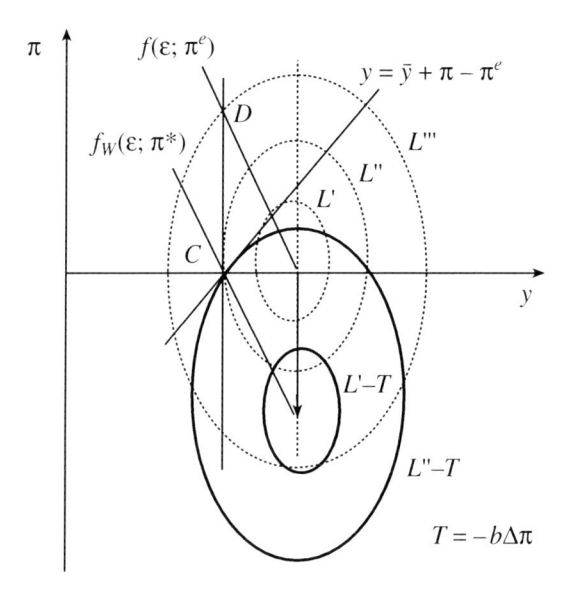

*Figure 23.7* The Walsh contract between the government and the central bank

optimal central bank contract induces the central banker to stabilize supply shocks according to a line $f_W(\varepsilon; \pi^e)$ which fully resembles the optimal stabilization line $f_C(\varepsilon)$ (compare Figure 23.4).

The transfer payments should be linear because expected inflation increases linearly with actual inflation. The extent to which deviations should be punished or rewarded (the power of the transfer) depends on the inflation bias $b\Delta$: the greater the bias, the more the payments should react to deviations. The good thing about the contract is that payments do not depend on the realization $\varepsilon$ of the shock. Transfer payments depend only on the inflation outcome $\pi$: $T(\pi, \varepsilon) = T(\pi)$. So if the central bank has private information about $\varepsilon$, the contract is not affected at all. Similarly, the nature of the contract is unchanged if inflation control is stochastic, as long as the central bank is risk neutral.

## 7 THE ADVANCED TRADE-OFF: CONSERVATIVE CENTRAL BANKER VERSUS OPTIMAL CENTRAL BANK CONTRACT

So far the preceding analysis seems rather conclusive. While an independent conservative central banker optimizes the trade-off between credibility and flexibility, the optimal central bank contract is most efficient in both dimensions. Moreover, the approach of a conservative central banker has a further drawback: as soon as private agents have formed their expectations, it would be in the interest of the representative agent to cancel the arrangement. There is a strong incentive for the government to renege on the delegation. Thus, delegation to a conservative banker makes sense only if, once appointed, the banker is free to do what he/she wants. The government should not be allowed to interfere with the banker's policy.

Certainly, the conditions derived show what could be achieved if the government continued with the delegation mechanism. But nothing can be inferred about why it will not renege on its commitment. More bluntly: why should it not be feasible for the government to abide by the announcement to preserve price stability, whereas it is feasible to continue with the process of delegation?

Of course, we can argue that there are costs of reneging on delegation.[2] If, for instance, the term length of the central bank appointment is written into a legal constitution, it may be very costly to cancel this arrangement. As Persson and Tabellini (1993) put it: 'Clearly, it is possible to change the central bank law, but only according to a preset procedure which requires time.' But now, implicitly, the structure of the game has been changed dramatically compared to the initial game. Presumably, there are also costs involved in not honouring an initial announcement. The whole story, even though intuitively appealing, is not fully convincing as long as the nature of commitment costs of different mechanisms is not specified. Rather than telling the story explicitly, the model resorts to some unspecified belief in the functioning of rules.

The fact that the nature of commitment costs is not modelled in a precise way is a serious drawback once we accept that there are also good arguments for at least some degree of accountability of monetary policy. To see that, the model has to be made more realistic. As shown above, the optimal degree of conservatism depends on the weight $b_m$ that the representative agent attaches to output stabilization. With decreasing weight $b_m$, policy should be delegated to an increasingly conservative banker. Assume now that, initially, there is some uncertainty about $b_m$ which will be resolved after stage 2, but before stage 3. If the actual $b_m$ deviates too much from expected value $E(b_m)$ (if there is a significant change in preferences), then there will be considerable gains from reneging on the delegation mechanism, the more so if the game is repeated for several periods. Now, the advantage of reduced inflation bias has to be traded off against inflexibility of the mechanism to respond to a change in the environment.

To summarize: Rogoff's approach is quite helpful as a first step in demonstrating the advantage of central bank independence; yet it is not much more than that. It certainly gives no justification for demanding that monetary policy should be completely resistant to democratic control, and it does not give much guidance as to how far independence should go. Thus, inflation targeting as the implementation of the optimal central bank contract seems to be the first choice. But this might be a short cut because it oversees some benefits of the conservative central banker and underestimates potential drawbacks of the optimal central bank contract in its operation.

Certainly, the government has a strong incentive to renege on its delegation to a conservative central banker. But it has an even stronger incentive to do so within an optimal central bank contract arrangement. In this framework after the public inflation expectations are incorporated into nominal contracts, both the central banker and the government would generate a surprisingly higher inflation and abandon the contract. So private arrangements between the government and the central banker are likely. In contrast, a conflict of interest occurs between the conservative central banker and the government whenever the latter tries to influence monetary policy decisions. Since the conservative central banker pursues his/her personally optimal monetary policy, he/she will not give in to political pressure. Thus, without public monitoring the institutional arrangement of an independent conservative central banker seems more stable than the optimal central bank contract.

Furthermore, as the analysis above showed, the transfer payments in an optimal central bank contract depend on the output gap. Thus, either the optimal central bank contract has to be contingent on the output gap, which would need a considerably more complex contract structure, or it has to be renewed quite frequently. But a frequent renewal of the contract could again be an opportunity for political inference.

## 8   THE REFLECTION OF THE IDEAS IN PRACTICE

Both frameworks for the institutional design of central banks described in Sections 5 and 6 have been applied in practice. While the legal structure of the ECB (like its prototype, the German Bundesbank) largely resembles the Rogoff approach, countries adapting inflation targeting, such as the UK and especially New Zealand, may be seen as implementing the optimal central bank contract in practice.

With respect to its legal structure, the ECB can be seen as the most independent central bank, even more than the Bundesbank was. The independence of the ECB and of the European System of Central Banks (ESCB) is laid down in the Maastricht Treaty, signed on 7 February 1992. The

Treaty sets only the overall objective of monetary policy, which is rather vaguely defined as preserving price stability. The ECB should conduct a policy that supports the general economic policy of the European Union only if this primary goal is achieved and not called into question.

In much more detail, the Maastricht Treaty defines the institutional, functional and personal independence of the ECB, the ESCB and its board members. Both the ECB and the national central banks of the member countries are strictly prohibited from following any directive of national governments or any other institution of the European Union to ensure institutional independence. Functional independence is guaranteed in the Maastricht Treaty by ruling out any responsibilities that potentially could conflict with the primary objective of the ECB. For instance, any financing of public deficits by the ECB or national central banks is strictly prohibited. Personal independence of the ECB board is achieved by overlapping and long but not renewable contracts. While the directors of the ECB are appointed for eight years, the presidents of the national central banks, who, together with the directors comprise the board of the ECB, hold office for at least five years.

Since the Maastricht Treaty is rather vague on the definition of price stability, the ECB has had the freedom to give a precise definition. In October 1998, the ECB board decided that price stability is achieved if the harmonized consumer price index (HICP) increases in the medium term at an annual rate of less than 2 per cent. For monetary policy strategy, the ECB chose a two-pillar framework. The first pillar consists of a flexible monetary targeting while the second is concerned with the analysis of all other indicators potentially relevant for future price developments. The ECB calculates a reference value for the annual growth rate of the broad monetary aggregate M3 that it considers to be consistent with price stability under 'normal' circumstances. The ECB will not react to deviations of the actual three-month average of the annual monetary growth rate from the reference value only if either the analysis of the components and counterparts of M3 indicates that the deviation is driven by portfolio shifts or the analysis of the second pillar indicates that the deviation does not cause any inflationary pressure. Furthermore, if the second pillar reveals threats to future price stability, the ECB will react even if actual monetary growth is in line with the reference value. In contrast to the ECB, central banks that follow the line of the optimal central bank contract do not have independence with respect to their primary objective. Both the Reserve Bank of New Zealand and the Bank of England are by law required to pursue a strict inflation targeting. Thus, neither of these banks has any goal independence; they are, however, independent with respect to the instruments they can choose in order to achieve the predetermined objective.

While the president of the Reserve Bank of New Zealand is held personally responsible for achieving the inflation target and may be dismissed by the government if this is not done, accountability of the Bank of England is guaranteed in a different way. In the UK, a broad transparency of the decision-making process of the Monetary Policy Committee (MPC) is expected to ensure public accountability. For example, the minutes of the MPC meeting and the individual voting behaviour of the members are published soon after the meeting. Moreover, the Bank of England publishes an Inflation Report which specifies in detail the inflation forecast, the probability of deviation of the future inflation from the target and all measures the Bank of England is taking in order to get future inflation in line with the target if there are any essential deviations to be expected. In addition to this transparency of the decision-making process, whenever it fails to meet the inflation target the Bank of England has to give reasons for the failure in an open letter to the government.

During the last decade, an increasing number of countries have adapted the inflation targeting regime. At the same time, inflation rates have been at an unprecedentedly low level. This, however, has been a worldwide trend, independent of the specific institutional design. Inflation targeting regimes have not yet been tested by inflationary shocks like those of the 1970s and 1980s. So at present, it is far from obvious which institutional setting is more efficient in practice.

## NOTES

1. To simplify the further analysis we standardize the slope of the supply curve to one ($a=1$).
2. In Rogoff (1985), these costs are assumed to be infinite. With finite costs, delegation would be cancelled in the case of large shocks. Lohmann (1992) shows that welfare increases if a conservative banker is appointed but threatened with dismissal if deviations from target inflation become too large. Given the threat, the central banker will adjust his/her policy in the case of large shocks more to the preferences $b_m$. Thus, if a policy could determine the cost for reneging on delegation, it would always incur some finite costs. Essentially, by mixing two commitment mechanisms (delegation and escape clause), a superior outcome is achieved.

## REFERENCES

Alesina, Alberto and Roberta Gatti (1995), 'Independent Central Banks: Low Inflation at No Cost?', *American Economic Review*, **85**(2), 196–200.
Barro, Robert J. and David B. Gordon (1983), 'Rules, Discretion, and Reputation in a Model of Monetary Policy', *Journal of Monetary Economics*, **12**, 101–20.
Cukiermann, Alex (1992), *Central Bank Strategy, Credibility, and Interpendence: Theory and Evidence*, Cambridge: MIT Press.

Eijffinger, Sylvester C.W. and Jakob De Haan (1996), 'The Political Economy of Central-Bank Independence', *Special Papers in International Economics*, **19**.

Fischer, Stanley (1995), 'Central-Bank Independence Revisited', *American Economic Review*, **85**(2), 201–6.

Friedman, Milton (1968), 'The Role of Monetary Policy', *American Economic Review*, **58**, 1–17.

Grilli, V., D. Masciandaro and G. Tabellini (1991), 'Political and Monetary Institutions, and Public Finance Policies in the Industrial Countries', *Economic Policy*, **13**, October, 341–92.

Kydland, Finn E. and Edward C. Prescott (1977), 'Rules Rather than Discretion: The Inconsistency of Optimal Plans', *Journal of Political Economy*, **85**(3).

Lohmann, Susanne (1992), 'Optimal Commitment in Monetary Policy: Credibility versus Flexibility', *American Economic Review*, **82**(1), 273–86.

Mangano, Gabriel (1998), 'Measuring Central Bank Independence: A Tale of Subjectivity and of Its Consequences', *Oxford Economic Papers*, **50**(3), July, 468–92.

McCallum, B.T. (1988), 'Robustness Properties of a Rule for Monetary Policy', *Carnegie-Rochester Conference Series on Public Policy*, **29**, 53–84.

Parkin, M. and R. Bade (1978), 'Central-bank laws and monetary policies: A preliminary investigation', in Porter, M. (ed.), *The Australian monetary system in the 1970s*, Clayton, Victoria: Monash University.

Persson, Torsen and Guido Tabellini (1993), 'Designing Institutions for Monetary Stability', *Carnegie-Rochester Conference Series on Public Policy*, **39**, 53–84.

Posen, Adam (1995), 'Declarations are not enough: Financial Sector Sources of Central Bank Independence', *NBER Macroeconomics Annual*, pp. 253–74.

Rogoff, Kenneth (1985), 'The Optimal Degree of Commitment to an Intermediate Monetary Target', *Quarterly Journal of Economics*, **100**, 1169–90.

Walsh, Carl E. (1995), 'Optimal Contracts for Central Bankers', *American Economic Review*, **85**(1), 150–67.

# 24. The International Monetary Fund: past, present and future
## Ian W. Marsh and Kate Phylaktis*

## 1 INTRODUCTION

The events of the 1990s, the European currency turmoil early in the decade, the subsequent introduction of the euro, the Mexican crisis of 1994, the Asian crisis of 1997 and the Russian crisis of 1998, have all provoked discussions of reform in the architecture of the international monetary system, and the role of the International Monetary Fund (IMF) in its orderly function. Since its inception in 1944, the IMF has had the responsibility of being the 'machinery' in charge of overseeing the international monetary and financial system (Camdessus, 2000). The IMF's role has changed over the years in response to the changes in the economic environment. The changes, however, have come in a piecemeal fashion and always after economic and financial shocks to the world economy. In this chapter, we shall trace its evolving role and discuss proposals for future changes, which will strengthen the global monetary system.

This discussion is structured as follows. In Section 2, we look at developments over the period from 1944 to 1990. In particular, we look at how the framework of conditionality practice has been shaped over the years, in conjunction with the various financial facilities. There are three distinct subperiods: the Bretton Woods System, a period characterized by small demands on the IMF's resources; the 1970s and the oil price shocks, which gave way to dramatic increases in credit; and in the 1980s the emergence of the international debt problem, which put further pressures on the Fund's resources.

In Section 3, we look at the decade of the 1990s. This period is characterized by a greater degree of capital market integration, by a renewal of capital inflows to emerging economies, and by financial instability as manifested by the financial crises in Mexico, South East Asia and Russia. These events have given way to crisis management by the IMF. At the same time, they have raised issues relating to the desirability of capital account

* This chapter reflects the opinions of the authors and does not necessarily reflect those of organizations with which the authors are associated.

convertibility, to the strengthening of countries' financial systems and to the prevention of crises. These issues and the possibility of the IMF acting as lender of last resort are discussed in Section 4.

## 2 PAST

### The Establishment of the IMF and its Role in the International Economy

The establishment of the IMF was agreed by the governments of the major Allied powers in 1944 with a mandate to promote economic and financial cooperation among its member countries. This cooperation would be the means to achieve the objectives considered essential for the economic welfare of the world community and laid out in Article I of the IMF's Articles of Agreement. Among these objectives were: the expansion and balanced growth of international trade; the promotion of exchange rate stability; and the elimination of foreign exchange restrictions through the establishment of a liberal multilateral system of current international payments and transfers. The member countries in pursuing these objectives were to have access to resources made available by the IMF, on a temporary basis and under adequate safeguards, in order to correct maladjustments in their balance of payments without resorting to measures destructive of national or international prosperity.

Thus, the IMF was seen from the very beginning as a source of financial support to member countries facing actual or potential balance of payments problems. This financial assistance, however, raised the spectre of moral hazard in the form of less determination on the part of member countries towards the adoption or maintenance of appropriate policies. The Fund, by making its resources conditional on the implementation of adjustment policies, was to contain the risk of moral hazard. These adjustment policies have come to be known by the term 'conditionality' and ensured that members are able to repay the IMF in a timely manner, which in turn allows the IMF's limited pool of financial resources to revolve and be made available to other members with balance of payments problems.

The operational framework for implementing conditionality has come to be based over time on the relationship between an external imbalance and the economic measures required to correct it. It involved an assessment of the nature and characteristics of the disequilibrium that requires correction. For example, is the disequilibrium the result of internal or external factors? Does it reflect exogenous or endogenous causes? Is it transitory or permanent?[1]

In adopting policies to adjust an external imbalance other objectives, such as sound growth rate, an appropriate level of employment and domestic price and exchange rate stability, are pursued. Equity and distributional consequences of economic policies are also taken into account. The Fund views the attainment of these other goals as important for the maintenance of a viable external payments position.

The Fund's recommended policies to achieve the above objectives have been based on both the fiscal and monetary dimensions of macroeconomic management. The fiscal policy measures include a reduction in fiscal spending or a rise in fiscal revenues. The former will tend to restore balance to the economy by lowering the weight of the public sector in aggregate demand, while the latter will reduce the share of private demand. The mix of fiscal measures will influence the speed of the adjustment process since a government's scope to control its outlays usually exceeds its ability to increase receipts.

The monetary dimension of macroeconomic management stresses the importance of the link between domestic credit expansion and money supply increases and their relationship with aggregate expenditure and income. It highlights the relationship between money market imbalance and goods market disequilibrium. This approach implies that in order to restore a sound relationship between expenditure and income, domestic credit expansion should be in line with the prospective path of desired money holdings in the economy. Thus, domestic credit expansion is a policy variable in the application of conditionality.

The fiscal and monetary dimensions of macroeconomic management are supplemented by appropriate foreign borrowing strategies, which can influence directly the expenditure income flow. Foreign borrowing can make it temporarily possible for an economy to keep demand and growth beyond the levels that it can sustain.

The emphasis of the above policies is in influencing absorption in the economy. A policy which aims to affect relative prices and restore competitiveness of domestic goods, and thereby improve the balance of payments, is exchange rate adjustment or flexibility in exchange rate management. That has also been an important policy of financial programmes recommended by the IMF. A complement to that is the liberalization of exchange and trade regimes in order to ensure that economic incentives and price signals fulfil their functions.

Various criticisms have been raised regarding the stabilization policies underlining conditionality. First, they may be criticized for being based on partial equilibrium rather than general equilibrium analysis. If a large number of countries pursue a combination of devaluation and deflation, then the competitive advantage sought by devaluation will be offset by other devaluations, while the attempt to reduce imports, on the assumption that exports are constant, will be undermined by the fact that exports fall (see Bird, 1990).

Second, the beneficial effects of devaluation on the balance of payments might not be substantial if foreign trade elasticities are low. This of course is an empirical issue and will differ from country to country. Similarly, in the case where countries are substantially open, the competitive advantage gained by devaluation will be short-lived. Finally, financial programmes have been criticized for having a short-term horizon, whereas many of the problems are of a structural nature and require long-term policies. In addition, they have been criticized for producing a deflationary overkill.

The analysis below shows that some of these criticisms have been taken on board over the years as conditionality has moved to promoting growth-orientated adjustment and efficient resource allocation through trade reforms. Another adjunct to conditionality in recent years has been the fostering of financial reforms and strengthening of banking supervision.

**The IMF under the Bretton Woods System**

The IMF in implementing conditionality developed the stand-by arrangement as the main instrument to provide members with conditional access to its financial resources. The arrangement outlined the circumstances under which a member could make drawings on the Fund and represented the first formal manifestation of the institution's belief that its assistance would be most effective if it were provided to support a member's policies designed to correct its external imbalance. This subsequently developed into a more specific economic policy programme with specific policy targets and instruments capable of relatively accurate measurement; for example, the expansion of domestic credit, public sector borrowing requirement and international reserves.

Two further developments took place. First, funds were made available over a period of time to provide incentives to policy implementation and to prevent unduly rapid rates of drawing. Second, the stand-by arrangements included performance criteria that had to be observed to ensure continued access to IMF resources. The rationale for that implied that failure to comply with these performance criteria served as a signal that the policy programme should be reviewed. These conditionality practices were formalized by the IMF Executive Board in 1968.

The UK's experience serves as an example of the implementation of the above procedures. The UK faced balance of payments problems in 1967 and the pound came under considerable pressure. The IMF management insisted on a devaluation of the pound, which took place in November, before giving a major loan of $1.4 billion – 50 per cent of the quota. The balance of payments problems persisted, however, because the Bank of England continued to support bond prices, which tended to fall, in order to limit the losses of commercial banks, which had taken on large bond-holdings with the Bank's encouragement. Thus, liquidity was expanding at a time when tightness was needed.

The Executive Board of the IMF decided, however, that all countries, developing and developed, should be treated the same and insisted that further IMF resources should be available in association with performance undertakings, which involved agreed quarterly limits on bank credit and on fiscal deficit. Both the Bank of England and the government agreed to these measures, which were implemented meticulously (see Finch, 1989). The policies were successful and the balance of payments recovered.

The UK faced another round of balance of payments problems in mid-1970s, and renewed approaches to the IMF. This time the problems stemmed from fiscal weakness and once again the IMF served as a catalyst for implementing the necessary fiscal measures the financial authorities knew were necessary. Following these measures the balance of payments recovered rapidly.

The involvement of the IMF with the UK highlighted two points. First, the importance of the IMF reaching an agreement with the government of the borrowing country on immediate measures necessary for the release of resources. This ensured an early response in the foreign exchange market, which eased the political problems of the implementation and helped the recovery programme. Second, both developed and developing countries were treated the same in terms of implementing policies in order to access IMF resources. The IMF had to ensure that the financial policies of the borrowing country would be adequate to guarantee timely repayment of the debt.

**The IMF during the 1970s**

The changing economic environment of the 1970s required further review of conditionality practices and financial facilities. The two oil price shocks, 1973–74 and 1979–80, were accompanied by balance of payments problems in the oil-importing countries. This implied, on the one hand, bigger imbalances, and on the other hand, structural adjustments to reduce oil consumption and to divert substantial resources to the external sector to pay for the sudden huge increase in imports. The large drawings that took place after the first oil price shock represented a turning point in the Fund's own history. At that point the Fund started to function as a 'financial intermediary' rather than a credit union, by using money borrowed from some members to make loans to others.

In 1974 it borrowed from 16 industrial countries and oil-producing countries and established an extended fund facility (EFF) to provide member countries with serious balance of payments difficulties with medium-term assistance, which covered periods of up to three years; the assistance had to be repaid within four and a half to ten years from its receipt. In 1979, the Fund borrowed further from 14 individual countries to establish the supplementary financing facility (SFF), which was committed by early 1981. It was replaced by an enlarged access to resources (EAR), which permitted the IMF to assist members in coping with 'payments imbalances that are large in relation to their quotas'.

Access to the EFF, created in 1974, was governed by somewhat different conditions. The EFF was designed to help countries adopting 'comprehensive' adjustment programmes, including policies to correct 'structural imbalances in production, trade and prices' as well as macroeconomic imbalances. That was accompanied by strict monitoring of performance. Access to the SFF was subject to certain limitations, relating to the increase in the member's oil-input bill, quota and reserves, but not to the usual forms of conditionality. Thus, there was an expansion in the amount of assistance as the external payments imbalances were becoming large and persistent, while conditionality practices were adapted to the required longer periods of adjustment.

These changes in the IMF's lending practices were formalized by the Executive Board in 1978-79. The revised guidelines acknowledged that the adjustment measures stretched over the medium term.[2]

**The IMF and the International Debt Crisis**

The developments in the foreign indebtedness of developing countries during the 1980s forced further modifications to the role of the IMF in the international community. The initial response to the second oil price increase seemed to mirror the first. In the first year, worldwide inflation accelerated, oil import countries' current accounts swung sharply negative, or more negative, and recession set in. But the similarity ended in 1980. Many countries at the time of the first oil price shock had sustainable current account positions and moderate levels of debt, and this was not true at the time of the second. In addition, the industrialized countries adopted anti-inflationary policies, which resulted in a prolonged recession and sharply higher nominal and real interest rates. The increase in interest payments and the reduction in exports resulted in a staggering increase in debt. Long-term debt rose from $359 billion in 1979 to $552 billion in 1982.

By 1982-83, many developing countries found themselves unable to continue servicing their debt. The first country to default was Mexico, an oil exporter, in 1982, and was quickly followed by other countries. In Mexico's case, however, the cause was highly expansionary macroeconomic policy, which was financed through unsustainable capital inflows based on its rapidly rising oil exports. In Brazil, appropriate policy changes were adopted, which would have improved the current account had worldwide recession not taken place.

The Fund believed that there was too much financing and too little adjustment after the first oil price shock and that a tougher stance was needed to deal with the second shock. The stock of Fund credit rose hugely with the start of the debt crisis, as a large number of countries resorted heavily to Fund credit. The Fund continued to apply conditionality in its support programmes, being optimistic about the prospects for growth and inflation in the debtor countries, and was heavily criticized at the time for putting its seal of approval on unrealistic policy packages.

The debt strategy was initially dominated by the prevention of a confidence crisis in the banking system. The debtors were thought to be facing a short-term problem reflecting the unusual combination of worldwide recession and high interest rates. There was a turning point in debt strategy following the 1985 Baker initiative, which recognized the need for long-term growth-orientated lending. The solution to the problem involved combining adjustment, financing and growth and that implied a concerted effort by debtors as well as creditors. The IMF became the vehicle of this cooperative strategy for the resolution of indebtedness problems.

The conditionality practices focused on structural reforms and microeconomic measures to ensure efficiency in resource allocation and the resumption of growth. At the same time, the IMF made sure that funds continued to flow to developing countries. This has led to the introduction of 'concerted' lending packages. The IMF required creditors to commit funds before agreeing its own support of the debtor adjustment programme. In this way the IMF became the catalyst for capital flows to countries willing and able to undertake an adjustment in their economies. This approach contained moral hazard on the part of debtors and creditors. On the part of debtors, the emphasis on adjustment implied a cost to imprudent borrowing and on the part of creditors the requirement that they support the process with new financing or debt relief or both served to contain it.

There was therefore a movement towards growth-orientated adjustment programmes, which would not impair growth prospects. Additional facilities were made available to support this approach, for example, the structural adjustment facility and the enhanced structural adjustment facility for low-income developing countries.

## 3  PRESENT

**Developments in the International Economy**

The above policies contributed to the relatively successful resolution of the less-developed country (LDC) debt crisis by the end of the 1980s. At the same time, the developing countries had been encouraged during the 1980s by the US, the World Bank and the IMF – the so-called Washington consensus – to change from being non-market economies into market economies. Each country had to take steps to integrate its economy with the rest of the world by the removal of domestic price controls, the establishment of free trade, financial deregulation and capital account convertibility. Each step could be summarized as 'free markets know best'. The IMF was criticized for using this oversimplified strategy, which failed to consider the initial conditions under which the countries were operating when they decided to move towards world integration. While the overall strategy might have been correct, the details had not been put in place. And it was the details that led to a succession of crises in the 1990s and to attempts to rethink the role of the IMF in the world economy.

This move towards greater deregulation and global integration, together with the relatively successful resolution of the LDC debt crisis, led to a renewal of capital flows into emerging economies. Between 1990 and 1996, net capital inflows to emerging markets climbed from $60 billion to $194 billion. However, not all economies were treated equally. The rapid development of the Asian economies and the recovery of some Latin American countries led them to receive the lion's share. Mexico was the biggest beneficiary, receiving $91 billion of net inflows between 1990 and 1993, equivalent to one-fifth of all flows to emerging markets. Sub-Saharan Africa, however, was still capital-starved.

Added to this, the fall of the Berlin Wall and collapse of communist regimes throughout Eastern Europe brought millions of people into the IMF's fold. Sheer proximity to Western Europe meant that for political and economic reasons these economies were recipients of massive flows of capital.

While many economies were becoming more financially integrated with the advanced economies by removing capital controls and developing their banking and financial sectors, several problems remained. One key difficulty was the outlet for investing capital flows into these economies. A large share of the capital inflows went on financial investments rather than on foreign direct investment (FDI), which are prone to being reversed, leading to reserve losses and/or lower current account deficits (see Calvo and Reinhart, 1999). The former increase the financial vulnerability of a country, while the latter affect output and employment in a standard Keynesian way. Calvo and Reinhart also argue that the economic slowdown causes a higher real interest rate, which induces financial distress due to the maturity and, in some cases, currency mismatch of bank portfolios. They term this the 'Fisherian channel' and argue that it contributes to the depth and length of the subsequent recession.

The vulnerability of countries to the sudden withdrawal of funds was first shown in Mexico in 1994 and subsequently in Asia and Russia. The way these crises were resolved implied a new role for the IMF, that of a crisis manager. In the rest of this section we shall examine these crises and discuss the evolving role of the IMF and of its conditionality approach.

**The Mexican Crisis**

The cornerstone of the Mexican economic management since 1988 was the pegging of the exchange rate to the US dollar. The assumption was that fixing the exchange rate would provide the nominal anchor for the Mexican economy and reduce inflation to US levels. The IMF gave a 'strong and unqualified endorsement of this economic management' in the spring of 1994. Consumer price inflation duly fell in Mexico from 180 per cent per annum in February 1988 to below 7 per cent in September 1994. The fiscal deficit was removed and the turnaround in the economy attracted huge capital flows into Mexico. In trying to stop the peso from appreciating, the Banco de Mexico was forced to accumulate reserves and to increase the monetary base. Attempts to sterilize the inflow were only partially successful and Mexican monetary aggregates grew much more rapidly than those in the US. Mexico's stock of reserves rose from $6.3 billion in 1989 to over $29 billion in early 1994. These reserves were viewed as evidence that Mexico could defend the fixed link. Some economists, including Milton Friedman, realized that the accumulating reserve stock was a symptom of a major problem (see Meigs, 1998).

Although Mexican inflation was falling towards US levels, the accumulated inflation differential was huge. Between 1988 and November 1994, Mexican consumer prices had climbed by 187 per cent, while US prices were up by only 29 per cent (see Meigs, 1997). Mexico's exchange rate policy meant that little of this differential was offset by a drop in the value of the peso, which made Mexican goods less competitive. The negative effect that this had on the Mexican economy was being offset by the monetary expansion, itself driven by capital inflows. The balance of the economy was wrong and the source of the problem was an exchange rate fixed at an inappropriately high level.

While the IMF felt the Mexican economy to be in good shape, political and external events contributed to a reversal of capital inflows. A string of political assassinations, civil war and US dithering over NAFTA (North American Free Trade Agreement) led foreign and domestic investors to withdraw capital from Mexico. It eventually became evident that this was not a temporary phenomenon and that capital flows were not going to reverse. Mexico was a classic example of a 'first generation' self-fulfilling speculative crisis where investors knew that reserves were dwindling and that to be late in the queue of investors seeking to get their money out at the current pegged exchange rate would mean facing large capital losses. Accordingly all investors tried to withdraw their money and the peso devalued, at first by 15 per cent and subsequently by a further 35 per cent.

The IMF rode to the rescue again, although it failed to take the lead (hamstrung by British and German reluctance to contribute to the support package). A total of about $40 billion was made available to Mexico but the economy still contracted by almost 10 per cent between 1994Q3 and 1995Q3. Mexican real income in dollar terms was the same in 1996 as in 1974. Meltzer (1998) notes that 'the Mexican people have been on a bumpy road, but they have gone nowhere'.

Besides failing to foresee the crisis, the IMF was criticized for bailing out private sector investors with public money. The money lent to Mexico was used to try to prop up the currency and to continue to pay off investors in Mexican government debt. Investors in government bonds and banks that had lent to the government could therefore get out of the market with minimal losses and even convert their pesos into dollars at the fixed rate. By the time the IMF and Mexico gave up and devalued, domestic and foreign investors had taken their money out of the economy. Equity-holders and those who failed to get their money out of Mexico quickly bore capital losses. But at least some investors, the critics argue, were subsidized by IMF money.

Possibly more importantly, the IMF's actions created a perception that they would continue to bail out investors in future crises. This created the much-discussed moral hazard problem. Since the international agencies could be expected to come to a country's aid in times of crisis, investors no longer had to worry so much about the creditworthiness of their counterparts and so took on riskier propositions than they would usually. This implication of the IMF's newly acquired role as crisis manager and lender would be a recurring theme in subsequent crises.

**The Asian Crisis**

While Mexico could be viewed as just another in a long line of Latin American nations whose reforms and economies failed, the next major round of emerging market financial crises was more serious. Although growth in the advanced Western nations had slowed to a trickle, the Tigers of the East were expanding their economies at double-digit rates. This was achieved through a combination of importing foreign technology and an effective set of sophisticated industrial policies and selective protectionism. The added incentive to overseas investors was that many countries in the region attempted to peg their exchange rates to the US dollar. When coupled with the high returns available from investments in these miracle economies, the apparent removal of exchange rate risk resulted in huge capital flows into these economies to take advantage of the investment opportunities offered.

Some economists began to question this 'miracle'. Paul Krugman (1994) argued that Asia's growth was not due to the more productive use of the inputs but to the heavy investment and a shift of labour from farms to factories. The Tiger economies were catching up with the West, and once they had expanded their capital stock sufficiently and used up the spare pool of rural labour, diminishing returns would set in and growth rates would slow.

Although controversial, his comments were well timed. The declining growth rates in output, export growth and industrial output that Krugman predicted in 1994 became apparent in 1996. And in 1997, a regional macroeconomic slowdown turned into a global financial crisis. The reasons for this implosion are by no means generally agreed, but the majority opinion is that the slowdown, combined with weaknesses in the financial systems and poor regulation, produced meltdown. A major contributory factor was the widespread use of relatively fixed exchange rates that prompted a capital inflow which was short term in nature, usually denominated in foreign currency and left unhedged. The dollar's 35 per cent appreciation against the yen in 1996 and 1997 dragged up the Thai baht and put pressure on Thai exporters since Japan was their main export market. Eventually, sufficient numbers of investors began to doubt the sustainability of the situation in Thailand and the baht fell to a huge speculative attack. The contagion effects may have been related to competitiveness issues, or financial linkages or simple investor panic. But whatever the reason, the crisis spread rapidly around South East Asia. Indonesia, Malaysia and the Philippines were all forced to abandon their currency pegs, and the South Korean won came under attack.

The IMF saw itself as 'charged with safeguarding the stability of the international monetary system' (IMF, 1999a). It thus saw its central role as clearly mandated and its main priority naturally followed, 'to help restore confidence to the economies affected by the crisis' (IMF, 1999a). It took a three-pronged approach to the problem. First, it introduced a stabilization package and series of reforms within affected countries. Second, it provided

South Korea, Indonesia and Thailand finance to the tune of $117 billion from its own coffers and from the treasuries of industrial nations. Third, it advised nations on how to avoid the contagion effects.

The packages of reforms aimed at stabilizing the affected countries were hugely controversial. Among the key elements were a tightening of monetary policy designed to slow the currency depreciations, and a maintenance of sound fiscal policies in anticipation of huge fiscal costs of financial sector restructuring. Putting the brakes on almost every economy in a region suffering an incalculably large crisis looks foolhardy with the benefit of hindsight. Higher interest rates did nothing to stabilize currencies that were falling through the floor. 'Prudent' fiscal policies designed to leave the governments with room to raise the necessary funds to recapitalize a collapsed banking system gave them no room to boost domestic demand with a Keynesian injection of spending.

The IMF was accused of having a single response to financial crises and of applying it regardless of the prevailing conditions. The IMF package had been initially tested on profligate governments in Latin America and Africa, whose fiscal deficits and willingness to print excessive amounts of money had provoked the crises. Monetary tightening and fiscal retrenchment were necessary in such cases to remove the root causes of the crises. However, the Asian governments were running fiscal surpluses rather than deficits, and were not facing spiralling prices as the highest inflation rate in the region was just 8 per cent. The suspicion that the IMF was recommending a one-policy-suits-all programme to combat crises is compelling.

The size of the loans packages put together was questioned on two counts. Massive amounts of monetary assistance were made available – Indonesia was pledged official finance equal to 20 per cent of 1997 GDP ($42 billion), while Korea and Thailand were pledged 13 and 11 per cent ($57 billion and $17 billion), respectively. Even so, these amounts were insufficient to cover the short-term liabilities of these nations, implying that the bailing-in of foreign creditors was required. For example, in October 1997 bankers estimated that Korea's short-term debts were $110 billion, more than three times Korea's reserves (Feldstein, 1998). However, Korea's total foreign debt was less than one-third of GDP.

Feldstein and others have argued that all Korea needed was coordinated action by creditor banks similar to the clubs set up in the 1980s to deal with Latin American debt. These economies were basically in good shape, but they were temporarily short of liquidity. The IMF could have assisted as it did in the debt crisis with temporary bridging loans and by organizing the commercial banks so that they could act in the collective interest by rescheduling the debts. To some extent this is what the IMF did. But by providing such large amounts of money it also ensured that the majority of foreign banks could get their money out of the region without sustaining massive losses. Once again, some private sector investors were bailed out with IMF and public cash. Those fearful of the moral hazard problem argue that the IMF pushed too much money at the problem and has only reinforced international lenders' beliefs that it will continue to act as a lender of last resort in future. There certainly appears to be some justification for this, as the discussion of the Russian crisis in the next subsection shows.

The alternative criticism is that the IMF should have given these economies all the money they needed to refinance their debts since they were fundamentally sound. A crisis of confidence brought down these economies because, in common with banks everywhere, there was a mismatch between short-term liabilities and long-term assets. As when any bank run occurs at a viable institution, the lender of last resort should step in to provide liquidity and avert the crisis. Critics who argue along these lines say that the IMF should not have imposed constraints in terms of fundamental reforms before lending, and that by even announcing that there were problems they prompted even more capital flight.

Both arguments are based on the assumption that the economies were fundamentally in good condition. The question then becomes whether the IMF should act as a lender of last resort to the world and provide liquidity without conditions, or whether the private sector should be forced to accept losses and rescheduling as a consequence of profligate lending, with the IMF merely having a coordination role.

The IMF behaved differently because it believed that the crisis was not one simply of liquidity. The Fund took the view that its financing was there to provide a cushion while necessary structural reforms were introduced. The validity of the IMF's argument is difficult to assess. The macroeconomies of the region were generally good immediately prior to the crisis and have mostly returned to reasonable states after the massive contractions they underwent as a result of the crises and the remedial policies introduced. The financial sectors of each have been massively overhauled and few can debate the necessity of that move. But whether this was a temporary liquidity crisis hinges on the Krugman question. Were these economies reaching stages at which slowdown was inevitable and problems hitherto disguised by rapid expansion would emerge, or did a regional recession and collapsing asset price bubbles bring down otherwise viable countries?

The IMF appears to have been swayed by the former view. Krugman had predicted that once the Asian economies raised capital-to-output ratios sufficiently they would run into diminishing returns, and as a result the foreign capital was applied to poorer-quality investments. Given the corruption and mismanagement that became apparent in some of these economies, some of the capital was applied to very poor-quality investments indeed, and in many cases served only to inflate asset price bubbles that burst so dramatically.

**The Russian Crisis**

The Asian crisis spread around the world and several emerging markets found interest rates rising as investors withdrew capital irrespective of the local economic conditions. Many countries withstood the effects, but the Russian economy, precarious despite seven years of IMF advice, was badly affected. The root problem was Russia's inability to collect taxes, which led to a large and growing fiscal deficit. In order to fund the deficit, the authorities took to borrowing in a newly established treasury bill market, known as GKOs. Here again, the moral hazard problem was apparent. The first deputy managing director of the IMF, Stanley Fischer, has admitted that if there was one country that could be expected to be supported by the international community it would be Russia. International investors were therefore not fazed by interest rates on GKOs of 50 per cent in dollar terms, extracted through the rouble's fixed exchange rate with the dollar. Although such high rates on government debt clearly indicated some degree of risk, the expectation that international support for Russia would be forthcoming in the event of a crisis kept investors in the market. However, such levels of interest payments were crippling a Russian economy already suffering from falling oil prices and could only be paid by the authorities engaging in a Ponzi scheme. In other words, Russia was experiencing a current account and fiscal deficit – 'twin deficit' – reminiscent of the Latin American problems of the 1980s. The Ponzi scheme worked because the 'greater fool' who was willing to lend the final amount of money so that all predecessors could be paid off was the IMF. A final $20 billion IMF loan package was used to pay off maturing debt in August 1998, as Russia ran out of foreign currency reserves. Investors refused to lend any more money to the government via the GKO market and the IMF could not raise another support package. Not surprisingly, the rouble devalued. Astonishingly, the Russians also defaulted on their short-term GKO debts denominated in roubles when all the government needed to do was roll the printing presses, albeit at the cost of a subsequent inflationary impulse. The shock affected all stock markets, brought down Long Term Capital Management and prompted fears of global meltdown.

Again the IMF was criticized. First, it had failed to bring about a satisfactory transition from a communist to a market-driven economy in Russia. This is a rather harsh assessment given that many of the key reforms suggested by the IMF and agreed by various Russian administrations were refused by the Duma. The failure of the IMF's programmes was as much due to incomplete implementation as inappropriate policies. Nevertheless, critics argue that the IMF gave poor policy advice and got its way because it was also willing to provide financial assistance alongside its advice, something that academic and private sector economists could never hope to match.

The second criticism regarded the very nature of the IMF. Somewhere between the debt crisis and the Russian crisis, the IMF metamorphosed into a crisis management organization willing to lend considerable sums of money from its own coffers and those of industrialized nations to nations facing financial problems. This is not so very removed from the IMF's initial role as a lender in times of balance of payments problems. There is little evidence to suggest that the IMF sought this role. Rather, it was forced by circumstance to become the world's crisis manager.

A major change from the IMF's original *modus operandi* is the nature of the conditionality applied to the loans. Prior to the recent crises, the IMF maintained strict conditionality. Funds would not be paid out until a nation had agreed to a detailed set of reforms, and successive tranches of money were dependent on successful implementation of policy changes. In a new role as crisis manager the IMF was forced to adapt. However, even up to the Russian crisis the IMF had insisted on immediate conditionality – a country must sign up to the IMF's structural reform programme before the funds would be released, even if the implementation of some of these reforms was less than perfect. For example, the IMF insisted that several financial institutions in Thailand were closed down as a precondition for disbursing money. With the Russians facing disaster, the IMF was essentially forced to lend on a medium-term conditionality basis, whereby the money is lent and the IMF can do little more than hope that reforms will be introduced. This is little removed from a lender of last resort that disburses money unconditionally, except that the IMF lends at subsidized low rates rather than punishingly high ones. The arguably involuntary assumption of a quasi-lender-of-last-resort function by the IMF is key to its future role.

## 4 FUTURE

There have been several repercussions of the 1990s crises. These can generally be collected under the title 'reforms of the international architecture' but each impinges on the operation of the IMF either in terms of the advice that it gives or in terms of the way the institution itself operates. The Washington consensus is under pressure. In particular, the then chief economist of the World Bank, Joseph Stiglitz, broke ranks in the aftermath of the Asian crisis to question the role of his own organization and, more notably, that of the IMF. In this section we review the changes in the financial environment and subsequently the developments in the operation of the IMF. We conclude with a discussion of the possibility of the IMF acting as a lender of last resort to the world.

**The World Economic Environment**

The Mexican, Asian and Russian crises were all characterized by rapid withdrawal of short-term international capital. Malaysia's response was to withdraw from the international capital markets by imposing capital controls. Every other affected nation has rejected this approach and accepted that the international mobility of capital is beneficial if handled correctly. Capital flows into emerging nations are increasing again after the sharp slowdown following the Asian crisis. The majority of the flows are in the form of equity investment with net bank lending still negative.

Sufficiently developed financial markets are necessary conditions for handling large, volatile international capital flows, something that the Asian crisis highlighted. The IMF is now emphasizing capital market developments as part of its supply-side-orientated policy recommendations. Rather belatedly, it is recognizing that the sequencing of reforms matters. It also now appears to favour Chilean-style controls to deter short-term capital inflows, and advises governments not to rush into removing outflow controls.[3] Ironically, more recently Chile has relaxed capital inflow controls. The effectiveness of capital controls is still debatable. Monteil and Reinhart (1999) find no statistically significant effect on the volume of capital flows. However, they do note that capital controls appear to change the composition of such flows so as to promote longer-term FDI flows at the expense of short-term portfolio flows. Calvo and Reinhart (1999) question the true effectiveness of capital restrictions and argue that the results may merely indicate a switch from foreign to domestic short-term debt. To the extent that domestic short-term debt is a claim on central bank reserves, it still remains a problem in the face of capital withdrawals. Severe maturity mismatch is a grave danger, even if it is not accompanied by currency mismatches. Similarly, Phylaktis (1997, 1999) raises doubts on the effectiveness of foreign exchange controls. In measuring the degree of capital market integration in the Pacific Basin region, extensive interest rate linkages were found even for countries like Taiwan and Korea, where foreign exchange controls were still in use. Furthermore, Phylaktis and Ravazzolo (2002) find that countries which are economically integrated, will see their financial markets move together even in the presence of foreign exchange controls.

Economic integration, if that is measured say by the contemporaneous movement of output growth of countries, provides a channel for financial integration through the effects of expected economic activity on the expected cash flows of firms and their stock prices. Thus, if two countries experience a movement in their output, then their cash flows will move together and so will their stock markets, irrespective of the existence of foreign exchange restrictions.

The IMF is also questioning the role of the exchange rate regime in contributing to financial crises. Another common characteristic of the 1990s crises was the presence of fixed exchange rates. Notably, countries operating floating regimes who might otherwise have been expected to be under pressure (such as Mexico and South Africa) were relatively unaffected by the later crises. There is now a greater willingness at the IMF to countenance floating regimes in emerging markets. Many Asian and Latin American nations have floated since the breakdown of their fixed systems. The floating has been dirty, however, with many countries boosting foreign currency reserves rather than letting their currencies appreciate as capital inflows returned. At the same time, there has been a great deal of enthusiasm for currency boards stemming from the experiences of Argentina and Hong Kong. Early in the Asian crisis, the high interest rates in those two countries seemed a small price to pay to avoid the turmoil affecting those economies that had led their exchange rates to float. But both Argentina and Hong Kong subsequently experienced recessions, while some of the early devaluers (Korea and Mexico) quickly returned to reasonable growth rates. In the case of Argentina the problem became worse with the mounting government debt forcing it to abandon the currency board. The enthusiasm for any boards has diminished accordingly since then. As Frenkel (1999) has pointed out, no single currency regime is right for all countries or at all times. The choice of the exchange rate regime at every stage is governed by how to ensure credibility. This becomes very difficult, however, when capital flows are free and exchange rates are fixed as the costs of an unfavourable shock may be too high in terms of real output.

**The Role of the IMF**

The IMF's greatest challenge remains to establish what role it wants in the new millennium. One approach recognizes that the IMF's ability to act decisively in a crisis is at best limited given the huge capital flows that it is facing. The Asian crisis showed that higher interest rates and macroeconomic policy changes cannot help stabilize currencies that are in free-fall. As a result, the IMF is trying to reinvent itself as a crisis prevention institution. The fact that it failed to publicly predict the crises discussed (although it claimed internal reports warned of Asian imbalances) has led the IMF to enhance its surveillance policies. It sought to improve data provision in the wake of the Mexican crisis and it has redoubled its efforts since. It has developed or is in the process of developing internationally accepted standards and codes of practice for economic, financial and business activities.[4] These data are to be publicly available and as widely disseminated as possible. For that purpose, it has strengthened the special data dissemination standards, notably with respect to international reserves and external debt. In a parallel move, the IMF and others are trying to revamp the Basle Committee agreements with the aim of preventing future crises. The primary initiative, which is still beset by disagreement, is to force banks to put aside capital depending on the riskiness of their loans. Since this is proving too problematic, the Basle Committee is also proposing higher levels of supervision and market discipline, particularly with respect to hedge funds. The US Congress is also proposing that the hedge funds disclose more about their investments, hoping that this will limit their lending excesses.

The second approach is for the IMF to enhance its resources with which it can combat crises. Despite its failure in Mexico, Asia and Russia, the IMF is still trying to increase its funding to allow it to lend yet more. It has introduced a new lending facility – the contingency credit line – aimed specifically at crisis-hit countries. Indeed, given its interventions in so many crises over the past decades, Meltzer (1998) argues that too much of the world has become too big and too indebted to fail in the eyes of world leaders. The IMF clearly still sees a role for itself in crisis resolution. However, to counter the claims that its policies lead to moral hazard problems, the IMF is trying to find ways to 'bail in' private sector lenders, that is, to involve the private sector in the resolutions of financial crises. This can take a variety of forms, including spontaneous new inflows, the direct provision of new money, and arrangements for creditors to maintain exposure, including coordinated rollover of interbank credit, bond exchanges and reschedulings, and restructurings. This is a direct response to criticisms that it has bailed banks out in previous crises. This is a step back towards its role in the debt crisis, where the IMF will act as coordinator of private sector creditors in discussions with crisis-hit countries looking to reschedule lending. It also recognizes that the overwhelming volume of capital flowing round the globe is too much for agencies to fight. The only way crises can be resolved is to bring the international financiers into the discussions too. Whether the banks will be allowed to incur losses in the event of imprudent lending, or whether the IMF will again try to bail them out as the price for bringing them to the rescheduling negotiation table remains to be seen. There are no hard and fast rules about how the private sector will be brought to the table and the IMF is proceeding on a case-by-case basis.

Camdessus (1999) argues against a one-size-fits-all approach and emphasizes alternative sources of funding in times of crisis, including both private sector and IMF contingent credit facilities. He also recognizes that it may not be possible to mobilize sufficient funds to resolve a crisis, and argues that all creditors must recognize that '*in extremis*, a country may have no orderly way out of [a] crisis other than a comprehensive debt restructuring that includes bonds'. His remarks clearly reflect the criticisms faced by the IMF through the recent crises. The bailing in of the private sector is a priority, and by altering the Basle Committee agreements to force banks to assess the risks of short-term lending more accurately while avoiding commitments to bail out lenders, the moral hazard problem is mitigated. Whether the financial community will take these comments to heart remains to be seen.

**The IMF as an International Lender of Last Resort**

In the context of the recent number of financial crises, the need for an international lender of last resort and whether the IMF can take that role for the countries facing an external financing crisis, that is, a massive demand for foreign currency, have been discussed extensively (see, for example, Fischer, 1999; Meltzer, 1998; Calomiris, 1998; and Giannini, 1998). According to the best-known classic writer on the lender of last resort, Walter Bagehot, 'in a crisis, the lender of last resort should lend freely, at a penalty rate, on the basis of collateral that is marketable in the ordinary course of business when there is no panic' (Bagehot, 1873). It is clear that the IMF cannot fulfil all of the above conditions. First of all, the IMF is not an international central bank and cannot freely create international money. In theory the IMF can create special drawing rights, but this is done infrequently, and never on short notice or to help specific problem debtors. However, the IMF has a financial structure, close to that of a credit union, which gives it access to a pool of resources which it can then lend to member countries. In addition, vast amounts of money are not required for managing a crisis. As Goodhart and Shoenmaker (1995) have pointed out, organizing a 'concerted lending operation' is the most common bail-out procedure for modern lenders of last resort.

The IMF cannot lend freely without limit without creating too much moral hazard. Borrower moral hazard has been deterred to some extent by the requirements of conditionality. In addition, the charging of penalty rates of interest introduced at the end of 1997 with the supplementary reserve facility loans, which can make large amounts available to countries in crisis, can also mitigate borrower moral hazard. What is more difficult to deal with is investor moral hazard – that a lender of last resort would encourage investors to lend unwisely. Involving the private sector in financing the resolution of crises will limit the moral hazard.

Bagehot's prescription that lending should take place on good collateral can actually be applied by the IMF as its Articles of Agreement permit it to ask for collateral. The IMF has rarely done so because it and the World Bank are regarded as preferred creditors and have first claim on payments made by countries in debt to them. Their collateral is the threat of denying access to global capital markets. Another of Bagehot's prescriptions, that lender-of-last-resort facilities should not be given to institutions which are bankrupt, is difficult to apply in the international context. There is no bankruptcy status for a sovereign, but workout procedures can play a similar role.

Thus, there are constraints for the IMF to act as international lender of last resort. However, the recent steps which have been taken to correct major weaknesses in the structure of the international economy, such as the improvements in transparency, the adoption of appropriate exchange rate systems, the development and monitoring of international standards, including a bankruptcy standard, the development of early warning systems to monitor country risks, and the development of precautionary lines of credit, will enable the IMF to play more successfully the two roles most relevant to a lender of last resort, those of crisis lender and crisis manager. Despite criticisms of how the recent crises were handled, no other national or international institution can play the role that the IMF has been playing in the global economy.

## NOTES

1. It should be noted that a slow correction of an imbalance might result in a transitory imbalance becoming less temporary than originally anticipated, or in an imbalance that was created exogenously to give rise to endogenous distortions that compound it (see Guitan, 1995).
2. For an evaluation of the Fund-supported adjustment programmes, see Conway (1994), Khan (1990, 1995) and Killick and Moazzam (1992).
3. That does not imply that Chile's controls on capital inflows have been effective. See Edwards (1999) for a discussion of the issue.
4. For example, Code of Good Practices on Fiscal Transparency: Declaration of Principles; Code of Good Practices on Transparency in Monetary and Financial Policies (see IMF, *Annual Report*, 1999b).

## REFERENCES

Bagehot W. (1873), '*Lombard Street: A Description of the Money Market*', London: William Clowes & Sons.

Bird, G. (1990), 'Evaluating the effects of IMF-supported adjustment programmes: an analytical commentary on interpreting the empirical evidence', in K. Phylaktis and M. Pradhan (eds), *International Finance and the Less Developed Countries*, Basingstoke: Macmillan, 28–41.

Calomiris, C.W. (1998), 'The IMF's imprudent role as lender of last resort', *Cato Journal*, **17**, 275–94.

Calvo, G.A. and C.M. Reinhart (1999), 'When capital inflows come to a sudden stop: consequences and policy options', mimeo, University of Maryland.

Camdessus, M. (1999), 'Preventing and resolving financial crises: the role of the private sector', *Speeches*, Washington, DC: IMF.

Camdessus, M. (2000), 'The IMF we need', *Speeches*, Washington, DC: IMF, February.

Conway, P. (1994), 'IMF lending programs: participation and impact', *Journal of Development Economics*, **45**, 365–91.

Edwards, S. (1999), 'How effective are capital controls?', *Journal of Economic Perspectives*, **13**, 65–84.

Feldstein, M. (1998), 'Refocusing the IMF', *Foreign Affairs*, **17**(2), 20–30.

Finch, C.D. (1989), 'The IMF: record and the prospect', *Essays in International Finance*, No. 175. Princeton University.

Fischer, S. (1999), 'On the need for an international lender of last resort', *Journal of Economic Perspectives*, **13**, 85–104.

Frenkel, J. (1999), 'No single currency regime is right for all countries or at all times', *Essays in International Finance*, Princeton University.

Giannini, C. (1999), 'Enemy of none but friend of all? An international perspective on the lender of last function', International Monetary Fund Working Paper WP/99/10, Washington, DC.

Goodhart, C. and D. Shoenmaker (1995), 'Should the functions of monetary policy and bank supervision be separated?', *Oxford Economic Papers*, **47**, 539–60.

Guitan, M. (1995), 'Conditionality: past, present, future', *IMF Staff Papers*, **42**, 792–835.

International Monetary Fund (IMF) (1999a), *The IMF's Response to the Asian Crisis*, Washington, DC: IMF.

International Monetary Fund (IMF) (1999), *Annual Report*, Washington, DC: IMF.

Khan, M., (1990), 'The microeconomics effects of fund-supported adjustment programs', *IMF Staff Papers*, **37**, 195–231.

Khan, M. (1995), 'Evaluating the effects of IMF-supported programmes: a survey', in K. Phylaktis and M. Pradhan (eds), *International Finance and the Less Developed Countries*, Basingstoke: Macmillan, 11–28.

Killick, T. and M. Moazzam (1992), 'Country experiences with IMF programmes in the 1980s', *World Economy*, **15**, 599–632.

Krugman, P. (1994), 'The myth of Asia's miracle: a cautionary fable', *Foreign Affairs*, **73**(6), 62–78.

Meigs, A.J. (1997), 'Mexican monetary lessons', *Cato Journal*, **17**(1).

Meigs, A.J. (1998), 'Lessons for Asia from Mexico' *Cato Journal*, **17**(3).

Meltzer, A. (1998), 'Asian problems and the IMF', *Cato Journal*, **17**(3).

Monteil, P. and C.M. Reinhart (1999), 'Do capital controls influence the volume and composition of capital flows? Evidence from the 1990s', *Journal of International Money and Finance*, **18**(4), 619–35.

Phylaktis, K. (1997), 'Capital market integration in the Pacific Basin countries: an analysis of real interest rate linkages', *Pacific Basin Finance Journal*, **5**.

Phylaktis, K. (1999), 'Capital market integration in the Pacific Region: an impulse response analysis', *Journal of International Money and Finance*, **18**.

Phylaktis, K. and F. Ravazzolo (2002), 'Measuring financial and economic integration with equity prices in emerging markets', *Journal of International Money and Finance*, **21** (forthcoming).

# 25. Reforming the privatized international monetary and financial architecture*

## Jane D'Arista

## 1 INTRODUCTION

Since the events of 1997, proposals for reforming the financial system have regularly punctuated public discussions of the global economy. But so far, neither these discussions nor a series of official multilateral initiatives have produced even modest changes in global finance or the monetary infrastructure on which it rides. During 1999, the momentum for reform has dissipated, despite the persistence of powerfully destabilizing features in the global system and the likelihood of future crises.

The most worrisome feature is, in many respects, the most deeply ingrained. After the worldwide removal of regulatory constraints, market forces have assumed a dominant role in the international monetary and payments system. With the ascendancy of liberalization as a governing paradigm for financial enterprise, the role of the public sector has been cut down if not cut out. As a result, what the public sector alone can do – manage liquidity, launch countercyclical initiatives and respond to crises at the international level – has become far less effective than in the past. Financial liberalization also poses a substantial threat to the sovereignty of nations, particularly those with emerging economies which stand most exposed to the punishing judgements of unrestrained market forces.

Ultimately, remedying these problems will require the public sector to reconstitute its powers to promote stability and growth in the global economy while enhancing the rights of individual countries to shape their own economic, social and political outcomes. The following three proposals suggest a framework through which old and new institutional arrangements could help reinvigorate these powers and rights.

- The first proposal puts forward a plan for establishing a public international investment fund for emerging markets. Structured as a closed-end mutual fund, this investment vehicle would address the problems that have emerged with the extraordinary growth in cross-border securities investment transactions in the 1990s. The proposal advocates a role for the public sector in managing those problems so that private portfolio investment – now the dominant channel for flows into emerging markets – can promote steady, sustainable growth rather than the boom and bust cycles that so far have been its primary contribution.[1]

- The second proposal recommends a new allocation of special drawing rights (SDRs), the international reserve asset issued by the International Monetary Fund (IMF). Issuing a new round of SDRs would provide substantial short-term relief from the debt burdens that aggravate imbalances in nations' access to international liquidity and perpetuate policies favouring lower wages, fiscal and monetary austerity and deflation.[2]
- The third proposal articulates an alternative to the privatized, dollar-based international monetary system that is a root cause of global instability and market failure. The proposal describes an international transactions and payments system managed by a public international agency in which cross-border monetary exchanges can be made in each country's own currency. This critical feature would help governments and central banks conduct effective economic policies, including countercyclical initiatives, at a national level. Equally important, it would allow all countries – not just a privileged few – to service external debt with wealth generated in their domestic markets. Thus it would help end the unsustainable paradigm of export-led growth that now governs the global economy.[3]

## 2 CREATING A PUBLIC INTERNATIONAL INVESTMENT FUND FOR EMERGING MARKETS

**The Rise of Foreign Portfolio Investment**

Of all the profound changes that shook the global financial order during the past two decades, none has had more dramatic effects than the rise of securities markets as the principal channel for private international investment flows. After the Second World War, international bank loans had been the pre-eminent medium for these flows. But beginning in the 1980s, three interrelated developments gradually established the supremacy of foreign portfolio investment.

Table 25.1  Assets of institutional investors

|  | 1980 | 1988 | 1990 | 1992 | 1995 |
|---|---|---|---|---|---|
| *In billions of US dollars* | | | | | |
| Canada | 93 | 257 | 326 | 376 | 493 |
| Germany | 165 | 443 | 627 | 764 | 1,113 |
| Japan | 244 | 1,459 | 1,650 | 1,972 | 3,035 |
| United Kingdom | 345 | 992 | 1,208 | 1,432 | 1,790 |
| United States | 1,607 | 4,316 | 5,221 | 7,183 | 10,501 |
| Total | 2,454 | 7,466 | 9,031 | 11,727 | 16,932 |
| *As percentage of GDP* | | | | | |
| Canada | 35 | 52 | 57 | 66 | 87 |
| Germany | 20 | 37 | 42 | 43 | 46 |
| Japan | 23 | 50 | 56 | 54 | 59 |
| United Kingdom | 64 | 118 | 124 | 137 | 162 |
| United States | 59 | 88 | 95 | 119 | 151 |

*Sources:* International Monetary Fund, *International Capital Markets*, 1995. Bank for International Settlements, *68th Annual Report, 1997–98*, June 1998.

First, patterns of saving and investment underwent a huge shift in major industrialized countries. Increasingly, individuals put their savings in pension plans and other institutional pools that invest those funds directly in securities rather than placing them in the hands of intermediaries such as depository institutions. In Canadian, German, Japanese and UK financial markets, assets of institutional investors doubled or nearly doubled as a percentage of GDP from 1980 through 1994. In the US, the share of total financial sector assets held by institutional investors rose from 32 per cent in 1978 to 54 per cent in 1998 as the share of depository institutions fell from 57 per cent to 27 per cent. (See Table 25.1.)

The rapid growth of these assets helped fuel a boom in cross-border investments. International transactions in bonds and equities among the G7 countries rose from 35 per cent of combined gross domestic product in 1985 to 140 per cent of combined GDP in 1995.[4]

The explosion in cross-border securities transactions was aided and abetted by a second key event – the dismantling of controls on capital movements by rich, poor and middle-income countries alike. The US took the lead in 1974, removing controls that had been imposed in the 1960s to halt capital outflows: the interest equalization tax on issues of foreign securities in US markets, restrictions on transfers of funds by US multinational corporations to their foreign affiliates and limits on new foreign lending by US banks.

In 1979, the UK eliminated controls on capital outflows and other European countries repealed limits on both outflows and inflows (such as reserve requirements and taxes on foreign borrowing) over the following decade to comply with the timetable set for unification and the implementation of the European Monetary System. Ending capital controls also became a prerequisite for membership in the Organization for Economic Cooperation and Development (OECD), which prompted their removal by Mexico and Korea in the 1990s. Under pressure from the US government and foreign investors, other emerging market countries lifted restrictions on inflows in the 1990s, too.

In many countries, the wholesale removal of capital controls took place against the backdrop of a vast privatization of state enterprise. The wave of privatization extended from the Thatcher government in the UK to the restructuring of centrally planned economies and it generated more securities issues in a wider range of national markets than in any previous period. This third critical development ensured the rise of portfolio investment worldwide. As cross-border securities transactions mushroomed in volume and scale, national capital markets expanded accordingly, markets grew more integrated worldwide, and capital mobility accelerated.

**Portfolio Investment Flows and Macroeconomic Leverage**

For most of the 1980s, America reigned as the primary recipient of foreign portfolio investment – initially as a result of easy fiscal and tight monetary policies that drove up real interest rates and the value of the dollar. As the Third World debt crisis (triggered in part by those same policies) stretched across the decade, debt service payments provided a large, continuing source of inflows to the US.

But the end-of-decade recession that sapped demand and depressed asset prices in the US and other industrialized countries caused investors to redirect funds into developing economies. Between 1989 and 1993, private investment flows into emerging markets multiplied more than 12 times over as a percentage of total foreign securities investment by industrial countries.

From a distance, this pattern superficially resembled earlier ebbs and flows in post-Bretton Woods economic and financial activity. During the 1970s, for example, rapid oil price increases produced recession and falling interest rates in industrialized countries, which set the stage for a wave of private lending to developing countries.

But international investment in the early 1990s differed from preceding periods in at least two important ways. First, developing countries absorbed a much larger volume of funds in much less time than ever before.

Table 25.2  Capital flows to developing countries[a] (in billions of US dollars)

|  | All developing countries | Asia | Western Hemisphere | Other developing countries[b] |
|---|---|---|---|---|
| *1977–1982* | | | | |
| Total net capital inflows | 183.0 | 94.8 | 157.8 | −69.6 |
| Net foreign direct investment | 67.2 | 16.2 | 31.8 | 19.2 |
| Net portfolio investment | −63.0 | 3.6 | 9.6 | −76.2 |
| Bank lending & other | 178.8 | 75.0 | 116.4 | −12.6 |
| *1983–1989* | | | | |
| Total net capital inflows | 61.6 | 116.9 | −116.2 | 60.9 |
| Net foreign direct investment | 93.1 | 36.4 | 30.8 | 25.9 |
| Net portfolio investment | 45.5 | 9.8 | −8.4 | 44.1 |
| Bank lending & other | −77.0 | 70.7 | −138.6 | −9.0 |
| *1990–1994* | | | | |
| Total net capital inflows | 625.5 | 195.3 | 203.8 | 226.4 |
| Net foreign direct investment | 224.6 | 116.8 | 68.8 | 39.0 |
| Net portfolio investment | 324.6 | 36.9 | 184.4 | 103.3 |
| Bank lending & other | 76.2 | 41.7 | −49.6 | 84.1 |
| *1995–1998* | | | | |
| Total net capital inflows | 618.9 | 143.7 | 276.6 | 198.6 |
| Net foreign direct investment | 482.7 | 217.5 | 169.9 | 95.3 |
| Net portfolio investment | 225.5 | 9.0 | 114.4 | 102.1 |
| Bank lending & other | −89.4 | −82.8 | −7.9 | 1.3 |

*Notes:*
[a] Flows exclude exceptional financing.
[b] Includes countries in Africa, Eastern Europe and the Middle East. Excludes capital exporting countries such as Kuwait and Saudi Arabia.

*Source:*  International Monetary Fund, *International Capital Markets*, 1995 and 1999 editions.

As unrestrained foreign portfolio investment poured into national markets, it bid up the prices of financial assets at unprecedented rates. Aggregate capital flows to Mexico from 1990 to 1993 totalled $91 billion, an amount equal to one-fifth of all net inflows to developing countries in those years. Two-thirds of the net inflow was portfolio investment, most of it channelled into a bubbling Mexican stock market, which rose 436 per cent between 1990 and 1993. (See Table 25.2.)

Second, the opening of financial markets to massive flows of foreign portfolio capital exposed countries to short investment horizons and hair-trigger investor judgements. Rather than residing as long-term assets on the books of banks, developing-nation investments became overnight guests on the constantly changing balance sheets of pension funds, mutual funds and hedge funds. Freed from restrictions on entry or exit, institutional investors could now shuffle their investments in bonds and equities from market to market in response to cyclical developments that raised and lowered returns – a privilege that subtly but inexorably weakened the impact of countercyclical monetary policies.

As the notion of 'hot money' entered the popular lexicon, central bankers discovered that the increasingly potent interest and exchange rate effects of capital flows were undermining their ability to control credit expansion and contraction. By lowering interest rates to revive economic activity, monetary authorities were likely instead to precipitate or intensify capital outflows and reduce credit availability in their national economy. By raising interest rates to cool economic activity, central banks would attract foreign inflows seeking higher returns. If large enough, the inflow might stimulate rather than suppress borrowing and lending.[5]

The danger of these procyclical pressures manifested itself with a vengeance in the mid-1990s, as industrialized countries pulled out of recession and increased their demand for credit. After skyrocketing from $29 billion to $142 billion between 1990 and 1993, the net value of foreign portfolio investment by US residents fell to $50 billion in 1994. The Federal Reserve played a decisive role in this reversal by initiating what became a seven-step monetary tightening in March 1994 and narrowing the spreads between US and emerging market debt issues.

As these spreads narrowed, equity prices fell in Mexico and other emerging markets, eroding their value as collateral for bank loans. Meanwhile, an appreciating peso lowered the cost of imported consumer goods and hammered Mexico's export sector, pushing the country's current account deficit to a whopping 8 per cent of GDP by the final quarter of 1994. As new foreign investment in private securities diminished, the Zedillo government attempted to finance the deficit by issuing dollar-indexed, short-term debt – so-called *tesobonos* which promised to protect their holders against the possibility of currency devaluation.

Although temporarily effective, this response only increased Mexico's vulnerability to a loss of confidence by foreign investors. Amid a series of political shocks and mounting concern over the country's dwindling international reserves, domestic and foreign investors began to take flight, forcing Mexico to devalue the peso in December 1994. Ultimately, the *tes-*

*obono* overhang contributed to the cost of a $50 billion bailout orchestrated by the Clinton administration.

In the wake of the peso crisis, many emerging market countries took measures to counter the propensity of heavy investment inflows to inflate exchange rates (thereby eroding the competitiveness of export sectors) and increase the volatility of capital markets (thereby heightening the vulnerability of their financial systems). According to the IMF, these remedial measures included increases in bank reserve requirements, increased exchange rate flexibility and the imposition of exchange controls. In 1995, the Bank for International Settlements (BIS) reported widespread agreement that short-term financial transactions should not be free from controls until developing nations could assure the soundness of their financial system.

This agreement, however, ran up against a far more powerful consensus in Washington. Leading American financial firms, the Democratic Administration, the Republican Congress, the Federal Reserve, the IMF and elite opinion makers all continued to press for unimpeded financial liberalization, insisting that greater freedom for capital movements was the solution, not the problem. Portraying capital inflows as wholly beneficial, these influential advocates claimed that mass outflows were an inevitable response to bad policies and an acceptable tool of market discipline.

As the 1994 Mexican crisis subsequently replayed itself in different forms throughout the world, the shortsightedness of this Washington consensus became clearer. When capital raced out of East Asia, Russia, Brazil and other emerging markets in successive waves of panic, the ripple effects on exchange rates, asset values, commodity prices, employment, incomes and financial systems brought the global economy to its knees.

Although partial recovery has begun, it is likely to take many years for these damaged national economies to repair their losses. And despite its role as the principal engine of recovery, America – with its bubbling equity prices, large current account deficits and unsustainable consumer debt burdens – may be increasingly susceptible to harsh judgements by the liberalized financial system that US policy elites have imposed on the rest of the world.

**Taming Portfolio Investment Flows to Emerging Markets**

With the phenomenal growth of institutional investors' assets, foreign portfolio capital could provide urgently needed financing for long-term economic expansion in developing countries. To achieve this beneficial result, however, emerging-market nations need portfolio investment inflows that are sizeable, stable and disciplined by the standards of public purpose.

Chile has been fairly successful in using capital controls to moderate these effects. During the 1990s, Chile has required foreign investors to hold securities for a year or more and Chilean companies to maintain reserve requirements on direct borrowing abroad. Similarly, Korea imposed strict limits on foreign borrowing by domestic companies for many years before its recent liberalization. Such controls may be fine as far as they go. But they do not go far enough towards accomplishing the dual task of injecting long-term private capital into emerging markets while deterring the destructive fluctuations in asset prices and exchange rates associated with procyclical surges in foreign portfolio flows.

One innovation that might be equal to this task is a closed-end investment fund for emerging-market securities. Such a fund could issue its own liabilities to private investors and buy stocks and bonds of private enterprises and public agencies in a wide spectrum of developing countries. Both the number of countries and the size of the investment pool would be large enough to ensure diversification. The fund's investment objectives would focus on the long-run economic performance of enterprises and countries rather than short-term financial returns. Selecting securities in consultation with host governments would help the fund meet these objectives.

Unlike open-end mutual funds, which must buy back an unlimited number of shares whenever investors demand it, closed-end investment pools issue a limited number of shares that trade on a stock exchange or in over-the-counter markets. This key structural difference makes the holdings in closed-end portfolios much less vulnerable to the waves of buying and redemptions that sometimes characterize open-end funds. Thus a closed-end fund would provide emerging markets a measure of protection by allowing the prices of shares in the fund to fluctuate without triggering destabilizing purchases and sales of the underlying investments.

To further balance the goals of market stability and economic dynamism, the closed-end fund should possess a solid capital cushion. Between 10 and 20 per cent of the value of shares sold to investors should be used to purchase and hold government securities of major industrial countries in amounts roughly proportional to the closed-end fund shares owned by residents of those countries. These holdings would provide investors a partial guaranteed return, denominated in their own currencies. And the government securities would explicitly guarantee the value of the fund's capital. This double-barrelled guarantee would moderate investors' concerns about potential risk.

Creating one or more closed-end funds on this model would reduce the need for capital controls, especially in countries that choose to accept foreign portfolio investment solely through this vehicle. The closed-end fund would have several additional benefits as well. It would help pension plans in developing and developed countries diversify their portfolios while minimizing country risk and transactions costs. And it would help institutional investors in developing countries share the cost of information and collectively combat the lack of disclosure by domestic issuers in these markets.

Despite the potential for promoting growth and stability, private investors are unlikely to inaugurate a closed-end fund on their own. For better or worse, these investors approach all markets with narrow interests, limited time horizons and a demonstrated willingness to externalize the costs of unsustainable economic activity and unstable financial markets through expensive, *ad hoc* public sector bail-outs. Therefore, like the modern public-purpose market innovations in the US that began with the Reconstruction Finance Corporation in the 1930s and culminated in the development of the secondary mortgage market in the 1970s, governments must take the lead in laying the institutional groundwork for a closed-end fund.

These arrangements need not reinvent the wheel. Just as the structural mechanisms and potential assets of an emerging-economies closed-end fund already exist in the marketplace, so the capacity for managing such a fund falls well within the reach of an existing public institution. Indeed, this management function is wholly consistent with the World Bank's mandate to facilitate private investment in developing countries. Moreover, the Bank's experience in issuing its own liabilities in global capital markets would expedite the start-up of a closed-end fund.

Like other Bretton Woods institutions, the World Bank ought to operate in a far more open, accountable and responsive fashion. Managing a closed-end fund would not in itself fully accomplish these goals. But it could play a substantial part in realigning the Bank's programme with the powers and functions enumerated in its charter. Properly structured (no small feat), the fund could make a significant downpayment on the democratic deficits that characterize governance and policy making in international financial institutions.

## 3 ISSUING A NEW ALLOCATION OF SDRs

In the unsettled aftermath of the cold war, Western responses to Russia's financial collapse spoke volumes about the political economy of US leadership. In April 1999, the International Monetary Fund (IMF) agreed to resume lending to Russia in return for renewed commitments to fiscal and banking reform. At the insistence of US and European officials, however, the IMF declined to provide cash and arranged merely to transfer moneys from one account to another to prevent default on Russia's outstanding debt to the Fund. The accounting was creative but it replicated the same technique used during the Third World debt crisis of the 1980s: piling debt on debt by capitalizing interest payments.

Compare the thrust of these policies to the reconstruction effort following the Second World War. Then, the US rebuilt Europe and Japan with Marshall Plan grants amounting to 2 per cent of annual GDP. By using US taxpayers' money to purchase US goods, Marshall Plan beneficiaries recycled funds back into the US economy, helping prevent the usual pattern of post-war recession. In addition to promoting mutual growth, the arrangement manifested a deeper understanding that nagging debts make enemies, not friends.

Now, of course, the US is in no position to repeat its mid-century largesse. America has become a debtor nation and provides stimulus to the global economy by going deeper into debt as it buys goods from others. And the US, like other debtors, is beginning to express its enmity toward those from whom it borrows to buy.

So what is a poor hegemonist to do? The US can still make war with taxpayers' money but finds it increasingly difficult to tap that source for lending, let alone grants. But more loans are not what Russia or any country trying to recover from financial crises needs. Nor does the world need the brand of medicine Alan Greenspan prescribed in an April 1999 speech to the World Bank.

Addressing the subject of 'Currency reserves and debt', the Fed chairman proposed that emerging-market nations adopt an 'external balance sheet rule' patterned on the ideal balance sheet configurations of the private international financial institutions that are their creditors. The rule for emerging-market countries would be to preserve a cushion of foreign exchange reserves while carefully managing the average maturity of foreign debt. Despite its ostensible emphasis on debt management for the sake of 'private sector burden-sharing', Greenspan's proposal simply reinforces the current paradigm that binds virtually every developing country to some combination of austerity, foreign borrowing and export-led growth.[6]

What the world needs instead is a dose of Marshall Plan-like creativity to remove debt's stranglehold on the global economy. One of the few existing resources available to this effort is the SDR, designed in the 1960s to deal with prospective global liquidity crunches. The following modest proposal describes how a new allocation of SDRs could contribute to solving current problems.

**SDRs: Some Background**

Special drawing rights are assets created by the IMF to supplement existing international reserves. The pool of existing reserves includes gold, member nations' positions in the IMF and financial assets denominated in foreign currencies (foreign exchange reserves).

Under a system created in 1969, the IMF allocates SDRs to member countries in proportion to their quota – their share of membership dues and voting power – in the Fund. SDRs are valued in relation to a basket of five currencies and serve as the unit of account in which all Fund transactions and obligations are denominated. Member countries' obligations to and claims on the Fund are also denominated in SDRs.

SDRs may be used as reserve assets by a member country in exchange for another country's currency in cases where the former needs to finance a balance of payments deficit and the latter has a strong balance of payments position. Such transactions can take place at the direction of the Fund or through the mutual consent of the two countries. In addition, SDRs can be used in swap arrangements, loans and the settlement of other financial obligations among member countries and between member countries and the Fund.

Although the Fund's Articles of Agreement state the intention of 'making the special drawing right the principal reserve asset in the international monetary system', this has not occurred. The last allocation of SDRs took place in 1981 and the cumulative value of total allocations is a modest SDR 21.4 billion or about $28 billion. By contrast, outstanding official foreign exchange reserves totalled $1.6 trillion at year-end 1997.

**Why a New Allocation Now?**

A 1987 IMF staff report affirmed that SDR allocations could serve as 'a "safety net" to cope with an international financial emergency of limited, though uncertain, duration'. Today, widening imbalances in the global economy have created a liquidity crisis for countries with 40 per cent or more of the world's population (see Table 25.3). In the absence of a true international lender of last resort, SDRs represent the single instrument in place at the global level to address the problem.

Given the unprecedented amount of IMF resources already committed to crisis-ridden member countries, new sources of funding are urgently needed. In theory, the IMF could obtain these funds by borrowing in private markets. But member country taxpayers would still remain the guarantor of IMF obligations. And the IMF would simply perpetuate the worst features of its current crisis-response operations if it reloaned privately raised funds to affected countries.

Debt owed to the IMF is no different from debt owed to the private sector in terms of the pressure it puts on countries to export their way out of massive loan obligations. New SDR allocations provide a uniquely benign alternative to bail-out loans which compound the underlying inequities –

*Table 25.3  Debt and the crisis countries*

|  | Total external debt ($ billions; year-end 1996) |
|---|---|
| Emerging markets | $2,095 |
| Russia | 125 |
| The Asian Five | 459 |
| Indonesia | 129 |
| Korea | 158 |
| Malaysia | 40 |
| Philippines | 41 |
| Thailand | 91 |

*Sources:* World Bank, *Global Development Finance*; International Monetary Fund, *World Economic Outlook and International Capital Markets: Interim Assessment*, December 1998.

not to mention the destructive trade practices, anti-Western resentments and growing inducements to violence – inherent in a global system organized around foreign currency-denominated debt.

**How a New SDR Allocation Should Be Structured**

By issuing a new allocation of SDRs, the IMF could accomplish three objectives. First, it could provide badly needed debt relief. Second, it would permit countries to shift from an export-led growth paradigm towards fostering deeper, stronger internal markets. Third, it could foster conditions for a resumption of growth in developing countries and in the global economy.

Ideally, new allocations should be directed only to highly indebted poor countries (HIPCs) (see Table 25.4 for a profile) and to those nations that have been hit hardest by the effects of financial crises. But changing the IMF's Articles of Agreement to direct allocations to particular countries would surely be contentious and time consuming. On the other hand, a general allocation based on quotas – a system that would distribute almost half the newly issued SDRs to G7 countries – could be done quickly, if agreed to by 85 per cent of the IMF Board.[7]

In any event, allocations for debt relief should supplement the so-called 'equity' allocations (adopted in April 1997 but not yet ratified) for countries that had not become members of the IMF when the last SDR allocations were made during 1979–81. Allocations to HIPCs should be sufficiently large to enable them to pay off public and private external debt. Allocations to other countries should be used to repay public debt and a needed portion of private debt.

Table 25.4  Highly indebted poor countries: a profile

| | |
|---|---:|
| Number of countries | 41 |
| Share of world's population | 20 per cent |
| Per capita annual income | less than $925 |
| Total debt | $221.0 billion |
|   US government's share | $6.8 billion |
|   Owed to private creditors | $55.2 billion |
|   Owed to other governments and multilateral financial institutions | $159.0 billion |
| Ratio of debt to annual exports | 250 per cent |
| Debt service in 1997 | $8.0 billion |
|   Share of budgetary revenues and expenditures (average) | 60 per cent |

Source: World Bank and International Monetary Fund. Data are for 1995 except as noted.

In the case of Russia, allocations should cover all debt incurred by the former USSR. In repaying private debt, SDR recipients would exchange the drawing rights with central banks of strong-currency countries for foreign exchange to pay off private lenders.

In addition, recipient countries should retain a portion of the new drawing rights as reserves to back a resumption of domestic bank lending. Adding reserves to their central banks' balance sheets would increase the countries' liquidity, enable monetary expansion and thereby allow domestic banks to lend at reasonable rates of interest.

The current reliance on high interest rates to attract foreign capital and raise currency values suppresses growth in crisis-battered countries. Borrowers cannot earn enough to repay their loans; hobbled banking systems drain public resources; credit crunches deter, rather than spur, new infusions of capital by foreign and domestic investors.

Moreover, unless newly allocated SDRs are also employed as domestic financial reserves, the export-led development paradigm will inevitably continue. Without an injection of liquidity in domestic markets, hard-hit countries must struggle to earn the reserves needed to rebuild financial systems capable of bankrolling job creation and income growth in the real sector. Under the prevailing system, increased exports provide their only way to earn those reserves.

**What a New Allocation Cannot Accomplish**

Issuing a new allocation of SDRs for use by a selected group of countries would provide badly needed relief for battered regions and the global economy. However, SDRs will not become the principal reserve asset in the international monetary system and will not provide a long-term solution to embedded global imbalances or growing financial fragility.

The SDR was designed for a system in which the preponderance of international liquidity was created, controlled and distributed among and between central banks and the Fund. With the collapse of the Bretton Woods system in 1971 and the private financial sector's emerging dominance over international liquidity-creation, the SDR was marginalized at birth. At present, the SDR is a hybrid instrument issued by a credit institution. Neither the SDR nor the Fund is adequate to the role of governing liquidity. That role requires the explicit structure of a bank of issue.

The 1987 IMF staff report on the role of the SDR correctly called for 'better international control of international liquidity and thus for making more active use of the reserve system for international stabilization policy conducted by the international community' (p. 24). Given the dominance of uncontrolled financial markets over trade flows and real-sector activity, stabilizing the global economy requires a full-scale revival of public sector influence over the creation of international liquidity.

## 4 CREATING AN INTERNATIONAL CLEARING SYSTEM

From the Mexican peso crisis through the collapse of Long Term Capital Management, every defining event in international finance during the 1990s has been rooted in a silent, if commanding, reality: the global system of monetary relations is not really a system at all. At the dawn of a new millennium and in the face of enormous economic dislocation, the fate of the world's money and, inevitably, the welfare of its people depend upon a web of privatized arrangements unaccountable to any larger public purpose.

During the past quarter-century, these anchorless arrangements effectively displaced the post-war foreign exchange system fashioned at Bretton Woods in response to devastating currency instability in the previous decade. Despite giving rise to an unprecedented era of economic growth and stability, the Bretton Woods system broke down in the face of its own flaws, rapid technological change, concerted ideological pressures and sustained efforts to create lucrative spot, forward and futures markets in freely floating currencies.

Western governments began yielding to these pressures when President Richard Nixon ended the convertibility of dollars into gold and subsequently allowed the dollar exchange rate to float in response to changes in global supply and demand for the US currency. These actions effectively signalled the end of any stable basis for the international monetary system. During the next two and a half decades, governments acquiesced to the growth of an unregulated offshore eurodollar market that usurped the role of public institutions in recycling OPEC surpluses and eventually forced the rollback of financial regulation in national markets. Meanwhile, the privatized international monetary system expanded in both scope and volume. Increasingly, market participants grew to depend on over-the-counter derivatives markets to offset the volatility created by the abandonment of exchange and interest rate controls and the weakening of other monetary policy tools.

Nevertheless, establishment debate over monetary matters remains narrow, generally contenting itself with rehashing the relative merits of fixed versus floating exchange rate regimes. The Clinton administration did propose that the International Monetary Fund provide foreign central banks more reserves to preclude traders' bets against their national currencies. But experience clearly shows that these kinds of injections only reassure investors if coupled with policies that constrain economic growth. When growth falters, the resources invariably wind up as profits for speculators. Modest, well-intentioned adjustments to the prevailing international monetary arrangements are not capable of restoring financial stability or facilitating sustainable economic activity. A new system of currency relations is needed.

**Key Features of the Clearing System**

To succeed, this new system must possess three essential attributes. First, it must enable national governments and central banks to reclaim from financial markets their sovereign capacities to conduct appropriate national economic policies. Second, it must promote the ability of governments and central banks to employ effective countercyclical policies at a national level. And third, it must support a symmetrical relationship between the creation of real wealth and the servicing of financial liabilities, regardless of the country of origin or currency of the creditor.

An international clearing agency (ICA) functioning as a clearinghouse and a repository for international reserves should be the keystone for this new system of monetary relations. (See Appendix 25A for the 'rules of the game' and the transactional framework for an ICS.) Although its creation would demand significant collaboration among nations, such an institution would not be a supranational central bank. It would not issue a single global currency. Indeed, it would not issue currency at all. That would remain the prerogative of national central banks. But, by providing a multinational structure for clearing payments, it would enable countries to engage in international trade and financial transactions in their own currencies.

The proposed ICA would hold debt securities of its member nations as assets and their international reserves as liabilities. Those assets and liabilities would allow the ICA to clear payments between countries. Exchange rates would be readjusted within a set range and over a set period of time in response to changes in levels of reserves held by the ICA. These periodic adjustments would reflect the valid role of market forces in shaping exchange rates through trade and investment flows. But speculators would no longer dominate the process.

The ICA's asset and liability structure would also allow it to conduct open market operations on an international basis, much as the Federal Reserve and other central banks do at the national level. By conducting these operations, the ICA would help smooth changes in international reserves caused by imbalances in trade or investment flows. For example, if a nation were experiencing excessive capital inflows, the ICA could help the national central bank absorb liquidity by selling its own holdings of that country's government securities to residents in the national market. In the case of a country experiencing excessive capital outflows, the ICA could assist the national central bank in supplying liquidity by buying government securities from residents in the national market and augmenting that country's supply of international reserves.

Thus, its ability to create liquidity would allow the ICA to act as a global lender of last resort – a role that neither the International Monetary Fund nor any other existing institution is structured to play effectively. In this capacity, the ICA could also help countries counter the effects of political shocks, commodity price gyrations and natural disasters on international payments.

Membership in the ICA would be open to national central banks of all participating countries and branches of the clearinghouse would conduct operations in every major financial centre in order to implement its critical role in international payments. The institution would fund its operations with earnings from the government securities on its balance sheet. Like the Federal Reserve System, the ICA would remit to the issuers of those securities (for example, the US Treasury in the case of America) annual earnings in excess of its expenses.

Like national central banks, the ICA should be equipped with a highly skilled transactional, policy and legal staff attuned to market dynamics and alert to the needs of commercial banks and other financial institutions. However, the ICA's mandate must focus on the interests of people and their institutions of self-government. Unlike national central banks such as the Fed, the ICA should not include commercial banks and other financial institutions among its primary constituents or as members of its advisory committees.

To guard against becoming a clubhouse for creditors or unrepresentative elites, the new ICA must level the central bank playing field upward. ICA eligibility standards should require member central banks to demonstrate genuine accountability to citizens in their own countries. The ICA itself would conform to tough disclosure and reporting standards that equal or exceed the best practices of government agencies (not just monetary authorities) worldwide.

Population as well as economic output would determine participating nations' governing power within the ICA. For example, the executive committee in charge of the Agency's operations and policy should be appointed on a rotating basis, with the requirement that its members represent countries that, in the aggregate, constitute over half the world's population and over half its total output. To ensure diverse inputs into policy deliberations, the ICA's staff and advisory bodies would represent a variety of regions, occupations and sectors and include constituencies that are frequently overlooked in the formulation of national policy.

While the ICA's independent directors would be the coequals of national central bank officials, their obligations and perspective must be mega-economic in scope. In seeking to influence the course of national economic policy, the ICA would operate primarily through persuasion and negotiation rather than resorting to unilateral exercise of its financial leverage in the open market. However, with a super-majority or consensus of member countries, the ICA would have the ability to redirect national policy in the long-term economic interests of all.

This aspect of the ICA's operations may seem radical, even with an unprecedented degree of transparency and accountability built in. In fact, it is far less radical and far more respectful of national sovereignty than financial markets' existing capacity to override national policy goals and undermine democratic institutions. Moreover, numerous precedents exist for international efforts to reshape economic policy in one country in the interests of global stability and widely shared prosperity. Among the most visible and recent precedents are attempts by the other six members of the G7 to redirect the course of Japan's macro policy.

**Main Benefits of the Clearing System: Developing Countries**

Restoring to the public sector its historic role as facilitator and guardian of the international payments system would have deep and lasting benefits. A stable regime of currency relations is key to reversing incentives in the current global economic system for lower wages and the export of goods and capital on ruinous terms.

In effect, an ICA would eliminate over-the-counter foreign exchange activities of large multinational banks, ending the wasteful reign of the vast

($1.5 trillion daily volume) foreign exchange casino and curbing the volatile movements in currency values that frustrate real economic activity. The new ICA would bar speculators from raiding the world's currency reserves by requiring that those reserves be held by the Agency and by periodically using changes in reserve levels to determine adjustments in exchange rates.

In such a system, no individual or firm could accumulate sufficient foreign exchange balances to influence the value of a currency. And restricting access to a national payments system only to authorized participants would radically diminish the ability of individuals, firms or unregulated havens to initiate or encourage off-market transactions. Most important, by requiring each country to pay for cross-border transactions in its own currency, an ICA-based system would allow national governments and central banks to focus on the needs of the domestic economy.

The current system requires that cross-border financing for development results in debt, most of which is not denominated in local currencies and cannot be serviced with local-currency income from domestic economic activity. Since external debt is denominated in foreign currencies, only export sales provide a means to earn the foreign exchange necessary for servicing it. During the past several decades, the debt-service imperative has relentlessly refocused international economic competition around labour costs rather than broader measures of comparative advantage.

At the same time, the spread of financial liberalization has exposed developing nations to the promise and perils of export strategies financed by hot money. Moreover, a deregulated environment dominated by portfolio investment flows fosters powerful, built-in incentives for austere monetary and fiscal policies in all nations – and corresponding disincentives for expansionary policy.

Today, the deflationary consequences of these trends have come home to roost. Emerging-market investment manias, the downward pull on global wages and debtor nations' forced export of goods and capital have fostered huge global imbalances in productive capacity and effective demand. Volatile movements in the foreign exchange casino compound the deflationary effect.

An international clearing system would help right these imbalances in several ways. If the ICA had been in existence for the past several years, it could have helped prevent the inflation of asset bubbles in Mexico, Thailand, Korea and other developing countries. These nations initially encouraged capital inflows in order to augment national savings and build the foreign exchange reserves needed to import production inputs and service external debt. But in many cases, emerging markets were overwhelmed by the volume of funds seeking outsized returns – and subsequently flattened by the wholesale withdrawal of those funds.

By pre-emptively absorbing some of the excess liquidity flooding into these countries, an ICA could have helped moderate their booms and prevent their busts. Emerging markets will still need foreign capital in order to develop. But by alleviating their need to build up foreign exchange reserves, the ICA's new monetary regime would allow developing countries to more effectively control capital flowing through their borders. Equally important, these nations will be able to turn their attention to developing broader, more diversified domestic markets for goods and services.

If, alternatively, a newly minted ICA had inherited the Asian crisis of pervasive asset bubbles and speculative attacks, it could have offset huge capital outflows by buying the beleaguered governments' securities and making sensible, incremental adjustments to their reserve positions. By making those adjustments, the ICA would have eliminated the precipitous change in currency values that drove up the cost of external debt for businesses in the affected countries.

In its capacity as a liquidity-absorber and liquidity-provider, the ICA would give nations greater freedom to run prudent expansionary policies based on their domestic needs. However, since exchange rates would be determined by a clearly articulated set of ICA rules as well as underlying trade and investment flows, the agency would not provide a blank cheque or unconditional safety net for wrongheaded policies. Moreover, the ICA's ability to help mop up excess liquidity or provide new liquidity would obviate the need for capital controls, which have proved to be of only limited and temporary effectiveness.

**Main Benefits of the Clearing System: Industrialized Countries**

Perhaps most important, the ICA would not benefit only developing nations. It would also be a boon to the industrialized world, especially the United States.

Despite its huge liabilities to foreign public and private investors, America's lack of foreign exchange reserves has caused barely a ripple of concern. Some say that continued use of the dollar as the dominant international reserve and transactions currency gives the US the equivalent of a platinum credit card that allows it to buy a great deal more than it sells to the rest of the world and run up debts on which it never has to pay principal, only interest. Perhaps, optimists suggest, foreign investors will be willing to perpetuate this arrangement for ever.

Perhaps. But more likely, the dollar's status as money of choice imposes costs as well as conferring benefits on America. Whether issued by US or foreign institutions, dollar-denominated debt increases the pressure on US markets to absorb the goods that generate income needed to service that debt – to function as a perennial buyer of last resort. These pressures compel growing trade deficits as peremptorily as would the most rigid command-and-control economic plan. US workers and firms in export-orientated sectors pay the price. And so do their counterparts, who compete with imports for domestic sales.

At the same time, the worldwide proliferation of dollar holdings as central bank reserves and in private hands has resulted in enormous capital inflows into the United States. These flows not only pushed the US current account into deficit but also transferred US financial assets to foreign owners, making the US more vulnerable to sudden swings in market sentiment about the dollar. What flows in can flow out.

In a privatized international monetary system where economic performance provides the measure of a store of value, it is unclear how long other nations will continue to use the currency of an economy that remains a chronic net international debtor. Given the interdependence of national and global financial markets and the scale of US liabilities to the rest of the world, a run on the dollar similar to the run in 1979 could produce global turmoil that dwarfs the dislocations of 1997–98. On the other hand, under the current monetary regime, preserving confidence in the dollar and all other currencies requires policies with a solidly deflationary bias – another, if perhaps slower, road to the same destination.

That is why Americans, as much as anyone, would benefit from genuine reform of the international monetary system.

## NOTES

\* First published in *Financial Markets and Society*, Financial Markets Centre, Philomont, VA, USA, November 1999, pp. 1–22.
1. The proposal for a closed-end investment fund was originally offered in a presentation to a conference on macroeconomic policy sponsored by the United Nations Development Programme and China's State Planning Commission in Beijing in 1995. It was subsequently included in a series of working papers for the Project on International Capital Markets and the Future of Economic Policy sponsored by the Center for Economic Policy Analysis at the New School for Social Research (available at www.newschool.edu/cepa). Sources for the data include the Bank for International Settlements, *Annual Report* (various issues); the International Monetary Fund, *International Capital Markets* (various issues), and the Bureau of Economic Analysis, US Department of Commerce, *Survey of Current Business* (various issues).
2. The proposal for a new allocation of SDRs was previously published in *FOMC Alert*, 18 May 1999. Much of the factual material on SDRs is drawn from the March 1987 International Monetary Fund study, *The Role of the SDR in the International Monetary System*. The discussion also benefited from 'Adequacy of liquidity in the current international financial environment', a paper prepared by Aziz Ali Mohammed for the Group of Twenty-Four in April 1999.
3. The proposal for an International Clearing System (ICS) was previously published in *FOMC Alert*, 22 December 1998. In that version, the proposed clearinghouse was called

a central bank. I am grateful to Nancy C. Alexander for suggesting that it be renamed. The international clearing agency proposed here would not issue a transactions currency that could be used by the general public. It would, however, create a non-national reserve asset similar to *bancor*, the reserve asset included in John Maynard Keynes's clearing-house proposal offered at the Bretton Woods conference. And, similar to a proposal by US Treasury official Harry Dexter White at Bretton Woods, the proposed Agency would have the power to conduct open market operations. The analysis of the problems inherent in a dollar exchange standard is indebted to the work of Robert Triffin. There are debts as well to Walter Russell Mead's essay, 'American economic policy in the antemillennial era' (*World Policy Journal*, Fall 1989) which introduced the concept of a 'mega-economic' perspective.

4. Cross-border transactions data for the G7 countries exclude the UK because of the uniquely international nature of its financial market.
5. In other cases, hiking interest rates may fail to attract foreign funds to finance a current account deficit or halt a drain on reserves if investors are not convinced the rate is high enough or will be maintained long enough to sustain the inflow and prevent a fall in the exchange rate.
6. Alan Greenspan, 'Currency reserves and debt', remarks before the World Bank Conference on Recent Trends in Reserves Management, 29 April 1999, Washington, DC.
7. David Lipton of the Carnegie Endowment for International Peace has suggested that a large general allocation be used to create a pool of funds to defend the international financial system in time of dire threat. Lipton's proposal constitutes a sensible use of SDRs allocated to countries that do not need debt relief or access to international liquidity.

# APPENDIX 25A

**The Rules of the Game for an International Clearing System**

The term 'rules of the game' refers to the practices and conditions that nations accept as the framework for participating in an international payments system. At the national level, such practices may be informally adapted to international transactions, as under the gold and gold/exchange standards, or may formally conform to multinational agreements, such as Bretton Woods. But any international monetary system that involves public sector institutions requires adherence to certain conventions. The rules of the game for the ICA system include the following:

1. All cross-border payments would be made in the payer's domestic currency.
2. Commercial banks in member countries would be required to accept cheques denominated in any other member country's currency. ('Commercial banks' means any financial institution that is part of a country's payments system).
3. Commercial banks in member countries would be required to present foreign currency-denominated cheques to their national central banks for payment. Payment would be made by crediting individual banks' reserve accounts to provide support for the creation of a domestic currency deposit of equal value. Thus, commercial banks would not be permitted to hold foreign currency deposits or make foreign currency payments.
4. National central banks in member countries would be required to present all foreign currency-denominated payments received by their national commercial banks to the international clearing agency for payment. Foreign currency payments received by the ICA would be processed through credits and debits to member countries' international reserve accounts. Thus, all international reserves would be held by the ICA.
5. International reserves would constitute bookkeeping entries on the asset side of the balance sheet of national central banks and on the liability side of the balance sheet of the ICA. The value of these reserves would reflect the aggregate value of all member countries' currencies – a comprehensive basket – rather than the value of individual currencies involved in specific transactions.
6. National central banks would be required to accept all cheques denominated in their currencies and finalize payment by debiting the domestic reserve accounts of the originating banks.

In summary, international payments would take place through the simultaneous debiting and crediting of: (a) reserve accounts held by commercial banks with their national central banks; and (b) the reserve accounts of national central banks held with the international clearing agency. No payments would be made directly between national central banks. Nor would national central banks provide foreign currency to private sector financial and non-financial institutions. All international reserves would be held by the international clearing agency and denominated in a weighted basket of currencies.

This structure would not prevent non-residents from holding domestic currency assets or deposits in a national market. Nor would it prevent foreign financial institutions from acting as authorized intermediaries for lending and investing transactions in the domestic currency within a national market. It would, however, restrict the use of a currency in transactions outside its national market, since only banks holding reserves with national central banks could accept payments in foreign currency or make payments to non-residents in the domestic currency. In other words, this framework would effectively disband and prevent the re-creation of external financial structures like the eurodollar and euroyen markets, which have become the main impediment to effective implementation of monetary policy and financial regulation by national authorities.

**The Transactional Framework for an International Clearing System**

The transactional work of the international clearing system (ICS) begins when a cheque is written in country B to pay for goods, services or investments purchased in country A. The buyer pays in his own currency. The seller deposits the foreign currency cheque in her own bank account. Her bank deposits the foreign currency cheque in its national central bank and receives a credit to its reserve account, which enables it to create a domestic currency deposit for the seller equivalent to the foreign currency she received.

Country A's central bank then submits the foreign currency cheque to the international clearing agency (ICA) and receives a credit in that amount to its international reserve account. The ICA, in turn, submits the cheque to country B's central bank and accepts payment for it by debiting country B's international reserve account. The final step in the process comes when country B's central bank submits the cheque to the buyer's bank and debits that institution's reserve account – exactly as the Fed and other central banks currently clear cheques on a domestic basis. The cheque is then cancelled and returned to the buyer.

During the course of a day, this kind of transaction would be repeated many times and involve many buyers and sellers in a number of countries. At the end of the day, however, countries A and B might end up in the same place as in the solitary transaction described in Figure 25A.1. Both the international reserves and domestic bank reserves of country A have increased while the international and domestic bank reserves of country B have declined. In the event of such symmetrical transactions, the ICA's balance sheet would reflect a shift in reserves. But neither the ICA's total assets and liabilities – nor, therefore, global liquidity – would change, as indicated by the balance of payments effects shown in the series of pluses, minuses and zeros below the line in Figure 25A.1.

Within the international clearing system, all member countries' international reserves will fluctuate as a result of payments for international trade and investment transactions – just as they do today. However, the job of the ICA will be to manage these fluctuations through a system of appropriate exchange rates determined at the inauguration of the system. Changes in international reserves that exceed an agreed-upon band in either direction (for example, plus or minus 5 per cent) and persist for a given amount of time (for example, more than 30 days) would signal the need for adjustments. Figure 25A.2 shows how the ICA would perform these adjustments.

Blocks one and two of Figure 25A.2 show the stock of assets and liabilities of the ICA before and after the transactions in Figure 25A.1. Assuming that changes in the reserves of countries A and B are large enough and have persisted long enough to trigger an adjustment in the exchange rates of these two countries, block three shows the ICA's response. It will increase or reduce its holdings of these countries' government securities to bring their values into line with the values of the two countries' reserves at the new exchange rates.

Again, these adjustments would produce no change in global liquidity. However if the ICA had to buy additional government securities from residents of country A or sell government securities to residents of country B in the process of making its adjustments, the agency's actions would reinforce the economic impacts of changes in reserve levels and exchange rates on these countries.

In most cases, the central banks of countries A and B would be able to deal with the expansionary or contractionary effects of changes in exchange rates in ways that promote their national policy objectives. In the absence of capital controls, however, the interest rate and asset price effects that follow an exchange rate adjustment could reinforce the procyclical response of capital flows. If flows become excessive and shocks occur, the ICA could prevent or moderate further exchange rate realignments by adjusting the international reserve holdings of one or more countries, as shown in Figure 25A.3.

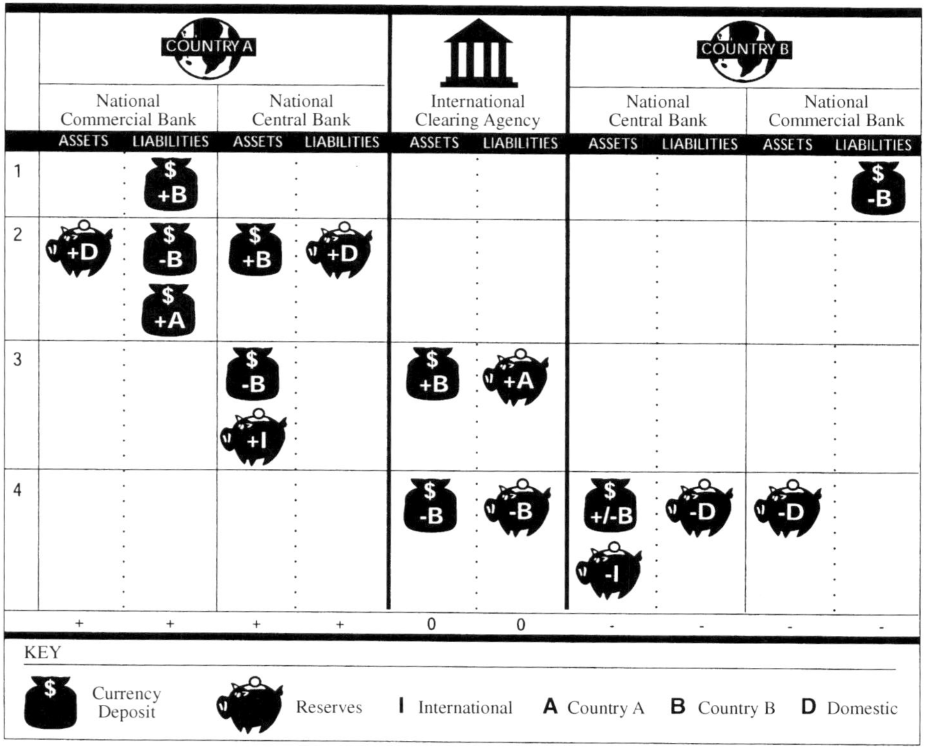

*Figure 25A.1  Clearing function*

| | International Clearing Agency | |
|---|---|---|
| | ASSETS | LIABILITIES |
| **Stocks** of assets and liablities (before transactions in Figure 25A.1) | A 100% / B 100% | A 100% / B 100% |
| **Stocks** of assets and liablities (after transactions in Figure 25A.1) | A 100% / B 100% | A 105% / B 95% |
| **Stocks** of assets and liablities after changes in reserve levels and exchange rates | A 105% / B 95% | A 105% / B 95% |

KEY: Government securities, Reserves, **A** Country A, **B** Country B

*Figure 25A.2   Exchange rate adjustment*

Again, block one shows the effects of the transactions in Figure 25A.1 on the stocks of assets and liabilities of the ICA and the central banks of countries A and B. The international reserves of country B have fallen by 5 per cent while those of country A have risen by 5 per cent. The resulting decline/increase in domestic bank reserves puts contractionary/expansionary pressure on the domestic economy in the two countries.

To cushion the impact of these pressures, the ICA reduces country A's reserves by selling some of its holdings of country A's government securities to its central bank and accepting payment for them by debiting its

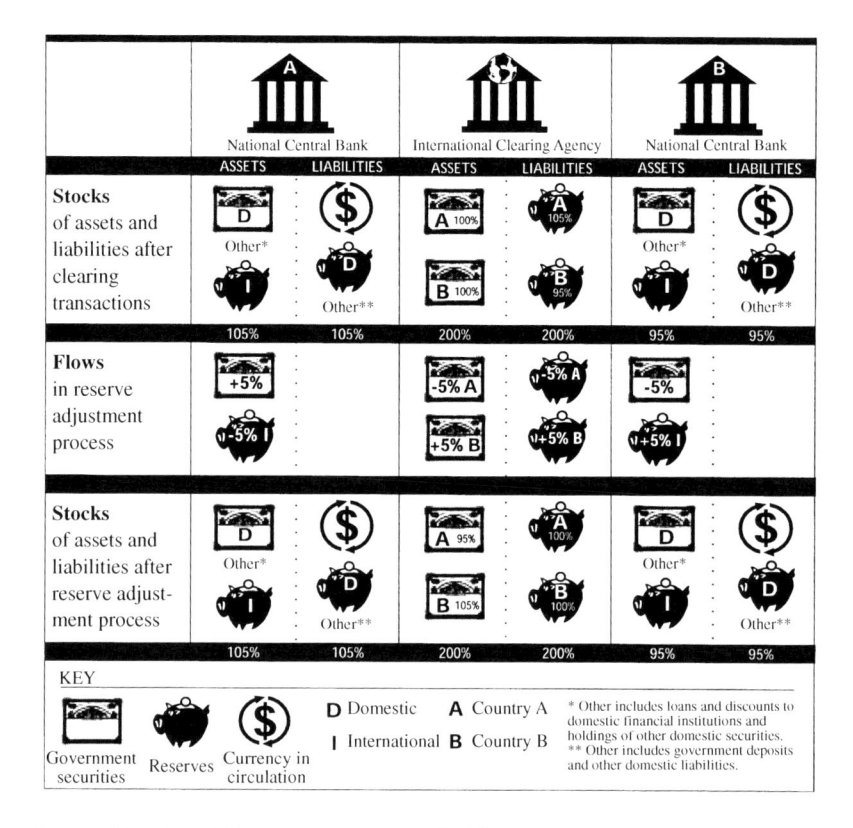

*Reforming the privatized international monetary and financial architecture* 747

*Figure 25A.3   Adjustment in reserve holdings*

international reserve account (see block two). At the same time, the ICA buys country B's government securities from its central bank and pays for them by crediting its international reserve account (also depicted in block two). As block three shows, these reserve adjustments alter the composition of assets and liabilities at the two central banks and the ICA – but do not change the aggregate level of assets and liabilities or alter international liquidity.

These transactions give the two central banks additional capacity to wrestle with the effects of international transactions on their domestic economies and financial sectors. The additional capacity does not guarantee a successful result. But it does enable national monetary authorities to use open market operations and other policy tools to cope more effectively with falling employment, rising prices or other domestic trends.

As Figure 25A.3 suggests, the ICA's transactional framework enables the agency itself to conduct open market operations at the international level

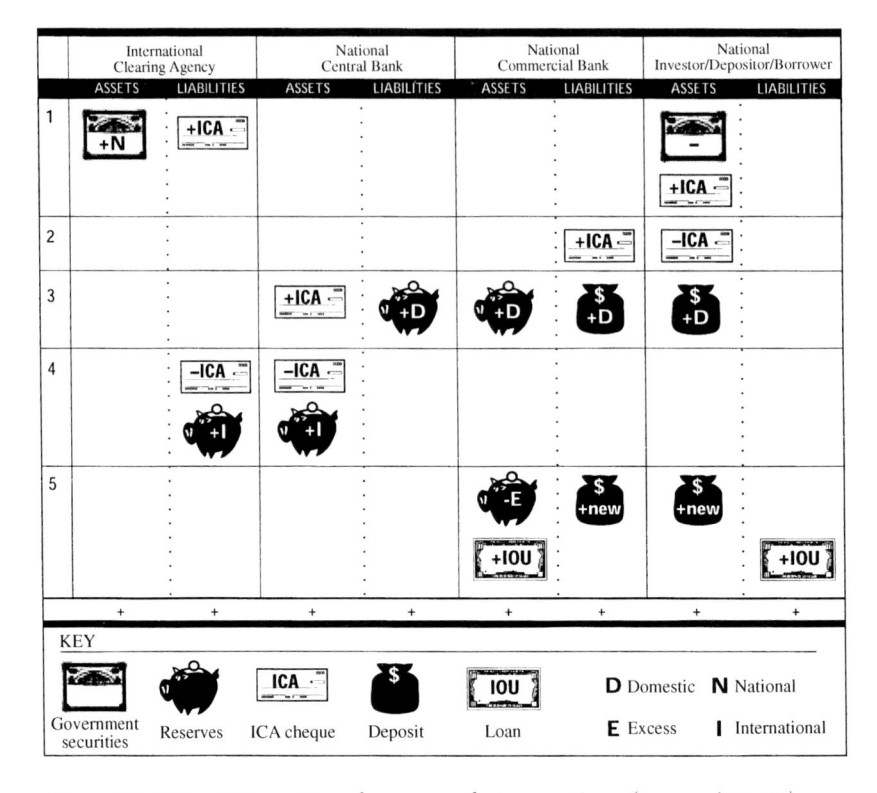

*Figure 25A.4a   International open market operations (expansionary)*

to reinforce national policy objectives, to stabilize global markets in ordinary circumstances or to act as a lender of last resort in crisis situations. Figures 25A.4a and 25A.4b outline the transactions involved in the conduct of international open market operations by the ICA.

The ICA would conduct international open market operations much as a central bank does in its national market by buying or selling government securities directly from or to residents of that country (block one, Figures 25A.4a and 25A.4b). When the ICA buys government securities, it would write a cheque denominated in the currency of that country for deposit in a commercial bank, which would submit the cheque to the country's central bank and receive credit in its reserve account (blocks two and three, Figure 25A.4a). The potential expansionary effects of the transaction are shown as increases in the assets and liabilities of both the central bank and the commercial bank.

The real expansion takes place after the central bank submits the cheque

*Figure 25A.4b  International open market operations (contractionary)*

to the ICA and is paid with an increase in its international reserve account (block 4, Figure 25A.4a). At this point, the commercial bank actually has excess reserves to make new loans that will expand economic activity (block 5, Figure 25A.4a). As the series of pluses below the line indicates, the increase in international and domestic reserves produces an increase in global liquidity.

If the ICA sold government securities to a resident of a member country, it would receive a cheque drawn on a commercial bank in the domestic currency (block one, Figure 25A.4b), present the cheque to the country's central bank, and accept payment by debiting the central bank's international reserve account (block two, Figure 25A.4b).

The loss of international reserves (assets) by the national central bank would automatically reduce its liabilities (domestic reserves). But the loss would be absorbed initially by the commercial bank on which the cheque had been drawn (block two, Figure 25A.4b). The reduction in the commercial bank's reserves and deposits would help rein in credit (block three, Figure 25A.4b) and lower the volume of economic activity. As the series of minuses below the line indicates, this tightening mechanism would shrink global liquidity.

# 26. Globalization, the WTO and GATS: implications for the banking sector in developing countries

**Victor Murinde and Cillian Ryan**

## 1 INTRODUCTION

Arguably, one main innovation of the World Trade Organization (WTO), compared to its predecessor the General Agreement on Tariffs and Trade (GATT), was that it took a much broader view of trade, and in particular, added to the trade negotiations issues such as trade-related intellectual property rights (TRIPS), trade-related investment measures (TRIMS), and the General Agreement on Trade in Services (GATS).[1] The provisions regarding trade in financial services, which are an integral element of the GATS, have proved to be a source of considerable anxiety for the non-industrialized countries generally. This concern arises, in part, because the consequences of the GATS are not well understood and there is a sense among these countries that they are being pressurized into signing up for something which may yet turn out to be to their detriment. There is some literature on the potential effects of the GATS on developing countries (see, for example, Murinde and Ryan, 2001 and 2002). For example, most developing countries are heavily dependent on oil imports and are largely vulnerable to exogenous shocks from the rest of the world, as noted by Collier and Gunning (1999). A few of the countries which are oil exporting, such as Nigeria, are acutely aware of the exhaustibility of their primary source of wealth but are unfortunately neither seeking to diversify their economies at home nor building up a suitable portfolio of interests abroad as a safeguard against future diminishing oil revenues.

There are many implications of the above for the financial sector, but we shall identify just four here.[2] First, most developing economies have very rudimentary and fragile financial sectors (Murinde, 1998). It is thus a matter of concern to the governments how the financial sector in these economies will respond to the increased competition brought about by the GATS. Moreover, the serious contagion effects from the recent Asian financial crisis have scared off some countries from embarking on the globalization trail. Second, developing countries also differ because their relative diverse colonial heritages, and the interests of transnational corporations (TNCs), have typically led to a significant, but sometimes restricted, foreign presence in these countries. Third, most developing economies are at the same stage of economic development and tend to produce similar goods and services. In order to diversify their economic base, these countries face the dilemma of linking their investment strategy to their trade regime; for example, investing in the key sectors such as manufacturing and services or the current main sectors such as agriculture and mining, or trying to export abroad versus investing in 'newly engineered' home industries. Finally, these countries have a particularly strong desire to see their financial industry survive and prosper. However, one of the difficulties faced by developing-country governments in choosing to diversify is to identify sectors that will yield sustainable economic growth. For this reason the financial sector, due to its appeal as a high-skilled, high-income industry, is sometimes identified by these countries as a potential source of future economic activity. Hence, the effects of freer trade in financial services under the GATS have special significance for developing economies.

This chapter assesses the implications of the GATS for the banking sector in developing countries, in the context of their membership benefits of the WTO as well as non-membership disadvantages. The idea is to review the relevant provisions of the GATS for banking services with emphasis on the free trade element and the implications for full liberalization of the banking sector. While the discussion is largely framed in the context of the GATS, we are aware that most developing countries have agreed in principle to allow the establishment of foreign banks in their countries, although this has yet to be implemented. Nevertheless, much of what we have to say relates to either liberalization policy and the regional initiative can be seen as an interim step towards the GATS.

In what follows, the remainder of this chapter is structured into four sections. Section 2 briefly considers the pure theory of international trade as it applies to trade in financial services, and identifies in broad terms the expected winners from liberalizing trade in this sector. The main provisions of the GATS as they apply to the financial sector are considered in Section 3. Section 4 concludes.

## 2  TRADE THEORY AND TRADE IN FINANCIAL SERVICES

It may be argued that the pressure for including financial services within the Uruguay Round came predominantly from the developed countries, and in particular, from those who currently have a major presence in the international banking market. The explanation for the dominance of these particular countries in international banking differs in each case, but a recurring theme is the distortionary impact of historical banking regulations resulting in the development or an enhancement of a comparative advantage in the provision of financial services.

It is instructive to briefly consider the traditional models of international trade, though, as we shall see, they are not particularly helpful in explaining patterns of international trade in banking and financial services. For example, we might look to technology as a source of comparative advantage. It may well be the case that we can identify differences in the technology, or the method of production of financial services from one country to another, but there is nothing intrinsically fixed about this advantage. Thus, unlike food production or coal- or mineral- or raw material-based industries, there is nothing about the physical environment which necessarily suggests that one country may have a technological advantage on the basis of its physical geography or infrastructure. There may of course be differences such as population density which effect branching costs; or the cost and efficiency of telephone and other electronic communication systems, but there is no discernible pattern internationally which might suggest that these factors are overwhelmingly important. Thus, if there is a difference in 'technology' it is invariably due to differences in 'ways of doing things'. The question is how do such differences in the level of 'know-how' arise and why are they not readily copied.

Factor intensity arguments lead us to a similar conclusion. In the case of trade in goods, we might readily accept that production might differ in relative capital and labour intensity from country to country. But that is harder to discern in financial services. Capital infrastructure, in terms of branch networks and so on, may be superficially important but financial capital is equally if not more important in the case of financial services. Overall capital requirements for banks and financial institutions did indeed differ in the past, and low capital/asset requirements are often cited as one of the principal reasons for the rapid international expansion of Japanese banks in the 1980s and early 1990s. However, this possible source of difference has systematically disappeared as a consequence of the Basle Agreement on the global capital/asset requirements and the increasing role of the Bank for International Settlements. Thus, while relative capital abundance might still be an issue, once again differences in production methods do not depend on differences in factor intensity *per se*, but rather on differences in 'ways of doing it' and the skills and know-how embodied in labour. Furthermore, the removal of barriers to capital flows particularly over the last two decades diminishes the issue of relative capital scarcity.

Thus, the main conventional explanations reduce to differences in knowhow. In the case of financial services this difference in skills and knowledge is usually attributed in part to investment in human capital, but even more importantly, to learning by doing (see Ryan, 1990).

The third major source of trade is trade attributable to economies of scale. However, while recent research is more supportive of returns to scale and scope, it is notoriously difficult to establish in financial services. Differences in tastes do not look particularly fruitful either, since they require some element of production specialization to be relevant, and as we have already seen, there is no obvious conventional argument for this.

A final source of trade is trade due to tax and regulatory distortions. For a huge variety of reasons this turns out to be vitally important in the context of financial services. We have already cited the case of Japanese international growth allegedly subsidized by low capital/asset requirements. By contrast, the importance of American banks is often attributed to the restrictive regulatory regime they faced in the US. Thus, they had an incentive to develop their international operations as a means of circumventing domestic restrictions. However, it was the very absence of restrictive regulations and an appropriate supervisory regime that reinforced the strength of certain financial centres such as London, and which enabled it to attract US and other banks attempting to circumvent their own restrictive domestic requirements. Of course while comparative regulatory regimes may be important in explaining the performance of London as a centre this century, its growth was initially determined by its location at the centre of the British Empire. However, its early growth as a financial centre owes much to the fact that there were restrictions on goods trade between colonies and third parties, forcing trade through the UK. Thus restrictions, this time on trade, also provide part of the explanation as to why London became the focus for the finance of international trade between third parties.

The key, however, is not the restriction itself. For if that were the only element in the story then the removal of the restriction or regulatory distortion would return the world to a level playing field. More importantly, the distortion not only allows a country to gain an advantage today, but also to capitalize on the learning-by-doing element of banking and thus to increase its 'know-how' and compound its comparative advantage.

By these historical factors, therefore, the existing major players have developed over many years specific banking skills and expertise which is seen as the most important ingredient in the provision of banking services. The generalized implementation of the GATS in addition to the Basle Agreement on capital ratios would have the effect of removing the distortionary regulations that led to the development of the comparative advantage in these countries. Thus, by eliminating distortionary regulatory factors, and the taxes and subsidies that encouraged and enabled existing market participants to acquire their specialist skills, the new agreement, when fully implemented, will remove the possibility of similar protection for new market entrants.

Thus, there is a general presumption that the GATS will largely enshrine historic comparative advantage and favour the existing market leaders at the expense of other countries with a less-developed presence in international financial markets. However, it would be wrong to imagine that the gains from financial liberalization will accrue only to the suppliers of international financial services or indeed that domestic production will be wiped out.

First it should be emphasized that a more efficient financial-service sector is beneficial not just because it yields static private-consumption benefits (which are typically quite low), but also because these services are important as an allocative intermediate input in production. Thus, an efficient financial-service sector is vital if a country is to enjoy the dynamic benefits of trade liberalization. Second, as we argue in more detail below, domestic presence is likely to remain an important form of supply for a considerable period yet. Thus, while liberalization might be expected to yield significant improvements, particularly in labour, process and managerial efficiency, the sector is unlikely to decline to the extent one would expect in the case of a goods sector at a similar comparative disadvantage. Thus, while theory might suggest that the current world leaders in international finance may have the most to gain (as suppliers), the implications for the retail banking, insurance and other financial services need to be qualified considerably at country level. Before we can do this, however, we need to review the main provisions of the GATS for the financial sector and to consider the current state of the Gulf financial industry. It is to these issues we now turn.

## 3  THE MAIN PROVISIONS OF THE GATS AND TRADE LIBERALIZATION

**The Main Provisions**

In its most general form the liberalization of financial trade under the GATS envisages that signatory states will (i) remove capital account restrictions to permit cross-border supply and consumption abroad;[3] (ii) grant 'market access' to all; that is, give everyone the right to establish in or to freely service the national market; and (iii) ensure 'national treatment'; that is, the authorities should seek to treat all banks, regardless of country of origin, on an equal basis, and make all banks subject to the same regulatory and tax regimes. The GATS also envisages that signatories will take steps to ensure that the regulatory and supervisory regime conforms with best international practice, though these requirements need not be specified in the agreement.[4]

By contrast with the GATT, the GATS agreement in the Uruguay Round stopped short of requiring full reciprocity in access, opting instead for the less stringent market-access and national-treatment requirements. Full reciprocity would require that foreign financial institutions should be allowed the same degree of market access in the domestic market as permitted to domestic firms in foreign markets. This provision would have effectively forced countries to liberalize their financial markets to a common standard. However, the consensus proved so difficult in this sector that this traditional approach was abandoned.

Instead, the initial agreement on financial services, as set out in 1995, required developed countries to implement the GATS within a year, but allowed emerging and developing countries to take exemptions, initially for five years. From a practical viewpoint the way these exemptions were established was very important. Instead of a general commitment to the agreement, with exemptions claimed for non-conforming measures as in the GATT (a so-called 'negative' list), the GATS followed what is called a 'hybrid' list. This required signatories to opt into specific sectors (and/or subsectors) and then to list a set of negative exemptions where appropriate. However, many countries disaggregated their sectors in such detail that their specific commitments amounted more to a positive list of 'opt-ins' for a particular mode, rather than any kind of general commitment to freer trade in financial services. Furthermore, many countries chose to be 'unbound' in a particular sector, meaning that they were making no commitments, and then specified what they would nevertheless allow. This further reinforced the perspective that the agreement was essentially a 'positive' list of low-level commitments.

This bottom-up approach had the effect of making the agreement a piecemeal collection of opt-ins which broadly corresponded with the *status quo ante* for many countries. Thus, for the most part non-Eastern European emerging and developing countries only agreed to continue what they were already doing. Furthermore, and in contrast to the GATT, there was nothing in the agreement to stop them putting in place further restrictive measures.[5] As a consequence of this outcome, the original aspiration in the agreement for an early move to eliminate exemptions was clearly not feasible and overly optimistic. In practice, emerging and developing countries had little idea what liberalization entailed and felt they were being rushed into a commitment they did not understand. Thus they had no clear vision of what the implications of the agreement might be, or even what full compliance might entail, and privately at least, did not take the proposed time schedule seriously. The subsequent financial crisis in the Far East has compounded this problem and many developing countries are now arguing that the effect of the GATS would be to leave them susceptible to a similar sort of crash.

As a consequence, the WTO appears to have conceded that progress will be slower than originally envisaged and Article XIX on Progressive Liberalization calls for a series of rounds to review exemptions be held at five-yearly intervals. The article also contains a considerable number of escape clauses which may 'facilitate' countries seeking further delays.

## The Effects of Liberalization in Principle

But what are the likely effects, in principle, of liberalizing trade in banking services in compliance with the long-term aspiration of the GATS both on the use and availability of funds in the region and on the banking sector within the countries themselves? In studying the effects of liberalization there are two distinct concepts to keep in mind. The first is the effect of GATS on the flow of funds in and out of countries, and the second is the effect on financial service provision. The former case relates to the issue of improved capital mobility, while the latter addresses the issue of who does the intermediation between borrowers and lenders both inside and outside the country.

## GATS and the Flow of Funds

GATS requires the removal of capital account restrictions in order to facilitate cross-border supplies and consumption abroad. Thus, in principle, by facilitating the international flow of capital, GATS ensures that investment flows internationally to those enterprises where it will be most productive in terms of risk and returns, in the new world trading regime. Thus, in theory, freer capital flows are an opportunity for producers to attract the new investment necessary for development, and an opportunity for domestic savers to invest in projects anywhere in the world.

Some developing countries (for example, the Gulf states of Bahrain, Kuwait, Qatar and the United Arab Emirates (UAE), and the African states of Ghana, Uganda and South Africa) have fairly liberal regimes regarding cross-border supply and consumption abroad with no regulatory restrictions on capital flows. However, the absence of regulations limiting capital flows does not necessarily mean that the market is operating efficiently. The extent of capital flows in and out of a country depends to a large extent on the ease with which domestic residents can gain access to projects abroad and foreign investors in turn can gain access to domestic projects. In the case of domestic investors this means the ease by which they can enter the international capital market. For wealthy individuals this may be relatively easy, but for the vast majority this depends on the financial intermediaries located in the domestic economy and is therefore predicated on their level of efficiency and/or biases. Similarly, in practice, local entrepreneurs are restricted in their access to funds by the extent to which foreign banks can locate in the domestic economy or by the exposure and efficiency of their local intermediary in operating in the international market. Thus, despite lack of prohibitions on the flows of funds, distortions and lack of efficiency in the local market may result in the misallocation of resources.

Another issue is the extent to which national and regional governments try to influence the financial sector in their efforts to promote (sometimes inappropriate) regional investment. As we observed before, natural-resource-rich developing countries, especially oil-exporting countries, are often in a good position to diversify their economic base. This could be by means of investing overseas, but more commonly they are choosing to develop industries and enterprises in their home economies. In the case of many of the African and South American nations, where there is a large source of labour, this policy is understandable; however, in the case of the Gulf states these new industries frequently require large immigrant communities to operate them. Nevertheless, these industries often require significant imports of factors, equipment and materials. The countries typically argue that such development is less risky (in both economic and especially political terms) than similar investment abroad either regionally or in Western economies. The continuing conflicts in parts of Africa and the wider Indian subcontinent are examples of the former, and even the Gulf states point to the succession of European wars as an argument for caution in investment in Western economies.

If national governments are really reflecting the tastes of the local population towards regional and political risk, and the population is well informed, then they will choose to invest their moneys in a bank which reflects this investment strategy without the need for political interference. However, it remains to be seen whether a competitive local banking system, whether domestic or foreign in ownership, would choose a similar level of domestic investment or whether it would opt to diversify more internationally either at a regional or global level. For example, in response to a recent UNCTAD report the UAE argued that the significant level of inward investment was an indication that the government's own preference for domestic investment was appropriate. Of course, appropriate diversification by foreign investors is neither evidence that domestic intermediaries are efficient nor a legitimate reason for biasing one's own investment towards the domestic economy.

**GATS and the Provision of Banking Services**

The second dimension to the GATS relates to the domestic provision of financial services and the possibility that foreign banks can enter domestic markets to compete with domestic banks. There are a number of ways this might happen:

1. banks could provide an arm's-length service directly to customers across borders without any domestic presence;
2. they might invest directly, establishing a new financial firm within a country;
3. they might purchase an existing financial services provider; or
4. they might enter into a partnership with an established domestic bank.

In the arm's-length scenario a foreign-based bank could bypass domestic banks and collect funds directly from domestic savers, provide them with payments instruments (credit cards and even cheques), and arrange loans using telephone and computer technology. In principle, all banking services could be provided in this manner, though in practice, consumers expect to have some direct contact, however occasional, with their financial service provider and, at present at least, even in developed economies (exclusive) e-bank entities only have a very limited share of the market.

The other scenarios all envisage a direct presence in the domestic economy. All these scenarios are similar to foreign direct investment in industry, in that the foreign bank invests money directly in the domestic economy. However, unlike other sectors, investment in substantial tangible assets such as plant and machinery is not necessary to conduct business, and even their property requirements may be quite limited. Furthermore, in principle, the labour requirements of such an operation might be quite modest, limited, in the extreme, to a handful of ex-patriot specialist advisers who provide the occasional contact alluded to above. At the other end of the spectrum, an incoming bank may establish or purchase an entire branch network and all its associated electronic payments systems and so on.

Given the presumption of comparative advantage of the major existing players, there is a theoretical possibility that a market could be completely dominated by low-cost foreign banks either providing cross-border financial services directly or with only a minimal domestic presence. There are two factors which tend to militate against this. In order to meet local demand for finance by domestic trading enterprises, banks will continue to maintain a sizeable staff with local knowledge to vet and monitor loans. Furthermore, despite the advances in arm's-length banking via telephone and computer, there is still a demand for personal contact with financial service providers. Indeed, deposit collection (traditionally the most costly element of banking services) is likely to remain branch intensive for some time to come. Taken together, these factors imply that the scenario whereby the market is serviced at arm's length by foreign banks is unlikely to develop in the foreseeable future.

The second piece of evidence relating to domestic versus foreign provision points to the developments in Europe in the wake of the Single European Market exercise, an initiative which most closely resembles the effects of implementing the GATS agreement in full. Prior to the implementation of the single market, measures of efficiency suggested widespread differences across member countries even after making adjustments for differences in levels and types of services (see Ryan, 1992). There was also considerable evidence of differences in levels of efficiency within countries. The European Single Market, like GATS, was designed to ensure that banks would have reciprocal rights of entry into domestic markets at no less favourable terms than domestic providers (the so-called 'National Treatment' provision). Given the pre-liberalization measures of efficiency, there might have a been a presumption of significant market entry by the more efficient providers, mainly in Belgium, Germany and to a lesser extent the UK and the Netherlands.

Significantly, this is not what happened. The advent of the single market provided an impetus for significant labour shedding and internal bank reorganization in the less efficient markets, rather than widespread takeovers or new entrants. There has been some evidence of joint ventures and buy-ins but; interestingly, the level of intra-EU (European Union) mergers and acquisitions has not been significantly higher than that of banks from outside the EU. Indeed, the level of activity between EU countries is probably less than the level within countries, where smaller banks have frequently merged to compete more effectively with their larger competitors in terms of regional coverage and product range. Murinde et al. (1999) suggest that levels of efficiency within the EU have converged in the wake of the 1992 Single Market, but the impetus for rationalization and efficiency gains was due as much to the *threat* of mergers, acquisitions and new competition as to actual outside entrants.

However, there are other factors which militate against potential mergers (and hence the efficiency benefits the threat such competition brings). Quite apart from political risk, potential entrants are hampered by a lack of transparency in accounting practices, leading to named-based rather than project-evaluation-based lending, as well as by judicial and enforcement risk on loan defaulters. For example, in some regimes foreign-owned banks have great difficulty in obtaining judgment against domestic defaulters, while in others an impartial judicial system is hampered by ineffective or biased enforcement processes, and even by limits by the central bank on foreign exchange transactions. In other cases, such as Uganda and Nigeria, the lack of transparency and corruption has led to widespread bank failures. While business surveys suggest that these unseen costs vary considerably, with some developing countries outperforming Western developed economies, the majority of developing countries lag considerably behind. Thus, to benefit from the potential allocative and efficiency gains that will spring from the GATS, developing economies also need to examine their financial regulatory and reporting regimes for both financial and commercial enterprises, and to establish the impartiality of their judicial and enforcement systems.

## 4 CONCLUSION

While liberalization may lead to a large shake-up of the banking industry in most developing countries, banks in these countries have little to fear from liberalization at least in terms of the continuing existence of a locally owned banking industry. Indeed, one might even argue that the disciplinary benefits of the market are more likely to benefit the owners at the expense of labour generally, and low-skilled foreign workers in particular. However, while the interests of the bank owners are undoubtedly important in the minds of the developing-country governments, that is not really the key issue. From their perspective it is the nature of the employment that these banks will provide which is the more strategic issue.

As with other sectors in developing countries generally, the banking sector employs significant numbers of non-local labour, with nationals often employed only in unskilled work or in a nominal capacity in management positions. This often leads to an implied restriction on the promotion of non-nationals within firms, which creates powerful disincentives within the context of banking organizations. These measures are unlikely to survive the increased competition which liberalization under the GATS will bring.

The development of a high-skilled cadre of national financial workers depends on investment in education and the acquisition of expertise through learning-by-doing by working alongside the existing skilled non-nationals. Thus, the real issue for regional governments is not whether to proceed with liberalization under the GATS but rather whether it should permit banks the freedom to develop their management cadre of overseas workers without discriminatory and educationally ineffective national quotas or alternatively to develop competitive national talent by a revision of social and educational policy within the states themselves.

The evidence from the European Single Market experiment is that a firm target date for the removal of restrictions relating to commercial presence will result in a rapid improvement in efficiency measures and training in advance of the deadline. This has to be tempered with the evidence on the length of time required to develop the knowledge associated with learning-by-doing which is unlikely to be less than five years and is more realistically ten (see Ryan, 1990). However, it is not clear that this window of opportunity exists. The sooner competitor economies respond to the prospect of the GATS, the lower the probability that an individual developing economy can reorganize and improve efficiency before the pressure from the WTO for full liberalization becomes overwhelming. In this regard, the move towards a pattern of regional free trade areas in financial services seems to be a sensible step.

Further problems within the sector are caused by a lack of transparency. There has been a recent trend towards providing appropriate accounts certified by qualified accountants, but the developing countries still lag behind developed-country standards in this regard. The absence of a series of certified accounts limits the ability of banks to assess returns and risks on new projects with respect to specific firms and whole sectors of the economy. Hence, lending decisions tend to be dominated by the reputation of the borrower and new entrepreneurs find it difficult to get start-up financing.

Increasing competition, especially from new foreign entrants, is likely to put further pressure on older-style lending policies, leading to more widespread use of auditing and accounting procedures and greater transparency.

A further impediment to trade in financial services which needs to be addressed is the provision of a comprehensive and transparent judicial superstructure for handling disputes, in particular bad loans and bankruptcy. For example, there is a belief that courts in some jurisdictions are unwilling to find against nationals in dispute with foreign banks, and there have been instances where central banks have prevented the effective award of damages by limiting foreign exchange transactions. While there are few restrictions on capital flows in most developing countries today generally, if these countries are to emerge as an international banking player, the judicial superstructure needs to pay attention to foreign as well as national interests.

# NOTES

1. Prior to the last set of trade negotiations under the GATT, the focus had been on the effect of tariffs, quotas and other non-tariff barriers on trade in goods. However, previous talks had assiduously eschewed some contentious areas where developed countries were at a comparative disadvantage *vis-à-vis* less developed countries, most notably textiles and agriculture. In return for concessions in these areas in the recent Uruguay Round, the developed nations urged the GATT to take a much broader view of trade, and in particular, added to the discussion issues such as TRIPS, TRIMS and GATS.
2. On the broad implications of WTO, rather than GATS, for developing countries, see Klein (1998).
3. In fact the agreement does not state this explicitly, but there are a variety of clauses in Article XI which essentially amounts to this. However, Footnote 8 in Article XVI appears to limit some of the obligations one would normally associate with these modes of supply. In particular it seems to relieve obligations on signatories regarding the outflow of funds under cross-border supply and commercial presence. Countries also have the right to impose restrictions in times of balance of payments crises and to take appropriate prudential and regulatory measures as they see fit.
4. Some countries have listed non-discriminatory exemptions (regarding licensing and so on) in their schedules which are essentially regulatory in nature.
5. The GATT originally worked on the basis of a general commitment combined with a negative list of exemptions. This approach made the trade restrictions in place transparent and thus allowed the GATT to monitor any attempt to engage in further restrictive practices and formed the basis for future negotiations. While in theory a positive list and a negative list could be the same, in practice, with a positive list, measures not made explicit are not transparent and there is essentially no means of preventing countries from implementing new restrictive measures.

# REFERENCES

Collier, P. and J.W. Gunning (1999), 'Explaining African economies' performance', *Journal of Economic Literature*, **37**(1).

Klein, L.R. (1998), 'Implication of WTO membership for the global economy', Emirates Lecture 9, Abu Dhabi: Emirates Center for Strategic Studies and Research.

Lensink, R., N. Hermes and V. Murinde (1998), 'The effect of financial liberalization on capital flight in African economies', *World Development*, **26**(7), 1349–68.

Murinde, V. (1998), 'Domestic sources of finance for Africa: what are the prospects?', *21st Century Policy Review*, **3**(3–4), 1–40.

Murinde, V., J. Agung and A. Mullineux (1999), 'Convergence of European financial systems: banks or equity markets?', in: M.M. Fischer and P. Nijkamp (eds), *Spatial Dynamics of European Integration*, Berlin: Springer, pp. 129–42.

Murinde, V. and C. Ryan (2001), 'The implications of WTO and GATS for the banking sector in Africa', in V. Murinde (ed.), *The Free Trade Area of the Common Market for Eastern and Central Africa*, Aldershot: Ashgate.

Murinde, V. and C. Ryan (2002), 'The implications of the General Agreement on Trade in Services for the banking sector in the Gulf region', in C. Milner and R. Read (eds), *Trade Liberalization, Competition and the WTO*, London: Macmillan.

Ryan, C. (1990), 'Trade liberalization and financial services', *The World Economy*, **13**(3), 349–66.

Ryan, C. (1992) 'The integration of financial services and economic welfare', in L. Alan Winters (ed.), *Trade Flows and Trade Policy after '1992'*, Cambridge: Cambridge University Press.

# Index

Abbey National 309, 310
ABN–AMRO Bank 118, 119, 122, 123, 214, 419, 511
ABS (asset-backed securitization)
  BIS 1999 proposals 95–6
  collaterized debt obligations (CDOs) 65–77
  credit derivatives 77–86
  European issuance by asset type 62
  overview 61–2
  process 63
  rationale behind 63–4
  release of capital 64
  see also asset management; mortgages
Accounting Standards Board (ASB) 100
acquisitions
  and eurobanking 120
  multinational banking 45, 46, 50
  see also conglomerates; economies of scale; mergers
adverse selection 78, 457
agencies, foreign 40, 41, 43, 44
agency theory, deregulation 644–5
air waybills 280
Al-Baraka Group 193–4
Albania 347
Alderney 346
Algeria 347, 590
Allfinance see bancassurance
allocated transfer risk reserves 340
AMC (Asset Management Corporation), Bank of Thailand 502–3
Andorra 346
Anglo-Saxon financial systems 16–17, 18
  see also capital market-orientated financial system
Angola 347

Antigua 550
Antilles 550
ANZ Bank 32, 46
  see also Australia; New Zealand
Argentina
  capital flight 529
  currency boards 156–7, 158, 160
  deposit insurance 666
  economic security ranking 348
  financial crises 334, 414, 431, 473, 475, 715
  loan leverage 441
  regulatory agencies 590
  sovereign ceilings 346
Argus, Don 33, 37, 46, 47, 51, 55, 56
  see also National Australia Bank
Asahi Bank 286
ASB (Accounting Standards Board) 100
Asian crisis
  bail-out 443–4
  balance of payments 431
  capital flight 516–17, 525, 714
  country risk 327, 328
  effects of 17, 22, 255–6, 752
  exchange rates 417, 419, 424
  factors behind 433, 434
  financial liberalization 414
  Financial Stability Forum response 10–11
  and IMF 708–12
  impact on financial reforms 501–2
  market discipline 447, 472
  regulation 416, 478, 591
  regulatory reform 502–13
  restructuring 502–13
  see also Bank of Thailand; individual countries
asset classification, Bank of Thailand 510–11
asset, institutional investor 729

765

asset management
  asset-backed securitization *see* ABS
  asset-swap market 79
  bank crises 417, 431–2, 434
  bank failures 375–7, 387
  companies, private 503–4
  in EU 138, 139
  foreign exchange market 237
  and globalization 9, 40
Asset Management Corporation (AMC), Bank of Thailand 502–3
asset measurement method, capital flight 522, 523, 529–30
asset price
  crash and banking crises 417
  swings 387, 417, 431–2, 434
asset risk 387
asset-backed securitization (ABS) *see* ABS
asset-swap market 79
auditors 380, 447, 461
Australia
  bank crises 413
  bank failures 388, 401
  banking regulation 572, 588, 590, 600–601
  central bank independence and inflation 690
  country risk 343, 346, 350
  economic security ranking 347
  and globalization 32, 33, 35, 44, 45
  international pool 401
  regulatory agencies 590
  sovereign ceilings 346
Austria
  cost–income ratios 136
  country risk 343, 346, 350
  deposit insurance 666
  economic security ranking 347
  equity return 136
  market concentration 124
  net interest margins 134
  non-interest income 135
  number of banks 131, 132
  regulatory agencies 590
  sovereign ceilings 346
avalization 267–8

back-to-back credits 273–5
bad banking practices 439–42
Bahamas 193, 346, 348, 550
Bahrain 346, 347, 757
bail-outs
  access to 221
  and contagion 122
  Crédit Lyonnais 378
  cross-border expansion 123–4
  financial crises 382, 442, 443, 444, 467
  SDR allocations 731–2
balance sheet performance, and CLOs 67, 74, 98
Banc-One 214, 220, 285
bancassurance companies 9, 13, 134, 284, 302, 319
Banco Ambrosiano 380, 415
Bangkok Bank 487, 511
Bangkok International Banking Facilities (BIBF) 490, 495, 499–500
Bangkok Metropolitan Bank 511, 512
Bangladesh 191, 348, 666
Bank America 123, 214, 220, 580
Bank of Ayuthaya 487
Bank of Boston 220
Bank of Credit and Commerce International (BCCI) 380, 381–2, 415, 474, 546–7
bank crises 403–27, 715
  assessment 471–2
  asset price crash 417
  bad banking practices 439–42
  and bank regulation 428–85
  commercial crises 408–9
  common elements in 432–3
  corporate governance 429, 447, 463, 477–9
  and currency boards 166
  fraud 415–16
  governance failure 414–16
  government involvement 433, 436, 438
  incentive structures 429, 433, 442–5, 453, 461–4
  international 404, 417–20, 424–5
  intervention 466–71
  and lending 406, 415, 431–2
  liberalization 448–52

looting 414–16
macroeconomic conditions 411–14
market discipline 429, 446–7
monitoring and supervision 429, 446, 464–6
moral hazard 414–16, 433, 442–5, 447
multidimensional problem 433–48
periodicity of 407–10
regulation 445–6, 455–60
regulatory regime 428–30, 453–81
risks, increasing 417–20
seasonality of 407
supervision failure 414–16
Bank of England
and bank failures 381, 382
financial crises study 411
inflation targeting 696
lender of last resort 423
Memorandum of Understanding 596
and money laundering 549
regulation 458
trading practices survey 246
bank failures
causes of 366–402
clustering 383–4
controversies 367–74
deposit insurance *see* deposit insurance
determinants of 374–96
fraud 379–80, 395
governance failures 414–16
managerial problems 367, 371, 377–9
and new financial products 383
quantitative models 384–95
regulators' role 380–82
too big to fail 382–3
bank funding, and CLOs 73
Bank Holding Company Act 285–6
Bank for International Settlements (BIS) *see* BIS
Bank Merger Act 613
Bank Muamalat 199–200
Bank of New York 547
bank runs 371, 372, 574–5, 646
Bank of Scotland 309
bank sector performance graph 332
Bank Thai 512

Bank of Thailand
and Asian financial crisis 486–7
asset classification 510–11
Asset Management Corporation (AMC) 502–4
BIBF licensing 499–500
capital adequacy 509–10
commercial bank loans 488
deposit insurance 505–6
equity holding guidelines 511
exchange rate system reform 489–91
extension of scope of banking 494–8
financial reforms impact 501–2
Financial Sector Restructuring Authority (FRA) 506–7
financial services, increased variety of 496–8
Financial System Master Plan 498–500
interest rate liberalization 492–4
mergers 512–13
offshore banking *see* BIBF
portfolio management relaxation 495, 496
post-crisis developments 511–13
privatization of state-owned banks 512–13
Property Loan Management Organization (PLMU) 507–8
Radanasin Bank 504, 506, 512
regulatory standards, international 509–10
reregulation 487–94
restructuring 502–13
rural credit policy 495–6
Secondary Mortgage Finance Corporation (SMC) 504–5
Thai Credit Bureau Company 508–9
*see also* Asian crisis; Thailand
Bank of Tokyo-Mitsubishi 286
bank-industry linkages, alternative 226
bank-orientated financial system 12, 13, 14, 15, 18
BankAmerica
mergers 229–30, 285, 286
and Nations Bank 285
price-to-book ratios 220
and systemic risk 122
Bankers Trust 53, 77–8, 152, 214, 220, 580

Bankhaus Herstatt 380, 383
banking
  costs and efficiency in 283–324
    cost function specification 294–6
    data envelopment analysis 288–9, 292
    Decision Making Units (DMUs) 289–92
    distribution free approach (DFA) 294
    Fourier's flexible form 296, 300, 317
    free disposal hull technique (FDH) 292
    methodology 288–96
    modelling the banking firm 296–7
    scale economies and X-efficiency 297–8
    stochastic frontier model 292–3
    thick frontier approach (TFA) 294
    translog cost function 294–5, 299, 302, 312–13, 315, 316, 317
    Young's theorem 295
  local 149–50
  representative offices 39–40, 42–3, 44
banking crises
  and balance of payments 431
  history of 405–10
  and inheritance problem 436–8
  international transmission 416–17
  lender of last resort (LOLR) 421–4
  and macro economy 434–6
  market discipline 472–6
  moral hazard 414–16, 465
  origins and transmissions of 410–20
  recent 430–32
  theory and history 285, 405–10
banking practices, bad 439–42
banking services provision and GATS 759–61
banking-orientated financial systems 13, 15, 227
bankruptcy-risk transfer 222
banks, number of, per country 131, 132
Banque Bruxelles Lambert (BBL) 117, 119
Banque de France 115, 117, 128
Banques Populaire 111
Barbados 346, 530, 590

Barclays Bank 111, 123, 208, 309, 419
Barings Bank
  and derivatives market 376
  fraud 395, 415
  and international mergers 119
  management of 378, 380, 416
  and new financial products 383
  profit-related bonuses 444
  regulators 22, 381
Basle Accord/Committee/Concordat
  capital adequacy 9, 10, 487, 509–10
  capital definition 87
  corporate governance 478–9, 481
  corporate loans 74
  credit risk 91
  deposit insurance 653
  financial crises 716, 717
  insolvent foreign subsidiaries 374
  market discipline 462, 476
  money laundering 549, 566
  regulators 382
  regulatory systems 12, 54, 56
  US banking 615, 618, 624, 625, 627
  see also BIS
Basle Banking Committee 653
Bayerische Hypo 123
BBL (Banque Bruxelles Lambert) 117, 119
BCCI (Bank of Credit and Commerce International) 380, 381–2, 415, 474, 546–7
Belgium
  banking history 29
  central bank independence and inflation 690
  cost–income ratios 136
  country risk 343, 346, 349
  deposit insurance 666
  economic security ranking 347
  equity return 136
  interest margins 115, 116, 134, 135, 136
  market concentration 124
  mergers 117, 118, 119, 151, 579
  non-interest income 135
  regulatory agencies 590
  sovereign ceilings 346
  strategic response 142, 759
Berger, Helge 156–72

Bermuda 346, 550, 590
BIBF (Bangkok International Banking Facilities) 490, 495, 499–500
Big Bang legislation 9, 11, 283–4, 287, 384
Bingham Report 546–7, 570
BIS (Bank for International Settlements)
  bank crises 419, 440, 445, 467, 481
  capital adequacy 460, 461, 582, 753
  capital arbitrage 90
  capital release 64
  country risk 330, 333, 335, 340
  Financial Stability Forum 24
  foreign exchange trading activities 237, 238, 256, 727
  proposals 88, 95–8
  see also Basle Accord/Committee/Concordat
BNP 111, 118, 123
Bolivia 346, 347, 590
bonds see corporate bonds
bonuses, incentive and Barings Bank 378–9
book value of equity (BVE) 210–29
Bosnia 156–7, 158
Botswana 348, 590
Brady bonds 328, 339, 342
branches, foreign 40, 41, 43–4
brand recognition 47–8
Brazil
  capital flight 516–17, 529
  country risk 339, 346, 347
  economic security ranking 347
  and IMF 705
  loan leverage 441
  regulatory agencies 590
  sovereign ceilings 346
Bretton Woods system
  abandonment of fixed exchange rates 237, 724, 734
  and IMF 702–3
  and rise of US dollar 113
  and World Bank 729
Brunei 158, 348, 495
bubble economy 254, 286, 287, 358, 376
building societies, UK 310–15
Building Societies Act 284, 309, 310, 311

Bulgaria
  currency boards 156–7, 158, 160
  economic security ranking 348
  financial crises 431
  flexible exchange rates 24
  regulatory agencies 590
  sovereign ceilings 346
Bundesbank 672, 695
Burkina Faso 347
'business of banking', redefining 616–17

Caisses d'Epargne 111
Cameroon 347
Canada
  bank branches 125
  bank crises 413
  bank failures 377
  central bank independence and inflation 690
  country risk 343, 346, 349
  deposit insurance 666
  economic security ranking 347
  free banking 176
  institutional investor assets 729
  loan leverage 441
  multinational banking 29
  regulatory agencies 590
  sovereign ceilings 346
  Task Force on the Future of the Canadian Financial Services Sector 59
capital, definition of 86–7
capital adequacy requirements (CARs)
  bank failure quantitative models 387, 395–6
  bank strategies, individual 458–9
  Basle capital adequacy recommendations 9, 460, 509–10
  country risk tree 345
  government intervention 177, 178
  insolvency regulation 91, 445–6, 573
  Miles argument 182–5
  and multinational banking 34
  regulation, arguments for 90–91, 181–2, 458–9, 460
  regulation, ineffective 445–6
  and strategic competition 90–91

capital arbitrage
  and CLOs 67, 69
  and credit ratings 251
  inadequate international standards 91
  and informationally efficient markets 239
  and risk management 90
  speculative behaviour at Barings Bank 383
capital asset pricing model (CAPM) 196, 250, 354
capital control relaxation 6–7
  and membership of OECD 724
capital flight
  asset measurement method 522, 523, 529–30
  capital inflow 533
  capital inflows 526–8
  concepts of 518–19
  determinants of 524–34
  and development aid 533
  Dooley measurement method 520–21, 522, 523, 524, 529, 530
  empirical studies 528–34
  history of 516–17
  hot money measurement method 522, 523, 524, 529, 530
  and IMF 711
  interest rate differentials 526, 533
  macroeconomic instability 525, 533
  magnitude of 523–4
  measurement of 519–23
  political instability 525, 533, 534–8
  residual measurement method 519–20, 522, 523, 529, 530
  stock of 528, 533–4
  trade misinvoicing measurement method 522
capital market-orientated system 11, 12, 13, 14, 15, 18
CAPM (capital asset pricing model) 196, 250, 354
CARs (capital adequacy requirements) *see* capital adequacy requirements
Cayman Islands 346, 495, 550
CDC-Trésor 111
CDO (collateralized debt obligation) 65–6

CEC (Council of the European Communities) 100
central banking 10, 174, 653
  conservative 685–91
  credibility versus flexibility 682–5
  independent versus currency board 156–72
  institutional design of 671–98
  monetary policy 672–5
  optimal contract 691–5
  time-inconsistency problem 675–82
CFTC (Commodity Futures Trading Commission) 627–9
CHAPS 415, 419
chartists 241, 254
Chase Manhattan 3, 214, 220, 229–31, 233, 285–6
Chemical Bank 230, 231
Chile
  bank crises 414
  and capital controls 728
  capital flight 529
  deposit insurance 666
  economic security ranking 348
  flexible exchange rates 24
  and IMF 714
  loan leverage 441
  regulatory agencies 590
  sovereign ceilings 346
China 348, 439, 440, 441, 495, 590
CIC-Banque 111
Citibank 3, 31, 36, 45, 46–9, 97
Citicorp 56, 57, 214, 220, 613
Citicorp–Travelers 285, 286, 580, 613
Citigroup 53, 119, 122, 123, 208, 214, 419
clearing system, international 734–40, 742–50
client activity theories and MNB 35–6
CLNs (credit-linked notes) 80–83
CLO (collateralized loan obligation)
  balance sheet performance 74
  bank funding 73
  and CDOs 65–6
  drawbacks to 76–7
  European issuance by asset type 62
  and investment-grade assets 75
  and investors 74–5
  issues, major 68
  market development potential 69

objectives of 72–3
origins of 66–7
regulation 86–98
and risk management 73
secondary markets 75
spread comparison 76
structuring 67–72
transactions 88, 89
*see also* risk management
closed-end investment 728–9
clustering
and bank failures 383–4
and Canadian banking system 125
Cobb–Douglas function 295
collateralized loan obligations (CLO)
*see* CLO
collateralized debt obligation (CDO) 65–6
collection accounts and money laundering 550
collection documentation in trade finance 262–7
Colombia 347, 441, 529, 590, 666
commercial banking
banking crises 419–20
CLO transactions 67, 74, 78, 82
country risk 340
crises, history of 409
cross-border mergers 117
diversification 302
interest margins 116
international clearing system 742
reregulation of, and Bank of Thailand 487–94
SME finance 7
structure and functions of 10, 208, 225, 262–3
*see also* international trade; retail banking
Commission Banquaire 115, 128
Commission of the European Communities 141, 155
Commodity Exchange Act 626
Commodity Futures Trading Commission (CTFC) 627–9
communications technology *see* IT
community banking institutions (US) 617–18
Community Reinvestment Act (CRA) 613

competitive banking
in EU 130–54
increased risk taking 452
and Japanese financial system 286
and mergers 126
and multinational banking theories 33–5
neutrality 458
and securitization 139
in SME financing 7
use of CLNs 81
*see also* leverage
conflict matrix, universal banking 222
conflicts of interest in universal banking 221–3
conglomerates
discounts 223–5, 232
multinational banking 53
regulatory policy 10, 54, 581, 582
and US banking 617
*see also* acquisitions; economies of scale; mergers
Congo 347
conservative central banking
advanced trade-off 693–5
optimizing trade-off 685–91
consolidation
community banking 617
Japan 316–17
market concentration 132, 133
multinational banking 48, 51, 53, 83
regulation 614
UK 284, 311
US 7, 150, 613–15
consumer protection 443, 573, 576
contagion effect
and Asian crisis 752
bank runs 177, 368–9, 370
country risk 357, 358–62
probit model 358–62
and regulation 573–4
Continental Illinois Bank 371, 377, 379, 381, 382
continental model *see* banking-orientated system
contingency credit line 716
contingent assignments 77
control systems 54, 465–6
*see also* regulation

convergence of banking systems and globalization 3–26, 581
convoy system 286
cooperative strategy 120–21
Coopers and Lybrand 381
Corestate Financial 220
corporate bonds
  bondholders 20
  convergence test 11–12
  and debt finance 18
  and EMU 13, 14, 15, 145, 147, 148
  market development 16
  and single currency 108–10
  sovereign ceilings 344, 346
  transactions, international, in 723
  *see also* equity; shareholding
corporate financing, patterns of 11–17
corporate governance
  and bank crises 447
  failures and bank failure 414–16
  and manager supervision 463
  reasons for 477–9
  trends in 18–20
  unsound agreements 447
corporate restructuring 8, 86
correspondent banking 39, 42–3, 148, 262
cost function specification 294–6, 312, 313, 316, 317
cost-cutting *see* efficiency measurement
cost–income ratio 134–5, 136
Costa Rica 348, 590
Côte d'Ivoire 348
Council of Europe Convention 566
Council of the European Communities (CEC) 100
Counter Party Risk Management Group (CRPMG) 624–5
Country Exposure Report 346
country risk 148, 327–65, 729
  analysis 21–2, 24
  contagion effect 358–62
  coping with changes 331–5
  models 336–41
  perspective on 328–31
  probit model 354–62
  qualitative models 342–51
  quantitative models 351–63
  tree 345

*see also* developing countries; moral hazard; risk management; systemic risk
CRA (Community Reinvestment Act) 613
Crédit Agricole 111, 118, 120, 123, 214
Credit Anstalt 404, 417
credit card loans 47, 48, 52, 61, 67, 76
credit derivatives
  and CLNs 72, 80–83
  credit default swaps 79
  origins of 77–8
  regulation of 88–9
  SBC Glacier Finance Ltd 84–6, 101, 214
  and single currency 115
  total return (TR)swaps 79, 80
Crédit Lyonnais 111, 119, 122, 214, 377, 378, 416
credit rating 96–8
credit risk
  analysis and management 21–2, 24, 73, 416
  and EMU 109–10, 114–15, 145–6, 148
  profiles 87–9
  and securitization 65
Crédit Suisse 123, 579
Crédit Suisse Private Banking 3, 214, 579
credit-linked notes (CLNs) 80–83
credits, back-to-back 273–5
crisis prevention and the IMF 715–16
CRMPG (Counter Party Risk Management Group) 624–5
cross-border banking *see* international banking
cross-border mergers
  competition 126
  and Euroland 150–51
  investor protection 121–2
  market concentration 124–5
  SME lending 125
  strategic issues 117–20
  systemic risk 122–4
  *see also* acquisitions; M&A; mergers
cross-border securities investment 723
cross-border transactions 4, 148, 359, 738

cross-selling 9, 212–13, 216, 217, 580
　see also economies of scope
cross-shareholding 8, 19, 20, 227
　see also keiretsu structures
CSFB 110, 119
Cuba 327, 347
currency, and home-country
　　relationship 108–9, 110, 111–12,
　　114
currency boards 156–72, 416
　see also developing countries
currency risk probit model 356–8
Curry, Elisa A. 27–59
Cyprus 343, 347, 550, 590
Czech Republic 347, 441, 590, 666

Dai-Ichi Kangyo 286, 288
Daiwa Bank fraud 23
Dale, Richard 444, 482, 572–611
Dar al-Mal al-Islami Trust (DMI) 193,
　　194
Dar, Hamayon A. 191–206
D'Arista, Jane 721–50
data envelopment analysis (DEA)
　　288–9, 292, 298, 300–301, 308,
　　316, 317
data transmission, enhanced 23
DBS Bank 511
de Haan, Jakob 156–72, 689, 698
DEA (data envelopment analysis)
　　288–9, 292, 298, 300–301, 308,
　　316, 317
debt see developing counties; lender of
　　last resort; lending
decision making units (DMU) 289–92
defensive expansion hypothesis 35
deferred payment L/Cs 272
DEG (German Investment and
　　Development Company) 344
Delors Report 105–6
Denmark
　bank failures 376–7, 383
　central bank independence and
　　inflation 690
　cost–income ratios 136
　country risk 343, 350
　deposit insurance 666
　economic security ranking 347
　equity return 136
　interest margins 115, 116, 134, 135
　Islamic banking in 191
　market concentration 124, 133
　market structures 142, 218
　mergers 118
　non-interest income 135
　number of banks 131, 132
　regulatory agencies 590
deposit insurance
　background to 638–9
　bank failures 370–71, 372
　and Bank of Thailand 505–6
　coverage limits 655–6
　and Diamond–Dybvig analysis
　　179–81, 407, 594, 641, 649
　and failed institutions 656–8
　and free banking 174, 177, 178–81,
　　182, 184
　and incentives 643–6
　institutional efficiency 654
　limiting of 468
　narrow banking 651
　origins and background 638–9
　policy implications 658–9
　premium pricing 646–50
　and regulation 473–4, 573, 574, 576,
　　577
　and risk-taking behaviour 640–46
　scheme design 650–58
　subordinated debt 651–2
　systems, design features 666–7
　and Thailand 505–6
　see also government intervention;
　　moral hazard
deregulation
　agency theory 644–5
　and bank crises 411
　bank failures 642–3
　and CLNs 81
　and competition 137
　globalization 12, 24, 52
　and IMF 706
　impact of 140–44
　international banking 581–2
　in Japan 286, 287
　in UK 284
　see also free banking; liberalization;
　　regulation
derivatives
　Barings Bank 376
　　see also Barings Bank

derivatives – *continued*
  Basle Committee recommendations 54
  and credit risk 88–9, 178, 625
  and globalization 6–11, 52–3
  and regulation 90, 645
  US banking regulation 626–9
Dermine, Jean 12, 14, 105–29
Deutsche Bank 119, 122, 123, 152, 208, 214, 419
developing countries
  banking crises 411, 414
  capital flight 529, 532
  clearing system 737–9
  creation of public international investment fund 722–9
  and debt 335
  financial exclusion 10
  foreign investment in 22, 722–9
  GATS (General Agreement on Trade in Services) 17, 755–61
  and globalization 4–5, 23, 24, 751–63
  independent central bank 156
  and international clearing house 737–9
  trade in financial services 17, 752–5
  *see also* country risk; currency boards; lending
DFA (distribution free approach) 294
Diamond–Dybvig analysis 179–81, 407, 594, 641, 649
  *see also* deposit insurance
direct banking 19–20, 137, 138, 151, 154, 314
  *see also* internet banking; IT; technological advances; telephone banking
*Directory of Financial Regulatory Agencies* 590, 594
*Directory of Islamic Banks and Financial Institutions* 191, 201, 206
disclosure 6, 54, 372–3, 432, 447
distribution free approach (DFA) 294
distribution network, control of 110–11
diversification
  benefits of 224
  and CLOs 73

country risk 338, 359
  and deposit insurance 639
  in EU 112, 115, 121, 126, 127, 145
  income-stream 218–20
  multinational banking 51
  and regulation 458
  SMP responses 143–4
  in UK 283–4, 311
  in US 37, 301–4
Djibouti 158
DMI (Dar al-Mal al-Islami Trust) 193, 194
DMU (decision making units) 289–92
documentary collections and trade finance 262–7
documentary credits and trade finance 268–82
  back-to-back L/Cs 275
  post-shipment finance 278–81
  pre-shipment finance 276, 277–8
  receipt and undertaking L/Cs 276
  red clause L/Cs 276
  revolving L/Cs 276–7
  transferable L/Cs 273–5, 294–5
Dominican Republic 347, 590, 666
Dooley measurement method, capital flight 520–21, 522, 523, 524, 529, 530
Dowd, Kevin 173–90, 651, 664
Drake, Leigh 283–304, 308–10, 311–12, 313–14, 317–18, 321–2
Dresdner 119, 123, 579
Dubai Islamic Bank 194

Eastern Caribbean Central Bank (ECCB) 158, 166
EC (European Commission) *see* European Commission
ECCB (Eastern Caribbean Central Bank) 158, 166
economic capital 74, 87
economic security, index of 344
economic security ranking 344, 347–8
economic theory, and foreign exchange trading 251–5
economies of scale
  financial services 141, 754
  in Japan 315–16, 319
  shareholder value 211–12, 231
  in UK 312–13, 319

in US 299–300, 319
and X-efficiency 213–17, 297–8, 300
*see also* acquisitions; conglomerates; mergers
economies of scope 212–17, 221, 231, 232, 301–4, 578
*see also* cross-selling
Economist Intelligence Unit, London 22
*Economist, The* 48, 57, 548, 569, 570
Ecuador 328, 347, 590
Edge Act Corporations 41
EEF (Exchange Equalization Scheme) 489
efficiency, Farrell 290
efficiency measurement 139, 288–92, 307
Farrell 290
scale and technical 291
efficient markets hypothesis 239
Egypt 191, 192–3, 348, 520, 590
Eichberger, Jürgen 237–58
El Salvador 330, 347, 357, 666
emerging markets *see* developing countries
EMU (European Monetary Union) *see* European Monetary Union
entry–exit equation 312
equity 644
allocations and debt relief 732
and convergence 11–16
corporate governance trends 18–20
and EMU 145, 148
international investment fund 723, 726
market-to-book value (UK) 219
returns on (EU) 136
and single currency 108–10
*see also* corporate bonds; shareholding
Eren, Ayse G. 259–82
ERM (European Exchange Rate Mechanism) 404, 419, 724
ESCB (European System of Central Banks) 106, 695–6
*see also* European Central Bank
ESF (European Securitisation Forum) 61, 92, 93, 98, 100
estimated cost function 303
Estonia 24, 156–7, 158, 160, 167

Ethiopia 347
EU *see* euro banking; Euroland; European Commission (EC); European Monetary Union (EMU); individual countries
euphoria speculation 432
Eureko 121
euro banking
balance sheet structure 83
corporate bonds 108–10
differences from US 146, 151–2, 153
EMU and credit risk 114–15
EMU, origins of 105–7
equity market 108–10
euro as international currency 113–14
euro-deposit market 112
eurobonds 108–10
foreign exchange markets 112
fund management 110–12
government bond market 107–8
impact of 144–6
low inflation 115–17
monetary policy discipline 48
and single currency 107–17, 420
single currency banking *see* single currency
strategic issues 117–21
euro-deposit market 112
eurobonds 108–10
Euroland
competitive strategies in 146–54
creation of 7, 14, 15
poor performance 152
strategic environment 137–40
*Euromoney* 246, 336, 339, 342, 343, 364
*Euromoney Ratings* 356
European ABS issuance by asset type 62
European American Bank 120
European Asian Bank 120
European banking, concentration in 133
European Central Bank (ECB)
and consolidation 151
corporate bonds 147
euro as international currency 114, 155
inflation 115
institutional design of 671, 672

European Central Bank (ECB) – *continued*
  local preferences 149, 418
  policy of 695–6
European Commission Banking Directive (1989) 9
European Commission (EC) 142, 150, 155
  Banking Directive (1989) 9
  country differences 153
  five-firm assets concentration 132
  marketization 138
  money laundering 549, 571
  SMP impact 143, 144, 150
European Community Directive 549
European Exchange Rate Mechanism (ERM) 404, 419, 724
European Investment Bank 108
European Monetary Institute 106
European Monetary Union (EMU)
  credit risk 114–15
  and financial integration 7
  impact on financial markets 144–6
  international transmission 416
  origins of 105–7
  and privatization 140
European Securitisation Forum (ESF) 61, 92, 93, 98, 100
European Single Market experiment 17
European System of Central Banks (ESCB) 106, 695–6
  *see also* European Central Bank
*Euroweek* 67, 100
Exchange Equalization Scheme (EEF) 489
exchange rate system
  alternative, and macroeconomic performance 161
  Bank of Thailand 489–91
  and capital controls 714
  central bank independence 157
  and convergence 12, 15
  and currency boards 156, 157, 162, 166–7, 168
  and EMU 106–7, 112
  fixed, and trade transaction costs 165
  movements and MNB 38
  overvaluation 525
  reform, and bank crises 416–17, 419

Export Import Bank 336
exporters *see* international trade
*Extraordinary Popular Delusions and the Madness of Crowds* 405

failed institutions, and deposit insurance 656–8
  *see also* bank failures
Farrell efficiency 290
FATF (Financial Action Task Force) 547–50, 551, 566–7, 569, 571
FDH (free disposal hull technique) 292
FDIC (Federal Deposit Insurance Corporation) 643, 646, 660
Fecht, Falko 671–98
Federal Deposit Insurance Corporation (FDIC) 73, 344, 379, 643, 646, 660
Federal Reserve Bank 643
Federal Reserve Bank of New York 107, 108, 128
Federal Reserve Board (FRB)
  and CLOs 88
  community banking 617
  Gramm–Leach–Bliley Act 630, 632–6
  Hedge Fund Report 621
  origins of 423
  and US banking supervision 615
  Working Groups 619
*Federal Reserve Bulletin* 346
Federal Reserve System 344, 346, 422
fee income 8, 133–4, 284, 302, 618
Fidelity Pensions Management 111
FIDF (Financial Institutions Development Fund) 493
Financial Action Task Force (FATF) 547–50, 551, 566–7, 569, 571
*Financial Havens, Banking and Money Laundering* 549
Financial Institution Reform, Recovery and Enforcement Act (FIRREA) 340
Financial Institutions Development Fund (FIDF) 493
financial *laissez-faire see* free banking
Financial Restructuring Authority Committee (FRAC) 512–13
Financial Services Authority (FSA) 10, 458, 461, 477, 588, 596, 597

Financial Services Modernization Act 285, 586
Financial Stability Forum 10–11, 24, 591
Financial System Inquiry 588, 594
Financial System Master Plan, Bank of Thailand 498–500
*Financial Times* 111, 548, 594
Finland
  bail-outs 221
  bank failures 376–7, 388
  convergence 16
  cost–income ratios 136
  country risk 343, 350
  deposit insurance 640, 666
  devaluation 114
  economic security ranking 347
  equity return 136
  financial crises 412, 414
  interest margins 134, 135, 136
  international pool 401
  market concentration 124–5, 133
  mergers 117, 118
  non-interest income 135
  number of banks 131, 132
  regulatory agencies 590
FIRREA (Financial Institution Reform, Recovery and Enforcement Act) 340
First Chicago 220, 285
First City 377
First Republic Bank 377
First Union 220, 580
Fisherian channel 707
Fitch IBCA ratings 342, 382, 390, 394–5
five-firm assets ratio 132, 133
fixed exchange rates *see* Bretton Woods system
Fleet Financial 220, 580
floating regimes 715
flow of funds, and GATS 757–9
Folk Theorem 680
Foreign & Colonial Institutional 111
*Foreign Affairs* 255
foreign agencies 40, 41, 43, 44
foreign banking *see* international banking
foreign branches 40, 41, 43–4

foreign exchange
  controls *see* exchange rate system
  dealers (US) 238
  market turnover (US) 238
foreign exchange trading activities
  of international banks 237–8
  security analysis techniques 239–46
  *see also* speculative trading
foreign market sophistication hypothesis 35
foreign portfolio investment 722–9
foreign subsidiaries 40
foreign taxation regimes 44–5
Fortis Bank 117, 118, 119, 579
Fourier flexible form 296, 300, 317
FRAC (Financial Restructuring Authority Committee) 512–13
France
  bank crises 418, 419, 422
  bank failures 366, 377, 382, 388, 389
  bank ratings 123
  Banque de 115, 117, 128
  central bank independence and inflation 690
  convergence 16
  cooperative strategy 120
  corporate bonds 108, 109
  cost–income ratios 136
  country risk 329–30, 343, 349
  deposit insurance 640, 666
  economic security rating 347
  equity returns 136
  foreign exchange market 248
  fund management 110–11
  globalization 8, 12, 13
  interest margins 116, 134, 135, 136
  international pool 401
  loan leverage 441
  and low inflation 115
  market concentration 124, 133
  mergers 118, 119, 151, 579
  mutual funds managers 111
  non-interest income 135
  number of banks 131, 132
  regulatory agencies 590
  state-centred approach 227
  strategy response to SMP 142
franchise values 228–9, 233, 452
Franklin National Bank 383
fraud 379–80, 395, 415–16, 655

FRB (Federal Reserve Board) *see* Federal Reserve Board
free banking
  case for 174–8, 371–2
  deposit insurance 651
  history of 173–4
  and state intervention 177–8
  *see also* deregulation; liberalization
free disposal hull technique (FDH) 292
Friedman, Milton
  deposit insurance 179, 185
  floating exchange rate 416
  Mexican crisis 707
  monetary target, strict 684
  speculative trading 251, 254
FSA (Financial Services Authority) 10, 458, 461, 477, 588, 596, 597
Fuji Bank 286
functional integration 578–81
fund management
  companies 576, 577–8
  and globalization 13, 47, 53
  and single currency 110–12
fundamental analysis and foreign exchange trading 239, 240, 244–7, 254
Fung, Justin G. 27–59
futures markets 53, 248, 342, 604–5

G7 countries 23, 329
G7 Paris Economic Summit 566
Gabon 348
Gambia 347
game-theoretic analysis 671–2, 680
Gardener, Edward P.M. 14, 130–55
Gastil Index 344
GATS (General Agreement on Trade in Services)
  banking services provision 759–61
  and developing countries 751–63
  effects of liberalization 757
  and flow of funds 757–9
  financial services trade 752–5
  and globalization 17
  main provisions of 173, 755–63
  and provision of banking services 759–61
  and Thailand 498
  and trade liberalization 755–61

German Investment and Development Company (DEG) 344
Germanic system *see* bank-orientated system
Germany
  bank crises 413, 414, 415
  bank rankings 123
  central bank independence 690
  central bank independence and inflation 690
  convergence 16
  corporate bonds 109
  cost–income ratios 136
  country risk 330, 331, 340, 343, 349
  deposit insurance 640, 666
  Deutsche Bank 122, 152, 208, 214, 419
  economic security ranking 347
  equity return 136
  foreign exchange trading 238, 246, 248, 250, 255
  globalization 8, 13, 14, 19, 20
  interest margins 134, 135, 136
  investor assets 723
  loan leverage 441
  market concentration 124, 133
  mergers 118, 119, 579
  multinational banking 29, 31, 45
  non-interest income 135
  number of banks 131, 132
  regulatory agencies 590
  reserve ratio 368
  single market entry 760
  strategy response to SMP 142
Ghana 348, 414, 757
Gibraltar 550
Glacier Finance Ltd, SBC 61, 84–6, 101, 214
Glass–Steagall Act 8, 11, 38, 208, 581, 586, 630
globalization and convergence of banking systems 3–26
  and EU 137, 139, 148
  and financial crises 20–21
  from multinational 46–9
  market structure change 53
  WTO and GATS 17
Goldman Sachs 110, 111
governance *see* corporate governance

government bonds and single currency 107–8, 145, 146, 148
government debt in EMU countries 145, 148
government involvement
  capital adequacy requirement 181–5
  in financial crises 433, 438, 443
  and free banking 177–8
  importance of 37–8
  non-financial shareholdings 227
  see also capital adequacy requirement; deposit insurance
Gramm–Leach–Bliley Act 208, 612, 629–36
Great Depression 416–17, 422
Greece
  bank crises 418
  country risk 348, 350
  economic security ranking 348
  loan leverage 441
  market concentration 124
  regulatory agencies 590
  strategy response to SMP 142
Group of Thirty 592, 595
Guatemala 347, 590
Guernsey 550
Guinea-Bissau 347
Gulf Cooperation Council see Islamic banking
Guyana 348

Haiti 347
Harper, Ian R. 27–59, 245, 257
Hausbank relationships 217
head-and-shoulders pattern 243, 244, 248, 250
hedge funds, US banking regulation 619–26
Heffernan, Shelagh 366–402
herd behaviour 444, 450, 517
Herfindahl–Hirshman index 218, 650
Hermes, Neils 6, 25, 515, 516–45, 763
Herstatt Bank 255, 404, 415, 417, 419
Herzegovina 156–7
Hill Samuel Asset Management 111
holding periods for traders 249
Holland see Netherlands
home loans see mortgages
HomeSide Inc. 35, 49
Honduras 330, 348, 357

Hong Kong
  bad banking practices 439
  country risk 347
  currency boards 158
  economic security ranking 347
  financial crises 436, 439, 440
  and IMF 715
  loan leverage 441
  regulatory agencies 590
  stock market price index 436
hot money measurement method, capital flight 522, 523, 524, 529, 530, 726
HSBC 123, 309, 419
Hungary 347, 431, 441, 530, 590, 666

IAIS (International Association of Insurance Supervisors) 11, 591
IBC (international business companies, offshore) 549
IBOS cash management system 120–21
Iceland 343, 347, 350, 666
IIF (Institute for International Finance) 22, 24, 333
Illing, Gerhard 671–98
IMF (International Monetary Fund)
  and Asian crisis 708–12, 714
  bail-out of South Korea 329
  and Bank of Thailand 493, 494, 515
  Bretton Woods system 702–3
  capital control relaxation 7
  country risk 330–31, 334, 335, 344
  and currency boards 167
  developments in international economy 706–7
  during 1970s 703–4
  establishment of 700–702
  exchange controls 489
  future role of 713–18
  history of 700–705
  international debt crisis 704–5
  international economy developments 706–7
  lender of last resort 422, 442, 443, 444, 591, 717–18, 729
  market supervision 11, 451
  and Mexican crisis 707–8, 716
  and Russian crisis 712–13, 716
  and world economic environment 714–15

*IMF Survey* 344
importers *see* international trade
incentives
  bank crises and moral hazard 442–5
  Barings Bank 378–9
  central bank crises 432, 433, 453, 461–4
  and deposit insurance 641, 643–6
  monitoring and supervision 464–6
income-stream diversification 218–20
independent central bank 156–72
index of economic security 344
India 347, 441, 590, 666
Indonesia
  bad banking practice 439–42
  country risk 329, 358, 732
  economic security ranking 348
  financial crises 21, 370, 416, 430–31, 434–7, 443
  and IMF 709–10
  Islamic banking in 191, 194, 199–200
  loan leverage 441
  regulatory agencies 590
  stock market price index 436
  supervision 446
Industrial Bank of Japan 286
industrialized countries, and international clearing house 739–40
inflation control
  and currency boards 160, 166
  and exchange rate 525
  and monetary policy 168, 672, 686
  PPP concept 247
  and single currency 115, 117
  time-inconsistency problem 675–82
  *see also* interest rates
information technology (IT) *see* IT
information transfer 223
ING (Internationale Nederland Groep) 117, 119, 123, 579
innovation versus regulation 89–92
insolvency 468–9, 475, 573, 645, 646
  *see also* bank failures
Institute of International Bankers 31, 41, 42, 44, 58
Institute for International Finance (IIF) 22, 24, 333

institutional design of central banks 671–98
institutional investor assets 729
*Institutional Investor, The* 356
insurance companies
  and globalization 4, 7, 9, 13, 18, 20
  income-stream diversification 218, 284
  regulation of 575–8
  total return swaps 79
integrated universal bank 208, 225
integration, functional 48, 578–81
Interagency Country Exposure Review Committee 340, 341, 351
interest margins 116, 134
interest parity theory and foreign exchange trading 245
interest rates
  and capital flows 726
  central banks, set by 10
  control, and EMU 106–7
  and country risk 338
  in EU 15
  liberalization, Bank of Thailand 492–4
  monetary policy 6
  PPP concept 247
  shortfalls, and CLO transaction 93
  *see also* inflation control
intermediation 51–2, 53, 54–5, 297
internal finance (retained earnings) 11–12, 15–16, 18, 19
International Association of Insurance Supervisors (IAIS) 11, 591
International Bank for Reconstruction and Development *see* World Bank
international banking crises *see* bank crises
international banking and foreign exchange trading activities
  background to 237–40
  fundamental analysis 244–6
  momentum rules 243–4
  moving averages analysis 242
  pattern recognition analysis 242–3
  security analysis techniques 240–46
  technical analysis, importance of 241, 246–50

trading strategies and economic
theory 251–5
trend recognition 241
international banking and
multinational banking 27–31
international banks, representative
operations in US 41
international business companies,
offshore (IBC) 549
*International Country Risk* 22, 356
international debt crisis and IMF
704–5
international economy developments
and IMF 706–7
International Lending Supervision Act
346
International Monetary Fund (IMF)
*see* IMF
International Organization of Security
Commissions (IOSCO) 10, 11,
56, 591, 594
International Pool, banks in 401–2
International Swap and Derivatives
Market (ISDA) 88, 625
international trade
documentary collections 262–7
documentary credits 268–81
financing 267–8
open account trading 260, 261
overview of 259–61
settlement 259–82
international transfer risk 341
Internationale Nederland Groep
(ING) 117, 119, 123, 579
internationalization 6–11, 131, 420
internet banking
in EMU 145, 151
and globalization 7, 9, 23–4
and mergers 314
money laundering 551
*see also* direct banking; IT;
technological advances;
telephone banking
intervention, bank crises 368–9, 453,
454, 466–71
investment banking
diversification into 7–8, 284, 302
in EU 139, 143, 146, 147, 153
and globalization 7–8, 53, 78, 81, 82
integrated universal bank 208, 225

investment firms, regulation of 575,
577–8
investment fund, international,
proposals for 721–9
investor protection, and cross-border
mergers 121–2
IOSCO (International Organization of
Security Commissions) 10, 11,
56, 591, 594, 595
Iran 191, 194, 201, 348
Iraq 347
Ireland
asset price boom 418
country risk 343, 347, 350
deposit insurance 666
economic security ranking 347
market concentration 124
regulatory agencies 590
strategy response to SMP 142
ISDA (International Swap and
Derivatives Market) 88, 625
Islamic banking 3, 191–206
future of 203–4
history of 192–4
organizational structure 200
practice 198–202
profit and loss sharing (PLS) 194–9,
201, 202–4
theory 194–8
Islamic Development Bank 191, 194
Israel 348, 590
IT, spend-levels in major banks 214
IT (information technology)
and economies of scale 213, 314
in Euroland 138, 140
globalization 11, 52, 53, 54
and single currency 119–20
in US 616–17
*see also* direct banking; internet
banking; technological
advances; telephone banking
Italy
bank crises 418, 422
bank failures 389
central bank independence and
inflation 690
cost–income ratios 136
country risk 329–30, 343, 349
deposit insurance 666
economic security ranking 348

Italy – *continued*
  equity return 136
  globalization 8
  interest margins 134, 135, 136, 579
  international pool 401
  market concentration 124, 133
  mergers 118, 119, 151
  non-interest income 135
  number of banks 131, 132
  regulatory agencies 590
  strategy response to SMP 142
Ivory Coast 590

Jamaica 348, 590
Japan
  asset management 375–6, 377
  assets of institutional investors 723
  bail-outs 221
  bank failures 366, 367, 368, 371, 372, 640, 653, 656–8
  bank fraud 380
  Big Bang 9, 11, 287
  central bank independence and inflation 690
  contagion effect 709
  corporate bonds 109
  costs and efficiency in 297, 315–20
  country risk 328, 343, 349
  deposit insurance 666
  economic security rating 347
  financial crises 404, 405, 412, 438
  financial market trends 286–8
  foreign exchange trading 248
  globalization 8, 10, 19, 20, 23, 38
  *keiretsu* networks 227, 286
    *see also* cross-shareholding
  loan leverage 441
  regulation 581, 602–3
  regulatory agencies 590
  risk premia 250
  too big to fail 382
  weak asset management 375–6, 377
Jersey 550
Johnson Matthey Bankers 380, 382
Jordan 348, 590
J.P. Morgan 3, 53, 214, 220, 285–6
junk bonds 18, 380, 383

*keiretsu* networks 227, 286
  *see also* cross-shareholding

Keller, Joachim 237–58
Kenya 348, 590, 666
Keynes, John Maynard 330, 338
Khoury, Sarkis Joseph 327–65
know your customer policy 550, 551
Korea *see* South Korea
Krung Thai Bank 487, 512
Kuwait 347, 666, 757

L/C (letter of credit) and trade finance 268–82
  *see also* documentary credit
La Poste 111
*laissez-faire see* free banking
Latin America
  banking crises 438, 447, 463
  capital flight 516, 532
  confirmed L/Cs 272
  currency boards 167
  globalization 21
  Japanese lending 375
  *see also* individual countries
Latvia 167, 441
LCTM (long-term capital management) 621–2, 625–6
Lebanon 348, 666
Leeson, Nick 378, 380
lender of last resort (LOLR)
  and bank crises 442, 443, 444
  capital adequacy regulation 182
  contagion prevention 176
  currency boards 165–6
  deposit insurance 468, 577, 645
  and IMF 442, 443, 591, 711, 717–18
  international banking crises 421–4, 444
  lifeboat rescues 382
  non-financial firms 8
  regulatory change, impact of 140, 182, 468, 577
  *see also* deposit insurance; moral hazard
lending
  bad banking practices 439, 440–42
  and bank crises 406, 415, 432, 439, 440, 443, 464
  concentration 124–5
  country risk 338–40, 445
  diversification in 9
  excessive 441–2

financial liberalization 450
  by foreign agencies 40
  incentive structures 464
  ineffective regulation 445
  loan securitization 52
  low inflation 115, 117
  and market concentration 124–5
  multinational banking 40, 41
  private sector 23, 335, 716
  and restructuring 471
  technological advances and 54
Lensink, Robert 25, 492, 514, 515, 516–45, 763
letter of credit (L/C) *see* documentary credit; L/C (letter of credit)
letter of pledge 279
leverage
  capital adequacy regulation 178
  credit derivatives 82
  deposit insurance 643
  double 625
  and globalization 64
  loan leverage ratios 441–2
  macroeconomic and portfolio investment flows 724–7
  MNB strengths 33–5, 49, 50
  in multinational banking 33–5, 49, 50
  *see also* risk management
liberalization
  Bank of Thailand 487–94
  and banking crises 448–52
  and developing countries 17
  and GATS 755–61
  public sector role 721
  steady state phase 451, 452
  stock-adjustment phase 449, 451
  transitional phase 449–51
  *see also* deregulation; free banking
Liberia 347
Libya 348
lifeboat rescues 382
liquidity ratio 368–9
Lithuania 156–7, 158, 160, 167, 441
Llewellyn, David T. 309, 321, 323, 428–85, 594
Lloyds Bank 118, 284, 309, 311
loan-back and money laundering 551, 560
loans *see* lending

local banks 149–50
logit analysis 22, 336, 384–93, 397
LOLR (lender of last resort) *see* lender of last resort
London Stock Exchange Big Bang 283–4
Long Term Credit Bank, Japan 286, 318
long-term capital management (LTCM) 621–2, 625–6
looting 369, 374, 380, 382, 395, 414–16
low-inflation environment, and single currency 115–17
Luxembourg
  and BCCI 381–2
  country risk 343, 344, 348
  deposit insurance 667
  economic security ranking 348
  market concentration 124
  mergers 119
  regulatory agencies 590

M&A (mergers and acquisitions) *see* acquisitions; conglomerates; economies of scale; mergers
Maastricht Treaty 106, 671, 695–6
Macau 590
macroeconomic leverage, and portfolio investment flows 724–7
macroeconomics and banking crises 22, 434–6
Madagascar 348
Malawi 347
Malaysia 348
  banking crises 430, 434–7, 439–41, 442, 443, 709, 732
  capital controls 714
  country risk 328, 329, 330, 348, 358
  economic security ranking 348
  globalization 24
  Islamic banking in 191, 193, 194
  loan leverage 441
  regulatory agencies 590
  stock market price index 436
Mali 347
Malmquist productivity indices 308, 310
Malta 347, 590
managed liabilities 297

management
　and bank failures 367, 371, 377–9, 380
　boards 19
　financial crises, lessons from 465–6, 478
　herd behaviour 444
　incentive structures 461–4, 644, 646
　poor, effects of 152, 166, 440
　see also bad banking practices
mark-up financing 201–2
market concentration 124–5, 133
market discipline
　and bank crises 446–7, 472–6
　and bank regulation 430, 453, 454, 455, 573
　in developing countries 23
　limitations of 475–6
　see also regulation
market failure see banking failure
market power and absolute size 218, 231
market spread analysis 336
market value of equity (MVE) 210–33
marketization of bank strategies 138–9
Marsh, Ian 699–720
Marshall Islands 667
Matthews, Kent 546–71
Mauritius 550
megamergers 284–5, 297, 299, 300, 319
Memorandum of Understanding, Bank of England 596
Mercury Asset Management 111
mergers (M&A)
　Bank of Thailand 512–13
　cost–income ratios 134, 135
　cross-border 286
　cross-functional 216–17, 579–80
　domestic 117–18
　in EMU 134–5, 145, 146, 148, 150, 151–3, 154
　and euro 83
　and foreign competition 143
　income-stream diversification 218, 220
　international 118–19
　management behaviour 13
　megamergers 284–6
　post-merger performance in US 304–8

　RBS and NatWest 309
　scale economies 297, 311
　scope economies 216–17, 301–2, 304
　in US 613–14
　see also acquisitions; conglomerates; economies of scale;
Meritabank 117, 118, 119, 151
Merrill Lynch 3, 68, 84, 87, 110, 119
Mexico
　bank crises 404, 415, 431, 443, 471–2, 738
　capital controls 724, 725, 726
　capital flight 516, 518, 529
　country risk 335, 339, 358
　deposit insurance 667
　economic security ranking 348
　globalization 21
　and IMF 705, 706, 707–8, 715
　loan leverage 441
　regulatory agencies 590
Michigan National Corporation 35, 51
Micronesia 667
Middle East see Islamic banking
Midland Bank 309
　see also HSBC
Miles argument, and CARs 182–5
Milne, Alistair 403–27
minimum retail rate (MRR) 493
misalignments and currency boards 166
Mit Ghamr Village Bank 192–3, 194
Mitsubishi Trust 286
MNB (multinational banking) 28
　client activity theories 35–6
　establishment of 45–6
　exchange rate movements 38
　foreign agencies, branches and subsidiaries 40, 41, 43, 44
　future of 51–5
　and geographic distances 38
　and globalization 46–9
　and government regulations 37–8, 44–5
　history of 29–31
　and international banking 27–31
　leveraging of strengths 33–5
　minimum capital requirements 54
　organizational forms 39–49
　performance of 49–51
　and profit opportunities 32–3

representative offices 39–40
resource requirements 44
and risk management 36–7
theories of 31–8
MNE (multinational enterprise) 28
Molyneux, Philip 14, 33, 38, 55, 57, 130–55, 320
momentum rules and foreign exchange trading 241, 243–4
*Monetary History of the United States* 179
monetary policy
　as a stabilization device 672–5
　*see also* central banking
money laundering 546–71
　collection account 550
　combating 565–7
　loan-back 551, 560
　macroeconomics of 556–65
　microeconomics of 553–6
　offshore business companies 549
　scale, scope and typology 547–52
　shell corporations 549, 551
　smurfing 549
　underground banking system 551
money-centre banks 218, 220
Mongolia 347
monitoring 6, 453, 657
monitoring and supervision
　and bank crises 446
　incentives 464–6
Moody's Investors Service 22, 67, 71, 87, 97, 328, 344
moral hazard
　bail-outs 382
　bank crises 414–16, 442–5, 447
　bank failures 368, 370–71
　capital adequacy regulation 182
　corporate governance 447, 465, 478
　credit derivatives 78
　currency boards 166
　and deposit insurance 370–71, 462, 468, 639, 640–46, 651–9
　and IMF 711
　regulation 574, 576
　*see also* country risk; deposit insurance; risk management; systemic risk
Morgan Grenfell 111, 119

Morgan Guaranty 520, 523–4, 535, 537, 538, 542
Morgan, J.P. 3, 53, 214, 220, 285–6
Morgan Stanley Dean Witter 3, 110, 119
Morocco 347
mortgage banks 311
mortgages 9, 35, 47, 49, 61, 76, 202, 283
　*see also* ABS
moving averages and foreign exchange trading 242, 243
Mozambique 348
MRR (minimum retail rate) 493
*Mudaraba* 202–3, 204
Mullineux, Andrew W. 3–26, 486–515, 763
Multi National Strategies of New York 22
multinational banking (MNB) *see* MNB
multinational enterprise (MNE) 28
Murinde, Victor 3–26, 259, 282, 486–515, 516–45, 751–63
Muslim countries *see* Islamic banking
Muslim Pilgrims Savings Corporation 193
mutual funds
　closed-end 224
　and globalization 7, 9, 18–19, 20
　managers in France 111
　and single currency 110–12
mutuality versus plc debate 309
MVE (market value of equity) 210–33
Myanmar 347

Namibia 348
narrow banking 651
Nasser Social Bank 194
NatWest Bank 67, 68, 123, 214, 284, 309, 311
national champions 9, 120
National Treatment provision 760
Nations Bank 68, 214, 220, 285, 580
net interest margins (EU) 133, 134
Net Present Value (NPV) projects 64
Netherlands
　bail-outs 127
　bank crises 413
　bank rankings 123

Netherlands – *continued*
  central bank independence and
    inflation 690
  cooperative strategy 120
  corporate bonds 109
  cost–income ratios 136
  country risk 343
  deposit insurance 667
  economic security ranking 347
  equity return 136
  globalization 16
  interest margins 116, 134, 135, 136
  market concentration 124, 133, 218
  mergers 117, 118, 119, 122, 151, 579
  non-interest income 135
  number of banks 131, 132
  regulatory agencies 590
  strategy response to SMP 142
network externalities 212–13
New Caledonia 348
New York Article XII Investment
    Companies 41
New York Safety Fund 642
New Zealand
  central bank independence and
    inflation 690
  country risk 343, 350
  economic security ranking 347
  globalization 32
  incentives 461, 463
  inflation targeting 672, 695, 696–7
  regulation 372–4, 586, 610–11
  regulatory agencies 590
NFCs (non-financial corporates)
    11–13, 15, 16
Nicaragua 347
Niger 347
Nigeria 347, 530, 590, 667, 751, 761
non-bank competition 644
non-bank financial companies 52, 125,
    137, 193
non-financial business sector 8, 18, 284
non-financial corporates (NFCs)
    11–12, 13, 15, 16
non-financial shareholdings 225–8
non-industrialized countries *see*
    developing countries
non-interest income/gross income (EU)
    135
Nordbanken 117, 118, 119, 151

Norton, Joseph J. 549, 571, 612–36
Norway
  bail-outs 221
  bank failures 376–7, 388
  banking crises 412, 414, 415
  central bank independence and
    inflation 690
  cost–income ratios 136
  country risk 343
  deposit insurance 640, 667
  economic security ranking 347
  equity return 136
  interest margins 134, 135, 136
  international pool 401
  non-interest income 135
  number of banks 131, 132
  regulatory agencies 590
Norwest-Wells Fargo 220, 285
NPV (Net Present Value) projects 64

OCC (Office of the Comptroller of the
    Currency) 344, 614, 636
OECD (Organization for Economic
    Cooperation and Development)
  bank crises 450
  capital controls 724
  country risk 335
  globalization 8, 11, 12–13, 15
  new market environment 578, 595
  tax havens and money laundering
    567, 570, 571
off-balance sheet trading 52, 53–4, 178,
    284, 302, 308
Office of the Comptroller of the
    Currency (OCC) 344, 614,
    636
offshore banking, Bank of Thailand
    490
offshore international business
    companies and money
    laundering 549
offshore investment *see* MNB
Okeahalam, C. Charles 637–67
Olive, Christopher D. 612–36
Oman 347
one-stop financial services 53, 216
OPEC (Organization of Petroleum-
    Exporting Countries) 338
open account trading 260, 261
open positions, closing of 249

Organization for Economic
    Cooperation and Development
    (OECD) 8
Organization of Islamic Conference
    194
Organization of Petroleum-Exporting
    Countries (OPEC) 338
OTC (over-the-counter) derivatives
    report, US banking regulation
    620–21, 626–9

Pakistan
    country risk 348
    deposit insurance 666
    economic security ranking 348
    Islamic banking in 191, 194, 201,
        203
    regulatory agencies 590
Panama 347
Papua New Guinea 347
Paraguay 347, 590
Paribas 111, 118, 119, 123
pattern recognition and foreign
    exchange trading 241, 242–3
payable-through-accounts 551
pension funds
    and globalization 6, 24, 48
    and investment changes 723
    managers, UK 111
    and single currency 110–12, 121
pension privatization 148
performance enhancement 63–4, 152
Peru 347, 441, 667
Philippines
    bad banking practices 442
    banking crises 414, 434–7, 732
    capital flight 520, 529, 530
    contagion effect 709
    country risk 329, 334, 335
    deposit insurance 667
    economic security ranking 347
    Islamic banking in 194
    loan leverage 441
    regulatory agencies 590
    stock market price index 436
Phillips & Drew 111, 286
Phylaktis, Kate 699–720
Pilgrims Management and Fund
    Board 193
Pinijkulviwat, Adisorn 486–515

pledge, letter of 279
PLMU (Property Loan Management
    Organization), Bank of
    Thailand 507–8
PLS (profit and loss sharing) and
    Islamic banking 194–9, 201,
    202–4
Poland 334, 347, 441, 530, 579, 590
political risk 328, 335, 338
    *see also* country risk
Political Risk Services of New York
    22, 344
political support and currency boards
    165
pooling equilibrium 680
portfolio investment
    and country risk 329, 339–40
    and emerging markets 724, 727–9
    flows 724–7
    foreign 145, 722–9
Portugal
    concentration 133
    cost–income ratios 136
    country risk 343
    deposit insurance 667
    economic security ranking 347
    equity return 136
    interest margins 134, 135, 136
    market concentration 124
    mergers 118
    monetary discipline 418
    non-interest income 135
    number of banks 131, 132
    regulatory agencies 590
    strategic response to SMP 142
post-merger performance 301–2, 304–8
post-shipment finance 277, 278–81
potential value of equity (PVE) 229–33
PPP (purchasing power parity) and
    foreign exchange trading 166,
    245, 247
pre-shipment finance 276, 277–8
precommitment strategy 469–70
premium pricing, deposit insurance
    646–50
Presley, John R. 191–206
price-to-book ratios (US) 220
principal components analysis 22
principal–agent problem 19, 367, 573,
    691

privatized international monetary architecture, reform of 721–50
probit models 22, 354–62, 384
productive process, model of 296–7, 309
profit and loss sharing (PLS) and Islamic banking 194–9, 201, 202–4
Property Loan Management Organization (PLMU), Bank of Thailand 507–8
Prudential Portfolio Managers 111
public debt 335
purchased funds reliance 50
purchasing power parity (PPP) and foreign exchange trading 166, 245, 247
PVE (potential value of equity) 229–33

'Q' ratio 211
Qatar 347, 757

Rabobank 123
Radanasin Bank 504, 506, 512
*Random Walk Down Wall Street, A* 239–40
ratio analysis 336
ratio-based standard 91
RBS (Royal Bank of Scotland) 120, 284, 309, 311
receipt and undertaking L/Cs 276
red clause L/Cs 276
regulation
  and bank crises 370, 428–85, 455–60
  BIS 1999 proposals 95–8
  consolidated supervision 582
  consumer protection 572–3, 574, 575–6, 587, 588
  contagion 573–4
  coordination of 22–3
  current overview 86–9
  deregulation 581–2
  and government intervention 178
  impact of, in EU 140–44
  implications for 584–9
  ineffective 445–6
  insurance companies 575–8
  international dimension 22–3, 589–92
  market integrity 573, 576
  moral hazard 574, 583, 587, 588
  and multinational banking 7–8 44–5, 53–4
  new market environment 578–84
  objectives 572–4
  risks, inherent 92–4
  self-regulation 94–5
  structural issues 572–95
  systemic risk 573–4, 575, 576, 583, 587, 591
  targets 574–6
  techniques 576–7
  US 612–36
  versus innovation 89–92
  *see also* CARs
Regulation Q 30, 38
regulators, role of 380–82
regulatory reform, Asian crisis *see* Asian crisis
regulatory regime, bank crises *see* bank crises
Repeat Offering Securitisation Entity (ROSE) 67
representative offices 39–40, 42–3, 44
reregulation of commercial banking, Bank of Thailand 487
reserve ratio 368
residual measurement method, capital flight 519–20, 522, 523, 529, 530
restructuring, Asian crisis 502–13
retail banking
  competitiveness 126
  conglomerate discount 225
  deposit insurance 638, 653
  in EU 111, 138, 139, 148, 149, 150, 153–4
  globalization 7–9, 28, 31
  *see also* commercial banking
retail customers, and deposit insurance 638, 653
retained earnings (internal finance) 11–12, 15–16, 18, 19
revolving L/Cs 276–7
risk management
  asset-backed securitization 63–5
  BIS 1999 proposals 95–8
  centralized approach to 580–81, 582, 583
  CLOs 73, 74, 81, 82, 83–4, 90–92
  country risk *see* country risk

and deposit insurance 640–46
disclosure system 373
diversification 123, 218–20
and financial crises 432, 433, 438,
  440, 458
franchise value 228–9
functional integration 580–82, 583
globalization 6, 7–9, 24, 28, 31, 48
importance of 465–6
and incentive structures 461
income-stream diversification
  218–20
letters of credit 272–3
and multinational banking 36–7
risk premia and technical trading
  250, 440
and securitization 63–5, 90–92
service provision 52–3
*see also* country risk; credit risk;
  leverage; supervision; systemic
  risk
risk premia and technical trading 250,
  440
risk-adjusted return measures 74
Romania 347
ROSE (Repeat Offering Securitisation
  Entity) 67, 68
Royal Bank of Scotland (RBS) 120,
  284, 309, 311
Rundt Associates of New York, S.J 22
rural credit policy, Bank of Thailand
  495–6
Russia
  banking crises 405, 712–13, 732, 733
  capital flight 516–17
  contagion effect 358
  country risk 38, 327, 329, 331,
    334–5, 340, 342
  currency boards 167
  economic security ranking 347
  globalization 5, 50
  and IMF 729–30
  loan leverage 441
  regulatory agencies 590
Ryan, Cillian 17, 751–63

S&L (savings and loans) crisis 640,
  642
S&P (Standard and Poor's) 22, 87, 230,
  250, 342, 344

Sakura Bank 286
salesman's stake and affiliates' products
  221
Salomon Smith Barney 110
Samuelson–Balassa effect 166
Santander–BCH 123
Sanwa Bank 286
Saudi Arabia 193-4, 348
savings and loans (S&L) crisis 640,
  642
SBC Glacier Finance Ltd 68, 84–6,
  101, 118, 214
scale and technical efficiency
  measurement 291
Scandinavia
  bad banking practices 439
  bank crises 404, 405, 434, 446, 451
  credit controls 419
  *see also* individual countries
scheme design, deposit insurance
  650–58
Schroder Investors 111
Scotland 176, 371
SDRs (special drawing rights) 722,
  729–34
SEC (Securities Exchange
  Commission) 619–20, 627–9
securities *see* ABS; securitization
Securities Exchange Commission
  (SEC) 619–20, 627–9
securities exchanges 576
securitization
  asset-backed 60–65, 76
  BIS 1999 proposals 95–7
  capital adequacy requirements 904
  CLOs 80–83, 92
  credit derivatives in 80–83
  and economies of scope 213
  in EU 138, 139, 145, 146, 147, 148,
    152–3
  globalization 6–11, 12, 90
  multinational banking 51, 52, 53–4
security analysis and foreign exchange
  trading 239–47
seigniorage 167–8, 357–8
self-regulation 94–5, 98
  *see also* regulation
Senegal 347
settlement and financing of
  international trade 259–82

shareholder value
  book value to market value 210–29
  and convergence 19–20
  economics of X-efficiency 213–17
  and management monitoring 367–8
  market value to potential value 229–33
  maximization 138
  Miles argument 184
  and universal banking 207–36
  and voting rights 13
  *see also* equity; investment; principal–agent problems
Shariah Supervisory Board 199
Sharpe ratio 250
shipping documents 279–80
Siam City Bank 511, 512
Siam Commercial Bank 487, 503, 511
Sierra Leone 347
Singapore
  bad banking practices 439, 440
  and Bank of Thailand 495
  country risk 343, 348
  economic security ranking 348
  loan leverage 441
  monopoly regulator 210
  regulatory agencies 590
  stock market price index 436
single currency
  corporate bond market 108–10
  and EMU 106–17
  euro as an international currency 113–14
  euro-deposit markets 112
  foreign exchange markets 112
  fund management 110–12
  government bond market 107–8
  in a low inflation environment 115–17
Single Market Programme (SMP) *see* SMP
size–efficiency relationships and building societies 313–15
size hypothesis 34, 148–9, 218
Slovak Republic 348, 441
Slovenia 441, 590
SMEs (small and medium-sized enterprises) 7, 11, 18, 19, 20, 125

SMP (Single Market Programme)
  cross-border mergers 151
  deregulation, effects of 141
  domestic consolidation 150
  and globalization 17
  market-orientated culture 140
  'National Treatment' provision 760
  opportunities 131
  strategy response to 142–4
smurfing 549
social security privatization 148
Société Générale 29, 111, 119, 123, 214, 579
Somalia 347
South Africa 191, 348, 441, 590, 715, 757
South East Asia
  bank crises 419
  globalization 5
  and IMF 443, 444, 447, 451, 472
  *see also* Asian crisis; individual countries
South Korea
  bad banking practices 439–42
  bail-out 329
  banking crises 416, 430–31, 435, 436, 437, 732
  capital flight 529
  clearing system, international 724, 728, 738
  country risk 329, 358
  economic security ranking 347
  foreign exchange controls 714–15, 724, 728
  globalization 21
  and IMF 329, 709–10
  loan leverage 441
  regulation 446, 590
  regulatory agencies 590
  stock market price index 436
  sovereign risk 96, 327, 336, 339, 415, 417
  *see also* country risk
Spain
  bank crises 404, 431
  bank failures 376–7, 383
  bank rankings 123
  central bank independence and inflation 690
  cost–income ratios 136

country risk 343
deposit insurance 667
economic security ranking 348
equity return 136
globalization 16
interest margins 115, 116, 134, 135, 136
international pool 401–2
market concentration 124
mergers 118, 151, 579
non-interest income 135
number of banks 131, 132
regulatory agencies 590
strategy response to SMP 142
special drawing rights (SDRs) 722, 729–34
Special Weapons Action Team (SWAT) 232
special-purpose vehicle (SPV) 62–3, 66, 69–72, 76, 77, 83, 87–8
speculative trading 167, 247, 251, 254–5
*see also* foreign exchange trading activities
SPV (special-purpose vehicle) 62–3, 66, 69–72, 76, 77, 83, 87–8
Sri Lanka 347, 590
Standard Chartered Bank 309, 310, 511
Standard and Poor's (S&P) 22, 87, 230, 250, 342, 344
standardization 93, 151
standby L/Cs 275–6
state intervention *see* government involvement
state-centred approach and non-financial shareholding 227
stochastic frontier model 292–3
stock market collapses 404
stock market price index, South East Asia 436
structured loans 259–60
stuffing fiduciary accounts 222
subordinated debt 651–2
subsidiaries, foreign 40
Sudan 191, 194, 334, 347, 520, 530
Sumitomo Bank 221, 286
supervision of banking system
consolidated 582–3
failures of 414–16, 432, 446, 451, 642

globalization 6, 9, 54
market discipline 473, 475
and regulatory scheme 453, 461, 463, 464–6, 467, 469
reserve bank responsibility 373
supervision by risk programme 614
Suriname 347
swaps
credit default 79–80, 81, 83
International Swap and Derivatives Market (ISDA) 88, 625
and multinational banking 53
total return 79, 80
SWAT teams (Special Weapons Action Team) 232
Sweden
bail-outs 221
bank failures 388
banking crises 412, 415
central bank independence and inflation 690
concentration 133
cost–income ratios 136
country risk 343, 349
economic security ranking 347
equity return 136
globalization 10, 15
interest margins 134, 135, 136
international pool 402
market concentration 124
mergers 117, 118, 119
non-interest income 135
number of banks 131, 132
regulatory agencies 590
Swiss Bank Corporation 61, 119, 286
Switzerland
bail-outs 221
bank failures 452
bank rankings 123
central bank independence and inflation 690
country risk 343, 349
deposit insurance 667
economic security ranking 348
foreign exchange trading 248
free banking 176
globalization 8, 44, 45
Islamic banking in 201
loan leverage 441
mergers 118, 119, 286, 579

Switzerland – *continued*
  regulatory agencies 590
  systemic risk 122, 127
synchronized business cycles 164
Syria 348
systemic failure 370
systemic risk
  and contagion 573–4
  and cross-border mergers 122–4
  and deposit insurance 370
  *see also* country risk; moral hazard; risk management
systemic stability and banking crises 430, 431, 432, 443

Tabung Hajj 193, 194
Taiwan
  bad banking practices 439–40
  country risk 329, 343, 348
  deposit insurance 667
  economic security ranking 348
  and IMF 714
  loan leverage 441
  regulatory agencies 590
  stock market price index 436
Tanzania 348, 666
Taranaki Savings Bank 373
TARGET system 148, 419
Task Force on the Future of the Canadian Financial Services Sector 59
tax constraints 82, 754
taxation regimes, foreign 44–5
TBTF (too-big-to-fail) *see* too-big-to-fail
technical analysis and foreign exchange trading 239, 241, 246–50
technical traders and security analysis 240–41
technological advances
  globalization 30, 48, 51, 53, 54
  and new strategic environment 137, 138
  *see also* direct banking; internet banking; IT; telephone banking
technological change specification 312, 313, 314
telephone banking *see* direct banking; internet banking; IT; technological advances

Tequila crisis *see* Mexico
TFA (thick frontier approach) 294
Thai Bankers Association 508–9
Thai Credit Bureau Company 508–9
Thai Farmers Bank 487, 502, 503, 511
Thailand
  bad banking practices 439–42
  bank crises 404, 430, 431, 434–7, 732
  bank failures 370
  Bank of Thailand *see* Bank of Thailand
  clearing system, international 738
  contagion effect and IMF 709, 710
  country risk 329, 357
  economic security ranking 347
  globalization 5, 21
  and IMF 443, 709, 710
  loan leverage 441
  regulatory agencies 590
  stock market price index 436
thick frontier approach (TFA) 294
third-party loans 222
Thomson Financial Securities 110, 579
thrifts 376, 379, 380, 381, 383
tie-ins 222
time-inconsistency problem and central banking 675–82
Togo 347
Tokai Bank 286
too-big-to-fail (TBTF)
  bail-outs 221
  deposit insurance 639
  equity potential 231, 232
  lifeboat rescues 382–3
  non-financial firms 8
  and regulatory change 140
total return (TR) swaps 79, 80
Tower Group 214
TR (total return swaps) 79, 80
trade finance hypothesis 35–6
trade finance, international 28, 259–82
trade liberalization and GATS 17, 755–61
trade misinvoicing measurement method, capital flight 522
trading interdependence and contagion 359

World Trade Organization (WTO) *see* WTO
WTO (World Trade Organization)
  and developing countries 751–63
  and globalization 17

X-efficiency 221, 231, 232, 293, 315, 317
  and economies of scale 213–17, 297–8, 300–301
X-inefficiency 141, 293–4, 303, 304–5, 307, 310, 317
  and economies of scope 213–17

Yasuda Life Assurance 288
Yemen 347
Young's theorem 295
Yugoslavia 347

Zaire 347
*zaitech* strategy 375–6, 383
*Zakah* accounts 193
Zambia 348, 590
Zhou, Chunsheng 78, 100, 327–65
Zimbabwe 348
Zions Bank 630
zombie banks 657–8